Federal Jurisdiction

Aspen Treatise Series

FEDERAL JURISDICTION

Ninth Edition

ERWIN CHEMERINSKY
Dean and Jesse H. Choper Distinguished Professor of Law
University of California, Berkeley School of Law

ASPEN
PUBLISHING

Cover image: Wil Etheredge/iStock.com

To contact Customer Service, e-mail customer.service@aspenpublishing.com, call 1-800-950-5259, or mail correspondence to:

Aspen Publishing
Attn: Order Department
1 Wall Street
Burlington, MA 01803

Printed in the United States of America.

1 2 3 4 5 6 7 8 9 0

ISBN 979-8-8920-7534-3

Library of Congress Cataloging-in-Publication Data

Names: Chemerinsky, Erwin, 1953- author.
Title: Federal jurisdiction / Erwin Chemerinsky, Dean and Jesse H. Choper Distinguished Professor of Law, University of California, Berkeley School of Law.
Description: Ninth edition. | Burlington : Aspen Publishing, 2025. | Includes bibliographical references and index. | Summary: "Treatise for law students on federal jurisdiction"—Provided by publisher.
Identifiers: LCCN 2025013723 | ISBN 9798892075343 (hardcover) | ISBN 9798892075367 (ebook)
Subjects: LCSH: Jurisdiction—United States. | Courts—United States.
Classification: LCC KF8858 .C48 2025 | DDC 347.73/2—dc23/eng/20250328
LC record available at https://lccn.loc.gov/2025013723

ABOUT ASPEN PUBLISHING

Aspen Publishing is a leading provider of legal education content and digital learning solutions in the United States and globally. Our innovative products and platforms—designed based on best practices in learning science—engage students and enhance outcomes. From textbooks and audiobooks authored by renowned experts to digital platforms and products like LEAF, Connected eBooks, Connected Quizzing, PracticePerfect, and JD-Next, we empower the next generation of legal professionals with innovative, trusted, and accessible resources.

The Aspen Casebook Series, affectionately known as the "red and black" casebooks among law faculty and students, includes hundreds of highly regarded textbooks across more than 80 disciplines. These range from foundational courses like Torts and Contracts to emerging electives such as Sustainability and the Law of Policing. Our study aids, including the popular *Examples & Explanations* series, help law students master complex topics with clarity and confidence.

Aspen's expertise extends to undergraduate education with our Paralegal, Criminal Justice, and Business Law series, offering the same hallmark quality to a broader audience. JD-Next, our groundbreaking online law school prep course and admissions test, provides a realistic preview of law school, equips students with essential skills for academic success, and evaluates their readiness for legal studies.

Aspen Publishing Is Proud to Be a UWorld Company

Since 2003, UWorld has been a global leader in developing high-quality learning tools for students preparing for high-stakes exams. With a commitment to excellence, UWorld has helped millions of students in undergraduate, graduate, and professional programs in fields such as medicine, nursing, finance, and law achieve their academic and career goals.

Founded by Chandra S. Pemmasani, M.D., during his medical residency, UWorld began focusing on medical education and has since expanded into various academic fields, including law. In 2020, UWorld launched its Legal vertical, starting with its comprehensive Multistate Bar Exam (MBE®) Question Bank, followed by the acquisition of Themis Bar Review, which integrated resources to provide a complete bar exam preparation experience. In 2024, UWorld expanded its offerings by acquiring Aspen Publishing, enhancing its suite of legal education products.

Today, UWorld offers an unparalleled range of study materials that blend active learning methods with expert content, ensuring students and educators can access the most effective resources. From bar preparation to law school success, UWorld is committed to supporting the next generation of legal professionals. Learn more at uworld.com.

In memory of my father, Arthur Chemerinsky

Summary of Contents

Contents

PART I

Constitutional and Statutory Limits on Federal Court Jurisdiction 33

CHAPTER 2

Justiciability: Constitutional and Prudential Limits on Federal Judicial Power 35

CHAPTER 3

Congressional Control of Federal and State Court Jurisdiction 173

CHAPTER 4

Congressional Power to Create Legislative Courts 217

CHAPTER 5

The Subject Matter Jurisdiction of the Federal Courts 267

CHAPTER 6

Federal Common Law 357

PART II

Federal Court Relief Against Governments and Government Officers 393

CHAPTER 7

Suits Against State Governments: The Eleventh Amendment and Sovereign Immunity 395

CHAPTER 8

Federal Court Relief Against Local Governments and State and Local Government Officers: 42 U.S.C. §1983 467

PART III

Federal Court Review of State Court Judgments and Proceedings 649

CHAPTER 10

U.S. Supreme Court Review 651

CHAPTER 11

Statutory Control of the Relationship Between Federal Courts and the States 721

CHAPTER 12

Federal Court Abstention Because of Unclear State Law 767

CHAPTER 13

Federal Court Abstention to Avoid Review of State Court Judgments or Interference with Pending State Proceedings 797

Preface

Defining the role of the federal courts poses some of the most difficult and some of the most interesting issues in American law. Underlying virtually all issues are basic questions of separation of powers and federalism. What is the proper role for the federal judiciary in the scheme of divided powers? What is the appropriate allocation of responsibility between federal courts and state courts? More fundamentally, what is the proper role for an unelected federal judiciary in American society? Not surprisingly, issues of federal jurisdiction generate intense debates among justices, lower courts, scholars, and hopefully students.

In this book I attempt to describe and analyze the doctrines and policies that shape the jurisdiction of the courts of the United States. Specifically, the book has three purposes. First, and most obviously, I seek to state clearly the current law defining the jurisdiction of the federal courts. Second, I wish to identify important unresolved issues and to describe the positions of the lower courts on these questions. Third, in discussing each area of the law, I want to examine the underlying, competing policy considerations. The law of federal jurisdiction is largely derived from opinions of the U.S. Supreme Court. The doctrines and principles reflect important choices about the nature of American government and the role of the federal courts. Although I often express my own views on particular topics, I try to identify them as such and present them only after summarizing the alternative positions as fairly as possible.

The law of federal jurisdiction changes rapidly. It is now thirty-two years since the first edition of this book was written. Over this time, and over the course of several editions, there have been changes in most areas and dramatic changes in many. Some of the most important changes since the publication of the previous edition include:

- Important decisions concerning justiciability, such as *TransUnion LLC v. Ramirez* on standing under federal statutes
- Significant decisions with regard to the use of non-Article III courts, such as *Securities and Exchange Commission v. Jarkesy*

- *Trump v. United States* on presidential immunity from criminal prosecutions
- New limits on *Bivens* suits in *Egbert v. Boule*

The ninth edition incorporates these new developments, while preserving the approach, style, and organization of the earlier eight editions. Every chapter has been revised to reflect new developments and new scholarship on the topic.

Covering a broad field in one volume of manageable size required many choices in topic selection, organization, and style. Before describing what is omitted, it is useful to summarize the contents and structure of the book.

- Chapter 1 is an introduction, considering the history of federal jurisdiction, describing the current structure of the federal judiciary, and identifying the two themes—separation of powers and federalism—that recur throughout this book.

The remainder of the book is divided into three major parts. Part I focuses on constitutional and statutory limits on the federal judicial power.

- Chapter 2 focuses on the justiciability doctrines that limit federal jurisdiction, including the prohibition against advisory opinions; the principles of standing, ripeness, and mootness; and the political question doctrine.
- Chapter 3 examines congressional power to control the jurisdiction of the Supreme Court and the lower federal courts. It also includes a new section on Congress's power to force state courts to hear federal law matters.
- Chapter 4 discusses congressional authority to create legislative courts—tribunals where the judges do not possess life tenure or protection against reduction in their salary.
- Chapter 5 considers the subject matter jurisdiction of the federal courts and examines both the constitutional and statutory provisions that define federal court authority. The chapter primarily focuses on federal question, diversity, ancillary, pendent, and removal jurisdiction. Also considered is the choice of law in diversity cases.
- Chapter 6 examines the power of the federal courts to fashion federal common law.

Part II concerns the ability of federal courts to give relief against governments and government officers.

- Chapter 7 discusses the Eleventh Amendment, which limits federal court relief against state governments.
- Chapter 8 examines 42 U.S.C. §1983, which is the basic vehicle for federal court review of the actions of local governments and state and local officials.
- Chapter 9 considers suits against federal officers and the federal government.

Part III focuses on federal court review of state court judgments and proceedings.

- Chapter 10 discusses Supreme Court review, both of state court decisions and of lower federal court rulings.
- Chapter 11 examines statutes limiting the jurisdiction of the federal courts and specifically considers the Anti-Injunction Act, the Tax Injunction Act, the Johnson Act, and the Civil Rights Removal Act.
- Chapters 12, 13, and 14 analyze the various abstention doctrines.
- Chapter 12 discusses abstention because of unclear state law, specifically focusing on *Pullman, Thibodaux,* and *Burford* abstention and the procedure followed when such abstention occurs.
- Chapter 13 considers abstention to avoid interference with pending state court proceedings, sometimes referred to as *Younger v. Harris* abstention, and abstention to avoid federal court review of state court decisions (the *Rooker-Feldman* doctrine).
- Chapter 14 examines abstention to avoid duplicative federal and state court proceedings, often termed *Colorado River* abstention.
- Finally, Chapter 15 focuses on federal court habeas corpus relief for state and federal prisoners.

Several related subjects are omitted or addressed only briefly. An arbitrary distinction has been drawn between matters of federal jurisdiction and issues of civil procedure. Hence, the topics addressed by the Federal Rules of Civil Procedure—matters such as service of process, pleading, joinder, discovery, and summary judgment—are beyond the scope of this book. The subject matter jurisdiction of the federal courts—a topic common to courses in both civil procedure and federal jurisdiction—is covered in detail in Chapter 5.

Also, some specialized areas of federal jurisdiction, most notably admiralty and maritime law, are not covered. Similarly, the topic of federal court review of federal agency decisions is not directly addressed.

In attempting to organize the material in what I believe to be the most comprehensible and useful manner, I made several choices. First, the choice of law in diversity cases—commonly known as the *Erie* problem—is considered in the treatment of diversity jurisdiction in Chapter 5. The development of federal common law in other contexts is discussed in Chapter 6 and also in Chapter 9, which focuses on federal court relief against federal government officers.

Second, the federal courts' duty to accord res judicata and collateral estoppel effect to state court judgments is not the subject of a separate chapter. However, such preclusion is discussed especially in Chapter 8, which focuses on §1983 suits, and in Chapter 14, which examines the problem of duplicative federal and state court litigation.

Third, appellate review of federal district court decisions by the U.S. Courts of Appeals is considered in Chapter 10, which focuses primarily on U.S. Supreme

Court review. The issues of appellate review are sufficiently similar to warrant treatment in a single chapter.

Stylistically, in discussing Supreme Court cases I have often chosen to quote directly from the Court's opinions. A primary objective of this book is to state the law. Thus, many cases announcing key legal principles are summarized, and I believe that the law often is best stated by using the Court's exact words. Also, I have tried to avoid the temptation to be encyclopedic in citations. Therefore, the reader should recognize that many law review articles and lower court cases are not included in the footnotes. References to statutory sources are usually undated. All such references are to compilations in force in 2024.

The book is complete through the conclusion of the Supreme Court's October 2023 Term, which ended on July 1, 2024.

In light of how rapidly this area of the law changes, I expect to continue to write new editions, as needed, for many years to come. The comments and suggestions from readers on the first eight editions have been most helpful, and I welcome responses to this ninth edition and ideas for future editions.

Erwin Chemerinsky

January 2025

Acknowledgments

It is hard for me to believe that this is the ninth edition of this book. I wrote the first edition during a sabbatical in the Spring 1988 semester. I was then a professor at the University of Southern California Law School. Subsequent editions have been written at my academic homes over the years: Duke Law School, University of California Irvine Law School, and now University of California Berkeley Law School. At each institution, I have been provided wonderful support by my deans, my provosts, and my chancellors.

Many friends offered very helpful suggestions on earlier drafts of particular chapters. I am particularly grateful to Tom Rowe for providing extensive comments on the first edition and its supplements. Bill Burnham offered detailed comments on the second edition. Their suggestions have been extremely helpful and are reflected throughout the book.

I also want to thank Susan Bandes, Ted Blumoff, David Cruz, Neal Devins, Don Doernberg, Catherine Fisk, John Jeffries, Judith Resnik, and Sharon Rush. I owe special thanks to William Marshall, who read and commented on a draft of virtually the entire book and has constantly challenged me to rethink my views about federal jurisdiction.

I also want to thank the editors who helped me so much over the years—Jessica Barmack, Rick Heuser, Elizabeth Kenny, Carol McGeehan, and Barbara Roth. Their encouragement, their assistance, and their patience mattered enormously and are very much remembered.

I am very grateful to a talented group of research assistants for their excellent work on the earlier editions: Penny Alexander, C.K. Alston, Bob Beauchamp, Sosi Biricik, Eric Blum, James Bozajian, Chelsea Brea, Lorrin Clark, Matt Collette, Saxon Cropper-Sykes, Jeanne Detch, Sherry DuPont, Cary Epstein, Jennifer Fercovich, Dave Fordyce, Eli Freedman, Karin Freeman, Laura Fry, Jeffrey Golden, Karen Grant, Autumn Gresowski, Christine Hayashi, Kelly Hickman, Julie Huffman, Alicia Ide, Jordan Liebman, Laura Lin, Laura Lively, Helen Machlovitz, Leslie McWilliams, Nancy Morgan, Barbara Murphy, Sue Odell, Beth Orsoff, Diana Palacios, Deana Pollard, Jamie Price, Lowell Reinstein, Lori Roos, Pam Rosenthal,

Adam Scott, Elizabeth Shaver, Carrie Steiner, Turner Swan, David Swift, Michael Tomasulo, Eleanor Walker, David Wang, and Steven Winters. For this edition, I was very much assisted by David Bernstein, Alice Choi, Michael Loughran, and Itai Tismanzky.

My work on this new edition, like all of my work, was tremendously helped by my terrific assistant, Whitney Mello.

Finally, and most important, I want to thank my family—my wife, Catherine Fisk, and Jeff, Kim, Adam, Katherine, Alex, Mara, Andrew, Sarah, and Amy. They are the greatest joys and the most wonderful part of my very blessed life.

This book is dedicated to the memory of my father, who died in the spring of 1993 while I was working on the second edition. Remembering his pride and excitement at the publication of the first edition was an inspiration as I have struggled to complete every edition since, including this one.

Federal Jurisdiction

CHAPTER 1

Introduction: Historical Background and Contemporary Themes

§1.1 ARTICLE III OF THE U.S. CONSTITUTION

Article III of the U.S. Constitution creates the federal judiciary and defines its powers. Many contemporary issues of federal jurisdiction are debated and decided as questions of how to interpret Article III.

Judicial Power Under the Articles of Confederation

Article III was a substantial departure from the Articles of Confederation. The Confederation Congress had very limited authority to create courts. The only national court established under the Articles of Confederation was the Court of Appeals in Cases of Capture. This court existed for admiralty cases, specifically for instances in which American ships seized vessels, termed *prizes,* belonging to enemy countries.[1] The Confederation Congress also had the authority to establish courts to punish piracies, but this power was immediately delegated to the states and never exercised at the national level.[2]

The Constitutional Convention recognized the need for a federal judiciary and, in fact, unanimously approved Edmund Randolph's resolution "that a National Judiciary be established."[3] Article III, as proposed by the Convention and ratified by the states, covers seven important topics concerning the federal judiciary.

Content of Article III

First, the initial words of Article III—"the judicial Power of the United States shall be vested"—create a federal judicial system. Although there was substantial disagreement about the appropriate structure and authority of the federal courts, there was a consensus that there should be a national judiciary. As Farrand remarked in his authoritative history of the proceedings of the Constitutional Convention, "[t]hat there should be a national judiciary was readily accepted by all."[4] In large part, federal courts were desired to effectively implement the powers of the national government; there was fear that state courts might not fully enforce and implement federal policies, especially where there was a conflict between federal and state interests.[5] At a minimum, a federal judiciary could help provide the uniform interpretation of the Constitution and laws of the United States. Additionally, federal courts were viewed by some, such as James Madison, as necessary to assure the protection of individual liberties.[6] Finally, there was agreement that a national tribunal was essential to resolve disputes between the states. A peaceful way to settle disagreements over matters such as borders was imperative, and state courts were obviously too parochial to perform this function.

§1.1 [1] John P. Frank, Historical Bases of the Federal Judicial System, 13 Law & Contemp. Probs. 3, 8 (1948).

[2] *Id.* Ad hoc tribunals were also created to resolve border disputes between the states. Richard H. Fallon, Jr., John F. Manning, Daniel J. Meltzer & David L. Shapiro, Hart & Wechsler's The Federal Courts and the Federal System 6 n.34 (7th ed. 2015). For example, a court was created by joint consent to resolve a border dispute between Connecticut and Pennsylvania. *Id.*

[3] 1 Max Farrand, The Records of the Federal Convention 20-23 (1913).

[4] Max Farrand, The Framing of the Constitution of the United States 79 (1913).

[5] Fallon et al., *supra* note 2, at 6 n.30.

[6] *Id.*

Creates Supreme Court and Permits Establishment of Lower Courts

Second, Article III vests the judicial power of the United States "in one supreme Court and in such inferior courts as Congress may from time to time ordain and establish." A major dispute at the Constitutional Convention was whether lower federal courts should exist. The Committee of the Whole, echoing resolutions offered by Randolph, proposed that there should be both a Supreme Court and inferior courts.[7] This proposal drew strong opposition from those who thought it was unnecessary and undesirable to create lower federal courts. Opponents of lower federal courts argued that they were unnecessary because state courts, subject to review by the Supreme Court, were sufficient to protect the interests of the national government. Furthermore, lower federal courts were perceived as an unnecessary expense and a likely intrusion on the sovereignty of the state governments. Farrand explains: "[Inferior courts] were regarded as an encroachment upon the rights of the individual states. It was claimed that the state courts were perfectly competent for the work required, and that it would be quite sufficient to grant an appeal from them to the national supreme court."[8]

But others expressed distrust in the ability and willingness of state courts to uphold federal law. James Madison stated, "Confidence cannot be put in the State Tribunals as guardians of the National authority and interests."[9] Madison argued that state judges were likely to be biased against federal law and could not be trusted, especially in instances where there were conflicting state and federal interests.[10] Appeal to the Supreme Court was claimed to be inadequate to protect federal interests because the number of such appeals would exceed the Court's limited capacity to hear and decide cases.

Thus, the question of whether state courts are equal to federal courts in their willingness and ability to uphold federal law—an issue that continues to be debated and that influences a great many aspects of the law of federal jurisdiction[11]—has its origins in the earliest discussions of the federal judicial power. The proposal to create lower federal courts was initially defeated five votes to four, with two states divided.[12]

Madison and James Wilson then proposed a compromise. They suggested that the Constitution mandate the existence of the Supreme Court, but leave it up to Congress whether to create inferior federal courts. They said that "there was a distinction between establishing such tribunals absolutely, and giving a discretion

[7] 1 Farrand, *supra* note 3, at 104-105.

[8] Farrand, *supra* note 4, at 79-80. For example, John Rutledge stated at the Convention, "[T]he State Tribunals might and ought to be left in all cases to decide in the first instance the right of appeal to the supreme national tribunal being sufficient to secure the national rights [and] uniformity of judgments." 1 Farrand, *supra* note 3, at 124.

[9] 2 Farrand, *supra* note 3, at 27.

[10] *Id.*

[11] This question of whether federal courts are equal to state courts in their ability and willingness to protect federal rights is often referred to as the question of the "parity" between federal and state courts. *See* Burt Neuborne, The Myth of Parity, 90 Harv. L. Rev. 1105 (1977). The issue of parity is discussed in §1.5 and recurs in discussions throughout this book.

[12] 1 Farrand, *supra* note 3, at 125.

to the Legislature to establish or not establish them."[13] Their proposal was adopted by a vote of eight states to two, with one state divided.[14] Congress, in its first judiciary act, established lower federal courts, and they have existed ever since.[15]

Insulates Federal Judges via Life Tenure and Salary Protections

Third, Article III assures the independence of the federal judiciary by according all federal judges life tenure, "during good Behaviour," and salaries that cannot be decreased during their time in office. In the American colonies, judges were appointed by the king of England and served at his pleasure.[16] There was great dissatisfaction with a court system beholden to the king and unresponsive to the needs of the colonists. The enumeration of grievances in the Declaration of Independence stated that the king "made judges dependent upon his will alone for the tenure of their offices and payment of their salaries."

Seeking to insulate federal judges from such direct control, the drafters of Article III granted life tenure to federal judges, assuming good behavior, and salaries that cannot be decreased. In fact, a crucial lasting difference between federal and state court judges is the electoral accountability of the latter. In thirty-nine states, state court judges are subject to some form of electoral review.[17] Some contend that this difference makes federal courts uniquely suited for the protection of constitutional rights.[18]

Important contemporary issues exist with regard to Article III's assurance of life tenure and salary protection.[19] For example, under what circumstances may Congress create tribunals, often termed "legislative courts," in which the judges do not have life tenure and guaranteed salary during their terms of office? This question is addressed in Chapter 4. Also, may Congress provide methods for

[13] *Id.*

[14] *Id.*

[15] The Judiciary Act of 1789 is discussed in §1.2, *infra.* There are revisionist views of Article III that argue that the Convention intended for lower federal courts to exist. *See* 1 Julius Goebel, History of the Supreme Court: Antecedents and Beginnings to 1801, at 247 (1971) (arguing that change in wording done by the Committee of Style is responsible for the language that appears to accord Congress discretion to decide whether to create lower federal courts); *see also* Robert N. Clinton, A Mandatory View of Federal Court Jurisdiction: A Guided Quest for the Original Understanding of Article III, 132 U. Pa. L. Rev. 741 (1984). Whether lower federal courts must exist, and under what circumstances, is discussed in §3.3, *infra.*

[16] Jerome R. Corsi, Judicial Politics: An Introduction 104 (1984).

[17] *See* Williams-Yulee v. Florida State Bar, 575 U.S. 433, 437 (2015) ("[i]n 39 States, voters elect trial or appellate judges at the polls").

[18] *See, e.g.,* Martin H. Redish, Constitutional Limitations on Congressional Power to Control Federal Jurisdiction: A Reaction to Professor Sager, 77 Nw. U. L. Rev. 143 (1982); Neuborne, *supra* note 11, at 1124; *but see* Michael E. Solimine & James L. Walker, Constitutional Litigation in Federal and State Courts: An Empirical Analysis of Judicial Parity, 10 Hastings Const. L.Q. 213, 230-231 (1983) ("[i]t does not follow, however, that elections of state judges. . . will influence subsequent decisions of elected judges"). *See* §1.5, discussing the issue of parity.

[19] Additionally, there is an ongoing debate over the meaning of judicial independence. *See, e.g.,* Charles G. Geyh, When Courts and Congress Collide: The Struggle for Control of America's Judicial System (2006).

disciplining judges short of impeachment? In 1980, Congress adopted a statute that allows federal judicial councils, composed of district and appeals court judges within a circuit, to discipline federal judges by private censure, public censure, temporary suspension of caseloads, and recommendation of impeachment.[20] The constitutionality of this act is uncertain and depends on whether impeachment will be regarded as the exclusive means for disciplining federal judges.[21] On the one hand, there is concern with preserving judicial independence, but on the other, there is a perceived need for a method to discipline judges short of impeachment, which is rarely used, as well as a process to deal with senile judges. Also, in recent years, there has been significant attention as to whether there should be term limits for Supreme Court justices and whether this would require a constitutional amendment.[22]

"Cases" and "Controversies" that Can Be Heard by Federal Courts

Fourth, Article III defines the federal judicial power in terms of nine categories of "cases" and "controversies." These nine categories fall into two major types of provisions.[23] One set of clauses authorizes the federal courts to vindicate and enforce the powers of the federal government. For example, the federal courts have the authority to decide all cases arising under the Constitution, treaties, and laws of the United States. Additionally, the federal courts have the ability to hear all cases in which the United States is a party. The federal government's powers in the area of foreign policy are protected by according the federal courts the authority to hear all cases affecting ambassadors, other public ministers, and consuls; to hear all cases of admiralty and maritime jurisdiction; and to hear cases between a state, or its citizens, and a foreign country or its citizens.

A second set of provisions authorizes the federal courts to serve an interstate umpiring function, resolving disputes between states and their citizens. Thus,

[20] Judicial Councils Reform and Judicial Conduct and Disability Act of 1980, Pub. L. No. 96-458, 94 Stat. 2035 (1980).

[21] *See, e.g.,* Hastings v. Judicial Conference of the United States, 593 F. Supp. 1371 (D.D.C. 1984) (holding the act constitutional), *rev'd,* 770 F.2d 1093 (D.C. Cir. 1985) (holding case was not ripe for adjudication), *cert. denied,* 477 U.S. 904 (1986); In the Matter of Certain Complaints Under Investigation by an Investigating Comm. of the Judicial Council of the Eleventh Circuit, 783 F.2d 1488 (11th Cir. 1986), *cert. denied,* 477 U.S. 904 (1986) (upholding the act as constitutional); Hastings v. Judicial Conference of the United States, 829 F.2d 91 (D.C. Cir. 1987) (holding that the act and recommendation of impeachment by judicial council are constitutional); *see also* Lynn A. Baker, Note, Unnecessary and Improper: The Judicial Councils Reform and Judicial Conduct and Disability Act of 1980, 94 Yale L.J. 1117 (1985).

[22] *See, e.g.,* Final Report, Presidential Commission on the Supreme Court (2021) https://www.whitehouse.gov/pcscotus/final-report/ (discussing the issue of term limits and whether it would require a constitutional amendment).

[23] Professor Frank divides the nine categories into three types of provisions: those relating to an effective national government, to international affairs, and to property and trade. Frank, *supra* note 1, at 12-14. Hart and Wechsler divide these nine categories into four types of provisions: vindication of federal authority, foreign affairs, interstate umpiring, and controversies between citizens of different states. Fallon et al., *supra* note 2, at 13-18.

Article III gives the federal courts the authority to decide controversies between two or more states, between a state and citizens of another state,[24] between citizens of different states, and between citizens of the same state claiming land in other states.

The Supreme Court has interpreted the terms "cases" and "controversies" as creating important limits on federal judicial power. These restrictions, often grouped under the label *justiciability*, are discussed in Chapter 2. Also, a central question concerning these provisions is whether they create the minimum or the maximum of federal court jurisdiction. Can Congress restrict the jurisdiction of the federal courts to hear controversial matters falling within Article III's enumeration of authority? Alternatively, may Congress expand the federal courts' authority to hear matters that previously were heard in state courts and are not mentioned in Article III? These questions are addressed in Chapter 3, which considers the ability of Congress to control the jurisdiction of the federal courts.

Allocates Authority Between Supreme Court and Lower Courts

Fifth, Article III allocates judicial power between the Supreme Court and the lower federal courts. Article III states that the Supreme Court has original jurisdiction over cases affecting ambassadors, other public ministers and consuls, and those in which a state shall be a party. In all other cases, the Supreme Court is granted appellate jurisdiction, both as to law and fact, subject to "such Exceptions and under such regulations as Congress shall make."

The Supreme Court has held that Congress can give the lower federal courts concurrent jurisdiction even over those matters where the Constitution specifies that the Supreme Court has original jurisdiction.[25] Under contemporary practice, the Supreme Court's original jurisdiction is limited to disputes between two or more states.[26] An unresolved controversial issue is whether Congress may use its power to create exceptions to the Supreme Court's appellate jurisdiction to prevent Supreme Court review in particular areas, such as over state laws regulating abortion or permitting school prayer. This question is discussed in §3.2.

Trial by Jury and Defines Treason

Sixth, Article III prescribes that the trial of all crimes, except in cases of impeachment, shall be by jury. Furthermore, it requires that the trial shall occur in the state where the crime was committed.

[24] Some of these provisions were modified by the Eleventh Amendment, which provides that the judicial power of the United States does not extend to cases between a state and citizens of a different state or citizens of foreign nations. The Eleventh Amendment and the issue of sovereign immunity are discussed in detail in Chapter 7.

[25] *See, e.g.*, Ames v. Kansas ex rel. Johnston, 111 U.S. 449, 464 (1884) (allowing concurrent jurisdiction over suits by ambassadors).

[26] *See* §10.3, *infra*.

Finally, Article III provides that treason shall consist only in "levying war" against the United States or giving aid or comfort to the enemy and that no person shall be convicted of treason except on testimony of two witnesses or on confession in open court. Article III concludes by stating that Congress has the power to prescribe the punishments for treason, but that "no Attainder of Treason shall work corruption of blood, or Forfeiture except during the Life of the Person attained." In other words, the traitor's heirs and descendants may be punished only for their own wrongdoing.

What the Framers Chose Not to Adopt

Having surveyed what is included in Article III, it is useful to note what the Framers chose not to adopt. Article III does not expressly accord federal courts the power to declare federal and state laws unconstitutional. There were proposals at the Constitutional Convention to create a Council of Revision, composed of the president and members of the national judiciary. The Council of Revision would have reviewed "every act of the National Legislature before it [went into effect]."[27] The proposal for a Council of Revision was defended as a check on legislative powers and as a vehicle to improve the legislative process,[28] but the proposal was defeated every time it was raised. Opponents successfully argued that it was undesirable to involve the judiciary directly in the lawmaking process.[29]

There have been over two centuries of debate as to whether the rejection of the Council of Revision also was an implicit rejection of the power of the federal courts to declare statutes unconstitutional.[30] Arguments are made on both sides, and Professor Monaghan expressed the view that it is "increasingly doubtful that any conclusive case can be made one way or the other."[31] However, after more than 200 years of constitutional judicial review, the power of the federal courts, and especially of the U.S. Supreme Court, to invalidate unconstitutional laws is seen as an established and integral part of American government.

Also, Article III does not specify the relationship between the jurisdiction of the federal and state courts. The Constitution is unclear whether federal jurisdiction was meant to be exclusive of the states or concurrent with state courts. As discussed in Chapter 5, the practice since 1789 has been to allow state courts

[27] 1 Farrand, *supra* note 3, at 21 (for a discussion of the proposed Council of Revision, *see id.* at 97-110).

[28] Fallon et al., *supra* note 2, at 12.

[29] 2 Farrand, *supra* note 3, at 328-329.

[30] For arguments that judicial review was intended by the Framers, *see, e.g.*, Raoul Berger, Congress v. The Supreme Court (1969); Gordon S. Wood, The Creation of the American Republic (1969); Saikrishna B. Prakash & John C. Yoo, The Origins of Judicial Review, 70 U. Chi. L. Rev. 887 (2003). For arguments that judicial review was not intended by the Framers, *see, e.g.*, 2 William Winslow Crosskey, Politics and the Constitution 1008-1046 (1953); Louis Boudianoff Boudin, Government by Judiciary (1932). For a contemporary argument against judicial review, *see* James MacGregor Burns, Packing the Court: The Rise of Judicial Power and the Coming Crisis of the Supreme Court 253 (2009).

[31] Henry Paul Monaghan, The Constitution Goes to Harvard, 13 Harv. C.R.-C.L. L. Rev. 117, 125 (1978).

to exercise concurrent jurisdiction with federal courts except in instances where Congress specifies that federal courts are to exercise exclusive jurisdiction.

During the ratification process, Article III attracted some opposition, but it was not one of the major targets for attack.[32] Critics focused on the absence of a provision requiring jury trials in civil cases, on the Supreme Court's authority to review on appeal matters of fact as well as issues of law, and especially on the authority for diversity jurisdiction.[33] In the *Federalist Papers,* written to persuade New York to ratify the Constitution, James Madison and Alexander Hamilton wrote five essays dealing with the federal courts, including Hamilton's famous declaration that the courts are the "least dangerous branch" of government.[34]

§1.2 THE JUDICIARY ACT OF 1789

Importance of the Judiciary Act of 1789

The first session of Congress adopted a statute creating lower federal courts and defining the jurisdiction of the federal judiciary. The Judiciary Act of 1789 was crucial in determining the nature of the federal courts.[1] Many decisions made by Congress in adopting this statute have been followed throughout American history. For example, lower federal courts have existed since 1789, although the Constitution leaves their creation up to Congress. Also, by vesting the federal courts with less than the full jurisdiction authorized in Article III, the Judiciary Act established that federal courts may hear a case only if there is both constitutional and statutory authority.[2]

Several provisions of the Judiciary Act have never been changed significantly. For example, the Rules of Decision Act, adopted as §34 of the 1789 law, provides that the "laws of the several states, except where the constitution or treaties of the United States or Acts of Congress shall otherwise require or decide, shall be regarded as rules of decision in civil actions in the courts of the United States."[3] Although the Supreme Court's interpretation of this law has changed markedly

[32] Frank, *supra* note 1, at 3 ("the judiciary clauses were almost immune from strenuous criticism or discussion").

[33] *Id.,* at 3 n.1.

[34] The Federalist No. 78, at 465 (A. Hamilton) (C. Rossiter ed. 1961).

§1.2 [1] The Judiciary Act of 1789, ch. 20, 1 Stat. 73, 92 (1789). For a particularly important and thorough history of the act, *see* Charles Warren, New Light on the History of the Federal Judiciary Act of 1789, 37 Harv. L. Rev. 49 (1923). *See also* Felix Frankfurter & James M. Landis, The Business of the Supreme Court (1927).

[2] The ability of Congress to control federal court jurisdiction is discussed in Chapter 3. The doctrines concerning federal subject matter jurisdiction are overviewed in §1.4 and discussed in Chapter 5.

[3] 28 U.S.C. §1652 (1982). The one change in the Rules of Decision Act since 1789 has been the substitution of the words "civil action" for "trial at common law."

over time, this provision is the key reason federal courts apply state law in diversity cases.[4]

Additionally, the Judiciary Act is especially important in understanding the federal court system because of the identity of its drafters. The Supreme Court observed that the act "was passed by the first Congress assembled under the Constitution, many members of which had taken part in framing that instrument, and is contemporaneous and weighty evidence of its true meaning."[5] The primary drafter of the statute was Oliver Ellsworth, previously an important delegate at the Constitutional Convention and later the second chief justice of the United States.

Structure of the Judiciary

The Judiciary Act reflected important choices as to both the structure of the federal court system and the appropriate content of its caseload. Structurally, the act created three levels of federal courts. The lowest tier was composed of the federal district courts. At least one such court was created for each state—a practice that continues to this day. The federal district courts had original jurisdiction of admiralty cases, minor civil matters, and civil cases brought by the United States exceeding more than $100.[6]

The middle level of the federal judiciary was termed the circuit courts. These tribunals were not assigned permanent judges. Rather, the courts were to hold two sessions a year, which were to be staffed by two Supreme Court justices and one district court judge. Soon after its adoption, the act was amended in 1793 to permit circuit courts to be staffed by one Supreme Court justice and one district court judge.[7] The practice of making the Supreme Court justices ride circuit rather than appointing permanent judges to the courts of appeals continued for more than 100 years. Without a doubt, from the time of its passage, the most criticized aspect of the Judiciary Act of 1789 was the requirement that Supreme Court justices travel around the country serving as circuit court judges.

Three such circuit courts were created for the entire country, encompassing all of the states except Kentucky and Maine, which were considered remote and were the subject of special arrangements.[8] The circuit courts had both original and appellate jurisdiction. These tribunals had original jurisdiction over most federal crimes and over diversity cases worth more than $500. Also, the circuit courts had original jurisdiction for suits brought by the United States with an amount in controversy greater than $500. The circuit courts had appellate jurisdiction from the district courts in civil cases where more than $50 was at stake, and in admiralty and maritime cases worth more than $300.

The act additionally specified that there would be six Supreme Court justices. The act granted the Court the original jurisdiction provided by the Constitution

[4] *See* §5.3.5, *infra* (discussing the law applied by the federal courts in diversity cases).

[5] Wisconsin v. Pelican Ins. Co., 127 U.S. 265, 297 (1888).

[6] 1 Stat. 73, §9.

[7] Act of Mar. 2, 1793, ch. 22, 1 Stat. 333.

[8] *Id.* §§3, 4.

and authorized the Supreme Court to hear appeals from the circuit courts in civil cases worth more than $2,000. No authority was granted for the Supreme Court to review criminal convictions. Additionally, in the famous §25, the act provided for judicial review of the final decisions of the highest state courts that ruled against a federal claimant. Specifically, the Supreme Court had the authority to review final judgments of a state court that ruled a federal treaty or statute invalid, upheld a state law against a claim that it violated federal law, or ruled against any right or privilege claimed under federal law.[9]

In other words, under the Judiciary Act of 1789, federal court review was not permitted of state court decisions ruling in favor of a person raising a federal law issue.

The creation of lower federal courts was an important decision that has been followed throughout American history. Another precedent-setting practice was the authorization for removal jurisdiction—the ability of the parties to remove certain cases from state to federal court. The Constitution does not speak of removal jurisdiction. Nonetheless, the Judiciary Act of 1789 allowed removal from state to federal courts of cases worth more than $500 involving an alien defendant and of cases where a plaintiff sues in his or her home state court against an out-of-state defendant.[10] Removal jurisdiction has existed ever since.[11]

The most notable omission from the Judiciary Act of 1789 was authority for the federal courts to hear cases arising under the Constitution, treaties, and laws of the United States. No provision created general federal question jurisdiction until 1875. However, congressional statutes on particular topics authorized judicial review of cases arising under those specific enactments.

Although much has changed in the structure of the federal judiciary since 1789, much has remained the same. The framework devised over 200 years ago has been remarkably resilient.

§1.3 *MARBURY V. MADISON* AND THE MEANING OF ARTICLE III

Factual Background

Marbury v. Madison is the single most important decision in American constitutional law and in defining the role of the federal courts.[1] The factual background is familiar.[2] The presidential election of 1800 was fiercely contested among four candidates: the incumbent, John Adams, Thomas Jefferson, Aaron Burr, and

[9] 1 Stat. 73, §25.

[10] *Id.* §12.

[11] Removal jurisdiction is currently provided for in 28 U.S.C. §§1441-1446 and is discussed in §5.5, *infra.*

§1.3 [1] 5 U.S. (1 Cranch) 137 (1803).

[2] For excellent reviews of the factual background and of the Supreme Court's decision, *see* Burt Neuborne, Madison's Music 146-194 (2015); Symposium: *Marbury* and Its Legacy: A Symposium to

Charles Pinckney. Jefferson received a majority of the popular vote but tied in the electoral vote with Burr. The clear losers were Adams and Pinckney.

In January 1801, Adams's secretary of state, John Marshall, was named to serve as the third chief justice of the U.S. Supreme Court. Throughout the remainder of Adams's presidency, Marshall served as both secretary of state and chief justice. Adams was a Federalist, and the Federalists in Congress were determined to exercise their influence before the Republican, Jefferson, took office. On February 13, 1801, Congress enacted the Circuit Court Act, which reduced the number of Supreme Court justices from six to five, decreasing the opportunity for Republican control of the Court.[3] The act also eliminated the Supreme Court justices' duty to serve as circuit court judges and created sixteen new judgeships on the circuit courts. However, this change was short-lived; in 1802, Congress repealed this statute, restoring the practice of circuit riding by Supreme Court justices and eliminating the newly created circuit court judgeships. The constitutionality of congressional abolition of judgeships was not tested in the courts.

On February 27, 1801, less than a week before the end of Adams's term, Congress adopted the Organic Act of the District of Columbia, which authorized the president to appoint forty-two justices of the peace. Adams announced his nominations on March 2, and on March 3, the day before Jefferson's inauguration, the Senate confirmed the nominees. Immediately, Secretary of State (and Chief Justice) John Marshall signed the commissions of these individuals and dispatched his brother, James Marshall, to deliver the commissions. A few commissions, including one for William Marbury, were not delivered before Jefferson's inauguration. President Jefferson instructed his secretary of state, James Madison, to withhold the commissions.

Marbury filed suit in the U.S. Supreme Court seeking a writ of mandamus to compel Madison, as secretary of state, to deliver the commission. Marbury claimed that the Judiciary Act of 1789 authorized the Supreme Court to grant mandamus in a proceeding filed originally in the Supreme Court. Although Marbury's petition was filed in December 1801, the Supreme Court did not hear the case until 1803 because Congress, by statute, abolished the June and December 1802 Terms of the Supreme Court.

The Supreme Court ruled against Marbury and held that it could not hear the case as a matter of original jurisdiction. The Court held that although the Judiciary Act of 1789 authorized such jurisdiction, the statute was unconstitutional and hence void.

The brilliance of John Marshall's opinion cannot be overstated. Politically, he had little choice but to deny Marbury relief. The Jefferson administration surely would have refused to obey a writ of mandamus, which would have undermined

---

Mark the 200th Anniversary of Marbury v. Madison, 72 Geo. Wash. L. Rev. 1 (2003); Symposium: Marbury v. Madison: A Bicentennial Symposium, 89 Va. L. Rev. 1105 (2003); Symposium: Judging Judicial Review: *Marbury* in the Modern Era, 101 Mich. L. Rev. 2557 (2003); William W. Van Alstyne, A Critical Guide to Marbury v. Madison, 1969 Duke L.J. 1.

[3] The Circuit Court Act, ch. 4, 2 Stat. 89 (1801). *See* Kathryn Turner, The Midnight Judges, 109 U. Pa. L. Rev. 494 (1961).

the Court's powers at the outset of American history. In addition, there was a real possibility that Jefferson might seek the impeachment of Federalist justices in an attempt to gain Republican control of the judiciary. One judge, albeit a clearly incompetent jurist, already had been impeached, and later, not long after his removal, the House of Representatives impeached Supreme Court Justice Samuel Chase on the grounds that he had made electioneering statements from the bench and had criticized the repeal of the 1801 Circuit Court Act.[4] Yet John Marshall did more than simply rule in favor of the Jefferson administration; he used the occasion of deciding *Marbury v. Madison* to establish the power of the judiciary and to articulate a role for the federal courts that survives to this day.

Marbury's Principles Concerning the Federal Judiciary

The Supreme Court's opinion in *Marbury v. Madison* established five important principles concerning the federal judiciary. First, *Marbury* established the power of the federal courts to review the actions of the executive branch of government. Chief Justice Marshall's opinion explained that the Court was authorized to give relief against the executive because "[t]he very essence of civil liberty certainly consists in the right of every individual to claim the protection of the laws, whenever he receives an injury."[5] The Court concluded that no person, not even the president or executive officials, can ignore the law. The Court stated: "But when the legislature proceeds to impose on that officer other duties; when he is directed peremptorily to perform certain acts; when the rights of individuals are dependent on the performance of those acts; he is so far the officer of the law; is amenable to the laws for his conduct; and cannot at his discretion sport away the vested rights of others."[6] Thus, the Court said that the judiciary could, assuming proper jurisdiction, issue a writ of mandamus to the executive.

The Court's claimed authority to review executive actions drew the most contemporary criticism.[7] But because the Court announced this power in a case in which it ruled in favor of the president, there was neither a confrontation nor an opportunity for the president to disregard a judicial order. The power of the federal courts to review presidential actions is responsible for many important Supreme Court decisions throughout American history. Perhaps most notably, in *United States v. Nixon*, the Court's holding—that the president had to comply with a subpoena to provide tapes of conversations for use in a criminal trial—led to the resignation of President Richard Nixon.[8]

[4] *See* William H. Rehnquist, Grand Inquests: The Historic Impeachments of Justice Samuel Chase and President Andrew Johnson (1992).

[5] 5 U.S. at 163.

[6] *Id.* at 166.

[7] 1 Charles Warren, The Supreme Court in United States History 232 (rev. ed. 1926) ("Contemporary writings make it very clear that the Republicans attacked the decision, not so much because it sustained the power of the Court to determine the validity of Congressional legislation, as because it announced the doctrine that the Court might issue mandamus to a Cabinet official who was acting by the direction of the President.").

[8] 418 U.S. 683 (1974).

Second, the Court in *Marbury* announced that there was a category of issues, termed "political questions," that were not reviewable by the federal courts. In explaining the judiciary's authority to review executive conduct, the Court drew a distinction between those matters committed solely to the executive's discretion and those where an individual right was at stake. The former, labeled political questions, were deemed not justiciable. Chief Justice Marshall wrote: "By the Constitution of the United States, the President is invested with certain important political powers, in the exercise of which he is to use his own discretion, and is accountable only to his country in his political character.... The subjects are political. They respect the nation, not individual rights."[9]

Thus, *Marbury v. Madison* can be credited with originating the political question doctrine: a principle that certain matters are not judicially reviewable because they are committed to the other branches of government. The political question doctrine is discussed in §2.6. As explained in that section, however, the modern political question doctrine is quite different from that articulated in *Marbury*. Under current law, the political question doctrine consigns certain allegations of constitutional violations to the other branches of government for adjudication and decision, even if all other jurisdictional and justiciability requirements are met.[10] But under *Marbury*, the Court is quite explicit that review is available for an allegation of an unconstitutional government action that harms an individual. Therefore, only if no individual claimed a personal injury could there be a political question. As such, the political question doctrine articulated in *Marbury* might be best understood as a predecessor of the modern standing doctrine, which requires individuals to allege an injury to obtain federal court review.[11]

Third, *Marbury* establishes that Article III creates the ceiling on the Supreme Court's original jurisdiction; that is, Congress cannot authorize original jurisdiction greater than that provided for within Article III. The Supreme Court read §13 of the Judiciary Act of 1789 as authorizing mandamus as part of the Court's original jurisdiction. It should be noted that this section did not explicitly provide such authority. Section 13 stated, in part:

> The Supreme Court shall also have appellate jurisdiction from the circuit courts and the courts of the several states, in the cases herein after specially provided for; and shall have power to issue writs of prohibition to the district courts, when proceeding as courts of admiralty and maritime jurisdiction, and writs of mandamus, in cases warranted by the principles and usages of law, to any courts appointed, or persons holding offices, under the authority of the United States.[12]

Although the Court viewed this statute as granting it original jurisdiction over requests for mandamus, alternative readings seem even more plausible.[13] For example, the statute might be read as pertaining only to the Court's appellate

[9] 5 U.S. at 165-166.
[10] *See* §2.6, *infra*.
[11] The standing requirements are discussed in detail in §2.3.
[12] The Judiciary Act of 1789, 1 Stat. 73, 81, §13.
[13] *See* Van Alstyne, *supra* note 2, at 14-16.

jurisdiction because that is the only type of jurisdiction mentioned. Alternatively, the statute might simply be understood as according the Court authority to issue mandamus, where appropriate, in cases properly within its jurisdiction. By this reading, the statute does not create original jurisdiction, but simply grants the Court remedial powers when it has jurisdiction. Under either of these approaches, Marbury still would have lost, but the Court would have avoided the question as to whether the statute was constitutional and thus would have lost the opportunity to announce its power to declare statutes unconstitutional.

The Court, however, said that the statute provided it original jurisdiction and held that this grant of authority was unconstitutional. The Court concluded that Article III enumerated its original jurisdiction and that Congress could not enlarge it. Chief Justice Marshall stated: "If it had been intended to leave it in the discretion of the legislature to apportion the judicial power between the supreme and inferior courts according to the will of that body, it would certainly have been useless to have proceeded further than to have defined the judicial power, and the tribunals in which it should be vested."[14]

Justice Marshall's analysis certainly is open to question. Article III's enumeration of the Court's original jurisdiction still has meaning even if Congress can increase it. Article III might be viewed as the floor, the minimum grant of original jurisdiction that cannot be reduced by Congress. Irrespective of possible alternative interpretations, the Court's holding that Congress cannot increase the Supreme Court's original jurisdiction remains the law to this day. However, the Court's statement that the categories of original and appellate jurisdiction are mutually exclusive has not been followed. The Supreme Court subsequently held that Congress could grant the district courts concurrent jurisdiction over matters within the Court's original jurisdiction.[15]

More generally, by viewing Article III as the ceiling of federal jurisdiction, *Marbury* helped establish the principle that federal courts are courts of limited jurisdiction. Federal courts may not hear matters unless there is constitutional authority, and Congress may not expand the jurisdiction granted in Article III of the Constitution. These principles survive to this day and are important in limiting congressional authority to override constitutional doctrines, such as standing, and to expand the subject matter jurisdiction of the federal courts.[16]

Fourth, and most important, *Marbury v. Madison* established the power of the federal courts to declare federal statutes unconstitutional. Chief Justice Marshall's opinion concluded that the grant of original jurisdiction to issue mandamus was inconsistent with the Constitution. He then stated: "The question, whether an act, repugnant to the constitution, can become the law of the land, is a question deeply interesting to the United States; but, happily, not of an intricacy proportioned to its interest."[17] Marshall offered several reasons why the Court could declare federal

[14] 5 U.S. at 174.

[15] *See, e.g.,* Ames v. Kansas ex rel. Johnston, 111 U.S. 449 (1884); *see* §10.3.1, *infra.*

[16] Standing is discussed in §2.3, and subject matter jurisdiction is discussed in Chapter 5, *see* §5.1.

[17] 5 U.S. at 176.

statutes unconstitutional; none of these arguments conclusively establishes his position.[18] In fact, there are arguments on both sides as to the legitimacy of constitutional judicial review under the Constitution.[19] However, after 190 years, it is a practice that is firmly entrenched and not open to serious debate.

Marshall argued, for example, that the Constitution imposes limits on government powers and that those limits are meaningless unless subject to judicial enforcement. Borrowing from Alexander Hamilton's arguments in *Federalist No. 78*, the Court stated: "The powers of the legislature are defined, and limited; and that those limits may not be mistaken, or forgotten, the constitution is written."[20] This is a powerful argument for judicial review, but it must be remembered that many other nations exist with written constitutions without according the judiciary the power to invalidate conflicting statutes.[21]

Marshall also argued that the Court's authority to decide cases arising under the Constitution implied the power to declare unconstitutional laws conflicting with the basic legal charter. But as Professor David Currie explains, "[J]urisdiction over 'cases arising under this Constitution' need not mean the Constitution is supreme over federal laws as well as over executive or state action."[22] In other words, the Court's power to decide cases under the Constitution still could have significant content even if the judiciary lacked the power to invalidate federal statutes. The Court would apply federal statutes to decide cases and could evaluate the constitutionality of state enactments.

Chief Justice Marshall additionally defended judicial review on the ground that judges take an oath of office and that they would violate this oath if they enforced unconstitutional laws. But this argument is question begging: judges would not violate their oath by enforcing unconstitutional laws if they did not have the power to strike down such statutes.[23] In a famous state court dissenting opinion that argued against judicial review, Justice Gibson stated: "[The] oath to support the constitution is not peculiar to the judges, but is taken indiscriminately by every officer of the government, and is designed rather as a test of the political principles of the man, than to bind the officer in the discharge of his duty."[24]

The point of this discussion is not, of course, to argue that Chief Justice Marshall was wrong or that judicial review is illegitimate. History has proven the opposite. Rather, the point is that constitutional judicial review was not axiomatic or unassailable; it had to be established by the Supreme Court, and John Marshall

[18] For an argument that the Constitution's text, structure, and history support judicial review, *see* Saikrishna B. Prakash & John C. Yoo, The Origins of Judicial Review, 70 U. Chi. L. Rev. 887 (2003).

[19] *See* §1.1, text accompanying notes 30-34 (explaining dispute over whether the Framers of the Constitution intended to allow constitutional judicial review). *See* John Harrison, The Constitutional Origins and Implications of Judicial Review, 84 Va. L. Rev. 333 (1998) (arguing that the text of the Constitution justifies judicial review).

[20] 5 U.S. at 176. *See* The Federalist No. 78, at 446-469 (A. Hamilton) (C. Rossiter ed. 1961).

[21] *See, e.g.*, Mauro Cappelletti & John Clarke Adams, Judicial Review of Legislation: European Antecedents and Adaptations, 79 Harv. L. Rev. 1207 (1966).

[22] David P. Currie, Federal Courts: Cases and Materials 27 (3d ed. 1982).

[23] *Id.*

[24] Eakin v. Raub, 12 Serg. & Rawls. 330 (Pa. 1825) (Gibson, J., dissenting), *reprinted in* Gerald Gunther, Constitutional Law 11 (11th ed. 1985).

found the ideal occasion. He established judicial review while declaring unconstitutional a statute that he read as expanding the Court's powers. The particular statutory provision invalidated was relatively minor, and Marshall's holding was a victory for his opponents.

Fifth and finally, *Marbury* appears to establish the Court as the authoritative interpreter of the Constitution. Perhaps the most frequently quoted part of the decision is the declaration: "It is emphatically the province and duty of the judicial department to say what the law is."[25] This statement is read as establishing not only that the Court gets a voice in evaluating the constitutionality of statutes but also that it has the decisive say.

Alternative Views as to Who Is Authoritative

Marbury actually is ambiguous about which branch is the authoritative interpreter of the Constitution.[26] In fact, there are three different positions concerning who is the authoritative interpreter of the Constitution, and *Marbury* can be read as supporting any of them.[27] One view is that there is no authoritative interpreter of the Constitution; each branch of government interprets the Constitution for itself, and disagreements are resolved through persuasion and power. Thomas Jefferson and Andrew Jackson expressed this position early in American history,[28] and former Attorney General Edwin Meese subsequently articulated it.[29] By this view, *Marbury* establishes only that the Court has a voice, not that the Court's views are binding on the other branches of government, which must independently interpret the Constitution.

A second position is that for each part of the Constitution, one branch of government is assigned the role of serving as the final arbiter of disputes as to the Constitution's meaning, but it is not the same branch for all parts of the Constitution. For example, when the Court declares that certain matters are political questions, it holds that constitutional interpretation of these questions is to be resolved by the other branches of government.[30] Arguably, *Marbury v. Madison* establishes only that the Court is authoritative in interpreting Article III of the Constitution, which determines the judiciary's power.

A third view is that the judiciary is the authoritative arbiter of the meaning of all constitutional provisions. Although each branch of government interprets the

[25] 5 U.S. at 177.

[26] *See* Laurence Tribe, American Constitutional Law 32-42 (2d ed. 1989).

[27] These three approaches are detailed in Erwin Chemerinsky, Interpreting the Constitution 82-85 (1987).

[28] Thomas Jefferson, letter to Abigail Adams (Sept. 11, 1804), 8 The Writings of Thomas Jefferson 310 (Ford ed. 1897), *quoted in* Gunther, *supra* note 24, at 22; Andrew Jackson, Veto Message (July 10, 1832), 2 Messages and Papers of the Presidents 576, 581 (Richardson ed. 1896), *quoted in* Gunther, *supra* note 24, at 22.

[29] Edwin Meese, The Law of the Constitution, 61 Tul. L. Rev. 979, 985-986 (1987). For a very different approach to defending the view that the Court is not authoritative, based on "popular constitutionalism," *see* Larry D. Kramer, The People Themselves: Popular Constitutionalism and Judicial Review (2004).

[30] *See* §2.6, *infra*.

Constitution in carrying out its responsibilities, the federal courts serve as the ultimate arbiter when disputes arise about the Constitution's meaning. In *United States v. Nixon,* for example, Chief Justice Burger, in rejecting the president's claim that it was for the executive to determine the scope of executive privilege, wrote: "The President's counsel . . . reads the Constitution as providing an absolute privilege of confidentiality for all Presidential communications. Many decisions of this Court, however, have unequivocally reaffirmed the holding of *Marbury v. Madison*. . . that '[i]t is emphatically the province and duty of the judicial department to say what the law is.'"[31] Similarly, in *Cooper v. Aaron,* in rejecting a state's claim that it could disregard federal court desegregation orders, the Supreme Court invoked *Marbury v. Madison* and stated: "[*Marbury*] declared the basic principle that the federal judiciary is supreme in the exposition of the law of the Constitution, and that principle ever since has been respected by this Court and the Country as a permanent and indispensable feature of our constitutional system."[32]

But *Nixon* also could be read as supporting the second approach, establishing that the judiciary has the final say in assuring the availability of evidence for criminal trials. *Cooper* is concerned with the obligation of state governments to follow Supreme Court decisions. Thus, *Marbury* did not resolve the question of who is the authoritative interpreter of the Constitution. Nor have the experiences of the past 200 years provided a conclusive choice among these three approaches.[33]

§1.4 THE STRUCTURE AND AUTHORITY OF THE FEDERAL COURTS: A HISTORY OF FEDERAL JURISDICTION SINCE THE JUDICIARY ACT OF 1789

§1.4.1 Introduction

Docket Pressure Motivates Reforms

The federal court system currently includes the Supreme Court, thirteen courts of appeals, ninety-four federal district courts, and several specialized federal courts and many administrative agencies that have the authority to decide matters included within Article III's enumeration of cases or controversies.[1] This structure,

[31] 418 U.S. 683, 703 (1974).

[32] 358 U.S. 1, 18 (1958). For an excellent defense of Cooper v. Aaron and the view that the Court should be the authoritative interpreter of the Constitution, *see* Larry Alexander & Frederick Schauer, On Extra Judicial Constitutional Interpretation, 110 Harv. L. Rev. 1359 (1997).

[33] For an argument that the judiciary should be the authoritative arbiter of the meaning of all constitutional provisions, *see* Chemerinsky, *supra* note 27, at 86-105.

§1.4 [1] For an excellent empirical examination of the federal courts and many aspects of their functioning, *see* Lee Epstein, William M. Landes & Richard A. Posner, The Behavior of Federal Judges: A Theoretical and Empirical Study of Rational Choice (2013).

as well as the current specification of the jurisdiction of these courts, is the product of numerous changes adopted in many statutes since the Judiciary Act of 1789. Repeatedly throughout American history there have been complaints of a crisis in the federal courts as a result of far more work than the judiciary can handle.[2] Revisions in the courts' structure and workload often have resulted. Again, today, there is attention to such a crisis in the federal court system.[3]

In 1990, the Federal Courts Study Committee issued a report declaring that a workload crisis was confronting the federal courts.[4] The committee noted that the federal courts' caseload tripled from 1958 to 1988 and that the number of federal district court and appeals judges doubled during this time period.[5] The committee stated that "[t]he federal courts' most pressing problem—today and for the immediate future—stems from the unprecedented number of federal narcotics prosecutions."[6] Federal criminal filings had increased by more than 50 percent since 1980, and drug cases had grown by 280 percent in the same time period.[7] Forty-four percent of all criminal trials in federal court and 50 percent of all criminal appeals were drug cases.[8] Because federal courts give criminal cases priority due to the Speedy Trial Act, "some districts with heavy drug caseloads are virtually unable to try civil cases and others will soon be at this point."[9]

The evolution of the federal courts can be best understood by examining the changes over time in each component of the system. Subsections 1.4.2-1.4.5 consider, respectively, the modifications in the structure and jurisdiction of the Supreme Court, the courts of appeals, the district courts, and the specialized federal courts.

§1.4.2 The Supreme Court of the United States

The jurisdiction of the Supreme Court is discussed in detail in Chapter 10.[10] In the following brief sketch of the evolution of the Supreme Court since 1789, four major changes are outlined.

[2] For a review of the changes in federal jurisdiction and what prompted these revisions, *see* Richard H. Fallon, Jr., John F. Manning, Daniel J. Meltzer & David L. Shapiro, Hart & Wechsler's The Federal Courts and the Federal System 24-30 (7th ed. 2015).

[3] In 1998, a Commission on Structural Alternatives for the Federal Courts of Appeals, created pursuant to federal statute and appointed by Chief Justice Rehnquist, was deliberating. For discussion of the workload of the federal courts and possible solutions, *see* Richard A. Posner, The Federal Courts: Crisis and Reform (1985); Samuel Estreicher & John Sexton, Redefining the Supreme Court's Role (1986); Report of the Federal Courts Study Committee (1990).

[4] The Federal Courts Study Committee was created by the Judicial Improvements and Access to Justice Act, Pub. L. No. 100-702, 102 Stat. 4642 (adopted Nov. 19, 1988).

[5] Report of the Federal Courts Study Committee, *supra* note 3, at 5.

[6] *Id.* at 36.

[7] *Id.*

[8] *Id.*

[9] *Id.*

[10] *See also* Paul Abraham Freund, The Supreme Court of the United States (1961); Felix Frankfurter & James Landis, The Business of the Supreme Court (1927); Charles Warren, The Supreme Court in United States History (1922).

Changes in Supreme Court Size

First, the number of Supreme Court justices fluctuated for the first seventy years of American history, but has remained constant at nine since 1869. Initially, six justices were on the Supreme Court. This number increased each time a new circuit court was added until ten justices were on the Court in 1864.[11] In 1866, in an effort to prevent beleaguered President Andrew Johnson from making appointments to the Court, the number of justices was reduced to seven.[12] In 1869, after Johnson left office, the number was increased to nine, where it has remained ever since.[13]

The only serious proposal for a change in size came during the mid-1930s, when President Franklin Roosevelt advocated his famous "court-packing plan."[14] Angry over the Supreme Court's invalidation of New Deal legislation in the midst of the Depression, Roosevelt proposed adding one new justice to the Court for each justice over the age of seventy, to a maximum of fifteen justices.[15] The effect would have been to allow Roosevelt immediately to appoint a majority of the Court, thus securing approval of his legislative programs. Despite Roosevelt's immense popularity at the time, the court-packing plan was severely criticized and even renounced by a Democrat-controlled Senate Judiciary Committee.[16] Ultimately, the plan became unnecessary when Justice Owen Roberts changed his position and voted to sustain important New Deal legislation. Whether his shift was in response to the pressure of the court-packing plan always will be in dispute; nonetheless, his change of mind will forever be known as "the 'switch in time' that 'saved the nine.'"[17] Soon thereafter many vacancies occurred on the Court, allowing Roosevelt to appoint seven new justices between 1937 and 1941, assuring a pro-New Deal majority.

Increases in Supreme Court Control Over Its Docket

Second, there has been a trend over the course of American history toward granting the Supreme Court discretion to determine what cases to hear and decide. Initially review was available in the Supreme Court by writ of error, and the Court was obligated to hear all such cases. In 1891, the Court was given discretion to decide whether to review diversity, admiralty, patent, and revenue cases.[18] The

[11] *See* Act of Mar. 3, 1863, ch. 100, 12 Stat. 784 (adding tenth justice to the Supreme Court).

[12] Act of July 23, 1866, ch. 210, 14 Stat. 209.

[13] Act of Apr. 10, 1869, ch. 22, 16 Stat. 44.

[14] For a discussion of the events surrounding the court-packing plan, *see* Jeff Shesol, Supreme Power: Franklin Roosevelt vs. The Supreme Court (2010).

[15] The plan is described, and Roosevelt's speech proposing it excerpted, in Gerald Gunther, Constitutional Law 128-130 (11th ed. 1985).

[16] Sen. Jud. Comm., S. 711, 75th Cong., 1st Sess. 13-14 (1937).

[17] *See* Gerald Gunther, Constitutional Law 11 (11th ed. 1985), at 130 n.2 (describing evidence that Justice Roberts actually decided to change positions prior to Roosevelt's announcement of his court-packing plan).

[18] Act of Mar. 3, 1891, ch. 517, 26 Stat. 826 (known as the Evarts Act).

statute adopted in 1891 provided that review in such cases was to be by a writ of certiorari, rather than the obligatory writ of error.

In 1925, Congress went further in giving the Supreme Court control over its own docket.[19] In an act known as the "Judges' Bill," Congress divided most of the Court's docket into two categories: appeal and certiorari jurisdiction. Appeals were cases that the Court would be obligated to take and decide. Appeals included instances where a state court rules against a claim of a federal right, either by invalidating a federal statute or upholding a challenged state law.[20] Also, a case came by appeal to the U.S. Supreme Court from a U.S. Court of Appeals if the court of appeals had invalidated a state statute or declared a federal statute unconstitutional in a civil action to which the United States is a party. Virtually all other cases came to the U.S. Supreme Court by certiorari, where the Court had discretion whether to grant review.

In 1988, Congress eliminated virtually all instances of Supreme Court review by appeal.[21] Now almost all cases come to the Supreme Court by certiorari, meaning that review is completely discretionary with the Court. This culminated the trend of giving the Supreme Court increasing control over its docket.

Enlargement of Supreme Court's Jurisdiction

A third change has been an enlargement of the Supreme Court's jurisdiction. Most notably, under the Judiciary Act of 1789, the Supreme Court could review state court judgments only when there was a final judgment ruling against a claim of a federal right. But in 1914, the Supreme Court was granted authority to hear, by writ of certiorari, cases in which the state court ruled in favor of a claim of a federal right, such as when it ruled a state law unconstitutional or upheld a federal statute.[22]

Elimination of Circuit Responsibilities

Finally, and perhaps most important, the responsibility for Supreme Court justices to sit as judges on the circuit courts was eliminated in 1891.[23] Without a doubt, the obligation for Supreme Court justices to "ride circuit" imposed an onerous burden, especially in an age when transportation was often quite difficult. The history of the circuit courts is discussed in §1.4.3.

§1.4.3 The U.S. Courts of Appeals

There are thirteen U.S. Courts of Appeals. In addition to eleven courts (known as the Courts of Appeals for the First Circuit through the Eleventh Circuit) each

[19] Act of Feb. 13, 1925, 43 Stat. 940. For a critical examination of the Judges' Act's enactment, *see* Edward A. Hartnett, Questioning Certiorari: Some Reflections Seventy-Five Years After the Judges' Bill, 100 Colum. L. Rev. 1643 (2000).

[20] *See* 28 U.S.C. §1257 (1982).

[21] Pub. L. No. 100-352, 102 Stat. 662.

[22] Act of Dec. 23, 1914, ch. 2, 38 Stat. 790.

[23] The Evarts Act, 26 Stat. 826, 827, §3.

reviewing several district courts, there is the United States Court of Appeals for the District of Columbia Circuit and the United States Court of Appeals for the Federal Circuit. The latter court has exclusive jurisdiction over appeals in patent, trademark, and plant variety protection cases, and also hears appeals from the Court of Claims as well as appeals in cases involving government employment and international trade.[24]

History of Development of Courts of Appeals

Undoubtedly, the most significant change in the structure of the federal courts during the past 200 years has involved the evolution of the courts of appeals. Initially, tribunals known as the circuit courts were created to occupy a place between the district courts and the Supreme Court. Under the Judiciary Act of 1789, the circuit courts exercised both appellate jurisdiction-reviewing decisions of the district courts and original jurisdiction for most criminal cases and for certain civil cases where the amount in controversy was more than $500.[25] There were no permanent circuit court judges; rather, two Supreme Court justices and one district court judge staffed the circuit courts.

In 1793, the composition of the circuit courts was modified so that a court consisted of one Supreme Court justice and one district court judge.[26] The obvious problem was unresolved disagreements between the two judges.

In 1801, during the last days of the administration of President John Adams, Congress abolished the practice of having the Supreme Court justices ride circuit and created sixteen permanent circuit court judgeships.[27] However, this change was short-lived. President Jefferson's administration succeeded in persuading Congress to abolish these new judgeships and to restore the use of Supreme Court justices as circuit court judges.[28] Also, the number of circuits was increased from three to six, and the statute permitted one judge to decide cases for the circuit court.[29]

As the country grew, the number of circuits was increased, but it was not until 1869 that the first permanent circuit judges were authorized.[30] Under the Act of 1869, one circuit judge was appointed for each circuit. This proved inadequate to deal with the workload, however, and the Supreme Court justices were still required to ride circuit.

[24] *See* 28 U.S.C. §1295 (1985). Also, there is the Temporary Emergency Court of Appeals, originally created by the 1971 amendments to the Economic Stabilization Act of 1970. Act of Dec. 22, 1971, 85 Stat. 843. The court is staffed by federal judges from other courts and has the authority to hear cases under several statutes, such as the Emergency Petroleum Act of 1973, the Energy Policy and Conservation Act of 1975, and the Emergency Natural Gas Act of 1977. Fallon et al., *supra* note 2, at 41 n.95(b).

[25] Act of Sept. 24, 1789, ch. 20, 1 Stat. 73, 78, §11.

[26] Act of Mar. 2, 1793, ch. 22, 1 Stat. 333.

[27] Act of Feb. 13, 1801, ch. 4, 2 Stat. 89.

[28] Act of Mar. 8, 1802, ch. 8, 2 Stat. 132.

[29] Act of Apr. 29, 1802, ch. 31, 2 Stat. 156.

[30] Act of Apr. 10, 1869, ch. 22, 16 Stat. 44.

In 1891, in the Evarts Act, Congress created new courts of appeals, establishing nine U.S. Courts of Appeals.[31] Each court was assigned two permanent judges, and the third judge in each case was to be either a district court judge or a Supreme Court justice. Also, for the first time, district court judges were prohibited from reviewing their own decisions when serving as appeals court judges. It should be noted that the Evarts Act did not abolish the circuit courts; it transferred their appellate jurisdiction to the courts of appeals, but retained the circuit courts for cases for which they had original jurisdiction. In 1911, the circuit courts were eliminated, and their original jurisdictions were transferred to the district courts.[32]

The structure for the courts of appeals has remained essentially the same since they were established in 1891. Today, there are thirteen circuits. Eleven, numbered the first through the eleventh, cover specific geographic areas, each including district courts in more than one state. The U.S. Court of Appeals for the District of Columbia Circuit hears appeals from the U.S. District Court for the District of Columbia and is assigned, by statute, the responsibility of reviewing the decisions of many administrative agencies.[33] Finally, in 1982, Congress created the U.S. Court of Appeals for the Federal Circuit.[34] This court assumed the appellate jurisdiction previously assigned to the Court of Customs and Patent Appeals and the Court of Claims.[35] Additionally, the Federal Circuit has exclusive jurisdiction to hear appeals in patent, trademark, and plant variety cases.[36] The Federal Circuit also decides a variety of other matters, including reviewing decisions of the U.S. Court of International Trade, decisions on matters of law made by the secretary of commerce under the Tariff Schedules, decisions of the Merit Systems Protection Board, and decisions of an agency board of contract appeals.[37]

At times there have been proposals to divide the Ninth Circuit into two circuits,[38] as was done when the Fifth Circuit was split into the current Fifth and Eleventh Circuits. Although the Ninth Circuit is the largest in terms of number of judges and covers a vast geographic area, dividing the circuit is controversial as there is disagreement over whether the large size presents a significant problem and over how the circuit could be best split.

[31] Act of Mar. 3, 1891, ch. 517, 26 Stat. 826.

[32] Act of Mar. 3, 1911, ch. 1, 36 Stat. 1087.

[33] *See* 28 U.S.C. §§41, 43 (1982).

[34] Federal Courts Improvement Act of 1982, Pub. L. No. 97-164, 96 Stat. 25.

[35] 28 U.S.C. §1295 (1982).

[36] *Id.*

[37] 28 U.S.C. §1295(a)(6), (7), (9), (10) (1982).

[38] In 1998, a Commission on Structural Alternatives for the Federal Courts of Appeals was considering the issue of splitting the Ninth Circuit. Created by federal law and with its members appointed by Chief Justice Rehnquist, the commission issued its report in 1998. The commission, chaired by former Supreme Court Justice Byron White, proposed retention of the Ninth Circuit's current size and boundaries, but proposed dividing the circuit into three regional divisions, with each having between seven and eleven judges. Commission on Structural Alternatives for the Federal Court of Appeals, Final Report (1998). For criticisms of this proposal, *see* Carl Tobias, The Unkindest Cut: The White Commission Proposal to Restructure the Ninth Circuit, 73 S. Cal. L. Rev. 377 (2000); Proctor Hug, The Commission on Structural Alternatives for the Federal Court of Appeals' Report: An Analysis of the Commission's Recommendations for the Ninth Circuit, 32 U.C. Davis L. Rev. 887 (1999).

The courts of appeals have obligatory jurisdiction to hear appeals from all final decisions of the district courts of the United States.[39] Although in limited instances the Supreme Court can directly review decisions of a district court, the usual practice is for appellate review to occur in the U.S. courts of appeals.[40]

§1.4.4 The U.S. District Courts

Federal district courts are the primary courts of original jurisdiction in the federal system. Cases are filed initially in the district courts, except for limited instances in which the Supreme Court has original jurisdiction and in which the courts of appeals directly review the decisions of federal administrative agencies.[41] There are ninety-four federal district courts.[42] Every state has at least one federal district court; larger states are divided into several districts. The territorial authority of federal district courts does not cross state lines.[43] Federal districts are often divided into divisions, but the divisions have little importance except, in some instances, as a specification of venue within the district.[44]

Changes in District Courts

There have been two major changes in the federal district courts over time. First, there have been revisions in their subject matter jurisdiction. For example, the amount in controversy requirement in diversity cases has been increased, and now requires that a claim be in excess of $75,000.[45] This change was in response to proposals to increase the amount in light of the substantial inflation that has occurred over the past thirty years.[46] More important, in 1875, federal district courts were given subject matter jurisdiction to hear cases arising under the Constitution, laws, and treaties of the United States.[47] The general federal question jurisdiction is widely regarded as the most important aspect of federal court authority. The subject matter jurisdiction of the federal district courts is discussed in detail in Chapter 5.

A second major modification in the federal district courts was the use of three-judge courts, especially in instances in which injunctions were sought to halt allegedly unconstitutional government practices. Three-judge district courts were first

[39] 28 U.S.C. §1291 (1982).

[40] *See* §10.3.4, *infra.*

[41] For a discussion of the original jurisdiction of the U.S. Supreme Court, *see* §10.3.1, *infra.*

[42] 28 U.S.C. §133 (1982).

[43] The only exception to this is the district court for Wyoming, which has jurisdiction over the parts of Yellowstone National Park that are in Montana and Idaho. *See* Charles Alan Wright, Law of Federal Courts 8 n.3 (4th ed. 1983).

[44] *Id.* at 8.

[45] Federal Courts Improvement Act of 1996, Pub. L. No. 104-317, §205, 110 Stat. 3847.

[46] *See, e.g.,* Posner, *supra* note 3, at 131-133.

[47] Act of Mar. 3, 1875, ch. 137, 18 Stat. 470.

authorized by the Expediting Act of 1903, which provided for these courts to be convened for antitrust suits brought by the U.S. government, litigation under acts regulating commerce, and instances where the U.S. attorney general deemed such courts to be appropriate.[48] A major expansion in the use of three-judge courts occurred in 1910, when Congress mandated their use in suits seeking to enjoin state officers from enforcing allegedly unconstitutional laws.[49] In 1937, the use of three-judge courts was expanded to include suits seeking injunctions to halt actions by federal officers enforcing allegedly unconstitutional federal laws.[50] The decisions of three-judge courts were reviewable, by appeal, to the U.S. Supreme Court.

In 1976, in response to many proposals to eliminate the multi-judge format, Congress repealed the statutes providing for three-judge courts in constitutional cases.[51] There remain, however, a few statutes directing the use of three-judge courts in specific circumstances. Federal laws require three-judge courts when there is a challenge to the apportionment of congressional districts or any statewide legislative body.[52] Also, the Civil Rights Act of 1964 provides for a three-judge court upon application of the attorney general of the United States.[53] The Voting Rights Act of 1965 provides for three-judge courts for several types of legal challenges to state and local election arrangements.[54] The Regional Rail Reorganization Act[55] and the Bipartisan Campaign Finance Reform Act of 2002 also have provisions authorizing the use of three-judge courts.[56] Decisions of these three-judge courts may be directly appealed to the U.S. Supreme Court.[57]

The major proposal for change in the district courts is the repeatedly advanced suggestion to eliminate diversity jurisdiction. Diversity jurisdiction, and the arguments for and against retaining it, are discussed in §5.3.

§1.4.5 Specialized Federal Courts

Many federal courts are authorized to adjudicate only specific matters, such as bankruptcy or tax cases. Additionally, independent regulatory agencies and administrative bodies often are empowered to adjudicate questions arising under federal law. Frequently, these judges or administrative officials are not accorded life tenure or the protection against decreases in salary guaranteed judges under

[48] Act of Feb. 11, 1903, ch. 544, 32 Stat. 823. Soon after the enactment of this law, three-judge courts were authorized for review of decisions of the Interstate Commerce Commission. Act of June 29, 1906, ch. 3591, 34 Stat. 584.

[49] Act of June 18, 1910, ch. 309, 36 Stat. 539, 557, §17.

[50] Act of Aug. 24, 1937, ch. 754, 50 Stat. 751.

[51] Act of Aug. 12, 1976, Pub. L. No. 94-381, 90 Stat. 1119.

[52] 28 U.S.C. §2284 (1985).

[53] 42 U.S.C. §2000a-5 (1985).

[54] *See, e.g.,* 42 U.S.C. §1971(g) (1982).

[55] 45 U.S.C. §701 (1982).

[56] Pub. L. No. 107-155, 116 Stat. 181 (2002).

[57] 28 U.S.C. §1253 (1982) provides for direct appeal from three-judge courts. Also, many of the specific statutes providing for three-judge courts also provide for appeal to the U.S. Supreme Court.

Article III. These tribunals in which decision makers lack life tenure or salary protections are termed "legislative courts." Chapter 4 focuses on the situations in which legislative courts are permissible.

Types of Legislative Courts

Four types of legislative courts exist. Each is briefly described here and discussed in detail in Chapter 4. First, legislative courts long have been used for federal territories and the District of Columbia.[58] For example, there are federal courts in which the judges lack life tenure in the Canal Zone, Guam, the Northern Mariana Islands, and the Virgin Islands.[59] In addition, the District of Columbia Superior Court and the District of Columbia Court of Appeals are courts created by Congress to handle matters arising in the District of Columbia that typically would be raised in state courts.[60]

Second, there are specialized courts for the military in which judges lack life tenure. Such courts have existed since early in America's history.

Third, there are legislative courts for civil disputes between the government and private citizens. For example, a Court of Claims has long existed to hear monetary claims, other than for torts, against the United States.[61] After some uncertainty, the Supreme Court decided that the Court of Claims was an Article III court because its judges were accorded life tenure and salary protections.[62] The Federal Courts Improvement Act of 1982 divided the Court of Claims' jurisdiction, giving its appellate jurisdiction to the new U.S. Court of Appeals for the Federal Circuit and according its trial jurisdiction to a new Claims Court, which is a legislative court.[63]

Another specialized court that exists to resolve civil disputes between the federal government and private citizens is the Court of International Trade, which exists to resolve disputes arising from import transactions.[64] The U.S. Tax Court is a legislative court whose judges sit for fifteen-year terms.[65] The Tax Court has jurisdiction to decide taxpayer challenges to deficiency determinations made by the Internal Revenue Service.

Fourth and finally, there are courts that exist as adjuncts to the federal district courts and resolve private civil disputes and even some criminal matters. For example, bankruptcy courts and federal magistrates decide a wide variety of federal law matters even though the bankruptcy judges and magistrates do not have

[58] *See, e.g.,* American Ins. Co. v. Canter, 26 U.S. (1 Pet.) 511 (1828); *see* §4.2, *infra.*

[59] 48 U.S.C. §§1406, 1424, 1694.

[60] District of Columbia Reform and Criminal Procedure Act of 1970, Pub. L. No. 91-358, 84 Stat. 473.

[61] 28 U.S.C. §§171-175 (1982). *See* §9.2, *infra* (discussing the authority of the Court of Claims).

[62] *See* Glidden Co. v. Zdanok, 370 U.S. 530 (1962); the earlier decision holding that the Court of Claims was a legislative court was Williams v. United States, 289 U.S. 553 (1933).

[63] Pub. L. No. 97-164, 96 Stat. 25.

[64] 28 U.S.C. §§1581-1585 (1985).

[65] 26 U.S.C. §§6213, 7441-7487 (1986).

life tenure, but instead sit for fourteen- and eight-year terms, respectively. The permissible scope of jurisdiction for these courts is discussed in detail in Chapter 4.

Some suggest that a partial solution to the federal courts' workload problem is to increase the number and type of specialized courts.[66] Others contend that the loss of generalist judges, and the danger of having judges likely drawn from the industry most affected by their decisions, outweighs the benefits of specialized courts.[67]

§1.5 SEPARATION OF POWERS AND FEDERALISM AS UNIFYING THEMES IN THE LAW AND STUDY OF FEDERAL JURISDICTION

Central Themes

In fashioning the doctrines determining federal court jurisdiction, the Supreme Court repeatedly has focused on two major policy considerations. First, what is the proper role of the federal courts relative to the other branches of the federal government? Second, what is the proper role of the federal courts relative to the states and especially to the state courts? Separation of powers and federalism issues underlie virtually every topic discussed in this volume. Quite often, the disagreement between the majority and the dissent in specific cases is a dispute over the proper allocation of power within the federal government or between the federal and state courts. Without a doubt, every doctrine determining access to the federal courts reflects choices about separation of powers and / or federalism.

Separation of Powers and Federal Jurisdiction

Every congressional restriction of judicial power, and even grants of authority that are not specifically provided for in the Constitution, raises separation of powers issues. For example, deciding whether Congress can limit federal court jurisdiction to hear specific controversial issues or whether Congress can create courts where judges lack life tenure requires analysis of the proper role of the national legislature relative to the judiciary. Some would accord Congress broad authority to determine the jurisdiction and powers of the federal courts, but others believe

[66] *See* Ellen R. Jordan, Specialized Courts: A Choice?, 76 Nw. U. L. Rev. 745 (1981). The Federal Courts Study Committee proposed creating an Article I court for disability claims and the creation of an Article III appellate division of the U.S. Tax Court with exclusive jurisdiction over appeals in federal income, estate, and gift taxation claims. Report of the Federal Courts Study Committee 55-60, 69-72 (1990).

[67] For a careful analysis of when specialized courts seem particularly useful and especially undesirable, *see* Richard L. Revesz, Specialized Courts and the Administrative Lawmaking System, 138 U. Pa. L. Rev. 1111 (1990). For an excellent criticism of the growth of Article I courts, *see* Judith Resnik, Trial as Error, Jurisdiction as Injury: Transforming the Meaning of Article III, 113 Harv. L. Rev. 924 (2000).

that there must be constitutional limits on congressional restrictions to preserve the judiciary's role in checking the other branches of government.[1] This issue is discussed in detail in Chapters 3 and 4, which examine, respectively, congressional authority to control federal court jurisdiction and congressional ability to create courts where judges lack the life tenure and salary protections assured in Article III.

Separation of powers issues also arise when the judiciary refuses to exercise authority granted to it or assumes power not clearly provided for in the Constitution. For instance, may the judiciary decline to hear cases in situations where Congress has expressly provided for judicial review? Some contend that it violates separation of powers for the federal court to decline to exercise jurisdiction;[2] but others argue that courts always have had equitable powers to refuse to hear cases, especially where declining jurisdiction would advance other important values.[3] This issue is considered in detail in Chapters 12, 13, and 14, which focus on the abstention doctrines.

At the same time, separation of powers issues often arise when the federal courts exercise their authority. For example, to what extent, if at all, should the judiciary formulate principles that minimize the occasion for judicial review, thus leaving resolution of issues to the political branches of government?[4] From one view, judicial review is to be avoided through techniques such as restrictive standing doctrines, so that decisions will be made not by the courts, but by the more directly politically accountable branches of government. But from another perspective, it is the federal courts' role to restrain and remedy unconstitutional government conduct, and separation of powers is enhanced, not infringed, when the judiciary hears and decides constitutional cases. Chapter 2, which focuses on the justiciability doctrines, examines this question of how separation of powers considerations should influence jurisdictional rules such as standing, ripeness, mootness, and the political question doctrine.

§1.5 [1] For arguments defending congressional control of federal court jurisdiction, *see, e.g.*, Michael J. Perry, The Constitution, the Courts, and Human Rights 134 (1982); Charles Lund Black, Decision According to Law 17-19, 37-39 (1981); Gerald Gunther, Congressional Power to Curtail Federal Court Jurisdiction: An Opinionated Guide to the Ongoing Debate, 36 Stan. L. Rev. 895, 917-922 (1984). For arguments that congressional control of federal court jurisdiction is constitutionally limited, *see, e.g.*, Akhil Reed Amar, The Two-Tiered Structure of the Judiciary Act of 1789, 138 U. Pa. L. Rev. 1499 (1990); Barry Friedman, A Different Dialogue: The Supreme Court, Congress, and Federal Jurisdiction, 85 Nw. U. L. Rev. 1 (1990); Lawrence Gene Sager, Foreword: Constitutional Limitations on Congress' Authority to Regulate the Jurisdiction of the Federal Courts, 95 Harv. L. Rev. 17 (1981); Henry M. Hart, The Power of Congress to Limit the Jurisdiction of the Federal Courts: An Exercise in Dialectic, 66 Harv. L. Rev. 1362 (1953).

[2] For an excellent discussion of how federal court refusal to exercise jurisdiction is a violation of separation of powers, *see* Martin H. Redish, Abstention, Separation of Powers, and the Limits of the Judicial Function, 94 Yale L.J. 71 (1984).

[3] *See, e.g.*, Michael Wells, Why Professor Redish Is Wrong About Abstention, 19 Ga. L. Rev. 1097 (1985).

[4] For example, the Supreme Court has restricted standing to sue in federal court, declaring that standing doctrines are "founded in concern about the proper—and properly limited—role of the [federal] courts in a democratic society." Warth v. Seldin, 422 U.S. 490, 498 (1975). Similarly, the Court concluded that "the law of Art. III standing is built on a single basic idea—the idea of separation of powers." Allen v. Wright, 468 U.S. 737, 752 (1984).

Similar separation of powers issues arise when the federal courts formulate federal common law. Some contend that the legislature alone has the authority to adopt rules that have the force of law and govern behavior; that judicially created law by the federal courts usurps congressional prerogatives. But others argue that federal common law must be developed in some areas to serve an interstitial function until Congress legislates. Also, it is maintained that in some areas federal common law is essential to implement the U.S. Constitution, such as where federal courts have created monetary remedies for violations of the Constitution by federal officers. The topic of federal common law, and this dispute over separation of powers, is discussed in Chapter 6, and the question of damage relief against federal officers is considered in §9.1.

Although the specific doctrines are diverse, the underlying questions are closely related. Ultimately, what is the proper role for the federal courts within the system of separated and shared federal powers? What congressional or judicial actions improperly usurp the prerogatives reserved to the other branch of government?

Parity and Comity

The other major underlying policy consideration concerns federalism and especially the proper relationship of federal and state courts.[5] Decisions and discussions about federal court jurisdiction often turn on the interrelated concepts of parity and comity.

Parity is the issue of whether, overall, state courts are equal to federal courts in their ability and willingness to protect federal rights.[6] Those favoring expansive federal court availability, particularly to decide constitutional claims, argue that state courts are not to be trusted to adequately safeguard federal rights.[7] They contend that in constitutional litigation between the government and private citizens, federal courts are more likely than state courts to rule in favor of individual liberties and against the government. Supporters of this position describe a history of state court hostility to federal claims.[8] Perhaps most important, those who deny the existence of

[5] In an important article, Professor Richard Fallon argues that there are two competing models of federal jurisdiction. Richard H. Fallon, The Ideologies of Federal Common Law, 74 Va. L. Rev. 1141 (1988). One, which he terms the "federalist" model, emphasizes the protection of state sovereignty and the parity between federal and state courts in deciding constitutional claims. The alternative approach, labeled the "nationalist model," emphasizes the supremacy of the national government and particularly the special role of the federal government in safeguarding federal rights. The nationalist model stresses the importance of access to the federal courts and the general superiority of the federal judiciary in resolving constitutional claims.

[6] *See, e.g.*, Burt Neuborne, The Myth of Parity, 90 Harv. L. Rev. 1105 (1977); for a review of the literature in the debate over parity, *see* Erwin Chemerinsky, Parity Reconsidered: Defining a Role for the Federal Judiciary, 36 UCLA L. Rev. 233 (1988).

[7] *See, e.g.*, Neuborne, *supra* note 6, at 1124-1127; Burt Neuborne, Toward Procedural Parity in Constitutional Litigation, 22 Wm. & Mary L. Rev. 725, 727 (1981).

[8] *See* Neuborne, *supra* note 6, at 1110-1115; Julie A. Davies, *Pullman* and *Burford* Abstention: Clarifying the Roles of State and Federal Courts in Constitutional Cases, 20 U.C. Davis L. Rev. 1, 31 (1986).

parity between federal and state courts point to the differing institutional characteristics of the two judicial systems.[9] For example, the federal judicial system has greater insulation from political pressure because federal judges have life tenure and salaries that cannot be decreased, whereas in thirty-eight states there is some form of judicial election. Also, some believe that federal courts attract superior judges, provide more institutional support, and are psychologically more committed to protecting federal rights than are state courts.[10]

Those who believe that federal courts are better than state courts in protecting federal rights seek to maximize access to the federal courts in constitutional cases and to insure federal court oversight of state court decisions. The Warren Court, for example, expanded federal court jurisdiction based on its explicit premise that federal courts often are necessary to assure adequate protection of constitutional rights. By increasing the availability of federal habeas corpus for state prisoners,[11] expanding the scope of relief under 42 U.S.C. §1983,[12] limiting the circumstances where federal courts must abstain,[13] and minimizing the preclusive effects of state court judgments in federal court,[14] the Warren Court implemented its belief that federal courts should be accessible to protect constitutional rights.

But others vehemently maintain that state courts are equal to federal courts in their ability and willingness to protect constitutional rights.[15] They argue that past differences between the state and federal judiciaries have been eliminated over time

[9] *See, e.g.,* Neuborne, *supra* note 6, at 1115-1130; Paul Carrington, Judicial Independence and Democratic Accountability in Highest State Courts, 61 Law & Contemp. Probs. 79 (1998); Donald A. Ziegler, Federal Court Reform of State Criminal Justice Systems: A Reassessment of the *Younger* Doctrine from a Modern Perspective, 19 U.C. Davis L. Rev. 31, 46-48 (1985); Gary Peller, In Defense of Federal Habeas Corpus Relitigation, 16 Harv. C.R.-C.L. L. Rev. 579, 677-685 (1982).

[10] *See, e.g.,* Richard A. Posner, The Federal Courts: Crisis and Reform 144 (1985) ("It is widely believed that federal judges are, on average (an important qualifier), of higher quality than their state counterparts."); Neuborne, *supra* note 6, at 1121-1125; Martin H. Redish, Judicial Parity, Litigant Choice, and Democratic Theory: A Comment on Federal Jurisdiction and Constitutional Rights, 36 UCLA L. Rev. 329 (1988) (arguing that institutional differences make federal courts superior for constitutional adjudication).

[11] *See, e.g.,* Fay v. Noia, 372 U.S. 391 (1963) (state court prisoners may raise matters on federal habeas corpus that were not raised in state court unless they deliberately bypassed state court procedures); Brown v. Allen, 344 U.S. 443 (1953) (state court prisoners can relitigate federal constitutional claims on habeas corpus). *See* Chapter 15 for a discussion of these issues concerning habeas corpus.

[12] *See, e.g.,* Monroe v. Pape, 365 U.S. 167 (1961) (state officers act under color of state law for purposes of 42 U.S.C. §1983 even if they are violating state statutes and rules); *see* Chapter 8 for a discussion of issues concerning §1983.

[13] *See, e.g.,* Dombrowski v. Pfister, 380 U.S. 479 (1965) (permitting federal courts to enjoin state court proceedings); *see* Chapter 13 for a discussion of this case and subsequent developments that prevent federal courts from enjoining pending state court proceedings.

[14] *See, e.g.,* England v. Louisiana State Bd. of Medical Examiners, 375 U.S. 411 (1964) (after federal court abstention, state court decisions on state law matters do not have res judicata effect in federal courts as to federal issues); *see* §12.3 *infra* for a discussion of the procedures followed in abstention cases.

[15] *See, e.g.,* Michael E. Solimine & James L. Walker, Respecting State Courts (1999); Michael E. Solimine & James L. Walker, Constitutional Litigation in Federal and State Courts: An Empirical Analysis of Judicial Parity, 10 Hastings Const. L.Q. 213 (1983) (arguing that state courts are as likely to rule in favor of constitutional claims as are federal courts).

and that the differing institutional characteristics do not affect decisions.[16] Some who deny the superiority of federal courts contend that even if federal and state courts might reach different results, there is no reason why one set of outcomes is more preferable than another.[17] They suggest that since both court systems offer equally acceptable processes, jurisdiction should not be determined based on an assumption of one court system's superiority.

In sharp contrast to the Warren Court, the Burger, Rehnquist, and Roberts Courts have frequently narrowed federal court jurisdiction based on its express declaration that state courts were equally trustworthy in deciding constitutional claims. The Burger and Rehnquist Courts' confidence in state courts is reflected in their restrictions on habeas corpus relief,[18] limitations on §1983 suits,[19] expansion of the abstention doctrines,[20] and increase in the preclusive effect of state court decisions on the federal courts.[21]

Simply put, decisions and discussions about the scope of federal jurisdiction frequently turn on beliefs about the comparative competence of federal and state courts. In fact, some suggest that the discussions about parity are really a subterfuge; conservatives who believe that state courts are more likely to favor the government over the individual may simply be using the parity argument as a tool to advance their ideological agenda.[22] Professor Neuborne explains that parity may be a "pretext for funneling federal constitutional decision making into state courts precisely because they are less likely to be receptive to vigorous enforcement of federal constitutional doctrine."[23]

The parity debate is probably unresolvable because parity is an empirical question—whether one court system is as good as another—for which it is

[16] Brett Christopher Gerry, Parity Revisited: An Empirical Comparison of State and Lower Federal Court Interpretations of Nollan v. California Coastal Commission, 23 Harv. J.L. & Pub. Poly. 233 (1999) (past state court hostility to federal rights has been eliminated).

[17] Paul M. Bator, Finality in Criminal Law and Federal Habeas Corpus for State Prisoners, 76 Harv. L. Rev. 441 (1963) (arguing that no set of results is preferable to any other; as long as there is a full and fair opportunity for a hearing, no relitigation of constitutional issues is necessary on habeas corpus).

[18] *See, e.g.*, McCleskey v. Zant, 499 U.S. 467 (1991) (limiting successive habeas corpus petitions); Teague v. Lane, 489 U.S. 288 (1989) (habeas petitions cannot seek recognition of new constitutional rights unless they are rights that would have retroactive application); Wainwright v. Sykes, 433 U.S. 72 (1977) (prisoners may not raise issues on habeas corpus that were not raised at trial unless they can demonstrate cause and prejudice for their procedural default); *see* Chapter 15 for a discussion of these issues concerning habeas corpus.

[19] *See, e.g.,* Parratt v. Taylor, 451 U.S. 527 (1981) (§1983 does not create a remedy when the plaintiff seeks only a postdeprivation remedy for loss of property and the state provides an adequate postdeprivation remedy). *See* Chapter 8 for a discussion of issues concerning §1983.

[20] *See, e.g.,* Younger v. Harris, 401 U.S. 37 (1971) (federal courts may not enjoin pending state court proceedings); *see* Chapter 13 for a discussion of federal court abstention when there are pending state court proceedings.

[21] *See, e.g.,* Allen v. McCurry, 449 U.S. 90 (1980) (state court decisions have preclusive effect on federal courts deciding claims under 42 U.S.C. §1983); *see* §8.10 for a discussion of res judicata and collateral estoppel in civil rights cases.

[22] Of course, this does not imply that all who proclaim that there is parity between federal and state courts do so as a subterfuge; rather, just that some might use parity as a tool to restrict federal court jurisdiction precisely because they believe that there is not parity and that state courts would produce results they prefer.

[23] Neuborne, *supra* note 6, at 1105-1106. *See also* Burt Neuborne, Parity Revisited: The Uses of a Judicial Forum of Excellence, 44 DePaul L. Rev. 797, 799 (1995) (arguing that despite changes in

unlikely there will ever be any meaningful empirical measure.[24] The problem with the parity debate partially stems from the difficulty in devising criteria by which federal and state courts are to be compared.[25] Also, there are enormous obstacles with devising a way to compare court systems because of the difficulty of matching cases and meaningfully comparing decisions.[26] Even if quality could be defined and even if it could be measured, at best the result would be a comparison of an aggregate of *all* state courts with *all* federal courts. As the term "parity" is used, it refers to an overall comparison of the federal courts with the composite of all of the state judiciaries, but the state courts differ from one another, just as the federal courts are not homogeneous. There is an enormous variance among the different states and many federal districts in their disposition toward protecting individual rights. Thus, an aggregate comparison is unlikely to be useful. Yet impressions about parity doubtless will continue to influence federal courts' doctrines.[27]

A related issue concerning federalism is comity—the deference federal courts owe to state courts as those of another sovereign.[28] For example, some contend that comity requires that federal courts minimize friction with state courts and avoid any doctrines or practices that will implicitly insult the competence of state courts.[29] Many decisions of the Burger Court expressly invoked comity as a justification for restricting federal court jurisdiction. Others argue that federal courts

recent decades "a relative institutional advantage for the plaintiff exists in federal court; an advantage resulting from a mix of political insulation, tradition, better resources and professional competence").

[24] For a detailed argument that parity is an empirical question for which no empirical measure is possible, *see* Chemerinsky, *supra* note 6, at 233; *but see* Solimine & Walker, *supra* note 15 (an empirical attempt to prove parity between federal and state courts); Thomas B. Marvell, The Rationales for Federal Question Jurisdiction: An Empirical Analysis of Student Rights Litigation, 1984 Wis. L. Rev. 1315 (an empirical attempt to prove that parity does not exist); both of these studies are analyzed in Chemerinsky, *supra* note 6, at 233. A subsequent empirical study is Gerry, *supra* note 16.

[25] *See, e.g.,* Bator, *supra* note 17, at 630-631 ("We are told that federal judges will be more receptive to constitutional values than state judges. What is really meant, however, is that federal judges will be more receptive to *some* constitutional values than state judges. And the hidden assumption of the argument is that the Constitution contains only one or two sorts of values: typically, those which protect the individual from the power of the state and those which assure the superiority of federal to state law.").

[26] For example, if one court system were better than another, self-selection would occur as litigants chose their forum accordingly; also, cases would be more likely to be settled in that system. For a detailed review of problems of measurement, *see* Chemerinsky, *supra* note 6, at 233.

[27] *See, e.g.,* William Rubenstein, The Myth of Superiority, 16 Const. Comment. 599 (1999) (arguing that state courts have been more receptive than federal courts to litigants seeking to establish and vindicate civil rights); Burt Neuborne, Parity Revisited: The Uses of a Judicial Forum of Excellence, 44 DePaul L. Rev. 797 (1995); Michael Wells, Behind the Parity Debate: The Decline of the Legal Process Tradition in the Law of Federal Courts, 71 B.U. L. Rev. 609 (1991); Akhil Reed Amar, Parity as a Constitutional Question, 71 B.U. L. Rev. 645 (1991); Susan N. Herman, Why Parity Matters, 71 B.U. L. Rev. 651 (1991).

[28] *See* Paul Finkelman, An Imperfect Union: Slavery, Federalism, and Comity 4 (1981) (defining comity as "the courtesy or consideration that one jurisdiction gives by enforcing the laws of another, granted out of respect and deference rather than obligation").

[29] *See, e.g.,* Younger v. Harris, 401 U.S. 37 (1971) (holding that because of comity federal courts may not enjoin pending state court proceedings); Railroad Commn. of Texas v. Pullman Co., 312 U.S. 496 (1941) (holding that federal courts should abstain when state court clarification of unclear state law might make a federal court ruling unnecessary, in part, to avoid friction with state courts); *see also* Michael Wells, The Role of Comity in the Law of Federal Courts, 60 N.C. L. Rev. 59 (1981).

should safeguard constitutional rights, irrespective of what friction or insult might be created.[30] They maintain that arguments about friction and insults are based on unsubstantiated theories about the reaction of state court judges and that, in any event, the protection of constitutional rights is more important than institutional harmony or judicial sensibilities.

Without a doubt, a justice's or a commentator's views about the appropriate content of jurisdictional rules often depend on his or her position on the substantive issues involved. A person is more willing to favor restricting federal court jurisdiction in situations where his or her preferences are more likely to be achieved in state courts. Conversely, an individual will favor expanding access to the federal courts when it is perceived that those courts will produce better substantive results. Jurisdictional rules often determine the outcome in specific cases; hence, it hardly is surprising that debates over the scope of federal court jurisdiction often turn on views about the appropriate nature of American government and, practically speaking, the best courses of action to achieve the desired outcomes. Separation of powers and federalism issues are thus discussed throughout this volume.

[30] *See, e.g.*, Donald H. Ziegler, Rights Require Remedies: A New Approach to the Enforcement of Rights in the Federal Courts, 38 Hastings L.J. 665, 688 (1987); Ann Althouse, How to Build a Separate Sphere: Federal Courts and State Power, 100 Harv. L. Rev. 1485, 1538 (1987).

Part I

Constitutional and Statutory Limits on Federal Court Jurisdiction

It is frequently stated and widely accepted that federal courts are courts of limited jurisdiction. There are two primary restrictions on federal judicial power. First, Article III of the Constitution defines the scope of federal court authority. For example, Article III circumscribes the maximum extent of federal court subject matter jurisdiction. Additionally, judicial interpretation of Article III has created crucial doctrines that restrict access to the federal courts. The principles of standing, ripeness, and mootness were created through judicial interpretation of Article III.

Second, Congress plays an important role in limiting federal court jurisdiction. The Supreme Court has held that a federal court may hear a matter only when there is *both* constitutional and statutory authorization. Thus, statutes limit the jurisdiction of the federal courts and the reach of the judiciary's power.

Part I of the book focuses on the constitutional and statutory limits on federal judicial power. Chapter 2 considers the justiciability doctrines—the prohibition against advisory opinions, standing, ripeness, mootness, and the political question doctrine—which serve as central constraints on access to the federal courts. Chapter 3 examines congressional control of federal court jurisdiction, including Congress's power to restrict the jurisdiction of the Supreme Court and the lower federal courts; it also covers Congress's ability to enlarge federal court jurisdiction beyond that authorized by Article III. Chapter 4 discusses Congress's authority to create specialized tribunals in which judges lack the life tenure and salary protections prescribed in Article III. Chapter 5 focuses on the subject matter jurisdiction of the federal courts, including federal question jurisdiction, diversity and alienage jurisdiction (including the choice of law in such cases), supplemental jurisdiction, and removal jurisdiction. Finally, Chapter 6 analyzes the federal courts' power to fashion federal common law.

Other limits on judicial power are discussed throughout the remainder of this book. For example, in Part II, Chapter 7 focuses on the Eleventh Amendment, which prevents suits against state governments in federal court. Also, there are many self-imposed restraints on federal judicial authority, such as the abstention doctrines, which are discussed in Chapters 12, 13, and 14 of Part III.

Examination of constitutional and statutory limits on the federal judicial power—like all topics in this book—inevitably entails consideration of separation of powers and federalism concerns. From a separation of powers perspective, a decision about the appropriate content of the constitutional and statutory limits on federal judicial power is a question about the proper role for the federal judiciary in the tripartite scheme of American government. Determining the courts' constitutional authority or deciding Congress's ability to control federal court jurisdiction inescapably involves separation of powers analysis.

Also, because state courts are the primary alternative to federal courts, the scope of federal judicial power is crucial in determining the authority of the state courts. Expansion of federal judicial authority may be defended on federalism grounds as necessary to protect the interests of the federal government from state intrusion. At the same time, however, increased federal court review can be opposed on federalism grounds as usurping power properly reserved to the states.

Ultimately, all of the materials in Part I concern what is the proper role of the federal courts in American society. Access to the federal courts is largely determined by the doctrines considered in the next several chapters.

CHAPTER 2

Justiciability: Constitutional and Prudential Limits on Federal Judicial Power

§2.1 INTRODUCTION

Perhaps the most important limit on the federal judicial power is imposed by a series of principles termed "justiciability" doctrines. The justiciability doctrines determine which matters federal courts can hear and decide and which must be dismissed. Specifically, justiciability includes the prohibition against advisory opinions, standing, ripeness, mootness, and the political question doctrine. Each of these justiciability doctrines was created and articulated by the U.S. Supreme Court. Neither the text of the Constitution, nor the Framers in drafting the document, expressly mentioned any of these limitations on the judicial power.

Constitutional Versus Prudential Requirements

Although all of these requirements for federal court adjudication were judicially created, the Supreme Court has distinguished two different sources for these rules. First, the Court has declared that some of the justiciability doctrines are a result of its interpretation of Article III of the U.S. Constitution. Article III, §2, defines the federal judicial power in terms of nine categories of "cases" and "controversies." The Supreme Court repeatedly has said that the requirement for cases and controversies imposes substantial constitutional limits on federal judicial power.

Second, the Court has said that other justiciability doctrines are derived not from the Constitution, but instead from prudent judicial administration. In other words, although the Constitution permits federal court adjudication, the Court has decided that in certain instances wise policy militates against judicial review. These justiciability doctrines are termed "prudential."

The distinction between constitutional and prudential limits on federal judicial power is important because Congress, by statute, may override prudential, but not constitutional, restrictions. Because Congress may not expand federal judicial power beyond what is authorized in Article III of the Constitution, a federal law may not change a constitutional limit on federal judicial review. But since prudential constraints are not derived from the Constitution, Congress may instruct the federal courts to disregard such a restriction.[1]

It must be emphasized that both constitutional and prudential limits on justiciability are the product of Supreme Court decisions. The Court determines whether a particular restriction is constitutional or prudential in its explanation of whether the rule derives from Article III or from its views of prudent judicial administration. Some justiciability doctrines, such as standing, have both constitutional and prudential components. In other instances—for example, the political question doctrine—the Court has not announced whether it views the limitation as constitutional or prudential.

Policies Underlying Justiciability Requirements

A clear separation of the constitutional and prudential aspects of the justiciability doctrines is often difficult because both reflect the same basic policy considerations. In fact, all of the justiciability doctrines are premised on several important concerns. First, the justiciability doctrines are closely tied to separation of powers. Chief Justice Warren explained that the "words [cases and controversies] define the role assigned to the judiciary in a tripartite allocation of power to assure that the federal courts will not intrude into areas committed to the other branches of government."[2] The justiciability doctrines define the judicial role; they determine when it is appropriate for the federal courts to review a matter and when it is necessary to defer to the other branches of government.

Second, the justiciability doctrines conserve judicial resources, allowing the federal courts to focus their attention on the matters most deserving of review. For example, the justiciability doctrine termed "mootness" conserves judicial resources by allowing the federal courts to dismiss cases where there no longer is a live controversy. Many influential commentators have argued not only that the federal courts have finite resources in terms of time and money but also that the federal judiciary has limited political capital.[3] That is, these commentators contend that

§2.1 [1] *See, e.g.,* Warth v. Seldin, 422 U.S. 490, 501 (1975) ("Congress may grant an express right of action to persons who otherwise would be barred by prudential standing rules."); *id.* at 500-501 (the requirements for injury and causation are constitutionally required; the ban on third-party standing and the prohibition against federal courts deciding generalized grievances are prudential); Bennett v. Spear, 520 U.S. 154, 167 (1997) (discussing the zone of interest test as a prudential requirement); *but see* Lujan v. Defenders of Wildlife, 504 U.S. 555 (1992) (declaring that the ban on generalized grievances is constitutional, not prudential).

[2] Flast v. Cohen, 392 U.S. 83, 95 (1968).

[3] Jesse Choper, Judicial Review and the National Political Process: A Functional Reconsideration of the Role of the Supreme Court 55-59 (1980); Alexander Bickel, The Least Dangerous Branch 201-268 (1962); *but see* Erwin Chemerinsky, Interpreting the Constitution 134-138 (1987) (arguing that the Court's legitimacy is not fragile and conserving judicial credibility should not be a primary objective in constitutional interpretation).

federal courts generally depend on the other branches to voluntarily comply with judicial orders and that such acquiescence depends on the judiciary's credibility. Justiciability doctrines permit the judiciary to expend its political capital only when necessary and not to squander it on matters inappropriate for judicial review.[4]

Third, the justiciability doctrines are intended to improve judicial decision-making by providing the federal courts with concrete controversies best suited for judicial resolution. The Supreme Court explained that the requirement for cases and controversies "limit[s] the business of federal courts to questions presented in an adversary context and in a form historically viewed as capable of resolution through the judicial process."[5] Because federal courts have limited ability to conduct independent investigations, they must depend on the parties to fully present all relevant information to them. It is thought that adverse parties, with a stake in the outcome of the litigation, will perform this task best. Many of the justiciability doctrines exist to ensure concrete controversies and adverse litigants.[6]

Finally, the justiciability doctrines also promote fairness, especially to individuals who are not litigants before the court. The justiciability doctrines generally prevent the federal courts from adjudicating the rights of those who are not parties to a lawsuit. It would be unfair to allow someone to raise a complaint on behalf of a person who is satisfied with a situation. Also, because judicial decisions almost inevitably affect many people other than the parties to the suit, it is thought fairest to reserve court review for situations where it is truly necessary.[7]

These policy considerations repeatedly recur in Supreme Court opinions concerning particular justiciability doctrines. Yet these justifications for limits on the judicial role must be balanced against the need for judicial review. Federal courts exist, in large part, to prevent and remedy violations of federal laws. Federal judicial review is particularly important in enjoining and redressing constitutional violations inflicted by all levels of government and government officers.[8] Thus, while justiciability doctrines serve the important goals described above, it is at least equally important that the doctrines not prevent the federal courts from performing their essential function in upholding the Constitution of the United States and preventing and redressing violations of federal laws.

The recurring issue is what should be the content of the justiciability doctrines to achieve this balance between restraint and review. Inevitably, the debate turns on a normative question concerning the proper role of the federal courts. Critics argue that the Court has gone too far in limiting justiciability and preventing federal courts from protecting and vindicating important constitutional rights.

[4] Bickel, *supra* note 3, at 116 (arguing that justiciability requirements create "a time lag between legislation and adjudication [and] strengthens the Court's hand in gaining acceptance for its principles").

[5] Flast v. Cohen, 392 U.S. at 95.

[6] *See, e.g.*, Baker v. Carr, 369 U.S. 186, 204 (1962) (standing ensures "concrete adverseness").

[7] Lea Brilmeyer, The Jurisprudence of Article III: Perspectives on the "Case or Controversy" Requirement, 93 Harv. L. Rev. 297, 306-310 (1979) (describing fairness as a basis for justiciability doctrines).

[8] *See* Erwin Chemerinsky, Closing the Courthouse Door: How Your Constitutional Rights Became Unenforceable 6 (2017); *see also* Susan Bandes, The Idea of a Case, 42 Stan. L. Rev. 227 (1990).

But the Court's defenders contend that the decisions have defined the properly limited role of the federal judiciary in a democratic society. This normative question about the appropriate role of the federal judiciary thus is common to discussions of each of the justiciability doctrines.

The debate over justiciability also centers on an issue of methodology: Should the rules of justiciability be as clear and predictable as possible, or should the doctrines be very flexible, permitting the federal courts discretion in choosing which cases to hear and which to decline? Some argue that the justiciability doctrines should be malleable, according judges great discretion in deciding which cases warrant federal judicial review. For example, the late Professor Alexander Bickel spoke of the "passive virtues"—the desirability of the Supreme Court using discretionary doctrines such as justiciability to decline review where prudence counsels judicial avoidance.[9]

But others contend that the rules defining jurisdiction should be as firm and predictable as possible.[10] They argue that it is undesirable for federal courts to be able to manipulate justiciability doctrines to avoid cases or to make decisions about the merits of disputes under the guise of rulings about justiciability. Thus, another recurring theme is whether the Supreme Court has been sufficiently specific and consistent in defining justiciability requirements—a question that, of course, depends on the normative question about the proper approach to justiciability.[11]

Other Limits on the Judicial Power

Additionally, there are other constitutional limits on federal judicial power, such as the Eleventh Amendment, which prevents federal court relief against state governments.[12] The Supreme Court also has identified a number of circumstances in which federal courts should abstain and refrain from deciding a matter even though it is justiciable and all jurisdictional requirements are met.[13]

Moreover, the Court has formulated other rules to guide its exercise of discretion. For example, the Court has stated that it will avoid deciding constitutional issues where there are nonconstitutional grounds for a decision, where the record is inadequate to permit effective judicial review, or where the federal issue is not properly presented.[14]

[9] Alexander Bickel, The Supreme Court 1960 Term: Foreword: The Passive Virtues, 75 Harv. L. Rev. 40 (1961).

[10] Gene R. Nichol, Jr., Rethinking Standing, 72 Cal. L. Rev. 68 (1984); Gerald Gunther, The Subtle Vices of the "Passive Virtues"—A Comment on Principle and Expediency in Judicial Review, 64 Colum. L. Rev. 1 (1964).

[11] Although the Supreme Court did not address the justiciability issue in Bush v. Gore, 531 U.S. 98 (2000), it can be asked whether the Court should have dismissed the case on justiciability grounds. *See* Erwin Chemerinsky, Bush v. Gore Was Not Justiciable, 76 Notre Dame L. Rev. 1073 (2001).

[12] The Eleventh Amendment is discussed in Chapter 7.

[13] For a discussion of the abstention doctrines, *see* Chapters 12-14.

[14] *See, e.g.,* Ashwander v. TVA, 297 U.S. 288, 346 (1936) (Brandeis, J., concurring) (articulating principles governing Supreme Court review, including avoiding constitutional decisions where possible). For an excellent criticism of these "avoidance" techniques, *see* Lisa Kloppenberg, Playing It Safe: How the Supreme Court Sidesteps Hard Cases and Stunts the Development of Law (2001).

But the justiciability doctrines are, without a doubt, among the most significant principles defining access to the federal courts. The doctrines are enormously important, especially in constitutional litigation, in determining whether a case can be heard and decided by a federal judge. As such, the doctrines are crucial in defining the role of the federal courts in American society.

§2.2 THE PROHIBITION AGAINST ADVISORY OPINIONS

The core of Article III's limitation on federal judicial power is that federal courts cannot issue advisory opinions. In many states, state courts are authorized to provide opinions about the constitutionality of pending legislation or on constitutional questions referred to them by other branches of government.[1] Such advisory opinions are in many ways beneficial. By providing guidance to the legislature, these rulings can prevent the enactment of unconstitutional laws. Also, an advisory opinion can spare a legislature the effort of adopting statutes soon to be invalidated by the courts and can save time by allowing the legislature to correct constitutional infirmities at the earliest possible time.

Justifications for Prohibiting Advisory Opinions

Despite these benefits, it is firmly established that federal courts cannot issue advisory opinions. Many of the policies described in the previous section are served by the prohibition of advisory opinions. First, separation of powers is maintained by keeping the courts out of the legislative process. The judicial role is limited to deciding actual disputes; it does not include giving advice to Congress or the president.

Second, judicial resources are conserved because advisory opinions might be requested in many instances in which the law ultimately would not pass the legislature. The federal courts can decide the matter if it turns into an actual dispute; otherwise, judicial review is unnecessary, a waste of political and financial capital.

Third, the prohibition against advisory opinions helps ensure that cases will be presented to the Court in terms of specific disputes, not as hypothetical legal questions. As the Court explained in *Flast v. Cohen*: "[T]he implicit policies embodied in Article III, and not history alone, impose the rule against advisory opinions. [The rule] implements the separation of powers [and] also recognizes that such suits often are not pressed before the Court with that clear concreteness provided when a question emerges precisely framed and necessary for decision from a clash

§2.2 [1] States permitting advisory opinions include Colorado, Florida, Maine, Massachusetts, New Hampshire, Rhode Island, and South Dakota. *See* Richard H. Fallon, Jr., John F. Manning, Daniel J. Meltzer & David L. Shapiro, Hart & Wechsler's The Federal Courts and the Federal System 58 (7th ed. 2015). For an excellent discussion of advisory opinions in state courts, *see* Helen Hershkoff, State Courts and the "Passive Virtues": Rethinking the Judicial Function, 114 Harv. L. Rev. 1833 (2001).

of adversary argument exploring every aspect of a multifaceted situation embracing conflicting and demanding interests."[2]

Criteria to Avoid Being an Advisory Opinion

For a case to be justiciable and not an advisory opinion, two criteria must be met. First, there must be an actual dispute between adverse litigants.[3] This requirement dates back to the earliest days of the nation. During the administration of President George Washington, then Secretary of State Thomas Jefferson asked the Supreme Court for its answers to a long list of questions concerning American neutrality in the war between France and England.[4] In his letter to the justices, Jefferson explained that the war between these countries had raised a number of important legal questions concerning the meaning of United States' treaties and laws. Jefferson's letter said that "[t]he President therefore would be much relieved if he found himself free to refer questions of this description to the opinions of the judges of the [Court], whose knowledge of the subject would secure us against errors dangerous to the peace of the United States."[5] For example, Jefferson asked the justices, "May we, within our own ports, sell ships to both parties, prepared merely for merchandise? May they be pierced for guns?"[6]

The justices wrote back to President Washington and declined to answer the questions asked. They explained that separation of powers would be violated if they were to give such advice to another branch of government. The justices, in their letter, stated: "[The] three departments of the government . . . being in certain respects checks upon each other, and our being judges of a court in the last resort, are considerations which afford strong arguments against the propriety of our extra-judicially deciding the questions alluded to."[7] The justices concluded their letter in a gracious tone: "We exceedingly regret every event that may cause embarrassment to your administration, but we derive consolation from the reflection that your judgment will discern what is right, and that your usual prudence, decision, and firmness will surmount every obstacle to the preservation of the rights, peace, and dignity of the United States."[8]

For over 200 years, then, it has been established that federal courts may not decide a case unless there is an actual dispute between adverse litigants. For example, federal courts must dismiss suits where the parties collude to bring the matter

[2] Flast v. Cohen, 392 U.S. 83, 96-97 (1968) (citations omitted).

[3] For a debate over whether this is a constitutional requirement, *see* James Pfander & Daniel Birk, Article III Power, the Adverse-Party Requirement, and Non-Contentious Jurisdiction, 124 Yale L.J. 1346 (2015); Ann Woolhandler, Adverse Interests and Article III, 111 Nw. U. L. Rev. 1025 (2017); James Pfander & Daniel Birk, Adverse Interests and Article III: A Reply, 111 Nw. U. L. Rev. 1067 (2017).

[4] *See* Fallon et al., *supra* note 1, at 50-52 (reprinting the correspondence between Jefferson and the Supreme Court).

[5] *Id.* at 51.

[6] *Id.* at 51.

[7] *Id.*

[8] *Id.* at 62.

to federal court in the absence of a real controversy between them. For instance, in *United States v. Johnson,* the Supreme Court held that a suit brought by the plaintiff at the request of the defendant, who also financed and directed the litigation, had to be dismissed.[9] The Court explained that "the absence of a genuine adversary issue between the parties" meant that the case was not justiciable.[10]

Another example of the Court's insistence on an actual dispute between adverse litigants is *Muskrat v. United States.*[11] Congress adopted a statute expanding the participants in an allotment of land that was made to certain Native American tribes. To facilitate resolution of constitutional questions about the law, Congress subsequently adopted a statute permitting the filing of two lawsuits in the Court of Claims to determine the validity of the earlier law. Pursuant to this statutory authorization, a suit was initiated, but the Supreme Court ruled that it was not justiciable. The interests of the Native Americans and the government were not at all adverse. In the Court's view, Congress simply had adopted a statute authorizing the federal courts to issue an advisory opinion on the constitutionality of a statute.

Many of the other justiciability doctrines seek to ensure the existence of an actual dispute between adverse litigants. For instance, the standing requirement that a plaintiff demonstrate that he or she has suffered or imminently will suffer an injury is crucial in determining whether there is an actual dispute that the federal courts can adjudicate. Likewise, the ripeness doctrine determines whether a dispute has occurred yet or whether the case is still premature for review. Also, the mootness requirement states that federal courts should dismiss cases where there no longer is an actual dispute between the parties, even though such a controversy might have existed at one time.

Second, for a case to be justiciable and not an advisory opinion, there must be a substantial likelihood that a federal court decision in favor of a claimant will bring about some change or have some effect. This requirement also dates back to the Supreme Court's earliest days. In *Hayburn's Case,* in 1792, the Court considered whether federal courts could express nonbinding opinions on the amount of benefits owed to Revolutionary War veterans.[12] Congress adopted a law permitting these veterans to file pension claims in the U.S. Circuit Courts. The judges of these courts were to inform the secretary of war of the nature of the claimant's disability and the amount of benefits to be paid. The secretary could refuse to follow the court's recommendation.

Although the Supreme Court never explicitly ruled the statute unconstitutional, five of the six Supreme Court justices, while serving as circuit court judges, found the assignment of these tasks to be unconstitutional. The justices explained that the duty of making recommendations regarding pensions was "not of a judicial nature."[13] They said that it would violate separation of powers because the judicial actions might be "revised and controuled by the legislature, and by an

[9] 319 U.S. 302 (1943).
[10] *Id.* at 304.
[11] 219 U.S. 346 (1911).
[12] 2 U.S. (2 Dall.) 409 (1792).
[13] *Id.* at 411.

officer in the executive department. Such revision and controul we deemed radically inconsistent with the independence of that judicial power which is vested in the courts."[14]

In other cases as well, the Supreme Court has said that a case is a nonjusticiable request for an advisory opinion if there is not a substantial likelihood that the federal court decision will have some effect. For example, in *Chicago & S. Air Lines v. Waterman Corp.*, the Supreme Court said federal courts could not review Civil Aeronautics Board decisions awarding international air routes because the president could disregard or modify judicial rulings.[15] The Court declared: "Judgments within the powers vested in courts by [Article III] may not lawfully be revised, overturned or refused faith and credit by another Department of Government. To revise or review an administrative decision which has only the force of a recommendation to the President would be to render an advisory opinion in its most obnoxious form."[16]

In *Plaut v. Spendthrift Farm, Inc.*, the Court applied the principle of *Hayburn's Case* to find unconstitutional a federal statute that overturned a Supreme Court decision dismissing certain cases.[17] In 1991, the Court ruled that actions brought under the securities laws, specifically §10(b) and Rule 10(b)(5), had to be brought within one year of discovering the facts giving rise to the violation and three years of the violation.[18] Congress then amended the law to allow cases to go forward that were filed before this decision if they could have been brought under the prior law.

In *Plaut,* the Supreme Court declared the new statute unconstitutional as violating separation of powers. Although the Court acknowledged that *Hayburn's Case* was distinguishable, the Court found *Hayburn*'s underlying principle of finality applicable. Justice Scalia, writing for the Court, said that the Constitution "gives the Federal Judiciary the power, not merely to rule on cases, but to decide them."[19] He said that because the "judicial power is one to render dispositive judgments," the federal law "effects a clear violation of separation-of-powers."[20] The statute was unconstitutional because it overturned a Supreme Court decision and gave relief to a party that the Court had said was entitled to none.

The difficulty with Justice Scalia's analysis is that Congress always has the ability to overturn Supreme Court statutory interpretation by amending the law. The Court's concern was that Congress was reinstating cases that had been dismissed by the judiciary. But it is not clear why Congress cannot give individuals a cause of action, even if the courts previously ruled that none existed. For example, if the Court ruled that a group of plaintiffs could not obtain relief under a particular civil rights law, Congress surely could amend the law to overturn the decision and

[14] *Id.*

[15] 333 U.S. 103 (1948); *see also* United States v. Ferreira, 54 U.S. (13 How.) 40 (1852) (denying jurisdiction because the secretary of treasury could refuse to pay claims under a treaty if they were deemed to not be just and equitable).

[16] 333 U.S. at 113.

[17] 514 U.S. 211 (1995).

[18] *See* Lampf, Pleva, Lipkind, Prupis & Petigrow v. Gilbertson, 501 U.S. 350 (1991).

[19] 514 U.S. at 244.

[20] *Id.* at 219, 225.

also could provide retroactive effect for the new statute. Critics of *Plaut* argue that this is exactly what Congress did with regard to the securities law after the Supreme Court's earlier ruling.

The Court refused to apply *Plaut* in a case concerning the Prison Litigation Reform Act (PLRA).[21] A provision of the PLRA provides that an injunction concerning prison conditions must be lifted by a federal court on a motion by the government after it has been in place for two years, unless the court finds that continuation of the order is needed to remedy ongoing constitutional violations. The section of the act also says that if the government moves to end the injunction, the federal court must act within thirty days; if it does not do so, then it must stay the injunction during the pendency of the proceedings.

The effect is that Congress, by statute, is ordering the suspension of a court injunction, essentially overturning a final judgment. But in *Miller v. French,*[22] the Court, in a five-to-four decision, distinguished *Plaut* and upheld this provision of the act. Justice O'Connor, writing for the majority, stressed that "[p]rospective relief under a continuing, executory decree remains subject to alteration due to changes in the underlying law."[23] Thus, unlike *Plaut,* it is not the "last word of the judicial department."[24] Therefore, even though the PLRA provision had the effect of retroactively overturning a court's order, it was permissible because Congress can require federal courts to revise their injunctions to be in compliance with changes in the law.

More generally, a federal court decision is purely advisory if it has no effect. In fact, several of the other justiciability doctrines prevent review where there is not a sufficient likelihood that the federal court decision will make some difference. One of the requirements for standing is termed redressability: there must be a substantial likelihood that a favorable federal court decision will remedy the claimed injury. Also, if a case is moot, then the federal court decision will not have any effect because the controversy already has been resolved.

The difficulty, however, is predicting in advance whether there is a substantial enough chance that a federal court decision will have an effect so as to avoid being an advisory opinion. As Professor Bickel expressed, "[T]he finality or lack of it in judicial judgments is rather a matter of degree."[28]

Therefore, for a case to be justiciable, and for it not to be a request for an advisory opinion, there must be an actual dispute between adverse litigants, and there must be a substantial likelihood that a favorable federal court decision will have some effect. These requirements must be met regardless of whether the plaintiff seeks monetary, injunctive, or declaratory relief.

[21] 18 U.S.C. §3626.

[22] 530 U.S. 327 (2000).

[23] *Id.*

[24] *Id.* at 329.

[28] Alexander Bickel, The Least Dangerous Branch 117 (1962). Professor Currie points out that the federal government can always refuse to pay money judgments against it; this does not, however, make such awards advisory opinions. *See* David Currie, Federal Courts 9 n.1 (4th ed. 1990).

Are Declaratory Judgments Impermissible Advisory Opinions?

For a time early in this century, the Supreme Court expressed doubts about whether suits for declaratory judgments could be justiciable.[29] In fact, at one point, Justice Brandeis said, "What the plaintiff seeks is simply a declaratory judgment. To grant that relief is beyond the power conferred upon the federal judiciary."[30]

Soon after this statement was uttered, the Supreme Court said that suits for declaratory judgments are justiciable as long as they meet the requirements for judicial review. In *Nashville, C. & St. L. Ry. v. Wallace*, the Court upheld the power of federal courts to issue declaratory judgments. A company sought a declaratory judgment that a tax was an unconstitutional burden on interstate commerce.[31] The Supreme Court explained that because the matter would have been justiciable as a request for an injunction, so was the suit for a declaratory judgment capable of federal court adjudication. Justice Stone, writing for the majority, explained, "The Constitution does not require that the case or controversy should be presented by traditional forms of procedure, invoking only traditional remedies. [Article III] did not crystallize into changeless form the procedure of 1789 as the only possible means for presenting a case or controversy."[32] The Court emphasized that the focus was on "substance" and "not with form" and that the case was justiciable "so long as the case retains the essentials of an adversary proceeding, involving a real, not a hypothetical, controversy."[33]

Wallace involved a request for relief pursuant to a state declaratory judgment statute. However, soon after *Wallace*, Congress adopted the Declaratory Judgment Act of 1934, authorizing a federal court to issue a declaratory judgment in a "case or actual controversy within its jurisdiction."[34] In *Aetna Life Insurance Co. v. Haworth*, the Supreme Court upheld the constitutionality of the act.[35] The Court concluded that "[w]here there is such a concrete case admitting of an immediate and definitive determination of the legal rights of the parties in an adversary proceeding upon the facts alleged, the judicial function may be appropriately exercised although the adjudication of the rights of the litigants may not require the award of process or the payment of damages."[36] In other words, federal courts can issue declaratory judgments if there is an actual dispute between adverse litigants and if there is a substantial likelihood that the favorable federal court decision will bring about some change.

An interesting case that found a request for a declaratory judgment to be nonjusticiable was *Calderon v. Ashmus*.[37] The Antiterrorism and Effective Death Penalty

[29] *See* Piedmont & Northern Ry. v. United States, 280 U.S. 469 (1930); Willing v. Chicago Auditorium Assn., 277 U.S. 274 (1928).

[30] *Id.* at 289.

[31] 288 U.S. 249 (1933).

[32] *Id.* at 264.

[33] *Id.*

[34] 28 U.S.C. §2201. *See also* 28 U.S.C. §2202 (authorizing federal courts to enforce declaratory judgments by appropriate further relief).

[35] 300 U.S. 227 (1937).

[36] *Id.* at 241.

[37] 523 U.S. 740 (1998).

Act of 1996 provides that there is a one-year statute of limitation for habeas corpus petitions, except in capital cases where the limitations period is reduced to six months if a state provides adequate counsel for collateral proceedings.[38] Death row inmates in California sought a declaratory judgment that California had not complied with the requirements for providing counsel, and thus the six-month statute of limitations for habeas corpus petitions did not apply.

The U.S. Supreme Court unanimously held that the request for a declaratory judgment was not justiciable. The Court explained that the determination of whether the statute of limitations was six months or a year would not resolve the key controversy between the inmate and the prison: whether the prisoner was entitled to collateral relief. The Court stated that the "disruptive effects of an action such as this are peculiarly great when the underlying claim must be adjudicated in a federal habeas proceeding."[39] The effect of *Calderon* is that prisoners may individually receive a determination of the statute of limitations in their case in the context of a ruling on their habeas corpus petition, but no declaratory relief will be available.

Although the Supreme Court was unanimous, this is a puzzling ruling. As explained above, declaratory judgments exist so that people can know their rights in advance. Prisoners obviously have a need to know whether they have six months or a year to file their habeas petitions. *Calderon* means that prisoners will need to guess, and if a prisoner guesses wrong, assuming a year when it is really six months, the court will deny the petition as time barred. In capital cases, that mistake can literally mean the difference between life and death. Although the determination of the statute of limitations would not resolve whether any particular prisoner was entitled to habeas corpus, it would have settled an important issue between the litigants and thus not have been an advisory opinion.

Importance of Prohibition of Advisory Opinions

Although the Supreme Court expressly refers to the ban on advisory opinions less frequently than the other justiciability doctrines, this should not be taken as an indication that it is less important. Quite the contrary, it is because the prohibition of advisory opinions is at the core of Article III that the other justiciability doctrines exist largely to ensure that federal courts will not issue advisory opinions. That is, it is because standing, ripeness, and mootness implement the policies and requirements contained in the advisory opinion doctrine that it is usually unnecessary for the Court to separately address the ban on advisory opinions.

[38] 110 Stat. 1214, Pub. L. No. 104-132, Apr. 24, 1996. The act is discussed in detail in Chapter 15.
[39] 523 U.S. at 747.

§2.3 STANDING

§2.3.1 Introduction

Standing is the determination of whether a specific person is the proper party to bring a matter to the court for adjudication. The Supreme Court has declared that "[i]n essence the question of standing is whether the litigant is entitled to have the court decide the merits of the dispute or of particular issues."[1]

Both justices and commentators have frequently identified standing as one of the most confused areas of the law.[2] Thus, it is hardly surprising that standing has been the topic of extensive academic scholarship and that the doctrines are frequently attacked. Many factors account for the seeming incoherence of the law of standing. The requirements for standing have changed greatly in the past fifty years as the Court has formulated new standing requirements and reformulated old ones. The Court has not consistently applied the tests for standing.[3] Moreover, many commentators believe that the Court has manipulated standing rules based on its views of the merits of particular cases.[4]

Most of all, though, the extensive attention to the standing doctrine reflects its importance in defining the role of the federal courts in American society. Basic policy considerations, about which there are strong arguments on both sides, are at the core of the law of standing. The Court has identified several values that are served by limiting who can sue in federal court.

Values Served By Limiting Standing

First, the standing doctrine promotes separation of powers by restricting the availability of judicial review.[5] The Supreme Court explained that standing "is founded in concern about the proper—and properly limited role—of the courts in a democratic society."[6] In *Allen v. Wright,* the Supreme Court declared that standing is "built on a single basic idea—the idea of separation of powers."[7]

§2.3 [1] Warth v. Seldin, 422 U.S. 490, 498 (1975).

[2] Joseph Vining, Legal Identity 1 (1978).

[3] The Court itself observed: "We need not mince words when we say that the concept of Art. III standing has not been defined with complete consistency in all of the various cases decided by this Court." Valley Forge Christian College v. Americans United for Separation of Church and State, 454 U.S. 464, 475 (1982).

[4] *See, e.g.,* Richard J. Pierce, Is Standing Law or Politics, 77 N.C. L. Rev. 1741 (1999); Gene R. Nichol, Jr., Abusing Standing: A Comment on Allen v. Wright, 133 U. Pa. L. Rev. 635, 650 (1985).

[5] *See* Antonin Scalia, The Doctrine of Standing as an Essential Element of the Separation of Powers, 17 Suffolk L. Rev. 881 (1983) (describing standing as a function of separation of powers). For a criticism of this view, *see* Nichol, *supra* note 4.

[6] Warth v. Seldin, 422 U.S. at 498.

[7] 468 U.S. 737, 752 (1984); *see also* Lewis v. Casey, 518 U.S. 343, 353 n.3 (1996) (Standing "has a separation of powers component, which keeps courts within certain traditional bounds vis-à-vis the other branches, concrete adverseness or not. That is where the 'actual injury' requirement comes from.").

Similarly, the Court explained: "The law of Article III standing, which is built on separation-of-powers principles, serves to prevent the judicial process from being used to usurp the powers of the political branches."[8] The notion is that by restricting who may sue in federal court, standing limits what matters the judiciary will address and minimizes judicial review of the actions of the other branches of government. Indeed, the Court had said that the "standing inquiry is especially rigorous [because of separation of powers concerns] when reaching the merits of a dispute would force [it] to decide whether an action taken by one of the other two branches of the federal government was unconstitutional."[9]

However, concern for separation of powers also must include preserving the federal judiciary's role in the system of government.[10] Separation of powers can be undermined either by overexpansion of the role of the federal courts or by undue restriction. Standing thus focuses attention directly on the question of what is the proper place of the judiciary in the American system of government.

Second, standing is said to serve judicial efficiency by preventing a flood of lawsuits by those who have only an ideological stake in the outcome.[11] In light of the high costs of litigation, however, one must wonder how large the burden really would be without the current standing restrictions. Standing also is justified in terms of conserving the Court's political capital. The Court once stated: "Should the courts seek to expand their power so as to bring under their jurisdiction ill-defined controversies over constitutional issues, they would become the organs of political theories. Such abuse of judicial power would properly meet rebuke and restriction from other branches."[12] The question, of course, is what constitutes judicial abuse and what is appropriate court behavior.

Third, standing is said to improve judicial decision making by ensuring that there is a specific controversy before the court and that there is an advocate with a sufficient personal concern to effectively litigate the matter. The Supreme Court has frequently quoted its words from *Baker v. Carr*, that standing requires that a plaintiff allege "such a personal stake in the outcome of the controversy as to assure that concrete adverseness which sharpens the presentation of issues upon which the court so largely depends for illumination of difficult constitutional questions."[14]

Yet the need for specificity is likely to vary; some cases present pure questions of law in which the factual context is largely irrelevant. For example, if a city

[8] Clapper v. Amnesty International, 568 U.S. 398, 408 (2013).

[9] Raines v. Byrd, 521 U.S. 811, 819-820 (1997). *See* Andrew Hessick, The Separation-of-Powers Theory of Standing, 95 N.C. L. Rev. 673 (2017) (arguing that standing exists to preserve separation of powers and that therefore no limit should exist on standing when separation of powers concerns are absent).

[10] *See* Susan Bandes, The Idea of a Case, 42 Stan. L. Rev. 227 (1990); *see also* Erwin Chemerinsky, Closing the Courthouse Door: How Your Constitutional Rights Became Unenforceable (2017) (arguing that separation of powers analysis must focus on the courts fulfilling their primary purposes under the Constitution).

[11] *See, e.g.*, United States v. Richardson, 418 U.S. 166, 192 (1974) (Powell, J., concurring).

[12] United Pub. Workers v. Mitchell, 330 U.S. 75, 90-91 (1947).

[14] 369 U.S. 186, 204 (1962).

government tomorrow banned all abortions within its borders, the surrounding facts in the legal challenge almost surely would be immaterial. Also, the insistence on a personal stake in the outcome of the litigation is a very uncertain guarantee of high-quality advocacy. The best litigator in the country who cared deeply about an issue could not raise it without a plaintiff with standing, but a pro se litigant with no legal training could pursue the matter on his or her own behalf.

Fourth, standing requirements are said to serve the value of fairness by ensuring that people will raise only their own rights and concerns and that people cannot be intermeddlers trying to protect others who do not want the protection offered. The Court explained, "[T]he courts should not adjudicate such rights unnecessarily, and it may be that in fact the holders of those rights either do not wish to assert them, or will be able to enjoy them regardless of whether the in-court litigant is successful or not."[15] But standing requirements might be quite unfair if they prevent people with serious injuries from securing judicial redress.[16]

Thus, although important values are served by the doctrine of standing, these same values also can often be furthered by expanding who has standing.[17] Ultimately, the law of standing turns on basic normative questions about which there is no consensus.[18]

Requirements for Standing

The Supreme Court has announced several requirements for standing, all of which must be met for a federal court to adjudicate a case. The Court has said that some of these requirements are constitutional; that is, they are derived from the Court's interpretation of Article III and as constitutional restrictions they cannot be overridden by statute. Specifically, the Supreme Court has identified three constitutional standing requirements.[19] First, the plaintiff must allege that he or she has suffered or imminently will suffer an injury. Second, the plaintiff must allege that the injury is fairly traceable to the defendant's conduct. Third, the plaintiff must allege that a favorable federal court decision is likely to redress the injury. The requirement for injury is discussed in §2.5.2. The latter two requirements—termed

[15] Singleton v. Wulff, 428 U.S. 106, 113-114 (1976). *See* Lea Brilmayer, The Jurisprudence of Article III: Perspectives on the "Case or Controversy" Requirement, 93 Harv. L. Rev. 297, 306-310 (1979) (explaining this fairness argument).

[16] *See* Richard H. Fallon, Jr., Of Justiciability, Remedies, and Public Law Litigation: Notes on the Jurisprudence of *Lyons*, 59 N.Y.U. L. Rev. 1 (1984).

[17] Heather Elliott, The Functions of Standing, 61 Stan. L. Rev. 459, 465-501 (2008) (arguing that standing doctrine serves some of its ostensible rationales only moderately well and others not at all).

[18] Indeed, some prominent commentators argue that the standing doctrine is unnecessary and that standing should simply be a question on the merits of the plaintiff's claim. *See* William Fletcher, The Structure of Standing, 98 Yale L.J. 221, 223 (1988) ("The essence of a true standing question is . . . [does] the plaintiff have a legal right to judicial enforcement of an asserted legal duty? This question should be seen as a question of substantive law, answerable by reference to the statutory or constitutional provision whose protection is invoked." *Id.* at 229).

[19] For the Court's articulation of these three constitutional standing requirements, *see, e.g.*, Murthy v. Missouri, 603 U.S. 43 (2024); Department of Education v. Brown, 600 U.S. 551 (2023).

causation and redressability—often have been treated by the Court as if they were a single test: Did the defendant cause the harm such that it can be concluded that limiting the defendant will remedy the injury?[20] Accordingly, these two requirements are considered together in §2.5.3.

In addition to these constitutional requirements, the Court also has identified three prudential standing principles. The Court has said that these are based not on the Constitution, but instead on prudent judicial administration. Unlike constitutional barriers, Congress may override prudential limits by statute.[21] First, a party generally may assert only his or her own rights and cannot raise the claims of third parties not before the court. Second, a plaintiff may not sue as a taxpayer who shares a grievance in common with all other taxpayers. However, in subsequent decisions the Supreme Court indicated that the bar on citizen suits, obviously quite similar to the limit on taxpayer suits, is constitutional and not prudential.[22] Third, a party must raise a claim within the zone of interests protected by the statute in question. These three standing requirements are discussed in §§2.3.4, 2.3.5, and 2.3.6, respectively.

Additionally, special standing problems arise that justify separate attention. For example, when may associations or groups sue on behalf of their members; when may legislators sue to protect their offices and interests; when may governments sue to protect their citizens? These questions are considered in §2.3.7.

Although the requirements for standing must be met in every lawsuit filed in federal court, the issue frequently arises in cases presenting important constitutional and public law statutory questions. As such, standing is crucial in defining the scope of judicial protection of constitutional rights. Because standing is jurisdictional, federal courts can raise it on their own, and it may be challenged at any point in the federal court proceedings.

§2.3.2 *Injury*

The Supreme Court has said that the core of Article III's requirement for cases and controversies is found in the rule that standing is limited to those who allege that they personally have suffered or imminently will suffer an injury. The Court explained, "The plaintiff must show that he has sustained or is immediately in danger of sustaining some direct injury as the result of the challenged official conduct and the injury or threat of injury must be both real and immediate, not conjectural or hypothetical."[23]

[20] It should be noted that the Supreme Court indicated that causation and redressability are separate and independent standing barriers. Allen v. Wright, 468 U.S. at 758-759.

[21] *See, e.g.,* Bennett v. Spear, 520 U.S. at 162 (1997) ("unlike their constitutional counterparts, [prudential standing requirements] can be modified or abrogated by Congress"); United Food & Com. Workers Union Loc. 751 v. Brown Grp., Inc., 517 U.S. 544 (1996) (Congress can override prudential standing requirements).

[22] Lujan v. Defenders of Wildlife, 504 U.S. 555 (1992), discussed below.

[23] *See, e.g.,* City of Los Angeles v. Lyons, 461 U.S. 95, 101-102 (1983) (citations omitted); *see also* Lujan v. Defenders of Wildlife, 504 U.S. at 560 (1992) ("[By injury in fact we mean] an invasion of a legally protected interest which is (a) concrete and particularized, . . . and (b) actual or imminent, not 'conjectural' or 'hypothetical.'"); McConnell v. Federal Election Commission, 540 U.S. 93, 225

The injury requirement is viewed as advancing the values underlying the standing and justiciability doctrines. Requiring an injury is a key to assuring that there is an actual dispute between adverse litigants and that the court is not being asked for an advisory opinion. The judicial role in the system of separation of powers is to prevent or redress particular injuries. Judicial resources are thought to be best saved for halting or remedying concrete injuries. An injury is said to give the plaintiff an incentive to vigorously litigate and present the matter to the court in the manner best suited for judicial resolution. An injury assures that the plaintiff is not an intermeddler but rather someone who truly has a personal stake in the outcome of the controversy.

Requirement for a Personally Suffered Injury

Two questions arise in implementing the injury requirement: What does it mean to say that a plaintiff must personally suffer an injury, and what types of injuries are sufficient for standing? Each issue warrants separate consideration.

The Supreme Court has declared that the "irreducible minimum" of Article III's limit on judicial power is a requirement that a party "show he personally has suffered some actual or threatened injury."[24] The Court has said that "we have repeatedly reiterated that 'threatened injury must be *certainly impending* to constitute injury in fact,' and that '[a]llegations of *possible* future injury' are not sufficient."[25]

Two environmental cases from the early 1970s illustrate this requirement. In *Sierra Club v. Morton,* the Sierra Club sought to prevent the construction of a ski resort in Mineral King Valley in California.[26] The issue was whether the plaintiff was "adversely affected or aggrieved" so as to be entitled to seek judicial review under the Administrative Procedure Act of the Interior Department's decision. The Sierra Club, a national membership organization dedicated to protecting the environment, asserted "a special interest in the conservation and the sound maintenance of the national parks, game refuges, and forests of the country."

The Supreme Court found this insufficient for standing purposes because there was no allegation that any of the Sierra Club's members ever had used Mineral King Valley. The Court stated: "The Sierra Club failed to allege that it or its members would be affected in any of their activities or pastimes by the . . . development. Nowhere in the pleadings or affidavits did the Club state that its members

---

(2003) (the injury must be both concrete and "actual or imminent"). For an argument challenging "injury" as a constitutional requirement, *see* F. Andrew Hessick, Standing, Injury in Facts, and Private Rights, 93 Cornell L. Rev. 275, 299 (2008) ("The absence of any mention of an injury-in-fact requirement for over one hundred years after the adoption of the Constitution suggests that the requirement is not essential to the exercise of the federal judicial power. If injury in fact is fundamental to ensuring the balance of power, one would expect the Court to have adopted the injury-in-fact requirement long before 1970.").

[24] Valley Forge Christian College v. Americans United for Separation of Church and State, 454 U.S. at 472 (1982).

[25] Clapper v. Amnesty International, 586 U.S. at 409.

[26] 405 U.S. 727 (1972).

use Mineral King for any purpose, much less that they use it in any way that would be significantly affected by the proposed actions of respondents."[27] The Court concluded that "a mere interest in a problem, no matter how long standing the interest and no matter how qualified the organization is in evaluating the problem, is not sufficient."[28] Justice White is quoted in *The Brethren* as saying, "Why didn't the Sierra Club have one goddamn member walk though the park and then there would have been standing to sue?"[29] In fact, on remand, the Sierra Club amended its complaint to allege that its members had used the park for activities that would be disrupted by the ski resort, and it was then accorded standing.

Sierra Club can be contrasted with another decision handed down a year later involving a group seeking to protect the environment. In *United States v. Students Challenging Regulatory Agency Procedures (SCRAP)*, the Supreme Court upheld the standing of a group of students to seek review under the Administrative Procedure Act of an Interstate Commerce Commission decision to increase freight rates.[30] A group of law students at George Washington University Law Center contended that the hike in railroad freight rates would discourage the use of recycled goods because of the extra cost of shipping them. The lawsuit claimed that a decrease in recycling would lead to more use of natural resources and thus more mining and pollution. The students maintained that their enjoyment of the forests, streams, and mountains in the Washington, D.C., area would be lessened as a result. The Supreme Court upheld the group's standing, concluding that aesthetic and environmental injuries are sufficient for standing as long as the plaintiff claims to suffer the harm personally.

A comparison of *Sierra Club* and *SCRAP* is revealing. The plaintiff's complaint must specifically allege that he or she has personally suffered an injury. Although what constitutes a sufficient injury is discussed in detail below, it is worth noting that these cases establish that an ideological interest in a matter is not enough for standing. Yet these cases also raise important policy questions. Why assume in *Sierra Club* that the only ones injured by the destruction of the park are those who already have used it? As Professor David Currie explained, why cannot a person upset by the destruction of the last grizzly bear be allowed to sue, even if he or she never has seen a grizzly?[31]

The Supreme Court has continued to apply *Sierra Club.*[32] In *Lujan v. National Wildlife Federation*, the plaintiffs challenged the federal government policy lessening the environmental protection of certain federal lands.[33] Two members of the

[27] *Id.* at 735.

[28] *Id.* at 739.

[29] Bob Woodward & Scott Armstrong, The Brethren 164 n.* (1979).

[30] 412 U.S. 669 (1973).

[31] David Currie, Federal Courts: Cases and Materials 42 (4th ed. 1990).

[32] *See also* Director, Office of Workers' Compensation Programs, Department of Labor v. Newport News Shipbuilding and Dry Dock Co., 514 U.S. 112 (1995) (holding that the director of the Office of Workers' Compensation Programs is not an aggrieved person under the Longshore and Harbor Workers' Compensation Act, and thus did not have standing to seek review of decisions by the Benefits Review Board that deny individuals benefits).

[33] 497 U.S. 871, 883 (1990).

National Wildlife Federation submitted affidavits that they used land "in the vicinity" of the reclassified land and that the increased mining activity would destroy the area's natural beauty. The Supreme Court, however, said that this allegation was too general to establish a particular injury, and thus the defendant was entitled to prevail on summary judgment because of the plaintiff's lack of standing. The Court quoted the district court's finding that thousands of acres were opened to development, and "[a]t a minimum, [the] . . . affidavit is ambiguous regarding whether the adversely affected lands are the ones she uses."[34] In other words, the plaintiffs were not entitled to standing unless they could demonstrate that they used specific federal land that was being mined under the new federal regulations.

The Supreme Court also applied this principle in *United States v. Hays* to hold that only a person residing within an election district may argue that the lines for the district were unconstitutionally drawn in violation of equal protection.[35] The Supreme Court has held that the government may use race in drawing election district lines only if it meets strict scrutiny, even if the purpose is to increase the likelihood of electing minority-race representatives.[36] In *Hays*, the Court held that only individuals residing within a district suffer an injury from how the lines for that district are drawn. The Court said that a "plaintiff [who] resides in a racially gerrymandered district . . . has standing to challenge the legislature's action," but a plaintiff who resides outside the district fails to suffer "the injury our standing doctrine requires."[37]

It is understandable that the Court would want to limit who has standing to challenge election district lines, but it seems hard to justify restricting standing to those who actually reside within the districts. Why shouldn't a voter residing in a contiguous district, who claims to have been excluded because of the race-based districting, also have standing?[38] Drawing lines for one election district inevitably affects the lines for neighboring districts. It therefore seems arbitrary to say that those within the district suffer an injury under the equal protection clause and all others do not.

The Court applied this principle in another voting case, *Gill v. Whitford*.[39] This case involved a constitutional challenge to the partisan gerrymandering of the Wisconsin legislature, where the Republican majority drew election districts to

[34] *Id.* at 888 (citation omitted).

[35] 515 U.S. 737 (1995). The Court reaffirmed and applied this limitation on standing to challenge election districts in Shaw v. Hunt, 517 U.S. 899, 904-905 (1996), and Bush v. Vera, 517 U.S. 952 (1996) (plurality opinion).

[36] *See, e.g.*, Miller v. Johnson, 515 U.S. 900 (1995); Shaw v. Reno, 509 U.S. 630 (1993).

[37] 515 U.S. at 745. Although the Court expressly said that the injury requirement was not met, the Court also said that the case presented a "generalized grievance." *Id.* at 745. This raises the question of whether the Court continues to believe that the generalized grievance requirement is a separate standing rule or simply another way of saying that there is not an injury sufficient for standing purposes.

[38] John Hart Ely, Standing to Challenge Pro-Minority Gerrymanders, 111 Harv. L. Rev. 576 (1997). *But see* Pamela S. Karlan, All Over the Map: The Supreme Court's Voting Rights Trilogy, 1993 Sup. Ct. Rev. 245 (arguing that even voters who live in majority-minority districts should not have standing).

[39] 585 U.S. 48 (2018). Subsequently, in Rucho v. Common Cause, 588 U.S. 684 (2019), the Court held that challenges to partisan gerrymandering are non-justiciable political questions. This case is discussed below in §2.6.3.

maximize safe seats for Republicans. A three-judge federal district court declared this unconstitutional. But the Supreme Court unanimously reversed on standing grounds.

Chief Justice John Roberts wrote the opinion for the Court and stressed that the plaintiffs had not proven that they lived in districts that were affected by partisan gerrymandering. Explicitly invoking *United States v. Hays,* the Court explained: "A plaintiff who complains of gerrymandering, but who does not live in a gerrymandered district, 'assert[s] only a generalized grievance against governmental conduct of which he or she does not approve.' Plaintiffs who complain of racial gerrymandering in their State cannot sue to invalidate the whole State's legislative districting map; such complaints must proceed 'district-by-district.'"[40] The plaintiffs in their complaint alleged that they lived in districts affected by partisan gerrymandering, but they had not proven this, and thus the Court found no standing.[41]

Although the Court found that the requirement for a personally suffered injury was not met in these cases, in other circumstances the Court has concluded that the plaintiffs adequately alleged a personally suffered injury. For example, in *Friends of the Earth v. Laidlaw,* the Court found that the plaintiffs had standing to challenge alleged mercury discharges because they used the affected area for recreational purposes.[42] The plaintiffs had filed affidavits that they lived near the area of the mercury discharges and that their ability to engage in activities such as hiking and fishing had been limited. The Court concluded that this was sufficient for standing and declared: "We have held that environmental plaintiffs adequately allege injury in fact when they aver that they use the affected area and are persons 'for whom the aesthetic and recreational values of the area will be lessened' by the challenged activity."[43]

The need for a personal stake in order to have standing is also reflected in two high-profile cases concerning challenges to laws prohibiting marriage equality.[44] In *Hollingsworth v. Perry,* the Court held, five to four, that the supporters of an initiative lack standing to appeal a federal district court decision invalidating the initiative when state officials refuse to appeal.[45] After the California Supreme

[40] *Id.* at 1930.

[41] Interestingly, the Court did not dismiss the case even though it reversed for lack of standing, but instead remanded it. The Court stated: "In cases where a plaintiff fails to demonstrate Article III standing, we usually direct the dismissal of the plaintiff's claims. This is not the usual case. It concerns an unsettled kind of claim this Court has not agreed upon, the contours and justiciability of which are unresolved. Under the circumstances, and in light of the plaintiffs' allegations that Donohue, Johnson, Mitchell, and Wallace live in districts where Democrats like them have been packed or cracked, we decline to direct dismissal. We therefore remand the case to the District Court so that the plaintiffs may have an opportunity to prove concrete and particularized injuries using evidence—unlike the bulk of the evidence presented thus far—that would tend to demonstrate a burden on their individual votes." *Id.* at 1933-1934.

[42] 528 U.S. 167 (2000).

[43] *Id.* at 183.

[44] The standing aspect of these decisions is discussed in Maxwell L. Stearns, Grains of Sand or Butterfly Effect: Standing, the Legitimacy of Precedent, and Reflections on *Hollingsworth* and *Windsor,* 65 Ala. L. Rev. 549 (2013).

[45] 570 U.S. 693 (2013).

Court found a right to marriage equality for gays and lesbians under the California Constitution, California voters in November 2008 passed Proposition 8. It amended the California Constitution to provide that marriage had to be between a man and a woman.

Two same-sex couples who wanted marriage licenses brought a challenge to the initiative. A federal district court ruled in their favor and held that Proposition 8 denied equal protection and violated the fundamental right to marry.[46] The Court enjoined the defendant state officials from enforcing Proposition 8. The defendants chose not to appeal, but the supporters of the initiative sought to appeal. After briefing and oral argument, the United States Court of Appeals for the Ninth Circuit certified the question to the California Supreme Court as to whether under California law the supporters of an initiative could defend it when public officials refuse to do so. The California Supreme Court found "the official proponents of the initiative are authorized under California law to appear and assert the state's interest in the initiative's validity and to appeal a judgment invalidating the measure when the public officials who ordinarily defend the measure or appeal such a judgment decline to do so."[47]

Nonetheless, the Court ruled, five to four, that the supporters of the initiative lacked standing to appeal under Article III. The Court, in an opinion by Chief Justice Roberts, stressed that "to have standing, a litigant must seek relief for an injury that affects him in a 'personal and individual way.'"[48] The Court explained that the supporters of Proposition 8 only have an ideological interest in having it enforced and that an ideological injury is insufficient for standing. Chief Justice Roberts explained: "Article III standing 'is not to be placed in the hands of concerned bystanders, who will use it simply as a vehicle for the vindication of value interests.' No matter how deeply committed petitioners may be to upholding Proposition 8 or how 'zealous [their] advocacy,' that is not a 'particularized' interest sufficient to create a case or controversy under Article III."[49]

By contrast, in a case decided the same day, *United States v. Windsor*, the Court allowed the Bipartisan Legal Advisory Group (BLAG) of the House of Representatives to defend the constitutionality of §3 of the Defense of Marriage Act (DOMA) when the president and the attorney general refused to do so.[50] When Thea Spyer died, her spouse, Edith Windsor, was required by federal law to pay $363,000 in estate taxes. If the federal government had recognized their marriage, as their home state of New York did, Windsor would owe no taxes. But §3 of DOMA requires that for federal law and federal benefits, marriages had to be

[46] Perry v. Schwarzenegger, 704 F. Supp. 2d 921 (N.D. Cal. 2010). For a detailed description of this litigation, *see* Jo Becker, Forcing the Spring: Inside the Fight for Marriage Equality (2014).

[47] Perry v. Brown, 52 Cal. 4th 1116, 1127 (2011).

[48] 570 U.S. at 705 (citations omitted).

[49] *Id.* at 707 (citations omitted). Justice Kennedy wrote the dissent, joined by Justices Thomas, Alito, and Sotomayor, and would have granted standing based on California law as interpreted by the California Supreme Court, which would allow the supporters of an initiative to defend it in court.

[50] 570 U.S. 744 (2013). The Court's analysis finding §3 of DOMA to violate equal protection is discussed in §9.7.4.

between a man and a woman. Windsor paid these taxes and then brought a challenge to §3 of DOMA.

The Obama administration's position was to enforce §3 of DOMA, as it did against Windsor, but not to defend it in court. The Bipartisan Legal Advisory Group of the House of Representatives voted three to two along party lines to intervene to defend §3 of DOMA.

In contrast to *Hollingsworth v. Perry,* the Court found that there was standing. The Court stressed that Windsor had suffered an economic injury—$363,000—and the outcome of the lawsuit would determine whether she would get the money back. The Court explained: "Windsor suffered a redressable injury when she was required to pay estate taxes from which, in her view, she was exempt but for the alleged invalidity of §3 of DOMA."[51] The Court said that the question of whether BLAG could defend the statute was prudential and not jurisdictional. The Court found that "BLAG's sharp adversarial presentation of the issues satisfies the prudential concerns that otherwise might counsel against hearing an appeal from a decision with which the principal parties agree."[52]

What explains why the Court did not find standing in *Hollingsworth,* but did in *Windsor*?[53] The Court saw *Hollingsworth* as involving solely an ideological interest on the part of the supporters of Proposition 8 who wanted to appeal to defend it. By contrast, in *Windsor,* the Court saw a concrete injury: a woman who had to pay $363,000 in estate taxes because of §3 of DOMA.

The requirement for a personally suffered injury is also illustrated by the Supreme Court's decision in *Clapper v. Amnesty International.*[54] Section 702 of the Foreign Intelligence Surveillance Act of 1978 (FISA), added by the FISA Amendments Act of 2008, permits the attorney general and the director of national intelligence to acquire foreign intelligence information by intercepting communications between persons in the United States and those in foreign countries.[55] A lawsuit was brought by attorneys, journalists, and business people who said that their communications were chilled by the possibility that their communications with individuals in foreign countries might be intercepted.

The Supreme Court, in a five-to-four decision, ordered that the case be dismissed for lack of standing. The Court, in an opinion by Justice Alito, stressed that none of the plaintiffs could show that their communications had been intercepted or were likely to be intercepted. Thus, they lacked the requisite injury required for standing. The Court explained: "First, it is speculative whether the Government will

[51] *Id.* at 755-56.

[52] *Id.* at 761, 784. Justice Scalia's dissent strongly disagreed that there was standing. *Id.* at 778-79 (Scalia, J., dissenting) ("The majority's discussion of the requirements of Article III bears no resemblance to our jurisprudence.").

[53] Of course, one explanation is that the majority of the justices wanted to reach the merits in *Windsor* and strike down §3 of DOMA, while a majority of the justices were not ready to declare unconstitutional all state laws prohibiting same-sex marriage.

[54] 568 U.S. 398 (2013). For an excellent criticism of the Court's decision in *Clapper, see* Vicki C. Jackson, Standing and the Role of Federal Courts: Triple Error Decisions in *Clapper v. Amnesty International USA* and *City of Los Angeles v. Lyons,* 23 Wm. & Mary Bill Rts. J. 127 (2014).

[55] 50 U.S.C. §1881a.

imminently target communications to which respondents are parties. . . . Second, even if respondents could demonstrate that the targeting of their foreign contacts is imminent, respondents can only speculate as to whether the Government will seek to use §1881a-authorized surveillance (rather than other methods) to do so. . . . Third, even if respondents could show that the Government will seek the Foreign Intelligence Surveillance Court's authorization to acquire the communications of respondents' foreign contacts under §1881a, respondents can only speculate as to whether that court will authorize such surveillance. . . . Fourth, even if the Government were to obtain the Foreign Intelligence Surveillance Court's approval to target respondents' foreign contacts under §1881a, it is unclear whether the Government would succeed in acquiring the communications of respondents' foreign contacts. And fifth, even if the Government were to conduct surveillance of respondents' foreign contacts, respondents can only speculate as to whether *their own communications* with their foreign contacts would be incidentally acquired."[56]

Justice Breyer, writing for the four dissenters, sharply disagreed and said that there was a sufficient likelihood that the plaintiffs' communications would be intercepted to meet the requirement for standing. He wrote: "The upshot is that (1) similarity of content, (2) strong motives, (3) prior behavior, and (4) capacity all point to a very strong likelihood that the Government will intercept at least some of the plaintiffs' communications. . . . Consequently, we need only assume that the Government is doing its job (to find out about, and combat, terrorism) in order to conclude that there is a high probability that the Government will intercept at least some electronic communication to which at least some of the plaintiffs are parties. The majority is wrong when it describes the harm threatened plaintiffs as 'speculative.'"[57]

A key difference between the majority and the dissent was how the test for future likelihood should be articulated. Justice Alito, writing for the Court, said that the injury has to be "certainly impending,"[58] while for the dissent what is required is a "reasonable probability" or "high probability."[59]

The Supreme Court, in *Spokeo v. Robins,* clarified that the requirements that the injury be "particularized" and "concrete" are distinct and that both must be met, though it left confusion as to how these requirements are different and what must be shown to meet each of them.[60] Spokeo owns and operates a website that provides in-depth reports containing personal information about individuals. Thomas Robins alleged that his Spokeo profile was filled with inaccuracies, including about his employment, his marital status, and whether he had children. Robins sued Spokeo for violating the Fair Credit Reporting Act.[61] Among other things,

[56] 568 U.S. at 411-15. The argument that the plaintiffs had an injury based on a claim that their speech was chilled is discussed below at text accompanying notes 102-103.

[57] 568 U.S. at 430-31 (Breyer, J., dissenting).

[58] *Id.* at 414.

[59] *Id.* at 447 (Breyer, J., dissenting).

[60] 578 U.S. 330 (2016). Subsequently, the Court clarified standing under this Act in TransUnion LLC v. Ramirez, 594 U.S. 413 (2021), which is discussed below in connection with when Congress, by statute, can create an injury sufficient for standing.

[61] Fair Credit Reporting Act of 1970 (FCRA or Act), 84 Stat. 1127, as amended, 15 U.S.C. §1681 et seq.

this law authorizes victims of "willful" violations to recover statutory damages of "not less than $100 and not more than $1,000."

The issue before the Court was whether Robins had standing to sue. The Ninth Circuit held that Robins had standing because Congress, by statute, had created a right and the infringement of that statutory right was sufficient for standing. The Court, in a 6-2 decision, reversed and remanded the case. Significantly, the Court did not change the law: Congress, by statute, can create rights the infringement of which is sufficient for standing to sue in federal courts. The Court approvingly quoted Justice Kennedy's concurring opinion in *Lujan v. Defenders of Wildlife* that "Congress has the power to define injuries and articulate chains of causation that will give rise to a case or controversy where none existed before."[62]

But the Court, in an opinion by Justice Alito, said that in order to have an injury sufficient for standing it must be "particularized" and "concrete." This, of course, is familiar language that has appeared in many Supreme Court cases about standing. The difference, though, is that never before has the Court treated these as two distinct requirements. The Court said that "[f]or an injury to be 'particularized,' it 'must affect the plaintiff in a personal and individual way,'" and the Court found that Robins met this requirement.[63]

The Court, however, said that a particularized injury is not sufficient for standing; it also must be a "concrete harm" and the Ninth Circuit had not considered whether the injury was "concrete." The issue for this case on remand, and for all other civil litigation in federal courts, is what does it mean for an injury to be "concrete." Here's what the Court says: "'[C]oncrete' injury must be '*de facto*'; that is, it must actually exist. When we have used the adjective 'concrete,' we have meant to convey the usual meaning of the term—'real,' and not 'abstract.' Concreteness, therefore, is quite different from particularization. 'Concrete' is not, however, necessarily synonymous with 'tangible.' Although tangible injuries are perhaps easier to recognize, we have confirmed in many of our previous cases that intangible injuries can nevertheless be concrete."[64] The Court said that in deciding whether an intangible injury is concrete, "both history and the judgment of Congress play important roles. Because the doctrine of standing derives from the case-or-controversy requirement, and because that requirement in turn is grounded in historical practice, it is instructive to consider whether an alleged intangible harm has a close relationship to a harm that has traditionally been regarded as providing a basis for a lawsuit in English or American courts."[65]

But this definition of "concrete" gives little guidance to lower courts. Moreover, though the Court says that being "particularized" and "concrete" are distinct requirements that must be met in order for there to be an injury sufficient for standing, the difference between these two is unclear.

The key point is that standing requires that a plaintiff allege and ultimately prove that he or she personally will suffer an injury. The Supreme Court continues

[62] 578 U.S. at 341.
[63] *Id.* at 339.
[64] *Id.* at 340.
[65] *Id.* at 340-341.

to enforce this basic requirement.[66] For example, in *Food and Drug Administration v. Alliance for Hippocratic Medicine,* the Supreme Court unanimously dismissed on standing grounds a challenge to the Food and Drug Administration's rules with regard to the availability of mifepristone, a drug that is used for medically induced abortions.[67] In 2000, the Food and Drug Administration approved a two-drug protocol for medically induced abortion using mifepristone and misoprostol. According to the Guttmacher Institute, in 2023, about 63 percent of all abortions were medically induced, rather than surgically performed.

The Alliance for Hippocratic Medicine, represented by the Alliance Defending Freedom, a conservative Christian organization, brought a challenge to the FDA's approval of mifepristone. The federal district court ruled in favor of the plaintiffs and would have invalidated the FDA's approval of the drug, but the United States Court of Appeals for the Fifth Circuit would have invalidated only more recent FDA actions that have made mifepristone more easily available.

The United States Supreme Court unanimously reversed the Fifth Circuit on standing grounds concluding: "But the plaintiffs do not prescribe or use mifepristone. And FDA is not requiring them to do or refrain from doing anything. Rather, the plaintiffs want FDA to make mifepristone more difficult for other doctors to prescribe and for pregnant women to obtain. Under Article III of the Constitution, a plaintiff 's desire to make a drug less available *for others* does not establish standing to sue."[68] The Court explained that no doctor would be injured because the "FDA is not requiring [doctors] to do or refrain from doing anything," and "federal law protects doctors from having to perform procedures that violate their conscience." Justice Kavanaugh noted that "plaintiffs have not shown—and cannot show—that FDA's actions will cause them to suffer any conscience injury."[69]

Application of Requirement for Personally Suffered Injury: *City of Los Angeles v. Lyons*

Perhaps the most important application of the requirement for a personally suffered injury is the requirement that a plaintiff seeking injunctive or declaratory relief must show a likelihood of future harm. This was the holding in *City of Los Angeles v. Lyons.*[70] *Lyons* involved a suit to enjoin as unconstitutional the use of chokeholds by the Los Angeles Police Department in instances where the police were not threatened with death or serious bodily injury. Adolph Lyons, a

[66] *See* Department of Education v. Brown, 600 U.S. 551 (2023) (dismissing a suit by borrowers to the Biden administration's loan forgiveness program because they were not injured by it); Carney v. Adams, 592 U.S. 53, 63 (2020) (dismissing a challenge to a Delaware requirement that appointments to Delaware courts have a partisan balance. The Court said that there was no standing because the "record evidence fails to show that, at the time he commenced the lawsuit, Adams was 'able and ready' to apply for a judgeship in the reasonably foreseeable future.")

[67] 602 U.S. 367 (2024).

[68] *Id.* at 374.

[69] *Id.* at 390.

[70] 461 U.S. 95 (1983).

twenty-four-year-old black man, was stopped by the police for having a burnt-out taillight on his car. Justice Marshall describes the uncontested facts:

> After one of the officers completed a patdown search, Lyons dropped his hands, but was ordered to place them back above his head, and one of the officers grabbed Lyons' hands and slammed them into his head. Lyons complained about the pain caused by the ring of keys he was holding in his hand. Within 5 to 10 seconds, the officer began to choke Lyons by applying a forearm against his throat. As Lyons struggled for air, the officer handcuffed him, but continued to apply the chokehold until he blacked out. When Lyons regained consciousness, he was lying facedown on the ground, choking, gasping for air, and spitting up blood and dirt. He had urinated and defecated. He was issued a traffic citation and released.[71]

At the time of the suit, sixteen people in Los Angeles had died from the chokehold—twelve of them black men.[72] Lyons's complaint alleged that it was the official policy of the Los Angeles Police Department to use the chokeholds in situations where officers were not faced with a threat of bodily injury or death.

The Supreme Court, in a five-to-four decision, ruled that Lyons did not have standing to seek injunctive relief. Although Lyons could bring a suit seeking damages for his injuries, he did not have standing to enjoin the police because he could not demonstrate a substantial likelihood that he, personally, would be choked again in the future. Justice White, writing for the Court, explained: "Lyons' standing to seek the injunction requested depended on whether he was likely to suffer future injury from the use of the chokeholds by police officers."[73] The Court concluded that "[a]bsent a sufficient likelihood that he will again be wronged in a similar way, Lyons is no more entitled to an injunction than any other citizen of Los Angeles; and a federal court may not entertain a claim by any or all citizens who no more than assert that certain practices of law enforcement officers are unconstitutional."[74] *Lyons* thus establishes that for a person to have standing to seek an injunction, the individual must allege a substantial likelihood that he or she will be subjected in the future to the allegedly illegal policy. Not surprisingly, the *Lyons* decision has been strongly criticized. First, some commentators have argued that the Court incorrectly assumed that Lyons would suffer an injury in the future only if he would be choked again. The Court's critics argue that Lyons would continue to suffer a psychological injury—fear of being subjected to a similar chokehold—as long as the police policy remained unchanged.[75]

Second, *Lyons* is criticized as representing a substantial departure from prior practice both with regard to standing and in terms of civil procedure. Never before had the Court determined standing on the basis of the remedy

[71] *Id.* at 115 (Marshall, J., dissenting).
[72] *Id.* at 115-116 (Marshall, J., dissenting).
[73] *Id.* at 105.
[74] *Id.* at 111.
[75] Gene R. Nichol, Jr., Rethinking Standing, 72 Cal. L. Rev. 68, 100-101 (1982).

sought.[76] In fact, under the Federal Rules of Civil Procedure, a plaintiff is not even required to request injunctive relief in the complaint to receive it as a remedy.[77]

Third, critics argue that the *Lyons* rationale, if strictly followed, would have a devastating effect on a substantial amount of public law litigation. Under the *Lyons* holding, plaintiffs would have standing to seek injunctions only of ongoing practices that were likely to directly harm them in the future. For example, a student would have standing to challenge an ongoing public school practice of holding prayer sessions every morning. But in many instances, plaintiffs seek injunctions—as Adolph Lyons did—of policies sure to affect someone in the future, but where a particular victim cannot be identified in advance.

Indeed, many lower courts have applied *Lyons* to prevent judicial review of allegedly unconstitutional government policies. For example, lower federal courts have dismissed the following for lack of standing: requesting an injunction against warrantless wiretaps, trying to stop certain TSA screening protocols, attempting to stop alleged unreasonable searches near the Mexican border, halting blanket policy of strip and cavity searching anyone detained, requests for injunctions to regulate the use of the chemical mace by police, challenges to a state practice of paying police officers a bonus if their arrest led to a conviction, and attempts to halt strip searches conducted at county jails of those arrested for minor crimes.[78] Additionally, lower courts consistently have applied *Lyons* to prevent standing in suits seeking declaratory judgments where standing for injunctive relief would be unavailable.[79]

[76] For a defense of distinguishing standing for damages as opposed to for injunctive relief, *see* Laura E. Little, It's About Time: Unraveling Standing and Equitable Ripeness, 41 Buff. L. Rev. 933 (1993).

[77] For an excellent development of this and other criticisms, *see* Richard H. Fallon, Jr., Of Justiciability, Remedies, and Public Law Litigation: Notes on the Jurisprudence of *Lyons*, 59 N.Y.U. L. Rev. 1 (1984).

[78] Corbett v. Transp. Sec. Admin., 930 F.3d 1225 (11th Cir. 2019) (holding no standing for traveler to challenge TSA screening protocol); J W by and through Tammy Williams v. Birmingham Bd. of Educ., 904 F.3d 1248 (11th Cir. 2018) (holding no standings against police use of chemical incapacitation spray); American Civil Liberties Union v. Nat'l Sec. Agency, 493 F.3d 644 (6th Cir. 2007) (holding no standing for challenging NSA warrantless wiretaps); Shain v. Ellison, 356 F.3d 211 (2d Cir. 2004) (ruling no standing for challenge blanket policy of strip / cavity searching); Hodgers-Durgin v. de la Vina, 199 F.3d 1037 (9th Cir. 1999) (holding no standing to challenge unreasonable searches for those stopped near the Mexican border); Curtis v. City of New Haven, 726 F.2d 65 (2d Cir. 1984) (no standing to challenge police use of mace); Brown v. Edwards, 721 F.2d 1442 (5th Cir. 1984) (no standing to challenge state policy awarding money to constables for each arrest they made that led to a conviction); Jones v. Bowman, 664 F. Supp. 433 (N.D. Ind. 1987) (no standing to challenge strip searches of women performed by county jail); John Does 1-100 v. Boyd, 613 F. Supp. 1514 (D. Minn. 1985) (no standing to challenge strip searches of people brought to the city jail for minor offenses).

[79] *See, e.g.*, J W, 904 F.3d 1248 (11th Cir. 2018) (holding that both declaratory and injunctive relief was unavailable); Cierco v. Mnuchin, 857 F.3d 407 (D.C. Cir. 2017) (ruling that no declaratory relief was available under *Lyons*); Fieger v. Mich. Sup. Ct., 553 F.3d 955 (6th Cir. 2009) (finding no standing for an attorney to challenge professional conduct rules); Fair Employment Council of Greater Washington, Inc. v. BMC Marketing Corp., 23 F.3d 1268 (D.C. Cir. 1994) (suit for injunctive and declaratory relief to halt discriminatory placement practices dismissed based on *Lyons*); Knox v. McGinnis, 998 F.2d 1405 (7th Cir. 1993) (prisoner's suit to stop prison officials from using "black box" restraining device dismissed based on *Lyons*).

Yet defenders of the *Lyons* decision argue that Lyons was not completely denied the ability to secure review of the police department's use of chokeholds. The Court did not deny his standing to pursue a damages claim and the constitutionality of the chokehold could be adjudicated there. The Court's rationale is that a person does not have standing to seek an injunction unless there is a reason to believe that he or she would directly benefit from the equitable relief. But critics of *Lyons* respond that unconstitutional government policies will remain in effect, especially in instances where damage suits cannot be brought or the government is willing to pay the damages in order to maintain its policy.

Since *Lyons*, the Supreme Court has reaffirmed that a plaintiff seeking injunctive or declaratory relief must show a likelihood of future injury. For example, in *County of Riverside v. McLaughlin*, the Court allowed plaintiffs standing to challenge a county arraignment policy that allowed long delays before arraignments over weekends and holidays.[80] The Court rejected a motion to dismiss based on *Lyons* and emphasized that plaintiffs were under arrest and in custody at the time that they filed their lawsuits. The plaintiffs' complaint alleged that they were suffering a current injury and that they "would continue to suffer that injury until they received the probable cause determination to which they were entitled."[81]

In contrast, in *Lujan v. Defenders of Wildlife*, the Supreme Court considered a challenge to a revision of a federal regulation that provided that the Endangered Species Act does not apply to U.S. government activities outside the United States or on the high seas.[82] The plaintiffs claimed that the failure to comply with the act "with respect to certain funded activities abroad increases the rate of extinction of endangered and threatened species."[83]

The Court expressly applied *Lyons* and held that the plaintiffs lacked standing because they could not show a sufficient likelihood that they would be injured in the future by a destruction of the endangered species abroad. Two of the plaintiffs had submitted detailed affidavits describing their trips abroad and their viewing of endangered animals such as the Nile crocodile, the elephant, and the leopard. The Court said that the fact that the women had visited the areas in the past "proves nothing," and their desire to return in the future—"someday"—is insufficient for standing "without any description of concrete plans or indeed any specification of when the some day will be."[84] Justice Blackmun wrote a vehement dissent and lamented that the requirement that a plaintiff have specific plans to return to a foreign country created only a silly formality that a plaintiff must purchase a plane ticket in order to sue.[85] Moreover, the dissent challenged the majority's assumption that a person is

---

[80] 500 U.S. 44 (1991).

[81] *Id.* at 51.

[82] 504 U.S. 555 (1992).

[83] *Id.* at 562 (citations omitted).

[84] *Id.* at 564. *See also* Steel Co. v. Citizens for a Better Environment, 523 U.S. 83 (1998) (relying on *Lujan* to deny standing to plaintiffs who sought relief for past violations of a federal law, but did not seek compensation for themselves, and did not allege that the company was likely to violate the statute in the future).

[85] *Id.* at 592 (Blackmun, J., dissenting). For a thorough criticism of *Lujan, see* Cass Sunstein, What's Standing After *Lujan*? Of Citizen Suits, "Injuries," and Article III, 91 Mich. L. Rev. 163 (1992).

harmed by the destruction of the environment only if the individual has concrete plans to visit the harmed place. Justice Blackmun stated: "It cannot be seriously contended that a litigant's failure to use the precise or exact site where animals are slaughtered or where toxic waste is dumped into a river means that he or she cannot show injury."[86]

What Injuries Are Sufficient?

The second major question concerning injury as a standing requirement is, what injuries are sufficient for standing? No formula exists for determining what types of injuries are adequate to allow a plaintiff standing to sue in federal court. It always has been understood that monetary harms are sufficient for standing. The law also is clear that injuries to common law, constitutional, and statutory rights are sufficient for standing. More than a half century ago, Justice Frankfurter wrote that "[a] litigant ordinarily has standing to challenge governmental action of a sort that, if taken by a private person, would create a right of action cognizable by the courts. Or standing may be based on an interest created by the Constitution or a statute."[87] Beyond these categories, however, it is difficult to do more than identify the types of interests that the Court has regarded as adequate bases for standing and those that have been deemed insufficient.

Monetary Harms

Dollars and cents injuries always have been thought sufficient for standing.[88] For example, in *Uzuegbunam v. Preczewski*, the Court held that a claim for nominal damages is sufficient for standing.[89]

By contrast, In *California v. Texas*, in 2021, the Court dismissed a challenge to the Patient Protection and Affordable Care Act on standing ground and stressed the lack of any monetary harm to the plaintiffs.[90] In 2012, in *National Federation of Independent Business v. Sebelius*, the Court in a 5-4 decision upheld the constitutionality of the Affordable Care Act (also known as Obamacare).[91] One of the key issues before the Court was the constitutionality of the individual mandate that required people to purchase insurance or pay a penalty. The Court, in an opinion

[86] 504 U.S. at 594 (Blackmun, J., dissenting).

[87] Joint Anti-Fascist Refugee Comm. v. McGrath, 341 U.S. 123, 152-153 (1951). Justice Frankfurter also expressed the view that only these categories could be a basis for standing; this certainly no longer is true, as discussed below.

[88] Also, the Supreme Court has ruled that "an assignee of a legal claim for money owed has standing, even when the assignee has promised to remit the proceeds of the litigation to the assignor." Sprint Communications Co. v. APCC Services, Inc., 554 U.S. 269 (2008). All of the Justices assumed that the claim for money was sufficient for standing, though split 5-4 as to whether the requirement for redressability is met when the plaintiff would not actually receive the funds. This is discussed below in the consideration of redressability.

[89] 592 U.S. 279 (2021).

[90] 593 U.S. 659 (2021).

[91] 567 U.S. 519 (2012).

by Chief Justice Roberts, held that the individual mandate was a valid exercise of Congress's power to impose a tax for the general welfare.

In December 2017, as part of the Tax Cuts and Jobs Act of 2017, Congress eliminated the individual mandate by setting the penalty amount at $0 for individuals not purchasing health insurance.[92] The requirement for having insurance still existed, but there were no consequences for refusing to enroll in a healthcare plan.

Texas, along with about a dozen other States and two individuals, brought suit against federal officials claiming that without the penalty, the ACA's minimum essential coverage provision is unconstitutional. They argued that the individual mandate had been upheld as a tax, but no longer could be characterized in that manner because Congress had eliminated the penalty for failing to purchase health insurance. Texas argued that this made the entire Act unconstitutional. The Trump administration agreed with the challengers and urged the federal court to strike down the entire healthcare statute. California and other "blue" states intervened to defend the law.

The lower courts ruled in favor of the plaintiffs. In a 7-2 decision, the Supreme Court dismissed the case for lack of standing. Justice Breyer wrote the opinion for the Court and said that none of the plaintiffs have shown an injury "fairly traceable" to the "allegedly unlawful conduct" that has been challenged.[93] The individual plaintiffs could not show any injury because, without a penalty for noncompliance, the Act is unenforceable. Thus, they could not show any injury resulting from the Affordable Care Act that would give them standing to sue in court.

Likewise, the Court said that Texas and the other states failed to demonstrate any monetary injuries as a result of the ACA's individual mandate penalty of $0. There was no showing that the change in federal law would cause more people to enroll in the program and thus increase their costs, nor had the states shown that their direct increase in administrative costs were a result of the change in the law.

Justice Alito, joined by Justice Gorsuch, dissented. Alito said: "The ACA imposes many burdensome obligations on States in their capacity as employers, and the 18 States in question collectively have more than a million employees. Even $1 in harm is enough to support standing. Yet no State has standing? In prior cases, the Court has been generous in allowing States to sue."[94]

Justice Alito argued that once the individual mandate penalty was reduced to zero, it could no longer be justified as a tax. Because the individual mandate could not be separated from the rest of the law, finding the provision unconstitutional meant that the remainder of the ACA was no longer enforceable. In other words, these two justices would have declared the entire Affordable Care Act unconstitutional.

[92] CCH Legislative Documents, Treaties (CCH) P P.L. 115-97, §11081.

[93] 593 U.S. at 669.

[94] *Id.* at 686-687 (Alito, J., dissenting).

Injuries to Common Law Rights

Injury to rights recognized at common law—property, contracts, and torts—are sufficient for standing purposes. In fact, for a time, the Court appeared to suggest that only such injuries would be enough for standing—that standing would be granted only if there would be a cause of action at common law for similar harms caused by a private actor. In *Tennessee Electric Power Co. v. Tennessee Valley Authority*, power companies attempted to enjoin the Tennessee Valley Authority from producing and selling electricity.[95] In denying the power companies standing to restrain their potential competitor, the Court explained that standing is unavailable "unless the right invaded is a legal right—one of property, one arising out of a contract, one protected against tortious invasion, or one founded on a statute which confers a privilege."[96] Although such injuries are obviously no longer exhaustive of those required for standing, violations of common law rights remain sufficient for standing purposes.[97]

Injuries to Constitutional Rights

Injuries to constitutional rights are also adequate to accord standing. Two qualifications are important. First, it is necessary to decide which constitutional provisions bestow rights. The Supreme Court has held that suits to halt the violation of certain constitutional provisions are nonjusticiable for lack of standing because they present "generalized grievances." For example, the Court refused to find standing for plaintiffs seeking to enjoin violations of constitutional clauses requiring a statement and account of all government expenditures and preventing members of Congress from serving in the executive branch.[98] These cases and the generalized grievance standing bar are discussed in detail in §2.3.5. In general, a person who claims discrimination or a violation of an individual liberty, such as freedom of speech or due process of law, will be accorded standing. But someone who seeks to prevent a violation of a constitutional provision dealing with the structure of government is unlikely to be accorded standing unless the person has suffered a particular harm distinct from the rest of the population.

Second, while an injury to a constitutional right is clearly a basis for standing, there remains the question of what facts are sufficient to establish such an injury. The Supreme Court's decision in *Laird v. Tatum* is illustrative.[99] In *Laird*, the

[95] 306 U.S. 118 (1939).

[96] *Id.* at 137-138.

[97] The Supreme Court ruled that "an assignee of a legal claim for money owed has standing, even when the assignee has promised to remit the proceeds of the litigation to the assignor." Sprint Communications Co. v. APCC Services, Inc., 554 U.S. 269 (2008). All of the justices assumed that the claim for money was sufficient for standing, though they split five to four as to whether the requirement for redressability is met when the plaintiff would not actually receive the funds. This is discussed below in the consideration of redressability.

[98] *See* Schlesinger v. Reservists Comm. to Stop the War, 418 U.S. 208 (1974); United States v. Richardson, 418 U.S. 166 (1974), discussed in §2.3.5, below.

[99] 408 U.S. 1 (1972).

plaintiffs contended that their First Amendment rights were violated because their expression was chilled by the army's surveillance of domestic groups. The Court said that "[a]llegations of a subjective 'chill' are not an adequate substitute for a claim of specific present objective harm or a threat of specific future harm."[100] However, it should be noted that in other instances the Court has found a chilling effect on speech to be a sufficient basis for standing. For example, in 1987, the Supreme Court accorded an exhibitor of foreign films standing to challenge the Department of Justice's labeling the films as "political propaganda" under the Foreign Agents Registration Act.[101] The Court accepted as a sufficient injury the allegation that the showing of films was chilled. The underlying point is that deciding whether there is an injury to a constitutional right often requires an inquiry into the merits of the case to determine whether a constitutional right was violated.

The Court reaffirmed *Laird v. Tatum* in *Clapper v. Amnesty International.*[102] As explained above, *Clapper* involved a challenge to a law enacted in 2008 to amend the Foreign Intelligence Surveillance Act to allow the gathering of foreign intelligence information by intercepting communications between persons in the United States and those in foreign countries. A lawsuit was brought by lawyers, journalists, and business people who said that their speech was chilled by the fear that their communications might be intercepted. The Court rejected this injury as being sufficient for standing and stated: "Because '[a]llegations of a subjective "chill" are not an adequate substitute for a claim of specific present objective harm or a threat of specific future harm,' the plaintiffs in—and respondents here—lack standing."[103]

Injuries to Statutory Rights

Violations of rights created by statute also are sufficient for standing purposes. The Supreme Court has explained that "Congress may create a statutory right or entitlement the alleged deprivation of which can confer standing to sue even where the plaintiff would have suffered no judicially cognizable injury in the absence of statute."[104] *Trafficante v. Metropolitan Life Insurance Co.* illustrates this type of injury.[105] In *Trafficante,* two white residents of an apartment complex were accorded standing to challenge the owner's discrimination against black applicants in violation of the Civil Rights Act of 1968.[106] The Supreme Court concluded that the statute created a right to be free from the adverse consequences of racial

[100] *Id.* at 13-14.

[101] Meese v. Keene, 481 U.S. 465 (1987).

[102] 568 U.S. 398 (2013).

[103] *Id.* at 418.

[104] Warth v. Seldin, 422 U.S. at 514 (1975). For an argument that Congress is inherently limited in its ability to solve standing problems, *see* Heather Elliott, Congress's Inability to Solve Standing Problems, 91 B.U. L. Rev. 159 (2011).

[105] 409 U.S. 205 (1972).

[106] 42 U.S.C. §3604.

discrimination and accepted the plaintiffs' claim that they were injured in being deprived of the right to live in an integrated community.[107]

The interesting question concerning injuries to statutory rights is how far Congress can expand standing pursuant to this authority. For instance, the Clean Air Act empowers "any person" to bring suit to enforce certain pollution control regulations.[108] In light of *Trafficante,* can Congress, by statute, create a right to clean air, the violation of which is a sufficient injury for standing purposes? The Court's decision in *Lujan v. Defenders of Wildlife* indicates that such broad authorizations for standing will not be allowed.[109]

In *Lujan,* the Court considered a challenge brought under the Endangered Species Act, which provides, in part, that "any person may commence a civil suit" to enjoin a violation of the act.[110] The Court held that Congress could not create standing in this manner. Justice Scalia, writing for the Court, stated: "To permit Congress to convert the undifferentiated public interest in executive officers' compliance with the law into an 'individual' right vindicable in the courts is to permit Congress to transfer from the president to the courts the Chief Executive's most important constitutional duty, to take care that the laws be faithfully executed."[111]

The relationship between *Lujan* and *Trafficante* is unclear. Perhaps the Court will draw a distinction between statutes that create a specific statutory right, such as a right to interracial housing, and those that are essentially procedural in creating a right for any person to sue. This distinction is troubling, however, because if Congress can create a right for all citizens, such as a right to have endangered animals protected, then Congress should be able to authorize enforcement of the right.

Alternatively, the Court may interpret statutes authorizing any citizen to sue to expand standing to the maximum allowed by Article III. In other words, Congress in expressly permitting such citizen suits is seen as abrogating prudential requirements and allowing standing as long as it is constitutionally permissible. Support for this view is found in the Court's decision in *Bennett v. Spear.*[112] Ranch operators and irrigation districts filed an action under the citizen-suit provision of the Endangered Species Act. The plaintiffs contended that the act was violated in the proposed use of reservoir water to protect certain species of fish. The Supreme Court upheld the plaintiffs' standing and cited *Trafficante* as an instance where "standing was expanded to the full extent permitted under Article III."[113] Although the Court did not discuss *Lujan,* its reasoning implies that in *Trafficante,* and in *Bennett* itself, the citizen-suit provision was a basis for standing because Article III's requirements also were met; in *Lujan,* the Article III standing requirements were not satisfied.

[107] *See, e.g.,* Havens Realty Corp. v. Coleman, 455 U.S. 363 (1982); Gladstone, Realtors v. Village of Bellwood, 441 U.S. 91 (1979).

[108] 42 U.S.C. §7604(a).

[109] 504 U.S. 555 (1992).

[110] 16 U.S.C. §1540(g).

[111] 504 U.S. at 555, 562-563.

[112] 520 U.S. 154 (1997). *Bennett's* discussion of the zone of interest test is discussed below in §2.3.6.

[113] *Id.* at 165.

The Court's subsequent standing cases seem to confirm that Congress retains broad authority to create injuries that are the basis for standing. In *Federal Election Commission v. Akins*, the Court held that Congress, by statute, could create a right to information and that the denial of such information was an injury sufficient to satisfy Article III.[114] A group of voters brought suit challenging a decision by the Federal Election Commission that the American Israel Public Affairs Committee is not a "political committee" subject to regulation and reporting requirements under the Federal Election Campaign Act of 1971. A federal statute authorizes suit by any person "aggrieved" by a Federal Election Commission decision.

The Court granted standing and concluded that Congress had created a right to information about political committees and that the plaintiffs were denied the information by virtue of the Federal Election Commission's decision. Justice Breyer, writing for the Court, explained: "The 'injury in fact' that respondents have suffered consists of their inability to obtain information—lists of AIPAC donors . . . and campaign-related contributions and expenditures—that on respondents' view of the law, the statute requires that AIPAC make public."[115] In other words, the statute created a right to information, albeit a right that would not exist without the statute, and the alleged infringement of that statutory right was deemed sufficient to meet Article III and to allow standing under the broad citizen-suit provision for any aggrieved person.

In *Friends of the Earth, Inc. v. Laidlaw Environmental Services, Inc.*, the Court also upheld a citizen-suit provision.[116] Friends of the Earth and other environmental groups sued under the citizen-suit provision of the Clean Water Act,[117] objecting to mercury discharges. The Supreme Court found that the plaintiffs had met the injury requirement because they had alleged that they used the area for recreational purposes and because the citizen-suit provision authorized litigation.

But the Court's most recent case, *TransUnion LLC v. Ramirez*, significantly limited Congress's power to create rights by statute that are the basis for standing.[118] The Fair Credit Reporting Act regulates the consumer reporting agencies that compile and disseminate personal information about consumers. The law requires that consumer reporting agencies "follow reasonable procedures to assure maximum possible accuracy" in consumer reports.[119] It provides that consumer reporting agencies must disclose to consumers all information in their file at the time of request. The Act also compels reporting agencies to "provide to a consumer, with each written disclosure by the agency to the consumer," a "summary of right" prepared by the Consumer Financial Protection Bureau.[120] Importantly for this case, the Act creates a cause of action for consumers to sue and recover damages for

[114] 524 U.S. 11 (1998).

[115] *Id.* at 21. *See* Cass R. Sunstein, Informational Regulation and Informational Standing: *Akins* and Beyond, 147 U. Pa. L. Rev. 613 (1999).

[116] 528 U.S. 167 (2000).

[117] 33 U.S.C. §1251.

[118] 594 U.S. 413 (2021).

[119] 15 U.S.C. § 1681e(b).

[120] 15 U.S.C. § 1681g(c)(2).

certain violations. The Court initially addressed standing under this law in *Spokeo, Inc. v. Robins* in 2016, which is discussed above.[121]

TransUnion is a credit reporting agency that compiles personal and financial information about individuals and creates consumer reports that are sold to entities that request information about the credit of consumers. In 2002 TransUnion introduced an add-on product called OFAC Name Screen Alert. When a business opted into OFAC, TransUnion would conduct its credit check and use a third-party software to compare a consumer's name against a list maintained by the United States Department of Treasury's Office of Foreign Assets Control (OFAC), hence the OFAC add-on. This list contained the OFAC's known terrorists, drug traffickers, and other serious criminals. If a consumer's first and last name matched a first and last name of someone on OFAC's list, then TransUnion would place an alert on the report to indicate a consumer was a potential "match" to an OFAC name. TransUnion at the time did not compare any data other than first and last names.

Sergio Ramirez learned the hard way that he was one of these individuals. Ramirez visited a car dealership in 2013 to purchase a vehicle. His credit check at the dealer returned an OFAC advisor alert. Due to matching on the terror list, the dealer refused to sell to Ramirez. Ramirez then called TransUnion to request a copy of his credit file, which was mailed to him. However, the first mailing did not include the OFAC alert, and the second mailing with the OFAC alert did not include a summary of his rights.

A class action suit was brought on behalf of 8,185 individuals with OFAC alerts in their credit files, including Ramirez, against TransUnion under the Fair Credit Reporting Act for failing to use reasonable procedures to ensure their credit files were accurate. The three claims included reputational harm based on these inaccurate credit files and two claims relating to formatting defects in mailings sent by TransUnion to the class members. Prior to trial, only 1,853 members had their misleading reports with OFAC alerts provided to third parties during the seven-month time period. The internal credit files of the rest of the 6,332 class members were not provided to third parties during that time period.

The Supreme Court ruled that this group lacked standing to sue, notwithstanding the federal law creating such a right and authorizing suits. The Court reiterated that, to have Article III standing to sue in federal court, plaintiffs must demonstrate that they suffered a "concrete" harm. The Court emphasized that a concrete harm is assessed based on whether it has a "close relationship" to a harm traditionally recognized as providing a basis for a lawsuit in American courts. The Court declared:

> What makes a harm concrete for purposes of Article III? As a general matter, the Court has explained that "history and tradition offer a meaningful guide to the types of cases that Article III empowers federal courts to consider." And with respect to the concrete-harm requirement in particular, this Court's opinion in *Spokeo* v. *Robins* indicated that courts should assess whether the alleged injury to the plaintiff has a "close relationship" to a harm "traditionally" recognized as providing a

[121] 578 U.S. 330 (2016).

> basis for a lawsuit in American courts. That inquiry asks whether plaintiffs have identified a close historical or common-law analogue for their asserted injury.[122]

The Court then spoke of the role of Congress in creating rights that are the basis for standing:

> In determining whether a harm is sufficiently concrete to qualify as an injury in fact, the Court in *Spokeo* said that Congress's views may be "instructive." . . . But even though "Congress may 'elevate' harms that 'exist' in the real world before Congress recognized them to actionable legal status, it may not simply enact an injury into existence, using its lawmaking power to transform something that is not remotely harmful into something that is." Importantly, this Court has rejected the proposition that "a plaintiff automatically satisfies the injury-in-fact requirement whenever a statute grants a person a statutory right and purports to authorize that person to sue to vindicate that right."[123]

The Court, in a 5-4 decision, applied this to hold that Ramirez lacked standing to sue. Justice Kavanaugh wrote the opinion for the Court, joined by Chief Justice Roberts and Justices Alito, Gorsuch, and Barrett. Even though Ramirez had been wrongly labelled a "terrorist," that was not a sufficient injury for standing purposes. The Court said that Ramirez did not suffer a harm with a close relationship to those harms traditionally recognized as providing a basis for a lawsuit.

Justice Thomas wrote a dissent joined by Justices Breyer, Sotomayor, and Kagan. It is not a combination of justices that has been seen very often. Justice Thomas argued that the violation of a statutory right is sufficient for standing: "[S]tatutes creat[e] legal rights, the invasion of which creates standing. And this understanding accords proper respect for the power of Congress and other legislatures to define legal rights . . . In light of this history, tradition, and common practice, our test should be clear: So long as a statute fixes a minimum of recovery. . . , there would seem to be no doubt of the right of one who establishes a technical ground of action to recover this minimum sum without any specific showing of loss."[124]

Thomas noted that "[n]ever before has this Court declared that legal injury is *inherently* insufficient to support standing. And never before has this Court declared that legislatures are constitutionally precluded from creating legal rights enforceable in federal courts if those rights deviate too far from their common-law roots."[125]

Justice Kagan wrote a separate dissent, joined by Justices Breyer and Sotomayor. She echoed the key point in Justice Thomas's dissent: never before had the Court limited standing to sue to enforce a statutory right based on whether it is one that existed at common law. She wrote: "The Court here transforms standing law from a doctrine of judicial modesty into a tool of judicial aggrandizement. It holds, for

[122] 594 U.S. at 424 (citations omitted).
[123] *Id.* at 425-426. (citations omitted).
[124] *Id.* at 448-449 (Thomas, J., dissenting) (citations omitted) (quotations omitted).
[125] *Id.* at 453-454 (Thomas, J., dissenting).

the first time, that a specific class of plaintiffs whom Congress allowed to bring a lawsuit cannot do so under Article III."[126]

TransUnion LLC v. Ramirez limits the ability to sue to enforce federal statutes creating rights. The Court's emphasis on the common law in determining whether it is a cognizable injury is a significant restriction on standing. For example, in *Trafficante v. Metropolitan Life Insurance*, the Court allowed standing to enforce the Fair Housing Act based on it seeing Congress as creating a right to interracial association.[127] But there was no such common law right.

Or consider standing to sue under the federal Freedom of Information Act. It creates a statutory right to all documents possessed by the federal government unless they fit into one of nine categories of exceptions. It authorizes standing to sue when documents are withheld. It is a statute that creates a right, albeit a right that did not exist at common law. After the Court's decision in *TransUnion* is such standing allowed to enforce this statute?

The requirement for injury under Article III has been created and enforced only in the last half century. Why should the common law be used to define something that did not exist then? There is no doubt that this case will cause great confusion over what federal laws creating rights can be enforced in the federal courts.

Other Injuries Sufficient for Standing

Injuries to common law, constitutional, and statutory rights are sufficient for standing. But these are not the only types of injuries that permit federal court review. The Supreme Court has considered many other interests, finding some to be a sufficient basis for a claim of injury, but concluding that others were inadequate. No ascertainable principle exists to rationalize these rulings. For example, the Court has ruled that a claim of an aesthetic or environmental harm is sufficient to constitute an injury.[128] In *Lujan*, for example, the Court conceded that the "desire to use or observe an animal species, even for purely aesthetic purposes, is undeniably a cognizable interest for purposes of standing."[129] In *Bennett*, the Court held that possible diminution of water allocations as a result of application of the Endangered Species Act was a sufficient injury for standing.[130] In *Massachusetts v. E.P.A.*, the Court ruled that the harms from global warming are sufficient to permit a state to sue the federal Environmental Protection Agency for failure to promulgate regulations to deal with greenhouse gas emissions.[131]

[126] *Id.* at 461 (Kagan, J., dissenting).

[127] Trafficante v. Metro. Life Ins. Co., 409 U.S. 205 (1972).

[128] *See* United States v. SCRAP, 412 U.S. 669, 686 (1973). For a creative approach to the problem of standing in environmental cases, *see* Christopher Stone, Should Trees Have Standing?—Toward Legal Rights for Natural Objects, 45 S. Cal. L. Rev. 450 (1972).

[129] 504 U.S. at 562-563.

[130] 520 U.S. at 154, 168.

[131] 549 U.S. 547 (2007).

Also, the Court has allowed standing for those suffering economic harms[132] or facing possible criminal prosecutions for their actions.[133] The Court has stated that "a person indicted for violating a federal statute has standing to challenge its validity on grounds that, by enacting it, Congress exceeded its powers under the Constitution, thus intruding upon the sovereignty and authority of the States."[134] As Justice Ginsburg explained, a "defendant has a personal right not to be convicted under a constitutionally invalid law."[135] The Court has held that the loss of the right to sue in the forum of one's choice is an injury sufficient to convey standing.[136]

In *Clinton v. City of New York*, an important decision that declared the line-item veto unconstitutional, the Court found that a change in market conditions was a sufficient injury to meet the standing requirement.[137] President Clinton used the line-item veto to cancel a tax provision that would have benefited sellers in a transaction, but not a cooperative that was purchasing their company. Nonetheless, the Court concluded that the cooperative had suffered an injury because of the change in market conditions.

In *Trump v. Hawaii*, the Court allowed standing to challenge President Trump's "travel ban"—his exclusion of immigration from designated countries—for family members who said that they were being kept from being with relatives.[138] The Court did not rule on the plaintiffs' claim of a dignitary injury based on President Trump's avowed desire to ban immigration by Muslims, but instead focused on the real-world injury of family separation: "We need not decide whether the claimed dignitary interest establishes an adequate ground for standing. The three individual plaintiffs assert another, more concrete injury: the alleged real-world effect that the Proclamation has had in keeping them separated from certain relatives who seek to enter the country. We agree that a person's interest in being united with his relatives is sufficiently concrete and particularized to form the basis of an Article III injury in fact."[139]

Also, in *Department of Commerce v. New York*, the Court found that there was a sufficient injury in terms of the possible loss of federal funds to challenge the choice of the federal government to ask a question about citizenship on the 2020 census.[140]

[132] Barlow v. Collins, 397 U.S. 159 (1970); Hardin v. Kentucky Utils. Co., 390 U.S. 1 (1968); FCC v. Sanders Bros. Radio Station, 309 U.S. 470 (1940).

[133] *See* Laurence Tribe, American Constitutional Law 115 (2d ed. 1988) ("A person subject to criminal prosecution, or faced with its imminent prospect, has clearly established the requisite 'injury in fact' to oppose such prosecution by asserting any relevant constitutional or federal rights.").

[134] Bond v. United States, 564 U.S. 211, 214 (2011).

[135] *Id.* at 226 (Ginsburg, J., concurring).

[136] *See* International Primate Protection League v. Administrators of Tulane Educ. Fund, 500 U.S. 72 (1991) (allowing plaintiffs standing to challenge removal of a case from state to federal court, even though plaintiffs lacked standing to challenge the government's action, which was the basis for the lawsuit). *See also* Asarco v. Kadish, 490 U.S. 605 (1989) (a state court decision can create an injury, and therefore be the basis for standing, even if plaintiffs initially would have lacked standing to sue in federal court).

[137] 524 U.S. 417 (1998).

[138] 585 U.S. 667 (2018).

[139] *Id.* at 698.

[140] 588 U.S. 752 (2019).

§2.3 Standing

The Trump administration decided to reverse past recent policy and have a question about citizenship on 2020 census forms. Challengers argued that this would cause noncitizens, and especially undocumented individuals, to be less likely to complete the census forms. Census data is used, among other purposes, for allocating federal funds. The Court, in a part of the opinion that was unanimous, found this sufficient: "Several state respondents here have shown that if noncitizen households are undercounted by as little as 2%—lower than the District Court's 5.8% prediction—they will lose out on federal funds that are distributed on the basis of state population. That is a sufficiently concrete and imminent injury to satisfy Article III, and there is no dispute that a ruling in favor of respondents would redress that harm."[141]

Other types of interests have been deemed insufficient for standing. For instance, in *Allen v. Wright*, the Supreme Court refused to allow standing to challenge the Internal Revenue Service's policy of providing tax exemptions to private schools that discriminated on the basis of race.[142] The Court said that the plaintiffs' claim that they were stigmatized by the government's policy was insufficient to constitute an injury for standing purposes. The Court explained: "[Stigmatic injury] accords a basis for standing only to those persons who are personally denied equal treatment. . . . If the abstract stigmatic injury were cognizable, standing would extend nationwide to all members of the particular racial groups against which the Government was alleged to be discriminating by its grant of a tax exemption to a racially discriminatory school."[143]

Another example where the Court deemed a harm as insufficient to meet the injury requirement was in one of the companion cases to *Roe v. Wade*.[144] Although the Court found the claim of another plaintiff to be justiciable, the Court refused to hear the challenge brought by a married couple to a law prohibiting abortion. The couple claimed that their "marital happiness" was adversely affected because they were "forced to the choice of refraining from normal sexual relations or of endangering Mary Doe's health through a possible pregnancy."[145] The Court deemed this injury insufficient to confer standing.

It is difficult to identify a principle that explains why aesthetic or economic injuries are sufficient for standing, but stigma or marital happiness are not. The only conclusion is that in addition to injuries to common law, constitutional, and statutory rights, a plaintiff has standing if he or she asserts an injury that the Court deems sufficient for standing purposes.[146]

[141] *Id.* at 767.

[142] 468 U.S. 737 (1984).

[143] *Id.* at 755-756. *Allen* also denied standing based on failure to meet the causation requirement; this is discussed below in §2.3.3.

[144] 410 U.S. 113 (1973).

[145] *Id.* at 128 (citations omitted).

[146] In an opinion concurring in the judgment, Justice Gorsuch (joined by Justice Thomas) argued that there is not a sufficient injury to allow plaintiffs to challenge religious symbols on government property. American Legion v. American Humanist Association, 588 U.S. 29, 79 (2019) (Gorsuch, J., concurring in the judgment). Justice Gorsuch argues that such a plaintiff is simply an "offended observer" and "suits like this one should be dismissed for lack of standing." *Id.*

§2.3.3 *Causation and Redressability*

Injury is necessary for standing, but not sufficient. A plaintiff also must allege and prove that the personal injury is "fairly traceable to the defendant's allegedly unlawful conduct and likely to be redressed by the requested relief."[147] These requirements have been labeled *causation* (the plaintiff must allege that the defendant's conduct caused the harm) and *redressability* (the plaintiff must allege that a favorable court decision is likely to remedy the injury). The Supreme Court has declared that both causation and redressability are constitutional requirements for standing.[148]

Initially, the Supreme Court treated causation and redressability as if they were a single test designed to determine whether a federal court decision would have some effect. Causation was deemed relevant because if the defendant is the cause of the plaintiff's injury, then it is likely that halting the defendant's behavior will stop the injury. Redressability focuses directly on the same inquiry: Will the federal court decision make a difference? Thus, in *Warth v. Seldin,* the Court said that in order to have standing a plaintiff must allege that "the asserted injury was the consequence of the defendants' actions, or that the prospective relief will remove the harm."[149]

In *Allen v. Wright,* however, the Court indicated that these are separate requirements for standing.[150] In its most recent articulations of the standing doctrine, the Court has consistently stated causation and redressability as distinct standing hurdles, both of which must be met for a federal court to hear a case.[151]

Key Cases Concerning Causation and Redressability

The causation and redressability tests are best understood in the context of the cases that first articulated the requirements: *Linda R.S. v. Richard D.,*[152] *Warth v. Seldin,*[153] *Simon v. Eastern Kentucky Welfare Rights Organization,*[154] *Duke Power Co. v. Carolina Environmental Study Group, Inc.,*[155] and *Allen v. Wright.*[156]

In *Linda R.S. v. Richard D.*, an unwed mother sought to have the father of her child prosecuted for failure to pay child support. The state of Texas had a policy of prosecuting fathers of legitimate children for not paying required child support, but did not prosecute fathers of illegitimate children. The plaintiff argued that this was unconstitutional discrimination on the basis of the child's legitimacy. The Supreme Court, however, dismissed the case for lack of standing. The

[147] Allen v. Wright, 468 U.S. at 751 (1984).

[148] *See, e.g.,* United States v. Hays, 515 U.S. at 743 (1995).

[149] 422 U.S. at 505 (1975).

[150] 468 U.S. at 753 n.19 (1984).

[151] *See, e.g.,* United States v. Hays, 515 U.S. at 743; Northeastern Fla. Chapter of Assoc. Gen. Contractors of Am. v. Jacksonville, 508 U.S. at 663 (1993); Lujan v. Defenders of Wildlife, 504 U.S. at 560-561 (1992).

[152] 410 U.S. 614 (1973).

[153] 422 U.S. 490 (1975).

[154] 426 U.S. 26 (1976).

[155] 438 U.S. 59 (1978).

[156] 468 U.S. 737 (1984).

Court reasoned that even an injunction commanding state prosecutions would not ensure that the mother would receive any additional child support money. The Court explained that "if appellant were granted the requested relief, it would result only in the jailing of the child's father. The prospect that prosecution, at least in the future, will result in payment of support can, at best, be termed only speculative."[157]

The importance of the causation and redressability doctrines as restrictions on federal jurisdiction was made clear in *Warth v. Seldin.* In *Warth,* several plaintiffs challenged the unconstitutionality of exclusionary zoning practices in Penfield, New York, a suburb of Rochester. The plaintiffs included Rochester residents who wanted to live in Penfield but claimed that they could not because of the zoning practices that prevented construction of multifamily dwellings and low-income housing. Also, an association of home builders that wanted to construct such housing joined as plaintiffs in the suit.[158]

The Supreme Court held that these plaintiffs lacked standing—even though they alleged violations of their constitutional rights—because they could not demonstrate that appropriate housing would be constructed without the exclusionary zoning ordinances. The Court felt that the low-income residents seeking to live in Penfield might not be able to afford to live there even if the town's zoning ordinances were invalidated. Also, the builders might not choose to construct new housing in Penfield, regardless of the outcome of the lawsuit. Justice Powell, writing for the Court, stated: "But the record is devoid of any indication that these projects, or other like projects, would have satisfied petitioners' needs at prices they could afford, or that, were the court to remove the obstructions attributable to respondents, such relief would benefit petitioners."[159]

Similarly, in *Simon v. Eastern Kentucky Welfare Rights Organization,* the Court denied standing to plaintiffs who were clearly injured because the Court concluded that the plaintiffs failed to meet the requirements for causation and redressability.[160] The plaintiffs challenged an Internal Revenue Service revision of a Revenue Ruling limiting the amount of free medical care that hospitals receiving tax-exempt status were required to provide. Whereas previously tax-exempt charitable hospitals had to provide free care for indigents, under the new provisions only emergency medical treatment of indigents was required. The plaintiffs were individuals who claimed that they were denied needed medical care, and hence injured, by hospitals receiving tax-exempt status.

Again, the Supreme Court denied standing, concluding that causation and redressability were lacking. The Court said that it was "purely speculative" whether the new Revenue Ruling was responsible for the denial of medical services to the plaintiffs and that "the complaint suggests no substantial likelihood that victory

[157] 410 U.S. at 618.

[158] Other plaintiffs included Rochester residents claiming injuries as taxpayers and an organization suing on behalf of its members who desired interracial association. Taxpayer standing is discussed in §2.3.5; standing for associations is discussed in §2.3.6.

[159] 422 U.S. at 505-506.

[160] 426 U.S. 26 (1976).

in this suit would result in respondents' receiving the hospital treatment they desire."[161]

In contrast, in *Duke Power Co. v. Carolina Environmental Study Group, Inc.*, the Supreme Court found the causation and redressability requirements to be satisfied. In *Duke Power*, forty individuals and two organizations challenged the constitutionality of the Price-Anderson Act, which limited the liability of utility companies in the event of a nuclear reactor accident.[162] The plaintiffs argued that the Price-Anderson Act violated the due process clause because it allowed injuries to occur without compensation. The Supreme Court found standing to exist because the construction of a nuclear reactor in the plaintiffs' area subjected them to many injuries, including exposure to radiation, thermal pollution, and fear of a major nuclear accident. Furthermore, the Court accepted the lower court's conclusion that the causation and redressability tests were met because *but for* the Price-Anderson Act the reactor would not be built and the plaintiffs would not suffer these harms. After finding standing, the Court held that the Price-Anderson Act was constitutional.

In *Allen v. Wright,* parents of Black public schoolchildren brought a class action suit challenging the failure of the Internal Revenue Service to carry out its statutory obligation to deny tax-exempt status to racially discriminatory private schools. The plaintiffs claimed two injuries. One was that they and their children were stigmatized by government financial aid to schools that discriminate. As described above, the Court held that this injury was too abstract to confer standing. The plaintiffs also claimed that their children's chances to receive an integrated education were diminished by the continued tax breaks to discriminatory schools. The parents argued that if the IRS enforced the law, the schools either would stop discriminating or have to charge more money because of the loss of the tax breaks. Either way, more white students likely would attend the public schools.

The Supreme Court acknowledged that this claim stated an injury, but denied standing based on an absence of "causation." The Court stated that "respondents' second claim of injury cannot support standing because the injury alleged is not fairly traceable to the Government conduct respondents challenge as unlawful. . . . From the perspective of the IRS, the injury to respondents is highly indirect and results from the independent action of some third party not before the court."[163] In an important footnote, the Court stated that even though a change in IRS policy might redress the injury, it would be insufficient for standing because the IRS did not cause the segregation. Justice O'Connor, writing for the Court, stated:

> The fairly traceable and redressability components of the constitutional standing inquiry were initially articulated by this Court as two facets of a single causation requirement. . . . Cases such as this, in which the relief requested goes well beyond

[161] *Id.* at 45-46.

[162] 42 U.S.C. §2210(e) (at the time *Duke Power* was decided, liability was limited to $560 million for a single nuclear accident).

[163] 468 U.S. at 757 (citations omitted).

> the violation of law alleged, illustrate why it is important to keep the inquiries separate if the redressability component is to focus on the requested relief. Even if the relief respondents request might have a substantial effect on the desegregation of public schools, whatever deficiencies exist in the opportunities for desegregated education for respondents' children might not be traceable to IRS violations of the law.[164]

These cases illustrate that the causation / redressability standing requirements are a powerful barrier to federal court review. Although in cases such as *Linda v. Richard, Warth, Simon,* and *Allen,* there were serious allegations of constitutional violations, access to the federal courts was denied.

The Court's subsequent decisions have sometimes found the causation and redressability requirements to be met, but sometimes have dismissed for failure to meet them. In *Massachusetts v. E.P.A.*, the Court held that Massachusetts could sue to challenge the Environmental Protection Agency's failure to promulgate rules to deal with greenhouse gas emissions even though it was uncertain how much such regulations would decrease the problem of global warming.[165] Justice Stevens, writing for a five-justice majority, explained: "While it may be true that regulating motor-vehicle emissions will not by itself *reverse* global warming, it by no means follows that we lack jurisdiction to decide whether EPA has a duty to take steps to *slow* or *reduce* it. Because of the enormity of the potential consequences associated with manmade climate change, the fact that the effectiveness of a remedy might be delayed during the (relatively short) time it takes for a new motor-vehicle fleet to replace an older one is essentially irrelevant. Nor is it dispositive that developing countries such as China and India are poised to increase greenhouse gas emissions substantially over the next century: A reduction in domestic emissions would slow the pace of global emissions increases, no matter what happens elsewhere."[166]

Chief Justice Roberts's dissent, which was joined by Justices Scalia, Thomas, and Alito, argued that global warming is too general a problem affecting the entire world to meet the requirement for a particularized injury. The dissent, however, focused especially on the redressability requirement and argued that it was not met. Chief Justice Roberts declared: "The Court's sleight of hand is in failing to link up the different elements of the three-part standing test. What must be *likely* to be redressed is the particular injury in fact. The injury the Court looks to is the asserted loss of land. The Court contends that regulating domestic motor vehicle emissions will reduce carbon dioxide in the atmosphere, *and therefore*

[164] *Id.* at 753 n.19.

[165] Similarly, in Sprint Communications Co. v. APCC Services, Inc., 549 U.S. 497 (2007), the Court split 5-4 and ruled that the assignee of a claim for money owed has standing to sue in federal court even when the assignee has promised to remit the proceeds of the litigation to the assignor. Justice Breyer, writing for the Court, said that "history and precedent are clear on the question before us: Assignees of a claim, including assignees for collection, have long been permitted to bring suit." The Court explained that redressability focuses "on whether the *injury* that a plaintiff alleges is likely to be redressed through the litigation—not on what the plaintiff ultimately intends to do with the money he recovers." *Id.* at 287.

[166] *Id.* at 525-526.

redress Massachusetts's injury. . . . The realities make it pure conjecture to suppose that EPA regulation of new automobile emissions will *likely* prevent the loss of Massachusetts coastal land."[167]

But the Supreme Court also has dismissed litigation for failing to meet the causation requirement for standing. *United States v. Texas* is a recent example of this.[168] In 2021, the Biden administration's Department of Homeland Security announced its priorities in arresting and deporting those who are illegally in the United States. There are over 11 million undocumented individuals in the country, but at most only several hundred thousand are deported each year.[169] Therefore, the Biden administration said that it would prioritize arresting and deporting those unlawfully present who are suspected terrorists or dangerous criminals, or who have unlawfully entered the country only recently.

Texas and Louisiana sued the Department of Homeland Security in federal court, claiming that federal laws require the federal government to arrest more non-citizens pending their deportation. As Justice Brett Kavanaugh said, "The States essentially want the Federal Judiciary to order the Executive Branch to alter its arrest policy so as to make more arrests."[170]

The Supreme Court in an 8-1 decision ruled that there is no standing to challenge the enforcement priorities of the executive branch of government. Justice Kavanaugh, writing for the Court, said: "The States have not cited any precedent, history, or tradition of courts ordering the Executive Branch to change its arrest or prosecution policies so that the Executive Branch makes more arrests or initiates more prosecutions. On the contrary, this Court has previously ruled that a plaintiff lacks standing to bring such a suit."[171]

The Court focused on its precedent from 1973 in *Linda R.S. v. Richard D.* Justice Kavanaugh said that "Court's Article III holding in *Linda R.S.* applies to challenges to the Executive Branch's exercise of enforcement discretion over whether to arrest or prosecute."[172] The Court stressed that this is particularly important in the context of immigration policy where there is great deference to the executive branch of government. Justice Kavanaugh declared: "That principle of enforcement discretion over arrests and prosecutions extends to the immigration context, where the Court has stressed that the Executive's enforcement discretion implicates not only 'normal domestic law enforcement priorities' but also 'foreign-policy objectives.'"[173] The Court stressed that allowing standing would put the Court in the untenable position of overseeing the enforcement priorities of the executive branch of government.

Murthy v. Missouri involved a suit brought by two state governments and five social media users against the Biden administration and many federal agencies

[167] *Id.* at 546 (Roberts, C.J., dissenting).

[168] 599 U.S. 670 (2023).

[169] Elma Mrkonjić, 37+ Remarkable Deportation Statistics [The View from 2021] (Jun. 30, 2021), https://thehighcourt.co/deportation-statistics/.

[170] 599 U.S. at 674.

[171] *Id.* at 677.

[172] *Id.*

[173] *Id.* at 679.

claiming that the First Amendment was violated by the government pressuring social media platforms to take down false speech.[174]

A conservative federal district court judge in Louisiana ruled in favor of the plaintiffs and issued an injunction against the White House and many federal agencies. But the United States Court of Appeals for the Fifth Circuit left much of the injunction in place and said that the federal government coerced and encouraged platforms to remove false speech.

In a 6-3 decision, with the majority opinion written by Justice Amy Coney Barrett, the Court reversed the Fifth Circuit and ordered the case dismissed for lack of standing, concluding that the plaintiffs failed to meet the causation requirement. The Court said that none of the plaintiffs could show that social media companies took down false speech because of coercion from the government. The Court stressed that "platforms had independent incentives to moderate content and often exercised their own judgment."[175] Justice Barrett wrote: "This evidence indicates that the platforms had independent incentives to moderate content and often exercised their own judgment. To be sure, the record reflects that the Government defendants played a role in at least some of the platforms' moderation choices. But the Fifth Circuit, by attributing *every* platform decision at least in part to the defendants, glossed over complexities in the evidence."[176]

Justice Samuel Alito, in his dissent, described this as "one of the most important free speech cases to reach this Court in years."[177] Justice Alito, joined by Justices Thomas and Gorsuch, concluded that the pressure from government officials clearly violated the First Amendment. He said that dismissing the case on standing grounds was "regrettable."[178]

Criticism and Defenses of the Requirement for Causation and Redressability

The causation / redressability standing requirement has been quite controversial. Its defenders argue that it simply implements the prohibition against advisory opinions; if a federal court decision will have little effect, if it will not redress the injuries, then it is an advisory opinion. But its critics contend that it imposes an unjustified and unprincipled limit on the availability of the federal forum.

One criticism of the redressability requirement is that it is undesirable because it is an improper determination to make on the basis of the pleadings. All decisions about standing initially are made on the basis of the pleadings, assuming all allegations within them to be true. The criticism is that redressability is inherently a factual question—how likely is it that a favorable court decision will have a particular effect—that should not be made at the outset of a lawsuit. Traditionally,

[174] 603 U.S. 43 (2024).
[175] 144 S. Ct. at 1987-88.
[176] *Id.* at 1988.
[177] *Id.* at 1997 (Alito, J., dissenting).
[178] *Id.* at 1999.

courts consider whether equitable relief will have the desired effect at the remedy stage, after there has been an opportunity for discovery and a hearing on the merits.

For example, in *Simon*, a plaintiff wanting to prove that the change in the Revenue Rulings was responsible for the lack of free care for indigents would seek to demonstrate that the hospitals economically would have little alternative but to provide free care rather than lose their tax-exempt status. But this would require discovery of the hospitals' financial records, something unavailable at the time standing is determined.

Similarly, in *Warth*, the Court implied that a plaintiff could have standing to challenge the exclusionary zoning only by producing specific plans for housing that the plaintiffs definitely could afford. But the more successful the exclusionary zoning, the less likely the plaintiffs could find a building company willing to go to the trouble and expense of drafting plans that are certain to be denied.

A second criticism of the causation / redressability requirement is that it is inherently unprincipled because it depends entirely upon how a court chooses to characterize the plaintiff's injury. If a court characterizes an injury one way, it is redressable, but if the court chooses a different characterization, redressability will be absent. For example, in *Linda v. Richard*, the Court characterized the plaintiff's injury as a lack of child support and concluded that there was not redressability because the plaintiff still might not receive payments even if her child's father was prosecuted. But if the Court characterized the plaintiff's injury as a denial of equal protection because of discrimination against mothers of illegitimate children, this injury would be remedied by a favorable court decision regardless of whether more money would be forthcoming as a result of the lawsuit.[179]

The Court's ability to manipulate the injury requirement is illustrated by comparing *Linda v. Richard* with *Orr v. Orr*.[180] In *Orr*, a man challenged an Alabama law that permitted courts to award alimony to women but not to men. Under the reasoning of *Linda v. Richard*, the case should have been dismissed for lack of standing: even if the Court declared the Alabama law unconstitutional, that would not ensure that Mr. Orr would receive more money. But the Court in *Orr* refused to dismiss the case on standing grounds, finding the injury to be a denial of equal protection that would be remedied by a favorable court decision.

The importance of how the injury is characterized is illustrated by *Northeastern Florida Chapter of the Associated General Contractors of America v. Jacksonville, Florida*.[181] A Jacksonville, Florida, ordinance had created a preference for minority businesses in receiving city contracts. The city moved to dismiss for lack of standing on the grounds that the plaintiffs could not demonstrate that they would have bid successfully on the contracts. The Supreme Court ruled that the plaintiffs had standing because their injury is the denial of the ability to compete equally for all contracts and a favorable court ruling will redress that injury. Justice Thomas, writing for

[179] Gene R. Nichol, Jr., Causation as a Standing Requirement: The Unprincipled Use of Judicial Restraint, 69 Ky. L.J. 185, 198 (1981).

[180] 440 U.S. 268 (1979).

[181] 508 U.S. 656 (1993).

the Court, explained: "When the government erects a barrier that makes it more difficult for members of one group to obtain a benefit than it is for members of another group, a member of the former group seeking to challenge the barrier need not allege that he would have obtained the benefit but for the barrier in order to establish standing."[182] The Court emphasized that the injury "is the denial of equal treatment resulting from the imposition of the barrier, not the ultimate inability to obtain the benefit."[183]

The Court relied on its earlier decision in *Regents of the University of California v. Bakke.*[184] Alan Bakke, a white male, was denied admission to the University of California at Davis Medical School and filed suit challenging the school's practice of setting aside 16 spots for minority students out of an entering class of 100. The state argued that Bakke lacked standing based on the redressability requirement. Even if the affirmative action program were declared unconstitutional, Bakke still might not be admitted to the medical school. In other words, if the Court characterized Bakke's injury as a denial of admission, there was no assurance that a favorable court decision would redress the injury. But the Court chose a different characterization of the harm. The Court stated that Bakke's injury was an inability to compete for all 100 slots and, therefore, a judicial decision declaring the set-aside of 16 spots unconstitutional would remedy the injury and give him a chance to compete for all the slots.[185]

The Court's reasoning in *Northeastern Florida,* and before that in *Bakke* and *Orr,* seems clearly correct. When a plaintiff alleges a denial of equal protection, the injury is the denial of the ability to evenly compete. Even if ultimately the plaintiff would not receive the benefit, a favorable court decision redresses the harm by providing equal opportunity. Yet *Linda v. Richard* seems inconsistent with this because there the claimed denial of equal protection was not deemed sufficient for standing.[186]

A third major criticism of the causation / redressability requirement is that it is inherently unprincipled in terms of what constitutes a sufficient likelihood of solution to justify standing. Causation and redressability are assessments of probability; how likely is it that the defendant is the cause of the plaintiff's injury and how likely is it that a favorable court decision will remedy the harm? But it is unclear where on the probability continuum it is sufficiently certain that a court should grant standing.

For example, in *Village of Arlington Heights v. Metropolitan Housing Development Corp.*, the Court allowed the plaintiffs standing to challenge a suburb's exclusionary

[182] *Id.* at 666.

[183] *Id.*

[184] 438 U.S. 265 (1978).

[185] *Id.* at 319-320.

[186] For example, when relief is ordered against the government, there is always the chance that the government will not comply. *See, e.g.,* Utah v. Evans, 536 U.S. 452 (2002), which allowed Utah standing to challenge census calculations in a suit against the Census Bureau and the Secretary of Commerce. The Court concluded that it was sufficiently likely that the president and congressional officials would act, if the lawsuit succeeded, to increase Utah's representation in the House of Representatives to make the case justiciable.

zoning.[187] *Arlington Heights* was distinguished from *Warth* because in Arlington Heights, Illinois, builders had developed specific plans for low-income housing that had been rejected, whereas no such plans existed in Penfield, New York. The Court stated that there was a "sufficient probability" that this housing project would be built, affording the plaintiff a chance to live in Arlington Heights.[188] But even if the Court declared the exclusionary zoning unconstitutional, the housing still might not have been built. The developers did not have financing and required substantial government subsidies that had not yet been appropriated. The Court's critics argue that a comparison of *Warth* and *Arlington Heights* reveals that courts make an arbitrary choice about what is a sufficient likelihood that a favorable court decision will remedy the harm.

Another illustration of this subjectivity is *Larson v. Valente*.[189] Minnesota law required charitable organizations to register with the state and to comply with detailed reporting requirements. An exemption was created for religious organizations that received at least 50 percent of their contributions from members. A group called the Holy Spirit Association for the Unification of World Christianity filed suit challenging the constitutionality of the 50 percent requirement.

The state argued to the Supreme Court that the group lacked standing because it was not a religious organization; thus, regardless of the outcome of the lawsuit, it would have to register. The Supreme Court acknowledged that the church's status was uncertain and it would need to be determined on remand whether the group was a religious organization. Thus, it was quite uncertain whether a favorable court decision would have any effect for the plaintiff. But the Court nonetheless found standing because it concluded that it is "substantial and meaningful relief" to make it clear that if the church is a religious organization it cannot be compelled to register. The Court said that "a plaintiff satisfies the redressability requirement when he shows that a favorable decision will relieve a discrete injury to himself. He need not show that a favorable decision will relieve his every injury."[190] The Court easily could have concluded either way in deciding whether there was a sufficient likelihood that the Court's decision would have an effect.

Subsequently, in *Lujan v. Defenders of Wildlife*, plaintiffs challenged a change in a federal regulation that provided that the Endangered Species Act would not be applied to federal government activity outside the United States.[191] The Court ruled that the plaintiffs lacked standing, in part because invalidating the new regulation might not change government behavior. Justice Scalia, writing for a plurality of four justices, said that agencies might not comply with a revised regulation in the future, thus preventing a federal court action from redressing the alleged harm. But if the possibility of noncompliance by government officials is sufficient to undermine redressability, countless cases would have to be dismissed, because noncompliance with a judicial order is always a possibility.

[187] 429 U.S. 252 (1977).
[188] *Id.* at 264.
[189] 456 U.S. 228 (1982).
[190] *Id.* at 244 n.15.
[191] 504 U.S. 555 (1992).

Critics argue that the Court manipulates causation and redressability based on its views of the merits.[192] For example, in *Duke Power* it is argued that the Court wanted to uphold the Price-Anderson Act and thus found standing. But in *Simon*, where the Court did not want to address the issue, it denied standing. Again, the Court's defenders might argue that this judicial discretion is desirable and question whether the causation/redressability requirement is more unprincipled than other legal rules that are inherently discretionary.

Initially, the Court treated causation and redressability as if they imposed a single requirement for standing. In *Duke Power*, the Court said that "[t]he more difficult step in the standing inquiry is establishing that these injuries 'fairly can be traced to the challenged action of the defendant,' . . . or put otherwise, that the exercise of the Court's remedial powers would redress the claimed injuries."[193] In *Arlington Heights*, the Court said that the standing requirement demanded no more than a showing that there was a substantial likelihood that a favorable federal court decision will redress the injury.[194] But in *Allen v. Wright*, the Court stated that causation and redressability are independent requirements that must both be met for a plaintiff to have standing.[195] In its most recent decisions, the Court has continued to articulate these as separate requirements.[196]

Commentators have criticized this separation of causation and redressability.[197] For example, commentators argue that in *Allen* the IRS could be said to be the cause of segregation through its tax policy to exactly the same degree that eliminating the exemptions would reduce segregation. More generally, commentators question why standing should be denied if the defendant acted illegally and restraining the defendant's wrongful behavior will cure the plaintiff's injury.

Even after *Allen*, in most cases, it would seem that causation and redressability would involve an identical inquiry. If it can be demonstrated that the defendant is the cause of the injury, then halting the defendant's conduct usually will remedy the harm.

§2.3.4 The Limitation on Third-Party Standing

While the requirements for injury, causation, and redressability are deemed to be constitutional limits on standing, the Court also has articulated prudential standing barriers.[198] One such nonconstitutional prudential limitation is the prohibition against third-party standing. The Court has explained that "even when the plaintiff

[192] *See, e.g.*, Laurence Tribe, Constitutional Choices 344-346 (1985).

[193] 438 U.S. at 74 (citations omitted).

[194] 429 U.S. at 262-263.

[195] 468 U.S. 737 (1984).

[196] United States v. Hays, 515 U.S. at 743; Northeastern Fla. Chapter of Assoc. Gen. Contractors of Am. v. Jacksonville, 508 U.S. at 663; Lujan v. Defenders of Wildlife, 504 U.S. at 562.

[197] *See, e.g.*, Gene R. Nichol, Jr., Abusing Standing: A Comment on *Allen v. Wright*, 133 U. Pa. L. Rev. 635 (1985).

[198] For a discussion of the concept of prudential standing, *see* S. Todd Brown, The Story of Prudential Standing, 42 Hastings Const. L.Q. 95 (2014).

has alleged injury sufficient to meet the 'case or controversy' requirement, the Court has held that the plaintiff generally must assert his own legal rights and interests, and cannot rest his claim to relief on the legal rights or interests of third parties."[199] In other words, a plaintiff can assert only injuries that he or she has suffered; a plaintiff cannot present the claims of third parties who are not part of the lawsuit.

It is important to note that there has been disagreement among the justices as to whether to consider the bar on third-party standing. *June Medical Services L.LC. v. Russo* involved a challenge by health care providers to a Louisiana law that required that doctors performing abortions have admitting privileges at a hospital within 30 miles of where the abortion is performed.[200] (This, of course, was before the Court overruled *Roe v. Wade.*) In the lower federal courts, the State of Louisiana did not challenge the standing of the doctors and health care providers to raise the claims of their patients, but they raised this issue in the Supreme Court. Justice Breyer, writing for the plurality, said that "the State has waived that argument," and that the Court long had allowed third-party standing in this context.[201] But Justice Thomas in dissent said that "[t]he rule against third-party standing is constitutional, not prudential" and thus as a jurisdictional rule could be raised at any time in the litigation.[202]

The prohibition against third-party standing—sometimes termed the rule against *jus tertii* standing—serves many of the underlying objectives of the standing doctrine.[203] The Court has emphasized that the people actually affected may be satisfied, and thus the ban on third-party standing avoids "the adjudication of rights which those before the Court may not wish to assert."[204] Also, the Court has stated that requiring people to assert only their own injuries improves the quality of litigation and judicial decision-making. In part, this is because the Court believes that the "third parties themselves usually will be the best proponents of their own rights."[205] Furthermore, it is thought that decisions might be improved in a concrete factual situation involving an injury to a party to the lawsuit.

The Supreme Court, however, has recognized three major exceptions to the prohibition against third-party standing. In these situations the Court has ruled that a person who has suffered an injury has standing to raise the interests of third

[199] Warth v. Seldin, 422 U.S. at 499. *See also* United Food & Com. Workers Union Loc. 751 v. Brown Grp., Inc., 517 U.S. at 557 (1996) (discussing the bar against third-party standing as prudential). *See* Curtis A. Bradley & Ernest A. Young, *Unpacking Third-Party Standing*, 131 Yale L.J. 1 (2021) (describing the basis for and use of the third party standing doctrine).

[200] 591 U.S. 299 (2020).

[201] *Id.* at 2117.

[202] *Id.* at 2145 (Thomas, J., dissenting).

[203] *See* Henry Monaghan, Third Party Standing, 84 Colum. L. Rev. 277, 278 n.6 (1984) (defining *jus tertii* standing).

[204] *See* Duke Power Co. v. Carolina Env't Study Grp., Inc., 438 U.S. at 80 (1978); *see also* Kowalski v. Tesmer, 543 U.S. 128, 129 (2004) ("This rule assumes that the party with the right has the appropriate incentive to challenge (or not challenge) governmental action and to do so with the necessary zeal and appropriate presentation.").

[205] Singleton v. Wulff, 428 U.S. 106, 114 (1976).

parties not before the court. It must be stressed that the person seeking to advocate the rights of third parties must meet the constitutional standing requirements of injury, causation, and redressability in addition to fitting within one of the four exceptions described below.

Exception: Where the Third Party Is Unlikely to Be Able to Sue

First, a person may assert the rights of a third party not before the court if there are substantial obstacles to the third party asserting his or her own rights and if there is reason to believe that the advocate will effectively represent the interests of the third party.[206] For example, in *Barrows v. Jackson,* the Court allowed third-party standing and permitted an individual sued for breaching a racially restrictive covenant to assert the rights of blacks in the community.[207] Barrows, a white person who had signed a racially restrictive covenant, was sued for breach of contract for allowing nonwhites to occupy the property. The defense was based on the rights of blacks, who were not parties to the lawsuit for breach of contract. The Court allowed third-party standing, permitting the white defendant to raise the interests of blacks to rent and own property in the community. The Court stated that "it would be difficult if not impossible for the persons whose rights are asserted to present their grievance before any court."[208] Because blacks were not parties to the covenant, they had no legal basis for participating in the breach of contract suit.

Another example of this exception permitting third-party standing where the third party is unlikely to assert his or her own rights is *Eisenstadt v. Baird.*[209] A Massachusetts law made it a felony to distribute contraceptives, except by physicians or pharmacists, and then only to married individuals. Baird was prosecuted for distributing contraceptive foam to unmarried individuals in violation of this statute. His defense centered on the rights of individuals to have access to and use contraceptives. In other words, he attempted to raise the rights of third parties not before the Court. The Supreme Court allowed Baird standing to present this argument, concluding that "unmarried persons denied access to contraceptives in Massachusetts . . . are not themselves subject to prosecution and, to that extent, are denied a forum in which to assert their own rights."[210]

Subsequently, the Supreme Court held that parties in a litigation may raise the claims of prospective jurors to be free from discrimination in the use of peremptory challenges. In *Powers v. Ohio,* the Supreme Court held that in addition to the constitutional interests of the parties in having a jury selected without discrimination, prospective jurors are denied equal protection if they are excluded because of their race.[211] In *Powers,* the Court ruled that a criminal defendant could represent the interests of the prospective jurors and in subsequent cases the Court

[206] Secretary of State v. J.H. Munson Co., 467 U.S. 947, 956 (1984).
[207] 346 U.S. 249 (1953).
[208] *Id.* at 257.
[209] 405 U.S. 438 (1972).
[210] *Id.* at 446.
[211] 499 U.S. 400 (1991).

extended this to civil litigants[212] and even to prosecutors.[213] In *Campbell v. Louisiana*, the Court applied *Powers* to find that a white defendant had standing to challenge the exclusion of African Americans from the grand jury that indicted him.[214]

This use of third-party standing fits within the well-recognized exception where individuals can represent the interests of parties who are unlikely to be able to represent their own interests. Prospective jurors who are struck on the basis of race will not know of the discriminatory pattern nor are they likely to have an incentive to bring a challenge on their own.[215]

Exception: Identity of Interests Between Plaintiff and Third Party

A second exception to the ban against third-party standing permits an individual to assert the rights of third parties where there is an identity of interests between the advocate and the third party. Usually, third-party standing is permitted in such circumstances where the individual seeking standing is part of the third party's constitutionally protected activity. For example, in *Pierce v. Society of Sisters*, a parochial school was accorded standing to challenge an Oregon law requiring all children to attend public school.[216] The parochial school argued that the law requiring public school attendance violated the rights of parents to control the upbringing of their children. The parochial school was allowed third-party standing because of the close relationship between the school and the parents and because the school was part of the regulated activity of providing parochial education.

Third-party standing based on this exception has been frequently allowed. For example, doctors often have been accorded standing to raise the rights of their patients in challenging laws limiting the patients' access to contraceptives and abortions.[217] In *Singleton v. Wulff*, two physicians were accorded standing to challenge a state statute that prohibited the use of state Medicaid benefits to pay for nontherapeutic abortions (abortions that were not necessary to protect the health or life of the mother).[218] The Court observed that the statute injured doctors because it denied them payments for particular medical services. Moreover, the Court emphasized the closeness of the doctors' relationship to the patient and that "the constitutionally protected abortion decision is one in which the physician is intimately involved."[219] The Court concluded that "it generally is appropriate to

[212] Edmonson v. Leesville Concrete Co., 500 U.S. 614 (1991).

[213] Georgia v. McCullom, 505 U.S. 42 (1992).

[214] 523 U.S. 392 (1998).

[215] The Court in *Powers* also said that allowing third-party standing to represent the interests of prospective jurors is justified under the second exception, discussed below: where there is a close relationship between the litigant and the injured third party. 499 U.S. at 413 (citations omitted). This rationale seems more questionable because, unlike other cases where this exception has been applied, there is no personal relationship between a litigant and prospective jurors.

[216] 268 U.S. 510 (1925).

[217] *But see* Tileston v. Ullman, 318 U.S. 44 (1943) (denying standing to doctor to raise challenges to law prohibiting use of contraceptives on behalf of patients).

[218] 428 U.S. 106 (1976).

[219] *Id.* at 117.

allow a physician to assert the rights of women patients as against governmental interference with the abortion decision."[220]

The Court also has allowed vendors to assert the rights of their customers based on this exception to the rule against third-party standing. The most famous example of this is *Craig v. Boren.*[221] Oklahoma adopted a law permitting women to buy 3.2 percent beer at age eighteen but denying men that privilege until age twenty-one.[222] A bartender sought to challenge the law on behalf of male customers between the ages of eighteen and twenty-one. The bartender suffered economic loss from the law, thus fulfilling the injury requirement. Furthermore, the Court observed that generally "vendors and those in like positions have been uniformly permitted to resist efforts at restricting their operations by acting as advocates for the rights of third parties who seek access to their market or function."[223]

A much publicized case in which the Court refused to allow third-party standing based on this exception was *Gilmore v. Utah.*[224] Gary Gilmore was sentenced to death in the state of Utah, but chose not to pursue collateral challenges in federal court. His mother sought a stay of execution on his behalf. In a five-to-four decision, the Court refused to hear his mother's claim. The Court's per curiam opinion said that the defendant had waived his rights by not pursuing them. Four justices, in a concurring opinion, said that the mother should be denied standing because there was no reason why her son could not protect and assert his own rights. The *Gilmore* case might be read as supporting the proposition that a close relationship is not enough for third-party standing; the advocate also must be part of the third party's exercise of the protected right. On the other hand, *Gilmore* might be thought of as a narrow decision in a unique factual context.

Gilmore was followed in *Whitmore v. Arkansas*, where the Supreme Court held that a death row inmate did not have standing to challenge the validity of a death sentence imposed on another inmate who elected to forgo his right of appeal to the state supreme court.[225] After Ronald Simmons chose not to appeal his death sentence, another inmate, James Whitmore, sought to intervene and appeal on Simmons's behalf. Additionally, Whitmore argued that under the Arkansas system of comparative review of death sentences, he could personally benefit from a change in Simmons's punishment. The Court rejected the assertion of third-party standing and held that "Whitmore provides no factual basis for us to conclude that the sentence imposed on a mass murderer like Simmons would even be relevant to a future comparative review of Whitmore's sentence."[226]

[220] *Id.* at 118.

[221] 429 U.S. 190 (1976).

[222] The equal protection aspect of the case is discussed in Erwin Chemerinsky, Constitutional Law: Principles and Policies §9.4.2 (7th ed. 2023).

[223] *Id.* at 195. *See also* Carey v. Population Servs. Int'l., 431 U.S. 678 (1977) (permitting vendor of contraceptives to challenge law on behalf of its customers).

[224] 429 U.S. 1012 (1976).

[225] 495 U.S. 149 (1990). For a discussion of *Gilmore* and *Whitmore*, *see* Ann Althouse, Standing, in Fluffy Slippers, 77 Va. L. Rev. 1177 (1991).

[226] 495 U.S. at 157.

Subsequently, the Court refused to allow third-party standing to a father who was suing on behalf of his daughter to challenge the use of the words "under God" in the Pledge of Allegiance in public schools.[227] In a 5-3 decision (Justice Scalia recused himself in response to a motion made by Newdow based on Justice Scalia's having given a speech in which he expressed his views on the case), the Court dismissed the case for lack of standing. The Court ruled that Michael Newdow lacked third-party standing to sue on behalf of his daughter. The Court stressed that the girl's mother, and not Newdow, had legal custody, and the Court also emphasized a traditional unwillingness of federal courts to get involved in domestic relations matters. Justice Stevens's majority opinion declared: "In our view, it is improper for the federal courts to entertain a claim by a plaintiff whose standing to sue is founded on family law rights that are in dispute when prosecution of the lawsuit may have an adverse effect on the person who is the source of the claimed standing. When hard questions of domestic relations are sure to affect the outcome, the prudent course is for the federal court to stay its hand rather than reach out to resolve a weighty question of federal constitutional law."[228]

It is difficult to fit the Court's decision in *Newdow* in the framework of traditional standing analysis. For example, apart from third-party standing, Michael Newdow could claim standing based on his own interests as a parent in the religious upbringing and education of his daughter. Also, it is longstanding practice that the Supreme Court defers to appellate courts' interpretations of state law, and the Ninth Circuit carefully considered California family law in concluding that the award of legal custody did not preclude a noncustodial parent from suing on behalf of a child. Perhaps the Court dismissed *Newdow* on standing grounds to avoid a highly controversial political issue, but the question then becomes whether that is an appropriate use of the justiciability doctrines.

The Court also rejected third-party standing in *Kowalski v. Tesmer*.[229] The issue was whether attorneys could sue to challenge a Michigan law that made appointment of counsel discretionary for indigent defendants who plead guilty or nolo contendere. The Court refused to allow attorneys to assert this claim and declared: "The attorneys before us do not have a 'close relationship' with their alleged clients; indeed, they have no relationship at all."[230] The Court stressed that the indigent defendants could have brought their own challenges to the denial of counsel. Indeed, a year later, the Court declared the Michigan law unconstitutional in response to a challenge brought by a criminal defendant.[231]

[227] Elk Grove Unified Sch. Dist. v. Newdow, 542 U.S. 1 (2004).
[228] *Id.* at 17.
[229] 543 U.S. 125 (2004).
[230] *Id.* at 131.
[231] Halbert v. Michigan, 545 U.S. 605 (2005).

Exception: The Overbreadth Doctrine

The third exception to the prohibition against third-party standing is termed the "overbreadth doctrine." A person generally can argue only that a statute is unconstitutional as it is applied to him or her; the individual cannot argue that a statute is unconstitutional as it is applied to third parties not before the court. For example, a defendant in a criminal trial can challenge the constitutionality of the law that is the basis for the prosecution solely on the claim that the statute unconstitutionally abridges his or her constitutional rights. The overbreadth doctrine is an exception to the prohibition against third-party standing. It permits a person to challenge a statute on the ground that it violates the First Amendment rights of third parties not before the court, even though the law is constitutional as applied to that defendant.[232] In other words, the overbreadth doctrine provides: "Given a case or controversy, a litigant whose own activities are unprotected may nevertheless challenge a statute by showing that it substantially abridges the First Amendment rights of other parties not before the court."[233]

The Court's decision in *Secretary of State of Maryland v. J.H. Munson Co.* illustrates the overbreadth doctrine.[234] A Maryland law prohibited charitable organizations from soliciting funds unless at least 75 percent of their revenues were used for "charitable purposes." The law was challenged by a professional fundraiser who raised the First Amendment rights of his clients, charities who were not parties to the lawsuit. The Supreme Court permitted the fundraiser standing to argue the constitutional claims of the charitable organizations. The state argued that third-party standing was inappropriate because the charities were fully able to litigate and protect their own rights. The Court rejected this contention, explaining that "where the claim is that a statute is overly broad in violation of the First Amendment, the Court has allowed a party to assert the rights of another without regard to the ability of the other to assert his own claims and with no requirement that the person making the attack demonstrate that his own conduct could not be regulated by a statute drawn with the requisite narrow specificity."[235]

The overbreadth doctrine appears limited to First Amendment cases.[236] This exception to the rule against third-party standing reflects a fear that an overbroad law will chill protected speech and that safeguarding expression justifies allowing third-party standing. The Court explained that "[l]itigants, therefore, are permitted to challenge a statute not because their own rights of free expression are

[232] The overbreadth doctrine is discussed in more detail in Chemerinsky, *supra* note 222, at §11.2.2.

[233] Village of Schaumburg v. Citizens for a Better Env't, 444 U.S. 620, 634 (1980). For an excellent discussion of the overbreadth doctrine, *see* Richard H. Fallon, Jr., Making Sense of Overbreadth, 100 Yale L.J. 853 (1991).

[234] 467 U.S. 947 (1984).

[235] *Id.* at 957 (citation omitted). *Accord* Village of Schaumburg v. Citizens for a Better Env't, 444 U.S. at 634 (1980) (also invalidating a statute regulating charitable solicitation on overbreadth grounds).

[236] For an excellent argument that the Court has used overbreadth outside the First Amendment context, *see* David H. Gans, Strategic Facial Challenges, 85 B.U. L. Rev. 1133 (2005).

violated, but because of a judicial prediction or assumption that the statute's very existence may cause others not before the court to refrain from constitutionally protected speech or expression."[237]

The Supreme Court has announced several limits on the overbreadth doctrine. For example, the Court has said that for a statute to be declared unconstitutional on overbreadth grounds, there must be "substantial overbreadth"; that is, the law's excessive regulation must "not only be real, but substantial as well, judged in relation to the statute's plainly legitimate sweep."[238] Also, the Court has held that when confronted with an overbreadth challenge, a court should attempt to construe the statute so as to avoid constitutional problems and failing that, should, if possible, attempt to sever the unconstitutional part of the law from the remainder of the statute.[239] Additionally, the Supreme Court has declared that overbreadth cannot be used in challenging regulations of commercial speech.[240] The Court apparently believes that the incentive to engage in advertising is sufficiently strong to lessen any worries that such speech will be chilled.

§2.3.5 The Prohibition Against Generalized Grievances

The Supreme Court has stated that there is a "prudential principle" preventing standing "when the asserted harm is a generalized grievance shared in a substantially equal measure by all or a large class of citizens."[241] The prohibition against generalized grievances prevents individuals from suing if their only injury is as a citizen or a taxpayer concerned with having the government follow the law.

The term "generalized grievance" is confusing because it implies that no one would have standing to challenge a blatantly unconstitutional law applicable to everyone in the country. For example, would it be a generalized grievance, and everyone denied the ability to sue, if Congress were to adopt a law prohibiting all religious worship? The answer is clearly that standing would exist in such an instance to challenge the denial of free exercise of religion even though it would

[237] Broadrick v. Oklahoma, 413 U.S. 601, 612 (1973); Dombrowski v. Pfister, 380 U.S. 479, 486 (1965).

[238] Broadrick v. Oklahoma, 413 U.S. at 615 (also suggesting that overbreadth is limited to "pure speech" and not conduct that is expressive); *see also* United States v. Hansen, 599 U.S. 762 (2023) (rejecting overbreadth challenge to federal law that makes it a crime for any person who "encourages or induces" a noncitizen to "come to, enter, or reside in the United States"); Virginia v. Hicks, 539 U.S. 113 (2003) (rejecting challenge to restrictions of trespassing in public housing project because there was not a showing of substantial overbreadth); New York v. Ferber, 458 U.S. 747, 770-771 (1982) (rejecting overbreadth challenge to law prohibiting distribution of child pornography because of the absence of substantial overbreadth).

[239] New York v. Ferber, 458 U.S. at 769 n.24.

[240] Village of Hoffman Estates v. Flipside, 455 U.S. 489, 497 (1982) ("the over-breadth doctrine does not apply to commercial speech").

[241] Warth v. Seldin, 422 U.S. at 499 (1975) (emphasis added) (citations omitted); Gladstone, Realtors v. Village of Bellwood, 441 U.S. at 99-100 (1979). However, in a subsequent decision the Supreme Court indicated that the ban on citizen standing is constitutional, not prudential. Lujan v. Defenders of Wildlife, 504 U.S. 555 (1992). *Lujan* is discussed below.

be an injury shared in substantially equal measure by all or a large class of citizens. In fact, the Court has explained, "Nor . . . could the fact that many persons shared the same injury be sufficient reason to disqualify from seeking review . . . any person who had in fact suffered injury. . . . To deny standing to persons who are in fact injured simply because many others are also injured, would mean that the most injurious and widespread Government actions could be questioned by nobody."[242] The Court has explained that "where a harm is concrete, though widely shared, the Court has found injury in fact."[243]

Thus, the number of people affected does not determine the existence of a generalized grievance. Rather, a generalized grievance is where the plaintiffs sue solely as citizens concerned with having the government follow the law or as taxpayers interested in restraining allegedly illegal government expenditures.

In other words, the bar against generalized grievance standing is inapplicable if a person claims that he or she has been denied freedom of speech or due process of law, even if everyone else in society has suffered the same harm. However, if the plaintiff alleges a violation of no specific constitutional right, but instead claims an interest only as a taxpayer or a citizen in having the government follow the law, standing is not allowed.

Sequence of Decisions: Four Sets of Cases

The prohibition against generalized grievances, and the current state of the law, can be best understood by examining four sets of cases: the initial decisions from about seventy years ago preventing taxpayer and citizen standing, the Warren Court's expansion of taxpayer standing, the Burger Court's rulings virtually eliminating taxpayer and citizen suits in federal court, and finally, decisions from the Rehnquist and Roberts Courts indicating that the bar on generalized grievances is constitutional and not prudential as previously declared.

The Supreme Court first articulated the barrier to taxpayer and citizen standing during the 1920s and 1930s. In *Frothingham v. Mellon*, the plaintiff, suing as a taxpayer, sought to restrain expenditures under the Federal Maternity Act of 1921, which provided financial grants to the states to reduce maternal and infant mortality.[244] The plaintiff asserted that the expenditures violated the Tenth Amendment's reservation of powers to the state governments. The Supreme Court ruled that the plaintiff lacked standing because her "interest in the moneys of the treasury . . . is comparatively minute and indeterminable."[245] The Court held that federal court review must be based on a plaintiff's alleging a direct injury and "not merely that he suffers in some indefinite way in common with people generally."[246]

[242] United States v. SCRAP, 412 U.S. at 686-688 (1973).

[243] Akins, 524 U.S. at 24 (1998).

[244] 262 U.S. 447 (1923). In a companion case, Massachusetts v. Mellon, 262 U.S. 447 (1923), the Supreme Court denied the state of Massachusetts standing to attack the constitutionality of the Maternity Act.

[245] 262 U.S. at 487.

[246] *Id.* at 488.

Similarly, a few years later in *Ex parte Levitt*, the Supreme Court ruled that a person could not gain standing as a citizen claiming a right to have the government follow the law.[247] Levitt involved a citizen's suit to have Justice Hugo Black's appointment to the U.S. Supreme Court declared unconstitutional. The plaintiff contended that Justice Black could not be appointed to the Court because Black had voted, while a senator, to increase Supreme Court justices' retirement benefits. This was alleged to violate Article I, §6, of the Constitution, which states that "[n]o Senator shall during the time for which he was elected, be appointed to any civil office the emoluments whereof shall have increased during such time." The Court, however, held that the plaintiff lacked standing because "it is not sufficient [for standing] that he has merely a general interest common to all members of the public."[248]

Frothingham and *Levitt* establish the bar to taxpayer and citizen standing. The primary case deviating from this rule was the Warren Court's decision in *Flast v. Cohen.*[249] In *Flast*, the Court upheld a taxpayer's standing to challenge federal subsidies to parochial schools as violating the First Amendment's prohibition against government establishment of religion. Under the Elementary and Secondary Education Act of 1965, the federal government provided funds for instruction in secular subjects in parochial schools. The lower court dismissed the plaintiff's challenge to the act based on *Frothingham*, concluding that the plaintiff's only claim was as a taxpayer and that such standing was not permitted.

The Supreme Court reversed, allowing standing. Both the majority and the dissent in *Flast* agreed that the rule preventing plaintiffs from asserting generalized grievances was prudential rather than constitutional in origin.[250] Chief Justice Warren, writing for the Court, said that the ability of the plaintiff to sue as a taxpayer depends on "whether there is a logical nexus between the status asserted and the claim sought to be adjudicated."[251]

Specifically, the Court said that in order to sue as a taxpayer the plaintiff needed to establish two factors. First, "the taxpayer must establish a logical link between that status and the type of legislative enactment attacked."[252] The Court said that this meant that a taxpayer could challenge only the expenditure of funds under the taxing and spending clause of the Constitution and not "an incidental expenditure of tax funds in the administration of an essentially regulatory statute."[253] Second, the "taxpayer must establish a nexus between that status and the precise nature of the constitutional infringement alleged."[254] In other words, the taxpayer must argue that Congress is violating a particular constitutional provision with the expenditure and not just that Congress is exceeding the scope of its powers under the Constitution.

[247] 302 U.S. 633 (1937).
[248] *Id.* at 634.
[249] 392 U.S. 83 (1968).
[250] *Id.* at 101; at 119-120 (Harlan, J., dissenting).
[251] *Id.* at 102.
[252] *Id.*
[253] *Id.*
[254] *Id.*

The Court distinguished *Flast* from *Frothingham* because although both involved challenges to government spending programs, the First Amendment is a limit on Congress's taxing and spending authority, whereas the Tenth Amendment, at issue in *Frothingham*, is not.[255] *Flast* raised speculation that the Court had substantially expanded the availability of taxpayer standing.[256]

However, the Burger Court consistently rejected attempts at taxpayer and citizen standing and essentially narrowed *Flast* to the facts of that case. In *United States v. Richardson*, the plaintiff claimed that the statutes providing for the secrecy of the Central Intelligence Agency budget violated the Constitution's requirement for a regular statement and accounting of all expenditures.[257] The Court ruled that the plaintiff lacked standing because his case presented a generalized grievance; the plaintiff did not allege a violation of a personal constitutional right, but instead claimed injury only as a citizen and taxpayer. The Court held that the plaintiff lacked standing because he was "seeking to employ a federal court as a forum in which to air his generalized grievances about the conduct of government."[258]

The Court deemed irrelevant the plaintiff's claim that if he could not sue, no one could. The Court stated: "It can be argued that if respondent is not permitted to litigate this issue, no one can do so. In a very real sense, the absence of any particular individual or class to litigate these claims gives support to the argument that the subject matter is committed to the surveillance of Congress, and ultimately to the political process."[259]

Similarly, in a decision handed down the same day as *Richardson*, in *Schlesinger v. Reservists Committee to Stop the War*, the Court denied citizen and taxpayer standing.[260] In *Schlesinger*, the plaintiffs sued to enjoin members of Congress from serving in the military reserves. Article I, §6, of the Constitution prevents a senator or representative from holding civil office. Again, the Court refused to rule on the plaintiff's claim of unconstitutionality, holding that the matter posed a generalized grievance. Standing was denied because the plaintiff alleged injury only as a citizen or taxpayer with an interest in having the government follow the law and not a violation of a specific constitutional right. The Court stated: "Respondents seek to have the Judicial Branch compel the Executive Branch to act in conformity with the Incompatibility Clause, an interest shared by all citizens. . . . Our system of government leaves many crucial decisions to the political processes. The assumption that if respondents have no standing to sue no one would have standing, is not a reason to find standing."[261]

After *Richardson* and *Schlesinger*, it appeared that taxpayer standing was restricted to the one area where it had been approved in *Flast*: for alleged violations of the establishment clause of the First Amendment. But a few years later, in

[255] *Id.* at 105.

[256] *See* Kenneth Davis, The Liberalized Law of Standing, 37 U. Chi. L. Rev. 450 (1970); Kenneth Davis, Standing: Taxpayers and Others, 35 U. Chi. L. Rev. 601 (1968).

[257] 418 U.S. 166 (1974).

[258] *Id.* at 175 (citations omitted).

[259] *Id.* at 179.

[260] 418 U.S. 208 (1974).

[261] *Id.* at 227.

Valley Forge Christian College v. Americans United for Separation of Church and State, the Court denied taxpayer standing to challenge a federal government grant of surplus property as violating the establishment clause of the First Amendment.[262] The U.S. Department of Health, Education, and Welfare gave a seventy-seven-acre tract of land, worth over $500 million, to Valley Forge Christian College. Americans United for Separation of Church and State sued to enjoin the transfer of the property on the ground that it was government aid to religion in violation of the establishment clause. The Supreme Court held that the plaintiffs lacked standing because they sued solely as taxpayers interested in having the government follow the law.[263]

Flast was distinguished from *Valley Forge* on two grounds. First, the plaintiffs in *Valley Forge* were challenging a decision by the Department of Health, Education, and Welfare to transfer property, not a congressional statute.[264] One might wonder why this distinction matters. Both Congress and the executive branch are bound to obey the First Amendment. In fact, in *Flast* the named defendant was Wilbur Cohen, secretary of the Department of Health, Education, and Welfare. Second, the *Valley Forge* Court said that unlike in *Flast*, the objection was to a government action pursuant to Congress's power over government property, Article IV, §3, and not to a spending program under Article I, §8.[265] Again, one must question why this distinction makes any difference. All congressional actions, whether pursuant to Article I or other provisions, must comply with the First Amendment and the entire Bill of Rights. If *Flast* establishes that taxpayers have standing to halt violations of the establishment clause, it is hard to see why it matters whether the objectionable action was taken under Article I or Article IV authority.

In 1988, the Supreme Court reaffirmed *Flast*'s holding that taxpayers have standing to challenge government expenditures as violating the establishment clause. In *Bowen v. Kendrick*, the Court allowed taxpayer standing to challenge the constitutionality of the Adolescent Family Life Act, which provided grants that required specific types of counseling to prevent teenage pregnancy.[266] The Court explained that it had continually adhered to *Flast* and the narrow exception it had created for taxpayer standing to challenge government expenditures that violate the establishment clause.

Two subsequent cases, however, have rejected taxpayer standing to enforce the establishment clause. In *Hein v. Freedom from Religion Found., Inc.*, the Court held that taxpayers lack standing to challenge expenditure of federal funds from general executive revenues.[267] Upon taking office, President George W. Bush created a White House office and several centers in executive branch offices to provide government funds to "faith-based institutions." This was designed to facilitate churches, synagogues, and mosques directly receiving federal money to provide

[262] 454 U.S. 464 (1982).

[263] *Id.* at 485-486.

[264] *Id.* at 479.

[265] *Id.* at 480.

[266] 487 U.S. 589 (1988).

[267] 551 U.S. 587 (2007). For a discussion of *Hein*, *see* Eric J. Segall, The Taxing Law of Taxpayer Standing, 43 Tulsa L. Rev. 673 (2008).

social services. The White House Office of Faith-Based and Community Initiatives was funded entirely through general executive revenue. Taxpayers brought a suit challenging this as violating the establishment clause.

The Court ruled, without a majority opinion, that the taxpayers lacked standing. Justice Alito announced the judgment for the Court and distinguished *Flast v. Cohen* as involving expenditures under a specific federal statute, whereas the money for the White House Office of Faith-Based and Community Initiatives came from general executive revenue. Justice Alito, in an opinion joined by Chief Justice Roberts and Justice Kennedy, explained: "The link between congressional action and constitutional violation that supported taxpayer standing in *Flast* is missing here. Respondents do not challenge any specific congressional action or appropriation; nor do they ask the Court to invalidate any congressional enactment or legislatively created program as unconstitutional. That is because the expenditures at issue here were not made pursuant to any Act of Congress. . . . Those expenditures resulted from executive discretion, not congressional action."[268] In other words, the plurality opinion in *Hein v. Freedom from Religion Found., Inc.* concludes that taxpayers lack standing to challenge expenditures of funds from general executive revenue as violating the establishment clause.

The other six justices sharply criticized the plurality's distinction of *Flast*. The executive branch, no less than Congress, must comply with the First Amendment. Besides, all federal spending is pursuant to a federal statute; Congress authorizes all executive branch revenues. Justices Scalia and Thomas concurred in the judgment and called for the overruling of *Flast v. Cohen*. Justice Scalia lamented the "meaningless distinctions" and wrote: "If this Court is to decide cases by rule of law rather than show of hands, we must surrender to logic and choose sides: Either *Flast v. Cohen* should be applied to (at a minimum) *all* challenges to the governmental expenditure of general tax revenues in a manner alleged to violate a constitutional provision specifically limiting the taxing and spending power, or *Flast* should be repudiated. For me, the choice is easy. *Flast* is wholly irreconcilable with the Article III restrictions on federal-court jurisdiction that this Court has repeatedly confirmed are embodied in the doctrine of standing."[269] By contrast, Justice Souter, in a dissent joined by Justices Stevens, Ginsburg, and Breyer, agreed that there was no meaningful distinction between money from general executive revenue and spending under a specific federal statute, but they would have followed *Flast* and allowed taxpayer standing.

It is difficult to understand the distinction drawn by the plurality in *Hein*. All federal revenue ultimately is spent pursuant to federal statutes. Besides, the executive, no less than Congress, must comply with the Constitution and the establishment clause. *Hein* can be understood as reflecting the desire of the Court's conservative majority to limit *Flast* but not having the votes to overrule it.

In *Arizona School Tuition Organization v. Winn*, the Court again distinguished *Flast* and rejected a claim of taxpayer standing.[270] The case involved a challenge to

[268] 551 U.S. at 605.
[269] *Id.* at 618 (Scalia, J., dissenting).
[270] 56 U.S. 125 (2011).

an Arizona law that allowed Arizona taxpayers who voluntarily contributed money to a "student tuition organization" (STO) to receive a dollar-for-dollar tax credit up to $500 of their annual tax liability. The Ninth Circuit concluded that this violated the establishment clause on the grounds that the program had the purpose and the effect of aiding religious schools; a disproportionate amount of the money went to evangelical Christian and Catholic schools.

The Supreme Court, in a five-to-four decision, reversed and concluded that taxpayers lacked standing to challenge the tax credits. Justice Kennedy, writing for the Court, distinguished *Flast v. Cohen.* He explained: "The distinction between governmental expenditures and tax credits refutes respondents' assertion of standing. When Arizona taxpayers choose to contribute to STOs, they spend their own money, not money the State has collected from respondents or from other taxpayers. . . . The STO tax credit is not tantamount to a religious tax or to a tithe and does not visit the injury identified in *Flast.* It follows that respondents have neither alleged an injury for standing purposes under general rules nor met the *Flast* exception. Finding standing under these circumstances would be more than the extension of *Flast* 'to the limits of its logic.' It would be a departure from *Flast*'s stated rationale."[271]

Justice Scalia concurred in an opinion joined by Justice Thomas and again expressed his desire to have *Flast v. Cohen* overturned.[272] Justice Kagan wrote a vehement dissent, joined by Justices Ginsburg, Breyer, and Sotomayor. She began by noting that since its inception, $350 million of tax revenue had been diverted to STOs, many of which discriminate based on religion.[273] She argued that there is no meaningful distinction between taxpayers being able to challenge a tax and their being able to challenge a tax credit. She wrote: "This novel distinction in standing law between appropriations and tax expenditures has as little basis in principle as it has in our precedent. Cash grants and targeted tax breaks are means of accomplishing the same government objective—to provide financial support to select individuals or organizations. Taxpayers who oppose state aid of religion have equal reason to protest whether that aid flows from the one form of subsidy or the other. Either way, the government has financed the religious activity. And so either way, taxpayers should be able to challenge the subsidy. Still worse, the Court's arbitrary distinction threatens to eliminate *all* occasions for a taxpayer to contest the government's monetary support of religion. Precisely because appropriations and tax breaks can achieve identical objectives, the government can easily substitute one for the other. . . . From now on, the government need follow just one simple rule—subsidize through the tax system—to preclude taxpayer challenges to state funding of religion."[274]

After *Richardson* and *Schlesinger* it was clear that the only situation in which taxpayer standing is permissible is if the plaintiff challenges a government expenditure

[271] *Id.* at 143.

[272] *Id.* at 147 (Scalia, J., concurring) ("I would repudiate that misguided decision and enforce the Constitution.").

[273] *Id.* at 1450 (Kagan, J., dissenting).

[274] *Id.*

as violating the establishment clause.[275] After *Valley Forge*, *Hein*, and *Winn*, taxpayer standing to enforce the establishment clause is significantly limited. *Flast* has not been overruled, but it would appear that it is confined to allowing taxpayers to challenge government expenditures pursuant to statutes as violating the establishment clause.[276]

Generalized Grievance as a Constitutional Bar

In *Warth v. Seldin*, the Supreme Court declared that the bar on citizen and taxpayer suits was "prudential," not constitutional.[277] The Court apparently believed that citizens and taxpayers are hurt when the government violates the law, but that it was prudent for the federal courts to refuse to hear such cases. However, in *Lujan v. Defenders of Wildlife*, the Court treated the bar on citizen standing as constitutional.[278] The Endangered Species Act provided that "any person may commence a civil suit on his own behalf (A) to enjoin any person, including the United States and any other governmental instrumentality or agency . . . who is alleged to be in violation of any provision of this chapter."[279] The plaintiffs invoked this authority as the basis for a suit challenging a federal regulation providing that the United States would not comply with the act outside the country except on the high seas.

The Court, in an opinion by Justice Scalia, held that the plaintiffs were asserting a generalized grievance and that Congress by statute cannot authorize standing in such an instance. The prohibition against citizen standing was characterized as being derived from Article III and therefore not susceptible to a statutory override.

Lujan has potentially dramatic implications for the many federal statutes that authorize "citizen suits" as an enforcement mechanism.[280] Such provisions are especially common in environmental statutes and are included in laws such as the Clean Water Act,[281] the Surface Mining Control and Reclamation Act of 1977,[282] the

[275] In DaimlerChrysler Corp. v. Cuno, 547 U.S. 332 (2006), the Court rejected the argument that *Flast* should be extended to allow taxpayer standing to challenge government actions that allegedly violate the dormant commerce clause. The Court thus dismissed a challenge to a state program to give tax benefits to businesses relocating from out of state.

[276] This allows challenges to state and local expenditures as well as those by the federal government. *See* Grand Rapids Sch. Dist. v. Ball, 473 U.S. 273 (1985) (allowing a challenge to local expenditures to parochial schools as violating the establishment clause and referring to "the numerous cases in which we have adjudicated Establishment Clause challenges by state taxpayers to programs for aiding nonpublic schools").

[277] 422 U.S. at 490. For a discussion of whether the generalized grievance bar should be regarded as constitutional or prudential, *see* Craig A. Stern, Another Sign from *Hein:* Does the Generalized Grievance Fail a Constitutional or a Prudential Test of Standing to Sue?, 12 Lewis & Clark L. Rev. 1169 (2008).

[278] 504 U.S. 555 (1992).

[279] 16 U.S.C. §1540(g).

[280] For a discussion of these implications, *see* Cass Sunstein, What's Standing After *Lujan*? Of Citizen Suits, "Injuries," and Article III, 91 Mich. L. Rev. 163 (1992).

[281] 33 U.S.C. §1365(e).

[282] 30 U.S.C. §1270.

Safe Drinking Water Act of 1974,[283] the Comprehensive Environmental Response, Compensation, and Liability Act,[284] the Clean Air Act,[285] the Noise Control Act,[286] and the Energy Conservation Act.[287] *Lujan* appears to mean that these provisions are unconstitutional except in instances where the plaintiff can otherwise demonstrate an injury sufficient for standing.

More generally, *Lujan* likely means that the bar against generalized grievances will be treated as constitutional and not prudential in the future. It is possible, though, that the Court might distinguish taxpayer suits from citizen suits and argue that the former involves a clearer injury because of the dollar and cents loss (although extremely small), thus justifying taxpayer standing continuing to be regarded as prudential.

However, it should be noted that in a subsequent case addressing the generalized grievance doctrine, the Court reaffirmed that plaintiffs have standing as long as they can show a personal, concrete injury. In *Federal Election Commission v. Akins*, the Court held that plaintiffs had standing to challenge a decision of the Federal Election Commission that the American Israel Political Affairs Committee is not a "political committee" subject to the regulation and reporting requirements under the Federal Election Campaign Act of 1971.[288] The federal statute permitted standing to any "aggrieved party." The dissent argued that plaintiffs presented a generalized grievance; their desire for enforcement of the federal law was the same as everyone else's in the world.[289]

Justice Breyer, writing for the majority, expressly rejected this argument and emphasized that the federal statute created a right to information and the denial of this right was a concrete injury sufficient for standing. The Court explained that unlike *Richardson*, "there is a statute which . . . does seek to protect individuals such as respondents from the kind of harm that they say that they have suffered, i.e., failing to receive particular information about campaign-related activities."[290] *Federal Election Commission v. Akins* is an important post-*Lujan* clarification of the generalized grievance requirement because it clearly holds that Congress by statute can create rights that would not otherwise exist and the alleged violation of those rights is sufficient for standing, even under a broad citizen-suit provision and even where the injury is widely shared in society.

Should There Be a Bar Against Generalized Grievances?

The generalized grievance standing doctrine can be defended on separation of powers grounds. This standing barrier reflects a belief that the judicial role is solely to prevent and remedy specific injuries suffered by individuals. The Court

[283] 42 U.S.C. §300j-8.
[284] 42 U.S.C. §6972.
[285] 42 U.S.C. §7604.
[286] 42 U.S.C. §4911.
[287] 42 U.S.C. §6305.
[288] 524 U.S. 11 (1998).
[289] *Id.* at 29.
[290] *Id.* at 22.

has no authority to halt government violations of the Constitution except when plaintiffs claim that their personal rights—be they rights created by common law, the Constitution, or statutes—are infringed. In *Richardson, Schlesinger, Valley Forge,* and *Lujan,* the Court expressly noted that the generalized grievance standing barrier reserves matters to the political branches of government, thereby promoting the separation of powers. Moreover, the generalized grievance standing barrier reflects a desire to exclude plaintiffs who sue entirely out of ideological interests and not on the basis of specific, concrete injuries.[291]

On the other hand, the generalized grievance standing doctrine can be criticized as the Court's abdicating the judicial role in upholding the Constitution. The argument is that the Court inappropriately deemed some parts of the Constitution to be enforceable only through the political process. No one is likely to have standing to challenge the practices objected to in *Richardson, Schlesinger,* and *Valley Forge.* The constitutional provisions involved there—the statements and accounts clause, the incompatibility clause, and the establishment clause—could be blatantly disregarded, and yet the courts would be powerless to halt the violations. This is deeply troubling because the purpose of the Constitution and judicial review is to safeguard matters from majority rule, a value that is lost when provisions are enforceable only through the political process. The effect of the generalized grievance doctrine is to read these clauses out of the Constitution except to the extent the political branches want to voluntarily comply with them.[292]

Also, critics argue that the Court's distinction between parts of the Constitution is unjustified. The Court draws a distinction between constitutional provisions creating individual rights—such as the equal protection clause, the violation of which creates standing—and provisions pertaining to the structure of government—such as the statements and accounts clause, the violation of which is a generalized grievance. But the desirability of drawing this distinction is open to question. Structural parts of the Constitution are integral to protecting individual rights. For example, if Congress were to adopt a law authorizing the current president a ten-year term, in violation of Article II, would anyone have standing to sue? Perhaps this might be challenged as infringing the right to vote. But under a strict reading of the generalized grievance cases, citizens would lack standing because any plaintiff would be presenting a claim common to all in society.

Ultimately, two competing visions of the role of the federal judiciary are at stake. Under one, the role of federal courts is limited to remedying specific injuries suffered by individuals. This position sees a need for great deference to the political branches of government and fears the powers of the federal courts as an

[291] Ideological plaintiffs are sometimes referred to as non-Hohfeldian plaintiffs. *See, e.g.*, Richard H. Fallon, Jr., Of Justiciability, Remedies, and Public Law Litigation: Notes on the Jurisprudence of *Lyons*, 59 N.Y.U. L. Rev. 1, 3 n.12 (1984). The term originates from the scholar Wesley Newcomb Hohfeld, who devised a taxonomy of legal rights. *See* Wesley Hohfeld, Some Fundamental Legal Conceptions as Applied in Judicial Reasoning, 23 Yale L.J. 16 (1913). Because the claims of ideological plaintiffs do not fit into any of Hohfeld's categories of legal rights, such plaintiffs are termed "non-Hohfeldian."

[292] This argument is more fully developed in Erwin Chemerinsky, Closing the Courthouse Door: How Your Constitutional Rights Became Unenforceable (2017).

antimajoritarian institution. An alternative view sees the federal judiciary as existing to ensure government compliance with the Constitution. Under this position, judicial deference does not include tolerating constitutional violations. The majority opinions in *Richardson, Schlesinger,* and *Valley Forge* endorsed the former view; the dissents expressed the latter position. The dispute is a fundamental disagreement over the role of the federal courts in American society.

§2.3.6 *The Requirement That the Plaintiff Be Within the Zone of Interests Protected by the Statute*

The Requirement Defined

A third prudential standing requirement, in addition to the ban on third-party standing and the prohibition against generalized grievances, is the rule that the plaintiff seeking standing must be within the zone of interests protected by the statute in question. This requirement applies when a person is challenging an administrative agency regulation that does not directly control the person's actions. Assuming that the constitutional standing requirements are met, the plaintiff may sue if it can show that it is within the group intended to benefit from the statute. For example, if there is a statute preventing widget companies from selling law books, a law book company might sue to challenge an administrative regulation permitting the widget company to sell law texts. Although the law book company is not directly controlled by the regulation, it may sue if it shows that it fulfills the constitutional standing requirements and that the statute limiting the widget company sales was intended to protect its interests.

The Supreme Court has stated that the plaintiff must allege that "the interest sought to be protected by the complainant is arguably within the zone of interests to be protected or regulated by the statute or constitutional guarantee in question."[293] In other words, if a plaintiff is suing pursuant to a statutory provision, to have standing the plaintiff must be part of the group intended to benefit from the law. Although the Court's statement of the test includes its application to constitutional provisions, for reasons discussed below, the zone of interests requirement is used only in statutory cases, usually involving administrative law issues.

The zone of interests test is particularly confusing, in part, because the Court has been inconsistent about whether it is a standing requirement. In some cases, in summarizing the law of standing, the Court has omitted the zone of interests test.[294] In other decisions, the test has been included in a listing of the prudential standing requirements.[295] In fact, the Supreme Court's failure to mention the zone of interests test for several years convinced some commentators and lower courts

[293] Association of Data Processing Serv. Orgs., Inc. v. Camp, 397 U.S. 150, 153 (1970).

[294] *See, e.g.,* Duke Power Co. v. Carolina Env't Study Grp., 438 U.S. 59 (1978); Warth v. Seldin, 422 U.S. 490 (1975) (summarizing the law of standing, but omitting the zone of interests test).

[295] *See, e.g.,* Valley Forge Christian College v. Americans United for Separation of Church and State, 454 U.S. 464 (1982); Gladstone, Realtors v. Village of Bellwood, 441 U.S. 91, 99-100 (1979).

that the Court had abandoned it as a separate standing requirement.[296] In a decision in 1987, however, the Court again reaffirmed the zone of interests test as a separate standing requirement, albeit one that the Court said is "not meant to be especially demanding."[297] Subsequently, in 2014, the Court again applied the zone of interests test and said that in the context of the Administrative Procedure Act "we have often 'conspicuously included the word "arguably" in the test to indicate that the benefit of any doubt goes to the plaintiff,' and have said that the test forecloses suit only when a plaintiff's 'interests are so marginally related to or inconsistent with the purposes implicit in the statute that it cannot reasonably be assumed that' Congress authorized that plaintiff to sue."[298] But despite these declarations that it is a relaxed standard, the Court has used this standing requirement to bar litigation.[299]

Creation of the Requirement

The zone of interests test was first articulated by the Supreme Court in *Association of Data Processing Service Organizations, Inc. v. Camp.*[300] The plaintiff challenged a ruling by the comptroller of the currency to allow banks to make data processing services available to other banks and bank customers. Although the data processors clearly were injured by the comptroller's decision, there was a question about whether they had standing to sue. Under the Administrative Procedure Act, persons may seek judicial review of an agency decision if they are "aggrieved by agency action within the meaning of a relevant statute."[301] The Court said that a person has standing under this provision if he or she has suffered an injury and if "the interest sought to be protected by the complainant is arguably within the zone of interests to be protected or regulated by the statute or constitutional guarantee in question."[302] The Court concluded that the data processors were arguably within the zone of interests protected by the Bank Service Corporation Act of 1962, which prohibited bank service corporations to "engage in any activity other than the performance of bank services for banks."[303]

The zone of interests test was applied by the Court in *Barlow v. Collins,*[304] decided the same day as *Camp. Barlow* also involved an attempt to secure judicial review of an agency decision under the Administrative Procedure Act. The

[296] *See, e.g.*, Robert Sedler, Standing, Justiciability, and All That: A Behavioral Analysis, 25 Vand. L. Rev. 479, 486-487 (1972); Department of Energy v. Louisiana, 690 F.2d 180, 187 (Emer. Ct. App. 1982).

[297] Clarke v. Securities Indus. Assn., 479 U.S. 388 (1987). *See also* Block v. Community Nutrition Inst., 467 U.S. 340 (1984).

[298] Lexmark Intl., Inc. v. Static Control Components, 527 U.S. 118, 130 (2014).

[299] *See* Air Courier Conference v. American Postal Workers Union, AFL-CIO, 498 U.S. 517 (1991), discussed below.

[300] 397 U.S. 150 (1970).

[301] 5 U.S.C. §702.

[302] 397 U.S. at 153.

[303] 12 U.S.C. §1864.

[304] 397 U.S. 159 (1970).

secretary of agriculture issued a regulation permitting tenant farmers to assign payments under the Upland Cotton Program as security for land they were renting. The farmers sought review, objecting that the new regulation caused landlords to coerce them into making exorbitant payments for rent and supplies. The Court again found the zone of interests test to be met, concluding that the pertinent statutory provision was adopted to protect the tenant farmers.

Is the Zone of Interests Test Desirable?

The zone of interests test has been defended on grounds similar to the prohibition against third-party standing. The idea is that those who invoke a statute's protections as a basis for standing should be the ones that the legislature intended to protect. Also, it is argued that the "zone of interests requirement . . . might improve the quality of adversary presentation, in part by providing a detailed fact setting that corresponds to the problems most likely to be encountered in the area of dispute, and in part by yielding parties sensitive to the perhaps conflicting interests of those most directly involved."[305]

But others have sharply criticized the zone of interests test.[306] Critics argue that the zone of interests test is unnecessary; if a person is asserting a judicially cognizable injury and fulfills all of the other standing requirements, there is no reason for the federal court to deny review. Moreover, critics argue that the Court never has articulated how a judge is to decide the zone of interests protected by a particular statute.

Inconsistent Application of the Test

Subsequent cases are inconsistent in applying the requirement. In *Clarke v. Securities Industries Association*, the Supreme Court applied the zone of interests test, but explained that it is a requirement that generally should not preclude standing.[307] In *Clarke*, a trade association of securities brokers challenged a decision by the comptroller of the currency to allow a bank to offer discount brokerage services at locations around the country. The association claimed that this violated a federal law preventing banks from creating branch banks in other states.

The Supreme Court said that the plaintiff had standing because it was injured and because it was within the zone of interests intended to be protected by the statute. The Court explained: "In cases where the plaintiff is not itself the subject of the contested regulatory action, the test denies a right of review if the plaintiff's interests are so marginally related to or inconsistent with the purposes implicit in the statute that it cannot reasonably be assumed that Congress intended to permit the suit."[308] The Court explained that the zone of interests test was "not meant to

[305] Charles Wright, Arthur Miller & Edward Cooper, 13 Federal Practice and Procedure 511-512 (1984).

[306] *See, e.g.*, Richard Stewart, The Reformation of American Administrative Law, 88 Harv. L. Rev. 1669, 1731-1734 (1975).

[307] 479 U.S. 388 (1987).

[308] *Id.* at 399.

be especially demanding; in particular, there need be no indication of congressional purpose to benefit the would-be plaintiff."[309] On the merits, the Court ruled in favor of the plaintiffs that the regulation was inconsistent with federal law.

The Court's subsequent applications of the zone of interests test, like *Clarke,* involved situations in which the Court found that its requirements were met. In *Bennett v. Spear,* the Court found that the authorization for citizen suits within the Endangered Species Act eliminated the requirement that the plaintiffs be within the zone of interests created by the statute.[310] In *Bennett,* ranch operators and irrigation districts sued under the citizen-suit provision of the Endangered Species Act to challenge the restriction of the use of reservoir water to protect two species of fish. Specifically, the Bureau of Reclamation determined that the operation of the Klamath Irrigation Project might affect two endangered species of fish and required the maintenance of water levels in the reservoir.

The ranch operators and irrigation districts sued and alleged an economic injury from the proposed federal action. The district court and court of appeals found that this was not within the zone of interests of the Endangered Species Act, which was intended to protect environmental interests. The U.S. Supreme Court reversed. Justice Scalia, writing for the Court, concluded that the authorization for citizen suits within the act was meant to expand federal court standing to the maximum permitted under Article III. Therefore, the statute overrides prudential standing requirements, such as the zone of interests test. The Court concluded: "It is true that the plaintiffs here are seeking to prevent application of environmental restrictions rather than to implement them. But the 'any person' formulation applies to all of the causes of action authorized by [the law]—not only to private violators of environmental restrictions, and not only to actions against the secretary asserting underenforcement. . . , but also to actions against the secretary asserting overenforcement."[311]

In *National Credit Union Administration v. First National Bank & Trust Co.*, the Court found that banks had standing to challenge a change in federal regulations that would have allowed credit unions to compete more directly with banks.[312] Although there was no indication that the federal law restricting credit union membership was intended to protect the economic interests of banks, the Court concluded that plaintiffs are not required to show that Congress intended to benefit them. Rather, plaintiffs need only demonstrate that the statute "arguably" protects their interests. Based on this relaxed standard, the Court concluded that the federal law restricting the operation of credit unions arguably protects the interests of their competitors.

In *Lexmark International, Inc. v. Static Control Components, Inc.*,[313] the Court found that the zone of interests test was met in a claim under the Lanham Act for false and deceptive advertising.[314] Lexmark makes toner cartridges and Static

[309] *Id.* at 399-400.
[310] 520 U.S. 154 (1997).
[311] 520 U.S. at 166.
[312] 522 U.S. 479 (1998).
[313] 572 U.S. 118 (2014).
[314] 15 U.S.C. §1125(a).

Control makes components for them. Static Control alleged that Lexmark engaged in false advertising and sued under the Lanham Act. The Court said: "We thus hold that to come within the zone of interests in a suit for false advertising under [the Lanham Act], a plaintiff must allege an injury to a commercial interest in reputation or sales. A consumer who is hoodwinked into purchasing a disappointing product may well have an injury-in-fact cognizable under Article III, but he cannot invoke the protection of the Lanham Act."[315] The Court thus found that Static Control's claim was within the zone of interests protected by the Lanham Act: "Static Control's alleged injuries—lost sales and damage to its business reputation—are injuries to precisely the sorts of commercial interests the Act protects. Static Control is suing not as a deceived consumer, but as a 'perso[n] engaged in' 'commerce within the control of Congress' whose position in the marketplace has been damaged by Lexmark's false advertising."[316]

In contrast, in *Air Courier Conference v. American Postal Workers Union,* the postal workers' union challenged the U.S. Postal Service's suspension of its monopoly over "extremely urgent" letters under the Postal Express Statutes.[317] After the Postal Service suspended the application of its monopoly over certain routes, postal unions challenged the decision. The Supreme Court ruled that the unions lacked standing because they were not within the zone of interests protected by the Postal Express statutes. In an opinion by Chief Justice Rehnquist, the Court began by noting that "[t]he particular language of the statutes provides no support for respondents' assertion that Congress intended to protect jobs with the Postal Service."[318] Additionally, the Court noted that the legislative history did not indicate an intent to benefit postal workers. The Court distinguished other cases where the zone of interests test had been met by pointing to statutory language or legislative history creating interests in those instances.

Air Courier is important in showing that the zone of interests test is not toothless. The Court concluded that a person or group can claim to be within the zone of interests protected by law only if the statute's text or history justifies such a conclusion.

Zone of Interests Test Likely Applies Only in Cases Under Administrative Procedure Act

There is a strong argument that the zone of interests test is an additional standing requirement only in cases seeking review of agency decisions under the Administrative Procedure Act. In *Clarke,* the Court explained that "[t]he principal cases in which the zone of interests test has been applied are those involving claims under the APA and the test is most usefully understood as a gloss on the meaning of §702 [which authorizes judicial review]."[319] The *Clarke* Court, however, spoke of the zone of interests protected both by statutory and constitutional provisions.

[315] 572 U.S. at 131-132.
[316] *Id.* at 137.
[317] 498 U.S. 517 (1991).
[318] *Id.* at 524-525.
[319] 479 U.S. at 400 n.16.

Furthermore, Professor Laurence Tribe persuasively argues that the zone of interests test is superfluous in constitutional litigation. Professor Tribe explains that in constitutional cases, the requirement that the plaintiff be within the zone of interests is "another way of saying that the right claimed is one possessed not by the party claiming it but by others."[320] If a person is asserting an injury to his or her constitutional rights, the zone of interests test is met. If an individual is not asserting a personally suffered wrong, then the requirement for injury or at least the bar against third-party standing would preclude review.

§2.3.7 Special Standing Problems: Organizations, Legislators, and Government Entities

The application of the standing rules discussed thus far pose special problems when applied to organizations, legislators, and government entities. Although each of these potential plaintiffs raises separate issues, a common theme is that each might sue on its own behalf or it might sue as a representative for others.[321] As Professor Tribe points out, "it is crucial to determine in what capacity" these possible plaintiffs are suing.[322] Is the plaintiff asserting harms to its own interests, in which case the traditional rules of standing apply, or is it suing in a representative capacity, in which case "special rules apply to ensure that the controversy is indeed genuine and the interests of the individuals alleged to be represented are indeed protected"?[323]

Standing for Organizations

An association or organization can sue based on injuries to itself or to its members.[324] An organization's mere concern about a problem, of course, is not enough to meet the requirement for injury; the organization has standing only if it or its members would be affected in a tangible way by the challenged action. For example, in *Sierra Club v. Morton,* discussed earlier in this chapter, a national environmental protection organization was denied standing to sue to halt the construction of a ski resort in a national park because it failed to allege harm to itself or that any of its members ever had used the park.[325]

[320] Laurence Tribe, American Constitutional Law 446 (3d ed. 2000). *See also* Bradford C. Mank, Prudential Standing and the Dormant Commerce Clause: Why the "Zone of Interests" Test Should Not Apply to Constitutional Cases, 48 Ariz. L. Rev. 23 (2006).

[321] Tribe, *supra* note 320, at 145. The idea of treating these three possible plaintiffs together is based on Professor Tribe's analysis.

[322] *Id.* (emphasis omitted).

[323] *Id.*

[324] In United Food & Com. Workers Loc. 751 v. Brown Grp., 517 U.S. at 557 (1996), the Court expressly discussed associational standing as an exception to the prohibition of third-party standing. It is worth noting that Justice Thomas has questioned whether associational standing should be allowed at all. Food and Drug Administration v. Alliance for Hippocratic Medicine, 602 U.S. 367 (2024).

[325] 405 U.S. at 735 (1972).

An organization has standing to sue on its own behalf if it has been injured as an entity. For example, an organization has standing to challenge conduct that impedes its ability to attract members, raise revenues, or fulfill its purposes.[326]

The Supreme Court's decision in *Havens Realty Corp. v. Coleman* is illustrative.[327] In *Havens*, several plaintiffs challenged a realty company's racial discrimination in providing information about housing. One of the plaintiffs was an organization dedicated to securing open housing. The organization claimed that the defendant's discriminatory practices undermined its ability to achieve its goals. The Court unanimously upheld standing for the organization, and for the other plaintiffs as well. The Court reasoned that the organization had standing because the defendant's practices injured the organization's ability to accomplish its purpose and required it to spend a great deal of its resources investigating and handling complaints of housing discrimination. The Court concluded that these injuries to the organization were sufficient for standing—that the organization successfully alleged "far more than simply a setback to the organization's abstract social interests."[328]

Alternatively, an organization might try to sue on behalf of its members. For example, in *NAACP v. Alabama*, the NAACP was allowed standing, in a representational capacity for its members, to challenge a state law requiring it to disclose its membership lists.[329] In addition to asserting its own interests as an organization, the NAACP raised the associational and speech rights of its members. The Court noted that the members who wish to remain anonymous might never come forward and thus it was desirable to allow the NAACP to assert its members' challenges to the constitutionality of the disclosure law.

In *Hunt v. Washington State Apple Advertising Commission*, the Supreme Court articulated a three-part test for determining when an organization may sue on behalf of its members.[330] In *Hunt*, an organization funded by apple growers in the state of Washington contended that a North Carolina law concerning the marketing of apples violated the dormant commerce clause, which limits state interference with interstate commerce.[331] The Supreme Court said that "[a]n association has standing to bring suit on behalf of its members when: (1) its members would otherwise have standing to sue in their own right; (2) the interests it seeks to protect are germane to the organization's purpose; and (3) neither the claim asserted nor the relief requested requires the participation in the lawsuit of the individual members."[332]

In *International Union, United Automobile Workers v. Brock*, the Court reaffirmed the *Hunt* three-part test for determining whether an organization may sue on

[326] Havens Realty Corp. v. Coleman, 455 U.S. at 379 (1982).

[327] *Id.*

[328] *Id.* at 379.

[329] 357 U.S. 449 (1958).

[330] 432 U.S. 333 (1977).

[331] The dormant commerce clause is discussed in Chemerinsky, *supra* note 222, at §5.3.

[332] 432 U.S. at 343.

behalf of its members.[333] The union, representing its members, sought to challenge the Trade Act of 1974, which limited the trade readjustment allowances that some individuals could receive in addition to unemployment compensation.

Under the *Hunt* three-part test, the organization was entitled to standing to represent its members. The members could have sued on their own behalf because they were injured by the denial of readjustment allowances. Also, the lawsuit was related to the organization's purpose because the union exists to protect the interests of its members with regard to their jobs and compensation. There is no reason why the individual members needed to be parties to the lawsuit; their interests were fully represented by the union.

The defendant argued that the Court should overrule the three-part *Hunt* test, prevent the organization from suing, and instead require the members to bring a class action suit. The Supreme Court expressly rejected this position, stating that it would not "abandon settled principles of associational standing."[334] The Court explained that there are many benefits to allowing an existing organization to sue that would be lost if class action suits were required instead. For example, the Court observed that "[w]hile a class action creates an ad hoc union of injured plaintiffs who may be linked only by their common claims, an association suing to vindicate the interests of its members can draw upon a pre-existing reservoir of expertise and capital."[335] People join associations to advance their interests; associations should be able to pursue their objectives through litigation on behalf of the members.

In *United Food and Commercial Workers v. Brown Group*, the Court again reaffirmed the *Hunt* test and clarified that its third prong—that neither the claim nor the relief requires the participation of the individual members—is prudential and not constitutional.[336] A federal law, the Worker Adjustment and Retraining Notification (WARN) Act,[337] grants a union the authority to sue for damages on behalf of its members. The Court upheld the constitutionality of the law and explained that the first part of the *Hunt* test—the requirement that the members of the association would otherwise have standing to sue in their own right—implemented the constitutional requirement for an injury. The Court concluded that the third part of the test is prudential and that Congress could therefore override it in allowing the association to sue for damages on behalf of its members.

Legislators' Standing

The question of when *legislators* have standing to sue is, in many ways, more complicated than the issue of associational standing. There is no doubt that legislators have standing for injuries that they personally suffer. For example, members

[333] 477 U.S. 274 (1986); *see also* New York State Club Assoc. v. City of New York, 487 U.S. 1 (1988) (reaffirming the *Hunt* test).

[334] 477 U.S. at 290.

[335] *Id.* at 289.

[336] 517 U.S. 544 (1996).

[337] 29 U.S.C. §2104(b).

of Congress certainly have standing to challenge a law that limits their salary in alleged violation of the Constitution.[338] In *Powell v. McCormack*, for instance, a member of Congress was allowed to sue for back pay as a result of the House of Representatives' refusal to seat him.[339]

The more difficult issue arises when the legislator sues on the basis of injuries to his or her ability to perform as a representative. The Supreme Court addressed this question in *Raines v. Byrd*,[340] a suit by individual members of Congress challenging the constitutionality of the Line Item Veto Act.[341] The act authorized the president to cancel certain spending and tax measures.[342] The day after the act went into effect, members of Congress sued and challenged its constitutionality. The Supreme Court ruled that the members lacked standing. The Court stressed that "[t]hey have not alleged that they voted for a specific bill, that there were sufficient votes to pass the bill, and that the bill was nonetheless deemed defeated. . . . Nor can they allege that the Act will nullify their votes in the future. . . . In the future, a majority of Senators and Congressmen can pass or reject the appropriations bills, the Act has no effect on this process."[343]

The Court expressly distinguished *Coleman v. Miller*, the only prior case that addressed legislators' standing. In *Coleman v. Miller*, twenty members of the Kansas legislature challenged the constitutionality of the legislature's decision to ratify a proposed constitutional amendment to prohibit child labor.[344] The Kansas legislature previously had rejected the amendment, which led to the claim that the later ratification was impermissible. The Supreme Court dismissed the case as posing a political question. But three justices indicated that they would accord the plaintiffs, state legislators, standing. Chief Justice Hughes wrote, "We think that these senators have a plain, direct and adequate interest in maintaining the effectiveness of their votes."[345] Four justices, in an opinion by Justice Frankfurter, contended that the legislators lacked standing. They maintained that the legislators lacked

[338] *See, e.g.*, Synar v. United States, 626 F. Supp. 1374, 1368, 1380 (D.D.C.), *aff'd sub nom.* Bowsher v. Synar, 478 U.S. 714 (1986) (members of Congress sued to challenge the Gramm-Rudman-Hollins Deficit Reduction Act that would limit their salaries; standing upheld for other plaintiffs).

[339] 395 U.S. 486 (1969).

[340] 521 U.S. 812 (1997).

[341] Pub. L. No. 104-130, 110 Stat. 1200, 2 U.S.C. §§691 et seq.

[342] The act was declared unconstitutional the following year in Clinton v. City of New York, 524 U.S. 417 (1998).

[343] 521 U.S. at 824.

[344] 307 U.S. 433 (1939). Although this discussion considers legislators' standing without separating members of Congress from members of state legislatures, there might be an important distinction between judicial review of these two groups' claims. Separation of powers concerns might justify limits on congressional standing that are inapplicable to suits brought by state legislators. On the other hand, there might be federalism concerns limiting review of state legislators' claims that are inapplicable to suits brought by members of Congress. The two topics are considered together because of the absence of cases distinguishing them and because they do raise common issues: When is a legislator injured, and when should the federal courts review claims of legislators as opposed to leaving the matter to the political process?

[345] *Id.* at 438.

a sufficiently personal interest to permit standing.[346] The remaining two justices expressed no position on the standing question.

In *Raines v. Byrd*, the Court characterized *Coleman* as involving the denial or nullification of a vote, something that it found to be absent with the line-item veto. The Court in *Raines* explained: "Just as appellees cannot show that their vote was denied or nullified as in *Coleman* (in the sense that a bill they voted for would have become law if their vote had not been stripped of its validity), so are they unable to show that their vote was denied or nullified in a discretionary manner (in the sense that their vote was denied its full validity in relation to the votes of their colleagues)."[347]

The Court found that the members of Congress did not allege a sufficient injury in claiming that their effectiveness was undermined. The Court pointed to several instances in which members of Congress might have sued had such a broad definition of standing been followed.[348]

After *Raines v. Byrd*, legislators have standing only if they allege either that they have been singled out for especially unfavorable treatment as opposed to other members of their bodies or that their votes have been denied or nullified. This is consistent with a large body of lower court precedent, primarily from the U.S. Court of Appeals for the District of Columbia Circuit, that required a showing of nullification of a vote as a prerequisite for standing. The court of appeals has stated that a member of Congress has standing only if "the alleged diminution in congressional influence . . . amount[s] to a disenfranchisement, a complete nullification or withdrawal of a voting opportunity."[349]

Raines v. Byrd leaves unclear whether there is any continuing significance to the District of Columbia Circuit's requirement that even a complete nullification is not sufficient to ensure standing, that the court can deny standing, even if all requirements are met, based on the doctrine of "equitable discretion." This doctrine was first articulated in *Riegle v. Federal Open Market Committee*.[350] A congressman sued, claiming that the Federal Open Market Committee was impermissibly headed by members who had not been confirmed by the Senate. The court of appeals agreed that the plaintiff had standing, but declined to hear the case as an exercise of its "equitable discretion."[351] "Equitable" discretion referred to the court's power to refuse to hear a case because it deemed it desirable to avoid review,

[346] *Id.* at 469-470 (Frankfurter, J., concurring in the judgment).

[347] 521 U.S. at 824 n.7.

[348] *Id.* at 824-828.

[349] Goldwater v. Carter, 617 F.2d 697, 702 (D.C. Cir.), *vacated and remanded on other grounds*, 444 U.S. 996 (1979); *see also* Harrington v. Bush, 553 F.2d 190, 213 (D.C. Cir. 1977). The issue of congressional standing arose in the context of whether members of Congress had standing to challenge the federal Deficit Reduction Act of 2005, Pub. L. No. 109-171, §10001, 120 Stat. 4, §183. The House and the Senate passed different versions of the bill, and the president signed the Senate version. Members of the House sued, but the district court, relying on Raines v. Byrd, ruled that they lacked standing. Conyers v. Bush, 2006 WL 3834224 (E.D. Mich. Nov. 6, 2006).

[350] 656 F.2d 873 (D.C. Cir.), *cert. denied*, 454 U.S. 1072 (1981). The same issue was raised and similarly dismissed in Melcher v. Federal Open Market Commn., 836 F.2d 561 (D.C. Cir. 1987).

[351] 656 F.2d at 882.

perhaps on separation of powers grounds. Subsequently, the court renamed this principle "remedial discretion."[352]

On several occasions, the court of appeals has invoked the doctrine of remedial discretion and has refused to hear constitutional issues brought by members of Congress. For example, in *Vander Jagt v. O'Neil*, the court refused to allow a Republican congressman to challenge the distribution of committee assignments in the House of Representatives.[353] Although the court agreed that the plaintiffs met the requirements for standing, the court dismissed the case under its equitable discretion. In *Moore v. United States House of Representatives*, the court of appeals used equitable discretion to dismiss a suit challenging the constitutionality of a bill to raise taxes on the ground that the bill had not originated in the House of Representatives as required by the Constitution.[354] In *Crockett v. Reagan*, the court of appeals relied on the doctrine of equitable discretion to dismiss a suit brought by twenty-nine members of Congress contending that the federal government's aid to El Salvador violated the Foreign Assistance Act of 1961.[355]

Raines did not discuss equitable discretion. Its silence might be interpreted as rejecting it as a requirement in analyzing legislators' standing. Alternatively, the absence of discussion might not be a rejection because the Court was able to deny standing without needing to consider equitable discretion.[356]

The Court returned to the issue of the standing of legislators in *Arizona State Legislature v. Arizona Independent Redistricting Commission*.[357] Arizona voters passed initiatives to create an independent commission to draw election district lines for congressional districts and both houses of the Arizona legislature. Members of the Arizona legislature sued arguing that this was unconstitutional for congressional districts because Article I of the Constitution requires that the "time, place, and manner of elections" be set by state legislatures.

The Court held, 5-4, that members of the Arizona legislature had standing to sue and that the Arizona initiative was constitutional. Justice Ginsburg, writing for the Court, reviewed the earlier decisions described above, *Coleman v. Miller* and *Raines v. Byrd*, and concluded that standing was justified under these precedents: "*Coleman*, as we later explained in *Raines*, stood 'for the proposition that legislators whose votes would have been sufficient to defeat (or enact) a specific legislative Act have standing to sue if that legislative action goes into effect (or does

[352] United Presbyterian Church v. Reagan, 738 F.2d 1375, 1381 n.5 (D.C. Cir. 1984) (citations omitted).

[353] 699 F.2d 1166 (D.C. Cir. 1982), *cert. denied*, 464 U.S. 823 (1983).

[354] 733 F.2d 946 (D.C. Cir. 1984), *cert. denied*, 469 U.S. 1106 (1985).

[355] 720 F.2d 1355, 1357 (D.C. Cir. 1983), *cert. denied*, 467 U.S. 1251 (1984); *see also* Gregg v. Barrett, 771 F.2d 539, 543-546 (D.C. Cir. 1985) (denying review based on remedial discretion of suit to compel verbatim transcripts in the Congressional Record of proceedings occurring on the floor of the House and Senate); Lowry v. Reagan, 676 F. Supp. 333 (D.D.C. 1987) (denying review of challenge to president's actions in the Persian Gulf as violating the War Powers Resolution).

[356] In Chenoweth v. Clinton, 997 F. Supp. 36 (D.D.C. 1998), the court denied congressional standing to a challenge to an executive order protecting historic rivers. The court focused on the lack of nullification of congressional votes, but did not discuss equitable discretion.

[357] 576 U.S. 787 (2015).

not go into effect), on the ground that their votes have been completely nullified.' Our conclusion that the Arizona Legislature has standing fits that bill. Proposition 106, together with the Arizona Constitution's ban on efforts to undermine the purposes of an initiative, would 'completely nullif[y]' any vote by the Legislature, now or 'in the future,' purporting to adopt a redistricting plan."[358] The Court thus did not change the test for legislator standing, but said that it was met in that the legislators claimed that their votes had been nullified.

Justice Scalia dissented and argued that there is not standing when it is a dispute between branches of a government. He wrote: "What history and judicial tradition show is that courts do not resolve direct disputes between two political branches of the same government regarding their respective powers. Nearly every separation-of-powers case presents questions like the ones in this case. But we have *never* passed on a separation-of-powers question raised directly by a governmental subunit's complaint. We have *always* resolved those questions in the context of a private lawsuit in which the claim or defense depends on the constitutional validity of action by one of the governmental subunits that has caused a private party concrete harm."[359] In *Virginia House of Delegates v. Bethune-Hill*, the Supreme Court held that the Virginia House of Delegates lacked standing to appeal from a lower court ruling that a state redistricting plan—adopted by both houses of the state legislature—constituted a racial gerrymander.[360] Virginia's Attorney General initially defended the plan in court, but decided not to pursue an appeal. The state House, which had participated in the case as an intervenor, sought to appeal to the Supreme Court. The Court, 5-4, said that it lacked standing and explained that Virginia could have "designated the House to represent its interests," but it had not done so.[361] The Court explained that one house of a bicameral legislature cannot claim a sufficient injury to permit standing.

The underlying normative question in all of these cases is whether and when legislators should be accorded standing. For example, some judges have argued that legislators' standing should be completely abolished. Most notably, then-Judge Antonin Scalia (while sitting on the District of Columbia Circuit) and former Judge Robert Bork argued that because of separation of powers, the court should not permit members of Congress to sue in court.[362] Judge Bork, for example, stated: "When the interest sought to be asserted is one of governmental power, there can be no congressional standing, however confined."[363] They contend that members of Congress can protect their own interests through the legislative process; resort to the courts is unnecessary and undesirable.

[358] *Id.* at 803.

[359] *Id.* at 856 (Scalia, J., dissenting).

[360] 587 U.S. 658 (2019).

[361] *Id.* at 663.

[362] Moore v. United States House of Reps., 733 F.2d at 959 (Scalia, J., concurring).

[363] Barnes v. Klein, 759 F.2d 21, 68 n.18 (D.C. Cir. 1984) (Bork, J., dissenting). *See also* Vicki C. Jackson, Congressional Standing to Sue: The Role of Courts and Congress in U.S. Constitutional Democracy, 93 Ind. L.J. 845 (2018).

Others argue that the court does not go far enough in allowing congressional standing. Their claim is that members of Congress should be able to challenge conduct that unconstitutionally usurps legislative powers or interferes with the legislature's ability to carry out its tasks.[364] If the Constitution is violated in a manner that adversely affects a legislator's performance, that individual should be able to sue to enjoin the illegality. Furthermore, the doctrine of equitable restraint is particularly subject to criticism; if all justiciability and jurisdictional requirements are met, it is questionable whether a court should be able to declare that it has discretion to refuse to hear a matter. Just as separation of powers issues are raised by judicial involvement in intrabranch disputes, so are separation of powers implicated when the court on its own declines to hear cases authorized by Congress and allowed by the Constitution.[365] Moreover, there already exists a political question doctrine limiting justiciability of certain claims—discussed in §2.6—making unnecessary the creation of the new principle of equitable discretion.

Yet the current law also has its defenders. The argument is that it is necessary to draw a balance. On the one hand, it would be undesirable for members of Congress to be able to turn to the federal courts whenever they lost a vote on an issue.[366] Courts should avoid interference in intrabranch disputes and, by some views, even avoid involvement in disputes between the branches of government. On the other hand, if there truly were an action precluding the Congress from voting or nullifying a vote, it should be reviewed and declared unconstitutional. The current law attempts to strike this balance, though its critics, depending on their position, would argue that it either goes too far or not far enough in allowing congressional standing.

Suits By Government Entities

The final topic concerns standing for suits by government entities. Again, a distinction must be drawn between a government entity suing to remedy injuries that it has suffered and suing in a representative capacity on behalf of its citizens. There is no doubt that a government can sue to protect its own interests. For example, a government certainly has standing to sue to enforce its laws or protect its activities as a sovereign government entity. The federal government, for instance, was accorded standing to enjoin state government violations of the federal Voting Rights Act.[367] Also, government entities have standing based on injuries

[364] Tom Campbell, Executive Action and Inaction, 95 N.C. L. Rev. 553 (2017); Jonathan Remy Nash, A Functional Theory of Congressional Standing, 114 Mich. L. Rev. 339 (2015).

[365] *See* Martin H. Redish, Abstention, Separation of Powers, and the Limits of the Judicial Function, 94 Yale L.J. 71 (1984) (arguing that it violates separation of powers for federal courts to refuse to exercise jurisdiction granted by Congress).

[366] *See, e.g.*, Carl McGowan, Congressman in Court: The New Plaintiffs, 15 Ga. L. Rev. 241 (1981); *see also* Vicki C. Jackson, Congressional Standing to Sue: The Role of Courts and Congress in U.S. Constitutional Democracy, 93 Ind. L.J. 845 (2018).

[367] Oregon v. Mitchell, 400 U.S. 112 (1970) (also reporting the decisions in United States v. Arizona and United States v. Idaho).

suffered when they act in a proprietary capacity.[368] State and local governments have standing to challenge interference with the performance of their duties as governments.[369]

As an example of this, in *Biden v. Nebraska,* the Court found that Missouri had standing to sue and that was sufficient for the justices to consider the merits of the case.[370] Chief Justice Roberts in a majority opinion focused on an agency in Missouri, the Missouri Higher Education Loan Authority, which was created to help state residents obtain student loans for college. The Court noted that the Biden plan would provide debt relief to over half of people with student loans and that the plan could cost the agency as much as $44 million a year. The Court stated: "The plan's harm to MOHELA is also a harm to Missouri. MOHELA is a 'public instrumentality' of the State."[371] He explained: "By law and function, MOHELA is an instrumentality of Missouri: It was created by the State to further a public purpose, is governed by state officials and state appointees, reports to the State, and may be dissolved by the State. The Secretary's plan will cut MOHELA's revenues, impairing its efforts to aid Missouri college students. This acknowledged harm to MOHELA in the performance of its public function is necessarily a direct injury to Missouri itself."[372]

Justice Kagan, in a dissent joined by Justices Sotomayor and Jackson, strongly disagreed that Missouri had standing. She said that the injury was to MOHELA, which is an independent entity that was not a party to the lawsuit. She wrote: "The plaintiffs in this case are six States that have no personal stake in the Secretary's loan forgiveness plan. They are classic ideological plaintiffs: They think the plan a very bad idea, but they are no worse off because the Secretary differs. In giving those States a forum—in adjudicating their complaint—the Court forgets its proper role. The Court acts as though it is an arbiter of political and policy disputes, rather than of cases and controversies."[373]

Having found standing, the Court reached the merits and struck down the Biden debt relief program.

Similarly, in *Wyoming v. Oklahoma,* the Supreme Court held that Wyoming had standing to challenge an Oklahoma law requiring Oklahoma utilities to burn coal

[368] *See, e.g.,* United States v. San Jacinto Tin Co., 125 U.S. 273, 278 (1888) (suit by the federal government to protect its interest in certain lands); City of Sausalito v. O'Neil, 386 F.3d 1186 (9th Cir. 2004) (holding that Sausalito had standing based on injury to its proprietary interests); Arkla Exploration Co. v. Texas Oil & Gas Corp., 734 F.2d 347, 354 (8th Cir. 1984), *cert. denied,* 469 U.S. 1158 (1985) (suit seeking revenues from oil and gas exploration revenues owed to the states).

[369] *See, e.g.,* Diamond v. Charles, 476 U.S. 54 (1986) (state's ability to sue to defend the constitutionality of its laws); Wyoming ex rel. Crank v. United States, 539 F.3d 1236 (10th Cir. 2008) (holding that Wyoming had standing to enforce its legal code); Dressman v. Costle, 759 F.2d 548, 555 n.8 (6th Cir. 1985) (standing of counties to challenge enforcement of the Clean Air Act); State of New York v. Heckler, 719 F.2d 1191 (2d Cir. 1983) (state's standing to challenge federal agency's limitation of grants to state governments).

[370] 600 U.S. 477 (2023).

[371] *Id.* at 2366.

[372] *Id.*

[373] *Id.* at 2381 (Kagan, J., dissenting).

containing at least 10 percent Oklahoma-mined coal.[374] Prior to the law, Oklahoma utilities relied almost exclusively on coal mined in Wyoming. Although the state of Wyoming itself did not engage in any mining or selling of coal, it nonetheless challenged the Oklahoma law as violating the dormant commerce clause. Wyoming argued that it suffered injury because of the loss of revenue from its severance tax on coal.

The Supreme Court held that Wyoming had standing because it would suffer a direct injury: the loss of tax revenue.[375] The Court rejected as immaterial the fact that Wyoming did not itself sell or mine coal. The economic harm Wyoming suffered from the Oklahoma law was a sufficient basis for standing.

The much harder issues arise when a government entity sues not to protect its sovereign or proprietary interests, but instead litigates as a representative for its citizens. In one sense this is an artificial distinction because everything a government does is as a representative for its constituents. But a distinction can and has been drawn between instances where the government is protecting its own sovereign or proprietary interests and where it is suing on behalf of the interests of its citizens. Such suits, where a government sues to protect its citizens, are often referred to as involving *parens patriae standing*.

The seminal case is *Missouri v. Illinois*, in which the Supreme Court allowed a state to sue to halt the dumping of sewage in interstate waters.[376] The Court said: "[I]f the health and comfort of inhabitants of a State are threatened, the State is the proper party to represent and defend them."[377] For a state to assert parens patriae standing, it must allege both a harm to its citizens and that the matter involved is the type that the state is likely to address through its lawmaking process.[378]

The Supreme Court's decision in *Alfred L. Snapp & Son, Inc. v. Puerto Rico* clarified the law concerning parens patriae standing.[379] Puerto Rico sued fifty-one private parties that grew apples in Virginia, claiming that the companies discriminated against temporary workers from Puerto Rico. The Court observed that a government cannot sue solely by asserting interests of its citizens. Rather, the Court identified two types of interests—termed *quasi-sovereign interests*—where a government has parens patriae standing.[380] One is where the government is suing based on its interest "in the health and well-being—both physical and economic—of its residents in general."[381] For example, in prior cases, the Court allowed states parens patriae standing to halt pollution[382] and to enforce federal antitrust laws on

[374] 502 U.S. 437 (1992).
[375] *Id.* at 448.
[376] 180 U.S. 208 (1901).
[377] *Id.* at 241.
[378] Alfred L. Snapp & Son, Inc. v. Puerto Rico, 458 U.S. 592, 607 (1982).
[379] 458 U.S. 592 (1982).
[380] *Id.* at 602.
[381] *Id.* at 607.
[382] *See, e.g.,* Georgia v. Tennessee Copper Co., 206 U.S. 230 (1907); Missouri v. Illinois, 180 U.S. 208 (1901).

behalf of their citizens.[383] The Court in *Snapp* stressed that the government entity must show both an injury to its citizens and that it is the type of harm "that the State, if it could, would likely attempt to address through its sovereign lawmaking powers."[384]

Second, the Court said that parens patriae standing exists to ensure that "the State and its residents are not excluded from the benefits that are to flow from participation in the federal system."[385] Under this rationale, the Court accorded Puerto Rico standing to challenge alleged discrimination against its citizens in interstate commerce by the apple companies.

One important limit on parens patriae standing of state and local governments is that they may not sue the federal government in this capacity, though they may sue the federal government to protect their own sovereign or proprietary interests. In *Massachusetts v. Mellon*, the Supreme Court denied a state standing to challenge a federal Maternity Act that provided aid to pregnant women and their newborn children.[386] The Court said that "[i]t cannot be conceded that a State, as *parens patriae*, may institute judicial proceedings to protect citizens of the United States from the operation of the statutes thereof."[387] This limitation might be questioned. Allowing states to sue the federal government on behalf of its citizens might provide essential protection, just as such suits are often important against private parties.

The ability of the federal government to sue in a parens patriae capacity is much more uncertain. The most famous Supreme Court decision on the subject is *In re Debs*, which upheld the ability of the federal government to seek an injunction to halt a labor strike.[388] The Supreme Court spoke expansively about the federal government's authority to sue. It stated: "Every government, entrusted, by the very terms of its being, with powers and duties to be exercised and discharged for the general welfare, has a right to apply to its own courts for any proper assistance. . . . [I]t is no sufficient answer to [say] that it has no pecuniary interest in the matter. The obligations which it is under to promote the interest of all, and to prevent the wrongdoing of one resulting in injury to the general welfare, is often of itself sufficient to give it standing in court."[389]

Relatively little has been made of this broad authorization to sue because in most instances, the federal government has sued pursuant to federal statutes and not based on its inherent interest in protecting its citizens. During the early 1960s,

[383] *See, e.g.,* Maryland v. Louisiana, 451 U.S. 725, 737 (1981); Georgia v. Pennsylvania R.R., 324 U.S. 439, 446-452 (1945).

[384] 458 U.S. at 607.

[385] *Id.* at 608.

[386] 262 U.S. 447, 485-486 (1923); *see also* South Carolina v. Katzenbach, 383 U.S. 301, 324 (1966) (relying on Massachusetts v. Mellon to limit state's ability as parens patriae to sue the federal government).

[387] 262 U.S. at 485.

[388] 158 U.S. 564 (1895).

[389] 158 U.S. at 584.

the federal government sued on behalf of blacks in the South challenging state laws mandating segregation of the races.[390]

In the 1970s, two federal courts of appeals denied the U.S. attorney general standing to sue to protect the constitutional rights of institutionalized mentally handicapped persons.[391] A subsequent federal statute, the Civil Rights of Institutionalized Persons Act, was adopted to provide the U.S. government standing in such circumstances.[392] Similarly, a federal court of appeals denied the United States standing to protect residents of Philadelphia from allegedly widespread police violations of civil liberties.[393] These decisions might be defended as reflecting many of the underlying values behind the standing doctrine: limiting the occasion for judicial review and insisting that injured individuals assert only their own rights. But in a society in which litigation costs are enormous and the protection of constitutional rights is imperative, allowing the government to sue on behalf of its citizens can provide essential safeguards that otherwise might be lacking.

§2.4 RIPENESS

§2.4.1 Introduction

Ripeness Defined

Ripeness, like mootness (discussed in the next section), is a justiciability doctrine determining when review is appropriate. While standing is concerned with who is a proper party to litigate a particular matter, ripeness and mootness determine when that litigation may occur. Specifically, the ripeness doctrine seeks to separate matters that are premature for review because the injury is speculative and may never occur from those cases that are appropriate for federal court action.[1]

Although the phrasing makes the questions of who may sue and when they may sue seem distinct, in practice there is an obvious overlap between the doctrines of standing and ripeness. If no injury has occurred, the plaintiff might be denied standing or the case might be dismissed as not ripe. For example, in *O'Shea v. Littleton,* the Supreme Court declared nonjusticiable a suit contending that the defendants, a magistrate and a judge, discriminated against blacks in setting bail

[390] *See, e.g.,* United States v. City of Jackson, 318 F.2d 1 (5th Cir. 1963); United States v. City of Shreveport, 210 F. Supp. 36 (W.D. La. 1962).

[391] United States v. Mattson, 600 F.2d 1295 (9th Cir. 1979); United States v. Solomon, 563 F.2d 1121 (4th Cir. 1977).

[392] Act of May 23, 1980, codified at 42 U.S.C. §1997.

[393] United States v. City of Philadelphia, 644 F.2d 187 (3d Cir. 1980).

§2.4 [1] Abbott Laboratories v. Gardner, 387 U.S. 136, 148 (1967). *See, e.g.,* Ohio Forestry Assn., Inc. v. Sierra Club, 523 U.S. 726 (1998) (environmental group's challenge is not ripe when permission to engage in logging has not yet been granted, modifications in the plan remain possible, and the plaintiffs have not raised claims that they will suffer immediate harms).

and imposing sentences.[2] The Court observed that none of the plaintiffs currently faced proceedings in the defendants' courtrooms, and hence "the threat of injury from the alleged course of conduct they attack is too remote to satisfy the case-or-controversy requirement."[3] This decision could be placed either under the label of standing—no injury was alleged—or ripeness—the type of injury was adequate but had not yet occurred.

Similarly, in *Susan B. Anthony List v. Driehaus,* the Court considered a challenge to an Ohio statute that criminalized making false statements about candidates during political campaigns.[4] The Susan B. Anthony List, a political group that previously had been threatened with prosecution under the law, brought a suit for a declaratory judgment to have the law declared unconstitutional. The Court found that the plaintiffs met the requirements of Article III because they alleged a credible threat of enforcement. The Court referred to this as being about standing and ripeness, but made no attempt to distinguish between these doctrines. In fact, the Court said: "As the parties acknowledge, the Article III standing and ripeness issues in this case 'boil down to the same question.' "[5]

Perhaps the distinction between standing and ripeness is that standing focuses on whether the type of injury alleged is qualitatively sufficient to fulfill the requirements of Article III and whether the plaintiff has personally suffered that harm, whereas ripeness centers on whether that injury has occurred yet. Again, while the distinction will work in some instances, in others it is problematic because the question of whether the plaintiff has suffered a harm is integral to both standing and ripeness concerns. For example, in *Sierra Club v. Morton,* the Supreme Court dismissed, on standing grounds, a challenge by an environmental group to the construction of a ski resort in a national park.[6] The Court emphasized the failure of the plaintiff to allege that it or its members ever had used the park. This standing decision could be viewed as a ripeness ruling as well, if ripeness is understood as focusing on whether an injury that is sufficient to meet Article III has been suffered yet.

To the extent that the substantive requirements overlap and the result will be the same regardless of whether the issue is characterized as ripeness or standing, little turns on the choice of the label. However, for the sake of clarity, especially in those cases where the law of standing and ripeness is not identical, ripeness can be given a narrower definition that distinguishes it from standing and explains the existing case law. Ripeness properly should be understood as involving the question of *when a party may seek preenforcement review of a statute or regulation.* Customarily, a person can challenge the legality of a statute or regulation only when he or she is prosecuted for violating it. At that time, a defense can be that the law is invalid, for example, as being unconstitutional.

[2] 414 U.S. 488 (1974).
[3] *Id.* at 489.
[4] 573 U.S. 149 (2014).
[5] *Id.* at 157 n.5.
[6] 405 U.S. 727 (1972), discussed in more detail in §2.3.2.

There is an unfairness, however, in requiring a person to violate a law in order to challenge it. A person might unnecessarily obey an unconstitutional law, refraining from the prohibited conduct, rather than risk criminal punishments. Alternatively, a person might violate a statute or regulation, confident that it will be invalidated, only to be punished when the law is upheld. A primary purpose of the Declaratory Judgment Act was to permit people to avoid this choice and obtain preenforcement review of statutes and regulations.

The Declaratory Judgment Act does not allow preenforcement review in all instances. Rather, it permits federal court decisions only "[i]n a case of actual controversy."[7] In upholding the constitutionality of the Declaratory Judgment Act, the Supreme Court emphasized that the statute did not permit advisory opinions because it limited federal court action to justiciable cases.[8] Ripeness, then, is best understood as the determination of whether a federal court can grant preenforcement review; for example, when may a court hear a request for a declaratory judgment, or when must it decline review?

The Supreme Court has stated that in deciding whether a case is ripe it looks primarily to two considerations: "the hardship to the parties of withholding court consideration" and "the fitness of the issues for judicial decision."[9] Ripeness is said to reflect both constitutional and prudential considerations. The focus on whether there is a sufficient injury without preenforcement review seems inextricably linked with the constitutional requirement for cases and controversies, whereas the focus on the quality of the record seems prudential.[10]

The ripeness doctrine, limiting preenforcement review, serves many of the purposes underlying the other justiciability doctrines. Ripeness advances separation of powers by avoiding judicial review in situations where it is unnecessary for the federal courts to become involved because there is not a substantial hardship to postponing review. In the leading case of *Abbott Laboratories v. Gardner*, the Court explained that the "basic rationale" of the ripeness requirement is "to prevent the courts, through avoidance of premature adjudication, from entangling themselves in abstract disagreements."[11]

Additionally, the ripeness requirement, like all justiciability doctrines, enhances judicial economy by limiting the occasion for federal court jurisdiction and the expenditure of judicial time and revenues. Perhaps most of all, ripeness is said to enhance the quality of judicial decision-making by ensuring that there is an adequate record to permit effective review.[12]

[7] 28 U.S.C. §2201.

[8] Aetna Life Ins. Co. v. Haworth, 300 U.S. 227, 241 (1937); for a discussion of the constitutionality of the Declaratory Judgment Act and why it is not an authorization for unconstitutional advisory opinions, *see* §2.2.

[9] Abbott Laboratories v. Gardner, 387 U.S. at 149.

[10] At times, the Court describes ripeness as constitutional; *see, e.g.*, Public Serv. Commn. of Utah v. Wycoff Co., 344 U.S. 237, 242-245 (1952); at other times, the Court describes the ripeness test as prudential; *see, e.g.*, Buckley v. Valeo, 424 U.S. 1, 114-118 (1976). In large part, this difference might reflect the aspects of ripeness at issue in particular cases.

[11] 387 U.S. at 148.

[12] *Id.*

As is reflected in the cases described below, the federal courts have a great deal of discretion in determining whether a case is ripe. The questions of whether there is sufficient hardship to permit preenforcement review and whether the record is adequately focused cannot be reduced to a formula. The result is that it is often difficult to distinguish why in some instances ripeness was found, but in other seemingly similar circumstances it was denied.

§2.4.2 *Criteria for Determining Ripeness: The Hardship to Denying Review*

The first part of the ripeness inquiry is, how significant is the harm to denying judicial review? The more a plaintiff can demonstrate substantial hardship to a denial of preenforcement review, the more likely a federal court is to find ripeness. Conversely, the more speculative and uncertain the harm, the less likely it is that review will be granted.[13]

Hardship from Choice Between Possibly Unnecessary Compliance and Possible Conviction

An examination of Supreme Court ripeness decisions reveals three situations in which the Court has found there to be enough hardship to justify preenforcement review. First, when an individual is faced with a choice between forgoing allegedly lawful behavior and risking likely prosecution with substantial consequences, the federal courts will deem the case ripe rather than insist that an individual violate the law and risk the consequences. *Abbott Laboratories v. Gardner* is illustrative.[14] The Food and Drug Administration (FDA) promulgated a regulation requiring the inclusion of generic names for prescription drugs on all labels and other printed materials. Violations of the regulation were punishable by civil and criminal sanctions. Thirty-seven drug companies, accounting for 90 percent of the supply of prescription drugs in the country, challenged the regulation as exceeding the scope of the FDA's authority under the pertinent statutes. The government argued that the case was not ripe until a drug company was prosecuted for violating the regulation.

The Supreme Court disagreed and permitted preenforcement review. The Court emphasized the substantial hardship to denying preenforcement review. The Court stated: "If petitioners wish to comply they must change all their labels, advertisements and promotional materials, they must destroy stocks of printed

[13] For example, in Texas v. United States, 523 U.S. 295 (1998), the Supreme Court refused to rule as to whether the preclearance provision of the Voting Rights Act of 1965 applied to the possible appointment of a magistrate to oversee school districts that failed to meet performance standards. The Court noted that no magistrate had yet been appointed and that the appointment of a magistrate was a last resort to be used only if all other means failed. The Court concluded that the case was not ripe because it was too speculative whether a magistrate ever would be appointed.

[14] 387 U.S. at 136.

matter; and they must invest heavily in new printing type and new supplies. The alternative to compliance . . . would risk serious criminal and civil penalties for the unlawful distribution of 'misbranded' drugs."[15]

The ripeness requirement can be understood by contrasting *Abbott Laboratories* with another case decided the same day, *Toilet Goods Association v. Gardner.*[16] An FDA regulation permitted the FDA free access to all manufacturing processes involved in the production of color additives and authorized the suspension of certifications for sales if access is denied. A cosmetic manufacturing company sought a declaratory judgment invalidating the regulation. Unlike *Abbott Laboratories,* the Court said that the matter was not ripe because there was minimal hardship to denying review. The Court explained that "a refusal to admit an inspector here would at most lead only to a suspension of certification services to the particular party, a determination that can then be promptly challenged through an administrative procedure, which in turn is reviewable by a court."[17]

In numerous other cases as well, the Supreme Court found substantial hardship in denying judicial review because of the choice that a person faced between refraining from allegedly protected conduct or risking sanctions. For instance, in *Steffel v. Thompson,* the plaintiff sought a declaratory judgment upholding his right to distribute handbills in a shopping center.[18] On two occasions, the plaintiff attempted to distribute anti-Vietnam War literature at a shopping center; both times, the owners of the property called the police. Although the plaintiff left to avoid arrest, his companions stayed and were arrested. The Supreme Court found the matter ripe because denying review would impose substantial hardship, forcing the plaintiff to choose between unnecessarily giving up possibly protected speech or risking arrest and criminal punishment. Justice Brennan, writing for the Court, spoke of the injury inflicted in placing "the hapless plaintiff between the Scylla of intentionally flouting state law and the Charybdis of forgoing what he believes to be constitutionally protected activity in order to avoid becoming enmeshed in a criminal proceeding."[19]

Similarly, in the earlier case of *Adler v. Board of Education of the City of New York,* the Court implicitly found ripe a challenge to a state law designed to eliminate "subversive persons from the public school system."[20] The state statute contained a list of subversive organizations, and membership in any of these groups was deemed a basis for disqualification from being employed in any school. Although Justice Frankfurter dissented, arguing that the case was not ripe, the Supreme Court upheld the statute on the merits. The Court's choice to decide the case apparently reflected a conclusion that there was substantial hardship to denying review, in that teachers had to either refrain from joining these organizations or risk loss of their jobs.

[15] *Id.* at 152-153.
[16] 387 U.S. 158 (1967).
[17] *Id.* at 165.
[18] 415 U.S. 452 (1974).
[19] *Id.* at 462.
[20] 342 U.S. 485, 488 n.4 (1952).

§2.4 Ripeness

In *Susan B. Anthony List v. Driehaus*, the Court considered whether a group had standing to challenge an Ohio statute that prohibits "false statements" during the course of a political campaign.[21] The Court explained that the "question in this case is whether their preenforcement challenge to that law is justiciable—and in particular, whether they have alleged a sufficiently imminent injury for the purposes of Article III."[22]

A member of Congress initiated proceedings against the Susan B. Anthony List in the Ohio Elections Commission, which found probable cause to proceed, but the matter was dismissed after the congressman lost his reelection bid. The Susan B. Anthony Fund had brought a challenge to the Ohio law in federal court and the issue before the Supreme Court was whether its challenge to the Ohio law could continue after the Ohio Elections Commission proceedings were dismissed.

The Supreme Court unanimously ruled in favor of the Susan B. Anthony Fund and held that the matter was justiciable. Justice Thomas, writing for a unanimous Court, noted that "[w]hen an individual is subject to such a threat, an actual arrest, prosecution, or other enforcement action is not a prerequisite to challenging the law."[23] The Court found that the matter was ripe for review because the plaintiffs "have alleged a credible threat of enforcement."[24] The Court stressed that "the threat of future enforcement of the false statement statute is substantial."[25]

Thus, it is well established that a case is ripe because of the substantial hardship to denying preenforcement review when a person is forced to choose between forgoing possibly lawful activity and risking substantial sanctions. People should not be forced to exercise their rights at peril of criminal sanctions or loss of employment.

However, some Supreme Court cases deviate from this principle. For example, in *International Longshoremen's and Warehousemen's Union Local 37 v. Boyd*, the Court dismissed as not ripe a case in which resident aliens were forced to choose between giving up a job and risking permanent exclusion from the country.[26] For many years, some resident aliens in the United States went to work in Alaska during the summer. Because the case arose before Alaska became a state, the aliens sued to enjoin immigration officers from preventing their return to the United States. The Supreme Court, in an opinion by Justice Frankfurter, held that their suit was not ripe. The Court found that the situation was "hypothetical" and concluded that "[d]etermination of the scope and constitutionality of legislation in advance of its immediate adverse effect in the context of a concrete case involves too remote and abstract an inquiry for the proper exercise of the judicial function."[27] But this ignores the enormous hardship in forcing a person to choose between unnecessarily giving up a job and risking permanent exclusion from the country.

[21] 573 U.S. 149 (2014).
[22] *Id.* at 152.
[23] *Id.* at 158.
[24] *Id.* at 159.
[25] *Id.* at 164.
[26] 347 U.S. 222 (1954).
[27] *Id.* at 224.

Like *Boyd,* the Supreme Court's decision in *United Public Workers v. Mitchell* is difficult to reconcile with the many cases holding that a case is ripe when a person is forced to choose between forgoing possibly constitutionally protected conduct and facing significant sanctions.[28] The issue in *Mitchell* was the ripeness of a challenge to the constitutionality of the Hatch Act of 1940, which prevented federal employees from taking "any active part in political management or political campaigns." The plaintiffs sought a declaratory judgment that the law violated their First Amendment rights and provided detailed affidavits listing the activities they wished to engage in. The Court found their claims to be not ripe. The Court said that the plaintiffs "seem clearly to seek advisory opinions upon broad claims. . . . A hypothetical threat is not enough. We can only speculate as to the kinds of political activity the appellants desire to engage in or as to the contents of their proposed public statements or the circumstances of their publication."[29] The Court found ripe the claims of one of the plaintiffs who was being fired for violating the act and upheld the statute as applied to him.

The *Mitchell* Court's holding that employees had to violate the Hatch Act in order to challenge its constitutionality is unjust and inconsistent with the decisions described above. The plaintiffs in *Mitchell* suffered substantial hardship because of the Court's denial of review: they had to choose between refraining from political speech and risking loss of their jobs. In fact, twenty-six years later, the Court was presented with another constitutional challenge to the Hatch Act and found ripeness based on almost the same facts that were insufficient in *Mitchell.* In *United States Civil Service Commission v. National Association of Letter Carriers, AFL-CIO,* the Court found the case ripe because the plaintiffs alleged that they desired to engage in specific political activity.[30]

With reasoning quite similar to that in *Mitchell,* in *Renne v. Geary,* the Court dismissed on ripeness grounds a challenge to a provision in the California constitution that prohibits political parties and political party central committees from endorsing, supporting, or opposing candidates for nonpartisan offices.[31] The Court concluded that there was insufficient evidence that the plaintiffs were prevented from engaging in specific constitutionally protected conduct because of the law. The Court noted that "[t]he affidavit provides no indication whom the Democratic committee wished to endorse, for which office, or in what election. Absent a contention that [the provision] prevented a particular endorsement, and that the controversy had not become moot prior to the litigation, this allegation will not support an action in federal court."[32]

But the question arises as to why the identity of particular candidates matters for a facial challenge to the law. The record documented past enforcement of the statute and the law undoubtedly would prevent endorsements in the future. As Justice Marshall argued in dissent: "Nothing in our analysis turn[s] on the identity

[28] 330 U.S. 75 (1947).
[29] *Id.* at 89-90.
[30] 413 U.S. 548 (1973).
[31] 501 U.S. 312 (1991).
[32] *Id.* at 320.

of the candidates to be endorsed, the nature or precise language of the endorsements, or the mode of publicizing endorsements."[33]

Hardship Where Enforcement Is Certain

Thus, generally although not always, the Court has found substantial hardship on the basis of forcing a person to choose between refraining from possibly protected conduct and risking significant sanctions. A second situation in which the Court has found substantial hardship is where the enforcement of a statute or regulation is certain and the only impediment to ripeness is simply a delay before the proceedings commence. Where the application of a law is inevitable and consequences attach to it, the Court will find the matter ripe before the actual proceedings occur.

For example, in the *Regional Rail Reorganization Act Cases*, the Court deemed ripe a lawsuit brought by eight major railroads challenging the conveyance of their property to Conrail.[34] The district court found the case not justiciable on ripeness grounds because the reorganization plan had not yet been formulated and a special court had not yet ordered the reconveyances. But the Supreme Court held that the case was ripe, concluding: "Where the inevitability of the operation of a statute against certain individuals is patent, it is irrelevant to the existence of a justiciable controversy that there will be a time delay before the disputed provisions will come into effect."[35]

Similarly, in *Lake Carriers Association v. MacMullan*, the Court found ripe a challenge to a statute forbidding discharge of sewage from boats, even though prosecutions were definitely not imminent.[36] State officials had announced that they would not enforce the law until land-based pump-out facilities would be available, a construction process that would take a substantial amount of time. Reversing a district court decision dismissing the case as not ripe, the Supreme Court unanimously concluded that the matter was justiciable. The Court reasoned that it was inevitable that the law would be enforced and that as a result the boat owners had to begin installing new facilities on their boats in anticipation of the time when the law was implemented. This was sufficient to make the case ripe.

In *Buckley v. Valeo*, the plaintiffs were allowed to challenge the method of appointing members to the Federal Election Commission in anticipation of "impending future rulings and determinations by the Commission."[37] There was no doubt that the rulings would be forthcoming; thus, the Court concluded that the plaintiffs' "claims as they bear upon the method of appointment of the Commission's members may be presently adjudicated."[38]

[33] *Id.* at 342 (Marshall, J., dissenting).

[34] 419 U.S. 102 (1974).

[35] *Id.* at 143.

[36] 406 U.S. 498, 507-508 (1972).

[37] 424 U.S. 1, 117 (1976).

[38] *Id.* at 118. *See also* Palazzolo v. Rhode Island, 533 U.S. 606 (2001) (finding a takings claim to be ripe for review though a plan for development had not been submitted to state court, because similar requests for development had been denied).

Hardship Because of Collateral Injuries

A third way in which the Court has found substantial hardship is based on collateral injuries that are not the primary focus of the lawsuit. *Duke Power Co. v. Carolina Environmental Study Group, Inc.* is illustrative.[39] The plaintiffs challenged the constitutionality of the Price-Anderson Act, which limited the liability of private nuclear power plants to $560 million in the event of a nuclear accident.[40] The plaintiffs contended that the statute violated the due process clause because it allowed injuries to occur without ensuring adequate compensation to the victims. There were obvious ripeness problems with this claim because it was uncertain whether an accident ever would occur, if it occurred whether the losses would exceed the limit on liability, and if it occurred and did exceed the limit whether Congress would pay the difference. Nonetheless, the Court found the matter ripe on the basis of other injuries imposed by the Price-Anderson Act. The Court explained that *but for* the Price-Anderson Act, nuclear power plants for electricity generation would not be constructed. Thus, because of the Price-Anderson Act, a reactor was about to be constructed in the plaintiffs' area and would subject them to harms such as the exposure to radiation, thermal pollution, and fear of a nuclear accident. In other words, while the primary injury that was the focus of the lawsuit was not ripe—uncompensated losses from a nuclear accident—other injuries existed to make the case justiciable.[41]

Hardship Is a Prerequisite for Ripeness

If hardship is demonstrated in any of these three ways, the case is likely to be found ripe. However, if there appears minimal harm to denying review, the case will be dismissed as not ripe. *Poe v. Ullman* is a classic example of a case dismissed for lack of ripeness.[42] Married women for whom pregnancy was medically unadvisable and their doctors filed a lawsuit challenging a Connecticut law preventing the distribution or use of contraceptives. The Court deemed the case nonjusticiable because there had been only one prosecution under the law in more than eighty years. The Court noted that "contraceptives are commonly and notoriously sold in Connecticut drug stores. . . . The undeviating policy of nullification by Connecticut of its anti-contraceptive laws throughout all the long years that they have been on the statute books bespeaks more than prosecutorial paralysis. . . . The fact that Connecticut has not chosen to press the enforcement of this statute deprives these controversies of the immediacy which is an indispensable condition of constitutional adjudication."[43] The Connecticut law was subsequently

[39] 438 U.S. 59 (1978). For an excellent analysis and criticism of this decision, *see* Jonathan Varat, Variable Justiciability and the Duke Power Case, 58 Tex. L. Rev. 273 (1980).

[40] 42 U.S.C. §2210.

[41] For a discussion of the standing aspects of *Duke Power*, *see* §2.3.3.

[42] 367 U.S. 497 (1961).

[43] *Id.* at 502, 508.

declared unconstitutional in *Griswold v. Connecticut* after the state prosecuted a Planned Parenthood clinic.[44]

Yet the Court's decision in *Poe* was subjected to substantial criticism. The effect of the Connecticut law was to limit the availability of contraceptives, especially by preventing the opening of Planned Parenthood clinics. Moreover, Justice Douglas, in dissent, argued that there was sufficient hardship to justify judicial review of the Connecticut statute: "What are these people—doctors and patients—to do? Flout the law and go to prison? Violate the law surreptitiously and hope they will not get caught? By today's decision we leave them no other alternatives. It is not the choice that they need have under the regime of the declaratory judgment and our constitutional system."[45]

In *Reno v. Catholic Social Services*, the Supreme Court held that a challenge to Immigration and Naturalization Service (INS) regulations had to be dismissed on ripeness grounds because it was too speculative that anyone would be injured by the rules.[46] The Immigration Reform and Control Act of 1986 provided that before illegal aliens residing in the United States could apply for legalization, they had to apply for temporary resident status. Temporary resident status required a showing that a person continually resided in the United States since January 1, 1982, and a continuous physical presence since November 6, 1986. The INS adopted many regulations to implement this law.

A class of plaintiffs, Catholic Social Services, challenged some of the INS regulations. The Supreme Court, in an opinion by Justice Souter, applied *Abbott Laboratories v. Gardner* and held that the case was not ripe for review. The Court said that it was entirely speculative whether any members of the class would be denied legalization because of the regulations. The Court said that the case might be ripe for review if the immigrants took the additional step of applying for legalization.

In *National Park Hospitality Assn. v. Department of Interior*,[47] the Court dismissed on ripeness grounds a challenge to a National Park Service rule that deems the federal Contract Disputes Act to be inapplicable to concession contracts. The Court expressly applied the two-part test from *Abbott Laboratories v. Gardner*. As to the first prong, the Court, in a majority opinion by Justice Thomas, concluded that the challengers would not suffer harms from the rule. The Court said that it was not a "legislative regulation with the force of law" and that contractors could continue to conduct their business in the same way as before the rule.[48] As to the second prong of the test, the Court said that the regulation might apply to some contracts, but not others, so that the federal courts were better off waiting for an actual enforcement effort, which would provide more concrete facts.[49]

In other words, *Poe v. Ullman*, *Reno v. Catholic Social Services*, and *National Park Hospitality Assn. v. Department of Interior* emphasize that a case will be dismissed on

[44] 381 U.S. 479 (1965), discussed in §10.3.2.
[45] 367 U.S. at 513 (Douglas, J., dissenting).
[46] 509 U.S. 43 (1993).
[47] 538 U.S. 803 (2003).
[48] *Id.* at 808.
[49] *Id.* at 812.

ripeness grounds if a federal court perceives the likelihood of harm as too speculative. Obviously, courts have a great deal of discretion in deciding what is a sufficient likelihood of hardship to meet the ripeness requirement.

§2.4.3 *Criteria for Determining Ripeness: The Fitness of the Issues and Record for Judicial Review*

Is There Significant Gain to Waiting for an Actual Prosecution?

The existence of substantial hardship without judicial review is one of the two criteria articulated by the Court for determining ripeness. The other issue concerns the fitness of the issues for judicial review. The more a question is purely a legal issue, the analysis of which does not depend on a particular factual context, the more likely it is that the Court will find ripeness. But the more judicial consideration of an issue would be enhanced by a specific set of facts, the greater the probability that a case seeking preenforcement review will be dismissed on ripeness grounds.

For example, in *Socialist Labor Party v. Gilligan*, the Supreme Court dismissed on ripeness grounds a challenge to a state law that allegedly limited the ability of the plaintiff to place candidates on the ballot for elections.[50] The law required candidates to sign an affidavit that they would not attempt to overthrow the government by force or violence. The Court concluded that "the record . . . now before this Court, is extraordinarily skimpy in the sort of proved or admitted facts that would enable us to adjudicate this claim."[51] The Court said that although the plaintiff might have standing to challenge the law, "their case has not given any particularity to the effect on them of Ohio's affidavit requirement."[52]

Another case in which the Court found an insufficient factual record to justify a conclusion of ripeness was *California Bankers Association v. Schultz*.[53] A bank, its customers, and bankers' organizations and associations sued to enjoin enforcement of a federal law that created recordkeeping and reporting requirements for banks and other financial institutions. The claim, in part, was that the reporting requirements violated the First Amendment rights of bank customers. The Court said that the claim was not ripe, emphasizing the need for a concrete factual situation to facilitate judicial review. The Court concluded: "This Court, in the absence of a concrete fact situation in which competing associational and governmental interests can be weighed, is simply not in a position to determine whether an effort to compel disclosure of such records would or would not be barred."[54]

[50] 406 U.S. 583 (1972).
[51] *Id.* at 587.
[52] *Id.* at 588.
[53] 416 U.S. 21 (1974).
[54] *Id.* at 56.

Relationship Between the Two Ripeness Criteria

The interaction of these two requirements for determining ripeness is not clear. Some commentators have suggested that ripeness can be found if either is met. Professor Tribe, for example, states that "[c]ases in which early legal challenges are held to be ripe normally present either or both of two features: significant present injuries . . . or legal questions that do not depend for their resolution on an extensive factual background."[55]

But the Court's decisions seem to indicate that both requirements must be met. For example, in *Poe v. Ullman*, the case was deemed not ripe even though it was a purely legal question that did not depend on an extensive factual background. In his dissenting opinion in *Poe*, Justice Harlan said, "I cannot see what further elaboration is required to enable us to decide the appellants' claims, and indeed neither the plurality nor the concurring opinion . . . suggests what more grist is needed before the judicial mill could turn."[56] Conversely, in *Socialist Labor Party v. Gilligan*, the Court admitted the existence of standing (and thus of an injury) but deemed the matter to be unripe because of the absence of an adequate record.[57]

Thus, while it appears that preenforcement review is possible only if there is both hardship to its denial and an adequate factual record, it is unclear whether a greater hardship might compensate for less in the way of a factual record or vice versa. Because the hardship requirement is constitutionally based, in all likelihood it is less flexible, whereas the prudential concern about the record is to be given less weight when there is a compelling need for immediate judicial review.

Finally, the relationship of ripeness to other doctrines should be noted. Ripeness is obviously closely related to requirements for exhaustion of administrative remedies before seeking federal court review; a case is not ripe until such exhaustion has occurred.[58] In a later decision, the Supreme Court overruled an earlier decision and held that a property owner could bring a takings challenge without the need to exhaust state administrative and judicial remedies.[59] In other words, the Court effectively said that such cases were ripe without the need to seek compensation in state administrative or judicial proceedings. Earlier, the Court had ruled that takings claims were not ripe until compensation has been sought and denied through the available administrative procedures.[60] But in *Knick v. Township of Scott, Pennsylvania*, the Court, 5-4, reversed these decisions and stated: "We now conclude that the state-litigation requirement imposes an unjustifiable burden on takings plaintiffs, conflicts with the rest of our takings jurisprudence, and must be overruled. A property owner has an actionable Fifth Amendment takings

[55] Laurence Tribe, American Constitutional Law 80 (3d ed. 2000).

[56] 367 U.S. at 528 (Harlan, J., dissenting).

[57] 406 U.S. at 588.

[58] Myers v. Bethlehem Shipbuilding Corp., 303 U.S. 41 (1938).

[59] Knick v. Township of Scott, Pennsylvania, 588 U.S. 180 (2019).

[60] *See, e.g.*, San Remo Hotel v. City and County of San Francisco, 545 U.S. 323 (2005); Williamson County Regional Planning Commn. v. Hamilton Bank, 473 U.S. 172 (1984).

claim when the government takes his property without paying for it."[61] The Court explained that no other constitutional claims required exhaustion of state remedies and nor should the taking clause: "The state-litigation requirement relegates the Takings Clause 'to the status of a poor relation' among the provisions of the Bill of Rights. Plaintiffs asserting any other constitutional claim are guaranteed a federal forum under §1983, but the state-litigation requirement 'hand[s] authority over federal takings claims to state courts.' Fidelity to the Takings Clause and our cases construing it requires overruling *Williamson County* and restoring takings claims to the full-fledged constitutional status the Framers envisioned when they included the Clause among the other protections in the Bill of Rights."[62]

Justice Kagan dissented and said that takings claims are different from other claims because the Constitution does not forbid the government from taking private property; it forbids takings *without just compensation.*[63] She wrote that "[i]n that way, the Takings Clause is unique among the Bill of Rights' guarantees."[64] It cannot be said that a state or local government has taken private property without just compensation so long as it has mechanisms available to provide this. For the dissent, as under *Williamson County*, a takings challenge should not be deemed ripe until there was an exhaustion of state administrative and judicial remedies that might have provided just compensation.

§2.5 MOOTNESS

§2.5.1 Description of the Mootness Doctrine

An actual controversy must exist at all stages of federal court proceedings, both at the trial and appellate levels. If events subsequent to the filing of the case resolve the dispute, the case should be dismissed as moot. The Supreme Court, quoting Professor Henry Monaghan, explained that "mootness [is] the 'doctrine of standing in a time frame. The requisite personal interest that must exist at the commencement of the litigation (standing) must continue throughout its existence (mootness).'"[1] The Court has declared that a "case that becomes moot at any point during the proceedings is 'no longer a Case or Controversy for purposes of Article III, and is outside the jurisdiction of the federal courts.'"[2]

[61] 588 U.S. at 185. The Supreme Court reaffirmed this in Pakdel v. City and County of San Francisco, 594 U.S. 474, 480 (2021) ("administrative 'exhaustion of state remedies' is not a prerequisite for a takings claim when the government has reached a conclusive position.")

[62] *Id.* at 189.

[63] *Id.* at 208 (Kagan, J., dissenting).

[64] *Id.* at 209.

§2.5 [1] United States Parole Commn. v. Geraghty, 445 U.S. 388, 397 (1980), quoting Henry Monaghan, Constitutional Adjudication: The Who and When, 82 Yale L.J. 1363, 1384 (1973).

[2] United States v. Sanchez-Gomez, 584 U.S. 381, 386-387 (2018).

Circumstances That Might Cause a Case to Be Moot

Many different types of events might render a case moot. For example, a case is moot if a criminal defendant dies during the appeals process or if a civil plaintiff dies where the cause of action does not survive death.[3] Also, if the parties settle the matter, a live controversy obviously no longer exists.[4] If a challenged law is repealed or expires, the case is moot.[5] Essentially, any change in the facts that ends the controversy renders the case moot. Thus, a defendant's challenge to a state law denying him pretrial bail was deemed moot after his conviction,[6] and a suit by students to enjoin a school's censorship of a student newspaper was dismissed as moot after the students graduated.[7]

Why Have a Mootness Doctrine?

The Supreme Court frequently has explained that the mootness doctrine is derived from Article III's prohibition against federal courts issuing advisory opinions.[8] By definition, if a case is moot, there no longer is an actual controversy between adverse litigants. Also, if events subsequent to the initiation of the lawsuit have resolved the matter, then a federal court decision is not likely to have any effect. Hence, neither of the prerequisites for federal court adjudication is fulfilled.[9]

Additionally, many of the values underlying the justiciability doctrines also explain the mootness rules. Mootness avoids unnecessary federal court decisions,

[3] Dove v. United States, 423 U.S. 325 (1976). In Tory v. Cochran, 544 U.S. 734 (2005), the Court held that the death of the plaintiff in a defamation suit, Johnny Cochran, did not moot a challenge to an injunction that prevented Ulysses Tory (and his wife or agents) from making any statements about Cochran or his law firm in any public forum. The Court stressed that the injunction remained in place even after Cochran's death.

[4] *See, e.g.*, United Airlines, Inc. v. McDonald, 432 U.S. 385, 400 (1977) (Powell, J., dissenting) ("The settlement of an individual claim typically moots any issues associated with it."); Stewart v. Southern Ry., 315 U.S. 283 (1942). Settlement must be distinguished from a situation in which the defendant voluntarily agrees to refrain from a practice, but is free to resume it at any time. As discussed below, the latter does not moot the case.

[5] *See, e.g.*, Burke v. Barnes, 479 U.S. 361, 365 (1987) (bill expired during pendency of appeal, rendering moot the question of whether the president's pocket veto prevented bill from becoming law); United States Dept. of Treasury v. Galioto, 477 U.S. 556 (1986) (amendment to federal statute rendered the case moot); Kremens v. Bartley, 431 U.S. 119, 128 (1977) (statutes providing for commitment of minors to institutions were repealed, rendering the case moot); *but see* City of Mesquite v. Aladdin's Castle, Inc., 455 U.S. 283 (1982) (repeal of a city ordinance was not moot where the city was likely to reenact it after completion of legal proceedings), discussed below.

[6] *See, e.g.*, Murphy v. Hunt, 455 U.S. 478, 481-482 (1982) (challenge to a state law denying bail to those accused of violent sex crimes dismissed as moot after the defendant's conviction).

[7] Board of School Commrs. of Indianapolis v. Jacobs, 420 U.S. 128, 130 (1975).

[8] *See, e.g.*, Genesis Healthcare Corp. v. Symczyk, 569 U.S. 66 (2013); SEC v. Medical Comm. for Human Rights, 404 U.S. 403, 406 (1972); Hall v. Beals, 396 U.S. 45, 48 (1969). *But see* Honig v. Doe, 484 U.S. 305, 330 (1988) (Rehnquist, C.J., concurring) (arguing that mootness doctrine is primarily prudential and not constitutionally based).

[9] *See* Church of Scientology of California v. United States, 506 U.S. 9, 11 (1992).

limiting the role of the judiciary and saving the courts' institutional capital for cases truly requiring decisions.[10] On the other hand, mootness might not save judicial resources, and it is not necessary to ensure a concrete factual setting in which to decide an issue. When a case is dismissed on appeal, there is a fully developed record and an opportunity for a definitive resolution of an issue. Dismissing such a case as moot might cause the same question to be litigated in many other courts until it is finally resolved by the Supreme Court.[11]

Perhaps it is because of these competing policy considerations that the Supreme Court has spoken of "the flexible character of the Article III mootness doctrine."[12] This flexibility is manifested in four exceptions to the mootness doctrine. Cases are not dismissed as moot if there are secondary or "collateral" injuries, if the issue is deemed a wrong capable of repetition yet evading review, if the defendant voluntarily ceases an allegedly illegal practice but is free to resume it at any time, and if it is a properly certified class action suit. These exceptions are discussed below.

Procedural Issues

Procedurally, a federal court on its own can raise mootness at any stage of the proceedings.[13] If the U.S. Supreme Court deems a case moot, the Court will vacate the lower court's decision and remand the case for dismissal.[14] By vacating the lower court's decision, the Supreme Court leaves the legal issue unresolved for future cases to decide.

However, in *U.S. Bancorp Mortgage Co. v. Bonner Mall Partnership*, the Court held that vacatur of a lower court opinion is not appropriate when a voluntary settlement of an underlying dispute makes a case moot.[15] The Court recognized that allowing such vacating of lower court opinions might facilitate settlements, as losing parties may choose to settle in order to vacate an unfavorable opinion that could harm their position in future litigation. Also, vacating the lower court opinion could prevent an erroneous decision from remaining on the books. Nonetheless, the Court unanimously held that voluntary settlement does not justify vacatur of a lower court opinion. Nothing about the settlement

[10] *See, e.g.*, Firefighter's Local 1784 v. Stotts, 467 U.S. 561, 596 (1984) (Blackmun, J., dissenting) (a central purpose of mootness doctrine is to avoid an unnecessary ruling on the merits).

[11] Chief Justice Rehnquist has urged an additional exception to the mootness doctrine for cases that become moot while pending before the Supreme Court. *See* Honig v. Doe, 484 U.S. 305, 330 (1988).

[12] United States Parole Commn. v. Geraghty, 445 U.S. at 400. For an excellent argument that mootness should be regarded as prudential and not constitutional, *see* Evan Lee, Deconstitutionalizing Justiciability: The Example of Mootness, 105 Harv. L. Rev. 605 (1992).

[13] *See, e.g.*, North Carolina v. Rice, 404 U.S. 244, 246 (1971).

[14] United States v. Munsingwear, Inc., 340 U.S. 36, 39 (1950) ("The established practice of the Court in dealing with a civil case from a court in the federal system which has become moot while on its way here or pending our decision on the merits is to reverse or vacate the judgment below and remand with a direction to dismiss.").

[15] 513 U.S. 18 (1994).

undermines the reasoning of the lower court and warrants the vacating of its decision.[16]

Overview of the Exceptions to the Mootness Doctrine

Most of the cases dealing with the mootness issue have focused on the exceptions to the mootness doctrine. These are situations where a federal court should not dismiss a case as moot even though the plaintiff's injuries have been resolved. The common issue concerning each of these exceptions is whether the policy considerations served by them justifies allowing review in a case where there is not an actual dispute between adverse litigants and where a favorable court decision will not effect a change. On the one hand, critics of these exceptions might argue that expediency does not justify a departure from Article III and that the Court wrongly has been much more flexible in carving exceptions to mootness than it has been in dealing with parallel doctrines, such as standing. But others might argue that important policy objectives are served by the exceptions and that the exceptions effectuate the underlying purpose of Article III in ensuring judicial review of allegedly illegal practices.

§2.5.2 *Exceptions to the Mootness Doctrine: Collateral Consequences*

The first exception is where a secondary or "collateral" injury survives after the plaintiff's primary injury has been resolved. Although this is referred to as an exception to the mootness doctrine,[17] actually the case is not moot because some injury remains that could be redressed by a favorable federal court decision. As the Supreme Court has explained, "[a]s long as the parties have a concrete interest, however small, in the outcome of the litigation, the case is not moot."[18]

Criminal Cases

For example, a challenge to a criminal conviction is not moot, even after the defendant has completed the sentence and is released from custody, when the defendant continues to face adverse consequences of the criminal conviction. Criminal convictions, especially for felonies, cause the permanent loss of voting privileges in many states, prevent individuals from obtaining certain occupational licenses, and increase the severity of sentences if there is a future offense. Thus, the Court has concluded that even if the primary injury, incarceration, no longer exists, the secondary or collateral harms are sufficient to prevent the case from being dismissed on mootness grounds.

[16] *See* Jill E. Fisch, Rewriting History: The Propriety of Eradicating Prior Decisional Law Through Settlement and Vacatur, 76 Cornell L. Rev. 589 (1991).

[17] Sibron v. New York, 392 U.S. 40, 53 (1968) (describing collateral consequences as an exception to the mootness doctrine); Laurence Tribe, American Constitutional Law 91-92 (2d ed. 1988).

[18] Chafin v. Chafin, 568 U.S. 165, 172 (2013) (citations omitted).

In *Sibron v. New York*, two defendants challenged the legality of evidence seized from them during a stop-and-frisk.[19] Although the defendants had completed their six-month sentences, the Court held that their challenge to the constitutionality of their convictions was not moot. The Court explained that "the obvious fact of life [is] that most criminal convictions do in fact entail adverse collateral legal consequences. The mere possibility that this will be the case is enough to preserve a criminal case from ending ignominiously in the limbo of mootness."[20]

Similarly, in *Carafas v. LaVallee*, a defendant convicted of burglary in state court was allowed to present a petition for habeas corpus in federal court challenging the constitutionality of his conviction despite the fact that he had been unconditionally released from custody.[21] The Court stated that "[i]n consequence of his conviction, he cannot engage in certain businesses; he cannot serve as an official of a labor union for a specified time; he cannot vote in any election held in New York State; he cannot serve as a juror. . . . On account of these 'collateral consequences,' the case is not moot."[22]

The Court has explained that a challenge to a criminal conviction should be dismissed as moot "only if it is shown that there is no possibility that any collateral legal consequences will be imposed on the basis of the challenged conviction."[23] Therefore, a defendant convicted of two crimes, but sentenced to concurrent sentences, may challenge one of the convictions even though its reversal would not hasten his or her release from custody.[24] The Court has reasoned that the additional conviction might have future collateral consequences, such as increasing the severity of a subsequent sentence if there is a new offense.

In fact, because the government has an interest in ensuring the conviction of criminals, the Supreme Court allows the state to continue to appeal matters even if the defendant has completed his or her sentence. In *Pennsylvania v. Mimms*, the Supreme Court granted the state's certiorari petition despite the fact that the defendant had completed the maximum three-year sentence.[25] The Court said that preventing the state from imposing the collateral consequences of a criminal conviction is of sufficient interest to the state to keep the case from being dismissed as moot.

Generally, a challenge to a particular sentence, as opposed to a challenge to the conviction, is moot after the sentence has been served because there are not collateral consequences to the sentence itself. For example, in *North Carolina v. Rice*, a defendant contended that the state courts acted unconstitutionally in increasing his sentence on appeal.[26] The Supreme Court dismissed the case as moot because the additional sentence had been served by the time the case came before the Court.

[19] 392 U.S. 40 (1968).
[20] *Id.* at 55 (citations omitted).
[21] 391 U.S. 234 (1968).
[22] *Id.* at 237-238.
[23] Sibron v. New York, 392 U.S. at 57.
[24] *See, e.g.,* Benton v. Maryland, 395 U.S. 784, 791 (1969).
[25] 434 U.S. 106, 108 (1977); *see also* United States v. Villamonte-Marquez, 462 U.S. 579, 581 (1983).
[26] 404 U.S. 244, 246 (1977).

Civil Cases

In civil litigation, a case is not moot, even if the plaintiff's primary injury is resolved, as long as the plaintiff continues to suffer some harm that a favorable court decision would remedy. For instance, a plaintiff seeking both reinstatement and back pay for alleged discrimination can continue to pursue the case even if reinstatement is granted or no longer sought.[27] The claim for back pay is adequate to keep the case from being moot. In fact, even if the amount of money damages sought is quite small, it is still sufficient to present a live controversy to the federal court. The Supreme Court explained: "Undoubtedly, not much money and seniority are involved, but the amount of money and seniority at stake does not determine mootness. As long as the parties have a concrete interest in the outcome of the litigation, the case is not moot."[28]

In *Moore v. Harper*, the Court considered whether state courts may enforce their state constitutions to limit partisan gerrymandering or whether this violates the Constitution in that the matter is entirely left to the legislature.[29] The North Carolina Supreme Court found that the legislature's gerrymandering violated the state constitution and had an independent commission draw congressional districts for the November 2022 election. After this occurred and while the case was pending in the Supreme Court, the political composition of the North Carolina Supreme Court changed as a result of the November 2022 election. It went from a 4-3 Democratic majority to a 5-2 Republican one. In 2023, the newly constituted North Carolina Supreme Court reversed the decision that had found the districting to violate the state constitution.

The Supreme Court asked for briefing about the significance of the reconsideration by the North Carolina Supreme Court. Chief Justice Roberts, writing for the Court, said that the North Carolina Supreme Court decision was a final judgment and thus reviewable by the United States Supreme Court, notwithstanding the change in the law in North Carolina. The Court said that if it reversed the North Carolina Supreme Court, the 2021 maps would go into effect, which was enough to make the case justiciable. Justice Thomas, in a dissent, strongly disagreed. He said that this "is a straightforward case of mootness" because the lower court decision had been reversed and the maps used in the 2022 election never would be used.[30]

Likewise, a plaintiff seeking both injunctive relief and money damages can continue to pursue the case, even after the request for an equitable remedy is rendered moot.[31] For example, the Supreme Court ruled that the release of plaintiffs

[27] *See, e.g.*, Firefighter's Local 1784 v. Stotts, 467 U.S. 561, 568 (1984).

[28] *Id.* at 571.

[29] 600 U.S. 1 (2023).

[30] *Id.* at 41-42 (Thomas, J., dissenting).

[31] Havens Realty Corp. v. Coleman, 455 U.S. 363, 370-371 (1982) (case not moot because plaintiffs would be entitled to $400 liquidated damages if defendants found liable); University of Texas v. Camenisch, 451 U.S. 390, 393 (1981) (case not moot when dispute for overpayment of money remained). In New York State Rifle & Pistol Ass'n, Inc. v. City of New York, New York, 590 U.S. 336 (2020), which is discussed below, the Court dismissed as moot a suit seeking to enjoin a New York law regulating firearms after that law had been repealed while the case was pending before the Supreme

on parole did not moot their suit when, in addition to a release from custody, they also sought money damages for the alleged violation of their constitutional rights.[32]

More generally, as long as the federal court's decision is likely to have some effect in the future, the case should not be dismissed even though the plaintiff's primary injury has passed. The Supreme Court's decision in *Super Tire Engineering Co. v. McCorkle* is particularly instructive.[33] During a labor strike, the employers whose plants were struck filed a lawsuit challenging a state law that permitted strikers to receive public assistance through state welfare programs. Although the strike ended before the completion of the federal court litigation, the Court held that the case was not moot because a federal court decision could substantially affect future labor-management negotiations.[34] Thus, while a plaintiff's emotional concern about the outcome of the case is not enough to keep it from being moot, any continuing injury means that there is a live controversy.[35]

The Court held that declining a settlement offer does not make the case moot. In *Campbell-Ewald v. Gomez*, the defendant offered the plaintiff the maximum amount he could recover if the matter went to trial.[36] The plaintiff refused the offer and the defendant then argued that made the case moot. The Court rejected that argument and said that "the unaccepted offer" was a "legal nullity, with no operative effect" and thus "an unaccepted settlement offer or offer of judgment does not moot a plaintiff's case."[37]

§2.5.3 *Exceptions to the Mootness Doctrine: Wrongs Capable of Repetition Yet Evading Review*

Definition

Perhaps the most important exception to the mootness doctrine is for "wrongs capable of repetition yet evading review." As the title of this exception implies, some injuries occur and are over so quickly that they always will be moot before

Court. The Court rejected the argument that a claim for money damages kept the case from being moot because the plaintiffs never had sought that relief: "Petitioners also argue that, even though they have not previously asked for damages with respect to the City's old rule, they still could do so in this lawsuit. Petitioners did not seek damages in their complaint; indeed, the possibility of a damages claim was not raised until well into the litigation in this Court." *Id.* at 1526. The case was remanded to allow the lower courts to rule on whether the plaintiffs could add a claim for monetary relief.

[32] Board of Pardons v. Allen, 482 U.S. 369, 371 n.1 (1987).

[33] 416 U.S. 115 (1974).

[34] The Court also reasoned that the case presented a wrong capable of repetition yet evading review, which is discussed below.

[35] *Id.* at 670, 672.

[36] 577 U.S. 153 (2016).

[37] *Id.* at 162, 165. The Court, however, said, "We need not, and do not, now decide whether the result would be different if a defendant deposits the full amount of the plaintiff's individual claim in an account payable to the plaintiff, and the court then enters judgment for the plaintiff in that amount. That question is appropriately reserved for a case in which it is not hypothetical." *Id.* at 166.

the federal court litigation process is completed. When such injuries are likely to recur, the federal court may continue to exercise jurisdiction over the plaintiff's claim notwithstanding the fact that it has become moot.[38] The Supreme Court has said that "[t]he exception applies where (1) the challenged action is in its duration too short to be fully litigated prior to cessation or expiration, and (2) there is a reasonable expectation that the same complaining party will be subject to the same action again."[39]

Roe v. Wade presented a paradigm example of a wrong capable of repetition yet evading review.[40] The plaintiff was pregnant when she filed her complaint challenging the constitutionality of a state law prohibiting abortion. Obviously, however, by the time the case reached the Supreme Court, her pregnancy was completed and she no longer sought an abortion. Hence, her case was moot; intervening circumstances meant that there no longer was a live controversy between the plaintiff and the state. The Supreme Court, however, refused a request to dismiss the case on mootness grounds. The Court explained that the duration of pregnancy was inherently likely to be shorter than the time required for federal court litigation. The Court concluded that the challenge to the state laws prohibiting abortions "truly could be 'capable of repetition yet evading review.' "[41]

Requirements for the Exception

Two criteria must be met for a matter to fit within the wrong capable of repetition yet evading review exception to the mootness doctrine. First, the injury must be of a type likely to happen to the plaintiff again. In other words, an injury is not deemed capable of repetition merely because someone, at some time, might suffer the same harm; there must be a reasonable chance that it will happen again to the plaintiff. The Court explained that there must be a "reasonable expectation that the same complaining party would be subjected to the same action again."[42] For instance, in *Murphy v. Hunt*, a defendant's challenge to a state law denying pretrial bail to those accused of violent sex crimes was dismissed as moot after the defendant's conviction.[43] The Court said that the case did not fit into the exception for wrongs capable of repetition yet evading review because there was no likelihood that the defendant would be arrested for a similar offense and denied bail in the future. The Court noted that "there must be a reasonable expectation or a demonstrated probability that the same controversy will recur involving the

[38] A seminal case articulating this exception to the mootness doctrine was Southern Pac. Terminal Co. v. ICC, 219 U.S. 498, 514-515 (1911) (allowing a challenge to an Interstate Commerce Commission order that had expired because the Court concluded that consideration of such orders should not be defeated, "as they might be, . . . by short term orders, capable of repetition, yet evading review").

[39] Federal Election Commn. v. Wisconsin Right to Life, Inc., 551 U.S. 449, 462 (2007).

[40] 410 U.S. 113 (1973).

[41] *Id.* at 125 (citations omitted).

[42] Weinstein v. Bradford, 423 U.S. 147, 149 (1975).

[43] 455 U.S. 478 (1982).

same complaining party. We detect no such level of probability in this case."[44] But it must be noted that in other cases—such as in *Roe* and the election cases described below—the Court did not specifically inquire whether the plaintiff in particular was likely to suffer the same harm in the future.

Second, it must be a type of injury of inherently limited duration so that it is likely to always become moot before federal court litigation is completed. For example, a ten-day restraining order on a protest demonstration was deemed to be capable of repetition but always likely to evade review because litigation never would be completed before the ten days expired.[45]

One area where the Court consistently has found cases to fit within the exception for wrongs capable of repetition yet evading review is court orders imposing prior restraints on speech. For example, in *Nebraska Press Association v. Stuart*, a trial judge imposed a limit on newspaper and broadcast reports concerning a pending murder trial.[46] Although the judge's order expired when the jury was empaneled, the Supreme Court held that it was a wrong capable of repetition yet evading review because similar orders might be imposed on the media again in the future, and they would escape judicial scrutiny because the restraints would be lifted long before the appellate process was completed.[47] Likewise, challenges to a court's order excluding the press from a pretrial hearing and to a court's order excluding the press from trial in a case involving a victim under age eighteen were deemed fit within this exception to the mootness doctrine.[48] In each instance, the Court reasoned that the media might be subjected to similar orders in the future and that the orders transpired so quickly as to prevent judicial review before they expired.

Another area where the Court often has applied this exception to the mootness doctrine is for challenges to election laws. Frequently, the election is over before the litigation is completed. For example, in *Moore v. Ogilvie*, a suit was brought challenging a state law requiring the obtaining of a certain number of signatures for an independent candidate to get on the ballot to run for president or vice president.[49] Although the election was held before the Supreme Court heard the case, the Court held that the case was not moot because it presented a "wrong capable of repetition, yet evading review."[50] The Court explained that the plaintiffs might again seek access to the ballot for independent candidates and that the matter would always escape review because litigation could never be completed before the election.

[44] *Id.* at 482 (citations omitted). *See also* United States v. Sanchez-Gomez, 584 U.S. 381 (2018), holding that criminal defendants could not challenge the policy of the United States Marshall Service for shackling in-custody defendants for court appearances because they could not show that it was likely to happen to them again in the future.

[45] Carroll v. President & Commrs. of Princess Anne, 393 U.S. 175 (1968).

[46] 427 U.S. 539 (1976).

[47] *Id.* at 546.

[48] Globe Newspaper Co. v. Superior Court, 457 U.S. 596, 602 (1982) (exclusion from trial of victim of sex crime who was under age eighteen); Gannett Co. v. DePasquale, 443 U.S. 368, 377 (1979) (exclusion from pretrial hearing).

[49] 394 U.S. 814 (1969).

[50] *Id.* at 816 (citation omitted).

Similarly, in *First National Bank of Boston v. Bellotti,* the plaintiffs were allowed to pursue their challenge to a law prohibiting corporations from spending money to influence voters with regard to pending ballot initiatives.[51] The Court reasoned that the issue would likely arise in the future and there would never be enough time for the matter to be fully litigated, appealed, and decided before the completion of the election.

In *Dunn v. Blumstein,* a voter was allowed to continue to challenge a state law imposing a one-year residency requirement in the state in order to vote in state elections.[52] Although the plaintiff could vote by the time the case got to the Supreme Court, the Court held that the matter was a wrong capable of repetition yet evading review and thus should not be dismissed on mootness grounds.

Subsequently, in *Norman v. Reed,* the Court applied this exception to the mootness doctrine to allow a challenge to a law that created obstacles for new parties getting on the ballot.[53] Although the challenge concerned the ability to get on the ballot for an election held in 1990, the Court concluded that "[t]here would be every reason to expect the same parties to generate a similar, future controversy subject to identical time constraints if we should fail to resolve the constitutional issues that arose in 1990."[54] Thus, it was justiciable as a wrong capable of repetition yet evading review.

The Court has continued to follow this in subsequent election cases. In *Federal Election Commn. v. Wisconsin Right to Life, Inc.,* the Court allowed a challenge to a provision of federal election law restricting expenditures by corporations even though the election was over. The Court explained: "We have recognized that the 'capable of repetition, yet evading review' doctrine, in the context of election cases, is appropriate when there are 'as applied' challenges as well as in the more typical case involving only facial attacks." Requiring repetition of every "legally relevant" characteristic of an as-applied challenge—down to the last detail—would effectively overrule this statement by making this exception unavailable for virtually all as-applied challenges."[55]

Similarly, in *Davis v. Federal Election Commission,* the Court allowed a challenge to a provision of the Federal Election Act to continue after the election was over.[56] Jack Davis twice ran for Congress, in 2004 and 2006, and spent enough of his own money for his campaign to trigger the so-called millionaire's provision of the McCain-Feingold Bipartisan Campaign Finance Reform Act of 2001. Under this provision, the opponent of a candidate who spends more than $350,000 of his or her own money receives the benefit of higher contribution and expenditure limits.

Davis filed his lawsuit challenging this provision while running for office, but the Supreme Court did not hear the case until after the election was over. Nonetheless, the Court unanimously rejected the government's argument that the

[51] 435 U.S. 765, 774 (1978).
[52] 405 U.S. 330 (1972).
[53] 502 U.S. 279 (1992).
[54] *Id.* at 288.
[55] 551 U.S. 449, 463 (2007).
[56] 554 U.S. 724 (2008).

case was moot (though it divided 5-4 in striking down the provision as violating the First Amendment). The Court found that this case was like others in which it held that challenges to laws regulating elections could continue after the elections were over.

Not all election cases fit within this exception to the mootness doctrine. For example, in *Illinois State Board of Elections v. Socialist Workers Party*, the plaintiffs challenged actions by the State Board of Elections that interfered with their getting on the ballot.[57] The Court held that the case was moot after the election was completed because there was "no evidence creating a reasonable expectation that the . . . Board will repeat its purportedly unauthorized actions in subsequent elections."[58]

Golden v. Zwickler is even more difficult to reconcile with the other election cases.[59] In *Golden*, the plaintiff filed a lawsuit in 1966 challenging a New York statute prohibiting the distribution of handbills that did not state the identity of the author. The plaintiff wanted to distribute anonymous leaflets in connection with the 1966 congressional election. The election was completed before the matter was fully resolved in the courts, but the plaintiff maintained that there was still a live controversy because he wanted to distribute anonymous handbills again in 1968. The Supreme Court deemed the case moot. The Court said that it was speculative whether the congressman whom the plaintiff sought to campaign for would run again.[60]

The question is whether it was more speculative that the plaintiff in *Golden* would want to distribute anonymous leaflets in the future than it was in *Moore v. Ogilvie* that the plaintiffs there would want to qualify independent candidates for the ballot in the future. Was it more speculative in *Socialist Workers Party* that the plaintiffs would be frustrated in gaining access to the ballot than it was in *Bellotti* that the corporation would want to spend money in the future to oppose ballot initiatives?

In other words, the election cases reflect that the "wrong capable of repetition yet evading review" exception requires a court to determine that there is a sufficient likelihood that the harm will recur. But the courts have a great deal of discretion in deciding what is sufficient.

Perhaps the case best illustrating this discretion is *DeFunis v. Odegaard*.[61] The plaintiff, a white male, applied for admission to the University of Washington Law School and was denied acceptance. He sued the school, contending that he was discriminated against because of the school's preferential treatment of minority candidates. The trial court issued a preliminary injunction admitting the plaintiff to law school while the case was pending. By the time the case reached the U.S. Supreme Court, the plaintiff was in his final year of school, and the school stipulated that the plaintiff would be allowed to complete his studies regardless of the

[57] 440 U.S. 173 (1979).
[58] *Id.* at 187.
[59] 394 U.S. 103 (1969).
[60] *Id.* at 109-110.
[61] 416 U.S. 312 (1974).

outcome of the litigation. The Supreme Court held that the case was moot because "the controversy between the parties has thus clearly ceased to be definite and concrete and no longer touches the legal relations of parties having adverse legal interests."[62]

Some criticize the Court for not finding the case to constitute a wrong capable of repetition yet evading review. Professor David Currie quotes one critic as remarking that *DeFunis* "announced a new principle: 'Difficult cases are moot.'"[63] On the other hand, the Court explained that there was no chance that DeFunis again would be subjected to the law school admissions process. Moreover, there was no reason to believe that the issue would evade review because not every challenger would obtain a preliminary injunction securing law school attendance while the case was pending.[64]

In sum, a case is not dismissed, although the plaintiff's claim is moot, if the injury is one likely to recur and if the injury is of an inherently short duration that would make complete federal court review impossible. Courts have substantial discretion in deciding what is a sufficient likelihood of future injury or a sufficiently short time span for the injury to justify invoking this exception.

§2.5.4 Exceptions to the Mootness Doctrine: Voluntary Cessation

Exception Defined

A case is not to be dismissed as moot if the defendant voluntarily ceases the allegedly improper behavior but is free to return to it at any time. Only if there is no reasonable chance that the defendant could resume the offending behavior is a case deemed moot on the basis of voluntary cessation.[65]

The Court explained these principles in *United States v. W.T. Grant Co.*[66] The United States sued to enjoin a practice of several corporations having similar boards of directors; the government claimed that the interlocking directorates violated federal antitrust laws. In response to the suit, the defendants said that they had eliminated the interlocking directorships and would not resume the practice. The Supreme Court said that this was not sufficient to justify dismissal of the case because the "defendant is free to return to his old ways."[67] The Court stated that "voluntary cessation of allegedly illegal conduct does not deprive the tribunal of power to hear and determine the case, i.e., does not make the case moot."[68] The Court said that "[t]he case may nevertheless be moot if the defendant

[62] *Id.* at 316-317.

[63] David Currie, Federal Courts: Cases and Materials 77 n.3 (4th ed. 1990).

[64] 416 U.S. at 316.

[65] Friends of the Earth, Inc. v. Laidlaw, 528 U.S. 167, 173, 179 (2000).

[66] 345 U.S. 629 (1953). *See also* United States v. Concentrated Phosphate Export Assn., 393 U.S. 199, 203 (1968) (citations omitted) (case not moot where defendant is "free to return to his old ways").

[67] *Id.* at 632.

[68] *Id.*

can demonstrate that there is no reasonable expectation that the wrong will be repeated. The burden is a heavy one."[69] The Court said the defendants' promise to not resume the offending practice is not enough to meet this burden and render the case moot.

The Court reaffirmed the narrowness of this exception in *Friends of the Earth, Inc. v. Laidlaw.*[70] Environmental groups brought a lawsuit pursuant to a citizen-suit provision of the Clean Water Act (CWA) against the holder of a National Pollutant Discharge Elimination System (NPDES) permit, alleging that it was violating mercury discharge limits. The plaintiffs sought declaratory and injunctive relief, civil penalties, costs, and attorneys' fees. The defendant sought to have the case dismissed as moot on the ground that it had changed its conduct and complied with the permit requirements and had closed one of the facilities.

The Court reiterated that voluntary changes in behavior by a defendant are not sufficient to make a case moot, because the defendant would be free to resume the behavior once the case was dismissed. Justice Ginsburg, writing for the Court, stated: "[T]he standard we have announced for determining whether a case has been mooted by the defendant's voluntary conduct is stringent: 'A case might become moot if subsequent events made it absolutely clear that the allegedly wrongful behavior could not reasonably be expected to recur.' The 'heavy burden of persua[ding]' the court that the challenged conduct cannot reasonably be expected to start up again lies with the party asserting mootness."[71] Indeed, Justice Ginsburg's statement of the test makes it clear that this is a very heavy burden: "[A] defendant claiming that its voluntary compliance moots a case bears the formidable burden of showing that it is absolutely clear the allegedly wrongful behavior could not reasonably be expected to recur."[72] This is quite different from standing, in which the burden is on the plaintiff to show that the constitutional and prudential requirements are met.[73] The Court, in *Laidlaw,* found that the defendant failed to meet its heavy burden and refused to dismiss the case based on its voluntary changes in behavior.

The Court has reaffirmed the narrowness of this exception. In *Federal Bureau of Investigation v. Fikre,* the Court said that a defendant seeking to dismiss a case as moot based on a change in practice must meet a "formidable burden."[74] Yonas Fikre, a United States citizen, brought suit alleging that the government placed him on the No Fly List unlawfully. Later, the government removed him from the

[69] *Id.* at 633 (citations omitted). *See* Iron Arrow Honor Socy. v. Heckler, 464 U.S. 67 (1983) (an exclusively male honorary society on campus sought to enjoin the Department of Health and Human Services from requiring the university to exclude it; while the case was pending, the university announced its decision to ban the club, regardless of the government's decision, rendering the case moot); Preiser v. Newkirk, 422 U.S. 395, 401-402 (1975) (case challenging transfer of prisoner to a medium- or maximum-security prison dismissed as moot because he had been moved back to a minimum-security unit and there was no likelihood that the wrong would be repeated).

[70] 528 U.S. 167 (2000).

[71] *Id.* at 189 (citation omitted).

[72] *Id.* at 170.

[73] *Id.*

[74] 601 U.S. 234 (2024).

list. The Court, though, said that the case should not be dismissed as moot. The Court said that "our precedents hold, a defendant's voluntary cessation of a challenged practice will moot a case only if the defendant can show that the practice cannot reasonably be expected to recur."[75]

An interesting application of this exception involved a party that had prevailed in the lower court, making the case moot while it was pending in the Supreme Court. In *City of Erie v. Pap's A.M.*,[76] the defendant, the owner of a nude dancing establishment, successfully challenged a city ordinance prohibiting public nudity that was adopted to close that business. While the case was pending in the Supreme Court, the business closed and the defendant moved for the Court to dismiss the matter on mootness grounds. The Court refused and said that the case was not moot because the company still had the license for the business and could reopen it at any time and because the city continued to be injured by the injunction of the ordinance entered by the state court.[77] The defendant also said that he was seventy-two years old and retired. The Court said that this was not sufficient: "Several members of this Court can attest, however, that the 'advanced age' of Pap's owner, 72, does not make it 'absolutely clear' that a life of quiet retirement is his only reasonable expectation."[78]

The Court applied this to decide a major environmental case, *West Virginia v. Environmental Protection Agency*.[79] The case concerns the authority of the EPA to regulate power plants to limit their greenhouse gas emissions. Coal-fired power plants are a major source of the pollution that significantly contributes to climate change.

The Obama administration adopted an aggressive approach, known as the Clean Power Plan, to limit these pollutants from coal-fired power plants across the country. The goal was to decrease the amount of energy produced by coal-fired power plants in the United States. The Trump administration rescinded the Clean Power Plan and adopted its own Affordable Clean Energy Plan, which was far more permissive in allowing pollution.

The United States Court of Appeals for the District of Columbia Circuit ruled that the Trump administration failed to follow proper procedures in rescinding the Obama-era plan and enacting its own approach. West Virginia and several coal companies sought Supreme Court review.

The Supreme Court, in a 6-3 decision, ruled that the EPA is limited in its ability to regulate greenhouse gas emissions from powerplants. Chief Justice John Roberts wrote the opinion for the majority, joined by the other conservative justices. Justice Elena Kagan wrote the dissent for the three liberal justices.

The Biden administration urged the Supreme Court not to take the case and then, once taken, urged the Court to dismiss it. The EPA has clarified that it does not intend to revive the Clean Power Plan or implement the Affordable Clean

[75] *Id.*
[76] 529 U.S. 277 (2000).
[77] *Id.* at 288.
[78] *Id.*
[79] 597 U.S. 697 (2022).

Energy Plan. The Biden administration announced that it would produce its own, new approach. In other words, the Obama Administration's Clean Power Plan is not law, the Trump Administration's Affordable Clean Energy (ACE) rule is not law, and the Biden Administration did not promulgate any rule on the subject. There are currently no regulations on powerplant greenhouse gas emissions. In light of this, the Biden administration argued that the case should not have been decided, asserting that the Court does not have the authority to judicially review future, potential, or hypothetical administrative regulations.

The Supreme Court expressly rejected this argument and drew a distinction between standing and mootness. The Court concluded that the states were injured by the earlier rule and thus had standing to challenge it. The question then, the Court observed, was whether the case should be dismissed on mootness grounds. There is an exception to the mootness doctrine, "voluntary cessation," which provides that cases will not be dismissed as moot if the defendant voluntarily halts that allegedly impermissible behavior but is free to resume it at any time. Chief Justice Roberts, writing for the majority, explained: "But 'voluntary cessation does not moot a case' unless it is 'absolutely clear that the allegedly wrongful behavior could not reasonably be expected to recur.' Here the Government 'nowhere suggests that if this litigation is resolved in its favor it will not' reimpose emissions limits predicated on generation shifting; indeed, it 'vigorously defends' the legality of such an approach. We do not dismiss a case as moot in such circumstances. The case thus remains justiciable, and we may turn to the merits."[80]

Statutory Change

Usually, a statutory change is enough to render a case moot, even though the legislature possesses the power to reinstate the allegedly invalid law after the lawsuit is dismissed. For example, in *Kremens v. Bartley*, the state repealed statutes challenged as unconstitutional in that they permitted involuntary commitment of juveniles.[81] The Supreme Court said that the legislative action made the case moot. Likewise, in *Massachusetts v. Oakes*, the Court dismissed a challenge to an overbreadth challenge to a Massachusetts law prohibiting nude photography of minors.[82] The law was amended while the case was pending, and the Court ruled that "overbreadth analysis is inappropriate if the statute being challenged has been amended or repealed."[83] In *New York State Rifle & Pistol Ass'n, Inc. v. City of New York, New York*, the Court dismissed as moot a challenge to a New York City ordinance that limited the ability of people to take guns out of their homes when they had permits that permitted them on the "premises."[84] After the federal district court and the court of appeals upheld the law, and after certiorari had been granted,

[80] 142 S. Ct. 2587 at 2607.

[81] 431 U.S. 119, 132 (1977).

[82] 491 U.S. 576 (1989).

[83] *Id.* at 582. *See also* Lewis v. Continental Bank Corp., 494 U.S. 472 (1990) (change in the law rendered the case moot).

[84] 590 U.S. 336 (2020).

New York City repealed the law, and New York State adopted a statute forbidding such city ordinances. The Court, in a per curiam opinion, held that the case was moot: "After we granted certiorari, the State of New York amended its firearm licensing statute, and the City amended the rule so that petitioners may now transport firearms to a second home or shooting range outside of the city, which is the precise relief that petitioners requested in the prayer for relief in their complaint. Petitioners' claim for declaratory and injunctive relief with respect to the City's old rule is therefore moot."[85]

However, the Court also has held that a repeal of a challenged law does not render a case moot if there is a reasonable possibility that the government would reenact the law if the proceedings were dismissed. In *City of Mesquite v. Aladdin's Castle, Inc.*, a city law limited licensing of video arcades and amusement centers.[86] The plaintiff challenged the ordinance as being unconstitutionally vague in prohibiting licensing of operations that have "connections with criminal elements." The city repealed this language from the ordinance while the case was pending. Nonetheless, the Court held that the case was not moot. Justice Stevens, writing for the majority, explained: "It is well settled that a defendant's voluntary cessation of a challenged practice does not deprive a federal court of its power to determine the legality of the practice. . . . In this case the City's repeal of the objectionable language would not preclude it from reenacting precisely the same provision if the District Court's judgment were vacated."[87]

Similarly, in *Northeastern Florida Contractors v. Jacksonville*, the Court refused to dismiss as moot a challenge to a city ordinance that provided preference in contracting for minority-owned businesses.[88] The Court explained that "[t]here is no mere risk that Jacksonville will repeat its allegedly wrongful conduct; it already has done so. Nor does it matter that the new ordinance differs in certain respects from the old one. . . . [I]f that were the rule, a defendant could moot a case by repealing the challenged statute and replacing it with one that differs only in some insignificant respect."[89] The Court said that the new statute posed the same basic constitutional question and thus the repeal of the earlier law did not moot the case.

The difficulty is determining why in some situations a legislative repeal is deemed to make a case moot, yet in other cases it does not. In all instances, the legislature is free to reenact the law. In *Aladdin's Castle*, the Court said that "[t]he test for mootness in cases such as this is a stringent one. Mere voluntary cessation of allegedly illegal conduct does not moot a case. . . . A case might become moot if subsequent events made it absolutely clear that the allegedly wrongful behavior could not reasonably be expected to recur."[90] Yet, in other cases described above, the Court concluded that legislative repeal was enough to make a case moot, although the law could have been readopted after the conclusion of the legal

[85] *Id.* at 338-339.
[86] 455 U.S. 283 (1982).
[87] *Id.* at 289.
[88] 508 U.S. 656 (1993). The standing aspects of the case are discussed in §2.3.3.
[89] *Id.* at 662.
[90] 455 U.S. at 289.

proceedings. The key appears to be that cases will not be dismissed as moot if the Court believes that there is a likelihood of reenactment of a substantially similar law if the lawsuit is dismissed.

Compliance with a Court Order

Compliance with a court order renders a case moot only if there is no possibility that the allegedly offending behavior will resume once the order expires or is lifted. For example, a case was not moot when a court order caused a union to end its boycott, because the union could resume the boycott as soon as the order was removed.[91] Similarly, the voluntary cessation exception was applied to prevent dismissal of a case when a union stopped its picketing in response to a court injunction but contested the constitutionality of that injunction and wished to challenge allegedly illegal harassment of its members.[92]

Vitek v. Jones illustrates the inability of court orders to render a case moot where the offending practices can resume if the orders are lifted.[93] In *Vitek*, the plaintiffs challenged the ability of state prisons to transfer prisoners to mental hospitals without providing adequate notice and an opportunity for a hearing. A court permanently enjoined these transfers imposed without due process protections. Although the transfers halted, the Court held that the case was not moot because "it is not absolutely clear absent the injunction that the allegedly wrongful behavior could not reasonably be expected to recur."[94]

But a case can be dismissed as moot if a court order produces a change in behavior and it is deemed unlikely that the offending conduct will resume. *County of Los Angeles v. Davis* is instructive.[95] The plaintiffs, representing present and future black and Mexican American applicants to the Los Angeles County Fire Department, brought a class action suit challenging alleged discriminatory hiring practices. The district court found a violation of federal civil rights statutes and permanently enjoined the discriminatory practices. The fire department complied with the injunction, discarding its preemployment screening test and hiring many new minority applicants.

The Supreme Court held that the case was moot. The Court explained that a case may become moot if "it can be said with assurance that there is no reasonable expectation that the alleged violation will recur, [and] interim relief or events have completely and irrevocably eradicated the effects of the alleged violation."[96] The Court said that the defendant had eliminated the use of the invalidated civil service exam and showed no propensity for reinstituting it and that the defendant had changed its hiring practices so that more than 50 percent of new recruits were racial minorities. As such, the Court deemed the case moot.

[91] Bakery Drivers v. Wagshal, 333 U.S. 437 (1948).
[92] Allee v. Medrano, 416 U.S. 802, 810 (1974).
[93] 445 U.S. 480 (1980).
[94] *Id.* at 487 (citations omitted).
[95] 440 U.S. 625 (1979).
[96] *Id.* at 631.

In short, under the voluntary cessation exception to the mootness doctrine, the central question is whether the defendant has the ability to resort to the allegedly improper behavior that was voluntarily stopped. Only if the defendant can show that there is no reasonable chance that the conduct can resume should a federal court dismiss a case as moot when a defendant voluntarily halts a challenged practice.

§2.5.5 *Exceptions to the Mootness Doctrine: Class Actions*

The Supreme Court has taken a particularly flexible approach to the mootness doctrine in class action suits. In a series of cases, the Supreme Court has held that a properly certified class action suit may continue even if the named plaintiff's claims are rendered moot. The Court has reasoned that the "class of unnamed persons described in the certification acquired a legal status separate from the interest asserted by the [plaintiff]," and thus the case can continue as long as the members of the class have a live controversy.[97] Furthermore, the Court has concluded that a plaintiff may continue to appeal the denial of class certification even after his or her particular claim is mooted. But the Court has subsequently refused to extend this exception beyond class actions to a situation where a statute allowed suits on behalf of "others similarly situated."[98]

Properly Certified Class Action Not Moot

Sosna v. Iowa was the first major departure from traditional mootness rules for class action suits.[99] The plaintiff, Mrs. Sosna, initiated a class action suit challenging an Iowa law requiring residence in the state for one year to obtain a divorce from an Iowa court. The class action was properly certified, and the district court ruled against the plaintiffs on the merits. While the appeals were pending, Mrs. Sosna satisfied the durational residency requirement, thus resolving her claim. The Supreme Court, in an opinion by Justice Rehnquist, held that the suit was not moot. The Court emphasized that the controversy "remains very much alive for the class of persons she has been certified to represent."[100] The Court explained that a class action suit should not be dismissed on mootness grounds as long as the named plaintiff had a live controversy when the suit was filed, there was a properly certified class action, and there are members of the class whose claims are not moot.

The Supreme Court applied *Sosna* in other cases involving class action suits. For example, in *Gerstein v. Pugh,* a properly certified class action suit challenged

[97] Sosna v. Iowa, 419 U.S. 393, 399 (1975).

[98] Genesis Healthcare Corp. v. Symczyk, 569 U.S. 66 (2013), discussed below.

[99] *Id.*

[100] *Id.* at 401. The Court also explained that the case could fit into the exception for wrongs capable of repetition yet evading review because of the fact that the residency requirement was shorter than the usual course of litigation. *Id.* at 401 n.9.

the constitutionality of a Florida practice of holding individuals without a judicial hearing determining probable cause.[101] Although the named plaintiff's claim was resolved because the pretrial detention ended, the case was not moot because there was a properly certified class action and the members of the class continued to present a live controversy.

In several cases decided the same year as *Sosna,* the Supreme Court concluded that the mootness doctrine required the dismissal of class action suits that were not properly certified when the named plaintiff's claim became moot.[102] The underlying rationale seems to be that when there is a properly certified class action, the entire class is the actual plaintiff, and as long as a live controversy exists for some of the plaintiffs, the case should not be deemed moot.

The Court expanded the exception for class action suits in *Franks v. Bowman Transportation Co.*[103] In *Franks,* the plaintiff brought a class action suit challenging alleged employment discrimination. By the time the case came to the Supreme Court, it was clear that the named plaintiff did not have a possible claim of discrimination even though other class members did. The Court said that even if the named plaintiff never had a legitimate claim for relief, a class action is not moot when it was properly certified and when some members continue to have live claims.

Appeals of Denial of Class Certification Not Moot

Sosna, Gerstein, and *Franks* all involved properly certified class actions. The Court first considered noncertified class actions in *United Airlines, Inc. v. McDonald.*[104] There the Court held that a member of the proposed class may intervene to challenge and appeal the denial of class certification after the named plaintiff's claims are mooted.

Subsequently, the Court held that a person seeking to initiate a class action suit may continue to appeal the denial of certification even after his or her own claims are rendered moot. In *United States Parole Commission v. Geraghty,* a prisoner who was denied parole on the basis of the Parole Commission's guidelines sought to bring a class action suit challenging the guidelines.[105] The district court refused to certify a class action and the plaintiff appealed. While the appeal was pending, the plaintiff was released from prison.

Even though a class action never was certified, the Court held that the case was not moot. The Court explained that the members of the proposed class still had a live controversy, justifying continued federal judicial consideration of whether the class should be certified. The Court stated "that an action brought on behalf of a

[101] 420 U.S. 103 (1975).

[102] *See, e.g.,* Board of School Commrs. of Indianapolis v. Jacobs, 420 U.S. 128 (1975); Weinstein v. Bradford, 423 U.S. 147 (1975); *see also* Pasadena City Bd. of Educ. v. Spangler, 427 U.S. 424 (1976); Franks v. Bowman Transportation Co., 424 U.S. 747 (1976).

[103] 424 U.S. 747 (1976).

[104] 432 U.S. 385, 393 (1977).

[105] 445 U.S. 388 (1980).

class does not become moot upon expiration of the named plaintiff's substantive claim, even though class certification has been denied. The proposed representative retains a 'personal stake' in obtaining class certification sufficient to assure that Art. III values are not undermined. If the appeal results in a reversal of the class certification denial, and a class subsequently is properly certified, the merits of the class claim then may be adjudicated pursuant to the holding in *Sosna*."[106]

Similarly, in *Deposit Guaranty National Bank v. Roper*, decided the same day as *Geraghty*, the Court held that the named plaintiffs in a proposed class action suit could continue to appeal the denial of class certification even after the plaintiffs settled their personal claims.[107] In *Roper*, the plaintiffs sought to bring a class action suit to challenge the interest charged by Bank Americard. The plaintiffs agreed to a settlement that paid them the full sum they claimed as damages. The Court said that the plaintiffs could continue to appeal the denial of class certification. The Court explained that the plaintiffs maintained a "personal stake in the appeal" because they had "a continuing individual interest in the resolution of the class certification question in their desire to shift part of the costs of litigation to those who will share in its benefits if the class is certified and ultimately prevails."[108] The Court explained that other class members had a live controversy, and allowing the settlement to end the litigation would give defendants an incentive to "buy off" named plaintiffs in class action litigation.[109]

The exception for class action suits makes sense in that it focuses on the interests of the class, rather than simply looking to the named plaintiff's claims. As long as the class presents a live controversy, the status of any particular member's claim is irrelevant. Thus, the Court has properly concluded that a properly certified class action is not moot simply because the named plaintiff's controversy is resolved. Nor should the mootness of the plaintiff's claim prevent an appeal of the denial of class certification. This mootness exception furthers the underlying purposes of the federal rules concerning class actions and is consistent with Article III because there is an actual dispute between adverse litigants and a favorable federal court decision will make a difference for the class members.

Refusal to Extend Exception Beyond Class Actions

The Fair Labor Standards Act of 1938 (FLSA)[110] provides that an employee may bring an action to recover damages for specified violations of the act on behalf of himself and other "similarly situated" employees.[111] The issue in *Genesis Healthcare Corp. v. Symczyk* was whether a class action is justiciable when the lone plaintiff's individual claim becomes moot. The Court, in a 5-4 decision, held that

[106] *Id.* at 404.
[107] 445 U.S. 326 (1980).
[108] *Id.* at 336.
[109] *Id.* at 339.
[110] 29 U.S.C. §201.
[111] 569 U.S. 66 (2013).

the case was moot and refused to extend the class action exception to the mootness doctrine to this situation.

Justice Thomas, writing for the Court, explained: "More fundamentally, essential to our decisions in *Sosna* and *Geraghty* was the fact that a putative class acquires an independent legal status once it is certified under Rule 23. Under the FLSA, by contrast, 'conditional certification' does not produce a class with an independent legal status, or join additional parties to the action. The sole consequence of conditional certification is the sending of court-approved written notice to employees, who in turn become parties to a collective action only by filing written consent with the court, §216(b). So even if respondent were to secure a conditional certification ruling on remand, nothing in that ruling would preserve her suit from mootness."[112] The Court thus "conclude[d] that respondent has no personal interest in representing putative, unnamed claimants, nor any other continuing interest that would preserve her suit from mootness."[113]

Nor was the Court willing to find an exception to mootness where there was a claim that there was a "functional class action." In *United States v. Sanchez-Gomez*, four criminal defendants challenged the United States Marshall Service policy of shackling in-custody defendants for some court proceedings.[114] The Supreme Court found the case moot, concluding that the class action exception is limited to when there is a formal mechanism, such as under Rule 23 of the Federal Rules of Civil Procedure. There is no such exception for "functional class actions."

§2.6 THE POLITICAL QUESTION DOCTRINE

§2.6.1 What Is the Political Question Doctrine?

Definition

The Supreme Court has held that federal courts should not rule on certain allegations of unconstitutional government conduct even though all of the jurisdictional and other justiciability requirements are met. The Court has said that constitutional interpretation in these areas should be left to the politically accountable branches of government, the president, and Congress. In other words, the "political question doctrine" refers to subject matter that the Court deems to be inappropriate for judicial review. Although there is an allegation that the Constitution has been violated, the federal courts refuse to rule and instead dismiss the case, leaving the constitutional question to be resolved in the political process. As the Court declared, "In such a case the claim is said to present a 'political question'

[112] *Id.* at 1530.
[113] *Id.* at 1532.
[114] 584 U.S. 381 (2018).

and to be nonjusticiable—outside the courts' competence and therefore beyond the courts' jurisdiction."[1]

Why Is the Political Question Doctrine Confusing?

In many ways, the political question doctrine is the most confusing of the justiciability doctrines. As Professor Martin Redish noted, "The doctrine has always proven to be an enigma to commentators. Not only have they disagreed about its wisdom and validity . . . , but they also have differed significantly over the doctrine's scope and rationale."[2] First, the confusion stems from the fact that the "political question doctrine" is a misnomer; the federal courts deal with political issues all of the time. For example, in *United States v. Nixon,* the Court decided that President Nixon had to comply with a subpoena to produce tapes of presidential conversations that were needed as evidence in a criminal trial, a decision with the ultimate political effect of causing a president to resign.[3] The Supreme Court's direct involvement in the political process has long included ending racial discrimination in political primaries and elections.[4]

Second, the political question doctrine is particularly confusing because the Court has defined it very differently over the course of American history. The Court first spoke of political questions in *Marbury v. Madison.*[5] Chief Justice John Marshall wrote: "By the Constitution of the United States, the President is invested with certain important political powers, in the exercise of which he is to use his own discretion, and is accountable only to his country in his political character and to his own conscience. . . . The subjects are political. [B]eing entrusted to the executive, the decision of the executive is conclusive. Questions, in their nature political, or which are by the constitution and laws, submitted to the executive can never be made in this court."[6] Chief Justice Marshall contrasted political questions with instances where individual rights were at stake; the latter, according to the Court, never could be political questions.[7]

The Court's definition of political questions in *Marbury v. Madison* was quite narrow. Included only were matters where the president had unlimited discretion, and there was thus no allegation of a constitutional violation. For example, presidents have the choice about whether to sign or veto a bill or who to appoint for a

§2.6 [1] Rucho v. Common Cause, 588 U.S. 684, 696 (2019). For an examination of how the political question doctrine has been used, especially in the lower federal courts, Curtis A. Bradley & Eric A. Posner, *The Real Political Question Doctrine,* 75 Stan. L. Rev. 1031 (2023).

[2] Martin Redish, Judicial Review and the Political Question, 79 Nw. U. L. Rev. 1031 (1985).

[3] 418 U.S. 683 (1974).

[4] *See, e.g.,* Nixon v. Herndon, 273 U.S. 536 (1927) (declaring unconstitutional racial discrimination in the Democratic political primary in Texas). The Court said that a claim that the matter was a political question because it involved the political process was "little more than a play upon words." *Id.* at 540.

[5] 5 U.S. (1 Cranch) 137 (1803), discussed above in §1.3.

[6] *Id.* at 165-170.

[7] *Id.* at 170.

vacancy on the federal judiciary. Because the Constitution vests the president with plenary authority in these areas, there is no basis for a claim of a constitutional violation regardless of how the president acts. But if there is a claim of an infringement of an individual rights—in other words, if the plaintiff has standing—there is not a political question under the formulation presented in *Marbury v. Madison.*[8]

In sharp contrast, the political question doctrine now includes instances where individuals allege that specific constitutional provisions have been violated and that they have suffered a concrete injury.[9] The political question doctrine definitely is not limited to instances in which the president is exercising discretion and there is no claim of unconstitutional conduct. But the Court never has explained the differing content given to the term "political question"; in fact, the Court even invokes *Marbury* in its modern, very different cases.[10]

The *Baker* Criteria and Their Limited Usefulness

Finally, and perhaps most important, the political question doctrine is confusing because of the Court's failure to articulate useful criteria for deciding what subject matter presents a nonjusticiable political question. The classic, oft-quoted statement of the political question doctrine was provided in *Baker v. Carr.*[11] The Court stated:

> Prominent on the surface of any case held to involve a political question is found a textually demonstrable commitment of the issue to a coordinate political department; or a lack of judicially discoverable and manageable standards for resolving it; or the impossibility of deciding without an initial policy determination of a kind clearly for nonjudicial discretion; or the impossibility of a court's undertaking independent resolution without expressing lack of the respect due coordinate branches of government; or an unusual need for unquestioning adherence to a political decision already made; or the potentiality of embarrassment from multifarious pronouncements by various departments on one question.[12]

Virtually every case considering the political question doctrine quotes this language, but these criteria seem useless in identifying what constitutes a political question. For example, nowhere in the Constitution does the text state that the legislature or executive should decide whether a particular action constitutes a constitutional violation. The Constitution does not mention judicial review, much less limit it by creating "textually demonstrable commitments" to other branches

[8] Howard Fink & Mark Tushnet, Federal Jurisdiction: Policy and Practice 231 (2d ed. 1987) ("But notice the effect of Marbury's classification: Standing is just the obverse of political questions. If a litigant claims that an individual right has been invaded, the lawsuit by definition does not involve a political question.").

[9] *See, e.g.,* Luther v. Borden, 48 U.S. (7 How.) 1 (1849) (declaring nonjusticiable a suit brought under the republican form of government clause even though the effect was to leave people in jail who contested the constitutionality of their conviction), discussed below in §2.6.3.

[10] *See, e.g.,* Rucho v. Common Cause, 588 U.S. at 695 (invoking Marbury v. Madison as the basis for the political question doctrine).

[11] 369 U.S. 186 (1962).

[12] *Id.* at 217.

of government. Similarly, most important constitutional provisions are written in broad, open-textured language and certainly do not include "judicially discoverable and manageable standards."[13] The Court also speaks of determinations of a kind "clearly for a nonjudicial determination," but that hardly is a criterion that can be used to separate political questions from justiciable cases.

In other words, it is impossible for a court or a commentator to apply the *Baker v. Carr* criteria to identify what cases are political questions. As such, it hardly is surprising that the doctrine is described as confusing and unsatisfactory.[14]

The political question doctrine can be understood only by examining the specific areas where the Supreme Court has invoked it. Specifically, the Court has considered the political question doctrine in the following areas: the republican form of government clause and the electoral process; foreign affairs; Congress's ability to regulate its internal processes; the process for ratifying constitutional amendments; instances where the federal court cannot shape effective equitable relief; and the impeachment process. Section 2.6.2 considers the basic normative question of whether there should be a political question doctrine. Sections 2.6.3-2.6.8 consider, in turn, each of the areas mentioned above.

§2.6.2 Should There Be a Political Question Doctrine?

Justifications for the Political Question Doctrine

The underlying normative issue is whether the political question doctrine should exist at all. Defenders of the doctrine make several arguments. First, and most commonly, it is argued that the political question doctrine accords the federal judiciary the ability to avoid controversial constitutional questions and limits the courts' role in a democratic society. Professor Alexander Bickel was the foremost advocate of this position.[15] Professor Bickel wrote:

> Such is the foundation, in both intellect and instinct, of the political question doctrine: the Court's sense of lack of capacity, compounded in unequal part of (a) the strangeness of the issue and its intractability to principled resolution; (b) the sheer momentousness of it, which tends to unbalance judicial judgment; (c) the anxiety, not so much that the judicial judgment will be ignored, as that perhaps it should but will not be; (d) finally ("in a mature democracy"), the inner vulnerability, the self-doubt of an institution which is electorally irresponsible and has no earth to draw strength from.[16]

[13] For an excellent discussion of this aspect of the political question doctrine, *see* Richard H. Fallon, Jr., Judicially Manageable Standards and Constitutional Meaning, 119 Harv. L. Rev. 1274 (2005).

[14] For an effort to reformulate the political question doctrine to focus on judicial competence in particular areas, *see* Jesse Choper, The Political Question Doctrine: Suggested Criteria, 54 Duke L.J. 1457 (2005).

[15] *See, e.g.,* Alexander Bickel, The Supreme Court, 1960 Term: Foreword: The Passive Virtues, 75 Harv. L. Rev. 40, 46 (1961); Alexander Bickel, The Least Dangerous Branch 184 (1962).

[16] Bickel, *id.*, The Least Dangerous Branch at 184. Based on these criteria, it can be asked whether the Court should have dismissed Bush v. Gore, 531 U.S. 98 (2000), as a political question. *See* Erwin Chemerinsky, Bush v. Gore Was Not Justiciable, 76 Notre Dame L. Rev. 1073 (2001); *see* also Louise

Professor Bickel contended that it was simply better for the federal courts to avoid deciding certain cases, especially so as to preserve what he perceived as the judiciary's fragile political legitimacy. Justice Felix Frankfurter argued, on this basis, that the Court should not have decided whether malapportionment violates the Constitution,[17] and many commentators have suggested that the federal courts should not review impeachment proceedings conducted by Congress because any ruling would jeopardize the Court's credibility and prestige.[18]

A second argument for the political question doctrine is that it allocates decisions to the branches of government that have superior expertise in particular areas. For example, some argue that the Court rightly has treated many constitutional issues concerning foreign policy to be political questions because of the greater information and expertise of the other branches of government.[19]

Third, the political question doctrine is defended on the ground that the federal courts' self-interest disqualifies them from ruling on certain matters. Specifically, it is argued that the courts should not become involved in reviewing the process for ratifying constitutional amendments because amendments are the only way to overturn the Supreme Court's constitutional interpretations.[20] Justice Powell, for example, spoke of the dangers of having the Court "oversee the very constitutional process used to reverse [its] decisions."[21]

Finally, the political question doctrine is justified on separation of powers grounds as minimizing judicial intrusion into the operations of the other branches of government. The argument is that in certain cases an effective remedy would require judicial oversight of day-to-day executive or legislative conduct. For example, a lawsuit contending that there were constitutional deficiencies in training the Ohio National Guard was deemed to be a political question because a remedy would involve judicial control and supervision over the Guard's activities.[22]

Criticisms of the Political Question Doctrine

On the other hand, critics such as Professor Martin Redish argue that "the political question doctrine should play no role whatsoever in the exercise of the

Weinberg, When Courts Decide Elections: The Constitutionality of Bush v. Gore, 82 B.U. L. Rev. 609 (2002).

[17] Baker v. Carr, 369 U.S. at 267 (Frankfurter, J., dissenting), discussed below.

[18] *See, e.g.,* Charles Black, Impeachment: A Handbook (1974) (discussing impeachment as a political question).

[19] *See, e.g.,* Fritz Scharpf, Judicial Review and the Political Question: A Functional Analysis, 75 Yale L.J. 517, 567 (1966).

[20] *See, e.g.,* Laurence Tribe, Constitutional Choices 22-23 (1985) (arguing that challenges to the constitutional amendment process should be treated as a political question).

[21] Quoted in Tribe, *id.*, at 23.

[22] Gilligan v. Morgan, 413 U.S. 1 (1973), discussed below. For an excellent defense of the political question doctrine and criticism of its nonuse by the Supreme Court, *see* Rachel E. Barkow, More Supreme Than Court? The Fall of the Political Question Doctrine and the Rise of Judicial Supremacy, 102 Colum. L. Rev. 237 (2002).

judicial review power."[23] Such critics contend, first, that the judicial role is to enforce the Constitution and that it is inappropriate to leave constitutional questions to the political branches of government.[24] The argument is that matters are placed in the Constitution to insulate them from majoritarian control; judicial review serves to effectuate and uphold the Constitution. Thus, it is inappropriate to relegate constitutional issues to the political branches of government. Politically accountable bodies should not be entrusted to enforce any part of a document that is meant to restrain them.

Second, critics of the political question doctrine question the premise of scholars such as Professor Bickel and justices such as Felix Frankfurter, who speak of the judiciary's fragile legitimacy. To the contrary, critics contend that the federal courts' credibility is quite robust, that there is no evidence that particular rulings have any effect on the judiciary's legitimacy, and that in any event, the courts' mission should be to uphold the Constitution and not worry about political capital.[25] The argument is that a judiciary that ducks controversial issues to preserve its credibility is likely to avoid judicial review where it is needed most—to restrain highly popular unconstitutional government actions.

Third, critics of the political question doctrine argue that it confuses deference with abdication. The claim is that in areas where the federal courts lack expertise, they should be more deferential to the other branches of government. Likewise, the courts should be particularly deferential in reviewing the process of ratifying constitutional amendments that seek to overturn the Supreme Court's judgments. But deference need not mean abdication. Many foreign policy questions do not involve matters of expertise, but instead pose interpretive questions like those constantly resolved by the courts.[26] Also, a blatant disregard of the Constitution's requirements—for example, an amendment deemed by Congress to have been ratified even though not approved by the requisite number of states—should not be tolerated by the federal courts.[27] In other words, critics of the political question doctrine argue that the doctrine's defenders demonstrate only that on the merits, the Court should hesitate in some areas before ruling against the other branches of government; it is wrong to deem those areas to be nonjusticiable.

Is it Constitutional or Prudential?

Perhaps as a reflection of this debate, important questions remain unsettled concerning the political question doctrine. For example, it is uncertain whether the

[23] Redish, *supra* note 2, at 1033; Erwin Chemerinsky, Closing the Courthouse Door: How Your Constitutional Rights Became Unenforceable 114-133 (2017).

[24] Redish, *supra* note 2, at 1045-1046; Chemerinsky, *supra* note 23, at 99-100.

[25] Chemerinsky, *supra* note 23, at 133-138; *see* also Laurence Tribe, American Constitutional Law viii (2d ed. 1988) ("The highest mission of the Supreme Court . . . is not to conserve judicial credibility, but in the Constitution's own phrase, 'to form a more perfect Union.' ").

[26] *See* Louis Henkin, Is There a Political Question Doctrine?, 85 Yale L.J. 597 (1976) (arguing against courts finding issues concerning foreign policy to be a political question).

[27] *See* Walter Dellinger, The Legitimacy of Constitutional Change: Rethinking the Amendment Process, 97 Harv. L. Rev. 386 (1983).

political question doctrine is constitutional, prudential, or both. Could Congress direct the federal courts to adjudicate a matter that the Supreme Court deemed to be a political question? Unlike the other justiciability doctrines, the political question doctrine is not derived from Article III's limitation of judicial power to "cases" and "controversies."

The political question doctrine might be treated as constitutional if it is thought to be based on separation of powers or textual commitments to other branches of government. On the other hand, the doctrine is prudential if it reflects the Court's concerns about preserving judicial credibility and limiting the role of an unelected judiciary in a democratic society.

§2.6.3 The "Republican Form of Government" Clause and Judicial Review of the Electoral Process

Article IV, §4, of the Constitution states: "The United States shall guarantee to every State in this Union a Republican form of government." The Supreme Court consistently has held that cases alleging a violation of this clause present nonjusticiable political questions. Some scholars have urged the Court to reconsider this rule and to find cases under the republican form of government clause to be justiciable.[28] Thus far, the Court has not done so, although Justice O'Connor remarked that "the Court has suggested that perhaps not all claims under the Guarantee Clause present nonjusticiable political questions" and acknowledged that "[c]ontemporary commentators have . . . suggested that courts should address the merits of such claims, at least in some circumstances."[29]

Luther v. Borden

Luther v. Borden is the seminal case.[30] In the 1840s, Rhode Island was the only state without a state constitution. The state governed pursuant to a state charter that had been granted to it by King Charles II in 1663. As a result, in 1840, the Rhode Island legislature was badly malapportioned and controlled by a rural minority. Jamestown, for example, had one representative in the state legislature for every 180 citizens, but Providence had one representative for every 6,000 citizens.

In 1841, a convention met to draft a state constitution. A constitution was proposed and ratified. The existing government, which was sure to lose power under

[28] *See, e.g.*, Erwin Chemerinsky, Cases Under the Guarantee Clause Should Be Justiciable, 65 U. Colo. L. Rev. 849 (1994); Deborah Merritt, The Guarantee Clause and State Autonomy: Federalism for a Third Century, 88 Colum. L. Rev. 1 (1988) (arguing that the guarantee clause should be seen as a basis for protecting federalism and states' rights from congressional interference); *but see* Ann Althouse, Time for Federal Courts to Enforce the Guarantee Clause—A Response to Professor Chemerinsky, 65 U. Colo. L. Rev. 881 (1994); Louise Weinberg, Political Questions and the Guarantee Clause, 65 U. Colo. L. Rev. 887 (1994).

[29] New York v. United States, 505 U.S. 144, 185 (1992).

[30] 48 U.S. (7 How.) 1 (1849).

the new document, enacted a law prohibiting the constitution from going into effect. Nonetheless, elections were held—even though the existing government had declared voting in them to be a crime. Relatively few people participated, but a new government was chosen, headed by Thomas Dorr, who was elected governor. Dorr's government met for two days in an abandoned foundry and then disbanded.

In April 1842, Sheriff Luther Borden broke into the house of one of the election commissioners, Martin Luther, to search for evidence of illegal participation in the prohibited election. Luther sued Borden for trespass. Borden claimed that the search was a lawful exercise of government power. Luther, however, contended that Borden acted pursuant to an unconstitutional government's orders; he maintained that the Rhode Island government violated the republican form of government clause.

The Supreme Court held that the case posed a political question that could not be decided by a federal court. The Court stated: "Under this article of the constitution it rests with Congress to decide what government is the established one in a State. For as the United States guarantee to each state a republican government, Congress must necessarily decide what government is established in the State before it can determine whether it is republican or not."[31] The Court also explained that the case posed a political question because if the state's government was declared unconstitutional, then all of its actions would be invalidated, creating chaos in Rhode Island.[32] Additionally, the Court spoke of a lack of criteria for deciding what constitutes a republican form of government.

Luther v. Borden has been followed consistently. There is not a single instance in which the Supreme Court has deemed a state government or state actions to violate the republican form of government clause.[33] In *Taylor & Marshall v. Beckham*, the Court refused to decide a claim that a state's resolution of a disputed gubernatorial race violated the republican form of government clause.[34] Similarly, in *Pacific States Telephone & Telegraph Co. v. Oregon*, the Court again held that cases under this clause are not justiciable.[35] *Pacific States* involved a challenge to a state law, passed through a voter initiative, that taxed certain corporations. The defendant was a corporation sued by the state of Oregon for failure to pay taxes due under this law. The corporation argued that the statute was unconstitutional because the initiative process violated the republican form of government clause. The claim was that a republican form of government is one in which people elect representatives, who then govern; direct democracy was said to be antithetical to a republican government. The Supreme Court held that the matter was not justiciable. The Court said that the issue was "political and governmental, and embraced within the scope of

[31] 48 U.S. at 10.

[32] *Id.* at 13-14.

[33] There are instances in which the Supreme Court decided cases on the merits under the republican form of government clause, upholding the challenged government action. *See, e.g.*, Forsyth v. Hammond, 166 U.S. 506 (1897); Foster v. Kansas ex rel. Johnson, 112 U.S. 201 (1884); Kennard v. Louisiana ex rel. Morgan, 92 U.S. 480 (1875).

[34] 178 U.S. 548 (1900).

[35] 223 U.S. 118 (1912).

powers conferred upon Congress, and not therefore within the reach of judicial power."[36]

Reapportionment

Following these precedents, the Court declared nonjusticiable the first challenges to malapportioned state legislatures. By the middle of this century, many state legislatures were badly malapportioned. Legislatures had not been reapportioned after substantial growth in urban areas, with the effect that rural residents were overrepresented and urban dwellers were substantially underrepresented in state legislatures. Legislators who benefited from this system were not about to voluntarily redraw districts at the expense of their seats. Also, the rurally dominated state legislatures drew district lines for electing members of the U.S. House of Representatives that obviously favored their areas.

In *Colegrove v. Green*, in 1946, the Supreme Court declared nonjusticiable a challenge to the congressional districting in Illinois.[37] In an opinion by Justice Frankfurter, the Court stated: "[T]he appellants ask of this Court what is beyond its competence to grant. . . . [E]ffective working of our government revealed this issue to be of a peculiarly political nature and therefore not fit for judicial determination. Authority for dealing with such problems resides elsewhere."[38] The Court concluded that "[c]ourts ought not to enter this political thicket."[39] Similarly, in *South v. Peters*, in 1950, the Court held that "[f]ederal courts consistently refuse to exercise their equity powers in cases posing political issues arising from a state's geographical distribution of electoral strength among its political subdivisions."[40] Only in cases alleging racial discrimination in the drawing of election districts or in holding elections did the Supreme Court approve federal court involvement.[41]

But in 1962, in the landmark decision of *Baker v. Carr*, the Supreme Court deemed justiciable claims that malapportionment violates the equal protection clause.[42] Interestingly, the Court did not overrule *Luther v. Borden*, but instead distinguished cases brought under the equal protection clause from those pursued under the republican form of government clause. Justice Brennan explained that whereas "the Guaranty Clause is not a repository of judicially manageable standards . . . [j]udicial standards under the Equal Protection Clause are well-developed and familiar."[43] This seems to be a fatuous distinction because both clauses are equally vague and the principle of one person, one vote could have been

[36] *Id.* at 151.

[37] 328 U.S. 549 (1946).

[38] *Id.* at 552-554.

[39] *Id.* at 556.

[40] 339 U.S. 276, 277 (1950).

[41] *See, e.g.*, Gomillion v. Lightfoot, 364 U.S. 339 (1960) (redrawing of Tuskegee, Alabama, districts to disenfranchise blacks); Terry v. Adams, 345 U.S. 461 (1953); Smith v. Allwright, 321 U.S. 649 (1944) (discrimination against blacks in political parties).

[42] 369 U.S. 186 (1962).

[43] *Id.* at 223-226.

articulated and enforced under either constitutional provision.[44] Nonetheless, the Court's holding that challenges to malapportionment are justiciable was one of the most important rulings in American history.[45] The political process was not likely to correct the constitutional violation and judicial review provided democratic rule.[46]

The Supreme Court and lower courts frequently have reaffirmed that challenges to election districts are justiciable.[47] For example, in *United States Department of Commerce v. Montana,* the Court found justiciable a challenge by Montana voters to the method of apportioning members to the U.S. House of Representatives.[48] The Court unanimously found the challenge to be justiciable, though it concluded that there was no constitutional violation. The Court explained that objections to apportionment by Congress should be treated no differently than challenges to state government districting decisions.

Likewise, the Supreme Court has not hesitated to decide the constitutionality of using race in drawing election districts to increase the likelihood of electing African American and Latino representatives.[49] Although the Supreme Court acknowledged that "[f]ederal court review of districting legislation represents a serious intrusion on the most vital of local functions," the Court has made it clear that strict scrutiny must be met for race to be used as a predominant factor in districting.[50]

Gerrymandering

In *Rucho v. Common Cause,* the Supreme Court held, 5-4, that challenges to partisan gerrymandering are non-justiciable political questions.[51] Partisan gerrymandering is where the political party that controls the legislature draws election districts to maximize safe seats for that party.

Rucho was not the first time the Court addressed whether federal courts could hear challenges to partisan gerrymandering. In *Davis v. Bandemer,* the Court held that challenges to gerrymandering are justiciable.[52] The Court said that "the issue is one of representation, and we decline to hold that such claims are never justiciable."[53] The plurality opinion by Justice White said that in order for a group

[44] *See* Reynolds v. Sims, 377 U.S. 533 (1964) (articulating the one person, one vote standard).

[45] Chief Justice Earl Warren remarked that the most important decisions during his tenure on the Court were those ordering reapportionment. The Warren Court: An Editorial Preface, 67 Mich. L. Rev. 219, 220 (1968).

[46] *See, e.g.,* Louis Pollak, Judicial Power and the Politics of the People, 72 Yale L.J. 81, 88 (1962).

[47] Justice Thomas, though, has recently argued that challenges to districting, including based on race, should not be decided by the courts. Alexander v. South Carolina State Conference of the NAACP, 602 U.S. 1, 1221, 1253 (2024).

[48] 503 U.S. 442 (1992).

[49] *See, e.g.,* Shaw v. Hunt, 517 U.S. 899 (1996); Bush v. Vera, 517 U.S. 952 (1996); Miller v. Johnson, 515 U.S. 900 (1995); Shaw v. Reno, 509 U.S. 630 (1993).

[50] Miller v. Johnson, 515 U.S. at 915.

[51] 588 U.S. 684 (2019).

[52] 478 U.S. 109 (1986).

[53] *Id.* at 125.

to prove a violation of equal protection it must prove "both intentional discrimination against an identifiable political group and an actual discriminatory effect on that group."[54] The plurality concluded that "unconstitutional discrimination occurs only when the electoral system is arranged in a manner that will consistently degrade a voter's or a group of voters' influence on the political process as a whole."[55]

But in *Vieth v. Jubelirer*,[56] the Court dismissed a challenge to partisan gerrymandering, and a plurality said that such suits are inherently nonjusticiable political questions. The issue was whether partisan gerrymandering violates equal protection. Republicans controlled the Pennsylvania legislature, and they drew election districts to maximize Republican seats. The plurality concluded that *Davis* had proven impossible to implement and the plurality opinion, written by Justice Scalia, concluded that challenges to partisan gerrymandering are nonjusticiable political questions. Justice Scalia, joined by Chief Justice Rehnquist and Justices O'Connor and Thomas, said that there are no judicially discoverable or manageable standards and no basis for courts to decide when partisan gerrymandering offends the Constitution.

Justice Kennedy, concurring in the judgment, provided the fifth vote for the majority. He agreed to dismiss the case because of the lack of judicially discoverable or manageable standards, but he said that he did not believe that such standards could not be developed in the future. Thus, he disagreed with the majority opinion that challenges to partisan gerrymandering are always political questions; he said that when standards are developed, such cases can be heard. Justices Stevens, Souter, and Breyer wrote dissenting opinions, which Justice Ginsburg joined, arguing that there are standards that courts can implement.

In *Rucho*, the Court resolved the uncertainty left by Justice Kennedy's opinion and held that challenges to partisan gerrymandering are non-justiciable political questions. *Rucho* involved two cases that came to the Court together, though they were decided in a single opinion. *Rucho v. Common Cause* arose in North Carolina. North Carolina is essentially a purple state, leaning red. Barack Obama carried it in 2008, but Mitt Romney won it in 2012 and Donald Trump in 2016, 2020, and 2024. Each election was decided by a narrow margin. Republicans got a slight majority of the votes cast for the North Carolina state legislature and drew election districts to give themselves a super-majority of both houses.

Republicans then drew districts for congressional districts using what they called "partisan advantage" criteria. They stated that their goal was to draw districts for the congressional delegation from North Carolina so that there would be 10 Republicans and three Democrats. They succeeded. In 2016, the statewide vote for members of Congress was nearly tied, but Republicans won 10 of 13 races.

Lamone v. Benisek, which arose in Maryland, involves a Democratically controlled state legislature drawing a district for a congressional seat to elect a Democrat. Like in *Rucho*, a three-judge federal district court found this to be

[54] *Id.* at 127.
[55] *Id.*
[56] 541 U.S. 267 (2004).

unconstitutional. The Court, in an opinion by Chief Justice Roberts, found both to be non-justiciable. He stressed that the issue for the judiciary in such cases inevitably is what is "too much" use of politics in districting, but there is no way for a court to decide that. He explained, "There are no legal standards discernible in the Constitution for making such judgments, let alone limited and precise standards that are clear, manageable, and politically neutral. Any judicial decision on what is 'fair' in this context would be an 'unmoored determination' of the sort characteristic of a political question beyond the competence of the federal courts."[57] The Court explicitly distinguished malapportionment cases and said: "But the one-person, one-vote rule is relatively easy to administer as a matter of math. The same cannot be said of partisan gerrymandering claims, because the Constitution supplies no objective measure for assessing whether a districting map treats a political party fairly."[58]

The Court said that there are other remedies for partisan gerrymandering. Congress can outlaw it for elections to the House of Representatives. State voters can mandate independent districting commissions. State courts can invalidate gerrymandering as violating state constitutions. The Court noted that it "express[es] no view on any of these pending proposals. We simply note that the avenue for reform established by the Framers, and used by Congress in the past, remains open."[59]

Justice Kagan wrote a vehement dissent, joined by Justices Ginsburg, Breyer, and Sotomayor. She began her dissent: "For the first time ever, this Court refuses to remedy a constitutional violation because it thinks the task beyond judicial capabilities.

"And not just any constitutional violation. The partisan gerrymanders in these cases deprived citizens of the most fundamental of their constitutional rights: the rights to participate equally in the political process, to join with others to advance political beliefs, and to choose their political representatives. In so doing, the partisan gerrymanders here debased and dishonored our democracy, turning upside-down the core American idea that all governmental power derives from the people."[60]

Justice Kagan argued that partisan gerrymandering undermines democracy, denies equal protection through vote dilution, and violates the First Amendment by discriminating on the basis of political party affiliation. In response to the majority's claim that there is no way to decide what is too much partisanship in drawing districts, Justice Kagan wrote: "This much is too much. By any measure, a map that produces a greater partisan skew than any of 3,000 randomly generated maps (all with the State's political geography and districting criteria built in) reflects 'too much' partisanship."[61] Justice Kagan said that tests have been developed and used in the lower courts for deciding when gerrymandering violates the Constitution;

[57] *Rucho*, 588 U.S. at 707.
[58] *Id.* at 708.
[59] *Id.* at 721.
[60] *Id.* at 721 (Kagan, J., dissenting).
[61] *Id.* at 721-722.

at the very least, she said that a test could be developed based on purpose, effect, and causation, as is so often done in legal tests. She concluded: "Of all times to abandon the Court's duty to declare the law, this was not the one. The practices challenged in these cases imperil our system of government. Part of the Court's role in that system is to defend its foundations. None is more important than free and fair elections. With respect but deep sadness, I dissent."[62]

Rucho v. Common Cause will have enormous practical effects. Legislatures can engage in partisan gerrymandering with impunity knowing that there is no possibility of a challenge in federal court. The difference between the majority and the dissent is over the role of the federal courts. The majority sees this as a matter where there is not the possibility of clear standards and therefore the federal courts should stay out. The dissent sees this as unconstitutional and a threat to democracy and essential for the federal court to provide a remedy.

Review of Political Parties

A final area where the Court has considered the application of the political question doctrine to the electoral process involves judicial review of the activities of political parties. The Court repeatedly has held that the federal judiciary will prevent racial discrimination by political parties.[63] But the courts have dismissed other challenges to political parties, especially suits concerning the seating of delegates at national conventions. In *O'Brien v. Brown*, the federal courts were asked to decide what group of delegates should be seated at the 1972 Democratic National Convention.[64] The case reached the Supreme Court three days before the convention began. Illinois delegates, led by Mayor Richard Daley, were excluded on the ground that they were not sufficiently representative of racial minorities. The Daley delegates argued that they were discriminated against and denied equal protection. Also, a group of California delegates pledged to Hubert Humphrey argued that the state's winner-take-all primary was unconstitutional. The court of appeals ruled that the case was not a political question and on the merits held for the California plaintiffs and against the Illinois plaintiffs.

The Supreme Court stayed the court of appeals decision. The Court cited *Luther v. Borden* and stated: "In light of the availability of the convention as a forum to review the recommendations of the Credentials Committee, in which process the complaining parties might obtain the relief they have sought from the federal courts, the lack of precedent to support the extraordinary relief granted by the Court of Appeals, and the large public interest in allowing the political process to function free from judicial supervision, we conclude the judgment of the Court of Appeals must be stayed."[65]

[62] *Id.* at 751.

[63] *See, e.g.*, Terry v. Adams, 345 U.S. 461 (1953); Smith v. Allwright, 321 U.S. 649 (1944) (discrimination against blacks in political parties).

[64] 409 U.S. 1 (1972).

[65] *Id.* at 5.

Subsequently, in *Cousins v. Wigoda*, the Court held that a state court should not interfere with the selection of delegates to a national political convention.[66] The Court did not expressly base its decision on the political question doctrine, but instead on the right of political association infringed by state oversight of the delegate selection process.

§2.6.4 Foreign Policy

The Supreme Court frequently has held that cases presenting issues related to the conduct of foreign affairs pose political questions.[67] In *Oetjen v. Central Leather Co.*, in 1918, the Court declared: "The conduct of the foreign relations of our Government is committed by the Constitution to the Executive and Legislature 'the political' Departments of the Government, and the propriety of what may be done in the exercise of this political power is not subject to judicial inquiry or decision."[68]

Yet the Court also has emphasized that "it is error to suppose that every case or controversy which touches foreign relations lies beyond judicial cognizance."[69] For example, the Court has upheld, on the merits, the constitutionality of the president's use of executive agreements instead of treaties to implement major foreign policy agreements.[70] Also, the Court has ruled in favor of the constitutionality of the use of the treaty power for specific subject matters.[71]

In *Zivotofsky v. Clinton*, the Court ruled that it was not a political question and the judiciary could rule on the constitutionality of a federal law that allows American parents who have a child born in Jerusalem to have the passport indicate Israel as the country of birth.[72] Since the establishment of Israel in 1948, American presidents have taken a position of neutrality over which sovereign controls Jerusalem.

In 2002, Congress passed a bill with a section titled, "United States Policy with Respect to Jerusalem as the Capital of Israel." Among other things, the section directed the State Department to record "Israel" as the place of birth on a passport of a citizen born in Jerusalem, if the parents or guardians of a U.S. citizen born in Jerusalem so requested. President Bush signed the bill into law, but issued a

[66] 419 U.S. 477 (1975). For a discussion of judicial review of the nominating process, *see, e.g.*, Ronald Rotunda, Constitutional and Statutory Restrictions on Political Parties in the Wake of Cousins v. Wigoda, 53 Tex. L. Rev. 935 (1975).

[67] For a defense of this use of the political question doctrine, *see* Theodore Blumoff, Judicial Review, Foreign Affairs, and Legislative Standing, 25 Ga. L. Rev. 227 (1991).

[68] 246 U.S. 297, 302 (1918). *See also* Chicago & S. Air Lines v. Waterman S.S. Corp., 333 U.S. 103, 111 (1948).

[69] Baker v. Carr, 369 U.S. at 211.

[70] *See, e.g.*, Dames & Moore v. Regan, 453 U.S. 654 (1981); United States v. Pink, 315 U.S. 203, 229 (1942); United States v. Belmont, 301 U.S. 324, 330 (1937).

[71] *See, e.g.*, Missouri v. Holland, 252 U.S. 416, 433 (1920) (approving the constitutionality of a treaty with Great Britain concerning migratory birds).

[72] 566 U.S. 189 (2012).

signing statement expressing the view that this was an unconstitutional encroachment on presidential power. The Obama administration took the same position.

Menachem Zivotofsky was born in 2002 in Jerusalem to parents who are United States citizens. Zivotofsky's mother applied for a United States passport, listing his place of birth as "Jerusalem, Israel." A lawsuit was brought on Zivotofsky's behalf, but the lower courts ordered it dismissed as a political question. The Supreme Court reversed. In an opinion by Chief Justice Roberts, the Court said that the matter was justiciable, even though it involved foreign policy. The Court explained: "Resolution of Zivotofsky's claim demands careful examination of the textual, structural, and historical evidence put forward by the parties regarding the nature of the statute and of the passport and recognition powers. This is what courts do. The political question doctrine poses no bar to judicial review of this case."[73]

Thus, it is difficult to identify any principle that determines which foreign policy issues are justiciable and which present political questions. The most that can be done is to describe the areas where the political question doctrine has been applied in the realm of foreign affairs.

Areas of Foreign Policy that Pose a Political Question

First, the Supreme Court has held that the determination of when war begins or when a war ends is left to the political branches of government. In *Commercial Trust Co. v. Miller*, the question presented was whether a congressional declaration that World War I had ended prevented application of the Trading with the Enemy Act.[74] In 1921, Congress, with the approval of the president, passed a joint resolution ending the war with Germany and proclaiming peace. Subsequently, the Alien Property Custodian attempted to invoke the Trading with the Enemy Act. The issue was whether the congressional proclamation suspended the application of the act. The Court stated that the power to decide when a war ends is vested exclusively in Congress.[75] Quite similarly, the Court has held that the political branches decide when hostilities begin, and hence when it is appropriate to call up the militia.[76]

Second, the Supreme Court has held that the recognition of foreign governments is a political question,[77] as are related questions concerning disputes about

[73] *Id.* at 201. On remand, the D.C. Circuit declared the federal law unconstitutional as infringing separation of powers and the Supreme Court, in a 5-4 decision, affirmed. Zivotofsky v. Kerry, 576 U.S. 1 (2015). (Because the power to recognize foreign states resides in the president alone, §214(d) of the Foreign Relations Authorization Act of 2003—which directs the secretary of state, upon request, to designate "Israel" as the place of birth on the passport of a U.S. citizen who is born in Jerusalem—infringes on the executive's consistent decision to withhold recognition with respect to Jerusalem.)

[74] 262 U.S. 51 (1923).

[75] *Id.* at 57.

[76] *See, e.g.,* Martin v. Mott, 25 U.S. (12 Wheat.) 19, 30 (1827).

[77] *See, e.g.,* United States v. Belmont, 301 U.S. 324, 330 (1937) (Court confirmed president's power to recognize and assume diplomatic relations with the Soviet Union); Oetjen v. Central Leather Co., 246 U.S. 297 (1918). The Court also has held that the recognition of Indian tribes is left to the political process. *See, e.g.,* United States v. Sandoval, 231 U.S. 28, 45-46 (1913).

the diplomatic status of individuals claiming immunity.[78] In other words, issues concerning who represents a foreign state, and in what capacity, are not justiciable.

Third, the Supreme Court has held that many issues concerning the ratification and interpretation of treaties pose political questions. For example, in *Terlinden v. Ames*, the Court held that it is a political question whether a treaty survives when one country becomes part of another.[79] Subsequently, a plurality of the Court held that a challenge to President Carter's rescission of the U.S. treaty with Taiwan posed a nonjusticiable political question. In *Goldwater v. Carter*, Senator Barry Goldwater argued that rescission of a treaty required approval of two-thirds of the Senate.[80] Senator Goldwater contended that just as the president cannot unilaterally repeal a law, neither is it constitutional for the president to rescind a treaty without the Senate's consent. Justice Rehnquist, writing for a plurality of four justices, said that the case posed a political question. The plurality said that there were no standards in the Constitution governing rescission of treaties and that the matter was a "dispute between coequal branches of our Government, each of which has resources available to protect and assert its interests."[81]

Fourth, federal courts frequently have declared challenges to the president's use of the war powers to constitute a political question. During the Vietnam War, several dozen cases were filed in the federal courts arguing that the war was unconstitutional because there was no congressional declaration of war. Although the Supreme Court did not rule in any of these cases, either as to justiciability or on the merits, most of the lower courts deemed the challenges to the war to constitute a political question.[82] In the same way, lower federal courts dismissed challenges to the constitutionality of the president's military activities in El Salvador as posing a political question.[83] Similarly, lower courts dismissed challenges to American involvement in the Persian Gulf War.[84] Subsequently, a federal court of appeals

[78] *See, e.g.*, In re Baiz, 135 U.S. 403 (1890).

[79] 184 U.S. 270 (1902).

[80] 444 U.S. 996 (1979).

[81] *Id.* at 1004. Justice Powell concurred in the result, arguing that the matter was not yet ripe because Congress had not taken a position on the issue. *Id.* at 997 (Powell, J., concurring in the judgment).

[82] *See, e.g.*, Holtzman v. Schlesinger, 484 F.2d 1307, 1309 (3d Cir.), *cert. denied*, 416 U.S. 936 (1973); DaCasta v. Laird, 471 F.2d 1146, 1147 (2d Cir. 1973); Sarnoff v. Connally, 457 F.2d 809, 810 (9th Cir. 1972), *cert. denied*, 409 U.S. 929 (1972); Orlando v. Laird, 443 F.2d 1039, 1043 (2d Cir.), *cert. denied*, 404 U.S. 869 (1971); Simmons v. United States, 406 F.2d 456, 460 (5th Cir.), *cert. denied*, 395 U.S. 982 (1969); *see also* Anthony D'Amato & Robert O'Neil, The Judiciary and Vietnam 51-58 (1972) (description of cases concerning the Vietnam War as a political question); Louis Henkin, Vietnam in the Courts of the United States: Political Questions, 63 Am. J. Intl. L. 284 (1969).

[83] *See, e.g.*, Crockett v. Reagan, 720 F.2d 1355 (D.C. Cir. 1983), *cert. denied*, 467 U.S. 1251 (1984); Sanchez-Espinoza v. Reagan, 770 F.2d 202 (D.C. Cir. 1985); Lowry v. Reagan, 676 F. Supp. 333 (D.D.C. 1987); *but cf.* Ramirez de Arellano v. Weinberger, 745 F.2d 1500 (D.C. Cir. 1984) (holding justiciable a claim by a U.S. citizen that the federal government had taken his property in Honduras for the purpose of using it as a military training site; no challenge to the legality of the military activities was present).

[84] *See, e.g.*, Ange v. Bush, 752 F. Supp. 509 (D.D.C. 1990).

dismissed a challenge to the constitutionality of the war in Iraq as posing a nonjusticiable political question.[85]

Should Foreign Policy Issues Be a Political Question?

The application of the political question doctrine to foreign policy is extremely controversial.[86] Some contend that it is appropriate for the judiciary to stay out of foreign policy because of the greater knowledge and expertise of the president and Congress in this area. The Supreme Court once stated: "[T]he very nature of executive decisions as to foreign policy is political, not judicial. Such decisions . . . are delicate, complex, and involve large elements of prophecy. . . . They are decisions of a kind for which the Judiciary has neither aptitude, facilities nor responsibility."[87] Furthermore, it is argued that the federal courts are particularly poorly suited to evaluating the constitutionality of a war and enforcing an order halting hostilities.

Yet critics of the political question doctrine argue that constitutional questions concerning foreign affairs should be adjudicated.[88] They contend that in many cases the constitutional questions do not depend on expert information. For example, deciding what constitutes a declaration of war is an interpretive question similar to others confronted by the Supreme Court. In instances that involve expertise, the Court can hear the case and defer to the other branches of government on the merits; there is no need to deem such matters to be nonjusticiable.

Critics of the political question doctrine argue that the constitutional provisions governing foreign policy are rendered essentially meaningless without judicial enforcement. Although in some instances the other branches of government might try to uphold the Constitution even in the absence of judicial review, at times this is likely impossible. For example, in *Goldwater v. Carter*, the plaintiffs contended that rescission of a treaty required approval of two-thirds of the Senate; that is, one-third of the senators should be able to block rescission.[89] Yet there is no way that one-third of the senators can have a voice or can enforce their position—even if it is impeccably correct constitutional law—without judicial review.

Because precedents concerning judicial review of constitutional issues pertaining to foreign affairs are conflicting and very controversial, it is inevitable that in the future the Court will need to decide again whether and when challenges to the conduct of foreign policy pose a political question.

[85] Doe v. Bush, 322 F.3d 109 (1st Cir. 2003).

[86] *See, e.g.*, Anne-Marie Slaughter Burley, Are Foreign Affairs Different?, 106 Harv. L. Rev. 1980 (1993); Thomas M. Franck, Political Questions/Judicial Answers: Does the Rule of Law Apply to Foreign Affairs? (1992).

[87] Chicago & S. Air Lines v. Waterman S.S. Corp., 333 U.S. 103, 111 (1948).

[88] *See, e.g.*, Redish, *supra* note 2, at 1052; Michael Tigar, Judicial Power, the Political Question Doctrine, and Foreign Relations, 17 UCLA L. Rev. 1135, 1141-1151 (1970).

[89] 444 U.S. 996 (1979).

§2.6.5 *Congressional Self-Governance*

On several occasions, the Court has considered whether the political question doctrine prevents federal court review of congressional decisions concerning its processes and members. Often, though certainly not always, the Court has held that the federal judiciary should not review congressional judgments pertaining to its internal governance.

For example, in *Field v. Clark*, the Court dismissed a claim that a section of a bill passed by Congress was omitted from the final version of the law authenticated by the speaker of the house and the vice president and signed by the president.[90] The Court emphasized that judicial review was unnecessary because Congress could protect its own interests by adopting additional legislation.

A key case rejecting the application of the political question doctrine to judicial review of internal congressional decisions is *Powell v. McCormack*.[91] In 1967, the House of Representatives refused to seat representative Adam Clayton Powell, even though he had been elected by his constituents. A House subcommittee found that Powell had deceived Congress by presenting false travel vouchers for reimbursements and had made illegal payments to his wife with government funds. Powell and thirteen of his constituents sued, arguing that the refusal to seat him was unconstitutional because he was properly elected and met all of the requirements stated in the Constitution for service as a representative. Although he was not seated at all during that term of Congress, he was reelected in 1968, and he was seated in 1969. Nonetheless, the Supreme Court held that his suit was not moot, because his claim for back pay for the time in which he was not seated remained a live controversy.

The Constitution specifically provides, in Article I, §5, that each house of Congress may, by a vote of two-thirds of its members, expel a member. However, the Court noted that the issue in *Powell v. McCormack* was not expulsion; he was excluded, not expelled.[92]

The defendants argued that the case posed a political question because the text of the Constitution in Article I, §5, provides that each house of Congress shall "be the Judge of the Qualifications of its Members." But the Court held that the House of Representatives had discretion only to determine if a member met the qualifications stated in Article I, §2—requirements of age, citizenship, and residence.[93] In declaring that the case was justiciable and did not pose a political question, the Court stressed the importance of allowing people to select their legislators. The Court "concluded that Art. 1, §5, is at most a 'textually demonstrable

[90] 143 U.S. 649 (1892).

[91] 395 U.S. 486 (1969).

[92] *Id.* at 506-512.

[93] The Court relied on *Powell* to declare unconstitutional a state law that limited access to the ballot for candidates for the U.S. House of Representatives or the U.S. Senate after they had served a specified number of terms. United States Term Limits v. Thornton, 514 U.S. 779 (1995). The Court again emphasized that Article I set the only permissible qualifications for a member of Congress.

commitment' to Congress to judge only the qualifications expressly set forth in the Constitution."[94]

The defendants urged the Court to dismiss the case rather than interfere with or risk conflict with another branch of government. The Court rejected that such considerations should influence its ruling. The Court stated: "Our system of government requires that federal courts on occasion interpret the Constitution in a manner at variance with the construction given the document by another branch. The alleged conflict that such an adjudication may cause cannot justify the courts' avoiding their constitutional responsibility."[95]

In *Roudebush v. Hartke,* the Court held that Article I's provision making the Senate the "judge of the elections . . . of its members" did not preclude the state from ordering a recount in a senatorial election.[96] But the Court did state that the determination of which "candidate is entitled to be seated in the Senate [poses] a non-justiciable political question."[97]

In *United States v. Munoz-Flores,* the Court refused to apply the political question doctrine to bar a challenge to a federal assessment as violating the origination clause of the Constitution, which provides that "[a]ll bills for raising revenue shall originate in the House of Representatives."[98] A federal statute required that courts collect a monetary assessment on any person convicted of a federal misdemeanor. The challenger argued that this was unconstitutional because the bill for the assessments arose in the Senate and not the House. The Court brushed aside concerns about the need for deference to Congress and the ability of the House of Representatives to protect its own interests. Justice Thurgood Marshall, writing for the Court, explained: "To be sure, the courts must develop standards for making the revenue and origination determinations, but the Government suggests no reason that developing such standards will be more difficult in this context than any other."[99]

The underlying normative question again is whether these decisions invoking the political question doctrine are proper deference to a coordinate branch of government or whether they are unjustified judicial abdication. From one view, the federal courts appropriately have refused to become involved in internal legislative matters. But from a different perspective, the courts have unjustifiably failed to enforce constitutional provisions and have eliminated an important check on Congress.

§2.6.6 The Process for Ratifying Constitutional Amendments

Article V of the Constitution prescribes the manner for amending the U.S. Constitution. When, if at all, should federal courts hear suits contending that

[94] 395 U.S. at 548.
[95] *Id.* at 549.
[96] 405 U.S. 15, 19 n.6 (1972) (citations omitted).
[97] *Id.* at 19.
[98] 495 U.S. 385 (1990).
[99] *Id.* at 395-396.

the process was improperly followed? Some scholars, such as Professor Laurence Tribe, argue that the courts generally should not become involved in the only mechanism that exists to directly overturn the judiciary's interpretation of the U.S. Constitution.[100] But others, such as Professor Walter Dellinger, contend that the federal courts must ensure that the proper procedures are followed in amending the Constitution.[101] The argument is that the very safeguards that protect the Constitution from easy alteration are rendered impotent if the political process is allowed to disregard Article V.

Nor is it fanciful to imagine that Congress might violate the procedures for ratifying amendments, as the history of the adoption of the Fourteenth Amendment demonstrates.[102] After the Civil War, Congress adopted the Fourteenth Amendment, but it was quickly rejected by enough southern and border states to prevent its passage. Congress, furious at what it perceived as an attempt to undo the outcome of the Civil War, enacted the Reconstruction Act, which provided, in part, for military rule of the rebel states and denied those states readmission into the Union until they had ratified the Fourteenth Amendment. After the southern states ratified the amendment, two other states that had previously approved it rescinded their ratification. Nonetheless, the Fourteenth Amendment was deemed adopted by counting all of the southern states that were coerced into ratifying it and including the two states that rescinded their earlier approval.

Inconsistency Among the Cases

The Supreme Court has not been consistent in deciding whether the process of ratifying amendments is a nonjusticiable political question. In some instances, the Court has allowed judicial review. In 1798, in *Hollingsworth v. Virginia*, the Court held that the president may not veto amendments passed by Congress.[103] The Court concluded that the veto power contained in Article I, §7, was confined to statutes and did not include amendments. In a case involving the ratification of the Nineteenth Amendment, *Leser v. Garnett*, the Court held that a state's certification that it had ratified an amendment was sufficient to allow it to be counted as having approved the proposed constitutional change.[104] In *Dillon v. Gloss*, the Court upheld the constitutionality of Congress's creating time limits for the ratification of amendments.[105]

Yet, on other occasions, the Court has indicated that the process of ratifying amendments poses a nonjusticiable political question. In *Coleman v. Miller*, a plurality of the Court declared that Congress has "sole and complete control

[100] *See, e.g.*, Laurence Tribe, Constitutional Choices 22-23 (1985).

[101] Walter Dellinger, The Legitimacy of Constitutional Change: Rethinking the Amendment Process, 97 Harv. L. Rev. 386 (1983).

[102] The history of the ratification of the Fourteenth Amendment is described in Coleman v. Miller, 307 U.S. 433 (1939).

[103] 3 U.S. (3 Dal.) 378, 382 (1798).

[104] 258 U.S. 130 (1922).

[105] 256 U.S. 368 (1921).

over the amending process, subject to no judicial review."[106] The issue in *Coleman* was whether the time period for ratifying an amendment had expired. In 1924, Congress passed a proposed amendment to prohibit the use of child labor. In 1925, the Kansas legislature rejected the proposal, but in 1937, it was approved by that state's legislature. Kansas legislators who opposed the amendment sued, arguing that the time period for ratification had lapsed and that the earlier rejection was controlling.

The Supreme Court denied review. A plurality opinion written by Justice Black stated that the process of amending the Constitution is a "political question . . . Article V . . . grants power over the amending of the Constitution to Congress alone. . . . The process itself is political in its entirety, from submission until an amendment becomes part of the Constitution, and is not subject to judicial guidance, control or interference at any point."[107]

An issue similar to that raised in *Coleman* was presented to the federal courts in *State of Idaho v. Freeman*.[108] Idaho ratified the proposed Equal Rights Amendment, but then rescinded its ratification. The plaintiffs filed suit arguing that the rescission was effective. Also, the plaintiffs contended that Congress had unconstitutionally extended the time period for ratification. The Amendment, as proposed, contained a seven-year time limit for ratification. At the expiration of this time period, Congress extended the limit by three years. The plaintiffs in *Idaho v. Freeman* argued that it was impermissible for Congress to approve the extension by majority vote; they argued that the Constitution requires a two-thirds vote of both houses of Congress to propose amendments.

The federal district court found that the case was justiciable and did not pose a political question. The court said that "the courts, as a neutral third party, and having the responsibility of guardian of the Constitution" should decide the issues presented.[109] On the merits, the court ruled that the extension of time for the ratification of the amendment was unconstitutional. Before appellate review of the district court's decision was completed, the three-year extension for the ratification of the Equal Rights Amendment expired without ratification by three-fourths of the states. Accordingly, the Supreme Court vacated the district court's decision and ordered the case dismissed on mootness grounds.[110]

In January 2020, Virginia became the 38th state to ratify the Equal Rights Amendment. Many issues arise: Is this sufficient to make the Twenty-Eighth Amendment part of the Constitution, or must Congress pass a resolution deeming it to be properly ratified? May the federal courts decide this question? If Congress passes such a resolution, is its constitutionality reviewable in the federal courts? What, if any, is the effect of the time period for ratification set out in the resolution accompanying the amendment and the earlier effort to extend it? What is the

[106] 307 U.S. 433, 459 (Black, J., concurring).
[107] *Id.* at 457-459.
[108] 529 F. Supp. 1107 (D. Idaho 1981), *vacated*, 459 U.S. 809 (1982).
[109] 529 F. Supp. at 1135 (citations omitted).
[110] 459 U.S. 809 (1982).

effect of states that rescinded their ratification? And most important, is it for the federal courts to decide these issues or for Congress?

The Proposed Balanced Budget Amendment

The reviewability of the process for ratifying amendments might soon come to the federal courts in connection with the proposed constitutional amendment to require a balanced federal budget. Article V of the Constitution provides a mechanism for amending the Constitution that never has been employed. If two-thirds of the states call for a constitutional convention, Congress shall call one into existence. The convention's proposals become amendments if approved by three-quarters of the states. There have been instances in which thirty-two states, two short of the necessary two-thirds, have called for a convention.[111]

A plethora of novel legal questions might arise if states call for such a convention.[112] For example, what if Congress does not call a convention into existence? Can the federal judiciary compel congressional action? Is the convention limited to considering the topic of a balanced budget, or is it free to propose amendments on any topic? If these problems arise, undoubtedly lawsuits will be filed asking for a judicial resolution, and the courts will need to decide whether the questions are justiciable. Perhaps *Coleman v. Miller* will be interpreted to preclude judicial review. On the other hand, because the convention process is meant to provide a way for states to initiate amendments when Congress does not act, the courts might be reluctant to allow Congress the final say as to the existence and nature of the convention process.[113] Also, the need for complete judicial restraint is lessened when the amendment does not seek to overturn a Supreme Court decision.

§2.6.7 *Excessive Interference with Coordinate Branches of Government*

Limiting Judicial Oversight and Intrusion

In many areas, the political question doctrine is intended to limit judicial oversight and control of the other branches of the federal government. For example, the Supreme Court's treatment of many aspects of foreign policy as political questions reflects a desire to avoid judicial intrusion into the domain of the other branches.

[111] *See* Dwight Connely, Amending the Constitution: Is This Any Way to Call for a Constitutional Convention?, 22 Ariz. L. Rev. 1011 (1980) (describing state resolutions for a constitutional convention to propose amendments prohibiting child labor and limiting judicial reapportionment).

[112] *See, e.g.*, Laurence Tribe, Issues Raised by Requesting Congress to Call a Constitutional Convention to Propose a Balanced Budget Amendment, 10 Pac. L.J. 627 (1979); *see also* Comment, A Constitutional Convention: Scouting Article Five's Undiscovered Country, 134 U. Pa. L. Rev. 939 (1986).

[113] Tribe, *supra* note 112, at 632-640.

In *Gilligan v. Morgan*, the Supreme Court deemed not justiciable a lawsuit claiming that the government was negligent in failing to adequately train the Ohio National Guard.[114] Students at Kent State University initiated the suit after the shooting of four students during an anti-Vietnam War protest on May 4, 1970. The plaintiffs contended that grossly inadequate training of the Guard was responsible for the unjustified use of lethal force and sought injunctive and declaratory relief.

The Supreme Court, in an opinion by Chief Justice Burger, dismissed the case as posing a political question. The Court said that allowing review "would plainly and explicitly require a judicial evaluation of a wide range of possibly dissimilar procedures and policies approved by different law enforcement agencies or other authorities. . . . It would be inappropriate for a district judge to undertake this responsibility, in the unlikely event that he possessed the requisite technical competence to do so."[115] The Court emphasized that relief would require ongoing supervision and control of the activities of the Ohio National Guard.

Lower courts have continued to find that there is a political question when there is a challenge to the exercise of executive discretion. For instance, in *United States v. Mandel*, the Ninth Circuit concluded that the decision of the secretary of interior to place an item on the commodity control list is not judicially reviewable.[116] The court of appeals explained that "[t]hese are quintessentially matters of policy entrusted by the Constitution to the Congress and the President, for which there are not meaningful standards of judicial review."[117]

A number of lower court cases, however, have refused to apply the political question doctrine on this basis. For example, in *Nation Magazine v. United States Department of Defense*, a federal district court found that the political question doctrine did not bar review of the method for issuing credentials to the press during the Persian Gulf War.[118]

The Supreme Court's use of the political question doctrine to deny review has been criticized.[119] For example, it is unclear why reviewing training of the Guard and requiring standards for improved training would be more intrusive than has been judicial review of school board or prison actions. Also, it is argued that the use of the political question doctrine was unnecessary—that courts always have had the power to deny equitable relief when supervision and enforcement of the equitable decree would be too difficult.[120]

[114] 413 U.S. 1 (1973).
[115] *Id.* at 8.
[116] 914 F.2d 1215 (9th Cir. 1990).
[117] *Id.* at 1223.
[118] 762 F. Supp. 1558 (S.D.N.Y. 1991).
[119] Redish, *supra* note 2, at 1055.
[120] *Id.* at 1055-1056.

§2.6.8 Impeachment and Removal From Office

Nixon v. United States

In 1993, the Court extended the use of the political question doctrine and resolved a previously undecided issue by holding that challenges to the impeachment process are nonjusticiable. *Nixon v. United States* involved federal district court judge Walter Nixon, who had been convicted of making false statements to a grand jury.[121] Judge Nixon refused to resign from the bench and continued to collect his judicial salary while in prison. The House of Representatives adopted articles of impeachment. The Senate, in accord with its rules, created a committee to hold a hearing and make a recommendation to the full Senate. The Committee recommended removal from office, and the entire Senate voted accordingly.

Nixon argued, however, that the Senate's procedure violated Article I, §3, of the Constitution, which provides that the "Senate shall have the sole Power to try all Impeachments." Nixon maintained that this meant that the entire Senate had to sit and hear the evidence; he contended that the use of a committee to hear testimony and make a recommendation was unconstitutional.

Chief Justice Rehnquist, writing for the Court, held that the language and structure of Article I, §3, demonstrate a textual commitment of impeachment to the Senate. The Court explained that the Framers intended that there would be two proceedings against office holders charged with wrongdoing: a judicial trial and legislative impeachment proceedings. Chief Justice Rehnquist noted that "[t]he Framers deliberately separated the two forums to avoid raising the specter of bias and to ensure independent judgments. . . . Certainly, judicial review of the Senate's trial would introduce the same risk of bias as would participation in the trial itself."[122]

Moreover, the Court stated that judicial review of impeachment would be inconsistent with the Framers' views of impeachment in the scheme of checks and balances. The Framers saw impeachment as the only legislative check on the judiciary; judicial involvement would undercut this independent check on judges.[123]

Nixon holds that the judiciary will not review the Senate's use of a committee to hold a hearing and make a recommendation on an impeachment. *Nixon* leaves open the question of whether all challenges to impeachment are nonjusticiable political questions. For example, what if the president were impeached and convicted for an act that was completely lawful and within his constitutional powers? Or what if the Senate declared the president to be convicted on the basis of a committee's determination or a vote of less than two-thirds of the senators? Although these events are certainly improbable, it also is unlikely that the Court would declare an impeachment unconstitutional in the absence of compelling circumstances.

[121] 506 U.S. 224 (1993).
[122] *Id.* at 234.
[123] *Id.* at 233-237.

Justice Souter, in an opinion concurring in the judgment, recognized the potential need for judicial review. He wrote: "If the Senate were to act in a manner seriously threatening the integrity of its results, convicting, say, upon a coin-toss, or upon a summary determination that an officer of the United States was simply a bad guy, judicial interference might well be appropriate."[124]

[124] *Id.* at 253 (Souter, J., concurring).

CHAPTER 3

Congressional Control of Federal and State Court Jurisdiction

§3.1 INTRODUCTION

What Is Congress's Power Over Federal Court Jurisdiction?

Article III of the Constitution defines the federal judicial power in terms of nine categories of "cases" and "controversies." To what extent, if at all, should Congress be able to add to or subtract from the federal courts' jurisdiction that is prescribed in Article III of the U.S. Constitution?

Phrased slightly differently, should Article III be viewed as the floor of federal jurisdiction, the ceiling of federal jurisdiction, both the floor and the ceiling, or neither the floor nor the ceiling? If Article III is the floor of federal jurisdiction, the minimum jurisdiction that must be vested in federal courts, then federal courts must be able to hear all of the matters described in Article III. Congress might add to this list, but cannot subtract from it. Alternatively, if Article III is the ceiling of federal jurisdiction, the maximum jurisdiction allowed, then Congress might remove matters from federal court authority but cannot add to it. If Article III is both the floor and the ceiling, then federal courts must be able to hear all matters outlined in Article III but no more; that is, Congress can neither add to nor subtract from federal jurisdiction under this view. Finally, if Article III is neither the floor nor the ceiling, then it is simply an initial allocation, and Congress may add to or subtract from federal jurisdiction as it deems appropriate.

This chapter discusses these issues concerning Congress's ability to control federal court jurisdiction. The question of congressional power to restrict federal court jurisdiction might arise in the particularly compelling and controversial circumstance of whether Congress may deny the federal courts the power to hear specific types of cases. For example, during the 1980s, there were proposals in Congress to prevent federal courts from hearing cases involving challenges to state laws permitting school prayers or state laws restricting access to abortions.[1] In the 1990s, there were significant restrictions on the authority of the federal courts to hear certain immigration matters.[2] Also, Congress enacted the Prison Litigation Reform Act of 1995, which limits the authority of federal courts to order systemic relief in prison condition cases, provides for the termination of injunctions issued by federal courts as remedies, and restricts the ability of federal courts to issue relief in prisoner cases.[3]

History of Attempts to Restrict Jurisdiction

Such proposals to restrict federal court jurisdiction over particular types of cases have been made at other times in American history. For example, during the 1950s, the Supreme Court invalidated some loyalty oaths for government workers and attorneys.[4] In response, the Jennings-Butler Bill was introduced in the U.S. Senate to prevent review of State Board of Bar Examiners' decisions concerning who could practice law in a state.[5] During the 1960s, jurisdictional stripping proposals were advanced in response to the Supreme Court's decision in *Miranda v. Arizona*, which held that confessions from criminal defendants would be admissible as evidence only if certain warnings were administered prior to interrogation.[6] A Senate proposal would have denied the Supreme Court or any lower federal court the authority "to review or to reverse, vacate, modify, or disturb in any way, a rule of any trial court of any State in any criminal prosecution admitting in evidence as voluntarily made an admission or confession of any accused."[7] Altogether,

§3.1 [1] *See, e.g.*, S. 158, 97th Cong., 1st Sess. (1981); H.R. 3225, 97th Cong., 1st Sess. (1981) (bills restricting federal court jurisdiction in abortion cases); S. 481, 97th Cong., 1st Sess. (1981); H.R. 4756, 97th Cong., 1st Sess. (1981) (bills restricting federal court jurisdiction over cases that involve voluntary school prayers).

[2] These restrictions are described below in text accompanying notes 56-63.

[3] Pub. L. No. 104-131, 110 Stat. 1321 (1996).

[4] *See, e.g.*, Schware v. Board of Bar Examiners, 353 U.S. 232 (1957); Konigsberg v. State Bar, 353 U.S. 252 (1957).

[5] S. 3386, 85th Cong., 2d Sess. (1958); *see also* Shelden D. Elliott, Court-Curbing Proposals in Congress, 33 Notre Dame L. Rev. 597 (1958).

[6] 384 U.S. 436 (1966).

[7] Gerald Gunther & Kathleen Sullivan, Constitutional Law 47 (20th ed. 2019).

between 1953 and 1968, more than sixty bills were introduced into Congress to restrict federal court jurisdiction over particular topics.[8]

In the 1990s, Congress enacted significant restrictions on federal court jurisdiction. For example, the Antiterrorism and Effective Death Penalty Act of 1996 limits the availability of federal habeas corpus relief, especially by precluding successive habeas corpus petitions without the express permission of the Court of Appeals.[9] As discussed below, in *Felker v. Turpin*, the Court upheld this provision's restriction on Supreme Court review of Court of Appeals decisions by concluding that there remained some opportunity for Supreme Court review: writs for habeas corpus filed directly in the Court.[10]

Additionally, the Antiterrorism and Effective Death Penalty Act,[11] the Illegal Immigration Reform and Immigrant Responsibility Act of 1996,[12] and the REAL ID Act of 2005[13] significantly restrict federal court jurisdiction over certain immigration matters.[14] The Antiterrorism and Effective Death Penalty Act greatly limits the ability of federal courts to review deportation orders. The act provides: "Any final order of deportation against an alien who is deportable by means of having committed a criminal offense [within the listed category] shall not be subject to review by any court."[15] Additionally, the act expressly deletes the prior provision in federal law that permitted habeas corpus review of claims by aliens who were held in custody pursuant to deportation orders.[16] The law thus appears to foreclose all judicial review of deportation orders.[17]

Congress further restricted judicial review in the Illegal Immigration Reform and Immigrant Responsibility Act of 1996. This law repealed a longstanding provision that authorized judicial review in the circuit courts of appeals and guaranteed habeas corpus upon detention. Additionally, the act limits review of removal orders directed at aliens by declaring that "all questions of law and fact . . . arising from any action taken or proceeding brought to remove an alien from the United

[8] Richard Fallon, Jr. et al., Hart and Wechsler's The Federal Courts and the Federal System 377 (7th ed. 2015).

[9] Pub. L. No. 104-132, 110 Stat. 1214 (Apr. 24, 1996) (amended 1996, 1997).

[10] 518 U.S. 651 (1996), discussed below in text accompanying notes 25-31.

[11] Pub. L. No. 104-132, 110 Stat. 1214.

[12] Pub. L. No. 104-208, 110 Stat. 3009, amended Pub. L. No. 104-302, 110 Stat. 3656 (Oct. 11, 1996).

[13] Pub. L. No. 109-13, 119 Stat. 302 (2005).

[14] For a discussion of these provisions and their constitutionality, *see* Lenni B. Benson, Back to the Future: Congress Attacks the Right to Judicial Review of Immigration Proceedings, 29 Conn. L. Rev. 1411 (1997).

[15] Antiterrorism and Effective Death Penalty Act §440(a).

[16] Antiterrorism and Effective Death Penalty Act §401(e). The act also provides that an alien convicted of an aggravated felony is to be "conclusively presumed" to be deportable. A petition for review or for habeas corpus on behalf of such an alien may only challenge whether the alien is in fact an alien. §242A(c).

[17] Lower courts generally have upheld the constitutionality of the restrictions found in the Antiterrorism and Effective Death Penalty Act. *See, e.g.,* Mansour v. INS, 123 F.3d 423 (6th Cir. 1997); Yang v. INS, 109 F.3d 1185 (7th Cir. 1997), *cert. denied,* 522 U.S. 1027 (1997).

States under this title . . . shall be available only in judicial review of a final order."[18] The act also limits court review of discretionary decisions by the attorney general, stating that no court has jurisdiction to review such rulings by the attorney general as cancellation of removal,[19] voluntary departure,[20] or adjustment of status.[21]

Most dramatically, Congress enacted laws that restrict the ability of the federal courts to hear challenges brought by those detained as enemy combatants. The Detainee Treatment Act of 2005 precluded federal courts from hearing writs of habeas corpus brought by those detained by the Department of Defense at Guantánamo Bay, Cuba.[22] The only access to federal courts available to such individuals would be in review by the District of Columbia Circuit of decisions by Combatant Status Review Tribunals or military commissions.

In June 2006, in *Hamdan v. Rumsfeld*,[23] the Supreme Court held that the restrictions on habeas corpus applied only prospectively and did not preclude judicial decisions concerning habeas petitions that were pending at the time the Detainee Treatment Act was adopted. In response to *Hamdan*, Congress passed and President Bush signed the Military Commissions Act of 2006.[24] The act makes clear that the restrictions on habeas corpus apply retroactively. The act states: "No court, justice or judge shall have jurisdiction to hear or consider an application for a writ of habeas corpus filed by or on behalf of an alien detained by the United States who has been determined by the United States to have been properly detained as an enemy combatant or is awaiting such determination."[25] Moreover, the act provides that this amendment "shall apply to all cases, without exception, pending on or after the date of the enactment of this Act which relate to any aspect of the detention, transfer, treatment, trial or conditions of an alien detained by the United States since September 11, 2001."[26]

This restriction of jurisdiction raises profound constitutional questions, especially as to whether this is an impermissible suspension of the writ of habeas corpus in violation of Article I, §9, of the Constitution. In *Boumediene v. Bush*, the Supreme Court held that the preclusion of habeas corpus petitions by those held as enemy combatants in Guantánamo Bay, Cuba, was an unconstitutional suspension of the writ of habeas corpus.[27] The Court, with Justice Kennedy writing for the Court in a 5-4 decision, ruled that the Military Commission Act was a suspension of the writ of habeas corpus and that this was unconstitutional because Article I, §9, allows Congress to suspend the writ of habeas corpus only in times of "rebellion or

[18] §242. In INS v. St. Cyr, 533 U.S. 289 (2001), the Court held that Congress's power to preclude review of the legality of executive detentions is limited by the constitutional provision that prevents suspension of the writ of habeas corpus. *St. Cyr* is discussed below in §3.3, notes 63-65.

[19] §240(a).

[20] §240(b).

[21] §245.

[22] Pub. L. No. 109-148, 119 Stat. 2680 (2005).

[23] 548 U.S. 557 (2006).

[24] Pub. L. No. 109-366, 120 Stat. 2600 (2006).

[25] Section 7 of the Military Commissions Act.

[26] Section 7(b) of the Military Commissions Act.

[27] 553 U.S. 723 (2008).

invasion." Chief Justice Roberts dissented and argued that the alternative provided for in the act—military tribunals with review in the U.S. Court of Appeals for the District of Columbia—was an adequate substitute for habeas corpus so that there was not a suspension of the writ.[28] Justice Scalia wrote an impassioned dissent in which he accused the majority of endangering American citizens and said that the judiciary should stay out of the matter and leave it to the president and Congress.[29] *Boumediene* is discussed in more detail in Chapter 15, which focuses on habeas corpus.

Other proposals for restricting federal court jurisdiction have not been adopted. For example, in 2004, the House of Representatives passed bills to prevent federal courts, including the Supreme Court, from hearing constitutional challenges to the Pledge of Allegiance or to the federal Defense of Marriage Act. The bills would have precluded federal district courts from exercising original jurisdiction or the Supreme Court from exercising appellate jurisdiction. Neither bill passed the Senate.

Although historically jurisdiction stripping has been proposed primarily by conservatives, in recent years some liberals have argued for it as a way of checking a conservative Supreme Court.[30] President Biden's commission on Supreme Court reform discussed jurisdiction stripping in detail, though without making specific recommendations.[31]

Purpose of Jurisdiction Stripping

The obvious purpose of most jurisdiction stripping bills is to achieve a change in the substantive law by a procedural device. Opponents of the Supreme Court's decisions in controversial areas such as abortion, school prayer, loyalty oaths, and criminal procedure would prefer to overturn the rulings by enacting constitutional amendments. Although amendments have been proposed, especially to ban abortions and permit school prayers, they have not attracted sufficient strength in Congress to be forwarded to the states for possible ratification. Unable to directly overrule the Supreme Court, opponents of these decisions believe that they might achieve a substantive change in the law by limiting federal court jurisdiction. Without lower federal courts or the Supreme Court to protect particular rights,

[28] *Id.* at 801 (Roberts, C.J., dissenting).

[29] *Id.* at 827-828 (Scalia, dissenting) ("The game of bait-and-switch that today's opinion plays upon the Nation's Commander in Chief will make the war harder on us. It will almost certainly cause more Americans to be killed. That consequence would be tolerable if necessary to preserve a time-honored legal principle vital to our constitutional Republic. But it is this Court's blatant *abandonment* of such a principle that produces the decision today.").

[30] *See, e.g.*, Joseph Fishkin & William E. Forbath, The Anti-Oligarchy Constitution: Reconstructing the Economic Foundations of American Democracy 431 (2022) (calling jurisdiction stripping a "tactical move[]" Congress might deploy against a hostile Supreme Court).

[31] *See* Presidential Comm'n on the Sup. Ct. of the U.S., Final Report 159-69 (2021), https://www.whitehouse.gov/wp-content/uploads/2021/12/SCOTUS-Report-Final-12.8.21-1.pdf [https://perma.cc/3DA4-CMBK].

the litigation would be entirely in state courts with no review in the federal judicial system.

Proponents of jurisdictional restrictions are hopeful that state courts, especially without the prospect of federal judicial oversight, will be more sympathetic to their causes and thus be more likely than federal courts to sustain state laws regulating abortion or permitting school prayers. Thus, the goal of jurisdictional restrictions is the "de facto reversal, by means far less burdensome than those required of a constitutional amendment, of several highly controversial Supreme Court decisions dealing with matters such as abortion, school prayer, and busing."[32]

Constitutionality Uncertain

Although such proposals to limit federal court jurisdiction over particular topics have been advanced for decades, their constitutionality is uncertain. The scholarly literature is rich with articles arguing both sides of whether, and when, Congress may restrict federal court jurisdiction.[33] Distinct, though certainly interrelated, issues arise in analyzing Congress's power over the Supreme Court's jurisdiction and that of the lower federal courts.

Congress's authority to prevent Supreme Court review of cases involving topics such as abortion is based on the language of Article III, which provides that the "Supreme Court shall have appellate jurisdiction, both as to Law and Fact, with such Exceptions, and under such Regulations as the Congress shall make." Proponents of limits on Supreme Court jurisdiction contend that this provision authorizes congressional restriction and that such restrictions are an important check on the federal judicial power.[34] Critics argue that Congress cannot exercise its power to limit jurisdiction, any more than it can exercise any authority, in a manner that violates the Constitution. Opponents of jurisdiction stripping maintain that limiting review in particular controversial areas would unconstitutionally infringe constitutional rights and that, in effect, it would allow Congress to disregard the Constitution and permit state courts to ignore federal law.[35] Section 3.2 considers the constitutionality of such restrictions on Supreme Court jurisdiction.

[32] Laurence Tribe, Jurisdictional Gerrymandering: Zoning Disfavored Rights Out of the Federal Courts, 16 Harv. C.R.-C.L. L. Rev. 129, 129-130 (1981); *see also* Lawrence Sager, Foreword: Constitutional Limitations on Congress' Authority to Regulate the Jurisdiction of the Federal Courts, 95 Harv. L. Rev. 17, 69 (1981).

[33] Scholarship on the issue includes Mark Tushnet, Court Reform for Progressives: A Primer on Constitutional Considerations, 2024 Wis. L. Rev. 79, 85-89; Daniel Birk, The Common-Law Exceptions Clause: Congressional Control of Supreme Court Appellate Jurisdiction in Light of British Precedent, 63 Vill. L. Rev. 189 (2018); Tara Grove, The Exceptions Clause as a Structural Safeguard, 113 Colum. L. Rev. 929 (2013); Joseph Blocher, Amending the Exceptions Clause, 92 Minn. L. Rev. 971 (2008).

[34] *See, e.g.,* Michael Perry, The Constitution, the Courts, and Human Rights 134 (1982); Charles Black, Decision According to Law, 17-19, 37-39 (1981); Gerald Gunther, Congressional Power to Curtail Federal Court Jurisdiction: An Opinionated Guide to the Ongoing Debate, 36 Stan. L. Rev. 895, 917-922 (1984).

[35] *See, e.g.,* Tribe, *supra* note 32; Sager, *supra* note 32; Henry Hart, The Power of Congress to Limit the Jurisdiction of Federal Courts: An Exercise in Dialectic, 66 Harv. L. Rev. 1362 (1953).

§3.1 Introduction

Congress's authority to limit the jurisdiction of lower federal courts raises somewhat different questions. Under Article III of the Constitution, Congress has discretion as to whether to create any lower federal courts. Congress never has vested the full jurisdiction of Article III in the lower federal courts. In fact, on several occasions the Court has upheld statutory limits on lower federal court jurisdiction, concluding that because Congress has discretion whether to create lower federal courts, Congress also has discretion to define their jurisdiction.[36]

But opponents of jurisdictional restrictions argue that these instances are not precedent for congressional limits on the ability of federal courts to decide cases in specific controversial areas.[37] Also, a compelling problem arises when the restriction on federal court jurisdiction would mean the unavailability of any court, state or federal, to hear a case. Under such circumstances, there is an often-made argument that due process considerations require the existence of a federal court. The ability of Congress to restrict the jurisdiction of the lower federal courts is discussed in §3.3.

While these questions concern whether Article III creates the floor of federal court jurisdiction, a far less controversial issue is whether Congress can add to federal court jurisdiction. This topic is discussed in §3.4.

Finally, §3.5 concludes by considering a closely related question: May Congress compel state courts to hear federal law matters? Although not a question directly concerning federal jurisdiction, the issue is important in assessing the constitutionality of restrictions on federal court jurisdiction, because such laws leave state courts as the only possible judicial forum for federal claims. But must state courts even hear these matters? Moreover, the obligation of state courts to hear federal law matters raises important issues of federalism. The Court has made it clear that Congress cannot compel state legislative or administrative action.[38] In light of these cases, can Congress compel state courts to hear federal law matters?

Importance of Congress's Authority to Control Federal Jurisdiction

Although few jurisdictional restrictions have been adopted thus far in American history, the topic of congressional control of federal court jurisdiction is extremely important.[39] Doubts about the constitutionality of jurisdictional

[36] *See, e.g.,* Yakus v. United States, 321 U.S. 414 (1944); Lockerty v. Phillips, 319 U.S. 182 (1943); Sheldon v. Sill, 49 U.S. (8 How.) 441 (1850); discussed below in §3.3.

[37] *See generally* Akhil Amar, A Neo-Federalist View of Article III: Separating the Two Tiers of Federal Jurisdiction, 65 B.U. L. Rev. 205 (1985); Robert Clinton, A Mandatory View of Federal Court Jurisdiction: A Guided Quest for the Original Understanding of Article III, 132 U. Pa. L. Rev. 741 (1984); Theodore Eisenberg, Congressional Authority to Restrict Lower Federal Court Jurisdiction, 83 Yale L.J. 498 (1974); discussed below in §3.3.

[38] *See* Printz v. United States, 521 U.S. 898 (1997); New York v. United States, 505 U.S. 144 (1992).

[39] One such law is Title I of 1996 Antiterrorism and Effective Death Penalty Act, which precludes Supreme Court review, by appeal or certiorari, of any decision by circuit courts of appeals granting or denying authorization for a state prisoner to file a second or successive application for habeas corpus relief. In Felker v. Turpin, 518 U.S. 651 (1996), the Supreme Court unanimously upheld the constitutionality of this provision on the grounds that it did not foreclose all Supreme Court review; for example, the Court still could hear successive habeas petitions as part of its original jurisdiction. *Felker* is discussed in more detail below.

limitations partially account for Congress's failure to adopt such statutes.[40] The issue of jurisdiction restrictions also raises important questions concerning the role of the federal courts relative to Congress and the states. The scope of Congress's power to define federal court jurisdiction focuses attention on separation of powers and the allocation of power among the branches of the federal government. Proposals to restrict federal court jurisdiction additionally require analysis of the importance of assuring the availability of a federal court to decide constitutional cases. Is it appropriate to trust state courts to have the final word in major constitutional litigation?[41]

Court Has Jurisdiction to Decide Constitutionality

At the outset in discussing congressional control of federal court jurisdiction, it is necessary to note that the federal courts undoubtedly would have jurisdiction to decide the constitutionality of statutes denying federal courts the authority to hear particular types of cases. *Marbury v. Madison* long ago established the power of the federal judiciary to rule on the constitutionality of federal statutes.[42] This would include the authority to determine the constitutionality of statutes restricting jurisdiction. More subtly, courts always have been accorded jurisdiction to determine whether they have jurisdiction. *Marbury* establishes that federal courts may not apply an unconstitutional law to decide a case. Hence, the federal courts must decide whether a statute restricting jurisdiction is constitutional before it can be applied to deny review in a particular case.

While this chapter directly focuses on congressional power to control federal court jurisdiction, the relationship of Congress to the federal courts recurs in the topics considered throughout this volume. For example, Chapter 4 discusses Congress's authority to create courts with judges who do not have the life tenure or salary protections prescribed in Article III. Chapter 5 examines federal subject matter jurisdiction, focusing in detail on the current statutes defining federal court authority. Chapter 10 considers the Supreme Court's jurisdiction, including an examination of the statutes defining the circumstances and availability of Supreme Court review. Chapter 11 discusses several statutes that define the relationship of federal and state courts—specifically, the Anti-Injunction Act, the Tax

[40] Mark Tushnet, Legal Realism, Structural Review, and Prophecy, 8 U. Dayton L. Rev. 809, 813 (1983) (a "scholarly consensus that such restrictions are unconstitutional has been a political force [keeping] . . . Congress from enacting such legislation"); *see also* Curtis Bradley & Neil Siegel, Historical Gloss, Constitutional Conventions, and Judicial Separation of Powers, 105 Geo. L.J. 255 (2017) (constitutional concerns have been a basis for rejecting jurisdiction stripping proposals). Professor Tara Grove argues that the rejection of these proposals for jurisdiction stripping may reflect political realities more than constitutional judgments about Congress's powers. Tara Grove, Article III in the Political Branches, 90 Notre Dame L. Rev. 1835 (2015).

[41] In an excellent recent article, Daniel Epps and Alan Trammel argue that jurisdiction stripping generally will accomplish little and indeed often would be counter-productive to what its sponsors seek. Daniel Epps & Alan Trammel, The False Promise of Jurisdiction Stripping, 123 Colum. L. Rev. 2077 (2023).

[42] 5 U.S. (1 Cranch) 137, 178 (1803), discussed above in §1.3.

Injunction Act, the Johnson Act (which prevents federal court injunctions of state rate-making procedures), and the Civil Rights Removal Act. Also, in many other chapters, separation of powers issues are discussed in considering whether the federal courts should fashion federal common law rules (Chapter 6) or whether the federal courts should abstain and refuse to exercise jurisdiction granted by Congress (Chapters 12, 13, and 14). In short, the relationship between Congress and the federal courts is a recurring theme in the law of federal jurisdiction.

§3.2 CONGRESSIONAL RESTRICTION OF THE JURISDICTION OF THE U.S. SUPREME COURT

The Issue

The jurisdiction of the U.S. Supreme Court is discussed in detail in Chapter 10. The focus here is on a specific question: Can Congress prevent the Supreme Court from hearing cases on particular topics? For example, would it be constitutional for Congress to prevent the Supreme Court from hearing, by appeal, certiorari, or any other mechanism, cases involving challenges to state laws regulating abortions or permitting school prayers?[1]

Despite decades of heated debate in the scholarly literature, there is no consensus on the constitutionality of such restrictions on jurisdiction. Because Congress rarely has attempted such jurisdiction stripping—and never in a manner that has been interpreted as precluding *all* Supreme Court review—the question of constitutionality is uncertain. Each side in the debate claims support for its position from the text of the Constitution, from precedents, and from policy arguments about the most desirable interpretation of the Constitution. Each type of argument—from the text, precedents, and policy considerations—warrants examination.

Throughout this discussion, it is assumed that even if Supreme Court jurisdiction is limited, some court would remain available to hear the claim. The absence of any court, state or federal, undoubtedly would raise a serious due process issue.[2] Additionally, in certain circumstances it can be argued that there must be some federal court available to hear the case.[3] Constitutional issues arising from the

§3.2 [1] *See, e.g.*, S. 158, 97th Cong., 1st Sess. (1981); H.R. 3225, 97th Cong., 1st Sess. (1981) (bills restricting federal court jurisdiction in abortion cases); S. 481, 97th Cong., 1st Sess. (1981); H.R. 4756, 97th Cong., 1st Sess. (1981) (bills restricting federal court jurisdiction over cases that involve voluntary school prayers).

[2] *See, e.g.*, Oestereich v. Selective Serv. Local Bd. No. 11, 393 U.S. 233, 243 n.6 (1968) (Harlan, J., concurring).

[3] *See generally* Akhil Amar, A Neo-Federalist View of Article III: Separating the Two Tiers of Federal Jurisdiction, 65 B.U. L. Rev. 205 (1985); Theodore Eisenberg, Congressional Authority to Restrict Lower Federal Court Jurisdiction, 83 Yale L.J. 498 (1974); discussed below in §3.3.

absence of any court and from the preclusion of all federal judicial review are discussed in §3.3. For the sake of clarity, this section focuses solely on the question of congressional power to restrict Supreme Court jurisdiction and assumes that other judicial forums would remain open to hear the case even if the nation's highest court could not.

Dispute Over Meaning of Constitutional Text

As is true of many constitutional arguments, the debate over congressional restrictions of Supreme Court jurisdiction begins with a dispute over the meaning of the text of the Constitution. Those who believe that Congress can limit Supreme Court jurisdiction to hear particular matters point to the language of Article III, §2: "[T]he supreme Court shall have appellate Jurisdiction, both as to Law and Fact, with such Exceptions, and under such Regulations as the Congress shall make." The claim is that the unambiguous language of Article III authorizes Congress to create exceptions to the Supreme Court's jurisdiction and that such exceptions include the ability to preclude review of particular topics, such as abortion or school prayer cases.[4]

Supporters of jurisdiction stripping proposals bolster their textual argument by claiming that the Framers of the Constitution intended such congressional control as a check on the judiciary's power.[5] Evidence of this intent, it is argued, is found in the fact that the first Congress did not vest the Supreme Court with appellate jurisdiction over all of the types of cases and controversies enumerated in Article III. For example, under the Judiciary Act of 1789, the Supreme Court had authority only to review decisions of a state's highest court that ruled against a federal constitutional claim.[6] It was not until the twentieth century that the Supreme Court was accorded power to review decisions of a state court that ruled in favor of a constitutional right.[7]

Opponents of jurisdiction stripping proposals take a very different view of the language of Article III. Some argue that the term "exceptions" in Article III was intended to modify the word "fact."[8] The contention is that the Framers were concerned about the Supreme Court's ability to overturn fact-finding by lower courts, especially when done by juries. Hence, Congress was given the authority to control the manner in which the Supreme Court reviews questions of fact. Under this view, Congress could create an exception to the Supreme Court's jurisdiction for review

[4] *See, e.g.,* Gerald Gunther, Congressional Power to Curtail Federal Court Jurisdiction: An Opinionated Guide to the Ongoing Debate, 36 Stan. L. Rev. 895 (1984); Paul M. Bator, Congressional Power over the Jurisdiction of the Federal Courts, 27 Vill. L. Rev. 1030 (1982).

[5] *See, e.g.,* Herbert Wechsler, The Courts and the Constitution, 65 Colum. L. Rev. 1001, 1005-1006 (1965).

[6] Act of Sept. 24, 1789, 1 Stat. 73; *see* Peter W. Low & John Calvin Jeffries, Federal Courts and the Law of Federal-State Relations 173 (9th ed. 2018).

[7] Act of Dec. 23, 1914, 38 Stat. 790.

[8] *See* Raoul Berger, Congress v. The Supreme Court 285-296 (1969).

of matters of fact, but Congress could not eliminate the Court's appellate jurisdiction for issues of law.[9]

Alternatively, it is argued that even though Congress is given authority to limit Supreme Court jurisdiction under the text of Article III, this power—like all congressional powers—cannot be used in a manner that violates the Constitution. Opponents of jurisdiction restriction contend that congressional preclusion of Supreme Court review of particular topics would violate other parts of the Constitution.[10] This issue, whether and to what extent there are constraints on jurisdiction restrictions imposed by other constitutional provisions, is discussed below.

Precedents for Both Arguments: *Ex Parte McCardle*

In addition to textual arguments, each side invokes a Supreme Court precedent in support of its position. Advocates of proposals to limit Supreme Court jurisdiction point to *Ex parte McCardle*.[11] McCardle was a newspaper editor in Vicksburg, Mississippi, whom federal officials arrested for writing a series of newspaper articles that were highly critical of Reconstruction and especially of the military rule of the South following the Civil War.[12] McCardle filed a petition for a writ of habeas corpus pursuant to a statute adopted in 1867 that permitted federal courts to grant habeas corpus relief to anyone held in custody in violation of the Constitution or laws of the United States by either a state government or the federal government. Under the 1867 law, the Supreme Court was empowered to hear appeals from lower federal courts in habeas corpus cases. Before 1867, under the Judiciary Act of 1789, which was supplemented but not replaced by the 1867 law, federal courts could hear habeas petitions only of those who were held in federal custody.

McCardle contended that the Military Reconstruction Act was unconstitutional in that it provided for military trials for civilians. He also claimed that his prosecution violated specific Bill of Rights provisions, including the First, Fifth, and Sixth Amendments. The U.S. government argued that the federal courts lacked jurisdiction to grant habeas corpus to McCardle under the 1867 Act. The federal government read the 1867 statute, despite its language to the contrary, as providing federal court relief only for state prisoners. The Supreme Court rejected

[9] *But see* Gunther, *supra* note 4, at 901 (rejecting view that exceptions and regulations refers to matters of fact).

[10] *See, e.g.*, Leonard Ratner, Congressional Power over the Appellate Jurisdiction of the Supreme Court, 109 U. Pa. L. Rev. 157 (1960); Larry Sager, Foreword: Constitutional Limitations on Congress's Authority to Regulate the Jurisdiction of the Federal Courts, 95 Harv. L. Rev. 17 (1981); Laurence Tribe, Jurisdictional Gerrymandering: Zoning Disfavored Rights Out of the Federal Courts, 16 Harv. C.R.-C.L. L. Rev. 129 (1981).

[11] 74 U.S. (7 Wall.) 506 (1869). For an excellent discussion of this case, *see* William Van Alstyne, A Critical Guide to Ex parte McCardle, 15 Ariz. L. Rev. 229 (1973). For a contemporary debate over the meaning of *McCardle*, *see* Patchak v. Zinke, 583 U.S. 244 (2018) (Thomas, J., plurality opinion); and *id.* at 920-921 (Roberts, C.J., dissenting).

[12] Among other things, McCardle urged whites to boycott elections of officials for state constitutional conventions. He offered $1 for the name of each white person who voted, with the names to be published in his newspaper. *See* Van Alstyne, *supra* note 11, at 236 n.42.

this contention and set the case for argument on the merits of McCardle's claim that the Military Reconstruction Act and his prosecution were unconstitutional.[13]

On March 9, 1868, the Supreme Court held oral arguments on McCardle's constitutional claims. Three days later, on March 12, 1868, Congress adopted a rider to an inconsequential tax bill that repealed that part of the 1867 statute that authorized Supreme Court appellate review of writs of habeas corpus. Members of Congress stated that their purpose was to remove the McCardle case from the Supreme Court's docket and thus prevent the Court from potentially invalidating Reconstruction. Representative Wilson declared that the "amendment [repealing Supreme Court authority under the 1867 Act is] aimed at striking at a branch of the jurisdiction of the Supreme Court . . . thereby sweeping the [McCardle] case from the docket by taking away the jurisdiction of the Court."[14]

On March 25, 1868, President Andrew Johnson vetoed the attempted repeal of Supreme Court jurisdiction. It should be noted that this was five days before the Senate was scheduled to begin its impeachment trial of President Johnson and that the grounds for impeachment focused solely on his alleged obstruction of Reconstruction. President Johnson declared: "I cannot give my assent to a measure which proposes to deprive any person restrained of his or her liberty in violation of the Constitution . . . , from the right of appeal to the highest judicial authority known to our government."[15] Congress immediately overrode President Johnson's veto on March 27, 1868.

The Supreme Court then considered whether it had jurisdiction to hear McCardle's constitutional claims in light of the recently adopted statute denying it authority to hear appeals under the 1867 Act that was the basis for jurisdiction in McCardle's petition. The Court held that it could not decide McCardle's case because of Congress's authority to create exceptions and regulations to the Court's appellate jurisdiction.

Chief Justice Chase, writing for the Court, began by noting that the "first question necessarily is that of jurisdiction," and that the case had to be dismissed for want of jurisdiction if the 1868 Act repealed the Court's authority under the 1867 statute.[16] Chief Justice Chase then observed that although the Court's authority stems from the Constitution, it "is conferred 'with such exceptions and under such regulations as Congress shall make.'"[17] The Court concluded that the 1868 Act was an unmistakable exception to the Court's appellate jurisdiction, thus mandating the dismissal of McCardle's appeal. The Court stated: "The provision of the Act of 1867, affirming the appellate jurisdiction of this court in cases of habeas corpus

[13] Ex parte McCardle, 73 U.S. (6 Wall.) 318 (1867).

[14] *Quoted in* Van Alstyne, *supra* note 11, at 239.

[15] *Quoted id.* at 239-240.

[16] 74 U.S. at 512.

[17] *Id.* at 513. Although Supreme Court jurisdiction is self-executing, the Court always has acted as if Congress confers jurisdiction on it. In Durousseau v. United States, 10 U.S. (6 Cranch) 307, 314 (1810), the Court stated: "The appellate powers of this court are not given by the judicial act. They are given by the Constitution. But they are limited and regulated by the judicial act, and by such other acts as have been passed on the subject."

is expressly repealed. It is hardly possible to imagine a plainer instance of positive exception."[18] Accordingly, the Court dismissed the case for lack of jurisdiction.

Thus, supporters of contemporary proposals to restrict Supreme Court jurisdiction cite *McCardle* as precedent. They contend that *McCardle* establishes that Congress may prevent Supreme Court review of constitutional issues. The fact that Congress intends to change the substantive law by limiting jurisdiction is deemed irrelevant, for they quote the *McCardle* Court's statement that "[w]e are not at liberty to inquire into the motives of the legislature. We can only examine into its power under the Constitution; and the power to make exceptions to the appellate jurisdiction of this court is given by express words."[19]

Opponents of jurisdiction stripping proposals contend that *McCardle* is easily distinguished from contemporary attempts to prevent Supreme Court review of topics such as abortion and school prayer. In *McCardle*, even after the repeal of the 1867 act, the Supreme Court still had authority to hear McCardle's claims under the 1789 Judiciary Act, which allowed federal courts to grant writs of habeas corpus to federal prisoners. In other words, in *McCardle*, the Supreme Court was considering the constitutionality of a statute that did not completely preclude Supreme Court review, but rather only eliminated one of two bases for its authority. The *McCardle* Court expressly indicated that it still had jurisdiction in habeas corpus cases notwithstanding the repeal of the 1867 act. The Court, at the conclusion of its opinion, declared: "Counsel seem to have supposed, if effect be given to the repealing act in question, that the whole appellate power of the court, in cases of habeas corpus, is denied. But this is an error. The act of 1868 does not except from that jurisdiction any cases but appeals from Circuit Courts under the act of 1867. It does not affect the jurisdiction which was previously exercised."[20]

Ex parte Yerger

In fact, a year after its decision in *McCardle*, the Supreme Court in *Ex parte Yerger* held that it had authority to review habeas corpus decisions of lower federal courts under the Judiciary Act of 1789.[21] Like *McCardle*, *Yerger* involved a newspaper editor's challenge to the constitutionality of the Military Reconstruction Act. After the Supreme Court upheld its jurisdiction to decide Yerger's constitutional claims, the federal military authorities dismissed all charges against him, thereby again preventing Supreme Court review of the constitutionality of Reconstruction.[22]

In light of *Yerger*, opponents of jurisdiction restrictions claim that *McCardle* only establishes the limited proposition that if there are two statutory grounds for Supreme Court jurisdiction, Congress may repeal one of them. The Court in

[18] 74 U.S. at 514.

[19] *Id.*

[20] *Id.* at 515.

[21] 75 U.S. (8 Wall.) 85 (1869).

[22] It should be noted that Chief Justice Chase indicated privately that had the Court reached the merits of McCardle's constitutional claims, "the Court would doubtless have held that this imprisonment for trial before a military commission was illegal." Van Alstyne, *supra* note 11, at 238 n.46.

McCardle did not review McCardle's habeas petition under the authority of the 1789 Act because he had not pled that act as the basis for federal court jurisdiction and because the Court was anxious to avoid ruling on the constitutionality of Reconstruction.[23] Moreover, McCardle was not in danger since he had been released from prison and even had resumed writing articles criticizing Reconstruction. Simply put, the opponents of jurisdiction stripping contend that *McCardle* is not a precedent for proposals that would eliminate all Supreme Court review of cases involving topics such as abortion or school prayer.[24]

Felker v. Turpin

In fact, the Supreme Court relied on this rationale in upholding a federal law that precluded Supreme Court review of some habeas corpus petitions.[25] Title I of the 1996 Antiterrorism and Effective Death Penalty Act prohibits state prisoners from bringing successive habeas corpus petitions unless approval is received from the U.S. Court of Appeals.[26] The law precluded U.S. Supreme Court review, by appeal or certiorari, of any decision by a court of appeals granting or denying authorization for a state prisoner to file a successive habeas corpus petition.[27]

In *Felker v. Turpin*, the Supreme Court unanimously upheld the constitutionality of this jurisdictional restriction.[28] Chief Justice Rehnquist, writing for the Court, emphasized that the law did not preclude *all* Supreme Court review of petitions from individuals denied the ability to file successive ones; the law did not repeal the Court's authority to entertain original habeas petitions.[29] The Court explained: "But since it does not repeal our authority to entertain a petition for habeas corpus, there can be no plausible argument that the Act has deprived this Court of appellate jurisdiction in violation of Article III, §2."[30]

The Supreme Court, however, has not granted an original habeas petition since 1925. *Felker* seems to stand for the proposition that any continuing basis for Supreme Court review, no matter how unlikely, is sufficient to make a restriction on jurisdiction constitutional.[31]

[23] *Id.* at 245-246.

[24] Some members of the Supreme Court have indicated that "there is a serious question whether the McCardle case could command a majority view today." Glidden Co. v. Zdanok, 370 U.S. 530, 605 n.11 (1962) (Douglas, J., and Black, J., dissenting).

[25] Felker v. Turpin, 518 U.S. 651 (1996).

[26] Pub. L. No. 104-132, 110 Stat. 1217, §106(b).

[27] §106(b)(3)(E).

[28] 518 U.S. 651 (1996).

[29] *Id.* at 662.

[30] *Id.*

[31] In a concurring opinion, Justice Stevens suggested that there might be other ways for the Supreme Court to review court of appeals decisions, such as through writs other than certiorari pursuant to the All Writs Act §28, U.S.C. §1651. *Id.* at 666 (Stevens, J., concurring). Justice Stevens, however, gave no examples as to what these writs might be.

United States v. Klein

On the other hand, opponents of jurisdiction stripping contend that *United States v. Klein* supports their position that Congress cannot restrict Supreme Court appellate review in an effort to direct particular substantive results.[32] *Klein,* like *McCardle,* arose during Reconstruction. In 1863, Congress adopted a statute providing that individuals whose property was seized during the Civil War could recover the property, or compensation for it, upon proof that they had not offered aid or comfort to the enemy during the war. The Supreme Court subsequently held that a presidential pardon fulfilled the statutory requirement of demonstrating that an individual was not a supporter of the rebellion.[33]

In response to this decision and frequent pardons issued by the president, Congress quickly adopted a statute providing that a pardon was inadmissible as evidence in a claim for return of seized property. Moreover, the statute provided that a pardon, without an express disclaimer of guilt, was proof that the person aided the rebellion and would deny the federal courts jurisdiction over the claims. The statute declared that upon "proof of such pardon . . . the jurisdiction of the court in the case shall cease, and the court shall forthwith dismiss the suit of such claimant."[34]

The Supreme Court held that the statute was unconstitutional. While acknowledging Congress's power to create exceptions and regulations to the Court's appellate jurisdiction, the Supreme Court said that Congress cannot direct the results in particular cases. The Court stated:

> It seems to us that this is not an exercise of the acknowledged power of Congress to make exceptions and prescribe regulations to the appellate power. . . . What is this but to prescribe a rule for the decision of a cause in a particular way? . . . Can we do so without allowing one party to the controversy to decide it in its own favor? Can we do so without allowing that the legislature may prescribe rules of decision to the judicial department in the cases pending before it?. . .
>
> We think not. . . . We must think that Congress has inadvertently passed the limit which separates the legislative power from the judicial power.[35]

Thus, opponents of proposals to restrict Supreme Court jurisdiction argue that *Klein* establishes that Congress may not restrict Supreme Court jurisdiction in an attempt to dictate substantive outcomes. By analogy, it would be unconstitutional for Congress to restrict Supreme Court jurisdiction in an attempt to undermine the Court's protections in abortion and school prayer cases.

Supporters of jurisdiction restriction argue that *Klein* establishes only that Congress may not restrict Supreme Court jurisdiction in a manner that violates

[32] 80 U.S. (13 Wall.) 128 (1872).
[33] United States v. Padelford, 76 U.S. (9 Wall.) 531 (1869).
[34] 92 Stat. 2076.
[35] 80 U.S. at 146-147.

other constitutional provisions.[36] Prior to *Klein*, the federal courts had the power to return seized property or award compensation pursuant to a federal statute. Why, then, could not Congress amend the statute to provide that a certain class of citizens, those pardoned, were not entitled to recover under the law? The answer cannot be a simple statement that Congress cannot direct substantive outcomes because Congress always is entitled to amend statutes and thereby determine subsequent results. For example, after the Supreme Court held that federal employment discrimination statutes did not require an employer to provide disability coverage for pregnancy, Congress amended the law to state that employers could not treat pregnancy different from other conditions.[37] The effect of the amendment was to change substantive outcomes, as all such amendments of statutes have that effect.

What is the difference between the statute in *Klein* and the statute reversing the Supreme Court's interpretation of Title VII? Both statutes, after all, reversed a Supreme Court holding and thereby determined the results in future litigation. Two features distinguish *Klein*. First, in the statute at issue in *Klein*, Congress was redefining the president's pardon power. The statute was arguably unconstitutional as an infringement of the executive's power under Article II of the Constitution.[38] Second, it can be argued that the statute in *Klein* unconstitutionally deprived property without just compensation or due process. Under the previous law, those pardoned had a vested right to the return of their property that had been seized, but the denial of jurisdiction prevented the federal courts from vindicating their protected property interest. Hence, the statute was unconstitutional.

Thus, supporters of jurisdiction stripping argue that despite the Court's broad language in *Klein*, that decision does not support the general proposition that Congress may not restrict jurisdiction in order to direct substantive outcomes. Rather, it stands for the much more limited principle that Congress cannot limit the Supreme Court's jurisdiction in a manner that violates other constitutional provisions.

Robertson v. Seattle Audubon Society

In 1992, in *Robertson v. Seattle Audubon Society*, the Supreme Court unanimously rejected a claim that a federal law—the Department of Interior and Related Agencies Appropriations Act of 1990—was unconstitutional under *Klein*.[39] The act

[36] For an exchange on the meaning of *Klein*, *see* Lawrence Sager, *Klein*'s First Principle: A Proposed Solution, 86 Geo. L.J. 2525 (1998) (arguing that *Klein* limits the ability of Congress to prevent the Supreme Court from deciding constitutional issues); Daniel J. Meltzer, Congress, Courts, and Constitutional Remedies, 86 Geo. L.J. 2537 (1998) (disagreeing with Sager and arguing that *Klein* does not prevent Congress from determining enforcement of statutory rights). *See also* Martin H. Redish & Christopher R. Pudelski, Legislative Deception, Separation of Powers, and the Democratic Process: Harnessing the Political Theory of United States v. Klein, 100 Nw. U. L. Rev. 437 (2006).

[37] General Elec. Co. v. Gilbert, 429 U.S. 125 (1976); Pregnancy Discrimination Act, 42 U.S.C. §2000e(k) (1978).

[38] 80 U.S. at 147.

[39] 503 U.S. 429 (1992).

both required the Bureau of Land Management to offer specified land for sale and imposed restrictions on harvesting from other land. Additionally, the act expressly noted two pending cases and said that "Congress hereby determines and directs that management of areas according to subsections (b)(3) and (b)(5) of this section on [the specified lands] is adequate consideration for the purpose of meeting the statutory requirements that are the basis for [the two lawsuits]."[40]

The Ninth Circuit held that this provision was unconstitutional under *Klein* because Congress was directing the outcome of the pending litigation. The Supreme Court disagreed, concluding that Congress had changed the law itself and did not direct findings or results under the old law.[41] The Court read *Klein* as applying in a situation where Congress directs the judiciary as to decision-making under an existing law and not applying when Congress adopts a new law. By placing the act into the latter category, the Court found *Klein* distinguishable and rejected the constitutional challenge.[42]

Plaut v. Spenthrift Farm, Inc.

In *Plaut v. Spendthrift Farm, Inc.*, the Court declared unconstitutional a federal statute that overturned a Supreme Court decision dismissing certain cases.[43] In 1991, the Court ruled that actions brought under the securities laws, specifically §10(b) and Rule 10(b)(5), had to be initiated within one year of discovering the facts giving rise to the violation and within three years of the violation.[44] Congress then amended the law to allow cases to go forward that were filed before this decision if they could have been brought under the prior law.

In *Plaut*, the Supreme Court declared the new statute unconstitutional as violating separation of powers. Justice Scalia, writing for the Court, said that the Constitution "gives the Federal Judiciary the power, not merely to rule on cases, but to decide them."[45] He said that because the "judicial power is one to render dispositive judgments," the federal law "effects a clear violation of separation-of-powers."[46] The statute was unconstitutional because it overturned a Supreme Court decision and gave relief to a party that the Court had said was entitled to none.

[40] 103 Stat. §318(b)(6)(a), *quoted in* 503 U.S. at 434.

[41] 503 U.S. at 437.

[42] For a strong argument that *Robertson* cannot be reconciled with *Klein*, *see* Amy D. Ronner, Judicial Self-Demise: The Test of When Congress Impermissibly Intrudes on Judicial Power after Robertson v. Seattle Audubon Society and the Federal Appellate Courts' Rejection of the Separation of Powers Challenges to the New Section of the Securities Exchange Act of 1934, 35 Ariz. L. Rev. 1037 (1993).

[43] 514 U.S. 211 (1995). *Plaut* is also discussed in §2.2, which considers the Court's conclusion that the federal statute overturning the earlier Supreme Court ruling is unconstitutional because it renders it an advisory opinion.

[44] *See* Lampf, Pleva, Lipkind, Prupis & Petigrow v. Gilbertson, 501 U.S. 350 (1991).

[45] 514 U.S. at 218.

[46] *Id.* at 219, 225.

Although *Plaut* was decided based on the principle of finality and the need to ensure that federal court rulings are not advisory opinions,[47] it can be analogized to *Klein*. In both cases, the federal statute commanded a result in federal court: in *Plaut*, it was hearing a case that the Court had ordered dismissed; in *Klein*, it was dismissing cases that the Court had allowed to be heard. In each case, the Court found a violation of separation of powers. Yet there also is a significant difference between the cases. *Plaut* did not involve any attempt by Congress to strip the federal courts of jurisdiction. Thus, its application to this area is only by analogy and in establishing separation of powers as a limit on Congress's ability to control results in federal court litigation.

Bank Markazi v. Peterson

A federal statute, the Iran Threat Reduction and Syria Human Rights Act of 2012, provides that assets held at a New York bank for Bank Markazi, the Central Bank of Iran, would be available to partially satisfy judgments gained in separate actions by over 1,000 victims of terrorist acts sponsored by Iran.[48] The judgments remain unpaid. As the Court explained, it "is an unusual statute: It designates a particular set of assets and renders them available to satisfy the liability and damages judgments underlying a consolidated enforcement proceeding that the statute identifies by the District Court's docket number."[49]

The issue before the Court was whether the federal law violates separation of powers by purporting to change the law for, and directing a particular result in, a single pending case? The Court, in an opinion by Justice Ginsburg, upheld the federal law. The Court explained that Congress can change the law prospectively, even for pending cases. The Court stated: "Section 8772, we hold, does not transgress constraints placed on Congress and the President by the Constitution. The statute, we point out, is not fairly portrayed as a 'one-case-only regime.' Rather, it covers a category of postjudgment execution claims filed by numerous plaintiffs who, in multiple civil actions, obtained evidence-based judgments against Iran together amounting to billions of dollars. . . . *Congress, our decisions make clear, may amend the law and make the change applicable to pending cases, even when the amendment is outcome determinative.*"[50]

The Court expressly distinguished *Klein* and *Plaut*, explaining that Section 8722 was a change in the law, but not Congress directing the courts as to how to

[47] In Miller v. French, 530 U.S. 327 (2000), the Court distinguished both *Plaut* and *Klein* and upheld a provision of the Prison Litigation Reform Act, 18 U.S.C. §3626, that required federal courts to stay injunctions that they had entered concerning prison conditions if they did not act within 30 days in response to a government's motion to end the injunction. The Court said that an injunction is not the "the last word of the judicial department" because it is always open to modification. Moreover, the Court said that Congress can change the substantive law and require that injunctions be modified to be in accord with the new law. The Court said that the change in the substantive law distinguished this act from the law in *Klein*.

[48] 22 U.S.C. §8772.

[49] 578 U.S. 212, 215 (2016).

[50] *Id.* (emphasis added).

decide specific cases. The Court also stressed that this was in the area of foreign policy, where there is traditionally deference to the President and Congress.[51]

It is clear from these cases that Congress cannot dictate how federal courts decide specific cases. But Congress can modify federal statutes in a way that determines the outcome in pending cases. This seems a difficult line to draw.

Patchak v. Zinke

In *Patchak v. Zinke,* the Court, without a majority opinion, reaffirmed that jurisdiction-stripping statutes violate Article III if they "compel . . . findings or results under old law," but not if they create new law.[52] The Court concluded that the statute was the latter and thus constitutional.

The federal government took into trust a parcel of land in Michigan known as the "Bradley Property" for the benefit of an American Indian tribe, which then could operate a gambling casino there. The government's action was based on a federal statute, the 1934 Indian Reorganization Act. Before the Secretary formally took the land into trust, a landowner, David Patchak, filed a lawsuit challenging the Secretary's decision, arguing that the Secretary lacked statutory authority to take the Bradley Property into trust for the Band because the Indian Reorganization Act does not allow the Secretary to take land into trust for tribes that were not under federal jurisdiction when the statute was enacted in 1934.

The Supreme Court, in *Match-E-Be-Nash-She-Wish Band of Pottawatomi Indians v. Patchak,* reversed the lower courts and held that Patchak had standing to sue and the suit was not barred by sovereign immunity.[53] In September 2014, while Patchak's suit was pending in the district court, Congress enacted the Gun Lake Act.[54] Section 2(a) of the Act states that the Bradley Property "is reaffirmed as trust land, and the actions of the Secretary of the Interior in taking that land into trust are ratified and confirmed." Section 2(b) then provided: "No Claims.—Notwithstanding any other provision of law, an action (including an action pending in a Federal court as of the date of enactment of this Act) relating to the land described in subsection (a) shall not be filed or maintained in a Federal court and shall be promptly dismissed."

The issue before the Supreme Court was whether this violated *Klein* in that Congress was specifying the outcome of the case. The Court, without a majority opinion, rejected the constitutional challenge. Justice Thomas, writing for the plurality, declared: "To distinguish between permissible exercises of the legislative power and impermissible infringements of the judicial power, this Court's precedents establish the following rule: Congress violates Article III when it 'compel[s] . . . findings or results under old law.' But Congress does not violate

[51] *Id.* at 235 ("Particularly pertinent, the Executive, prior to the enactment of the FSIA, regularly made case-specific determinations whether sovereign immunity should be recognized, and courts accepted those determinations as binding.").

[52] 583 U.S. 244 (2018).

[53] 567 U.S. 209 (2012).

[54] 128 Stat. 1913.

Article III when it 'changes the law.'"[55] Justice Thomas said this was the latter, a change in the law: "Section 2(b) changes the law. Specifically, it strips federal courts of jurisdiction over actions 'relating to' the Bradley Property. Before the Gun Lake Act, federal courts had jurisdiction to hear these actions. Now they do not. This kind of legal change is well within Congress' authority and does not violate Article III."[56]

Justice Ginsburg, joined by Justice Sotomayor, concurred in the judgment and said that this was simply Congress withdrawing its waiver of sovereign immunity. She wrote: "Just as it is Congress's prerogative to consent to suit, so too is it within Congress's authority to withdraw consent once given."[57]

Chief Justice Roberts dissented, joined by Justices Kennedy and Gorsuch. He saw this as Congress impermissibly stripping jurisdiction to direct the result in a particular case. He wrote: "Contrary to the plurality, I would hold that Congress exercises the judicial power when it manipulates jurisdictional rules to decide the outcome of a particular pending case. Because the Legislature has no authority to direct entry of judgment for a party, it cannot achieve the same result by stripping jurisdiction over a particular proceeding."[58]

Policy Arguments and Responses

Because neither the text nor precedents conclusively resolve the debate over congressional authority to restrict jurisdiction, the issue turns on competing policy considerations and ultimately the question of when jurisdictional restrictions violate other constitutional provisions. Supporters of proposals to limit Supreme Court jurisdiction under the "exceptions and regulations" clause argue that such congressional power is an essential democratic check on the power of an unelected judiciary. Professor Michael Perry, for example, argues that "the legislative power of Congress . . . to define, and therefore to limit, the appellate jurisdiction of the Supreme Court and the original and appellate jurisdiction of lower federal courts" is essential to reconcile judicial review with principles of democracy.[59] Professor Perry, and other commentators as well, argue that in a democracy all value choices should be subject to control by electorally accountable officials, and congressional restrictions on jurisdiction are an essential majoritarian check on the judiciary.[60]

Opponents of restrictions on the Supreme Court's jurisdiction contend that this argument is based on a misdefinition of democracy and is inconsistent with the purposes of the Constitution. Professor Perry's argument is premised on a definition of democracy in purely procedural terms as majority rule. Others argue that the correct definition of American democracy must include substantive values,

[55] 578 U.S. at 250.

[56] *Id.* at 250-251.

[57] *Id.* at 263 (Ginsburg, J., concurring in the judgment).

[58] *Id.* at 275 (Roberts, C.J., dissenting).

[59] Michael Perry, The Constitution, the Courts, and Human Rights 138 (1982).

[60] *See, e.g.*, Charles Black, Decision According to Law 17-19, 37-39 (1981) (Congressional power to restrict jurisdiction is a necessary democratic check).

such as those contained in the Constitution.[61] The claim is that the purpose of the Constitution is to protect crucial values from majority rule and that it is undesirable to accord Congress the power to undermine Supreme Court decisions.

More specifically, opponents of Professor Perry's position argue that he is in a dilemma. On the one hand, jurisdiction restrictions may not achieve the desired effect of a majoritarian check on the federal judiciary. Limiting the federal courts' jurisdiction does not overrule prior judicial decisions.[62] For example, an act of Congress restricting Supreme Court jurisdiction to hear challenges to state laws regulating abortion would not overturn the precedents protecting women's right to choose whether to have an abortion. The Supreme Court's prior decisions would remain the law, and both Congress and the states would be obligated to uphold them. In fact, because the Court could not hear additional cases on the subject, the effect of the jurisdiction restriction would be to freeze the existing law. Assuming state judges remain true to their oath of office and follow the Court's precedents, restrictions on jurisdiction will not achieve the hoped-for democratic check on the judiciary.

Alternatively, the restrictions on jurisdiction might bring about a substantive change in the law. The limit on federal court power might be perceived by some state legislatures as an open invitation to adopt laws disregarding Supreme Court precedents and some state courts, without the prospect of Supreme Court review, might sustain such statutes. Although the defenders of jurisdiction restriction proposals might applaud this as desirable in a democracy, opponents of such bills contend that such disregard of the Constitution is repugnant. They maintain that the Constitution's ultimate purpose and the Court's primary function is to protect minorities and individual rights from majoritarian interference, and that this is lost if the majority can overrule Supreme Court precedents through the technique of jurisdiction restrictions.[63]

Thus, in terms of policy considerations, supporters of jurisdiction restrictions see the tool as a desirable democratic check on the judiciary. Opponents argue that the Constitution and the Court are intentionally antimajoritarian and that it is undesirable to create a majoritarian check on the process of constitutional interpretation.

Finally, critics of proposals to limit Supreme Court review argue that Congress cannot use its power to control jurisdiction in a way that violates other constitutional provisions. The claim is that congressional authority to create exceptions and regulations is limited, as is all congressional power, by the other parts of the Constitution. There are two primary ways in which it is argued that jurisdictional restrictions would violate the Constitution: they would undermine the Court's

[61] *See, e.g.,* Erwin Chemerinsky, Interpreting the Constitution 6-21 (1987).

[62] *See* Richard Kay, Limiting Federal Court Jurisdiction: The Unforeseen Impact on Courts and Congress, 65 Judicature 185, 187 (1981).

[63] *See, e.g.,* Larry Alexander, Painting Without the Numbers: Noninterpretive Judicial Review, 8 U. Dayton L. Rev. 447, 456-457 (1983) ("There is very little difference between legislative overrules of judicial decisions and legislative withdrawals of jurisdiction.").

essential function in the system of government, and they would infringe specific constitutional rights.

In a famous article written as a dialogue, the late Professor Henry Hart said, "[T]he exceptions must not be such as will destroy the essential role of the Supreme Court in the constitutional system."[64] Other commentators as well have argued that there is a limit on Congress's power to create exceptions: Congress cannot use its power to interfere with the Court's essential functions under the Constitution.[65] For example, it is argued that restrictions on jurisdiction would undermine the Court's essential function of ensuring the supremacy of federal law. If Congress were to restrict the Supreme Court's jurisdiction, states could ignore Supreme Court precedents with impunity, even though they remained the law of the land, and thus make state law supreme over federal. The notion of a national Constitution with uniform meaning throughout the country would be lost.[66]

Additionally, the Court's essential function in checking the legislature would be lost if Congress could enact an unconstitutional statute and immunize the law from judicial review. The power of the federal courts to review the constitutionality of federal statutes, established in *Marbury v. Madison*, would be largely meaningless if Congress could enact unconstitutional laws and also restrict jurisdiction to prevent federal court review.

Other prominent commentators who support the constitutionality of jurisdiction restrictions challenge the essential functions thesis. Professor Gerald Gunther calls it "question-begging" that confuses the familiar with the necessary.[67] Likewise, Professor Martin Redish terms it constitutional wishful thinking.[68] Their contention is that Article III gives Congress plenary power to create exceptions and make regulations and that this is as much a part of the Constitution as separation of powers and federalism.

Opponents of jurisdiction restriction also argue that Congress cannot limit Supreme Court review in a manner that violates specific constitutional rights. The paradigm example is that it obviously would be unconstitutional if Congress were to create an exception to Supreme Court jurisdiction for appeals brought by Black people. Such a jurisdictional restriction would violate the guarantee of equal protection that is applied to the federal government through the Fifth Amendment. Similarly, it is argued that a restriction on jurisdiction that is designed to limit abortion or permit school prayers would violate these constitutional rights. The

[64] Henry Hart, The Power of Congress to Limit Jurisdiction of Federal Courts: An Exercise in Dialectic, 66 Harv. L. Rev. 1362, 1402 (1953).

[65] *See, e.g.,* Leonard Ratner, Majoritarian Constraints on Judicial Review: Congressional Control of Supreme Court Jurisdiction, 27 Vill. L. Rev. 929 (1982); Leonard Ratner, Congressional Power over the Appellate Jurisdiction of the Supreme Court, 109 U. Pa. L. Rev. 157 (1960); Sager, *supra* note 10, at 37-42.

[66] On several occasions, the Supreme Court has stated that the central purpose of judicial review is to ensure the uniform application and enforcement of the Constitution. *See, e.g.,* Dodge v. Woolsey, 59 U.S. (18 How.) 331, 335 (1855); Cohens v. Virginia, 19 U.S. (6 Wheat.) 264, 386-387 (1821).

[67] Gunther, *supra* note 4, at 920.

[68] Martin H. Redish, Constitutional Limitations on Congressional Power to Control Federal Jurisdiction: A Reaction to Professor Sager, 77 Nw. U. L. Rev. 143, 145 (1982).

argument is that when Congress acts with the purpose and effect of limiting a constitutionally protected right, at a minimum its enactment should be subjected to strict scrutiny. A law that is intended to undermine a constitutional right and that has the potential impact of lessening that right should be sustained only if it is necessary to achieve a compelling government purpose. Because the restrictions on jurisdiction are motivated only by a desire to undermine the protection of the right, they would fail strict scrutiny.

Those who defend the constitutionality of jurisdictional restrictions contend that Congress may exempt particular areas from Supreme Court review. Professor Paul Bator, for example, argued that although Congress could not restrict jurisdiction in a racially discriminatory manner, "[i]t is, however, a fundamental and egregious mistake to broaden this argument into an assertion that Congress is not free to differentiate among different subject matters, and to specify categories of cases arising under federal law which [cannot be reviewed in federal courts]."[69] The argument is that racial discrimination in itself violates the Constitution, but nothing in the Constitution requires the availability of Supreme Court review for particular types of claims. In fact, it is argued that the "exceptions and regulations" clause of Article III expressly authorizes Congress to remove particular matters from federal court jurisdiction.[70]

Thus, the debate over the constitutionality of congressional control of Supreme Court jurisdiction will rage on unsettled until Congress uses its authority and sets the stage for a definitive Supreme Court ruling. Even then, the context of the law likely will make a great deal of difference. For example, it is difficult to imagine the Court upholding a congressional enactment that blatantly violated the Constitution and simultaneously precluded Supreme Court review. Permitting such legislative disregard of the Constitution would mean that judicial review exists at the pleasure of Congress, and it would cast grave doubt on the holding in *Marbury v. Madison* that "[i]t is emphatically the province and duty of the judicial department to say what the law is."[71]

Similarly, a congressional restriction on jurisdiction that resulted in state court disregard of Supreme Court precedents would be unlikely to be upheld by the Court. Precluding review in such cases would mean upholding, in effect, state law that conflicted with federal law. State law then would be supreme; this would be a blatant violation of the supremacy clause in Article VI of the Constitution.

These predictions, like all of the above analysis, must wait for their validation or refutation until the day comes when the Court considers the constitutionality of congressional limits on Supreme Court jurisdiction. Depending on one's views, it might be much better if that day never arrives.

[69] Bator, *supra* note 4, at 1034.
[70] *See* Gunther, *supra* note 4, at 916-921.
[71] 5 U.S. (1 Cranch) 137, 177 (1803).

§3.3 CONGRESSIONAL RESTRICTION OF LOWER FEDERAL COURT JURISDICTION

Would a statute precluding lower federal courts from hearing challenges to state laws regulating abortion or permitting voluntary school prayer be constitutional? Again, the debate in the scholarly literature has been heated and lengthy; yet here, too, no consensus has emerged.[1] In fact, four different positions might be identified as to the constitutionality of congressional restrictions of lower federal court jurisdiction.

Approach 1: Federal Courts Must Have the Full Judicial Power

The first approach, and the only one that seems clearly untenable, is that lower federal courts created by Congress must have the full judicial power described in Article III. The text of Article III seems to support this view. Article III, §1, says that the judicial power of the United States shall be vested in one Supreme Court and such inferior courts as Congress shall establish. Article III, §2, states that the judicial power "shall extend to" nine categories of cases and controversies. Hence, the conclusion is that although Congress has a choice regarding whether to establish lower federal courts, once they are created they must have the judicial power to decide all matters described in Article III. By this view, all attempts to restrict jurisdiction would be unconstitutional.[2]

The problem with this theory is that it has not been followed at any point in American history. The first Judiciary Act did not vest in federal courts the power to hear all matters outlined in Article III. For example, federal courts did not have the authority to hear all cases arising under the Constitution, treaties, and laws of the United States until 1875. In fact, under the first theory, amount in controversy requirements would be unconstitutional because they are a restriction on federal court jurisdiction not provided for in Article III. Yet such requirements have existed since the Judiciary Act of 1789. Thus, after 200 years of contrary practice, it no longer is possible to argue persuasively that the lower federal courts' jurisdiction cannot be limited in any way.

§3.3 [1] *See, e.g.*, John Harrison, The Power of Congress to Limit the Jurisdiction of Federal Courts and the Text of Article III, 64 U. Chi. L. Rev. 203 (1997); Robert J. Pushaw, Jr., Congressional Power over Federal Court Jurisdiction: A Defense of the Neo-Federalist Interpretation of Article III, 1997 BYU L. Rev. 847; Akhil Amar, A Neo-Federalist View of Article III: Separating the Two Tiers of Federal Jurisdiction, 65 B.U. L. Rev. 205 (1985); Robert Clinton, A Mandatory View of Federal Court Jurisdiction: A Guided Quest for the Original Understanding of Article III, 132 U. Pa. L. Rev. 741 (1984).

[2] *See* Gordon G. Young, A Critical Reassessment of the Case Law Bearing on Congress's Power to Restrict the Jurisdiction of the Lower Federal Courts, 54 Md. L. Rev. 132 (1995) (arguing that Supreme Court precedents limit Congress's ability to restrict lower federal court jurisdiction).

Approach 2: Congressional Discretion to Decide Jurisdiction

A second approach is that Congress has authority to determine the jurisdiction of the federal courts because Congress has discretion as to whether to establish such tribunals.[3] Article III, §1, provides that the judicial power of the United States shall be vested in one Supreme Court and in "such inferior courts as the Congress may from time to time ordain and establish." Therefore, in light of this literal language, Congress need not create lower federal courts at all. Some conclude from this that because Congress need not even establish such courts, Congress can create them with whatever jurisdiction it desires. In short, the second approach accords Congress virtually plenary authority to define the jurisdiction of the lower federal courts.[4]

This second position finds strong support in Supreme Court precedents. *Sheldon v. Sill,* decided in 1850, is a seminal case concerning congressional power to determine the jurisdiction of the lower federal courts.[5] The Judiciary Act of 1789 prohibited diversity jurisdiction from being created by the assignment of a debt.[6] Under this principle, when there has been an assignment, a federal court may take the case under its diversity jurisdiction only if the case properly could have been brought to federal court prior to the assignment. Article III, which authorizes diversity jurisdiction, creates no such limitation precluding jurisdiction based on assignment.

The issue in *Sheldon v. Sill* was whether Congress could restrict diversity jurisdiction in this manner. Sheldon, a Michigan resident, owed money to Hastings, also a Michigan resident, on a bond and a mortgage. Hastings assigned the debt owed to him to Sill, a New York resident. Pursuant to this assignment, Sill sued Sheldon in federal court to recover the sum due. Sheldon moved to dismiss because under the Judiciary Act of 1789, federal courts could not hear cases where diversity was created by an assignment. Sill contended that because Article III authorizes diversity jurisdiction and does not contain a limitation for diversity gained by assignment, this section of the Judiciary Act was unconstitutional.

The Supreme Court upheld the Judiciary Act's restriction on diversity jurisdiction. The Court declared: "Congress may withhold from any court of its creation jurisdiction of any of the enumerated controversies. Courts created by statute can have no jurisdiction but such as the statute confers."[7] The Court continued in even broader language: "The political truth is, that the disposal of the judicial power (except in a few specified instances) belongs to Congress; and Congress is not

[3] *See, e.g.,* Charles E. Rice, Congress and the Supreme Court's Jurisdiction, 27 Vill. L. Rev. 959, 960-962 (1982).

[4] Even under this approach, there is a strong argument that Congress could not use its power to determine jurisdiction in a manner that restricts other constitutional provisions. For example, it certainly would be unconstitutional if Congress were to adopt a law saying that no African Americans could file suit in a federal court. The nature of constitutional limits on the power to restrict federal jurisdiction is discussed below.

[5] 49 U.S. (8 How.) 441 (1850).

[6] 1 Stat. 73, §11.

[7] 49 U.S. at 449.

bound to enlarge the jurisdiction of the Federal courts to every subject, in every form which the Constitution might warrant."[8] *Sheldon v. Sill* thus stands as a strong precedent for the proposition that because Congress has discretion to create lower federal courts, Congress also possesses authority to determine their jurisdiction.

The Supreme Court has adopted this position in a number of other decisions. In *Kline v. Burke Construction Co.*, the Supreme Court held that the Anti-Injunction Act precluded a federal court from enjoining a simultaneous state court proceeding for breach of contract.[9] In upholding this limit on federal court power, the Court stated: "Only the jurisdiction of the Supreme Court is derived directly from the Constitution. Every other court created by the general government derives its jurisdiction wholly from the authority of Congress. That body may give, withhold or restrict such jurisdiction at its discretion, provided it be not extended beyond the boundaries fixed by the Constitution."[10]

In *Lauf v. E. G. Shinner & Co.*, the Court considered the constitutionality of the Norris-LaGuardia Act, which limited the ability of the federal courts to issue injunctions in labor disputes and prevented federal courts from enforcing contracts whereby employees agreed to not join a union.[11] During the first decades of the twentieth century, the federal courts were hostile to the labor movement and often enjoined labor protests. Moreover, the Supreme Court held that states could not prohibit employers from requiring employees to agree to refrain from joining a union as a condition for employment.[12] The Norris-LaGuardia Act sought to protect labor by limiting the power of the federal courts.

In *Lauf*, an employer sought an injunction to prevent an unincorporated labor union from picketing an employer that refused to require employees to join the union. The federal district court ruled in favor of the employer and issued the injunction. The Supreme Court reversed. The Court held that the Norris-LaGuardia Act restricted the district's court authority to hear the matter or issue the remedy. The Court found the constitutional issue untroubling. Justice Roberts, writing for the Court, declared: "There can be no question of the power of Congress thus to define and limit the jurisdiction of the inferior courts of the United States."[13]

Additional litigation concerning congressional power to control lower federal court jurisdiction emerged as a result of the Emergency Price Control Act, which was adopted during World War II.[14] Under the Act, price controls adopted by the government could be challenged by filing a protest with the price control administrator.[15] Appeals from the administrator's decisions could be taken, within 30 days, to an Emergency Court of Appeals, composed of three federal judges.

[8] *Id.* (citations omitted).

[9] 260 U.S. 226 (1922). The Anti-Injunction Act is discussed in §11.2; the issue of simultaneous federal and state proceedings is discussed in Chapter 14.

[10] *Id.* at 234.

[11] 303 U.S. 323 (1938).

[12] *See, e.g.,* Coppage v. Kansas, 236 U.S. 1 (1915).

[13] 303 U.S. at 330.

[14] 56 Stat. 23 (1942).

[15] *Id.* §203(a), described in Lockerty v. Phillips, 319 U.S. 182, 186 (1943).

No other federal court, except for the U.S. Supreme Court, had authority to determine the validity of a regulation or provide injunctive relief.

In *Lockerty v. Phillips,* the Court held that a federal district court lacked jurisdiction to hear challenges to price controls promulgated under the Emergency Price Control Act.[16] Without filing an administrative protest or seeking review in the Emergency Court of Appeals, a group of wholesale meat dealers initiated suit in federal court to enjoin the enforcement of price controls. The plaintiffs contended that the Act was an unconstitutional delegation of legislative power to an administrative agency and that the price regulations denied them due process of law. The Supreme Court held that the federal court lacked jurisdiction to hear the suit. The Court stated that "[t]here is nothing in the Constitution which requires Congress to confer equity jurisdiction on any particular inferior federal court."[17] Furthermore, the Court spoke broadly of Congress's authority to prescribe the jurisdiction of the lower federal courts: "The Congressional power to ordain and establish inferior federal courts includes the power of investing them with jurisdiction either limited, concurrent, or exclusive, and of withholding jurisdiction from them in the exact degrees and character which to Congress may seem proper for the public good."[18]

An even more serious challenge to the constitutionality of the Emergency Price Control Act arose in *Yakus v. United States.*[19] In *Yakus,* the government initiated a criminal prosecution in federal district court for the sale of beef for an amount in excess of that specified in the price controls. The defendant in the criminal proceeding argued that the price controls were unconstitutional. The government contended that the federal district court had no jurisdiction to hear this defense because the defendant had not raised the constitutional issue in a protest to the administrator or in the Emergency Court of Appeals.

The Supreme Court agreed with the government and precluded the defendant from challenging the constitutionality of the price controls as a defense in the criminal action. The Court said that the defendant "forfeited" the opportunity to bring such a constitutional challenge by failing to use the prescribed administrative and judicial procedures.[20] The Court said that *Lockerty* had established the power of Congress to restrict the jurisdiction of the federal courts and to specify the Emergency Court of Appeals as the only forum to hear challenges to price controls.

Justices Rutledge and Murphy filed a vehement dissent in *Yakus.* They argued that under *Marbury v. Madison,* a federal court had the inherent power to determine the constitutionality of a statute that it was asked to apply. The dissenters stated: "It is one thing for Congress to withhold jurisdiction. It is entirely another to confer it and direct that it be exercised in a manner inconsistent with constitutional requirements or, what in some instances may be the same thing, without

[16] 319 U.S. 182 (1943).
[17] *Id.* at 187.
[18] *Id.*
[19] 321 U.S. 414 (1944).
[20] *Id.* at 444.

regard to them."[21] They explained, "Once it is held that Congress can require the courts criminally to enforce unconstitutional laws or statutes, including regulations, or to do so without regard to their validity the way will have been found to circumvent the supreme law, and what is more, to make the courts party to doing so. This Congress cannot do."[22]

Most recently, in *Bouarfa v. Mayorkas,* the Court unanimously held that Congress had constitutionally stripped federal courts of jurisdiction to review a decision by the Secretary of the Department of Homeland Security to revoke an approved visa petition.[23] The Court explained that "Congress granted the Secretary broad authority to revoke an approved visa petition 'at any time, for what he deems to be good and sufficient cause.' Such a revocation is thus 'in the discretion of' the agency."[24] Although the Court acknowledged in general the presumption in favor of judicial review of agency actions, the Court said that this presumption can be overcome by "clear and convincing evidence of congressional intent to preclude judicial review."[25] The Court said that the law in this case met that requirement because it was "a jurisdiction-stripping statute."[26]

Supporters of the constitutionality of jurisdiction restrictions maintain that these decisions establish Congress's power to determine the scope of federal court authority. Opponents of jurisdiction stripping proposals contend that none of these cases are precedents for Congress to identify particular rights, such as abortion, and deny federal court jurisdiction over claims of government infringement. *Sheldon* and *Kline* did not involve constitutional claims. In *Lockerty* and *Yakus,* Congress specified one federal court to hear a particular issue; it did not preclude all federal court jurisdiction. *Lauf* is the hardest case to distinguish, but it is possible to argue that in the Norris-LaGuardia Act, Congress only limited the federal courts' ability to award a particular *remedy*: injunctions.[27] Congress did not foreclose all lower federal court review as is done in the contemporary proposals to strip jurisdiction in areas such as abortion or school prayer. Opponents of attempts to restrict lower federal court jurisdiction over matters such as abortion and school prayer argue that such congressional legislation is unprecedented and unconstitutional for the reasons described below.

[21] *Id.* at 468 (Rutledge, J., dissenting).

[22] *Id.*

[23] 604 U.S. 6 (2024).

[24] *Id.* at 8.

[25] *Id.* at 7.

[26] *Id.*

[27] A distinction might be drawn between Congress's ability to restrict jurisdiction and Congress's ability to foreclose certain remedies from being used by federal courts. This issue emerged especially with regard to proposals for Congress to prevent lower federal courts from using busing as a remedy in school desegregation cases. *See* Ronald D. Rotunda, Congressional Power to Restrict the Jurisdiction of the Lower Federal Courts and the Problem of School Busing, 64 Geo. L.J. 839 (1976); Sharon Susser Harzenski, Jurisdictional Limitations and Suspicious Motives: Why Congress Cannot Forbid Court-Ordered Busing, 50 Temp. L.Q. 14 (1976). The possible distinction between restrictions on jurisdiction and limits on remedies is discussed below at text accompanying notes 77-79, *infra.*

Approach 3: Constitutional Requirement for Some Federal Courts

A third major approach urged by some commentators is that the existence of lower federal courts is constitutionally required, at least for some types of claims. While the first two approaches begin with the assumption that Congress has complete discretion as to whether to create lower federal courts, this position is premised on the contrary claim that, at least for some issues, lower federal courts must exist. Justice Joseph Story advanced the most famous version of this theory in dictum in *Martin v. Hunter's Lessee.*[28]

Justice Story stated that the full judicial power must be vested in some federal court. Justice Story argued that "[t]he language of the article throughout is manifestly designed to be mandatory upon the legislature. . . . The judicial power of the United States *shall be vested* (not may be vested). . . . If then, it is the duty of congress to vest the judicial power of the United States, it is a duty to vest the *whole judicial power.*"[29] Justice Story explained that if Congress could refuse to create lower federal courts, there would be at least some categories of cases that never could be heard in federal court. For instance, there are some matters that cannot be heard by state courts and that cannot be heard by the Supreme Court in its original jurisdiction. In such instances, lower federal courts must exist or no federal judicial tribunal would be available. Justice Story stated, "It would seem, therefore, to follow, that congress [is] bound to create some inferior courts, in which to vest all that jurisdiction which, under the constitution, is *exclusively* vested in the United States and of which the supreme court cannot take original cognizance."[30]

For example, under Supreme Court precedents, state courts may not grant habeas corpus to federal prisoners or issue writs of mandamus compelling performance by federal officers.[31] If there were no lower federal courts, there could be no federal court review of claims arising under the Constitution pursuant to a writ of habeas corpus or a writ of mandamus. The Supreme Court could not hear such matters as part of its original jurisdiction under Article III, and *Marbury v. Madison* conclusively establishes that Congress may not increase the Court's original jurisdiction.[32] Because state courts could not hear the claims, the Supreme Court could not gain appellate jurisdiction by reviewing state court decisions. In other words, without lower federal courts, no federal judicial tribunal would be able to hear the matter. This clearly conflicts with Justice Story's conclusion: "[Congress] might establish one or more inferior courts; they might parcel out the jurisdiction among

[28] 14 U.S. (1 Wheat.) 304, 328-331 (1816). *See* Michael G. Collins, Article III Cases, State Court Duties, and the Madisonian Compromise, 1995 Wis. L. Rev. 39 (arguing that history supports Justice Story's theory, that the Framers thought that state courts would not adjudicate federal issues, and that Congress was required to create lower federal courts to hear these claims).

[29] 14 U.S. at 328-329 (emphasis in original).

[30] *Id.* at 331 (emphasis in original).

[31] Tarble's Case, 80 U.S. (13 Wall.) 397 (1871) (state courts cannot grant habeas corpus to federal prisoners); M'Clung v. Sillman, 19 U.S. (6 Wheat.) 598 (1821); *see also* Richard S. Arnold, The Power of State Courts to Enjoin Federal Officers, 73 Yale L.J. 1385 (1964).

[32] 5 U.S. (1 Cranch) 137 (1803). In fact, in *Marbury,* the Court ruled that it could not grant mandamus as part of its original jurisdiction.

such courts, from time to time, at their own pleasure. But the whole judicial power of the United States should be, at all times, vested either in an original or appellate form, in some courts created under its authority."[33]

There is one instance in which a lower federal court followed this theory. In *Eisentrager v. Forrestal*, the U.S. Court of Appeals for the District of Columbia Circuit considered a habeas corpus petition from an individual who was imprisoned by U.S. military authorities in Germany.[34] The federal habeas corpus statute as then interpreted provided that a federal court could grant habeas relief only to prisoners held within the jurisdiction of the court.[35] Therefore, no federal court had jurisdiction to hear Eisentrager's claim that he was held in custody in violation of the U.S. Constitution. No state court could hear his habeas petition because of the Supreme Court's decision in *Tarble's Case* preventing state courts from granting habeas to federal prisoners.[36] The Supreme Court lacked original jurisdiction and could not hear the matter on appeal because there was no lower court from which an appeal could be taken.

The District of Columbia Circuit found the complete preclusion of jurisdiction to be unconstitutional and heard the case. The court said that because a state court cannot inquire into the validity of federal custody, federal jurisdiction must exist or else the government's action would be completely unreviewable. The court said that this is impermissible both under Justice Story's theory and because it would allow the government to suspend the writ of habeas corpus in violation of the Constitution. But the Supreme Court disagreed and held that the federal courts could not hear these claims by noncitizens held outside the United States.[37]

Justice Story's argument and the view of the D.C. Circuit in *Eisentrager* would require the existence of lower federal courts in two situations. In instances where the Supreme Court cannot exercise original jurisdiction and where state courts cannot hear the matter, lower federal courts must exist to ensure jurisdiction in some federal court. Additionally, if Congress simultaneously restricts Supreme Court and lower federal court jurisdiction, the law would be unconstitutional because under Justice Story's theory some federal court must exist to hear cases and controversies specified in Article III. The proposals to prevent federal court jurisdiction in abortion or school prayer cases would be unconstitutional under this approach because they would preclude both the Supreme Court and the lower federal courts from hearing such matters.

[33] 14 U.S. at 331. In addition to Justice Story's argument, it is possible to argue that restrictions on jurisdiction in such circumstances would deny due process of law; *see* the discussion below, text accompanying notes 48-49, *infra.*

[34] 174 F.2d 961 (D.C. Cir. 1949), *rev'd,* Johnson v. Eisentrager, 339 U.S. 763 (1950).

[35] *See* Ahrens v. Clark, 335 U.S. 188 (1948); *but see* Braden v. 30th Judicial Circuit Court of Kentucky, 410 U.S. 484 (1973); discussed in §15.4, *infra.*

[36] 80 U.S. (13 Wall.) 397 (1871).

[37] Johnson v. Eisentrager, 339 U.S. 763 (1950). In Rasul v. Bush, 542 U.S. 466 (2004), the Supreme Court distinguished Johnson v. Eisentrager and held that those held in Guantánamo Bay, Cuba, could have their habeas corpus petitions heard in federal court. In Boumediene v. Bush, 553 U.S. 723 (2008), the Court reaffirmed this distinction and held that the denial of access to habeas corpus to those held as enemy combatants in Guantánamo was an impermissible suspension of the writ of habeas corpus.

Contemporary commentators have advanced several alternative versions of Justice Story's approach. In an article, Professor Akhil Amar argued that it is necessary to focus carefully on the text of Article III, §2.[38] This section says that the federal judicial power extends to "all" cases arising under the Constitution and laws of the United States, to "all" cases affecting ambassadors and public ministers, and to "all" cases of admiralty or maritime jurisdiction. But the other categories of cases and controversies are not preceded by the word "all." Professor Amar concluded that Justice Story's theory is accurate as to those categories where the Constitution is explicit that the federal judicial power exists to *all* such matters. In such instances, most notably for cases arising under federal law, jurisdiction must exist in some federal court.[39]

Professor Theodor Eisenberg advanced an even more expansive argument that lower federal courts are constitutionally required.[40] Professor Eisenberg argued that the Framers of the Constitution intended that a federal court would be available, either via original jurisdiction or on appeal, to hear virtually every constitutional claim. The Framers assumed that even if lower federal courts did not exist, the Supreme Court could perform the important task of ensuring compliance with the Constitution. But Professor Eisenberg contended that now, given the growth in the size of the country and rise in the volume of litigation, the Supreme Court cannot perform this function by itself. He maintained that Congress must create lower federal courts to ensure the existence of a federal forum for constitutional claims. He stated: "It is thus no longer reasonable to assert that Congress may simply abolish the lower federal courts. When Supreme Court review of all cases within Article III jurisdiction was possible, lower federal courts were perhaps unnecessary. As federal caseloads grew, however, lower federal courts became necessary components of the national judiciary."[41] He concluded that "[i]t can now be asserted that their existence in some form is constitutionally required."[42]

Professor Lawrence Sager developed yet another version of the argument that lower federal courts must exist where otherwise Supreme Court review would be impossible.[43] Professor Sager argued that the essential function of the federal judiciary is the "supervision of state conduct to ensure general compliance with the Constitution."[44] He contended that state courts cannot be fully trusted to perform this function because they lack the assurance of life tenure and salary protections accorded the federal judiciary. His conclusion is that a federal court must exist to hear constitutional challenges to state government actions.

[38] Amar, *supra* note 1; *but see* John Harrison, The Power of Congress to Limit the Jurisdiction of Federal Courts and the Text of Article III, 64 U. Chi. L. Rev. 203 (1997) (responding to and critiquing Amar's theory).

[39] *Id.* at 271-272.

[40] Theodore Eisenberg, Congressional Authority to Restrict Lower Federal Court Jurisdiction, 83 Yale L.J. 498 (1974).

[41] *Id.* at 513.

[42] *Id.*

[43] Lawrence Gene Sager, Foreword: Constitutional Limitations on Congress' Authority to Regulate the Jurisdiction of the Federal Courts, 95 Harv. L. Rev. 17 (1981).

[44] *Id.* at 45. Also, other commentators base an argument for a constitutional requirement that federal courts exist on the intent of the Constitution's Framers, *see, e.g.,* Clinton, *supra* note 1; 1 Julius Goebel, History of the Supreme Court of the United States: Antecedents and Beginnings to 1801, at 246 (1971).

Other commentators strongly disagree with the positions advanced by Justice Story and contemporary scholars such as Professors Amar, Eisenberg, and Sager. Supporters of the constitutionality of jurisdiction restrictions contend that the language of Article III is unequivocal: Congress has complete discretion as to whether lower federal courts should exist.[45] Article III represented a compromise. Whereas one group at the Constitutional Convention wanted to ensure the existence of lower federal courts, another faction wanted the Supreme Court to be the exclusive federal judicial tribunal.[46] The compromise was to create a Supreme Court and to leave it to Congress to decide whether and under what circumstances lower federal courts should exist. Any argument that lower federal courts are required to exist disregards this history.[47]

If anything, there might be a due process argument that state courts must be able to hear matters where the effect of jurisdiction stripping would mean that no court would be available. For example, there might be an argument that *Tarble's Case* cannot be applied to prevent a person held in prison in violation of the Constitution from securing some judicial remedy. This due process argument is discussed below, but it should be remembered that due process in this context would require only that some court exist, not that it necessarily would require a federal forum.

Approach 4: Specific Constitutional Limits

There is a fourth and final approach to the issue of congressional restriction of lower federal court jurisdiction. Congress has discretion both to create lower federal courts and to determine their jurisdiction, but Congress may not restrict the jurisdiction in a manner that violates other constitutional provisions. As in the previous section's discussion concerning congressional limitations on Supreme Court jurisdiction, the argument is that Congress's power to restrict jurisdiction—like all congressional powers—cannot be exercised in a manner that violates constitutional rights.

For example, Congress cannot restrict jurisdiction in a manner that would deny due process of law. There is a strong argument that due process would be violated if the effect of the jurisdictional restriction is that no court, state or federal, could hear a constitutional claim.[48] In fact, on several occasions the Supreme

[45] *See, e.g.,* Martin H. Redish & Curtis Woods, Congressional Power to Control the Jurisdiction of Lower Federal Courts: A Critical Review and New Synthesis, 124 U. Pa. L. Rev. 45, 90 (1975); Gerald Gunther, Congressional Power to Curtail Federal Court Jurisdiction: An Opinionated Guide to the Ongoing Debate, 36 Stan. L. Rev. 895, 916 (1984).

[46] This history is described in §1.1, *supra.*

[47] Redish & Woods, *supra* note 45, at 70.

[48] A distinction might be drawn between statutes that preclude review of statutory claims and those that preclude review of constitutional claims. In Dalton v. Specter, 511 U.S. 462 (1994), the Court upheld a federal law that precluded review of the president's closure of military bases under the Defense Base Closure and Realignment Act of 1990. The Court found that Congress could preclude all review of statutory claims, but suggested that Congress may not prevent all federal court review of constitutional claims. *See* Richard H. Fallon, Jr., Some Confusions About Due Process, Judicial Review, and Constitutional Remedies, 93 Colum. L. Rev. 309 (1993) (arguing that the issue of whether there is a constitutional right to judicial review depends on the underlying substantive law).

Court went out of its way to narrowly construe federal statutes that appeared to preclude all judicial review.[49]

In *Johnson v. Robison*, the Court refused to interpret a statute limiting review of Veterans Administration decisions in a manner that would have foreclosed all judicial review.[50] Robison, a conscientious objector who had performed alternative service, challenged a federal statute that provided educational benefits to veterans but excluded conscientious objectors. A federal law appeared to preclude federal court review of Robison's claim. The statute provided: "[T]he decisions of the Administrator on any question of law or fact under any law administered by the Veterans Administration providing benefits for veterans . . . shall be final and conclusive and no official or any court of the United States shall have power or jurisdiction to review any such decision."[51]

The Court observed that there would be "serious question" about the constitutionality of this provision if it precluded all review. The Court, however, narrowly interpreted the statute and said that it did not apply in this case because this was not an objection to a decision made by the Veterans Administration, but instead a challenge to a statute adopted by Congress. The Court said that the purposes for the limit on judicial review—deference to the agency in awarding benefits—would not be undermined by allowing jurisdiction to hear challenges to the statute.

Similarly, in *Oestereich v. Selective Service System Local Board No. 11*, the Court narrowly interpreted a provision limiting review of Selective Service decisions.[52] During the 1960s, the Selective Service Commission retaliated against students involved in anti-Vietnam War protests by revoking their student deferments and classifying them as ready for induction. After the federal courts held that this was impermissible and enjoined the Selective Service Commission, Congress responded by adopting a statute limiting judicial review. The act provided that "no judicial review shall be made of the classification or processing of any registrant . . . except as a defense to a criminal prosecution . . . after the registrant has responded affirmatively or negatively to an order to report for induction."[53] The statute appeared to limit challenges to its validity to two contexts: defenses to a criminal prosecution and habeas corpus.

Oestereich was a full-time student at a theological school preparing for the ministry and was therefore entitled to a draft exemption under federal statutes. After he participated in an antiwar protest, however, he was reclassified as I-A, ready for induction. Despite the federal statute appearing to preclude jurisdiction, the Court held that Oestereich could bring a suit challenging the legality of

[49] For an excellent defense of the Court's interpretation of statutes to preserve jurisdiction and avoid the constitutional issue, *see* Ernest A. Young, Constitutional Avoidance, Resistance Norms, and the Preservation of Judicial Review, 78 Tex. L. Rev. 1549 (2000).

[50] 415 U.S. 361 (1974). *See also* Webster v. Doe, 486 U.S. 592 (1988) (refusing to find statute to preclude review of a claim by an employee of the CIA who alleged that he was fired because he was a homosexual).

[51] 38 U.S.C. §211(a) (1982).

[52] 393 U.S. 233 (1968).

[53] Military Selective Service Act of 1967, 50 U.S.C. §10(b)(3) (1982).

his reclassification. The Court held that the law limiting judicial review was not meant to apply to a clearly lawless action by a draft board. Justice Harlan, in a concurring opinion, stated that it "is doubtful whether a person may be deprived of his personal liberty without the prior opportunity to be heard by some tribunal competent fully to adjudicate his claims."[54]

In *United States v. Mendoza-Lopez,* the Court held that an alien who is prosecuted for illegal entry following deportation may assert in the constitutional proceeding the invalidity of the underlying administrative deportation order.[55] In narrowly construing statutes that appeared to preclude judicial review, the Court declared: "[W]here the defects in an administrative proceeding foreclose judicial review of that proceeding, an alternative means of obtaining judicial review must be made available before the administrative order may be used to conclusively establish an element of a criminal offense."[56]

In *McNary v. Haitian Refugee Center, Inc.*, the Supreme Court interpreted a federal statute to avoid finding that it precluded judicial review.[57] The Immigration Reform and Control Act of 1986 created a special amnesty program for specified alien farmworkers and barred judicial review of "a determination respecting an application," except in the federal court of appeals as part of judicial review of a deportation order.

The Supreme Court declared that there is a "well-settled presumption favoring interpretations of statutes that allow judicial review of administrative action."[58] The Court noted that it assumed that Congress was aware of this presumption, and therefore "it is most unlikely that Congress intended to foreclose all forms of meaningful judicial review."[59] Hence, the Court concluded that the statute should be interpreted as not precluding judicial review.

Likewise, in *Reno v. Catholic Social Services,* the Court refused to find a preclusion of jurisdiction in INS regulations implementing the legalization program for illegal immigrants under the Immigration Reform and Control Act.[60] The Court explained that to find preclusion of review it "would have to impute to Congress an intent to preclude judicial review of the legality of the INS action entirely under those circumstances."[61] The Court noted that there is a "well-settled presumption" in favor of interpreting statutes to allow judicial review and that it "accordingly will find an intent to preclude such review only if presented with clear and convincing evidence."[62]

Subsequently, in *INS v. St. Cyr,* the Court interpreted jurisdictional preclusion in a federal immigration law as still permitting challenges in federal court

[54] 393 U.S. at 243-244 n.6.
[55] 481 U.S. 828 (1987).
[56] *Id.* at 838-839.
[57] 498 U.S. 479 (1991).
[58] *Id.* at 480.
[59] *Id.*
[60] 509 U.S. 43 (1993).
[61] *Id.* at 63.
[62] *Id.*

via habeas corpus petitions.[63] In the Illegal Immigration Reform and Immigrant Responsibility Act of 1996 (IIRIRA), Congress limited both the attorney general's authority to waive deportation in certain cases and federal court jurisdiction over challenges to deportation. St. Cyr sought to argue that the limitation of waivers by the attorney general did not apply to him, but the statute precluded his seeking judicial review of the deportation order.

The Supreme Court, in a 5-4 decision, held that the express statutory preclusion of judicial review of deportation proceedings did not bar a challenge from being brought through a writ of habeas corpus. Justice Stevens, writing for the Court, emphasized "the strong presumption in favor of judicial review of administrative action."[64] The Court recognized the statutory preclusion of direct judicial review of INS deportation orders, but said that this did not bar habeas corpus proceedings. Justice Stevens said that Congress "must articulate specific and unambiguous statutory directives" to repeal the availability of habeas jurisdiction.[65]

These cases establish that the Court will go out of its way to read statutes so that they do not foreclose all judicial review. In one instance, a lower federal court declared unconstitutional a federal statute that prevented any court from hearing a matter. In *Battaglia v. General Motors Corp.*, the U.S. Court of Appeals for the Second Circuit considered a federal statute that precluded all judicial review.[66] Previously, the Supreme Court held that employees were allowed to consider as part of their workweek time spent walking to their workstations, washing after work, and changing clothes.[67] Congress responded by adopting a statute, the Portal-to-Portal Act, specifying that time spent on such activities did not count as part of the workweek.[68] Moreover, the act provided that "[n]o court of the United States, of any State, Territory or possession of the United States, or of the District of Columbia shall have jurisdiction . . . to enforce liability or impose punishments" for failure of the employer to pay for work time spent on such activities.[69]

The Second Circuit indicated that Congress could not restrict jurisdiction in a manner that prevented all courts from hearing claims. The court explained that "while Congress has the undoubted power to give, withhold, and restrict the jurisdiction of courts other than the Supreme Court, it must not so exercise that power

[63] 530 U.S. 289 (2001). Also, in Calcano-Martinez v. Immigration and Naturalization Service, 533 U.S. 348 (2001), the Court upheld a provision of the IIRIRA, 8 U.S.C. §1252(a)(1), limiting direct appellate review of final INS removal orders based on past criminal convictions because of the existence of the writ of habeas corpus. The Court concluded: "Finding no support in the text or history of §1252 for concluding that the court of appeals retain jurisdiction to hear petitions such as those brought in this case, but concluding that Congress has not spoken with sufficient clarity to strip the district courts of jurisdiction to hear habeas petitions raising identical claims, we affirm the judgment of the Court of Appeals in all particulars [upholding the restriction on direct review by the Court of Appeals]." 533 U.S. at 351-352.

[64] 530 U.S. at 298.

[65] *Id.* at 299.

[66] 169 F.2d 254 (2d Cir. 1948).

[67] Tennessee Coal, Iron & R.R. v. Muscoda Local 123, 321 U.S. 590 (1944).

[68] 61 Stat. 84 (1947), 29 U.S.C. §251.

[69] *Id.* §2(d).

as to deprive any person of life, liberty, or property without due process of law or to take private property without just compensation."[70]

This due process argument states only that *some* court, state or federal, must be available to hear claims. Proposals to restrict federal court jurisdiction to hear abortion and school prayer cases would not violate this requirement because state courts would remain open to decide constitutional challenges to state laws. Due process claims, however, might arise from jurisdiction restrictions in two circumstances.

One is if the state courts would refuse to hear federal constitutional claims in an instance where federal court jurisdiction was precluded. However, in numerous cases the Supreme Court has held that state courts cannot discriminate against federal claims and refuse to hear cases arising under federal law.[71]

Alternatively, due process problems might arise in the face of federal jurisdictional restrictions in circumstances where state courts are precluded from hearing certain matters altogether by federal law. For example, as mentioned earlier, state courts cannot grant habeas corpus petitions of federal prisoners or issue mandamus to federal officers.[72] Under such circumstances, a restriction on federal court jurisdiction would foreclose all court review and pose due process problems.[73] Some commentators have argued that limits on federal court jurisdiction are thus unconstitutional when they have the effect of precluding *all* judicial review, state and federal.[74] This, however, would not be the case with proposals to limit federal court jurisdiction over, for example, abortion or school prayer cases because state courts would remain available. Also, it might be argued that due process requires the state courts to hear the case, not that the restriction on federal jurisdiction is unconstitutional.

In addition to due process as a limit on Congress's power to restrict federal court jurisdiction, it is argued that other constitutional rights as well cannot be violated by jurisdictional restrictions. As was discussed in the previous section with regard to limits on Supreme Court jurisdiction, the paradigm example of an unconstitutional jurisdictional limitation would be a law that prevents Black people from suing in federal court. Some argue similarly that Congress cannot restrict jurisdiction with the purpose and effect of lessening the protection of constitutional rights, such as abortion or school prayer.[75]

[70] 169 F.2d at 257.

[71] These cases are discussed in detail in §3.5 below.

[72] *See, e.g.*, Tarble's Case, 80 U.S. (13 Wall.) 397 (1871) (state courts cannot grant habeas corpus to federal prisoners); M'Clung v. Sillman, 19 U.S. (6 Wheat.) 598 (1821) (state courts cannot issue mandamus to federal officers).

[73] Earlier it was argued that restrictions on all federal court jurisdiction in such circumstances would violate Article III. This is a distinct argument that such jurisdictional limitations would violate due process.

[74] *See, e.g.*, Redish & Woods, *supra* note 45, at 102-109.

[75] Laurence Tribe, Jurisdictional Gerrymandering: Zoning Disfavored Rights out of the Federal Courts, 16 Harv. C.R.-C.L. L. Rev. 129 (1981) (arguing strict scrutiny is used for laws that burden fundamental rights).

Other commentators, who believe that jurisdictional restrictions are constitutional, challenge the analogy between racist restrictions on jurisdiction and those that prevent lower federal courts from hearing specific types of issues. They argue that while the Constitution forbids Congress from discriminating, it does not forbid Congress from singling out particular topics and assigning them to state court rather than federal court.[76] To the contrary, they maintain that the Constitution expressly authorizes Congress to determine the jurisdiction of the federal courts.

Congressional Restriction of Remedies

A related question is whether Congress can limit the remedies federal courts may employ even though it is not completely precluding jurisdiction. For example, can Congress prevent federal courts from using busing as a remedy in school desegregation cases? Some argue that this is unconstitutional because limiting remedies can have the effect of undermining the protection of a constitutional right unless other equally effective remedies are available.[77] Others argue that Congress has even greater power to limit remedies than to restrict jurisdiction. They claim that "Congress has plenary authority to structure remedies,"[78] as well as the authority to confer federal jurisdiction on the condition that certain remedies not be used.

In *United States v. Dickerson*,[79] the Supreme Court declared unconstitutional a federal law that sought to overrule *Miranda v. Arizona*.[80] Congress, in a 1968 law, provided that confessions should be admissible in a federal court as long as they were voluntarily obtained, even if *Miranda* warnings were not properly administered. The challenge to the law was based in part on the argument that Congress could alter the remedies that federal courts could use for Fifth Amendment violations. The Supreme Court, in a 7-2 decision, declared the law unconstitutional. Chief Justice Rehnquist, writing for the Court, said that *Miranda* is a "constitutional rule" and that Congress by statute cannot overturn constitutional rules.

Dickerson does not resolve the question that long has been unresolved as to Congress's ability to limit remedies. But it does make clear that Congress cannot modify remedies that are deemed to be themselves constitutional rules.

[76] *See, e.g.*, Gunther, *supra* note 45, at 918-919; Paul M. Bator, Congressional Power over the Jurisdiction of the Federal Courts, 27 Vill. L. Rev. 1030, 1034 (1982).

[77] *See* Rotunda, *supra* note 27, at 839; Harzenski, *supra* note 27, at 14.

[78] Mark V. Tushnet & Jennifer Jaff, Why the Debate over Congress' Power to Restrict the Jurisdiction of the Federal Courts Is Unending, 72 Geo. L.J. 1311, 1322 (1984).

[79] 530 U.S. 428 (2000).

[80] 18 U.S.C. §3501.

§3.4 CONGRESSIONAL POWER TO ENLARGE THE JURISDICTION OF THE FEDERAL COURTS

Can Congress Authorize Jurisdiction in Excess of Article III?

A far less controversial issue than Congress's power to curtail federal court jurisdiction is whether Congress may expand federal jurisdiction beyond the scope of the cases and controversies enumerated in Article III. There is, of course, no doubt that Congress could, if it chose, vest in federal courts the power to hear all matters described in Article III. But could Congress go even further and add other matters to the jurisdiction of the federal courts? Because Article III specifically authorizes federal courts to hear matters arising under the Constitution and all federal laws, this question rarely arises.

Marbury v. Madison established that Article III is the ceiling of the Supreme Court's original jurisdiction.[1] The Court held that Congress could not authorize the Supreme Court to issue a writ of mandamus as part of its original jurisdiction because this power was not included in Article III. The Court said that the enumeration of types of jurisdiction would be meaningless if Congress could add to the Supreme Court's authority. There is, of course, a strong response to this argument. Even if Congress could add to the Court's jurisdiction, Article III still would have meaning if it were read as the floor of Supreme Court authority, the minimum that Congress could not reduce.[2] Nonetheless, *Marbury* long has been read as establishing that Congress cannot enlarge the Supreme Court's jurisdiction.

By analogy, it could be argued that Congress also cannot increase the jurisdiction of the lower federal courts. That is, just as Article III sets the ceiling on Supreme Court jurisdiction, so does it prevent enlargement of lower federal court authority. In *Hodgson v. Bowerbank*, Chief Justice John Marshall, in a short opinion, held that a federal statute could not authorize suits between aliens because the Constitution extends the judicial power only to suits between aliens and American citizens.[3] *Hodgson* thus can be read as establishing that Congress may not expand federal court jurisdiction beyond what is authorized in Article III.[4]

National Mutual Insurance Co. v. Tidewater Transfer Co.

Additionally, the contention that Congress cannot increase federal court jurisdiction finds support in the Supreme Court's decision in *National Mutual Insurance Co. v. Tidewater Transfer Co.*[5] *Tidewater* is a confusing case because of the absence of a majority opinion. Yet six justices clearly voted that Congress cannot expand

§3.4 [1] 5 U.S. (1 Cranch) 137 (1803).

[2] *See* William W. Van Alstyne, A Critical Guide to Marbury v. Madison, 1969 Duke L.J. 1.

[3] 9 U.S. (5 Cranch) 303 (1809).

[4] *But see* Dennis J. Nahoney, A Historical Note on Hodgson v. Bowerbank, 49 U. Chi. L. Rev. 725 (1982) (arguing that the decision was based on an interpretation of the jurisdictional statute).

[5] 337 U.S. 582 (1949).

federal court jurisdiction beyond that provided in Article III. In *Tidewater*, the issue was the constitutionality of a federal statute providing that citizens of the District of Columbia should be treated as citizens of a state for purposes of determining whether there is diversity jurisdiction. In 1804, the Supreme Court held that citizens of the District of Columbia were not citizens of a state and therefore could not sue or be sued in diversity cases.[6] In 1940, Congress amended the diversity statute to provide that citizens of the District of Columbia should be treated as citizens of a state for diversity purposes.[7] The constitutionality of this law was the issue in *Tidewater*.

There were several opinions, none attracting a majority. Three justices—Justices Jackson, Black, and Vinson—argued that the federal law was constitutional because Congress could enlarge the jurisdiction of the federal courts. These justices contended that Congress could authorize federal courts to hear matters beyond those authorized in Article III if such an expansion was "necessary and proper" to effectuate a congressional power.[8]

Two justices—Justices Rutledge and Murphy—concurred in the judgment. They also voted to uphold the statute, but disagreed that Congress could expand federal court jurisdiction beyond what is enumerated in Article III. Justices Rutledge and Murphy argued that logically it made sense to treat citizens of the District of Columbia as citizens of a state for diversity purposes. They observed that such an approach would fulfill the underlying purposes of diversity jurisdiction. In other words, they concluded that the law was constitutional, not because Congress could expand jurisdiction beyond Article III, but because it was permissible under Article III to treat the District of Columbia like a state.

Four justices—Chief Justice Vinson and Justices Douglas, Frankfurter, and Reed—dissented. They argued that Congress could not expand the judicial power beyond what was provided in Article III and that the District of Columbia should not be treated like a state under the Constitution.

Thus, there were five votes to uphold the statute, though there was no agreement as to the basis for finding the law constitutional, but there were six votes that Congress may not expand federal court jurisdiction. Hence, the *Tidewater* case is seen as affirming *Marbury v. Madison*: Congress may not enlarge the jurisdiction of the federal courts.[9]

Examples of Congress Increasing Federal Court Jurisdiction

There are, however, some instances in which the Supreme Court has held that specialized Article III courts can hear matters in addition to those specified in the Constitution.[10] For example, during the 1930s, the Supreme Court held that

[6] Hepburn & Dundas v. Ellzey, 6 U.S. (2 Cranch) 445 (1805).

[7] 28 U.S.C. §1332(d) (1982).

[8] 337 U.S. at 588-589.

[9] For a discussion of the jurisdiction of the federal courts under the Constitution and current jurisdictional statutes, *see* Chapter 5.

[10] An Article III court is simply a court where the judges have life tenure, salaries that cannot be decreased during their terms of office, and responsibilities that are primarily deciding Article III

it was permissible for Congress to assign the U.S. Court of Appeals for the District of Columbia administrative tasks, such as reviewing public utility rates.[11] The Supreme Court considered the District of Columbia court as a "hybrid" because it performed both judicial and administrative tasks.[12] Subsequently, the Court held that the Court of Claims and Court of Customs and Patent Appeals are Article III courts even though they were assigned some additional functions besides deciding cases and controversies.[13]

These cases seem to be exceptions that emerged from longstanding historical practices. The general rule is that Congress cannot assign to Article III courts additional duties beyond deciding Article III cases and controversies.[14] The most important implication of this principle is that Congress cannot override constitutional limits on federal court jurisdiction. For example, if the Court finds that certain standing requirements are constitutionally required, Congress may not eliminate them by statute because the effect of doing so would be to expand federal jurisdiction beyond the limits set in Article III.[15] Likewise, this principle makes it important to determine whether other jurisdictional rules announced by the Court—such as abstention doctrines—are constitutional or prudential.[16] Because Congress cannot expand jurisdiction, it can eliminate only prudential limits by statute; it cannot override constitutional restrictions.

§3.5 CONGRESSIONAL POWER TO HAVE STATE COURTS DECIDE FEDERAL LAW MATTERS

Authority for State Courts to Hear Federal Law Matters

It is clearly established that state courts may decide questions of federal law unless a federal statute mandates exclusive federal court jurisdiction. The Supreme Court has explained: "The general principle of state-court jurisdiction over cases

cases and controversies. *See* Glidden Co. v. Zdanok, 370 U.S. 530, 533-534 (1962) (defining Article III courts). For a discussion of Article III courts as opposed to courts where judges do not have life tenure and salary protections, *see* Chapter 4.

[11] O'Donoghue v. United States, 289 U.S. 516 (1933) (courts are Article III tribunals though they have administrative tasks); Keller v. Potomac Elec. Power Co., 261 U.S. 428 (1923) (Supreme Court cannot review U.S. Court of Appeals for the District of Columbia's review of Public Utility Commission rates because it is an administrative task). These cases are discussed more fully in §4.2, *infra.*

[12] O'Donoghue v. United States, 289 U.S. at 546.

[13] Glidden Co. v. Zdanok, 370 U.S. 530 (1962).

[14] Commentators have developed an additional theory justifying congressional expansion of federal court jurisdiction, termed "protective jurisdiction." This theory is that Congress may authorize jurisdiction to protect federal interests. Protective jurisdiction is discussed in §5.2.2, *infra.*

[15] For a discussion of constitutional limits on standing, *see* §2.3, *supra.*

[16] For example, for a discussion of whether the judicially created rule preventing federal courts from enjoining pending state court proceedings is constitutional or prudential, *see* §13.3, *infra.*

arising under federal law is straightforward: state courts may assume subject matter jurisdiction over a federal cause of action absent provision by Congress to the contrary or disabling incompatibility between the federal claim and the state-court adjudication."[1]

Indeed, the Supreme Court has spoken of a "deeply rooted presumption in favor of concurrent state court jurisdiction."[2] Therefore, state courts have the authority to hear all cases, including ones arising under federal law, unless Congress has vested exclusive jurisdiction in the federal courts over a matter.

Must State Courts Hear Federal Law Claims?

While it is clear that state courts *may* hear federal law matters absent a federal statute to the contrary, *must* state courts do so? There is strong authority from the Supreme Court that state courts cannot discriminate against federal claims. For example, in a series of decisions arising under the Federal Employers' Liability Act, the Court declared that state courts could not decline to hear the federal claims. In *Mondou v. New York, New Haven & H. R.R.*, the Supreme Court reversed a state court's refusal to hear a suit brought under the Federal Employers' Liability Act.[3] The Court stated: "We conclude that matters arising under the act in question may be enforced as of right, in the courts of the States when their jurisdiction, as prescribed by local laws, is adequate to the occasion."[4] Likewise, in a similar case arising under the same act, the Court stated: "[T]he Federal Constitution prohibits state courts of general jurisdiction from refusing to do so solely because the suit is brought under a federal law. . . . A state may not discriminate against rights arising under federal laws."[5]

Likewise, *Testa v. Katt* precludes state courts from discriminating against federal law claims.[6] In *Testa*, the Rhode Island Supreme Court dismissed a claim filed under the Emergency Price Control Act, a statute that gave concurrent jurisdiction to state and federal courts. The U.S. Supreme Court reversed the state court decision and held that state courts cannot refuse to hear federal claims, at least in circumstances where state courts would hear similar state law claims.[7]

§3.5 [1] Gulf Offshore Oil Co. v. Mobil Oil Co., 453 U.S. 473, 477 (1981).

[2] Tafflin v. Levitt, 493 U.S. 455, 459 (1990) (holding that state courts have concurrent jurisdiction over RICO cases); *see also* Yellow Freight System, Inc. v. Donnelly, 494 U.S. 820 (1990) (state courts have concurrent jurisdiction to hear Title VII cases).

[3] 223 U.S. 1 (1912).

[4] *Id.* at 59.

[5] McKnett v. St. Louis & S.F. Ry., 292 U.S. 230, 233-234 (1934).

[6] 330 U.S. 386 (1947). For an argument that these cases prevent Congress from discriminating against certain constitutional claims and thus limit the congressional power to restrict federal court jurisdiction, *see* Lea B. Brilmayer & Stefan Underhill, Congressional Obligation to Provide a Forum for Constitutional Claims: Discriminatory Jurisdictional Rules and Conflict of Laws, 69 Va. L. Rev. 819 (1983).

[7] *See* Nicole A. Gordon & Douglas Gross, Justiciability of Federal Claims in State Court, 59 Notre Dame L. Rev. 1145 (1984) (arguing that the supremacy clause requires state courts to hear federal claims even if similar rights under state law would not be heard in state court); Terrance Sandalow, Henry v. Mississippi and the Adequate State Ground: Proposals for a Revised Doctrine, 1965 Sup. Ct. Rev. 187, 206-207 (discussing state courts' obligations to hear federal claims).

In *Howlett v. Rose*, the Court reviewed these precedents and concluded that a state court could not apply a state law defense to defeat a federal law claim.[8] Howlett involved a claim by a former high school student against school officials challenging both an allegedly illegal search and wrongful suspension from school. The suit was brought in Florida state court pursuant to 42 U.S.C. §1983, the federal statute that creates a cause of action against those acting under color of state law who violate the Constitution or laws of the United States.[9] The Florida Court of Appeal found that the suit was barred by state law sovereign immunity.

The U.S. Supreme Court reversed. The Court summarized the law in this area:

> Three corollaries follow from the proposition that "federal" law is part of the law of the land in the state: 1. A state court may not deny a federal right, when the parties and controversy are properly before it, in the absence of a "valid excuse." 2. An excuse that is inconsistent with or violates federal law is not a valid excuse: the supremacy clause forbids state courts to disassociate themselves from federal law because of disagreement with its content or a refusal to recognize the superior authority of its source.... 3. When a state court refuses jurisdiction because of a neutral state rule regarding the administration of the courts, we must act with utmost caution before deciding that it is obligated to entertain the claim. The requirement that a state court of competent jurisdiction treat federal law as the law of the land does not necessarily include within it a requirement that the state create a court competent to hear the case in which the federal claim is presented.[10]

In *Howlett*, the Court concluded that a state court could not use state law sovereign immunity to deny recovery under §1983. *Howlett* is important for reaffirming that state courts cannot discriminate against federal law claims. However, *Howlett* does not answer what constitutes a valid excuse that would permit a state court to refuse to hear a federal law matter. It remains unclear as to when, if ever, state courts can refuse to hear federal law claims. Indeed, although *Howlett* would seem to create a duty for state courts to hear §1983 claims, subsequently Justice Thomas in a footnote in a majority opinion stated: "We have never held that state courts must entertain §1983 claims."[11]

Subsequently, in *Haywood v. Drown*, the Court reaffirmed the duty of state court to hear federal claims, but notably, it was a 5-4 decision, split along ideological lines.[12] Under New York law, corrections officers could not be sued in state court for money damages. This barred New York state courts from hearing §1983 claims for money damages against state officers.

Justice Stevens, writing for the majority, explained that states may have "neutral rules of judicial administration" but declared, "[A]lthough States retain substantial leeway to establish the contours of their judicial systems, they lack authority

[8] 496 U.S. 356 (1990).

[9] Section 1983 is discussed in detail in Chapter 8.

[10] 496 U.S. at 356.

[11] National Private Truck Council, Inc. v. Oklahoma Tax Commission, 515 U.S. 582, 588 n.4 (1995).

[12] 556 U.S. 729 (2009).

to nullify a federal right or cause of action they believe is inconsistent with their local policies."[13] The fact that New York precluded jurisdiction in state court over both federal and state law claims was irrelevant; barring the state courts from hearing federal claims was deemed unconstitutional. The Court stated, "We therefore hold that, having made the decision to create courts of general jurisdiction that regularly sit to entertain analogous suits, New York is not at liberty to shut the courthouse door to federal claims that it considers at odds with its local policy."[14]

Justice Thomas wrote for the four dissenting justices and argued that the supremacy of federal law "is not impugned by a State's decision to strip its local courts of subject-matter jurisdiction to hear certain federal claims."[15] Justice Thomas distinguished cases such as *Howlett v. Rose* on the ground that they involved statutes precluding only federal claims, whereas the New York law barred all claims against state corrections officers. He concluded his dissent by declaring, "By imposing on state courts a duty to accept subject-matter jurisdiction over federal §1983 actions, the Court has stretched the Supremacy Clause beyond all reasonable bounds and upended a compromise struck by the Framers in Article III of the Constitution."[16]

Must State Courts Follow Federal Procedures?

If a state court is hearing a case arising under federal law, must it also follow the federal procedures? If the federal law expressly specifies the procedures to be used with regard to a particular cause of action, then, of course, states must follow it. In *Dice v. Akron, Canton & Youngstown Railroad Co.*, the Court concluded that the federal law, the Federal Employers' Liability Act, expressly provided for jury trials and thus state courts hearing cases under it had to comply with this requirement.[17]

Absent such clear statutory intent, the Supreme Court generally has held that state courts are not obligated to follow federal procedural rules as long as the state procedures do not unduly burden the federal rights. For example, in *Johnson v. Fankell*, the Supreme Court ruled that states need not allow interlocutory appeals for the denial of immunity in suits against government officials.[18] The Supreme

[13] *Id.* at 736.

[14] *Id.* at 740-741.

[15] *Id.* at 755 (Thomas, J., dissenting).

[16] *Id.* at 777. Interestingly, the dissent did not rely on Supreme Court cases holding that Congress cannot compel state legislative or administrative activity. In New York v. United States, 505 U.S. 144 (1992), the Court declared unconstitutional as violating the Tenth Amendment a federal statute that commanded states to clean up their nuclear wastes. In Printz v. United States, 521 U.S. 898 (1997), the Court similarly invalidated a federal law that required that state and local law enforcement personnel conduct background checks before issuing permits for firearms. In each case, the Court found it unconstitutional for Congress to commandeer the states and compel actions. Although Justice Thomas did not expressly invoke these decisions, the underlying issue is the same: When may Congress compel states to act, such as to compel state courts to hear federal law matters? For an excellent discussion of this issue, *see* Evan H. Caminker, State Sovereignty and Subordinancy: May Congress Commandeer State Officials to Implement Federal Law?, 95 Colum. L. Rev. 1001, 1022-1060 (1995).

[17] 342 U.S. 359 (1952).

[18] 520 U.S. 911 (1997).

Court has held that government officers sued for constitutional violations may raise an affirmative defense of immunity.[19] In *Mitchell v. Forsyth,* the Court ruled that a trial court's denial of immunity is subject to an interlocutory appeal.[20] The issue in *Johnson v. Fankell* was whether state courts must allow interlocutory appeals when they hear suits against individual officials under §1983. The Court ruled that state courts need not follow this aspect of federal procedure because the denial of interlocutory review was not likely to be "outcome determinative" and because Congress "has mentioned nothing about interlocutory appeals in §1983."[21]

In contrast, in *Felder v. Casey*, the Court held that failure to comply with a state notice of claim rule could not be used to deny relief under §1983.[22] The state law required that claims against government entities or officials be filed in writing within 120 days of the incident. A state court used this statute to dismiss a suit under §1983. The Supreme Court found that the application of this state procedural requirement was unconstitutional. The Court explained that "application of the notice requirement burdens the exercise of the federal right" in a manner that is "inconsistent in both design and effect with the compensatory aims of federal civil rights law."[23]

Thus, state courts generally need not follow federal procedures when hearing federal law claims. However, state courts must do so if Congress specifies the procedure for a particular matter. Additionally, states must follow federal procedures if the application of state procedures would be "outcome determinative" or significantly "burden the exercise of federal rights."

[19] Absolute and qualified immunities are discussed in detail in Chapter 8.
[20] 472 U.S. 511 (1985).
[21] 520 U.S. at 918-921, 921 n.12.
[22] 487 U.S. 131 (1988).
[23] *Id.* at 141.

CHAPTER 4

Congressional Power to Create Legislative Courts

§4.1 INTRODUCTION

Article III versus Article I courts

Article III of the U.S. Constitution provides that federal judges shall have life tenure, assuming good behavior, and salaries that cannot be decreased during their terms of office.[1] This protection was intended to insulate federal judges from

§4.1 [1] U.S. Const., Art. III, §1.

direct political pressure and ensure that they would uphold the Constitution and federal laws without regard to the popularity of their actions. In the *Federalist Papers*, Alexander Hamilton wrote that "[t]he standard of good behavior for the continuance in office of the judicial magistracy is certainly one of the most valuable of the modern improvements in the practice of government."[2] Hamilton explained that "[i]n a monarchy it is an excellent barrier to the despotism of the prince; in a republic it is no less excellent barrier to the encroachments and oppressions of the representative body. And it is the best expedient which can be devised in any government to secure a steady, upright, and impartial administration of the laws."[3]

Yet throughout virtually all of American history, Congress has created tribunals in which the judges do not have life tenure and protected salary to decide cases and controversies enumerated in Article III. Sometimes, Congress creates courts for particular matters and specifies that the judges will sit for fixed terms. The Tax Court, for instance, has judges who sit for 15-year terms.[4] In other instances, Congress empowers administrative agencies to decide particular matters that also fit within the nine categories of cases and controversies enumerated in Article III.[5]

These tribunals that have judges or other decision makers who are not accorded life tenure or salary guarantees are termed "legislative courts" or "Article I courts." In other words, an Article III court is one where the judges hold their positions for life, unless impeached, and where the judges' salaries may not be decreased during their terms of office. A legislative or Article I court is one where the judges do not have these protections.[6] The term "legislative court," as used throughout this chapter, includes judicial tribunals and administrative agencies that decide Article III judicial matters but whose decision makers lack life tenure and salary protections.[7]

Reasons for Creating Article I Courts

Congress might choose to create legislative courts for a number of reasons. Desiring to keep the federal judiciary small and prestigious, Congress might want to avoid establishing large numbers of additional judgeships to deal with the countless matters handled in administrative agencies and in specialized tribunals like bankruptcy courts. Moreover, Congress might want to allow agencies that also possess rule-making and investigative powers to decide particular controversies

[2] The Federalist No. 78, at 465 (A. Hamilton) (C. Rossiter ed. 1961).

[3] *Id.*

[4] 26 U.S.C. §§7441, 7446 (1982).

[5] *See, e.g.*, Atlas Roofing Co. v. Occupational Safety & Health Review Comm'n., 430 U.S. 442 (1977) (constitutionality of Occupational Safety and Health Commission imposition of civil penalties).

[6] *See, e.g.*, Glidden Co. v. Zdanok, 370 U.S. 530 (1962) (describing the meaning of the term "legislative courts"). The terms "legislative courts" and "Article I" courts are used synonymously throughout this chapter. They include both administrative agencies that perform adjudicative functions and those designated as courts in which the judges do not have life tenure and a guaranteed salary.

[7] *See* Laura K. Donohue & Jeremy McCabe, Federal Courts: Article I, II, III, and IV Adjudication, 71 Cath. U. L. Rev. 543, 545 (2022) (offering labels to clarify these types of tribunals).

within their expertise.[8] Using agencies, rather than courts, to decide issues offers the advantages of efficiency and cost savings.[9] In some instances, Congress might prefer legislative courts precisely because the judges are less likely to be independent because they lack life tenure and salary protections.

This chapter focuses on this question: When is it constitutional for Congress to vest Article III cases and controversies—matters that are part of the federal judicial power and may be heard by an Article III court—in a legislative court?

Should All Federal Courts Be Article III Tribunals?

A tempting answer is that under the text of Article III, Congress is never permitted to create judges who lack life tenure and salary assurances. Article III states that "[t]he judicial power of the United States shall be vested in one Supreme Court, and in such inferior courts as the Congress may from time to time ordain and establish." The next sentence of Article III provides that "[t]he Judges, both of the Supreme and inferior courts, shall hold their Offices during good Behavior, and shall, at stated Times, receive for the Services, a Compensation, which shall not be diminished during their Continuation in Office."

These provisions seem unambiguously to require that the judicial power be vested only in courts where the judges have life tenure and salary protection. Any court created by Congress, by definition, is an inferior court because it is subordinate to the U.S. Supreme Court. All such judges, like Supreme Court justices, must be allowed to sit for life, assuming good behavior. Moreover, Article III specifies that the judicial power be vested only in the Supreme Court or in the inferior courts created by Congress. The Constitution offers no authority for granting other bodies the power to decide Article III judicial matters.[10]

Despite the apparent clarity of the text, however, it no longer is realistic to argue that it is always unconstitutional for Congress to create legislative courts to decide Article III judicial business. For over 200 years, legislative courts have been permitted. The first Congress authorized executive officers in the Treasury Department to decide matters, such as claims to veterans' benefits, that fell within Article III.[11] The Supreme Court has upheld the constitutionality of legislative courts since 1828.[12] Declaring all legislative courts unconstitutional would invalidate hundreds of tribunals and agencies. In light of this background, it is highly unlikely that the Supreme Court ever would declare all legislative courts to be unconstitutional.[13]

[8] *See* Richard Fallon, Of Legislative Courts, Administrative Agencies and Article III, 101 Harv. L. Rev. 916, 935-936 (1988).

[9] *Id.*

[10] For an argument that there is no clear textual prohibition against legislative courts, *see* Craig A. Stern, What's a Legislative Court Among Friends: Unbalancing Article III, 146 U. Pa. L. Rev. 1043 (1998) (arguing that the text of Article III permits legislative courts).

[11] Fallon, *supra* note 8, at 919.

[12] American Ins. Co. v. Canter, 26 U.S. (1 Pet.) 511 (1828).

[13] For an excellent discussion of why Article III literalism is impossible in this context, *see* Fallon, *supra* note 8, at 918-926. For a defense of a more literal approach to Article III, *see* David P. Currie,

Nor is it likely that the Court ever would rule that all legislative courts, regardless of the circumstances, are permissible. For example, it is doubtful that the Court would permit Congress to circumvent Article III's assurance of an independent judiciary by creating legislative courts to hear all constitutional matters or to decide particular controversial cases according to Congress's wishes.[14] The assurances of life tenure and stable judicial salaries are the core of the Constitution's assurance of an independent judiciary.

Thus, because legislative courts are neither likely to be always invalidated nor always approved, a line-drawing problem emerges. Under what circumstances may Congress authorize legislative courts to decide Article III cases and controversies? The law in this area long has been regarded as complex and confusing. More than a half-century ago, Justice Harlan remarked that the problem of legislative courts "has been productive of much confusion and controversy."[15] Three major decisions on the topic during the 1980s only exacerbated the confusion.[16] The issue reemerged because of the Supreme Court's decision in 2011 in *Stern v. Marshall,* which concerned the authority of the bankruptcy courts to issue final judgments over state law counterclaims and which potentially could affect the powers of other non-Article III courts as well.[17] But just four years later, in 2015, the Court limited the importance of *Stern v. Marshall* and took a completely different approach to when non-Article III courts are permissible in *Wellness International Network Ltd. v. Sharif.*[18] Most recently, in 2024, in *Securities and Exchange Commission v. Jarkesy,* the Supreme Court held that it violates the Seventh Amendment for agencies to impose civil penalties for fraud, potentially imposing a significant new limit on adjudications in non-Article III tribunals.[19]

Current Law Summarized

To the extent that the law in this area can be simply summarized, there are four situations in which legislative courts are permissible: (1) for U.S. possessions and territories, (2) for military matters, (3) for civil disputes between the United States and private citizens,[20] and (4) for criminal matters or for disputes between

---

Bankruptcy Judges and the Independent Judiciary, 16 Creighton L. Rev. 441 (1983); Martin H. Redish, Legislative Courts, Administrative Agencies, and the *Northern Pipeline* Decision, 1983 Duke L.J. 197.

[14] The Supreme Court's decision in Northern Pipeline Constr. Co. v. Marathon Pipe Line Co., 458 U.S. 50 (1982), demonstrates that the Court is not about to approve all legislative courts. This case is discussed in detail in §4.5.3, *infra.*

[15] Glidden Co. v. Zdanok, 370 U.S. at 534 (Harlan, J., concurring).

[16] Commodity Futures Trading Comm'n. v. Schor, 478 U.S. 833 (1986); Thomas v. Union Carbide Agric. Prods. Co., 473 U.S. 568 (1985); Northern Pipeline Constr. Co. v. Marathon Pipe Line Co., 458 U.S. 50 (1982). These cases are discussed in §§4.5.3 and 4.5.4, *infra.*

[17] 564 U.S. 462 (2011). Stern v. Marshall is discussed in detail in §4.5.5, *infra.*

[18] 575 U.S. 665 (2015), discussed in detail in §4.5.5, *infra.*

[19] 603 U.S. 109 (2024), discussed below at text accompanying notes 38-44, *infra.*

[20] It is here that Securities and Exchange Commission v. Jarkesy, *id.* imposes a significant limit, concluding that the Seventh Amendment requires that civil penalties for fraud be adjudicated in a federal court.

private citizens where the legislative court serves as an adjunct to an Article III court that can review the legislative court's decisions. A legislative court can be considered an adjunct of the federal district court if the former lacks the ability to enforce its own judgments and if there is de novo review of its decisions by an Article III judge.[21]

Each of these four areas is considered, in turn, in §§4.2-4.5. This topic of legislative courts is important because it raises basic questions of separation of powers as to the proper relationship between Congress and the federal courts. What is Congress's power to control federal jurisdiction by directing Article III judicial business to legislative courts?[22] In fact, one of the major objections to legislative courts is based on separation of powers: the fear that Congress will attempt to influence the outcome of cases by channeling matters to tribunals where judges are less insulated from direct political pressure.[23] Additionally, examination of the problem of legislative courts focuses attention on the importance of life tenure and salary protection for judges. Because a primary difference between the federal and state courts is the life tenure of federal judges, it is important to consider whether this factor really matters in ensuring fairness and justice.[24]

The Roberts Court is in the midst of making substantial changes to administrative law.[25] Although most of these have not been about the constitutionality of using agencies to adjudicate matters, some such as *Securities and Exchange Commission v. Jarkesy*, have been about this. And others certainly affect how agencies operate and how they are reviewed by Article III courts.

[21] For an excellent article discussing the situations in which Article I courts are permissible, *see* James E. Pfander, Article I Tribunals, Article III Courts, and the Judicial Power of the United States, 118 Harv. L. Rev. 643 (2004) (emphasizing the importance of Article I's reference to "inferior tribunals" compared with Article III's reference to "inferior courts").

[22] The distinct, though obviously related, question of Congress's power to restrict federal jurisdiction and thereby direct matters to state courts (rather than to legislative courts) is discussed in Chapter 3.

[23] *See* Fallon, *supra* note 8, at 937.

[24] *See generally* Judith Resnik, The Mythic Meaning of Article III Courts, 56 U. Colo. L. Rev. 581 (1985). It should be noted that the importance of life tenure and salary protections is a recurring theme in the debate over whether there is parity between federal and state courts in constitutional cases; that is, whether state judges, who usually face some electoral review, should be regarded as equal to federal judges in their ability and willingness to protect federal constitutional rights. *See* §1.5, *supra*.

[25] In an important article, Professor William Baude argues non-Article III courts might exercise three types of power, including "judicial power, but not the judicial power of the United States. Rather, they exercise the judicial power of some other government. The obvious example is state courts, but the same logic explains adjudication by territorial courts, tribal courts, and foreign courts. Some exercise executive power, not judicial power. The main constitutional constraint on this form of executive power is the longstanding principle, codified by the Due Process Clause, that requires judicial process before one can be deprived of life, liberty, or property. This power, and this proviso, explains the administrative adjudication of public rights. Executive power also explains military courts, although they have a historically different relationship to due process.

"Finally, some adjudication is done in bodies that are vested with no governmental power at all. These bodies must derive their ability to adjudicate either from a nongovernmental source, such as the consent of the parties, or from their close relationship as an 'adjunct' of a true court vested with judicial power." William Baude, Adjudication Outside Article III, 133 Harv. L. Rev. 1511, 1513-14 (2020).

§4.2 LEGISLATIVE COURTS FOR THE TERRITORIES AND THE DISTRICT OF COLUMBIA

Legislative Courts for Territories

Territorial courts posed the first instance in which the Supreme Court considered the constitutionality of federal courts where judges were appointed without life tenure. In *American Insurance Co. v. Canter*, in 1828, the Supreme Court considered the constitutionality of a court created for the territory of Florida, which was not yet a state.[1] Judges on this territorial court were appointed for four-year terms. The territorial court had authorized the sale of a cargo of cotton salvaged off the coast of Florida. An insurance company that claimed ownership interests in the cotton challenged the sale, arguing, in part, that the court's judgment was invalid because a court exercising admiralty jurisdiction under Article III had to be staffed with judges possessing life tenure.

Chief Justice Marshall, writing for the Court, upheld the constitutionality of the territorial courts. The Court contrasted "constitutional courts" established by Congress pursuant to Article III, with "legislative courts," which were created pursuant to Congress's legislative powers under Articles I and IV of the Constitution. Chief Justice Marshall declared: "These Courts, then, are not constitutional Courts. . . . They are legislative Courts, created in virtue of that general right of sovereignty which exists in the government, or in virtue of the clause which enables Congress to make all needful rules and regulations, respecting the territory belonging to the United States."[2] The Court reasoned that Congress's plenary power to govern the territories, granted by Article IV, included the authority to establish courts that did not have to conform to Article III, but that could exercise jurisdiction over matters enumerated in Article III.

The primary reason Congress created territorial courts with judges lacking life tenure was to avoid a surplus of federal judges after the territories were admitted into statehood.[3] The territorial courts decided all judicial matters—both federal and state law questions—arising in the territories. Thus, there was a need for more territorial judges than there would be for federal judges once the territory became a state. In Florida, for example, there were five territorial judges, but after it became a state, there was only one federal court judge.[4] The Supreme Court later explained that "[i]t would have been doctrinaire in the extreme to deny the right of Congress to invest judges of its creation with authority to dispose of the judicial business of the territories. It would have been at least as dogmatic . . . to fashion on those judges a guarantee of tenure that

§4.2 [1] 26 U.S. (1 Pet.) 511 (1828).

[2] *Id.* at 546.

[3] *See* Glidden Co. v. Zdanok, 370 U.S. 530, 544-547 (1962) (explaining rationale behind territorial courts).

[4] *Id.*

Congress could not put to use and that the exigencies of the territories did not require."[5]

An argument can be made that this policy argument did not justify the Court's permitting a departure from the literal language of Article III. Article III says that all inferior federal courts—that is, all federal courts subordinate to the U.S. Supreme Court—shall have judges with life tenure who are protected against reductions in salary. By definition, the territorial courts are inferior courts of the United States. It might be argued that Congress was obligated under Article III to create two classes of judges: one group with life tenure to hear Article III cases and controversies, and the other with limited terms to decide state law matters.

Nonetheless, Chief Justice Marshall's opinion established the constitutionality of courts where judges are appointed for fixed terms and coined the phrase "legislative courts."[6] Legislative courts for the territories remain in existence to this day. For example, the district courts for Guam, the Virgin Islands, the Northern Mariana Islands, and the Canal Zone are considered to be legislative courts whose judges serve for fixed terms.[7]

In *Nguyen v. United States*,[8] the Court held that it was impermissible for a U.S. Court of Appeals hearing an appeal from a territorial court to be comprised of two Article III judges and one Article I territorial court judge. An individual was convicted in federal court in Guam of drug offenses and his appeal was heard by a panel composed of two Ninth Circuit judges and the chief district judge for the Northern Mariana Islands. The latter is not an Article III judge, and the Court held that an Article I judge was not allowed under federal statutes to sit on an appellate panel.

District of Columbia Courts

The courts for the District of Columbia are in many ways analogous to the territorial courts because for much of American history they decided both state and federal law questions and performed administrative tasks as well. For example, during the early part of the twentieth century, the Court of Appeals for the District of Columbia had broad authority to review rates set by the Public Utilities Commission for the District of Columbia and licensing orders issued by the Federal Radio Commission.

The Supreme Court initially held that rulings by the District of Columbia Court of Appeals in these areas were administrative and not judicial and thus were not subject to review by the U.S. Supreme Court.[9] The Court reasoned that the District of Columbia Court was created pursuant to Congress's powers under

[5] *Id.*

[6] Corporation of the Presiding Bishop of the Church of Latter Day Saints v. Hodel, 830 F.2d 374 (D.C. Cir. 1987), *cert. denied,* 486 U.S. 1015 (1988) (upholding the constitutionality of the High Court for the American Samoa).

[7] Judges for the federal district court in Puerto Rico, however, are accorded life tenure. 28 U.S.C. §134(a) (1982).

[8] 539 U.S. 69 (2003).

[9] Federal Radio Commn. v. General Elec. Co., 281 U.S. 464 (1930); Keller v. Potomac Elec. Power Co., 261 U.S. 428 (1923).

Article I of the Constitution and hence could decide nonjudicial matters assigned to it by the legislature.

This view of the U.S. Court of Appeals for the District of Columbia was short-lived. Just a few years after labeling the District of Columbia court a legislative court, the Supreme Court concluded that it was an Article III court and that its judges had to be accorded life tenure and salary protection. In 1932, in the midst of the Depression, Congress adopted a law reducing the salaries of all judges who were not protected from such a decrease by Article III. In *O'Donoghue v. United States*, the Supreme Court held that the District of Columbia Court of Appeals was an Article III court and therefore its judges' salaries could not be lowered.[10]

But the Court ruled that it was permissible for Congress to vest in this Article III court the responsibility for handling administrative matters not included within the Article III judicial power.[11] The Court reasoned that the District of Columbia Court of Appeals properly should be characterized as a "hybrid court."[12] The Court said that the District of Columbia Court was an Article III tribunal because its judges possessed life tenure and salary protection, but that Congress's plenary power to govern the district allowed it to authorize the District of Columbia court to hear matters in addition to those enumerated in Article III.[13]

The Supreme Court returned to the problem of the District of Columbia Courts in *Palmore v. United States.*[14] In the District of Columbia Court Reform and Criminal Procedure Act, Congress stripped the U.S. District Court for the District of Columbia and the U.S. Court of Appeals for the District of Columbia Circuit of all of their local jurisdictions.[15] Congress created a new District of Columbia Superior Court (with appeals to a District of Columbia Court of Appeals) that was expressly said to be "established pursuant to article I," and whose judges serve a 15-year term. Under the law restructuring the District of Columbia courts, violations of federal criminal laws that apply throughout the country are tried in federal court, but infractions of criminal statutes applying only in the District of Columbia are tried in the Superior Court.

In *Palmore,* the Supreme Court considered the constitutionality of permitting a legislative court, the District of Columbia Superior Court, to decide federal criminal law cases.[16] Palmore argued that because he was prosecuted under a federal law, albeit one applicable only in the District of Columbia, and tried in

[10] 289 U.S. 516 (1933).

[11] For a discussion of Congress's power to vest Article III courts with authority greater than that enumerated in Article III, *see* §3.4, *supra.*

[12] 289 U.S. at 546.

[13] *Id.*

[14] 411 U.S. 389 (1973). Three justices also addressed implicitly the issue of the District of Columbia courts in National Mut. Ins. Co. v. Tidewater Transfer Co., 337 U.S. 582 (1949). The issue in *Tidewater* was whether Congress could permit residents of the District of Columbia to be treated as citizens for the purpose of diversity jurisdiction. Three justices (Justices Jackson, Black, and Burton) argued that Congress could use its powers under Article I to turn all federal courts into hybrid courts and permit them to hear matters in addition to those arising under Article III. Six justices rejected this position. The *Tidewater* case is discussed in more detail in §3.4, *supra.*

[15] 84 Stat. 473.

[16] 411 U.S. 389 (1973).

a court created by Congress, it was unconstitutional for the judge not to have life tenure. The Supreme Court rejected this contention. The Court concluded that "the requirements of Article III, which are applicable where laws of national applicability and affairs of national concern are at stake, must in proper circumstances give way to accommodate plenary grants of power to Congress to legislate with respect to specialized areas having particularized needs and warranting distinctive treatment."[17] The Court reasoned that a criminal defendant tried in the District of Columbia court for violating a local law was "no more disadvantaged and no more entitled to an Article III judge than any other citizen of any of the 50 states who is tried for a strictly local crime."[18]

Thus, the use of legislative courts for the territories and for the District of Columbia is firmly established. The underlying constitutional rationale is that Congress created these courts not pursuant to its power under Article III but rather as an exercise of its authority granted by Article IV to regulate the territories and by Article I to govern the nation's capital.

Legislative Courts for Foreign Countries

Also, the Supreme Court has held that Congress can create legislative courts in foreign countries.[19] The Court reasoned that the Constitution has no application outside the United States and hence permits the creation, when necessary, of judicial tribunals in which judges are not accorded life tenure. Because these courts are likely to be transitory, such as courts for the territories, a permanent judiciary would be undesirable.

§4.3 LEGISLATIVE COURTS FOR THE MILITARY

Initial Authority for Military Courts

Although military tribunals have the power to deprive military personnel of their liberty by imprisonment and even to impose capital punishment, the Court has permitted these courts to be staffed with judges who lack life tenure and salary protections. In *Dynes v. Hoover*, in 1858, the Supreme Court upheld Congress's

[17] *Id.* at 408.

[18] *Id.* at 410. For a criticism of *Palmore*, *see* James Durling, The District of Columbia and Article III, 107 Geo. L.J. 1205 (2019).

[19] In re Ross, 140 U.S. 453 (1891); *see also* Herbert Jay Stern, Judgment in Berlin (1984) (description of the creation of a special U.S. court in Berlin to try an East German hijacker); Thomas G. Becker, Justice on the Far Side of the World: The Continuing Problem of Misconduct by Civilians Accompanying the Armed Forces in Foreign Countries, 18 Hastings Intl. & Comp. L. Rev. 277 (1995).

power to create legislative courts for the military.[1] The Court explained that Congress's authority under Article I permitted it "to provide for the trial and punishment of military and naval offences . . . without any connection between it and the 3d article of the Constitution defining the judicial power of the United States."[2]

Military courts lack not only judges with life tenure but also crucial constitutional protections otherwise required by the Bill of Rights: grand jury indictment;[3] trial by jury;[4] and in some instances, the right to counsel.[5] For much of American history, no Article III court—including the U.S. Supreme Court—had authority to review on appeal the decisions of military courts.[6] Thus, it is hardly surprising that the military courts had been strongly criticized as antithetical to the American system of justice: criticism perhaps best summarized in the title of Robert Sherrill's famous book, *Military Justice Is to Justice as Military Music Is to Music.*[7]

Although it is well established that legislative courts for the military are constitutional, it still might be argued that the Court has erred in permitting Congress to deviate from the requirements of Article III in this area. The argument for separate courts for the military is that specialized tribunals and procedures are justified by the need for discipline and order in the armed services. But this only explains the need for a distinct military court system and some differences in procedures; it does not explain why judges in military courts should not be accorded life tenure and salary protections. Some might argue that to ensure an independent judiciary for the military, the specialized military courts should have the protections required in Article III for all U.S. courts.[8]

Jurisdiction of Military Courts Limited

The Supreme Court has limited the jurisdiction of the military courts. First, military courts lack authority to try civilians. In *Ex parte Milligan,* the Supreme

§4.3 [1] 61 U.S. (20 How.) 65 (1858). In Weiss v. United States, 510 U.S. 163 (1994), the Supreme Court held that the due process clause does not require that military judges have fixed terms of office. For a criticism of the constitutional basis for non-Article III military courts, *see* Stephen Vladeck, Military Courts and Article III, 103 Geo. L.J. 933 (2015).

[2] 61 U.S. at 79.

[3] The Fifth Amendment itself expressly says that grand jury indictment is unnecessary in "cases arising in the land or naval forces, or in the Militia, when in actual service in time of War or public danger."

[4] *See* Ex parte Quirin, 317 U.S. 1, 40 (1942); Ex parte Milligan, 71 U.S. (4 Wall.) 2, 123 (1866).

[5] *See* Middendorf v. Henry, 425 U.S. 25 (1976) (no right to counsel in summary court-martial proceedings).

[6] The Military Justice Act of 1983, 28 U.S.C. §1259, provides for certiorari to the U.S. Supreme Court from the Court of Military Appeals in certain cases. Federal district courts do have limited authority to review military court decisions pursuant to a writ of habeas corpus. *See, e.g.,* Burns v. Wilson, 346 U.S. 137 (1953); Humphrey v. Smith, 336 U.S. 695 (1949).

[7] Robert Sherrill, Military Justice Is to Justice as Military Music Is to Music (1970).

[8] *See, e.g.,* Robinson O. Everett, Some Observations on Appellate Review of Court Martial Convictions: Past, Present, and Future, 31 Fed. B. News & J., 420, 421-423 (1984) (proposing life tenure for judges on the Military Court of Appeals).

Court considered the case of a civilian who was sentenced to death by a military commission during the Civil War.[9] The Court reversed the conviction and ordered the prisoner released. The Court explained that "[o]ne of the plainest constitutional provisions was . . . infringed when Milligan was tried by a court not ordained and established by Congress, and not composed of judges appointed during good behavior."[10]

Subsequently, the Supreme Court held that as civilians, the spouses of service personnel could not be tried in military courts.[11] The Uniform Code of Military Justice subjected to military jurisdiction "all persons serving with, employed by, or accompanying the armed forces without the constitutional limits of the United States." In *Reid v. Covert,* the Supreme Court held that the dependents of service personnel could not be tried for capital crimes in military courts.[12] The Court reasoned that Congress's power to create military courts relates to its authority to make rules for the "land and naval Forces," and "not to their civilian wives, children, and other dependents."[13] In *Kinsella v. United States ex rel. Singleton,* the Court expanded this holding and concluded that for noncapital crimes as well, military courts had no authority to try civilians.[14] Similarly, the Court ruled that military courts may not try civilian employees of the armed forces working abroad.[15]

Second, military courts have jurisdiction over service personnel only while the individuals remain in the service. In *United States ex rel. Toth v. Quarles,* the Supreme Court held that former service personnel could not be tried in a military court even for offenses they committed while in the service.[16] The Court explained that "[i]t is impossible to think that the discipline of the Army is going to be disrupted, its morale impaired, or its orderly processes disturbed, by giving ex-servicemen the benefit of a civilian court trial when they are actually civilians."[17]

Finally, the Court has held that the military has authority to try service personnel even for crimes that are not service related. In *O'Callahan v. Parker,* the Supreme Court held that a serviceman could not be court-martialed by a military court for an attempted rape committed off the military base because the crime was not service related.[18] But in 1987, in *Solorio v. United States,* the Supreme Court overruled *O'Callahan.*[19] In *Solorio,* the Coast Guard attempted to court-martial one of its servicemen for sexually abusing the children of a fellow Coast Guardsman. The issue presented in the military courts was whether the offense was service related and thus a basis for court-martial under *O'Callahan.* But the Supreme Court held

[9] 71 U.S. (4 Wall.) 2 (1866).

[10] *Id.* at 122.

[11] Kinsella v. United States, 361 U.S. 234 (1960); Reid v. Covert, 354 U.S. 1 (1957).

[12] 354 U.S. 1 (1957).

[13] *Id.* at 19-20.

[14] 361 U.S. 234 (1960).

[15] *See* McElroy v. United States ex rel. Guagliardo, 361 U.S. 281 (1960).

[16] 350 U.S. 11 (1955).

[17] *Id.* at 22.

[18] 395 U.S. 258 (1969); *see also* Relford v. Commandant, United States Disciplinary Barracks, 401 U.S. 355 (1971).

[19] 483 U.S. 435 (1987).

that a military court's jurisdiction does not depend on the service connection of the offenses charged and expressly overruled *O'Callahan.*[20] The Court emphasized that civilian courts are "ill-equipped" to deal with matters of military concern.[21] Also, the Court stressed that the service-connection test of *O'Callahan* was confusing and difficult to apply.[22]

Justices Marshall, Brennan, and Blackmun dissented.[23] They argued that military court jurisdiction and procedure should be limited to service-related offenses. If a matter is not service related, then the government's interest in military order and discipline is not implicated. Moreover, because many constitutionally mandated procedural protections are inapplicable in military proceedings, it is desirable to confine rather than expand the jurisdiction of military tribunals. The dissent explained that under the holding in *Solorio,* "every member of our armed forces . . . can now be subjected to court-martial jurisdiction—without grand jury indictment or trial by jury—for *any* offense, from tax fraud to passing a bad check, regardless of its lack of relation to 'military discipline, morale and fitness.'"[24] In *Ortiz v. United States,* the Court concluded that it is constitutional for Congress to provide for Supreme Court review of decisions by the Court of Appeals for the Armed Forces, a non-Article III military court.[25] The Court, in an opinion by Justice Kagan, stressed that military courts are adjudicatory; the "essential character" of the military court system is judicial.[26] Justice Kagan then explained that the Supreme Court long has been able to review the decisions of non-Article III judicial tribunals, such as state courts, territorial courts, and the District of Columbia's courts. She wrote: "But this Court's appellate jurisdiction, as Justice Story made clear ages ago, covers more than the decisions of Article III courts."[27]

The Court rejected the argument that the location of the military courts in the executive branch precluded judicial review. But the Court concluded its discussion by leaving issues open for the future: "But finally . . . we say nothing about whether we could exercise appellate jurisdiction over cases from other adjudicative bodies in the Executive Branch, including those in administrative agencies. Our resolution of the jurisdictional issue here has rested on the judicial character, as well as the constitutional foundations and history, of the court-martial system. We have relied, too, on the connections that our cases have long drawn between that judicial system and those of the territories and the District. If Congress were to grant us appellate jurisdiction over decisions of newer entities advancing an administrative (rather than judicial) mission, the question would be different—and the answer not found in this opinion."[28]

[20] *Id.* at 437.

[21] *Id.* at 440.

[22] *Id.*

[23] Justice Stevens concurred in the result because he believed that the conduct was service related. Justice Stevens indicated that he would not overrule *O'Callahan. Id.* at 442 (Stevens, J., concurring).

[24] *Id.* at 445 (Marshall, J., dissenting) (emphasis in original).

[25] 585 U.S. 427 (2018).

[26] *Id.* at 437.

[27] *Id.* at 441.

[28] *Id.* at 448.

Military Tribunals

An important issue concerning non-Article III courts concerns the constitutionality of military tribunals for those accused of terrorist acts or of supporting terrorism. In November 2001, President George W. Bush issued an executive order authorizing the use of military tribunals to try noncitizens accused of terrorism or supporting terrorism.[29] In the executive order, President Bush declared: "Having fully considered the magnitude of the potential deaths, injuries, and property destruction that would result from potential acts of terrorism against the United States, and the probability that such acts will occur, I have determined that an extraordinary emergency exists for national defense purposes, that this emergency constitutes an urgent and compelling government interest, and that issuance of this order is necessary to meet the emergency." The order authorized the use of military tribunals for *noncitizens* accused of terrorist acts or of assisting terrorists. The order provided: "Any individual subject to this order shall, when tried, be tried by military commission for any and all offenses triable by military commission that such individual is alleged to have committed, and may be punished in accordance with the penalties provided under applicable law, including life imprisonment or death."

The executive order did not prescribe procedures for military tribunals, but it instructed the secretary of defense to promulgate relevant regulations. On March 21, 2002, the Department of Defense issued Military Commission Order No. 1, "Procedures for Trials by Military Commissions of Certain Non-United States Citizens in the War Against Terrorism." The order provides that military commissions shall have between three and seven judges, each of whom "shall be a commissioned officer of the United States Armed Forces." Additionally, both prosecutors and defense counsel shall be military officers, though the order also provides that the accused "may also retain the services of a civilian attorney of the Accused's own choosing and at no expense to the United States."

The procedures provide that the accused shall have notice of the charges and "be presumed innocent until proven guilty." A commission member may vote for a guilty verdict "if and only if that member is convinced beyond a reasonable doubt, based on the evidence admitted at trial that the Accused is guilty of the crime." An accused cannot be required to testify at trial, and no adverse inference can be drawn from a defendant's choice not to testify. The accused may obtain witnesses and documents and may present evidence and cross-examine adverse witnesses. There is a presumption of openness for trials, but the presiding officer may close them when deemed necessary.

If there is a conviction, the secretary of defense shall designate a review panel consisting of three military officers. The review panel makes a recommendation to the secretary of defense, who makes the final decision, unless the matter is referred to the president for the final decision. The order provides: "After review by the Secretary of Defense, the record of trial and recommendations will be forwarded

[29] Detention, Treatment, and Trial of Certain Non-Citizens in the War Against Terrorism, 66 Fed. Reg. 57,833 (Nov. 13, 2001).

to the President for review and final decision (unless the President has designated the Secretary of Defense to perform this function)." No judicial review in any court is provided for or authorized.

There has been significant scholarly debate over the constitutionality and desirability of military tribuunals.[30] On the one hand, opponents point to the Supreme Court's decision in *Ex parte Milligan*,[31] where the Supreme Court held that a military tribunal lacked the authority to try a U.S. citizen for conspiracy to aid the Confederacy. The Court stressed that military tribunals were impermissible because federal courts were "always open to hear criminal accusations and redress grievances; and no usage of war could sanction a military trial there for any offense whatever of a citizen in civil life, in nowise connected with the military service."[32]

On the other hand, in *Ex parte Quirin*,[33] the Supreme Court upheld the use of military tribunals during World War II. Eight German saboteurs were arrested in the United States during World War II. They arrived on a German submarine and came wearing German uniforms. They were tried, convicted, and sentenced to death by military tribunal for violating the law of war. The Supreme Court upheld the convictions and the sentences.

The Supreme Court found that Congress, by statute, and the president, by proclamation, had authorized the use of military tribunals.[34] The Court said that the issue before it "concerned only . . . the question whether it is within the constitutional power of the National Government to place petitioners upon trial before a military commission for the offenses with which they are charged."[35] The Court answered in the affirmative and drew a distinction between lawful and unlawful combatants, a distinction that could be very relevant in the current detentions of suspected terrorists. The Court said: "By universal agreement and practice, the law of war draws a distinction between . . . lawful and unlawful combatants. Lawful combatants are subject to capture and detention as prisoners of war by opposing military forces. Unlawful combatants are likewise subject to capture and detention, but in addition they are subject to trial and punishment by military tribunals for acts which render their belligerency unlawful."[36]

The Court said that it did not matter that one of the individuals tried claimed to be an American citizen, and the Court rejected the argument that the use of military tribunals violated the Constitution. The Court declared: "[W]e must conclude that §2 of Article III and the Fifth and Sixth Amendments cannot be taken to have extended the right to demand a jury to trials by military commissions, or to have required that offenses against the law of war not triable by jury at common law be tried only in the civil courts."[37]

[30] *See* Neal Katyal & Laurence Tribe, Waging War, Deciding Guilty: Trying the Military Tribunals, 111 Yale L.J. 1259 (2002) (arguing that military tribunals require congressional authorization).

[31] 71 U.S. (4 Wall.) 2 (1866).

[32] *Id.* at 122.

[33] 317 U.S. 1 (1942).

[34] *Id.* at 29.

[35] *Id.*

[36] *Id.* at 30-31.

[37] *Id.* at 40.

In *Hamdan v. Rumsfeld*,[38] in June 2006, the Supreme Court invalidated the military commissions created by the presidential executive order. The Court held that the military commissions were not adequately authorized by statute and that they violated the requirements of the Uniform Code of Military Justice and the Geneva Accords. The Court distinguished *Quirin* on the basis of more specific statutory authority existing for military commissions during World War II. The Court also emphasized that the military commissions created by presidential executive order to try those held in the war on terrorism violated specific provisions of the Uniform Code of Military Justice and the Geneva Accords, especially in allowing individuals to be convicted without being allowed to know the evidence against them.

Subsequently, Congress enacted the Military Commissions Act of 2006, which creates statutory authority for military commissions to try those accused of being enemy combatants.[39] The act also prescribes the procedures to be used in these military commissions and precludes the federal courts from hearing habeas corpus petitions on behalf of those held as enemy combatants. In *Boumediene v. Bush*, the Court declared this aspect of the Military Commissions Act to be an unconstitutional suspension of the writ of habeas corpus.[40] The Court in *Boumediene* did not address the permissibility of the procedures provided for military tribunals in the Military Commissions Act, and it has not done so subsequently. There has been an ongoing debate over whether terrorists should be tried in Article III federal courts or military tribunals. On the one hand, there is the sense that a verdict in an Article III court will have more credibility, and that Article III courts have handled sensitive matters, including trials for terrorism, throughout American history. On the other hand, supporters of military tribunals for trials of terrorists believe that this method will offer greater security and that it would be more consistent with tradition to try an enemy combatant in a military as opposed to a civilian tribunal.

§4.4 LEGISLATIVE COURTS FOR CIVIL DISPUTES BETWEEN THE GOVERNMENT AND PRIVATE CITIZENS

Public Rights Matters

The most important category of cases handled by legislative courts, in terms of the number of such courts and the volume of cases, is civil disputes between the

[38] 548 U.S. 557 (2006).

[39] Pub. L. No. 109-366, 120 Stat. 2600 (2006).

[40] 553 U.S. 723 (2008). *Boumediene* is discussed in detail in Chapter 15, which focuses on habeas corpus. For an excellent discussion of habeas corpus and these cases, *see* Amanda Tyler, Habeas Corpus in Wartime: From the Tower of London to Guantanamo Bay (2018).

government and private citizens. The Supreme Court long has held that legislative courts can be used for these matters, often termed "public rights" cases.[1]

The use of legislative courts for civil disputes between the government and private citizens was first approved by the Supreme Court in *Murray's Lessee v. Hoboken Land & Improvement Co.*[2] In *Murray's Lessee*, the Court stated that Congress could not withdraw from federal "judicial cognizance any matter which, from its nature, is the subject of a suit at the common law, or in equity, or admiralty."[3] But the Court said that "there are matters, involving public rights, which may be presented in such form that the judicial power is capable of acting on them, and which are susceptible of judicial determination, but which Congress may or may not bring within the cognizance of the Courts of the United States."[4]

Under the public rights doctrine, many disputes between the government and private citizens are decided, at least initially, in administrative agencies or Article I courts. The Tax Court, for example, has judges who sit for fifteen-year terms.[5] Because the Tax Court resolves disputes between the government and citizens, Article I judges are permitted.[6]

Similarly, administrative agencies often perform adjudicatory tasks. For instance, the Federal Trade Commission has the authority to decide whether unfair or deceptive methods of competition have been used. Although these cases arising under federal law are decided by administrative law judges and by commissioners who do not have life tenure, the practice is constitutional under the public rights doctrine.[7] Federal agencies, employing administrative law judges, decide a large volume of cases involving benefits under government entitlement programs, such as the Social Security Act.[8] Immigration cases are yet another category of civil

§4.4 [1] *See, e.g.*, Northern Pipeline Constr. Co. v. Marathon Pipe Line Co., 458 U.S. 50, 51 (1982). In *Northern Pipeline*, the Court defined public rights matters as disputes between the government and others, excluding criminal matters. *Id.* at 69-70 n.24. For an excellent discussion of the use of legislative courts for public rights matters, *see* John M. Golden & Thomas H. Lee, Federalism, Private Rights, and Article III Adjudication, 108 Va. L. Rev. 1547, 1549 (2022); Richard H. Fallon, Of Legislative Courts, Administrative Agencies, and Article III, 101 Harv. L. Rev. 915, 951-974 (1988).

[2] 59 U.S. (18 How.) 272 (1856).

[3] *Id.* at 284.

[4] *Id.* It should be noted that *Murray's Lessee* did not actually involve a legislative court. The holding was that Congress could authorize summary distraint of property to satisfy debts owed to the United States.

[5] In Freytag v. Commissioner of Internal Revenue, 501 U.S. 868 (1991), the Supreme Court held that the chief judge of the Tax Court may appoint special judges for specified proceedings. The Supreme Court reasoned that the Tax Court, although an Article I tribunal, is a "Court of Law," and thus Congress could authorize it to appoint special judges under the authority granted in Article II that Congress may vest the appointment of inferior officers in "the President alone, in the Courts of Law, or in the Heads of Departments."

[6] For example, a constitutional challenge to the Tax Court was rejected on the ground that the Tax Court fit into the traditional public rights exception because it adjudicated disputes between the government and private citizens. Simanonok v. Commissioner of Internal Revenue, 731 F.2d 743 (11th Cir. 1984).

[7] *See, e.g.*, National Harness Mfrs. Assn. v. FTC, 268 F. 705 (6th Cir. 1920).

[8] *See* Fallon, *supra* note 1, at 963-967 (discussing entitlement cases). The Federal Courts Study Committee proposed creating a new Article I court to hear Social Security Disability cases because

cases arising under federal law, albeit ones where the consequences of decisions are usually great, that are handled in administrative proceedings.[9] These are just a few of countless instances in which legislative courts decide civil disputes between the government and private citizens.[10]

Reasons for Allowing Legislative Courts for Public Law Matters

The Supreme Court has offered several explanations for why public law matters can be decided in non-Article III tribunals. One rationale is based on sovereign immunity. Because the U.S. government has sovereign immunity, it may be sued only if Congress authorizes such suit. Also, the federal government has the power to sue only if Congress grants it such authority. The argument is that because Congress has discretion whether to permit such litigation, it can choose to authorize the suits on the condition that they be brought in a particular tribunal, such as a legislative court.[11]

Another justification for the public rights doctrine is that the Framers intended that Congress should be able to create legislative courts for such matters. Justice Brennan explained that "the framers expected that Congress would be free to commit such matters completely to nonjudicial executive determination, and that as a result there can be no constitutional objection to Congress' employing the less drastic expedient of committing their determination to a legislative court or administrative agency."[12]

An additional explanation offered by the Supreme Court for the assignment of public rights matters to legislative courts is historical. The Court said that there is "a historically recognized distinction" between inherently judicial matters, which must be decided by an Article III court, and those that can be decided in other tribunals.[13] The Court stated that "[p]rivate rights disputes . . . lie at the core of the historically recognized judicial power."[14] But according to the Court, public law matters—civil disputes between the government and private citizens—are not inherently judicial and may be assigned to legislative courts.

---

of the large volume of such cases currently in federal courts. Report of the Federal Courts Study Committee 55 (1990).

[9] *Id.* at 967-970.

[10] Similarly, a federal court of appeals upheld the authority of the Benefits Review Board, which reviews the award of benefits for conditions such as black lung disease. The court emphasized the ability of Congress to assign the adjudication of statutorily created rights to administrative agencies. Gibas v. Saginaw Mining Co., 748 F.2d 1112 (6th Cir.), *cert. denied,* 471 U.S. 1116 (1984).

[11] Northern Pipeline Constr. Co. v. Marathon Pipe Line Co., 458 U.S. at 67 ("The doctrine may be explained in part by reference to the traditional principle of sovereign immunity, which recognizes that the Government may attach conditions to its consent to be sued.").

[12] *Id.* at 68.

[13] *Id.*

[14] *Id.* at 70.

Criticism of Allowing Legislative Courts for Public Law Matters

These rationales, however, are open to question. A strong argument can be made that an independent judiciary is especially important in a dispute between the government and a private citizen.[15] A primary purpose of the Constitution is to protect people from the arbitrary exercise of power by the federal government. Judges with life tenure and salary protection are more likely to perform this checking function than are those answerable to the legislature and executive branches.[16] Moreover, it can be argued that although Congress has discretion to allow the United States to be sued, once such suits are authorized it would be an "unconstitutional condition" to require the litigation be brought in courts that are otherwise unconstitutional.[17] Under this view, Congress can choose only whether the suit will be permitted; once litigation is allowed, it must be in an Article III court.

Thus, many commentators urge the reversal, or at least the narrowing, of the public rights doctrine.[18] Alternatively, it is argued that when legislative courts are used for public law matters, their decisions should be subjected to close appellate review by an Article III court.[19]

Key Cases Approving of Legislative Courts for Public Rights Matters: *Bakelite, Williams, Glidden,* and *Oil States Energy Services*

The Supreme Court approved the use of legislative courts for public rights matters in several cases. Some of the most important decisions in this area have concerned the U.S. Court of Customs Appeals (renamed U.S. Court of Customs and Patent Appeals in 1929) and the U.S. Court of Claims. In *Ex parte Bakelite Corp.*, the Supreme Court considered the constitutionality of the U.S. Court of Customs Appeals.[20] In 1909, Congress created the Court of Customs Appeals to hear appeals from the Board of General Appraisers (later termed the Customs Court) respecting the classification of merchandise and the rate of duty applied to it.[21] Also, the Court of Customs Appeals was later given authority to review certain

[15] *See* Martin H. Redish & Austin Piatt, Cutting the Gordian Knot: Legislative Courts and Due Process, 99 Ind. L.J. 675, 677 (2024) ("the public-private rights dichotomy seems upside down. Common sense, as well as the constitutional principles put in place by the Framers, should tell us the exact opposite: the need for protection of judicial salary and tenure is logically at its greatest in cases where the government is a party or at the very least has a strong interest in the outcome.")

[16] *See, e.g.,* Kenneth S. Klein, The Public Rights Doctrine in Light of the Historical Rationale of the Seventh Amendment, 21 Hastings Const. L.Q. 1013 (1994); Mary Ellen Fullerton, No Light at the End of the Pipeline: Confusion Surrounds Legislative Courts, 49 Brook. L. Rev. 207, 230-231 (1983).

[17] *See, e.g.,* Martin H. Redish, Legislative Courts, Administrative Agencies, and the *Northern Pipeline* Decision, 1983 Duke L.J. 197, 214.

[18] *See, e.g., id.* (arguing to reverse it); Fallon, *supra* note 1, at 953 (arguing for "narrowing construction").

[19] *See* Fallon, *supra* note 1, at 953.

[20] 279 U.S. 438 (1929).

[21] Since 1980, it has been known as the Court of International Trade.

findings of the Tariff Commission that would not fit within any of the categories of cases or controversies enumerated in Article III.

In *Bakelite,* the Supreme Court held that the Court of Customs Appeals was a legislative court. Even though the statute creating the court did not specify a fixed term for the judges and therefore appeared to accord them life tenure, the Supreme Court nonetheless characterized it as a legislative tribunal primarily because it existed to decide public law matters. Justice Van Devanter, writing for a unanimous Court, said that the Court of Customs Appeals' jurisdiction included "nothing which inherently or necessarily requires judicial determination, but only matters the determination of which may be, and at times has been, committed exclusively to executive officers."[22]

In *Williams v. United States,* the Supreme Court held that the Court of Claims was a legislative court and therefore Congress was permitted to reduce the salary of judges on the Court of Claims.[23] The Court of Claims was created in 1855 to resolve monetary claims against the U.S. government.[24] In *Williams,* the Supreme Court said that because the matters involved disputes between the government and private citizens, they were outside the scope of Article III.[25] The Court said that Article III could not include suits against the government because of "the limitation fundamentally implicit in the constitutional separation of powers, namely, that a power definitely assigned by the Constitution to one department can neither be surrendered nor delegated by that department."[26] In other words, because Congress had discretion to permit suits against the United States, such litigation was inherently legislative, not judicial.

However, in *Glidden Co. v. Zdanok,* the Supreme Court reversed *Bakelite* and *Williams,* holding that the Court of Customs and Patent Appeals and the Court of Claims are Article III courts.[27] Subsequent to the decisions in *Bakelite* and *Williams,* Congress enacted a statute declaring these courts to "be established under Article III of the Constitution."[28] In *Glidden,* the Court considered two consolidated cases. In one, there was an objection to a retired judge of the Court of Customs and Patent Appeals serving, by designation, as the trial judge in a criminal case. In the other, a party objected to a judge of the Court of Claims sitting, by designation, as a judge on the U.S. Court of Appeals for the Second Circuit. The challengers argued that they were entitled to have Article III judges decide their cases and that under *Bakelite* and *Williams,* these judges were not Article III judges.

The Supreme Court, in *Glidden,* overturned *Bakelite* and *Williams* and held that these courts were Article III tribunals. The Court explained that *Bakelite* and *Williams* should be understood as establishing only that Congress could, if it desired, allow legislative courts to hear disputes between the government and private citizens. However, the Court said that the earlier decisions were overturned

[22] 279 U.S. at 458.
[23] 289 U.S. 553 (1933).
[24] The current jurisdiction of the Court of Claims is discussed in §9.2, *infra.*
[25] 289 U.S. at 577.
[26] *Id.* at 580.
[27] 370 U.S. 530 (1962).
[28] 28 U.S.C. §§171, 211 (1982).

insofar as they implied that only legislative courts could decide such disputes as those arising in the Court of Customs and Patent Appeals or the Court of Claims. Although each of these courts performed some tasks not authorized by Article III, this was not enough to convince the Supreme Court that they should not be regarded as Article III courts.

The Court of Customs and Patent Appeals and the appellate jurisdiction of the Court of Claims are now part of the U.S. Court of Appeals for the Federal Circuit, also an Article III court.[29] As part of creating the Federal Circuit, a new legislative court—the U.S. Claims Court—was established to assume the trial jurisdiction of the Court of Claims.

In *Northern Pipeline Construction Co. v. Marathon Pipe Line Co.*, the Supreme Court reviewed the law concerning legislative courts and again stated that Congress may create such tribunals to decide public law matters.[30] Subsequently, in *Stern v. Marshall*, which is discussed below in detail, the Court reaffirmed that Congress may use non-Article III courts to decide public law matters and concluded that a state law counterclaim in a dispute between two private parties did not fit within this category.[31] The Court applied the public rights doctrine in the patent law context in *Oil States Energy Services, LLC v. Greene's Energy Group, LLC.*[32] Pursuant to a federal statute, the Patent and Trademark Office (PTO) can hear challenges to a patent. Under this procedure, "inter partes review," the PTO may hear requests to cancel a patent on the ground that it fails requirements for a patent, such as novelty or non-obviousness. The proceedings are adjudicatory in nature. As the Court explained: "Once inter partes review is instituted, the Patent Trial and Appeal Board—an adjudicatory body within the PTO created to conduct inter partes review—examines the patent's validity. The Board sits in three-member panels of administrative patent judges. During the inter partes review, the petitioner and the patent owner are entitled to certain discovery; to file affidavits, declarations, and written memoranda; and to receive an oral hearing before the Board. The petitioner has the burden of proving unpatentability by a preponderance of the evidence."[33] A party dissatisfied with the Board's decision can appeal to the United States Court of Appeals for the Federal Circuit.

The issue was whether it violated the Constitution for Congress to have this adjudication done by the PTO, a non-Article III court. The Court found this constitutional, concluding: "Inter partes review falls squarely within the public-rights doctrine. This Court has recognized, and the parties do not dispute, that the decision to *grant* a patent is a matter involving public rights—specifically, the grant of a public franchise."[34] Although the dispute is between private parties who are disputing the validity of a patent, the Court said that the public-rights doctrine

[29] Federal Courts Improvement Act of 1982, Pub. L. No. 97-164, 96 Stat. 25 (1982).

[30] 458 U.S. at 70.

[31] 564 U.S. 462, 488 (2011) ("Vickie's counterclaim cannot be deemed a matter of 'public right' that can be decided outside the Judicial Branch.").

[32] 584 U.S. 325 (2018).

[33] *Id.* at 333.

[34] *Id.* at 334-35.

applied because "the grant of a patent involves a matter 'arising between the government and others.' By issuing patents, the PTO 'take[s] from the public rights of immense value, and bestow[s] them upon the patentee.'"[35] The Court concluded: "the determination to grant a patent is a 'matte[r] involving public rights.' It need not be adjudicated in Article III court. Inter partes review involves the same basic matter as the grant of a patent. So it, too, falls on the public-rights side of the line."[36]

Oil States Energy does not provide a precise definition of what makes a matter a "public right" that can be adjudicated in a non-Article III court. But the Court indicates that the bestowal of a benefit by the government pursuant to federal law and the historical practice surrounding a particular type of claim are relevant in making something a public right.[37]

A Seventh Amendment Limit on Agency Adjudication: *Securities and Exchange Commission v. Jarkesy*

In *Securities and Exchange Commission v. Jarkesy*, the Supreme Court created a significant new limit on the public rights doctrine and specifically on the ability of agencies to impose civil penalties.[38] The Court ruled that the Seventh Amendment right to jury trial requires that civil penalties, at least for fraud claims, be brought to federal court and not adjudicated within a federal agency. As Justice Sotomayor pointed out in a dissent, there are "more than 200 statutes authorizing dozens of agencies to impose civil penalties for violations of statutory obligations."[39] This is therefore a major curtailment of the power of non-Article III courts.

[35] *Id.* at 335.

[36] *Id.* at 336.

[37] *In United States v. Arthrex, Inc.*, 594 U.S. 1 (2021), the Court held that it violated the Constitution to have the Secretary of Commerce appoint Administrative Patent Judges to the Patent Trial and Appeal Board. Chief Justice Roberts wrote the majority opinion and ruled that these individuals were officers of the United States and thus needed to be appointed by the President. The Court found that "Congress [had] assigned APJs 'significant authority' in adjudicating the public rights of private parties, while also insulating their decisions from review and their offices from removal" and is thus unconstitutional. *Id.* at 23. The Court's solution was to give the Director authority over APJ actions to remedy the violation, as the Director is appointed by the President and consented to by the Senate. The Director now has the discretion to review APJ decisions, where "the President remains responsible for the exercise of executive power—and through him, the exercise of executive power remains accountable to the people." *Id.* at 27.

Although the case does not directly involve the authority of legislative courts, it is important in clarifying the appointment power for administrative law judges who exercise power of the sort involved in this case. There is already a substantial literature on this case and its significance. *See* Tejas M. Narechania, Arthrex and the Politics of Patents, 12 Calif. L. Rev. Online 65, 69 (2022); Laura Stanley, Supervising Guantanamo Tribunals: Appointments Clause Challenges After Arthrex, 90 Geo. Wash. L. Rev. 1265, 1268-69 (2022); Jennifer Mascott & John F. Duffy, Executive Decisions After Arthrex, 2021 Sup. Ct. Rev. 225, 227 (2021).

[38] 603 U.S. 109 (2024).

[39] *Id.* at 167-168 (Sotomayor, J., dissenting).

The Securities and Exchange Commission (SEC) has statutory authority to seek civil penalties in administrative proceedings (which ultimately can be reviewed in a court) or in a federal district court. A jury trial is available in court, but not in an agency.

The SEC launched an investigation against George Jarkesy and his company, Patriot28. The SEC chose to proceed in an administrative proceeding before an administrative law judge. There was a finding against Jarkesy and his company. The SEC reviewed the decision and issued a final order that levied a civil penalty of $300,000 against Jarkesy and Patriot28, directed them to cease and desist committing or causing violations of the antifraud provisions, ordered Patriot28 to disgorge earnings, and prohibited Jarkesy from participating in the securities industry and in offerings of penny stocks.

The Supreme Court, in a 6-3 decision, found that the administrative proceedings violated the Seventh Amendment. Chief Justice Roberts wrote for the majority and declared: "This case poses a straightforward question: whether the Seventh Amendment entitles a defendant to a jury trial when the SEC seeks civil penalties against him for securities fraud. The threshold issue is whether this action implicates the Seventh Amendment. It does. The SEC's antifraud provisions replicate common law fraud, and it is well established that common law claims must be heard by a jury."[40] The Court stressed, under an originalist and history-focused analysis, that fraud was a type of claim that was heard by juries in England and at common law in the United States, so the SEC's claim similarly required a jury trial.

The Court acknowledged that there is a doctrine for "public rights" that allows Congress to assign some matters to agencies rather than Article III courts. The effect, of course, is that there is not a jury trial available in the agency. Prior cases, described above, indicated that public rights matters are those between the government and private parties. But the Court rejected this broad definition of public rights. It said instead: "The Constitution prohibits Congress from 'withdraw[ing] from judicial cognizance any matter which, from its nature, is the subject of a suit at the common law.' Once such a suit 'is brought within the bounds of federal jurisdiction,' an Article III court must decide it, with a jury if the Seventh Amendment applies. These propositions are critical to maintaining the proper role of the Judiciary in the Constitution."[41]

Chief Justice Roberts made clear that this case was not only about the Seventh Amendment, but also about separation of powers. He concluded his majority opinion: "A defendant facing a fraud suit has the right to be tried by a jury of his peers before a neutral adjudicator. Rather than recognize that right, the dissent would permit Congress to concentrate the roles of prosecutor, judge, and jury in the hands of the Executive Branch. That is the very opposite of the separation of powers that the Constitution demands."[42]

Justice Sotomayor wrote a scathing dissent, joined by Justices Kagan and Jackson. She stressed that this was the first time that the Court ever had imposed

[40] *Id.* at 120.
[41] *Jarkesy*, 603 U.S. at 127.
[42] *Id.* at 140.

this limit on Congress and federal agencies. She explained that Congress long has had the authority to assign disputes between the government and private parties to federal agencies where there is not a right to trial by jury. She said the Court was "plainly wrong. This Court has held, without exception, that Congress has broad latitude to create statutory obligations that entitle the Government to civil penalties, and then to assign their enforcement outside the regular courts of law where there are no juries."[43]

Justice Sotomayor identified over two dozen agencies that have statutory power to impose penalties in agency proceedings. For some, there is no statutory authority to go to court. She was blunt in saying: "Make no mistake: Today's decision is a power grab. Once again, the majority arrogates Congress's policymaking role to itself. . . . Judicial aggrandizement is as pernicious to the separation of powers as any aggrandizing action from either of the political branches."[44]

There are a number of questions left unanswered by the Court's decision in *Jarkesy*. First, can agencies ever impose civil penalties? The Court's opinion stresses that they cannot do so for fraud because that is a matter that could have gone to a jury at common law. But that leaves open whether it will be permissible for agencies to impose civil penalties for any other type of claim. Second, what about agencies that don't have the statutory authority to bring court proceedings? Will it take an act of Congress for these agencies to be able to recover civil penalties? Third, what will this mean for the public rights doctrine and the ability of non-Article III courts to hear other matters? The Court in *Jarkesy* has narrowed the public rights doctrine, the contours of which are not clear.

§4.5 LEGISLATIVE COURTS FOR PRIVATE LAW AND CRIMINAL MATTERS

§4.5.1 Introduction: Inherently Judicial Matters

Overview

The Supreme Court held that certain matters were "inherently judicial" and hence must be decided by an Article III court; that is, they have to be decided by a judge with life tenure whose salary could not be decreased. Federal criminal prosecutions and civil cases between private parties were considered to be inherently judicial matters. However, the Supreme Court ruled that even in these areas legislative courts could be used as *adjuncts* to Article III courts. These decisions, authorizing legislative courts for "inherently judicial" matters, are reviewed in §4.5.2.

[43] *Id.* at 168 (Sotomayor, J., dissenting).
[44] *Id.* at 202-203.

In 1982, in the extremely important decision of *Northern Pipeline Construction Co. v. Marathon Pipe Line Co.*, the Supreme Court declared the bankruptcy courts unconstitutional because they were legislative courts entrusted with deciding private law matters.[1] This case is discussed in §4.5.3.

In two subsequent decisions—*Thomas v. Union Carbide Agricultural Products Co.*[2] and *Commodity Futures Trading Commission v. Schor*[3]—the Court upheld the use of legislative courts to decide particular private law matters. These cases are discussed in §4.5.4. These cases, unlike *Northern Pipeline,* took a very functional approach to legislative courts, concluding that they are permissible unless they undermine the independence of the federal judiciary.

But in 2011, in *Stern v. Marshall,* the Court held that a bankruptcy court cannot issue a final judgment as to a state law counterclaim and reverted to the more formalistic approach of *Northern Pipeline.*[4] Subsequently, in 2015, in *Wellness International Network Ltd. v. Sharif,* the Court limited the effects of *Stern v. Marshall* by holding that parties can consent to allowing a bankruptcy court to issue a final judgment over a state law claim and by shifting back to the functional approach of *Thomas* and *Schor.*[5] *Stern v. Marshall* and *Wellness International Network Ltd v. Sharif* are discussed in §4.5.5.

In summary, the analysis that follows reveals that the Supreme Court has approved the use of legislative courts for private and criminal law matters where the tribunal is an adjunct to an Article III court, where the matter involves private litigation that is closely related to a public regulatory scheme, or, generally, where the benefits of using a legislative court exceed the disadvantages.[6] Also, the Court has allowed parties to consent to a non-Article III court even when otherwise it would be impermissible.

However, there is an underlying difference in approach in these cases that makes the law uncertain and that makes it very difficult to predict in any particular case whether the use of a legislative court for a private law matter is unconstitutional. In *Northern Pipeline,* the Court used a formalistic approach to deciding the permissibility of non-Article III courts. In *Thomas* and *Schor,* the Court shifted to a functional approach and focused on whether use of a non-Article III tribunal would undermine judicial independence and the goals of Article III. In *Stern v. Marshall,* however, the Court eschewed this functional approach and returned to a formalistic way of determining if a non-Article III court is permissible. But then in *Wellness International Network Ltd. v. Sharif,* the Court expressly followed the functional approach of *Thomas* and *Schor.*

§4.5 [1] 458 U.S. 50.

[2] 473 U.S. 568 (1985).

[3] 478 U.S. 833 (1986).

[4] 564 U.S. 462 (2011).

[5] 575 U.S. 6651932 (2015).

[6] For a criticism of this balancing test and an argument that the Constitution broadly authorizes the creation of Article I courts, *see* Craig A. Stern, What's a Constitution Among Friends: Unbalancing Article III, 146 U. Pa. L. Rev. 1043 (1998).

§4.5.2 *The Approval of Legislative Courts for Criminal and Private Law Matters*

Crowell v. Benson

The Supreme Court has approved the use of legislative courts for private law matters when those tribunals serve as "adjuncts" to Article III courts.[7] *Crowell v. Benson* was the Supreme Court's first approval of non-Article III courts for the adjudication of private civil disputes.[8] The issue in *Crowell* involved the requirement, created by federal law, that workers injured in maritime accidents file their claims with a U.S. Employees' Compensation Commission.[9] A worker named Knudson was hurt in a maritime accident while working for Benson. Crowell, a deputy commissioner of the U.S. Employees' Compensation Commission, held a hearing and ruled in favor of the claimant, Knudson. Benson then appealed the decision to federal district court, contending that the underlying statute was unconstitutional and that Knudson was not an employee when injured and thus not entitled to compensation.

The federal district court ruled that the Constitution mandated that a de novo hearing be available before an Article III court. The district court held such a proceeding and concluded that Knudson was not Benson's employee at the time of the accident. The U.S. Court of Appeals affirmed the district court's decision reversing Crowell's ruling in favor of Knudson.

An issue before the Supreme Court was whether Congress was permitted to create government bodies to resolve disputes between private citizens. In *Crowell*, for example, the suit was between two private parties, an employer and an employee. Workers' compensation boards were created throughout the country early in the twentieth century to replace court adjudication of employee injury cases. The use of administrative agencies to resolve these private disputes was favored partially for efficiency; workers' compensation boards provided more informal, faster proceedings than did courts. Also, there was a belief that the boards would develop expertise that would improve their decisions. Political considerations were a factor, too. Some suggest that workers' compensation boards were created because courts were hostile to workers' claims, using tort law doctrines such as assumption of risk, contributory negligence, and the fellow servant rule to deny recovery to injured individuals. Others argue that workers' compensation schemes were created just as these tort law defenses began to erode and that workers' compensation boards were favored by businesses that sought to transfer the cases away from juries and thereby limit recoveries.[10]

[7] *See* Northern Pipeline Constr. Co. v. Marathon Pipe Line Co., 458 U.S. at 53 (speaking of legislative courts as adjuncts).

[8] 285 U.S. 22 (1932).

[9] Longshoremen's and Harbor Workers' Compensation Act, Act of Mar. 4, 1927, 44 Stat. 1424, 33 U.S.C. §§901 et seq.

[10] *See, e.g.*, Joseph A. Page, Bitter Wages (1973); Chester Arthur Williams, Compendium on Workmen's Compensation (1973); Earl Frank Cheit, Injury and Recovery in the Course of Employment (1961).

The Supreme Court in *Crowell v. Benson* agreed with the federal district court and held that in private law matters, ultimate decision-making authority must rest in Article III courts. Legislative courts, such as the Employees' Compensation Commission, could resolve private law disputes only if there was substantial oversight by an Article III court. The Supreme Court said that Article III courts must be able to decide de novo all questions of law, constitutional facts, and jurisdictional facts.

The Supreme Court has declared that "[t]he supremacy of law demands that there shall be an opportunity to have some court decide whether an erroneous rule of law was applied."[11] De novo review of questions of law decided by legislative courts, such as administrative agencies, is the norm.

Constitutional facts are those facts that are the basis for a claim of a constitutional violation. In general, *Crowell* remains good law in that such facts may be relitigated, de novo, in an Article III federal court.[12]

Jurisdictional facts are those facts that are the basis for the agency's legal authority to hear a matter. For example, the Employees' Compensation Commission had authority to award compensation to those injured in the course of maritime employment. A jurisdictional fact would be whether a person was injured in the course of maritime employment; the commission's authority depended on this premise. Allowing de novo review of jurisdictional facts was based on the notion that courts should check agencies to ensure that they do not improperly assume jurisdiction. The jurisdictional fact doctrine, however, is no longer followed and has seldom been mentioned since *Crowell.*[13]

Crowell is important because it both allows legislative courts for private law disputes and sets limits on their use. *Crowell* requires that such tribunals be subject to close oversight in Article III courts. Also, in *Crowell,* the commission could be viewed as an adjunct of a federal court because the commission had no independent authority to enforce its compensation orders. Rather, the commission's compensation orders were appealable to federal district courts that possessed the authority to implement the orders or set them aside. The Court in *Crowell* analogized the commission to the "familiar practice" of using commissioners or assessors to determine the extent of damages in civil cases.[14]

Justice Brandeis's dissent in *Crowell* took a different approach to the question of the constitutionality of legislative courts. Justice Brandeis argued, in part, that because Congress might have left these workers' compensation claims to state courts, where judges generally lack life tenure and salary protection, Congress could choose to have them decided in legislative courts.[15] This position would

[11] St. Joseph Stock Yards Co. v. United States, 298 U.S. 38, 84 (1936) (Brandeis, J., concurring).

[12] *See, e.g.,* Eschbach v. Brown, 84 F. Supp. 825, 827 (N.D. Ill. 1949), *rev'd on other grounds,* 181 F.2d 860 (7th Cir. 1950); Perkins v. Endicott Johnson Corp., 128 F.2d 208, 224 (2d Cir. 1942), *aff'd,* 317 U.S. 501 (1943).

[13] Laurence H. Tribe, American Constitutional Law 54 (2d ed. 1988) (the jurisdictional fact doctrine has fallen into "desuetude"); Louis L. Jaffe, Judicial Review: Constitutional and Jurisdictional Facts, 70 Harv. L. Rev. 953, 973 (1957).

[14] 285 U.S. at 54.

[15] *Id.* at 87 (Brandeis, J., dissenting).

authorize virtually unlimited use of legislative courts because Congress has broad discretion to control the jurisdiction of the federal courts and to leave matters to state courts for adjudication.[16]

This position ignores a crucial difference between legislative courts and state judiciaries: legislative courts are more likely to be influenced by Congress than are state courts. Legislative judges, who depend on Congress for their salary and for confirmation of their reappointment, are less likely to be independent than are state judiciaries, which are not subject to congressional control. Thus, legislative courts pose separation of powers problems not present when matters are assigned to state courts for adjudication. Also, the Constitution clearly presumed the existence of state courts; the constitutional status of legislative courts is far more questionable.

Magistrate Judges

The Supreme Court further expanded the permissible use of non-Article III tribunals for "inherently judicial matters" in *United States v. Raddatz*.[17] The issue in *Raddatz* was the constitutionality of the use of federal magistrates to decide important issues in criminal cases as an adjunct to federal district courts.

The position of magistrate was created in the first Judiciary Act, which authorized these officials to set bail for persons accused of federal crimes.[18] In 1817, Congress designated these individuals as "commissioners" and expanded their duties to include taking affidavits and depositions in civil cases.[19] Over the next 150 years, the commissioner system underwent continuous revision and expansion, fueled by an increasing concern for judicial efficiency. As early as 1940, Congress granted general jurisdiction to U.S. commissioners to try all petty offenses committed on federal property, contingent on the defendant's consent.[20]

The Federal Magistrate's Act of 1968 established the magistrate system in order to "reform the first echelon of the federal judiciary into an effective component of a modern system of justice."[21] The statute provided magistrates with the authority to exercise all powers and duties formerly possessed by U.S. commissioners: to try to dispose of misdemeanor offenses; to assist district courts by conducting pretrial proceedings, discovery proceedings, and preliminary review of habeas corpus petitions; and to perform such additional duties as are consistent with the Constitution of the United States. Magistrates are appointed for eight-year terms.

The Magistrate Act spawned a great deal of litigation concerning the scope of the magistrates' powers.[22] In *Wingo v. Wedding*, the Supreme Court in 1974 said that

[16] The authority of Congress to restrict federal court jurisdiction is discussed in Chapter 3.

[17] 447 U.S. 667, 687 (1980).

[18] Judiciary Act of 1789, ch. 20, §33. For a history of the magistrates, *see* Linda J. Silberman, Masters and Magistrates, Parts I and II, 50 N.Y.U. L. Rev. 1070 and 1297 (1975).

[19] Act of Mar. 1, 1817, 3 Stat. 350, ch. 25.

[20] Act of Oct. 9, 1940, ch. 785, 54 Stat. 1058-1059.

[21] H.R. Rep. No. 1629, 90th Cong., 2d Sess. (1968).

[22] *See, e.g.*, T.P.O., Inc. v. McMillen, 460 F.2d 348, 359 (7th Cir. 1972); Ingram v. Richardson, 471 F.2d 1268, 1270 (6th Cir. 1972); *see also* Peter G. McCabe, The Federal Magistrate Act of 1979, 16 Harv. J. on Legis. 343, 351 (1979).

magistrates lacked the power under the act to conduct evidentiary hearings in connection with habeas corpus petitions.[23] In response to this decision, Congress in 1976 amended the Federal Magistrates Act of 1968 and, more specifically, defined the tasks that magistrates could perform.[24]

Under the 1976 amendments, which remain in effect, magistrates exercise substantial authority. First, they may decide any pretrial motion in a civil or criminal case upon reference by the judge, except for eight specified case-dispositive pretrial motions. Second, magistrates may hear any case-dispositive motion or prisoner case and file proposed findings of fact and a recommended decision. Third, magistrates may be appointed by a judge as a special master with the parties' consent, or without it in exceptional cases. Fourth, magistrates may be assigned and may perform any other duties not inconsistent with the U.S. Constitution.

The magistrates' authority was again expanded in the Federal Magistrate's Act of 1979.[25] The act granted magistrates the authority, with consent of all parties, to conduct all pretrial and trial proceedings in jury or nonjury civil matters and to order entry of final judgments. The act also expanded the authority of magistrates to hear criminal trials for all federal misdemeanor offenses.

In *Raddatz*, the defendant was indicted for violating a federal firearms statute. Prior to trial, the defendant moved to suppress certain incriminating evidence. The federal district court judge referred the motion to a magistrate, who conducted the suppression hearing and submitted to the judge proposed findings of fact and a recommendation that the motion be denied. The defendant then filed with the judge an objection to the magistrate's decision. The federal judge heard oral argument from counsel on the motion and also reviewed the transcript of the magistrate's hearing, the parties' papers, and the magistrate's report. The judge, however, did not rehear the testimony presented to the magistrate in connection with the suppression motion. The district court accepted the magistrate's recommendation and denied the suppression motion.

The Court of Appeals, however, reversed the district court's decision, holding that the defendant's due process rights were violated by the district court's failure to rehear controverted testimony. The U.S. Supreme Court reversed the Court of Appeals and upheld the constitutionality of the magistrates as used in this case.

Chief Justice Burger, writing for the Court, concluded that Congress did not intend for the district court to rehear the evidence on contested issues. Chief Justice Burger said that "[i]n providing for a 'de novo determination,' rather than de novo hearing, Congress intended to permit whatever reliance a district judge, in the exercise of sound judicial discretion, chose to place on a magistrate's proposed findings and recommendations."[26] The Court also rejected the defendant's due process claim. The Court emphasized the procedural safeguards that are provided in the hearing before the magistrate. More important, the Court stressed

[23] 418 U.S. 461 (1974).

[24] The changes enacted in the 1976 Amendments are codified in 28 U.S.C. §636(b).

[25] The changes adopted in the 1979 Act are found in 28 U.S.C. §636(c).

[26] 447 U.S. at 676.

that the district court judge had the authority to hold additional hearings if that was deemed appropriate in a particular case. The Court concluded that because "the entire process takes place under the district court's total control and jurisdiction . . . [the Act] strikes the proper balance between the demands of due process and the constraints of Art. III."[27]

Justices Stewart, Brennan, Marshall, and Powell dissented. The dissenters argued that where witness credibility was the central issue in evaluating a suppression motion, it violated due process for a judge to decide the motion without hearing the testimony.[28] Justice Marshall, for example, explicitly recognized the general permissibility of legislative courts, but said that suppression hearings were "one of the admittedly few contexts in which independent fact-finding by an Art. III judge is constitutionally required."[29] Likewise, Justice Powell argued that due process requires a court to "rehear crucial witnesses when, as in this case, a suppression hearing turns *only* on credibility."[30]

Raddatz is important because it again expanded the circumstances in which non-Article III judges could decide matters previously labeled "inherently judicial." Also, it raised an important question of whether an Article III judge was required, not just because of the text of the Constitution and separation of powers, but also based on due process considerations.[31]

Decisions Clarifying Role for Magistrate Judges

Subsequent Supreme Court cases have further defined the power of magistrate judges. In *Gomez v. United States*, the Supreme Court held that the Magistrates Act did not authorize the U.S. magistrates to preside over jury selection at felony trials.[32] The Federal Magistrates Act provides that a "magistrate may be assigned such additional duties as are not inconsistent with the Constitution and laws of the United States."[33] The Court concluded, however, that there was no evidence in the legislative history of the Magistrates Act that Congress intended for magistrates to preside over jury selection in federal trials. Moreover, the Court noted that allowing magistrates such authority would raise a substantial constitutional question because of the improbability of meaningful district court review of what occurred at voir dire.

However, in *Peretz v. United States*, the Supreme Court held that magistrates may supervise jury selection in felony cases with the consent of the parties.[34] The Court did not address whether a defendant has a right to have an Article III judge

[27] *Id.* at 681, 683-684.

[28] *Id.* at 694-695, 702 (Marshall, J., dissenting); *id.* at 686-687 (Powell, J., dissenting).

[29] *Id.* at 712 (Marshall, J., dissenting).

[30] *Id.* at 686 (Powell, J., dissenting) (emphasis in original).

[31] For a discussion of the fairness basis for criticizing legislative courts, *see* Richard H. Fallon, Of Legislative Courts, Administrative Agencies, and Article III, 101 Harv. L. Rev. 915, 941-942 (1988).

[32] 490 U.S. 858 (1989).

[33] 28 U.S.C. §636(b)(3).

[34] 501 U.S. 923 (1991).

preside over the jury selection process. Rather, the Court reasoned that even if such a right exists, "litigants may waive their personal right to have an Article III judge preside over a civil trial."[35] The Court further explained that although litigants may not waive the structural protections afforded by Article III, these are met because of the district court's general control over magistrates' conduct.

In *McCarthy v. Bronson*, the Court ruled that magistrate judges may hear challenge to conditions of confinement, whether in a claim of a specific instance of unconstitutional conduct or in a systematic challenge to ongoing prison conditions.[36] Federal law specifically authorizes the nonconsensual referral to magistrates for a hearing and recommended findings on "prisoner petitions challenging conditions of confinement."[37] In *McCarthy*, a prisoner brought a suit claiming that excessive force had been used to move him from one cell to another. Although the plaintiff objected to having the magistrate conduct the trial, the Supreme Court ruled that it was permissible for magistrates to perform this task.[38]

Finally, in *Roell v. Withrow*, the Court held that consent to trial by a magistrate judge can be implied from a party's conduct during litigation.[39] In other words, consent can be inferred and need not be explicitly stated for a magistrate judge to try a civil case.

As docket pressures increase in federal district courts, so will the responsibilities assigned to magistrate judges.[40] Inevitably, there will continue to be litigation about the scope of the powers allowed under the Magistrates Act and about what is permissible under Article III.

[35] 501 U.S. at 936.

[36] 500 U.S. 136 (1991).

[37] 28 U.S.C. §636(b)(1)(B).

[38] *McCarthy* involved a nonjury trial. The Supreme Court did not address the question of whether magistrates constitutionally can preside over jury trials. The Court noted: "No constitutional question arises in cases like this one, in which the plaintiff has waived the right to a jury trial. And, in cases in which the jury right exists and is not waived, the lower courts, guided by the principle of constitutional avoidance, have consistently held that the statute does not authorize reference to a magistrate." 500 U.S. at 144. *See* Jones v. Johnson, 134 F.3d 309 (5th Cir. 1998) (a district court may not delegate to a magistrate judge conclusive authority to grant or deny a "certificate of applicability" necessary to appeal the denial of a habeas corpus petition).

[39] 538 U.S. 580 (2003).

[40] *See, e.g.*, United States v. Harden, 758 F.3d 886 (7th Cir. 2014) (magistrates cannot accept guilty pleas in felony cases and determine a defendant guilty); In re United States of America, 10 F.3d 931 (2d Cir.), *cert. denied*, 513 U.S. 812 (1993) (statute does not allow district courts to delegate to magistrate judges issuing wiretap warrants); Ward v. Rutherford, 921 F.2d 286 (D.C. Cir. 1990) (permissible for magistrates to conduct international extradition proceedings because the magistrates' decisions are subject to habeas corpus review by an Article III judge); Minerex Evloel, Inc. v. Sina, Inc., 838 F.2d 781 (5th Cir. 1988) (unconstitutional to use magistrates in bankruptcy cases); United States v. Curry, 767 F.2d 328 (7th Cir. 1985) (unconstitutional to have magistrates preside over probation hearings).

§4.5.3 Northern Pipeline Construction Co. v. Marathon Pipe Line Co.[41]

Bankruptcy Act of 1978

Without a doubt, the *Northern Pipeline* case is one of the most important Supreme Court decisions limiting the power of Congress to create legislative courts. In *Northern Pipeline*, the Supreme Court—without a majority opinion—declared unconstitutional the bankruptcy courts created by the Bankruptcy Act of 1978. Under the Bankruptcy Act of 1978, bankruptcy judges appointed to 14-year terms had broad jurisdiction to decide private civil disputes. The Supreme Court held that this authority violated Article III of the Constitution.

The Bankruptcy Act of 1978 changed the structure of the bankruptcy courts and substantially enlarged their jurisdiction. Prior to the act, bankruptcy proceedings generally were held before referees appointed by federal district court judges.[42] A federal district court judge could withdraw any case from a referee and could review the referee's decisions on appeal. Also, prior to the 1978 act, a distinction was drawn between *summary* and *plenary* jurisdiction. Summary jurisdiction referred to property within the bankrupt's possession or within the court's jurisdiction. Plenary jurisdiction referred to claims regarding other property. For example, the bankrupt's assets were part of the summary jurisdiction, but the bankrupt's claims against third parties were part of the plenary jurisdiction. The district courts, and derivatively the referees, had summary jurisdiction—power to dispose of all assets within their jurisdiction—but plenary jurisdiction could be gained only by consent of the parties.

The 1978 act changed this. It created the U.S. Bankruptcy Courts, with judges appointed by the president and confirmed by the Senate. Bankruptcy court judges were to sit for 14-year terms and were removable by the judicial council of a circuit on account of "incompetency, misconduct, negligence, neglect of duty or physical or mental disability." The salaries of bankruptcy judges were set by statute and subject to adjustment under the Federal Salary Act.

Perhaps most important, the act eliminated the summary / plenary distinction and gave the new bankruptcy courts jurisdiction over both property in their jurisdiction and all other claims by or against the bankrupt. The act accorded the new courts jurisdiction over all "civil proceedings arising under [the Bankruptcy Act] or arising in or related to cases arising under [it]."[43]

The bankruptcy courts were given virtually all of the "powers of a court of equity, law and admiralty." This included the ability to issue declaratory judgments, to hold jury trials, to issue writs of habeas corpus under certain circumstances, and to issue any orders necessary to carry out its duties.[44] The act also created an appeals process, primarily using appellate panels of bankruptcy judges whose decisions were then reviewable in the U.S. Courts of Appeals.

[41] 458 U.S. 50 (1982).

[42] In 1973, these referees were retitled "judges." *Id.* at 53 n.2.

[43] *Id.* at 54.

[44] These powers are summarized in the *Northern Pipeline* decision, *id.* at 55.

A major issue in the congressional debates was the proper status for the bankruptcy judges. The House of Representatives, expressing concern about whether a legislative bankruptcy court would be constitutional, passed a bill according the bankruptcy judges life tenure and salary protection,[45] but the Senate provided these judges only a fixed term. The Senate, at the urging of Chief Justice Burger, did not want to substantially expand the number of Article III judges, thereby perhaps diluting the prestige of the office, by providing bankruptcy judges with life tenure.[46] The Senate's version was adopted in the Conference Committee.

Facts and Opinions in *Northern Pipeline*

The Supreme Court considered the constitutionality of this Act in *Northern Pipeline Construction Co. v. Marathon Pipe Line Co.* The facts of the case were simple. The Northern Pipeline Construction Company sued the Marathon Pipe Line Company in the U.S. District Court for the Western District of Kentucky. Subsequently, Northern Pipeline filed for bankruptcy in the U.S. Bankruptcy Court for the District of Minnesota. Northern Pipeline also filed a claim against Marathon Pipe Line for breach of contract in the bankruptcy court. This was identical to the suit filed in federal court in Kentucky. Marathon Pipe Line argued that it was unconstitutional for the breach of contract claim to be tried in the bankruptcy court because the judges lacked life tenure and the salary protections required under Article III.

The Supreme Court agreed with the defendant and ruled that the bankruptcy courts were unconstitutional. There were three major opinions, none of which were joined by a majority of the Court. Justice Brennan wrote for a plurality, including Justices Marshall, Blackmun, and Stevens. Justices Rehnquist and O'Connor concurred in the judgment. Justice White wrote a lengthy dissent, in which Chief Justice Burger and Justice Powell concurred. Understanding the *Northern Pipeline* decision and the current law concerning legislative courts requires consideration of each of these opinions.

Justice Brennan's plurality opinion stressed that legislative courts were permitted only in a few instances—for territories, the military, and public rights disputes—and that bankruptcy did not fit into these exceptions.[47] Moreover, the plurality opinion said that legislative courts could be used as an adjunct to Article III courts only under limited circumstances. The existence of review by an Article III court was deemed insufficient to permit the use of a legislative court. Justice Brennan wrote: "Appellants suggest that *Crowell* and *Raddatz* stand for the proposition that Art. III is satisfied so long as some degree of appellate review is provided. But that suggestion is directly contrary to the text of our Constitution. . . . Our precedents make it clear that the constitutional requirements for the exercise of the judicial power must be met at all stages of adjudication."[48]

[45] *Id.* at 61 n.12.
[46] *Id.*
[47] 458 U.S. at 63-76.
[48] *Id.* at 86 n.39.

The plurality emphasized that unlike in *Crowell* and *Raddatz*, the bankruptcy courts could not be characterized as adjuncts of Article III courts. For example, while the agency in *Crowell* was limited to jurisdiction over a particular area of law, the bankruptcy courts had jurisdiction over all civil matters.[49] Whereas the agency in *Crowell* could not enforce its own orders, bankruptcy courts were empowered to exercise all of the powers of federal district courts.[50] Although the agency's decisions in *Crowell* could be set aside if not supported by the evidence, the bankruptcy courts' rulings could be overturned only if they were "clearly erroneous," a much narrower basis for appellate review.[51] The plurality thus concluded that the bankruptcy courts "are exercising powers far greater than those lodged in the adjuncts approved in either *Crowell* or *Raddatz*."[52]

The plurality did not limit its ruling to holding the plenary jurisdiction of the bankruptcy courts unconstitutional. The plurality believed that this grant of jurisdiction could not be severed from the remainder of its authority because it was uncertain what Congress would have done had it known of the constitutional defects in the statute. Accordingly, the entire grant of jurisdiction to the bankruptcy courts was declared unconstitutional.

Justices Rehnquist and O'Connor concurred in the judgment. Their position was that it was unconstitutional for Congress to vest in the bankruptcy courts broad authority to adjudicate state law matters that were only tangentially related to the adjudication of bankruptcy under federal law.[53] They agreed with the plurality that appellate review in an Article III court was insufficient to cure this constitutional defect.[54] Unlike the plurality, the concurrence said that it was unnecessary to express an opinion on anything other than this aspect of the bankruptcy courts' jurisdiction. However, because Justices Rehnquist and O'Connor agreed that it was uncertain what Congress would have enacted had it been unable to vest plenary jurisdiction in the bankruptcy courts, they concurred in declaring the courts unconstitutional.

Justice White wrote a lengthy dissent joined by Chief Justice Burger and Justice Powell.[55] The dissent emphasized a functional approach to analyzing the constitutionality of legislative courts focusing on whether the particular court undermines separation of powers and checks and balances. Justice White explained: "The inquiry should, rather, focus equally on those Art. III values and ask whether and to what extent the legislative scheme accommodates them or, conversely, substantially undermines them. The burden on Art. III values should then be measured

[49] *Id.* at 81-86.

[50] *Id.* at 85.

[51] *Id.*

[52] *Id.* at 86.

[53] *Id.* at 90 (Rehnquist, J., concurring).

[54] *Id.* at 91 (bankruptcy courts are not an adjunct to Article III courts).

[55] Chief Justice Burger also wrote a short, separate dissenting opinion to emphasize the narrowness of the concurring opinion authored by Justices Rehnquist and O'Connor and hence the narrowness of the ultimate holding in *Northern Pipeline*. *Id.* at 92 (Burger, C.J., dissenting).

against the values Congress hopes to serve through the use of Art. I courts."[56] Justice White's approach would openly balance the benefits of a legislative court against its effects on separation of powers and judicial independence.

In this instance, the dissent found little reason to object to the use of a legislative court. Justice White emphasized that when a legislative court is "designed to deal with issues likely to be of little interest to the political branches," there is no fear that Congress is creating such tribunals to aggrandize its own power.[57] Moreover, Justice White explained that for the sake of flexibility, Congress understandably did not want to create several hundred bankruptcy judges with life tenure. In light of the existence of appellate review by Article III courts, the dissent would have upheld the constitutionality of the bankruptcy courts.

Issues Raised by *Northern Pipeline*

The *Northern Pipeline* decision raised far more questions than it answered. First, why did the plurality draw the line at legislative courts for the territories, the military, and public rights disputes? In *Palmore v. United States*, the Court spoke of the constitutionality of legislative courts for "specialized areas having particularized needs and warranting distinctive treatment."[58] The plurality found legislative courts for the territories, the military, and public rights matters to fit within this exception, but not bankruptcy courts. Yet the justices gave little explanation for why they were drawing the line at this point.[59]

Second, the plurality left it uncertain when a legislative court could be used as an adjunct to an Article III court and what factors must be present in order for the legislative tribunal to be labeled an "adjunct." Justice Brennan's statement in a footnote that the "requirements for the exercise of the judicial power must be met at all stages of adjudication" raises questions about all legislative courts in private rights disputes.[60] Professor Martin Redish suggests that Justice Brennan's opinion "lead[s] to the conclusion that much of the work of most federal administrative agencies is unconstitutional."[61]

The plurality opinion, however, implicitly reaffirmed the earlier decisions in *Crowell* and *Raddatz* that legislative courts could be used as adjuncts of Article III courts. The plurality did not define what relationship must exist between a legislative court and an Article III court for the latter to be considered an adjunct. Instead, the plurality pointed to many factors as distinguishing the bankruptcy

[56] *Id.* at 115 (White, J., dissenting).

[57] *Id.*

[58] 411 U.S. 389, 408 (1973).

[59] One commentator suggested that the plurality was delivering a message to Congress about the likely unconstitutionality of restrictions on federal court jurisdiction in areas such as abortion or school prayer that were then pending before Congress. *See* Judith Resnik, The Mythic Meaning of Article III Courts, 56 U. Colo. L. Rev. 581, 599 (1985).

[60] 458 U.S. at 86 n.39.

[61] Martin H. Redish, Legislative Courts, Administrative Agencies, and the *Northern Pipeline* Decision, 1983 Duke L.J. 197, 200.

courts from *Crowell* and *Raddatz* without explaining which of these characteristics were essential for a legislative court to pass constitutional muster.

Also, it should be noted that the plurality and the concurrence agreed only that the bankruptcy courts' jurisdiction was unconstitutional insofar as it permitted adjudication of *state law* claims unrelated to federal law. Yet, if the state law matters were tried in state courts, they generally would be heard before state judges without life tenure and salary guarantees. Although state courts are more independent of Congress than are legislative courts, this seemed irrelevant to the majority because there was no indication that bankruptcy courts were made legislative courts to allow Congress to influence their decisions.

Perhaps the decision could be read as resting on federalism grounds in its ruling that it is unconstitutional for the bankruptcy courts to hear the state law matters.[62] The Court's decision could be reinterpreted as protecting state courts by preventing federal usurpation of state law litigation. None of the justices, however, mentioned this concern, nor did any of the justices indicate that it would be unconstitutional to vest an Article III judge with the bankruptcy courts' power to decide state law claims.

Another issue left unresolved is what type of appellate review is sufficient to meet the Constitution's requirements. Would it be constitutionally permissible to have direct appeal from the bankruptcy courts to the U.S. Courts of Appeals, or must there be the opportunity for review in the district courts?[63]

Subsequent History of the Bankruptcy Courts

Following *Northern Pipeline,* Congress amended the Bankruptcy Act of 1978 to make the bankruptcy courts adjuncts of Article III courts when they adjudicate state law matters.[64] In the *Northern Pipeline* decision, the Court stayed its order, dated June 28, 1982, declaring the bankruptcy courts unconstitutional until October 4, 1982. When Congress did not amend the law in time to meet this deadline, the Court extended its order until December 24, 1982. After Congress again failed to amend the law, the Court refused further extensions. Confusion reigned as to whether the bankruptcy courts could exist at all and, if so, what jurisdiction could be exercised. The Judicial Conference of the United States promulgated emergency guidelines.

It was not until 1984 that Congress enacted a statute to reconstitute the bankruptcy courts and address the constitutional defects identified in *Northern Pipeline.*

[62] *Cf.* Lucinda M. Finley, Article III Limits on Article I Courts: The Constitutionality of the Bankruptcy Court and the 1979 Magistrate Act, 80 Colum. L. Rev. 560, 582 (1980) (a pre-*Northern Pipeline* article discussing federalism problems with according the bankruptcy courts' authority to decide state law matters).

[63] *See* Erwin Chemerinsky, Decision-Makers: In Defense of Courts, 71 Am. Bankr. L.J. 109 (1997) (arguing that direct appeal to the courts of appeals from the bankruptcy courts is unconstitutional); *but see* Barbara J. Crabb, In Defense of Direct Appeals: A Further Reply to Professor Chemerinsky, 71 Am. Bankr. L.J. 137 (1997) (arguing that direct appeals would be constitutional).

[64] For an argument that *Northern Pipeline* should be overruled, *see* Erwin Chemerinsky, Ending the Marathon: It Is Time to Overrule *Northern Pipeline,* 65 Am. Bankr. L.J. 311 (1991).

Under the Bankruptcy Amendments and Federal Judgeship Act of 1984, bankruptcy judges are appointed for 14-year terms by the U.S. Courts of Appeals.[65] Bankruptcy judges are said to be officers of the district courts.

Also, the 1984 act changed the jurisdiction of the bankruptcy courts. The new law drew a distinction between "core" and "noncore" bankruptcy proceedings. Core matters are those that would have fit within the bankruptcy courts' summary jurisdiction prior to 1978; that is, core matters are those involving the bankrupt's property or assets within the jurisdiction of the bankruptcy court. Bankruptcy courts may "hear and decide" these core proceedings.

Noncore matters are those that earlier would have been within the bankruptcy courts' plenary jurisdiction. Here, the 1984 act draws a further distinction between noncore matters that would have fit within federal court jurisdiction absent the bankruptcy act (e.g., because of diversity or federal question jurisdiction) and those that a federal court could not otherwise have heard. As to noncore matters for which there is an independent basis for federal jurisdiction, the bankruptcy courts make proposed findings of fact and conclusions of law to the federal district court. A final order is not entered until after the district court engages in de novo review of any matters to which an objection was made. But noncore matters, for which there is not a separate basis for federal jurisdiction, should be dismissed upon a motion if state proceedings exist that can provide a timely resolution of the issue. Also, the bankruptcy courts specifically are prevented from exercising jurisdiction over personal injury tort and wrongful death claims.

Jury Trials in Bankruptcy Courts

An important question, ultimately resolved by statute, is the constitutionality of bankruptcy judges conducting jury trials. In *Granfinanceria, S.A. v. Nordberg*, the Court concluded that a jury trial must be provided in bankruptcy court when the relief sought is of a legal nature, such as money damages, and the matter involves private rights.[66] The Court, however, did not address the question of whether it violates Article III for Congress to authorize Article I bankruptcy courts to conduct jury trials.[67]

The specific question presented in *Granfinanceria* was whether a person who has not submitted a claim against a bankruptcy estate has a right to a jury trial when sued by the trustee in bankruptcy to recover an allegedly fraudulent monetary transfer. The Court concluded that the suit was properly denominated as being of a "legal" nature because of its historical treatment and because it was a claim for money. The Court thus held that there was a Seventh Amendment right to a jury trial, notwithstanding Congress's denomination of fraudulent conveyances as "core proceedings" in the bankruptcy act. Furthermore, the Court ruled

[65] Under Article II of the Constitution, Congress may vest the appointment of inferior officers in the federal courts. *See* Morrison v. Olsen, 487 U.S. 654 (1988) (upholding the constitutionality of permitting the courts of appeals to appoint independent special prosecutors).

[66] 492 U.S. 33 (1989).

[67] *Id.* at 64.

that the issue presented was not a "public right" because it neither involved the government as a party nor was so closely related to a public regulatory scheme as to allow treatment without a jury.

The *Granfinanceria* Court said that it did not face the question whether it violates Article III for Congress to authorize Article I bankruptcy courts to preside over jury trials subject to review in the district courts.[68] The Bankruptcy Reform Act of 1994 clarified this and grants bankruptcy courts authority to conduct jury trials with approval of the district court and consent of the parties. Specifically, the law provides: "If the right to a jury trial applies in a proceeding that may be heard under this section by a bankruptcy judge, the bankruptcy judge may conduct the jury trial if specially designated to exercise such jurisdiction by the district court and with the express consent of all the parties."[69]

§4.5.4 The Law After Northern Pipeline*: The Supreme Court's Decisions in* Thomas *and* Schor

Soon after *Northern Pipeline*, there were two Supreme Court decisions considering the constitutionality of legislative courts for matters once labeled "inherently judicial." In both instances the Court distinguished *Northern Pipeline* and upheld the constitutionality of the tribunal. Most dramatically, the Court appears to have adopted the approach that Justice White advocated in his dissent in *Northern Pipeline*: balancing the adverse impact on Article III values with the justification for use of a legislative court.[70]

Thomas v. Union Carbide Agricultural Products Co.

The first post-*Northern Pipeline* decision was *Thomas v. Union Carbide Agricultural Products Co.*[71] In *Thomas*, the Supreme Court upheld the constitutionality of an arbitration system designed to resolve valuation disputes among participants in a pesticide registration program. Federal law required that manufacturers submit research data regarding the health, safety, and environmental effects of all pesticides. The law permitted the data submitted by one company to be used by another that sought to register the same or a similar product, but a company using another's data had to pay for the costs of the data generation. The Environmental Protection Agency (EPA) was entrusted with determining the appropriate amount of compensation owed and resolving disputes. To relieve the EPA of this burden, Congress shifted the task of valuation for compensation purposes to a system of

[68] *Id.* at 65. Justice Scalia, in a concurring opinion, expressed the view that "public rights" involve only cases with the United States as a party. *Id.* at 69-71 (Scalia, J., concurring).

[69] 28 U.S.C. §157(e), Bankruptcy Reform Act of 1994, Pub. L. No. 1-3-394, §112.

[70] National Bankruptcy Commission, Bankruptcy: The Next Twenty Years (1997).

[71] 473 U.S. 568 (1985).

negotiations and binding arbitrations. Judicial review was limited to instances of "fraud, misrepresentation, or other misconduct."[72]

The issue in *Thomas* was whether Congress could assign this private law dispute to a non-Article III court. In upholding the constitutionality of the arbitration system, the Court narrowly stated what it understood to be the holding of *Northern Pipeline.* Justice O'Connor, writing for the majority, said that the earlier decision established only "that Congress may not vest in a non-Article III court the power to adjudicate, render final judgment, and issue binding orders in a traditional contract action arising under state law, without consent of the litigants, and subject only to ordinary appellate review."[73]

The Court said that legislative courts were permissible for private disputes that were closely related to government regulatory activities. In perhaps the most important language of the majority opinion, Justice O'Connor stated: "Congress, acting for a valid legislative purpose pursuant to its constitutional powers under article I, may create a seemingly 'private' right that is so closely integrated into a public regulatory scheme as to be a matter appropriate for agency resolution."[74]

The Court emphasized the "public" nature of the regulatory scheme and the public interest served by the arbitration procedure.[75] The matter was handled by a government agency pursuant to congressional authority and was not a substitute for any existing common law proceeding.[76] The Court also stressed that appellate review, albeit limited in scope, was provided and that there was no indication that the arbitration system threatened Article III courts or implicated separation of powers concerns.[77]

At minimum, *Thomas* recognized a new category of cases where legislative courts could be constitutionally employed: private law disputes closely related to government regulatory programs. Professor Resnik termed this category "agency adjudication of private rights that the public cares about."[78] But *Thomas* potentially has even greater importance in representing a new approach to judicial analysis of legislative courts. In the *Northern Pipeline* decision, the plurality opinion indicated that there were four, and only four, situations in which legislative courts could be used: for territories, the military, public rights matters, and as adjuncts to Article III courts. In *Thomas,* the Court rejected the claim that these categories are exhaustive of the situations in which legislative courts are constitutional.[79] Instead, the Court adopted a functional approach, considering the desirability of a non-Article III tribunal and the degree of encroachment on the federal judiciary. In this way, the Court's approach seems similar to the balancing test endorsed by Justice White in *Northern Pipeline.*[80]

[72] 7 U.S.C. §136a(c)(1)(D)(ii).

[73] 473 U.S. at 584.

[74] *Id.* at 593-594.

[75] *Id.* at 589-590, 593-594.

[76] *Id.* at 587, 589.

[77] *Id.* at 591.

[78] Resnik, *supra* note 59, at 598.

[79] 473 U.S. at 585-586.

[80] The *Northern Pipeline* plurality concurred in the judgment in *Thomas. See id.* at 594 (Brennan, J., concurring); and *id.* at 602 (Stevens, J., concurring).

Commodity Futures Trading Commission v. Schor

The Court's other post-*Northern Pipeline* decision approving legislative courts is *Commodity Futures Trading Commission v. Schor.*[81] The Commodity Futures Trading Commission has the statutory authority to provide reparations to individuals who are injured by fraudulent or illegally manipulative conduct by brokers.[82] The commission has also promulgated regulations that enabled it to hear all counterclaims arising out of the same allegedly impermissible transactions.

The Court separately considered these two aspects of the commission's jurisdiction: the authority to provide reparations and the power to adjudicate counterclaims. As to the former, the Court found that the commission's jurisdiction to order reparations to injured consumers was "of unquestioned constitutional validity."[83] Because the commission could not enforce its own orders, which instead required federal court action, the Court concluded that the commission served as an adjunct to the federal court in a manner approved in *Crowell v. Benson.*[84]

The more difficult question was whether the commission could hear state law counterclaims. In *Northern Pipeline,* both the plurality and the concurrence found objectionable the bankruptcy courts' authority to decide state law matters. However, in *Schor,* the Court approved the commission's authority to rule on the state law counterclaims. The Court expressly endorsed a balancing test in appraising the constitutionality of legislative courts.[85]

The Court identified the benefits of an administrative alternative to federal court litigation in terms of efficiency and expertise.[86] At the same time, the Court said that these interests had to be balanced against "the purposes underlying the requirements of Article III."[87] The Court considered two goals of Article III: ensuring fairness to litigants by providing an independent judiciary and maintaining the "structural" role of the judiciary in the scheme of separation of powers. As to fairness, the Court said that the defendant had consented to the administrative proceedings as an alternative to federal court litigation and hence could not claim that the commission adjudication was inherently unfair.[88]

As to separation of powers, the Court declared: "In determining the extent to which a given congressional decision to authorize the adjudication of article III business in a non-article III tribunal impermissibly threatens the institutional integrity of the Judicial Branch, the Court has declined to adopt formalistic and unbending rules."[89] Justice O'Connor, writing for the majority, said that instead the Court focuses on several factors including "the extent to which the 'essential attributes of judicial power' are reserved to article III courts, and conversely, the

[81] 478 U.S. 833 (1986).
[82] 7 U.S.C. §18.
[83] 478 U.S. at 856.
[84] *Id.*
[85] *Id.* at 851.
[86] *Id.* at 856.
[87] *Id.* at 847.
[88] *Id.* at 849-850.
[89] *Id.* at 851.

extent to which the non-article III forum exercises the range of jurisdiction and powers normally vested only in article III courts, the origins and importance of the right to be adjudicated, and the concerns that drove Congress to depart from the requirements of article III."[90] Justice O'Connor emphasized that no single factor is likely to be determinative of constitutionality.

In *Schor*, the Court said that the commission's authority is quite similar to that traditionally exercised by agencies, except for the jurisdiction to hear counterclaims. The Court felt that this aspect of agency jurisdiction did not create constitutional infirmities. The Court concluded that "the magnitude of any intrusion on the Judicial Branch can only be termed *de minimis*."[91]

Justices Brennan and Marshall dissented. They argued that legislative courts should be permitted only in the narrow circumstances outlined in the plurality opinion in *Northern Pipeline*. Because the commission's authority exceeded these limits, they would have found its ability to decide private law disputes unconstitutional.

Unresolved Questions

Schor answered some questions, but raised others. After *Thomas* and *Schor* it appeared that the *Northern Pipeline* plurality's view is not controlling. Legislative courts are permitted in situations in addition to territorial and military courts, public rights disputes, and as adjuncts to Article III courts. The Court's approach in these latter cases was to balance the benefit of using a legislative court with the harms in terms of fairness to litigants and to the structure of separation of powers.

What is unclear is how this balancing will be done. By identifying several factors that will be considered in the weighing process, and by expressly refusing to identify any of the factors as more important than others, the Court has adopted an approach that inevitably requires case-by-case decision-making. Moreover, the decision-making is inherently unpredictable because it is uncertain what factors the Court will consider decisive in any particular instance.[92] These questions are even more important after the Court's decision in *Wellness International Network Ltd. v. Sharif*—discussed below—which shifts back to the balancing approach of *Thomas* and *Schor*.

§4.5.5 *Subsequent Developments:* Stern v. Marshall, Executive Benefits v. Arkison, *and* Wellness International Network Ltd. v. Sharif

The Court's decisions in *Stern v. Marshall, Executive Benefits v. Arkison*, and *Wellness International Network Ltd. v. Sharif* have only added to the confusion about bankruptcy courts and the overall law in this area. In *Stern*, the Court relied on *Northern Pipeline* and indeed returned to the formalistic approach of that opinion as

[90] *Id.*

[91] *Id.* at 856.

[92] Fallon, *supra* note 31, at 933-992.

compared to the functional approach in *Thomas* and *Schor*. But four years later, in *Wellness*, the Court relied on *Schor* and embraced a functional approach to deciding when non-Article III courts are permissible.

Stern v. Marshall

Chief Justice Roberts began his majority opinion in *Stern v. Marshall* by quoting from Charles Dickens's novel *Bleak House*, and the analogy certainly seems apt.[93] Vickie Lynn Marshall and J. Howard Marshall met in October 1991 and were married on June 27, 1994. Although he lavished gifts and significant sums of money on Vickie during their courtship and marriage, J. Howard did not include anything for Vickie in his will.[94] Before J. Howard passed away in August 1995, Vickie filed suit in Texas probate court, claiming that Pierce Marshall—J. Howard's younger son—fraudulently induced his father to sign a living trust that did not include her. She maintained that J. Howard meant to leave her half of his estate. Pierce denied any fraudulent activity and defended the trust and, after his father's death, the will.

Soon after J. Howard died, in January 1996, Vickie filed a petition for bankruptcy in the U.S. District Court for the Central District of California. In June 1996, Pierce filed a proof of claim in the federal bankruptcy proceeding, alleging that Vickie had defamed him when attorneys representing Vickie told members of the press that Pierce had engaged in forgery, fraud, and overreaching to gain control of his father's assets. Vickie answered, asserting truth as a defense. She also filed counterclaims, among them a claim that Pierce had tortiously interfered with a gift she expected. She contended that Pierce essentially imprisoned J. Howard against his wishes, surrounded him with hired guards for the purpose of preventing contact with Vickie, made misrepresentations to J. Howard, and transferred property against J. Howard's expressed wishes.[95]

The bankruptcy court granted summary judgment in favor of Vickie on Pierce's claim and, after a trial on the merits, entered judgment for Vickie on her tortious interference counterclaim.[96] The bankruptcy court also held that both Vickie's objection to Pierce's claim and Vickie's counterclaim qualified as "core proceedings" under the Bankruptcy Act, which meant that the court had authority to enter a final judgment disposing of those claims.[97] The court awarded Vickie compensatory damages of more than $449 million—less whatever she recovered in the ongoing probate action in Texas—as well as $25 million in punitive damages.[98]

The district court concluded that the bankruptcy court lacked the authority to issue a final judgment on Vickie's counterclaim and thus said that it would treat

[93] 564 U.S. at 468.

[94] Because there are three different individuals named Marshall involved—J. Howard Marshall, Pierce Marshall, and Vickie Lynn Marshall—it is easiest to refer to them by first names.

[95] Marshall v. Marshall, 547 U.S. 293, 301 (2006).

[96] 253 B.R. 550, 558-559 (Bankr. C.D. Cal. 2000).

[97] 257 B.R. 35, 39-40 (Bankr. C.D. Cal. 2000).

[98] *Id.* at 40.

the bankruptcy court's judgment as "proposed rather than final" and engaged in an "independent review of the record."[99]

However, subsequent to the bankruptcy court decision, but prior to the decision of the district court, the Texas probate court had conducted a jury trial and ruled in favor of Pierce Marshall. The district court, however, did not give preclusive effect to this decision and agreed with the bankruptcy court that Pierce had tortiously interfered with Vickie's inheritance. The district court reduced the damages to approximately $88 million, divided equally between compensatory and punitive damages.

The Ninth Circuit reversed the district court based on the matter falling within the probate exception to federal jurisdiction, but the Supreme Court unanimously reversed and remanded the case back to the Ninth Circuit.[100] The Ninth Circuit then ruled in favor of Pierce, holding that the counterclaim was not properly within the core jurisdiction of the bankruptcy court and thus that it lacked the authority to issue a final judgment.[101] Because the bankruptcy court could not issue a final judgment, its ruling lacked preclusive effect; thus, the Texas probate court decision was binding.

That was the issue before the Supreme Court. If the bankruptcy court had the authority to issue a final judgment, then its ruling was preclusive of the Texas probate court's decision and Vickie's estate wins. But if the bankruptcy court lacked the authority to issue a final judgment, then there was no preclusion of the Texas probate court and Pierce's estate wins. The Court, 5-4, took the latter approach.

Chief Justice Roberts wrote for the Court. The Court said that the Bankruptcy Act in §157(b)(2)(c) expressly makes counterclaims "core" proceedings over which the bankruptcy court could issue a final judgment.[102] The Court found, however, that this violated the Constitution because bankruptcy judges do not have life tenure. Chief Justice Roberts's majority opinion began by stressing the essential nature of Article III protections for separation of powers and the protection of individual liberties. He wrote:

> Article III protects liberty not only through its role in implementing the separation of powers, but also by specifying the defining characteristics of Article III judges. . . . Article III could neither serve its purpose in the system of checks and

[99] 264 B.R. 609, 633 (C.D. Cal. 2001) ("[A] counterclaim should not be characterized as core [if it] is only somewhat related to the claim against which it is asserted, and when the unique characteristics and context of the counterclaim place it outside the normal type of set-off or other counterclaims that customarily arise.").

[100] Marshall v. Marshall, 547 U.S. 293 (2006). The Supreme Court held that the "probate exception" to federal court jurisdiction did not bar a federal court, including a bankruptcy court, from deciding a claim of tortious interference with recovery from an estate.

[101] In re Marshall, 600 F.3d 1037, 1058-1059 (9th Cir. 2010).

[102] 564 U.S. at 489-490. The Bankruptcy Act designates some matters as core, over which the bankruptcy court can issue a final judgment and some matters as noncore, over which the bankruptcy court can issue a final judgment with consent of the parties or otherwise makes a report and recommendation to the federal district court.

> balances nor preserve the integrity of judicial decisionmaking if the other branches of the Federal Government could confer the Government's "judicial Power" on entities outside Article III. That is why we have long recognized that, in general, Congress may not "withdraw from judicial cognizance any matter which, from its nature, is the subject of a suit at the common law, or in equity, or admiralty."[103]

The Court concluded that it violated Article III for Congress to authorize the bankruptcy court to issue a final judgment over the state law counterclaim. The Court explained that this did not fit into any of the traditional exceptions where non-Article III courts are allowed, such as for "public rights" matters where it is a claim against the United States and Congress has waived its sovereign immunity, but with the condition that the matter be heard in a non-Article III court.[104] Nor, the Court said, could the bankruptcy court be seen as an "adjunct" of the district court. Chief Justice Roberts explained that given its expansive authority, "a bankruptcy court can no more be deemed a mere 'adjunct' of the district court than a district court can be deemed such an 'adjunct' of the court of appeals."[105]

In what is likely the most important language of the opinion in terms of when bankruptcy courts can issue final judgments, the Court said that "the question is whether the action at issue stems from the bankruptcy itself or would necessarily be resolved in the claims allowance process."[106] Vickie's counterclaim for tortious interference did not fit within this definition, and thus the bankruptcy court decision was not a final judgment and had no preclusive effect over the Texas probate court decision.

The basis for the Court's decision was that it was unconstitutional for Congress to give non-Article III judges the authority to issue a final judgment over the state law counterclaim. But it is questionable as to why this is unconstitutional. Chief Justice Roberts focused, at some length, on the importance of Article III in ensuring the independence of the federal judiciary.[107]

The Court's emphasis on the importance of an independent judiciary would make sense if this were an issue of federal constitutional law, especially one where life tenure might make judges more inclined to withstand popular pressure and uphold the Constitution. The issue in *Stern v. Marshall*, however, was a state law claim that by itself would not even fit within the scope of the matters that federal courts are allowed to hear under Article III, §2 of the Constitution. State law claims are generally adjudicated by state law judges who rarely have life tenure. What then was so objectionable about Congress authorizing bankruptcy judges without life tenure to hear the matters?

Chief Justice Roberts's only answer to this question comes at the end of the majority opinion. He writes: "Is there really a threat to the separation of powers where Congress has conferred the judicial power outside Article III only over

[103] *Id.* at 483-484. (citations omitted).

[104] *Id.* at 488 ("Vickie's counterclaim cannot be deemed a matter of 'public right' that can be decided outside the Judicial Branch.").

[105] *Id.* at 500.

[106] *Id.* at 499.

[107] *Id.* at 482-485.

certain counterclaims in bankruptcy? The short but emphatic answer is yes. A statute may no more lawfully chip away at the authority of the Judicial Branch than it may eliminate it entirely."[108]

But Congress has "chipped away" at the "authority of the Judicial Branch" by assigning judicial matters to non-Article III courts in many different situations since the earliest days of American history. The question, which the Court does not answer, is what is objectionable about this matter being assigned to a non-Article III court in light of all that preceded it in terms of situations in which non-Article III judges were allowed.

It seems difficult to reconcile the functional approach in *Thomas* and *Schor* with the formalistic approach in *Stern v. Marshall*. The Court in *Stern v. Marshall* returned to the earlier formalism of *Northern Pipeline* but without ever acknowledging that the cases subsequent to it had taken a dramatically different method of analyzing when Congress can give authority to non-Article III courts.

Chief Justice Roberts's majority opinion in *Stern v. Marshall* distinguished *Thomas* and *Schor* but without acknowledging or addressing their expressly functional approach to determining when non-Article III courts are permissible. The Court said that *Thomas* was different because "any right to compensation result[ed] from the statute" and did not "depend on or replace a right to compensation under state law."[109] As for *Schor*, the Court said the Vickie's claim to relief "is not 'completely dependent upon' adjudication of a claim created by federal law, as in *Schor*."[110] Pierce did not truly consent to resolution of Vickie's claim in the bankruptcy court proceedings. He had nowhere else to go if he wished to recover from Vickie's estate.

Although these are distinctions between *Stern v. Marshall* and *Thomas* and *Schor*, they miss the point that the Court was departing from the functional and pragmatic approach of the earlier decisions. This was the central point of the dissent. Justice Breyer, writing for the dissenting justices, declared:

> Rather than leaning so heavily on the approach taken by the plurality in *Northern Pipeline*, I would look to this Court's more recent Article III cases *Thomas* and *Schor*—cases that commanded a clear majority. In both cases the Court took a more pragmatic approach to the constitutional question. It sought to determine whether, in the particular instance, the challenged delegation of adjudicatory authority posed a genuine and serious threat that one branch of Government sought to aggrandize its own constitutionally delegated authority by encroaching upon a field of authority that the Constitution assigns exclusively to another branch.[111]

Stern v. Marshall immediately caused enormous litigation as to its scope and application. Two questions are crucial: What other matters will be outside the

[108] *Id.* at 502-503.
[109] *Id.* at 491, quoting *Thomas*, 473 U.S. at 584.
[110] *Id.* at 493.
[111] *Id.* at 510 (Breyer, J., dissenting).

power of bankruptcy courts to issue final judgments, and can consent cure the defect?

As for the scope of the holding, Chief Justice Roberts concluded the majority opinion by saying that the Court was holding only that in "one isolated respect" Congress had violated Article III.[112] But it is impossible to see the decision in such a narrow way; if bankruptcy courts cannot issue a final judgment as to state law counterclaims, what other state law claims are outside the scope of bankruptcy courts power to issue final judgments? Simple examples illustrate the importance of this question. Justice Breyer, in dissent, gives the example of a tenant who files for bankruptcy.[113] The landlord files a claim for unpaid rent, and the tenant then presents various state law counterclaims against the landlord. After *Stern v. Marshall*, it is hard to see how the bankruptcy court can issue a final judgment as to those state law counterclaims. Also, in the months after *Stern* was decided, a number of bankruptcy courts ruled that they no longer could issue final judgments as to claims of fraudulent conveyance, an issue that arises with great frequency in bankruptcy court proceedings.[114]

The majority opinion in *Stern v. Marshall* gives a clear indication of its scope, and it is far broader than Chief Justice Roberts's conclusion acknowledged. The Court stated: "[T]he question is whether the action at issue stems from the bankruptcy itself or would necessarily be allowed in the claims allowance process."[115] This rule is quite restrictive and would place most state law counterclaims, and many other matters, outside the scope of bankruptcy courts to issue final judgments.

What difference would this make? It would seem that bankruptcy courts would have to make "reports and recommendations" to the district courts so that they could issue final judgments.[116] As Justice Breyer points out in dissent, there are 1.6 million bankruptcy filings every year (as compared to 280,000 civil cases and 78,000 criminal cases), and to require that a significant portion of these now be reviewed by the federal district courts would have a staggering impact.[117] As Justice Breyer explains in his conclusion, "[U]nder these circumstances, a constitutionally required game of jurisdictional ping-pong between courts would lead to inefficiency, increased cost, delay, and needless additional suffering among those faced with bankruptcy."[118]

[112] *Id.* at 503.

[113] *Id.* at 518-520 (Breyer, J., dissenting).

[114] *See* Sitka Enters., Inc. v. Segarra-Miranda, No. 10-1847CCC, 2011 U.S. Dist. LEXIS 90243, at *8 (D.P.R. Aug. 12, 2011) ("[T]he fraudulent conveyance action brought by the trustee cannot by adjudicated by the Bankruptcy Court, a non-Article III court, for lack of constitutional authority to do so."); Samson v. Blixseth, 456 B.R. 318 (Bankr. W.D. Mich. 2011); Meoli v. Huntington National Bank, No. HG-05-00690, 2011 WL 3610050, at *14 (Bankr. W.D. Mich. Aug. 17, 2011).

[115] 564 U.S. at 499.

[116] There actually is a statutory problem with this: the Bankruptcy Act recognizes two kinds of cases—core and noncore proceedings. It provides for bankruptcy courts to issue reports and recommendations as to the latter. But Stern v. Marshall creates a third category: core proceedings where bankruptcy courts cannot issue final judgments. Are these to be treated as noncore proceedings under the statute?

[117] 564 U.S. at 520 (Breyer, J., dissenting).

[118] *Id.*

The crucial practical question after *Stern v. Marshall* was whether consent could cure the problem. If bankruptcy courts could issue final judgments over state law claims with consent of the parties, *Stern v. Marshall* is relatively unimportant. But if consent is not permissible, then its effects on the bankruptcy courts would be great and it would have implications for magistrate judges and other non-Article III courts. The circuits quickly split on this issue,[119] and the Supreme Court granted review in *Executive Benefits v. Arkison,* which did not resolve the question, and then *Wellness International Network Ltd. v. Sharif,* which held that consent is permissible and that it even can be implied consent.

Executive Benefits v. Arkison

Following *Stern v. Marshall,* the Ninth Circuit, in *In re Bellingham Insurance,* asked for briefing on the question of whether a bankruptcy court could issue a final judgment over a state law claim—in this case a fraudulent conveyance claim—with consent of the parties.[120] The Supreme Court granted review on the question of whether consent is permissible, but then did not decide the issue. Rather, the Supreme Court held that there was de novo review in this case in the federal district court and that was sufficient to meet the requirements of Article III.

Justice Thomas wrote the opinion for a unanimous Court. The Court indicated that the state law claim for fraudulent transfer was one over which a bankruptcy court cannot issue a final judgment after *Stern v. Marshall.* The Court said that "when a bankruptcy court is presented with such a claim, the proper course is to issue proposed findings of fact and conclusions of law. The district court will then review the claim *de novo* and enter judgment. This approach accords with the bankruptcy statute and does not implicate the constitutional defect identified by *Stern.*"[121] The Court concluded that the "District Court conducted *de novo* review" and that this was therefore sufficient to meet the requirements of Article III.[122] Having decided the case on this basis, the Court said that there was no need to decide the question of whether consent was permissible.

Although *Executive Benefits v. Arkison* did not resolve the crucial issue of the permissibility of consent, it still has significance for the law in this area. First, the Supreme Court never has defined what it means for a non-Article III court to be an "adjunct" to a district court, and *Executive Benefits v. Arkison* says that de novo review in a district court is sufficient for this. Second, the Court held that "core" matters under the Bankruptcy Act for which the bankruptcy court cannot issue a final judgment under *Stern v. Marshall* should be treated like noncore matters. The Bankruptcy Act divides matters into "core" and "noncore," but *Stern v. Marshall*

[119] *Compare* Waldman v. Stone, 698 F.3d 910 (6th Cir. 2012), *cert. denied,* 568 U.S. 1231 (2013) (bankruptcy courts cannot issue final judgments where otherwise it would be impermissible with consent of the parties), *with* In re Bellingham Insurance, 702 F.3d 553 (9th Cir. 2012), *aff'd on other grounds, and* Executive Benefits v. Arkison, 573 U.S. 25 (2014) (consent is permissible).

[120] 702 F.3d 553 (9th Cir. 2012), *aff'd on other grounds sub nom.* Executive Benefits v. Arkison, 573 U.S. 25 (2014) (consent is permissible).

[121] Executive Benefits v. Arkison, 573 U.S. at 31.

[122] *Id.* at 39-40.

created a third category: core matters, such as state law counterclaims, over which bankruptcy courts cannot issue final judgments. *Executive Benefits v. Arkison* resolved a split among the circuits and held that they are to be treated the same as noncore matters.

Wellness International Network Ltd. v. Sharif

Almost immediately after not resolving the question concerning consent in *Executive Benefits v. Arkison,* the Court granted review on that issue in *Wellness International Network Ltd. v Sharif.*[123] The Court, in a 6-3 decision, held that consent is permissible and that it can be implied consent. Two of the justices from the majority in *Stern*—Justices Kennedy and Alito—joined the four *Stern* dissenters to create the majority.

Wellness International Network is a manufacturer of health and nutrition products. Wellness and Sharif entered into a contract under which Sharif would distribute Wellness's products. A dispute developed and Sharif sued Wellness in the United States District Court for the Northern District of Texas. Sharif repeatedly ignored Wellness's discovery requests and other litigation obligations, resulting in an entry of default judgment for Wellness. The District Court eventually sanctioned Sharif by awarding Wellness over $650,000 in attorneys' fees.

Sharif filed for Chapter 7 bankruptcy in the Northern District of Illinois. The bankruptcy petition listed Wellness as a creditor. Wellness requested documents concerning Sharif's assets, which Sharif did not provide. Wellness later obtained a loan application Sharif had filed in 2002, listing more than $5 million in assets. When confronted, Sharif informed Wellness and the Chapter 7 trustee that he had lied on the loan application. The listed assets, Sharif claimed, were actually owned by the Soad Wattar Living Trust (Trust), an entity Sharif said he administered on behalf of his mother, and for the benefit of his sister. The bankruptcy court ruled in favor of Wellness, but Sharif objected in the district court based on *Stern v. Marshall.* The district court found that Sharif had waived this objection and consented to the authority of the bankruptcy court. But the United States Court of Appeals for the Seventh Circuit reversed and concluded that "a litigant may not waive" a *Stern* objection.[124]

The Supreme Court reversed and held "that Article III is not violated when the parties knowingly and voluntarily consent to adjudication by a bankruptcy judge."[125] Justice Sotomayor, writing for the majority, said that "the foundational case in the modern era is *Commodity Futures Trading Comm'n v. Schor.*"[126] The Court explained that "the entitlement to an Article III adjudicator is 'a personal right' and thus ordinarily 'subject to waiver.'" Article III also serves a structural purpose, "barring congressional attempts 'to transfer jurisdiction [to non-Article III tribunals] for the purpose of emasculating' constitutional courts and thereby prevent[ing]

[123] 575 U.S. 665 (2015).
[124] 727 F.3d 751, 773 (2013).
[125] 575 U.S. at 669.
[126] *Id.* at 675 (citations omitted).

'the encroachment or aggrandizement of one branch at the expense of the other.' But allowing Article I adjudicators to decide claims submitted to them by consent does not offend the separation of powers so long as Article III courts retain supervisory authority over the process."[127]

The Court expressly embraced the functional approach to determining the permissibility of non-Article III courts that had been followed in *Schor* and *Thomas*. The Court stated: "The question here, then, is whether allowing bankruptcy courts to decide *Stern* claims by consent would 'impermissibly threate[n] the institutional integrity of the Judicial Branch.' And that question must be decided not by 'formalistic and unbending rules,' but 'with an eye to the practical effect that the' practice 'will have on the constitutionally assigned role of the federal judiciary.'"[128] The Court found no threat to judicial independence from having bankruptcy courts decide state law questions, explaining that "[s]o long as those judges are subject to control by the Article III courts, their work poses no threat to the separation of powers."[129]

The Court also concluded that consent need not be express; implied consent is permissible. The Court stated: "Nothing in the Constitution requires that consent to adjudication by a bankruptcy court be express. . . . '[T]he Article III right is substantially honored' by permitting waiver based on 'actions rather than words.'"[130]

Justice Alito in a concurring opinion said that he would not reach the question of whether implied consent is permissible.[131] Chief Justice Roberts wrote a dissent, joined by Justices Scalia and Thomas, in which he objected to the functional approach of the majority and argued that Article III imposes structural limits on the use of non-Article III courts and that structural limits cannot be overcome by consent. He wrote: "'[P]arties cannot by consent cure' an Article III violation implicating the structural separation of powers. . . . The Court justifies its decision largely on pragmatic grounds. I would not yield so fully to functionalism."[132]

In one sense, *Stern v. Marshall* and *Wellness International Network Ltd. v. Sharif* are consistent. *Stern* says that bankruptcy courts cannot issue final judgments over state law claims that do not arise from the bankruptcy itself. *Wellness* does not question this holding, but instead says that bankruptcy courts can do this with consent of the parties.

In another sense, though, *Stern* and *Wellness* are very different in their approach to when non-Article III courts are permissible. *Stern* takes the formalistic approach of *Northern Pipeline* and expressly rejects practical considerations. But *Wellness* takes

[127] *Id.* at 678 (citations omitted).
[128] *Id.* (citations omitted).
[129] *Id.* at 681.
[130] *Id.* at 684.
[131] *Id.* at 686 (Alito, J., concurring in part and concurring in the judgment).
[132] *Id.* at 687 (Roberts, C.J., dissenting). Justice Thomas also wrote a separate dissent. *Id.* at 706 (Thomas, J., dissenting).

the functional approach of *Schor* and *Thomas*—even declaring that the "modern era" begins with *Schor* (and notably not *Northern Pipeline*).

Ultimately, *Wellness* means that *Stern v. Marshall* is far less important than it seemed when decided. Parties overwhelmingly will consent to bankruptcy courts issuing final judgments and even implied consent is sufficient. The question sure to be litigated is what is sufficient for implied consent.

CHAPTER 5

The Subject Matter Jurisdiction of the Federal Courts

§5.1 INTRODUCTION

Subject matter jurisdiction is the legal authority of a court to hear and decide a particular type of case. State judiciaries have general jurisdiction and may therefore hear all causes of action unless there is a statute denying them subject matter jurisdiction. Federal courts have limited subject matter jurisdiction; that is, they are restricted in what cases they may adjudicate and may exercise jurisdiction only if it is specifically authorized.

Need for Both Constitutional and Statutory Authority

Several important principles arise from this well-established maxim that federal courts are courts of limited jurisdiction. First, a federal court may adjudicate a case only if there is *both* constitutional and statutory authority for federal jurisdiction. Constitutional authority derives from Article III of the Constitution, which provides for federal judicial power over nine categories of "cases" and "controversies." These nine categories fall into two major types of provisions. One set of clauses provides the federal courts with the authority to vindicate and enforce the powers of the federal government. For example, the federal courts have the power to decide all cases arising under the Constitution, treaties, and laws of the United States. Additionally, the federal courts have the authority to hear all cases in which the United States is a party. The federal government's powers in the area of foreign policy are protected by giving the federal courts the authority to hear all cases affecting ambassadors, other public ministers, and consuls; all cases of admiralty and maritime jurisdiction; and cases between a state, or its citizens, and a foreign country or its citizens.

A second set of provisions grants the federal courts the authority to serve an interstate umpiring function, resolving disputes between states and their citizens. Thus, Article III accords the federal courts the authority to decide controversies between two or more states, between a state and citizens of another state, between citizens of different states, and between citizens of the same state claiming land in other states. However, the Eleventh Amendment modifies Article III by denying federal courts the ability to hear suits between a state and citizens of another state or a foreign country.[1]

The existence of a constitutional provision, although necessary, is not sufficient to create federal court subject matter jurisdiction. There also must be a federal statute authorizing jurisdiction. In large part, the additional statutory requirement reflects Congress's power to determine the jurisdiction of the lower federal courts. Under Article III, Congress has discretion whether to create lower federal courts and to define the jurisdiction of the tribunals it establishes.[2] Ever since the first statute creating federal courts, the Judiciary Act of 1789, federal

§5.1 [1] The Eleventh Amendment is discussed in detail in Chapter 7. As interpreted, the Eleventh Amendment precludes suits against state governments both by their own citizens and by citizens of other states.

[2] *See, e.g.,* Sheldon v. Sill, 49 U.S. (8 How.) 441 (1850) (Congress creates lower federal courts and thus has discretion to vest them with less than the full jurisdiction allowed in Article III). For a discussion of congressional authority to control lower federal court jurisdiction, *see* §3.3, *supra.* The requirement that there be a statutory provision for jurisdiction applies only to lower federal courts; that is, a constitutional provision is sufficient for Supreme Court jurisdiction, which is said to be "self-executing." The Supreme Court nonetheless always has acted as if Congress confers jurisdiction on it. *See* Durousseau v. United States, 10 U.S. (6 Cranch) 307, 314 (1810).

jurisdiction never has included the authority to adjudicate all matters allowed by Article III.[3]

Many federal statutes concerning specific topics contain provisions allowing federal court subject matter jurisdiction over matters arising under them. Additionally, many jurisdictional statutes allow federal court adjudication in particular situations.[4] Some provisions are quite broad in authorizing federal court jurisdiction. For example, 28 U.S.C. §1331 grants federal district courts original jurisdiction over "all civil actions arising under the Constitution, laws, or treaties of the United States." This expansive language makes many of the specific grants of jurisdiction superfluous. Until 1980, §1331 contained an amount in controversy requirement. Thus, prior to this revision, statutes creating subject matter jurisdiction over particular matters without regard to the amount in controversy were quite important.[5]

Presumption Against Federal Court Jurisdiction

A second significant principle arising from the maxim that federal courts are courts of limited jurisdiction is the presumption against federal court jurisdiction. A person seeking to invoke federal jurisdiction has the burden of proof to demonstrate at the outset that the federal court has the authority to hear the case.[6]

Subject Matter Jurisdiction Cannot Be Gained by Consent

Third, federal court jurisdiction cannot be gained by consent of the parties. The restrictions on federal court jurisdiction advance the important values of federalism and separation of powers. For example, limiting federal court authority preserves the role of the state courts. Also, constraining federal judicial power helps to limit the role of the judiciary in the federal system. Accordingly, parties cannot bring matters to federal court where constitutional or statutory authority is lacking. Therefore, consent is never adequate to permit federal jurisdiction where none otherwise would exist.[7] In fact, subject matter jurisdiction may be challenged at any point and by either party. Thus, subject matter jurisdiction may be challenged on appeal and even by the party that initially brought the case to federal

[3] For example, federal courts did not have general federal question jurisdiction to hear matters arising under the Constitution and laws of the United States until 1875. *See* §1.2, *supra* (describing the history of federal jurisdiction).

[4] *See* 28 U.S.C. §§1330-1364.

[5] For example, 28 U.S.C. §1343 creates subject matter jurisdiction for civil rights cases. This jurisdictional provision was important because of the difficulty of ascertaining the monetary value of civil rights and liberties. However, the elimination of the amount in controversy requirement in §1331 made §1343 superfluous.

[6] *See* McNutt v. General Motors Acceptance Corp., 298 U.S. 178 (1936).

[7] *See, e.g.,* Sosna v. Iowa, 419 U.S. 393, 398 (1975); Mitchell v. Maurer, 293 U.S. 237, 244 (1934). For a criticism of the inability to gain subject matter jurisdiction by consent, *see* Dan B. Dobbs, The Decline of Jurisdiction by Consent, 40 N.C. L. Rev. 49 (1961).

court.[8] However, except in very limited circumstances, subject matter jurisdiction is not a basis for a collateral attack on a judgment; that is, once a judgment is entered it cannot be attacked, except on appeal, on the ground that the court lacked subject matter jurisdiction.[9]

Federal Courts May Challenge Their Own Jurisdiction

Fourth, federal courts, on their own, may raise objections to subject matter jurisdiction. In American courts that are committed to the adversary system, generally judges are supposed to rule only on motions brought by the parties. But subject matter jurisdiction is one of the few matters that courts can raise on their own. Moreover, because subject matter jurisdiction must exist at every level of appeal, all federal courts—trial and appellate—can challenge the existence of federal subject matter jurisdiction.[10]

State Courts Generally Have Concurrent Jurisdiction

Fifth, it should be noted that state courts have concurrent jurisdiction with federal courts over all matters within federal jurisdiction, unless there is a specific federal statute creating exclusive federal jurisdiction.[11] For example, federal law provides exclusive federal jurisdiction over copyright and patent cases.[12]

The Supreme Court has made it clear that there is a strong presumption in favor of concurrent state court jurisdiction. In *Tafflin v. Levitt*, the Court stated that concurrent state court jurisdiction over civil RICO claims would be denied only "by an explicit statutory directive, by unmistakable implication from legislative history, or by clear incompatibility between state-court jurisdiction and federal interests."[13] The Court concluded that state courts could hear civil RICO claims because there was "[n]othing in the language, structure, legislative history, or underlying policies of RICO" precluding state court jurisdiction.[14]

In *Yellow Freight System, Inc. v. Donnelly*, the Court relied expressly on *Tafflin* and unanimously held that state courts had concurrent jurisdiction to decide employment discrimination claims brought under the Civil Rights Act of 1964.[15] The Court premised its decision on "the presumption of concurrent jurisdiction

[8] *See, e.g.*, American Fire & Casualty Co. v. Finn, 341 U.S. 6 (1951) (party that invoked federal court jurisdiction may challenge it); Capron v. Van Noorden, 6 U.S. (2 Cranch) 126 (1804) (party that invoked federal jurisdiction may challenge it).

[9] *See, e.g.*, McCormick v. Sullivan, 23 U.S. (10 Wheat.) 192 (1825) (no collateral attacks for lack of subject matter jurisdiction).

[10] *See, e.g.*, Louisville & Nashville R.R. v. Mottley, 211 U.S. 149 (1908) (Supreme Court raising objection to federal court jurisdiction).

[11] The Moses Taylor, 71 U.S. (4 Wall.) 411, 430 (1866) (approving exclusive federal jurisdiction in admiralty cases).

[12] 28 U.S.C. §§1337, 1338.

[13] 493 U.S. 455, 459-460 (1990).

[14] *Id.* at 467.

[15] 494 U.S. 820 (1990).

that lies at the core of our federal system."[16] The Court concluded that "Title VII contains no language that expressly confines jurisdiction to federal courts or ousts state courts of presumptive jurisdiction. The omission of any such provision is strong, and arguably sufficient, evidence that Congress had no such intent."[17]

Sixth, if both personal jurisdiction and subject matter jurisdiction are disputed in a case, a federal court may dismiss the matter for lack of personal jurisdiction without reaching the issue of whether there is subject matter jurisdiction. In *Ruhrgas AG v. Marathon Oil Co.*, a case was removed from state to federal court and the defendant moved to dismiss for lack of personal jurisdiction or, in the alternative, to remand for lack of diversity jurisdiction.[18] The district court took the former approach, concluding that it was clear that there was no personal jurisdiction, while the subject matter jurisdiction issue posed a much harder question that did not need to be reached. For the plaintiff, the basis for dismissal mattered enormously: if the case was dismissed for lack of personal jurisdiction, it could not proceed in state court, but a federal court dismissal for lack of subject matter jurisdiction obviously would not bar a state court suit.

The Supreme Court, in an opinion by Justice Ginsburg, stressed that personal jurisdiction and subject matter jurisdiction are both constitutional requirements and that either can be considered first. The Court stated: "We hold that in cases removed from state court to federal court, as in cases originating in federal court, there is no unyielding jurisdictional hierarchy. Customarily, a federal court first resolves doubt about its jurisdiction over the subject matter, but there are circumstances in which a district court appropriately accords priority to a personal jurisdiction inquiry. The proceeding before us is such a case."[19] The Court explained that if a case can be easily resolved and dismissed for lack of personal jurisdiction, a federal court should do so, particularly if there is a difficult question concerning subject matter jurisdiction.

Similarly, the Court has held that a case can be dismissed on forum non conveniens grounds without a court needing to decide issues of personal or subject matter jurisdiction. In *Sinochem International v. Malaysia International Shipping*, a Malaysian corporation sued a Chinese corporation in a federal district court over a matter that was being litigated in a Chinese court.[20] Difficult issues were raised concerning personal and subject matter jurisdiction, but it was clear that the case ultimately would have been dismissed on forum non conveniens grounds. Justice Ginsburg, writing for a unanimous Court, concluded, "[W]here subject-matter or personal jurisdiction is difficult to determine, and forum non conveniens considerations weigh heavily in favor of dismissal, the court properly takes the less burdensome course."[21]

[16] *Id.* at 826.
[17] *Id.* at 823.
[18] 526 U.S. 574 (1999).
[19] *Id.* at 578.
[20] 549 U.S. 422 (2007).
[21] *Id.* at 436.

Once Case Is Dismissed, No Subject Matter Jurisdiction Remains

Finally, it should be noted that if a federal court dismisses a case pursuant to a settlement, the court lacks subject matter jurisdiction to have continuing involvement in the matter, such as to enforce the settlement. In *Kokkonen v. Guardian Life Insurance Company of America*, a case was removed from state to federal court based on diversity jurisdiction and then was settled.[22] The federal court dismissed the case, with the consent of the parties, pursuant to Rule 41 of the Federal Rules of Civil Procedure. Subsequently, when the defendant did not meet the terms of the settlement, the plaintiff sought to invoke federal court jurisdiction.

The Supreme Court, however, ruled that the federal court lacked authority to hear the matter. The Court explained that there was no case properly before the federal court and the enforcement action would require a separate suit that properly invoked federal court jurisdiction. The Court observed that the situation would have been different if there had been a clause in the settlement that provided for the continuing jurisdiction of the federal court to enforce it.

Organization of the Chapter

The two most important areas of federal court jurisdiction are federal question jurisdiction (the ability to hear suits arising under the Constitution, laws, and treaties of the United States) and diversity jurisdiction (the authority to adjudicate suits between citizens of different states). These two types of jurisdiction are discussed in §§5.2 and 5.3, respectively. Section 5.4 considers the ability of a federal court to decide issues or claims against parties that otherwise would not be within federal jurisdiction but are closely related to a case properly before the court. This is the concept of "supplemental jurisdiction," codified into statute by the Judicial Improvements Act of 1990. Finally, under certain circumstances cases can be removed from state to federal court. Termed "removal jurisdiction," this authority is discussed in §5.5.

Although these are the major types of subject matter jurisdiction, they are not exhaustive. For instance, federal courts continue to have exclusive jurisdiction to adjudicate admiralty, maritime, and prize cases.[23] Also, federal courts have subject matter jurisdiction to hear all suits brought by the United States or its agencies or officers.[24] Additionally, suits against the United States or its officers may be brought in federal court or, if initiated in state court, may be removed to a federal forum.[25] Suits against the United States are limited by the doctrine of sovereign

[22] 511 U.S. 375 (1994).

[23] 28 U.S.C. §1333. For a discussion of admiralty jurisdiction, *see* David W. Robertson, Steven F. Friedell & Michael F. Sturley, Admiralty and Maritime Law in the United States: Cases and Materials (4th ed. 2020); Jo Desha Lucas and Randall Schmidt, Admiralty Cases and Materials (6th ed. 2012); Grant Gilmore & Charles L. Black, The Law of Admiralty (2d ed. 1975).

[24] 28 U.S.C. §1345 (United States as plaintiff).

[25] 28 U.S.C. §1346 (United States as defendant); 28 U.S.C. §1361 (action to compel an officer of the United States to perform his or her duty); 28 U.S.C. §1442 (removal of suits against federal officers in state courts).

immunity, discussed in §9.2, and suits against federal officers are limited by immunity doctrines discussed in §8.6.

§5.2 FEDERAL QUESTION JURISDICTION

§5.2.1 *Introduction*

Justifications for Federal Question Jurisdiction

The core of modern federal court jurisdiction is cases arising under the Constitution and laws of the United States. Termed "federal question jurisdiction," these cases comprise the largest component of the federal courts' docket and are widely viewed as the most important component of the federal courts' workload. The existence of federal question jurisdiction is not controversial. At a minimum, no one questions a government's ability to create courts to enforce its laws. Interestingly, many of the arguments supporting federal question jurisdiction focus on distrust of the state courts. The American Law Institute, for example, declared that federal question jurisdiction should exist "to protect litigants relying on federal law from the danger that the state courts will not properly apply that law, either through misunderstanding or lack of sympathy."[1] But the assumption that there is a lack of parity between federal and state courts in upholding federal law is highly disputed in other contexts.[2] In fact, the Supreme Court often has proclaimed that state courts are equal to federal courts in their ability and willingness to protect federal rights.[3]

Another frequently offered justification for federal question jurisdiction is the need to ensure uniformity in the interpretation of federal law.[4] This rationale is even more problematic. It is not clear that 94 federal judicial districts will produce more uniformity than 50 state judiciaries. It might be argued that 13 federal courts of appeals will produce more uniformity than 50 state judiciaries, but this conclusion is less obvious than it might seem. On a controversial issue, there are likely to be two or three different positions adopted among the 13 federal courts of appeals. Even if all 50 state judiciaries consider the issue, there still are likely to be just two or three different positions taken on a given legal question. In other words, it is not clear that a greater number of courts will produce more variance in the law.

§5.2 [1] American Law Institute, Study of the Division of Jurisdiction Between State and Federal Courts 168 (1969).

[2] *See* §1.5, *supra,* discussing the parity debate.

[3] *See, e.g.,* Stone v. Powell, 428 U.S. 465, 493-494 n.35 (1976) (We are "unwilling to assume that there now exists a general lack of appropriate sensitivity to constitutional rights in the trial and appellate courts of the several States.").

[4] American Law Institute, *supra* note 1, at 164-168.

Nonetheless, federal question jurisdiction is firmly entrenched and not questioned.[5] Perhaps this reflects that even those proclaiming parity between federal and state courts actually harbor distrust of state judiciaries. Or perhaps the acceptance of federal question jurisdiction reflects an uncritical acceptance that a federal forum should exist for federal law matters and that Supreme Court review of state court decisions is insufficient to adequately ensure such a forum.

Constitutional and Statutory Authority

Article III of the Constitution states that the judicial power of the United States "shall extend to all Cases, in Law and Equity, arising under this Constitution, the Laws of the United States, and Treaties made, or which shall be made, under their Authority." For the first 86 years of American history, no federal statute empowering federal courts to hear all federal question cases was enacted. Many specific federal statutes concerning particular topics authorized federal court jurisdiction as to matters arising under those statutes. It was not until 1875 that Congress authorized general federal question jurisdiction.[6] Except for the deletion of an amount in controversy requirement in 1980, the federal question jurisdiction statute has remained essentially unchanged. As now codified in 28 U.S.C. §1331, the law provides that "[t]he district courts shall have original jurisdiction of all civil actions arising under the Constitution, laws, or treaties of the United States."[7]

Constitutional and Statutory Provisions Interpreted Differently

Although the statutory language is virtually identical to that found in the Constitution, the Supreme Court has adopted markedly different interpretations of these two provisions. The Court has interpreted the constitutional provision very expansively, allowing federal jurisdiction whenever federal law is a potentially

[5] For powerful criticism that the Supreme Court has not fulfilled the purpose of federal question jurisdiction, *see* Arthur D. Hellman, The Federal Question Jurisdiction Under Article III: "First in the Minds of the Framers," But Today, Perhaps, Falling Short of the Framers' Expectations, 104 Boston University Law Review 3 (2024); Helen Hershkoff & Luke Norris, The Oligarchic Courthouse: Jurisdiction, Corporate Power, and Democratic Decline, 122 Mich. L. Rev. 1 (2023).

[6] Act of Mar. 3, 1875, ch. 137, 18 Stat. 470. The Judiciary Act of 1801 briefly created general federal question jurisdiction. The provision was repealed, however, in 1802. The law had been enacted in the final days of President Adams's term and was repealed by the Jeffersonians who subsequently controlled the White House and Congress. *See* Howard P. Fink & Mark V. Tushnet, Federal Jurisdiction Policy and Practice 7 (2d ed. 1987).

[7] Additionally, specific federal statutes can create federal question jurisdiction over particular matters if the statutes are clear in authorizing federal court jurisdiction. For example, the Supreme Court has held that a congressional charter for a corporation confers federal court jurisdiction only if it specifically mentions the federal courts. *See* American National Red Cross v. S.G., 505 U.S. 247 (1992); *see also* Lightfoot v. Cendant Mortgage Corp., 580 U.S. 82 (2017) (holding that the authority to "sue or be sued" in a federal corporate charter is not a separate grant of jurisdiction, but allows suit only in a "state or federal court already endowed with subject-matter jurisdiction.").

important ingredient of a case.[8] But the Court has taken a much narrower view in interpreting §1331. The current law appears to be that a case arises under federal law if it is apparent from the face of the plaintiff's complaint either (1) that the plaintiff's cause of action was created by federal law, or (2) that the plaintiff's cause of action is based on state law, but a federal law that creates a cause of action is an essential component of the plaintiff's complaint.[9] The Supreme Court explained:

> Although the language of §1331 parallels that of the "Arising Under" clause of Art. III, this Court never has held that statutory "arising under" jurisdiction is identical to Art. III "arising under" jurisdiction. Quite the contrary is true. . . . [T]he many limitations which have been placed on jurisdiction under §1331 are not limitations upon the constitutional power of Congress to confer jurisdiction on the federal courts. . . . Art. III "arising under" jurisdiction is broader than federal question jurisdiction under §1331.[10]

Section 5.2.2 examines the Court's interpretation of the constitutional provision, and §5.2.3 considers the Court's construction of the jurisdictional statute.

Is the Differing Interpretation of the Same Language Justified?

The underlying policy question is whether the Court was justified in adopting differing interpretations of identical language. The legislative history of §1331 is skimpy and, if anything, indicates Congress's desire to authorize expansive jurisdiction equal to that allowed by the Constitution. The 1875 law was adopted quickly at the end of a congressional session as a Senate amendment to a House bill dealing with removal jurisdiction.[11] Senator Carpenter, the floor manager of the bill, declared: "The act of 1789 did not confer the whole power which the Constitution conferred. . . . This bill does. . . . This bill gives precisely the power which the Constitution confers—nothing more, nothing less."[12] Thus, many commentators argue that the Court has erred as a matter of statutory construction in interpreting §1331 differently from Article III.[13]

But other commentators argue that the Court was justified in giving §1331 a narrower meaning than Article III. These scholars contend that under the Court's broad construction of Article III, virtually any case could come to federal court

[8] *See* Osborn v. Bank of the United States, 22 U.S. (9 Wheat.) 738 (1824); *see* discussion in §5.2.2, *infra.*

[9] As discussed below, in Grable & Sons Metal Products, Inc. v. Darue Engineering & Manufacturing, 545 U.S. 308 (2005), the Court held that there can be federal question jurisdiction even in the absence of a federal statute creating a cause of action if there is a national interest in providing a federal forum and a federal law is an essential part of the claim.

[10] Verlinden B. V. v. Central Bank of Nigeria, 461 U.S. 480, 494-495 (1983).

[11] Richard H. Fallon, John F. Manning, Daniel J. Meltzer, & David L. Shapiro, Hart & Wechsler's The Federal Courts and the Federal System 782 (7th ed. 2015).

[12] *Id.*

[13] *See, e.g.,* Roy Forrester, The Nature of a "Federal Question," 16 Tul. L. Rev. 362 (1942); James H. Chadbourn & A. Leo Levin, Original Jurisdiction of Federal Questions, 90 U. Pa. L. Rev. 639 (1942).

because some ingredient of a case will involve federal law, even if only remotely related to the actual matter in dispute. Professor Paul Mishkin, for example, argued that it is desirable to retain a broad interpretation of Article III and employ a narrower construction of the jurisdictional statute. Professor Mishkin wrote:

> The potential judicial power of the United States over federal question cases must necessarily be extremely broad. The situations in which a sympathetic forum may be required for the vindication of national rights cannot always be foreseen, and there must be power under the Constitution to provide for those eventualities. . . . [B]ut to include within the jurisdiction of the lower federal courts all cases which might conceivably turn finally upon an issue of national law would create an impossible situation.[14]

The law concerning federal question jurisdiction is particularly confusing because identical language is given different meanings. Moreover, the confusion is exacerbated because the Court frequently has failed to differentiate clearly whether it is interpreting the constitutional or statutory provision, and at times it has purported to apply the broad constitutional perspective in justifying narrow results under the statute.[15] Additionally, while a broad interpretation of the constitutional provision is firmly established, the Court has not adopted a clear or consistent definition to determine when cases arise under federal law for purposes of the jurisdictional statute.[16]

Key Issue: Defining "Arising Under"

Thus, the crucial issue in interpreting both the constitutional and the statutory provision is, what does it mean to say that a case "arises under" the Constitution and laws of the United States? There is no doubt that jurisdiction exists under both the constitutional and statutory provisions when the cause of action is created by federal law. Jurisdiction for claims under the Constitution of the United States has been held to include all constitutional provisions except for the full faith and credit clause of Article IV, §1. The Court has held that this provision creates a rule of decision to be applied, requiring a state to honor the judgments entered by other states' courts. The full faith and credit clause does not independently justify

[14] Paul J. Mishkin, The Federal "Question" in the District Courts, 53 Colum. L. Rev. 157, 162-163 (1953).

[15] *See, e.g.,* Starin v. New York, 115 U.S. 248 (1885); *see also* Pacific Railroad Removal Cases, 115 U.S. 1 (1885) (interpreting statute in same manner as constitutional provision to allow federal court jurisdiction over tort actions against railroads with federal charters). On other occasions, the Court has expressly indicated that the constitutional and statutory provisions are to be given different interpretations. *See, e.g.,* Shoshone Mining Co. v. Rutter, 177 U.S. 505 (1900).

[16] *Compare* American Well Works Co. v. Layne & Bowler Co., 241 U.S. 257, 260 (1916) (federal question exists only if the cause of action arises under federal law), *with* Smith v. Kansas City Title & Trust Co., 255 U.S. 180 (1921) (allowing federal question jurisdiction for a cause of action created by state law because federal law was an essential component of the claim). These cases and the interpretation of the jurisdictional statute are discussed in §5.2.3, *infra.*

federal court jurisdiction every time a person seeks to compel a state to respect the judgment of another state's courts.[17] Federal laws include all federal statutes, federal administrative regulations, and federal common law as well. The Court explained: "We see no reason not to give 'laws' its natural meaning . . . and therefore conclude that §1331 jurisdiction will support claims founded upon federal common law as well as those of a statutory origin."[18]

The difficult question is, when do matters "arise under" federal law when there is a state law cause of action but federal law is an ingredient of the case? It is here that the constitutional and statutory interpretations diverge.

§5.2.2 The Meaning of "Arising Under" Federal Law for Purposes of Article III

Osborn v. Bank of the United States

The seminal case interpreting federal question jurisdiction under Article III is *Osborn v. Bank of the United States.*[19] In the landmark decision of *McCulloch v. Maryland,* the Supreme Court held that it was constitutional for Congress to create the Bank of the United States and that it was unconstitutional for the state of Maryland to tax the bank.[20] Several states declared that they disagreed with this ruling and that they would continue to tax the Bank of the United States. Ohio, for example, announced that it intended to collect a $50,000 tax owed to it by the bank. The bank went to federal court and enjoined the Ohio state auditor from collecting the tax, but the state sent its officers to raid the Bank of the United States in Chillicothe, Ohio, and seized more than $120,000 of the bank's money. Federal officers then raided the state treasury and recaptured $98,000. The bank sued in federal court to recover the additional monies and received a judgment in its favor.

The issue before the Supreme Court was whether the federal court had jurisdiction to hear the bank's suit. Chief Justice John Marshall, writing for the Court, said that two questions were presented: whether the act of Congress had created federal jurisdiction and whether, under the Constitution, Congress had the power to create jurisdiction.

The Court found the resolution of the first issue to be an easy task. A federal statute provided that the bank shall be "made able and capable in law . . . to sue and be sued, plead and be impleaded, answer and be answered, defend and be defended, in all State Courts having competent jurisdiction, and in any Circuit Court of the United States."[21] The Court found this statute to be a clear

[17] *See* Minnesota v. Northern Sec. Co., 194 U.S. 48 (1904).
[18] Illinois v. Milwaukee, 406 U.S. 91, 100 (1972).
[19] 22 U.S. (9 Wheat.) 738 (1824).
[20] 17 U.S. (4 Wheat.) 316 (1819).
[21] 22 U.S. at 817.

authorization for federal court jurisdiction. Chief Justice Marshall wrote: "These words seem to the Court to admit of but one interpretation. They cannot be made plainer by explanation. They give, expressly, the right 'to sue and be sued,' in every Circuit Court of the United States' and it would be difficult to substitute other terms which would be more direct and appropriate for the purpose."[22]

In addressing the latter question, concerning the meaning of the constitutional provision, the Court adopted a broad construction of what cases arise under federal law. The Court began by explaining that the federal judicial power is coextensive with the federal legislative power and that the federal judiciary may be given authority to construe and enforce every federal statute.[23] The Court then explained that under the Constitution, a case arises under federal law whenever federal law "forms an ingredient of the original cause . . . [even though] other questions of fact or of law may be involved in it."[24] Chief Justice Marshall wrote: "A cause may depend on several questions of fact and law. Some of these may depend on the construction of a law of the United States; others on principles unconnected with that law. . . . [It is] a sufficient foundation for jurisdiction, that the title or right set up by the party, may be defeated by one construction of the constitution or law of the United States, and sustained by the opposite construction."[25] The Court concluded that because the Bank of the United States was created by federal law, any action brought by it arose under federal law.[26] In fact, in a companion case decided the same day as *Osborn*, the Supreme Court in *Bank of the United States v. Planter's Bank* allowed the Bank of the United States to sue in federal court to recover money owed on notes issued by a state bank.[27]

Justice Johnson wrote a persuasive dissent in *Osborn*. He especially objected to the breadth of the Court's definition of the possible scope of federal court jurisdiction. For example, he asked whether the Court's reasoning meant that every naturalized citizen of the United States could bring any suit to federal court because, like the bank, which was created by federal law, naturalized citizens owe their status to an act of Congress.[28] Justice Johnson also pointed out that Chief Justice Marshall's reasoning would allow Congress to transfer all lawsuits for breach of contract to federal court simply by enacting law requiring contracts to be written on a certain form of stamped paper.[29]

[22] *Id.* There is an alternative interpretation of this statutory provision: the statute creates the capacity for the bank to sue or be sued, but it does not create jurisdiction. *See* Charles Alan Wright, Law of Federal Courts 101 n.6 (5th ed. 1994).

[23] 22 U.S. at 818-819.

[24] *Id.* at 823. For an excellent analysis of what Chief Justice Marshall intended, *see* Anthony J. Bellia, Jr., Article III and the Cause of Action, 89 Iowa L. Rev. 777 (2004).

[25] *Id.* at 821-822.

[26] *Id.* at 828.

[27] 22 U.S. (9 Wheat.) 904 (1824).

[28] *Id.* at 875 (Johnson, J., dissenting). Chief Justice Marshall explicitly responded to this argument in his majority opinion. He stated: "A naturalized citizen is indeed made a citizen under an act of Congress, but the act does not proceed to give, to regulate, or to prescribe his capacities. . . . There is, then, no resemblance between the act incorporating the Bank, and the general naturalization law." 17 U.S. at 827-828.

[29] *Id.* at 874 (Johnson, J., dissenting).

§5.2 Federal Question Jurisdiction

The breadth of Chief Justice Marshall's interpretation of federal question jurisdiction in *Osborn* cannot be overstated. According to his opinion for the Court, the Constitution permits Congress to create federal court jurisdiction whenever federal law is a potential ingredient of a case. Not only does federal jurisdiction extend beyond situations where there are federal causes of action, but it also includes all instances where the case might turn on a question of federal law, no matter how unlikely it is that federal law will be an actual basis for the decision. Commentators have explained that Chief Justice Marshall, ever the federalist concerned with expanding the powers of the national government, "was construing for the future, and characteristically he construed broadly in order to allow future change and growth."[30]

Broad Definition Continues

Because no general federal question jurisdiction statute existed until 1875, the Court's opinion in *Osborn* indicated the potential scope of federal jurisdiction; it did not actually enlarge jurisdiction to that extreme. As is explained in detail in §5.2.3, the Court has adopted a much narrower construction of the federal question jurisdiction statute. But although this issue has been addressed infrequently, the Court has never backed away from its broad interpretation of the constitutional authorization of federal question jurisdiction. For example, in 1983, the Supreme Court reaffirmed the Court's decision in *Osborn.* In *Verlinden B.V. v. Central Bank of Nigeria,* the Court again explained the scope of Article III's authorization for jurisdiction for cases arising under federal law.[31]

Verlinden B.V. v. Central Bank of Nigeria

In *Verlinden,* a Dutch corporation brought suit in federal court against Nigeria claiming breach of contract. Jurisdiction was based on the Foreign Sovereign Immunities Act of 1976, which grants federal courts the authority to hear suits by an alien against a foreign state.[32] The U.S. Court of Appeals for the Second Circuit held that federal courts lacked authority to hear the case because the cause of action was based either on international or state law; there was no federal law basis for recovery.[33]

The Supreme Court reversed and held that Article III permitted jurisdiction, even though there was no federal cause of action. The Court explained: "The controlling decision on the scope of Art. III 'arising under' jurisdiction is Chief Justice Marshall's opinion for the Court in *Osborn v. Bank of the United States. . . . Osborn . . .* reflects a broad conception of 'arising under' jurisdiction, according to which Congress may confer on the federal courts jurisdiction over any case or controversy

[30] Chadbourn & Levin, *supra* note 13, at 649.

[31] 461 U.S. 480 (1983).

[32] 28 U.S.C. §1330(a).

[33] 647 F.2d 320, 329 (2d Cir. 1981), *rev'd,* 461 U.S. 480 (1983).

that might call for the application of federal law."[34] Although it acknowledged scholarly criticisms of *Osborn,* the Court unanimously held that Congress could create federal court jurisdiction for suits involving foreign commerce. The Court wrote: "By reason of its authority over foreign commerce and foreign relations, Congress has the undisputed power to decide, as a matter of federal law, whether and under what circumstances foreign nations should be amenable to suit in the United States."[35]

It might be argued that under the Court's holding in *Verlinden,* the requirements of Article III would be met by any congressional statute creating jurisdiction because cases could be said to arise under the jurisdictional law. However, the Court said that the statute creating federal court jurisdiction in *Verlinden* reflected an important policy decision by Congress concerning foreign sovereign immunity. Accordingly, Congress could advance that policy by enacting a statute authorizing federal court jurisdiction. The Court explained: "[T]he jurisdictional provisions of the Act are simply one part of this comprehensive scheme. The Act thus does not merely concern access to the federal courts. Rather, it governs the types of actions for which foreign sovereigns may be held liable in court in the United States, federal or state. The Act codifies the standards governing foreign sovereign immunity as an aspect of substantive federal law . . . and applying those standards will generally require interpretation of numerous points of federal law."[36]

Verlinden thus reaffirmed *Osborn* and a broad interpretation of the Constitution's authorization for federal court jurisdiction for cases arising under federal law. As long as the federal law to be applied does more than merely create jurisdiction, it is a basis for federal court jurisdiction if it is potentially important in the outcome of the litigation.

Protective Jurisdiction

Scholars have developed an intriguing theory to explain the Supreme Court's decision in *Osborn v. Bank of the United States.* They argue that the decision can best be understood as authorizing Congress to create "protective jurisdiction"—that is, Congress may authorize federal court jurisdiction where it believes that federal court availability is necessary to protect important federal interests.[37] Professor Paul Mishkin, for example, argued that "where there is an articulated and active federal policy regulating a field, the 'arising under' clause of Article III apparently permits the conferring of jurisdiction on the national courts of all cases in the

[34] 461 U.S. at 492.

[35] *Id.* at 493.

[36] *Id.* at 496-497.

[37] Seminal articles advancing the theory of protective jurisdiction include Mishkin, *supra* note 14; Herbert Wechsler, Federal Jurisdiction and the Revision of the Judicial Code, 13 Law & Contemp. Probs. 216 (1948). Subsequent discussions of protective jurisdiction can be found in George D. Brown, Beyond *Pennhurst*: Protective Jurisdiction, the Eleventh Amendment, and the Power of Congress to Enlarge Federal Jurisdiction in Response to the Burger Court, 71 Va. L. Rev. 343 (1985); Carole E. Goldberg-Ambrose, The Protective Jurisdiction of the Federal Courts, 30 UCLA L. Rev. 542 (1983).

area—including those substantively governed by state law."[38] By this view of *Osborn v. Bank of the United States*, Congress created federal court jurisdiction, even as to state law claims litigated by the Bank of the United States, to protect the bank from potential state court hostility.[39]

There has been little consideration of the concept of protective jurisdiction by the U.S. Supreme Court. For example, in *Verlinden, B.V. v. Bank of Nigeria*, the Supreme Court found jurisdiction based on the federal statutes pertaining to foreign sovereign immunity and thus concluded that it did not need to "consider petitioner's alternative argument that the Act is constitutional as an aspect of so-called 'protective jurisdiction.'"[40]

The only Supreme Court case expressly discussing protective jurisdiction is *Textile Workers Union v. Lincoln Mills*.[41] The case involved the constitutionality of §301 of the Taft-Hartley Act, which grants jurisdiction over breach of contract suits for violations of labor management agreements in industries affecting interstate commerce.[42] The Taft-Hartley Act does not create substantive law, though it does authorize federal court jurisdiction.

The majority in *Lincoln Mills*, in an opinion by Justice Douglas, found that federal court jurisdiction was appropriate because Congress intended for the federal courts to create a federal common law of labor-management contracts. As such, cases under the act arose under federal common law and thus jurisdiction was permissible under Article III.

Justices Harlan and Burton concurred in the result; they disagreed that federal law was to be applied, but argued that jurisdiction was appropriate based on the theory of protective jurisdiction.[43] Taking an approach previously adopted by the First Circuit, Justices Harlan and Burton contended that state law was to be applied in contract cases brought to federal court under the Taft-Hartley Act.[44] However, they argued that Congress could constitutionally authorize federal court jurisdiction out of a desire to protect the federal interest in labor cases.

Justice Frankfurter dissented and strongly argued against the concept of protective jurisdiction. After a careful review of the cases and the scholarly literature, Justice Frankfurter concluded that "'[p]rotective jurisdiction,' once the label is discarded, cannot be justified under any view of the allowable scope to be given to Article III . . . The theory must have as its sole justification a belief in the inadequacy of state tribunals in determining state law. The Constitution reflects such a belief in the specific situation within which the Diversity Clause was confined. The intention to remedy such supposed defects was exhausted in this provision of Article III."[45]

[38] Mishkin, *supra* note 14, at 192.
[39] *Id.* at 187; Goldberg-Ambrose, *supra* note 37, at 547-551.
[40] 461 U.S. at 491.
[41] 353 U.S. 448 (1957).
[42] 29 U.S.C. §185.
[43] 353 U.S. at 460 (Harlan, J., concurring in the result).
[44] *See* International Bhd. of Teamsters v. W. L. Mead, Inc., 230 F.2d 576, 580-581 (1st Cir. 1956).
[45] 353 U.S. at 474-475 (Frankfurter, J., dissenting).

The status of protective jurisdiction remains disputed by scholars. Some argue that Congress should be able to create federal court jurisdiction in any situation in which it possesses the power to legislate.[46] Contrary to Justice Frankfurter's argument that state courts are trusted in all instances except diversity cases, supporters of protective jurisdiction contend that the very existence of federal courts reflects a distrust of state courts. If state courts were fully trusted, federal courts and federal jurisdiction would be unnecessary. Therefore, Congress should be able to create federal jurisdiction wherever necessary to protect federal interests. If nothing else, the Constitution's jurisdictional requirement would be met because the case arises under the statute creating federal jurisdiction.

There is strong criticism of the concept of protective jurisdiction.[47] It is argued that Congress cannot expand federal jurisdiction beyond the bounds of the Constitution and that allowing protective jurisdiction would give Congress limitless power to enlarge federal subject matter jurisdiction. Furthermore, the critics contend that protective jurisdiction cannot be reconciled with the text of Article III. Professor David Currie wrote: "What is the federal law under which the case arises? The only federal law in the picture is the federal law creating federal jurisdiction. To say that a case arises under federal law whenever a federal statute gives jurisdiction is to destroy all limitations on federal jurisdiction."[48]

The topic of protective jurisdiction is likely to remain of interest primarily to scholars because few cases pose questions about the meaning of federal question jurisdiction under Article III. In light of the Court's much narrower interpretation of §1331, virtually all cases present questions of statutory and not constitutional interpretation. Moreover, the broad definition of "arising under" the Court adopted in *Osborn* means that most matters will fit within the scope of Article III's authorization for jurisdiction.

§5.2.3 The Meaning of "Arising Under" Federal Law for Purposes of the Federal Question Jurisdiction Statute

Principle for Determining if a Case Arises Under Federal Law

28 U.S.C. §1331 provides that the "district courts shall have original jurisdiction of all civil actions arising under the Constitution, laws, or treaties of the United States." As described earlier, the Supreme Court repeatedly has held that this provision has a much narrower meaning than does the corresponding language in Article III.[49] But the Court never has formulated a clear test for deciding

[46] *See* Wechsler, *supra* note 37, at 225; Goldberg-Ambrose, *supra* note 37, at 583-595.

[47] *See, e.g.,* Martin H. Redish, Federal Jurisdiction: Tensions in the Allocation of Judicial Power 94-95 (2d ed. 1990).

[48] David P. Currie, Federal Jurisdiction in a Nutshell 103 (3d ed. 1990). For a discussion of Congress's power to expand federal court jurisdiction beyond that authorized in Article III, *see* §3.4, *supra.*

[49] *See* text accompanying notes 19-31, *supra.*

when a case "arises under" federal law for purposes of §1331. In fact, some of the Court's interpretations of §1331 are inconsistent.[50]

The decisions interpreting §1331 can be best summarized by the following principle: a case arises under federal law if it is apparent from the face of the plaintiff's complaint either that the plaintiff's cause of action was created by federal law or, if the plaintiff's cause of action is based on state law, that a federal law that creates a cause of action or that reflects an important national interest is an essential component of the plaintiff's claim. There are three parts to this rule.

Well-Pleaded Complaint Rule

First, it must be clear from the face of the plaintiff's complaint that there is a federal question. *Louisville & Nashville Railroad v. Mottley* is the leading case articulating the well-pleaded complaint rule.[51] The Mottleys were injured in a railroad accident, and as part of the settlement of their suit, they were given free railroad passes for the rest of their lives. In 1907, Congress adopted a law prohibiting free railroad passes. The railroad then refused to reissue the passes to the Mottleys.

The Mottleys sued for breach of contract, seeking specific performance of the railroad's obligation to provide them with free passes. The Mottleys argued that it would be an unconstitutional taking of their property to apply the statute and deny them the passes to which they were entitled. The trial court ruled for the plaintiffs, but the U.S. Supreme Court reversed. The Supreme Court held that the federal court lacked subject matter jurisdiction under §1331. The Court explained that the plaintiffs' complaint presented a state law claim for breach of contract. The federal issue arose only from the plaintiffs' anticipation of a defense based on the federal statute. The Court explained: "It is not enough that the plaintiff alleges some anticipated defense to his cause of action and asserts that the defense is invalidated by some provision of the Constitution of the United States."[52] The Court said that a plaintiff's cause of action must be based on federal law in order for the case to arise under federal law for purposes of §1331.[53]

The *Mottley* well-pleaded complaint rule has been repeatedly reaffirmed by the U.S. Supreme Court.[54] Thus, federal court jurisdiction cannot be based on a federal

[50] *Compare* Smith v. Kansas City Title & Trust Co., 255 U.S. 180 (1921) *with* Moore v. Chesapeake & Ohio Ry., 291 U.S. 205 (1934). In fact, the Supreme Court expressly referred to the "widely perceived 'irreconcilable' conflict" between *Smith* and *Moore*. Merrell Dow Pharmaceuticals, Inc. v. Thompson, 478 U.S. 804, 814 n.12 (1986). For a discussion of these two decisions, *see* text accompanying notes 95-103, *infra*.

[51] 211 U.S. 149 (1908).

[52] *Id.* at 152.

[53] After dismissal by the Supreme Court, the Mottleys filed suit in state court. The railroad raised the federal statute as a defense, and the Mottleys argued that the statute could not constitutionally be applied to take away their passes. The state court ruled in favor of the plaintiffs, but the Supreme Court reversed, concluding that it was not unconstitutional to deny the Mottleys free railroad passes. Louisville & N.R.R. v. Mottley, 219 U.S. 467 (1911).

[54] *See, e.g.*, Franchise Tax Bd. v. Construction Laborers Vacation Trust, 463 U.S. 1, 9-10 (1983); Verlinden, B.V. v. Central Bank of Nigeria, 461 U.S. 480, 494 (1983). Subsequently, in Holmes Group,

law defense or on the plaintiff's anticipation of a federal law defense. A plaintiff cannot file suit in federal court, and a defendant may not remove a case from state to federal court unless it is clear from the face of the plaintiff's complaint that there is a federal question. A federal law issue raised in the defendant's answer or counterclaim is not a basis for removal of a case from state to federal court if there is not a federal question presented in the plaintiff's complaint. Also, if a plaintiff chooses not to present a federal claim, even though one is potentially available, the defendant may not remove the case from state to federal court.[55] However, "a plaintiff may not defeat removal by omitting to plead necessary federal questions in a complaint."[56]

Application in Declaratory Judgment Cases

A plaintiff may not circumvent this rule by seeking a declaratory judgment that the federal law is unconstitutional or inapplicable if the complaint in a lawsuit for redress would not state a federal question. *Skelly Oil Co. v. Phillips Petroleum Co.*[57] established that "if, but for the availability of the declaratory judgment procedure, the federal claim would arise only as a defense to a state created action, jurisdiction is lacking."[58] Phillips Petroleum contracted with Skelly Oil to purchase natural gas, subject to the condition that Phillips obtain a certificate from the Federal Power Commission. Phillips obtained the required certificate, but the Federal Power Commission imposed several unanticipated requirements in issuing it. Skelly Oil contended that the conditional certificate did not meet the requirements of the contract and gave notice that it was terminating the contract.

Phillips then brought an action in federal court seeking a declaratory judgment that a proper certificate had been issued by the Federal Power Commission and that the contract therefore had to be performed. The Supreme Court held that there was no federal question jurisdiction because the federal issue arose

---

Inc. v. Vornado Circulation Sys., 535 U.S. 826 (2002), the Supreme Court held that a federal counterclaim, even a compulsory counterclaim, does not provide for "arising under" jurisdiction. The Court explained that this would allow a defendant to defeat the plaintiff's choice of forum and prevent determination of jurisdiction based on the complaint.

[55] *See, e.g.,* Fair v. Kohler Die & Specialty Co., 228 U.S. 22, 25 (1913) ("The party who brings a suit is master to decide what law he will rely upon and therefore does determine whether he will bring a 'suit arising under' . . . [the] law of the United States.").

[56] Franchise Tax Bd. v. Construction Laborers Vacation Trust, 463 U.S. at 22.

[57] 339 U.S. 667 (1950).

[58] Franchise Tax Bd. v. Construction Laborers Vacation Trust, 463 U.S. at 16 (stating holding of Skelly Oil Co. v. Phillips Petroleum Co.). The Supreme Court recognized but did not decide the question of whether a declaratory judgment complaint raising a nonfederal defense to a federal claim would be a basis for jurisdiction under §1331. In Textron Lycoming Reciprocating Engine Div. v. AW, 523 U.S. 653 (1998), the Court suggested, without deciding, that federal question jurisdiction does not exist when the declaratory judgment complaint asserts a nonfederal defense to possible federal claim. The Court said that *Skelly Oil* "suggests that the declaratory-judgment plaintiff must himself have a federal claim." *Id.* at 659. But the Court did not decide the issue, instead dismissing the case on justiciability grounds. The Court applied the principle of *Skelly Oil* and stated that the burden of proving patent infringement is on the party asserting infringement and does not change based on who files the suit for a declaratory judgment. Medtronic, Inc. v. Mikrowski Family Ventures, 571 U.S. 191 (2014).

solely as an anticipation of a federal law defense. The Court said that if the case had been properly presented, there would have been a state law claim for breach of contract by Phillips against Skelly, and Skelly's defense would then have rested on the nature of the certificate issued by the Federal Power Commission. The Court explained that it would "distort the limited procedural purpose of the Declaratory Judgment Act" to allow federal jurisdiction based on requests for declaratory judgments that are actually anticipations of federal defenses.[59]

Franchise Tax Board v. Construction Laborers Vacation Trust

The principles of *Mottley* and *Skelly Oil* were reaffirmed by the Supreme Court in *Franchise Tax Board v. Construction Laborers Vacation Trust.*[60] Pursuant to a collective bargaining agreement, the Construction Laborers Vacation Trust administered a fund that provided for paid vacations for construction workers. Because the laborers often worked for several employers over the course of a year, a centralized vacation fund was established and administered. The trust fund was an "employee welfare benefit plan" and thus was regulated by the Employee Retirement Income Security Act of 1974 (ERISA).[61]

The California Franchise Tax Board is a state agency responsible for collecting personal income taxes within the state of California. The board sought unpaid taxes from three union members and requested the trust to pay the sums due from money held in the individuals' vacation accounts. The trust claimed that under the federal ERISA statute the state could not seek payment from funds held by the trust for the individuals.

The board filed suit in California state court against the trust to recover the money owed by the three individuals. The complaint stated two causes of action. The first simply sought the $380 in taxes that the trust had refused to pay from the three members' funds. The second cause of action requested a declaratory judgment that the federal ERISA statute did not preempt the ability of the state to obtain payment from the trust. The trust removed the case from state to federal court. The district court ruled in favor of the board on the merits, but the U.S. Court of Appeals reversed, finding the state's ability to obtain payment to be preempted by federal law.

The Supreme Court held that the federal court should have dismissed the case for lack of subject matter jurisdiction. Justice Brennan, writing for the Court, began by strongly reaffirming the well-pleaded complaint rule and the precedents of *Mottley* and *Skelly.*[62] The Court ruled that California had a state law cause of action to collect money and that federal law arose only as a defense based on preemption. The request for the declaratory judgment on the federal law issue did not state a federal question and thus did not permit the defendant to remove the case to federal court. The Court said that subject matter jurisdiction exists if either party could have brought a federal

[59] 339 U.S. at 673-674.
[60] 463 U.S. 1 (1983).
[61] *Id.* at 4-5.
[62] *Id.* at 9-22.

law claim—not a federal defense or a request for a declaratory judgment. The Court explained: "Federal courts have regularly taken original jurisdiction over declaratory judgment suits in which, if the declaratory judgment defendant brought a coercive action to enforce its rights, that suit would necessarily present a federal question."[63] Because the state's claim was entirely founded on state law and the federal issue could arise only as a defense, federal question jurisdiction was absent.

The trust maintained, however, that there was a federal law claim under ERISA. The trust argued that "ERISA . . . was meant to create a body of federal common law, and that 'any state court action which would require the interpretation or application of ERISA to a plan document "arises under" the laws of the United States.'"[64] The Supreme Court rejected this contention. The Court stated that "it is clear that a suit by state tax authorities . . . does not 'arise under' ERISA. . . . [T]he state's right to enforce its tax levies is not of central concern to the federal statute."[65]

Preemption as a Basis for Federal Court Jurisdiction Where Congress Has Created a Cause of Action

However, in a subsequent case—*Metropolitan Life Insurance Co. v. Taylor*—the Supreme Court held that preemption defenses based on ERISA could be the basis for federal question jurisdiction where Congress has created a cause of action under the statute.[66] The Court explained that "[i]n *Franchise Tax Board*, the Court held that ERISA preemption, without more, does not convert a state claim into an action arising under federal law."[67] However, for the matter involved in *Taylor*, Congress had "clearly manifested an intent to make causes of action within the scope of the civil enforcement provisions . . . removable to a federal court."[68] After *Franchise Tax Board* and *Taylor*, it appears that a state court suit is removable to federal court based on a claim of preemption if Congress created a cause of action in the allegedly preemptive statute. This approach is similar to that proposed by Professor Mary Twitchell, who argued that federal question jurisdiction should exist if Congress has created a cause of action, if the defendant argues that Congress intended to preempt the state law claims, and if the state law claims are, in fact, preempted.[69]

[63] *Id.* at 19.

[64] *Id.* at 24.

[65] *Id.* at 25-26.

[66] 481 U.S. 58 (1987); *see also* Pilot Life Ins. Co. v. Dedeaux, 481 U.S. 41 (1987) (holding that the type of claims presented in *Taylor* are preempted by federal law). For a defense of broad federal jurisdiction based on preemption, *see* Karen A. Jordan, The Complete Preemption Dilemma: A Legal Process Perspective, 31 Wake Forest L. Rev. 927 (1996).

[67] 481 U.S. at 64. Previously, the Supreme Court had ruled in Avco Corp. v. Aero Lodge No. 735, Intl. Assn. of Machinists & Aerospace Workers, 390 U.S. 557 (1968), that a state law claim for breach of a labor-management contract could be removed to federal court because "the preemptive force of §301 [of the Labor Management Relations Act of 1947] is so powerful as to displace entirely any state cause of action." 463 U.S. at 23. *See also* Caterpillar, Inc. v. Williams, 482 U.S. 386 (1987) (holding that a particular labor dispute did not fit within the *Avco Corp.* decision).

[68] 481 U.S. at 66.

[69] Mary P. Twitchell, Characterizing Federal Claims: Preemption, Removal, and the Arising-Under Jurisdiction of the Federal Courts, 54 Geo. Wash. L. Rev. 812, 865 (1986).

The Court's subsequent decisions on the relationship of preemption and federal question jurisdiction are consistent with this approach. In *Vaden v. Discover Bank,* the Court concluded that there was not federal question jurisdiction based on a preemption claim.[70] Discover Bank filed an action in state court against Vaden seeking to recover past-due charges on a credit card. Vaden counterclaimed, saying that the finance charges and interest violated state law, and presented this as a class action against Discover Bank. Discover Bank then filed a petition in federal court seeking arbitration under the Federal Arbitration Act, which provides that "[a] party aggrieved by the alleged failure, neglect, or refusal of another to arbitrate under a written agreement for arbitration may petition any United States District Court which, save for such agreement, would have jurisdiction under title 28 . . . for an order directing that such arbitration proceed in the manner provided for in such agreement."[71]

The Supreme Court ruled 5-4 that this was insufficient to create federal court jurisdiction. The Court stressed that a *counterclaim* cannot be the basis for federal court jurisdiction under the well-pleaded complaint rule. Justice Ginsburg, writing for the Court, explained, "Under our precedent construing §1331 . . . counterclaims, even if they rely exclusively on federal substantive law, do not qualify a case for federal-court cognizance."[72] She further explained, "Under the well-pleaded complaint rule, a completely preempted counterclaim remains a counterclaim and thus does not provide a key capable of opening a federal court's door."[73]

Criticism and Defense of the Well-Pleaded Complaint Rule

The well-pleaded complaint rule articulated in *Mottley*, applied in *Skelly Oil*, and reaffirmed in *Franchise Tax Board* is strongly criticized by many scholars. The primary criticism is that federal courts should be able to decide cases that turn on federal law.[74] The federal interest in having federal courts adjudicate federal issues is just as great when the federal question arises in a defense, or in a response to a defense, as when it is presented in the plaintiff's complaint. The desirability of having federal

[70] 556 U.S. 49 (2009).

[71] 9 U.S.C. §4.

[72] 556 U.S. at 60.

[73] *Id.* at 66. Subsequently, in Badgerow v. Walters, 596 U.S. 1 (2022), the Court evaluated the notion of "look-through jurisdiction," a principle in Vaden v. Discover Bank, which held "there was a jurisdictional basis to decide a Section 4 petition to compel arbitration by means of examining the parties' underlying dispute." In *Badgerow*, the Court declined to expand this jurisdictional principle, finding that Congress did not intend to extend the Court's subject matter jurisdiction over additional arbitration proceedings.

[74] For excellent criticism of the well-pleaded complaint rule, *see* Larry W. Yackle, Reclaiming the Federal Courts 102-105 (1994); Donald L. Doernberg, There's No Reason for It; It's Just Our Policy: Why the Well-Pleaded Complaint Rule Sabotages the Purposes of Federal Question Jurisdiction, 38 Hastings L.J. 597 (1987). *See also* William Cohen, The Broken Compass: The Requirement That a Case Arise "Directly" Under Federal Law, 115 U. Pa. L. Rev. 890 (1967).

courts hear and decide federal questions is "independent of which party introduces the federal question . . . [or] where in the structure of the case the issue is technically located."[75] Thus, commentators argue that federal question jurisdiction should exist whenever a federal law issue is likely to be dispositive, irrespective of whether it is presented in the plaintiff's complaint.[76]

The well-pleaded complaint rule also has its defenders. Professors Friedenthal, Kane, and Miller observe: "The well-pleaded complaint rule fulfills a useful and necessary function. Given the limited nature of federal subject matter jurisdiction, it is essential that the existence of jurisdiction be determined at the outset, rather than being contingent upon what *may* occur at later stages in the litigation. By demanding that a federal issue be raised in the complaint, the rule accomplishes this goal."[77]

Although the critics of the well-pleaded complaint rule seem to have the better of the argument—allowing federal court adjudication of dispositive federal issues regardless of who raises them fulfills the purposes of federal question—the Court shows no indication of discarding or modifying the rule. In *Franchise Tax Board,* the Court admitted that the rule is based more on "history than logic," but reaffirmed it nonetheless.[78] Thus, the first part of the principle concerning federal question jurisdiction under §1331 is firmly established: it must be clear from the face of the plaintiff's complaint that there is a federal question.

Cause of Action Based on Federal Law

The second major part of the principle is that a case arises under federal law if it is based on a cause of action created by federal law. This is the least difficult aspect of the Court's interpretation of §1331. Justice Oliver Wendell Holmes declared that "[a] suit arises under the law that creates the cause of action."[79] There is little dispute that there is a federal question if the plaintiff's complaint states a claim under a federal law that provides a legal entitlement to a remedy.

Occasionally, in cases in the early part of this century, the Supreme Court refused to find federal question jurisdiction even though there was a federal cause of action. One such case was *Shoshone Mining Co. v. Rutter.*[80]

[75] Doernberg, *supra* note 74, at 650-651, 661.

[76] *Id.* at 657-658 (describing how federal question jurisdiction would be determined in the absence of the well-pleaded complaint rule).

[77] Jack H. Friedenthal, Mary Kay Kane & Arthur R. Miller, Civil Procedure 22 (2d ed. 1993) (emphasis in original). But Professors Friedenthal, Kane, and Miller recognize that this benefit "may be overshadowed" by the disadvantage in precluding federal courts from adjudicating federal issues raised as defenses or in response to defenses. *Id.*

[78] 463 U.S. at 4.

[79] American Well Works Co. v. Layne & Bowler Co., 241 U.S. 257, 260 (1916).

[80] 177 U.S. 505 (1900). Another such case was Shulthis v. McDougal, 225 U.S. 561, 569 (1912), where the Court declared:

> A suit to enforce a right which takes its origins in the laws of the United States is not necessarily, or for that reason alone, one arising under those laws, for a suit does not so arise unless it really and substantially involves a dispute or controversy respecting the validity, construction or effect of such a law, upon the determination of which the result depends.

§5.2 Federal Question Jurisdiction

A federal statute was enacted permitting federal courts to resolve disputes among miners concerning conflicting claims on federal lands. The statute provided that the disputes were to be resolved by "local customs or rules of miners in the several mining districts, so far as the same are applicable and not inconsistent with the laws of the United States." The Supreme Court said that a suit brought under the statute did not present a federal question. The Court explained that the suit "may not involve any question as to the construction or effect of the Constitution or laws of the United States, but may present simply a question of fact as to the time of the discovery of mineral, the location of the claim on the ground, or a determination of the meaning and effect of certain local rules."[81]

The Supreme Court never has overruled the *Shoshone* decision, and federal judges continue to treat it as good law,[82] but there are no decisions in which the Court has denied the existence of a federal question when a federal law created a cause of action. Furthermore, in its subsequent holdings, the Court has stated that there is a federal question if "federal law creates the cause of action."[83]

In *Mims v. Arrow Financial Services, Inc.*, the Court held that a federal statute authorizing damage suits in state courts does not preclude federal question jurisdiction under §1331.[84] The Telephone Consumer Protection Act authorizes private actions for damages in state courts to enforce the federal rights created by the law. The issue was whether a plaintiff also could bring a damages action in federal court under §1331.

The Court concluded that federal question jurisdiction existed. Justice Ginsburg, writing for a unanimous Court, explained that "[b]ecause federal law creates the right of action and provides the rules of decision, Mims's TCPA claim, in 28 U.S.C. §1331's words, plainly 'aris[es] under' the 'laws . . . of the United States.' 'A suit arises under the law that creates the cause of action.' "[85] The Court stressed that federal courts have concurrent jurisdiction with state courts over federal causes of action unless Congress expressly divests the federal courts of jurisdiction. The Court explained: "Section 1331, our decisions indicate, is not swept away so easily. When federal law creates a private right of action and furnishes the substantive rules of decision, the claim arises under federal law, and district courts possess federal-question jurisdiction under §1331. That principle endures unless Congress divests federal courts of their §1331 adjudicatory authority."[86] The Court concluded that "[i]n the absence of direction from Congress . . . we apply the familiar default rule: Federal courts have §1331 jurisdiction over claims that arise under federal law."[87]

[81] 177 U.S. at 509.

[82] *See, e.g.*, Redish, *supra* note 47, at 103; Cohen, *supra* note 74, at 906-907, 916; *see also* Merrell Dow Pharmaceuticals, Inc. v. Thompson, 478 U.S. 804, 814 n.12 (1986) (citing *Shoshone* with approval).

[83] Franchise Tax Bd. v. Construction Laborers Vacation Trust, 463 U.S. at 27-28.

[84] 565 U.S. 368 (2012).

[85] *Id.* at 377.

[86] *Id.* at 378-79.

[87] *Id.* at 387.

Federal Questions in Suits Based on State Causes of Action

Although Justice Holmes believed that there was a federal question *only* when a federal law created a cause of action, the Supreme Court has not taken such a restrictive view. It has been explained that Justice Holmes's "formula is more useful for inclusion than for the exclusion for which it was intended."[88] The Supreme Court observed that "it is well settled that Justice Holmes's test is more useful for describing the vast majority of cases that come within the district courts' original jurisdiction than it is for describing which cases are beyond district court jurisdiction."[89]

Thus, the third part of the rule stated at the beginning of this section: even if the plaintiff does not allege a cause of action based on federal law, there is a federal question if it is clear from the face of the plaintiff's complaint that a federal law that creates a cause of action or that reflects an important national interest is an essential component of the plaintiff's state law claim. The issue is: When, if at all, does a state law cause of action present a federal question? Under *Osborn v. Bank of the United States*, for purposes of Article III, there is a federal question whenever federal law is a potential ingredient of the litigation.[90] But for §1331, more is required than just a federal ingredient. Unfortunately, the Supreme Court has not formulated a clear test to determine when the presence of a federal law in a state law action constitutes a federal question.

Justice Cardozo provided the most famous explanation in *Gully v. First National Bank in Meridian*: "To bring a case within the statute, a right or immunity created by the Constitution or laws of the United States must be an element and an essential one, of the plaintiff's cause of action. . . . The right or immunity must be such that it will be supported if the Constitution or laws of the United States are given one construction or effect and defeated if they receive another."[91] Subsequently, in the *Franchise Tax Board* decision, the Court stated that under §1331, federal courts have jurisdiction to hear "only those cases in which a well-pleaded complaint establishes either that federal law creates the cause of action or that the plaintiff's right to relief necessarily depends on resolution of a substantial question of federal law."[92] In *City of Chicago v. International College of Surgeons*, the Court applied *Franchise Tax Board* and found that a case could be removed to federal court because the plaintiff's "federal constitutional claims . . . turn[ed] exclusively on federal law."[93] The Court reaffirmed that "[e]ven though state law creates [a party's] cause of action, its case might still 'arise under' the laws of the United States if a well-pleaded

[88] T. B. Harms Co. v. Eliscu, 339 F.2d 823, 827 (2d Cir. 1964), *cert. denied,* 381 U.S. 915 (1965).

[89] 463 U.S. at 9. For an argument that the Holmes test should be controlling and exhaustive, *see* Linda R. Hirshman, Whose Law Is It Anyway?: A Reconsideration of Federal Question Jurisdiction over Cases of Mixed State and Federal Law, 60 Ind. L.J. 17 (1984).

[90] *See* text accompanying notes 19-30, *supra.*

[91] 299 U.S. 109, 112 (1936).

[92] Franchise Tax Bd. v. Construction Laborers Vacation Trust, 463 U.S. at 27-28. The most famous academic formulation of the test is Professor Mishkin's: "the criterion for original federal jurisdiction [is] a substantial claim founded 'directly' upon federal law." Mishkin, *supra* note 14, at 168.

[93] 522 U.S. 156, 164 (1997).

complaint established that its right to relief under state law requires resolution of a substantial question of federal law."[94]

Because the Court has not been more specific than these abstract formulations, it is useful to examine the specific cases in which the Court considered the existence of a federal question because of the importance of federal law to a state law claim. The seminal case is *Smith v. Kansas City Title & Trust Co.*[95] In *Smith,* a shareholder in a corporation sued to enjoin the corporation from purchasing bonds issued by the federal government. The shareholder alleged that the bonds were issued in violation of the Constitution, and thus the corporation could not lawfully purchase them because of a state statute delineating permissible investments. The shareholders presented a state law cause of action. Nonetheless, the Supreme Court ruled that a federal question was presented because the challenge to the federal statute was an integral component of the plaintiff's complaint. The Court wrote: "The general rule is that, where it appears from the bill or statement of the plaintiff that the right to relief depends upon the construction or application of the Constitution or laws of the United States, and that such federal claim is not merely colorable, and rests upon a reasonable foundation, the District Court has jurisdiction."[96]

Although without a doubt *Smith* remains good law to this day,[97] commentators long have been troubled by its seeming inconsistency with the Court's decision in *Moore v. Chesapeake & Ohio Railway.*[98] An injured railroad worker sought damages under a state statute providing a remedy for injuries suffered while working on an intrastate railroad. The state's law provided that an employee could not be found liable of contributory negligence if the employer's violation of any safety law contributed to the worker's death or injury. A federal statute regulated the safety of railroads, including intrastate railroad cars that also operated in interstate commerce. Thus, a key question in the case was whether the railroad violated the federal law regulating the safety of railroads. The plaintiff contended that the presence of this federal question justified the existence of federal question jurisdiction.

The Supreme Court disagreed and denied the existence of jurisdiction. The Court stated: "[I]t does not follow that a suit brought under the state statute which defines liability to employees who are injured while engaged in intrastate commerce, and brings within the purview of the statute a breach of duty imposed by the federal statute, should be regarded as a suit arising under the laws of the United States and cognizable in the federal court in the absence of diversity of citizenship."[99]

[94] *Id.*

[95] 255 U.S. 180 (1921). For a fascinating discussion of the historical context of *Smith, see* Larry Yackle, Federal Banks and Federal Jurisdiction in the Progressive Era: A Case Study of Smith v. K.C. Title & Trust Co., 62 Kan. L. Rev. 255 (2013).

[96] 255 U.S. at 199.

[97] *See, e.g.,* Merrell Dow Pharmaceuticals, Inc. v. Thompson, 478 U.S. 804, 820 (1986) ("The continuing vitality of *Smith* is beyond challenge. We have cited it approvingly on numerous occasions, and reaffirmed its holding several times.") (Brennan, J., dissenting).

[98] 291 U.S. 205 (1934).

[99] *Id.* at 214-215.

In both *Smith* and *Moore*, an interpretation of a federal law was likely to decide a state law cause of action, but in the former, though not the latter, a federal question was deemed to exist. There is an obvious conflict between these decisions.[100] In the Supreme Court's 1986 decision in *Merrell Dow Pharmaceuticals, Inc. v. Thompson*, both the majority and dissenting opinions directly addressed this seeming inconsistency.

The majority opinion, written by Justice Stevens, argued that the difference between the two decisions was in the nature of the federal interest present. Justice Stevens explained: "Focusing on the nature of the federal interest, moreover, suggests that the widely perceived 'irreconcilable' conflict between the finding of federal jurisdiction in *Smith v. Kansas City Title & Trust Co.* and the finding of no jurisdiction in *Moore v. Chesapeake & Ohio R. Co.*, is far from clear. For the difference in results can be seen as manifestations of the differences in the nature of the federal issues at stake."[101] Justice Stevens said that while the issue in *Smith* was the constitutionality of a federal statute, in *Moore* the "violation of the federal standard as an element of state tort recovery did not fundamentally change the state tort nature of the action."[102]

The dissenting justices in *Merrell Dow* felt that *Smith* and *Moore* could not be reconciled and that *Moore* was simply anomalous. Justice Brennan wrote: "My own view is in accord with those commentators who view the results in *Smith* and *Moore* as irreconcilable. That fact does not trouble me greatly, however, for I view *Moore* as having been a 'sport' at the time it was decided and having long been in a state of innocuous desuetude. . . . *Moore* simply has not survived the test of time . . . [and] it ought to be overruled."[103]

The important underlying issue, of course, is when does the presence of a federal issue in a state law claim present a federal question? Unfortunately, no formula or criteria exist; the Court never has done better than Justice Cardozo's explanation in the *Gully* case quoted above. A majority of the Court now has endorsed the position advanced by commentators that the existence of a federal question depends on "an evaluation of the nature of the federal interest at stake."[104] But the Court has not elaborated on the content or structure of that evaluation. Moreover, such an approach to defining federal question jurisdiction inherently is unpredictable, vesting great discretion in the district court to determine the nature of the federal interest and to decide whether that interest merits federal jurisdiction for the state law claim. The malleability of this evaluation can be criticized on the grounds that jurisdictional rules should be firmer and more predictable.[105]

[100] Redish, *supra* note 47, at 98-99.

[101] Merrell Dow Pharmaceuticals, Inc. v. Thompson, 478 U.S. at 816.

[102] *Id.*

[103] *Id.* at 821 n.1 (Brennan, J., dissenting).

[104] *Id.* at 814 n.12; *see* David L. Shapiro, Jurisdiction and Discretion, 60 N.Y.U. L. Rev. 543, 568 (1985); Cohen, *supra* note 74, at 916.

[105] *See* Merrell Dow Pharmaceuticals, Inc. v. Thompson, 478 U.S. at 821 n.1 (Brennan, J., dissenting).

Federal Statute Must Itself Create a Cause of Action or Reflect an Important National Interest

Furthermore, in *Merrell Dow*, the Supreme Court added another important limitation about when state law claims can be the basis for federal question jurisdiction. The Court held that it is not enough for a federal law to be an essential component of a state law cause of action; federal question jurisdiction exists only if the *federal law itself* creates a cause of action, albeit one not relied on by the plaintiff. In *Merrell Dow*, the plaintiffs sought recovery, based on state law causes of action, for birth defects allegedly caused by the use of the drug Bendectin by a pregnant woman. The plaintiffs argued, in part, that the drug company's violation of the federal Food, Drug, and Cosmetic Act created a presumption of negligence. Hence, they argued that there was a federal question because the outcome of the suit was likely to depend on the construction of this federal law.

The Supreme Court held that there was no federal question jurisdiction. A state law claim could be the basis for jurisdiction under §1331 only if it relied on a federal statute that itself created a cause of action. Justice Stevens, writing for the Court, stated: "We conclude that a complaint alleging a violation of a federal statute as an element of a state cause of action, when Congress has determined that there should be no private, federal cause of action for the violation does not state a claim 'arising under' the Constitution, laws, or treaties of the United States."[106] The Court explained that if Congress had wanted the matter tried in federal court, it would have created a federal cause of action. Therefore, without a federal cause of action, a federal law cannot be the basis for federal question jurisdiction.

A great many federal laws do not create private causes of action; government benefit programs and regulatory statutes are prominent examples of such laws.[107] After *Merrell Dow*, it appeared that none of these statutes could be the basis for federal question jurisdiction.[108] *Merrell Dow* narrows the *Smith* authorization for federal question jurisdiction for certain state claims: a plaintiff's state law claim must depend on a federal statute that creates a cause of action. It can be questioned, however, whether the absence of a federal cause of action means that Congress intended to foreclose federal jurisdiction when the construction of the federal law will be decisive in a state lawsuit. Congress may have thought it unnecessary to authorize suits for recovery; it does not follow that Congress decided it was unnecessary to have a federal court interpret the federal law in every instance.

[106] *Id.* at 817.

[107] *See* §6.3, *infra.*

[108] *See, e.g.,* International Science & Technology Institute, Inc. v. Inacom Communications, Inc., 106 F.3d 1146 (4th Cir. 1997) (denying subject matter jurisdiction based on *Merrell Dow* even though Telephone Consumer Protection Act of 1991 created a cause of action because it only authorizes suits in state court); Seinfeld v. Austen, 39 F.3d 761 (7th Cir. 1994) (federal antitrust laws used by the plaintiff as part of its state law breach of fiduciary duty claims could not be the basis for federal question jurisdiction because they do not create a cause of action); Mulcahey v. Columbia Organic Chemicals Co., Inc., 29 F.3d 148 (4th Cir. 1994) (not allowing federal question jurisdiction based on state law cause of action that relied on duties created by several federal environmental statutes because there was not a showing of congressional intent to create federal question jurisdiction).

After *Merrell Dow*, courts and commentators thought that federal question jurisdiction under §1331 always would require a federal law that created a cause of action, either for the plaintiff to sue directly under or as an essential part of the plaintiff's state law claim. In *Grable & Sons Metal Products, Inc. v. Darue Engineering & Manufacturing*, the Court held that there can be federal question jurisdiction in the absence of a federal law creating a cause of action if there is an important national interest to be served by allowing federal question jurisdiction.[109]

The case involved whether a case could be removed from state court to federal court based on federal question jurisdiction, even though there was no federal cause of action, because of the important national interest in providing a federal forum for federal tax litigation. In 1994, the Internal Revenue Service seized property from Grable & Sons Metal Products, Inc., to satisfy an unpaid tax delinquency. Grable was given notice of the seizure and also notice when the property was placed for sale. Grable did not attempt to challenge the seizure or the sale. The IRS sold the property to Darue Engineering and Manufacturing.

Five years later, Grable brought an action to quiet title in state court. Grable claimed that Darue's title was invalid because the IRS failed to provide the notice required by the statute. Grable argued that the statute required personal notice, not the service by certified mail that the government used. Darue sought to remove the case from state to federal court. The district court and the federal court of appeals allowed removal, and the Supreme Court granted review "to resolve a split within the Courts of Appeals on whether *Merrell Dow* always requires a federal cause of action as a condition for exercising federal question jurisdiction."[110]

The Supreme Court ruled in favor of the existence of federal question jurisdiction. Justice Souter, writing for the Court, noted that the case turned on an issue of federal law. He explained that "[w]hether Grable was given notice within the meaning of the federal statute is thus an essential element of its quiet title claim, and the meaning of the federal statute is actually in dispute; it appears to be the only legal or factual interest contested in the case."[111] The Court then stressed the national interest in having the matter adjudicated in federal court: "The meaning of the federal tax provision is an important issue of federal law that sensibly belongs in federal court. The Government has a strong interest in the 'prompt and certain collection of delinquent taxes.'"[112] Also, "[t]he Government has a direct interest in the availability of a federal forum to vindicate its administrative action, and buyers (as well as tax delinquents) may find it valuable to come before judges used to federal tax matters."[113]

The Court expressly rejected the view that a federal law always must create a cause of action in order to be a basis for federal court jurisdiction.[114] The Court said that "*Merrell Dow* should be read in its entirety as treating the absence of a

[109] 545 U.S. 308 (2005).
[110] *Id.* at 311-312.
[111] *Id.* at 315.
[112] *Id.* at 315.
[113] *Id.*
[114] *Id.* at 317.

federal statute as evidence relevant to, but not dispositive of, 'the sensitive judgments about congressional intent' that §1331 requires."[115]

On the one hand, *Grable* opens the door to federal question jurisdiction where it has not been thought to exist since *Merrell Dow*; it allows federal question jurisdiction in the absence of federal law authorizing it if there is an important national interest. *Grable* is an invitation to lawyers in a wide array of cases to claim that their cases, which turn on an issue of federal law, reflect an important national interest and federal question jurisdiction should be allowed. On the other hand, Justice Souter's majority opinion stressed the narrowness of the holding. The Court stressed that such instances would be "rare" and that this would not affect usual litigation.[116]

The Court applied its *Grable* analysis in *Gunn v. Minton* to conclude that a malpractice claim stemming from the mishandling of a patent claim does not arise under federal law.[117] The Court did not dispute that resolution of a question of federal patent law was an indispensable element of the plaintiff's claim of malpractice.[118] But Chief Justice Roberts, writing for a unanimous Court, said that this is not enough for federal question jurisdiction under *Grable*. The Court explained: "Applying *Grable*'s inquiry here, it is clear that Minton's legal malpractice claim does not arise under federal patent law. Indeed, for the reasons we discuss, we are comfortable concluding that state legal malpractice claims based on underlying patent matters will rarely, if ever, arise under federal patent law for purposes of §1338(a). Although such cases may necessarily raise disputed questions of patent law, those cases are by their nature unlikely to have the sort of significance for the federal system necessary to establish jurisdiction."[119]

The Court said that *Grable* requires a substantial federal interest and declared: "The substantiality inquiry under *Grable* looks instead to the importance of the issue to the federal system as a whole."[120] The Court found that there is not such an interest in malpractice claims arising from the handling of a patent claim.

Summary

Thus, as stated at the beginning of this section, the current law concerning when cases arise under federal law for purposes of §1331 can be summarized by the following principle: A case arises under federal law if it is apparent from the

[115] *Id.* at 318.

[116] For a discussion of *Grable*, *see* Lumen N. Mulligan, A Unified Theory of U.S.C. Section 1331 Jurisdiction, 61 Vand. L. Rev. 1667 (2008); Richard D. Freer, Of Rules and Standards: Reconciling Statutory Limits on "Arising Under" Jurisdiction, 82 Ind. L.J. 309 (2007).

[117] 568 U.S. 251 (2013). This case is criticized in Amelia Smith Rinehart, The Federal Question in Patent-Licensee Cases, 90 Ind. L.J. 659 (2015); Simona Grossi, A Modified Theory of the Law of Federal Courts: The Case of Arising-Under Jurisdiction, 88 Wash. L. Rev. 961 (2013).

[118] 568 U.S. at 258-59.

[119] *Id.*

[120] *Id.* at 260.

face of the plaintiff's complaint either that the plaintiff's cause of action was created by federal law or, if the plaintiff's cause of action is based on state law, that a federal law that creates a cause of action or reflects an important national interest is an essential component of the plaintiff's claim. Until the Court provides additional clarification, a more precise statement is impossible.

§5.3 DIVERSITY AND ALIENAGE JURISDICTION[1]

§5.3.1 Introduction

Article III of the Constitution authorizes federal court jurisdiction for suits between citizens of different states. The necessary statutory authorization for such jurisdiction, termed "diversity jurisdiction," is found in 28 U.S.C. §1332. That provision states: "The district courts shall have original jurisdiction of all civil actions where the matter in controversy exceeds the sum or value of $75,000, exclusive of interest and costs, and is between . . . citizens of different States." Additionally, both Article III and §1332 authorize "alienage jurisdiction"—federal court jurisdiction for suits between citizens of a state and citizens or subjects of a foreign state.[2]

Subsection 5.3.2 considers the continuous debate over whether diversity jurisdiction should be abolished. Subsection 5.3.3 examines the rules for determining whether there is diversity of citizenship in a particular case. Subsection 5.3.4 focuses on the amount in controversy requirement and what needs to be alleged to meet this prerequisite for diversity and alienage jurisdiction. Finally, §5.3.5 discusses the choice of law in diversity cases.

§5.3 [1] The statute involving non-citizens in federal court refers to this as "alienage" jurisdiction and thus that terminology is used here. But it would be preferable if courts and commentators would shift to referring to it as "non-citizen jurisdiction" and if the statute is changed.

[2] 128 U.S.C. §1332(a)(2). The statute also allows federal court jurisdiction for suits between "citizens of different States and in which citizens or subjects of a foreign state are additional parties" and for suits between "a foreign state . . . as plaintiff and citizens of a State or of different states." §1332(a)(3) and (4). *See* Molinos Valle Del Cibao, C. por A. v. Lama, 633 F.3d 1330 (11th Cir. 2011) ("alienage" jurisdiction exists if non-citizens are on either side of the controversy). Traditionally, diversity and "alienage" jurisdiction are considered together because both stem from the same statutory authority. *But see* Kevin Johnson, Why Alienage Jurisdiction? Historical Foundations and Modern Justifications for Federal Jurisdiction over Disputes Involving Noncitizens, 21 Yale J. Intl. L. 1 (1996) (arguing that there is a conceptual difference between alienage and diversity jurisdiction and that a separate alienage jurisdiction statute should exist).

§5.3.2 *The Debate Over the Retention or Elimination of Diversity Jurisdiction*

Initial Justifications for Diversity Jurisdiction

Diversity and alienage jurisdiction have existed since the adoption of the Judiciary Act of 1789, but there is little agreement about why diversity jurisdiction was created. The traditional theory is that diversity jurisdiction was intended to protect out-of-state residents from the bias that they might experience, or at least fear that they might face, in state courts. The most famous explanation of this rationale for diversity jurisdiction is Chief Justice John Marshall's statement: "However true the fact may be, that the tribunals of the states will administer justice as impartially as those of the nation, to parties of every description, it is not less true that the constitution itself either entertains apprehensions on this subject, or views with such indulgence the possible fears and apprehensions of suitors, that it has established national tribunals for the decision of controversies between aliens and a citizen, or between citizens of different states."[3]

But some commentators—most notably Judge Henry Friendly—challenged this rationale for diversity jurisdiction. Friendly argued that the diversity clause "was not a product of difficulties that had been acutely felt under the Confederation" and that "such information as we are able to gather . . . entirely fails to show the existence of prejudice on the part of the state judges."[4] It should be noted, however, that this argument only partially refutes the traditional explanation for the creation of diversity jurisdiction. Even if prejudice did not actually exist, perhaps prejudice was feared and diversity jurisdiction was established to provide an alternative to state courts, which might be distrusted in diversity cases.[5]

Judge Friendly offered an alternative explanation for the authorization for diversity jurisdiction. Judge Friendly argued that there was fear of populist state legislatures adopting antibusiness laws; federal court jurisdiction and the development of federal common law rules provided protection for interstate commerce and business. Friendly wrote that "a careful reading of the arguments of the time will show that the real fear was not of state courts so much as of state legislatures."[6] Additionally, Friendly contended that there was fear that state judges who lacked life tenure would be more likely to be influenced by populist sentiments and be biased against merchants.[7] By this theory, diversity jurisdiction initially was based less on the existence of state court hostility to out-of-staters and more on the fear of state court hostility to commercial interests.[8]

[3] Bank of United States v. Deveaux, 9 U.S. (5 Cranch) 61, 87 (1809).

[4] Henry J. Friendly, The Historic Basis of Diversity Jurisdiction, 41 Harv. L. Rev. 483, 484, 493 (1928).

[5] *See* John P. Frank, The Case for Diversity Jurisdiction, 16 Harv. J. on Legis. 403, 406 (1979).

[6] Friendly, *supra* note 4, at 495.

[7] *Id.* at 497-499.

[8] *See* Felix Frankfurter, Distribution of Judicial Power Between United States and State Courts, 13 Cornell L.Q. 499, 521-522 (1928).

These explanations, of course, are not mutually exclusive; both could have influenced the creation of diversity jurisdiction. Although diversity jurisdiction has existed for 200 years, it remains very controversial. There have been repeated proposals to abolish, or at least greatly restrict, federal court diversity jurisdiction. In 1978, a bill to abolish diversity jurisdiction passed the House of Representatives but died in the Senate Judiciary Committee.[9] Nor are proposals to eliminate diversity jurisdiction new. Influential justices such as Chief Justices Warren and Burger and Justices Frankfurter and Jackson long have argued that diversity jurisdiction should be abolished.[10] Justice Jackson expressed these sentiments when he declared: "[I]n my judgment the greatest contribution that Congress could make to the orderly administration of justice in the United States would be to abolish the jurisdiction of the federal courts which is based solely on the ground that the litigants are citizens of different states."[11]

Arguments for Abolishing Diversity Jurisdiction

The primary argument for the abolition of diversity jurisdiction is that it is unnecessary and costly. Those who believe that its original justifications are no longer valid perceive diversity jurisdiction as an anachronistic relic.[12] Critics of diversity jurisdiction argue that there is insufficient proof of bias against out-of-staters in state courts and indeed say that studies show that there no longer is bias to justify diversity jurisdiction.[13] Moreover, ever since the landmark decision in *Erie Railroad v. Tompkins*,[14] federal courts have applied state law in diversity cases, lessening the possibility of federal court protection of business from populist state legislatures.

A related argument for abolishing diversity jurisdiction is that it creates a bias against rural areas because matters often are removed from state courts in rural areas to federal courts in urban areas. Professor Debra Lyn Bassett argues that "far from being an antidote to local bias, diversity jurisdiction today embodies, and indeed promotes, a form of bias by its very existence—a bias against rural areas so pervasive as to require the abolition of diversity jurisdiction."[15]

[9] H.R. 9622, 95th Cong., 2d Sess. (1978).

[10] *See, e.g.*, Earl Warren, 36th Annual Meeting, 1959 A.L.I. Proc. 27-43; Warren E. Burger, Annual Report on the State of the Judiciary, 62 A.B.A. J. 443, 444 (1976); Lumbermen's Mutual Casualty Co. v. Elbert, 348 U.S. 48, 54 (1954) (Frankfurter, J., concurring); Robert Houghwout Jackson, The Supreme Court in the American System of Government 38 (1955).

[11] Jackson, *supra* note 10, at 38.

[12] *See, e.g.*, Thomas D. Rowe, Abolishing Diversity Jurisdiction: Positive Side Effects and Potential for Further Reforms, 92 Harv. L. Rev. 963, 966 (1979) ("the lack of positive reasons for it, the need for a reduction in federal caseloads and jury trials, and the appropriateness of merging more fully the power to interpret state law with the responsibility of applying it").

[13] *See* Scott DeVito, On the Death of Diversity Jurisdiction: An Empirical Study Establishing That Diversity Jurisdiction Is No Longer Justified, 55 Ind. L. Rev. 233, 234 (2022); Kyle C. Kopko & Christopher J. Devine, Home Court Advantage? An Empirical Analysis of Local Bias in U.S. District Court Diversity Jurisdiction Cases, 125 W. Va. L. Rev. 543, 545 (2022).

[14] 304 U.S. 64 (1938). *Erie* is discussed in detail in §5.3.5, *infra*.

[15] Debra Lyn Bassett, The Hidden Bias in Diversity Jurisdiction, 81 Wash. U. L.Q. 119 (2003).

Furthermore, diversity jurisdiction is costly. A study by the Federal Judicial Center, done over 35 years ago, found that diversity jurisdiction costs the federal government $131 million and that even a limited reform of preventing plaintiffs from relying on diversity as a basis for federal court jurisdiction in their home states would save almost $59 million.[16] Professor Scott DeVito recently has estimated "that the elimination of diversity jurisdiction for simple actions would, on average, save the federal courts $2.7 billion per year."[17]

Because of ever-increasing concern about reducing federal court docket congestion, eliminating diversity jurisdiction is an attractive option. In 1990, the Federal Courts Study Committee recommended abolishing most diversity jurisdiction, in large part because it accounts for 10 percent of all expenditures in the federal system, one-fourth of the cases in the district court, and one-half of the civil trials.[18]

Abolishing diversity jurisdiction also could simplify many aspects of federal court procedure. Federal courts no longer would have to speculate on the meaning of state law, as they often must do in diversity cases. Additionally, many complex rules, such as those governing venue in diversity actions, would be unnecessary if diversity jurisdiction were abolished.[19]

Arguments for Retaining Diversity Jurisdiction

Diversity jurisdiction has its staunch defenders, especially among the organized bar.[20] The defenders contend that bias still exists against out-of-staters and that even the perception of possible bias in state courts is a sufficient justification for the continuance of diversity jurisdiction.[21] Professor Wright, although an advocate of abolishing diversity jurisdiction, summarized the argument for its retention: "The key question is not whether out-of-state investors will in fact receive fair treatment from state courts, but whether they think they will. If abolition, or significant curtailment, of diversity jurisdiction would give rise to irrational fears by investors, and inhibit their willingness to invest in different parts of the country, then

[16] Anthony Partridge, The Budgetary Impact of Possible Changes in Diversity Jurisdiction 8, 35 (1988).

[17] Scott DeVito, The Federal Courts Are Not Bias Free Zones: An Argument for Eliminating Diversity Jurisdiction, 84 U. Pitt. L. Rev. 873, 883 (2023).

[18] Report of the Federal Court Study Committee 38-39 (1990). The committee recommended retaining diversity jurisdiction for cases involving complex multistate litigation, interpleader, and aliens.

[19] Rowe, *supra* note 12, at 966.

[20] *See* Frank, *supra* note 5, at 404. Not surprisingly, attorneys favor diversity jurisdiction because it offers them a choice of forums for litigation. Charles Alan Wright, Restructuring Federal Jurisdiction: The American Law Institute Proposals, 26 Wash. & Lee L. Rev. 185, 207 (1969) ("I believe the basis for their position is not that they love the state courts less but that they love a choice of forum more."). Recent studies have confirmed this. *See* Jason A. Cantone & Emery G. Lee III, Federal and State Forum Preferences: A Survey of Attorneys in Recently Closed Diversity Jurisdiction Cases, Prepared for the Judicial Conference Committee on Federal-State Jurisdiction, ii (November 2021).

[21] *See, e.g.*, William E. Betz, For the Retention of Diversity Jurisdiction, 56 N.Y. St. B.J., July 1984, at 35; Richard D. Freer, The Political Reality of Diversity Jurisdiction, 94 S. Cal. L. Rev. 1083, 1121 (2021).

diversity serves a useful purpose and should be retained."[22] Defenders of diversity jurisdiction also argue that it facilitates national commercial transactions by making available the federal court system with its uniform rules. Furthermore, diversity jurisdiction allows litigants to transfer cases from county courthouses, which are sometimes in rural areas, to federal courts in more easily accessible large cities.[23]

Supporters of diversity jurisdiction contend that the benefits of its elimination are overstated. Abolishing diversity jurisdiction would not decrease the amount of litigation; it simply would transfer cases from overcrowded federal courts to overcrowded state courts. Moreover, supporters of diversity jurisdiction argue that there are benefits to be derived from allowing concurrent jurisdiction in state and federal courts over diversity cases. They maintain that having two court systems focus on the same issue will produce more ideas and improve decisions.[24]

Is Diversity Jurisdiction Still Necessary?

Ultimately, much of the disagreement in the debate over diversity jurisdiction centers on whether state courts are likely to be biased against out-of-staters. If prejudice is minimal or nonexistent, then an irrational fear does not justify diversity jurisdiction; it simply calls for greater publicity of the studies establishing the lack of bias. On the other hand, if bias can be proven, then there is a strong reason to maintain diversity jurisdiction.[25]

Unfortunately, the question of whether state courts are biased against out-of-staters is an empirical question, and it is extremely difficult to devise studies that can adequately measure the differences between court systems. Methodological problems, such as self-selection, difficulties in matching cases, and settlements based on perceived likely outcomes, all make empirical measurement very difficult. Several studies have attempted to measure the need for diversity jurisdiction. These studies all have involved questioning attorneys as to their choice of forum in particular cases or their overall perception of the state and federal systems. One such survey found that in Cook County, Illinois, 40 percent of attorneys who had filed diversity cases in federal court said that "[local] bias against an out-of-state resident" was a factor in their decision to invoke federal jurisdiction.[26]

[22] Wright, *supra* note 20, at 136-137.

[23] Adrienne J. Marsh, Diversity Jurisdiction: Scapegoat of Overcrowded Federal Courts, 48 Brook. L. Rev. 197, 208-209 (1982).

[24] *See, e.g.*, Betz, *supra* note 21, at 51-52; Frank, *supra* note 5, at 409.

[25] For an argument that those who argue for and against bias as a basis for diversity jurisdiction are "wrong" and there are other reasons for diversity jurisdiction, *see* Scott Dodson, Beyond Bias in Diversity Jurisdiction, 69 Duke LJ. 267, 269 (2019).

[26] Jerry Goldman & Kenneth S. Marks, Diversity Jurisdiction and Local Bias: A Preliminary Empirical Inquiry, 9 J. Legal Stud. 93, 97-99 (1980). For recent studies, *see* Jason A. Cantone & Emery G. Lee III, Federal and State Forum Preferences: A Survey of Attorneys in Recently Closed Diversity Jurisdiction Cases, Prepared for the Judicial Conference Committee on Federal-State Jurisdiction, ii (November 2021).

Other surveys have found less perception of prejudice. One study found a perception of bias only in rural districts.[27] An earlier study in Wisconsin found that attorneys rarely cited local prejudice as a basis for invoking federal court jurisdiction; a much more common basis was convenience or difference in the rules between the jurisdictions.[28]

Perhaps the difference in results simply reflects geographic variances: in some states there is more bias against out-of-staters than in other places. Or maybe the differences really indicate variations in the way the studies were administered. Regardless, the debate over whether diversity jurisdiction is necessary is likely to rage on.

Some commentators have suggested a compromise between eliminating and retaining diversity jurisdiction. The American Law Institute, for example, proposed restricting diversity jurisdiction by preventing a plaintiff from filing such a suit in a federal court in his or her own state.[29] It has been estimated that this change could decrease the number of diversity cases in federal courts by 50 percent.[30] The American Law Institute also proposed defining a corporation as a citizen of every place where it maintains a local establishment of business.[31] Additionally, others have proposed a substantial increase in the jurisdictional amount,[32] a change that was implemented in 1988 when Congress raised the amount in controversy to cases in excess of $50,000 and again in 1996 when the amount was raised to the current $75,000.[33] Some scholars have criticized these proposals, either for not going far enough toward eliminating diversity jurisdiction or for restricting it too much.[34]

Neither side of the debate over the desirability of diversity jurisdiction is likely to persuade the other. There are simply competing perceptions about the need for diversity jurisdiction, and neither available empirical measures nor normative arguments seem capable of resolving the impasse. For the time being, diversity jurisdiction seems safe, but as federal court caseloads increase and as the attack

[27] Kristin Bumiller, Choice of Forum in Diversity Cases: Analysis of a Survey and Implications for Reform, 15 Law & Socy. Rev. 749 (1981); *see also* Scott DeVito, On the Death of Diversity Jurisdiction: An Empirical Study Establishing That Diversity Jurisdiction Is No Longer Justified, 55 Ind. L. Rev. 233, 234 (2022).

[28] Marvin R. Summers, Analysis of Factors That Influence Choice of Forum in Diversity Cases, 47 Iowa L. Rev. 933 (1962).

[29] American Law Institute, Study of the Division of Jurisdiction Between State and Federal Courts 10-14, 99-108 (1969).

[30] Marsh, *supra* note 23, at 222; Partridge, *supra* note 16, at 35 (preventing plaintiffs from invoking diversity jurisdiction in their home states would save almost $59 million).

[31] American Law Institute, *supra* note 29, at 10-14.

[32] *See* Richard A. Posner, The Federal Courts: Crisis and Reform 139-147 (1985) (also proposing changes similar to those endorsed by the American Law Institute); *see also* David L. Shapiro, Federal Diversity Jurisdiction: A Survey and a Proposal, 91 Harv. L. Rev. 317 (1977); James William Moore & Jere Charles Wicker, Federal Jurisdiction: A Proposal to Simplify the System to Meet the Needs of a Complex Society, 1 Fla. St. U. L. Rev. 1 (1973).

[33] Federal Courts Improvement Act of 1996, Pub. L. No. 104-317, §205, 110 Stat. 3847.

[34] *See* David P. Currie, The Federal Courts and the American Law Institute, 36 U. Chi. L. Rev. 1 (1968) (criticizing the ALI proposals).

by scholars and judges continues, it only may be a matter of time before diversity jurisdiction is eliminated or substantially curtailed.[35]

§5.3.3 *The Determination of Whether There is Diversity of Citizenship*

Some of the rules for determining the existence of diversity and alienage jurisdiction are found in §1332, but the Supreme Court has imposed many others over the past 200 years. Many of the rules seem supported by little except their longevity; it is difficult to see how they advance any of the underlying policies behind the existence of diversity jurisdiction.

The Requirement for Complete Diversity

First, for diversity jurisdiction to exist, there must be complete diversity—that is, no plaintiff can be a citizen of the same state as any of the defendants.[36] This rule was first articulated in *Strawbridge v. Curtiss,* in 1806, and it has been followed ever since.[37] In a very brief opinion written by Chief Justice John Marshall, the Court quoted the diversity statute and concluded: "The court understands these expressions to mean, that each distinct interest should be represented by persons, all of whom are entitled to sue, or may be sued in the federal courts. That is, that where the interest is joint, each of the persons concerned in that interest must be competent to sue, or liable to be sued, in those courts."[38] In short, as the Court later explained, "diversity jurisdiction does not exist unless *each* defendant is a citizen of a different State from *each* plaintiff."[39] The complete diversity rule does not prevent co-plaintiffs (or codefendants) from being from the same state; rather, it requires that all of the plaintiffs be from different states than all of the defendants.

There are many persuasive criticisms of the requirement for complete diversity. In fact, John Marshall is said to have later regretted creating the rule.[40] Although the Court purported to base the requirement on the jurisdictional statute, nothing in its language or history supports the requirement for complete diversity. Nor is

[35] Dean Freer argues that the political realities are that diversity jurisdiction will not be eliminated. Richard D. Freer, The Political Reality of Diversity Jurisdiction, 94 S. Cal. L. Rev. 1083, 1121 (2021).

[36] A major exception to the requirement for complete diversity is the Class Action Fairness Act of 2005, Pub. L. No. 109-2, 119 Stat. 4, which provides for diversity jurisdiction in some class action suits with incomplete diversity. This act is discussed below.

[37] 7 U.S. (3 Cranch) 267 (1806).

[38] *Id.*

[39] Owen Equip. & Erection Co. v. Kroger, 437 U.S. 365, 373 (1978). An important exception to the requirement for complete diversity is the Federal Interpleader Statute, 28 U.S.C. §1335, which allows a federal court to decide all claims to a single sum put within its jurisdiction as long as there is minimal diversity (at least one plaintiff from a different state than one defendant). *See, e.g.,* State Farm Fire & Casualty Co. v. Tashire, 386 U.S. 523 (1967).

[40] *See* Louisville, C. & C. R. Co. v. Letson, 43 U.S. (2 How.) 497, 555 (1844).

the rule supported by the underlying policies that justify the existence of diversity jurisdiction.

Moreover, the requirement has many pernicious effects. A plaintiff desiring a federal forum may omit parties from his or her state and sue them separately in a state court proceeding.[41] The result is concurrent litigation involving the same subject matter in two different courts. Also, if a plaintiff sues several defendants who are from the same state in federal court, one of the defendants might bring a state court proceeding against the plaintiff and the other defendants. Because complete diversity does not exist in the latter situation, the case cannot be removed to federal court. This results in simultaneous litigation of the same transaction or occurrence in state and federal court, and whichever court decides first will preclude the other court from rendering a judgment.[42] Alternatively, a plaintiff trying to avoid removal to federal court might add defendants who are from the same state.

Nonetheless, after 200 years, the requirement for complete diversity is unlikely to change unless Congress chooses to abolish it.[43] However, since there is little support for expanding diversity jurisdiction, the rule probably will remain in effect as long as diversity jurisdiction exists.

A major federal statute, the Class Action Fairness Act of 2005,[44] creates an exception to the requirement for complete diversity. Section 4 of the act creates original jurisdiction in the federal courts for any class action suits in which the matter in controversy (after aggregating the claims of all class members) exceeds $5 million and in which any member of the class of plaintiffs is from a state different from any defendant.[45] The section also authorizes a federal court to decline to exercise jurisdiction if more than one-third, but less than two-thirds, of the plaintiffs and the primary defendants are from the forum state.[46] The section requires federal courts to refuse to exercise jurisdiction if more than two-thirds of the plaintiff class members and at least one defendant against whom significant relief is sought are from the forum state. Section 5 of the act provides for removal from state court to federal court of class actions meeting the requirements of §4.

[41] *See* Rowe, *supra* note 12, at 967-968.

[42] The problem of pending concurrent state and federal court litigation is discussed in Chapter 14.

[43] The complete diversity requirement is entirely a product of statutory interpretation, and thus Congress could abolish it. *See* Owen Equip. & Erection Co. v. Kroger, Administrix, 437 U.S. at 373 n.13 ("It is settled that complete diversity is not a constitutional requirement."); *see also* State Farm Fire & Casualty Co. v. Tashire, 386 U.S. 523, 530-531 (1967).

[44] Pub. L. No. 109-2, 119 Stat. 4.

[45] This also applies if the defendant is a foreign country or a citizen of a foreign country.

[46] In deciding whether to exercise or decline jurisdiction in such circumstances, the federal court is to consider six factors: whether the claims asserted involve matters of national or interstate interest; whether the claims asserted will be governed by laws of the state in which the action was originally filed or by the laws of other states; whether the class action has been pleaded in a manner that seeks to avoid federal jurisdiction; whether the action was brought in a forum with a distinct nexus with the class members, the alleged forum, or the defendants; whether the number of plaintiffs of the state in which the action was filed is substantially larger than the number of citizens from any other state; and whether during the three-year period preceding the filing of the class action, one or more other class actions asserting the same or similar claims on behalf of the same or other persons have been filed.

Simply put, the act allows federal courts to hear class actions with an amount in controversy greater than $5 million with minimal diversity. The act raises important questions, both normative and practical. From a normative perspective, there is the question of whether it is desirable to bring to federal courts many class action suits that previously had been handled in state courts. Section 2 of the act details Congress's findings that class action suits are often abused and that federalizing is seen as a remedy. Others, of course, dispute that serious abuse occurs and believe that this was simply an attempt by business to shift from state courts, which often were more sympathetic to plaintiffs, to federal courts, which were seen as a more hospitable forum.[47]

In the area of civil liberties, it traditionally has been liberals who argue that there is not parity between federal and state courts and that federal jurisdiction should be expanded to enhance the protection of rights.[48] Here, though, conservatives and businesses sought to expand federal jurisdiction to move class actions from state to federal court.

There also are many practical questions in applying the act that will need to be resolved. How is the percentage of in-state residents to be determined? How is it to be decided who is a "primary defendant"? These and other issues in interpreting the act will be litigated for many years to come.

Each Party Must Be a Citizen of a State or Foreign Country

Second, for diversity jurisdiction to exist, each party must be a citizen of a state or a citizen only of a foreign country. For a person to be a citizen of a state, he or she must be a U.S. citizen. This proposition was established in the infamous decision of *Dred Scott v. Sandford,* in which the Supreme Court held that a slave could not invoke diversity jurisdiction because he was not a citizen of the United States.[49]

Additionally, a person may not sue or be sued in a diversity case if he or she is a citizen of the United States but not a citizen of a particular state. The U.S. Court of Appeals for the Seventh Circuit's decision in *Sadat v. Mertes* is widely cited as reflecting this principle.[50] An American citizen who also was a citizen of Egypt was domiciled abroad and sought to sue in federal court to recover for injuries suffered in an automobile accident. The court held that diversity jurisdiction was unavailable because the plaintiff was not a citizen of a particular state. Furthermore, the

[47] For a discussion of the Class Action Fairness Act and its desirability, *see* Stephen B. Burbank, The Class Action Fairness Act of 2005 in Historical Context: A Preliminary View, 156 U. Pa. L. Rev. 1439 (2008); Kevin M. Clermont & Theodore Eisenberg, CAFA Judicata: A Tale of Waste and Politics, 156 U. Pa. L. Rev. 1553 (2008); Emery G. Lee & Thomas Willging, The Impact of the Class Action Fairness Act on the Federal Courts: An Empirical Analysis of Filings and Removals, 156 U. Pa. L. Rev. 1723 (2008).

[48] *See, e.g.,* Burt Neuborne, The Myth of Parity, 90 Harv. L. Rev. 1105 (1977). The issue of parity is discussed in §1.5.

[49] 60 U.S. (19 How.) 393 (1856).

[50] 615 F.2d 1176 (7th Cir. 1980). *See also* Aly v. Hanzada for Imp. & Exp. Co., 864 F.3d 844 (8th Cir. 2017); Molinos Valle Del Cibao, C. por A. v. Lama, 633 F.3d 1330 (11th Cir. 2011); Buchel-Ruegsegger v. Buchel, 576 F.3d 451 (7th Cir. 2009).

court ruled that an American citizen cannot invoke alienage jurisdiction based on dual citizenship.

Again, this rule seems unjustified in light of the underlying purposes behind diversity jurisdiction. A person who is not a citizen of any state seems just as likely to be a victim of prejudice against out-of-staters as a citizen of another state. In fact, a court might be reluctant to discriminate against citizens of other states for fear that their state courts might retaliate. Individuals who are not citizens of any state, however, seem to be the most vulnerable to potential discrimination.

Although the Supreme Court originally held that citizens of the District of Columbia were not citizens of a state for diversity purposes, Congress amended the diversity statute to allow citizens of the District of Columbia to sue and be sued in diversity.[51] The Supreme Court upheld the constitutionality of this statute.[52]

Domicile Determines Individual's Citizenship

Third, specific rules determine the citizenship of individuals, corporations, unincorporated associations, and class actions.[53] An individual is deemed to be a citizen of the state where he or she is "domiciled"—that is, the one "place where he has his true, fixed, and permanent home and principal establishment, and to which he has the intention of returning whenever he is absent therefrom."[54] Although a person may have many residences, he or she has only one domicile.[55] Hence, an individual is considered to be a citizen of only one state for purposes of determining diversity jurisdiction.[56] Ultimately, the question of domicile is one of intent: Where does the person intend to make his or her permanent home? Relevant evidence of intent might include the place of employment; voting or automobile registration; location of personal or real property, including location of bank accounts; and membership in churches or other associations.[57]

The diversity jurisdiction statute provides that a corporation is a citizen *both* of any state where it is incorporated and of the state where it has its principal place of business.[58] Originally, the Supreme Court ruled that corporations were not citizens for purposes of the diversity jurisdiction statute.[59] In 1844, however, the Court

[51] Hepburn v. Ellzey, 6 U.S. (2 Cranch) 445 (1805).

[52] National Mut. Ins. Co. v. Tidewater Transfer Co., 337 U.S. 582 (1949). There was not a majority opinion in this case. Three justices said that the statute was constitutional because Congress could enlarge the jurisdiction of the federal courts; six justices rejected this position. Two justices concurred in the result on the ground that citizens of the District of Columbia should be treated as citizens of a state. This decision is discussed in §3.4, *supra*.

[53] For an argument that from an originalist perspective, corporations should not be able to invoke diversity jurisdiction, *see* Mark Moller & Lawrence B. Solum, The Article III "Party" and the Originalist Case against Corporate Diversity Jurisdiction, 64 Wm. & Mary L. Rev. 1345, 1351 (2023).

[54] Wright, *supra* note 20, at 146.

[55] *See* Steigleder v. McQuesten, 198 U.S. 141 (1905) (distinguishing residence from domicile).

[56] *See* Williamson v. Osenton, 232 U.S. 619 (1914).

[57] *See* 13B Charles Alan Wright, Arthur R. Miller & Edward H. Cooper, Federal Practice and Procedure 530-533 (1984).

[58] 28 U.S.C. §1332(c).

[59] Bank of the United States v. Deveaux, 9 U.S. (5 Cranch) 61 (1809).

reversed itself and held that a corporation was a citizen of the state that created it.[60] A decade later, the Court said that although a corporation is not a citizen, its shareholders would be presumed to be citizens of the incorporating state.[61] This fiction continued until Congress amended the diversity statute to make corporations citizens of both the states where they are incorporated and where they have their principal place of business.[62] Thus, a corporation cannot sue or be sued in diversity if any of the opposing parties are from the same state where it is incorporated or where it has its principal place of business.

Both determining the place of incorporation and the principal place of business pose potential problems. For example, some corporations are incorporated in more than one state; is such a business deemed a citizen of every state where it is incorporated? In general, until 1958, the answer was that a corporation was deemed to have only one place of incorporation, even if, in fact, it was incorporated in more than one state. The Court ruled that if a corporation sued or was sued in a state where it was incorporated, then that state was deemed to be the state of its incorporation and all other places of incorporation were irrelevant for purposes of determining diversity.[63] However, some commentators, such as Professor Wright, have suggested that this approach did not survive the 1958 amendment of the diversity statute and that now a corporation is a citizen of every state where it is incorporated.[64] Courts seem to be split between those that continue to adhere to the pre-1958 rules and those that accept Professor Wright's view that a corporation cannot sue or be sued in diversity by individuals who are citizens of any of the states where it is incorporated.[65]

Even more difficult questions arise in determining a company's principal place of business. There had been a split among the circuits as to whether this determination should focus on the location of a corporation's "nerve center"—the primary place where corporate policy is formulated—or on the location of the corporation's assets, such as where its principal service or sales activities are centered. In *Hertz Corp. v. Friend,* the Court resolved this and unanimously held that the "nerve center" will typically be found at a corporation's headquarters.[66]

The issue in the case was whether Hertz Corp. should be deemed to have its principal place of business in New Jersey, where it had its corporate headquarters, or in California, where it did the most business. The Supreme Court said the nerve center test had the advantage of providing a clearer rule that would be easier to apply, something of great benefit for jurisdictional rules: "A 'nerve center' approach, which ordinarily equates that 'center' with a corporation's

[60] Louisville, C. & C. R. v. Letson, 43 U.S. (2 How.) 497 (1844).

[61] Marshall v. Baltimore & O. R.R., 57 U.S. (16 How.) 314 (1853).

[62] Act of July 25, 1958, Pub. L. No. 85-554, 72 Stat. 415.

[63] *See, e.g.,* Patch v. Wabash R.R., 207 U.S. 277 (1907); Railway Co. v. Whitton's Admr., 80 U.S. (13 Wall.) 270 (1871).

[64] Wright, *supra* note 20, at 151.

[65] *See* Yancoskie v. Delaware River Port Auth., 528 F.2d 722, 727 n.17 (3d Cir. 1975); Oslick v. Port Auth., 83 F.R.D. 494 (S.D.N.Y. 1979); *but see* Hudak v. Port Auth. Trans-Hudson Corp., 238 F. Supp. 790 (S.D.N.Y. 1965) (adhering to the earlier view).

[66] 559 U.S. 77, 81 (2010).

headquarters, is simple to apply *comparatively speaking*. The metaphor of a corporate 'brain,' while not precise, suggests a single location. By contrast, a corporation's general business activities more often lack a single principal place where they take place. That is to say, the corporation may have several plants, many sales locations, and employees located in many different places. If so, it will not be as easy to determine which of these different business locales is the 'principal' or most important 'place.' "[67]

However, the Court left open the possibility of allowing a showing that a corporate headquarters is really a sham created for the purposes of creating or frustrating diversity jurisdiction. Justice Breyer, writing for the Court, explained, "Indeed, if the record reveals attempts at manipulation—for example, that the alleged 'nerve center' is nothing more than a mail drop box, a bare office with a computer, or the location of an annual executive retreat—the courts should instead take as the 'nerve center' the place of actual direction, control, and coordination, in the absence of such manipulation."[68]

Also, §1332(c) states that in a direct action against an insurance company, the company is deemed to be a citizen not only of the state of its incorporation and its principal place of business but also of the "State of which the insured is a citizen." The legislative history behind this provision, which was adopted in 1964, suggests a belief that diversity jurisdiction should not be created simply because the insurance company is the defendant rather than the responsible individual or entity.[69] Also, interestingly, a major purpose of the revision was to decrease docket congestion in federal courts in Louisiana as a result of a Louisiana statute that permitted direct actions against insurance companies.[70]

An unincorporated association is considered to be a citizen of every state where one of its members is a citizen. In other words, an unincorporated association cannot sue or be sued in diversity by citizens from any state where a member of the unincorporated association is a citizen. For example, in *United Steelworkers v. R. H. Bouligny*, the Supreme Court held that a labor union is to be considered a citizen of every state where one of its members is a citizen.[71] The Court emphasized that it was for Congress and not the judiciary to decide whether unincorporated associations, such as unions, should be able to sue or be sued in diversity as an entity. Again, there seems little justification for the continued obstacles imposed on diversity jurisdiction for unincorporated associations. A better approach would be to accord an unincorporated association a distinct identity and treat it as a citizen where it has its principal place of business.[72]

The Supreme Court has held that citizenship of both general and limited partners must be taken into account in determining whether there is diversity

[67] *Id.* at 94-95.

[68] *Id.* at 97.

[69] S. Rep. No. 1308, 88th Cong., 2d Sess. (1964).

[70] *Id.*; *see also* Donald T. Weckstein, The 1964 Diversity Amendment: Congressional Indirect Action Against State "Direct Action" Laws, 1965 Wis. L. Rev. 268.

[71] 382 U.S. 145 (1965).

[72] The American Law Institute proposed this change; *see supra* note 29, at 10.

among the parties. In *Carden v. Arkoma Associates*, the Court ruled that the citizenship of limited partners must be considered because of the "oft-repeated rule that diversity jurisdiction in a suit by or against the entity depends on the citizenship of 'all the members.'"[73] The Court noted that strictly enforcing the requirement for complete diversity limited federal court jurisdiction "at a time when our federal courts are already seriously overburdened."[74]

Finally, it long has been established that in class action suits diversity is determined based on the citizenship of the named representative.[75] As discussed above, the Class Action Fairness Act of 2005 allows minimal diversity for some class actions where the amount in controversy is more than $5 million.[76]

Burden on Party Seeking to Invoke Diversity Jurisdiction

A fourth major principle concerning the determination of diversity jurisdiction is that the party seeking to invoke federal court jurisdiction must allege its existence and, if there is a dispute, that party has the burden of proof.[77] Thus, diversity of citizenship must be alleged on the face of the plaintiff's complaint or the defendant's removal petition. However, 28 U.S.C. §1653 states that "[d]efective allegations of jurisdiction may be amended, upon terms, in the trial or appellate courts."

If a plaintiff initiates a diversity suit in federal court, diversity is determined at the time the action is filed; neither citizenship when the cause of action arose nor citizenship at the time of judgment matter.[78] Thus, if diversity properly exists when a lawsuit is filed, subsequent moves by the parties cannot destroy diversity. However, for a defendant to remove a case from state to federal court, diversity must exist both at the time the complaint is filed and at the time the removal petition is presented to the federal court.[79]

In *Caterpillar, Inc. v. Lewis*, however, the Supreme Court ruled that if a federal court improperly grants removal jurisdiction in the absence of complete diversity, the judgment shall stand as long as diversity properly existed at the time of the judgment.[80] A case was removed from state to federal court and should have been remanded for lack of complete diversity. The federal court, however, accepted jurisdiction. While the case was being litigated, a settlement was reached with one of the parties, who then dropped out of the lawsuit. At that point, there was

[73] 494 U.S. 185, 195 (1990).

[74] *Id.* at 207.

[75] *See* Supreme Tribe of Ben Hur v. Cauble, 255 U.S. 356 (1921).

[76] Pub. L. No. 109-2, 119 Stat. 4.

[77] *See* Cameron v. Hodges, 127 U.S. 322 (1888) (burden of pleading citizenship is on the party seeking to invoke jurisdiction); Hertz Corp. v. Friend, 559 U.S. at 96 ("The burden of persuasion for establishing diversity jurisdiction, of course, remains on the party asserting it.").

[78] *See, e.g.*, Louisville, N.A. & C.R. Co. v. Louisville Trust Co., 174 U.S. 552 (1899); Mollan v. Torrance, 22 U.S. (9 Wheat.) 537 (1824).

[79] *See* Jackson v. Allen, 132 U.S. 27 (1889); Jack H. Friedenthal, Mary Kay Kane & Arthur R. Miller, Civil Procedure 59 (2d ed. 1993).

[80] 519 U.S. 61 (1996), discussed more fully below in §5.5.

complete diversity. The Supreme Court said that this judgment should stand, even though the federal court did not properly have jurisdiction at the time of the removal from state court. The Court stressed "considerations of finality, efficiency, and economy" in coming to this conclusion.[81]

By contrast, in *Grupo Dataflux v. Atlas Global Group, L.P.*, the Court held that a change in citizenship after the lawsuit was filed could not cure the absence of diversity and thus the judgment could not stand.[82] Diversity did not exist when the suit was filed, but a month before the trial a member of the partnership who precluded complete diversity left the partnership. The result was complete diversity at the date of trial and the judgment, though not when the case was filed. The Supreme Court rejected this as insufficient. Justice Scalia, writing for the Court in a 5-4 decision, said that "jurisdiction . . . depends on the state of things at the time of the action brought."[83]

Is there a meaningful distinction between these two cases? The technical distinction is that a party leaving the lawsuit to create diversity that otherwise did not exist can save the judgment, but a change in the residency of a party cannot cure a defect in diversity and save the judgment. On the other hand, it is hard to see why this distinction matters. In both cases, a person dropping out of the lawsuit cured the defect in diversity. In one case this was enough to save the judgment, but not in the other.

Diversity Cannot Be Gained by Collusion

Fifth, diversity cannot be gained by collusion. In fact, 28 U.S.C. §1359 specifically provides: "A district court shall not have original jurisdiction of a civil action in which any party, by assignment or otherwise, has been improperly or collusively made or joined to invoke the jurisdiction of such court." The major case interpreting this provision is *Kramer v. Caribbean Mills, Inc.*[84] A Panamanian corporation assigned, for the price of one dollar, its entire interest in a breach of contract suit to a Texas attorney. The attorney promised to pay back to the corporation 95 percent of the money recovered in the suit. The attorney then initiated a diversity suit in federal court in which he was the named plaintiff. The Supreme Court found that diversity jurisdiction was inappropriate because of improper collusion in violation of §1359. The Court stated: "When the assignment to Kramer is considered together with his total lack of previous connection with the matter and his simultaneous assignment of a 95% interest back to Panama, there can be little doubt that the assignment was for purposes of collection. . . . Moreover, Kramer candidly admits that the 'assignment was in substantial part motivated by a desire . . . to make diversity jurisdiction available.' "[85]

[81] *Id.* at 76.
[82] 541 U.S. 567 (2004).
[83] *Id.* at 570.
[84] 394 U.S. 823 (1969).
[85] *Id.* at 827-828.

Collusion is not determined simply by the motives of those invoking federal jurisdiction.[86] Crucial to the analysis is an identification of who are the real parties in interest in the litigation and whether they are diverse to each other. Thus, generally the citizenship of an administrator of an estate or a trustee is used for determining whether there is diversity of citizenship.[87] But the citizenship of the administrator or the trustee is not employed in determining the existence of diversity jurisdiction if the appointment was done solely to create or frustrate diversity jurisdiction.[88]

Not all actions intended to manufacture diversity are considered to be impermissible collusion. Because diversity is determined at the time the complaint is filed, a person can move from one state to another before initiating a lawsuit to create diversity jurisdiction where it otherwise would be lacking. In fact, in one case, the Supreme Court upheld diversity jurisdiction where a Kentucky corporation dissolved and reincorporated itself in Tennessee entirely for the purpose of creating diversity of citizenship with the Kentucky defendant.[89]

Also, the Supreme Court has held that the plaintiff's alignment of the parties is not determinative; a federal court, in determining whether there is complete diversity, should realign parties according to their real interests. In *City of Indianapolis v. Chase National Bank*, the Court held that a New York bank's suit against two Indiana defendants did not meet the requirements of diversity jurisdiction because one of the Indiana defendants had the same interests as the bank in the lawsuit.[90] The Supreme Court has explained that a federal court must "look beyond the pleadings and arrange the parties according to their sides in the dispute."[91]

No Diversity Jurisdiction for Domestic Relations or Probate Cases

Sixth, and finally, diversity jurisdiction does not exist for two major types of cases: probate matters and domestic relations cases involving divorce, alimony, and child custody matters. Long ago, the Supreme Court declared that "[t]he whole

[86] For example, valid assignments of claims can be a basis for diversity jurisdiction, *see* Ambrosia Coal & Constr. Co. v. Pages Morales, 482 F.3d 1309 (11th Cir. 2007); Attorneys Trust v. Videotape Computer Products, 93 F.3d 593 (9th Cir. 1996), but an invalid assignment cannot be the grounds for jurisdiction, *see* Nat'l Fitness Holdings, Inc. v. Grand View Corporate Center, LLC, 749 F.3d 1202 (10th Cir. 2014); Airlines Reporting Corp. v. S and N Travel, Inc., 58 F.3d 857 (2d Cir. 1995).

[87] *See* Navarro Sav. Assn. v. Lee, 446 U.S. 458 (1980) (citizenship of trustee used for determining existence of diversity). For a detailed discussion of this issue, *see* Linda S. Mullenix, Creative Manipulation of Federal Jurisdiction: Is There Diversity After Death?, 70 Cornell L. Rev. 1011 (1985).

[88] *See, e.g.*, Chemical Leaman Tank Lines, Inc. v. Aetna Cas. and Sur. Co., 177 F.3d 210, 223 n.16 (3d Cir. 1999); Pallazola v. Rucker, 797 F.2d 1116 (1st Cir. 1986); McSparran v. Weist, 402 F.2d 867 (3d Cir.), *cert. denied*, 395 U.S. 903 (1968); O'Brien v. AVCO Corp., 425 F.2d 1030 (2d Cir. 1969); Lester v. McFadden, 415 F.2d 1101 (4th Cir. 1969). *See also* Hackney v. Newman Memorial Hosp., 621 F.2d 1069 (10th Cir.), *cert. denied*, 449 U.S. 982 (1980) (collusion determined not by motive but by the interest of the plaintiffs).

[89] Black & White Taxicab & Transfer Co. v. Brown & Yellow Taxicab Co., 276 U.S. 518, 524 (1928).

[90] 314 U.S. 63 (1941).

[91] City of Dawson v. Columbia Ave. Sav. Fund, 197 U.S. 178, 180 (1905).

subject of the domestic relations of husband and wife, parent and child, belongs to the laws of the States and not to the laws of the United States."[92] The Supreme Court has reaffirmed this limitation on federal court jurisdiction. In *Thompson v. Thompson*, the Court held that the Parental Kidnapping Prevention Act of 1980 did not create a private cause of action in federal court.[93] The act requires a state court to enforce child custody decrees entered by other states' courts. In refusing to allow federal court suits, the Court spoke of the "long-standing tradition of reserving domestic-relations matters to the States."[94] The Court especially emphasized Congress's rejection of a proposal to allow diversity jurisdiction in actions seeking to enforce state custody decrees.

In *Ankenbrandt v. Richards*, the Supreme Court further clarified the domestic relations exception to diversity jurisdiction.[95] A mother of two daughters sued, on their behalf, their father and his female companion for having sexually and physically abused the girls. The suit was brought in federal court pursuant to diversity jurisdiction, but the court dismissed the action based on the domestic relations exception to diversity jurisdiction.

The Supreme Court held that the federal court properly had jurisdiction over the matter. The Court explained that neither Article III nor the diversity jurisdiction statute, §1332, carve out an exception for domestic relations cases. The Court, however, recognized a more limited exception, concluding that federal courts may not hear cases "involving the issuance of a divorce, alimony, or child custody decree."[96] The Court explained that these areas have been traditionally left to state courts and are therefore an area where state courts have developed expertise. The Court also noted that "[i]ssuance of decrees of this type not infrequently involve retention of jurisdiction by the court and deployment of social workers to monitor compliance."[97] State courts are thus in a better position to handle divorce, alimony, and child custody matters.[98]

Also, federal courts may not hear probate matters as part of their diversity jurisdiction.[99] For example, federal courts may not probate wills or administer estates.

[92] In re Burrus, 136 U.S. 586, 593-594 (1890); *see also* Williams v. North Carolina, 325 U.S. 226, 233 (1945).

[93] 484 U.S. 174 (1988).

[94] *Id.* at 187 n.4.

[95] 504 U.S. 689 (1992). In Elk Grove Unified School District v. Newdow, 542 U.S. 1 (2004), the Supreme Court cited *Ankenbrandt* approvingly in explaining why a federal court should defer to state law in determining the right of a noncustodial father to sue on behalf of his daughter to challenge the words "under God" in the Pledge of Allegiance. The Court ruled that the father lacked standing. This case is discussed above in §2.3.4.

[96] 504 U.S. at 703.

[97] *Id.* at 703-704.

[98] Some scholars have challenged this rationale for excluding domestic relations cases from federal courts and contend that the refusal of federal courts to hear these matters reflects gender bias and the undervaluing of matters dealing with women and the family. *See, e.g.*, Naomi R. Cahn, Family Law, Federalism, and the Federal Courts, 79 Iowa L. Rev. 1073 (1994); Judith Resnik, "Naturally" Without Gender: Women, Jurisdiction, and the Federal Courts, 66 N.Y.U. L. Rev. 1682 (1991).

[99] *See, e.g.*, Markham, Alien Property Custodian v. Allen, 326 U.S. 490 (1945); Byers v. McAuley, 149 U.S. 608 (1893); In re Broaderick's Will, 88 U.S. (21 Wall.) 503 (1875).

The Court considered and rejected the application of the probate exception in an unusual and highly publicized context. *Marshall v. Marshall* involved a claim by Anna Nicole Smith, also known as Vickie Lynn Marshall, against Pierce Marshall for his tortiously interfering with her right to receive a gift from her late husband, J. Howard Marshall,[100] who was much older than Smith and had lavished gifts on her during his life but had not designated her as a beneficiary in his will. The will was probated in Texas, and the probate court found that Smith was not entitled to any inheritance.

Pierce Marshall filed a claim for libel against Smith in the California bankruptcy court proceedings. Smith counterclaimed for tortious interference with her right to receive a gift from J. Howard Marshall. The bankruptcy court ruled in her favor, as did the federal district court, but the Ninth Circuit reversed based on the probate exception.

The Supreme Court found that the probate exception was inapplicable. The Court said that the probate exception is based on the need for one court to relinquish jurisdiction to another when there is an issue of real property. Justice Ginsburg, writing for the Court, explained: "Thus, the probate exception reserves to state probate courts the probate or annulment of a will and the administration of a decedent's estate; it also precludes federal courts from endeavoring to dispose of property that is in the custody of a state probate court. But it does not bar federal courts from adjudicating matters outside those confines and otherwise within federal jurisdiction."[101]

The Court stressed that Smith was seeking "an *in personam* judgment against Pierce, not the probate or annulment of a will. Nor does she seek to reach a *res* in the custody of a state court."[102] Thus, the Court held that the probate exception does not bar a separate tort suit for tortious interference with recovery from an estate.

The exclusion from diversity jurisdiction of domestic relations and probate matters has been strongly criticized.[103] In part, the critics contend that it is inappropriate for the Court to establish an exception to diversity jurisdiction; if such an exception is desired, it is argued, Congress should create it. For example, in *Ankenbrandt*, the Supreme Court emphasized the absence of statutory exclusion of domestic relations cases as the reason federal courts can hear tort suits arising from family situations, but nonetheless recognized an exception for divorce, alimony, and child custody matters even though the statute is equally silent about these. Also, it is suggested that there is no reason to exempt domestic relations and

[100] 547 U.S. 293 (2006). The matter returned to the Supreme Court in 2011 on another issue: whether the bankruptcy court could issue a final judgment on the state law counterclaim. Stern v. Marshall, 564 U.S. 462 (2011). This case is discussed in detail in Chapter 4.

[101] 547 U.S. at 311-312.

[102] *Id.*

[103] *See, e.g.*, Barbara Freedman Wand, A Call for the Repudiation of the Domestic Relations Exception to Federal Jurisdiction, 30 Vill. L. Rev. 307 (1985); Sharon Elizabeth Rush, Domestic Relations Law: Federal Jurisdiction and State Sovereignty in Perspective, 60 Notre Dame L. Rev. 1 (1984).

probate matters from federal court review because they are no more linked to core aspects of state sovereignty than are many other types of suits that federal courts may adjudicate. Justice Stevens declared, "I do not believe that there is any 'probate exception' that ousts a federal court of jurisdiction it otherwise possesses."[104]

Others, however, support the continuation of this exemption. One federal court explained that "the strong state interest in domestic relations matters, the competence of state courts in settling family disputes, the possibility of incompatible federal and state court decrees in cases of continuing judicial supervision by the state, and the problem of congested dockets in federal courts" all justified denial of federal court jurisdiction over such matters.[105]

§5.3.4 The Determination of the Amount in Controversy

History of the Jurisdictional Amount Requirement

Diversity and alienage jurisdiction exist under §1332 only "where the matter in controversy exceeds the sum or value of $75,000, exclusive of interest and costs." Although the Constitution does not mention a jurisdictional amount, an amount in controversy requirement has existed for diversity and alienage jurisdiction since the Judiciary Act of 1789. Originally, the amount in controversy was $500;[106] it was increased to $10,000 in 1958 and raised to $50,000 in 1988.[107] It was increased to the current level of $75,000 in 1996.[108] In explaining the jurisdictional amount, the Senate Report in 1958 said that the goal was to set a figure "not so high as to convert the Federal courts into courts of big business nor so low as to fritter away their time in the trial of petty controversies."[109]

The jurisdictional amount requirement was unchanged from 1958 until 1988. Not surprisingly, there were many proposals to change the amount in controversy requirement. Until it was eliminated in 1980, there also was an amount in controversy requirement for federal question cases.[110] Some have suggested that the amount in controversy requirement should be eliminated in diversity cases as well.[111] The dollar value of a case does not necessarily measure its importance to the parties or to society. For an individual, $5,000 may represent a life's savings, but for a multibillion-dollar corporation, $75,000 is a mere pittance. If the goal is limiting suits in federal court, a better approach might be to exclude diversity cases involving particular types of claims that are least likely to benefit from federal

[104] Marshall v. Marshall, 547 U.S. at 1752 (Stevens, J., dissenting).

[105] Ruffalo by Ruffalo v. Civilleti, 702 F.2d 710, 717 (8th Cir. 1983) (citations omitted).

[106] 1 Stat. 73, 78.

[107] Act of July 25, 1958, Pub. L. No. 85-554, 72 Stat. 415; Act of Nov. 19, 1988, Pub. L. No. 100-72.

[108] Federal Courts Improvement Act of 1996, Pub. L. No. 104-317, §205, 110 Stat. 3487.

[109] S. Rep. No. 1830, 85th Cong., 2d Sess., *reprinted in* 1958 U.S. Code Cong. & Admin. News 3099, 3101.

[110] Act of Dec. 1, 1980, 94 Stat. 2369.

[111] *See* Daniel J. Meador, A New Approach to Limiting Diversity Jurisdiction, 46 A.B.A. J. 383 (1960).

jurisdiction.[112]Others, though, have suggested increasing the amount in controversy requirement as a way of further limiting diversity cases in federal court.[113]

Case Dismissed Only if Legal Certainty Amount Not Met

The Supreme Court has articulated several important principles in determining the amount in controversy in a case. First, a case should be dismissed for failing to meet the jurisdictional amount requirement only if there is a *legal certainty* that the plaintiff cannot recover in excess of $75,000. In *St. Paul Mercury Indemnity Co. v. Red Cab Co.*, the Court declared: "The rule governing dismissal for want of jurisdiction in cases brought in the federal court is that, unless the law gives a different rule, the sum claimed by the plaintiff controls if the claim is apparently made in good faith. It must appear to a legal certainty that the claim is really for less than the jurisdictional amount to justify dismissal."[114]

At first, this rule might seem curious because of the usual strong presumption against federal court jurisdiction. However, it would be undesirable for the federal court to try to measure the plaintiff's likely recovery in advance of the litigation. The court either would need to hold a mini-trial at the start of the litigation to determine probable damages, or the court would be left to make an impressionistic guess about the plaintiff's likely damages. To avoid these alternatives, the rule is that a plaintiff's allegation that more than the jurisdictional amount is at stake is accepted unless there is a legal certainty that the plaintiff cannot recover that amount. If necessary, the court can request affidavits to assist it in evaluating the jurisdictional amount; a trial-type hearing is extremely rare in the determination of the amount in controversy.[115]

The plaintiff must allege that *more* than $75,000 is in controversy, exclusive of interest and costs that might be recovered. However, if there is a statutory or contractual provision allowing a prevailing plaintiff to recover attorneys' fees, this possible recovery may be counted in calculating the jurisdictional amount.[116] The failure of the plaintiff to actually recover in excess of $75,000 does not deny a federal court jurisdiction, but §1332 does provide for an assessment of costs against a plaintiff who recovers less than the jurisdictional amount.[117] Generally, there is no jurisdiction if the plaintiff seeks less than the amount in controversy.[118] However, a

[112] *Id.* at 384.

[113] *See* Steven Gensler & Roger Michalski, The Million-Dollar Diversity Docket, 47 BYU L. Rev. 1653, 1711-1722 (2022) (describing the effects of increasing the amount in controversy requirement).

[114] 303 U.S. 283, 288 (1938).

[115] *See, e.g.,* Tanzymore v. Bethlehem Steel Corp., 457 F.2d 1320 (3d Cir. 1972) (no right to an evidentiary hearing in the determination of diversity jurisdiction).

[116] *See, e.g.,* Missouri State Life Ins. Co. v. Jones, 290 U.S. 199 (1933).

[117] *See, e.g.,* Rosado v. Wyman, 397 U.S. 397, 405 n.6 (1970); Smith v. Greystone Alliance, LLC, 772 F.3d 448 (7th Cir. 2014); Pratt v. Central Park Ltd. Partnership v. Dames & Moore, Inc., 60 F.3d 350 (7th Cir. 1995); 28 U.S.C. §1332(b).

[118] *See, e.g.,* Federated Mut. Ins. Co. v. McKinnon Motors, LLC, 329 F.3d 805 (11th Cir. 2003); Burns v. Windsor Insurance Co., 31 F.3d 1092 (11th Cir. 1994).

federal court can exercise jurisdiction if it can be shown that the plaintiff did this in state court in an effort to frustrate removal, knowing that the claims were actually for a greater amount that still could be recovered in state court notwithstanding the complaint. The Fifth Circuit explained: "[I]f a defendant can show that the amount in controversy actually exceeds the jurisdictional amount, the plaintiff must be able to show that, as a matter of law, it is certain that he will not be able to recover more than the damages for which he has prayed in the state court complaint. Such a rule is necessary to avoid the sort of manipulation that occurred in the instant case."[119]

Valuation of Claims

Second, in terms of valuation, problems arise primarily in suits for injunctions and declaratory judgments. When the plaintiff is seeking money damages, the plaintiff's request for damages determines the amount in controversy unless there is a legal certainty that the plaintiff could not recover in excess of $75,000. For injunctions and declaratory relief, the Court stated that "the amount in controversy is measured by the value of the object of the litigation."[120] For example, in *Healy v. Ratta,* the Court considered the amount in controversy in a suit where the plaintiff sought to enjoin the application of a tax to his business.[121] The Court said that the amount in controversy was not the penalty for failure to pay the tax, but the amount of the tax, "since payment of it would avoid the penalty and end the dispute."[122]

The problem that arises in valuing suits for injunctive or declaratory remedies is that the amount in controversy varies depending on the perspective: Is it the monetary harms the plaintiff will incur without court relief, the costs the court's remedy will impose on the defendant, or the combination of the plaintiff's harms and the defendant's costs? Some authority can be found to support many different approaches. Many decisions hold that the jurisdictional amount in a suit for a declaratory judgment or injunction is determined by the harm the plaintiff will incur without court relief. In *Glenwood Light & Water Co. v. Mutual Light, Heat & Power Co.,* the Court considered a suit to enjoin the defendant from interfering with the plaintiff's utility poles and wires.[123] Although compliance would cost the defendant only $500, the Court found the jurisdictional amount requirement to be met based on allegations of the expenses that the plaintiff would incur without a favorable court decision.

[119] Corral v. Select Portfolio Servicing Inc., 878 F.3d 770 (9th Cir. 2017); In re Exxon Chemical Fire, 558 F.3d 378 (5th Cir. 2009); De Aguillar v. Boeing Co., 47 F.3d 1404 (5th Cir.), *cert. denied,* 516 U.S. 865 (1995).

[120] Hunt v. Washington State Apple Advertising Commn., 432 U.S. 333, 347-348 (1977).

[121] 292 U.S. 263 (1934).

[122] *Id.* at 268.

[123] 239 U.S. 121 (1915). *See also* Hunt v. Washington State Apple Advertising Com'n, 432 U.S. 333 (1977) (holding that for these circumstances the amount in controversy was the amount plaintiffs would suffer if law was enacted); Western & A. R.R. v. Railroad Commn. of Ga., 261 U.S. 264 (1923).

Other courts have said that the amount in controversy is determined by looking to the sum at stake for the party invoking federal court jurisdiction.[124] Thus, if the plaintiff files a suit for declaratory or injunctive relief in federal court, the plaintiff's harms without the remedy determine the amount, but if the defendant is removing the case to federal court, then the cost to the defendant of complying with the proposed relief determines the amount.

The trend seems to be that the amount in controversy is met if *either* the plaintiff's harms or the defendant's costs of compliance will exceed $75,000.[125] This rule makes the most sense, because the amount in controversy in a lawsuit exceeds $75,000 if either the plaintiff or defendant will have to pay that amount.

One of the more complex and confusing valuation issues arises when there are installment contracts or payments. Under these circumstances, the court's judgment will not immediately award more than $75,000 to the plaintiff, but its long-term effect could far exceed that sum. The Supreme Court said, "[W]here an injunction commanding future payments is sought, there is no need to await accrual of [the full jurisdictional amount] in back benefits to bring suit."[126]

Other precedents are seemingly in conflict. In *Elgin v. Marshall*, a plaintiff sought to recover interest due on certain bonds.[127] The Supreme Court denied jurisdiction because the sum due on the bond's coupons to that date was less than the amount in controversy requirement, even though the total amount of payments would exceed the jurisdictional amount.

The best way to reconcile these seemingly conflicting precedents is that if the suit involves an issue concerning the entire contract, then the amount in controversy is the total value of the contract, including future payments. In other cases, only the amount due at the time of the initiation of the suit is relevant in determining the jurisdictional amount.[128]

Aggregation of Claims

Finally, there is the problem of whether claims can be aggregated to meet the jurisdictional amount. It is firmly established that a single plaintiff may aggregate the value of all of the claims presented against a single defendant, even if the claims arise from completely separate transactions or occurrences.[129] However, when there are

[124] *See, e.g.*, Fastcase, Inc. v. Lawriter LLC, 907 F.3d 1335 (11th Cir. 2018); Auto-Owners Ins. Co. v. Stevens & Riccie, Inc., 835 F.3d 388, 398 n.15 (3d Cir. 2016).

[125] *See, e.g.*, Horton v. Liberty Mut. Ins. Co., 367 U.S. 348 (1961); Frye v. Anadarko Petroleum Corp., 953 F.3d 285 (5th Cir. 2019); Corral v. Select Portfolio Servicing, Inc., 878 F.3d 770 (9th Cir. 2017); McCarty v. Amoco Pipeline Co., 595 F.2d 389 (7th Cir. 1979); Smith v. Washington, 593 F.2d 1097 (D.C. Cir. 1978).

[126] Weinberger v. Wiesenfeld, 420 U.S. 636, 642 n.10 (1975) (allowing jurisdiction in an action to recover survivor's benefits under the Social Security Act). *See also* Aetna Casualty & Sur. Co. v. Flowers, 330 U.S. 464 (1947).

[127] 106 U.S. (16 Otto) 578 (1882).

[128] Wright, *supra* note 20, at 188.

[129] *See* Edwards v. Bates County, 163 U.S. 269 (1896) (permitting aggregation of tort and contract claims).

multiple plaintiffs, one must allege a claim that is in excess of $75,000.[130] No longer is it the rule that each plaintiff must independently meet the jurisdictional amount requirement.

The same analysis is followed in class action suits.[131] This rule requiring each plaintiff to meet the amount in controversy has been applied to class action suits. In *Snyder v. Harris*, the Supreme Court said that the members of a class action could not aggregate their claims to meet the jurisdictional amount.[132] The Court held that a class action could not invoke diversity jurisdiction unless one member met the amount in controversy requirement. In *Zahn v. International Paper Co.*, the Court went even further and held that every member of a class action suit must independently meet the jurisdictional amount requirement.[133]

However, in *Exxon Mobil Corp. v. Allapattah Services*,[134] the Supreme Court found that the supplemental jurisdiction statute, 28 U.S.C. §1367, effectively overturned *Zahn* and that a federal court could hear claims, including class action suits, as long as one plaintiff met the amount in controversy requirement. There were actually two companion cases before the Supreme Court. *Exxon Mobil* involved a class action in which at least one of the plaintiffs did not meet the amount in controversy requirement. The other case, *Ortega v. Star-Kist Foods, Inc.*, was not a class action; it involved a child, who claimed damages in excess of the amount in controversy requirement from consuming tainted foods, and her family members, whose claims for emotional distress and expenses did not meet the amount in controversy requirement.

In a 5-4 decision, the Supreme Court held that the federal court had jurisdiction to hear all of the claims in both cases. Justice Kennedy wrote the opinion for the Court. He stressed that the cases fit within the scope of §1367: "When the well-pleaded complaint contains at least one claim that satisfies the amount-in-controversy requirement, and there are no other relevant jurisdictional defects, the district court, beyond all question, has original jurisdiction over that claim."[135] Justice Kennedy said that none of the exceptions found in §1367(b) applied to prevent the exercise of jurisdiction.

A seeming problem with Justice Kennedy's approach is that it also would negate the requirement for complete diversity; as long as one plaintiff and one defendant are diverse, that would seem to be enough. Justice Kennedy answered this expressly and said that the absence of complete diversity, "unlike the failure to meet some claims to meet the requisite amount in controversy, contaminates every claim in the action."[136] It is unclear, however, why the presence of nondiverse

[130] *See* Exxon Mobil Corp. v. Allapattah Services, Inc., 545 U.S. 546 (2005).

[131] In fact, in shareholder derivative suits, a completely different rule for determining the amount in controversy is used. The focus is not on the potential benefit to the plaintiff shareholder, but on the alleged damages suffered by the corporation. *See* Koster v. American Lumbermens Mut. Casualty Co., 330 U.S. 518 (1947).

[132] 394 U.S. 332 (1969).

[133] 414 U.S. 291 (1974).

[134] 545 U.S. 546 (2005).

[135] *Id.* at 559.

[136] *Id.* at 560.

defendants contaminates diversity any more than the presence of some parties who do not meet the amount in controversy contaminates that requirement.

The majority and the dissent disagreed over the clarity and relevance of the legislative history. Justices Stevens and Breyer in separate dissenting opinions focused on statements in the legislative history that §1367 was not meant to change diversity jurisdiction. Justice Kennedy's majority opinion found it unnecessary to look at the legislative history because the statutory provision was clear and in any event found the legislative history "far murkier" than the dissent made it seem.[137]

There is no doubt that *Exxon Mobil* is a major change in the law concerning determination of the amount in controversy requirement. Its importance in class action suits is lessened somewhat by the Class Action Fairness Act, which allows aggregation of claims, but the decision remains quite significant in joinder situations.

Finally, it remains unclear whether a counterclaim can be the basis for meeting the amount in controversy requirement. For example, the courts are split as to whether a defendant can remove a case from state to federal court based on the value of a compulsory counterclaim where the plaintiff's claim is for less than the jurisdictional amount.[138] The main Supreme Court decision concerning counterclaims is *Horton v. Liberty Mutual Insurance Co.*[139] Horton was injured in an industrial accident and sought $14,035 from the insurance company. The Texas Industrial Accident Board awarded only $1,050. The insurance company then filed a suit in federal court, based on diversity jurisdiction, to have the board's award set aside. The insurance company alleged that the amount in controversy was $14,035, sufficient to meet the amount in controversy requirement at the time, because that was the amount that Horton was seeking. Horton moved to dismiss the federal court suit for failing to meet the jurisdictional amount requirement, and he also filed a suit in state court seeking to have the board's award increased to $14,000.

The Supreme Court held that the insurance company's suit met the amount in controversy requirement. Even though the company was faced only with a $1,050 judgment against it by the Industrial Accident Board, the Court concluded that the actual amount at stake in the suit was $14,035 because that was the amount the plaintiff might recover in a trial de novo in state court. Justice Black, writing for the Court, stated: "Thus the record before us shows beyond a doubt that the award is challenged by both parties and is binding on neither; that petitioner claims more than $10,000 from the respondent and the respondent denies it should have to pay petitioner anything at all. No matter which party brings it into court, the controversy remains the same; it involves the same amount of money and is to be

[137] *Id.* at 569 (Stevens, J. dissenting).

[138] *See, e.g.*, Spectacor Management Group v. Brown, 131 F.3d 120 (3d Cir. 1997) (holding compulsory counter-claim could be used to meet amount in controversy); Royal Cosmopolitan, LLC v. Star Real Estate Group, LLC, 620 F. Supp. 2d 594 (E.D. La. 2008) (holding that counterclaims were for clearing ambiguity and not for meeting amount in controversy); Independent Machine Co. v. International Tray Pads & Packaging, Inc., 991 F. Supp. 687, 692-693 (D.N.J. 1998) (removal not allowed); National Upholstery Co. v. Corley, 144 F. Supp. 658 (M.D.N.C. 1956) (removal allowed).

[139] 367 U.S. 348 (1961).

adjudicated and determined under the same rules. Unquestionably, therefore, the amount in controversy is in excess of $10,000."[140]

Even after more than a half-century, the significance of *Horton* is unclear. Perhaps the case reflects a unique fact situation because of the trial de novo procedure in state court that made it clear that $14,035 was really at stake.[141] Or perhaps the case reflects a more general proposition still to be developed by the Supreme Court: that the amount in controversy should be determined on the basis of the sum that is actually at stake in the lawsuit.[142]

§5.3.5 The Choice of Law in Diversity Cases

Few topics concerning federal court jurisdiction have attracted more sustained attention from scholars than the question of what law is to be applied by federal courts in diversity cases. The shift from having federal courts develop federal common law to requiring federal courts to apply state law reflected major changes in jurisprudence and the legal system. For the 60 years since the Supreme Court held that federal courts should apply state law in diversity cases, commentators and justices have struggled to develop an approach that permits uniform procedural rules to be applied in federal court while still allowing state substantive law to govern.

Swift v. Tyson

In *Swift v. Tyson*, in 1842, the Supreme Court held that in diversity cases, in the absence of a state statutory or constitutional provision, or a particular local interest, federal courts should fashion federal common law.[143] *Swift* involved a question of commercial law, where there was no controlling state statutory or constitutional provision, but there was state common law on point. The issue in *Swift* was whether the federal court should follow the state court's precedents or whether the federal court could develop its own law.

The Rules of Decision Act—a provision adopted originally as part of the Judiciary Act of 1789 and that has continued largely unchanged to this day—states: "[T]he laws of the several states, except where the constitution, treaties or statutes of the United States shall otherwise require or provide, shall be regarded as rules of decisions in trials at common law in the courts of the United States in cases where they apply."[144] However, Justice Story, writing for the Court in *Swift v. Tyson*, concluded that the Rules of Decision Act only required federal

[140] *Id.* at 354.

[141] *See* Wright, *supra* note 20, at 207-208 (discussing significance of the *Horton* decision).

[142] *See* Spectacor Management Group v. Brown, 131 F.3d 120 (3d Cir.), *cert. denied,* 523 U.S. 1120 (1997) (counterclaim as basis for removal because defendant did not challenge jurisdiction).

[143] 41 U.S. (16 Pet.) 1 (1842).

[144] 28 U.S.C. §1652. The only modification in this provision since the Judiciary Act of 1789 has been to substitute the words "civil action" for "trials at common law."

courts to apply state constitutional and statutory provisions, not state common law. Justice Story wrote: "The laws of a state are more usually understood to mean the rules and enactments promulgated by the legislative authority thereof, or long-established local customs having the force of laws. . . . In the ordinary use of language it will hardly be contended that the decisions of courts constitute laws."[145] In fashioning their own common law rules, federal courts could examine how state courts have dealt with a particular issue, but such state decisions "cannot furnish positive rules, or conclusive authority, by which our own judgments are to be bound up and governed."[146]

The Court's holding in *Swift v. Tyson* providing for the development of federal common law in diversity cases was motivated by several concerns. In large part, there was a desire to create uniform national law to facilitate commercial transactions.[147] Federal common law not only would help encourage a national economy by providing a uniform set of legal rules but also could provide a model for the states to use that would be copied and thus further increase uniformity. Additionally, Justice Story undoubtedly was motivated by a view that there were objectively correct legal principles and that federal courts should not be bound to follow wrong state court decisions. Justice Story observed that the Rules of Decision Act did not apply to contracts and commercial transactions: "[T]he true interpretation and effect whereof are to be sought, not in the decisions of local tribunals, but in the general principles and doctrines of commercial jurisprudence."[148]

For almost 100 years, federal courts followed the holding of *Swift v. Tyson* and developed an elaborate body of federal common law in areas such as torts, as well as contracts and commercial law. *Swift* recognized that for certain "local" matters, state decisions should control.[149] Primarily, this meant that state court interpretations of state statutory and constitutional provisions were binding on federal courts, but there also were areas, such as real property, where state common law was given effect.[150]

Criticisms of *Swift v. Tyson*

By the late nineteenth and early twentieth centuries, the development of federal common law in diversity cases was subjected to substantial criticism.[151] In part, the attack on *Swift v. Tyson* centered on the enormous problems created by having one set of legal rules applied in federal court and another in state court. Instead

[145] 41 U.S. at 12-13, 18.

[146] *Id.* at 19.

[147] *Id.*; *see also* Tony Allan Freyer, Harmony and Dissonance: The *Swift* and *Erie* Cases in American Federalism (1981) (arguing that Swift v. Tyson was primarily concerned with commercial law).

[148] 41 U.S. at 2.

[149] *Id.* at 18.

[150] *See* Wright, *supra* note 20, at 349-350.

[151] *See, e.g.*, Harry Shulman, The Demise of Swift v. Tyson, 47 Yale L.J. 1336 (1938); Felix Frankfurter, Distribution of Federal Judicial Power Between Federal and State Courts, 13 Cornell L.Q. 499 (1928); Charles Warren, New Light on the History of the Federal Judiciary Act of 1789, 37 Harv. L. Rev. 49 (1923).

of promoting the development of uniform law, *Swift* caused enormous variances between the laws applied by federal courts and those followed in state judiciaries. The law for a transaction depended on whether the parties were from the same state or different states. Forum shopping was encouraged as parties tried to get the case into the court that would apply the most favorable law. The facts in *Black & White Taxicab & Transfer Co. v. Brown & Yellow Taxicab & Transfer Co.* are illustrative.[152] A Kentucky corporation dissolved and reincorporated in Tennessee so that it could sue a Kentucky defendant in federal court. Had the suit been brought in Kentucky state court, the plaintiff likely would have lost, but the completely different federal common law principles were highly favorable to the plaintiff.

Also, there was an attack on the jurisprudential underpinnings of *Swift*—the assumption that there are objectively true principles of law for the federal courts to apply. Belief in natural law had waned and had been replaced by a view that common law rules are chosen, not divined, by judges. As Justice Frankfurter later explained, "The overruling [of] *Swift v. Tyson* . . . did not merely overrule a venerable case. It overruled a particular way of looking at law which dominated the judicial process long after its inadequacies had been laid bare. . . . Law was conceived as a 'brooding omnipresence' of Reason, of which decisions were merely evidence and not themselves the controlling formulations."[153] But especially after the Legal Realist movement early in this century, such a view of law held little sway among commentators or justices.

Erie Railroad v. Tompkins

Swift v. Tyson was expressly overruled by the Supreme Court in the landmark decision of *Erie Railroad v. Tompkins.*[154] Tompkins, a citizen of Pennsylvania, was walking next to railroad tracks and was injured by an open door on a railcar. Tompkins sued the Erie Railroad, a New York corporation, in the U.S. District Court for the Southern District of New York, alleging that the railroad's negligence caused his injuries. Under Pennsylvania common law, those who use pathways along railroad tracks are deemed trespassers and are not able to recover for negligence, unless it is wanton and willful. The federal district court, however, said that it was "to exercise their independent judgment as to what the law is."[155] The district court concluded that the federal common law of torts permitted recovery for negligence.

Neither side argued to the Supreme Court that *Swift v. Tyson* should be overruled. Each believed that it could prevail under federal common law. Nor was there any reason to believe that the Court was about to overrule a century-old precedent. Apparently, the suggestion for overruling *Swift v. Tyson* came from Chief Justice Charles Evans Hughes, who began the justices' conference after

[152] 276 U.S. 518 (1928).
[153] Guaranty Trust Co. v. York, 326 U.S. 99, 101-102 (1945).
[154] 304 U.S. 64 (1938).
[155] Tompkins v. Erie R.R., 90 F.2d 603, 604 (2d Cir. 1937).

Erie was argued by stating: "If we wish to overrule *Swift v. Tyson,* here is our opportunity."[156]

Justice Brandeis wrote the opinion for the Court and offered three reasons why *Swift v. Tyson* was overruled. First, the Court said that new historical research cast doubts on the validity of the holding in *Swift v. Tyson.* Specifically, Justice Brandeis cited the research of Charles Warren.[157] Warren said that he had found an earlier handwritten draft of the Judiciary Act of 1789. The original phrasing of the Rules of Decision Act provided "[t]hat the Statute law of the several States in force for the time being and their unwritten or common law now in use, whether by adoption from the common law of England, the ancient statutes of the same or otherwise, except where the constitution, Treaties or Statutes of the United States shall otherwise require or provide, shall be regarded as the rules of decision in the trials at common law in the courts of the United States in cases where they apply."[158] Warren contended that the drafters of the Judiciary Act intended for state common law to be followed and that the modification in the language was only stylistic.

Many question whether this argument, by itself, justified overruling *Swift v. Tyson.* Some contend that Warren misinterpreted the language that was deleted; the original phrasing simply provided that the state's common law would control only until federal courts developed federal common law to replace it.[159] An even more powerful criticism is that the Court generally should not overrule its interpretation of a statute; if Congress disagrees with the Court, Congress can revise the law on its own. Judge Henry Friendly explained: "If ever Congress's reenactment of a statute or failure to alter it could fairly be taken as approving a prior judicial interpretation, the unchanged existence of Section 34 for a century after Story's construction was such a case."[160]

Second, the Court explained that *Swift v. Tyson* was overruled because "[e]xperience in applying [it] . . . had revealed its defects, political and social; and the benefits expected to flow from the rule did not accrue. Persistence of state courts in their own opinions on questions of common law prevented uniformity; and the impossibility of discovering a satisfactory line of demarcation between the province of general law and that of local law developed a new well of uncertainties."[161] Justice Brandeis discussed the unfairness of having the law vary depending on whether the lawsuit was between in-staters or based on diversity and decried the forum shopping that resulted. Interestingly, Justice Brandeis phrased this argument, in part, in terms of discrimination and equal protection. He wrote: "*Swift*

[156] Howard P. Fink & Mark V. Tushnet, Federal Jurisdiction: Policy and Practice 188 (1987), *quoting* II Merlo John Pusey, Charles Evans Hughes 710 (1951).

[157] 304 U.S. at 73 n.5.

[158] Charles Warren, New Light on the History of the Federal Judiciary Act of 1789, 37 Harv. L. Rev. 49, 51-52, 81-88, 108 (1923).

[159] William Winslow Crosskey, Politics and the Constitution in the History of the United States vol. I, 626-628; vol. II, 866-871 (1953).

[160] Henry J. Friendly, In Praise of *Erie*: And of the New Federal Common Law, 39 N.Y.U. L. Rev. 383, 390 (1964).

[161] 304 U.S. at 74.

v. Tyson introduced grave discrimination by noncitizens against citizens. It made rights enjoyed under the unwritten 'general law' vary according to whether enforcement was sought in the state or in the federal court. . . . Thus, the doctrine rendered impossible equal protection of the law."[162] This appears to be a rhetorical rather than a constitutional argument because the Supreme Court had not yet applied the requirements of equal protection to the federal government.

Without a doubt, the strongest argument for overruling *Swift* was its pernicious effects on the fair administration of civil justice. *Swift* encouraged forum shopping, and it was unjust that the result in a case depended on the citizenship of the parties. Yet even here a separation of powers argument could be made that any change should come from congressional amendment of the Rules of Decision Act.

Third and finally, Justice Brandeis stated that *Swift* was overruled because it was inconsistent with the Constitution. He wrote: "*There is no general federal common law.* Congress has no power to declare substantive rules of common law applicable in a State whether they be local in their nature or 'general,' be they commercial law or a part of the law of torts. And no clause in the Constitution purports to confer such a power upon the federal courts."[163] Quoting Justice Holmes, the Court said that *Swift v. Tyson* represented an "unconstitutional assumption of powers by courts of the United States."[164] Justice Brandeis made it clear that the constitutional argument was integral to the Court's holding when he stated: "If only a question of statutory construction were involved, we should not be prepared to abandon a doctrine so widely applied throughout nearly a century. But the unconstitutionality of the course pursued has now been made clear and compels us to do so."[165]

The constitutional basis for the *Erie* decision has confounded scholars.[166] The Court appears to have invoked a restrictive view of congressional power that already had been eroded and soon would be overruled. From approximately 1887 until 1937, the Supreme Court held that the Tenth Amendment reserved a zone of activities for the states' exclusive control, and it narrowly interpreted the scope of federal powers under provisions such as the commerce and spending clauses.[167] Beginning in 1937, the Court departed from these precedents, and by the early 1940s the Court had expansively interpreted Congress's authority and declared that the Tenth Amendment states "but a truism."[168] Under these latter precedents, there is no doubt that Congress could prescribe a national commercial law. In his concurring opinion, Justice Reed argued that Congress, pursuant to the necessary

[162] *Id.* at 74-75.

[163] *Id.* at 78 (emphasis added).

[164] *Id.* at 79.

[165] *Id.* at 77-78.

[166] *See, e.g.,* Stewart Jay, Origins of Federal Common Law: Part Two, 133 U. Pa. L. Rev. 1231 (1985); Martin H. Redish & Carter G. Phillips, *Erie* and the Rules of Decision Act: In Search of the Appropriate Dilemma, 91 Harv. L. Rev. 356 (1977); John Hart Ely, The Irrepressible Myth of *Erie,* 87 Harv. L. Rev. 693 (1974).

[167] *See, e.g.,* Carter v. Carter Coal Co., 298 U.S. 238 (1936); Hammer v. Dagenhart, 247 U.S. 251 (1918); United States v. E.C. Knight Co., 156 U.S. 1 (1895) (narrowly interpreting the scope of Congress's commerce power and protecting state sovereignty).

[168] United States v. Darby, 312 U.S. 100, 124 (1941); *see also* Wickard v. Filburn, 317 U.S. 111 (1942); NLRB v. Jones & Laughlin Steel Corp., 301 U.S. 1 (1937).

and proper clause of Article I, certainly could enact substantive rules to be applied by the federal courts.[169] Thus, the constitutional argument in *Erie*, especially since it is based on a premise of very limited congressional power, is quite questionable. It is curious that *Swift* was overruled not during the era of dual federalism, but at the beginning of its demise and at the inception of a time of Supreme Court approval of expansive federal powers.

Although some of the reasoning in the *Erie* decision has been questioned, its holding now is widely accepted: in diversity cases, federal courts are to apply state law, including state common law. The importance of the decision cannot be overstated. *Erie* substantially altered the nature of law practice. A huge body of federal common law was simply wiped from the books. Attorneys' choice of forum decisions were radically altered. Also, the decision marked a significant change in terms of federal and state relations. Unless there is a federal constitutional, treaty, or statutory provision, state law controls all transactions. Moreover, as discussed above, the decision reflected a major shift in jurisprudence away from a belief that courts simply apply preexisting objectively true natural law principles.

Issues in Applying *Erie*

Applying the *Erie* holding has posed many problems. Two issues have been of particular importance: Under what circumstances may federal courts apply federal procedural law, and how should a federal court determine the content of a state's law? Each of these issues has been considered in numerous Supreme Court decisions and has provoked a voluminous body of scholarly articles. Each is discussed in turn.

Erie held that state law is to be used by federal courts in deciding diversity cases. However, that does not mean that federal courts must apply state procedural rules. The Supreme Court long has recognized the need for uniform rules of procedure in federal courts.[170] The adoption of the Federal Rules of Civil Procedure in 1938—coincidentally the same year *Erie* was decided—reflected many choices about how cases should be conducted in federal court. Virtually all would agree that it would be extremely undesirable if the rules in federal court for matters such as service of process, pleading, joinder, and discovery varied in each case depending on the state's law to be applied.

Therefore, a simple principle emerges after *Erie*: Federal courts are to apply state substantive law and federal procedural law. The problem is that distinctions between substance and procedure are inherently ephemeral and thus difficult to draw. For example, is a statute of limitations or a rule concerning the burden of proof to be considered substantive or procedural? Ever since *Erie*, the Court has struggled to provide criteria to determine when federal law may be used in diversity cases.

[169] 304 U.S. at 90-92 (Reed, J., concurring).

[170] The ability of the federal government to prescribe procedural rules for federal court cases has been established since Wayman v. Southard, 23 U.S. (10 Wheat.) 1 (1825).

Test Summarized

Rather than present the cases in the chronological order in which they were decided, the current law can be best understood as involving a three-question inquiry.[171] If there is no conflict between state and federal law, both are to be applied. But if state and federal law are inconsistent, the following questions must be asked. First, is there a valid federal statute or federal rule of procedure on point, such as a provision of the Federal Rules of Civil Procedure or the Federal Rules of Appellate Procedure? If so, then the federal law is to be applied, even if there is conflicting state law. If there is no valid statute or rule of procedure, the second question is whether the application of the state law in question is likely to determine the outcome of the lawsuit. If the state law is not outcome determinative, then federal law is used. But if the state law is deemed to be outcome determinative, then the third question is asked: Is there an overriding federal interest justifying the application of federal law? If state law is outcome determinative and there is no countervailing federal interest, then state law controls. Otherwise, federal law is applied. In applying this test, federal courts are to be guided by the goals of the *Erie* doctrine, which are to prevent forum shopping and the inequitable administration of justice.

Is there a Valid Federal Law?

Each part of this three-part test warrants separate consideration. The first question is whether there is a valid federal statute or rule of procedure concerning the issue in question. The Rules of Decision Act requires that state law be applied only when there is not a federal statute or constitutional provision on point. As the Supreme Court declared, "Although state law generally supplies the rules of decision in federal diversity cases, . . . it does not control the resolution of issues governed by federal statute."[172] If there is a federal statute, then the only question is whether "the statute covers the point in dispute and whether the statute represents a valid exercise of Congress' authority under the Constitution."[173]

The Federal Rules of Civil Procedure and the Federal Rules of Appellate Procedure were adopted pursuant to authority created by a federal statute—the Rules Enabling Act.[174] Accordingly, it is now clearly established that the Federal Rules of Civil Procedure and the Federal Rules of Appellate Procedure are to be applied by the federal court, even if there is a conflicting state requirement and even if the application of the federal rule might determine the outcome of the case. The key decision establishing this proposition is *Hanna v. Plumer*.[175]

[171] The three-question inquiry presented here is loosely based on that suggested by John Hart Ely in his superb article on *Erie*. *See* Ely, *supra* note 166.

[172] Budinich v. Becton Dickinson & Co., 486 U.S. 196, 199 (1988) (federal statute determines appealability, not state law).

[173] Stewart Org., Inc. v. Ricoh Corp., 487 U.S. 22, 27 (1988) (federal statutes determine venue and thus application of forum selection clause in a contract).

[174] 28 U.S.C. §2072.

[175] 380 U.S. 460 (1965).

The issue in *Hanna,* decided in 1965, was whether service of process in a diversity case should be in accord with the Federal Rules of Civil Procedure or with state law. Federal and state law conflicted concerning the permissible manner of service of process, and it was undisputed that this issue was likely to determine the outcome of the lawsuit.

Chief Justice Warren, writing for the Court, observed that "[t]he broad command of *Erie* was therefore . . . [that] federal courts are to apply state substantive law and federal procedural law."[176] The Supreme Court held that a valid rule promulgated under the Rules Enabling Act is to be applied by the federal courts in diversity actions.[177] Chief Justice Warren wrote: "*Erie* and its offspring cast no doubt on the long-recognized power of Congress to prescribe housekeeping rules for federal courts even though some of those rules will inevitably differ from comparable state rules. . . . To hold that a Federal Rule of Civil Procedure must cease to function whenever it alters the mode of enforcing state-created rights would be to disembowel either the constitution's grant of power over federal procedure or Congress' attempt to exercise that power in the Enabling Act."[178]

In part, the Court justified its conclusion by relying on its earlier decision in *Sibbach v. Wilson & Co.*[179] In *Sibbach,* the issue was whether medical examinations could be required by a federal court pursuant to Rule 35 of the Federal Rules of Civil Procedure or whether the federal court should apply the state law, which prohibited such examinations. The Supreme Court held that Rule 35 was a valid exercise of power under the Rules Enabling Act and thus was to be applied by the federal court. Similarly, in *Hanna,* the Court concluded that the federal rule concerning service of process was to be applied because it is a valid exercise of authority under the Rules Enabling Act.

Thus, as long as the rule applies, and as long as it is a valid exercise of authority under the Rules Enabling Act, the rule must be followed by the federal court in a diversity case.[180] Although scholars have paid substantial attention to the Rules Enabling Act, there are no cases declaring any of the federal rules to be invalid as

[176] *Id.* at 465.

[177] 28 U.S.C. §2072, Act of June 19, 1934, ch. 651, 48 Stat. 1064. *See, e.g.,* Klocke v. Watson, 936 F.3d 240 (5th Cir. 2019); Royalty Network, Inc. v. Harris, 756 F.3d 1351 (11th Cir. 2014).

[178] 380 U.S. at 473-474.

[179] 312 U.S. 1 (1941). For a criticism of *Sibbach* on the grounds that federal rules should be deemed invalid if they control substantive matters, *see* Ely, *supra* note 166, at 718-738. For an excellent article criticizing *Hanna* and *Sibbach, see* Stephen B. Burbank, The Rules Enabling Act of 1934, 130 U. Pa. L. Rev. 1015 (1982).

[180] The Rules Enabling Act specifies that "[s]uch rules shall not abridge, enlarge or modify any substantive right and shall preserve the right of trial by jury as at common law and as declared by the Seventh Amendment to the Constitution." 28 U.S.C. §2072. Thus, a federal rule might be challenged as invalid as an impermissible substantive alteration of the law. This, again, would require analysis of the elusive substantive-procedure distinction. For an excellent description of the useful content of this analysis, *see* Ely, *supra* note 166, at 724-725 (defining rules as procedural if they are designed to improve the fairness or efficiency of the litigation process). However, in light of *Hanna*'s broad approval of the Federal Rules, there is a strong presumption that the Federal Rules are valid and should be applied when they are on point.

exceeding the authority of the Rules Enabling Act.[181] As such, it can be safely stated that where there is an applicable federal rule, it is to be applied by federal courts in diversity actions.[182]

The Court followed this principle in *Burlington Northern Railroad v. Woods.*[183] A state statute imposed fixed penalties on losing appellants who obtained stays of judgment pending appeals. The Supreme Court determined that this law conflicted with a rule of the Federal Rules of Appellate Procedure that provided for judicial discretion in assessing costs and penalties in such circumstances. The Court explained, "In *Hanna v. Plumer* we set forth the appropriate test for resolving conflicts between state law and the Federal Rules. The initial step is to determine whether, when fairly construed, the scope of [the Rule] . . . is 'sufficiently broad' to cause a 'direct collision' with the state law or, implicitly, to 'control the issue' before the court, thereby leaving no room for the operation of that law. The Rule must then be applied if it represents a valid exercise of Congress' rule-making authority."[184] Because the state law was found to conflict with a valid federal rule of appellate procedure, the federal rule was to be applied.

The key inquiry under this first question is whether a federal rule conflicts with state law. Sometimes that is quite unclear. For example, in *Walker v. Armco Steel Corp.*, a lawsuit was filed before the expiration of the statute of limitations, but service of process was not done until after the limitations period had expired.[185] Under Oklahoma law, an action is commenced by service of process. The question was whether Federal Rule of Civil Procedure 3, providing that a civil action is commenced with the filing of a complaint, conflicted with and therefore superseded state law. The Supreme Court held that the federal rule did not speak to the question of when an action commences for the purpose of a statute of limitations; thus, because there was no federal rule on point, state law was to be applied. The Court explained: "Since there is no direct conflict between the Federal Rule and the state law, the *Hanna* analysis does not apply."[186]

In *Semtek International v. Lockheed Martin Corp.*, the Court also considered the question of when there is federal law "on point" in deciding the appropriate law to apply in determining res judicata.[187] Semtek sued Lockheed in federal district court in California; jurisdiction was based on diversity of citizenship. The court dismissed the case based on California's two-year statute of limitations for such claims. Semtek then filed an identical claim in the Maryland state courts because

[181] Richard H. Fallon, Daniel J. Meltzer & David L. Shapiro, Hart & Wechsler's The Federal Courts and the Federal System 769 (7th ed. 2015) ("To date the Court has never squarely held a provision of the civil rules to be invalid on its face or as applied.").

[182] The Court has declared that "a Rule made law by Congress supersedes conflicting laws no less than a Rule this Court prescribes." Henderson v. United States, 517 U.S. 654, 668 (1996) (holding that the shorter time for service of process prescribed in Rule 4 of the Federal Rules of Civil Procedure supersedes the provision in the Suits in Admiralty Act, which required service "forthwith").

[183] 480 U.S. 1 (1987).

[184] *Id.* at 4. The rule involved was Rule 38, Federal Rules of Appellate Procedure.

[185] 446 U.S. 740 (1980).

[186] *Id.* at 752.

[187] 531 U.S. 497 (2001).

Maryland had a three-year statute of limitations. The Maryland courts held that the preclusive effect of the federal court's judgment was to be determined by federal law, not California state law, and that the action was precluded.

The Supreme Court unanimously reversed and held that the res judicata effect of a federal court decision in a diversity case is to be determined by state law. Justice Scalia, writing for the Court, looked to whether there is federal law on point. He noted that there is no federal rule of civil procedure concerning the question, nor does any federal constitutional or statutory provision address the issue. He wrote: "Neither the Full Faith and Credit Clause, U.S. Const. Art. IV, §1, nor the full faith and credit statute, 28 U.S.C. §1738, addresses the question. By their terms they govern the effects to be given only to state-court judgments. . . . And no other federal textual provision, neither of the Constitution nor of any statute, addresses the claim-preclusive effect of a judgment in a federal diversity action."[188]

Interestingly, finding no federal law on point, the Court then concluded that "federal common law governs the claim-preclusive effect of a dismissal by a federal court sitting in diversity. . . . It is left to us, then, to determine the appropriate federal rule." But the Court then said that the appropriate federal rule was to follow state law. Justice Scalia wrote, "[T]here is no conceivable federal interest in giving that time bar more effect in other courts than California courts would themselves impose." The Court remanded the case back to the Maryland courts to determine the preclusive effect of the earlier dismissal under California law.

Semtek is not strictly an *Erie* case because it involves what rule should be followed in a state court. Yet the Court's analysis of whether there was a federal law on point is identical to the first step in *Erie* analysis. Also, as with *Erie*, the case is very much about the choice between federal and state law. What makes the decision puzzling is the Court's choice to say it was relying on federal common law and then to hold that the federal common law rule is to follow state law. A more direct approach, which would have been more consistent with *Erie* analysis, would have been simply to hold that state law is to be used to decide the preclusive effect of a decision based on state law.

The Court's later decision concerning *Erie*, *Shady Grove Orthopedic Associates v. Allstate Insurance Co.*, also focused on the first part of the *Hanna* analysis and when a federal rule is controlling.[189] Shady Grove provided medical care to a patient and then submitted its claim for payment to Allstate Insurance Co. Under New York law, the company had 30 days to pay but did not do so within this time and also refused to pay interest, which was required by New York law. Shady Grove then filed a class action against Allstate in federal court, with jurisdiction based on diversity of citizenship, claiming that Allstate routinely refused to pay the interest required under New York law.

[188] Justice Scalia also noted that the only Supreme Court decision to address the issue, Dupasseur v. Rochereau, 88 U.S. (21 Wall.) 130 (1875), was based on interpretation of the Conformity Act, which required federal courts to apply the procedural rules of the states. This, of course, was replaced by the Federal Rules of Civil Procedure.

[189] 559 U.S. 393 (2010).

The federal district court said that the case could not go forward as a class action because New York law does not allow class actions to recover "penalties," and the unpaid interest was deemed a penalty. The question was which law should apply: Rule 23 of the Federal Rules of Civil Procedure, which allows for class actions in federal court, or the New York law, which would not allow class actions under these circumstances?

The Supreme Court, in a 5-4 decision, held that the federal court under *Erie* and *Hanna* should apply Rule 23 and allow the class action. Justice Scalia, writing for the majority, followed the framework described above and stated: "We must first determine whether Rule 23 answers the question in dispute. If it does, it governs—New York's law notwithstanding—unless it exceeds statutory authorization or Congress's rule-making power. We do not wade into *Erie*'s murky waters unless the federal rule is inapplicable or invalid."[190]

The Court concluded that Rule 23 applied in that it provided for a class action in diversity suits and its requirements were met. Justice Scalia wrote: "The question in dispute is whether Shady Grove's suit may proceed as a class action. Rule 23 provides an answer. It states that '[a] class action may be maintained' if two conditions are met: The suit must satisfy the criteria set forth in subdivision (a) (*i.e.*, numerosity, commonality, typicality, and adequacy of representation), and it also must fit into one of the three categories described in subdivision (b). By its terms this creates a categorical rule entitling a plaintiff whose suit meets the specified criteria to pursue his claim as a class action."[191]

Thus, as long as Rule 23 fits within the scope of the Rules Enabling Act, it was to be applied. As with every case since *Hanna*, the Court found that this requirement was met. Justice Scalia, in a part of the opinion joined by Chief Justice Roberts and Justices Thomas and Sotomayor, noted, "[W]e have rejected every statutory challenge to a Federal Rule that has come before us."[192] Likewise, Justice Scalia said that Rule 23, authorizing class actions, was permissible under the Rules Enabling Act. He wrote: "[W]e think it obvious that rules allowing multiple claims (and claims by or against multiple parties) to be litigated together are also valid. Such rules neither change plaintiffs' separate entitlements to relief nor abridge defendants' rights; they alter only how the claims are processed. For the same reason, Rule 23—at least insofar as it allows willing plaintiffs to join their separate claims against the same defendants in a class action—falls within §2072(b)'s authorization. A class action, no less than traditional joinder (of which it is a species), merely enables a federal court to adjudicate claims of multiple parties at once, instead of in separate suits. And like traditional joinder, it leaves the parties' legal rights and duties intact and the rules of decision unchanged."[193]

Justice Stevens concurred in the judgment and was the fifth vote to hold that Rule 23 applied. He concluded that Rule 23 is valid under the Rules Enabling Act and was controlling, but he recognized that there might be some instances in

[190] *Id.* at 398.
[191] *Id.*
[192] *Id.* at 407.
[193] *Id.* at 408.

which state procedural rules should be followed notwithstanding a Federal Rule of Civil Procedure. He wrote that "there are some state procedural rules that federal courts must apply in diversity cases because they function as a part of the State's definition of substantive rights and remedies."[194] For Justice Stevens, the analysis "turns on whether the state law actually is part of a State's framework of substantive rights or remedies."[195] Justice Stevens concluded that applying Rule 23 would not "abridge, enlarge, or modify New York's rights or remedies," and therefore Rule 23 should be applied.[196]

Justice Ginsburg wrote a dissent joined by Justices Kennedy, Breyer, and Alito. She would have interpreted New York law as not conflicting with Rule 23 and thus allowed the New York law to be applied without needing to go any further. At the outset of her dissent, she stressed that the Court should "interpret Federal Rules with awareness of, and sensitivity to, important state regulatory policies."[197] She said that "[s]ensibly read, Rule 23 governs procedural aspects of class litigation, but allows state law to control the size of a monetary award a class plaintiff may pursue. . . . In other words, Rule 23 describes a method of enforcing a claim for relief, while §901(b) defines the dimensions of the claim itself."[198]

In one sense, *Shady Grove* simply follows the law since *Hanna*: when there is a federal rule of civil procedure on point, it is followed in diversity cases. But in another sense, *Shady Grove* is important because it illustrates the difficulty of deciding when a federal rule of civil procedure is "on point." The majority saw Rule 23's authorization of class actions as controlling and preventing New York law from precluding a class action; the dissent saw New York as imposing a limit on damages and thus not being in conflict with the federal rule. Underlying the dispute are questions about the scope of the Rules Enabling Act and the role of federalism in making these determinations.[199]

Outcome Determinative Test

Thus, if there is a valid federal statute or rule *on point*, it is to be applied in diversity cases. If there is not a valid statute or federal rule, the second question is then asked: Is the application of state law likely to be determinative of the outcome of the lawsuit? The outcome determinative test was articulated by the Supreme Court in its first major post-*Erie* decision concerning choice of law, *Guaranty Trust Co. v. York*.[200]

[194] *Id.* at 416-17 (Stevens, J., concurring in part and concurring in the judgment in part).

[195] *Id.* at 419.

[196] *Id.* at 430.

[197] *Id.* at 437 (Ginsburg, J., dissenting).

[198] *Id.* at 447.

[199] *See* William H.J. Hubbard, An Empirical Study of the Effect of Shady Grove v. Allstate on Forum Shopping, 10 J.L. Econ & Poly. 151 (2013); Stephen B. Burbank & Tobias Barrington Wolff, Redeeming the Missed Opportunities of *Shady Grove*, 159 U. Pa. L. Rev. 17 (2010).

[200] 326 U.S. 99 (1945).

The issue in *Guaranty Trust* was whether the federal court should have applied a state statute of limitations, which would have barred the lawsuit, or whether it should have applied equitable principles, which would have permitted the action. Justice Frankfurter, writing for the Court, said that the distinction between substance and procedure was inadequate for deciding when state law was to be applied. Justice Frankfurter explained that "[m]atters of 'substance' and matters of 'procedure' are much talked about in the books as though they defined a great divide cutting across the whole domain of law. But, of course, 'substance' and 'procedure' are the same key words to very different problems. . . . Each implies different variables depending upon the particular problem for which it is used."[201]

Justice Frankfurter stated that instead of focusing on the substance-procedure distinction, a federal court should focus on whether the state law in question is likely to determine the outcome of the case. If so, state law should be applied. The Court concluded that the federal court should use the state statute of limitations because it was likely to determine the result in the litigation. The Court explained that "[a]s to consequences that so intimately affect recovery or non-recovery a federal court in a diversity case should follow State law."[202]

The problem with the outcome determinative test is that virtually any rule can determine the outcome of a case.[203] For many years after *Guaranty Trust*, the Court struggled to define and apply the outcome determinative test.

In *Palmer v. Hoffman*, the Supreme Court concluded that in diversity suits federal courts should apply state rules concerning burdens of proof because such rules often determine the results in the litigation.[204] In *Angel v. Bullington*, the Supreme Court held that the federal court had to apply a state law preventing a mortgage holder from suing to recover unpaid sums after foreclosure of the mortgage.[205] Although the state expressly characterized this rule as "procedural," the Supreme Court concluded that because it was outcome determinative, the state law precluding the suit was to be followed by the federal court.

In 1949, the Supreme Court handed down three decisions on the same day applying the outcome determinative test. In *Cohen v. Beneficial Industrial Loan Corp.*, the Court said that the federal court should apply a state law that made an unsuccessful plaintiff in a shareholder derivative suit liable for the costs of the defense.[206] Because the state law was likely to be outcome determinative, the Court said that it could not be dismissed as a "mere procedural device."[207]

In *Ragan v. Merchants Transfer & Warehouse Co.*, the Court held that the federal court should apply a state rule that the statute of limitations is not tolled until there is service of process, rather than the federal rule that the action commences

[201] *Id.* at 108.

[202] *Id.* at 110.

[203] *See, e.g.*, Henry M. Hart, The Relations Between State and Federal Law, 54 Colum. L. Rev. 489, 512 (1954).

[204] 318 U.S. 109 (1943).

[205] 330 U.S. 183 (1947).

[206] 337 U.S. 541 (1949).

[207] *Id.* at 556.

with the filing of the complaint.[208] Again, the Court emphasized the outcome determinative test and concluded that state law should govern. As described above, the Supreme Court reaffirmed this holding in the subsequent decision of *Walker v. Armco Steel Corp.*, concluding that the federal rule did not speak to the question of tolling the running of a statute of limitations.[209]

In *Woods v. Interstate Realty Co.*, the Court held that the federal court should dismiss a company's diversity suit. Under the state's law, the company was not allowed to sue in state court because it had not properly registered to do business in the state.[210] The Court emphasized that a contrary result would return to the pre-*Erie* situation where the result would vary depending on whether the case was brought in federal or state court.

After these decisions, there was great concern that the outcome determinative test articulated in *Guaranty Trust* and applied in *Cohen*, *Ragan*, and *Woods* ultimately would preclude the use of the Federal Rules of Civil Procedure in diversity cases because the rules certainly can determine the outcome of litigation.[211] However, *Hanna v. Plumer*, described above, resolved that concern and made it clear that a valid federal rule is to be applied by a federal court in a diversity action even if it is outcome determinative. *Hanna*, however, did not eliminate the use of the outcome determinative test but instead clarified its role. The outcome determinative test is used if there is no federal statute or rule on point. In the absence of federal law, if the state law is found to be not outcome determinative, then federal law is applied. In *Hanna*, the Court emphasized that federal courts applying the outcome determinative test should be guided by the underlying purposes of *Erie*: avoiding forum shopping and avoiding the unfairness that occurs when the result in a case depends on the citizenship of the litigants.[212]

Is There an Overriding Federal Interest?

However, if the state law is outcome determinative, then the third question is asked: whether an overriding federal interest justifies application of federal law, even though state law is outcome determinative. The seminal case here is *Byrd v. Blue Ridge Rural Electric Cooperative, Inc.*[213] The issue was whether a person had a right to a jury trial in a diversity case in federal court where federal law accorded a jury trial, but state law permitted only a bench trial. The Supreme Court recognized that the availability of a jury trial could be outcome determinative. The Court stated: "It may well be that in the instant personal injury case the outcome would be substantially affected by whether the issue of immunity is decided by a

[208] 337 U.S. 530 (1949).

[209] 446 U.S. 740 (1980); *see* discussion accompanying notes 185-186, *supra*.

[210] 337 U.S. 535, 538 (1949).

[211] *See, e.g.*, Charles E. Clark, The *Tompkins* Case and the Federal Rules, 1 F.R.D. 417 (1940); Charles E. Clark, State Law in the Federal Courts: The Brooding Omnipresence of Erie v. Tompkins, 55 Yale L.J. 267 (1946).

[212] Hanna v. Plumer, 380 U.S. 460 (1965).

[213] 356 U.S. 525 (1958).

judge or a jury. Therefore, were 'outcome' the only consideration, a strong case might appear for saying that the federal court should follow state practice."[214]

The Court concluded that a jury trial should be provided because of the overriding federal interest in complying with the Seventh Amendment's assurance of jury trial in civil cases. The Court wrote: "But there are affirmative countervailing considerations at work here. The federal system is an independent system for administering justice to litigants who properly invoke its jurisdiction. An essential characteristic of that system is the manner in which, in civil common-law actions, it distributes trial functions between judge and jury, and under the influence—if not the command—of the Seventh Amendment, assigns the decisions of disputed questions of fact to the jury."[215] Thus, the Court held that even where state law is outcome determinative, federal law should be applied where there is an important, overriding federal interest.

An interesting case concerning the relationship of the Seventh Amendment and state law was *Gasperini v. Center for Humanities, Inc.*[216] The plaintiff, a photographer, sued in federal court based on diversity jurisdiction to recover for the defendant's loss of transparencies of pictures taken in Central America. The jury awarded the plaintiff $450,000, and the district court judge, without explanation, denied the defendant's motion to set aside the verdict as excessive.

New York law provides that appellate courts may set aside a jury's verdict when it "deviates materially from what would be reasonable compensation."[217] The U.S. Court of Appeals for the Second Circuit applies this law to reduce the jury award to $150,000. The plaintiff objected, however, and argued to the Supreme Court that this violated the Seventh Amendment, which states that "no fact tried by a jury shall be otherwise reexamined in any Court of the United States, than according to the rules of the common law."

The U.S. Supreme Court, in an opinion written by Justice Ruth Bader Ginsburg, held that under *Erie*, state law should govern the amount of damages recoverable in federal court in a diversity action. Justice Ginsburg explained that if New York had a statutory cap on damages, federal courts would be obliged to follow it. New York's preclusion of damages that "deviate materially from what would be reasonable compensation" is a cap that procedurally operates on a case-by-case basis. Justice Ginsburg stated that federal courts must follow such state law because *Erie* "precludes a recovery in federal court significantly larger than the recovery that would have been tolerated in state court."[218] In other words, state law must be followed in determining damages because the choice of law is "outcome determinative."

The Court then considered whether the Seventh Amendment's limit of appellate review precluded the application of New York law. The Court noted that the New York standard was to be applied both by trial courts in reviewing jury awards and by courts of appeals. The Court said that application of the New York test by

[214] *Id.* at 537.
[215] *Id.*
[216] 518 U.S. 415 (1996).
[217] N.Y. Civ. Prac. Law & Rules, §5501(c).
[218] 518 U.S. at 416.

a trial court would not violate the Seventh Amendment, but that a federal court of appeals was limited to determining whether the district court's ruling was an abuse of discretion. The Court thus remanded the case to the district court for application of the New York standard concerning jury verdicts, and review in the U.S. Court of Appeals would then be confined to whether the district court abused its discretion in upholding or modifying the jury's verdict.

There appears to be a tension between the Court's holdings in *Byrd* and in *Gasperini.* As Justice Scalia argued in dissent, *Byrd* provides that federal law governs the relationship between judges and juries in diversity cases because of the overriding importance of the Seventh Amendment.[219] *Gasperini* says that state law limits on damages must be followed in federal court and govern review of damage awards, especially in the district court. On the other hand, *Gasperini* can be seen as a classic application of the *Erie* rule: state law limiting damages is to be applied because it is outcome determinative and it is to be followed to the extent that it is consistent with the Seventh Amendment.

The Court has done little in the years since *Byrd* to clarify what types of federal interests are sufficient to override the application of state law. In *Byrd* and in *Gasperini,* there was a constitutional interest involved—the Seventh Amendment right to jury trials in civil cases.[220] It is not clear what other interests justify the application of federal law instead of outcome determinative state legal principles. However, as mentioned before, the Supreme Court has emphasized that in deciding whether to apply state law, federal courts should be guided by the twin purposes of *Erie*: preventing forum shopping and avoiding the inequities that occur when results depend on the citizenship of the parties.[221]

Thus, if there is a conflict between federal and state law in deciding whether to apply state or federal law, a three-step inquiry is used. First, is there a valid federal statute or rule of civil or appellate procedure on point? If so, the federal law is to be applied by the federal court deciding a diversity action. If there is not a valid, on-point federal law, the second inquiry is whether the application of the state law is likely to determine the outcome of the litigation. If state law is not outcome determinative, then federal law is applied. But once it is concluded that state law is likely to determine the results, then the third question is whether there is an overriding federal interest. If so, then federal law controls; otherwise, the state law that is outcome determinative is applied. Of course, at each step there are unanswered questions, and federal courts possess discretion to decide what constitutes

[219] *Id.* at 465 (Scalia, J., dissenting); *see also* Douglas Floyd, *Erie* Awry: A Comment on Gasperini v. Center for Humanities, Inc., 1997 BYU L. Rev. 267.

[220] Hanna v. Plumer, 380 U.S. 460 (1965).

[221] For cases applying the *Byrd* balancing test, *see, e.g.,* In re Orange County, 784 F.3d 520 (9th Cir. 2015) (holding that federal law applies to pre-dispute jury trial waivers in diversity actions); G-I Holdings, Inc. v. Reliance Ins. Co., 586 F.3d 247 (3d Cir. 2009) (ruling that federal judicial estoppel rules apply in diversity cases); Shropshire v. Laidlaw Transit, Inc., 550 F.3d 570 (6th Cir. 2008) (holding that federal law overruled a state law about judge-jury division of responsibility); Alternative Systems Concepts, Inc. v. Synopsys, Inc., 374 F.3d 23 (1st Cir. 2004) (holding that federal judicial estoppel rules apply).

an on-point federal law in a particular case, when a state law is outcome determinative, and what federal interests outweigh the need to use state law.

How Is State Law Determined?

The second major problem posed by *Erie* concerns how a federal court is to decide the content of a state's law. A state's highest court is the authoritative interpreter of a state's law. Thus, if the state's highest court has a decision on point, federal courts must apply it because *Erie* holds that federal courts are to apply state common law principles. But what if a federal court is confronted with a state law question on which the state's highest court has not yet ruled?

The law is now settled that a federal court must try to predict how the state's highest court is likely to decide the case; the federal court is not obligated to follow lower state court precedents. At first, the Supreme Court took a contrary approach and required federal courts to follow whatever state law was in existence. *Fidelity Union Trust Co. v. Field,* decided in 1940, reflected the high point of Supreme Court deference to lower state courts.[222] In a diversity case, there was an issue concerning the permissibility of a certain type of trust agreement. There were no state supreme court or even court of appeals decisions on point; the law consisted of two opinions written by state trial court judges. The U.S. Court of Appeals held that these decisions did not have to be followed by the federal court, but the Supreme Court reversed.

Not surprisingly, the *Field* decision was sharply criticized. U.S. Court of Appeals Judge Jerome Frank wrote that federal judges were now "to play the role of ventriloquist's dummy to the courts of some particular state."[223] But in the face of substantial criticism, the Court has backed away from the approach it took in *Field.* In *King v. Order of United Commercial Travelers,* the Supreme Court held that the federal court was not obligated to follow unreported decisions of a lower state court.[224] The Court said that "[i]t would be incongruous indeed to hold the federal court bound by a decision which would not be binding on any state court."[225]

In *Bernhardt v. Polygraphic Co. of America,* the question was whether the federal court was obligated to apply a state court decision deeming certain arbitration agreements to be unenforceable.[226] Although the Court ruled that state law should be applied, it emphasized the existence of a clear, on-point decision of the state's supreme court. The Court explained that "there appears to be no confusion in the Vermont decisions, no developing line of authorities that casts a shadow over the established ones, no dicta, doubts or ambiguities in the opinions of Vermont judges on the question, no legislative development that promises to undermine the judicial rule."[227]

[222] 311 U.S. 169 (1940).
[223] Richardson v. C.I.R., 126 F.2d 562, 567 (2d Cir. 1942).
[224] 333 U.S. 153 (1948).
[225] *Id.* at 161.
[226] 350 U.S. 198 (1956).
[227] *Id.* at 205.

The current law is best stated in *Commissioner of Internal Revenue v. Bosch*, where the Court declared: "[T]he State's highest court is the best authority on its own law. If there be no decision by that court then federal authorities must apply what they find to be the state law after giving 'proper regard' to relevant rulings of other courts of the State. In this respect, it may be said to be, in effect, sitting as a state court."[228] In other words, a federal court in a diversity case is to apply the law the state's highest court likely would apply. The federal court should consider lower state court decisions, but is not bound to apply and follow them if the federal court believes that they would not be affirmed by that state's highest court. The federal court may consider all available material in deciding what law would be followed by a state.[229]

In fact, the Supreme Court has held that a federal court in a diversity action should follow the conflicts of law principles that it believes the state court would apply. In *Klaxon Co. v. Stentor Electric Manufacturing Co.*, the question was whether New York or Delaware law should be applied.[230] The Supreme Court held that the federal court should use the same choice of law principles that the state court in that state would use. The Court said that "[i]t is not for the federal courts to thwart . . . local policies by enforcing an independent 'general law' of conflicts of laws."[231] In several decisions, the Supreme Court has reaffirmed *Klaxon*'s holding that federal courts in diversity actions should determine the conflict of law principles likely to be applied by the forum state's highest court and follow the same law that would be applied there.[232]

Many have criticized the *Klaxon* rule, contending that there should be uniform conflicts of law principles applied by federal courts.[233] They argue, in part, that *Klaxon* has the effect of encouraging forum shopping among federal courts, as parties will seek the court where the state conflict of law principles will lead to the application of the most favorable law. But it now appears settled, for conflicts of law as well as all topics, that a federal court should apply the same legal principles that it believes that the state's highest court would follow.

The Court has held that when there is a transfer of venue pursuant to 28 U.S.C. §1404(a), the court to which the matter is transferred must apply the choice of law rules that would have been followed in the initial court. In *Van Dusen v. Barrack*, the Court held that when the defendant successfully moves for a change of venue under §1404(a), the transferee court must apply the choice of law rule that would

[228] 387 U.S. 456, 465 (1967).

[229] Except in rare circumstances, federal courts may not abstain in diversity cases because of unclear state law. Meredith v. City of Winter Haven, 320 U.S. 228 (1943). *See* §12.2, *infra*.

[230] 313 U.S. 487 (1941).

[231] *Id.* at 496.

[232] *See, e.g.,* Day & Zimmerman, Inc. v. Challoner, 423 U.S. 3 (1975); Bernhardt v. Polygraphic Co. of Am., 350 U.S. 198 (1956); Griffin v. McCoach, 313 U.S. 498 (1941).

[233] *See, e.g.,* Patrick J. Borchers, The Origins of Diversity Jurisdiction, the Rise of Legal Positivism, and a Brave New World for *Erie* and *Klaxon*, 72 Tex. L. Rev. 79 (1993); William F. Baxter, Choice of Law and the Federal System, 16 Stan. L. Rev. 1, 22-42 (1963); Alfred Hill, The *Erie* Doctrine and the Constitution, 53 Nw. U. L. Rev. 427, 561 (1958).

have been followed in the transferor court.[234] In *Ferens v. John Deere Co.*, the Court held that the same rule applies when it is the plaintiff that requests a transfer of venue.[235] The Court explained that the central goal of *Erie* was preventing forum shopping and that "[a]n opportunity for forum shopping exists whenever a party has a choice of forums that will apply different laws."[236]

Issues concerning the *Erie* doctrine will exist as long as there is diversity jurisdiction. Indeed, even if diversity jurisdiction is abolished, there still will be the need for federal courts to decide state law questions such as when there are supplemental state law claims. There are simply too many conflicting values, such as the desire to have uniform federal procedural rules but still follow state substantive law, and too many inherently difficult questions, such as the problem of having a federal court apply state law where none exists, for *Erie* issues ever to be completely resolved.

§5.4 SUPPLEMENTAL JURISDICTION

Need for Supplemental Jurisdiction

Many cases that are properly within a federal court's jurisdiction include issues or claims against parties that would not independently meet the requirements for federal jurisdiction. For example, a plaintiff with a federal claim might also have a state law cause of action arising from the same facts. Another common example is that in a diversity case a defendant might wish to implead a third-party defendant who is not diverse to the plaintiff, thus seemingly destroying complete diversity.

It is extremely desirable for federal courts to have the authority to decide the entire case, including the matters that are not part of federal jurisdiction. Judicial economy is served by having a matter litigated in one court rather than in two or more tribunals. The splitting of lawsuits increases costs to the parties, wastes social resources, and risks inconsistent verdicts from the different courts. Additionally, allowing all aspects of a case to be tried in federal court preserves the attractiveness of the federal forum for litigants. If the entire case could be tried in state court, but only part of it could be litigated in federal court, then parties would have a strong incentive to eschew the federal forum.

The constitutional basis for such jurisdiction stems from Article III's authorization for federal courts to decide "cases" and "controversies." A case or controversy is said

[234] 376 U.S. 612 (1964). *See* Robert A. Ragazzo, Transfer and Choice of Federal Law: The Appellate Model, 93 Mich. L. Rev. 703 (1995) (arguing that *Van Dusen* should apply to cases permanently transferred, but not to those transferred by the Judicial Panel on Multidistrict Litigation, which only provides for handling of pretrial proceedings).

[235] 494 U.S. 516 (1990).

[236] *Id.* at 527.

to refer to a single set of facts. A case or controversy includes all claims arising from a set of facts, and thus a federal court may decide the entire matter, even though only part of it meets the requirements for federal court jurisdiction. The Supreme Court first approved of the constitutionality of such supplemental jurisdiction in an opinion by Chief Justice John Marshall, in which he stated: "[W]hen a question to which the judicial power of the Union is extended by the constitution, forms an ingredient of the original cause, it is in the power of Congress to give the Circuit Courts jurisdiction of that cause, although other questions of fact or of law may be involved in it."[1]

Until 1990, there was no express statutory authority for federal courts to hear such additional claims and issues. Rather, the judicially created doctrines of ancillary and pendent jurisdiction were the basis for federal court authority. Although the terms "ancillary and pendent jurisdiction" have been replaced by the new statutory provision for supplemental jurisdiction, the earlier decisions concerning ancillary and pendent jurisdiction continue to be quite important.

Ancillary and Pendent Jurisdiction Defined

Ancillary jurisdiction referred to the authority of a federal court to hear claims that otherwise would not be within federal jurisdiction because the claims arise from the same set of facts as a case properly before the federal court.[2] A simple example of ancillary jurisdiction is that a defendant in a diversity suit may present a compulsory counterclaim against the plaintiff, even though the counterclaim is for less than the jurisdictional amount. The plaintiff properly invokes federal jurisdiction—there is diversity of citizenship, and the plaintiff alleges more than $75,000 as the amount in controversy. The defendant could not independently bring his or her claim to federal court; however, because it arises from the same facts as the plaintiff's claim, ancillary jurisdiction exists.

The seminal case concerning ancillary jurisdiction was *Freeman v. Howe.*[3] In *Freeman,* a federal official seized certain property pursuant to a federal court action. Others, who were not diverse to the defendant, had claims for the seized property. The Supreme Court held that the third parties could intervene and present their claims in federal court, even though there was no separate basis for federal court jurisdiction. The Court explained that the third parties' suit was "not an original suit, but ancillary and dependent, supplementary merely to the original suit, out of which it had arisen."[4]

After *Freeman,* the Court expanded the concept of ancillary jurisdiction to permit individuals to intervene, even though their presence eliminated complete

§5.4 [1] Osborn v. Bank of the United States, 22 U.S. (9 Wheat.) 738, 823 (1824).

[2] The Court has emphasized that ancillary jurisdiction only exists if there is a case properly before the federal court. *See* Kokkonen v. Guardian Life Insurance Company of America, 511 U.S. 375 (1994) (once a case is dismissed from federal court pursuant to a settlement, the federal court cannot exercise ancillary jurisdiction to enforce the settlement; ancillary jurisdiction requires that there be a case properly before the federal court).

[3] 65 U.S. (24 How.) 450 (1860).

[4] *Id.* at 460.

diversity, because intervention "did not oust the jurisdiction of the court, already lawfully acquired, as between the original parties."[5] Similarly, in *Moore v. New York Cotton Exchange,* the Supreme Court upheld federal court jurisdiction over the defendant's counterclaim because it arose from the same set of facts as the plaintiff's claims, even though there was no independent basis for federal court jurisdiction.[6]

In other words, under ancillary jurisdiction, federal courts were allowed to hear claims that arise from a common nucleus of operative fact—or as it is sometimes phrased, from the same transaction or occurrence—even though there was no other basis for federal jurisdiction. For example, federal courts could exercise ancillary jurisdiction over a defendant's counterclaim arising from the same set of facts, even if the counterclaim is based on state law and fails to meet the amount in controversy.[7] Similarly, ancillary jurisdiction existed when a defendant impleads a third-party defendant, even though the defendant's claims against the third party do not fulfill the requirements for federal court jurisdiction.[8] Ancillary jurisdiction existed when there was intervention as of right, but not for permissive intervention.[9] Generally, ancillary jurisdiction existed for cross-claims, such as for claims between co-plaintiffs or codefendants.[10]

Pendent jurisdiction was one specific type of ancillary jurisdiction. A federal court plaintiff presenting a federal question also may litigate state law claims that arise from the same facts as the federal law claim. For example, if a city police officer beats someone, the injured individual might bring a federal court suit for damages under 42 U.S.C. §1983, and, at the same time, seek recovery under state law for the tort of battery. Assuming a lack of diversity of citizenship, the state law claim would not independently justify federal court jurisdiction. However, because it arises from the same set of facts as the federal law claim, the federal court may exercise pendent jurisdiction over the state law matter.

As such, pendent jurisdiction was best understood as a particular, especially important type of ancillary jurisdiction. Some have suggested another distinction between pendent and ancillary jurisdiction. Pendent jurisdiction can be thought of as claims contained in the *plaintiff's complaint* for which there are not independent bases for federal court jurisdiction. In contrast, ancillary jurisdiction can be understood as claims that are asserted *after the filing of the original complaint* that do not independently meet the requirements for federal court jurisdiction.[11]

[5] Stewart v. Dunham, 115 U.S. 61, 64 (1885).

[6] 270 U.S. 593 (1926).

[7] Under the Federal Rules of Civil Procedure, a counterclaim arising from the same set of facts is termed a "compulsory counterclaim," whereas a counterclaim arising from a different set of facts is termed a "permissive counterclaim." *See* Rule 13, Federal Rules of Civil Procedure. By definition, ancillary jurisdiction exists only for compulsory counterclaims.

[8] *See* Charles Alan Wright, Law of Federal Courts 37 (5th ed. 1994).

[9] *Id.*

[10] *Id.*

[11] *See* Corporacion Venezolana De Fometo v. Vintero Sales Corp., 477 F. Supp. 615, 622 n.13 (S.D.N.Y. 1979). For discussions of ancillary and pendent jurisdiction, *see* Richard D. Freer, A Principled Statutory Approach to Supplemental Jurisdiction, 1987 Duke L.J. 34; Arthur R. Miller, Ancillary and Pendent Jurisdiction, 26 S. Tex. L.J. 1 (1985).

The seminal case concerning pendent jurisdiction was *Siler v. Louisville & Nashville Railroad.*[12] In *Siler,* a state agency's regulation of railroad rates was challenged both as violating the U.S. Constitution and as exceeding the agency's authority under state law. The federal court lacked independent jurisdiction over the latter claim because the agency's authority under state law did not present a federal question and there was no diversity of citizenship. Nonetheless, the Supreme Court upheld the authority of the federal court to decide the state law claim. The Court explained: "The Federal questions, as to the invalidity of the state statute because, as alleged, it was in violation of the Federal Constitution, gave the Circuit Court jurisdiction, and, having properly obtained it, that court had the right to decide all the questions in the case, even though it decided the Federal questions adversely to the party raising them, or even if it omitted to decide them at all, but decided the case on local or state questions only."[13]

In other words, a federal court may decide a state law claim arising from the same set of facts as a federal question regardless of whether the court decides the federal claim or even if the plaintiff loses the federal claim. In fact, the Supreme Court has said that because federal courts should avoid unnecessary constitutional rulings, federal courts generally should decide pendent state law claims before reaching the federal constitutional issues.[14]

In *Hurn v. Oursler,* in 1933, the Supreme Court first attempted to formulate a test for determining the existence of pendent jurisdiction.[15] In *Hurn,* the plaintiffs sued in federal court to enjoin the performance of a play. The plaintiffs presented a federal claim under the federal copyright laws, claiming that the play infringed a copyright that they had on another play. The plaintiffs also presented a state law claim for unfair competition through the unauthorized use of the copyrighted play. Additionally, the plaintiffs sought recovery for unfair competition for alleged improper use of a noncopyrighted version of their play.

The Supreme Court held that the unfair competition claim arising from the use of the copyrighted material was properly within the federal court's pendent jurisdiction, but that pendent jurisdiction did not exist for the unfair competition claim for use of the noncopyrighted play. The Court reasoned that the alleged improper use of copyrighted materials presented a single cause of action and that both a federal copyright claim and a state law claim arising from it could be litigated in federal court. However, since the suit to recover for the use of the play that was not copyrighted was deemed to present a separate cause of action, the Court denied pendent jurisdiction. In other words, under *Hurn,* a federal court could hear a pendent state law claim if the state law claim formed a separate but parallel ground for relief as the claim based on federal law.

[12] 213 U.S. 175 (1909).

[13] *Id.* at 191.

[14] *See* Schmidt v. Oakland Unified School Dist., 457 U.S. 594 (1982); Hagans v. Lavine, 415 U.S. 528 (1974); *see also* §12.2 (discussing policy of avoiding unnecessary constitutional rulings).

[15] 289 U.S. 238 (1933).

United Mine Workers v. Gibbs Test for Pendent Jurisdiction

Not surprisingly, lower courts struggled to apply the *Hurn* test. The Court offered little guidance for deciding whether a state law claim was part of a cause of action, and therefore was within pendent jurisdiction, or whether it was a separate cause of action. In *United Mine Workers v. Gibbs*, the Supreme Court noted the "considerable confusion" engendered by *Hurn* and completely reformulated the test for pendent jurisdiction.[16]

Gibbs grew out of a dispute between two unions—the United Mine Workers and the Southern Labor Union—that were competing to represent mine workers in the southern Appalachian coalfields. United Mine Workers represented workers at the Tennessee Consolidated Coal Company. Consolidated laid off 100 workers as a result of closing a mine. Soon after the layoff, a wholly owned subsidiary company hired Gibbs as a mine superintendent, awarded him a contract for shipping the coal, and attempted to open a new mine on Consolidated's property using Southern Labor Union members. Allegedly, members of the United Mine Workers threatened Gibbs and prevented the opening of the new mine. Gibbs lost his job as a mine superintendent and other contracts in the area. Gibbs sued the United Mine Workers in federal court, alleging both a violation of a federal labor statute and a state law cause of action based on tortious interference with contracts.

The Supreme Court upheld the existence of pendent jurisdiction and replaced the *Hurn* test with a much simpler approach.[17] The Supreme Court explained: "Pendent jurisdiction, in the sense of judicial *power*, exists whenever there is a claim arising under [federal law] . . . and the relationship between that claim and the state claim permits the conclusion that the entire action before the court comprises but one constitutional 'case.' The federal claim must have substance sufficient to confer subject matter jurisdiction on the court. The state and federal claims must derive from a common nucleus of operative fact."[18] In other words, pendent jurisdiction may be exercised when there is a federal claim properly before a federal court and a state claim arises from a common nucleus of operative fact.

The Court went further and explained that federal courts need not exercise pendent jurisdiction in all instances where it is allowed. The Court stated that "pendent jurisdiction is a doctrine of discretion, not of plaintiff's right. Its justification lies in considerations of judicial economy, convenience, and fairness to litigants; if these are not present a federal court should hesitate to exercise jurisdiction over state claims."[19] The Court suggested as an example of the discretionary nature of pendent jurisdiction that a federal court should dismiss pendent state law claims if the federal claims are dismissed before trial or if "state issues substantially predominate."[20]

[16] 383 U.S. 715, 724 (1966).

[17] The Court, however, reversed the lower court based on the Norris-LaGuardia Act, 29 U.S.C. §106, which limits liability of unions and their officers for the actions of individual members.

[18] 383 U.S. at 725 (emphasis in original).

[19] *Id.* at 726.

[20] *Id.*

Statutory Authority for Supplemental Jurisdiction

The Judicial Improvements Act of 1990 provided the first statutory authority for ancillary and pendent jurisdiction, created the new concept of "supplemental jurisdiction," which encompasses both ancillary and pendent jurisdiction, and changed several aspects of the law.[21] The act, as now codified in 28 U.S.C. §1367, provides that, subject to stated exceptions:

> [I]n any civil action of which the district courts have original jurisdiction, the district courts shall have supplemental jurisdiction over all other claims that are so related to claims in the action within such original jurisdiction that they form part of the same case or controversy under Article III of the United States Constitution. Such supplemental jurisdiction shall include claims that involve the joinder or intervention of additional parties.

This statutory provision changes the preexisting law in that it seems to make supplemental jurisdiction mandatory not discretionary.[22] The court, however, has observed that the "supplemental jurisdiction statute codifies [the] principles" from *Gibbs* and other cases decided before the enactment of §1367.[23]

Exception to Preserve the Rule of Complete Diversity

One exception provided for in the statute is designed to preserve the rule of complete diversity. Specifically, the law prohibits supplemental jurisdiction over persons made parties or seeking to be made parties under Federal Rules of Civil Procedure 14, 19, 20, or 24 "when exercising jurisdiction over such claims would be inconsistent with the jurisdictional requirements of section 1332."[24]

This provision was intended to preserve the Supreme Court's ruling in *Owen Equipment & Erection Co. v. Kroger*, which held that a plaintiff, suing in federal court based on diversity, may not assert claims against nondiverse third-party defendants.[25] An Iowa resident was electrocuted at work when a crane he was working

[21] Pub. L. No. 101-650, 104 Stat. 5089. For a comprehensive analysis of §1367 and its implications, *see* Denis F. McLaughlin, Federal Supplemental Jurisdiction: A Constitutional and Statutory Analysis, 24 Arizona St. L.J. 849 (1992); John B. Oakley, Recent Statutory Changes in the Law of Federal Jurisdiction and Venue: The Judicial Improvements Acts of 1988 and 1990, 24 U.C. Davis L. Rev. 735 (1991).

[22] For example, the Supreme Court ruled that a federal court could review a state administrative decision, using the deferential state law standard of review, if there also was a federal question that provided a basis for removal. City of Chicago v. International College of Surgeons, 522 U.S. 156 (1997). The Court stated, "The whole point of supplemental jurisdiction is to allow the district courts to exercise pendent jurisdiction over claims as to which original jurisdiction is lacking." *Id.* at 170.

[23] City of Chicago v. International College of Surgeons, 522 U.S. at 172-173.

[24] 28 U.S.C. §1367(b).

[25] 437 U.S. 365 (1978). Some commentators are very critical of the act's preservation of supplemental jurisdiction. *See, e.g.,* Richard D. Freer, Compounding Confusion and Hampering Diversity: Life After *Finley* and the Supplemental Jurisdiction Statute, 40 Emory L.J. 445, 469-470, 475-476 (1991). For a scholarly debate over supplemental jurisdiction and §1367, *see, e.g.,* Robert G. Bone, Revisiting the

on touched a power line. His estate sued a Nebraska company, the Omaha Public Power District, in federal court based on diversity of citizenship, claiming that its negligence caused the death. The Power District impleaded the deceased's employer, the Owen Equipment & Erection Co. (Owen Co.), and alleged that the employer's negligence was responsible for the action. The plaintiff then filed an amended complaint naming Owen Co. as an additional defendant. The complaint alleged diversity of citizenship on the ground that Owen Co. was a Nebraska corporation with its principal place of business in Nebraska. The defendant's answer admitted the jurisdictional allegations in the plaintiff's complaint.

The court granted summary judgment in favor of the Power District, thus leaving for trial the claim of the estate against the employer. On the third day of trial it was disclosed that the Owen Co.'s principal place of business was in Iowa and not Nebraska. The defendant moved to dismiss for lack of subject matter jurisdiction because of the absence of complete diversity. The court denied the motion because there was ancillary jurisdiction over the plaintiff's claim against the third-party defendant. Judgment was entered for the plaintiff and affirmed by the court of appeals.

The Supreme Court reversed and held that ancillary jurisdiction was not permissible. The specific issue before the Court was quite narrow: whether ancillary jurisdiction permitted a federal court to hear a claim against a nondiverse third-party defendant *when the diverse defendant was dismissed from the suit.* However, the Court stated the question as being much broader. At the beginning of his opinion for the Court, Justice Stewart wrote: "In an action in which federal jurisdiction is based on diversity of citizenship, may the plaintiff assert a claim against a third-party defendant when there is no independent basis for federal jurisdiction over that claim?"[26] Furthermore, the Court's conclusion was that ancillary jurisdiction does not exist for a plaintiff's claim against nondiverse third-party defendants; the Court did not limit this ruling to instances where the diverse defendant was dismissed from the action.

The Court reasoned that to allow a plaintiff to bring a claim against a nondiverse third-party defendant would circumvent the rule requiring complete diversity. The Court stated: "But neither the convenience of litigants nor considerations of judicial economy can suffice to justify extension of the doctrine of ancillary jurisdiction to a plaintiff's cause of action against a citizen of the same State in a diversity case. Congress has established the basic rule that diversity jurisdiction exists under 28 U.S.C. §1332 only when there is complete diversity of citizenship. . . . To allow the requirement of complete diversity to be circumvented as it was in this case would simply flout the congressional command."[27] The problem with this holding is the weight that it gives to preserving the requirement for

Policy Case for Supplemental Jurisdiction, 74 Ind. L.J. 139 (1998); Edward H. Cooper, An Alternative and Discretionary §1367, 74 Ind. L.J. 153 (1998); Howard P. Fink, Supplemental Jurisdiction! Take It to the Limit, 74 Ind. L.J. 161 (1998).

[26] 437 U.S. at 367.

[27] *Id.* at 377. For a discussion of *Kroger, see* John B. Oakley, *Kroger* Redux, 51 Duke L.J. 663 (2001); Edward A. Hartnett, Would the *Kroger* Rule Survive the ALI's Proposed Revision of 1367?, 51 Duke L.J. 647 (2001).

complete diversity. As explained in §5.3.3, this longstanding requirement is dubious in its origin and justification. Yet §1367 clearly preserves the *Owen* rule and its protection of the requirement for complete diversity.

Exceptions to Supplemental Jurisdiction

One exception in §1367 is designed to preserve the rule of complete diversity; the other exception codifies the situations under *Gibbs* where federal courts could choose not to exercise pendent jurisdiction.[28] Specifically, the statute provides:

> The district courts may decline to exercise supplemental jurisdiction over a claim under subsection (a) if:
> (1) the claim raises a novel or complex issue of state law;
> (2) the claim substantially predominates over the claim or claims over which the district court has original jurisdiction;
> (3) the district court has dismissed all claims over which it has original jurisdiction;
> (4) in exceptional circumstances, where there are other compelling reasons for declining jurisdiction.

Courts applying this provision follow the same reasoning as under the *Gibbs* test. For example, if federal claims are dismissed at an early stage in the proceedings, the federal court declines to adjudicate the remaining state claims.[29] Likewise, federal courts, pursuant to the new statutory provision, decline to exercise supplemental jurisdiction if state claims predominate.[30] The Supreme Court recently has explained that this provision "reflects the understanding that, when deciding whether to exercise supplemental jurisdiction, a federal court should consider and weigh in each case, and at every stage in the litigation, the values of judicial economy, convenience, fairness, and comity."[31]

Section 1367 does not, of course, change a constitutional limit on supplemental jurisdiction created by the Supreme Court: a federal court may not hear pendent state law claims against a state government officer who has been sued for

[28] In 1988, in *Carnegie-Mellon Univ. v. Cohill*, the Supreme Court held, however, that the presumption in favor of pendent jurisdiction is not absolute and that federal courts possess discretion under *Gibbs* to decline pendent jurisdiction when there are substantial reasons for doing so. Section 1367 continues this in its specifically stated exceptions.

[29] *See, e.g.*, Zubrod v. Hoch, 907 F.3d 568 (8th Cir. 2018); Dietchweiler by Dietchweiler v. Lucas, 827 F.3d 622 (7th Cir. 2016); Glaziers and Glassworkers Union Local 252 Annuity Fund v. Newbridge Securities, Inc., 823 F. Supp. 1191 (E.D. Pa. 1993) (dismissing state claims because federal claims were dismissed early in the proceedings).

[30] *See, e.g.*, Ameritox, Ltd. v. Millennium Laboratories, Inc., 803 F.3d 518, 537 n.28 (11th Cir. 2015); Oneida Indian Nation of New York v. Madison County, 665 F.3d 408 (2d Cir. 2011); James v. Sun Glass Hut, Inc., 799 F. Supp. 1083 (D. Colo. 1992).

[31] City of Chicago v. International College of Surgeons, 522 U.S. at 173. Prior to this statement by the Supreme Court, federal courts of appeals had split as to whether §1367 codified or changed the *Gibbs* standard. For a description of this split among the circuits, *see* Itar-Tass Russian News Agency v. Russian Kurier, Inc., 140 F.3d 442, 446-447 (2d Cir. 1998).

violating federal law. In *Pennhurst State School & Hospital v. Halderman,* the Supreme Court held that the Eleventh Amendment, which bars suits against state governments in federal court, precludes pendent state law claims against state government officers.[32] *Pennhurst* is discussed in detail in §7.5.

Section 1367 does not specify whether the entire case or only the state law claims are to be remanded when supplemental jurisdiction is not exercised. However, lower federal courts are in agreement that the federal court should retain jurisdiction over the federal claims that are properly before it.[33] This seems clearly correct because a party should not lose federal court jurisdiction over matters properly before the federal court because of the presence of other claims.

Pendent Party Jurisdiction

One of the most important changes in the law as a result of the 1990 act is the specific allowance of pendent party jurisdiction. Pendent party jurisdiction is the authority of the federal court to hear claims against additional parties, over which it would not otherwise have jurisdiction, because those claims arise from a common nucleus of operative facts. For example, if a plaintiff presents a federal question and another possible plaintiff presents a state law claim arising from the same set of facts, may the federal court entertain the latter suit? Or if a plaintiff brings a federal claim against one defendant and a state law claim, arising from the same set of facts, against a second defendant, may the federal court entertain the second claim? These types of situations have been termed "pendent party jurisdiction."[34]

The 1990 act was specifically intended to overrule *Finley v. United States,* where the Supreme Court held that pendent party jurisdiction is not permitted without specific statutory authorization.[35] In *Finley,* the plaintiff was a woman whose husband and children died when an airplane struck electric power lines. Initially, the plaintiff filed suit in state court against the San Diego Gas and Electric Company for negligently maintaining the lights on the airport runway. Subsequently, the plaintiff learned that the Federal Aviation Administration (FAA) was responsible for the runway lights. The plaintiff then sued the FAA in federal court under the Federal Tort Claims Act. She sought to amend her federal court complaint to include as a defendant the utility company against whom she only had state law claims. In other words, *Finley* presented a classic case of pendent party jurisdiction: an attempt to invoke federal court jurisdiction over an additional party (over whom there is no independent basis for federal court jurisdiction) because the claim arises from the same facts as a federal question properly before the federal court.

The Supreme Court, in a 5-4 decision, held that pendent party jurisdiction is not permissible unless there is an express statutory authorization for it. The Court

[32] 465 U.S. 89 (1984).

[33] *See* Lloyd v. Benton, 686 F.3d 1225 (11th Cir. 2012); Poche v. Texas Air Corps, Inc., 549 F.3d 999 (5th Cir. 2008); Baker v. Kingsley, 387 F.3d 649 (7th Cir. 2004).

[34] For a discussion of pendent party jurisdiction, *see* David P. Currie, Pendent Parties, 45 U. Chi. L. Rev. 753 (1978).

[35] 490 U.S. 545 (1989).

concluded that nothing in the Federal Tort Claims Act authorizes jurisdiction over pendent parties. The Court distinguished pendent claim jurisdiction, which it reaffirmed as permissible, from what it viewed as the "much more radical" concept of pendent party jurisdiction.[36]

The Federal Courts Study Committee proposed overruling *Finley* to allow pendent party jurisdiction. Congress adopted this recommendation, and §1367(a) expressly provides that "supplemental jurisdiction shall include claims that involve the joinder or intervention of additional parties." Lower courts have followed this and now allow pendent party jurisdiction under the statutory authorization for supplemental jurisdiction.[37]

The change to allow pendent party jurisdiction is a desirable one. The purpose of supplemental jurisdiction is to permit a case—one common nucleus of operative facts—to be tried in a single court. Pendent party jurisdiction facilitates this goal. Moreover, pendent jurisdiction exists to preserve the attractiveness of the federal forum. Pendent party jurisdiction accomplishes this goal because without pendent party jurisdiction a plaintiff with claims against two defendants—one defendant to be sued based on federal law and the other on state law—either would have to sue in two different courts or else forgo the federal forum.[38]

It should be noted, however, that the Court generally has rejected the concept of pendent appellate jurisdiction; that is, federal courts of appeals do not have the authority to hear appeals by additional parties that otherwise would not be properly before them on the grounds that the issues arise from the same facts as matters appropriately within their jurisdiction. In *Swint v. Chambers County Commission*, plaintiffs sued a local government and its officials after police raids on a nightclub.[39] The district court denied the individual defendant's motion to have the suit against them dismissed based on qualified immunity, and the defendants exercised their right to an interlocutory appeal of this order. The local government defendants were not entitled to interlocutory appeal and sought review in the Court of Appeals based on pendent appellate jurisdiction. The U.S. Court of Appeals for the Eleventh Circuit granted review on this basis and issued summary judgment in the defendants' favor.

The Supreme Court reversed. The Court observed that the there was no final judgment against the municipal governments and that none of the exceptions to the final judgment rule applied.[40] The Court noted that the federal district

[36] *Id.* at 555. The Court relied, in part, on Aldinger v. Howard, 427 U.S. 1 (1976), where the Court refused to allow a pendent party claim against a county at a time when §1983 was interpreted to prevent suits against local governments.

[37] *See, e.g.*, PTA-FLA, Inc. v. ZTE USA Inc., 844 F.3d 1299 (11th Cir. 2016); Allstate Interiors & Exteriors, Inc. v. Stonestreet Constr. LLC, 730 F.3d 67 (1st Cir. 2013); Godfrey v. Perkin-Elmer Corp., 794 F. Supp. 1179 (D.N.H. 1992); American Pfauter, Ltd. v. Freeman Decorating Co., 772 F. Supp. 1071 (N.D. Ill. 1991).

[38] As discussed above in §5.3, Exxon Mobil Corp. v. Allapattah Services, Inc., 545 U.S. 546 (2005), the Court held that only one plaintiff in a diversity action, including a class action, need meet the amount in controversy requirement.

[39] 514 U.S. 35 (1995).

[40] The final judgment rule and its exceptions are discussed in §10.4.

court had indicated that it would reconsider these defendants' summary judgment motion before the case was submitted to the jury. The Supreme Court expressly rejected the concept of pendent appellate jurisdiction. The notion of pendent party jurisdiction contained in §1367 authorizes the federal courts to hear claims against additional parties, but it does not override the final judgment rule and provide a basis for federal courts of appeals to hear matters that otherwise would not be appropriate for appellate review.

Tolling Provision

Finally, §1367 provides that if the federal court dismisses a claim, the statute of limitations will be deemed tolled during the time the action was pending in federal court and "for a period of 30 days after it is dismissed unless State law provides for a longer tolling provision."[41] This provision preserves the ability of parties to proceed in state court if the federal court does not exercise supplemental jurisdiction.

In *Raygor v. Regents of the University of Minnesota*,[42] the question presented was whether this tolling provision is constitutional when the claims are against a state government. Lance Raygor and James Goodchild sued the University of Minnesota in federal court for age discrimination. They alleged a violation of the federal Age Discrimination in Employment Act,[43] and of state antidiscrimination laws. In January 2000, while their case was pending, the Supreme Court decided *Kimel v. Florida Board of Regents*[44] and held that state governments cannot be sued for violations of the Age Discrimination in Employment Act without their consent.

The federal district court then exercised its discretion under §1367 to dismiss Raygor's and Goodchild's suit because only state law claims remained. Raygor and Goodchild filed suit in state court under them, but the state moved to dismiss, contending that the statute of limitations had expired in the meantime. Raygor and Goodchild pointed to §1367(d), which tolled the statute of limitations while the claims were pending in federal court. The Minnesota Supreme Court, however, declared this provision unconstitutional, concluding that Congress constitutionally could not toll the statute of limitations on state claims in state court.

The Supreme Court, in a 6-3 decision, affirmed. Justice Sandra Day O'Connor wrote for the Court and emphasized that "with respect to suits against a state sovereign in its own courts, . . . a state may prescribe the terms and conditions on which it may be sued." Justice O'Connor said that §1367(d) does not clearly state that it was meant to apply to claims against state governments. She therefore concluded that to avoid serious constitutional questions, the Court would interpret it to not apply to state claims filed against a state government in state court.[45]

[41] 28 U.S.C. §1367(d).

[42] 534 U.S. 533 (2002).

[43] 29 U.S.C. §621 et seq.

[44] 528 U.S. 62 (2000). *Kimel* is discussed in detail in §7.7.

[45] In Artis v. District of Columbia, 583 U.S. 71 (2018), the Court held "that §1367(d)'s instruction to 'toll' a state limitations period means to hold it in abeyance, i.e., to stop the clock." This generally makes it easier for plaintiffs to file in state court should their federal court challenges fail.

From a practical perspective, this case is very troubling in terms of the choices it will pose for litigants. A lawyer having both federal and state law claims will have several options, none desirable. One approach would be to file both the federal and state claims in state court and forgo federal court entirely. This, of course, undermines the availability of federal courts and is especially undesirable in areas where the federal court is perceived as more hospitable to civil rights claims than the state court. Another possibility would be to file suit in both federal and state court, or at least to file in state court right before the statute of limitations on the state courts is about to run. This is certainly permissible, but the problem is that whichever court decides first, federal or state, will completely preclude the other from deciding the matter. Res judicata, claim preclusion, will apply once one court renders a decision.[46]

Conclusion

Overall, §1367 provides a statutory basis for the judicially created doctrines of pendent and ancillary jurisdiction, simplifies vocabulary by providing the new label "supplemental jurisdiction" to replace the often confusing definitions of ancillary and pendent jurisdiction, and clarifies the availability of such jurisdiction. Although the new provision has its critics, it is generally regarded as a positive change in the law.[47]

§5.5 REMOVAL JURISDICTION

Authority for Removal Jurisdiction

Thus far, this chapter has focused primarily on how plaintiffs may invoke federal court jurisdiction based on diversity of citizenship or a federal question, as well as supplemental claims that may be brought in cases properly before a federal court. Additionally, defendants may invoke federal court jurisdiction by removing

[46] In Jinks v. Richland County, S.C., 538 U.S. 456 (2003), the Supreme Court held that §1367(d) applies to local governments and that it ensures that plaintiffs with both federal and state claims can take advantage of the federal forum.

[47] There has been a heated scholarly exchange as to the desirability of §1367. *See* Richard D. Freer, Compounding Confusion and Hampering Diversity: Life After *Finley* and the Supplemental Jurisdiction Statute, 40 Emory L.J. 445 (1991); Thomas D. Rowe, Stephen Burbank & Thomas Mengler, Compounding or Creating Confusion About Supplemental Jurisdiction: A Reply to Professor Freer, 40 Emory L.J. 943 (1991); Thomas C. Arthur & Richard D. Freer, Grasping at Burnt Straws: The Disaster of the Supplemental Jurisdiction Statute, 40 Emory L.J. 963 (1991); Thomas D. Rowe, Stephen Burbank & Thomas Mengler, A Coda on Supplemental Jurisdiction, 40 Emory L.J. 993 (1991); Thomas C. Arthur & Richard D. Freer, Close Enough for Government Work: What Happens When Congress Doesn't Do Its Job, 40 Emory L.J. 1007 (1991).

a case from state to federal court. Although removal jurisdiction is not expressly mentioned in Article III, statutes have authorized removal ever since the Judiciary Act of 1789.[1] The constitutionality of removal jurisdiction was established long ago.[2] Article III defines the matters that federal courts may hear, but it is silent as to the procedures that may be used to initiate federal court jurisdiction. Accordingly, the Supreme Court always has permitted Congress to define such procedures, such as the availability of removal jurisdiction.

The existence of removal jurisdiction reflects the belief that both the plaintiff and the defendant should have the opportunity to benefit from the availability of a federal forum. For example, if a plaintiff sues in his or her home state court, removal by the defendant to a federal court effectuates a primary purpose of diversity jurisdiction in providing a seemingly more neutral forum.

The primary statutory provision authorizing removal jurisdiction is 28 U.S.C. §1441.[3] This section focuses on three questions concerning removal under §1441: When is removal allowed under §1441; what is the procedure followed when a case is removed; and what, if anything, can a plaintiff do to prevent removal?[4]

Removal Only if Case Could Have Been Filed in Federal Court

First, defendants generally may remove a case from state to federal court if the plaintiff could have brought the matter to federal court. Section 1441(a) provides: "Except as otherwise expressly provided by Act of Congress, any civil action brought in a State court of which the district courts of the United States have original jurisdiction, may be removed by the defendant or the defendants, to the district court of the United States for the district and division embracing the place where such action is pending." Many separate requirements are contained in this provision.

The statute makes it plain that defendants may remove a case to federal court only if the suit initially could have been filed in federal court. Thus, generally, the plaintiff's complaint must present either a federal question or diversity of

§5.5 [1] Ch. 29, 21 Stat. 73, 79-80.

[2] Tennessee v. Davis, 100 U.S. (10 Otto) 257 (1879); Railway Co. v. Whitton's Admr., 80 U.S. (13 Wall.) 270 (1871).

[3] Other removal statutes include provisions allowing federal officers to remove suits against them from state to federal court, 28 U.S.C. §1442, and permitting removal of certain civil rights cases from state to federal court, 28 U.S.C. §1443. Both of these provisions are different from §1441 in that they allow removal of civil or criminal actions. The Civil Rights Removal Act is discussed in detail in §11.5, *infra*.

[4] Section 1441 is not the only statutory provision providing for removal of cases from state to federal court. For example, §1442 provides for removal of cases by federal officers sued as defendants in state courts. *See* Mesa v. California, 489 U.S. 121 (1989) (federal officers can remove a case to federal court only if they are asserting a federal law defense). Section 1442 was amended to authorize removal by the United States and federal agencies, as well as by federal officers. §1442(a)(1). Federal Courts Improvement Act of 1996, Pub. L. No. 104-317, §206, 110 Stat. 3847. This provision overrules International Primate Protection League v. Administrators of Tulane Educ. Fund, 500 U.S. 72 (1991), which held that statutory authorization for removal of cases by federal officers does not allow removal by federal agencies.

citizenship must exist for a case to be removed to federal court under §1441(a). For example, a federal law defense is insufficient by itself to permit removal because of the well-pleaded complaint rule requiring that the federal question be on the face of the complaint for federal jurisdiction to exist.[5]

In *Rivet v. Regions Bank of Louisiana,* the Supreme Court held that a federal court cannot exercise removal jurisdiction solely to enforce an earlier federal court ruling if the case then pending in state court could not have been brought in federal court.[6] A case was brought in state court involving mortgage rights in real property. The defendant sought to remove the case based on the ground that the plaintiffs' state litigation was barred by a prior federal bankruptcy judgment. The Supreme Court held that removal was inappropriate because the state court action did not meet the requirements for federal court jurisdiction, and thus it was not a case that properly could have been initiated in federal court.

Only Defendant May Remove and Only from State to Federal Court

Section 1441(a) also clearly states that only a defendant may remove a case from state to federal court. A plaintiff may never remove the case to federal court after filing suit in state court. This principle was announced by the Court in *Shamrock Oil & Gas Corp. v. Sheets.*[7] In *Shamrock Oil,* the Court held that a plaintiff could not remove a case to federal court in response to a counterclaim filed by a defendant. The Court focused primarily on the language of the removal statute and its lack of authorization for removal by plaintiffs. The Court stated: "We can find no basis for saying that Congress, by omitting from the present statute all reference to 'plaintiffs,' intended to save a right of removal to some plaintiffs and not to others."[8] The rationale for not allowing plaintiffs to remove the case to federal court is that the plaintiffs chose the state forum and thus implicitly waived their right of access to a federal court.

Also, the statute provides only for removal of cases from state to federal court. No provision permits the removal of a case properly before a federal court to a state court. Thus, removal jurisdiction reflects the policy that federal court jurisdiction should be available to either party where it properly can be invoked.

[5] *See, e.g.,* Louisville & Nashville R.R. v. Mottley, 211 U.S. 149 (1908); *see* §5.2.3, *supra* (discussing the well-pleaded complaint rule).

[6] 522 U.S. 470 (1998).

[7] 313 U.S. 100 (1941). In Home Depot U.S.A., Inc. v. Jackson, 587 U.S. 435 (2019), the Court held that a third-party counterclaim defendant cannot remove a suit from state to federal court because it is not a "defendant" under the removal statutes. This is a party brought into a lawsuit by the defendant who is asserting a counter-claim against the plaintiff. The Court held that the removal statute, §1441(a), permits removal only by defendants. The Court concluded that the Class Action Fairness Doctrine did not change this.

[8] 313 U.S. at 108.

Limits on Removal in Diversity Cases

There are, however, several important exceptions to the availability of removal jurisdiction. First, removal of a diversity case from state to federal court is not permitted if any of the defendants are residents of the state where the action was filed. Section 1441(b) specifically provides that federal question cases are removable without regard to citizenship of the parties, but diversity cases "shall be removable only if none of the parties in interest properly joined and served as defendants is a citizen of the State in which such action is brought." The exception reflects the belief that diversity jurisdiction is unnecessary because there is less reason to fear state court prejudice against the defendants if one or more of them is from the forum state.

If the plaintiff voluntarily dismisses the resident defendants from the suit, then the nonresident defendants may remove the case, but if the state court dismisses the resident defendants over the plaintiff's objection, the case may not be removed.[9] The rationale for this distinction is unclear. Professors Friedenthal, Kane, and Miller explain that it "serve[s] the purpose of preventing removal when the resident defendant's dismissal has not been determined finally in the state courts, and may be reversed on appeal. A voluntary dismissal is final, and there can be no doubt that original federal jurisdiction over the remaining parties exists."[10]

Another limitation on removal is where there are specific statutory provisions prohibiting removal. For example, 28 U.S.C. §1445 provides that workers' compensation cases in state courts under state workers' compensation laws may not be removed to federal court.[11]Also, §1445 states that certain claims against railroads and common carriers, primarily workers' compensation claims, may not be removed.[12]

In *Syngenta Crop Protection, Inc. v. Henson,*[13] the Supreme Court held that removal must be pursuant to the removal statutes and cannot be based on the All Writs Act.[14] Lawsuits were simultaneously filed in a dispute in both federal and state courts. The federal court litigation was settled, and a hearing was held in state court as to whether that lawsuit should be dismissed. One of the parties misrepresented to the state court that only some of the claims had been settled. The state court decided to allow the litigation before it to proceed.

[9] Jack H. Friedenthal, Mary Kay Kane & Arthur R. Miller, Civil Procedure 59-60 (2d ed. 1993) (citing Powers v. Chesapeake & Ohio Ry., 169 U.S. 92 (1898)); Southern Ry. v. Lloyd, 239 U.S. 496 (1916); Knudson v. Systems Painters, Inc., 634 F.3d 968 (8th Cir. 2011); Pretka v. Kolter City Plaza II, Inc., 608 F.3d 744, 761 n.17 (11th Cir. 2010).

[10] Friedenthal et al., *supra* note 9, at 60.

[11] 28 U.S.C. §1445(c). This provision was based especially on the fact that the "workload of the federal courts has greatly increased because of the removal of workmen's compensation cases from the State courts." S. Rep. No. 1830, 85th Cong., 2d Sess., *reprinted in* 1958 U.S. Code Cong. & Admin. News 3099, 3105.

[12] 28 U.S.C. §1445(a), (b) (primarily cases under the Federal Employees' Liability Act and the Jones Act).

[13] 537 U.S. 28 (2002).

[14] 28 U.S.C. §1651.

The other side, upon learning of this, attempted to remove the state court action to federal court pursuant to the All Writs Act. The U.S. Court of Appeals for the Fifth Circuit upheld this, but the Supreme Court unanimously reversed and held that the All Writs Act did not provide a basis for removal jurisdiction; all removal must be pursuant to the removal statutes.

Removable Claim Linked with Nonremovable Claim

There is also the question, addressed in a statutory revision, concerning whether removal is permissible when removable claims are joined with nonremovable ones. Section 1441(c) directly addresses this issue: "Whenever a separate and independent claim or cause of action, within the jurisdiction conferred by section 1331 of this title is joined with one or more otherwise nonremovable claims or causes of action, the entire case may be removed and the district court may determine all issues therein, or, in its discretion, may remand all matters in which state law predominates." In part, this section serves to prevent state court plaintiffs from attempting to frustrate removal by trying to join separate claims against nondiverse defendants.

Also, §1441(c) serves the same values as supplemental jurisdiction: It allows an entire case to be tried in one forum.[15] If there are claims properly before a federal court, it is more efficient to allow other claims not within federal jurisdiction to be tried at the same time. Section 1441(c) also serves to preserve the attractiveness of the federal forum. If the defendant could remove only part of a case to federal court but would still have to try the remainder in state court, there would be a strong disincentive to invoking federal jurisdiction. As is true with regard to pendent jurisdiction, under §1441(c), a federal court has discretion to decide whether it will hear the removed claims that would not independently fit within its jurisdiction.

There are two important limits within §1441(c). The provision, as amended in 1990, applies only in federal question cases; it no longer applies in diversity litigation.[16] Also, the 1990 revision permits remand only as to matters in which "State law predominates."

Section 1441(c) provides for removal if there is "a separate and independent claim." The most important decision construing this phrase is *American Fire & Casualty Co. v. Finn.*[17] Although *Finn* is a diversity case and diversity cases no longer are covered by §1441(c), *Finn* remains important in understanding the phrase "separate and independent claim." The plaintiff, a Texas citizen, sued two insurance companies—one from Florida and one from Indiana—to recover on a fire insurance policy. The plaintiff also sued an insurance agent who was a Texas resident. The plaintiff argued that the insurance companies were liable to him, but

[15] For a discussion of the relationship between §1441(c) and §1367, the supplemental removal statute, *see* Joan Steinman, Supplemental Jurisdiction in §1441 Removal Cases: An Unsurveyed Frontier of Congress' Handiwork, 35 Ariz. L. Rev. 305 (1993).

[16] Judicial Improvements Act of 1990, Pub. L. No. 101-650, 104 Stat. 5089.

[17] 341 U.S. 6 (1951).

if not, it was because the agent was negligent in obtaining a policy, and thus the agent was liable.

The insurance company defendants removed the case from state to federal court based on §1441(c). They argued that a separate and independent claim against them was joined with a nonremovable claim against a nondiverse defendant. Hence, the defendants contended that under §1441(c) the entire case could be removed to federal court.

The Supreme Court held that removal was not proper under §1441(c) because there was no "separate and independent" claim that was removable. The Court concluded that there was one claim to recover for losses suffered in the fire, and thus the presence of a nondiverse defendant precluded removal. The Court explained: "The single wrong for which relief is sought is the failure to pay compensation for the loss on the property. Liability lay among three parties, but it was uncertain which one was responsible. Therefore, all were joined as defendants in one petition."[18]

The Supreme Court offered guidance to lower courts applying §1441(c). The Court stated that "where there is a single wrong to plaintiff, for which relief is sought, arising from an interlocked series of transactions, there is no separate and independent claim or cause of action under §1441(c)."[19]

Procedures for Removal

The second major topic concerning removal involves the procedures followed when there is removal. Section 1446 provides that removal can be accomplished by filing a notice of removal in federal court. The notice is to be filed in the federal court for the district in which the state court action is pending. The notice of removal must set forth the facts supporting the existence of federal jurisdiction that would entitle the defendant to remove the case to federal court. Also, the notice of removal must be accompanied by all pleadings and orders that have been filed in the state court proceeding. Once the petition is filed in federal court, the state court is divested of jurisdiction over the case. The federal court can take whatever action is needed to effectuate its jurisdiction, including, if necessary, enjoining further state court proceedings.[20]

A defendant must file the notice of removal within thirty days after being served with the plaintiff's complaint.[21] If a pleading, motion, or order makes it possible to remove a case that otherwise was not removable—for example, if the state court plaintiff dismisses claims against nondiverse defendants—the notice of removal must be filed within 30 days of receipt of the particular document.[22]

[18] *Id.* at 14.

[19] *Id.*

[20] One of the exceptions to the Anti-Injunction Act specifically permits injunctions to effectuate federal court jurisdiction. 28 U.S.C. §2283. The Anti-Injunction Act and this exception are discussed in §11.2, *infra.*

[21] 28 U.S.C. §1446(b).

[22] *Id.*

However, a defendant will be deemed to waive removal if he or she engages in substantial defensive action in the state court during these 30 days, such as by filing a motion to dismiss or engaging in discovery.[23] The rationale for this waiver rule is that a defendant should not be able to try part of the case in state court and then, perhaps after some unfavorable rulings, seek a new forum. If there are multiple defendants, all must request removal or the case remains in state court.[24]

After removal, a party can object to federal court jurisdiction by making a motion to remand the case to state court. Although customarily the plaintiff would file the motion to remand, any party—including the one who removed the case—can object to federal court jurisdiction. For example, in the *Finn* case, described above, jurisdiction was challenged by one of the defendants who had removed the case to federal court. Section 1447(c) states that "[i]f at any time before final judgment it appears that the case was removed improvidently and without jurisdiction, the district court shall remand the case, and may order the payment of just costs." A federal court may remand only on the ground that it lacks subject matter jurisdiction; it may not remand simply because of an overcrowded docket.[25]

The Supreme Court has held that remand orders by a district court are not subject to appellate review.[26] *Things Remembered, Inc. v. Petraca* was removed by the defendants from state court to federal bankruptcy court.[27] The federal district court, reviewing the bankruptcy court's decision, found that the case was not properly removed under either §1441 or §1452(a), which provides for removal of cases to bankruptcy court. The district court remanded the case to state court, and the defendants sought appellate review of this order. The U.S. Supreme Court found that §1447(d) expressly "precludes appellate review of any order 'remanding a case to the State court from which it was removed.'"[28]

How Plaintiffs Can Prevent Removal

The final major topic concerning removal involves the steps that a plaintiff can take to prevent removal. A plaintiff who wishes to keep a matter in state court can preclude removal by ensuring that no federal questions are presented in the complaint or, if it is potentially a diversity action, that nondiverse defendants are included in the suit. A plaintiff is the master of his or her lawsuit and can prevent removal, for example, by choosing not to pursue federal claims that are potentially

[23] Friedenthal et al., *supra* note 9, at 63.

[24] *See, e.g.,* Chicago, R.I. & P. Ry. v. Martin, 178 U.S. 245 (1900).

[25] *See* Thermtron Prods., Inc. v. Hermansdorfer, 423 U.S. 336, 351-352 (1976). The Court in *Thermtron* said that §1441(d) precludes appeal of remand orders pursuant to §1441(c) but not other remand orders.

[26] For a criticism of this rule, *see* Rhonda Wasserman, Rethinking Review of Remands: Proposed Amendments to the Federal Removal Statute, 43 Emory L.J. 83 (1994); Michael E. Solimine, Removal, Remands, and Reforming Federal Appellate Review, 58 Mo. L. Rev. 287 (1993).

[27] 516 U.S. 124 (1995).

[28] *Id.* at 127.

available. However, if the plaintiff presents a federal question, then an attempt to hide it by artful pleading will not prevent removal.[29]

After a case is properly removed to federal court, the plaintiff can attempt to frustrate federal court jurisdiction by dismissing the part of the suit that permitted federal jurisdiction to be invoked.[30] However, generally such actions after removal are insufficient to justify a remand to state court. In *St. Paul Mercury Indemnity Co. v. Red Cab Co.*, after a defendant removed a diversity case to federal court, the plaintiff amended the complaint to allege less than the jurisdictional amount.[31] The Supreme Court held that remand to state court under such circumstances was inappropriate. The Court said that "events occurring subsequent to removal which reduce the amount recoverable . . . do not oust the district court's [diversity] jurisdiction."[32]

However, the Supreme Court has said that in federal question cases, if a plaintiff dismisses the federal claims after removal, the federal court has discretion as to whether to retain or remand the state law claims. In the decision of *Carnegie-Mellon University v. Cohill*, the Supreme Court upheld a district court's remand to state court after the plaintiff dismissed all of the federal claims in the case.[33] A plaintiff sued in state court for violations of the federal age discrimination statute and for recovery under several state law causes of action. After the defendant properly removed the case to federal court, the plaintiff then dismissed the federal law claim and requested that the case be remanded to state court. The federal district court granted the motion to remand and the Supreme Court upheld this decision as being a permissible exercise of discretion. The Court stated: "We conclude that a district court has discretion to remand to state court a removed case involving pendent claims upon a proper determination that retaining jurisdiction over the case would be inappropriate. The discretion to remand enables district courts to deal with cases involving pendent claims in the manner that best serves the principles of economy, convenience, fairness, and comity which underlie the pendent jurisdiction doctrine."[34]

This holding makes sense in light of the doctrine of pendent jurisdiction. On the one hand, as the dissent emphasized, the Court's decision in *Cohill* has the undesirable effect of permitting a plaintiff to frustrate a defendant's right to

[29] *See, e.g.,* Federated Dept. Stores v. Moitie, 452 U.S. 394, 397 n.2 (1981).

[30] In January 2025, in Royal Canin U.S.A., Inc. v. Wullschleger, 604 U.S. 22 (2025), the Supreme Court unanimously held that federal court jurisdiction is defeated if a case is removed from state court to federal court and the plaintiff amends the complaint to dismiss all of the federal claims. The Court stated: "What happens if, after removal, the plaintiff amends her complaint to delete all the federal-law claims, leaving nothing but state-law claims behind? May the federal court still adjudicate the now purely state-law suit? We hold that it may not. When an amendment excises the federal-law claims that enabled removal, the federal court loses its supplemental jurisdiction over the related state-law claims. The case must therefore return to state court." *Id.* at 25-26.

[31] 303 U.S. 283 (1938).

[32] *Id.* at 293.

[33] 484 U.S. 343 (1988).

[34] *Id.* at 357.

remove a case to federal court.[35] Under the removal statute, if a case is properly removed, the case is within federal jurisdiction and subsequent events do not eliminate jurisdiction. On the other hand, an opposite ruling in *Cohill* would have had the effect of forcing federal courts to try cases presenting only state law claims in situations where pendent jurisdiction is inappropriate.[36]

Interestingly, the Supreme Court has held that even if a federal court improperly exercises removal jurisdiction, its judgment should be upheld if jurisdiction properly existed at the time of the judgment. In *Caterpillar v. Lewis,* a federal district clearly erred in exercising jurisdiction because there was not complete diversity at the time of removal.[37] However, by the time of the judgment, the nondiverse party had settled and complete diversity existed. Nonetheless, application of the traditional rule that jurisdiction is determined at the time the case comes to federal court would justify overturning the judgment. The U.S. Supreme Court disagreed and, emphasizing the inefficiency of having the case tried all over again, concluded that the judgment should stand as long as jurisdiction properly existed at the time of judgment, even though it did not exist at the time of removal. The Court said that "[o]nce a diversity case has been tried in federal court . . . considerations of finality, efficiency, and economy become overwhelming."[38]

[35] *Id.* at 362 (White, J., dissenting).

[36] In 1998, the Supreme Court ruled that if some claims are nonremovable because they are barred by the Eleventh Amendment, the case can be removed, with the precluded claims remanded to state court. Wisconsin Department of Corrections v. Schacht, 524 U.S. 381 (1998).

[37] 519 U.S. 61 (1996).

[38] *Id.* at 76. As discussed in §5.3, Grupo Dataflux v. Atlas Global Group, L.P., 541 U.S. 567 (2004), the Court held that if diversity jurisdiction is not proper when the case is filed, a subsequent change in state residency by a party does not validate jurisdiction and allow the judgment to be upheld.

CHAPTER 6

Federal Common Law

§6.1 INTRODUCTION

The phrase "federal common law" refers to the development of legally binding federal law by the federal courts in the absence of directly controlling constitutional or statutory provisions. Professor Martha Field explains that " 'federal common law' . . . refer[s] to any rule of federal law created by a court . . . when the substance of that rule is not clearly suggested by federal enactments—constitutional or congressional."[1]

Presumption Against Federal Common Law

There long has been a strong presumption against the federal courts fashioning common law to decide cases. The Rules of Decision Act, which was part of the Judiciary Act of 1789 and remains largely unchanged to this day, states that "the laws of the several states, except where the Constitution or treaties of the United States or Acts of Congress otherwise require or provide, shall be regarded as rules of decisions in civil actions in the courts of the United States, in cases where they apply."[2] This law, by its very terms, seems to deny the existence of federal common law; the Rules of Decision Act commands that in the absence of positive federal law, federal courts must apply state law.[3]

Early in American history, the Supreme Court refused requests to create a federal common law of crimes. In *United States v. Hudson & Goodwin*, the Court held that federal trial courts lacked the authority to punish common law crimes against the United States.[4] The Court emphasized that both separation of powers and federalism considerations prevented the federal judiciary from creating such common law. In terms of separation of powers, the Court explained that federal courts possess only the authority Congress confers on them.[5] Because no statutory basis existed for creating a common law for criminal prosecutions, the Court could not do so. Additionally, the Court emphasized that creating such common

§6.1 [1] Martha A. Field, Sources of Law: The Scope of Federal Common Law, 99 Harv. L. Rev. 881, 890 (1986) (emphasis omitted); *see also* Thomas W. Merrill, The Common Law Powers of Federal Courts, 52 U. Chi. L. Rev. 1, 5 (1985) ("'Federal common law' . . . means any federal rule of decision that is not mandated on the face of some authoritative federal text—whether or not that rule can be described as the product of 'interpretation' in either a conventional or an unconventional sense."). Professor Caleb Nelson wrote: "In modern parlance, the phrase 'federal common law' has become an umbrella term for many different types of unwritten law, regardless of their sources. Thus, what we currently call 'federal common law' might include (1) traditional principles of common law, admiralty, or equity jurisprudence; (2) rules that reflect customary practices of other sorts; (3) rules that reflect common themes in the written laws of the fifty states; (4) rules that the federal courts have developed in light of the purposes behind specific federal statutes; and (5) rules that federal judges simply make up out of whole cloth." Caleb Nelson, The Legitimacy of (Some) Federal Common Law, 101 Va. L. Rev. 1, 63 (2015).

[2] 28 U.S.C. §1652. As originally enacted in the Judiciary Act of 1789, the Rules of Decision Act was identical, except the words "in trials at common law" were used instead of the current phrase "civil actions." 1 Stat. 92 (1789).

[3] Professor Martin Redish argues that the terms of the Rules of Decision Act prohibit any federal common law. Martin H. Redish, Federal Common Law, Political Legitimacy, and the Interpretive Process: An "Institutionalist" Perspective, 83 Nw. U. L. Rev. 761 (1989). *But see* Louise Weinberg, Federal Common Law, 83 Nw. U. L. Rev. 805 (1989) (arguing for the legitimacy of federal common law).

[4] 11 U.S. (7 Cranch) 32 (1812). *See also* United States v. Coolidge, 14 U.S. (1 Wheat.) 415 (1816) (reaffirming *Hudson & Goodwin* and denying federal common law power to punish crimes committed on the high seas).

[5] 11 U.S. at 32.

law would infringe on the states' prerogatives. Justice Johnson, writing for the Court, observed that "[t]he powers of the general Government are made up of concessions from the several states—whatever is not expressly given to the former, the latter expressly reserve."[6] To this day, no federal common law creates criminal offenses against the United States.

Similarly, it long has been established that the existence of federal question jurisdiction does not authorize the creation of federal common law. The Court often has declared that "[t]he vesting of jurisdiction in the federal courts does not in and of itself give rise to authority to formulate federal common law."[7]

The most dramatic statement that federal courts should not create common law is found in *Erie R.R. v. Tompkins*.[8] For almost 100 years, federal courts did fashion federal common law in diversity cases in the absence of a state constitutional or statutory provision. In *Swift v. Tyson*, the Supreme Court held that the Rules of Decision Act only required the application of state constitutional or statutory law, not state common law.[9] In overruling *Swift*, the Court in *Erie* flatly declared that "[t]here is no federal general common law."[10]

Limited Scope of Federal Common Law

Despite this declaration and the presumption against federal common law, federal courts have fashioned common law in limited circumstances throughout American history.[11] As discussed in this chapter, a substantial body of federal common law concerns topics such as the rights and duties of the federal government, international law, conflicts among the states, and admiralty. In fact, on the very same day the *Erie* Court declared that there is no federal common law, it also expressly approved the creation of federal common law principles to apportion an interstate stream between two states.[12]

Federal common law has developed out of necessity. In some instances, there are simply gaps in the law; the application of statutory and constitutional provisions often requires the development of legal rules.[13] The fashioning of federal common law for deciding disputes between states, which has occurred throughout

[6] *Id.* at 33. For an excellent discussion of the political background of the *Hudson & Goodwin* decision and how that background likely affected the decision, *see* Stewart Jay, Origins of Federal Common Law: Part Two, 133 U. Pa. L. Rev. 1231, 1233 (1985).

[7] Texas Indus., Inc. v. Radcliff Materials, Inc., 451 U.S. 630, 640-641 (1981) (citation omitted); *see also* United States v. Little Lake Misere Land Co., 412 U.S. 580, 591 (1973).

[8] 304 U.S. 64 (1938); *Erie* is discussed in detail in §5.3.5, *supra*.

[9] 41 U.S. (16 Pet.) 1 (1842); *Swift* is discussed in detail in §5.3.5, *supra*.

[10] 304 U.S. at 78.

[11] *See* Stewart Jay, Origins of Federal Common Law: Part One, 133 U. Pa. L. Rev. 1003 (1985); Jay, *supra* note 6, at 1231.

[12] Hinderlider v. La Plata River & Cherry Creek Ditch Co., 304 U.S. 92 (1938).

[13] *See* D'Oench, Duhme & Co. v. Federal Deposit Ins. Corp., 315 U.S. 447, 472 (1942) ("Federal common law implements the federal Constitution and statutes, and is conditioned by them. Within these limits, federal courts are free to apply the traditional common-law technique of decision and to draw upon sources of the common law in cases such as the present.") (citation omitted).

American history, is a classic example of this.[14] The Supreme Court's original jurisdiction to hear cases between states is very important in that it provides a neutral forum to resolve conflicts.[15] Where federal statutory rules do not exist for particular disputes, the Supreme Court often has no alternative except to fashion common law principles.

In some instances, federal courts create common law to fulfill congressional intent. For example, sometimes Congress expressly has desired that federal courts develop a body of common law principles under a particular statute.[16] In other situations, the Supreme Court has concluded that creating a cause of action under a congressional statute that does not contain one would best effectuate the legislature's purpose.[17]

Also, federal common law especially has developed to protect the interests of the federal government. There are instances in which the application of state law would frustrate important federal interests and objectives, yet there are no federal statutory provisions on point. In these circumstances, federal courts have created common law rules. Important examples of this include the development of federal common law in cases involving the proprietary interests of the federal government and in matters involving international law.[18]

Separation of Powers and Federalism Issues

Thus, the issue is not whether federal common law should exist. Federal common law always has existed and always will exist. In fact, it is often difficult to separate where statutory or constitutional interpretation ends and where federal common law begins.[19] Professor Louise Weinberg suggests that "in all cases along the continuum, courts obviously glean what they can from legislative action or

[14] *See, e.g.,* Illinois v. City of Milwaukee, Wis., 406 U.S. 91, 103 (1972); Hinderlider v. La Plata River & Cherry Creek Ditch Co., 304 U.S. 92, 110 (1938); Kansas v. Colorado, 206 U.S. 46, 98 (1907). The development of federal common law to resolve disputes between states is discussed in §6.2.5, *infra.*

[15] The original, exclusive jurisdiction of the Supreme Court to hear disputes between states is provided for in 28 U.S.C. §1251(a) and is discussed in §10.3.1, *infra.*

[16] *See* §6.3.2, *infra.*

[17] *See* §6.3.3, *infra.*

[18] *See* §§6.2.1-6.2.3, *infra.* In an excellent article, Professor Seth Davis has argued that federal courts should be willing to create a right of action when it is the federal government suing to protect its interests. Seth Davis, 114 Colum. L. Rev. 1, 9 (2014) ("A public right of action gives the United States or a state (or a federal or state agency or state subdivision) the right to sue for judicial relief to enforce federal statutory or constitutional law. A public remedy is the form judicial relief takes when a public litigant succeeds on the merits of its suit.").

[19] *See* Peter Westen & Jeffrey S. Lehman, Is There Life for *Erie* After the Death of Diversity?, 78 Mich. L. Rev. 311, 332 (1980) ("The difference between 'common law' and 'statutory interpretation' is a difference in emphasis rather than a difference in kind. The more definite and explicit the prevailing legislative policy, the more likely a court will describe its lawmaking as statutory interpretation; the less precise and less explicit the perceived legislative policy, the more likely a court will speak of common law. The distinction, however, is entirely one of degree."). *See also* Donald H. Zeigler, Rights, Rights of Action, and Remedies: An Integrated Approach, 76 Wash. L. Rev. 67 (2001) (the issue of rights, private rights of action, and remedies is about whether the statutory provision entitles the plaintiff to a remedy).

inaction. It is a waste of time to try to isolate the former as somehow 'legitimate' in a way that the latter is not."[20] The relevant inquiry is, when is it appropriate for federal courts to create federal common law?[21]

Like most topics throughout this book, the question of when federal common law should be created raises important issues about federalism and separation of powers.[22] With regard to federalism, the creation of federal common law often displaces state laws, generating objections that it usurps state prerogatives. On the other hand, the failure to fashion federal common law can offend the values of federalism if the effect is to allow state law to frustrate federal interests.

Similarly, the development of federal common law can be challenged on the separation of powers grounds that Congress has the sole power to decide the existence and content of federal laws. Under certain circumstances, however, developing common law principles is an inherent part of the judicial role of deciding cases. Additionally, federal common law often is created to effectuate congressional intent, undermining any separation of powers objection. The underlying issue is whether federal courts should possess the power judicial tribunals traditionally have to develop common law, or whether because of separation of powers, federal courts should be denied this authority.

In short, consideration of federal common law is integrally related to issues of federalism and separation of powers. However, neither value provides any clear guidance as to when federal courts should create or refrain from creating federal common law.

Two Categories Where Federal Common Law Has Developed

The topic of federal common law is particularly difficult because the label falsely implies that a coherent body of legal principles exists. Quite the contrary, federal common law has developed in an ad hoc fashion in a number of different areas. The Court has devoted little attention to developing general principles for when federal common law may or may not be created. The many areas where federal common law exists can be grouped into two major categories.

[20] Louise Weinberg, Federal Common Law, 83 Nw. U. L. Rev. 805, 807 (1989). *See also* Jane Schacter, The Confounding Common Law Originalism in Recent Supreme Court Statutory Interpretation: Implications for the Legislative History Debate and Beyond, 51 Stan. L. Rev. 1 (1998) (arguing that courts have many tools to give meaning to statutory language).

[21] An argument might be made that the Rules of Decision Act prohibits the development of any federal common law. *See* Martin H. Redish, Federal Jurisdiction: Tensions in the Allocation of Judicial Power 121 (2d ed. 1990) ("Potentially, the most significant obstacle to the creation of federal common law is the Rules of Decision Act."). First, however, history provides an answer to this argument. Federal courts have fashioned common law for over 200 years, notwithstanding the literal dictate of the Rules of Decision Act. The statute must be read in light of this history in the absence of congressional modification or objection. Second, as Professor Redish points out, a textual answer is possible to objections based on the Rules of Decision Act. The act dictates that state law shall be used "in cases where they apply." It can be argued that where there is federal common law, state law does not apply. *Id.* at 121.

[22] For a summary of the federalism and separation of powers objections to federal common law, *see* Merrill, *supra* note 1, at 13-23.

First, federal common law has developed where the Supreme Court has decided that federal rules are "necessary to protect uniquely federal interests."[23] Included in this category is the creation of federal common law to protect federal proprietary interests in cases involving the U.S. government, to safeguard federal interests in litigation between private parties, to uphold federal interests in international law, and to resolve conflicts among the states. Section 6.2 examines this category and these specific areas of federal common law.

The second major area of federal common law rules is where the Court has acted to effectuate congressional intent. Sometimes this has occurred when Congress has desired that the federal courts develop a body of common law principles in a particular area. Furthermore, in some situations, the Court has inferred a private right of action under federal statutes in order to fulfill Congress's purpose. Section 6.3 considers these uses of federal common law.

The major area of federal common law not considered in this chapter concerns the creation of a cause of action for money damages directly under constitutional provisions against federal government officers who violate federal rights. Termed "*Bivens* actions," this topic is discussed in detail in §9.1, which focuses on relief against federal officers.[24]

One other area of federal common law not discussed in this chapter concerns federal common law for admiralty and maritime cases. Admiralty and maritime jurisdiction and law is a highly specialized, complex body of law that is beyond the scope of this book.[25] It suffices here to point out that the Supreme Court long has ruled that admiralty and maritime cases are governed by federal common law because of the strong federal interest in such matters.[26]

[23] Texas Indus., Inc. v. Radcliff Materials, Inc., 451 U.S. 630, 640 (1981), *quoting* Banco Nacional de Cuba v. Sabbatino, 376 U.S. 398, 426 (1964).

[24] The term "*Bivens* action" comes from the seminal case where the Court inferred a private cause of action for money damages under the Fourth Amendment, Bivens v. Six Unknown Named Agents of Fed. Bureau of Narcotics, 403 U.S. 388 (1971). *Bivens* and decisions that follow it are discussed in detail in §9.1.

[25] The Supreme Court recently reaffirmed that "[i]n maritime tort cases, we act as a common-law court, subject to any controlling statutes enacted by Congress." Air & Liquid Sys. Corp. v. DeVries, 586 U.S. 446 (2019). For a discussion of admiralty and maritime law, *see* Jo Desha Lucas, Cases and Materials on Admiralty Law (6th ed. 2012); Grant Gilmore & Charles L. Black, The Law of Admiralty (2d ed. 1975).

[26] *See, e.g.,* Kossick v. United Fruit Co., 365 U.S. 731 (1961); Chelentis v. Luckenbach Steamship Co., 247 U.S. 372 (1918); Southern Pac. Co. v. Jensen, 244 U.S. 205 (1917). For an excellent review of these cases and an argument for limiting federal common law in admiralty and maritime cases, *see* Redish, *supra* note 21, at 140-147.

§6.2 THE DEVELOPMENT OF FEDERAL COMMON LAW TO PROTECT FEDERAL INTERESTS

§6.2.1 Introduction

In many instances, federal common law has been created to protect the federal government's interests. The Supreme Court has articulated a two-part inquiry in deciding whether to create federal law to safeguard federal interests.[1] First, the Court considers whether the matter justifies creating federal law. Second, if federal law is to be developed, the Court decides its content; specifically, the Court determines whether to copy existing state law principles or to formulate new rules.

Does the Matter Warrant Creation of Federal Common Law?

A classic example of the first inquiry—whether a matter warrants the creation of federal law—is found in *Clearfield Trust Co. v. United States.*[2] A check issued by the federal government was cashed in a department store, which then endorsed it over to Clearfield Trust for payment. Clearfield Trust received payment for the check from the Federal Reserve System. The person to whom the original check was issued objected to the government that he never received it, so a second check was issued to him. The federal government then sued Clearfield Trust for recovery on the first check. The question was whether the federal government's delay in notifying Clearfield Trust of the theft and forgery of the first check precluded the government from recovering. The lower federal court applied Pennsylvania law and ruled against the United States because of its excessive delay in providing notice to Clearfield Trust that a stolen check with a forged endorsement had been cashed.

The Supreme Court held that the federal court should have fashioned a federal common law rule. The Court concluded that "the rule of *Erie R. Co. v. Tompkins* does not apply to this action. The rights and duties of the United States on commercial paper which it issues are governed by federal rather than local law."[3] The Court explained: "The authority to issue the check had its origin in the Constitution and the statutes of the United States and was in no way dependent on the laws of Pennsylvania or of any other state. The duties imposed upon the

§6.2 [1] The separation of the inquiry into two parts was first articulated in Henry J. Friendly, In Praise of *Erie*—and of the New Federal Common Law, 39 N.Y.U. L. Rev. 383, 410 (1964). Professor Martha Field has phrased the two-part inquiry as follows: "[F]irst, a court should ask whether the issue before it is properly subject to the exercise of federal power; if it is, the court should go on to determine whether, in light of the competing state and federal interests involved, it is wise as a matter of policy to adopt a federal substantive rule to govern the issue." Martha A. Field, Sources of Law: The Scope of Federal Common Law, 99 Harv. L. Rev. 881, 886 (1986). Professor Field's article is largely devoted to criticizing this two-prong test. *See* text accompanying notes 11-12, *infra.*

[2] 318 U.S. 363 (1943).

[3] *Id.* at 366.

United States and the rights acquired by it as a result of the issuance find their roots in the same federal sources. In absence of an applicable Act of Congress it is for the federal courts to fashion the governing rule of law according to their own standards."[4]

In other words, the core of the first inquiry is whether a federal interest exists that justifies the Court's creation of federal law. No clear criteria guide this determination. The Court often looks to whether the underlying purpose of a constitutional or statutory provision warrants the development of federal common law. §§6.2.2-6.2.5 examine the areas in which the Court has considered whether there is a sufficient federal interest justifying the fashioning of federal law.

What Should Be the Content of Federal Common Law?

If the Court decides that there should be federal law in an area, then its content must be determined. The Court can base the federal law on already existing state law principles—sometimes termed "incorporat[ing] or borrow[ing] state law as the federal rule of decision."[5] Alternatively, the Court can create a new legal rule to serve the federal government's interests. For example, in *Clearfield Trust*, the Court stated: "In our choice of the applicable federal rule we have occasionally selected state law. But reasons which may make state law at times the appropriate federal rule are singularly inappropriate here."[6] The Court explained that the need for a uniform rule concerning commercial paper issued by the United States justified fashioning new legal rules, rather than borrowing from existing state law.

The Court has articulated a balancing test for deciding whether to incorporate state law as the federal rule of decision or whether to create federal law. In *United States v. Kimbell Foods, Inc.*, the Court described the relevant considerations.[7] The issue in *Kimbell Foods* was whether the federal government's liens take priority over private liens when the federal government seeks recovery on defaulted federal loans. The Court discussed the inquiry in deciding whether to base federal law on existing state rules. The Court stated:

> Undoubtedly, federal programs that "by their nature are and must be uniform in character throughout the Nation" necessitate formulation of controlling federal rules. Conversely, when there is little need for a nationally uniform body of law, state law may be incorporated as the federal rule of decision. Apart from considerations of uniformity, we must also determine whether application of state law would frustrate specific objectives of the federal programs. If so, we must fashion special rules solicitous of those federal interests. Finally, our choice-of-law inquiry must consider the extent to which application of a federal rule would disrupt commercial relationships predicated on state law.[8]

[4] *Id.* at 366-367.

[5] Peter W. Low, John C. Jeffries, Jr., and Curtis A. Bradley, Federal Courts and the Law of Federal State Relations 127 (10th ed. 2022).

[6] 318 U.S. at 367.

[7] 440 U.S. 715 (1979).

[8] *Id.* at 728-729 (citations omitted).

In other words, in deciding whether to incorporate state law or to fashion new federal law, the Court balances the need for federal uniformity and for special rules to protect federal interests against the disruption that will come from creating new legal rules. For example, in *DeSylva v. Ballentine*, the question was whether the federal court should "borrow" state law principles in deciding whether illegitimate children should be allowed to exercise the statutory right of children to renew the copyrights of their deceased parents.[9] The Supreme Court held that state law should be applied because the federal government had no particular interest in matters concerning family relationships and because a well-developed body of state law existed that dealt with family law and inheritance.[10]

Two-Part Test for Federal Common Law and Its Critics

Thus, a two-part inquiry is used when there is a claim of a need for federal common law to protect the federal government's interests. First, does the issue fall within federal common law power, and should the federal court create federal common law to decide the matter? Second, if so, what should its content be—should it be based on existing state law rules, or should new principles be fashioned?

Professor Martha Field has persuasively criticized the two-prong test.[11] She argued that the two inquiries are rarely distinct and ultimately involve the same basic question regarding the need for federal law to replace existing state law. She contended that even in instances where federal law should be developed but its content should be based on state law, a single inquiry would suffice. She wrote: "[A] two-fold inquiry is unnecessary. . . . If one starts with the question whether there is any need to displace state law with federal law . . . , surely every case in which a need can be found is also one in which the court can cite a federal enactment that it interprets as supporting federal rulemaking."[12]

The use of federal common law to protect federal interests, and the application of the two-part test described above, can be best understood by examining the specific areas in which common law has been developed to safeguard the interests of the United States. Specifically, §§6.2.2-6.2.5, respectively, examine federal common law to protect federal proprietary interests in suits involving the United States or its officers, to safeguard federal interests in cases between private parties, to protect federal interests in litigation pertaining to international relations, and to resolve disputes between state governments.

[9] 351 U.S. 570 (1956).

[10] In the Copyright Act of 1976, Congress specifically amended the law to provide that "children" includes legitimate and illegitimate children. 17 U.S.C. §101.

[11] Field, *supra* note 1, at 950-953.

[12] *Id.* at 952.

§6.2.2 *Federal Common Law to Protect Federal Proprietary Interests in Suits Involving the United States or Its Officers*

Initial Rejection of Federal Common Law

Initially, the Supreme Court held that federal courts were to apply state law in deciding cases involving the proprietary interests of the U.S. government. For example, in *Cotton v. United States,* the federal government brought an action for trespass against an individual who, without permission, cut timber from federal land.[13] The defendant argued that there was no federal law permitting recovery by the United States, but the Supreme Court disagreed, stating that "[a]s an owner of property in almost every State of the Union, [the United States has] the same right to have it protected by the local laws that other persons have."[14] The Court did not fashion common law to protect the federal interests, but rather simply applied state law.

Similarly, in *Mason v. United States,* the federal government sought damages from individuals who wrongly took oil and natural gas from federal lands.[15] The United States asserted that the federal court should fashion common law to determine the proper measure for damages. The Supreme Court disagreed and concluded that the "entire cause of action is . . . local . . . and the matter of damages within the controlling scope of state legislation."[16] In *United States v. San Jacinto Tin Co.,* the Supreme Court upheld the authority of the attorney general to sue in order to protect the interests of the United States, but emphasized that "the right of the government of the United States to institute such a suit depends upon the same general principles which would authorize a private citizen to apply to a court of justice for relief against an instrument obtained from him by fraud or deceit."[17]

However, the early law was not completely consistent. In some instances the Supreme Court created common law for transactions involving the United States. For example, in two decisions, the Supreme Court held that the liability of parties on a bond issued by the U.S. government was to be determined not according to the law of the state where the bond was executed, but by the "rules of the civil law."[18] In these cases, the Supreme Court refused to apply Louisiana's state law, which was based on the civil law of France, and instead fashioned common law rules to decide the issues.

[13] 52 U.S. (11 How.) 229 (1850).

[14] *Id.* at 231.

[15] 260 U.S. 545 (1923).

[16] *Id.* at 558. *See also* United States v. Burnison, 339 U.S. 87 (1950); United States v. Fox, 94 U.S. (4 Otto) 315 (1877) (using state law to decide probate matters involving the federal government).

[17] 125 U.S. 273, 285 (1888).

[18] Duncan v. United States, 32 U.S. (7 Pet.) 435, 449 (1833); Cox v. United States, 31 U.S. (6 Pet.) 172, 202 (1832).

Development of Federal Common Law

The modern era concerning the development of the federal common law began in the 1930s. In a series of cases culminating in *Clearfield Trust*, described above, the Supreme Court held that federal common law should be created for transactions involving banking and the rights of the United States with regard to commercial paper. In *Deitrick v. Greaney*, a receiver of a national bank brought a suit to recover on a note issued by one of the bank's directors in violation of the National Bank Act.[19] The Supreme Court said that the state's law where the bank was located was irrelevant and that the "extent and nature of the legal consequences of this condemnation, though left by the [federal] statute to judicial determination, are nevertheless to be derived from it and the federal policy which it has adopted."[20]

In *D'Oench, Duhme & Co. v. Federal Deposit Insurance Corp.*, a company executed a note, payable on demand, to a bank with the understanding that the note would not be called for payment.[21] The Federal Deposit Insurance Corporation subsequently acquired the note as collateral for a loan but was not informed of the original understanding that payment would not be demanded on the note. The Supreme Court held that federal law would determine the question of whether the federal government could collect on the note. The Court declared that "the liability of petitioner on the note involves decision of a federal, not a state, question. . . . [Under federal statutes there is] a federal policy to protect respondent, and the public funds which it administers, against misrepresentations as to the securities or other assets in the portfolios of the banks which respondent insures or to which it makes loans."[22]

In *Clearfield Trust*, described above, the Supreme Court clearly expressed that questions concerning the rights of the United States in recovering on commercial paper are to be determined by federal common law.[23] *Clearfield Trust* is widely cited for the proposition that federal courts may develop federal common law to protect the proprietary interests of the United States.[24]

This proposition has been extended beyond matters involving commercial paper. For example, it is firmly established that federal common law is to be fashioned to protect the federal government's interest in real property. In *United States v. Little Lake Misere Land Co.*, the Supreme Court held that state law may not be used to abrogate federal government contracts that acquire land for public uses.[25] The United States brought a suit to quiet title on two parcels of land that it had

[19] 309 U.S. 190 (1940).

[20] *Id.* at 200-201.

[21] 315 U.S. 447 (1942).

[22] *Id.* at 456-457. Justice Jackson wrote a famous concurring opinion in which he discussed the need for federal courts to fashion common law rules to implement federal statutes. *See id.* at 473-475.

[23] *See* text accompanying notes 2-4, *supra.*

[24] *See, e.g.*, United States v. Little Lake Misere Land Co., 412 U.S. 580, 594 (1973); Friendly, *supra* note 1, at 410; Martin H. Redish, Federal Jurisdiction: Tensions in the Allocation of Judicial Power 125-126 (2d ed. 1990).

[25] 412 U.S. 580 (1973).

obtained pursuant to a federal statute. A provision in a state law seemingly invalidated some of the terms in the land acquisition agreement. The Supreme Court, however, held that federal law, not the state's, governed the matter.

The Court engaged in the two-step inquiry described above. First, the Court concluded that the matter was one that should be governed by federal common law. The Court explained that "[t]here will often be no specific federal legislation governing a particular transaction to which the United States is a party. . . . But silence on that score in federal legislation is no reason for limiting the reach of federal law. . . . To the contrary, the inevitable incompleteness presented by all legislation means that interstitial federal lawmaking is a basic responsibility of the federal courts."[26] The Court held that federal common law was needed to protect the interests of the United States and in order to effectuate Congress's purpose in enacting the statute authorizing the acquisition of the land in question.[27]

The Court then considered the second part of the analysis and concluded that the federal common law principles should not be borrowed from state law. The Court reasoned that the specific state provisions run counter to the interests of the federal government under the statute and thus should not be applied.[28] The Court quoted, with approval, Professor Paul Mishkin's statement that when the United States is a party to a contract and "the issue's outcome bears some relationship to a federal program, no rule may be applied which would not be wholly in accord with that program."[29]

Federal Common Law for Tort Claims Involving Federal Government

In tort cases as well, the Court has developed federal common law to protect the interests of the United States. In *United States v. Standard Oil Co. of California*, the Court held that a tort suit brought by a U.S. soldier against a private tortfeasor was to be determined by federal common law and not state tort law rules.[30] In *Howard v. Lyons*, the Court concluded that a suit for a tort against a federal officer was to be decided by federal common law rather than by state tort law.[31] The officer was sued for defamation and libel for statements made in the course of duty. In rejecting the application of state law, the Court explained that "[t]he authority of a federal officer to act derives from federal sources, and the rule which recognizes a privilege under appropriate circumstances as to statements made in the course of duty is one designed to promote the efficient functioning of the Federal Government."[32]

[26] *Id.* at 593.

[27] *Id.* at 595-596.

[28] *Id.* at 596-597.

[29] *Id.* at 604, *quoting* Paul J. Mishkin, The Variousness of "Federal Law": Competence and Discretion in the Choice of National and State Rules for Decision, 105 U. Pa. L. Rev. 797, 805-806 (1957).

[30] 332 U.S. 301 (1947).

[31] 360 U.S. 593 (1959) (the matter involved a libel suit against a former Navy officer and commander of the Boston Naval Shipyard).

[32] *Id.* at 597.

The Federal Tort Claims Act creates liability against the United States for actions that would be torts in the state where they occur, subject to a number of specified exceptions.[33] Although the legislative history indicates that the exceptions are to be exclusive, the Supreme Court has fashioned an additional exception preventing suit against the United States for injuries incurred by armed forces personnel incident to service. Termed the "*Feres* doctrine," because it was first articulated in *Feres v. United States*,[34] the prohibition against such suits is best understood as a principle of common law immunity created by the Supreme Court. The *Feres* doctrine is discussed in detail in §9.2.

Cases Refusing to Create Federal Common Law

Thus, the presence of a proprietary interest of the United States—in contract, property, and torts contexts—has been held to justify the creation of federal common law. There are, however, exceptional cases where the Supreme Court has found the development of federal law unnecessary even for commercial transactions involving the United States. For example, in *United States v. Yazell*, the Supreme Court applied state law to prevent recovery by the U.S. Small Business Administration on a loan that it had issued.[35] The United States sued a woman to recover on a loan that the Small Business Administration had made to the woman and her husband. The woman invoked the state's law of coverture, an anachronistic, sexist principle that prevented married women from binding their property without a court order.

The Supreme Court held that although the matter involved the proprietary interests of the federal government, federal common law should not be developed and, instead, state law was to be applied. The Court emphasized that "this was a custom-made, hand-tailored, specifically negotiated transaction. It was not a nationwide act of the Federal Government, emanating in a single form from a single source."[36] Thus, *Yazell* simply reinforces that even in commercial transactions involving the United States, the two-part inquiry described above is to be used, and federal common law should be developed only if there is an interest of the United States warranting its creation. Likewise, even where federal common law is developed, the second part of the balancing test will lead to the use of existing state law as the federal standard where there are not federal interests justifying the creation of new law.[37]

[33] 28 U.S.C. §1346(b); this statute is discussed in detail in §9.2, *infra*.

[34] 340 U.S. 135 (1950).

[35] 382 U.S. 341 (1966).

[36] *Id.* at 348.

[37] *See, e.g.*, United States v. Kimbell Foods, Inc., 440 U.S. 715 (1979); DeSylva v. Ballentine, 351 U.S. 570 (1956), *supra*.

Regulation of Banking

The Supreme Court also considered whether to create federal common law when a federal agency is a party in a case involving the Federal Deposit Insurance Corporation and the Resolution Trust Corporation. In *O'Melveny & Myers v. FDIC, as receiver for American Diversified Savings Bank, et al.*, the FDIC, as receiver for an insolvent savings and loan, sued a law firm that had given legal advice to the savings and loan.[38] The issue was whether federal common law or state law should apply in a suit by the FDIC as receiver of a federally insured bank.

The Supreme Court rejected the application of federal common law. The Court concluded that state law should be applied when the FDIC sues in the shoes of an insolvent savings and loan. The Court said, "What is fatal to respondent's position in the present case is that it has identified *no* significant conflict with an identifiable federal policy or interest. . . . The rules of decision here do not govern the primary conduct of the United States or any of its agents or contractors."

Similarly, *Atherton v. FDIC* involved a suit by the Resolution Trust Corporation against officers of a failed savings and loan on account of their negligent decisions.[39] The Court unanimously ruled that absent any federal statutory regulation, state law rather than federal common law governs. The key issue, according to the Court, is whether there is a need for state law to be displaced by federal common law. Justice Breyer, writing for the Court, explained that "a significant conflict between some federal policy or interest and the use of state law . . . must first be specifically shown before federal common law is fashioned."[40]

Summary

The cases involving the FDIC and the RTC are unusual because these institutions are suing on behalf of private institutions, rather than to protect the interests of the federal government. Therefore, courts have not fashioned and applied federal common law.[41] Generally, however, the Supreme Court has shown a great proclivity to create federal common law to protect the proprietary interests of the United States and, where necessary, to establish new legal principles rather than just borrowing existing state law as the federal rule of decision.

[38] 512 U.S. 79 (1994).

[39] 519 U.S. 213 (1997).

[40] *Id.* at 670.

[41] *See, e.g.,* DiVall Insured Income Fund Limited Partnership v. Boatman's First National Bank, 69 F.3d 1398 (8th Cir. 1995); RTC v. City Savings Bank, 57 F.3d 1231 (3d Cir. 1995), *judgment vacated on other grounds, sub nom* Atherton v. FDIC, 519 U.S. 213 (1997); RTC v. Everhart, 37 F.3d 151 (4th Cir. 1994) (rejecting application of federal common law).

§6.2.3 Federal Common Law to Protect Federal Interests in Suits Between Private Parties

Refusal to Create Federal Common Law

Although the Court has been quite willing to fashion common law to protect federal interests in suits involving the United States or its officers, it has been quite reluctant to do so in litigation involving private parties. The Court has made it clear that federal common law will be developed in suits between private parties only if applying state law will frustrate federal interests. This reluctance to create federal common law in suits involving private parties is reflected in several important decisions.

In *Bank of America National Trust & Savings Association v. Parnell*, the Court said that state law should be used to decide the ability of private parties to recover for conversion of a bond issued by the United States.[42] *Parnell* was a diversity suit in which a bank sued to recover funds an individual obtained by cashing bonds issued by the U.S. Home Owner's Loan Corporation. The federal court of appeals applied *Clearfield Trust* and ruled that federal law should be created because federal bonds were involved. The Supreme Court disagreed and held that the presence of federal commercial interests was not sufficient to justify creating federal common law. The Court explained that "[t]he present litigation is purely between private parties and does not touch the rights and duties of the United States."[43] The Court emphasized that applying state law did not harm the interests of the United States. The Court stated that it did not preclude the development of federal common law principles in future private litigation where it is necessary to protect federal interests.

In *Wallis v. Pan American Petroleum Corp.*, the Court articulated the relevant inquiry in deciding whether federal common law should be created in litigation involving private parties.[44] The case involved a suit between two private parties over a lease to recover oil and natural gas from federal lands. Two separate applications for permission to recover the petroleum were filed, and the issue was whether the lease covered both or just the first application. The court of appeals ruled that federal law should be created to resolve the contracts question because of pervasive federal regulation and because of the danger that state law could thwart federal policy concerning the lease and development of the land.

The Supreme Court disagreed and reversed. The Court stated that the issue was "whether in general federal or state law should govern the dealings of private parties in an oil and gas lease validly issued under the Mineral Leasing Act of 1920."[45] The Court explained that state law should be used unless there is "a significant conflict between some federal policy or interest and the use of state law."[46]

[42] 352 U.S. 29 (1956).
[43] *Id.* at 33.
[44] 384 U.S. 63 (1966).
[45] *Id.* at 67.
[46] *Id.* at 68.

The existence of gaps in a federal statutory structure is not sufficient by itself to warrant the creation of federal common law in suits between private parties. State law should perform the interstitial task, unless the state law will frustrate the federal government's objectives.

Although not articulated as such, the test seems identical to that used for determining whether federal law preempts state law. Essentially, the Court stated that if a state's law is preempted, and if there is no federal statute on the matter, then the federal court will fashion federal common law.

The Supreme Court relied on *Parnell* and *Wallis* in refusing to create federal common law in *Miree v. DeKalb County, Georgia.*[47] A victim of a plane crash and the survivors of deceased passengers sued, based on diversity of citizenship, to recover from the county that maintained the airport from which the plane had taken off. The plaintiffs alleged that the county breached its contract with the Federal Aviation Administration by maintaining a garbage dump near the airport's runways. The plaintiffs said that the plane crash was caused by birds, which were attracted to the garbage in large numbers, being drawn into the plane's engines. In other words, the plaintiffs sued as third-party beneficiaries of the contract between the Federal Aviation Administration and the county, which contained clauses requiring a safe environment for the airport.

The plaintiffs urged the Court to create federal common law to uphold the federal regulatory interest in aviation safety represented in the contract in question. The Court refused, concluding that there was no showing that the application of state law would frustrate the federal interests at stake. The Court emphasized that the suit was between private parties and that it would create federal common law under such circumstances only if there is a "significant conflict between some federal policy or interest and the use of state law."[48] The presence of a strong federal interest in aviation safety was not sufficient to justify the creation of federal common law; there also had to be a showing that state law would impair the interests of the federal government. The Court concluded that there was no evidence of such a conflict and, hence, refused to create federal common law.

Similarly, in *Kamen v. Kemper Financial Services, Inc.*, the Supreme Court held that federal courts developing federal common law under the Investment Company Act of 1940 should use the law of the state of incorporation.[49] The plaintiff was an investor in a mutual fund administered by Kemper Financial Services, Inc. The mutual fund is regulated under the Investment Company Act of 1940, which requires that at least 40 percent of the company's directors be financially independent of the investment advisor, that the shareholders approve the contract between the fund and the advisor, and that the advisor perform as a fiduciary. The plaintiff brought a shareholder's derivative suit alleging violations of these provisions.

The issue before the Supreme Court was whether the plaintiff's suit should be dismissed because of the failure to comply with state law and make a

[47] 433 U.S. 25 (1977).

[48] *Id.* at 31, *quoting* Wallis v. Pan Am. Petroleum Corp., 384 U.S. at 68 (emphasis omitted).

[49] 500 U.S. 90 (1991).

demand of the corporation or to demonstrate that the suit was futile. Because the federal statute is silent on the issue, the specific question was whether the federal court should have created independent federal common law or applied state law.

Justice Thurgood Marshall, writing for a unanimous Court, held that federal law should apply, but concluded that "[i]t does not follow . . . that the content of such a rule must be wholly the product of a federal court's own devising."[50] Justice Marshall said that "[t]he presumption that state law should be incorporated into federal common law is particularly strong in areas in which private parties have entered legal relationships with the expectation that their rights and obligations would be governed by state-law standards. . . . Corporation law is one such area."[51] Thus, the Court concluded that "a court entertaining a derivative action under the Investment Company Act must apply the futility exception as it is defined by the law of the state of incorporation."

Most recently, in *Empire Health Choice Assurance, Inc. v. McVeigh*,[52] the Supreme Court refused to allow the creation of federal common law in a suit between private parties that implicated a contract to which the government was a party. A federal statute provides for health care plans for federal employees. One provision of the plan, negotiated between the federal government and health care providers, requires that insured individuals who receive payments for their medical bills in tort suits must reimburse the insurance company for payments that it made. This case involved a suit by an insurance company for reimbursement after there was recovery in a state court tort action.

The Supreme Court, in a 5-4 decision, held that federal law did not govern the reimbursement action. The Court explained that its precedents "made clear that uniform federal law need not be applied to all questions in federal government litigation, even in cases involving government contracts."[53] The Court concluded that state law, and not federal common law, should be used to determine issues concerning the obligations for the insured to reimburse the insurance company out of tort recoveries.

Justice Breyer, writing for the four dissenters, sharply disagreed. He said, "There is little about this case that is not federal. . . . In sum, the statute is federal, the program it creates is federal, the program's beneficiaries are federal employees working throughout the country, the Federal Government pays all relevant costs, and the Federal Government receives all relevant payments. The private carrier's only role in this scheme is to administer the health benefits plan for the federal agency in exchange for a fixed service charge."[54]

[50] *Id.* at 98.
[51] *Id.*
[52] 547 U.S. 677 (2006).
[53] *Id.* at 679.
[54] *Id.* at 702-704.

Federal Common Law in Cases Involving Private Parties

In some instances, however, the Supreme Court has been willing to develop federal common law in suits between private parties in order to protect federal interests. Most such cases have involved claims by family members to payments under federal insurance policies. In such instances, the Court has justified a refusal to apply state law because of its inconsistency with federal law. For example, *Wissner v. Wissner* involved recovery under a life insurance policy issued by the federal government.[55] A serviceman, estranged from his wife, designated his mother as the beneficiary. Under California's community property law, however, the widow was entitled to half of the proceeds of the policy, in large part because the premiums on the policy were paid with his army salary that was received during the marriage. The Supreme Court, however, refused to apply the state's community property law because of a provision in the act that stated the "insured shall have the right to designate the beneficiary . . . and shall . . . at all times have the right to change the beneficiary."[56] In essence, the Court found the state law to be preempted by federal law.

However, where a conflict between federal and state law does not exist, state law has been applied in determining recovery under federal bonds and insurance policies. For example, in *Rose v. Rose,* the Supreme Court said that a state court had the authority to order a veteran to pay child support out of the benefits paid to him by the Veterans Administration.[57] Although a statutory provision exempted such disability benefits from the claims of creditors, the Court found that the state court's order was not in conflict with federal law because the "benefits are intended to support not only the veteran, but the veteran's family as well."[58]

In *Boyle v. United Technologies Corp.*, the Supreme Court held that federal common law should determine the liability of a contractor providing military equipment to the federal government.[59] The issue in *Boyle* was whether a contractor could be held liable under state tort law for injuries caused by design defects in products supplied to the military. In a 5-4 decision, the Court concluded that there is a uniquely federal interest in obtaining equipment for the military and that the application of state tort law would impair this federal activity. Thus, the Court chose to fashion federal common law and declared that a contractor is not liable where the United States approved precise specifications for the equipment, the equipment met those specifications, and the supplier warned the United States

[55] 338 U.S. 655 (1950).

[56] *Id.* at 658-659. *See also* Ridgway v. Ridgway, 454 U.S. 46 (1981) (state court could not prevent a former serviceman from changing the beneficiary in his life insurance policy).

[57] 481 U.S. 619 (1987); *see also* Yiatchos v. Yiatchos, 376 U.S. 306 (1964) (permitting state law to determine rights of widows under federal bonds).

[58] 481 U.S. at 634.

[59] 487 U.S. 500 (1988).

about dangers in the use of the equipment known to the supplier but not to the United States.[60]

Federal Common Law Only if Federal Law Preempts State Law

These decisions reflect that in cases involving private parties, federal common law will be developed only if federal law is deemed to preempt state law. Preemption traditionally is found if a state law imposes obligations that are mutually exclusive with federal law, if a state law frustrates the achievement of a federal objective, or if there is a clear congressional intent to preempt state law.[61]

The underlying question is whether the Court has been correct in its greater reluctance to create federal common law in suits involving private parties than in litigation involving the government. Although preemption certainly is sufficient to justify creation of common law in suits where the United States is a party, it has not been necessary. The key issue is really a substantive one concerning whether the Court's holdings in cases such as *Parnell, Wallis,* and *Miree* adequately protected the federal government's specific interests in those instances.

§6.2.4 *Federal Common Law to Protect Federal Interests in International Relations*

Foreign Policy Interests Justify Federal Common Law

The Supreme Court often has declared that matters concerning foreign policy pose a nonjusticiable political question.[62] In some instances, however, the Court has found questions involving international relations to be justiciable and has developed federal common law to decide the cases. Federal common law is created because of the uniquely federal interest in foreign affairs and because the application of state law would frustrate the uniformity needed in the United States' relations with other countries.[63]

The most important example of the development of federal common law to protect federal interests in international relations is *Banco Nacional de Cuba v. Sabbatino.*[64] An American commodity broker contracted to purchase sugar from a subsidiary of a Cuban corporation that was largely owned by U.S. residents. The day the sugar

[60] *See* Michael D. Green & Richard A. Matasar, The Supreme Court and the Products Liability Crisis: Lessons from *Boyle*'s Government Contractor Defense, 63 S. Cal. L. Rev. 637 (1990) (criticizing *Boyle*'s reasoning and its failure to rely on state law defenses).

[61] For a discussion of the law concerning preemption, *see* Erwin Chemerinsky, Constitutional Law: Principles and Policies, ch. 5 (7th ed. 2022).

[62] *See* §2.6, *supra.*

[63] Martin H. Redish, Federal Jurisdiction: Tensions in the Allocation of Judicial Power 135-136 (2d ed. 1990); *see also* James M. Edwards, The *Erie* Doctrine in Foreign Affairs Cases, 42 N.Y.U. L. Rev. 674 (1967); John Norton Moore, Federalism and Foreign Relations, 1965 Duke L.J. 248.

[64] 376 U.S. 398 (1964).

was loaded aboard a ship in Cuba, the Cuban government nationalized all property of the Cuban corporation. Ultimately, the question before the Supreme Court was who had title to the sugar. Cuba claimed legal possession pursuant to its nationalization; the American business asserted that the federal courts should not honor the expropriation.

The Supreme Court ruled in favor of the Cuban government. At the outset, the Court explained that federal law must be formulated to resolve the matter. The Court stated that "the competence and function of the Judiciary and the National Executive in ordering our relationships with other members of the international community must be treated exclusively as an aspect of federal law."[65] The Court analogized the creation of federal law in this area to other instances in which federal common law was developed to protect unique federal interests.

The Court concluded that Cuba had title to the sugar under the "act of state doctrine," which "precludes the courts of this country from inquiring into the validity of the public acts a recognized foreign sovereign power committed within its own territory."[66] The Court explained that although the act of state doctrine was not compelled by the Constitution, federal statutes, or international law, it was the principle most suited to protect the interests of the federal government.[67] The Court stated that applying the act of state doctrine would minimize conflicts with a foreign nation and would avoid interference with negotiations carried on by the executive branch.[68]

Although both Congress and the Court subsequently have restricted the application of the act of state doctrine,[69] *Sabbatino* still stands for the important proposition that in cases related to foreign affairs, federal courts may fashion federal common law. However, because of the application of the political question doctrine in many cases related to foreign policy, the development of federal common law in this area is likely to be minimal.

§6.2.5 Federal Common Law to Resolve Disputes Between States

Need for Federal Common Law for Suits Between States

The development of federal common law is particularly important in resolving disputes between state governments. A crucial function of the federal courts,

[65] *Id.* at 425.

[66] *Id.* at 401.

[67] *Id.* at 421-423.

[68] *Id.* at 437-438.

[69] *See* 22 U.S.C. §2370(e) (limiting application of the act of state doctrine); First Natl. City Bank v. Banco Nacional de Cuba, 406 U.S. 759 (1972) (act of state doctrine should not be applied against the wishes of the executive branch of government); Alfred Dunhill of London, Inc. v. Republic of Cuba, 425 U.S. 682 (1976) (act of state doctrine does not apply to the commercial activities of a foreign government).

and particularly the U.S. Supreme Court, is to provide a forum for the peaceful resolution of disputes between the states.[70] Obviously, in a conflict between two states, neither state's laws can be applied to resolve the dispute. Therefore, in the absence of a pertinent federal statute, federal common law must be created to protect the federal government's interest in interstate harmony.

The Supreme Court has expressly recognized its authority to create federal common law to resolve such disputes. In *Kansas v. Colorado,* the Court explained that when two states conflict, "[the] court is called upon to settle that dispute in such a way as will recognize the equal rights of both and at the same time establish justice between them."[71] The Court said that through its "successive . . . decisions this court is practically building up what may not improperly be called interstate common law."[72]

For example, the Court has developed federal common law to resolve disputes between states concerning interstate waters. In *Hinderlider v. La Plata River & Cherry Creek Ditch Co.*, the Supreme Court held that federal common law should be created to apportion water from an interstate stream between two states.[73] In *Hinderlider,* decided the same day as *Erie R.R. v. Tompkins,* the Court declared: "For whether the water of an interstate stream must be apportioned between two States is a question of 'federal common law' upon which neither the statutes nor the decisions of either State can be conclusive."[74]

Another decision concerning the use of federal common law to resolve a dispute concerning interstate waters is *Illinois v. City of Milwaukee, Wisconsin.*[75] Four Wisconsin cities sued the state of Illinois to halt pollution of Lake Michigan. An earlier Supreme Court case had implied that state law would cover such actions.[76] However, in *Illinois v. City of Milwaukee,* the Court held that federal common law should be developed to resolve the case concerning pollution of interstate waters. The Court stressed the existence of many federal statutes dealing with pollution, evidencing Congress's intent that this was a matter of national concern. Justice Douglas, writing for the majority, stated: "The remedy sought by Illinois is not within the precise scope of remedies prescribed by Congress. Yet the remedies which Congress provides are not necessarily the only federal remedies available. . . . *When we deal with air and water in their ambient or interstate aspects, there is a federal common law.*"[77]

Subsequently, the Supreme Court held that the 1972 Amendments to the Water Pollution Control Act prevented a federal common law action for nuisance as a result of pollution of interstate waters.[78] The Court, in an opinion by Justice Rehnquist, reasoned that the comprehensive statutory structure established

[70] The Supreme Court has original and exclusive jurisdiction for suits between states. 28 U.S.C. §1251(a). This aspect of federal court jurisdiction, and its importance, is discussed in §10.3.1, *infra.*

[71] 206 U.S. 46, 98 (1907).

[72] *Id.*

[73] 304 U.S. 92 (1938).

[74] *Id.* at 110 (citations omitted).

[75] 406 U.S. 91 (1972).

[76] Ohio v. Wyandotte Chemicals Corp., 401 U.S. 493, 498-499 n.3 (1971).

[77] 406 U.S. at 103 (emphasis added).

[78] Milwaukee v. Illinois, 451 U.S. 304 (1981).

liability for water pollution; federal common law that serves an interstitial function was unnecessary and improper.[79] Subsequently, in *Virginia v. Maryland*, the Supreme Court explained, "Federal common law governs interstate bodies of water, ensuring that the water is equitably apportioned between the states and that neither state harms the other's interest in the river."[80]

The development of federal common law to resolve disputes among the states is extremely desirable simply because it often is essential if such conflicts are to be adjudicated. Some commentators have urged that the creation of federal common law should be extended to include mass tort cases involving claims throughout the country and where conflicting state laws make adjudication extremely problematic.[81] Although such cases do not involve disputes between the states, a persuasive argument exists for creating federal common law in federal court litigation over disasters, such as asbestos, where conflicts among state laws will lead to inconsistent recoveries and enormous problems in terms of preclusion. The difficulties in creating federal common law for mass tort cases will be in deciding what types of cases qualify and in determining the content of the appropriate law. Congress could aid this process by enacting a statute specifically permitting the creation of federal common law for such cases.[82]

§6.3 THE DEVELOPMENT OF FEDERAL COMMON LAW TO EFFECTUATE CONGRESSIONAL INTENT

§6.3.1 Introduction

Is Federal Common Law Necessary to Effectuate Congressional Intent?

The Supreme Court has created federal common law when it believes it necessary to effectuate the intent behind a federal statute. Unlike the first category

[79] The Court explained that "the appropriate analysis in determining if federal statutory law governs a question previously the subject of federal common law is not the same as that employed in deciding if federal law pre-empts state law." 451 U.S. at 316. Although clear congressional intent is necessary to preempt state law, the Court reasoned that the existence of legislation in an area presumptively makes federal common law unnecessary and inappropriate.

[80] 540 U.S. 5 (2003).

[81] *See, e.g.,* Linda S. Mullenix, Federalizing Choice of Law for Mass Tort Litigation, 70 Tex. L. Rev. 1623 (1992); Linda S. Mullenix, Class Resolution of the Mass-Tort Case: A Proposed Federal Procedure Act, 64 Tex. L. Rev. 1039, 1077 (1986); *but see* Jackson v. Johns-Manville Sales Corp., 750 F.2d 1314, 1325 (5th Cir. 1985) (en banc); In re Joint Eastern and Southern Dist. Asbestos Litig., 129 B.R. 710 (E. and S.D.N.Y. 1991) (refusing to create federal common law for asbestos cases).

[82] Mullenix, *supra* note 81, Class Resolution, at 1077-1079; Benjamin E. Haller, Death in the Air: Federal Regulation of Tort Liability a Must, 54 A.B.A. J. 382 (1968); Jackson v. Johns-Manville Sales Corp., 750 F.2d at 1329-1335 (Clark, J., dissenting).

described above, which focuses primarily on whether federal common law is needed to protect the interests of the U.S. government, here the central question is whether common law is needed to fulfill Congress's purposes in adopting a particular statute.

This type of federal common law is easily justified. In adopting statutes, Congress cannot foresee every possibility. Inevitably, statutes have gaps, and the application of statutes to specific situations requires the development of rules not created within the laws. Justice Jackson explained this in his famous concurrence in *D'Oench, Duhme & Co. v. Federal Deposit Insurance Corp.*: "The federal courts have no general federal common law. . . . But this is not to say that wherever we have occasion to decide a federal question which cannot be answered from federal statutes alone we may not resort to all of the source materials of the common law, or that when we have fashioned an answer it does not become a part of the federal non-statutory or common law. . . . Were we bereft of the common law, our federal system would be impotent. This follows from the recognized futility of attempting all-complete statutory codes, and is apparent from the terms of the Constitution itself."[1] In fact, separating statutory interpretation from the creation of this type of federal common law is often difficult.[2]

The development of federal common law to effectuate congressional intent occurs in two situations. One is where Congress wants federal courts to develop a body of common law rules under a particular statute. The second and more controversial area concerns the creation of private rights of action under federal statutes. These two situations are discussed in §6.3.2 and §6.3.3, respectively.

§6.3.2 Congressional Authorization for Federal Courts to Create a Body of Common Law Rules

In most statutes, Congress provides detailed provisions of substantive law regulating particular conduct. Occasionally, Congress has decided that state law is to be incorporated as the substantive law under a federal statute. For example, the Federal Tort Claims Act makes the United States liable for actions that would be torts in the states where they occur.[3] In other words, rather than create a body of federal tort law, the act incorporates state law, subject to a series of exceptions stated in the statute.[4]

§6.3 [1] 315 U.S. 447, 469-470 (1942).

[2] *See* Peter Westen & Jeffrey S. Lehman, Is There Life for *Erie* After the Death of Diversity?, 78 Mich. L. Rev. 311, 332 (1980) (distinction between interpretation and development of federal common law is one of degree).

[3] 8 U.S.C. §§1346(b), 2672. The Federal Tort Claims Act is discussed in detail in §9.2.2, *infra*.

[4] Of course, questions still will arise where both the statute and the state's law are silent, requiring a federal court to decide whether to fashion federal common law or predict the likely course of state law. *See* Holmberg v. Armbrecht, 327 U.S. 392 (1946) (need to decide when statute of limitations begins to run for action under Federal Farm Loan Act).

In other instances, the Supreme Court has concluded that Congress intended for the federal courts to develop a body of federal common law rules under particular statutes. Congress might provide a broad statutory mandate with the expectation that the federal judiciary will develop specific standards through a series of decisions. The Court has explained that "[f]ederal common law also may come into play when Congress has vested jurisdiction in the federal courts and empowered them to create governing rules of law."[5]

Textile Workers Union of America v. Lincoln Mills of Alabama

The most famous decision in this area is *Textile Workers Union of America v. Lincoln Mills of Alabama.*[6] An employer sued a union for an injunction to enforce an arbitration agreement. Section 301 of the Taft-Hartley Act grants the federal courts jurisdiction to decide disputes under labor-management contracts in industries that affect interstate commerce.[7] The law does not, however, enact any substantive principles for the federal courts to use in deciding such cases. The issue in *Lincoln Mills* was whether the case arose under federal law, since a jurisdictional authorization existed without any substantive federal provisions.

Justice Douglas, writing for the Court, upheld federal jurisdiction on the ground that Congress intended for the federal courts to develop a body of common law principles to resolve such labor-management disputes. As such, jurisdiction was appropriate because the case arose under the federal common law.[8] In a subsequent case, the Court held that state courts must apply this body of federal common law in deciding cases under §301.[9]

Statutes Interpreted As Authorizing Federal Common Law

The Supreme Court also has approved the development of federal common law under the federal Employee Retirement and Income Security Act (ERISA). The Court declared that "courts are to develop a federal common law of rights and obligations under ERISA plans."[10] Thus, "[w]hen ERISA is silent on an issue, a federal court must fashion federal common law to govern ERISA suits."[11] For example, federal courts have developed federal common law to determine the accrual date for causes of action under ERISA,[12] the nonavailability of a defense of equitable

[5] Texas Indus., Inc. v. Radcliff Materials, Inc., 451 U.S. 630, 642 (1981).

[6] 353 U.S. 448 (1957).

[7] 9 U.S.C. §185.

[8] An alternative ground of decision, relied on in the concurring opinion of Justices Harlan and Burton, was that Congress used its authority to create "protective jurisdiction." 353 U.S. at 460. Protective jurisdiction refers to creating jurisdiction to safeguard federal interests that Congress believes would be compromised in state courts. Protective jurisdiction is discussed in §5.2.2, *supra.*

[9] *See* Local 174, Teamsters of Am. v. Lucas Flour Co., 369 U.S. 95 (1962).

[10] Firestone Tire & Rubber Co. v. Bruch, 489 U.S. 101, 110 (1989).

[11] Fox Valley & Vicinity Constr. Workers Pension Fund v. Brown, 897 F.2d 275, 281 (7th Cir.) (en banc) *cert. denied,* 498 U.S. 820 (1990).

[12] Tolle v. Carroll Touch, Inc., 977 F.2d 1129 (7th Cir. 1992).

estoppel to ERISA-based claims,[13] and how benefits should be coordinated among plans.[14]

Similarly, the Court has held that the first two sections of the Sherman Antitrust Act authorize the federal courts to create a body of common law rules.[15] These statutory provisions forbid "[e]very contract, combination . . . or conspiracy, in restraint of trade" and "monopoliz[ing], or attempt[ing] to monopolize . . . any part of trade or commerce."[16] The Supreme Court has ruled that Congress intended for the federal courts to create common law rules under this provision. The Court declared: "Congress, however, did not intend the text of the Sherman Act to delineate the full meaning of the statute or its application in concrete situations. The legislative history makes it perfectly clear that it expected the courts to give shape to the statute's broad mandate by drawing on common-law tradition."[17]

The Court held that its authority to formulate common law rules under the Sherman Act did not include the authority to create a right of contribution allowing a defendant to recover from others who were part of an unlawful conspiracy. In *Texas Industries, Inc. v. Radcliff Materials, Inc.*, the Court explained that "[t]he intent to allow courts to develop governing principles of law, so unmistakably clear with regard to substantive violations, does not appear in debates on the treble-damages action created in §7 of the original act."[18] The Court said that it had developed federal common law defining liability under the act pursuant to congressional authorization and to effectuate the purposes of §§1 and 2 of the Sherman Act. The Court found no such authorization with regard to the liability section, or under the Clayton Act, and concluded that failing to create a rule of contribution would not harm federal interests. The Court said that it is for Congress, not the judiciary, to establish such a right.[19]

Texas Industries thus reaffirms the basic principle: the federal judiciary will formulate a body of common law rules only pursuant to clear congressional intent for such action. Although numerically the number of statutes authorizing such judicial actions is relatively small, this type of federal common law is quite important in terms of the significance of the statutes involved. Some of the most important federal laws—such as the labor, ERISA, and antitrust statutes described above—are instances in which the federal courts have been authorized to create common law rules.

The Supreme Court found that a federal statute authorizes federal courts to create and use federal common law in *Sosa v. Alvarez-Machain*.[20] The Court held that the Alien Tort Statute authorizes the federal courts to apply federal common law in limited circumstances.[21]

[13] Greany v. Western Farm Bureau Life Ins. Co., 973 F.2d 812 (9th Cir. 1992).

[14] PM Group Life Ins. Co. v. Western Growers Assur. Trust, 953 F.2d 543 (9th Cir. 1991).

[15] 15 U.S.C. §§1, 2.

[16] *Id.*

[17] National Socy. of Professional Engrs. v. United States, 435 U.S. 679, 688 (1978).

[18] 451 U.S. at 643-644.

[19] *Id.* at 647.

[20] 542 U.S. 692 (2004).

[21] 28 U.S.C. §1350.

The case involved a doctor, Humberto Alvarez-Machain, who was kidnapped in Mexico by federal authorities and brought to the United States to be tried for his role in the murder of a federal drug enforcement agent. Subsequently, a federal court dismissed the charges against Alvarez-Machain as lacking any basis. Alvarez-Machain then sued his kidnappers, in part, under the Alien Tort Statute, a federal law that was part of the Judiciary Act of 1789. The Alien Tort Statute provides that the "district courts shall have original jurisdiction of any civil action by an alien for a tort only, committed in violation of law of nations or a treaty of the United States."

The Supreme Court unanimously ruled against Alvarez-Machain and rejected his claim that the Alien Tort Statute was "authority for the creation of a new cause of action for torts in violation of international law."[22] Although the Court saw the provision as jurisdictional, it was clear that the statute can be used for civil actions in limited circumstances. Justice Souter, writing for the Court, explained that the Alien Tort Statute was enacted based "on the understanding that the common law would provide a cause of action for the most number of international law violations with a potential for personal liability at the time."[23] Justice Souter, in a part of the opinion joined by five other justices, said that three examples of this were violation of safe conducts, infringement of the rights of ambassadors, and piracy.[24]

Thus, the Court in *Alvarez-Machain* expressly left open the ability of plaintiffs to bring claims under the Alien Tort Statute, but such suits are allowed only in the limited circumstances where the offense is similar to those that provided a basis for an action in the late eighteenth century. The crucial issue for litigation after *Alvarez-Machain* is what circumstances will meet this standard. But the Court was clear that there are instances in which federal courts may use federal common law in carrying out this important federal statute.

Subsequently, the Court has consistently narrowed the availability of the Alien Tort Statute. In *Kiobel v. Royal Dutch Petroleum Co.*, the Court held that a cause of action does not exist under the Alien Tort Statute for actions arising in foreign countries of non-United States parties. The Court concluded that the statute did not disrupt the presumption against extraterritorial application.[25] And in *Jesner v. Arab Bank, PLC*, the Court ruled, 5-4, that foreign corporations cannot be sued under the Alien Tort Statute.[26] Justice Kennedy, writing for the majority, spoke of the "Court's general reluctance to extend judicially created private rights of action. The Court's recent precedents cast doubt on the authority of courts to extend or create private rights of action even in the realm of domestic law, where this Court has 'recently and repeatedly said that a decision to create a private right of action is one better left to legislative judgment in the great majority of cases.' "[27]

[22] 542 U.S. at 713.
[23] *Id.* at 724.
[24] *Id.*
[25] 569 U.S. 108 (2013).
[26] 584 U.S. 241 (2018).
[27] *Id.* at 264.

In *Nestle USA, Inc. v. Doe,* the Supreme Court held that litigants cannot sue American corporations under the Alien Tort Statute (ATS) when the alleged injury occurred entirely abroad.[28] Six individuals from Mali who had been trafficked into Ivory Coast as child slaves to produce cocoa sued American companies Nestle USA and Cargill for aiding and abetting child slavery. The companies did not own or operate the farms in Ivory Coast, but maintained close business relations with these establishments. The companies bought cocoa from these farms, provided the farmers with technical and financial resources, and held the exclusive right to purchase their cocoa. The plaintiffs sued under the ATS, claiming that the defendants aided and abetted forced overseas labor.

The Court stressed that the alleged human right violations occurred outside the United States and therefore could not be a basis for a suit in federal court. Justice Thomas, writing for the majority, said that the actions in the United States, namely corporate presence and decision-making, are not sufficient for a domestic application of the ATS.[29]

The justices, though, disagreed about the scope of the ATS. In a section of the opinion joined only by Justices Gorsuch and Kavanaugh, Justice Thomas suggests that since *Sosa,* "courts must refrain from creating a cause of action whenever there is even a single sound reason to defer to Congress."[30] He said that the ATS should be limited to just causes of action for torts recognized when it was adopted: "violation of safe conducts, infringement of the rights of ambassadors, and piracy."[31]

Justice Sotomayor, joined by Justices Breyer and Kagan, suggests that Justice Thomas's plurality opinion would "overrule *Sosa v. Alvarez-Machain* in all but name."[32] She wrote: "The First Congress enacted the ATS to ensure that federal courts are available to foreign citizens who suffer international law violations for which other nations may expect the United States to provide a forum for redress. Justice Thomas would limit the ATS' reach to only the three international law torts that were recognized in 1789. That reading contravenes both this Court's express holding in *Sosa* and the text and history of the ATS."[33]

There is no doubt that the Court has consistently narrowed the availability of the ATS, though it has not gone as far as Justice Thomas urged.

§6.3.3 Private Rights of Action

Reluctance to Create Private Rights of Action

One of the most controversial issues concerning federal common law concerns when federal courts may create private rights of action to enforce federal

[28] 593 U.S. 628, 630-631 (2021).
[29] *Id.* at 634.
[30] *Id.* at 635.
[31] *Id.* at 636 (citation omitted).
[32] *Id.* at 646 (Sotomayor, J., concurring in part and concurring in the judgment).
[33] *Id.*

laws that do not contain them. In general, the Supreme Court has been reluctant to create new causes of action, even in areas where it has been willing to develop common law rules. For example, in *Wheeldin v. Wheeler*, the Supreme Court refused to create a cause of action against a federal officer for abuse of the federal subpoena power.[34] Although the Court has developed federal common law principles to decide cases involving torts by federal officers, the Court refused to extend this to creating a right of action. The Court stated: "As respects the creation by the federal courts of common law rights, it is perhaps needless to state that we are not in the free-wheeling days antedating *Erie R. Co. v. Tompkins*. . . . [I]t is difficult for us to see how the present statute, which only grants power to issue subpoenas, implies a cause of action for abuse of that power."[35]

Similarly, in *United States v. Gilman*, the Supreme Court refused to create a cause of action by the United States for contribution under the Federal Tort Claims Act.[36] In *Gilman*, the United States had been sued for the negligence of its employee, and the government brought a third-party complaint against the individual for indemnity. Although a private employer would have been able to bring such an action, the Court unanimously ruled that the United States could not do so without express congressional authorization of the cause of action.

The Supreme Court refused to allow a private right of action to enforce the supremacy clause of Article VI of the Constitution, which provides that the Constitution and laws and treaties made pursuant to it are the supreme law of the land. In *Armstrong v. Exceptional Child Center*, the Court considered whether Medicaid providers could sue to enforce a provision of the Medicaid Act by suing under the supremacy clause.[37] The Ninth Circuit had ruled that there is "an implied right of action under the Supremacy Clause to seek injunctive relief against the enforcement or implementation of state legislation."[38]

But the Supreme Court, in an opinion by Justice Scalia, reversed. The Court explained that it is equally apparent that the supremacy clause is not the "‘"source of any federal rights,"' . . . and certainly does not create a cause of action."[39] The Court explained that "[i]f the Supremacy Clause includes a private right of action, then the Constitution *requires* Congress to permit the enforcement of its laws by private actors, significantly curtailing its ability to guide the implementation of federal law. It would be strange indeed to give a clause that makes federal law supreme a reading that *limits* Congress's power to enforce that law, by imposing mandatory private enforcement—a limitation unheard-of with regard to state legislatures."[40] For the Court, the supremacy clause provides a rule of decision in cases, like those involving preemption, where it is implicated. But it does not provide a cause of action where the federal law does not do so.

[34] 373 U.S. 647 (1963).
[35] *Id.* at 651.
[36] 347 U.S. 507 (1954).
[37] 575 U.S. 320 (2015).
[38] Inclusion, Inc. v. Armstrong, 567 Fed. Appx. 496, 497 (9th Cir. 2014).
[39] 575 U.S. at 324-325.
[40] *Id.* at 326.

The Court's reluctance to create causes of action reflects both separation of powers and federalism concerns. Separation of powers is implicated because of the Court's conviction that the legislature, not the judiciary, should authorize recovery.[41] Furthermore, the absence of federal legislation means that state law controls the conduct; the creation of federal common law means that the states no longer have exclusive authority in an area.

Nonetheless, in some instances the Supreme Court has created causes of action in the absence of express statutory authorization. By far, the most important example is the existence of private rights of action against federal officers for violations of constitutional rights. The Court has inferred a cause of action for money damages against federal officers directly from constitutional provisions, such as the Fourth, Fifth, and Eighth Amendments.[42] This topic—often referred to as *Bivens* actions after the seminal case in the area[43]—is discussed in detail in §9.1.

Statutes Without Private Rights of Action

The Court also has created a cause of action under statutes where it believes that a private right of action would fulfill congressional intent. Many federal statutes, especially criminal and regulatory laws, specify standards for conduct but do not expressly authorize suits for money damages. For example, many government benefit programs, many federal regulatory acts administered by government agencies, and most criminal laws do not authorize civil causes of action.[44] Not surprisingly, individuals injured by violations of these laws have asked the federal courts to create a private right of action.

The Supreme Court has held that it is willing to create such causes of action under federal statutes where it is necessary to effectuate Congress's intent.[45] As the Court stated: "The question whether a statute creates a cause of action, either expressly or by implication, is basically a matter of statutory construction . . . [and] what must ultimately be determined is whether Congress intended to create the private remedy asserted."[46]

There is no dispute that the basic inquiry is whether Congress intended, explicitly or implicitly, to create a private right of action. The controversy has centered on what constitutes sufficient evidence of intent and how restrictive or

[41] *See, e.g.,* H. Miles Foy, Some Reflections on Legislation, Adjudication, and Implied Private Actions in the State and Federal Courts, 71 Cornell L. Rev. 501 (1986); Thomas W. Merrill, The Common Law Powers of Federal Courts, 52 U. Chi. L. Rev. 1 (1985).

[42] *See, e.g.,* Carlson v. Green, 446 U.S. 14 (1980); Davis v. Passman, 442 U.S. 228 (1979) (Fifth Amendment); Bivens v. Six Unknown Named Agents of Fed. Bureau of Narcotics, 403 U.S. 388 (1971) (Fourth Amendment). These cases are discussed in detail in §9.1, *infra.*

[43] Bivens v. Six Unknown Named Agents of Fed. Bureau of Narcotics, 403 U.S. 388 (1971).

[44] For a description, with many examples, of the kinds of statutes that do not create causes of action, *see* Peter W. Low & John Calvin Jeffries, Federal Courts and the Law of Federal State Relations 1081-1082 (4th ed. 1998).

[45] *See, e.g.,* Cannon v. University of Chicago, 441 U.S. 677, 688 (1979); J.I. Case Co. v. Borak, 377 U.S. 426 (1964). These cases are discussed *infra.*

[46] Transamerica Mortgage Advisors, Inc. v. Lewis, 444 U.S. 11, 16 (1979).

liberal the Court should be in creating causes of action under statutes. The law in this area is difficult to summarize because there are a great many cases that are not completely consistent either in their methodology or in their results. The trend has been for the Supreme Court to be less willing to create private rights of action.

Approaches in Creating Private Rights of Action

Over the past 40 years, the Court has taken three different approaches, each more restrictive than the prior, in deciding when to create private rights of action. One approach was when the Court seemed willing to create a private right of action where it would help effectuate the purpose for a statute and if no legislative history mitigated against authorizing such a remedy. *J.I. Case Co. v. Borak* is a paradigm example of this approach.[47] The Securities Exchange Act of 1934 states that it is unlawful for a person to solicit proxies in violation of rules prescribed by the Securities and Exchange Commission.[48] Rule 14(a) prohibits proxy statements that contain false or misleading information. Federal courts are given exclusive jurisdiction under the statute. The issue in *Borak* was whether a shareholder had a private right of action for damages for violation of §14(a) of the Act.

The Supreme Court concluded that "it appears clear that private parties have a right . . . to bring suit for violation of §14(a) of the Act."[49] Although recognizing that the act does not create such a cause of action, the Court explained that the purposes of the statute would be best accomplished by allowing private actions for money damages. The Court said that the legislative history revealed that Congress wanted to prevent false proxy statements that inherently frustrated the rights of shareholders. The Court said that "[p]rivate enforcement of the proxy rules provides a necessary supplement to Commission action."[50] Contrary to any assertion that it was usurping legislative powers by creating a cause of action, the Court observed that "under the circumstances here it is the duty of the courts to be alert to provide such remedies as are necessary to make effective the congressional purpose."[51]

The *Borak* approach allows federal courts to create a private right of action, in the absence of any express congressional authorization, if damage suits would help accomplish the legislative purpose for a statute. This approach represents

[47] 377 U.S. 426 (1964). The issue of whether a statute creates a "right" enforceable via a private right of action has become even more important in light of Gonzaga University v. Doe, 536 U.S. 273 (2002), which held that the question of whether a statute creates an enforceable right, so as to be enforceable under §1983, is identical to the issue of whether a statute creates an enforceable right for determining whether there is a private right of action. Gonzaga University v. Doe is discussed in detail in §8.8.

[48] Section 14(a) of the Securities Exchange Act of 1934, 48 Stat. 895, 15 U.S.C. §78(n)(a).

[49] 377 U.S. at 430-431.

[50] *Id.* at 432.

[51] *Id.* at 433.

the high point in the Court's willingness to create private rights of action under federal statutes.[52]

Cort v. Ash Approach

A decade later, after the Burger Court had replaced the Warren Court, the Supreme Court shifted its approach and required a detailed inquiry into congressional intent in deciding whether to create private rights of action. Unlike the first approach, the second did not permit causes of action to be established simply because they advanced the legislative purpose behind a statute; the second approach consisted of a structured inquiry into Congress's intent. In *Cort v. Ash,* which represents the second approach, the Supreme Court articulated a four-part test for determining whether private rights of action should be created under federal statutes.[53]

The issue in *Cort* was whether a civil cause of action existed under a criminal statute prohibiting corporations from making contributions in connection with any presidential or vice presidential campaign. In a unanimous decision, the Court declined to allow such a suit and explained the appropriate inquiry:

> In determining whether a private remedy is implicit in a statute not expressly providing one, several factors are relevant. First, is the plaintiff "one of the class for whose especial benefit the statute was enacted"—that is, does the statute create a federal right in favor of the plaintiff? Second, is there any indication of legislative intent, explicit or implicit, either to create such a remedy or to deny one? Third, is it consistent with the underlying purposes of the legislative scheme to imply such a remedy for the plaintiff? And finally, is the cause of action one traditionally relegated to state law, in an area basically of concern of the States, so that it would be inappropriate to infer a cause of action based solely on federal law?[54]

Applying the four criteria, the Supreme Court refused to create a cause of action under the laws regulating campaign contributions by corporations. The Court reasoned that no evidence proved that the plaintiff was part of the class especially benefiting from the law, that no legislative history supported such a right of action, that the Court had no reason to believe that such actions would further

[52] *See, e.g.,* Allen v. State Bd. of Elections, 393 U.S. 544 (1969) (creating a cause of action under the Voting Rights Act of 1965); Superintendent of Ins. v. Bankers Life & Casualty Co., 404 U.S. 6 (1971) (creating a cause of action for violations of Rule 10(b)(5) promulgated by the Securities and Exchange Commission). By contrast, in Stoneridge Investment Partners, LLC v. Scientific Atlanta, Inc., 552 U.S. 148 (2008), the Court held that there was not a private right of action for investors who do not rely on the inaccurate statements or representations.

[53] 422 U.S. 66 (1975). Other cases shortly before Cort v. Ash foreshadowed this shift in approach. *See, e.g.,* Securities Investor Protection Corp. v. Barbour, 421 U.S. 412 (1975) (no private right of action for brokers to compel government agency to enforce the law for their benefit); National R.R. Passenger Corp. v. National Assn. of R.R. Passengers, 414 U.S. 453 (1974) (no private right of action under Amtrak Act).

[54] 422 U.S. at 78 (citations omitted).

the legislative purpose, and that regulation of corporations was generally left to state governments.[55]

For several years, the Supreme Court used the four-part *Cort v. Ash* approach when it was asked to create private rights of action to enforce federal statutes. For the most part, the Court refused to create causes of action.[56] *Cannon v. University of Chicago* is a particularly important decision in which the Court used the *Cort v. Ash* test to permit a private right of action.[57] In part, *Cannon* is noteworthy because of Justice Powell's dissent, which urged a more restrictive approach and was the basis for a future shift in the law.

Cannon involved Title IX of the Education Amendments of 1972, which provides: "No person in the United States shall, on the basis of sex, be excluded from participation in, be denied the benefits of, or be subjected to discrimination under any education program or activity receiving Federal financial assistance."[58] The Court said that it was appropriate to create a private right of action under the statute because the plaintiff, who claimed that she was wrongly denied admission to medical school on account of her gender, was part of the special class designed to benefit from the law. Additionally, the Court found that Congress intended a broad remedial scheme, including lawsuits, and that private actions would effectuate the statute's objective of ending discrimination.

Justice Powell wrote a dissent criticizing both the Court's approach and its result. Justice Powell contended that the "mode of analysis we have applied in the recent past cannot be squared with the doctrine of separation of powers. The time has come to reappraise our standards for the judicial implication of private causes of action."[59] According to Justice Powell, Congress alone has the authority to create causes of action and courts should establish them only in very rare circumstances. Justice Powell explained: "The 'four factor' analysis of [*Cort*] is an open invitation to federal courts to legislate causes of action not authorized by Congress. It is an analysis not faithful to constitutional principles and should be rejected. *Absent the most compelling evidence of affirmative congressional intent, a federal court should not infer a private cause of action.*"[60]

Touche Ross Approach

Soon after *Cannon*, the Court shifted to a third approach, adopting Justice Powell's method: the Court will create a private right of action only if there is affirmative evidence of Congress's intent to create a private right of action. In

[55] *Id.* at 80-85.

[56] *See, e.g.*, Piper v. Chris-Craft Indus., Inc., 430 U.S. 1 (1977) (no private right of action under §14(e) of the Securities Exchange Act).

[57] 441 U.S. 677 (1979). The Supreme Court reaffirmed *Cannon*'s recognition of a private right of action under Title IX in Gebser v. Lago Vista Independent School Dist., 524 U.S. 274 (1998). The Court also reaffirmed *Cannon* in Alexander v. Sandoval, 532 U.S. 275 (2001).

[58] 20 U.S.C. §1681(a).

[59] 441 U.S. at 730 (Powell, J., dissenting).

[60] *Id.* at 731 (emphasis added).

Touche Ross & Co. v. Redington, a majority of the Court first articulated this approach.[61] Although the Court did not expressly discard the *Cort v. Ash* test, commentators read *Touche Ross* as an unmistakable departure in methodology.[62] In fact, Justices Scalia and O'Connor stated that they believed that *Touche Ross* had "effectively overruled the *Cort v. Ash* analysis."[63]

In *Touche Ross,* the Court considered whether a cause of action could be brought under §17(a) of the Securities Exchange Act of 1934, which imposes a duty for maintenance of records as required by the Securities and Exchange Commission.[64] The Supreme Court refused to create a cause of action and declared that "our task is limited solely to determining whether Congress intended to create the private right of action asserted."[65] The Court said that "the statute by its terms grants no private rights to any identifiable class and proscribes no conduct as unlawful. And . . . legislative history of the 1934 Act simply does not speak to the issue of private remedies under §17(a). At least in such a case as this, the inquiry ends there."[66]

In many decisions since *Touche Ross,* the Supreme Court has reaffirmed its use of the third approach: private rights of action will be created only if there is affirmative evidence that Congress intended to create a private right of action. For example, in *Transamerica Mortgage Advisors, Inc. v. Lewis,* the Court reinforced that the "dispositive question remains whether Congress intended to create any such remedy."[67] In *Lewis,* the Court refused to allow a cause of action for damages for violations of the Investment Advisers Act of 1940, which prohibits fraudulent practices by investment advisors.[68] The Court reasoned that the existence of other remedies in the statute reflected a lack of intent to allow private actions. In light of the absence of affirmative authorization for private suits, the Court refused to permit them.

Similarly, in *Karahalios v. National Federation of Federal Employees,* the Court unanimously held that the statutorily created right to fair representation does not justify a private right of action by a federal employee.[69] The Court noted that Congress in enacting the statute did not create a private right of action and that Congress was aware that the Court was unwilling to infer a cause of action unless there was a clear indication of legislative intent to justify such suits. The Court emphasized that Congress knew "that such issues [judicial creation of private rights of action]

[61] 442 U.S. 560 (1979).

[62] *See, e.g.,* Low & Jeffries, *supra* note 44, at 165.

[63] Thompson v. Thompson, 484 U.S. 174 (1988).

[64] Securities Exchange Act of 1934, 48 Stat. 897, as amended, 15 U.S.C. §78q(a).

[65] 442 U.S. at 568.

[66] *Id.* at 576.

[67] 444 U.S. 11 (1979).

[68] 15 U.S.C. §§80b-1 et seq. The act also provides that contracts in violation of the act are void and the Court approved equitable actions, such as rescission and restitution, to enforce this part of the statute.

[69] 489 U.S. 527 (1989).

were being resolved by a straight-forward inquiry into whether Congress intended to provide a private right of action."[70]

Subsequently, in *Alexander v. Sandoval*, the Supreme Court rejected an implied right of action to enforce the regulations enacted under Title VI of the Civil Rights Act of 1964.[71] Title VI prohibits racial discrimination by recipients of federal funds. The Supreme Court has interpreted this as being coextensive with the equal protection clause of the Fourteenth Amendment and thus as requiring discriminatory intent for a violation.[72] The Department of Justice, however, enacted regulations under Title VI that prohibit recipients of federal funds from engaging in practices that have a racially discriminatory impact. The issue in *Alexander v. Sandoval* was whether there is a private right of action to enforce these regulations.

Alexander v. Sandoval involved a challenge to Alabama's administering driver's license tests only in English; it was claimed that this has a racially disparate impact against Hispanics. The Supreme Court, however, ruled 5-4 that there is no private right of action to enforce the Title VI regulations. The Court accepted that there is a private right of action to enforce Title VI and that Title VI requires intentional discrimination, whereas the regulations do not. But the Court said that there was nothing in the statute that supported a private right of action to enforce the Title VI regulations. Justice Scalia, writing for the Court, noted that the statute provides methods for its enforcement, such as fund cutoffs for noncompliance, and that "[t]he express provision of one method of enforcing a substantive rule suggests that Congress intended to preclude others."[73] The Court expressly rejected the idea that laws adopted between 1964 and 1975—the period between *J.I. Case v. Borak* and *Cort v. Ash*—should be considered under an approach that is more permissive for creating private rights of action.

Alexander v. Sandoval is particularly important because the Title VI regulations are often crucial for civil rights litigants challenging practices with a racially discriminatory impact. These will be much more difficult to challenge in light of the Court's holding that there is no private right of action to enforce the Title VI regulations.[74]

Although there have been many decisions in which the Court has refused to create private rights of action because of the absence of congressional intent,[75]

[70] *Id.* at 536.

[71] 532 U.S. 275 (2001).

[72] *See* Regents of the University of California v. Bakke, 438 U.S. 265 (1978). In Guardians Assn. v. Civil Service Commn. of New York, 463 U.S. 582 (1983), the Court indicated that there is a cause of action under Title VI only for intentional discrimination.

[73] 532 U.S. at 290.

[74] There is uncertainty as to whether §1983 can be used to enforce these regulations against government recipients of federal funds. Justice Stevens, dissenting in Alexander v. Sandoval, argues that §1983 suits can be brought to enforce these rules. 532 U.S. at 305 (Stevens, J., dissenting). Section 1983, and its use to enforce federal statutes, is discussed in Chapter 8.

[75] *See, e.g.*, Thompson v. Thompson, 484 U.S. 174 (1988) (refusing to create a cause of action under the Parental Kidnapping Prevention Act); California v. Sierra Club, 451 U.S. 287 (1981) (refusing to create a cause of action under the Rivers and Harbors Appropriation Act of 1899); Northwest Airlines, Inc. v. Transport Workers Union of Am., 451 U.S. 77 (1981) (refusing to create a cause of action for contribution under the Equal Pay Act of 1963 and Title VII of the Civil Rights Act of 1964).

in a few cases the Court has established such causes of action under the third approach. In *Merrill Lynch, Pierce, Fenner & Smith, Inc. v. Curran*, the Court, by a 5-4 vote, permitted a cause of action for damages under the Commodities Futures Trading Commission Act.[76] The majority emphasized that a private right of action existed under the act when Congress amended it in 1974. The Court reasoned that it was "simply assumed the remedy was available," and said that Congress's failure to eliminate it or amend the statutory provisions from which it was inferred justified its maintenance.[77]

Also, in *Herman & MacLean v. Huddleston*, the Court unanimously held that a private right of action existed under §10(b) of the Securities Exchange Act of 1934.[78] The Court stressed that private actions had been allowed under this provision for more than 35 years and concluded that "[t]he existence of this implied remedy is simply beyond peradventure."[79]

Curran and *Huddleston* share in common the fact that the Court was continuing existing causes of action, rather than creating new ones. Under current law, it appears that the Court will establish private rights of action only if affirmative evidence shows that Congress intended to allow such suits.

Admittedly, the above description makes the law appear neater than it actually is. Even today, when the Court uses the third approach, it cites cases decided under earlier approaches, and no decisions have been expressly overruled. But undoubtedly there has been a marked shift by the Court away from creating federal common law in the form of private rights of action under federal statutes.

Debate Over Creating Private Rights of Action

The desirability of the Court's shift is heatedly debated in the voluminous scholarly literature.[80] On the one hand, the Court's defenders argue that separation of powers requires a highly restrictive approach in creating causes of action. Advocates of this position maintain that Congress alone has the power to authorize private rights of action and that the Court oversteps its bounds when it both creates the basis for the suit and awards the remedy under it.[81] Others, however, take a very different approach. The Court's critics maintain that judicial abdication is itself a violation of separation of powers. This position is that the Court's role includes effectuating congressional intent and that the judiciary should create a private right of action where it will advance the purposes behind a statute.[82] Those

[76] 456 U.S. 353 (1982).

[77] *Id.* at 380.

[78] 459 U.S. 375 (1983).

[79] *Id.* at 380.

[80] *See, e.g.*, Merrill, *supra* note 41, at 1; Seth Davis, Implied Public Rights of Action, 114 Colum. L. Rev. 1 (2014). Robert H.A. Ashford, Implied Causes of Action Under Federal Laws: Calling the Court Back to *Borak*, 79 Nw. U. L. Rev. 227 (1984); George D. Brown, Of Activism and *Erie:* The Implication Doctrine's Implications for the Nature and Role of the Federal Courts, 69 Iowa L. Rev. 617 (1984).

[81] *See, e.g.*, Brown, *supra* note 80, at 644-649.

[82] Tamar Frankel, Implied Rights of Action, 67 Va. L. Rev. 553, 565-566 (1981).

who favor a greater judicial willingness to create causes of action under federal laws maintain that the Court wrongly has assumed that congressional silence is an implicit rejection of private rights of action. Professors Stewart and Sunstein persuasively argued, "When Congress is simply silent on the question of remedies for defective administrative performance, that silence cannot automatically be read to negate judicial authority to create such remedies."[83] At minimum, it would be desirable if the Court engaged in a richer inquiry than has been evident in its cases when it determines whether a private right of action would further Congress's intent.

[83] *See, e.g.,* Richard B. Stewart & Cass R. Sunstein, Public Programs and Private Rights, 95 Harv. L. Rev. 1193, 1317 (1982).

Part II

Federal Court Relief Against Governments and Government Officers

The most important function of the federal courts is to uphold the Constitution and the laws of the United States. Part II considers the federal courts' power, as well as the limits on federal court authority, to review the actions of federal, state, and local governments and their officers. Chapter 7 examines federal court relief against state governments, specifically focusing on the Eleventh Amendment, which has been interpreted as a bar to virtually all suits brought directly against state governments. Chapter 8 considers suits brought pursuant to 42 U.S.C. §1983, which is the basic vehicle for litigation against local governments and state and local officers to prevent and remedy violations of the Constitution and federal statutes. Chapter 9 focuses on suits against federal officers, especially pursuant to Supreme Court created causes of action, and against the federal government.

Several themes unite these chapters. First, what is the proper role of sovereign immunity in the American constitutional structure? Is sovereign immunity an anachronistic relic of English common law that provided that the king could do no wrong, or is sovereign immunity a crucial doctrine protecting government and taxpayers from potentially devastating lawsuits and constant supervision by the judiciary?

Second, what is the proper allocation of liability between government entities and government officers? Some liability is required to compensate individuals injured by government action and to deter wrongdoing. But where should this liability be placed? Is it better to shift all liability to government entities and completely immunize the officers, or is it better to make both government entities and the government officers liable under some circumstances? And in the latter case, when should each be liable?

Third, as is true throughout this book, the chapters in Part II raise the issue of whether it is important that *federal* courts and federal law remedies be available. For example, the Eleventh Amendment's preclusion of suits against state governments means that suits against state governments must be brought in state court. Additionally, a narrow construction of §1983 and the absence of federal law damage remedies against government officers would leave only state law remedies. Would requiring such recourse to state law remedies be a desirable promotion of federalism or an unjustified absence of adequate safeguards for federal interests?

CHAPTER 7

Suits Against State Governments: The Eleventh Amendment and Sovereign Immunity

§7.1 INTRODUCTION

Importance of Sovereign Immunity

A major limit on the federal judicial power—and now on the authority of state courts as well—is the doctrine of sovereign immunity. Sovereign immunity in the federal courts is based on the Supreme Court's interpretation of the Eleventh Amendment, which states, "The Judicial power of the United States shall not be construed to extend to any suit in law or equity, commenced or prosecuted against one of the United States by Citizens of another State, or by Citizens or Subjects of any foreign state." As interpreted, the Eleventh Amendment prohibits suits in federal courts against state governments in law, equity, or admiralty, by a state's own citizens, by citizens of another state, or by citizens of foreign countries.

Additionally, the Supreme Court held that sovereign immunity bars suits against state governments in state court without their consent.[1] The Court thus has ruled that there is a broad principle of sovereign immunity that applies in both federal and state courts; the Eleventh Amendment is a reflection and embodiment of part of that principle. As Justice Kennedy, writing for the Court in *Alden v. Maine*, declared, "[S]overeign immunity derives not from the Eleventh Amendment but from the structure of the original Constitution itself."[2]

The Eleventh Amendment and sovereign immunity are particularly important in defining the relationship between the federal and state governments and in determining the scope of constitutional protections. An expansive reading of the Eleventh Amendment effectively immunizes the actions of state governments from federal court review, even when a state violates the most fundamental constitutional rights. Hence, the Eleventh Amendment protects state autonomy by immunizing states from suits in federal court, but it provides this independence by risking the ability to enforce basic federal rights. As Professors Low and Jeffries observed: "The stakes involved in interpreting the Eleventh Amendment are potentially very high. Virtually the entire class of modern civil rights litigation plausibly might be barred by an expansive reading of the immunity of the states from suit in federal court."[3]

Unwilling, however, to trust state courts completely to uphold and enforce the Constitution and federal laws, the Supreme Court has devised a number of ways to avoid the broad prohibition of the Eleventh Amendment and to ensure federal court review of allegedly illegal state actions.[4] The case law concerning the Eleventh Amendment often has been conflicting and inconsistent, as the Court has struggled to articulate a standard that protects state autonomy while still ensuring state compliance with federal law. Commentators have labeled these decisions as a "tortuous line of Supreme Court cases"[5] and as "little more than a hodgepodge of confusing and intellectually indefensible judge-made law."[6]

§7.1 [1] Alden v. Maine, 527 U.S. 706 (1999). Also, the Court has held that sovereign immunity bars actions against states in federal administrative agencies. Federal Maritime Commission v. South Carolina Ports Authority, 535 U.S. 743 (2002).

[2] 527 U.S. at 728.

[3] Peter W. Low & John C. Jeffries, Jr., Federal Courts and the Law of Federal-State Relations (9th ed. 2018).

[4] These techniques for avoiding the Eleventh Amendment are discussed in §§7.5, 7.6, and 7.7.

[5] John R. Pagan, Eleventh Amendment Analysis, 39 Ark. L. Rev. 447, 449 (1986).

[6] John J. Gibbons, The Eleventh Amendment and State Sovereign Immunity: A Reinterpretation, 83 Colum. L. Rev. 1889, 1891 (1983).

§7.1 Introduction

In examining the Eleventh Amendment and sovereign immunity, §7.2 begins by describing the history of its ratification—a history that continues to be examined and relied on in modern interpretations.[7] Although the Eleventh Amendment has been part of the Constitution for more than 215 years, there still is no agreement as to its proper scope. In fact, several very different theories have been offered as to the appropriate meaning of the amendment. The choice of theory is likely to be determinative of most questions that arise concerning the effect of the Eleventh Amendment. These competing theories are described in §7.3.

The Supreme Court has addressed many particular issues concerning the application of the Eleventh Amendment. Section 7.4 details this law and discusses which suits are prohibited by the amendment, as well as what type of litigation is allowed.

The Supreme Court has devised three primary mechanisms allowing federal courts to ensure state compliance with federal law. Specifically, the Court has allowed suits against state officers, permitted states to waive their Eleventh Amendment immunity and consent to suit, and sanctioned litigation against the states pursuant to statutes adopted under the Fourteenth Amendment. These techniques are described in §§7.5, 7.6, and 7.7, respectively.

Underlying Policy Issues

Sovereign immunity is a topic of great significance in current law. From a practical perspective, there remains uncertainty in the current law concerning the details of when state governments may be sued and which actions are barred. From a policy perspective, it raises profound questions about the appropriate role of the judiciary. On the one hand, supporters of sovereign immunity argue that it was a principle that predates the Constitution and is part of the very structure of that document. They maintain that safeguarding state governments, and particularly their treasuries, is deeply embedded in the Constitution. For example, the Court has stated, "[T]he preeminent purpose of [sovereign immunity] is to accord States the dignity that is consistent with their status as sovereign entities."[8] Supporters maintain that there are other adequate ways of holding state governments accountable, such as suits against state officers and suits by the federal government.[9]

Critics of sovereign immunity argue that it is a principle not found in the text of the Constitution or intended by the Framers. Opponents of sovereign immunity

[7] *See, e.g.,* Atascadero State Hosp. v. Scanlon, 473 U.S. 234, 247-302 (1985) (Brennan, J., dissenting); William A. Fletcher, A Historical Interpretation of the Eleventh Amendment: A Narrow Construction of an Affirmative Grant of Jurisdiction Rather Than a Prohibition Against Jurisdiction, 35 Stan. L. Rev. 1033 (1983) (detailing the history of the ratification of the Eleventh Amendment as a basis for an argument about its proper scope).

[8] Federal Maritime Commission v. South Carolina State Ports Authority, 535 U.S. at 760. For an excellent critique of the dignity rationale for sovereign immunity, *see* Judith Resnik & Julie Chi-hye Suk, Adding Insult to Injury: Questioning the Role of Dignity in Conceptions of Sovereignty, 55 Stan. L. Rev. 1921 (2003).

[9] *See* Jesse H. Choper & John C. Yoo, Who's Afraid of the Eleventh Amendment: The Limited Impact of the Court's Sovereign Immunity Rulings, 106 Colum. L. Rev. 213 (2006).

argue that it wrongly favors government immunity over accountability and is inconsistent with the very notion of a government under law.[10] People can be deprived of life, liberty, or property, but be left with no remedy and thus no due process. State governments can violate the Constitution and nowhere be held accountable. In *Alden v. Maine*, Justice Kennedy expressly addressed concerns about accountability and declared:

> The constitutional privilege of a State to assert its sovereign immunity in its own courts does not confer upon the State a concomitant right to disregard the Constitution or valid federal law. The States and their officers are bound by obligations imposed by the Constitution and by federal statutes that comport with the constitutional design. We are unwilling to assume the States will refuse to honor the Constitution or obey the binding laws of the United States. The good faith of the States thus provides an important assurance that "[t]his Constitution, and the Laws of the United States which shall be made in Pursuance thereof . . . shall be the supreme Law of the Land." U.S. Const., Art. VI.[11]

Defenders of sovereign immunity say that the doctrine properly puts trust in governments. Critics argue that such trust has no role in constitutional jurisprudence; government at times will violate the law and must be held accountable.

In addition to strengthening the Eleventh Amendment's protections for state governments, the Supreme Court in the past two decades also has used other doctrines to limit federal power and protect state governments. For example, in *New York v. United States*,[12] *Printz v. United States*,[13] *National Federation of Independent Business v. Sebelius*,[14] and *Murphy v. NCAA*,[15] the Supreme Court held that Congress violates the Tenth Amendment if it compels state legislative or regulatory activity. In *United States v. Lopez*[16] and *United States v. Morrison*,[17] the Court invalidated federal statutes as exceeding the scope of Congress's commerce clause authority.

All of these decisions reflect the Court's commitment to protecting state sovereignty by limiting federal power. All also reveal the ideological dimension of federalism. Virtually every major sovereign immunity case in the last several decades has split along ideological lines, with conservative justices favoring protecting sovereign immunity and liberal justices rejecting it.

[10] *See* Erwin Chemerinsky, Against Sovereign Immunity, 53 Stan. L. Rev. 1201 (2001).
[11] 527 U.S. at 755.
[12] 505 U.S. 144 (1992).
[13] 521 U.S. 898 (1997).
[14] 567 U.S. 519 (2012).
[15] 584 U.S. 453 (2018).
[16] 514 U.S. 549 (1995).
[17] 529 U.S. 598 (2000).

§7.2 HISTORY OF THE RATIFICATION OF THE ELEVENTH AMENDMENT

Justices and commentators continue to base their arguments about the proper interpretation of the Eleventh Amendment on claims about the history of its ratification.[1] Therefore, a brief description of this history is appropriate.[2]

Did Article III Override Sovereign Immunity? The Early Debate

As described previously, Article III of the Constitution defined the federal judicial power in terms of nine categories of cases and controversies. Two of the clauses of Article III, §2, specifically deal with suits against state governments. These provisions permit suits "between a State and Citizens of another state" and "between a State . . . and foreign . . . Citizens." These are the clauses that the Eleventh Amendment modified, and these are the provisions that are frequently discussed in interpretations of the Eleventh Amendment.

A key matter in dispute is whether the above-quoted language of Article III was meant to override the sovereign immunity that kept states from being sued in state courts. As Justice Souter observed, "The 1787 draft in fact said nothing on the subject, and it was this very silence that occasioned some, though apparently not widespread, dispute among the framers and others over whether ratification of the Constitution would preclude a State sued in federal court from asserting sovereign immunity as it could have done on any nonfederal matter litigated in its own courts."[3] There is no record of any debate about this issue or these clauses at the Constitutional Convention.

However, at the state ratification conventions, the question of suits against state governments in federal court was raised and received a great deal of attention. States had incurred substantial debts, especially during the Revolutionary

§7.2 [1] For example, in Seminole Tribe of Florida v. Florida, 517 U.S. 44 (1996), both the majority and the dissent argue over the historical understanding of sovereign immunity and the meaning of the Eleventh Amendment. Justice Souter's dissent, in particular, focuses at length on the history surrounding the adoption of Article III and the ratification of the Eleventh Amendment. *See id.* at 100 (Souter, J., dissenting). Commentators, too, argue at length over the proper historical understanding of the Eleventh Amendment. *See, e.g.,* Caleb Nelson, Sovereign Immunity as a Doctrine of Personal Jurisdiction, 115 Harv. L. Rev. 1561 (2002); Carlos Manuel Vazquez, What Is Eleventh Amendment Immunity, 106 Yale L.J. 1683 (1997); Vicki C. Jackson, The Supreme Court, the Eleventh Amendment, and State Sovereign Immunity, 98 Yale L.J. 1 (1988); William A. Fletcher, A Historical Interpretation of the Eleventh Amendment: A Narrow Construction of an Affirmative Grant of Jurisdiction Rather Than a Prohibition Against Jurisdiction, 35 Stan. L. Rev. 1033 (1983). For an argument that interpretation of the Eleventh Amendment should focus on the text and not on its history and purpose, *see* John F. Manning, The Eleventh Amendment and the Precise Reading of Constitutional Texts, 113 Yale L.J. 1663 (2004).

[2] For more detailed histories of the ratification of the Eleventh Amendment, *see* Clyde E. Jacobs, The Eleventh Amendment and Sovereign Immunity (1972); James E. Pfander, History and State Suability: An Explanatory Account of the Eleventh Amendment, 83 Cornell L. Rev. 1269 (1998).

[3] Seminole Tribe of Florida v. Florida, 517 U.S. at 100 (Souter, J., dissenting).

War, and there was a great fear of suits being brought against the states in federal court to collect on these debts. More generally, the concern was expressed that although sovereign immunity was a defense to state law claims in state court, it would be unavailable if the same matter were raised against a state in a diversity suit in federal court.

Thus, at the state ratification conventions there was a debate over whether states could be sued in federal court without their consent.[4] One group argued that the text of Article III clearly made states subject to suit in federal court. In Virginia, George Mason opposed ratification of the Constitution and particularly disliked the provisions that made the states liable in federal court:

> Claims respecting those lands, every liquidated account, or other claim against this state, will be tried before the federal court. Is not this disgraceful? Is this state to be brought to the bar of justice like a delinquent individual? Is the sovereignty of the state to be arraigned like a culprit, or private offender?[5]

Mason believed that Article III's explicit provision for suits against the states would have the effect of abrogating the states' sovereign immunity defense.[6]

Likewise, Patrick Henry opposed the Constitution at the Virginia convention, in part based on his belief that Article III unmistakably permitted litigation against states in federal court. He labeled as "incomprehensible" the claim that Article III allowed states to be plaintiffs but not defendants.[7] Henry said, "There is nothing to warrant such an assertion. . . . What says the paper? That it shall have cognizance of controversies between a state and citizens of another state, without discriminating between plaintiff and defendant."[8]

Nor was this view that Article III overrides state sovereignty and permits suits against unconsenting states in federal court held only in Virginia or only by opponents of ratification. In Pennsylvania, North Carolina, and New York, there were major objections to this part of the Constitution.[9] Many of the Constitution's supporters also agreed that Article III permitted states to be sued in federal court. In fact, they argued that this lack of immunity was desirable to ensure that states could not escape their liabilities or avoid litigation that was necessary to hold states properly accountable. Edmund Randolph, a member of the Committee of Detail at the Constitutional Convention, argued: "I ask the Convention of the free people of Virginia if there can be honesty in rejecting the government because justice is to be done by it? . . . Are we to say that we shall discard this government because

[4] *See, e.g.,* Jacobs, *supra* note 2, at 27-40; John J. Gibbons, The Eleventh Amendment and State Sovereign Immunity: A Reinterpretation, 83 Colum. L. Rev. 1889, 1902-1914 (1983).

[5] 3 The Debates in the Several States Conventions on the Adoption of the Federal Constitution 526-527 (Jonathan Elliot ed. 1937).

[6] Atascadero State Hosp. v. Scanlon, 473 U.S. 234, 265 (1985) (Brennan, J., dissenting) (describing Mason's opposition to Article III).

[7] Elliot, *supra* note 5, at 543.

[8] *Id.*

[9] Gibbons, *supra* note 4, at 1902-1914.

it would make us all honest?"[10] In Pennsylvania, Thomas Pickering argued that it was important for federal courts to be able to give relief against states to citizens of other states or nations who had been wronged and might be unable to receive fair treatment in a state's own courts.[11]

In sharp contrast, many other supporters of the Constitution argued that Article III did not override state sovereignty and that, notwithstanding its provisions, states could be sued in federal court only if they consented to be a party to the litigation. Alexander Hamilton wrote in the *Federalist Papers*:

> It is inherent in the nature of sovereignty not to be amenable to the suit of an individual *without its consent.* This is the general sense and the general practice of mankind; and the exemption, as one of the attributes of sovereignty, is now enjoyed by the government of every State in the Union. Unless, therefore, there is a surrender of this immunity . . . it will remain with the States.[12]

Similarly, Madison argued that states have sovereign immunity and that Article III serves only to allow states to come to federal court as plaintiffs, not that it allows them to be sued as defendants without their consent.[13] Madison said that "jurisdiction in controversies between a state and citizens of another state is much objected to, and perhaps without reason. It is not in the power of individuals to call any state into court."[14]

This recounting of the ratification debates reveals that there was no consensus, even among the Constitution's supporters, about whether state sovereign immunity survived Article III.[15] Yet, as discussed more fully below, the Supreme Court has barred states from being sued by their own citizens, in large part, based on its belief, supported by quotations from Madison and Hamilton, that Article III was not intended to authorize states to be sued without their consent.[16] In reviewing the Eleventh Amendment's history, the Supreme Court observed that "[a]t most, then, the historical materials show that . . . the intentions of the Framers and Ratifiers were ambiguous."[17]

[10] Elliot, *supra* note 5, at 575.

[11] 14 John P. Kaminsky & Gaspare J. Saladino, The Documentary History of the Ratification of the Constitution 204 (1983).

[12] The Federalist Papers No. 81, at 487-488 (A. Hamilton) (C. Rossiter ed. 1961) (emphasis in original).

[13] Elliot, *supra* note 5, at 533.

[14] *Id.*

[15] Justice Souter, after a detailed recounting of this history, observed: "[T]he framers and their contemporaries did not agree about the place of common-law state sovereign immunity even as to federal jurisdiction resting on the citizen-state diversity clause." Seminole Tribe of Florida v. Florida, 517 U.S. at 142-143 (Souter, J., dissenting).

[16] *See* Hans v. Louisiana, 134 U.S. 1 (1890); *see also* Seminole Tribe of Florida v. Florida, 517 U.S. at 69-70 (reaffirming *Hans,* in part, by defending the views of Marshall, Madison, and Hamilton). *See* discussion in §7.4, *infra.*

[17] Welch v. Texas Dept. of Highways & Pub. Transp., 483 U.S. 468 (1987).

Chisholm v. Georgia

The dispute over whether sovereign immunity survived Article III was presented to the U.S. Supreme Court soon after ratification of the Constitution. The Judiciary Act of 1789 gave the Supreme Court original jurisdiction in cases between states and citizens of another state or citizens of foreign states.[18] In fact, the first case filed in the U.S. Supreme Court involved a suit by Dutch creditors trying to collect on Revolutionary War debts owed to them by Maryland.[19] The Supreme Court, however, did not address the question of Article III and its relation to sovereign immunity until 1794 in *Chisholm v. Georgia.*[20] This decision is particularly important because the Eleventh Amendment was ratified specifically to overrule the Court's holding in *Chisholm.*

Chisholm involved an attempt by a South Carolina citizen to recover money owed by the state of Georgia. Robert Farquhar, a South Carolina citizen, had supplied materials to Georgia during the Revolutionary War. Although the Georgia legislature appropriated the funds for this debt, the Georgia commissaries refused to pay for the purchases. Farquhar died, and Alexander Chisholm, the executor of his estate, sued Georgia to recover the money owed. Chisholm, also a South Carolinian, sued in the Supreme Court based on the provision in the Judiciary Act of 1789 that created original jurisdiction for suits against a state by citizens of other states.

Chisholm was represented before the Supreme Court by Edmund Randolph, who was also serving at the time as attorney general of the United States. Randolph, who had been a delegate at the Constitutional Convention, argued that Article III of the Constitution clearly permitted suits against states by citizens of other states. The state of Georgia chose not to appear, believing that federal courts had no jurisdiction over it unless it consented to be sued.

The Supreme Court, in a 4-1 decision, ruled in Chisholm's favor. Announcing their decisions *seriatim,* four justices seemed to have easily concluded that the unmistakable language of Article III authorized suits against a state by citizens of another state. Although later decisions criticized this view of Article III and the decision in *Chisholm,*[21] it must be remembered that the four justices in the majority in *Chisholm* had impeccable credentials, especially in discussing the intent behind constitutional provisions. Justices John Blair and James Wilson had been delegates to the Constitutional Convention. Justice William Cushing presided over the state ratification convention in Massachusetts. Chief Justice John Jay was a delegate to the New York ratification convention and one of the authors of the *Federalist Papers.*[22]

[18] The Judiciary Act of 1789, ch. 20, 1 Stat. 73, 80, §13.

[19] Vanstophorst v. Maryland, 2 U.S. (2 Dall.) 401 (1791).

[20] 2 U.S. (2 Dall.) 419 (1793).

[21] *See, e.g.,* Hans v. Louisiana, 134 U.S. 1 (1890) (criticizing the decision in Chisholm v. Georgia).

[22] John V. Orth, The Judicial Power of the United States: The Eleventh Amendment in American History 22-23 (1987).

Only Justice Iredell dissented in *Chisholm.* He argued that the Judiciary Act did not specifically authorize suits in assumpsit against states and that such suits were not permitted against the government in English common law. Thus, he concluded that the general language of Article III was insufficient to authorize such a suit against the state of Georgia without its consent.

State legislators and governors were outraged by the Supreme Court's decision in *Chisholm v. Georgia.* Georgia adopted a statute declaring that anyone attempting to enforce the Supreme Court's decision is "hereby declared to be guilty of a felony, and shall suffer death, without the benefit of clergy by being hanged."[23] The intense reaction to *Chisholm* is reflected in the speed with which a constitutional amendment to overturn the decision was adopted. The Supreme Court decided *Chisholm* on February 14, 1794. By March 4, 1794, fewer than three weeks later, both houses of Congress had approved the Eleventh Amendment. Within a year, the requisite number of states ratified it, although it was three more years until the president issued a proclamation declaring the Eleventh Amendment to have been properly ratified.[24]

The consensus among historians is that states were particularly concerned about the *Chisholm* decision because they feared suits against them to collect unpaid Revolutionary War debts.[25] Also, there was fear that British creditors and American Tories whose property was seized during the war would sue the states to recover their assets.[26] The fact that such suits already had been filed in South Carolina, Georgia, Virginia, and Massachusetts indicated that it was not a baseless fear.[27] Thus, within a few years after *Chisholm,* the Eleventh Amendment was adopted to prohibit federal courts from hearing suits against a state by citizens of another state or of a foreign country.

§7.3 WHAT DOES THE ELEVENTH AMENDMENT MEAN? COMPETING THEORIES

Competing Theories of the Eleventh Amendment

Although the Eleventh Amendment is well over 200 years old, there still is no agreement as to what it means or what it prohibits. In fact, several different

[23] Peter W. Low, John C. Jeffries, Jr., and Curtis A. Bradley, Federal Courts and the Law of Federal-State Relations 1096 (9th ed. 2018).

[24] For a description of this history and a discussion of why there was such a delay in the issuance of the presidential proclamation, *see* Orth, *supra* note 22, at 20-21.

[25] 1 Charles Warren, The Supreme Court in United States History 99 (1922); Orth, *supra* note 22, at 7-8. *But see* Jacobs, *supra* note 2, at 70 ("There is practically no evidence that Congress proposed and the legislatures ratified the Eleventh Amendment to permit the states to escape payment of existing obligations.").

[26] Orth, *supra* note 22, at 7.

[27] Warren, *supra* note 25, at 99.

theories have been developed to interpret it. The theory chosen determines the scope of the Eleventh Amendment and the circumstances under which states may be sued in federal courts.

The Rehnquist Court was split between two different theories. One theory—supported by a majority composed of Chief Justice Rehnquist and Justices O'Connor, Scalia, Kennedy, and Thomas—saw the Eleventh Amendment as a restriction on the subject matter jurisdiction of the federal courts that bars all suits against state governments. The competing theory—supported by Justices Stevens, Souter, Ginsburg, and Breyer—viewed the Eleventh Amendment as restricting the federal courts' subject matter jurisdiction only in precluding cases being brought against states that are founded solely on diversity jurisdiction.[1] The Roberts Court appeared to be split along exactly the same ideological lines—with Chief Justice Roberts and Justices Thomas, Alito, Gorsuch, Kavanaugh, and Barrett taking the former position, while the more liberal Justices—Sotomayor, Kagan, and Jackson—likely taking the latter.[2]

Hans v. Louisiana

To understand the alternative theories, it is important to note that the Supreme Court has interpreted the Eleventh Amendment as prohibiting suits against a state by its own citizens, as well as by citizens of other states and foreign

§7.3 [1] Another theory of the Eleventh Amendment is that it reinstates the common law immunity from suit enjoyed by states prior to the adoption of Article III and, perhaps, prior to the Supreme Court's decision in Chisholm v. Georgia. For a thorough defense of this theory, *see* Vicki C. Jackson, The Supreme Court, the Eleventh Amendment, and State Sovereign Immunity, 98 Yale L.J. 1 (1988); *see also* Vicki C. Jackson, One Hundred Years of Folly: The Eleventh Amendment and the 1988 Term, 64 S. Cal. L. Rev. 51 (1990). In *Chisholm,* the Court held that Article III of the Constitution permits states to be sued by citizens of other states. Thus, some believe that the Eleventh Amendment in reversing *Chisholm* reinstated the common law immunity that states had previously possessed. The claim is that originally states had common law immunity as to all suits against them. Article III and *Chisholm* denied immunity to the states from suits brought by citizens of other states. Thus, the Eleventh Amendment reinstituted the previously existing sovereign immunity. Under this theory, the Eleventh Amendment does not create a constitutional bar to suits against a state by its own citizens. The Eleventh Amendment by its terms and history has nothing to do with such suits. States had sovereign immunity to suits by their own citizens prior to the adoption of the Constitution and Article III did not change this by authorizing suits against a state by citizens of other states and foreign countries. *Chisholm* and the Eleventh Amendment leave untouched a state's common law immunity to suits by citizens against their own states. Therefore, according to this view, the Court in *Hans* was not using the Eleventh Amendment as a constitutional bar, but was stating only the unchanged principle of common law immunity. In earlier cases, Justice Brennan advocated this second theory. Employees of the Dept. of Pub. Health & Welfare v. Department of Pub. Health & Welfare, 411 U.S. 279, 309-322 (1973) (Brennan, J., dissenting). However, in his later opinions, Justice Brennan shifted to the third approach discussed below. *See, e.g.,* Pennsylvania v. Union Gas Co., 491 U.S. 1, 5 (1989); Atascadero State Hosp. v. Scanlon, 473 U.S. 234, 258-259 (1985) (Brennan, J., dissenting). No other justice has expressly advocated this view in recent decisions.

[2] *See* Whole Woman's Health v. Jackson, 595 U.S. 30 (2021); Franchise Tax Board v. Hyatt, 587 U.S. 230 (2019).

countries.[3] Although the terms of the amendment only prohibit suits against a state by citizens of other states and foreign countries, the Supreme Court, in 1890, in *Hans v. Louisiana,* held that it would be "anomalous" to allow states to be sued by their own citizens.[4] Thus, since *Hans,* states have been immune to suits both by their own citizens and by citizens of other states.[5]

The underlying basis for the decision in *Hans,* and of the entire Eleventh Amendment, remains very much in dispute. In fact, the justices have disagreed over whether *Hans* was decided correctly or whether it should be overruled. For example, in *Seminole Tribe of Florida v. Florida,* the Court's majority reaffirmed *Hans* and declared that the "decision found its roots not solely in the common law of England, but in the much more fundamental 'jurisprudence of all civilized nations.' "[6] In contrast, the dissent identified "three critical errors in *Hans*: . . . the *Hans* Court misread the Eleventh Amendment; [i]t also misunderstood the conditions under which common-law doctrines were received or rejected at the time of the founding, and it fundamentally mistook the very nature of sovereignty in the young republic that was supposed to entail a state's immunity to federal question jurisdiction in federal court."[7] The majority views *Hans* as reflecting a constitutional principle, embodied in the Eleventh Amendment, that states have sovereign immunity when sued in federal court. The dissent sees *Hans* as wrongly decided and at most only recognizing common law immunity for state governments.

First Theory: Constitutional Limit on Subject Matter Jurisdiction for All Suits Against State Governments

One theory is that sovereign immunity creates a constitutional restriction on federal court subject matter jurisdiction for all suits against state governments. By this view, the Eleventh Amendment is part of a broader constitutional limitation on federal court jurisdiction created by sovereign immunity. Proponents of this view point to the initial language of the amendment, which appears to express a constitutional limitation on federal subject matter jurisdiction: "The Judicial power of the United States shall not be construed to extend to. . . ." In articulating this view, the Supreme Court declared that the Eleventh Amendment "affirm[s]

[3] *See* discussion in §7.4, *infra.*

[4] 134 U.S. 1, 18 (1890). For an excellent critique of *Hans, see* Edward R. Purcell, Jr., The Particularly Dubious Case of Hans v. Louisiana: An Essay on Law, Race, History, and Federal Courts, 81 N.C. L. Rev. 1927 (2003). *See also* Bradford H. Clark, The Eleventh Amendment and the Nature of the Union, 123 Harv. L. Rev. 1817 (2010) (arguing that allowing suits by citizens of a state, but not citizens of other states, made historical sense because the Framers did not anticipate that suits against states would arise under the laws of the United States.)

[5] *See, e.g.,* Employees of the Dept. of Pub. Health & Welfare v. Department of Pub. Health & Welfare, 411 U.S. 279, 280 (1973) ("[A]n unconsenting State is immune from suits brought in federal courts by her own citizens as well as by citizens of another State."); In re New York, 256 U.S. 490, 497 (1921) (federal courts may not hear suits "brought by citizens of another state, or by citizens or subjects of a foreign state, because of the Eleventh Amendment; and not even one brought by its own citizens, because of the fundamental rule of which the Amendment is but an exemplification").

[6] 517 U.S. 44, 69 (1996).

[7] *Id.* at 130 (Souter, J., dissenting).

that the fundamental principle of sovereign immunity limits the grant of judicial authority in Art. III."[8]

Although it is possible to argue that the constitutional bar only applies to suits brought by citizens of other states, those who advocate this first theory believe that *Hans* establishes sovereign immunity limits on federal court jurisdiction barring suits against a state by its own citizens. In cases involving suits against a state by its own citizens, the Supreme Court has declared that "the principle of sovereign immunity is a constitutional limitation on the federal judicial power established in Art. III"[9] and that "[t]he Eleventh Amendment is an explicit limitation of the judicial power of the United States."[10] In *Edelman v. Jordan*, for instance, the Supreme Court held that defendants could raise the Eleventh Amendment in the court of appeals, although it had not been argued in the trial court.[11] Generally, except for jurisdictional arguments, matters may not be raised on appeal if they were not presented in the lower court. The Court concluded that the Eleventh Amendment partakes sufficiently of the characteristics of a jurisdictional bar that it may be raised for the first time on appeal.

In other words, the first approach to the Eleventh Amendment is that federal court subject matter jurisdiction is limited by the states' sovereign immunity. Justices holding this view have declared that the Eleventh Amendment reflects a "broad constitutional principle of sovereign immunity."[12] The principle of sovereign immunity is explicitly articulated in the text of the Eleventh Amendment for suits against a state by citizens of other states and was recognized by the Supreme Court in *Hans v. Louisiana* for suits against a state by its own citizens.

The Supreme Court, however, has not been completely consistent in treating the Eleventh Amendment as a restriction on subject matter jurisdiction. For example, it is firmly established that subject matter jurisdiction may not be gained in federal court by consent or waiver.[13] Agreement of the parties is never sufficient to create federal court jurisdiction when it otherwise would not be allowed. Yet the Supreme Court repeatedly and consistently has held that a state may waive its Eleventh Amendment immunity.[14] In *Hans*, for instance, the Court observed that a state is immune "*unless the State consents to be sued.*"[15] But waiver should not be possible if the Eleventh Amendment is a restriction on subject matter jurisdiction.

[8] Pennhurst State School & Hosp. v. Halderman, 465 U.S. 89, 98 (1984).

[9] *Id.*

[10] Missouri v. Fiske, 290 U.S. 18, 25 (1933).

[11] 415 U.S. 651, 677-678 (1974) (*Edelman* involved a suit against the Illinois Commissioner of the Department of Public Welfare brought by Illinois citizens).

[12] Pennsylvania v. Union Gas Co., 491 U.S. 1, 39 (1989) (Scalia, J., concurring in part and dissenting in part) (citations omitted).

[13] *See, e.g.*, Sosna v. Iowa, 419 U.S. 393, 398 (1975); Mitchell v. Maurer, 293 U.S. 237 (1934); Mansfield, C. & L. M. Ry. v. Swan, 111 U.S. 379, 382 (1884).

[14] Port Authority Trans-Hudson Corp. v. Feeney, 495 U.S. 299, 305-306 (1990); *Pennhurst*, 465 U.S. at 99; Ashton v. Cameron County Water Improvement Dist., 298 U.S. 513, 531 (1936). *See* discussion in §7.6, *infra*.

[15] 134 U.S. at 20 (emphasis added).

Also, federal courts are required to raise objections to subject matter jurisdiction on their own when defects in jurisdiction become apparent. Subject matter jurisdiction is different from almost all other areas where courts must wait for the parties to raise objections. Yet the Supreme Court concluded, "[W]e have never held that [the Eleventh Amendment] is jurisdictional in the sense that it must be raised and decided by this Court on its own motion."[16]

More fundamentally, it is difficult to justify the view that the Eleventh Amendment constitutionally prohibits federal courts from hearing suits against a state by its own citizens, and that sovereign immunity bars suits against state governments in state courts and in federal administrative proceedings. The terms of the amendment only speak to suits against a state by citizens of other states and foreign countries.[17] The amendment was added to the Constitution to overrule the Supreme Court's decision in *Chisholm v. Georgia*,[18] which had upheld the right of a South Carolina resident to sue the state of Georgia. The focus was on protecting a state from suits by citizens of other states. Thus, neither the language nor the history of the Eleventh Amendment justify reading it as creating a constitutional bar to suits against states by their own citizens.[19] Moreover, if sovereign immunity is a limit on federal judicial power even when not expressed in the text of the Constitution, then it is a principle of even greater significance than the document itself. This theory seems inconsistent with the supremacy clause, which declares that the Constitution is the supreme law of the land.

On the other hand, the advantage of this first approach is that it provides a clear rule: federal courts may not hear suits against state governments regardless of the citizenship of the plaintiffs. Additionally, it is a view based on a need for federal court deference to state governments and for the use of federalism to protect states from federal encroachments. In fact, the Supreme Court has spoken of "the vital role of the doctrine of sovereign immunity in our federal system."[20]

Second Theory: Limit Only Diversity Suits

A second view of the Eleventh Amendment treats it as restricting only the diversity jurisdiction of federal courts.[21] Article III of the Constitution permits subject matter jurisdiction based on either the content of the litigation—for example,

[16] Patsy v. Board of Regents of Fla., 457 U.S. 496, 516 n.19 (1982).

[17] The Supreme Court acknowledged this, but declared: "Although the text of the amendment would appear to restrict only the Article III diversity jurisdiction of the federal courts, we have understood the 11th Amendment to stand not so much for what it says, but for the presupposition which it confirms." Seminole Tribe of Florida v. Florida, 517 U.S. 44, 54 (1996).

[18] 2 U.S. (2 Dall.) 419 (1793). *See* discussion in §7.2, *supra.*

[19] *See* Lawrence Marshall, Fighting the Words of the Eleventh Amendment, 102 Harv. L. Rev. 1342 (1989) (arguing from the text of the Eleventh Amendment that it is a prohibition against states being sued by citizens of other states).

[20] *Pennhurst*, 465 U.S. at 99.

[21] *See* John J. Gibbons, The Eleventh Amendment and State Sovereign Immunity: A Reinterpretation, 83 Colum. L. Rev. 1889 (1983); William A. Fletcher, A Historical Interpretation of the Eleventh Amendment: A Narrow Construction of an Affirmative Grant of Jurisdiction Rather Than a Prohibition Against Jurisdiction, 35 Stan. L. Rev. 1033 (1983).

federal question jurisdiction, or based on the identity of the parties—for example, diversity jurisdiction. Article III, §2, identifies nine categories of cases and controversies that might be heard in federal court. One of these is "Cases, in Law and Equity, arising under this Constitution, the Laws of the United States, and Treaties made, or which shall be made, under their Authority." This is the provision that authorizes federal question jurisdiction. A different, later passage of Article III, §2, allows for "Controversies . . . between a State and Citizens of another state." This is an authorization for suits against a state based on diversity of citizenship.

The language of the Eleventh Amendment clearly is directed at modifying this latter provision. In fact, the amendment simply states: "The Judicial Power of the United States shall not be construed to extend to any suit . . . against one of the United States by Citizens of another state." Because *Chisholm* only involved this latter part of Article III, it makes sense to view the Eleventh Amendment as restricting only diversity suits against state governments. Therefore, according to this view, the Eleventh Amendment does not bar suits against states based on other parts of Article III. Most notably, the amendment does not preclude suits based on federal question jurisdiction. Thus, all claims of state violations of the U.S. Constitution or federal laws could be heard in federal courts.[22] Those who take this view also reject the Court's conclusion in *Alden v. Maine* that state governments cannot be sued in state court without their consent.

However, it should be noted that this view is inconsistent with the Supreme Court's decision in *Hans v. Louisiana.*[23] In *Hans*, a federal question was presented in a suit by a Louisiana resident against Louisiana; the issue was whether Louisiana had unconstitutionally impaired the obligation of contracts by refusing to pay interest owed on bonds it had issued. If the Eleventh Amendment only restricts diversity suits and does not affect federal question jurisdiction, then *Hans* was wrongly decided and the suit should not have been dismissed.[24] Several prominent scholars, such as William Fletcher and David Shapiro, and four Supreme Court justices, in dissenting opinions, have taken exactly this position and contended that the decision in *Hans* was an error.[25]

[22] There are alternative versions of the diversity theory. Professor William Fletcher argues that the amendment prohibits only suits founded solely on diversity jurisdiction; federal question suits against states are allowed. William A. Fletcher, The Diversity Explanation of the Eleventh Amendment: A Reply to Critics, 56 U. Chi. L. Rev. 1261 (1989). In contrast, Professor Larry Marshall contends that states may not be sued by citizens of other states in federal court under either diversity or federal question jurisdiction. Lawrence C. Marshall, Fighting the Words of the Eleventh Amendment, 102 Harv. L. Rev. 1342 (1989).

[23] 134 U.S. 1 (1890).

[24] Professor William Marshall argues that neither the text of the Eleventh Amendment nor its history supports the claims for the diversity theory and that those who advocate this approach have failed to meet their burden of overcoming the 100 years of precedent since *Hans.* William P. Marshall, The Diversity Theory of the Eleventh Amendment: A Critical Evaluation, 102 Harv. L. Rev. 1372 (1989).

[25] Fletcher, *supra* note 21, at 1087-1091; David L. Shapiro, Wrong Turns: The Eleventh Amendment and the *Pennhurst* Case, 98 Harv. L. Rev. 61, 70 (1984); Seminole Tribe of Florida v. Florida, 517 U.S. at 100 (Stevens, J., dissenting); at 76 (Souter, Ginsburg, and Breyer, JJ., dissenting). *See also* Atascadero State Hosp. v. Scanlon, 472 U.S. at 301-302 (Brennan, Marshall, Blackmun, and Stevens, JJ., dissenting).

Underlying Value Question

Ultimately, the choice among the three theories is, in large part, a value question: How should state sovereignty be weighed against federal supremacy? For instance, the first theory accords great importance to sovereign immunity and federalism, but less weight to ensuring state compliance with the Constitution. In contrast, the second theory makes the opposite choice: subjecting states to liability whenever they violate federal law but according relatively little weight to state sovereign immunity. Eleventh Amendment doctrines—and sovereign immunity more generally—thus reflect baseline assumptions about both the need for court review to ensure state compliance with federal law and the importance of immunizing state governments from federal jurisdiction.

At least since 1996, when the Court decided *Seminole Tribe v. Florida*,[26] it has split along ideological lines, with the conservative majority favoring the former, broad view of sovereign immunity, and the liberal dissenters taking the latter narrow approach.

§7.4 THE APPLICATION OF THE ELEVENTH AMENDMENT AND SOVEREIGN IMMUNITY: WHAT'S BARRED AND WHAT'S ALLOWED

There have been literally dozens of Supreme Court decisions defining the scope of the Eleventh Amendment and delineating what suits are prohibited in federal court and what suits are permissible. This section describes this law. Postponed for consideration until the subsequent sections is discussion of three major ways around the Eleventh Amendment: suits against state officers for injunctive relief or money damages;[1] suits based on state consent to federal court jurisdiction; and suits pursuant to congressional statutes, especially pursuant to civil rights laws.

Suits Barred

Most consistently, the Supreme Court has held that the Eleventh Amendment precludes suits against a state government by citizens of another state or citizens of a foreign country.[2] The very terms of the amendment clearly prohibit federal

[26] 517 U.S. 44 (1996).

§7.4 [1] The distinction between "official capacity" and "individual capacity" suits is discussed in §7.5.2 in the text accompanying notes 45-52, *infra*.

[2] *See, e.g.*, In re New York, 256 U.S. 490 (1921); Smith v. Reeves, 178 U.S. 436 (1900); Fitts v. McGhee, 172 U.S. 516 (1899). The protection of states against suits in federal court also applies to territories of the United States. *See, e.g.*, McCormick v. Miami University, 693 F.3d 654 (6th Cir. 2012); Fred v. Rogue, 916 F.2d 37, 38 (1st Cir. 1990); Rodriguez-Garcia v. Davila, 904 F.2d 90, 98 (1st Cir. 1990).

court jurisdiction over such litigation. Based on this provision, the Court has held that the Eleventh Amendment bars Indian tribes from suing state governments in federal court without their consent.[3]

Additionally, the Supreme Court repeatedly has held that the Eleventh Amendment bars suits against a state by its own citizens.[4] As described above, in *Hans v. Louisiana*, the Supreme Court applied the Eleventh Amendment to preclude a suit by a Louisiana resident against Louisiana to compel officials to pay money owed under state-issued bonds and coupons.[5] The Court held that a suit against an unconsenting state, even when brought by a citizen of that state, was "unknown to the law . . . [and] not contemplated by the Constitution when establishing the judicial power of the United States."[6] The Court concluded that it would be "anomalous" to allow a state to be sued by its own citizens in federal court when it cannot be sued by citizens of other states or nations. Although many commentators urged the overruling of *Hans*,[7] the Court repeatedly has reaffirmed it over the past decade.

Although the terms of the Eleventh Amendment speak only about federal jurisdiction over "suits in law or equity," the Supreme Court also has found admiralty suits against the states to be barred.[8] Likewise, despite the language of the amendment discussing suits by "Citizens of another State, or by Citizens or Subjects of any Foreign State," the Court has held that the Eleventh Amendment prohibits suits against a state by foreign nations[9] or Native American tribes.[10]

Additionally, although the Eleventh Amendment speaks only of restrictions on the federal judicial power, in *Alden v. Maine* the Court held that state governments cannot be sued in state court without their consent.[11] Probation officers in Maine sued, claiming that they were owed overtime pay under the federal Fair Labor Standards Act. The suit was initially filed in federal court, but was dismissed based on the Eleventh Amendment. The probation officers then sued in Maine state court. The Supreme Court, in a 5-4 decision, ruled that the state had

[3] Seminole Tribe of Florida v. Florida, 517 U.S. 44 (1996); Blatchford v. Native Village of Noatak, 501 U.S. 775 (1991).

[4] Edelman v. Jordan, 415 U.S. 651 (1974); Missouri v. Fiske, 290 U.S. 18, 28 (1933); Hans v. Louisiana, 134 U.S. 1, 15 (1890).

[5] 134 U.S. 1 (1890). For an excellent discussion of the background of this case and the development of the Eleventh Amendment doctrines, *see* John V. Orth, The Judicial Power of the United States: The Eleventh Amendment in American History (1987).

[6] 134 U.S. at 15.

[7] *Id.* at 18. For detailed criticism of the *Hans* decision, *see* William Fletcher, A Historical Interpretation of the Eleventh Amendment: A Narrow Construction of an Affirmative Grant of Jurisdiction Rather Than a Prohibition Against Jurisdiction, 35 Stan. L. Rev. 1033, 1087-1091 (1983); Seminole Tribe of Florida v. Florida, 517 U.S. at 100 (Souter, J., dissenting); Atascadero State Hosp. v. Scanlon, 473 U.S. 234, 259-260, 299-302 (1985) (Brennan, Marshall, Blackmun, and Stevens, JJ., dissenting).

[8] *See, e.g.,* Florida Dept. of State v. Treasure Salvors, Inc., 458 U.S. 670 (1982); In re New York, 256 U.S. 490 (1921).

[9] *See, e.g.,* Monaco v. Mississippi, 292 U.S. 313 (1934).

[10] *See, e.g.,* Seminole Tribe of Florida v. Florida, 517 U.S. at 44.

[11] 527 U.S. 706 (1999).

sovereign immunity and could not be sued in state court, even on a federal claim, without its consent. Justice Kennedy wrote for the Court and acknowledged that the Constitution and its Framers were silent about the ability to sue state governments in state courts. Justice Kennedy said, though, that it was unthinkable that the states would have ratified the Constitution had they thought that it made them subject to suit without their consent. The Court declared: "We hold that the powers delegated to Congress under Article I of the United States Constitution do not include the power to subject nonconsenting States to private suits for damages in state courts."[12]

Subsequently, in *Federal Maritime Commission v. South Carolina State Ports Authority*, the Supreme Court held that states cannot be named as defendants in federal administrative agency proceedings.[13] A cruise ship company brought a claim against a state agency in the Federal Maritime Commission, claiming that it had been discriminated against in violation of federal maritime law. The Supreme Court, in a 5-4 decision, held that such actions are barred by sovereign immunity.

The Court relied on *Alden v. Maine*'s conclusion that sovereign immunity is broader than the protections of the Eleventh Amendment. Justice Thomas, writing for the majority, stressed that the Eleventh Amendment "is but one exemplification" of state sovereign immunity.[14] The Court said that the "preeminent purpose" of sovereign immunity is to protect the "dignity" of state governments and that such dignity would be impermissibly offended by allowing states to be named as defendants in agency proceedings without their consent.[15]

In *Franchise Tax Board v. Hyatt*, in 2019, the Court held that a state cannot be sued in another state court.[16] In *Nevada v. Hall*, 40 years earlier, the Court came to the opposite conclusion.[17] Relying on *Nevada v. Hall*, Gilbert Hyatt sued the Franchise Tax Board of California in Nevada state court for its harassing conduct. Hyatt, an inventor, moved from California to Nevada in 1991. Employees of the Franchise Tax Board, believing that Hyatt had not actually moved, went to Nevada and broke into his house, sent letters with private information, including his Social Security number, and spread false rumors about him. The state court jury ruled in favor of Hyatt and awarded him $385 million in damages. After decades of proceedings and two prior trips to the Supreme Court, the judgment had been reduced to $100,000.

But the Supreme Court, in a 5-4 decision, overruled *Nevada v. Hall* and held that a state government cannot be sued in another state's court. Justice Clarence Thomas wrote the opinion for the Court. He wrote that: "*Hall*'s determination that the Constitution does not contemplate sovereign immunity for each State

[12] *Id.* at 712. By contrast, 20 years before Alden v. Maine, in Nevada v. Hall, 440 U.S. 410 (1979), the Court held that a state could be sued in another state's courts. But in Franchise Tax Board v. Hyatt, 139 S. Ct. 1485 (2019), the Court overruled *Nevada v. Hall* and held that a state cannot be sued in another state's courts.

[13] 535 U.S. 743 (2002).

[14] *Id.* at 753.

[15] *Id.* at 760.

[16] 587 U.S. 230 (2019).

[17] 440 U.S. 410 (1979).

in a sister State's courts misreads the historical record and misapprehends the 'implicit ordering of relationships within the federal system necessary to make the Constitution a workable governing charter and to give each provision within that document the full effect intended by the Framers.'"[18] Justice Thomas said that the absence of a constitutional provision creating such sovereign immunity did not matter: "Hyatt argues that we should find no right to sovereign immunity in another State's courts because no constitutional provision explicitly grants that immunity. But this is precisely the type of 'ahistorical literalism' that we have rejected when 'interpreting the scope of the States' sovereign immunity.'"[19] He concluded: "*Nevada v. Hall* is irreconcilable with our constitutional structure and with the historical evidence showing a widespread preratification understanding that States retained immunity from private suits, both in their own courts and in other courts."[20]

Suits Allowed

In contrast, the Supreme Court has refused to apply the Eleventh Amendment in many instances. For example, the Eleventh Amendment does not bar federal court suits by the U.S. government against a state.[21]

Also, the Eleventh Amendment does not bar suits against a state by another state.[22] However, for such suits to be allowed the state must be suing to protect its own interests. If the state is suing to collect debts owed to individual citizens, the litigation is barred from the federal courts by the Eleventh Amendment.[23] The apparent rationale is that it is important for there to be a neutral forum to resolve disagreements between the states, but the Court will not allow circumvention of the Eleventh Amendment by allowing states to litigate their citizens' claims.

Significantly, the Eleventh Amendment does not prevent the U.S. Supreme Court from hearing claims against the state as part of its appellate jurisdiction.[24] The Court has concluded that the Eleventh Amendment bars suits "commenced or prosecuted" in federal court, thus barring original jurisdiction before the Supreme Court or other federal courts but not appellate jurisdiction in the form of Supreme Court review of state court decisions when the state is a party.[25] Thus,

[18] 587 U.S. at 237.

[19] *Id.* at 247.

[20] *Id.* at 249.

[21] *See, e.g.,* United States v. Mississippi, 380 U.S. 128, 140-141 (1965); United States v. Texas, 143 U.S. 621 (1892).

[22] *See, e.g.,* Colorado v. New Mexico, 459 U.S. 176, 182 n.9 (1982).

[23] *See, e.g.,* Maryland v. Louisiana, 451 U.S. 725, 745 n.21 (1981). In Kansas v. Colorado, 533 U.S. 1 (2001), the Court ruled that as long as the state, as a state, has been injured and has an interest in the suit, the Eleventh Amendment does not bar an award in which damages are measured by the losses suffered by its citizens.

[24] *See, e.g.,* McKesson Corp. v. Division of Alcoholic Beverages & Tobacco, Department of Business Regulation of Florida, 496 U.S. 18, 26 (1990); Maine v. Thiboutot, 448 U.S. 1, 9 n.7 (1980); Nevada v. Hall, 440 U.S. 410, 418-421 (1979).

[25] Monaco v. Mississippi, 292 U.S. 313 (1934) (Supreme Court cannot hear on its original jurisdiction claims against state governments).

the declared: "We recognize what has long been implied in our consistent practice and uniformly endorsed in our cases: the Eleventh Amendment does not constrain the appellate jurisdiction of the Supreme Court over cases arising from state courts."[26]

The Supreme Court also has carved an exception for suits in admiralty. In *Florida Department of State v. Treasure Salvors, Inc.*, the Supreme Court held that the Eleventh Amendment did not bar a federal court from issuing a warrant in an in rem action for a wreckage in an admiralty suit.[27] In *California v. Deep Sea Research*, the Court ruled that the Eleventh Amendment does not bar jurisdiction over an in rem admiralty suit when the state is not in possession of the property.[28]

The Court applied this in *Tennessee Student Assistance Corp. v. Hood* to hold that states can be sued in bankruptcy proceedings to discharge debts since they are in rem in nature.[29] Two years later, in *Central Virginia Community College v. Katz*, the Supreme Court went even further and held that the Eleventh Amendment and sovereign immunity do not apply in bankruptcy proceedings at all.[30] Justice Stevens wrote for the Court in a 5-4 decision.[31] He concluded that the clause in Article I, §8 of the Constitution, empowering Congress to create uniform rules for bankruptcy, was meant to override considerations of sovereign immunity. This case is discussed below in considering Congress's authority to override sovereign immunity and permit suits against states.[32]

Suits Against Cities

Perhaps most important, the Court long has held that the Eleventh Amendment does not bar suits against municipalities or political subdivisions of a state.[33] The ability to sue local governments in federal court is significant because it is this level of government that provides most social services in this country, such as police and fire protection, education, and sanitation. Therefore, if the Eleventh Amendment barred suits against municipalities, federal courts could not ensure compliance with the Constitution by those who are most likely to violate it.

The Supreme Court, however, has said that the state's Eleventh Amendment immunity does extend to local governments when there is so much state involvement

[26] McKesson Corp. v. Div. of Alcohol Beverages & Tobacco, Dept. of Bus. Reg. of Fla., 496 U.S. at 26.

[27] 458 U.S. 670 (1982). Four justices indicated that the Eleventh Amendment might bar determination of the state's ownership of the wreckage.

[28] 523 U.S. 491 (1998).

[29] 541 U.S. 440 (2004).

[30] 546 U.S. 356 (2006).

[31] Justice Stevens's majority opinion was joined by Justices O'Connor, Souter, Ginsburg, and Breyer. The case came down soon before Justice O'Connor left the bench and was replaced by Justice Alito.

[32] *See* §7.7, *infra.*

[33] *See, e.g.,* Northern Ins. Co. v. Chatham County, Georgia, 547 U.S. 189 (2006); Mt. Healthy City School Dist. Bd. of Educ. v. Doyle, 429 U.S. 274 (1977); Lincoln County v. Luning, 133 U.S. 529 (1890).

in the municipalities' actions that the relief, in essence, runs against the state. In *Pennhurst State School & Hospital v. Halderman*, the Court held that the Eleventh Amendment barred relief against the county as well as against state officers.[34] The Court concluded that the county could not be sued in federal court because "funding for the county mental retardation programs comes almost entirely from the State . . . and the costs of the Masters have been borne by the State. . . . Finally, the MH/MR Act contemplates that the state and county officials will cooperate in operating the mental retardation programs."[35] Thus, the state's funding of a county program and cooperation were deemed sufficient to create an Eleventh Amendment barrier to suits against the county.

This holding is a potentially marked expansion of local government immunity. Interestingly, the Court supported its conclusion by citation to only one Supreme Court precedent, *Lake County Estates, Inc. v. Tahoe Regional Planning Agency*.[36] In that case, however, the Supreme Court reached exactly the opposite result, holding that state funding of an interstate agency did not confer the protection of the Eleventh Amendment upon the agency.[37] The Court stated that it "has consistently refused to construe the amendment to afford protection to political subdivisions such as counties and municipalities, even though such entities exercise a 'slice of state power.'"[38] The Eleventh Amendment prevents suits against local governments only if a money judgment has to be paid directly by the state treasury. In *Pennhurst*, the state was not obligated to pay any money judgment issued against the county. Nor is it clear why state cooperation is sufficient to immunize municipalities, because in the *Lake County Estates* case the Supreme Court explicitly held that state cooperation in regional compacts did not bestow immunity on those entities.[39] But thus far, the Supreme Court has not used *Pennhurst* to expand municipal immunity.

Immunity of State Agencies

Finally, the law concerning the immunity of state agencies, boards, and other entities from suit in federal courts is quite inconsistent. It is clear, however, that an agency of state government, such as the department of health or treasury, is a part of the state for purposes of the Eleventh Amendment.[40] The Court most directly confronted the question of when a suit is against a state in *Regents of University of California v. Doe*.[41] An individual worked for the Lawrence Livermore National Laboratory of the University of California pursuant to a contract with the U.S. Department of Energy. Under the terms of the contract, the federal government was responsible for any

[34] 465 U.S. 89, 123-124 (1979).
[35] *Id.* at 124.
[36] 440 U.S. 391 (1979).
[37] *Id.* at 400-402.
[38] *Id.* at 401.
[39] *Id.* at 400-402.
[40] *See, e.g.*, Florida Dept. of Health & Rehabilitative Servs. v. Florida Nursing Home Assn., 450 U.S. 147 (1981); Ford Motor Co. v. Department of Treasury, 323 U.S. 459 (1945).
[41] 519 U.S. 425 (1997).

liabilities incurred by the state of California. The Ninth Circuit held that the Eleventh Amendment did not bar the plaintiff's suit against the state university because there was no possibility of state financial liability.

The U.S. Supreme Court unanimously reversed. The Court stated that "it is the entity's potential legal liability, rather than its ability or inability to require a third party to reimburse it, or to discharge the liability in the first instance, that is relevant."[42] The Court thus concluded that "[t]he Eleventh Amendment protects the State from the risk of adverse judgments even though the State may be indemnified by a third party."[43] In other words, if it is a suit against the state—and the University of California is clearly a part of the state—then the Eleventh Amendment bars the suit even if there is no risk of actual state financial responsibility.

The Court did not completely reject possible state monetary liability as a factor to consider in evaluating whether a particular agency should be regarded as state rather than local. In fact, in *Regents of the University of California v. Doe*, the Court declared, "Of course, the question whether a money judgment against a state instrumentality or official would be enforceable against the State is of considerable importance to any evaluation of the relationship between the State and the entity or individual being sued."[44] Shortly after its decision in *Doe*, the Court concluded that the St. Louis Board of Police Commissioners is not the state for purposes of the Eleventh Amendment, even though the governor appoints a majority of its members.[45] In a footnote, the Court noted that financial responsibility rests with the local government, and thus it should be regarded as part of local rather than state government.

For state boards, corporations, and other entities, when the law is uncertain, the courts look to several factors. Professor Pagan suggests that four criteria are used:

(1) Will a judgment against the entity be satisfied with funds in the state treasury?[46]
(2) Does the state government exert significant control over the entity's decisions and actions?
(3) Does the state executive branch or legislature appoint the entity's policymakers?
(4) Does the state law characterize the entity as a state agency rather than as a subdivision?[47]

Affirmative answers to these questions, especially the first, indicate that the Eleventh Amendment will protect the entity; negative answers suggest that the governing body will be deemed sufficiently independent of the state so that the Eleventh Amendment does not apply. Thus, Professor Pagan observes that public universities are properly considered to be part of the state for Eleventh Amendment purposes

[42] *Id.* at 431.
[43] *Id.*
[44] *Id.*
[45] Auer v. Robbins, 519 U.S. 905, 908 n.1 (1997).
[46] As noted above, Regents of the University of California v. Doe is clear that a suit against a state is barred even if the state will be reimbursed from other funds.
[47] John R. Pagan, Eleventh Amendment Analysis, 39 Ark. L. Rev. 447, 461 (1986).

because the state treasury usually funds them and because the governor appoints the members of the governing authority.[48] In contrast, school districts are found to be separate from the state for Eleventh Amendment purposes because citizens usually select the board members, who then make decisions concerning budget, personnel, and curriculum.[49]

Suits Against Local Officials Deemed State Officers

The issue of whether it is a suit against the state is likely to come up more frequently in light of the Supreme Court's decision in *McMillian v. Monroe County, Alabama.*[50] In *McMillian,* the Court held that a county sheriff in Alabama is a state official, not a local official, even though sheriffs are elected locally and paid by the county. Although the Court's holding was narrow and emphasized the Alabama Constitution's definition of sheriffs' responsibility, the reasoning in *McMillian* has potentially much broader applications. A key factor for the majority in *McMillian* was that the county sheriff in Alabama enforces state law. This is true in most states and is also so for other county officials, such as coroners.

While *McMillian* arose in the context of whether a sheriff's decisions establish local policy for purposes of §1983 and the Court did not discuss the Eleventh Amendment, the obvious implication is that the Eleventh Amendment applies once the sheriff is deemed a state officer. In fact, even before *McMillian,* the Fourth Circuit ruled that South Carolina sheriffs are state officials for Eleventh Amendment purposes.[51] It is likely after *McMillian* that many county officials will attempt to claim that they should be treated as state officers and that the Eleventh Amendment applies in the litigation.[52]

Denial of Eleventh Amendment Immunity Immediately Appealable

The Supreme Court has ruled that a denial of Eleventh Amendment immunity is immediately appealable. In *Puerto Rico Aqueduct and Sewer Authority v. Metcalf & Eddy,* the Court held that the Eleventh Amendment creates a constitutional immunity from suit and not simply an affirmative defense.[53] Accordingly, a denial of Eleventh Amendment immunity is immediately appealable in the

[48] Pagan, *supra* note 50, at 461.

[49] *Id.* at 461-462.

[50] 520 U.S. 781 (1997).

[51] Cromer v. Brown, 88 F.3d 1315 (4th Cir. 1996).

[52] *See, e.g.,* Huminski v. Corsones, 396 F.3d 53 (2d Cir. 2005) (sheriffs in Vermont are state officials); Johnson v. Karnes, 398 F.3d 868 (6th Cir. 2005) (sheriffs in Kentucky are local officials); Venegas v. County of Los Angeles, 11 Cal. Rptr. 692 (2004) (county sheriff is a state official in California); Brewster v. Shasta County, 275 F.3d 803 (9th Cir. 2004) (county sheriff is a local official in California); Cash v. Granville County, 242 F.3d 219 (4th Cir. 2001) (school board is county and not state entity); Freeman v. Oakland Unified School Dist., 179 F.3d 846 (9th Cir. 1999) (school board in California is a state agency and protected by the Eleventh Amendment).

[53] 506 U.S. 139 (1993).

same way that the denial of immunity to an individual officer can be immediately appealed.[54]

The three most significant limitations on the scope of the Eleventh Amendment are its inapplicability to suits against state officers, to situations in which states waive their immunity, and to suits brought under some federal civil rights laws. The first of these is considered in this section and the other two exceptions are considered, respectively, in the next sections.

§7.5 WAYS AROUND THE ELEVENTH AMENDMENT: SUITS AGAINST STATE OFFICERS

Origins of Permitting Suits Against Officers

In *Osborn v. Bank of the United States*, the Supreme Court concluded that the Eleventh Amendment precludes suits against a state only when the state is actually named as the defendant in the litigation.[1] Chief Justice John Marshall concluded that "in all cases where jurisdiction depends on the party, it is the party named in the record" that matters.[2] Thus, the Eleventh Amendment could be circumvented by naming a state officer as defendant instead of the state government itself. This principle actually was derived from English common law, under which the king had sovereign immunity but other officials could be sued to remedy wrongs done by the government.[3]

Although the general rule is that suits against state officers are not barred by the Eleventh Amendment, the law is much more complicated, and the ability to sue the state officer in a particular case depends, to a large extent, on the nature of the relief sought and the claim presented. For example, suits for money damages to be paid from the state treasury are barred, even if the officer is named as the defendant.[4] Also, the Eleventh Amendment prohibits federal court pendent jurisdiction over state law claims against state officers.[5]

Overview of Section

These principles are examined in detail in this section, which considers the ability to sue state officers in federal court. Subsection 7.5.1 discusses suits against

[54] Mitchell v. Forsyth, 472 U.S. 511 (1985), discussed in §8.6.2, *infra*.

§7.5 [1] 22 U.S. (9 Wheat.) 738 (1824).

[2] *Id.* at 857.

[3] John V. Orth, The Judicial Power of the United States: The Eleventh Amendment in American History 41 (1987).

[4] *See, e.g.*, Ford Motor Co. v. Department of Treasury, 323 U.S. 459, 464 (1945) (court looks to "essential nature and effect of the proceeding").

[5] Pennhurst State School & Hosp. v. Halderman, 465 U.S. 89 (1984).

state officers for injunctive relief in federal court. Monetary relief in suits against state officers is examined in §7.5.2. Finally, exceptions to the ability to sue officers are discussed in §7.5.3. These exceptions include a bar against suing officers if they are not involved in enforcing the law, the prohibition against pendent state law claims against state officers, the preclusion of suits against officers to enforce federal laws that have a comprehensive enforcement mechanism, and a narrow exception for suits against state officers to quiet title to submerged land. Because state governments always act through their officers, suits against officers are clearly the most important way around the Eleventh Amendment.

§7.5.1 *Suits Against State Officers for Injunctive Relief*

Ex parte Young

The Eleventh Amendment does not preclude suits against state officers for injunctive relief, even when the remedy will enjoin the implementation of an official state policy. *Ex parte Young* is widely credited with establishing this principle,[6] and it has been heralded as "one of the three most important decisions the Supreme Court of the United States has ever handed down."[7]

Like many states around the turn of the century, Minnesota adopted a law limiting railroad rates. The railroads and their shareholders believed that such regulations were unconstitutional and sought to enjoin their enforcement. The railroads and shareholders could have violated the law and raised their constitutional challenge as a defense to prosecution. The statute, however, had severe penalties—a $2,500 fine for each violation and imprisonment of the railroad's agents for as long as five years.[8] Thus, shareholders in the Northern Pacific Railway instead instituted an action in federal court against the company and state officials responsible for enforcing the law to prevent compliance with the limits on railroad rates. Specifically, the plaintiffs sought an injunction against the attorney general of Minnesota, Edward T. Young, to prevent him from beginning any proceedings to enforce the challenged legislation.

While the lawsuit was pending, the federal district court issued a preliminary order enjoining Young from enforcing the law. Young, however, ignored the court's order and immediately filed a mandamus action against the railroad in state court to compel its compliance with the state law. Young then was cited by the federal court for contempt for disregarding its order. He was informed that he would be held in federal custody until such time as he dismissed the state action he

[6] 209 U.S. 123 (1908). Actually, several earlier cases had held similarly that the Eleventh Amendment did not preclude suits against state officers. *See, e.g.,* Tindal v. Wesley, 167 U.S. 204 (1897); Osborn v. Bank of the United States, 22 U.S. (9 Wheat.) 738 (1824).

[7] Allied Artists Pictures Corp. v. Rhodes, 473 F. Supp. 560, 564 (E.D. Ohio 1979) (citations omitted).

[8] Clyde E. Jacobs, The Eleventh Amendment and Sovereign Immunity 139 (1972).

had initiated against the railroads. Young petitioned for habeas corpus to the U.S. Supreme Court, claiming that the injunction violated the Eleventh Amendment.

The Supreme Court ruled against Young, holding that the Eleventh Amendment does not bar suits against state officers to enjoin violations of federal law.[9] In reaching this holding, the Court concluded that state officers have no authority to violate the Constitution and laws of the United States. Hence, their illegal acts are stripped of state authority, and the Eleventh Amendment does not preclude such suits. The Court wrote:

> The act to be enforced is alleged to be unconstitutional, and if it be so, the use of the name of the State to enforce an unconstitutional act to the injury of complainants is a proceeding without the authority of and one which does not affect the State in its sovereign or governmental capacity. It is simply an illegal act upon the part of a state official in attempting to use the name of the State to enforce a legislative enactment which is void because unconstitutional. If the act which the state Attorney General seeks to enforce be a violation of the Federal Constitution, the officer in proceeding under such enactment comes into conflict with the superior authority of that Constitution, and he is in that case stripped of his official or representative character and is subjected in his person to the consequences of his individual conduct. The State has no power to impart to him any immunity from responsibility to the supreme authority of the United States.[10]

Criticism and Defense of *Ex Parte Young*

Thus, if a state government is acting in violation of federal law, pursuant to an unconstitutional statute or otherwise, suit to enjoin the impermissible behavior may be brought in federal court by naming the state officer as the defendant. The decision in *Ex parte Young* long has been recognized as a primary method of limiting the effect of the Eleventh Amendment and of ensuring state compliance with federal law. As Professor Charles Alan Wright noted, "[T]he doctrine of *Ex parte Young* seems indispensable to the establishment of constitutional government and the rule of law."[11] Similarly, Professor Kenneth Culp Davis remarked, "From that day to this . . . *Young* has been the mainstay in challenging [state] governmental action[s]."[12] Because state governments always act through officers, state conduct in violation of the Constitution or federal laws can be halted by enjoining the state officers responsible for executing the state policy.

Many commentators have criticized the *Young* decision as creating a fictional distinction between the state and its officers.[13] Indeed, a majority of the Court has

[9] Ex parte Young, 209 U.S. at 159-160.

[10] *Id.*

[11] Charles Alan Wright & Mary Kay Kane, Law of Federal Courts (8th ed. 2017).

[12] Kenneth Culp Davis, Suing the Government by Falsely Pretending to Sue an Officer, 29 U. Chi. L. Rev. 435, 437 (1962).

[13] Charles Alan Wright, Arthur R. Miller & Edward H. Cooper, 13 Federal Practice and Procedure §3524, at 154 (1984); Davis, *supra* note 12, at 437.

called *Young* "an obvious fiction."[14] The argument is that when a state officer is sued to enjoin the enforcement of an official state policy, the state is the real party in interest. The result—an injunction against enforcement of a state law—is the same as if the state had been sued directly. The infringement on state sovereignty is the same as if the state had been sued directly. Especially when the officer is acting in the scope of his or her duties, pursuant to an official state policy, it seems fictitious to say that the officer is "stripped" of state authority and the Eleventh Amendment's protection of the state is inapplicable.

Although the result in *Young* certainly has a fictional quality, this criticism is somewhat overstated. First, the state officer is the proper defendant in a lawsuit to prevent the officer's unconstitutional conduct. As Professor Orth explains, "*Ex parte Young* was nonfictional in that Young was really and truly about to damage the interests of plaintiffs."[15] Second, *Young* distinguishes between the state and its officers in much the same way as the common law always has distinguished between a principal and its agent.[16] For example, a corporate officer who is performing acts that the corporation cannot legally authorize is said to be acting "ultra vires," or beyond the powers conferred by the corporation.[17] Such an officer cannot claim the authority of the corporation. Similarly, in *Young*, the Court concluded that an officer acting illegally is stripped of state authority, and therefore the Eleventh Amendment does not bar suits against officers.

The caution against dismissing *Young* as a fiction is because of the importance of that decision in ensuring state compliance with the U.S. Constitution. As Professors Wright, Miller, and Cooper remarked: "To be sure the doctrine of *Ex parte Young* has a fictive quality to it; nonetheless, it serves as an effective mechanism for providing relief against unconstitutional conduct by state officers and for testing, in the federal courts, the constitutionality of the state statutes under which they act."[18] Without *Young*, federal courts often would be powerless to prevent state violations of the Constitution and federal laws.[19]

[14] Idaho v. Coeur d'Alene Tribe, 521 U.S. 261, 270 (1997). The Court stated: "This doctrine has existed alongside our sovereign-immunity jurisprudence for more than a century, accepted as necessary to 'permit the federal courts to vindicate federal rights.' It rests on the premise—less delicately called a fiction that when a federal court commands a state official to do nothing more than refrain from violating federal law, he is not the State for sovereign-immunity purposes." Virginia Office for Protection and Advocacy v. Stewart, 563 U.S. 247, 255 (2011).

[15] Orth, *supra* note 3, at 133.

[16] *See, e.g.,* Restatement (Second) of Agency Authority §7, at 228, 383 (1958); Harold G. Reuschlein & William A. Gregory, Handbook on the Law of Agency and Partnership §13 (1979); Van Arsdale v. Metropolitan Title Guar. Co., 103 Misc. 2d 104, 425 N.Y.S.2d 482 (1980); Webb v. Webb, 602 S.W.2d 127 (Tex. Civ. App. 1980) (distinguishing between authority of agent and principal).

[17] Orth, *supra* note 3, at 133.

[18] Wright, Miller & Cooper, *supra* note 13.

[19] As discussed below, the Court has imposed a new limit on Ex parte Young suits: they cannot be used to enjoin laws creating civil liability because state officers are not involved in enforcing them. Whole Woman's Health v. Jackson, 595 U.S. 30 (2021); *see* text accompanying notes 53-65, *infra*.

Is There State Action If an Officer Is Stripped of State Authority?

Allowing plaintiffs to circumvent the Eleventh Amendment by suing state officers creates a number of problems. First, if officers are stripped of the state's authority, is there state action for purposes of the Fourteenth Amendment? It is clearly established that the Fourteenth Amendment only applies to state action; private conduct is not prohibited by the Constitution.[20] *Young* holds that officers acting in violation of the Constitution cannot claim to be the state for purposes of the Eleventh Amendment and, in fact, are stripped of all state authority. Therefore, a dilemma seems to arise: either the officers are part of the state, in which case the Eleventh Amendment should apply, or the officers are not part of the state, in which case there is no state action and therefore no constitutional violation.

The Supreme Court addressed this problem a few years after *Young* in *Home Telephone & Telegraph v. Los Angeles*.[21] There the Court held that individual conduct not entitled to Eleventh Amendment immunity is nonetheless state action for purposes of the Fourteenth Amendment. In other words, under *Ex parte Young*, the officer is stripped of state authority solely for purposes of Eleventh Amendment analysis, a result that does not affect the determination of state action under the Fourteenth Amendment. Undoubtedly, this too seems fictional, manipulating the definition of state action to achieve the essential result of remedying unconstitutional conduct.

A second problem concerns injunctive relief that has the effect of awarding money damages against the state treasury. For example, equitable relief in the form of orders for restitution or injunctions that require substantial expenditures pose special Eleventh Amendment problems because of the underlying purpose of the amendment to protect state treasuries from federal courts. This issue is discussed in the next subsection, which focuses on monetary relief issues against state officers.

§7.5.2 *Suits Against State Officers for Monetary Relief*

What Monetary Consequences Against a State Are Permitted?

The Supreme Court is very concerned about federal court relief against state officers that has the effect of forcing state governments to pay money damages. Thus, the Court has held that the Eleventh Amendment prevents an award of monetary relief from the state treasury even when the individual officer is the named defendant in the lawsuit. In *Ford Motor Co. v. Department of the Treasury*, the Court said, "[W]hen the action is in essence one for the recovery of money from the state, the state is the real, substantial party in interest and is entitled to

[20] *See, e.g.*, The Civil Rights Cases, 109 U.S. 3 (1883).
[21] 227 U.S. 278 (1913).

invoke its sovereign immunity from suit even though individual officials are nominal defendants."[22]

A complex set of doctrines has developed for determining what monetary relief is allowed and what is prohibited. The current law in this regard can be summarized in three parts. First, the Eleventh Amendment does not prevent suits against state officers for money damages to be paid out of the officers' own pockets, even when the damages are retrospective compensation for past harms.[23] The Eleventh Amendment is concerned with protecting state treasuries, not individual officers. Hence, there is no reason to apply the amendment if the relief is to be paid by an officer to the injured victim of the officer's actions. Often this is described as a suit against the officer in his or her "individual capacity."

State indemnification policies are irrelevant for Eleventh Amendment analysis and do not prevent federal court relief against individual officers. That is, an officer of the state cannot claim Eleventh Amendment immunity on the grounds that state law requires that the officer be indemnified with funds from the state treasury.[24] In part, this is because the state has voluntarily chosen to indemnify the officer and should not be able to invoke the Eleventh Amendment because of its choice to provide compensation out of state resources. Also, in part, there is real concern that states could eliminate all relief against state and local government officers and even against local governments simply by enacting laws requiring indemnification from state funds. If the Eleventh Amendment prohibited awards against state officers where indemnification policies exist, states would lose nothing by adopting such policies because they never could be required to pay a penny. At the same time, injured victims would be wholly without federal remedies because they would be prohibited from suing both the state officers and the state government in federal court.

It should be noted that to successfully sue an officer for money damages it is necessary to overcome common law immunities that all individual officers possess, which protect them from money damage awards except under limited circumstances. These immunities, which are not based on the Eleventh Amendment, are discussed in detail in §8.6.

Prospective Versus Retroactive Relief

Second, the Eleventh Amendment does not prohibit a federal court from giving injunctive relief against a state officer even though compliance with the injunction will cost the state a great deal of money in the future.[25] This is termed "prospective

[22] 323 U.S. 459, 464 (1945).

[23] *See, e.g.*, Kentucky v. Graham, 473 U.S. 159 (1985) (discussing distinction between suits against an officer in an individual as opposed to an official capacity).

[24] *See, e.g.*, Maliandi v. Montclair State Univ., 845 F.3d 77 (3d Cir. 2016); Ernst v. Rising, 427 F.3d 351 (6th Cir. 2005); Chestnut v. Lowell, 305 F.3d 18 (1st Cir. 2002); Sales v. Court, 224 F.3d 293 (4th Cir. 2000); Leeds v. Sexson, 1 F.3d 1246 (9th Cir. 1993).

[25] *See, e.g.*, Quern v. Jordan, 440 U.S. 332 (1979); Milliken v. Bradley, 433 U.S. 267 (1977); Edelman v. Jordan, 415 U.S. 651 (1974).

relief," or sometimes "ancillary relief." For example, in *Graham v. Richardson,* the Supreme Court held that Arizona and Pennsylvania officials were prohibited from denying welfare benefits to otherwise qualified recipients who were aliens.[26] The injunction compelling state officers to allow aliens access to welfare benefits cost the state treasuries large sums of money. The funds obviously would be paid from state resources and not out of the officers' own pockets. Nonetheless, the relief was permitted because it is firmly established that the Eleventh Amendment does not forbid a federal court from issuing an injunction, even when compliance will cause the state to expend substantial amounts of money.

Third, the Eleventh Amendment prevents a federal court from awarding retroactive relief—damages to compensate past injuries—when those damages will be paid by the state treasury.[27] Under such circumstances, it is irrelevant that the individual officer is the named defendant rather than the state itself.

The seminal case articulating the distinction between retroactive and prospective relief is *Edelman v. Jordan.*[28] In that case the plaintiffs sued Edelman, the Illinois Commissioner of the Department of Public Welfare, objecting to the state's failure to comply with federal standards for processing welfare applications. The plaintiffs sought two types of relief: an injunction requiring the state to comply with federal guidelines in the future, and an injunction requiring the state to give back payments of all the funds that were previously improperly withheld.

The Supreme Court held that the Eleventh Amendment does not bar the order compelling state compliance in the future. The Court said that *Ex parte Young* establishes that federal courts may give injunctive relief against state officers, even when compliance will cost the state money.

The Court, however, refused to allow the injunction ordering payment of the previously owed sums. The Court said that the Eleventh Amendment bars such relief even though the officer and not the state is named as the defendant because the money obviously would be paid from the state treasury and not from the officer's own pocket. Furthermore, the fact that the relief is characterized as equitable does not matter; the Eleventh Amendment prohibits all awards of retroactive damages to be paid from the state treasury.

Thus, *Edelman* draws the extremely important distinction between prospective and retroactive relief. A federal court may order future compliance by state officials, but it may not compel payment of damages to compensate for past violations.[29]

Criticism and Defense of the Prospective/Retroactive Distinction

Does the distinction between prospective and retroactive relief make sense in determining the application of the Eleventh Amendment? Both prospective and retroactive relief can involve the expenditure of funds from the state treasury.

[26] 403 U.S. 365 (1971).

[27] *See, e.g.,* Edelman v. Jordan, 415 U.S. 651 (1974); Ford Motor Co. v. Department of the Treasury, 323 U.S. 459 (1945).

[28] 415 U.S. 651 (1974).

[29] *See, e.g.,* Cory v. White, 457 U.S. 85 (1982).

In fact, in some cases, prospective compliance might cost much more than back payments.[30] Justice Rehnquist recognized this in *Edelman* when he stated that "the difference between the type of relief barred by the Eleventh Amendment and that permitted under *Ex parte Young* will not in many instances be that between day and night."[31] Nonetheless, Justice Rehnquist said that there was a difference when the expenditure of funds was "ancillary" to compliance with an injunction.

Furthermore, there are conceptual problems in trying to distinguish between retroactive and prospective relief. If an injury occurred in the past, is preventing it from continuing prospective or retroactive? For example, in *Edelman,* is the payment of the previously wrongfully withheld funds prospective in the sense that it is preventing individuals from being harmed in the future by the continued denial of funds that are owed to them, or is it retroactive in that it is compensation for a previous wrongful act?

Perhaps the difference between prospective and retroactive relief is primarily one of appearance. When a federal court issues retroactive relief that will be paid by the state, it appears that the court is taking a sum directly out of the state treasury. This is what the Eleventh Amendment seemed concerned with preventing. In contrast, prospective relief appears to be simply an order to comply with the law; the costs are incidental to the state's obligation to act in accordance with federal law.

Application of the Distinction

Not surprisingly, since *Edelman* the Supreme Court has struggled with determining whether relief is prospective and permitted or whether orders constitute retroactive awards and are therefore prohibited. For example, in *Milliken v. Bradley* the Court upheld a school desegregation order requiring the expenditure of state funds for educational aspects of a desegregation plan, including several remedial and compensatory education programs.[32] The Court found the remedy prospective and not barred by the Eleventh Amendment, concluding:

> The decree to share the future costs of educational components in this case fits squarely within the prospective-compliance exception reaffirmed by *Edelman*. . . . The educational components, which the District Court ordered into effect *prospectively*, are plainly designed to wipe out continuing conditions of inequality produced by the inherently unequal dual school system long maintained by Detroit. . . . That the programs are also "compensatory" in nature does not change the fact that they are part of a plan that operates *prospectively* to bring about the delayed benefits of a unitary school system. We therefore hold that such prospective relief is not barred by the Eleventh Amendment.[33]

[30] *See, e.g.*, Milliken v. Bradley, 433 U.S. 267 (1977) (relief that required substantial state expenditures on education deemed to be prospective and not barred by the Eleventh Amendment).

[31] 415 U.S. at 667.

[32] 433 U.S. 267 (1977).

[33] 433 U.S. at 289-290 (emphasis in original).

Milliken powerfully illustrates the difficulty in distinguishing prospective from retroactive relief. The orders were designed to remedy past injustices and hence could have been labeled retroactive, yet they will go into effect in the future and could be termed prospective. As Professor David Currie explains, "*Milliken* was no more 'prospective' than that condemned in *Edelman* itself. In both cases the money was to be paid in the future in order to right a past wrong. If that is enough to make the order 'prospective,' there is no such thing as a retrospective order; nobody is ever ordered to have paid yesterday."[34]

In *Frew v. Hawkins*, the Supreme Court unanimously held that state officials may be sued to enforce the terms of a consent decree.[35] Texas state officials were sued for their failure to comply with the requirements of the federal Medicaid law. The suit was settled with a consent decree, which contained some requirements that went beyond the dictates of the federal law. When the Texas officials breached this agreement, the plaintiffs sued to gain compliance. The Supreme Court, in an opinion by Justice Kennedy, concluded that under *Ex parte Young*, the suit against the officials to gain compliance with the terms of the consent decree was not barred by the Eleventh Amendment.

Ancillary Relief

In applying the prospective-retroactive distinction, the Court has placed a great deal of emphasis on the language in *Edelman* that "ancillary" relief against state treasuries is not barred by the Eleventh Amendment. In *Hutto v. Finney*, the Supreme Court held that federal courts may award attorneys' fees to be paid from state treasuries to successful plaintiffs in civil rights actions pursuant to 42 U.S.C. §1988.[36] In *Hutto*, plaintiffs successfully challenged the conditions of confinement in Arkansas prisons as violating the Eighth Amendment's prohibition against cruel and unusual punishment. The district court awarded attorneys' fees to the plaintiffs to be paid by the state. The Supreme Court held that the fee award did not violate the Eleventh Amendment. In part, the Court justified this conclusion by holding that the fee award was ancillary to the injunctive relief ordered in favor of the plaintiffs.[37] *Hutto* thus expanded the notion of permissible ancillary relief because in *Edelman* the Court spoke "not of ancillary orders to pay money but of orders having ancillary effects on the treasury."[38]

The concept of ancillary relief also was crucial in two other Supreme Court decisions, *Quern v. Jordan*[39] and *Green v. Mansour*.[40] After the Supreme Court

[34] David P. Currie, Sovereign Immunity and Suits Against Government Officers, 1984 Sup. Ct. Rev. 149, 162.

[35] 540 U.S. 431 (2004).

[36] 437 U.S. 678 (1978).

[37] The Court also based its decision on the ability of Congress to override the Eleventh Amendment pursuant to statutes adopted under §5 of the Fourteenth Amendment. *See* §7.7, *infra*.

[38] Currie, *supra* note 35, at 162.

[39] 440 U.S. 332 (1979).

[40] 474 U.S. 64 (1985).

decided *Edelman v. Jordan,* the federal district court ordered the state of Illinois to send to every member of the plaintiff's class a notice that they were denied money owed to them and informing them of the administrative procedures available for collecting the funds. In *Quern v. Jordan,* the Supreme Court held that the order to send such notices did not violate the Eleventh Amendment. The Court concluded that the notice was "properly viewed as ancillary to the prospective relief already ordered by the court."[41] It did not matter that the notices would have the effect of encouraging claims for retroactive benefits because the availability of such payments would rest "entirely with the state, its agencies, courts, and legislature, not with the federal court."[42]

In sharp contrast, the Supreme Court, in *Green v. Mansour,* held that the Eleventh Amendment barred a federal court from compelling the state to send notices informing welfare recipients that they might wrongfully have been denied benefits. In response to a class action challenging Michigan's calculation of welfare benefits, the state voluntarily changed its practices to conform with federal requirements. The Supreme Court, in a 5-4 decision, said that under such circumstances notice relief was barred because it was not ancillary to other prospective relief. Unlike the situation in *Quern,* in *Green* there was "no claimed continuing violation of federal law, and therefore no occasion to issue an injunction."[43] The dissent, however, was not persuaded by this distinction and argued that the notice relief requested by the plaintiffs in *Green* was permissible because it was prospective and needed to remedy past illegal state practices.[44]

Thus, the Court has struggled with determining what is prospective or retroactive and what is ancillary. This difficulty inevitably will continue; most remedies can be characterized either way. Nonetheless, a great deal depends on how such relief is labeled because the Eleventh Amendment bars retroactive expenditures to be paid by the state treasury, but not injunctions that result in prospective or ancillary costs to the state.

Official Versus Individual Capacity Suits

If the recovery is from the individual officer's pocket, the suit can be said to be against the officer in an "individual capacity." If the recovery will be from the state treasury, however, the suit is against the officer in an "official capacity." As described above, official capacity suits are barred unless the plaintiff is seeking prospective relief. In *Will v. Michigan Department of State Police,* the Supreme Court held that suits against state governments, even in state courts, are not permitted under §1983 and that suits against state officers in their official capacity are barred under

[41] 440 U.S. at 349.

[42] *Id.* at 348.

[43] 474 U.S. at 73.

[44] *Id.* at 76-77. *See also* Papasan v. Allain, 478 U.S. 265 (1986) (state possesses Eleventh Amendment immunity in suit against it for failure to apply the profits acquired from land granted by the federal government to education as it was required to do under the terms of the federal land grant).

this rule.[45] However, in a footnote, the Court made it clear that this holding did not disturb the well-established rule of *Ex parte Young*: State officers may be sued, even in an official capacity, for injunctive relief.[46]

The key question, which frequently has perplexed lower courts, is when should a suit be regarded as an official capacity suit, and when is it an individual capacity suit. The Court provided clarification in *Hafer v. Melo*.[47] After being elected to the position of auditor general in Pennsylvania, Barbara Hafer fired 18 individuals. These individuals sued Hafer, contending that they were fired because of their Democratic political affiliation. Hafer, in defense, argued that *Will* barred the claims against her because in dismissing the employees, she acted in an official capacity.

The Supreme Court unanimously held that the Eleventh Amendment did not bar the suit against Hafer. The Court reaffirmed the distinction between official capacity and individual capacity suits. Official capacity suits are an attempt to sue the government entity by naming the officer as a defendant, whereas personal capacity suits "seek to impose individual liability upon a government officer for actions taken under color of state law."[48]

The Court explained that a suit is not to be regarded as an official capacity suit simply because the government officer was acting in an official capacity. The Court stated that "the phrase 'acting in their official capacities' is best understood as a reference to the capacity in which the state officer is sued, not the capacity in which the officer inflicts the alleged injury."[49]

In other words, if the suit against a state officer is for injunctive relief, under *Ex parte Young* as reaffirmed in *Will*, there is no Eleventh Amendment bar to federal court jurisdiction. Likewise, if the suit is against an officer for money damages when the relief would come from the officer's own pocket, there is no Eleventh Amendment bar even though the conduct was part of the officer's official duties. In such a suit, the officer could claim absolute or qualified immunity as a defense. The state's choice to indemnify the officer would not convert the suit from individual to official capacity.[50] However, there is an Eleventh Amendment bar if the suit against the officer would lead to monetary relief against the state treasury other than through indemnification.

The practical difficulty for judges is deciding whether a suit is official or individual capacity at the outset of the litigation. Some courts look to how the complaint is drafted,[51] and some look to the defenses raised in determining the

[45] 491 U.S. 58 (1989). *Will* is discussed in detail in §8.7, *infra*.

[46] 491 U.S. at 71 n.10.

[47] 502 U.S. 21 (1991).

[48] 502 U.S. at 25.

[49] *Id.* at 26.

[50] *See, e.g.*, Stoner v. Santa Clara County Office of Educ., 502 F.3d 1116 (9th Cir. 2007); Andrews v. Daw, 201 F.3d 521 (4th Cir. 2000); Darul-Islam v. Dubois, 997 F. Supp. 176 (D. Mass. 1998); Blaylock v. Schwinden, 862 F.2d 1352, 1354 (9th Cir. 1988); Wilson v. Beebe, 770 F.2d 578 (6th Cir. 1985) (en banc); Duckworth v. Franzen, 780 F.2d 645, 650 (7th Cir. 1985).

[51] *See, e.g.*, Moore v. City of Harriman, 272 F.3d 769 (6th Cir. 2001); Egerdahl v. Hibbing Community College, 72 F.3d 615 (8th Cir. 1995); Arab African International Bank v. Epstein, 958 F.2d 532 (3d Cir. 1992); Gregory v. Chehi, 843 F.2d 111 (3d Cir. 1988); Shabazz v. Coughlin, 852 F.2d 697 (2d Cir. 1988).

capacity in which the person is sued.[52] *Hafer* has not ended the confusion over the distinction between official capacity and individual capacity, but it has helped by making it clear that the fact that a government officer is acting in the scope of official duties is not enough to bar a suit as being in "official capacity."

§7.5.3 *Exceptions to* Ex Parte Young

There are four major exceptions to *Ex parte Young*. First, there cannot be suits against state officers to enjoin unconstitutional laws that create civil liability that are not enforced by the government. Second, state officers may not be sued on pendent state law claims. Third, state officers may not be sued to enforce federal statutes that contain comprehensive enforcement mechanisms. Fourth, state officers cannot be sued to quiet title to submerged lands. Each of these exceptions is discussed in turn. Finally, the section concludes by considering an opinion from almost three decades ago by Justice Anthony Kennedy, joined only by Chief Justice Rehnquist, which would have dramatically limited the ability to sue state officers in federal court.

Bar on Suits Against State Officers to Enjoin Laws Creating Civil Liability That Are Not Enforced by the State

Texas adopted a law, S. B. 8, which prohibits abortion once the fetal heartbeat can be detected, which is about six weeks after a woman's last menstrual period. It thus prohibits abortions significantly before viability, which is about the 24th week of pregnancy, and before many women even know that they are pregnant. At the time Texas enacted this law, before the Court overruled *Roe v. Wade*, it was clearly unconstitutional.[53]

The Texas law is not enforced by state or local government officials, but instead authorizes civil suits against doctors who perform abortions or against those who aid or abet abortions. Such individuals can be sued for $10,000. Thus S. B. 8 is enforced by private civil suits, not by government action.

Whole Women's Health v. Jackson involved whether state officials can be sued to enjoin an unconstitutional state law if they play no role in enforcing it.[54] The Court, in a 5-4 decision, ruled that state officers may be sued for injunctive relief only if they have a role in enforcing the law.[55] The Court also held, 8-1, that licensing officials in Texas play a role in enforcing S. B. 8 and thus could be sued to enjoin it.

[52] *See, e.g.*, Colvin v. McDougall, 62 F.3d 1316 (11th Cir. 1995); Powell v. Alexander, 391 F.3d 1 (1st Cir. 2004); Pinaud v. County of Suffolk, 52 F.3d 1139 (2d Cir. 1995); Shabazz v. Coughlin, 852 F.2d 697 (7th Cir. 1988); Shockley v. James, 823 F.2d 1068 (7th Cir. 1987).

[53] *See* Dobbs v. Jackson Woman's Health Org., 597 U.S. 215 (2022) (overruling Roe v. Wade).

[54] 595 U.S. 30 (2021). In a companion case, United States v. Texas, 595 U.S. 74 (2021), the Court granted certiorari to decide whether the United States government had standing to challenge the Texas law. The Court dismissed the case as certiorari improvidently granted.

[55] 595 U.S. at 43-44.

Justice Gorsuch wrote the opinion for the Court and focused on what suits are permissible against state officials. He said that Texas state judges and court clerks could not be sued to enjoin S. B. 8: "But as *Ex parte Young* explained, this traditional exception does not normally permit federal courts to issue injunctions against state-court judges or clerks. Usually, those individuals do not enforce state laws as executive officials might; instead, they work to resolve disputes between parties. If a state court errs in its rulings, too, the traditional remedy has been some form of appeal, including to this Court, not the entry of an *ex ante* injunction preventing the state court from hearing cases."[56] The Court explained that the state court judges and clerks are not adverse parties and thus not appropriate as defendants in a suit seeking injunctive relief.

The Court next said that the Texas Attorney General could not be sued for an injunction because he plays no role in enforcing the law. While *Ex parte Young* authorizes federal courts to enjoin certain state officials from enforcing state laws, the Court emphasized that the attorney general of Texas does not have any enforcement in connection with S. B. 8 that a federal court might enjoin him from exercising. Justice Gorsuch wrote: "While *Ex parte Young* authorizes federal courts to enjoin certain state officials from enforcing state laws, the petitioners do not direct this Court to any enforcement authority the attorney general possesses in connection with S. B. 8 that a federal court might enjoin him from exercising."[57] Justice Gorsuch explained that an injunction is to restrain a person from acting; if state officials play no role in enforcing the law, then an injunction against them does not make sense.

The effect of this decision precludes suits against state officials for injunctions to enjoin laws that authorize money damages for exercising a constitutional right. Justice Gorsuch addressed this and said that remedies still exist. A person sued under S. B. 8, or any law authorizing civil suits, can argue as a defense that it is unconstitutional. Also, the Court said that challenges seeking injunctive relief might be brought in state court.[58] Justice Gorsuch said, "This Court has never recognized an unqualified right to pre-enforcement review of constitutional claims in federal court."[59]

Eight justices, all but Justice Thomas, agreed that the state licensing officials could be sued for injunctive relief because they play a role in enforcing the law. Justice Thomas said that "even when there is an appropriate defendant to sue, a plaintiff may bring an action under *Ex parte Young* only when the defendant 'threaten[s] and [is] about to commence proceedings.' Our later cases explain that 'the prospect of state suit must be imminent.' Here, none of the licensing officials has threatened enforcement proceedings against petitioners because none has authority to bring them. Petitioners do not and cannot dispute this point."[60]

[56] *Id.* at 39.
[57] *Id.* at 43.
[58] *Id.* at 48-50.
[59] *Id.* at 49.
[60] *Id.* at 56-57 (Thomas, J., concurring in part and dissenting in part) (internal citations omitted).

That issue was remanded to the Fifth Circuit, which then certified the question to the Texas State Supreme Court to decide whether medical licensing boards play a role in enforcing S. B. 8. Of course, the importance of this issue changed dramatically after June 24, 2022, when the Court overruled *Roe v. Wade.* This means the Texas law prohibiting abortions after the sixth week of pregnancy is constitutional.

Chief Justice Roberts strongly disagreed and stressed the importance of an injunction against an unconstitutional law. He wrote: "These provisions, among others, effectively chill the provision of abortions in Texas. Texas says that the law also blocks any pre-enforcement judicial review in federal court. On that latter contention, Texas is wrong. As eight Members of the Court agree, petitioners may bring a pre-enforcement suit challenging the Texas law in federal court under *Ex parte Young,* because there exist state executive officials who retain authority to enforce it. Given the ongoing chilling effect of the state law, the District Court should resolve this litigation and enter appropriate relief without delay."[61]

Roberts would have allowed the Attorney General to be sued, because "the Attorney General maintains authority coextensive with the Texas Medical Board to address violations of S. B. 8. The Attorney General may 'institute an action for a civil penalty' if a physician violates a rule or order of the Board."[62] He also would have allowed the court clerk to be sued for injunctive relief.

Most importantly, Roberts emphasized the importance of federal courts being available to hear challenges to the constitutionality of laws. He forcefully concluded: "The clear purpose and actual effect of S. B. 8 has been to nullify this Court's rulings. It is, however, a basic principle that the Constitution is the 'fundamental and paramount law of the nation,' and '[i]t is emphatically the province and duty of the judicial department to say what the law is.' *Marbury v. Madison* (1803). Indeed, '[i]f the legislatures of the several states may, at will, annul the judgments of the courts of the United States, and destroy the rights acquired under those judgments, the constitution itself becomes a solemn mockery.' The nature of the federal right infringed does not matter; it is the role of the Supreme Court in our constitutional system that is at stake."[63]

Justice Sotomayor in her opinion said, "The Court should have put an end to this madness months ago, before S. B. 8 first went into effect."[64] Justice Sotomayor said that *Ex parte Young* allows suits against state officers to enjoin unconstitutional laws and can be applied to permit a suit for an injunction in these circumstances. She expressed grave concerns about the implications of the Court's holding for the future. She wrote: "The dispute is over whether States may nullify federal constitutional rights by employing schemes like the one at hand. The Court indicates that they can, so long as they write their laws to more thoroughly disclaim all enforcement by state officials, including licensing officials. This choice to shrink from Texas' challenge to federal supremacy will have far-reaching repercussions.

[61] *Id.* at 59-60 (Roberts, C.J., concurring in the judgment in part and dissenting in part) (internal citations omitted).

[62] *Id.* at 60.

[63] *Id.* at 61-62 (internal citation omitted).

[64] *Id.* at 62 (Sotomayor, J., concurring in the judgment in part and dissenting in part).

I doubt the Court, let alone the country, is prepared for them. . . . This is a brazen challenge to our federal structure."[65]

The implications for federal jurisdiction extend far beyond the abortion context. A state can create civil liability for any constitutionally protected behavior and so long as no state official plays any role in enforcing it, the law will remain on the books until someone violates it, is sued, and challenges it. For instance, a state can create civil liability for anyone who performs a same-sex wedding or owns a gun or criticizes the governor. The state conceivably could set civil liability at a million dollars, so that no one would risk being sued. To be clear, a person who violates the law and is sued can argue as a defense that the law is unconstitutional. But state officers may be sued for injunctive relief only if they play a role in enforcing the law.

Bar on Suits Against State Officers Based on Pendent State Claims

Pendent jurisdiction—now called supplemental jurisdiction—provides that a federal court may hear state law claims that would otherwise not be within the federal judiciary's subject matter jurisdiction if those claims arise from a "common nucleus of operative fact" with a claim properly within the court's jurisdiction.[66] Therefore, under the traditional rule for pendent jurisdiction, a federal court could hear and decide state law claims against state officers that arose from the same matter as federal law claims. The Supreme Court, however, in *Pennhurst State School & Hospital v. Halderman,* held that the Eleventh Amendment bars federal courts from enjoining state officers from violating state law.[67] The Court ruled that although federal courts may hear federal claims against state officers, they may not hear pendent state law claims. Justice Powell, writing for the majority, stated: "[A] claim that state officials violated state law in carrying out their official responsibilities is a claim against the State that is protected by the Eleventh Amendment. . . . We now hold that this principle applies as well to state law claims brought into federal court under pendent jurisdiction."[68]

The *Pennhurst* litigation began in 1974 when a resident of the Pennhurst State School and Hospital filed a lawsuit challenging conditions in this institution for the care of people with mental disabilities operated by the state of Pennsylvania.[69] The class action suit claimed that inhumane and inadequate conditions violated

[65] *Id.* at 71.

[66] 28 U.S.C. §1367; United Mine Workers v. Gibbs, 383 U.S. 715, 725 (1966) (articulating the test for pendent jurisdiction). *See* discussion in §5.4, *supra.*

[67] 465 U.S. 89 (1984). For excellent criticisms of the Court's decision in *Pennhurst, see* David L. Shapiro, Wrong Turns: The Eleventh Amendment and the *Pennhurst* Case, 98 Harv. L. Rev. 61 (1984); George D. Brown, Beyond *Pennhurst*: Protective Jurisdiction, the Eleventh Amendment, and the Power of Congress to Enlarge Federal Jurisdiction in Response to the Burger Court, 71 Va. L. Rev. 343 (1985). For a defense of *Pennhurst, see* Ann Althouse, How to Build a Separate Sphere: Federal Courts and State Power, 100 Harv. L. Rev. 1485 (1987).

[68] 597 U.S. 580.

[69] The Supreme Court provides a detailed description of the factual history of the *Pennhurst* litigation at *id.* at 92-97.

the class members' rights under the Eighth and Fourteenth Amendments to the U.S. Constitution, as well as federal statutes[70] and state laws.[71] Defendants included the hospital and various hospital officials, the Pennsylvania Department of Welfare and several of its officials, and various county commissioners and county officials responsible for people with mental disabilities.

In 1977, after a lengthy trial, the district court rendered its decision in favor of the plaintiffs.[72] It concluded that "[c]onditions at Pennhurst are not only dangerous, with the residents often physically abused or drugged by staff members, but also inadequate for the 'habilitation' of the retarded."[73] The Court concluded that conditions violated the U.S. Constitution, federal law, and state law. The U.S. Court of Appeals for the Third Circuit affirmed, basing its decision entirely on the conclusion that the state was violating a federal statute—the "bill of rights" included in the Developmentally Disabled Assistance and Bill of Rights Act.[74] The appeals court found it unnecessary to determine whether there were also violations of the U.S. Constitution or other federal or state laws.

The U.S. Supreme Court reversed the decision of the Third Circuit.[75] The Court held that states were not required to comply with the "bill of rights" in the Developmentally Disabled Assistance and Bill of Rights Act. The Court said that Congress may require state compliance with conditions in federal grants only if the conditions are clear and unequivocal; this degree of clarity was absent in this act.[76]

On remand, the Third Circuit again affirmed the district court's decision, concluding that the plaintiffs were entitled to relief because of violations of Pennsylvania law.[77] The case again went to the U.S. Supreme Court, and again the Court reversed the Third Circuit's decision. The Court held that the Eleventh Amendment bars relief against state officers on the basis of state law.[78] The Court concluded that federal courts can give relief against state officers on federal law grounds because of the importance of securing compliance with federal law. Because the federal system has no such need to ensure enforcement of state law, there is no reason to create an exception to the Eleventh Amendment and allow suits against state officers on pendent state law claims in federal court.

Many commentators have criticized the Court's reasoning in the *Pennhurst* decision. First, the holding in *Ex parte Young*[79]—that officers who act illegally are stripped of state authority and may be sued in federal court—should apply no

[70] Rehabilitation Act of 1973, 29 U.S.C. §794 (1983), Assistance and Bill of Rights Act, Pub. L. No. 94-103, 89 Stat. 496 (1975), 42 U.S.C. §§6000-6083 (Supp. 1985).

[71] Pennsylvania Mental Health and Mental Retardation Act of 1966, 50 Pa. Cons. Stat. Ann. §§4101-4704 (Purdon 1985).

[72] Halderman v. Pennhurst State School & Hosp., 446 F. Supp. 1295 (E.D. Pa. 1977).

[73] 612 F.2d 84, 107 (3d Cir. 1979) (en banc). The Third Circuit reversed and remanded, however, on the issue of appropriate relief.

[74] 451 U.S. 1 (1981).

[75] *Id.* at 7.

[76] *Id.* at 17.

[77] 673 F.2d 647 (3d Cir. 1982) (en banc).

[78] 465 U.S. at 120-121.

[79] 209 U.S. 123 (1908). The Court's decision in Ex parte Young is discussed in detail in §7.5.1, *supra.*

less forcefully when the violation is of state as opposed to federal law. *Young* distinguishes between the state and its officers, much as the common law distinguishes between a principal and agent. The decision states that the agent, the officer who acts illegally, is powerless to try to protect such actions by invoking the immunity of the principal, the state.

Because state authority protects only lawful actions of state officers, it follows directly that a state officer who violates state law also is stripped of state authority for purposes of the Eleventh Amendment. This is exactly what the Third Circuit held on remand in *Pennhurst*, concluding that it could give relief against state officers based on their violation of state statutes.[80] In fact, the basis for federal relief is even stronger in *Pennhurst* than in *Ex parte Young*. In *Young*, the state officer—the attorney general—was enforcing a statute adopted by the Minnesota legislature, while in *Pennhurst*, the officers were violating a statute adopted by the legislature. In *Ex parte Young*, the state authorized the officer's conduct, while in *Pennhurst* it proscribed it. Thus, if there was no finding of state authority in *Young*, then none existed in *Pennhurst*.

Second, the Court's decision in *Pennhurst* substantially undermines the attractiveness of the federal forum for litigants and might have the effect of forcing many cases out of federal court. After *Pennhurst*, how should a litigant with both federal and state claims against a state officer proceed? There are three possible choices. One approach is to bring both the federal claims and the state claims in state court, in which case the federal forum would be lost. Alternatively, a litigant could bring the federal claims in federal court and the state claims in state court. This approach, however, risks having the federal claims completely barred by res judicata should the state court decide its case first.[81] If a state court decides in favor of the defendant on the state law claims, the defendant could then go to federal court and assert res judicata or collateral estoppel as a bar to a federal court decision on the federal claims. Because the claims arise from the same subject matter, and because all the federal claims could have been raised in state court, all litigants who split their claims after *Pennhurst* risk the res judicata bar if the state court decides first.

The final possibility is for plaintiffs to file their claims sequentially—first going to federal court and, if unsuccessful, then going to state court with the state law claim. This approach, like splitting the claims, is wasteful of court and litigant resources. Moreover, the federal court's fact-finding would have collateral estoppel effect in the state court proceeding.

Litigants seeking to raise both federal and state claims against state officers in federal court possibly still have a few avenues open to them after *Pennhurst*. One way is to argue that *Pennhurst* does not preclude state claims based on a contention that the state officer acted in excess of his or her authority. The Court in *Pennhurst* said that sovereign immunity precludes injunctive relief "against state officials for

[80] 673 F.2d 647 (3d Cir. 1982) (en banc).

[81] *See, e.g.*, Migra v. Warren City Sch. Dist. Bd. of Educ., 465 U.S. 75 (1984); Kremer v. Chemical Constr. Corp., 456 U.S. 461 (1982); Allen v. McCurry, 449 U.S. 90 (1980) (state court decisions are accorded collateral estoppel and res judicata effects in federal court). *See* discussion in §8.10, *infra*.

failing to carry out their duties under state statutes" or "on violations of state statutes that command purely discretionary duties."[82] The Court stated: "Since it cannot be doubted that the statutes at issue here gave petitioners broad discretion in operating Pennhurst, the conduct alleged in this case would not be ultra vires even under the standards of the dissent's cases."[83] Therefore, the Court in *Pennhurst* does not address the situation in which the state officer violates a state law that creates a nondiscretionary duty or acts in excess of lawful authority. Accordingly, *Pennhurst* might be construed as not precluding pendent state law claims against state officers in those circumstances.

An alternative way for litigants to bring state law claims into federal court after *Pennhurst* is to argue that the state law in question gives rise to a liberty or property interest protected by the due process clause of the Fourteenth Amendment. Under the Burger Court's procedural due process doctrines, state law can create both liberty and property rights, either explicitly or by creating an expectation that gives rise to a vested right.[84] For example, in *Pennhurst*, the court of appeals found that state law required the state "to adopt the 'least restrictive environment' approach for the care of the mentally retarded."[85] That is, under the Burger Court's approach to procedural due process, the state law has created a liberty interest, and thus the state's violation of its own law constitutes a denial of liberty without due process.[86] In this manner, it appears that some state law claims can be construed as federal claims and therefore can be brought into federal court, avoiding the need for litigants to split their claims.

Suits Enforcing Federal Laws with Comprehensive Enforcement

In *Seminole Tribe v. Florida*,[87] the Court recognized an additional exception to *Ex parte Young*: state officers cannot be sued to enforce federal statutes that contain comprehensive enforcement mechanisms. The Indian Gaming Regulatory Act provides that an Indian tribe may conduct gambling activities only in accord with a valid compact between the tribe and the state where the tribe is located.[88] The law, enacted by Congress pursuant to its authority to regulate commerce with Indian tribes, requires that states negotiate in good faith with tribes for the formation of such compacts. The statute specifically authorizes suits against states to enforce its provisions.[89]

[82] 465 U.S. at 109-110.

[83] *Id.* at 110-111.

[84] *See, e.g.*, Paul v. Davis, 424 U.S. 693 (1976); Board of Regents v. Roth, 408 U.S. 564 (1972) (state law defines the existence of property and liberty for the purposes of procedural due process).

[85] 463 U.S. at 1251; *see also* John P. Dwyer, Pendent Jurisdiction and the Eleventh Amendment, 75 Cal. L. Rev. 129 (1987) (*Pennhurst* should be understood as preventing only suits for structural relief requiring ongoing federal court supervision of state officers).

[86] *See, e.g.*, Jackson v. Ylst, 921 F.2d 882, 886 (9th Cir. 1990); Toussaint v. McCarthy, 801 F.2d 1080 (9th Cir. 1986); Spruyette v. Walters, 753 F.2d 498 (6th Cir. 1985).

[87] 517 U.S. 44 (1996).

[88] 25 U.S.C. §2710(d)(1)(C).

[89] 25 U.S.C. §2710(d)(7).

The Seminole Tribe of Indians sued the state of Florida and its governor, Lawton Chiles, for failing to negotiate to create a compact allowing gambling. The tribe offered two theories as to why the suit was not barred by the Eleventh Amendment. First, a federal statute expressly abrogated the Eleventh Amendment and authorized a suit against the state government. The Court's rejection of this argument, and its narrowing of the ability of Congress to override the Eleventh Amendment, is discussed below in §7.7.

Second, the tribe argued that *Ex parte Young* permitted the suit against the governor to enforce the federal statute. The Supreme Court carved a new exception to *Ex parte Young* and held that a state officer cannot be sued to enforce a federal law that contains a comprehensive enforcement mechanism. Chief Justice Rehnquist, writing for the Court, stated: "[W]here Congress has prescribed a detailed remedial scheme for the enforcement against a state of a statutorily created right, a court should hesitate before casting aside those limitations and permitting an action against a state officer based on *Ex parte Young*."[90] The Court found that the Indian Gaming Regulatory Act contained a detailed remedial scheme in that it provided for court-ordered negotiation and the submission of claims to a mediator.

This aspect of the *Seminole Tribe* decision raises two questions: one descriptive and the other normative. Regarding the descriptive question, what is sufficient to justify a finding that a statute has a detailed remedial scheme sufficient to preclude suits against individual officers under *Ex parte Young*? Chief Justice Rehnquist's opinion offers no criteria and little discussion to guide lower courts. It should be noted that the primary enforcement mechanism in the Indian Gaming Regulatory Act was the ability to sue states in federal court, a provision declared unconstitutional in *Seminole Tribe*. Perhaps courts will analogize to a line of cases that hold that §1983 cannot be used as a cause of action to enforce federal statutes that contain comprehensive enforcement mechanisms.[91] As discussed in §8.8, the Supreme Court has interpreted this to be a narrow exception that applies when federal statutes intend an alternative to court enforcement to ensure compliance.

The normative question is whether this exception to *Ex parte Young* is justified. *Young* is based on the premise that state officers are stripped of authority if they violate federal law. It is clearly established that suits against officers are permitted for violations of both federal statutes and the U.S. Constitution.[92] Therefore, under the reasoning of *Young*, a state officer is stripped of state authority, and is amenable to suit, for violating any federal law, regardless of whether it has a detailed remedial scheme.

Moreover, the exception created by the Supreme Court assumes that Congress can choose to eliminate suits against officers to enforce federal laws. Even accepting this as true, the inquiry for each statute must be whether Congress intended to allow or preclude federal court review—does the remedial scheme for the law indicate that Congress wanted it to supplant suits in federal court for enforcement?

[90] 517 U.S. at 74.

[91] *See* Middlesex County Sewage Authority v. National Sea Clammers Assn., 453 U.S. 1 (1981), discussed in §8.8.

[92] *See, e.g.*, Green v. Mansour, 474 U.S. at 68 (injunctive relief is available to enforce federal laws).

Congress clearly chose to permit federal court enforcement of the Indian Gaming Regulatory Act, as evidenced by its explicit authorization for suits against state governments. Therefore, it is puzzling that the Court would find that the remedial scheme in the statute evidences an intent by Congress to preclude suits under *Ex parte Young* to enforce the statute in federal court.

Exception for Suits to Quiet Title to Submerged Lands

In *Idaho v. Coeur d'Alene Tribe*, the Court carved a new, quite narrow exception to *Ex parte Young*: State officers cannot be sued to quiet title to submerged lands.[93] The case involved a dispute over whether the tribe's ownership of lands extends to the banks and submerged lands of Lake Coeur d'Alene or is vested in the state of Idaho. The Supreme Court found that the suit against the state was barred by the Eleventh Amendment and that the suit against the state officials was precluded because "if the tribe were to prevail, Idaho's sovereign interest in its lands and waters would be affected to a degree fully as intrusive as almost any conceivable retroactive levy upon funds in its treasury."[94] Justice Kennedy, writing this part of the opinion on behalf of the Court's majority, explained that "[t]he requested injunctive relief would bar the state's principal officers from exercising their governmental powers and authority over the disputed lands and waters. The suit would diminish, even extinguish, the state's control over a vast reach of lands and waters long deemed by the state to be an integral part of its territory."[95]

On the one hand, *Idaho v. Coeur d'Alene Tribe* can be viewed as a narrow case, involving an interest of particular importance to the State of Idaho. Indeed, Justice Kennedy's opinion concluded by speaking of the case's "particular and special circumstances."[96] On the other hand, the Court's decision precludes the tribe from any federal court remedy for its claims; it can sue neither the state nor its officers. Preclusion of federal court jurisdiction is especially troubling in this context because of the special federal role in mediating disputes between Native American tribes and state governments. Moreover, the case opens the door to the Court finding other exceptions to *Ex parte Young* when the relief would have significant impact on a state government.

The Court has refused to extend *Idaho v. Coeur d'Alene Tribe* and held that state officers may be sued by an agency of the state government to ensure compliance with federal law. In *Virginia Office for Protection and Advocacy v. Stewart*, the Court, in an opinion by Justice Scalia, rejected the argument that permitting a state agency to sue an officer of that state would undermine important sovereign interests of the state or impermissibly impugn the integrity of the state.[97] The Court said that

[93] 521 U.S. 261 (1997).
[94] *Id.* at 287.
[95] *Id.* at 281.
[96] *Id.* at 287.
[97] 563 U.S. 247 (2011).

the state failed to show that allowing such suits would "threaten any similar invasion of Virginia's sovereignty,"[98] as occurred in *Idaho v. Coeur d'Alene Tribe.*

A Broader Exception to *Ex Parte Young*?

Justice Kennedy, in a part of the opinion in *Idaho v. Coeur d'Alene Tribe* joined only by Chief Justice Rehnquist, urged a much broader new exception to *Ex parte Young.* Declaring *Young* "an obvious fiction,"[99] Justice Kennedy argued that state officers should be subject to suit in federal court only in two narrow circumstances. First, state officers could be sued if "there is no state forum available to vindicate federal interests."[100] Second, state officers could be sued in federal court when there is a showing of a particular need for federal court interpretation and enforcement of federal law. Justice Kennedy observed that this concern could lead "to expansive application of the *Young* exception" and that there was no indication that "states consented to these types of suits in the plan of the convention."[101] Justice Kennedy stated that such claims against state officers generally could be brought in state court and noted that "[n]either in theory nor in practice has it been shown problematic to have federal claims resolved in state courts."[102] Thus, Justice Kennedy advocated a case-by-case balancing approach, with federal courts exercising jurisdiction in a suit against a state officer only if there was a showing in that instance that one of the above two circumstances was present.

Justice Kennedy's approach, had it attracted support from a majority of the Court, would have radically altered constitutional litigation in the United States. Virtually all constitutional challenges to state laws and state government actions, now brought to federal court pursuant to *Ex parte Young,* would have been shifted to state courts. Rarely is a state forum unavailable and seldom under Justice Kennedy's approach could it be shown that there was a special need for federal court review. Justice Kennedy's approach would do no less than largely overrule *Ex parte Young.* Although this would have the virtue of furthering federalism by expanding state immunity from federal court review, it would undermine state accountability by eliminating the primary mechanism used to ensure state compliance with federal law.

Seven justices rejected Justice Kennedy's attempt to reformulate *Ex parte Young.* In an opinion concurring in the judgment, Justice O'Connor, joined by Justices Scalia and Thomas, rejected replacing *Young*'s bright-line rule with a case-by-case balancing approach.[103] Additionally, the four dissenting justices—Justices

[98] *Id* at 257. Chief Justice Roberts and Justice Alito dissented and emphasized the importance of sovereign immunity and the need to narrowly construe any exceptions. This certainly indicates that they are likely to be consistent votes in favor of expansively construing sovereign immunity and limiting exceptions.

[99] 521 U.S. at 270.

[100] *Id.*

[101] *Id.* at 274. The "plan of the Convention" as a basis for congressional power to override sovereign immunity is discussed in §7.7 below.

[102] *Id.* at 274-275.

[103] *Id.* at 288 (O'Connor, J., concurring and concurring in the judgment).

Stevens, Souter, Ginsburg, and Breyer—also rejected Justice Kennedy's attempt to carve a new, dramatic exception to *Ex parte Young*.[104]

Indeed, in a subsequent decision concerning *Ex parte Young*, the Supreme Court unanimously reaffirmed its holding. In *Verizon Maryland, Inc. v. Public Service Commission of Maryland*, the Court held that the Eleventh Amendment does not bar suits against officers when it is alleged that there is a violation of federal law.[105] Verizon sued the Maryland Public Service Commission and its officers to challenge an order that Verizon was required, as a matter of state law, to pay a competitor after the Federal Communications Commission ruled that no such compensation was required under federal law.

The Supreme Court said that it had no need to consider the ability to sue the state agency because relief was available against the individual officers pursuant to *Ex parte Young*. Justice Scalia, writing for a unanimous Court, explained: "In determining whether the doctrine of *Ex parte Young* avoids an Eleventh Amendment bar to suit, a court need only conduct a 'straightforward inquiry into whether [the] complaint alleges an ongoing violation of federal law and seeks relief properly characterized as prospective.' "[106]

This is an emphatic reaffirmation of *Ex parte Young*. No justices have returned to Justice Kennedy's suggested balancing approach since *Idaho v. Coeur d'Alene Tribe* in 1997.

§7.6 WAYS AROUND THE ELEVENTH AMENDMENT: WAIVER

Is Waiver Consistent with a Limit on Subject Matter Jurisdiction?

A second major way around the Eleventh Amendment is the state waiving its immunity and consenting to be sued in federal court. Although allowing such waivers seems inconsistent with viewing the Eleventh Amendment as a restriction on the federal courts' subject matter jurisdiction, it is firmly established that "if a State waives its immunity and consents to suit in federal court, the Eleventh Amendment does not bar the action."[1] Permitting states to waive their Eleventh Amendment immunity reflects the close relationship between the amendment and sovereign immunity.[2] Traditionally, sovereign immunity could be waived, and that principle has carried over to Eleventh Amendment jurisprudence. Professor Pagan suggests that "[w]hen

[104] *Id.* at 298 (Souter, J., dissenting).

[105] 535 U.S. 635 (2002).

[106] *Id.* at 645.

7.6 [1] Atascadero State Hosp. v. Scanlon, 473 U.S. 234, 238 (1985).

[2] John V. Orth, The Judicial Power of the United States: The Eleventh Amendment in American History 123 (1987). For an excellent history and discussion of waivers of sovereign immunity, *see* Jonathan R. Siegel, Waivers of State Sovereign Immunity and the Ideology of the Eleventh Amendment, 523 Duke L.J. 1167 (2003).

a state consents to federal adjudication, it waives not the lack of subject matter jurisdiction, which a litigant never can waive, but rather the privilege of enforcing a limitation on the exercise of jurisdiction otherwise possessed by the court."[3] Although this distinction seems ephemeral and is not followed in other areas of subject matter jurisdiction, nevertheless the Supreme Court consistently has held that consenting states may be sued in federal court.[4]

If a state waives its Eleventh Amendment immunity, it may be sued directly in federal court, even for retroactive relief to be paid out of the state treasury. However, the Court has stated clearly that the "test for determining whether a state has waived its [Eleventh Amendment] immunity from federal-court jurisdiction is a stringent one."[5] In *Edelman v. Jordan,* the Court declared that a state will be deemed to have waived its immunity "only where stated 'by the most express language or by such overwhelming implications from the text as [will] leave no room for any other reasonable construction.' "[6]

Explicit and Constructive Waivers

Two types of waivers exist: explicit waivers and constructive waivers. To be effective, an explicit waiver requires the state expressly to agree to be sued in federal court. A state's consent to be sued in its state courts is not sufficient to constitute a waiver of its Eleventh Amendment immunity.[7] Nor is a state's general waiver of its sovereign immunity enough. For example, a state statute authorizing the state to be sued "in any court of competent jurisdiction" is not an adequate waiver of Eleventh Amendment immunity.[8] The Court declared that "[a]lthough a State's general waiver of sovereign immunity may subject it to suit in state court, it is not enough to waive the immunity guaranteed by the Eleventh Amendment."[9] Rather, for a state statute or constitutional provision to constitute a waiver of Eleventh Amendment immunity, "it must specify the State's intention to subject itself to suit in *federal court.*"[10] Thus, the Supreme Court's test is so stringent that it is quite unlikely that very many explicit state waivers of Eleventh Amendment immunity will be found.

In *Port Authority Trans-Hudson Corp. v. Feeney,* the Court found an express waiver by a state of its Eleventh Amendment immunity.[11] The issue in *Feeney* was whether the Eleventh Amendment barred a suit against the Port Authority Trans-Hudson

[3] John R. Pagan, Eleventh Amendment Analysis, 39 Ark. L. Rev. 447, 488-489 (1986).

[4] *See, e.g.,* Florida Dept. of Health & Rehabilitative Servs. v. Florida Nursing Home Assn., 450 U.S. 147, 149-150 (1981); Edelman v. Jordan, 415 U.S. 651 (1974); Clark v. Barnard, 108 U.S. 436 (1883).

[5] Atascadero State Hosp. v. Scanlon, 473 U.S. at 241.

[6] 415 U.S. at 673 (citation omitted). *See also* Port Auth. Trans-Hudson Corp. v. Feeney, 495 U.S. 299, 305-306 (1990).

[7] *See, e.g.,* Florida Dept. of Health & Rehabilitative Servs. v. Florida Nursing Home Assn., 450 U.S. 147, 149-150 (1981).

[8] Kennecott Copper Corp. v. State Tax Commn., 327 U.S. 573, 578-580 (1946).

[9] Atascadero State Hosp. v. Scanlon, 473 U.S. at 241.

[10] *Id.* at 241 (emphasis in original).

[11] 495 U.S. 299 (1990).

Corporation (PATH), an entity created by New York and New Jersey to operate transportation facilities. The Supreme Court assumed that PATH is a state agency entitled to Eleventh Amendment immunity.

The Court concluded that the states had waived their Eleventh Amendment immunity. Each state had adopted a law stating that it "consent[s] to suits, actions, or proceedings of any form or nature at law, in equity, or otherwise . . . against the Port Authority of New York."[12] Although this provision alone was insufficient to constitute a waiver, because it did not consent to suit in *federal* court, there was another provision that was specific. The venue provision stated that "the foregoing consent is granted on the condition that venue . . . shall be within a county or judicial district, established by one of said States or by the United States, and situated wholly or partially within the Port of New York District."[13] Because the venue provision was part of the same law that consented to suit and because it clearly indicated that the states envisioned federal court litigation, the Court found that it was sufficient to waive the states' Eleventh Amendment immunity.

Subsequent cases have made clear that express waiver provisions are to be narrowly construed. In *Sossamon v. Texas*,[14] the Court construed a provision of the Religious Land Use and Institutionalized Persons Act, which prohibits state and local governments from imposing a substantial burden on the religious exercise of an institutionalized person absent a compelling state interest.[15] The statute applies to programs that "receive federal assistance," and the act creates an express private cause of action for "appropriate relief against a government."[16]

The Supreme Court, however, ruled that this was not sufficient to constitute a waiver of sovereign immunity. Justice Thomas wrote for the Court and said that a federal law that conditions receipt of federal funds on a waiver of sovereign immunity must be explicit and that the authorization in the Religious Land Use and Institutionalized Persons Act was not sufficiently specific. He explained: " 'Appropriate relief' is open-ended and ambiguous about what types of relief it includes, as many lower courts have recognized. Far from clearly identifying money damages, the word 'appropriate' is inherently context-dependent. The context here—where the defendant is a sovereign—suggests, if anything, that monetary damages are not 'suitable' or 'proper.' "[17]

Justice Sotomayor, in a dissent joined by Justice Breyer, said that a federal law authorizing any "appropriate relief" certainly should be seen as including claims for money damages. She wrote: "No one disputes that, in accepting federal funds, the States consent to suit for violations of RLUIPA's substantive provisions; the only question is what relief is available to plaintiffs asserting injury from such violations. That monetary damages are 'appropriate relief' is, in my view, self-evident. Under general remedies principles, the usual remedy for a violation of a legal

[12] *Id.* at 306, *quoting* N.J. Stat. Ann. §32:1-157 (1963); N.Y. Unconsol. Laws §7101 (McKinney 1979).
[13] *Id.* at 307, *quoting* N.J. Stat. Ann. §32:1-162; N.Y. Unconsol. Laws §7106 (McKinney 1979).
[14] 563 U.S. 277 (2011).
[15] 42 U.S.C. §2000cc-1.
[16] 42 U.S.C. §2000cc-2(a).
[17] 563 U.S. at 286.

right is damages. Consistent with these principles, our precedents make clear that the phrase 'appropriate relief' includes monetary relief."[18]

Constructive Waivers Not Allowed

Alternatively, there is the possibility of directly suing a state in federal court based on the state's constructive waiver of its Eleventh Amendment immunity. After some uncertainty in the law, it now appears that constructive waivers are disfavored and rarely will be found by the Court. As Justice Rehnquist declared, writing for the majority in *Edelman v. Jordan*, "Constructive consent is not a doctrine commonly associated with the surrender of constitutional rights and we see no place for it here."[19] The height of the doctrine of constructive consent was in *Parden v. Terminal Railway of Alabama State Docks Department.*[20] The issue in *Parden* was whether the state could be sued for violating provisions of the Federal Employers' Liability Act in the operation of a state railroad. The Court held that the state's choice to operate a railroad in light of the federal statute reflected constructive consent by the state to be sued in federal court. Although the state had said explicitly it did not consent to be sued, waiver was nonetheless found. Justice Brennan, writing for the majority, stated:

> Our conclusion is simply that Alabama, when it began operation of an interstate railroad approximately 20 years after enactment of the FELA, necessarily consented to such suit as was authorized by that Act. By adopting and ratifying the Commerce Clause, the States empowered Congress to create such a right of action against interstate railroads; by enacting the FELA in the exercise of this power, Congress conditioned the right to operate a railroad in interstate commerce upon amenability to suit in federal court as provided by the Act; by thereafter operating a railroad in interstate commerce, Alabama must be taken to have accepted that condition and thus to have consented to suit.[21]

Four justices dissented, arguing that constructive waiver should be found only if there is an explicit statement from Congress that it intended to make states liable if they engaged in particular activities.

Subsequently, in *Employees of the Department of Public Health & Welfare v. Department of Public Health & Welfare*, the dissenting position in *Parden* was adopted by a majority of the Court.[22] The *Employees* case involved a suit against the state of Missouri to enforce the state's compliance with the Fair Labor Standards Act, which had been amended to apply to state and local governments. The majority distinguished

[18] *Id.* at 293 (Sotomayor, J., dissenting).

[19] Edelman v. Jordan, 415 U.S. 651, 653 (1974). It is interesting that Justice Rehnquist analogized a state's Eleventh Amendment immunity to an individual's constitutional rights.

[20] 377 U.S. 184 (1964). The Supreme Court overruled *Parden* in Welch v. Texas Dept. of Highways & Pub. Transp., 483 U.S. 468 (1987). *Welch* is discussed in detail at the text accompanying notes 29-32, *infra.*

[21] 377 U.S. at 192.

[22] 411 U.S. 279 (1973).

Parden on the grounds that whereas states have a choice whether or not to operate railroads, they have little discretion in deciding whether to provide basic public services such as public hospitals and police protection. Especially absent a clear declaration from Congress that it intended to make states liable for violations of the act, there is no basis for finding a constructive waiver.[23]

The Court's refusal to find constructive waivers became even clearer a year after the *Employees* decision, in *Edelman v. Jordan*.[24] In addition to trying to avoid the Eleventh Amendment by suing the state officers,[25] the plaintiffs also claimed that Illinois had waived its immunity to suits over its welfare program by voluntarily choosing to receive federal funds. Under the Social Security Act, states are not obligated to participate in the program of Aid to the Aged, Blind, and Disabled. If, however, a state decides to participate, it receives federal funds but must comply with federal standards. The Court said that there was not a sufficient declaration of Congress's desire to permit suits against states in federal courts when states choose to receive federal welfare money. The Court concluded that the "mere fact that a State participates in a program through which the Federal Government provides assistance for the operation by the State of a system of public aid is not sufficient to establish consent on the part of the State to be sued in the federal courts."[26]

The holding in *Edelman* has been reaffirmed and applied by the Court in rulings that a state does not waive its Eleventh Amendment immunity by receiving federal funds under the Rehabilitation Act of 1973[27] or by agreeing to be bound by the requirements of the federal Medicaid Act.[28]

In 1987, the Supreme Court explicitly overruled its earlier decision in *Parden*. In *Welch v. Texas Department of Highways & Public Transportation*, the Court considered whether the Jones Act can be the basis for state liability in federal court.[29] The Jones Act is a federal statute creating remedies for injured seamen like those for injured railroad employees involved in the *Parden* case. Welch was injured while working for the state of Texas on the docks and sued to recover for his injuries.

The Supreme Court held that the Eleventh Amendment barred Welch's suit against Texas. The Court stated, "Congress has not expressed in unmistakable statutory language its intention to allow States to be sued in federal court under the Jones Act."[30] The Court emphasized that waiver will be found only if Congress clearly and unequivocally expresses its intent to make states liable. The Court

[23] *Id.* at 285. Justices Brennan and Marshall wrote dissenting opinions, in which they set out their views of the Eleventh Amendment, including the view that the Eleventh Amendment does not prevent a citizen's suit against his or her own state and that the Eleventh Amendment is a reinstatement of common law immunity.

[24] 415 U.S. 651 (1974).

[25] This aspect of Edelman v. Jordan is discussed in §7.5.2, *supra*.

[26] 415 U.S. at 673.

[27] Atascadero State Hosp. v. Scanlon, 473 U.S. 234 (1985).

[28] Florida Dept. of Health & Rehabilitative Servs. v. Florida Nursing Home Assn., 450 U.S. 147 (1981).

[29] Welch v. Texas Dept. of Highways & Pub. Transp., 483 U.S. 468 (1987).

[30] *Id.* at 475.

declared that *Parden* was overruled to the extent that it was inconsistent with its holding in *Welch.*[31]

However, subsequent to *Welch,* the Supreme Court held that *Parden* was overruled only insofar as its holding that FELA constituted a waiver of the Eleventh Amendment. The Court ruled that suits still may be brought against states in state courts under FELA.[32]

Subsequently, in *College Savings Bank v. Florida Prepaid Postsecondary Expense Board,* the Supreme Court, in a 5-4 decision, again ruled that there is no constructive waiver of the Eleventh Amendment.[33] College Savings Bank is a company that devised a system for students to use to save money for their college education. Florida Prepaid, a Florida state agency, copied this system. College Savings Bank sued for patent infringement and for deceptive business practices in violation of the Lanham Act.[34] In *College Savings Bank v. Florida Prepaid,* the Court dealt with the latter claim and rejected the argument that the state had waived its sovereign immunity by engaging in the impermissible conduct. Justice Scalia, writing for the Court, stressed that there is no such thing as constructive waiver of the Eleventh Amendment.

In short, constructive waiver of Eleventh Amendment immunity is virtually nonexistent.[35] If it ever will exist, it will be in situations in which Congress indicates a clear intent to make states liable in federal court if they engage in a particular activity, and then a state voluntarily chooses to engage in that conduct.[36] The congressional desire to make states liable must be in "unmistakable language in the statute itself,"[37] and it must be an area where the state realistically could choose not to engage in the activity.[38]

Nonetheless, there are important unresolved questions concerning waiver. Is the removal of a case from state to federal court a waiver? The Supreme Court addressed but did not fully resolve this issue in *Lapides v. Board of Regents of University System of Georgia.*[39] The Court began by stating that the issue before it was "whether the State's act of removing a lawsuit from state court to federal court waives this immunity."[40] The Court declared: "We hold that it does,"[41] but actually

[31] *Id.* at 476.

[32] Hilton v. South Carolina Public Railways Commn., 502 U.S. 197, 202 (1991).

[33] 527 U.S. 786 (1999).

[34] In a separate decision, Florida Prepaid Postsecondary Education Expense Board v. College Savings Bank, 527 U.S. 627 (1999), the Court held that the state could not be sued for patent infringement because Congress lacked the authority to permit such suits. This decision is discussed below.

[35] In Wisconsin Department of Corrections v. Schacht, 524 U.S. 381, 394 (1998) (Kennedy, J., concurring), Justice Kennedy suggested that a state's choice to remove a case from state to federal court can be regarded as a waiver. In *Schacht,* the Supreme Court held that the presence of a state defendant and claims barred by the Eleventh Amendment do not preclude removal of a suit from state to federal court, but it did not need to reach the issue of whether removal constitutes a waiver.

[36] Pagan, *supra* note 3, at 491-492. *See also* Kit Kinports, Implied Waiver After *Seminole Tribe,* 82 Minn. L. Rev. 793 (1998).

[37] 473 U.S. at 243.

[38] Pagan, *supra* note 3, at 494-495.

[39] 535 U.S. 613 (2002).

[40] *Id.* at 616.

[41] *Id.*

only decided a much narrower question. The case involved a suit by a professor in the Georgia state university system filed in state court against the university and several of its officials. The state removed the case from state to federal court and then moved to dismiss based on the Eleventh Amendment. There were no viable federal claims because state governments cannot be sued under 42 U.S.C. §1983,[42] and all that remained were state claims. Georgia had waived sovereign immunity for these state claims in state court.

The Supreme Court ruled that the state's choice to remove the case to federal court was a waiver of its sovereign immunity. The Court's actual holding was narrow: A state's choice to remove a case from state to federal court is a waiver when there are state law claims and the state has waived its immunity as to these claims in state court. The Court declared: "It has become clear that we must limit our answer to the context of state-law claims, in respect to which the State has explicitly waived immunity from state-court proceedings. That is because Lapides' only federal claim against the State arises under 42 U.S.C. §1983, that claim seeks only monetary damages, and we have held that a State is not a 'person' against whom a §1983 claim for money damages might be asserted. Hence this case does not present a valid federal claim against the State. Nor need we address the scope of waiver by removal in a situation where the State's underlying sovereign immunity from suit has not been waived or abrogated in state court."[43]

The Court's reasoning means that the case likely has broader implications: if the state removes a case from state to federal court, it has made the choice to invoke federal jurisdiction, and thus waives its sovereign immunity. The Court explained: "It would seem anomalous or inconsistent for a State both (1) to invoke federal jurisdiction, thereby contending that the 'Judicial power of the United States' extends to the case at hand, and (2) to claim Eleventh Amendment immunity, thereby denying that the 'Judicial power of the United States' extends to the case at hand. And a Constitution that permitted States to follow their litigation interests by freely asserting both claims in the same case could generate seriously unfair results. Thus, it is not surprising that more than a century ago this Court indicated that a State's voluntary appearance in federal court amounted to a waiver of its Eleventh Amendment immunity."[44] This reasoning suggests that the state waives its sovereign immunity if it makes the voluntary choice to invoke federal court jurisdiction by removing a case from federal to state court.[45] But because the holding in *Lapides* was narrower than this, it remains unresolved whether a state's removal always constitutes a waiver of sovereign immunity.

[42] Will v. Michigan Dept. of State Police, 491 U.S. 58 (1989) (holding that state governments are not "persons" and thus cannot be sued under §1983).

[43] 535 U.S. at 617.

[44] *Id.* at 619.

[45] *See, e.g.,* Utah School for the Deaf and Blind v. Sutton, 173 F.3d 1226 (10th Cir. 1999) (state by removing case from state court to federal court has waived its Eleventh Amendment immunity). *But see* Stewart v. North Carolina, 393 F.3d 484 (4th Cir. 2005) (removal by a state government from state to federal court is not a concern of sovereign immunity).

Likewise, it is unsettled whether a state's participation in pretrial proceedings constitutes a waiver.[46] Underlying these questions are issues concerning who within the state may waive its sovereign immunity; can the state attorney general do this, such as by removal, or can waiver be done only by a state legislature? Also, what is sufficient to constitute a waiver?

§7.7 WAYS AROUND THE ELEVENTH AMENDMENT: SUITS PURSUANT TO FEDERAL LAWS

Should Congress Be Able to Abrogate the Eleventh Amendment?

Many scholars have argued that Congress should be able to override the Eleventh Amendment and authorize suits against states in federal court. For example, Professors John Nowak and Laurence Tribe wrote articles contending that the Eleventh Amendment is a limit on the federal judiciary's powers, not on Congress's authority.[1] Both argue that questions of federalism are best resolved through the political process; therefore, Congress should have authority to balance federal and state interests and, where necessary, create state liability in federal court.[2]

Additionally, if the Eleventh Amendment is viewed as reinstating common law immunity,[3] then federal laws can authorize suits against the states because statutes can override the common law and federal statutes are supreme over the states.[4] Similarly, if the Eleventh Amendment is solely a prohibition of diversity suits against states in federal court, states may be sued pursuant to any congressional statute.[5] But if the Eleventh Amendment is viewed as a limit on federal court subject matter jurisdiction, then, under traditional constitutional principles, statutes should not be able to authorize suits against the states. It has been established since *Marbury v. Madison* that Congress may not expand federal jurisdiction beyond the outer boundary created by the Constitution.[6]

[46] Hill v. Blind Industries and Services of Maryland, 179 F.3d 754 (9th Cir. 1999). Participation in pretrial proceedings in federal court is a waiver of sovereign immunity.

§7.7 [1] *See* John E. Nowak, The Scope of Congressional Power to Create Causes of Action Against State Governments and the History of the Eleventh and Fourteenth Amendments, 75 Colum. L. Rev. 1413 (1975); Laurence H. Tribe, Intergovernmental Immunities in Litigation, Taxation, and Regulation: Separation of Powers Issues in Controversies About Federalism, 89 Harv. L. Rev. 682 (1976).

[2] For a criticism of the Nowak and Tribe positions, *see* Martha A. Field, The Eleventh Amendment and Other Sovereign Immunity Doctrines: Congressional Imposition of Suits upon the States, 126 U. Pa. L. Rev. 1203, 1258-1261 (1978).

[3] *See* discussion in §7.3, *supra*.

[4] For a development of this position, *see* Field, *supra* note 2, at 1253-1257.

[5] *See, e.g.,* William A. Fletcher, A Historical Interpretation of the Eleventh Amendment: A Narrow Construction of an Affirmative Grant of Jurisdiction Rather Than a Prohibition Against Jurisdiction, 35 Stan. L. Rev. 1033 (1983).

[6] 5 U.S. (1 Cranch) 137 (1803).

The current law is that there are limited areas where the "plan of the Convention" allows Congress to override sovereign immunity, and also Congress may authorize suits against state governments when it is acting pursuant to §5 of the Fourteenth Amendment, but Congress may not override the Eleventh Amendment when acting under any other constitutional authority.

Congress's Power to Override Sovereign Immunity Based on the "Plan of the Convention"

In three cases, the Supreme Court has found that Congress has power under Article I to override sovereign immunity because that was "the plan of the Convention." In *Central Virginia Community College v. Katz*, the Supreme Court held that sovereign immunity does not apply in bankruptcy proceedings.[7]

Justice Stevens wrote for the Court in a 5-4 decision. He concluded that the clause in Article I, §8 of the Constitution, empowering Congress to create uniform rules for bankruptcy, was meant to override considerations of sovereign immunity. The Court declared that the clause, its history, and the initial bankruptcy legislation enacted by Congress all "demonstrate that [the Bankruptcy Clause] was intended not just as a grant of legislative authority to Congress, but also to authorize limited subordination of state sovereign immunity in the bankruptcy arena."[8]

In other words, the Court did not hold that the Bankruptcy Act's authorization of suits against states was sufficient to override sovereign immunity. Rather, more broadly, the Court concluded that sovereign immunity does not apply at all in proceedings properly arising under the bankruptcy powers of Congress.[9]

In *PennEast Pipeline Co., LLC v. New Jersey*, the argument emerged that in ratifying the Constitution, states implicitly waived sovereign immunity in the face of certain powers designated completely to the federal government, including eminent domain power.[10] The issue was whether a private party, empowered by the federal government to condemn state property, could exercise this ability in court. While neither the Constitution nor the Bill of Rights explicitly creates the federal government's eminent domain power, the Takings Clause of the Fifth Amendment implicitly recognizes this power.

[7] 546 U.S. 356 (2006).

[8] 546 U.S. at 363. For a discussion of *Katz, see, e.g.*, Martin H. Redish & Daniel M. Greenfield, Bankruptcy, Sovereign Immunity and the Dilemma of Principled Decision-Making: The Curious Case of Central Virginia Community College v. Katz, 15 Am. Bankr. Inst. L. Rev. 13 (2007); Ralph Brubaker, Explaining *Katz*'s New Bankruptcy Exception to State Sovereign Immunity: The Bankruptcy Power as a Federal Forum Power, 15 Am. Bankr. Inst. L. Rev. 95 (2007); Randolph J. Haines, Federalism Principles in Bankruptcy After *Katz*, 15 Am. Bankr. Inst. L. Rev. 135 (2007).

[9] The Court declared: "Insofar as orders ancillary to the bankruptcy courts' in rem jurisdiction, like orders directing turnover of preferential transfers, implicate States' sovereign immunity from suit, the States agreed in the plan of the Convention not to assert that immunity. So much is evidenced not only by the history of the Bankruptcy Clause, which shows that the Framers' primary goal was to prevent competing sovereigns' interference with the debtor's discharge, but also by legislation considered and enacted in the immediate wake of the Constitution's ratification." 546 U.S. at 374.

[10] 594 U.S. 482, 500 (2021).

§7.7 Ways Around the Eleventh Amendment: Suits Pursuant to Federal Laws

In 1947, Congress amended an existing statute, the Natural Gas Act (NGA), to allow natural gas companies that obtain authorization certificates from the Federal Energy Regulatory Commission (FERC) to exercise federal eminent domain power. In 2018, the FERC granted PennEast Pipeline Co. a certificate to construct a pipeline from Pennsylvania to New Jersey. Soon thereafter, PennEast filed suits in Federal District Court in New Jersey to exercise federal eminent domain power under the statute to obtain possession of numerous properties, including two parcels of land in which New Jersey asserted a possessory interest. New Jersey moved to dismiss the suits on sovereign immunity grounds.

The Court, in an opinion authored by Chief Justice Roberts and joined by Justices Breyer, Alito, Sotomayor, and Kavanaugh, held that private parties may condemn state property in court. The Court reasoned that a state may be sued if it has agreed to a suit in the "plan of the Convention," referring to implicit waivers found in the structure of the Constitution itself.[11] Under the plan of the Convention doctrine, states implicitly consented to certain waivers of immunity at the country's founding (or when joining the union). The Court analogized to bankruptcy proceedings, suits by other states, and suits by the Federal Government. Notably, the majority argued that the carve-out enabling the exercise of eminent domain via private parties is not a congressional abrogation of sovereign immunity, but rather an application of consent / waiver.[12]

Justice Gorsuch in dissent argued that the states "never waived that immunity in the summer months of 1787."[13] Justice Barrett's dissent, joined by Justices Thomas, Kagan, and Gorsuch, rested on the premise that the Natural Gas Act is an exercise of Congress's Article I power to regulate interstate commerce and that the Commerce Clause "does not permit Congress to strip the States of their sovereign immunity."[14]

In *Torres v. Texas Department of Public Safety*, the Court recognized another area where Congress may authorize suits against state governments: Congress's power to raise an army and a navy.[15] The Uniformed Services Employment and Reemployment Rights Act of 1994 gives returning veterans the right to reclaim their prior jobs with state employers and requires that state governments use "reasonable efforts" to accommodate any service-related disability, or find an "equivalent" position (or its "nearest approximation") where such disability prevents the veteran from holding their prior position.[16] The statute authorizes suit if those employers refuse to accommodate them.

Le Roy Torres enlisted in the Army Reserves in 1989. In 2007, he was called to active duty and deployed to Iraq. While serving, Torres was exposed to toxic burn pits, a method of garbage disposal that sets open fire to all manner of trash, human waste, and military equipment.

[11] *Id.*
[12] *Id.* at 501.
[13] *Id.* at 509 (Gorsuch, J., dissenting).
[14] *Id.* at 512 (Barrett, J., dissenting).
[15] 597 U.S. 580 (2022).
[16] 38 U.S.C. §4313(a)(3).

Torres received an honorable discharge. He returned home with constrictive bronchitis, a respiratory condition that narrowed his airways and made breathing difficult. These ailments, Torres alleged, changed his life and left him unable to work at his old job as a state trooper. Torres asked his former employer, the Texas Department of Public Safety, to accommodate his condition by reemploying him in a different role. Texas refused to do so.

Torres sued Texas, contending that the state had violated the Uniformed Services Employment and Reemployment Rights Act of 1994's (USERRA) mandate that state employers rehire returning servicemembers, using "reasonable efforts" to accommodate any service-related disability. Texas claimed that sovereign immunity protected it from suit and that Congress had acted unconstitutionally in authorizing suits against states.

The issue was whether Congress could abrogate sovereign immunity in acting under its power to regulate armies and navies. The Court ruled that Congress could do so. It was a 5-4 decision, with Justice Breyer writing the majority opinion and joined by Chief Justice Roberts and Justices Sotomayor, Kagan, and Kavanaugh. Justice Breyer emphasized Congress's broad powers to provide for the military. He wrote: "The Constitution vests in Congress the power '[t]o raise and support Armies' and '[t]o provide and maintain a Navy.' Pursuant to that authority, Congress enacted a federal law that gives returning veterans the right to reclaim their prior jobs with state employers and authorizes suit if those employers refuse to accommodate them. See Uniformed Services Employment and Reemployment Rights Act of 1994 (USERRA)."[17] Justice Breyer explained that this case asks whether States may invoke sovereign immunity as a legal defense to block such suits. He concluded: "In our view, they cannot. Upon entering the Union, the States implicitly agreed that their sovereignty would yield to federal policy to build and keep a national military. States thus gave up their immunity from congressionally authorized suits pursuant to the 'plan of the Convention,' as part of 'the structure of the original Constitution itself.' "[18]

The Court stressed that the "Constitution's text, its history, and this Court's precedents show that 'when the States entered the federal system, they renounced their right' to interfere with national policy in this area."[19]

Justice Thomas wrote for the dissenting justices and strongly disagreed that Congress had the power to authorize suits against the states. He said that "constitutional text, history, and precedent all show that when the States ratified the Constitution, they did not implicitly consent to private damages actions filed in their own courts—whether authorized by Congress' war powers or any other Article I power."[20]

These three areas—bankruptcy, eminent domain power, and the authority to raise armies and navies—are the only ones where the Court has found that "the plan of the Convention" was to allow Congress pursuant to its Article I powers to abrogate

[17] 597 U.S. at 584 (internal citations omitted).

[18] *Id.* at 584-585 (internal citations omitted).

[19] *Id.* at 590 (internal citations omitted).

[20] *Id.* at 601 (Thomas, J., dissenting).

state sovereign immunity.[21] The interesting question is why sovereign immunity is not implicated as to these powers of Congress, but is present when Congress acts under other powers found in Article I, §8, such as those pursuant to its authority to create patents and copyrights.[22]

Statutes Adopted Under §5 of the Fourteenth Amendment

The seminal case holding that Congress can make states liable to suit in federal court pursuant to its powers under the post-Civil War amendments was *Fitzpatrick v. Bitzer*.[23] *Fitzpatrick* involved a suit brought directly against a state government pursuant to Title VII of the Civil Rights Act of 1964, which prohibits employment discrimination. Congress applied Title VII to the states pursuant to its powers under §5 of the Fourteenth Amendment. The Court reasoned that the Fourteenth Amendment specifically was intended to limit state sovereignty, and therefore congressional legislation under the Fourteenth Amendment can authorize suits directly against the states in federal court. Justice Rehnquist, writing for the majority, stated:

> When Congress acts pursuant to §5, not only is it exercising legislative authority that is plenary within the terms of the constitutional grant, it is exercising that authority under one section of a constitutional Amendment whose other sections by their own terms embody limitations on state authority. We think that Congress may, in determining what is "appropriate legislation" for the purpose of enforcing the provisions of the Fourteenth Amendment, provide for private suits against States or state officials which are constitutionally impermissible in other contexts.[24]

Soon after *Fitzpatrick*, the Supreme Court held, in *Hutto v. Finney*, that states may be sued for attorneys' fees pursuant to 42 U.S.C. §1988, a statute allowing successful plaintiffs in civil rights cases to recover attorneys' fees.[25] Despite the absence of an explicit authorization of suits against states in that statute, the Court said attorneys' fees against states are appropriate because of the clear congressional

[21] For a defense of the plan of the convention approach and an argument that it should be expanded, *see* Richard E. Welch III, A Flickering Light in the Wilderness: Could the Recent "Plan of the Convention" Cases Correct and Simplify the Supreme Court's State Sovereignty Doctrine?, 57 New Eng. L. Rev. 171 (2023). For a criticism of the plan of the convention approach, *see* Ernest A. Young, State Sovereign Immunity After the Revolution, 102 Tex. L. Rev. 697, 699 (2024); Katherine Mims Crocker, Constitutional Rights and Remedial Consistency, 110 Va. L. Rev. 521, 528 (2024).

[22] *See* Allen v. Cooper, 589 U.S. 248 (2020) (holding that Congress could not authorize suits against state governments for copyright infringement); Florida Prepaid Postsecondary Ed. Expense Bd. v. College Savings Bank, 527 U.S. 627 (1999) (Congress could not authorize suits against states for patent infringement).

[23] 427 U.S. 445 (1976).

[24] *Id.* at 456.

[25] 437 U.S. 678 (1978). In *Hutto*, the Court also said that attorneys' fees are permissible as a form of ancillary relief. *See* discussion in §7.5, *supra*.

intent to include states and the statutory language that seemingly allows attorneys' fees to be awarded against all defendants.[26]

In subsequent cases, the Supreme Court has required Congress's intent to be very explicit in order to override state sovereignty pursuant to the Fourteenth Amendment. In *Quern v. Jordan,* the Court discussed whether 42 U.S.C. §1983 overrides the Eleventh Amendment.[27] Section 1983 is the basic civil rights law, creating an action in federal court against those acting under color of state law who violate the Constitution or federal laws.[28] If the Eleventh Amendment does not bar §1983 suits, any allegation of a state violation of federal law, statutory or constitutional, could be brought into federal court.

In *Quern v. Jordan,* Justice Rehnquist concluded that although §1983 was adopted pursuant to §5 of the Fourteenth Amendment, there was insufficient indication of an express congressional desire to make state governments liable under that statute. Justice Rehnquist wrote:

> [Section] 1983 does not explicitly and by clear language indicate on its face an intent to sweep away the immunity of the States; nor does it have a history which focuses directly on the question of state liability and which shows that Congress considered and firmly decided to abrogate the Eleventh Amendment immunity of the States.[29]

Justices Brennan and Marshall vehemently disagreed with this part of Justice Rehnquist's opinion, although they concurred in the result that it was permissible to compel Illinois to send notification to those who had been wrongfully denied welfare benefits. First, they argued that it was unnecessary to reach the question in *Quern* of whether §1983 overrides the Eleventh Amendment, because the Court already had ruled that the notice ordered by the district court did not violate the Eleventh Amendment.[30] Thus, the majority's discussion of the relationship of §1983 to the Eleventh Amendment is completely unnecessary to the result and is therefore dicta. Second, the dissent objected to Justice Rehnquist's reliance on *Alabama v. Pugh*[31] as authority that §1983 does not override the Eleventh Amendment, because that question had not been briefed or argued in *Pugh.*[32] Third, and perhaps most important, the dissenters argued that §1983 was meant to override state sovereignty and that the states are persons for purposes of liability under §1983.[33] Nonetheless, the Supreme Court subsequently stated that the "holding" in *Quern* was that §1983 does not

[26] 437 U.S. at 693-698. *Hutto* was reaffirmed in Missouri v. Jenkins, 491 U.S. 274, 284 (1989) ("We reaffirm our holding in *Hutto v. Finney* that the Eleventh Amendment has no application to an award of attorneys' fees, ancillary to a grant of prospective relief, against a state.").

[27] 440 U.S. 332 (1979).

[28] Section 1983 is discussed in detail in Chapter 8.

[29] 440 U.S. at 345.

[30] *Id.* at 350 (Brennan, J., dissenting).

[31] 438 U.S. 781 (1978).

[32] 440 U.S. at 354 (Brennan, J., dissenting).

[33] *Id.* at 354-366.

abrogate the Eleventh Amendment.[34] In fact, the Supreme Court held that Eleventh Amendment principles mean that states may not even be sued in state court under §1983.[35]

Thus, although Congress may override the Eleventh Amendment pursuant to statutes adopted under §5 of the Fourteenth Amendment, there must be a clearer expression of congressional intent than existed for §1983. However, as *Hutto* indicates, the expression of congressional intent does not have to be in the text of the statute. Section 1988, in its text, does not expressly authorize attorneys' fees against states, but the Court found that the legislative history was sufficiently clear to permit this.

Statutes Adopted Under Other Congressional Powers

In 1996, in *Seminole Tribe of Florida v. Florida,* the Supreme Court held that Congress may abrogate the Eleventh Amendment only when acting under its §5 powers and not under any other constitutional authority.[36] This overruled a series of cases decided in the late 1980s in which the Supreme Court held that Congress may authorize suits when acting pursuant to other constitutional powers as long as the federal law, in its text, clearly and expressly permits federal court jurisdiction over state governments.

This principle, overruled in *Seminole Tribe,* was first expressed in *Atascadero State Hospital v. Scanlon,* in which the Supreme Court refused to allow suits against a state pursuant to the Rehabilitation Act of 1973.[37] The act prohibits employment discrimination against an "otherwise qualified" "individual with handicaps" by any recipient of federal assistance.[38] There was strong evidence from the legislative history that Congress intended for states to be liable under the act. Nonetheless, the Court, in a 5-4 decision, refused to allow a suit against the state of California, on the grounds that Congress was not sufficiently explicit concerning its desire to make states liable in federal courts. The Court stated:

> We . . . affirm that Congress may abrogate the States' constitutionally secured immunity from suit in federal court only by making its intention unmistakably clear in the language of the statute. . . . A general authorization for suit in federal court is not the kind of unequivocal statutory language sufficient to abrogate the Eleventh

[34] Pennhurst State School & Hosp. v. Halderman, 465 U.S. 89, 99 (1984).

[35] Will v. Michigan Dept. of State Police, 491 U.S. 58 (1989), discussed in §8.7, *infra.*

[36] 517 U.S. 44 (1996).

[37] 473 U.S. 234 (1985). In *Atascadero,* the Court also discussed the requirements for a state's waiver of its Eleventh Amendment immunity, an aspect of the case discussed in §7.6, *supra.*

[38] 29 U.S.C. §794 (1985). Rehabilitation Act Amendments of 1986, Pub. L. No. 99-506, 100 Stat. 1810, 29 U.S.C. §794 (1985) (The amendments replaced each occurrence of the words "handicapped individual" with the words "individuals with handicaps."). *See also* 1986 U.S. Code Cong. & Admin. News 3471, 3487.

Amendment. When Congress chooses to subject the States to federal jurisdiction, it must do so specifically.[39]

In *Pennsylvania v. Union Gas Co.*,[40] the Supreme Court held that Congress may authorize suits against states, as long as the law does so expressly in its text. In *Pennsylvania v. Union Gas Co.*, the Supreme Court confronted two questions: (1) Does the Comprehensive Environmental Response, Compensation, and Liability Act of 1980 (CERCLA),[41] as amended by the Superfund Amendments and Reauthorization Act of 1986 (SARA), authorize suits against state governments in federal court?[42] (2) If so, does Congress, when legislating pursuant to the commerce clause, have the authority to create such state government liability?

The Court answered both questions affirmatively. However, the Court did so without a majority opinion and was very splintered. Four justices—Brennan, Marshall, Blackmun, and Stevens—concluded that the statute permits suits against states[43] and that Congress may authorize such litigation under its commerce power.[44] These justices ruled that CERCLA expressly defines "persons" to include states, and other parts of the statute explicitly exclude states where Congress wanted to protect them from liability.

Three justices—Chief Justice Rehnquist and Justices O'Connor and Kennedy—concluded that CERCLA did not expressly authorize suits against state governments.[45] Moreover, these justices stated that even if CERCLA authorized such suits, the federal courts lacked jurisdiction because Congress could not override the Eleventh Amendment pursuant to its commerce power.[46]

Justice White agreed with the dissenters that the statute was not sufficiently specific to permit state governments to be sued in federal court. He reasoned that federal courts lacked jurisdiction because CERCLA "did not include an *unmistakable* declaration of abrogation of state immunity."[47] However, Justice White agreed with Justices Brennan, Marshall, Blackmun, and Stevens that Congress has the constitutional power to abrogate the states' immunity pursuant to its commerce power.

[39] 473 U.S. at 245. The dissenting justices argued that the Eleventh Amendment should be regarded only as limiting diversity suits against state governments; thus, all actions pursuant to federal statutes present federal questions and would be allowed to proceed in federal court. 473 U.S. at 247-248 (Brennan, J., dissenting). This aspect of the *Atascadero* dissent is discussed in §7.3, *supra.*

[40] 491 U.S. 1 (1989).

[41] 642 U.S.C. §9601.

[42] 100 Stat. 1613 (codified as 42 U.S.C. §9601).

[43] *Union Gas,* 491 U.S. at 13 (Congress intended to permit suits brought by private citizens against the state under CERCLA).

[44] *Id.* at 19 (Congress may abrogate states' immunity from suit when legislating pursuant to the plenary powers granted it by the Constitution).

[45] These three justices concurred in Justice White's opinion stating that CERCLA did not clearly authorize suits against state governments in federal court. *Id.* at 50 (White, J., concurring).

[46] These three justices concurred in Justice Scalia's opinion that Congress may not, pursuant to its commerce power, abrogate a state's Eleventh Amendment immunity. *Id.* at 42 (Scalia, J., concurring in part and dissenting in part).

[47] *Id.* at 46-47 (White, J., concurring) (emphasis in original).

In a short paragraph, Justice White stated that he concurred in the conclusion, although he said, "I do not agree with much of [Justice Brennan's] reasoning."[48]

Justice Scalia's position was exactly the opposite of Justice White's. Justice Scalia stated that he believed that CERCLA clearly expressed a desire to impose liability on state governments in federal court. However, he forcefully argued that Congress should not be able to authorize suits against states under the commerce clause.[49]

Thus, there were five votes that CERCLA permits states to be sued for monetary liability in federal court: Justices Brennan, Marshall, Blackmun, Stevens, and Scalia. There also were five votes that Congress, acting pursuant to its commerce clause authority, can create such federal court jurisdiction: Justices Brennan, Marshall, Blackmun, Stevens, and White.[50]

Thus, *Pennsylvania v. Union Gas* clearly held that Congress could override the Eleventh Amendment pursuant to any of its constitutional powers, as long as the law was explicit in its text in authorizing suits against state governments. This was overruled in *Seminole Tribe.* As described previously, *Seminole Tribe* involved a suit under the Indian Gaming Regulatory Act, which required that states negotiate with American Indian tribes to form compacts to allow gambling on American Indian land. The act specifically authorized suits against states in federal court as an enforcement mechanism.[51]

The Supreme Court held that the federal statute authorizing suits against states in federal court was unconstitutional. Congress may authorize suits against states only when acting pursuant to §5 of the Fourteenth Amendment and not pursuant to other federal powers, such as the Indian commerce clause. Chief Justice Rehnquist, writing for the majority in the 5-4 decision, emphasized that *Pennsylvania v. Union Gas* was a plurality opinion. Chief Justice Rehnquist declared that "[t]he plurality's rationale . . . deviated sharply from our established federalism jurisprudence and essentially eviscerated our decision in *Hans.*"[52] The Court concluded: "Reconsidering the decision in *Union Gas,* we conclude that none of the policies underlying stare decisis require our continuing adherence of its holding."[53]

[48] *Id.* at 57 (White, J., concurring).

[49] *Id.* at 42 (Scalia, J., concurring in part and dissenting in part).

[50] In two cases decided the same Term, the Court applied Pennsylvania v. Union Gas, but found that Congress had not authorized suits against the states. In Dellmuth v. Muth, 491 U.S. 223 (1989), the Court ruled that states cannot be sued in federal court pursuant to the Education for All Handicapped Children Act, a federal law that assures that disabled children may receive a free public education appropriate for their needs. The Supreme Court, in a 5-4 decision, ruled that the act does not authorize suits against state governments in federal court. In Hoffman v. Connecticut Department of Income Maintenance, 492 U.S. 96 (1989), by the same 5-4 margin, the Court held that states could not be sued in federal court pursuant to the then-existing provisions of the Bankruptcy Code.

[51] 25 U.S.C. §2710(d)(7).

[52] 517 U.S. at 45.

[53] *Id.* at 66.

Seminole Tribe produced a heated debate among scholars.[54] Many questions can be raised about the decision. First, was the Court justified in overruling the earlier, recent decisions that Congress could authorize suits against states under any constitutional power? What, after all, had changed in only seven years since the earlier rulings? The obvious answer is that in the intervening several years, Justice Thomas joined the Court, and he joined with the four dissenters in *Pennsylvania v. Union Gas*—Chief Justice Rehnquist and Justices O'Connor, Kennedy, and Scalia—to create the majority to overrule it. The issue in evaluating *Seminole Tribe*, in part, is about the proper role of stare decisis.

Second, is there a meaningful distinction between Congress's authority under §5 and other constitutional powers? The majority claims that §5 is different because it was meant as a limit on states and that the Fourteenth Amendment modifies the previously enacted Eleventh Amendment. The dissent argues that there is nothing in the history of the Eleventh Amendment that suggests that it was meant to preclude suits against states pursuant to federal statutes.[55] The dissent maintains that states consented to the exercise of congressional power in ratifying the Constitution.

Third, and most fundamentally, *Seminole Tribe* raises basic questions about federalism. Should the protection of state governments be left to Congress, and should the need to ensure state compliance with federal law justify allowing Congress to authorize suits against states in federal court? This was the view underlying cases such as *Pennsylvania v. Union Gas*. Or is it the role of the Supreme Court to protect state sovereignty, especially from congressional encroachment? This is the assumption of *Seminole Tribe*. Ultimately, it is a choice about the meaning of federalism and the respective roles of Congress and the Supreme Court in defining and protecting it.

Which Statutes Were Validly Enacted Under §5 of the Fourteenth Amendment? *City of Boerne v. Flores*

The key question after *Seminole Tribe* is whether a statute was a proper exercise of Congress's powers under §5. A state can be sued in federal court only if the Court concludes that the law was enacted under §5 and only if it expressly authorizes suits against state governments.

In *City of Boerne v. Flores*, the Court sharply limited the scope of Congress's power under §5 of the Fourteenth Amendment.[56] The Court ruled that pursuant to §5, Congress may act only to prevent or remedy rights recognized by the courts

[54] *See, e.g.*, Vicki Jackson, *Seminole Tribe*, the Eleventh Amendment, and the Potential Evisceration of *Ex parte Young*, 72 N.Y.U. L. Rev. 495 (1997); Carlos Manuel Vasquez, What Is Eleventh Amendment Immunity?, 106 Yale L.J. 1683 (1997); Herbert Hovenkamp, Judicial Restraint and Constitutional Federalism: The Supreme Court's *Lopez* and *Seminole Tribe* Decisions, 96 Colum. L. Rev. 2213 (1996); Daniel J. Meltzer, The *Seminole* Decision and State Sovereign Immunity, 1996 Sup. Ct. Rev. 1; Henry Paul Monaghan, The Sovereign Immunity "Exception," 110 Harv. L. Rev. 102 (1996).

[55] 517 U.S. at 111 (Souter, J., dissenting).

[56] 521 U.S. 507 (1997).

and that Congress may not create new rights or expand the scope of rights. Any law must be narrowly tailored to solving constitutional violations; it must be "proportionate" and "congruent" to preventing and remedying constitutional violations. Thus, in assessing whether a state government can be sued pursuant to a federal statute, the inquiry is whether that law fits within the scope of §5 as construed in *City of Boerne v. Flores.*

In *City of Boerne v. Flores,* the Supreme Court, in a 6-3 decision, declared the Religious Freedom Restoration Act (RFRA) unconstitutional as exceeding the scope of Congress's §5 powers.[57] The act was adopted in 1993 to overturn a recent Supreme Court decision that had narrowly interpreted the free exercise clause of the First Amendment. In *Employment Div., Dept. of Human Resources of Oregon v. Smith,* in 1990, the Supreme Court significantly lessened the protections of the free exercise clause.[58] Oregon law prohibited the consumption of peyote, a hallucinogenic substance. Native Americans challenged this law, claiming that it infringed free exercise of religion because their religious rituals required the use of peyote. Under prior Supreme Court precedents, government actions burdening religion would be upheld only if they were necessary to achieve a compelling government purpose.[59] The Supreme Court, in *Smith,* changed the law and held that the free exercise clause cannot be used to challenge neutral laws of general applicability. The Oregon law prohibiting consumption of peyote was deemed neutral because it was not motivated by a desire to interfere with religion, and it was a law of general applicability since it applied to everyone.

In response to this decision, in 1993, Congress overwhelmingly adopted the Religious Freedom Restoration Act, which was signed into law by President Clinton. The Religious Freedom Restoration Act was express in stating that its goal was to overturn *Smith* and restore the test that was followed before that decision. The act requires courts considering free exercise challenges, including to neutral laws of general applicability, to uphold the government's actions only if they are necessary to achieve a compelling purpose. Specifically, RFRA prohibited "[g]overnment" from "substantially burden[ing]" a person's exercise of religion, even if the burden results from a rule of general applicability, unless the government can demonstrate that the burden "(1) is in furtherance of a compelling governmental interest; and (2) is the least restrictive means of furthering that compelling governmental interest."[60]

City of Boerne v. Flores involved a church in Texas that was prevented from constructing a new facility because its building was classified a historic landmark. The church sued under the Religious Freedom Restoration Act, and the city challenged the constitutionality of the law. Justice Kennedy, writing for the Court, held that the act is unconstitutional. The Court held that Congress under §5 of the Fourteenth Amendment may not create new rights or expand the scope of rights; rather, Congress is limited to laws that prevent or remedy violations of rights recognized

[57] 42 U.S.C. §2000b.
[58] 494 U.S. 872 (1990).
[59] *See, e.g.,* Sherbert v. Verner, 374 U.S. 398 (1963).
[60] 42 U.S.C. §2000bb-1.

by the Supreme Court, and these must be narrowly tailored—"proportionate" and "congruent"—to the constitutional violation.[61]

Justice Kennedy explained that §5 gives Congress power to enact laws "to enforce" the provisions of the Fourteenth Amendment. He stated, "Legislation which alters the meaning of the Free Exercise Clause cannot be said to be enforcing the Clause. Congress does not enforce a constitutional right by changing what the right is. It has been given the power 'to enforce,' not the power to determine what constitutes a constitutional violation. Were it not so, what Congress would be enforcing would no longer be, in any meaningful sense, the 'provisions of [the Fourteenth Amendment].'"[62]

Congress thus is limited to enacting laws that prevent or remedy violations of rights already recognized by the Supreme Court. Moreover, the Court said that "[t]here must be a congruence and proportionality between the injury to be prevented or remedied and the means adopted to that end."[63]

Justice Kennedy defended this conclusion by invoking the need to preserve the Court as the authoritative interpreter of the Constitution. Justice Kennedy quoted *Marbury v. Madison* and wrote: "If Congress could define its own powers by altering the Fourteenth Amendment's meaning, no longer would the Constitution be 'superior paramount law unchangeable by ordinary means.' It would be 'on a level with ordinary legislative acts, and like other acts, . . . alterable when the legislature shall please to alter it.'"[64] Justice Kennedy concluded this part of the majority opinion by declaring: "Shifting legislative majorities could change the Constitution and effectively circumvent the difficult and detailed amendment process contained in Article V."[65]

Justice Kennedy's majority opinion then declared RFRA unconstitutional on the grounds that it impermissibly expanded the scope of rights and that it was not proportionate or congruent as a preventive or remedial measure. He wrote: "RFRA is not so confined. Sweeping coverage ensures its intrusion at every level of government, displacing laws and prohibiting official actions of almost every description and regardless of subject matter. . . . Any law is subject to challenge at any time by any individual who alleges a substantial burden on his or her free exercise of religion. The reach and scope of RFRA distinguish it from other measures passed under Congress' enforcement power, even in the area of voting rights. The stringent test RFRA demands of state laws reflects a lack of proportionality or congruence between the means adopted and the legitimate end to be achieved."[66] RFRA prohibits much that would not violate the Constitution and thus was deemed to exceed the scope of Congress's §5 powers.[67]

[61] 521 U.S. at 519-520.

[62] *Id.* at 519.

[63] *Id.* at 520.

[64] *Id.* at 529, *quoting* Marbury v. Madison, 5 U.S. (1 Cranch) 137, 177 (1803).

[65] 521 U.S. at 529.

[66] *Id.* at 532.

[67] Many excellent articles have been written discussing the scope of Congress's §5 powers in light of these decisions. *See, e.g.,* Evan H. Caminker, "Appropriate" Means-Ends Constraints on Section 5 Powers, 53 Stan. L. Rev. 1127 (2001); Robert C. Post & Reva B. Siegel, Protecting the Constitution from the People: Juricentric Restrictions on Section 5 Power, 78 Ind. L.J. 1 (2003); Ernest A. Young, Is the Sky Falling on the Federal Government?: State Sovereign Immunity, the Section Five Power, and the Federal Balance, 81 Tex. L. Rev. 1551 (2003).

The Intersection of *Seminole Tribe* and *City of Boerne*

Seminole Tribe holds that Congress can authorize suits against states only when acting pursuant to §5 of the Fourteenth Amendment, and *City of Boerne*, a year later, greatly narrows when Congress may act under §5. Thus, the issue in deciding whether a state may be sued pursuant to a federal law is whether it meets the restrictive test articulated in *City of Boerne v. Flores.*

In the more than two decades since *City of Boerne v. Flores,* there have been a number of Supreme Court decisions considering which laws can be used to sue state governments. In the first three cases, the Court found that federal laws were not valid exercises of power under §5 of the Fourteenth Amendment and could not be used to sue state governments: *Florida Prepaid Postsecondary Education Expense Board v. College Savings Bank,*[68] *Kimel v. Florida Board of Regents,*[69] and *University of Alabama v. Garrett.*[70] In each case, by a 5-4 margin, the Court found that a law adopted by Congress exceeded the scope of Congress's §5 power and thus could not be used to sue state governments.

But then, in three subsequent cases—*Nevada Department of Human Resources v. Hibbs,*[71] *Tennessee v. Lane,*[72] and *United States v. Georgia*[73]—the Court found that laws were within the scope of Congress's power under §5 because they dealt with fundamental rights and types of discrimination that receive heightened scrutiny. Each of these cases is described below. Together they seem to establish the proposition that Congress has broad powers under §5 in dealing with types of decision-making and rights that receive heightened scrutiny, and thus may authorize suits against strikes. In other situations, Congress's powers are greatly limited, and it cannot act under §5 or authorize suits against states unless there is proof before Congress of pervasive unconstitutional state conduct.

In a subsequent decision, *Coleman v. Maryland Court of Appeals,* the Court, 5-4, found that a statute did not fit within §5 of the Fourteenth Amendment and could not be used to sue state governments.[74] The Court did not change the law in this area, but the case does reflect the continuing ideological division of the Court concerning Congress's power to authorize suits against state governments and more generally about sovereign immunity.

The underlying question is whether the distinction drawn in these cases makes sense. Why should Congress's power under §5 vary and depend on the level of scrutiny prescribed by the Supreme Court?

[68] 527 U.S. 627 (1999).
[69] 528 U.S. 62 (2000).
[70] 531 U.S. 356 (2001).
[71] 538 U.S. 721 (2003).
[72] 541 U.S. 509 (2004).
[73] 546 U.S. 151 (2006).
[74] 566 U.S. 30 (2012).

Cases Rejecting Suits Against States

Florida Prepaid involved College Savings Bank, a New Jersey company that devised a system, which it patented, for students to use to save money to later pay for their college education. Florida Prepaid, an agency of the Florida government, copied this system for use by Florida residents to save money to attend Florida schools. College Savings Bank sued Florida Prepaid for, among other things,[75] patent infringement.

In 1992, Congress expressly amended the patent laws to authorize suits against state governments for patent infringement.[76] The Supreme Court, however, held that the law was not a valid exercise of power under §5 of the Fourteenth Amendment and thus could not be used to sue the state government. Although patents unquestionably are property and the Fourteenth Amendment protects property from being taken by state governments without due process, the Court found that the authorization of suits was impermissible because it was not "proportionate" or "congruent" to remedy constitutional violations.

Chief Justice Rehnquist, writing for the Court, stated: "In enacting the Patent Remedy Act, however, Congress identified no pattern of patent infringement by the States, let alone a pattern of constitutional violations. Unlike the undisputed record of racial discrimination confronting Congress in the voting rights cases, Congress came up with little evidence of infringing conduct on the part of the States."[77] The Court held that the law was not valid under §5 because "[t]he legislative record thus suggests that the Patent Remedy Act does not respond to a history of 'widespread and persisting deprivation of constitutional rights' of the sort Congress has faced in enacting proper prophylactic §5 legislation."[78]

Florida Prepaid follows from *Seminole Tribe* and *City of Boerne*. The Court reaffirmed that Congress can authorize suits against states only pursuant to §5, and it concluded, based on *City of Boerne*, that the law authorizing suits for patent infringement did not fit within this power. However, what is striking about *Florida Prepaid* is that it involved patent law, an area in which federal courts have exclusive jurisdiction. Barring patent infringement suits against state governments in federal court means that a state government can infringe patents without ever facing a lawsuit.[79]

The Court next considered the scope of Congress's §5 powers in the context of its power to authorize suits against state governments in *Kimel v. Florida Board of Regents*.[80] *Kimel* involved a suit by current and former faculty and librarians

[75] College Savings Bank also sued for a violation of the Lanham Act, but the Supreme Court, in a separate opinion, also found that this was barred by sovereign immunity. College Savings Bank v. Florida Prepaid Postsecondary Expense Education Board, 527 U.S. 666 (1999).

[76] 35 U.S.C. §271.

[77] 527 U.S. at 639.

[78] *Id.*

[79] Although the state government cannot be sued, a state official may be sued. Ex parte Young, 209 U.S. 123 (1908). Thus, the state official may be sued for an injunction to stop future infringements, but the state government may not be sued for damages.

[80] 528 U.S. 62 (2000).

at Florida State University, including Daniel Kimel, Jr. They alleged that the university's failure to provide promised pay adjustments discriminated against older workers and thus violated the Age Discrimination in Employment Act (ADEA). A companion case was brought by Wellington Dickson, an employee of the Florida Department of Corrections who claimed that he was denied promotions because of his age. Another of the consolidated cases involved faculty members at a state university in Alabama who claimed age discrimination.

The Supreme Court held that all of these claims against state agencies are barred by the Eleventh Amendment. By a 7-2 margin, with only Kennedy and Thomas dissenting, the Court concluded that the ADEA is an express authorization of suit against the states. The Court then ruled 5-4 that the ADEA is not a valid exercise of Congress's power under §5 and that therefore it cannot be used to sue state governments.

Justice O'Connor wrote the majority opinion and was joined by Chief Justice Rehnquist and Justices Scalia, Kennedy, and Thomas. The Court concluded that the burdens the ADEA imposes on state and local governments are disproportionate to any unconstitutional behavior that might exist. The Court emphasized that under prior decisions, only rational basis review is used for age discrimination.[81] The Court explained that there is not a "history of purposeful discrimination" based on age and that "age also does not define a discrete and insular minority because all persons, if they live out their normal life spans," will experience it.[82] Indeed, the Court said that states "may discriminate based on age without offending the Fourteenth Amendment if the age classification is rationally related to a legitimate state interest."[83] The Court said that age often is a relevant criterion for employers.

Therefore, the Court concluded that the broad prohibition of age discrimination in the ADEA was deemed to exceed the scope of Congress's power. The Court declared: "Judged against the backdrop of our equal protection jurisprudence, it is clear that the ADEA is so out of proportion to a supposed remedial or preventive object that it cannot be understood as responsive to, or designed to prevent, unconstitutional behavior."[84]

The Court stressed that the ADEA prohibits a great deal of conduct that is otherwise constitutional. The Court also emphasized that there were not "findings" by Congress of substantial age discrimination by state governments. Therefore, the Court stated that because of "the lack of evidence of widespread and unconstitutional age discrimination by the States, we hold that the ADEA is not a valid exercise of power under section five of the Fourteenth Amendment."[85]

Where does this leave state employees who are victims of age discrimination? Justice O'Connor concludes the majority opinion by saying that their recourse is under state law in state courts. She states: "Our decision does not signal the end

[81] *See, e.g.*, Vance v. Bradley, 440 U.S. 93 (1979); Massachusetts Bd. of Retirement v. Murgia, 427 U.S. 307 (1976).

[82] 528 U.S. at 83.

[83] *Id.*

[84] *Id.* at 86.

[85] *Id.* at 65.

of the line for employees who find themselves subject to age discrimination at the hands of state employers. . . . State employees are protected by state age discrimination statutes, and may recover money damages from their state employers, in almost every State of the Union. Those avenues of relief remain available today, just as they were before the decision."[86] State courts and state law are the only recourse for an attorney seeking redress for a state employee who has suffered age discrimination.

Subsequently, in *University of Alabama v. Garrett*,[87] the Court considered whether state governments may be sued for violating Title I of the Americans with Disabilities Act (ADA), which prohibits employment discrimination against the disabled and requires reasonable accommodation for disabilities by employers. The plaintiff's key argument to the Court was that the elaborate legislative history documenting government discrimination against the disabled made the Americans with Disabilities Act different from other laws the Court had considered in the last few years. The Supreme Court, in a 5-4 decision, rejected this argument and held that state governments may not be sued for violating Title I of the ADA.

Patricia Garrett was the director of nursing at the University of Alabama, Birmingham hospital. She was diagnosed with breast cancer and took time off work to have surgery, chemotherapy, and radiation. When she returned to work, she was informed that her position as director of nursing was no longer available. She sued under Title I of the Americans with Disabilities Act (ADA).

Chief Justice Rehnquist's majority opinion began by stating that the ADA was a substantial expansion of rights compared to the Constitution. He explained that under equal protection, discrimination based on disability need meet only a rational basis test, being rationally related to a legitimate government purpose.[88] The ADA prohibits much more than would fail a rational basis test, and its requirement for reasonable accommodation of disabilities is significantly greater than the Constitution requires.

The Court then concluded that Title I of the ADA is not "proportionate" or "congruent" to preventing and remedying constitutional violations. Chief Justice Rehnquist declared: "The legislative record of the ADA, however, simply fails to show that Congress did in fact identify a pattern of irrational state discrimination in employment against the disabled."[89] Justice Breyer attached a 39-page appendix to his dissenting opinion in which he listed the numerous references in the legislative history to government discrimination against the disabled.[90] Chief Justice Rehnquist's majority opinion found these insufficient. He said that some were just anecdotes.[91] He said that most involved local governments, not state governments, and local governments are not protected by state sovereign immunity.[92]

[86] *Id.*
[87] 531 U.S. 356 (2001).
[88] *Id.* at 366, citing City of Cleburne v. Cleburne Living Center, 473 U.S. 432 (1985).
[89] 531 U.S. at 365.
[90] *Id.* at 388-389 (Breyer, J., dissenting).
[91] *Id.* at 370-371.
[92] *Id.*

He said that some of the evidence concerns government discrimination against the disabled in providing services and that is Title II, not Title I, of the ADA. He observed: "In 1990, the States alone employed more than 4.5 million people. It is telling, we think, that given these large numbers, Congress assembled only such minimal evidence of unconstitutional state discrimination in employment against the disabled."[93]

Chief Justice Rehnquist contrasted the legislative record for the Voting Rights Act of 1965, which he said was in "stark" contrast to the ADA. He noted the statistical findings by Congress in enacting the Voting Rights Act, such as "an otherwise inexplicable 50-percentage-point gap in the registration of white and African-American voters in some States."[94] He concluded that the congressional findings for the ADA were insufficient in comparison. He wrote: "[I]n order to authorize private individuals to recover money damages against the States, there must be a pattern of discrimination by the States which violates the Fourteenth Amendment, and the remedy imposed by Congress must be congruent and proportional to the targeted violation. Those requirements are not met here, and to uphold the Act's application to the States would allow Congress to rewrite the Fourteenth Amendment law laid down by this Court in *Cleburne.* Section 5 does not so broadly enlarge congressional authority."[95]

Chief Justice Rehnquist, however, added a footnote to make clear that the Court was not declaring the ADA unconstitutional as applied to state governments, but rather only holding that state governments could not be sued by individuals for violations.[96] He explained that the federal government still could sue the states to enforce the law and that suits against individual government officers for injunctive relief were also permissible,[97] but damages actions against state governments are barred.

Cases Allowing Suits Against States Pursuant to Federal Statutes

However, in three subsequent cases, the Supreme Court has allowed suits against states by finding that the federal statutes fit within the scope of Congress's §5 powers. The court stressed that these cases involved claims that receive heightened judicial scrutiny because of the type of discrimination involved or because a fundamental right was implicated. The Court held that Congress has greater latitude to legislate under §5 in such circumstances and thus more authority to permit suits against state governments.

In *Nevada Department of Human Resources v. Hibbs,*[98] the Supreme Court held that the family leave provision of the Family and Medical Leave Act (FMLA) fits

[93] *Id.* at 370.
[94] *Id.* at 373.
[95] *Id.* at 374.
[96] *Id.* at 374 n.9.
[97] *Id.*
[98] 538 U.S. 721 (2003).

within the scope of Congress's §5 powers and can be used to sue state governments. The FMLA requires that employers, including government employers, provide their employees with unpaid leave time for family and medical care. The Supreme Court in *Hibbs,* by a 6-3 margin, held that the family leave provision is a valid congressional abrogation of state sovereign immunity.[99]

Chief Justice Rehnquist, writing for the Court, stressed that the "FMLA aims to protect the right to be free from gender-based discrimination in the workplace."[100] The Court said that Congress, recognizing social realities, found that the absence of family leave policies disadvantaged women in the workplace. Although the FMLA is gender-neutral in that it requires leaves be granted to both men and women, and Hibbs was male, the Court said that Congress clearly intended the law to prevent gender discrimination in employment.

Chief Justice Rehnquist distinguished *Kimel* and *Garrett* on the grounds that they involved types of discrimination that receive only rational basis review, whereas gender discrimination triggers intermediate scrutiny under equal protection. The Court explained: "Here, however, Congress directed its attention to state gender discrimination, which triggers a heightened level of scrutiny. Because the standard for demonstrating the constitutionality of a gender-based classification is more difficult to meet than our rational basis test, . . . it was easier for Congress to show a pattern of constitutional violations."[101]

The Court followed and extended *Hibbs* in *Tennessee v. Lane.*[102] The case involved a criminal defendant who literally climbed on his hands and knees to get to a second-floor courtroom because it was not accessible to those with disabilities. He sued the state government pursuant to Title II of the Americans with Disabilities Act,[103] which prohibits state and local governments from discriminating against people with disabilities in government programs, services, and activities.

The Court, in a 5-4 decision, held that Lane's suit against the state was not barred by sovereign immunity. The Court, in an opinion by Justice Stevens, emphasized that there is a well-established fundamental right of access to the courts. The Court recognized that Congress has greater latitude to legislate under §5 when dealing with a claim that receives heightened judicial scrutiny, whether because it is a fundamental right or a type of discrimination that receives heightened scrutiny. The majority opinion was joined by Justices O'Connor, Souter, Ginsburg, and Breyer.

Tennessee v. Lane does not address whether states can be sued under Title II when there is no fundamental right that is implicated. The Court returned to the question of when states may be sued under Title II in *United States v. Georgia.*[104] Tom Goodman, a paraplegic inmate in the Georgia correctional system, was housed in a

[99] For an excellent discussion of the issue presented in *Hibbs, see* Robert C. Post & Reva B. Siegel, Legislative Constitutionalism and Section Five Power: Policentric Interpretation of the Family and Medical Leave Act, 112 Yale L.J. 1943 (2003).

[100] 538 U.S. at 728.

[101] *Id.* at 736.

[102] 541 U.S. 509 (2004).

[103] 42 U.S.C. §12131.

[104] 546 U.S. 151 (2006).

prison that was not accessible to those with disabilities. As a result, he could not use the toilet in his cell without assistance, and other prison facilities were inaccessible to him. The issue was whether he could sue the state under Title II of the ADA.

The Supreme Court unanimously ruled in Goodman's favor. Justice Scalia wrote the opinion for the Court and stressed that Goodman alleged a constitutional violation: cruel and unusual punishment because of the degrading incidents suffered as a result of the lack of access to toilet facilities. In a brief opinion, the Court explained that "insofar as Title II creates a private cause of action for damages against the States for conduct that actually violates the Fourteenth Amendment, Title II validly abrogates state sovereign immunity."[105]

Thus, it appears after *United States v. Georgia,* in considering whether a state government can be sued for violating a federal law that authorizes such suits, the initial question is whether the plaintiff alleges a constitutional violation. If so, a state can be sued. If not, the question becomes whether the statute is dealing with a type of discrimination that receives heightened scrutiny or a fundamental right, in which case the lawsuit against the state likely can go forward. But if the plaintiff is not alleging a constitutional violation and the case does not involve a type of discrimination or a right receiving heightened scrutiny, the state can be sued only if Congress found pervasive unconstitutional state conduct.

Rejection of Allowing Suits Pursuant to a Federal Statute

Subsequent cases have not overruled *Hibbs* or *Lane,* but have not extended them and have rejected efforts to allow suits against states based on federal statutes.

In *Coleman v. Court of Appeals of Maryland,*[106] the issue was whether state governments could be sued under the self-care provisions of the Family and Medical Leave Act. In *Nevada Department of Human Resources v. Hibbs,* discussed above, the Court held that state governments could be sued under the family care provisions of this law because they were intended to lessen the sex discrimination in employment that results from traditional gender roles. But in *Coleman,* the Court ruled that the self-care provisions were not about lessening sex discrimination in the workplace and thus are within Congress's power under §5 of the Fourteenth Amendment. Justice Kennedy wrote for a plurality of four and concluded that "suits against States under this provision are barred by the States' immunity as sovereigns in our federal system."[107]

Justice Scalia concurred in the judgment and would have discarded any inquiry as to "proportionality and congruence." He said that he "would limit Congress's power to the regulation of conduct that *itself* violates the Fourteenth Amendment. Failing to grant state employees leave for the purpose of self-care—or any other purpose, for that matter—does not come close."[108]

[105] *Id.* at 159.
[106] 566 U.S. 30 (2012).
[107] *Id.* at 33.
[108] *Id.* at 45 (Scalia, J., concurring in the judgment).

Justice Ginsburg wrote the dissent, joined by Justices Breyer, Sotomayor, and Kagan, and would have found *Hibbs* to be controlling. The dissenters would have held "that the self-care provision, §2612(a)(1)(D), validly enforces the right to be free from gender discrimination in the workplace."

Coleman does not change the law as to Congress's power to abrogate sovereign immunity. But it does reflect that the Roberts Court, like its predecessor the Rehnquist Court, was ideologically split on questions of sovereign immunity and Congress's power to abrogate it and authorize suits against state governments.

In *Allen v. Cooper*, the Court ruled that state governments could not be sued for copyright infringement.[109] The Court concluded that *Florida Prepaid*, discussed above, which held that Congress could not authorize suits for patent infringement, effectively resolved the issue of claims for copyright infringement. Justice Kagan, writing for the Court, declared: "In two basically identical statutes passed in the early 1990s, Congress sought to strip the States of their sovereign immunity from patent and copyright infringement suits. Not long after, this Court held in *Florida Prepaid Postsecondary Ed. Expense Bd. v. College Savings Bank* that the patent statute lacked a valid constitutional basis. Today, we take up the copyright statute. We find that our decision in *Florida Prepaid* compels the same conclusion."[110]

Future Implications

There are two key questions in appraising these decisions: Descriptively, what are they likely to mean in terms of the ability to sue state governments to enforce other federal civil rights laws? Normatively, are they desirable in their protection of state sovereign immunity and in the distinctions drawn as to when state governments may be sued?

Descriptively, the law seems to be that if it is a claim that receives heightened scrutiny, based on the type of discrimination or the presence of a fundamental right, Congress has broad authority to legislate. Indeed, based on *Hibbs*, there is no need for a congressional finding of pervasive constitutional violations when Congress is dealing with areas that receive heightened judicial scrutiny. In *Hibbs*, Congress never found any *unconstitutional* gender discrimination. On the other hand, if it is a claim that receives only rational basis review, then even an elaborate legislative record, as in *Garrett*, is unlikely to be enough to allow suits against state governments. Unless Congress finds pervasive unconstitutional state conduct, it cannot authorize suits against the states. But given the Supreme Court having become decidedly more conservative, there is the question of whether *Hibbs* and *Lane* still will be regarded as good law.

Normatively, there are questions as to whether the distinctions drawn in these cases are desirable, and, more generally, whether Congress should be able to authorize suits against state governments. The Court offered little explanation as to why

[109] 589 U.S. 248 (2020).
[110] *Id.* at 251.

the level of scrutiny matters in determining the scope of Congress's powers under §5. Perhaps it is that in areas receiving heightened scrutiny, there already are sufficient findings of historical violations, so that there is no need for congressional documentation. Critics, including the dissenting justices, argue that Congress's power under §5 is not altered by the level of scrutiny used by the courts.

Defenders of the Court's decisions in *Florida Prepaid*, *Kimel*, and *Garrett* contend that the rulings are an appropriate protection of state sovereign immunity and a proper limit on Congress's §5 powers.[111] They argue that sovereign immunity is an important aspect of the Constitution's protection of state governments and that Congress's power to authorize suits against state governments must be limited. As explained above in the discussion of *City of Boerne v. Flores*, its defenders argue that the decision properly interpreted §5 based on the text of the provision, its framers' intent, and the need to preserve the Supreme Court's role in determining the meaning of the Constitution.

Critics of these decisions disagree with their premise that the sovereign immunity is an inherent part of the Constitution's design. Indeed, those objecting to the decisions contend that sovereign immunity is not authorized by the text of the Constitution and that such immunity undermines the basic constitutional principle of government accountability.[112] Critics also argue, as discussed above, that *City of Boerne* was wrongly decided, and that Congress should have the authority under §5 to expand the scope of rights. The critics contend that all of these decisions are undue conservative judicial activism: the five most conservative justices struck down important federal laws on the basis of principles found nowhere in the Constitution.

This debate is likely to continue for the foreseeable future as the federal courts continue to apply *City of Boerne* and *Seminole Tribe*. Ultimately, the disagreement is over basic constitutional principles concerning separation of powers, federalism, and the protection of individual rights under the Constitution.

[111] *See, e.g.*, James Eugene Fitzgerald, State Sovereign Immunity: Searching for Stability, 48 UCLA L. Rev. 1203 (2001); Alfred Hill, In Defense of Our Law of Sovereign Immunity, 42 B.C. L. Rev. 485 (2001).

[112] *See, e.g.*, Erwin Chemerinsky, Against Sovereign Immunity, 53 Stan. L. Rev. 1201 (2001).

CHAPTER 8

Federal Court Relief Against Local Governments and State and Local Government Officers: 42 U.S.C. §1983

§8.1 INTRODUCTION

A primary function of the federal courts is to provide relief against governments and government officers for their violations of the Constitution and laws of the United States. The previous chapter discussed the Eleventh Amendment's limits on federal court review of state government actions. This chapter considers the federal statute, 42 U.S.C. §1983, which is the basis for most suits in federal courts against local governments and state and local government officers to redress violations of federal law.

Section 1983 creates a cause of action against any person who, acting under color of state law, abridges rights created by the Constitution and laws of the United States. Specifically, the text of this important statute provides:

> Every person who, under color of any statute, ordinance, regulation, custom, or usage of any State or Territory or the District of Columbia, subjects, or causes to be subjected, any citizen of the United States or other person within the jurisdiction thereof to the deprivation of any rights, privileges, or immunities secured by the Constitution and laws, shall be liable to the party injured in an action at law, suit in equity, or other proper proceeding for redress, except that in any action brought against a judicial officer for an act or omission taken in such officer's judicial capacity, injunctive relief shall not be granted unless a declaratory decree was violated or declaratory relief was unavailable. For the purposes of this section, any Act of Congress applicable exclusively to the District of Columbia shall be considered to be a statute of the District of Columbia.[1]

Jurisdiction for §1983 Suits

Section 1983 does not create federal court jurisdiction. Rather, it creates a cause of action, a legal entitlement to relief, against those who, acting pursuant to state government authority, violate federal law. Federal court jurisdiction to hear §1983 suits exists under the general federal question jurisdiction statute, 28 U.S.C. §1331, and pursuant to 28 U.S.C. §1343(3), which grants jurisdiction for suits redressing violations of the federal laws that provide for equal rights of citizens.[2] Section 1343(3) was part of the original statute that contained §1983.[3] The absence of an amount in controversy requirement in §1343(3) made that statute important at a time when the general federal question jurisdiction statute had a

§8.1 [1] 42 U.S.C. §1983.

[2] For a detailed discussion of §1331, *see* §5.2, *supra*. The text of 28 U.S.C. §1343(3) provides: "(3) To redress the deprivation, under color of any State law, statute, ordinance, regulation, custom or usage, of any right, privilege or immunity secured by the Constitution of the United States or by any Act of Congress providing for equal rights of citizens or of all persons within the jurisdiction of the United States. The district courts shall have original jurisdiction of any civil action authorized by law to be commenced by any person: . . ."

[3] Both statutes were part of §1 of the Civil Rights Act of 1871, 17 Stat. 13; §1 of the Ku Klux Klan Act of April 20, 1871; R.S. §1979.

minimum amount requirement.[4] The elimination, in 1980, of the amount in controversy requirement for §1331 rendered §1343(3) superfluous.[5]

Rooker-Feldman Doctrine: No Appellate Review of State Decisions

Although §1331 and §1343(3) appear to create federal court subject matter jurisdiction for all §1983 cases, there are a few situations where jurisdiction does not exist. The most important exception is that federal courts do not have jurisdiction pursuant to §1983 to review the judgments and decisions of state courts. This principle is often referred to as the Rooker-Feldman doctrine, based on the two Supreme Court cases that held that §1983 may not be used in federal court to review state court decisions.

In *Rooker v. Fidelity Trust Co.*, the plaintiffs attempted to have a state court judgment declared "null and void" and the Supreme Court ruled that federal district courts have no jurisdiction to "entertain a proceeding to reverse or modify" a state court judgment.[6] In *District of Columbia Court of Appeals v. Feldman,* the Supreme Court again ruled that a district court has "no authority to review final judgments of a state court in judicial proceedings."[7] Thus, the Supreme Court has explained that the *Rooker-Feldman* doctrine provides that "a party losing in state court is barred from seeking what in substance would be appellate review of the state judgment in a United States District Court based on the losing party's claim that the state judgment itself violates the loser's federal rights."[8] The Rooker-Feldman doctrine is discussed in detail in §13.2.

Importance of §1983

Even though §1983 is not a grant of jurisdiction, detailed consideration of it in a text on federal jurisdiction is necessary. Section 1983 serves as the basic vehicle for federal court review of alleged state and local violations of federal law.

[4] *See, e.g.,* Chapman v. Houston Welfare Rights Org., 441 U.S. 600 (1979) (considering whether violations of the Social Security Act are within the jurisdiction created by §1343(3); the issue was important because the case did not meet the jurisdictional amount requirement then contained in §1331).

[5] Federal Question Jurisdictional Amendment Act of 1980, 28 U.S.C. §1331, Pub. L. No. 96-486, 94 Stat. 2369.

[6] Rooker v. Fidelity Trust Co., 263 U.S. 413 (1923). *See also* Hagerty v. Succession of Clement, 749 F.2d 217, 220 (5th Cir. 1984), *cert. denied,* 474 U.S. 968 (1985) ("well-settled rule that a plaintiff may not seek a reversal of a state court judgment simply by recasting his complaint in the form of a civil rights action"). The Rooker-Feldman doctrine is discussed in detail in §13.2.

[7] 460 U.S. 462 (1983).

[8] Johnson v. De Grandy, 512 U.S. 997, 1005-1006 (1994). In two cases, the Supreme Court limited the application of the Rooker-Feldman doctrine. In Exxon Mobil Corporation v. Saudi Basic Industries Corp., 544 U.S. 280 (2005), the Court held that *Rooker-Feldman* applies only when a losing party in state court seeks to relitigate the same matter in an action in federal district court. In Lance v. Dennis, 546 U.S. 459 (2006), the Court held that *Rooker-Feldman* does not bar actions by nonparties to the state court judgment, even if they were in privity with a party to the judgment. These cases are discussed in detail in Chapter 13.

Its importance in defining the role of the federal courts cannot be overstated. In terms of sheer quantity, although there were only 270 §1983 suits in 1961, in 1985 there were 36,582 such cases in federal court, of which 19,000 were brought by prisoners; by 1999, 41,304 civil rights suits were filed in the federal courts, plus 14,083 civil rights claims by prisoners.[9] In 2024, there were 45,781 civil rights suits in federal court, not counting prison suits; it is estimated that more than 10 percent of the federal court docket consists of §1983 suits.[10]

Section 1983 is the basis for almost all constitutional rulings arising from the actions of state and local governments and their officers. Most of the other doctrines discussed in this book—such diverse topics as standing, the Eleventh Amendment, and abstention—frequently arise in the context of §1983 litigation. Some commentators have flatly declared that "[n]o statute is more important in contemporary America" than §1983.[11] Certainly, none is more important in defining the role of the federal judiciary.

Prison Litigation Reform Act as a Limit on §1983 Suits

As indicated in the statistics above, prisoner suits traditionally have been a significant percentage of litigation brought under §1983. This has changed as a result of the Prison Litigation Reform Act.[12] Among other requirements, the Act mandates that all inmates pay filing fees for initiating lawsuits and precludes in forma pauperis status to inmates who have filed three or more frivolous suits unless the prisoner is "under imminent danger of serious physical injury."[13] The act directs federal district courts to screen complaints by inmates before filing and to dismiss those that are frivolous. Also, the act provides for the revocation of good-time credits for inmates who are found to have filed malicious or false claims. The act additionally bars suits for mental or emotional injury unless there is a showing of a physical injury and limits attorneys' fees. The statute also mandates the expiration of court orders dealing with prison conditions. Perhaps most importantly, the act requires that prisoners exhaust administrative remedies before filing suits in court.[14] Individually and cumulatively, these reforms are a very substantial limit on the ability of prisoners to sue in federal court.

[9] *See, e.g.*, Cooper v. Schriro, 189 F.3d 781 (8th Cir. 1999); Jenkins v. Haubert, 179 F.3d 19 (2d Cir. 1999). Martin A. Schwartz, Section 1983 Litigation: Claims and Defenses 1-7 (4th ed. 2019).

[10] *See* Administrative Office of the U.S. Courts, "U.S. District Courts - Civil Cases Filed, by Nature of Suit" 2 (Sep. 30, 2024). *See e.g.*, Aucoin v. Cupil, 958 F.3d 379 (5th Cir. 2020); Stearns v. Inmate Services Corp, 957 F.3d 902 (8th Cir. 2020); Swain v. Junior, 958 F.3d 1081 (11th Cir. 2020). George C. Pratt, Foreword to M. Schwartz & J. Kirklin, Section 1983 Litigation: Claims, Defenses, and Fees at xviii (4th ed. 2003).

[11] *See, e.g.*, Levin v. Madigan, 692 F.3d 607 (7th Cir. 2012) (holding that §1983 is a means for vindicating federal rights); Communities for Equity v. Mich. High School Athletic Ass'n, 459 F.3d 676, 681 (6th Cir. 2006) ("§1983 serves as a vehicle to obtain damages for violations of both the Constitution and of federal statutes."). Martin A. Schwartz & John E. Kirklin, Section 1983 Litigation: Claims, Defenses, and Fees 2 (3d ed. 1997).

[12] Pub. L. No. 104-134, 110 Stat. 1321. A detailed examination of the act is beyond the scope of this book.

[13] §804(d).

[14] *See* Woodford v. Ngo, 548 U.S. 81 (2006) (exhaustion requirement of the PLRA requires dismissal by the federal court of cases where there was not proper exhaustion); Porter v. Nussle, 534

On the one hand, the Prison Litigation Reform Act is defended as a needed response to an explosion of prisoner suits, many frivolous, and the burden they placed on the federal dockets. Initial statistics indicate that the act is succeeding in this goal. The number of prisoner suits filed in federal court fell from 41,215 in fiscal year 1996 to 28,635 for fiscal year 1997.[15] This is a drop of 31 percent in the year immediately following the enactment of the act.

However, the act can be criticized as limiting access to the federal courts to the group that most needs its protection: Prisoners who have no meaningful influence in the political process. Statistics about the increased number of suits by prisoners are misleading because they fail to account for the dramatic increase in the number incarcerated. Controlling for this factor reveals that prison litigation has not increased.[16] Moreover, truly frivolous prisoner suits take relatively little court time before being dismissed.

Whichever perspective one adopts, it is clear that the Prison Litigation Reform Act is a substantial limit on the ability of prisoners to file §1983 suits in federal court. Although a detailed examination of its provisions is beyond the scope of this book, it is discussed below in connection with its requirement that prisoners exhaust administrative remedies before filing challenges to prison conditions.[17]

Organization and Coverage of the Chapter

In examining §1983, §8.2 of this text begins by describing the historical background of the statute, a history that frequently is relied on by the Supreme Court in deciding particular issues. The remainder of the chapter considers five major questions concerning the meaning and scope of §1983. First, what does it mean to say that an officer acts "under color of state law"? Section 8.3 examines the landmark decision in *Monroe v. Pape* that dramatically expanded the definition of this phrase and hence is largely responsible for the explosion of §1983 litigation.[18] Section 8.4 considers an important corollary of this broad definition: litigants need not exhaust state administrative or judicial proceedings before bringing a §1983 claim to federal court.

The second major topic considered concerns who may be sued under §1983. Section 8.5 examines whether municipalities are persons and, if so, under what circumstances they are liable under §1983. Section 8.6 considers the liability of individual government officers under §1983, especially considering the important topic of officer immunities. Finally, §8.7 briefly discusses the question of whether

---

U.S. 516 (2002) (PLRA requires exhaustion for excessive force claims brought by prisoners); Booth v. Churner, 532 U.S. 731 (2001) (PLRA exhaustion requirement applies even if administrative remedies cannot provide what the plaintiff seeks as long as it can provide something of value).

[15] Administrative Office of the United States Courts, Judicial Business of the United States Courts: 1997 Report of the Director 131-132 (1997).

[16] Theodore Eisenberg & Stewart Schwab, The Reality of Constitutional Tort Litigation, 72 Cornell L. Rev. 641, 667 (1987).

[17] *See* §8.4, text accompanying notes 5-24.

[18] 365 U.S. 167 (1961).

state governments are persons for purposes of §1983 litigation. In *Will v. Michigan Department of State Police*, the Court resolved this issue by holding that state governments are not persons and cannot be sued in a §1983 action.[19]

The third major question concerns what constitutes a violation of the laws and Constitution of the United States for purposes of §1983. Section 8.8 examines the violations of federal statutes that are actionable via §1983 suits. Section 8.9 considers the constitutional claims that can be raised in §1983 suits. The focus is on the Court's attempt to limit the use of the Constitution and §1983 as a basis for litigating matters that also are torts under state law.

The fourth topic considered in this chapter, discussed in §8.10, concerns preclusion of §1983 suits as a result of state court decisions. The fifth and final topic, examined in §8.11, is the remedies that are available under §1983.

Two important, related subjects are largely omitted from consideration. First, there is little discussion of the availability of attorneys' fees for prevailing plaintiffs in §1983 lawsuits pursuant to 42 U.S.C. §1988. Although the availability of attorneys' fees is frequently contested and it is of obvious significance in determining the nature of §1983 litigation, space considerations and the focus of this book on topics more closely related to jurisdiction prevent consideration of attorneys' fees questions here.[20]

Second, except for considering whether state governments may be sued in state courts pursuant to §1983, there is little discussion of §1983 litigation in state courts. The Supreme Court has explicitly held that federal courts do not have exclusive jurisdiction over §1983 lawsuits.[21] Moreover, *Howlett v. Rose*[22] and *Haywood v. Drown* held that state courts generally must hear §1983 suits and may not apply state law immunities as a defense.[23] Although all of the principles discussed in this chapter apply in §1983 suits in both state and federal courts, any discussion of special problems of state court treatment of federal law issues, including §1983, is beyond the scope of this book.[24]

[19] 491 U.S. 58 (1989). Earlier, in Quern v. Jordan, 440 U.S. 332 (1979), the Court had ruled that §1983 did not override the Eleventh Amendment and could not be used to sue a state in federal court.

[20] *See, e.g.*, Montanez v. Simon, 755 F.3d 547 (7th Cir. 2014) (holding that the district court did not abuse its discretion by awarding substantially less attorney's fees than the plaintiff requested); McAfee v. Boczar, 781 F.3d 81 (4th Cir. 2013) (holding that attorney's fees 109 times more than the verdict itself was not justified); Mahach-Watkins v. Deepee, 593 F.3d 1054 (9th Cir. 2010) (affirming the district court's decision to award plaintiff attorneys' fees). For an excellent, comprehensive treatment of the attorneys' fees issues, *see* Schwartz & Kirklin, *supra* note 11, at 11-124.

[21] Maine v. Thiboutot, 448 U.S. 1, 10-11 (1980).

[22] 496 U.S. 356 (1990). *Howlett* is discussed in §3.5, concerning the duty of state courts to hear federal claims.

[23] 556 U.S. 729 (2009). *Haywood* also is discussed in §3.5.

[24] For an excellent review of state court §1983 litigation, *see* Steven H. Steinglass, Section 1983 Litigation in State Courts (2004 and yearly inserts). The obligation of state courts to hear federal law issues is discussed in §3.3, *supra*.

§8.2 THE HISTORICAL BACKGROUND OF §1983 LITIGATION

Legislative History of §1983

Following the Civil War and the adoption of the Thirteenth, Fourteenth, and Fifteenth Amendments, violence against Black people was endemic throughout the South. The U.S. Senate conducted extensive investigations on this lawlessness, especially focusing on the role of the Ku Klux Klan. A 600-page Senate report detailed the unwillingness or inability of Southern states to control the activities of the Klan.[1] In response to this report, Congress adopted the Civil Rights Act of 1871, §1 of which is now embodied in §1983. The law, titled "An Act to enforce the Provisions of the Fourteenth Amendment to the Constitution, and for other Purposes," was a direct result of "the campaign of violence and deception in the South, fomented by the Ku Klux Klan, which was denying decent citizens their civil and political rights."[2]

In considering the Act, there were lengthy discussions in Congress concerning the uncontrolled violence in the South and the failure of state police and state courts to adequately control the problem. The Supreme Court frequently has summarized this testimony in supporting its conclusion that §1983 was meant "to give a broad remedy for violations of federally protected civil rights."[3] As the Court declared in *Monroe v. Pape*:

> The debates were long and extensive. It is abundantly clear that one reason the legislation was passed was to afford a federal right in federal courts because, by reason of prejudice, passion, neglect, intolerance, or otherwise, state laws might not be enforced and the claims of citizens to the enjoyment of rights, privileges, and immunities guaranteed by the Fourteenth Amendment might be denied by the state agencies.[4]

Section 1983 was meant to substantially alter the relationship of the federal government to the states.[5] The statute empowered the federal government, and most especially the federal courts, with the authority necessary to prevent and redress violations of federal rights. As the Supreme Court declared: "The very

§8.2 [1] S. Rep. No. 1, 42d Cong., 1st Sess. (1871).

[2] Wilson v. Garcia, 471 U.S. 261, 276 (1985).

[3] Monell v. Department of Social Servs., 436 U.S. 658, 685 (1978). For other discussions by the Supreme Court of the historical background of §1983, *see* Patsy v. Board of Regents of Fla., 457 U.S. 496 (1982); Allen v. McCurry, 449 U.S. 90 (1980); Mitchum v. Foster, 407 U.S. 225 (1972); Monroe v. Pape, 365 U.S. 167 (1961). For a discussion of the history of §1983 and the Supreme Court's inconsistent uses of it, *see* Gene R. Nichol, Federalism, State Courts, and Section 1983, 73 Va. L. Rev. 959 (1987).

[4] 365 U.S. at 180.

[5] Patsy v. Board of Regents of Fla., 457 U.S. at 502-503 (§1983 as a "basic alteration" of our federal system).

purpose of §1983 was to interpose the federal courts between the States and the people, as guardians of the people's federal rights—to protect the people from unconstitutional action under color of state law, whether that action be executive, legislative, or judicial."[6]

A constant theme throughout this book is the question of parity—whether state courts should be treated as equal to federal courts in their ability and willingness to protect federal rights.[7] The congressional testimony concerning §1983 reveals that in 1871 Congress did not believe that state courts in the South could be trusted to protect the constitutional rights of Black people.[8]

Sparing use of §1983 Before 1961

Despite the broad aspirations for §1983, for decades it was largely moribund. Between its enactment in 1871 and 1920, only 21 cases were decided under §1983.[9] Many factors combined to render §1983 meaningless during this time period. The end of Reconstruction brought a halt to Northern attempts to protect the rights of Black people in the South.[10] Federal judges in the South appeared no more willing to stop racism and discrimination than were state judges.[11] Repeatedly during this time, the Supreme Court refused to invalidate discriminatory state laws and, in fact, gave a narrow construction to the federal government's authority to protect civil rights.[12]

Section 1983 was used so infrequently that early in this century, Justice Oliver Wendell Holmes clarified that the Court assumed that Congress had not repealed the statute.[13] During the first half of the twentieth century, §1983 litigation remained relatively rare. The most notable use of the statute was as a vehicle for

[6] Mitchum v. Foster, 407 U.S. at 242 (citations omitted).

[7] *See* discussion in §1.5, *supra; see also* Susan N. Herman, Beyond Parity: Section 1983 and the State Courts, 54 Brook. L. Rev. 1057 (1989).

[8] *See* Burt Neuborne, The Myth of Parity, 90 Harv. L. Rev. 1105, 1108 (1977) (reviewing post-Civil War history).

[9] Comment, The Civil Rights Act: Emergence of an Adequate Federal Civil Remedy?, 26 Ind. L.J. 361, 363 (1951).

[10] *See* C. Vann Woodward, Reunion and Reaction: The Compromise of 1877 and the End of Reconstruction 245 (1951); John P. Frank & Robert F. Munro, The Original Understanding of Equal Protection of the Laws, 50 Colum. L. Rev. 131, 167 (1950) (describing the Compromise of 1877 whereby Democrats agreed to support the election of Rutherford Hayes over Samuel Tilden for president in exchange for the end of Reconstruction and Northern control of the South).

[11] *See* Eugene Gressman, The Unhappy History of Civil Rights Legislation, 50 Mich. L. Rev. 1323 (1952); Robert J. Harris, The Quest for Equality 56, 82-89 (1960).

[12] *See, e.g.,* Plessy v. Ferguson, 163 U.S. 537 (1896) (upholding state laws mandating separate accommodations for whites and Black people); The Civil Rights Cases, 109 U.S. 3 (1883) (holding unconstitutional the Civil Rights Act of 1875 as exceeding Congress's authority on account of its regulation of private conduct); The Slaughterhouse Cases, 83 U.S. (16 Wall.) 36 (1873) (narrowly construing the provisions of the Fourteenth Amendment).

[13] Giles v. Harris, 189 U.S. 475, 485 (1903).

invalidating several state laws that disenfranchised Black voters.[14] Still, as recently as 1960, in the entire country, there were only 287 civil rights suits against state and local governments and their officers filed in, or removed to, federal court.[15]

Growth in §1983 Litigation

Since 1961, however, the growth in §1983 litigation has been phenomenal. In 1977, there were more than 20,000 such suits; in 1985, the number grew to over 36,000; by 1995, the number had increased to more than 57,000. Today, over 60,000 suits are filed each year, including prisoner suits.[16] In fact, even by the end of the 1960s, commentators were examining possible ways of limiting the volume of §1983 litigation.[17]

The marked increase in §1983 suits can be linked to many factors. First, the Supreme Court's decision in *Monroe v. Pape*, discussed in the next section, greatly expanded the scope of §1983 by permitting suits both for official government actions that violate the Constitution and for unauthorized actions by individual officers in excess or even in violation of state law.[18] Historically, the marked increase in §1983 litigation began immediately after the *Monroe* decision.

Second, the adoption of the Civil Rights Attorney's Fees Awards Act of 1976 added to the §1983 litigation by allowing prevailing plaintiffs to recover the costs of their attorneys' fees.[19] Individuals who were unable to afford an attorney often could gain representation because of the availability of attorneys' fees upon the plaintiff's victory. Also, the growth in §1983 litigation must be linked to a substantial change in society's attitudes toward civil rights and civil liberties litigation. The 1960s were a time of great attention to protecting civil rights, and constitutional litigation has been growing ever since.

Third, and perhaps most importantly, there has been a general increase in the amount of federal court litigation. Analyzing the volume of §1983 litigation requires more than recitation of statistics about the number of civil rights cases on federal dockets. Empirical studies reveal that the quantity of §1983 litigation has not grown more rapidly than other types of federal court cases. For example, a study by Professors Eisenberg and Schwab indicates that much of the increase in civil rights litigation involves employment discrimination claims, often under

[14] Peter W. Low & John C. Jeffries, Federal Courts and the Law of Federal-State Relations 917 (4th ed. 1998). *See, e.g.*, Smith v. Allwright, 321 U.S. 649 (1944); Lane v. Wilson, 307 U.S. 268 (1939); Rice v. Elmore, 165 F.2d 387 (4th Cir. 1947); Chapman v. King, 154 F.2d 460 (5th Cir. 1946).

[15] Theodore Eisenberg, Civil Rights Legislation: Cases and Materials 86 (2d ed. 1987), citing statistics from the Administrative Office of the United States Courts, Annual Report of the Director 232 (1960).

[16] Administrative Office of the U.S. Courts, Annual Report of the Director: Judicial Business of the United States 2023.

[17] Note, Limiting the Section 1983 Action in the Wake of Monroe v. Pape, 82 Harv. L. Rev. 1486 (1969).

[18] 365 U.S. 167 (1961).

[19] 42 U.S.C. §1988; Pub. L. No. 94-559.

Title VII of the Civil Rights Act of 1964.[20] Apart from employment discrimination suits and prisoner litigation (discussed below), civil rights cases increased by 94 percent from 1975 to 1984, compared with an increase of all other types of cases of 125 percent.[21] Although the amount of prisoner litigation has risen markedly, this must be placed in the context of a substantial increase in the number of prisoners throughout the country. Controlling for the growth in prison populations, prisoner litigation rose by 100 percent between 1975 and 1984, less than the increase for non-civil rights cases.[22] In an earlier empirical study, which also documented that the burden of §1983 litigation is often overstated, Professor Eisenberg observed, "[S]ection 1983 cases are not overwhelming the federal courts; trivial claims, involving little if any federal policy, do not dominate district court dockets, and courts are not, at the behest of state prisoners, eagerly overseeing minute details of prison life."[23]

These factors, taken together, along with other Supreme Court decisions discussed in subsequent sections that expanded the scope of §1983 remedies, made §1983 the centerpiece of federal court relief against local governments and state and local officers.

Inconsistent Reading of History

Finally, in discussing the historical background of §1983 litigation, it must be noted that the Court has been quite inconsistent in its use of this history.[24] As is discussed in the subsequent sections, at times the Court has read the legislative history as broadly authorizing federal courts to supplant state courts in civil rights matters.[25] At other times, the Court has interpreted §1983 against a background of comity and deference to state courts.[26] A recurring issue throughout this chapter is the meaning of the legislative history of §1983 and its relevance to contemporary interpretation of the statute.[27]

[20] Theodore Eisenberg & Stewart Schwab, The Reality of Constitutional Tort Litigation, 72 Cornell L. Rev. 641, 662-665 (1987).

[21] *Id.* at 666.

[22] *Id.* at 667.

[23] Theodore Eisenberg, Section 1983: Doctrinal Foundations and an Empirical Study, 67 Cornell L. Rev. 483, 484 (1982). As discussed above, the Prison Litigation Reform Act, Pub. L. No. 104-134, 110 Stat. 1321, has caused a significant decrease in prisoner litigation.

[24] *See, e.g.,* Nichol, *supra* note 3, at 978-983 (Court's inconsistency in interpreting the history of §1983).

[25] *See, e.g.,* Mitchum v. Foster, 407 U.S. 225 (1972) (§1983 was based on distrust of state courts); *Mitchum* is discussed in detail in §11.2, *infra.*

[26] *See, e.g.,* Allen v. McCurry, 449 U.S. 90 (1980) (federal courts in §1983 litigation must accord collateral estoppel effect to state court judgments); *Allen* is discussed in detail in §8.10, *infra.*

[27] *See, e.g.,* Nichol, *supra* note 3, at 959-964, 978-983; Richard A. Matasar, Personal Immunities Under Section 1983: The Limits of the Court's Historical Analysis, 40 Ark. L. Rev. 741 (1987).

§8.3 THE MEANING OF "UNDER COLOR OF STATE LAW"

Interpretations Before *Monroe v. Pape*

Section 1983 creates liability against any person who violates the Constitution or laws of the United States while acting "under color of any statute, ordinance, regulation, custom, or usage of any state or territory." This language usually is phrased more simply as a requirement that the plaintiff demonstrate that the defendant acted "under color of state law."

In defining "under color of state law," the central question is whether §1983 applies only to actions taken pursuant to official government policies or whether §1983 suits also may be brought against the unauthorized or even illegal acts by government officers. Before *Monroe v. Pape* was decided in 1961,[1] there was a "longstanding assumption that §1983 reached only misconduct either officially authorized or so widely tolerated as to amount to a 'custom or usage.'"[2]

However, it should be noted that prior to *Monroe*, the Court broadly interpreted *criminal* statutes containing language similar or identical to that found in §1983. For example, in *United States v. Classic*, the Supreme Court considered a prosecution under a criminal statute authorizing punishment for anyone who "under color of any law, statute, ordinance, regulation, or custom" subjects any person to the deprivation of "any rights, privileges, or immunities secured or protected by the Constitution of the United States."[3] *Classic* involved a prosecution of election officials in Louisiana who failed to count ballots cast by Black voters. The Supreme Court broadly interpreted the statute's language, concluding that "[m]isuse of power, possessed by virtue of state law and made possible only because the wrongdoer is clothed with the authority of state law, is action taken 'under color' of state law."[4]

Similarly, in *Screws v. United States*, the Supreme Court held that for purposes of the criminal statutes prohibiting violations of civil rights, officers act under color of state law as long as they are performing in an official capacity.[5] In *Screws*, three state law enforcement officers—a county sheriff, a special deputy, and a city policeman—arrested a Black man on a minor crime and then, while the prisoner was in handcuffs, beat him to death. The Court concluded that the officers could be prosecuted because their actions were "under color of state law," even though they were not expressly or impliedly authorized by the state.[6]

§8.3 [1] 365 U.S. 167 (1961).

[2] Peter W. Low & John C. Jeffries, Federal Courts and the Law of Federal-State Relations 917 (4th ed. 1998).

[3] 313 U.S. 299 (1941); 18 U.S.C. §242; adopted as §2 of the Civil Rights Act of April 9, 1866, 14 Stat. 27.

[4] 313 U.S. at 326.

[5] 325 U.S. 91 (1945).

[6] *See also* Williams v. United States, 341 U.S. 97 (1951).

Monroe v. Pape

Monroe v. Pape, however, was the Supreme Court's first occasion to directly consider the meaning of "under color of law" under §1983. In *Monroe,* the plaintiff's complaint alleged that 13 Chicago police officers broke into his home early in the morning, subjected his family to humiliation by making them stand naked in the living room, and ransacked every room of the house.[7] Monroe's complaint further alleged that he was taken to the police station and held for 10 hours without arraignment and without being given the chance to contact an attorney. No charges ever were filed against Monroe.

A central question before the Supreme Court was whether the actions of the Chicago police officers could be deemed to have occurred "under color of law" because the conduct obviously was not authorized by the government.[8] The Supreme Court ruled that actions taken by an officer in his or her official capacity are deemed to have occurred "under color of law" even if they are not in pursuance of any official state policy and even if they violate state law. The Court concluded that "[m]isuse of power, possessed by virtue of state law and made possible only because the wrongdoer is clothed with the authority of state law, is action taken 'under color of' state law."[9]

The Court held that a §1983 suit was available even though adequate state judicial remedies were potentially available. Justice Douglas, writing for the majority, declared:

> It is no answer that the state has a law which if enforced would give relief. The federal remedy is supplementary to the state remedy, and the latter need not be first sought and refused before the federal one is invoked. *Hence the fact that Illinois by its constitution and laws outlaws unreasonable searches and seizures is no barrier to the present suit in the federal court.*[10]

The Court explained that §1983 was intended to provide a remedy in situations where states prohibit practices, but provide inadequate remedies, and in instances where state remedies, theoretically adequate, are unavailable in practice.[11] The Court realized that a narrow definition of "under color of law"—limiting liability to officials acting pursuant to official policies—would permit state governments to substantially immunize their officers from §1983 liability simply by enacting general statutes prohibiting officers from violating the Constitution or laws of the United States.

Similarly, the Court was unwilling to permit §1983 actions only upon proof that state remedies are inadequate. The Court recognized that it often would

[7] 365 U.S. at 169.

[8] Another issue before the Court was whether local governments could be sued under §1983. In *Monroe,* the Supreme Court held that municipalities were not persons for purposes of §1983. This aspect of the *Monroe* decision was subsequently overruled in Monell v. Department of Social Servs., 436 U.S. 658 (1978). *See* discussion in §8.5, *infra.*

[9] 365 U.S at 184.

[10] *Id.* at 183 (emphasis added).

[11] *Id.* at 173-174.

be difficult or impossible to *prove* state court hostility to federal rights. Instead, the *Monroe* Court held that a government officer acts under color of law for all actions taken as an official that violate the Constitution and laws of the United States.

Justice Frankfurter wrote a vehement dissent in *Monroe.*[12] His contention was that an officer who acts in excess of his or her authority, or in violation of state law, cannot be deemed to act "under color of state law." Justice Frankfurter maintained that "[i]n the face of Illinois decisions holding such intrusions [by the police] unlawful . . . such a complaint fails to state a claim under §1983."[13] Justice Frankfurter would have reserved §1983 for instances of official state and local policies or customs that violate federal laws or situations where state remedies are proven to be inadequate.

Although Justice Frankfurter's position never has attracted majority support on the Court,[14] the Court has relied upon the distinction between official policy and unauthorized acts of government officers in decisions concerning other aspects of §1983 liability. For example, as discussed in detail in §8.5, the Court held that municipalities are liable under §1983 only for their official policies in violation of the Constitution and laws of the United States; respondeat superior liability of cities is not permitted.[15] Also, as considered in §8.9, the Court has held that there is no violation of due process when the plaintiff seeks a post-deprivation remedy for the random and unauthorized acts of government officials, if the state provides an adequate post-deprivation remedy.[16] Nonetheless, the broad definition of "under color of law" adopted in *Monroe* remains unaltered: §1983 liability exists for all actions taken in an officer's official capacity, whether authorized by state law or in violation of it.

"Under Color of Law" Satisfied If There is State Action

In essence, the test for determining whether someone is acting under "color of law" is virtually identical to evaluating whether there is state action. The Supreme Court long has held that the Constitution only applies to actions by

[12] *Id.* at 236 (Frankfurter, J., dissenting).

[13] *Id.* at 258.

[14] Justice Scalia has lamented the Court's failure to accept Justice Frankfurter's position in *Monroe.* Justice Scalia stated: "*Monroe* changed a statute that generated only 21 cases in the first 50 years of its existence into one that pours into the federal courts tens of thousands of suits each year, and engaged this Court into a losing struggle to prevent the Constitution from degenerating into a general tort law." Crawford-El v. Britton, 523 U.S. 574, 611 (1998) (Scalia, J., dissenting).

[15] Monell v. Department of Social Servs., 436 U.S. 658 (1978).

[16] Parratt v. Taylor, 451 U.S. 527 (1981). *Parratt* applies to random and unauthorized acts depriving an individual of property in situations where the plaintiff seeks a postdeprivation remedy and the state provides one. The application of *Parratt* to liberty is unresolved. *See* discussion in §8.9, *infra.* For an excellent discussion explaining how both *Parratt* and *Monell* create a similar distinction between random and unauthorized acts and official policy, *see* Susan Bandes, *Monell, Parratt, Daniels,* and *Davidson*: Distinguishing a Custom or Policy from a Random, Unauthorized Act, 72 Iowa L. Rev. 101 (1986). *See* discussion in §8.9.

governments and their employees; private conduct generally is not regulated by the Constitution.[17] This is termed the "state action" requirement. The Supreme Court declared in *United States v. Price*: "In cases under §1983, 'under color' of law has consistently been treated as the same thing as the 'state action' required under the Fourteenth Amendment."[18] Subsequently, in *Lugar v. Edmondson Oil Co.*, the Supreme Court reiterated this position by stating: "[I]t is clear that in a §1983 action brought against a state official, the statutory requirement of action 'under color of state law' and the 'state action' requirement of the Fourteenth Amendment are identical."[19]

Problems in Defining "Under Color of Law"

Although an examination of the state action doctrine is beyond the scope of this book, several specific problems arise in using it to determine whether an officer acts under "color of law" for purposes of §1983.[20] First, some might argue that there is not state action when a public officer is acting without the authority of the government and even may be violating the law.[21] The Court, however, has routinely rejected this position. In the landmark case of *Home Telephone and Telegraph Co. v. Los Angeles*, the Supreme Court ruled that actions taken by an officer in his or her official capacity constitute state action, whether or not the conduct is authorized by state law.[22]

Second, problems arise in deciding when off-duty government officers are acting under color of law, as opposed to in a purely private nongovernmental role. The Supreme Court has held that "state employment is generally sufficient to render the defendant a state actor. . . . [G]enerally, a public employee acts under color of state law while acting in his official capacity or while exercising his responsibilities pursuant to state law."[23] But definitional questions frequently occur, especially in cases involving off-duty police officers, in deciding whether a person was acting as a government officer or in a private capacity.[24] Martin Schwartz and John Kirklin correctly summarized the factors that courts consider in determining whether the officer exercised state authority: "[W]hether there is a policy requiring officers to

[17] *See, e.g.,* Rendell-Baker v. Kohn, 457 U.S. 830 (1982); Jackson v. Metropolitan Edison Co., 419 U.S. 345 (1974); The Civil Rights Cases, 109 U.S. 3 (1883).

[18] 383 U.S. 787, 794 n.7 (1966).

[19] 457 U.S. 922, 929 (1982). *See also* West v. Atkins, 487 U.S. 42 (1988) ("If a defendant's conduct satisfies the state action requirement of the Fourteenth Amendment that conduct is also action under color of law and will support a suit under §1983.") (citations omitted).

[20] For a summary of the state action doctrines, *see* Erwin Chemerinsky, Constitutional Law: Principles and Policies, ch. 5 (7th ed. 2023).

[21] For an early decision suggesting that there is not state action when officers violate the law, *see* Barney v. City of New York, 193 U.S. 430 (1904).

[22] 227 U.S. 278 (1913); *see also* Mosher v. City of Phoenix, 287 U.S. 29 (1932).

[23] West v. Atkins, 487 U.S. at 49-50.

[24] *See, e.g.,* United States v. Day, 591 F.3d 679 (4th Cir. 2010) (Virginia's conferral of authority on armed security officers to effect an arrest did not make them state actors for purposes of §1983); Bustos v. Martini Club, 599 F.3d 458 (5th Cir. 2010) (assault and excessive force by off-duty police officers is not under color of law).

be on-duty at all times; whether the officer displayed a badge or an identification card, identified himself as a police officer, or carried or used a service revolver or other weapon or device issued by the police department; and whether the officer purported to place the individual under arrest."[25]

Public Employees with Independent Duties to Clients

A third problem in defining "under color of law" concerns public employees who have independent duties to a client, such as doctors, lawyers, and public guardians. The law in this area is inconsistent and difficult to reconcile. In *O'Connor v. Donaldson* a prisoner sued a psychiatrist, who also was the administrator of a state mental health facility.[26] In *Estelle v. Gamble,* a prisoner sued a doctor, who also was the chief medical officer at the prison hospital, for malpractice.[27] Subsequently, in *West v. Atkins,* a prisoner sued a private physician who provided medical care in the prison pursuant to a contract with the state.[28] In all of these instances the Supreme Court found that the doctors were acting under color of state law.

In sharp contrast, the Supreme Court held that a public defender, employed by the state to represent indigent criminal defendants, does not act under color of state law. In *Polk County v. Dodson,* the Court concluded that a public defender performs a function indistinguishable from that provided by private attorneys.[29] The Court found that the public defender should not be thought of as a government employee because the public defender's loyalties are not to the government, but rather to the client. Accordingly, the Court held that although the public defender is a government officer performing in an official capacity, nonetheless, the public defender cannot be said to act under color of state law.[30]

It is difficult to reconcile *Polk County* with *O'Connor, Estelle,* and *West.* A doctor employed by the government provides the same care as a private physician. Just as the attorney's primary loyalties are to the client, so are the psychiatrist's or physician's fundamental duties to the patient and not to the government employer. In *Polk County,* the Supreme Court distinguished the public defender from the doctors in *O'Connor* and *Estelle* by noting that the psychiatrist and the physician in the former cases also were prison administrators—the director of the state mental hospital and the medical director of the prison hospital.[31] However, this distinction is misleading because in *O'Connor* and *Estelle* the suits concerned the doctors' alleged negligence in providing medical care to the individual prisoners; the litigation was not a challenge to their administrative decisions.

Subsequently, in *West v. Atkins,* the Supreme Court explained that a public defender is different from a doctor because a doctor's "professional and ethical

[25] Martin A. Schwartz & John E. Kirklin, Section 1983 Litigation: Claims, Defenses, and Fees 496 (3d ed. 1997).

[26] 422 U.S. 563 (1975).

[27] 429 U.S. 97 (1976).

[28] 487 U.S. 42 (1988).

[29] 454 U.S. 312 (1981).

[30] *Id.* at 325.

[31] *Id.* at 320.

obligation to make independent medical judgments [does] not set him in conflict with the State and other prison authorities."[32] A public defender is deemed not to act under color of law because his or her role is inherently adverse to the state.

But it is unclear why a professional employed by the government does not act under color of law simply because the individual has other professional obligations or opposes the state. The Court has created a false dichotomy. Despite the attorney's responsibilities for the client, a public defender, fully salaried by the state, acts by virtue of the authority granted by the government.

The Court's decision in *Polk County v. Dodson* raises the question of whether other professionals employed by the government can claim that they do not act under color of law because of their independent professional obligations. For instance, the lower federal courts are divided as to whether a guardian appointed and paid by the state acts under color of state law.[33] But *West v. Atkins* strongly indicates that *Polk County* creates a narrow exception to the under color of law analysis. The Court stated that "[d]efendants are not removed from the purview of §1983 simply because they are professionals acting in accordance with professional discretion and judgment."[34] Thus, it appears that a professional employed by the government does not act under color of law only if the individual employee is placed in a role inherently adverse to the government.

Liability of Private Individuals

Fourth and finally, courts often confront the question of when private actions, such as pursuant to a conspiracy, should be deemed to occur under color of law because of their close relationship to the acts of government officers.[35] In *Adickes v. S.H. Kress & Co.*, a group of seven people, one white and six Black, was refused service at the Kress Store in Hattiesburg, Mississippi.[36] The plaintiff, a white schoolteacher, sued, claiming in part that the restaurant conspired with the police to prevent Black people from being served and that there was a custom of discriminating within the state. The Court concluded that proof of such a conspiracy would establish that the restaurant acted under color of law, and thus the private entity could be held liable under §1983.

In *Dennis v. Sparks*, the Supreme Court held that private individuals who conspire with government officials may be sued under §1983.[37] In *Dennis*, the defendant was accused of conspiring with a judge to corruptly issue injunctions that denied the plaintiffs of their property without due process of law. A unanimous

[32] 487 U.S. at 51.

[33] *Compare* Schaffrath v. Thomas, 993 F. Supp. 842 (D. Utah 1998); Holley v. Deal, 948 F. Supp. 711 (M.D. Tenn. 1996), *with* Thomas S. v. Morrow, 781 F.2d 367 (4th Cir.), *cert. denied,* 476 U.S. 1124 (1986) (guardian does act under color of state law).

[34] 487 U.S. at 52.

[35] Additionally, there is the possibility for recovery against those conspiring to violate civil rights pursuant to 42 U.S.C. §1985.

[36] 398 U.S. 144 (1970).

[37] 449 U.S. 24 (1980).

Court concluded that a private person is deemed to act under color of state law if he or she is a "willful participant in joint action with the State or its agents."[38]

An important issue arises in situations where tasks traditionally performed by the government have been privatized. For example, many jurisdictions now contract with private prisons to incarcerate inmates. A strong argument exists that there is state action when private entities perform such public functions.[39] State authority is used to incarcerate the individuals and empower the private prisons.[40] In *Richardson v. McKnight*, the Supreme Court assumed, but did not decide, that private prison guards act under color of state law for purposes of §1983.[41]

Suits Against Federal Officers

In fact, although §1983 generally does not create liability for federal officers,[42] the lower federal courts consistently have held that federal officers may be sued under §1983 "when [they] are engaged in a conspiracy with state officials to deprive constitutional rights."[43] This expansive definition of "under color of law," which includes private parties participating in conspiracies with government officers, reflects the broad remedial goals of §1983 to redress all violations of constitutional rights that occur under the aegis of state authority and power.

§8.4 EXHAUSTION OF STATE REMEDIES IS NOT REQUIRED FOR §1983 LITIGATION

State Judicial Remedies Need Not Be Exhausted

As described in the previous section, *Monroe v. Pape* establishes that a plaintiff may properly bring a §1983 suit to federal court even if the state provides judicial remedies that appear completely adequate to redress the injuries.[1] In other words, a plaintiff need not exhaust state remedies before initiating a §1983 suit in federal court. The Court explicitly declared: "The federal remedy is supplementary to the

[38] *Id.* at 27. The Supreme Court has held that private individuals sued under §1983 generally can claim qualified immunity. See Filarsky v. Delia, 566 U.S. 377 (2012), discussed *infra* at §8.6.3.

[39] *See* Jackson v. Metropolitan Edison Co., 419 U.S. 345, 352 (1974) (there is state action "in the exercise by a private entity of powers traditionally exclusively reserved to the State").

[40] *See id.* at 403-414, discussing the entanglement exception to the state action doctrine.

[41] 521 U.S. 399 (1997) (holding that private prison guards are not entitled to qualified immunity), discussed below in §8.6.3.

[42] For a discussion of the liability of federal officers, *see* §9.1, *infra.* L. Xia v. Tillerson, 865 F.3d 643, 658 (D.C. Cir. 2017); Doe v. United States, 831 F.3d 309, 314 (5th Cir. 2016) (emphasizing that §1983 does not apply to "federal officials acting under color of federal law").

[43] Hampton v. Hanrahan, 600 F.2d 600, 623 (7th Cir. 1979); *see also* Big Cats of Serenity Springs, Inc. v. Rhodes, 843 F.3d 853 (10th Cir. 2016); Arar v. Ashcroft, 585 F.3d 559 (2d Cir. 2009).

§8.4 [1] 365 U.S. 167, 183 (1961).

state remedy, and the latter need not be first sought and refused before the federal one is invoked."[2]

In large part, the absence of an exhaustion requirement is based on the Court's reading of the legislative history of §1983. As described earlier, §1983 was adopted because of substantial distrust of the ability and willingness of state courts to protect the rights of Black people.[3] Also, if there was an exhaustion requirement for §1983 suits, and if federal courts were obligated to accord res judicata and collateral estoppel effect to state court rulings, then federal district court jurisdiction in §1983 cases would be virtually meaningless.[4] State court rulings would be controlling and preclude federal court review, except for appellate review by the U.S. Supreme Court.

State Administrative Remedies Need Not Be Exhausted

The holding in *Monroe*, that plaintiffs need not exhaust state judicial remedies before filing federal §1983 suits, was soon extended so that exhaustion of state administrative remedies was also not a prerequisite to federal court §1983 litigation. In non-civil rights litigation, a plaintiff generally must exhaust state administrative remedies, but not judicial remedies, before filing suit in federal court. In 1963, in *McNeese v. Board of Education*, the Court considered an Illinois administrative remedy for segregated public schools.[5] Under an Illinois statute, whenever at least 50 residents believed a school district to be segregated, they could file a complaint with the superintendent of public instruction. The superintendent then would hold a hearing on the matter. If he or she found the complaint to be "substantially correct," the superintendent would request the attorney general to file suit. The superintendent's request did not obligate the attorney general to initiate litigation.

The plaintiffs in *McNeese* filed suit in federal court without using the state's administrative scheme. The state moved for dismissal on the ground that the plaintiffs were required to exhaust their state administrative remedies before suing under §1983. The Court disagreed. Relying on *Monroe v. Pape*, the Court held that "relief under the Civil Rights Act may not be defeated because relief was not first sought under state law which provided a remedy."[6] The Court based its conclusion on the legislative history of §1983. The statute was passed, the Court argued, to "provide a remedy where state law was inadequate . . . and to provide a remedy in the federal courts supplementary to any remedy any State might have."[7] The Court also reasoned that "[t]he First Congress created federal courts as the chief—though

[2] *Id.*

[3] *See* §8.3, *supra.*

[4] The Supreme Court has held that federal courts, in hearing §1983 actions, must give res judicata and collateral estoppel effect to state judicial and some state administrative proceedings. *See, e.g.*, Migra v. Warren City Sch. Dist. Bd. of Educ., 465 U.S. 75 (1984); Allen v. McCurry, 449 U.S. 90 (1980); *see* discussion in §8.10, *infra.*

[5] 373 U.S. 668 (1963).

[6] *Id.* at 671.

[7] *Id.* at 672.

always the exclusive—tribunals for enforcement of federal rights."[8] To require exhaustion of state remedies would subvert that goal.

On several occasions, the Supreme Court has reiterated its conclusion that plaintiffs need not exhaust state administrative remedies before initiating federal court §1983 litigation.[9] In 1982, in *Patsy v. Board of Regents*, the Court reconsidered the exhaustion issue.[10] Once again, the Court concluded that "exhaustion of state administrative remedies should not be required as a prerequisite to bringing an action pursuant to section 1983."[11]

In *Patsy*, the plaintiff filed an employment discrimination claim alleging that her employer, Florida International University, had denied her employment opportunities on account of her race and gender. The state of Florida provided an administrative remedy for employment discrimination claims against state agencies. The Court reiterated its position that the legislative history of §1983 reveals Congress's intent that plaintiffs need not exhaust state remedies before filing federal civil rights litigation. The Court stated that §1983 granted the federal courts a "paramount role in protecting constitutional rights."[12] Section 1983 created "dual or concurrent forums in the state and federal system, enabling the plaintiff to choose the forum in which to seek relief."[13]

Finally, the Court noted that Congress had recently rejected a bill that would have created an exhaustion requirement in civil rights cases. Instead, Congress passed the Civil Rights of Institutionalized Persons Act, which contains a limited exhaustion requirement for a carefully defined class of litigants.[14] The Court concluded that since Congress did not impose an exhaustion requirement, the Court would not do so on its own.

Justices Powell and Burger dissented in *Patsy*, contending that the Supreme Court erred in not applying the traditional rule requiring exhaustion of state administrative remedies prior to the initiation of federal litigation.[15] The dissent emphasized the enormous burden §1983 suits impose on the federal judiciary and the ability of an exhaustion requirement to conserve scarce judicial resources by

[8] *Id.*

[9] *See, e.g.,* King v. Smith, 392 U.S. 309 (1968); Houghton v. Shafer, 392 U.S. 639 (1968); Damico v. California, 389 U.S. 416 (1967).

[10] 457 U.S. 496 (1982).

[11] *Id.* at 516.

[12] *Id.* at 503.

[13] *Id.* at 506.

[14] 42 U.S.C. §1997e. Under the statute, the exhaustion requirement is expressly limited to §1983 actions brought by an adult convicted of a crime. 42 U.S.C. §1997e(a)(1). The statute instructs the attorney general to "promulgate minimum standards for the development and implementation of a plain, speedy and effective system for the resolution of grievances of adults confined in any jail, prison, or other correctional facility." 42 U.S.C. §1997e(b)(1). A court may require exhaustion of administrative remedies only if "the Attorney General has certified or the court has determined that such administrative remedies are in substantial compliance" with the minimum standards created by the Act. 42 U.S.C. §1997e(a)(2). Also, before requiring exhaustion the court must determine that such an action would "be appropriate and in the interests of justice." 42 U.S.C. §1997e(a)(1). Finally, when this statute is applied, the court is not to dismiss the case, but instead to continue the case for no more than 90 days to permit use of the administrative mechanism. 42 U.S.C. §1997e(a)(1).

[15] 457 U.S. at 532 (Powell, J., dissenting).

screening out a large number of frivolous claims.[16] Ultimately, Justices Powell and Burger argued that an exhaustion requirement was "dictated in §1983 actions by common sense, as well as by comity and federalism."[17]

In *Knick v. Township of Scott, Pennsylvania,* the Court held that there is no need to exhaust state administrative or judicial remedies before bringing a takings claim under §1983.[18] Earlier the Court had ruled that takings claims were not ripe until compensation has been sought and denied through the available administrative procedures.[19]

But in *Knick,* the Court, 5-4, reversed these decisions and stated: "A property owner has an actionable Fifth Amendment takings claim when the government takes his property without paying for it."[20] The Court said that there was no reason to treat takings claims differently from other constitutional rights.

However, it should be noted that the Prison Litigation Reform Act (PLRA) created an exhaustion requirement before prisoners can bring lawsuits challenging prison conditions.[21] This is a significant statutory exception to the general rule that there is no requirement for exhaustion of administrative procedures before bringing a §1983 suit.

Indeed, the Supreme Court has enforced the exhaustion requirement of the PLRA strictly. In *Booth v. Churner,* the Court held that a prisoner seeking money damages must exhaust administrative proceedings even if they cannot award such damages, as long as they can provide something of value to the inmate.[22] In *Porter v. Nussle,* the Court held that an individual inmate complaining of excessive force by a guard must meet the exhaustion requirements of the PLRA.[23] In *Woodford v. Ngo,* the Court said that a suit by a prisoner must be dismissed if the inmate failed to exhaust administrative remedies even if none were available at the time the lawsuit was filed.[24] Together, these cases impose a stringent exhaustion requirement and reveal a Court committed to strictly enforcing it.

Relationship to Other Federal Jurisdiction Doctrines

The absence of an exhaustion requirement for §1983 suits has a close relationship to several other federal jurisdiction doctrines. First, cases such as *Monroe,*

[16] *Id.* at 534-535.

[17] *Id.* at 536.

[18] Knick v. Township of Scott, Pennsylvania, 588 U.S. 180 (2019); *see also* Pakdel v. City & Cty. of S.F., 594 U.S. 474, 475 (2021) ("exhaustion of state remedies is not a prerequisite to an action under 42 U.S.C. §1983."). In Williams v. Reed, 145 S.Ct. 465 (February 21, 2025), the Court again reaffirmed that there is no need to exhaust state administrative remedies before bringing a §1983 suit in state court.

Knick is discussed in §2.4 to its implications for ripeness.

[19] *See, e.g.,* San Remo Hotel v. City and County of San Francisco, 545 U.S. 323 (2005); Williamson County Regional Planning Commn. v. Hamilton Bank, 473 U.S. 172 (1984).

[20] 588 U.S. at 185.

[21] Pub. L. No. 104-134, 110 Stat. 1321 (1996).

[22] 532 U.S. 731 (2001).

[23] 534 U.S. 516 (2002).

[24] 548 U.S. 81 (2006).

McNeese, and *Patsy* only establish that §1983 plaintiffs are not required to use state administrative or judicial forums; the decisions do not preclude plaintiffs from presenting their claims in such tribunals. Federal courts do not have exclusive jurisdiction over §1983 claims.[25] Plaintiffs may present §1983 claims in state court and use other state administrative remedies, as well. However, as discussed in detail in §8.10, decisions by state courts and agencies likely will have preclusive res judicata and collateral estoppel effects in federal court.[26] In other words, by choosing to litigate in a state forum, the plaintiff essentially relinquishes access to the lower federal courts.

A second issue that is implicated by the no exhaustion rule in §1983 suits is its relationship to the Supreme Court's holding in *Parratt v. Taylor*.[27] As is discussed in detail in §8.9, in *Parratt* the Supreme Court held that a plaintiff does not allege a due process violation when the complaint seeks a post-deprivation remedy for the random and unauthorized deprivation of property by a government officer and the state provides an adequate post-deprivation remedy. In *Parratt*, the plaintiff, a state prisoner, sought damages for a hobby kit lost by prison authorities. The Court held that there was no denial of due process because the plaintiff was seeking only a damage remedy, which the state provided.

Parratt, however, should not be understood as imposing an exhaustion requirement. *Monroe* and its progeny hold that if the plaintiff presents a constitutional claim, state remedies need not be sought before initiating §1983 litigation. *Parratt* holds that under certain circumstances there is no claim of a constitutional violation because of the existence of adequate state remedies. Moreover, under *Parratt*, plaintiffs are consigned to state court proceedings when they seek post-deprivation remedies for the random and unauthorized deprivation of property by government officers. An unsuccessful state court plaintiff cannot go to federal court after exhausting the state appeals unless there is some claim that the state proceedings were themselves constitutionally inadequate. Although the reach of *Parratt* is uncertain,[28] the decision does not disturb the general rule: exhaustion of state judicial and administrative remedies is not a prerequisite to initiating a federal court §1983 suit.

Third, there is a tension between the no exhaustion rule for §1983 suits and the requirement that habeas corpus petitioners must exhaust all state appeals before securing review in federal court.[29] Until 1973, a state prisoner challenging the constitutionality of his or her confinement could bring a §1983 action for an injunction to obtain release, thereby avoiding the need to file a habeas corpus petition and circumventing the exhaustion requirement.

The Supreme Court resolved this issue in *Preiser v. Rodriguez* by holding that §1983 suits cannot be used by individuals seeking to end or shorten their

[25] *See, e.g.*, Maine v. Thiboutot, 448 U.S. 1, 10-11 (1980).

[26] *See, e.g.*, Migra v. Warren City Sch. Dist. Bd. of Educ., 465 U.S. 75 (1984); Allen v. McCurry, 449 U.S. 90 (1980); *see* discussion in §8.10, *infra*.

[27] 451 U.S. 527 (1981). *Parratt* is discussed more fully in §8.9, *infra*.

[28] *See* discussion in §8.9, *infra*.

[29] For a discussion of the exhaustion requirement in habeas corpus cases, *see* discussion in §15.4, *infra*.

confinement.[30] In *Preiser*, New York State prisoners sought concurrent §1983 and habeas actions for restoration of good time credits that they claimed were unconstitutionally revoked by state officials. The Court held that the prisoners' sole remedy was through habeas corpus: "[W]hen a state prisoner is challenging the very fact or duration of his physical imprisonment, and the relief he seeks is a determination that he is entitled to immediate release or a speedier release . . . his sole federal remedy is a writ of habeas corpus."[31] The Court emphasized that challenges to the *conditions* of confinement are actionable under §1983 without exhaustion of state remedies; it is only challenges seeking "immediate or more speedy release" that cannot be brought via §1983 litigation.[32]

Since *Preiser*, the Supreme Court has adhered to this distinction between suits seeking to remedy the conditions of confinement and litigation seeking to end or shorten the period of confinement. For example, in *Wolff v. McDonnell*, the Supreme Court concluded that state prisoners may bring an action for damages in federal court, without exhausting state remedies, for allegedly unconstitutional deprivation of good time credits.[33]

The Supreme Court has consistently held that inmates sentenced to death who are challenging the manner of their execution may bring §1983 suits. In *Nelson v. Campbell*, the Court unanimously held that an inmate could bring a §1983 action to challenge the procedure used for cutting veins to administer a lethal injection.[34] Similarly, in *Hill v. McDonough*, the Court ruled that an inmate facing death by lethal injection could bring a §1983 action to challenge the drugs that would be used as cruel and unusual punishment.[35] The Court reaffirmed this in *Nance v. Ward*.[36] In all of these cases, the Court emphasized that the inmate was not challenging the sentence itself, but rather the method of its being implemented.

An Additional Exhaustion Requirement: *Heck v. Humphrey* and *Edwards v. Balisok*

In *Heck v. Humphrey*, in 1994, the Supreme Court extended *Preiser* to create a new exhaustion requirement: to recover damages for an allegedly unconstitutional conviction or imprisonment, a plaintiff must first have the conviction or sentence reversed on appeal or expunged by executive pardon.[37]

In *Heck*, a state prison inmate who had been convicted of voluntary manslaughter and was serving a 15-year sentence brought a civil suit for money damages against the state prosecutor and police investigator for malicious prosecution. The plaintiff alleged that the defendants, while acting under color of state law,

[30] 411 U.S. 475 (1973).

[31] *Id.* at 500.

[32] *Id.* at 494. *See* Wilwording v. Swenson, 404 U.S. 249, 251 (1971); Houghton v. Shafer, 392 U.S. 639, 640 (1968).

[33] 418 U.S. 539 (1974).

[34] 541 U.S. 637 (2004).

[35] 547 U.S. 573 (2006).

[36] 597 U.S. 159, 165 (2022).

[37] 512 U.S. 477 (1994).

"had engaged in an 'unlawful, unreasonable, and arbitrary investigation' leading to petitioner's arrest; 'knowingly destroyed' evidence which was exculpatory in nature. . .; and caused 'an illegal and unlawful voice identification procedure' to be used at petitioner's trial."[38]

Because the plaintiff sought money damages and not a release from custody, *Preiser v. Rodriguez* was inapplicable. However, the Supreme Court nonetheless held that the suit was barred and announced a new rule of exhaustion in §1983 litigation. The Court held that "in order to recover damages for allegedly unconstitutional conviction or imprisonment, or for other harms caused by actions whose unlawfulness would render a conviction or sentence invalid, a §1983 plaintiff must prove that the conviction or sentence has been reversed on direct appeal, expunged by executive order, declared invalid by a state tribunal authorized to make such determination, or called into question by a federal court's issuance of a writ of habeas corpus."[39] Simply put, an individual convicted of a crime cannot bring a civil suit challenging the conviction until and unless it is overturned. This might be viewed as a rule of preclusion because the conviction has the effect of barring the subsequent litigation or as a rule of exhaustion in the sense that the §1983 suit cannot be brought unless and until challenges to the conviction are successfully exhausted.

In the *Edwards v. Balisok* decision, the Court extended *Heck* to lawsuits brought by inmates against prison officers.[40] Jerry Balisok was an inmate in a Washington prison serving a 20-year sentence for attempted murder. In 1993, while incarcerated, Balisok was charged with violating the prison's disciplinary code by blackmailing another inmate. After a hearing, Balisok was found guilty of the rule infractions. The sanctions included revocation of 30 days of good-time credits. Balisok unsuccessfully appealed the finding of misconduct to the prison warden.

Balisok then filed a §1983 suit for money damages against the hearing officer, Gary Edwards, contending that due process had been violated. Balisok often served as a jailhouse lawyer and helped other inmates with their suits against the prison, and he contended that in retaliation for this, Edwards refused to consider key evidence at the hearing. Balisok maintained that he was told at the time of the hearing that the inmate-witnesses that he wanted to testify had refused to provide statements or answer questions. Subsequently, he discovered that three statements were in his file. Although the hearing officer could preclude the statements from being used as evidence if they were not filed in a timely fashion, Balisok contended that they intentionally were not date-stamped. Balisok's amended complaint did not seek restoration of the good-time credits, but rather money damages for the alleged violation of his rights.

The Supreme Court unanimously held that Balisok's claim was not cognizable under §1983 until he first succeeded in having the good-time credits restored.[41]

[38] *Id.* at 479.

[39] *Id.* at 486-487.

[40] 520 U.S. 641 (1997).

[41] Justice Ginsburg, joined by Justices Souter and Breyer, wrote a short concurring opinion to emphasize that the Court's holding applies only to civil suits that "necessarily imply the invalidity of the punishment imposed." *Id.* at 650.

Balisok had argued that *Heck* was distinguishable, in part, because he was challenging the *procedures* followed and not the results of the hearing; in *Heck*, in contrast, the civil suit directly attacked the validity of the conviction. The Court was not persuaded by this distinction. Justice Scalia's majority opinion said that the argument was incorrect, "since it disregards the possibility, clearly envisioned by *Heck*, that the nature of the challenge to the procedures could be such as necessarily to imply the invalidity of the judgment."[42]

Justice Scalia explained that "[t]he principal procedural defect complained of by respondent would, if established, necessarily imply the invalidity of his good-time credits."[43] Thus, the Court concluded that the "claim for declaratory relief and money damages, based on allegations of deceit and bias on the part of the decision-maker that necessarily imply the invalidity of the punishment imposed is not cognizable under §1983."[44] In other words, a prison disciplinary proceeding revoking good-time credits precludes a civil suit for money damages based on a claim that the proceeding denied due process.

Although unanimous, *Edwards* raises serious concerns about the appropriate reach of *Heck v. Humphrey. Heck* was based on a desire to prevent individuals from collaterally attacking their convictions in civil suits. The Court justified its holding in *Heck* on the grounds that a key element in a civil suit for malicious prosecution "is termination of the prior criminal proceeding in favor of the accused."[45] Although the Court did not use the language of issue preclusion, that principle seems to underlie *Heck*. The Court said that a key issue, the validity of the conviction, was litigated and resolved in the earlier court proceeding and thus was taken as established for the civil suit. This issue negated a basic element of the civil cause of action and thus precluded relief.

However, *Edwards* was not a case about issue preclusion at all. The issue of whether the prison disciplinary proceeding violated due process had not ever been litigated. Nor had there ever been the opportunity to do so. Furthermore, Balisok was not seeking to collaterally attack the revocation of the good-time credits, but instead wanted damages for procedural violations. If the latter implied fundamental unfairness of the prison hearing, it is an even stronger reason for allowing §1983 relief.

In *Wilkinson v. Dotson*, the Court refused to extend *Heck* and *Edwards* to cases where inmates were challenging parole board determinations that they were not eligible for consideration for parole.[46] The Court explained that the prior decisions had focused "on the need to ensure that state prisoners use only habeas corpus (or similar state) remedies when they seek to invalidate the duration of their confinement—either *directly* through an injunction compelling speedier release or *indirectly* through a judicial determination that necessarily implies the

[42] *Id.* at 645.

[43] *Id.* at 646.

[44] *Id.* at 648.

[45] 512 U.S. at 484. In Spencer v. Kenna, 523 U.S. 1 (1998), five justices, though not in any single opinion, took the position that *Heck* and *Edwards* do not apply if the prisoner is no longer in custody. By this view, *Heck* and *Edwards* apply only when habeas corpus is available.

[46] 544 U.S. 74 (2005).

unlawfulness of the State's custody."[47] But in this case, the Court explained that the inmates were not seeking an injunction ordering immediate or speedier release. Rather, the Court said that they were just seeking to have their parole applications heard and thus were not barred by the principles of *Heck* and *Edwards*.

The Court also declined to apply *Heck* to bar a challenge to Texas refusing to allow a challenge to a denial of access to DNA testing by a person who was convicted of murder and sentenced to death. In *Skinner v. Switzer*, the Court said that *Heck* did not preclude the §1983 suit seeking access to biological evidence for the purpose of DNA testing.[48] The Court distinguished *Heck* and said: "Measured against our prior holdings, Skinner has properly invoked §1983. Success in his suit for DNA testing would not 'necessarily imply' the invalidity of his conviction. While test results might prove exculpatory, that outcome is hardly inevitable; as earlier observed, results might prove inconclusive or they might further incriminate Skinner."[49]

State and local officials are likely to try to use *Heck* and *Edwards* to preclude many §1983 claims.[50] For example, there is now a split between the circuits as to whether *Heck* applies in suits for excessive force against police officers when brought by individuals who have been convicted.[51] However, *Heck* would not seem to apply to such claims: whether the police used excessive force is completely distinct from whether the defendant committed the crime.

§8.5 WHO IS A "PERSON" FOR PURPOSES OF §1983 LIABILITY? MUNICIPAL GOVERNMENTS; SUPERVISORY LIABILITY

§8.5.1 Are Municipalities "Persons" and, If So, When are They Liable?

Because municipalities provide important basic government services—police, fire, education, sanitation—there is substantial opportunity for local governments to violate federal law. Hence, a question of major importance is whether local governments are liable under §1983.

[47] *Id.* at 81.

[48] 562 U.S. 521 (2011).

[49] *Id.* at 534.

[50] *See, e.g.*, Morgan v. Schott, 914 F.3d 1115 (7th Cir. 2019) (ruling that *Edwards* and *Heck* barred prisoners' due process claim against prison disciplinary hearing); Smith v. Hood, 900 F.3d 180 (5th Cir. 2018) (holding that *Heck* does not apply to challenging condition of confinement); Wilson v. Ill. Dep't of Fin. and Prof'l Regulation, 871 F.3d 509 (7th Cir. 2017) (holding that *Heck* did not extend to state administrative proceedings); Clay v. Allen, 242 F.3d 679 (5th Cir. 2001) (*Heck* does not apply to claim that court clerk and court reporter conspired to tamper with court documents); Moore v. Sims, 200 F.3d 1170 (8th Cir. 2000) (*Heck* does not apply to claim of illegal detention and search without probable cause).

[51] *Compare* Aucoin v. Cupil, 958 F.3d 379 (5th Cir. 2020) (ruling that *Heck* did not bar an excessive force claim); Schreiber v. Moe, 596 F.3d 323 (6th Cir. 2010) (*Heck* does not bar an excessive force claim), *with* O'Brien v. Town of Bellingham, 943 F.3d 514 (1st Cir. 2019) (holding that *Heck* barred an excessive force claim); Connors v. Graves, 538 F.3d 373 (5th Cir. 2008) (*Heck* bars excessive force claim).

Monroe: No Municipal Liability

In 1961, in *Monroe v. Pape*, the Supreme Court held that municipal governments may not be sued under §1983.[1] In *Monroe*, the plaintiffs sought damages for allegedly unconstitutional police conduct from both individual officers and from their employer, the city of Chicago. Although the Court upheld the potential liability of the officers,[2] it concluded that "Congress did not undertake to bring municipal corporations within the ambit of [§1983]."[3]

The *Monroe* Court based this conclusion on its reading of the legislative history of §1983. When the statute that contained §1983 was debated before the Senate, Senator Sherman of Ohio proposed an amendment that would have created municipal liability for certain acts of violence occurring within their borders. Essentially, the Sherman Amendment would have imposed strict liability on cities for specified violent acts, even though the city and its officials did not participate and were not directly responsible. The apparent objective of the Sherman Amendment was to overcome municipal inaction in the face of widespread Klan activities by giving cities a powerful monetary incentive to prevent violence. Although the Senate approved the Sherman Amendment, the House rejected it and it was deleted in a Conference Committee.[4]

Justice Douglas, writing for the majority in *Monroe*, concluded that the rejection of the Sherman Amendment reflected a desire to immunize cities from liability. Furthermore, the Court rejected the argument that the Dictionary Act, which defined "person" to include "bodies politic and corporate," was a basis for holding cities liable.[5] Justice Douglas concluded that the definition in the Dictionary Act was "merely an allowable, not a mandatory one."[6] Thus, the *Monroe* Court precluded all municipal liability under §1983, whether for damages or equitable relief.[7]

In the years following *Monroe*, its review of §1983's legislative history was subjected to sharp criticism.[8] Additionally, lower courts developed techniques for circumventing *Monroe*'s holding and creating municipal liability for constitutional violations. For example, lower courts permitted liability based on other civil rights

§8.5 [1] 365 U.S. 167 (1961).

[2] *See* discussion in §8.3, *supra* (describing *Monroe*'s holding concerning the liability of individual officers).

[3] 365 U.S. at 187.

[4] *Id.* at 188.

[5] Act of Feb. 25, 1871, §2, 16 Stat. 431. The Dictionary Act was enacted a few months before the Civil Rights Act of 1871, which contained §1983.

[6] 365 U.S. at 191.

[7] *See* City of Kenosha v. Bruno, 412 U.S. 507 (1973) (equitable relief not allowed); Moor v. County of Alameda, 411 U.S. 693 (1973) (monetary relief not allowed); *see also* Aldinger v. Howard, 427 U.S. 1 (1976) (pendent party jurisdiction could not be the basis for §1983 suits in federal court against municipalities).

[8] *See, e.g.,* Ronald M. Levin, The Section 1983 Municipal Immunity Doctrine, 65 Geo. L.J. 1483 (1977); Don B. Kates & J. Anthony Kouba, Liability of Public Entities Under Section 1983 of the Civil Rights Act, 45 S. Cal. L. Rev. 131 (1972).

laws,[9] and some courts allowed suits against cities based on causes of action inferred directly from the Constitution.[10]

Monell v. Department of Social Services: Yes Municipal Liability

In 1978, in the landmark decision of *Monell v. Department of Social Services*, the Supreme Court expressly overruled *Monroe*'s limitation on municipal liability.[11] *Monell* involved a suit against the city of New York challenging a policy requiring pregnant teachers to take unpaid leaves of absences. The Supreme Court again reviewed the legislative history of §1983 and concluded that it had erred in preventing municipal liability. Justice Brennan, writing for the majority, stated that the rejection of the Sherman Amendment was meant to prevent municipal liability for the wrongful acts of others; it was not intended to preclude municipalities from being held liable for their own violations of the Fourteenth Amendment.[12] The Sherman Amendment would have created an affirmative duty on cities to stop violence within their borders; its defeat was meant to prevent new liability from being created, not to totally immunize cities. Furthermore, the Court emphasized that the Dictionary Act of 1871, enacted only months before the Civil Rights Act containing §1983, defined "persons" to include "bodies politic and corporate."[13]

Thus, the *Monell* Court declared that "Congress *did* intend municipalities and other local government units to be included among those persons to whom §1983 applies."[14] However, the Court imposed a substantial limitation on this liability: municipal governments may be sued only for their own unconstitutional or illegal policies. Municipalities may not be sued for the acts of their employees. The Court stated:

> [T]he language of §1983, read against the background of the same legislative history, compels the conclusion that Congress did not intend municipalities to be held liable unless action pursuant to official municipal policy of some nature caused a constitutional tort. In particular, we conclude that a municipality cannot be held liable *solely* because it employs a tortfeasor—or, in other words, a municipality cannot be held liable under §1983 on a *respondeat superior* theory.[15]

In limiting municipal liability to instances of official policy or custom, the Court focused on the language of §1983, which specifies: "Every person who . . . subjects or causes to be subjected, any citizen . . . to the deprivation of any rights, privileges, or immunities." The Court concluded that this language meant that cities

[9] *See, e.g.,* Mahone v. Waddle, 564 F.2d 1018 (3d Cir. 1977), *cert. denied,* 438 U.S. 904 (1978) (using §1981 to create liability for racial discrimination by police officers).

[10] *See, e.g.,* Hanna v. Drobnick, 514 F.2d 393 (6th Cir. 1975); *but see* Cale v. City of Covington, 586 F.2d 311 (4th Cir. 1978).

[11] 436 U.S 658 (1978).

[12] *Id.* at 683.

[13] *Id.* at 688-689.

[14] *Id.* at 690 (emphasis included).

[15] *Id.* at 691 (emphasis included).

only could be held responsible for the actions they caused. Additionally, the Court said that although respondeat superior liability might deter wrongdoing or spread costs among the larger community, the rejection of the Sherman Amendment properly should be understood as a repudiation of deterrence and risk spreading as the goals for §1983.[16] Thus, the *Monell* Court's holding was clear: "[A] local government may not be sued under §1983 for an injury inflicted solely by its employees or agents. Instead it is when execution of a government's policy or custom, whether made by its lawmakers or by those whose edicts or acts may fairly be said to represent official policy, inflicts the injury that the government as an entity is responsible under §1983."[17]

The Court also has held that the requirement for proof of municipal policy applies in all suits against local governments, whether they are for money or for injunctive or declaratory relief. In *Los Angeles County, California v. Humphries*, the Court unanimously concluded: "The language of §1983 read in light of *Monell*'s understanding of the legislative history explains why claims for prospective relief, like claims for money damages, fall within the scope of the 'policy or custom' requirement. Nothing in the text of §1983 suggests that the causation requirement contained in the statute should change with the form of relief sought."[18]

Criticisms of the *Monell* Decision

The *Monell* Court's conclusion and reasoning have been criticized both by those who disagree with its overruling of *Monroe* and by those who would prefer more expansive municipal liability. On the one hand, the dissent argued that there was not adequate justification for overruling *Monroe*'s interpretation of §1983's legislative history.[19] Justice Rehnquist argued that in light of Congress's failure to amend §1983 after *Monroe*, the Court should overrule *Monroe* only if it was clear "beyond doubt" that the earlier Court made a mistake in reading the legislative history.[20] Justice Rehnquist argued that, at most, there were differing interpretations of an unclear record; there was not evidence that the Court had erred in its earlier interpretation of the legislative history. Ultimately, the underlying issue dividing the dissent and the majority concerned the role of precedent and when it is appropriate for a later Court to overrule an earlier decision based on a differing view of a statute's purpose.

On the other hand, limiting municipal liability to official policies also has been criticized.[21] The Court in *Monell* employed exactly the same distinction that it

[16] *Id.* at 693-694.

[17] *Id.* at 694.

[18] 562 U.S. 29, 37 (2010).

[19] 436 U.S. at 714 (Rehnquist, J., dissenting).

[20] *Id.* at 724.

[21] *See, e.g.,* David Jacks Achtenberg, Taking History Seriously: Municipal Liability Under 42 U.S.C. §1983 and the Debate over Respondeat Superior, 73 Fordham L. Rev. 2183 (2005); Karen M. Blum, From *Monroe* to *Monell*: Defining the Scope of Municipal Liability in Federal Courts, 51 Temp. L.Q. 409 (1978); Christina B. Whitman, Government Responsibility for Constitutional Torts, 85 Mich. L. Rev. 225, 236 n.43 (1986).

had rejected in *Monroe* in interpreting the meaning of "under color of law": the distinction between unauthorized acts and official policies. Furthermore, the Court's rejection of the deterrence and risk-spreading arguments for broader liability is especially subject to criticism. In *Monell*, the Court concluded that although deterrence and risk spreading would be served by allowing respondeat superior liability, the defeat of the Sherman Amendment evidences a rejection of these policies. However, the defeat of the Sherman Amendment, as the *Monell* Court noted, only was a refusal to create an affirmative duty for cities to keep the peace by making them monetarily liable for the actions of private citizens. Just because deterrence and risk spreading were not accepted as sufficient to justify municipal liability for private actions does not mean that deterrence and risk spreading were completely repudiated as underlying objectives of §1983. In fact, two years after *Monell*, the Court held that municipalities do not have good-faith immunity under §1983 because such immunity would frustrate the objectives of deterrence and risk spreading.[22]

Justice Breyer, in a dissenting opinion joined by Justices Stevens and Ginsburg, sharply criticized *Monell* and declared that the "case for reexamination is a strong one."[23] Justice Breyer argued that neither the language of §1983 nor its legislative history supports *Monell's* preclusion of vicarious liability.[24] Moreover, Justice Breyer stated, "*Monell's* basic effort to distinguish between vicarious liability and liability derived from 'policy or custom' has produced a body of liability and liability derived from 'policy or custom' that is neither readily understandable nor easy to apply."[25] Justice Breyer also argued that "relevant legal and factual circumstances may have changed in a way that affects likely reliance upon *Monell's* liability limitation. The legal complexity . . . makes it difficult for municipalities to predict just when they will be held liable for policy or custom."[26]

[22] Owen v. City of Independence, 445 U.S. 622 (1980); *see* discussion in §8.5.3, *infra*. For a criticism of the argument that liability of local governments deters misconduct, *see* Daryl Levinson, In Making Government Pay: Markets, Politics, and the Allocation of Constitutional Costs, 67 U. Chi. L. Rev. 345 (2000); *but see* Myriam E. Gilles, In Defense of Making Government Pay: The Deterrent Effect of Constitutional Tort Remedies, 35 Ga. L. Rev. 845 (2001). Professor Joanna Schwartz has made the point that police officers are virtually always indemnified by the government entity and this decreases the deterrent effect of damage judgments. Joanna C. Schwartz, Police Indemnification, 89 N.Y.U. L. Rev. 895 (2014) ("During the study period, governments paid approximately 99.98% of the dollars that plaintiffs recovered in lawsuits alleging civil rights violations by law enforcement. Law enforcement officers in my study never satisfied a punitive damages award entered against them and almost never contributed anything to settlements or judgments—even when indemnification was prohibited by law or policy, and even when officers were disciplined, terminated, or prosecuted for their conduct.").

[23] Board of the County Commissioners of Bryan County v. Brown, 520 U.S. 397, 437 (1997) (Breyer, J., dissenting).

[24] *Id.* at 431-433.

[25] *Id.* at 433.

[26] *Id.* at 436.

Unresolved Issues

Monell left unresolved three important questions that are considered in the next two sections: How is a municipal policy or custom proven, do municipalities have a good-faith defense to liability, and are municipalities liable for punitive damages in suits under §1983?

§8.5.2 How is the Existence of an Official Municipal Policy Proven?

Monell is clear in its holding that cities are liable only for constitutional violations resulting from their official policies and customs. *Monell*, however, does not say much about what must be demonstrated to establish the existence of a municipal policy or custom. Although the Supreme Court has clarified this issue somewhat since *Monell*, many major questions remain unresolved. The question is when a municipality can be deemed to have "subject[ed] or cause[d] to be subjected" a person to a violation of his or her constitutional rights.

Actions of Municipal Legislative Bodies

After *Monell*, there are at least five possible ways to establish the existence of a policy or custom sufficient to impose §1983 liability on a municipal government. First, and most obviously, actions by the municipal legislative body constitute official policies. As the Supreme Court observed in *Pembaur v. City of Cincinnati*, "No one has ever doubted . . . that a municipality may be liable under §1983 for a single decision by its properly constituted legislative body—whether or not that body had taken similar action in the past or intended to do so in the future—because even a single decision by such a body unquestionably constitutes an act of official government policy."[27] Thus, a city council's firing of a government official without providing procedural due process[28] and a city council's cancellation of a concert in violation of the First Amendment were properly the basis for §1983 liability.[29]

Agencies Exercising Delegated Authority

Second, official policy exists when there are actions by municipal agencies or boards that exercise authority delegated by the municipal legislative body. In *Monell*, for example, the plaintiffs challenged regulations adopted by the Department of Social Services and the Board of Education requiring pregnant employees to take unpaid leaves of absence.[30] The Court found that actions of these agencies "unquestionably involve[] official policy."[31]

[27] 475 U.S. 469, 480 (1986).
[28] Owen v. City of Independence, 445 U.S. 622 (1980).
[29] City of Newport v. Fact Concerts, 453 U.S. 247 (1981).
[30] Monell v. Department of Social Servs., 436 U.S. 658, 661 (1978).
[31] *Id.* at 694.

Individuals with Final Decision-Making Authority

Third, actions by those with final authority for making a decision in the municipality constitute official policy for purposes of §1983. In *Pembaur v. City of Cincinnati*, the Court held that an order by a prosecutor to break down a doctor's door constituted the city's official policy.[32] In *Pembaur*, police officers who were frustrated in trying to serve subpoenas called an assistant prosecutor for further instructions. The assistant prosecutor conferred with the county prosecutor, who issued instructions "to go in and get [the witnesses]."[33] The police then obtained an axe and chopped down the door, which was the basis for the subsequent §1983 suit.

The Supreme Court held that "municipal liability under §1983 attaches where—and only where—a deliberate choice to follow a course of action is made from among various alternatives by the official or officials responsible for establishing final policy with respect to the subject matter in question."[34] In other words, the Court reasoned that municipal liability could not be imposed merely because an employee had discretion in the discharge of his or her duties. An official must "be responsible for establishing final government policy" for municipal liability to attach to his or her decision.[35] Such authority could be granted legislatively or be delegated from higher officials. Its existence is a question of state law. Based on the relevant Ohio law, the Court concluded that the prosecutor had authority for making the final decision and, hence, his decision constituted the city's official policy.

In *City of St. Louis v. Praprotnik*, a plurality of the Supreme Court concluded that the determination of whether a person has final decision-making authority in a particular area is a question of state law for the judge to decide, not a question of fact for the jury to resolve.[36] In *Jett v. Dallas Independent School District*, a majority of the Court endorsed the position taken by the plurality in *Praprotnik* and held that the determination of who has final decision-making authority is to be based on state law.[37]

Jett involved claims brought by a former high school football coach against a city for alleged racial discrimination.[38] The Court stated that the question of whether a person has final decision-making authority is "a legal question to be resolved by the trial judge *before* the case is submitted to the jury."[39] In determining which individuals have final decision-making authority for a city, courts can consider state and local laws and "custom or usage having the force of law."[40] Once

[32] 475 U.S. 469 (1986).

[33] *Id.* at 473.

[34] *Id.* at 483-484.

[35] *Id.* at 483.

[36] 485 U.S. 112 (1988).

[37] 491 U.S. 701 (1989).

[38] The football coach sued under both §1981 and §1983. The Court rejected the claim under §1981 and held that §1983 "provides the exclusive federal damage remedy for the violation of rights guaranteed by §1983 when the claim is pressed against a state actor." *Id.* at 735.

[39] *Id.* at 737 (emphasis in original).

[40] *Id. See, e.g.*, Bellamy v. City of New York, 914 F.3d 727 (2d Cir. 2019) (ruling that New York City was the final policymaking authority citing that "New York appellate courts have expressly affirmed our conclusions"); Hunter v. Town of Mocksville, N.C., 897 F.3d 538 (4th Cir. 2018) (holding, by

the court has identified the policymakers in a specific area, "it is for the jury to determine whether *their* decisions have caused the deprivation of rights at issue by policies which command that it occur . . . or by acquiescence in a long-standing practice or custom which constitutes the standard operating procedure of the local government entity."[41]

Pembaur, Praprotnik, and *Jett* clearly establish that decisions by individuals with final decision-making authority establish municipal policy and that the scope of an officer's authority is to be determined by state and local law. Subsequently, the Court applied this rule and interpreted a state's law to deem a county official to be a state officer and his acts therefore not a basis for local government liability. In *McMillian v. Monroe County, Alabama,* the Court held that a county sheriff in Alabama is a state official, not a local official, and therefore is not a final decision maker for the local government.[42]

Walter McMillian was convicted of murder and spent six years on death row in Alabama. After the Alabama Supreme Court reversed his conviction and ordered his release, McMillian brought a §1983 action against the county and county sheriff alleging that his constitutional rights were violated by the sheriff's intimidating witnesses into making false statements and by suppressing exculpatory evidence. McMillian claimed that the county was liable because the sheriff had final decision-making authority for the acts taken.

The Supreme Court, in a 5-4 decision, ruled that under Alabama law, the county sheriff was acting as a state official and thus was not a policymaker for the county. In Alabama, the sheriff is elected locally by the voters in each county and is paid and equipped with county funds. Moreover, the sheriff's authority exists only within the borders of the county. Nonetheless, the Court affirmed the Eleventh Circuit's holding that under Alabama law, "a sheriff acting in his law enforcement capacity is not a policymaker for the county."[43]

Chief Justice Rehnquist, writing for the Court, stressed that the Alabama Constitution designates the sheriff as exercising the executive power of the state.[44] Additionally, the sheriff enforces state law and can be removed from office only by the Alabama Supreme Court.[45] The Court concluded that "Alabama sheriffs, when

---

examining town ordinances, that the town manager was the final policymaking authority manager); McGreevy v. Stroup, 413 F.3d 359, 368 (3d Cir. 2005) ("[T]he fact that the Pennsylvania Code provides that the school board is the final policymaker regarding dismissal of employees does not mean that a school board action is a prerequisite for imposition of liability on the district."); Mandel v. Doe, 888 F.2d 783, 793 (11th Cir. 1989) (After *Jett,* the determination of who is a policymaker for the city looks "not only [at] the relevant positive law, . . . but also the relevant customs and practices having the force of law."). There is a tension inherent in this standard. Determining whether there is a custom is likely a factual question, yet the Supreme Court has ruled that determining whether a particular individual has final decision-making authority is a question of law.

[41] 491 U.S. at 737 (emphasis in original) (citations omitted).

[42] 520 U.S. 781 (1997).

[43] *Id.* at 784.

[44] *Id.* at 788.

[45] *Id.*

executing their law enforcement duties, represent the State of Alabama, not their counties."[46]

McMillian appears to be a narrow decision based on the Court's interpretation of Alabama law, but its implications may be much broader. First, the Court's reasoning is likely to mean that county sheriffs in many other states are not municipal policymakers. As in Alabama, it is common in other places for sheriffs to be elected and paid by the county but be responsible for enforcing state law and thus to exercise state executive power.[47] Second, other county officials besides sheriffs, such as coroners and educators, might be regarded as state officers under *McMillian* because they implement state law and are regarded as carrying out state policy. Finally, deeming a county official to be a state officer has very significant procedural implications for a suit in federal court because it means that the Eleventh Amendment, and all of its restrictions, applies.[48] For instance, state officers, unlike local government officials, cannot be sued in federal court on supplemental state law claims.[49] Perhaps *McMillian* will be limited to Alabama sheriffs, but it seems more likely that it will have much broader implications.

Even after the four major Supreme Court cases concerning municipal liability for acts by those with final decision-making authority, much remains unclear as to which municipal officials should be deemed to possess final decision-making authority. Lower courts are struggling with this issue. Many lower courts have emphasized whether the particular city official is responsible for making the ultimate decision, in which case it constitutes municipal policy, or whether the decision is subject to review, in which case it cannot be the basis for city liability.[50]

[46] *Id.* at 792.

[47] *See, e.g.*, Couser v. Gay, 959 F.3d 1018 (10th Cir. 2020) (ruling that Kansas sheriffs are county officials); United States v. County of Maricopa, Ariz., 889 F.3d 648 (9th Cir. 2018) (ruling that Arizona sheriffs are county officials); Dean v. County of Gage, Neb., 807 F.3d 931 (8th Cir. 2015) (holding that Nebraska sheriffs are county officials); Jones v. Hamilton County Sheriff, 838 F.3d 782 (6th Cir. 2016) (ruling that sheriff was a state official while transporting arrestee); Mercado v. Dart, 604 F.3d 360 (7th Cir. 2010) (sheriff in Illinois is not a state official); Huminski v. Corsones, 396 F.3d 53 (2d Cir. 2005) (county sheriff in Vermont is a state official); Abusaid v. Hillsborough County Bd. of County Commissioners, 405 F.3d 1298 (11th Cir. 2005) (Florida sheriff acts for the county and is not an arm of the state); Johnson v. Karnes, 398 F.3d 868 (6th Cir. 2005) (a suit against a sheriff in Kentucky is a suit against a local government); *cf.* Venegas v. County of Los Angeles, 32 Cal. 4th 820 (2004) (county sheriff is a state official in California), *with* Brewster v. Shasta County, 275 F.3d 803 (9th Cir. 2004) (county sheriff is a local official in California).

[48] The Eleventh Amendment is discussed in detail in Chapter 7.

[49] Pennhurst State School & Hospital v. Halderman, 465 U.S. 89 (1984), discussed in §7.5; Candillo v. North Carolina Dept. of Corrections, 199 F. Supp. 342 (M.D.N.C. 2002) (head of department of corrections not final decision maker because she "did not make the decision alone").

[50] *See, e.g.*, B.S. v. Somerset County, 704 F.3d 250, 275 n.36 (3d Cir. 2013); Atkinson v. City of Mountain View, Mo., 709 F.3d 1201 (8th Cir. 2013) (ruling that the sheriff was not the final decision maker because Missouri law stipulated that the mayor and the board were the final policy makers); Bolton v. City of Dallas, Tex., 541 F.3d 545 (5th Cir. 2008) (holding that the city manager was not the final policymaker for terminating police chief); Auriemma v. Rice, 957 F.2d 397, 401 (7th Cir. 1992) (holding that the Chicago Superintendent of Police is not a final decision-maker because he or she has "no power to countermand the statutes regulating the operation of the department"); Greensboro Professional Fire Fighters Assn., Local 3157 v. City of Greensboro, 64 F.3d 962, 965-966 (4th Cir. 1995) (fire chief not a final decision maker); Riddick v. School Board of Portsmouth, 238 F.3d

For example, in *Vodak v. City of Chicago*, the Seventh Circuit found that the superintendent was the final decision-making authority with regards to an event because the "police superintendent ha[d] sole responsibility to make policy regarding control of demonstrations."[51] In *Dean v. County of Gage, Nebraska*, the Eighth Circuit held that the county sheriff had final decision-making authority with regard to law enforcement and investigations in the county.[52] In *Hunter v. Town of Mocksville, North Carolina*, the Fourth Circuit concluded that, for firing plaintiffs, the town manager was the final policymaker as the Town Board had conferred on her "unfettered final policymaking authority with respect to almost all personnel matters."[53] In each instance, the court emphasized the finality of the officials' decisions.

In contrast, in *Webb v. Town of Saint Joseph*, the Fifth Circuit found that the Town Attorney, despite the Mayor giving him "decision-making authority," was not the final policymaker.[54] In *Brown v. Sessoms*, the D.C. Circuit found a university's Board of Trustees was not the final decision-maker, as D.C. code vested this power in the university president.[55] In *Walden v. City of Providence, Rhode Island*, the First Circuit held that the director of communications, despite having the ability to "influence general substantive parameters," was not the final decision-maker for a program that recorded phone calls because the City Charter made clear that authority lay elsewhere.[56] In *Riddick v. School Board of Portsmouth*, the Fourth Circuit said that the school board and not the superintendent had final policymaking authority over personnel decisions.[57]

The Tenth Circuit, after examining the many cases considering when an official has final decision-making authority, observed: "[W]e can identify three elements that help determine whether an individual is a 'final policymaker': (1) whether the official is meaningfully constrained by policies not of that official's own making; (2) whether the official's decisions are final—i.e., are they subject to any meaningful review; and (3) whether the policy decision purportedly made by the official is within the realm of the official's grant of authority."[58]

Although the Tenth Circuit's summary is accurate and useful, no formula or simple test is likely to be developed. The crucial question in determining whether an official has final decision-making authority is whether under state or local law, including relevant customs or practices, the person has policymaking authority for the city.[59]

---

518 (4th Cir. 2000) (school board, not principal, had final authority over personnel decisions); Soto v. Schembri, 960 F. Supp. 751 (S.D.N.Y. 1997) (the mayor of the City of New York, the city council, and the personnel director are the final decision-makers in personnel decisions, not the heads of agencies).

[51] 639 F.3d 738, 748 (7th Cir. 2011).

[52] 807 F.3d 931 (8th Cir. 2015).

[53] 897 F.3d 538, 561 (4th Cir. 2018).

[54] 925 F.3d 209, 217 (5th Cir. 2019).

[55] 774 F.3d 1016 (D.C. Cir. 2014).

[56] 596 F.3d 38, 56-58 (1st Cir. 2010).

[57] 238 F.3d 518 (4th Cir. 2000).

[58] Randle v. City of Aurora, 69 F.3d 441, 448 (10th Cir. 1995).

[59] *See* Steven Stein Cushman, Municipal Liability Under §1983: Toward a New Definition of Municipal Policymaker, 34 B.C. L. Rev. 693 (1993) (arguing for expanded liability for local governments based on acts of officials).

Policy of Inadequate Training or Supervision

A fourth way of demonstrating an official policy is by establishing a government policy of inadequate training or supervision. When, if at all, is the failure to train officers adequately, or the lack of supervision, or the failure to respond to complaints a municipal policy?

The first Supreme Court case dealing with establishing policy on the basis of government inaction was *City of Oklahoma City v. Tuttle.*[60] In *Tuttle,* an individual was shot and killed by the police; his family sued, claiming that the officer's excessive use of force was caused by a municipal policy of inadequate training of officers. The Supreme Court, in a plurality opinion written by Justice Rehnquist, stated that the district court erred in its instructions to the jury, which allowed a finding that there was a policy of inadequate training on the basis of the one incident. Thus, *Tuttle* resolves relatively little about when there can be a policy based on government inaction; it simply holds that one instance is an insufficient basis for inferring the existence of a policy.[61]

In *City of Canton, Ohio v. Harris,* the Supreme Court resolved the uncertainty as to the legal standard and held that demonstrating a policy of inadequate training requires proof of deliberate indifference by the local government.[62] The plaintiff, Geraldine Harris, claimed she had been injured by the failure of the city to instruct police officers to recognize medical ailments and to summon treatment. She was ill at the police station following her arrest, but the officers did not provide or summon any medical assistance.

The Supreme Court rejected the municipality's contention that §1983 liability can be imposed only where the municipal policy in question is itself unconstitutional.[63] A municipal policy that causes constitutional violations can be the basis for §1983 liability. Furthermore, the Court held that "the inadequacy of police training may serve as the basis for §1983 liability only where the failure to train amounts to deliberate indifference to the rights of persons with whom the police come into contact."[64] The Court declared: "Only where a failure to train reflects a 'deliberate' or 'conscious' choice by a municipality—a policy as defined by our prior cases—can a city be liable for such a failure under section 1983."[65]

The Court indicated at least two types of situations that would justify a conclusion of deliberate indifference in the failure to train police officers. One is failure to provide adequate training in light of foreseeable serious consequences that could result from the lack of instruction. For example, the Court indicated that

[60] 471 U.S. 808 (1985).

[61] Justice Rehnquist's opinion suggested another limit in establishing a municipal policy establishing liability under §1983: that the municipal policy must itself be unconstitutional. 471 U.S. at 824. Justice Brennan, concurring in the judgment, disagreed and contended that it is sufficient that the municipality's policy caused the unconstitutional actions. *Id.* at 832.

[62] 489 U.S. 378 (1989).

[63] *Id.* at 387.

[64] *Id.* at 388.

[65] *Id.* at 389.

lack of instruction in the use of firearms or in the use of deadly force could constitute "deliberate indifference."[66] A second type of situation justifying a conclusion of deliberate indifference is where the city fails to act in response to repeated complaints of constitutional violations by its officers.[67]

In its most important ruling since *Canton*, in *Board of County Commissioners of Bryan County, Oklahoma v. Brown*,[68] the Supreme Court made it significantly more difficult to prove municipal policy based on deliberate indifference. In *Brown*, the Court ruled that a county's liability was not established by proving that its sheriff acted improperly in hiring a deputy with a criminal record. The Bryan County sheriff hired his nephew's son as a deputy without adequately reviewing the individual's criminal record, which included driving infractions and guilty pleas for misdemeanors such as assault and battery, resisting arrest, and public drunkenness.[69] After a high-speed chase, the deputy violently pulled a woman, Jill Brown, from the automobile where she was a passenger and caused serious and permanent damage to her knees.

Justice O'Connor wrote for the Court in a 5-4 decision and said that there was not sufficient proof that the local government caused the injuries to Jill Brown. O'Connor explained that "[w]here a plaintiff claims that the municipality has not directly inflicted an injury, but nonetheless has caused an employee to do so, rigorous standards of culpability and causation must be applied to ensure that the municipality is not held liable solely for the actions of its employees."[70]

The Court concluded that the single instance of inadequate screening was not sufficient to prove that the municipality caused the injuries. The Court said that "a finding of culpability simply cannot depend on the mere probability that any officer inadequately screened will inflict constitutional injury. Rather, it must depend on a finding that this officer was highly likely to inflict the particular injury suffered by the plaintiff. The connection between the background of the particular applicant and the specific constitutional violation must be strong."[71] Justice O'Connor's majority opinion said that federalism concerns required that rigorous causation requirements be applied before creating municipal liability. The Court concluded that "Bryan County is not liable for Sheriff Moore's isolated decision to hire Burns without adequate screening, because respondent has not demonstrated that his decision reflected a conscious disregard for a high risk that Burns would use excessive force in violation of respondent's federally protected right."[72]

[66] *Id.* at 390; *see also* 489 U.S. at 398 (O'Connor, J., concurring in part and dissenting in part).

[67] The Supreme Court has indicated, in dicta, that the deliberate indifference test under *Canton* is objective, not subjective. In Farmer v. Brennan, 511 U.S. 825, 840 (1994), the Court, in setting forth a subjective test for deliberate indifference for the cruel and unusual punishment clause of the Eighth Amendment, contrasted *Canton* and said: "It would be hard to describe the *Canton* understanding of deliberate indifference, permitting liability to be premised on obviousness or constructive notice, as anything but objective."

[68] 520 U.S. 397 (1997).

[69] *Id.* at 400.

[70] *Id.* at 405.

[71] *Id.* at 412.

[72] *Id.* at 415.

The Court's decision is troubling because the jury had found that the sheriff's deliberate indifference in hiring caused the injuries to Brown. The jury's decision was supported by the record: failing to review a prospective deputy's criminal records risks hiring violent individuals who can cause great harm. It is unclear how much worse the criminal record would have needed to be for the Supreme Court to allow the verdict of liability to stand. *Brown* articulates a heightened requirement for causation but does not define it with any precision. After *Brown,* it is unclear as to how much evidence there must be to support a jury's verdict finding causation, but it is clear that the Court sees it as a legal question to be vigilantly monitored by the appellate courts. After *Brown,* it will be very difficult to establish municipal liability based on inadequacies in the hiring process.[73]

Subsequent to *Brown,* the Supreme Court held that deliberate indifference sufficient to establish municipal liability rarely can be found on the basis of a single incident. In *Connick v. Thompson,*[74] the Court held that a local government could not be held liable for a failure to train its prosecutors to comply with their constitutional obligation to turn over potentially exculpatory evidence to criminal defendants. Thompson spent 18 years in prison, most of them on death row, for murder. At his trial, the prosecutors failed to disclose key blood evidence to the defense as clearly required by *Brady v. Maryland.*[75] After the *Brady* violation was discovered, Thompson was retried and acquitted. He sued, claiming that the local district attorney's office was "deliberately indifferent" to its obligations to adequately train its attorneys to comply with *Brady* and thus liable. The jury ruled in favor of Thompson and awarded him $14 million in damages.

The Supreme Court, in a 5-4 decision, reversed. Justice Thomas wrote for the Court and explained that "[a] pattern of similar constitutional violations by untrained employees is 'ordinarily necessary' to demonstrate deliberate indifference for purposes of failure to train."[76] He said that although a single incident can in unusual circumstances establish a policy, that was not present in this case: "In *Canton,* the Court left open the possibility that, 'in a narrow range of circumstances,' a pattern of similar violations might not be necessary to show deliberate indifference. . . . Failure to train prosecutors in their *Brady* obligations does not fall within the narrow range of *Canton*'s hypothesized single-incident liability. The obvious need for specific legal training that was present in the *Canton* scenario is absent here."[77]

Justice Ginsburg, in a dissent joined by Justices Breyer, Sotomayor, and Kagan, vehemently disagreed with the majority's conclusion. She said: "What happened here, the Court's opinion obscures, was no momentary oversight, no single

[73] *See, e.g.,* Hyun Ju Park v. City and County of Honolulu, 952 F.3d 1136 (9th Cir. 2020); Waller v. City and County of Denver, 932 F.3d 1277 (10th Cir. 2019); Estate of Davis by and through Dyann v. City of North Richland Hills, 406 F.3d 375 (5th Cir. 2005) (rejecting municipal liability based on *Brown*). *But see* J.K.J. v. Polk County, 960 F.3d 367 (7th Cir. 2020) (finding the county liable).

[74] 563 U.S. 51 (2011).

[75] 373 U.S. 83 (1963).

[76] 563 U.S. at 62.

[77] *Id.* at 63-64.

incident of a lone officer's misconduct. Instead, the evidence demonstrated that misperception and disregard of *Brady*'s disclosure requirements were pervasive in Orleans Parish. That evidence, I would hold, established persistent, deliberately indifferent conduct for which the District Attorney's Office bears responsibility under §1983."[78] She said that "abundant evidence" demonstrated the deliberate indifference in the prosecutor's office, which had led to multiple violations of its constitutional duties under *Brady*.[79]

The Court in *Connick v. Thompson* acknowledged that there could be instances where a single incident might be a basis for showing deliberate indifference and thus establishing municipal liability, but such circumstances will be exceptional.

Since *Canton*, hundreds of lower court decisions have applied it to allegations of inadequate training and supervision. Several courts have found "deliberate indifference" based on the failure to train in light of the consequences of the conduct. The Tenth Circuit found that there was a need for police departments to provide training on how to deal with armed, suicidal, emotionally disturbed persons.[80] The Tenth Circuit, ruling after *Brown*, said that the case fit into "the 'narrow range of circumstances' recognized by *Canton* and left intact by *Brown*, under which a single violation of federal rights may be a highly predictable consequence of failure to train officers to handle recurring situations with an obvious potential for a violation."[81] In *Young v. City of Providence*, the First Circuit found that the absence of training of officers on preventing harms from "friendly fire" amounted to deliberate indifference.[82] In *Flores v. Morgan Hill Unified School District*, the Ninth Circuit found that the failure to train teachers to deal with harassment based on sexual orientation amounted to deliberate indifference.[83] In *Conn v. City of Reno*, the Ninth Circuit held that the failure to train officers on how to identify and when to report suicide risks constituted deliberate indifference.[84]

Other courts have found deliberate indifference in light of a city's failure to respond to complaints. For example, in *Oviatt by and through Waugh v. Pearce*, when an individual was incarcerated 114 days before arraignment, the Ninth Circuit found deliberate indifference because of nineteen similar instances between 1981 and 1989.[85] Similarly, in *Gentile v. County of Suffolk*, the Second Circuit found that a failure to respond to repeated complaints of police abuse is a basis for finding municipal liability.[86] In *Chew v. Gates*, the Ninth Circuit found that the failure to train police officers in the handling of police dogs could be the basis for liability.[87]

[78] *Id.* at 80 (Ginsburg, J., dissenting).

[79] *Id.* at 93.

[80] Allen v. Muskogee, 119 F.3d 837, 843-844 (10th Cir. 1997).

[81] *Id.* at 845.

[82] 404 F.3d 4 (1st Cir. 2005).

[83] 324 F.3d 1130 (9th Cir. 2003).

[84] 591 F.3d 1081 (9th Cir. 2010).

[85] 954 F.2d 1470 (9th Cir. 1992); *see also* Parrish v. Luckie, 963 F.2d 201 (8th Cir. 1992) (failure to respond to several complaints about a police officer's conduct is sufficient to state a complaint against the city for the officer's behavior).

[86] 926 F.2d 142 (2d Cir. 1991).

[87] 27 F.3d 1432 (9th Cir. 1994).

The court explained: "Where the city equips its police officers with potentially dangerous animals, and evidence is adduced that those animals inflict injury in a significant percentage of the cases in which they are used, a failure to adopt a departmental policy governing their use, or to implement rules or regulations regarding the constitutional limits of that use, evidences a 'deliberate indifference' to constitutional rights."[88]

Many other lower courts have rejected claims of "deliberate indifference." Some courts have rejected claims of deliberate indifference in the failure of prisons to prevent suicides by inmates, absent evidence of specific failings by the officials.[89] For instance, in *Mateyko v. Felix*, the Ninth Circuit found that a few hours' training in the use of the Taser stun gun was not deliberate indifference.[90]

City of Canton, Ohio v. Harris is quite important because it articulates a standard for when local governments may be sued for inadequate training and supervision: When there is deliberate indifference. Although the definition of "deliberate indifference" is uncertain, it is clear that local governments are liable when their deliberate indifference in training and supervising officers results in violations of federal law that creates injuries. In *Collins v. Harker Heights, Texas*, the Supreme Court concluded that there need not be proof of an abuse of government power to sue a city under §1983 for inadequate training; a cause of action exists as long as the deliberate indifference results in a violation of the Constitution and laws of the United States.[91]

Custom

A fifth and final way to establish municipal liability under §1983 would be to demonstrate the existence of a "custom." The Supreme Court, however, has provided little guidance as to what constitutes a "custom" for purposes of §1983. In *Pembaur* and *Praprotnik*, the Court explicitly reaffirmed that municipal governments could be sued for their customs that cause constitutional violations, even though such customs had not received formal approval from the official legislative body.[92] But because the plaintiffs did not allege a municipal custom, the

[88] *Id.* at 1445.

[89] Barrie v. Grand County, 119 F.3d 862 (10th Cir. 1997); Hare v. City of Corinth, 74 F.3d 633 (5th Cir. 1996) (en banc) (jails liable for suicides only if proof of subjective deliberate indifference); *but see* Greason v. Kemp, 891 F.2d 829 (11th Cir. 1990); Dorman v. District of Columbia, 888 F.2d 159 (D.C. Cir. 1989).

[90] 924 F.2d 824 (9th Cir. 1990).

[91] *See* 503 U.S. 115 (1992) (*Collins* involved a claim by the estate of an asphyxiated sanitation worker alleging deliberate indifference in training and equipping the worker. The Fifth Circuit ruled in favor of the city because of the absence of abuse of government power. The Supreme Court held that abuse of government power is not required, but that there was no allegation of a constitutional violation by the plaintiff).

[92] 475 U.S. 469, 481-482 n.10 (1986). For an excellent discussion of the use of custom to establish municipal liability, *see* George Rutherglen, Custom and Usage as Action Under Color of State Law: An Essay on the Forgotten Terms of Section 1983, 89 Va. L. Rev. 925 (2003); Myriam E. Gilles, Breaking the Code of Silence: Rediscovering "Custom" in Section 1983 Municipal Liability, 80 B.U. L. Rev. 17 (2000).

Court did not reach the issue. A federal district court articulated an approach to understanding "custom" as a basis for liability, explaining that "[u]nlike a 'policy,' which comes into existence because of the top-down affirmative decision of a policymaker, a custom develops from the bottom-up. Thus, the liability of the municipality for customary constitutional violations derives not from its creation of the custom, but from its tolerance or acquiescence in it."[93]

Generally, courts of appeals have found that a custom exists if "policymakers knew about the widespread practice but failed to stop it."[94] For example, the Sixth Circuit has held that proving a custom requires demonstrating: (1) a clear and persistent pattern of illegal activity, (2) which the department knew or should have known about, (3) yet remained deliberately indifferent about, and (4) that the department's custom was the direct cause of the harm.[95] In an important application, some circuit courts have found that the "code of silence" in police departments is a custom and is a basis for municipal liability.[96]

Pleading Requirements

The above discussion has considered five alternative ways to establish the existence of a municipal policy. A related but separate question concerns what must be alleged to withstand a motion to dismiss for failure to state a claim upon which relief can be granted. The issue is whether it is sufficient for the plaintiff to generally allege that there is a municipal policy or whether the complaint must plead specific facts indicating the existence of an official policy. If conclusory allegations are enough—literally magic words in the complaint contending there is a municipal policy—then plaintiffs have every incentive to include the talismanic phrases and hope that discovery will produce actual evidence supporting government liability. Many frivolous claims are inevitable. Alternatively, a requirement that the plaintiff must plead specific facts supporting the existence of a municipal policy is inconsistent with the philosophy of notice pleading underlying the Federal Rules of Civil Procedure. Exclusion of many meritorious claims seems inescapable if plaintiffs must present facts supporting the existence of a municipal policy even before they engage in discovery.

A split among the circuits existed as to this issue until the Supreme Court's decision in *Leatherman v. Tarrant County Narcotics Intelligence and Coordination Unit.*[97] In *Leatherman,* the district court dismissed a suit against the city for inadequate

[93] Britton v. Maloney, 901 F. Supp. 444, 450 (D. Mass. 1995).

[94] Floyd v. Walters, 133 F.3d 786, 795 (11th Cir. 1998).

[95] D'Ambrosio v. Marino, 747 F.3d 378 (6th Cir. 2014); Thomas v. City of Chattanooga, 398 F.3d 426 (6th Cir. 2005); *see also* Okin v. Cornwall-on-Hudson Police Department, 577 F.3d 415 (2d Cir. 2009) (finding municipal liability based on custom).

[96] Barron v. Suffolk County Sheriff's Dept., 402 F.3d 225 (1st Cir. 2005) (finding proof of a pattern of ongoing harassment that the department knew of and did not stop could lead the jury to conclude that there was sufficient evidence of a code of silence); Sharp v. City of Houston, 164 F.3d 923 (5th Cir. 1999) (finding a custom within the Houston Police Department of a "code of silence" based, in part, on retaliation against officers who report misconduct).

[97] 507 U.S. 163 (1993).

training even though the complaint declared that there had been deliberate indifference, because there had not been sufficient pleading with particularity as to the basis for believing that training was insufficient. The Supreme Court reversed, unanimously holding that notice pleading is sufficient for §1983 suits against local governments. Chief Justice Rehnquist, writing for the Court, reaffirmed the standard of notice pleading under the Federal Rules of Civil Procedure and emphasized the absence of a specific rule or statute requiring heightened pleading for suits against local governments.[98]

In *Swierkiewicz v. Sorema N.A.*, the Supreme Court emphatically reaffirmed that notice pleading is the standard under the Federal Rules of Civil Procedure, unless there is a specific rule or statutory provision requiring heightened pleading.[99] In a case involving Title VII and the Age Discrimination in Employment Act, the Court reaffirmed *Leatherman*'s holding: Courts may not impose heightened pleading requirements in civil rights cases.

However, in *Bell Atlantic Corp. v. Twombly*[100] and *Ashcroft v. Iqbal*,[101] the Supreme Court significantly changed the law regarding pleading. No longer is it enough that the plaintiff allege sufficient facts so that it cannot be said that it is impossible that the plaintiff can recover.[102] Now a plaintiff must plead sufficient facts so that a federal court can conclude that it is "plausible" that the plaintiff can recover. The Court declared in *Ashcroft v. Iqbal*:

> To survive a motion to dismiss, a complaint must contain sufficient factual matter, accepted as true, to "state a claim to relief that is plausible on its face." A claim has facial plausibility when the plaintiff pleads factual content that allows the court to draw the reasonable inference that the defendant is liable for the misconduct alleged. The plausibility standard is not akin to a "probability requirement," but it asks for more than a sheer possibility that a defendant has acted unlawfully. Where a complaint pleads facts that are "merely consistent with" a defendant's liability, it "stops short of the line between possibility and plausibility of 'entitlement to relief.' "[103]

Some federal courts of appeals have ruled that these cases implicitly overrule *Swierkiewicz*.[104] *Leatherman* has not been expressly overruled by the Court; it never

[98] The Court specifically left open the question of whether heightened pleading can be required in suits against individual government officers. *See id.* at 166-167. This is discussed below in §8.6.1, text accompanying notes 45-46.

[99] 534 U.S. 506 (2002).

[100] 550 U.S. 544 (2007).

[101] 556 U.S. 662 (2009).

[102] This was the standard under Conley v. Gibson, 355 U.S. 41 (1957), but this decision was effectively overruled in *Bell Atlantic*, 550 U.S. at 563 ("The phrase is best forgotten as an incomplete, negative gloss on an accepted pleading standard: once a claim has been stated adequately, it may be supported by showing any set of facts consistent with the allegations in the complaint.").

[103] 556 U.S. at 678.

[104] *See, e.g.*, Fowler v. UPMC Shadyside, 578 F.3d 203 (3d Cir. 2010); Francis v. Giacomelli, 588 F.3d 186 (4th Cir. 2009) ("The standard that the plaintiffs quoted from *Swierkiewicz* . . . was explicitly overruled in *Twombly*."); *but see* Arista Records, LLC v. Doe 3, 604 F.3d 110 (2d Cir. 2010); Swanson v. Citibank, N.A., 614 F.3d 400 (7th Cir. 2010).

has discussed *Leatherman* in light of *Bell Atlantic* and *Iqbal*, but there is an obvious tension between *Leatherman*'s emphasis on notice pleading and the later cases' shift to plausibility as the standard of pleading.[105]

Studies have shown that *Bell Atlantic* and *Iqbal* have had an effect, especially in civil rights cases, in that more cases are dismissed at the pleading stage. A study by Professor Raymond H. Brescia focused on the effects of *Bell Atlantic* and *Iqbal* in civil rights cases, and found that "motions to dismiss challenging the sufficiency of the pleadings are much more common since *Iqbal*, and far more cases are being dismissed after the release of that decision than before."[106] He concluded that "there did appear to be an *Iqbal* effect, both in terms of dismissal rates and in the frequency of motions to dismiss based on challenges to the sufficiency of the pleadings. Not only were cases dismissed at a higher rate since *Iqbal*, but also, plaintiffs were forced to defend themselves on these grounds far more often than before, meaning significant transactions costs."[107]

Professor Patricia Hatamyar Moore conducted a statistical analysis and came to similar conclusions, specifically with regard to constitutional claims: "In constitutional civil rights cases, even excluding pro se plaintiffs, courts granted 12(b)(6) motions at a higher-than-average rate under *Iqbal*."[108] The statistical increase in dismissals in constitutional cases is disturbing: "Combining grants in full with and without leave to amend means courts granted 64% of the 12(b)(6) motions in the database in constitutional civil rights cases under *Iqbal*, even when the plaintiff was represented by counsel. Comparatively, under *Conley*, courts granted in full 41% of the motions in constitutional civil rights cases with represented plaintiffs (35% without and 6% with leave to amend)."[109] Put another way, "constitutional civil rights cases courts were 3.77 times more likely to grant motions to dismiss in full without leave to amend, as compared to deny, under *Iqbal* than under *Conley*."[110]

[105] Morris v. Philadelphia Housing Authority, No. 10-5431, 2011 WL 1661506, at *3-5 (E.D. Pa. Apr. 28, 2011) ("The difficulty in following *Leatherman* is that its holding appears to be significantly undermined by *Iqbal*, yet *Leatherman* is not cited in either the majority or dissenting opinions of *Iqbal*.").

[106] Raymond H. Brescia, The *Iqbal* Effect: The Impact of New Pleading Standards in Employment and Housing Discrimination Litigation, 100 Ky. L.J. 235, 241 (2012).

[107] *Id.* at 284.

[108] Patricia Hatamyar Moore, An Updated Quantitative Study of *Iqbal*'s Impact on 12(b)(6) Motions, 46 Rich. L. Rev. 603, 618 (2012).

[109] *Id.* at 619.

[110] *Id.* at 623. A study by the Federal Judicial Center came to an opposite conclusion and did not find this effect of *Twombly* and *Iqbal*. *See* Joe S. Cecil, George W. Cort, Margaret S. Williams & Jared J. Bataillon, Motions to Dismiss for Failure to State a Claim After *Iqbal*: Report to the Judicial Conference Advisory Committee on Civil Rules, Federal Judicial Center (March 2011). Professor Moore, however, pointed out significant methodological problems with this study. Overall, the article finds that the FJC's study was under-inclusive in its methods for collecting cases for its database. *Id.* at 633. "Most critically, the FJC excluded all cases brought by pro se plaintiffs (which constitute 29% of my database and 26% of all civil cases in federal district court). The FJC also excluded all cases in which the 12(b)(6) motion was granted on the basis of sovereign or qualified immunity (as in *Iqbal* itself)." *Id.* at 634. "Further, the FJC database is limited to orders entered in two six-month periods from twenty-three of the ninety-four district courts." *Id.* at 634-635.

§8.5.3 *Municipal Immunities*

Monell left open the question of whether municipal governments could invoke immunity as a defense. The Court considered this issue in two cases in the early 1980s.

No Qualified Immunity for Local Governments

In *Owen v. City of Independence*, the Supreme Court held that local governments are liable even when their constitutional violations are a result of actions taken in good faith.[111] In *Owen*, a city council fired the police chief without providing him any procedural due process protections. The firing occurred shortly before the Supreme Court's major procedural due process decisions established a right to protections under such circumstances.[112] The city claimed immunity because its actions were done in good faith.

The Court, however, held that the fact that city officials acted in good faith will not protect a municipal government from liability under §1983. The Court emphasized that there is no indication in the legislative history that Congress meant to accord municipal governments any form of immunity; in fact, local governments generally had no such immunity under the common law in 1871. Furthermore, the Court noted that allowing cities good-faith immunity would frustrate the underlying purposes of §1983 in terms of deterrence and risk spreading.[113] The Court rejected the assertion that municipal officials would be chilled in the exercise of their discretion unless there was good-faith immunity. Because the individual officials had good-faith immunity to their personal liability, the existence of damage remedies against the municipality should not have an adverse effect on government operations. The Court reasoned that allowing municipal liability would create an incentive for local governments to prevent constitutional violations.

The Court's reasoning in *Owen* is open to criticism. In a situation such as that present in *Owen*, it is not clear how liability could have a deterrent effect, because there is no way the officers could have known that their actions were unconstitutional. Moreover, the Court seems caught in a dilemma. If municipal liability influences how officers perform, then there is some risk of chilling the exercise of discretion; on the other hand, if officers are unaffected by government liability as long as they have personal immunity, then municipal liability will have no deterrent effect.[114] The Court cannot have it both ways, simultaneously contending that municipal liability deters individual officer wrongdoing and that it has no effect on individual officers.

[111] 445 U.S. 622 (1980).

[112] *See* Board of Regents v. Roth, 408 U.S. 564 (1972); Perry v. Sinderman, 408 U.S. 593 (1972).

[113] 445 U.S. at 651.

[114] *Id.* at 669 n.9 (Powell, J., dissenting).

No Punitive Damages

A year after *Owen,* the Supreme Court held that municipal governments do have immunity to claims for punitive damages. In *City of Newport v. Fact Concerts,* the Court rejected punitive damages in the context of a First Amendment suit against a city that canceled a rock concert because of its objections to the content of the music.[115] The Court emphasized the absence of municipal liability for punitive damages at common law when §1983 was adopted. Furthermore, the Court concluded that punitive damages exist to punish and that it would be unfair to punish the city's taxpayers because of the officer's wrongdoing.

There is tension between the Court's reasoning in *Owen* and *Fact Concerts.* If deterrence is the goal, as *Owen* concluded, then greater costs through punitive damages likely would lead to additional care, supervision, and control. Furthermore, the objective of compensation would be advanced by allowing punitive damages because it would provide a remedy for serious constitutional violations where there was no monetary loss. As the Supreme Court noted in another context, "punitive damages may be the only significant remedy available in some §1983 actions where constitutional rights are maliciously violated but the victim cannot prove compensable injury."[116] Alternatively, if the goal is protecting the innocent taxpayers, then denying municipalities good-faith immunity is unfair because taxpayers will have to absorb the costs by increased taxes or decreased government services.

Nonetheless, the immunity issues are settled: municipalities cannot invoke a defense of good-faith immunity, but they are immune to claims for punitive damages.

§8.5.4 Municipal Liability: Conclusion

The discussion of municipal liability suits raises major questions concerning the interpretation and scope of §1983. First, what role should the legislative history of §1983 play in contemporary decisions? In all of the major cases—*Monroe, Monell, Owen,* and *Fact Concerts*—the Court based its decision, in part, on a review of Congress's intent and the common law as it existed in 1871. In light of an unclear legislative record and the passage of time, some have questioned whether such historical analysis is useful or desirable.

Second, what are the purposes of §1983? In *Monell* the Court expressly rejects deterrence and risk spreading as a basis for §1983 decision-making.[117] Yet in *Owen* the Court embraces them as the primary basis for its decision. If the goals really

[115] 453 U.S. 247 (1981).

[116] Carlson v. Green, 446 U.S. 14, 22 n.9 (1980); *Carlson* is discussed in more detail in §9.1, *infra.*

[117] For discussion of the appropriate goals of §1983 litigation, *see* Symposium, Municipal Liability in Civil Rights Litigation, 48 DePaul L. Rev. 619 (1999); John C. Jeffries, Compensation for Constitutional Torts: Reflections on the Significance of Fault, 88 Mich. L. Rev. 82 (1989); Charles F. Abernathy, Section 1983 and Constitutional Torts, 77 Geo. L.J. 1441 (1989); Sheldon Nahmod, Section 1983 Discourse: The Move from Constitution to Tort, 77 Geo. L.J. 1719 (1989).

are deterrence and risk spreading, then the current doctrines are open to question. Allowing suits against municipalities for their officers' actions likely would increase both deterrence and risk spreading. At the same time, it is not clear how deterrence is achieved in circumstances where no reasonable officer could know that the action was wrongful. Hence, there is an argument that *Monell* and *Owen* have it backwards as to how to best deter wrongdoing: Respondeat superior liability should be allowed against local governments, but a good-faith defense should be permitted.

Third, and perhaps most important, there is an unarticulated tension between wanting to protect taxpayers from liability and desiring to compensate injured individuals and protect citizens by deterring violations of federal law. On the one hand, all municipal liability imposes costs on governments that must meet the expense either by increasing taxes or cutting social services. Damage judgments are proving devastating, especially for smaller cities.

However, unless municipal governments are liable, injured individuals may receive no compensation because officers may be immune or often judgment proof. Also, municipal liability gives cities an incentive to prevent wrongdoing. Ideally, voters would be angry at large judgments and use the democratic process to elect more law-abiding officials.

This tension explains the split in the Court. The majority in *Monell* and *Owen*, and the dissent in *Fact Concerts*, emphasized the latter values in arguing for broader municipal liability. In contrast, the majority in *Fact Concerts* and the dissents in *Monell* and *Owen* relied on the former values in arguing for greater protection of municipal governments from liability. Ultimately, the question is both a normative one about what values to prefer and an empirical one about what kinds of liability will best deter unconstitutional conduct.[118]

§8.5.5 Supervisory Liability

Closely related to the issue of holding local governments liable is the question of when there can be supervisory liability: When may government officials be held liable because of their role as supervisors of those who violate the Constitution? Like for local governments, the Supreme Court has been clear that there cannot be supervisory liability based on respondeat superior liability. But also, as for local governments, supervisors can be held liable for their own misconduct, including as supervisors.

The Court expressed this in *Ashcroft v. Iqbal.*[119] This decision is best known for its holding that to withstand a motion to dismiss, a plaintiff must plead sufficient

[118] *See generally* Peter H. Schuck, Suing Government: Citizen Remedies for Official Wrongs (1983); Jon O. Newman, Suing the Lawbreakers: Proposals to Strengthen the Section 1983 Damage Remedy for Law Enforcers' Misconduct, 87 Yale L.J. 447 (1978) (discussing the objectives for liability and proposals for how to best meet the goals).

[119] 556 U.S. 662 (2009).

facts so that the court can conclude that it is "plausible" that the plaintiff can recover.[120] Additionally, the Court expressed when supervisory liability is permitted.

Iqbal, a man of Pakistani descent, was detained after September 11, 2001, and subsequently filed suit against the attorney general and others, contending that his detention and treatment were unconstitutional. The claim against the attorney general, in part, rested on a claim of supervisory liability. The Court rejected this claim and stated: "[Iqbal] argues that, under a theory of 'supervisory liability,' petitioners can be liable for 'knowledge and acquiescence in their subordinates' use of discriminatory criteria to make classification decisions among detainees.' . . . We reject this argument. Respondent's conception of 'supervisory liability' is inconsistent with his accurate stipulation that petitioners may not be held accountable for the misdeeds of their agents. In a §1983 suit or a *Bivens* action—where masters do not answer for the torts of their servants—the term 'supervisory liability' is a misnomer. Absent vicarious liability, each Government official, his or her title notwithstanding, is only liable for his or her own misconduct."[121]

This does *not* eliminate the possibility of supervisory liability.[122] Rather, after *Iqbal*, supervisors can be held liable if their own actions violate the Constitution.[123] The difficult cases likely will arise in situations where the supervisors' inaction is alleged to violate the Constitution. As Professor Karen Blum explained: "So, if a supervisor takes part in an unlawful search or seizure or gives an order to make an unlawful entry into someone's home or to use excessive force on a suspect, or adopts or implements an unconstitutional strip search policy, the supervisor should be liable for the unreasonable search or seizure under the same Fourth Amendment standard that would apply to the line officers. . . . When supervisors are not direct participants, however, as when they are not on the scene nor directly involved through the giving of an order to engage in unconstitutional conduct or through the adoption or implementation of an unconstitutional policy, their liability, if any, will be based on inaction or acts of omission."[124]

[120] This is discussed in §8.5.2.

[121] 556 U.S. at 677.

[122] *See, e.g.,* T.E. v. Grindle, 599 F.3d 583 (7th Cir. 2010) (a supervisor may be held liable for an equal protection violation if it is shown that the supervisor, like the subordinate, intended to discriminate based on a protected class; claim that supervisor concealed sexual abuse of girls was sufficient to withstand motion to dismiss and motion for summary judgment); Nelson v. Correctional Medical Services, 583 F.3d 522 (8th Cir. 2009) (en banc) (supervisor is liable for keeping a female prisoner in shackles during labor only if the supervisor personally displayed deliberate indifference to the hazards and pain of doing so; supervisor had no personal involvement in having this woman kept in shackles, so no supervisory liability); Sanchez v. Peirera-Castilla, 590 F.3d 3 (1st Cir. 2009) (supervisory liability can exist in two ways: the supervisor was a primary violator or a direct participant in the rights-violating incident, or the supervisor supervises, hires, or trains a subordinate with deliberate indifference toward the possibility of a civil rights violation. The latter requires proof of a causal connection to harm. Plaintiff's complaint was conclusory as to the latter and should have been dismissed.).

[123] *See* Sheldon Nahmod, Constitutional Torts, Over-Deterrence and Supervisory Liability After *Iqbal*, 14 Lewis & Clark L. Rev. 279 (2010).

[124] Karen Blum, Supervisory Liability After *Iqbal*: Misunderstood but Not Misnamed, 43 Urb. L. Rev. 541, 555 (2011).

§8.6 WHO IS A "PERSON" FOR PURPOSES OF §1983 LIABILITY? THE LIABILITY OF INDIVIDUAL OFFICERS

§8.6.1 Introduction to Individual Officers' Immunities

Importance of Immunities

Section 1983 is written in absolute terms: it creates liability for any person, acting under color of state law, who violates the Constitution and laws of the United States. No exceptions are mentioned in the statute. However, the Supreme Court consistently has held that all officers possess some degree of immunity from liability.

Immunity doctrines are extremely important. The availability of relief against individual officers is often crucial because the governmental entity frequently is completely protected from liability. State governments generally cannot be sued in federal court because of the Eleventh Amendment, and municipal governments are not liable unless their official policy caused the unconstitutional conduct. Hence, if injured individuals are to receive compensation, and if there is to be deterrence of wrongdoing through federal court liability, it frequently must take the form of suits against the individual officers.

However, it is widely believed that some degree of immunity for individual officers is imperative. At minimum, it seems unfair to hold an officer personally liable if he or she had no reason to know that the actions taken were illegal. As the Supreme Court remarked, official immunity reflects "the injustice, particularly in the absence of bad faith, of subjecting to liability an officer who is required by the legal obligations of his position, to exercise discretion."[1] Additionally, there is concern that the absence of immunity might make it more difficult to attract people into government service, or at least would chill the exercise of discretion.[2]

Historical Approach to Immunities

Thus, there is a need to strike a balance; the standard must provide sufficient liability to ensure compensation and deterrence, while according immunities adequate to encourage government employees to perform their duties. Interestingly, although the Supreme Court addresses this functional question, the emphasis in the decisions has been more historical. The Court repeatedly has stated that in determining the immunity accorded to a particular government officer, the inquiry must focus on the "immunity historically accorded the relevant official at common law."[3] That is, the nature of an officer's immunity is determined, in

§8.6 [1] Scheuer v. Rhodes, 416 U.S. 232, 240 (1974).

[2] *Id.* (Noting "the danger that the threat of such liability would deter his willingness to execute his office with the decisiveness and the judgment required by the public good".) *See* Peter H. Schuck, Suing Government: Citizen Remedies for Official Wrongs 60-77 (1983) (personal liability will cause excessive defensive behavior on the part of individual officers).

[3] Imbler v. Pachtman, 424 U.S. 409, 421 (1976).

part, by an examination of the law as it existed in 1871. The Court stated that its approach is based on the "important assumption . . . that members of the 42nd Congress were familiar with common law principles, including defenses previously recognized in ordinary tort litigation, and that they likely intended these common law principles to obtain, absent specific provision to the contrary."[4] The Supreme Court reaffirmed this saying that questions of immunity must "be construed in light of common-law principles that were well settled at the time of its enactment."[5]

In numerous specific cases—ranging from the scope of judicial immunity[6] to the availability of punitive damages[7]—the Court has focused extensively on the common law of immunities as it existed when §1983 was adopted. This historical approach is subject to substantial criticism. First, it assumes that the common law was clear about the nature of the immunity to be accorded to particular government officers. Yet usually there was great divergence among the states, and there were no firmly established rules. For instance, the Court has emphasized the common law immunity of judges in according them absolute immunity to suits for damages under §1983.[8] However, in 1871, only 13 of 37 states accorded judges such immunity for suits.[9] In fact, in adopting §1983, many members of Congress were particularly concerned about unconstitutional conduct by judges.[10]

As a result of the historical uncertainty, immunity decisions are likely to produce conflicting majority and dissenting opinions, each citing to cases supporting their view of the law as it existed in 1871. Justice O'Connor powerfully expressed this point in her dissent in *Smith v. Wade.*[11] The majority in allowing punitive damages against individual officers under §1983 focused on the common law, as did the dissenting opinion of Justice Rehnquist. Justice O'Connor, although agreeing with Justice Rehnquist's conclusion, took issue with the approach used by both the majority and the dissent. She said, "Both opinions engage in exhausting, but ultimately unilluminating exegesis of the common law of the availability of punitive damages in 1871. Although both the Court and Justice Rehnquist display admirable skills in legal research and analysis of great numbers of musty cases, the results do not significantly further the goal of the inquiry."[12] In Justice O'Connor's words, "The battle of the string citations can have no winner."[13]

[4] City of Newport v. Fact Concerts, 453 U.S. 247, 258 (1981); *see also* Pierson v. Ray, 386 U.S. 547, 554 (1967).

[5] Kalina v. Fletcher, 522 U.S. 118, 123 (1997).

[6] *See, e.g.,* Antoine v. Byers & Anderson, Inc., 508 U.S. 429 (1993); Pulliam v. Allen, 466 U.S. 522, 529 (1984) ("The starting place in our own analysis is the common law"; holding that judges do not have immunity in suits for injunctive relief.); Pierson v. Ray, 386 U.S. 547 (1967).

[7] Smith v. Wade, 461 U.S. 30 (1983).

[8] *See* Pulliam v. Allen, 466 U.S. 522, 529 (1984); Stump v. Sparkman, 435 U.S. 349 (1978); Pierson v. Ray, 386 U.S. 547 (1967).

[9] Note, Liability of Judicial Officers Under Section 1983, 79 Yale L.J. 322, 326-327 (1969).

[10] Mitchum v. Foster, 407 U.S. 225, 240 (1972) ("Proponents of the legislation noted that state courts were being used to harass and injure individuals.")

[11] 461 U.S. 30 (1983).

[12] *Id.* at 92 (O'Connor, J., dissenting).

[13] *Id.*

Additionally, even if the common law principles were clear and discoverable, their relevance to modern doctrines is questionable. The fundamental premises of tort law have changed dramatically over the past 150 years, as have views about the Constitution and individual rights. Undoubtedly, many officers occupy far different positions than they did in 1871. Furthermore, there is a strong argument that common law tort immunities have little relevance in determining the scope of responsibility for constitutional violations. Some suggest that the Court should abandon the immunity inquiry and leave the entire issue of immunities to the legislature.[14] Others would prefer a more functional approach to determining the nature of immunities.[15] In Spring 2020, after the death of George Floyd, proposals were introduced into Congress to eliminate immunity for police officers accused of excessive force.

The Supreme Court has recognized two basic types of immunity: absolute immunity and good-faith immunity. Section 8.6.2 examines who has absolute immunity and under what circumstances. Good-faith immunity, usually termed "qualified immunity," is explored in §8.6.3.

In considering individual officer immunities it is worth remembering that most governments have indemnification policies to repay some of the costs and losses incurred by their employees in defending suits related to their job performance.[16] The content of the indemnification policies is determined by state and local law and hence varies enormously among jurisdictions.[17] However, the existence of indemnification does not change the law applied in determining an officer's liability. For example, a state government's decision to indemnify officers does not create an Eleventh Amendment bar to suits in situations where indemnification is available.[18]

Issues in Litigating Immunity

Five general points about immunity should be noted. First, the determination of the immunity to be accorded as a defense in a §1983 suit is entirely a question of federal law.[19] State immunities and defenses are not relevant in §1983 litigation, even when the §1983 suit is brought in state court.[20] In *Howlett v. Rose*, the Supreme

[14] Jon O. Newman, Suing the Lawbreakers: Proposals to Strengthen the Section 1983 Damage Remedy for Law Enforcers' Misconduct, 87 Yale L.J. 447 (1978).

[15] Schuck, *supra* note 2, at 60-77.

[16] Joanna C. Schwartz, Police Indemnification, 89 N.Y.U. Rev. 895 (2014) ("During the study period, governments paid approximately 99.98% of the dollars that plaintiffs recovered in lawsuits alleging civil rights violations by law enforcement.").

[17] Peter W. Low & John C. Jeffries, Federal Courts and the Law of Federal-State Relations 924 (2d ed. 1989) ("the availability of counsel, indemnification and insurance depends on the statutes, ordinances, and practices obtaining in each jurisdiction").

[18] *See* Duckworth v. Franzen, 780 F.2d 645, 650 (7th Cir. 1985), *cert. denied,* 479 U.S. 816 (1986) ("every court that has considered this issue has rejected, rightly in our view, the argument that an indemnity statute brings the Eleventh Amendment into play"). *See also* Stoner v. Wisconsin Department of Agriculture, Trade and Consumer Products, 50 F.3d 481 (7th Cir. 1995).

[19] Wood v. Strickland, 420 U.S. 308, 314 (1975).

[20] Howlett v. Rose, 496 U.S. 356 (1990); Martinez v. California, 444 U.S. 277, 285 n.11 (1980).

Court unanimously ruled that because of the supremacy clause of Article VI, state law immunities cannot frustrate the enforcement of a federal law.[21]

Second, the Supreme Court held that a court ruling denying immunity is immediately appealable.[22] The Court concluded that immunity is an "entitlement not to stand trial or face the other burdens of litigation."[23] Because the "entitlement is an *immunity from suit* rather than a mere defense to liability, . . . it is effectively lost if a case is erroneously permitted to go to trial."[24] This decision likely will have a deleterious effect on civil rights litigation. In a large number of cases, officials denied immunity will choose to appeal immediately. The plaintiff then will need to litigate that issue in the court of appeals, substantially increasing the costs and delaying the litigation.[25]

Indeed, the Supreme Court subsequently held that defendant officials can obtain interlocutory appeals twice in the same case, both when a motion for qualified immunity is denied and when a motion for summary judgment is denied. *Behrens v. Pelletier* involved a defendant who filed an unsuccessful interlocutory appeal of the denial of a motion to dismiss based on qualified immunity.[26] After remand by the court of appeals, the district court denied the defendant's motion for summary judgment based on qualified immunity. The defendant then filed a second interlocutory appeal. The U.S. Court of Appeals for the Ninth Circuit ruled that defendants can bring only one interlocutory appeal in a case, but the U.S. Supreme Court disagreed. In an opinion by Justice Scalia, the Court explained that the issues at the motion to dismiss and the summary judgment stages are different and thus interlocutory appeals should be available at both times. The result is an even greater ability of defendants to delay §1983 litigation.[27]

It should be emphasized that interlocutory appeal exists so that the court of appeals can determine whether as a matter of law a defendant is entitled to qualified immunity. In *Johnson v. Jones*, the court held that a district court judge's determination of whether there is a triable issue of fact is not subject to interlocutory appeal.[28] In other words, a defendant can appeal the denial of summary judgment based on qualified immunity if the defendant is challenging the district court's conclusions as to the law, but not if the defendant is disagreeing with the district court's decision that there are genuine issues of fact for trial.

Third, although this chapter focuses on suits against state and local officers pursuant to §1983, the Supreme Court has held that the law is identical concerning

[21] 496 U.S. at 372. *Howlett* also is discussed in §3.5.

[22] Mitchell v. Forsyth, 472 U.S. 511 (1985).

[23] *Id.* at 526.

[24] *Id.* (emphasis included).

[25] However, it is notable that the Supreme Court held that state courts hearing §1983 claims need not follow *Mitchell.* Johnson v. Fankell, 520 U.S. 91 (1997). In other words, whether to allow an interlocutory appeal in state court of the denial of qualified immunity is left to state law.

[26] 516 U.S. 299 (1996).

[27] For an excellent discussion of the proper scope of interlocutory review of qualified immunity decisions, *see* Kathryn R. Urbonya, Interlocutory Appeals from Orders Denying Qualified Immunity: Determining the Proper Scope of Appellate Jurisdiction, 55 Wash. & Lee L. Rev. 3 (1998).

[28] 515 U.S. 304 (1995).

the immunities accorded to federal officers. The Court concluded that it would be "untenable to draw a distinction for purposes of immunity law between suits brought against state officials under §1983 and suits brought directly under the Constitution against federal officers."[29] Thus, although the law concerning suits against federal officers is discussed in detail in §9.1, this section will discuss the immunities accorded to government officers at all levels.

Fourth, immunities are a defense to liability, not an element of the plaintiff's prima facie case.[30] Thus, technically, a plaintiff's complaint need not include allegations necessary to overcome immunities, but because immunities are determined early in the lawsuit and often decide the litigation, plaintiffs must be prepared to address the immunities issue. Nonetheless, there is a split among the circuits as to who has the burden of proof as to qualified immunity. Five circuits place the burden of persuasion on the plaintiff regarding both as to whether there is a constitutional violation and as to whether there is clearly established law: the Fifth,[31] Sixth,[32] Seventh,[33] Tenth,[34] and Eleventh[35] Circuits. Conversely, it appears that five circuits place the burden of persuasion in a qualified immunity inquiry on the defendant: the First,[36] Second,[37] Third,[38] Ninth,[39] and D.C.[40] circuits.

Fifth, the pleading standard in suits against individual officers is uncertain in light of the Court's decisions in *Bell Atlantic Corp. v. Twombly*[41] and *Ashcroft v. Iqbal*,[42] in which the Supreme Court significantly changed the law regarding pleading.

[29] Harlow v. Fitzgerald, 457 U.S. 800, 809 (1982); Butz v. Economou, 438 U.S. 478, 504 (1978).

[30] Siegert v. Gilley, 500 U.S. 226 (1991); Gomez v. Toledo, 446 U.S. 635 (1980).

[31] Collier v. Montgomery, 569 F.3d 214, 217 (5th Cir. 2009) ("Although nominally an affirmative defense, the plaintiff has the burden to negate the assertion of qualified immunity once properly raised.").

[32] Tindle v. Enochs, 420 F. App'x 561, 563 (6th Cir. 2011).

[33] Erwin v. Daley, 92 F.3d 521, 525 (7th Cir. 1996) ("Once a public official raises the defense of qualified immunity, the plaintiff bears the burden of proof on the issue.").

[34] Justus v. Maynard, 1994 WL 237513, at *1-2 (10th Cir. 1994) ("Although qualified immunity is a defense which must be pleaded by the defendant, once the defendant raises qualified immunity, the burden of proof is on the plaintiff to show that the right allegedly violated was clearly established at the time of the challenged conduct.").

[35] Montoute v. Carr, 114 F.3d 181, 184 (11th Cir. 1997) ("Once an officer or official has raised the defense of qualified immunity, the burden of persuasion as to that issue is on the plaintiff").

[36] DiMarco-Zappa v. Cabanillas, 238 F.3d 25, 35 (1st Cir. 2001) ("Qualified immunity is an affirmative defense, and thus the burden of proof is on defendants-appellants.").

[37] Jackler v. Byrne, 658 F.3d 225, 242 (2d Cir. 2011) ("Qualified immunity, an affirmative defense as to which the defendants have the burden of proof. . . .").

[38] Reiff v. Marks, No. 08-CV-5963, 2011 WL 666139, at *5 (E.D. Pa. Feb. 23, 2011) ("Qualified immunity is an affirmative defense for which the defendants bear the burden of proof.").

[39] Moreno v. Baca, 431 F.3d 633, 638 (9th Cir. 2005) ("Because the moving defendant bears the burden of proof on the issue of qualified immunity, he or she must produce sufficient evidence to require the plaintiff to go beyond his or her pleadings.").

[40] Reuber v. United States, 750 F.2d 1039, 1057 n.25 (D.C. Cir. 1984) ("Qualified immunity is an affirmative defense based on the good faith and reasonableness of the actions taken and the burden of proof is on the defendant officials.").

[41] 550 U.S. 544 (2007).

[42] 556 U.S. 662 (2009).

As discussed above, a plaintiff must plead sufficient facts so that a federal court can conclude that it is "plausible" that the plaintiff can recover. In *Swierkiewicz v. Sorema N.A.*, the Supreme Court held that heightened pleading is permitted in federal court only where prescribed by a specific Federal Rule of Civil Procedure or a federal statute.[43] Following *Swierkiewicz*, courts of appeals across the country held that there is not a heightened pleading requirement in suits against individual officers.[44]

But in *Bell Atlantic* and *Iqbal*, the Court articulated a new standard for pleading in federal courts: plausibility.[45] It is unclear what this standard will mean in the context of suits against individual officers and whether circuits will return to the heightened pleading requirements that had been imposed before *Swierkiewicz*.[46] There is no doubt, though, that *Bell Atlantic* and *Iqbal* increase the pleading burdens on plaintiffs and require that plaintiffs allege sufficient facts that the federal district court can conclude that it is plausible that the plaintiff can recover.

Sixth, a distinction frequently is drawn between suits against an officer in his or her "official" as opposed to "individual" capacity. The Supreme Court has recognized that this distinction "continues to confuse lawyers and confound lower courts."[47] The issue is whether the plaintiff seeks money damages directly from the individual officer who is named as the defendant in the action, or whether the remedy actually is sought against the government entity that employs the officer. If the former—that is, if the damages are to be paid by the officer (or by the government through an indemnification policy)—the defendant can invoke the immunities discussed in this section. If the latter—that is, if the suit actually seeks money damages from the government's treasury—the Eleventh Amendment bars the suit when the defendant is a state officer and municipal policy or custom must be proven to establish liability when the defendant is a local official.[48] In other words, as the Supreme Court explained in *Hafer v. Melo*, an official capacity suit attempts to sue the government entity by naming the officer as a defendant, whereas personal capacity suits "seek to impose individual liability upon a government officer for actions taken under color of law."[49]

[43] 534 U.S. 506 (2002).

[44] *See, e.g.,* Kolupa v. Ruselle Park Dist., 438 F.3d 713 (7th Cir. 2005); Doe v. Cassell, 403 F.3d 986 (8th Cir. 2004); Galbraith v. County of Santa Clara, 307 F.3d 1119 (9th Cir. 2002).

[45] In fact, some courts have held that *Swierkiewicz* has been implicitly, or even explicitly, overruled. Francis v. Giacomelli, 588 F.3d 186 (4th Cir. 2009) ("The standard that the plaintiffs quoted from *Swierkiewicz* . . . was explicitly overruled in *Twombly*.").

[46] *See, e.g.,* Yamashita v. Scholastic, Inc., 936 F.3d 98 (2d Cir. 2019) (rejecting the idea that *Iqbal* heightened pleading requirements); Arista Records, LLC v. Doe 3, 604 F.3d 110 (2d Cir. 2010) (*Iqbal* did not increase the pleading requirements); Woods v. City of Greensboro, 855 F.3d 639 (4th Cir. 2017) (holding that *Iqbal* heightened pleading requirements); Francis v. Giacomelli, 588 F.3d 186 (4th Cir. 2009) (seeing *Twombly* and *Iqbal* as increasing the pleading requirements).

[47] Kentucky v. Graham, 457 U.S. 159, 165 (1985).

[48] The Eleventh Amendment is discussed in Chapter 7, *supra,* and the need to prove a municipal policy to establish municipal liability is discussed in §8.5, *supra. See also* Brandon v. Holt, 469 U.S. 464 (1985) (if municipal policy is proven, and municipality participated in the lawsuit, it can be required to pay damages even though it was not named as a party to the suit).

[49] 502 U.S. 21, 25 (1991). *See also* Will v. Michigan Dept. of State Police, 491 U.S. 58, 67 (1989) ("A suit against a state official in his or her official capacity is not a suit against the official but rather a suit against the official's office.").

§8.6.2 Absolute Immunity

The Supreme Court has held that individuals performing certain functions have absolute immunity from liability under §1983. Specifically, as described below, the Court has recognized absolute immunity for those performing judicial, legislative, and prosecutorial functions. The Court also has determined that police officers serving as witnesses and the President of the United States possess absolute immunity.

Because of the harsh consequences of absolute immunity, the Supreme Court has explained that "[t]he presumption is that qualified rather than absolute immunity is sufficient to protect government officials in the exercise of their duties."[50] Indeed, the Court has declared that it is "quite sparing in our recognition of absolute immunity, and have refused to extend it any further than its justification would warrant."[51]

Function, Not Title, Receives Absolute Immunity

In applying absolute immunity for judges, legislators, and prosecutors, the focus is on the *function* performed, rather than the title possessed. For example, judges have absolute immunity for their judicial functions, but not when they act in an administrative or executive capacity. Also, it should be noted that absolute immunity varies in scope among the officers protected. For some of the above-mentioned officers, such as judges, the immunity only is for suits for money damages; for others, such as legislators, the immunity includes protection from litigation for prospective relief as well as monetary remedies. When absolute immunity does not exist, government officers are accorded good-faith immunity to suits for money damages, discussed in the next section.

The Supreme Court has said that absolute immunity is necessary for certain functions because it is especially important that these tasks be carried out without fear of lawsuits.[52] Also, the Court has distinguished those functions accorded absolute immunity by the likelihood that disgruntled individuals will file suits that would occupy a great deal of the official's time.[53] Yet another factor determining what tasks are accorded absolute immunity is the availability of alternative checks on the exercise of discretion. For instance, most judicial decisions are subject to appellate review, legislators are reviewed through the electoral process, and prosecutors are checked by judges.[54]

[50] Burns v. Reed, 500 U.S. 478, 487 (1991).

[51] *Id.*

[52] *See, e.g.,* Nixon v. Fitzgerald, 457 U.S. 731, 751-752 (1982) (discussing presidential immunity); Stump v. Sparkman, 435 U.S. 349, 363 (1978) (discussing judicial immunity); Imbler v. Pachtman, 424 U.S. 409, 430 (1976) (discussing prosecutorial immunity). For a summary of the factors justifying absolute immunity, *see* Schuck, *supra* note 2, at 90.

[53] *See, e.g.,* Mireles v. Waco, 502 U.S. 9, 11 (1991); *see also* Nixon v. Fitzgerald, 457 U.S. at 753; Stump v. Sparkman, 435 U.S. at 363; Imbler v. Pachtman, 424 U.S. at 425.

[54] *See* Ronald A. Cass, Damage Suits Against Public Officers, 129 U. Pa. L. Rev. 1110 (1981).

Criticism of Absolute Immunities

Still the question arises as to whether *absolute* immunity is necessary to achieve these goals.[55] The choice is not limited to selecting between absolute immunity and good-faith immunity. For example, certain functions could be protected by according immunity except for malicious acts, or immunity except for intentional violations of rights. Admittedly, such a standard would open the door to litigation, but it might be preferable to protect officials from meritless suits by employing strict pleading requirements or aggressive use of summary judgment rather than by according them absolute immunity for even egregious actions.

Because the scope of absolute immunity varies, it is useful to examine each of the instances in which the Supreme Court has upheld absolute immunity and also to consider officers whose claims of absolute immunity have not yet been resolved by the Court. The Court has recognized absolute immunity in five instances.

Absolute Immunity for Judicial Acts

First, judges have absolute immunity to suits for monetary damages for their judicial acts.[56] Absolute immunity exists even when there are charges that the judge acted maliciously; it exists "however erroneous the act may have been, and however injurious in its consequences it may have proved to the plaintiff."[57]

The Supreme Court has held that immunity does not exist if judges act in the "clear absence of all jurisdiction."[58] The Court, however, has given a narrow construction to this limitation on absolute immunity. In *Stump v. Sparkman*, a state court judge was sued for issuing an order to sterilize a 15-year-old girl.[59] The girl's mother went to the judge in his chambers and asked him to sign an order approving a tubal ligation for her daughter. The mother said that the girl was "somewhat retarded" (although she attended public school and was promoted each year with her class) and that she was staying out overnight with older men. The mother said that sterilizing the girl would "prevent unfortunate circumstances."

Although the judge lacked statutory authority to issue such an order, he did so. The girl was told that her appendix was being taken out, when actually she was surgically sterilized. She learned the true nature of the operation two years later when she

[55] For a criticism of absolute immunity, *see* Michael L. Wells, Absolute Official Immunity in Constitutional Litigation, 57 Ga. Law. Rev. 919 (2023).

[56] *See, e.g.*, Stump v. Sparkman, 435 U.S. 349 (1978); Pierson v. Ray, 386 U.S. 547 (1967); Bradley v. Fisher, 80 U.S. 335 (1871). Administrative law judges also are accorded absolute immunity for their adjudicatory functions. Butz v. Economou, 438 U.S. 478 (1978).

[57] Bradley v. Fisher, 80 U.S. at 347; Pierson v. Ray, 386 U.S. at 554 (a judge should not have to "fear that unsatisfied litigants may hound him with litigation charging malice or corruption"); *see also* Mireles v. Waco, 502 U.S. 9 (1991) (upholding absolute immunity for a judge that allegedly ordered excessive force be used in arresting a suspect).

[58] Stump v. Sparkman, 435 U.S. at 357. For excellent discussion of this case and explorations of the justifications for judicial immunity, *see* Randolph J. Block, Stump v. Sparkman and the History of Judicial Immunity, 1980 Duke L.J. 879.

[59] 435 U.S. 349 (1978).

was married and unable to conceive a child. She then sued, among others, the judge who approved the operation.

A compelling case can be made that the judge was acting without jurisdiction. There was no authority for the judge to hear such a case or issue such an order. No case was filed with the court; there were no pleadings and no docket number was assigned. The matter was handled entirely ex parte; neither the girl nor any representative for her was present or allowed to respond. Nonetheless, the Court said that the judge had absolute immunity to the suit for money damages. The Court emphasized that because the judge sat in a court of general jurisdiction, he was acting in excess of jurisdiction but not in the absence of it.[60] As such, the judge was protected by absolute immunity. *Stump* is a very troublesome decision because it involves a judge acting without any legal authority, inflicting great harm, without the barest rudiments of procedural due process.

Additionally, a federal statute extended absolute judicial immunity to suits for injunctive relief. The Federal Courts Improvement Act of 1996 provides that injunctive relief cannot be granted under §1983 against a judicial officer based upon action or inaction in a judicial capacity unless a declaratory decree was violated or declaratory relief was unavailable.[61] Additionally, attorneys' fees may not be awarded against a judicial officer based upon action taken in a judicial capacity unless the judge's act was in clear excess of his or her jurisdiction.[62]

This statutory provision overrules the Supreme Court's decision in *Pulliam v. Allen.*[63] In *Pulliam,* a state court judge was sued for her practice of requiring bond for nonjailable offenses and incarcerating those who could not make bail. A federal district court found the practice unconstitutional, enjoined its continuation, and awarded attorneys' fees against the judge. The Supreme Court upheld the district court's ruling. The Court reviewed the common law history and concluded that injunctive relief is similar to the prerogative writ system, which existed to provide review of judicial conduct. The Court emphasized that "injunctive relief against a judge raises concerns different from those addressed by the protection of judges from damage awards."[64] Furthermore, the Court held that the judge could not claim absolute immunity to a claim for attorneys' fees resulting from the successful suit for injunctive relief. Many years of attempts by judges' groups to have *Pulliam* overruled by statute succeeded in 1996.

An important limitation on the absolute immunity accorded to judges is that immunity only extends to judicial tasks, not to administrative or executive ones.[65] The Supreme Court reaffirmed this distinction in *Forrester v. White.*[66] A state court

[60] *Id.* at 358.

[61] Pub. L. No. 104-317, (b)-(c), 110 Stat. 3847.

[62] *Id.*

[63] 466 U.S. 522 (1984).

[64] *Id.* at 537.

[65] Judges do have absolute immunity when they are performing legislative or prosecutorial tasks, as those are functions that also are accorded absolute immunity. *See* Supreme Court of Va. v. Consumers Union, 446 U.S. 719 (1980).

[66] 484 U.S. 219 (1988).

judge was sued for firing a probation officer on account of her gender in violation of the equal protection clause of the Fourteenth Amendment. The Court held that judges possess absolute immunity for their judicial or adjudicatory functions, but not for their executive or administrative actions.[67] A unanimous Court ruled that the state court judge did not have absolute immunity because the firing of the probation officer was administrative in nature. Although the distinction between a judicial function and an administrative one is often clear, there are many instances in which the characterization of the task is problematic. For instance, when a judge takes security measures in the courtroom, are they to be considered as part of the judicial or administrative function?[68] Is a chief judge's assignment of cases administrative or judicial?[69]

Several questions remain open concerning the scope of judicial immunity. For example, it is unclear as to when court personnel, such as clerks, can invoke the judge's absolute immunity.[70] However, in *Antoine v. Byers & Anderson*, the Supreme Court held that court reporters are entitled to qualified, not absolute, immunity.[71] The Court emphasized the historical absence of absolute immunity for court reporters and the fact that court reporters are not in any way engaged in the function of judging.

An important issue concerns what other officials conducting adjudicative proceedings can invoke absolute judicial immunity. In *Cleavinger v. Saxner*, the Supreme Court found that senior corrections officers who sat as members of prison disciplinary committees were not entitled to absolute immunity.[72]

Many lower courts, however, have extended absolute judicial immunity to government officials performing administrative adjudicatory tasks. For example, in *Capra v. Cook County Board of Review*, the Seventh Circuit held that members of a property tax board of review were protected by absolute immunity when sued

[67] *Id.* at 227.

[68] *See, e.g.*, Martinez v. Winner, 771 F.2d 424, 434-435 (10th Cir. 1985), *cert. granted, vacated, and remanded*, 475 U.S. 1138 (1986) (concluding that they are judicial); *see also* Davis v. Tarrant County, Tex., 565 F.3d 214 (5th Cir. 2009).

[69] Winner, 771 F.3d at 434 (concluding that they are judicial); *see also* Roth v. King, 449 F.3d 1272 (D.C. Cir. 2006) (holding it was a judicial act for a judge to create a panel system for appointing attorneys).

[70] *See, e.g.*, Hamilton v. City of Hayti, Mo., 948 F.3d 921 (8th Cir. 2020) (ruling that clerk was entitled to quasi-judicial immunity); Hamilton v. Murray, 648 Fed. Appx. 344 (4th Cir. 2016) (holding that clerks have immunity when acting under court direction); Snyder v. Nolan, 380 F.3d 279 (7th Cir. 2004) (holding that clerk was not entitled to immunity because he was not acting on the judge's direction); Clay v. Allen, 242 F.3d 679 (5th Cir. 2001) (court clerk protected by absolute immunity); Rodriguez v. Weprin, 116 F.3d 62, 66-67 (2d Cir. 1997) (court clerks protected by absolute immunity); Moore v. Brewster, 96 F.3d 1240 (9th Cir. 1996), *cert. denied*, 519 U.S. 1118 (1997) (law clerk assisting judge in carrying out judicial functions is protected by absolute immunity); Martin v. Board of County Commissioners of the County of Pueblo, 909 F.2d 402, 404-405 (10th Cir. 1990) (court officers are entitled to absolute immunity when executing orders of the court); Smith v. Tandy, 897 F.2d 355 (8th Cir. 1990) (court personnel get absolute immunity). It is clear, however, that private individuals who conspire with judges to violate rights cannot invoke the judge's immunity. *See* Dennis v. Sparks, 449 U.S. 24 (1980).

[71] 508 U.S. 429 (1993).

[72] 474 U.S. 193 (1985).

on a claim that they had violated equal protection and the First Amendment in their decisions.[73] In *Killinger v. Johnson,* the Seventh Circuit also held that a mayor's actions in suspending a liquor license and closing a bar were adjudicatory in nature and thus protected by absolute immunity.[74] In *Keystone Redevelopment Partners v. Decker,* the Third Circuit found that members of the state gaming board perform quasi-judicial functions and are thus protected by absolute judicial immunity.[75] In *Sinapi v. Rhode Island Board of Bar Examiners,* the First Circuit held that members of the Rhode Island Board of Bar Examiners were protected by absolute quasi-judicial immunity for denial of a request for accommodations.[76] In *Buckles v. King County,* the Ninth Circuit held that members of a growth management board, which adjudicates land use disputes, were protected by absolute immunity.[77] Similarly, in *Heyde v. Pittinger,* the Seventh Circuit ruled that members of county board of tax review were protected by absolute judicial immunity because their task was "quasi-judicial" in nature.[78]

Absolute Immunity for the Legislative Function

The legislative function is a second major area in which absolute immunity exists. Members of the U.S. Congress, and their aides, have absolute immunity to suits for damages and prospective relief because of the "speech and debate clause" of Article I, §6.[79] The Supreme Court has accorded state and local legislators similar absolute immunity, both to suits for money damages and equitable remedies.[80] For example, in the landmark case of *Tenney v. Brandhove,* the plaintiffs sought damages from legislators and their aides who operated the California Senate's Fact-Finding Committee on Un-American Activities.[81] Although the plaintiffs alleged a violation of their constitutional rights, the Court concluded that state legislators have absolute immunity when they act "in a field where legislators traditionally have power to act."[82]

[73] 733 F.3d 705 (7th Cir. 2013).
[74] 389 F.3d 765 (7th Cir. 2005).
[75] 631 F.3d 89 (3d Cir. 2011).
[76] 910 F.3d 544 (1st Cir. 2018).
[77] 191 F.3d 119 (9th Cir. 1999).
[78] 633 F.3d 512 (7th Cir. 2011).
[79] *See* Eastland v. United States Servicemen's Fund, 421 U.S. 491 (1975) (absolute immunity extends to suits for prospective relief); for a general discussion of the speech and debate clause, *see* Robert J. Reinstein & Harvey A. Silverglate, Legislative Privilege and the Separation of Powers, 86 Harv. L. Rev. 1113 (1973).
[80] *See* Supreme Court of Virginia v. Consumers Union, 446 U.S. 719 (1980) (absolute immunity from prospective relief; also equating immunity of state and local legislators with that accorded members of Congress under the speech and debate clause); Lake County Estates v. Tahoe Regional Planning Agency, 440 U.S. 391 (1979) (immunity for local and regional legislators); Tenney v. Brandhove, 341 U.S. 367 (1951) (absolute immunity from damages).
[81] 341 U.S. 367 (1951).
[82] *Id.* at 379.

The Supreme Court reaffirmed absolute immunity for legislators and made it clear that this extends to local legislators in *Bogan v. Scott-Harris.*[83] *Bogan* involved the decision of the mayor and the city council to eliminate a particular position as part of the budget process. The individual whose job was eliminated sued and alleged race discrimination and retaliation for speech activities. The U.S. Supreme Court found that the suit against both the mayor and the member of the city council had to be dismissed based on absolute legislative immunity. The Court unanimously concluded that the process of proposing, voting for, and signing a budget are "integral steps in the legislative process" and thus safeguarded by absolute immunity. The case is most remarkable in extending absolute legislative immunity to the acts of the mayor in the budget process. The mayor obviously is an executive official, and it is notable that the Court found all aspects of the budget process, even those traditionally done in the executive branch, should be deemed legislative in nature.

It must be emphasized that absolute immunity exists for *legislative* tasks; legislators do not have absolute immunity for their nonlegislative functions. In speaking of the immunity possessed by members of Congress, the Court remarked that for absolute immunity to exist, the activity "must be an integral part of the deliberative and communicative processes by which members participate in committee and House proceedings with respect to the consideration and passage or rejection of proposed legislation or with respect to other matters which the Constitution places within the jurisdiction of either house."[84] Again, line drawing often is a problem. The Court has recognized absolute immunity for all committee-related activities of legislators, but not for public statements and press releases.[85] There is a split in lower court authority as to whether the hiring and firing of legislative personnel should be considered a legislative task for which absolute immunity exists.[86] There also is the issue of who is entitled to absolute legislative immunity. For example, the Third Circuit held that the decision by a salary board to fire an individual was not protected by absolute immunity.[87] Similarly, the Eighth Circuit ruled that members of a university board of regents were not protected by absolute immunity.[88]

[83] 523 U.S. 44 (1998).

[84] Gravel v. United States, 408 U.S. 606, 625 (1972) (holding that a congressman who arranges for public printing and distribution of committee materials—here, the Pentagon Papers—could not invoke the speech and debate clause).

[85] *Compare* Tenney v. Brandhove, 341 U.S. 367, 377 (1951); Eastland v. United States Servicemen's Fund, 421 U.S. 491 (1975) (committee-related acts immunized) *with* Hutchinson v. Proxmire, 443 U.S. 111 (1979) (press statements not immunized).

[86] *Compare* Fowler-Nash v. Democratic Caucus of Pa. House of Representatives, 469 F.3d 328 (3d Cir. 2006) (denying legislative immunity); Davis v. Passman, 544 F.2d 865 (5th Cir. 1977), *rev'd on other grounds,* 442 U.S. 228 (1979) (denying legislative immunity); Chateaubriand v. Gaspard, 97 F.3d 1218 (9th Cir. 1996); Carver v. Foerster, 102 F.3d 96 (3d Cir. 1996) (denying legislative immunity), *with* Leapheart v. Williamson, 705 F.3d 310 (8th Cir. 2013) (according legislative immunity); Carlos v. Santos, 123 F.3d 61 (2d Cir. 1997); Agromayor v. Colberg, 738 F.2d 55 (1st Cir.), *cert. denied,* 469 U.S. 1037 (1984) (according legislative immunity).

[87] In re Montgomery County, 215 F.3d 367 (3d Cir. 2000).

[88] Maitland v. University of Minnesota, 260 F.3d 959 (8th Cir. 2001).

Prosecutorial Immunity

Third, the prosecutorial function is accorded absolute immunity to suits for money damages. The Supreme Court long has allowed prosecutors to be sued for injunctive relief.[89] However, in *Imbler v. Pachtman*, the Supreme Court accorded absolute immunity to a prosecutor who was sued for damages for knowingly using perjured testimony that resulted in an innocent person's conviction and incarceration for nine years.[90] The Court concluded that anything less than absolute immunity risked "harassment by unfounded litigation [that] would cause a deflection of the prosecutor's energies from his public duties, and the possibility that he would shade his decisions instead of exercising the independence of judgment required by his public trust."[91] However, it again must be asked whether something less than absolute immunity might have achieved this goal. For example, would prosecutorial liability for intentional use of known perjured testimony chill discretion in an undesirable way?[92]

The Court in *Imbler* specified that absolute immunity exists for prosecutorial tasks, but not for administrative functions carried out by prosecutors.[93] The Court admitted that "[d]rawing a proper line between these functions may present difficult questions."[94] In giving guidance to lower courts, the Court specified that absolute immunity exists for prosecutors when they decide whether to present a case to a grand jury, decide who or whether to prosecute, or decide what evidence and witnesses to present.[95]

In five post-*Imbler* cases, the Supreme Court has emphasized that investigative acts by a prosecutor are protected only by qualified immunity and has clarified the line between investigation and prosecution. In *Mitchell v. Forsyth*, the Court held that former Attorney General John Mitchell could claim only qualified, good-faith immunity for his decision to wiretap.[96] The Court concluded that such conduct was not prosecutorial in nature, and thus not a basis for absolute immunity.[97]

Burns v. Reed is a particularly important case in clarifying the scope of absolute prosecutorial immunity.[98] After Cathy Burns's children were shot in their sleep (both recovered), the police had no suspects. The police focused their investigation on Burns even though she passed a lie detector test and a voice stress test. A police officer thought that maybe she had a multiple personality disorder and an alternative personality was responsible for the shootings. The officer called the

[89] *See, e.g.*, Ex parte Young, 209 U.S. 123 (1908).

[90] 424 U.S. 409 (1976).

[91] *Id.* at 423.

[92] For a criticism of absolute prosecutorial immunity for such wrongdoing by prosecutors, *see* Douglas J. McNamara, *Buckley*, *Imbler* and Stare Decisis: The Present Predicament of Prosecutorial Immunity and an End to Its Absolute Means, 59 Alb. L. Rev. 1135 (1996).

[93] 424 U.S. at 431 n.33.

[94] *Id.*

[95] *Id.*

[96] 472 U.S. 511 (1985).

[97] *Id.* at 521.

[98] 500 U.S. 478 (1991).

Chief Deputy Prosecutor Rick Reed, who authorized putting Burns under hypnosis to discover possible alternative personalities. Under hypnosis, Burns at one point appeared to refer to the assailant as "Katie" and also seemed to refer to herself by that name. Based on this, the police officer told that prosecutor that there was probable cause for an arrest. The prosecutor obtained a warrant from a judge but did not disclose how the information was obtained.

Cathy Burns was arrested, spent four months in a psychiatric ward of a state hospital, and temporarily lost custody of her children. Repeated examinations found no evidence of a multiple personality disorder. Nor was there any evidence that she had been involved in the shootings.

The issue before the Supreme Court was whether the prosecutor had absolute immunity. The Court followed the line drawn in *Imbler v. Pachtman.* The Court held that prosecutors have absolute immunity for their in-court behavior, but not for their advice to police officers. Thus, the prosecutor, Reed, had absolute immunity for statements at the probable cause hearing. However, he had only qualified immunity for approving the hypnosis by the police officers. The Court explained that, historically, absolute immunity did not exist for prosecutors advising law enforcement officers and that the risk of vexatious suits did not justify absolute immunity for such conduct.

In *Buckley v. Fitzsimmons,* the Court emphasized the narrow scope of absolute prosecutorial immunity.[99] In a case involving a rape and murder, the prosecutor was sued for fabricating evidence by shopping for a favorable expert witness and for allegedly making false statements at a press conference. The plaintiff spent almost three years in jail, despite protests from a police officer who, feeling that the plaintiff was innocent, resigned from the police force in protest of the prosecution.

The Supreme Court unanimously held that the prosecutor's statements to the press were not protected by absolute immunity. Moreover, the Court ruled, 5-4, that the alleged fabrication of evidence was protected only by qualified immunity. The Court followed its historical approach and concluded that there is no authority that "a prosecutor's fabrication of false evidence during the preliminary investigation of an unsolved crime was immune from liability at common law, either in 1871, or at any date before the enactment of §1983. It therefore remains protected only by qualified immunity."[100]

The Court again applied the distinction between prosecutorial and investigative acts in *Kalina v. Fletcher.*[101] Rodney Fletcher was arrested for burglary based on three documents that the prosecutor filed in state court: an unsworn information charging him with burglary; an unsworn motion for an arrest warrant; and a declaration by the prosecutor summarizing the evidence supporting the charge. In the latter, the prosecutor swore to the truth of the facts alleged "[u]nder penalty of perjury." Based on these documents, an arrest warrant was issued, and the defendant was arrested and held in jail for a day. Subsequently, all charges were dropped.

[99] 509 U.S. 259 (1993).
[100] *Id.* at 275.
[101] 522 U.S. 118 (1997).

The defendant sued the prosecutor under 42 U.S.C. §1983 for violating his constitutional right to be free from unreasonable seizures. The defendant focused on two false factual statements contained in the prosecutor's declaration. The defendant was charged with stealing computers from a school. The prosecutor's declaration stated that the defendant's fingerprint was found on a glass partition in the school, and it stated that the defendant had "never been associated with the school in any manner and did not have permission to enter the school or take any property."[102] In fact, the defendant had installed partitions in the school and was authorized to be on the premises. The prosecutor's declaration also stated that an employee in an electronics store had identified the defendant as a person who came to the store and asked for an appraisal of a computer stolen from the school. However, this was false; the employee did not identify the defendant.

The Supreme Court held that the prosecutor's filing of the unsworn information and the unsworn motion for an arrest warrant were protected by absolute immunity. The Court, though, concluded that the filing of the sworn certificate was not protected by absolute immunity, but instead only qualified immunity. After reviewing its prior decisions concerning prosecutorial immunity, the Court concluded: "These cases make it quite clear that the petitioner's activities in connection with the preparation and filing of two of the three charging documents—the information and the motion for an arrest warrant—are protected by absolute immunity. Indeed, except for her act in personally attesting to the truth of the averments in the certification, it seems equally clear that the preparation and filing of the third document in the package was part of the advocate's function as well."[103]

The Court explained that neither federal nor state law required that the prosecutor file a declaration under penalty of perjury to obtain an arrest warrant. The Court said that by doing so, the prosecutor was acting as a witness, not as an advocate. In *Malley v. Briggs*, the Court had ruled that a police officer who obtains an arrest warrant based on a declaration containing false statements is not entitled to absolute immunity.[104] The Court said that the same principle applies to a prosecutor who files a declaration, under penalty of perjury, containing false allegations. The Court concluded that allowing liability for prosecutors acting as complaining witnesses does not "depart from our prior cases that have recognized that the prosecutor is fully protected by absolute immunity when performing the traditional functions of an advocate."[105]

Finally, in *Van de Kamp v. Goldstein*,[106] the Court found that the failure of a district attorney to develop policies to ensure compliance with *Brady v. Maryland* was prosecutorial in nature and thus protected by absolute immunity.[107] Tommy Lee Goldstein spent 23 years in prison for murders that he almost certainly did not commit. At his trial, there was no physical evidence linking him to the crimes,

[102] *Id.* at 121.
[103] *Id.* at 129.
[104] 475 U.S. 335 (1986).
[105] 522 U.S. at 131.
[106] 555 U.S. 355 (2009).
[107] 373 U.S. 83 (1963).

no eyewitnesses, and no incriminating statements. The key evidence against him was the testimony of two police informants who said that they had heard Goldstein admit to the crimes. One recanted his testimony, and the other had a long history of making deals with prosecutors for reduced charges and sentences in exchange for giving testimony. The prosecutors were obligated to turn over this information because of its potential usefulness in impeaching the witness,[108] but they did not do so.

Goldstein sued the then-district attorney, John Van de Kamp, on the ground that there had been an administrative failure to adequately train and supervise assistant district attorneys as to their obligations under *Brady*. The Supreme Court, however, unanimously held that the failure was *prosecutorial*, and therefore absolute immunity barred the suit. Justice Breyer, writing for the Court, explained that the inadequacies all directly related to what would happen in court and thus were properly deemed prosecutorial and not administrative. He wrote that there is "an intimate connection between prosecutorial activity and the trial process. The management tasks at issue, insofar as they are relevant, concern how and when to make impeachment information available at a trial. They are thereby directly connected with the prosecutor's basic trial advocacy duties."[109]

Although there is still some uncertainty as to the precise scope of prosecutorial immunity, *Imbler*, *Burns*, *Buckley*, *Kalina*, and *Van de Kamp* indicate that absolute immunity is reserved for traditional prosecutorial activities. In general, in-court activities by a prosecutor—such as the use of perjured testimony in *Imbler* and the request for the warrant in *Burns*—are protected by absolute immunity.[110] But out-of-court activities—such as authorizing the hypnosis in *Burns* and allegedly seeking a biased expert witness and making false statements at a press conference in *Buckley*—are generally covered only by qualified immunity. Likewise, under *Kalina*, the obtaining of warrants is protected only by qualified immunity. *Van de Kamp* indicates that out-of-court activities that have an "intimate connection" to what goes on in court are also protected by absolute immunity.

The Supreme Court has not yet ruled whether prosecutors are protected by absolute immunity when engaged in civil enforcement actions. In *Torres v. Goddard*, the Ninth Circuit ruled as a matter of first impression that absolute immunity is available to prosecutors in the context of civil forfeiture proceedings.[111] Similarly, in *Knowlton v. Shaw*, the First Circuit found that a prosecutor was protected by absolute immunity in negotiating a civil settlement.[112] However, the Ninth Circuit, in *Stapley v. Pestalozzi*, ruled that prosecutors are not protected by absolute immunity for civil RICO suits they initiated.[113] The court explained that because the

[108] Giglio v. United States, 405 U.S. 150 (1972).

[109] 555 U.S. at 862-863.

[110] *See, e.g.*, Spurlock v. Thompson, 330 F.3d 791 (6th Cir. 2003) (prosecutor's actions to have witnesses testify falsely are protected by absolute immunity); Cooper v. Parrish, 203 F.3d 937 (6th Cir. 2000) (initiation of civil forfeiture proceedings is protected by absolute immunity).

[111] 793 F.3d 1046 (9th Cir. 2015).

[112] 704 F.3d 1 (1st Cir. 2013).

[113] 733 F.3d 804 (9th Cir. 2013).

RICO suit was civil, it was not "intimately associated with the judicial phase of the *criminal* process."[114]

Police Officers As Witnesses

Fourth, the Supreme Court has held that police officers have absolute immunity for the testimony they give as witnesses, even if the police officers commit perjury. In general, police officers have only qualified, good-faith immunity to suits against them pursuant to §1983.[115] However, in *Briscoe v. LaHue*, the Court concluded that police officers who commit perjury have absolute immunity in suits against them for money damages.[116] The Court contended that officers should testify as witnesses without worry about possible civil litigation and argued that if absolute immunity did not exist, officers would be sued frequently. Thus, the Court concluded that allowing officers to be sued for their testimony as witnesses "might undermine not only their contribution to the judicial process but also the effective performance of their other public duties."[117] The Court emphasized that police officers, like all other witnesses, could be criminally prosecuted for perjury, and believed that this provided an adequate deterrent to perjury.

The Court extended this logic in *Rehberg v. Paulk*.[118] An investigator in a district attorney's office three times went before grand juries and allegedly lied and caused a person to be wrongly indicted three times. Each of the indictments was dismissed. The investigator was sued and raised absolute immunity as a defense. The Court ruled unanimously that the investigator was protected by absolute immunity.

Justice Alito wrote the opinion for a unanimous Court and began the opinion by stating: "This case requires us to decide whether a 'complaining witness' in a grand jury proceeding is entitled to the same immunity in an action under 42 U.S.C. §1983 as a witness who testifies at trial. We see no sound reason to draw a distinction for this purpose between grand jury and trial witnesses."[119] The Court explained: "The factors that justify absolute immunity for trial witnesses apply with equal force to grand jury witnesses. In both contexts, a witness' fear of retaliatory litigation may deprive the tribunal of critical evidence. . . . Neither is there any reason to distinguish law enforcement witnesses from lay witnesses."[120]

President of the United States

Fifth and finally, the Supreme Court has held that the president of the United States has absolute immunity to suits for money damages for acts done

[114] *Id.* at 810.

[115] *See, e.g.*, Pierson v. Ray, 386 U.S. 547 (1967) (police officers have qualified immunity in suits for damages).

[116] 460 U.S. 325 (1983).

[117] *Id.* at 343.

[118] 566 U.S. 356 (2012).

[119] *Id.* at 359.

[120] *Id.* at 367.

while carrying out the presidency and absolute immunity from criminal prosecution. Although previously the Court concluded that state governors can claim only good-faith immunity,[121] *Nixon v. Fitzgerald* accorded the president absolute immunity.[122] In a 5-4 decision, the Court held that the president's "unique status under the Constitution" and the "singular importance" of the duties of the office justified absolute immunity.[123] As in other cases according absolute immunity, the Court emphasized the likelihood of frequent suits as a justification for providing more than good-faith immunity.

It is important to note, however, that the Court's approach in *Nixon v. Fitzgerald* was substantially different from its customary approach to absolute immunities. As described above, absolute immunities generally attach to the function performed, not to the office. Hence, a more consistent approach would have been to hold that certain presidential tasks have absolute immunity, not that all presidential conduct is completely immunized. This was the position of the dissent.[124] The majority, however, felt that the unique nature of the presidency justified absolute immunity for actions of the office.

In *Clinton v. Jones*, the Court clarified the scope of presidential absolute immunity and ruled that the president has no immunity to suits for acts that allegedly occurred prior to taking office.[125] Paula Jones sued Bill Clinton for sexual harassment that allegedly occurred when he was governor of Arkansas. Clinton sought to have the suit dismissed or at least stayed until after the completion of his presidency. The U.S. Supreme Court disagreed and ruled that presidential immunity extends only to acts while in office. The Court stressed that no person, not even the president, is above the law. Moreover, immunities exist to protect the exercise of discretion in office; therefore, they do not extend to conduct before taking office. The Court said that trial courts should manage litigation against a president to minimize interference with presidential tasks. Of course, it was the Court's ruling in *Clinton v. Jones* that led to President Clinton being deposed in the Paula Jones case and to Clinton's denial of a sexual relationship with Monica Lewinsky.

The Court relied on *Nixon v. Fitzgerald* in holding, in *Trump v. United States*, that the president has absolute immunity from criminal prosecutions for official acts taken pursuant to constitutional or statutory authority.[126] The issue was whether and to what extent Donald Trump had immunity from criminal prosecution for actions taken to allegedly undermine the outcome of the 2020 presidential election. Jack Smith, the special counsel, sought an indictment, and a federal grand jury indicted Donald Trump on four counts for conduct that occurred while he was president that was intended to keep him in office and to deny the presidency to Joe Biden.

[121] Scheuer v. Rhodes, 416 U.S. 232 (1974).
[122] 457 U.S. 731 (1982).
[123] *Id.* at 750-751.
[124] *Id.* at 764 (White, J., dissenting).
[125] 520 U.S. 681 (1997).
[126] 603 U.S. 593 (2024).

Trump moved to dismiss the indictment, claiming absolute immunity from criminal prosecution for actions he took while president of the United States. The district court denied President Trump's motion to dismiss and the court of appeals affirmed the district court, denying Trump immunity from prosecution.

It was a 6-3 decision, with Chief Justice Roberts writing for the Court. Justices Thomas and Barrett each wrote concurring opinions. And Justices Sotomayor and Jackson each wrote blistering dissenting opinions.

Chief Justice Roberts's majority opinion began with the premise of a general need to protect the presidency from judicial scrutiny. He wrote: "The President occupies a unique position in the constitutional scheme, as 'the only person who alone composes a branch of government.' The Framers 'sought to encourage energetic, vigorous, decisive, and speedy execution of the laws by placing in the hands of a single, constitutionally indispensable, individual the ultimate authority that, in respect to the other branches, the Constitution divides among many.'"[127] The Court expressed concern that allowing criminal prosecutions of actions while in office could chill necessary presidential conduct. But the Court also recognized the importance of holding presidents accountable. Chief Justice Roberts observed: "The President, charged with enforcing federal criminal laws, is not above them."[128]

The Court then divided presidential acts into three categories. First, there are presidential acts carrying out official powers bestowed by the Constitution or federal statutes. For these, the president has absolute immunity from criminal prosecution. The Court said that "[w]hen the President exercises such authority, he may act even when the measures he takes are 'incompatible with the expressed or implied will of Congress.' The exclusive constitutional authority of the President 'disabl[es] the Congress from acting upon the subject.'"[129] In this realm, Congress cannot create criminal liability.[130]

The Court was explicit that the motives of the president are irrelevant and cannot be examined by a court. The Court declared: "In dividing official from unofficial conduct, courts may not inquire into the President's motives."[131] In fact, the Court went even further and said that evidence from these official acts could not be used to establish criminal liability in areas where the president does not have absolute immunity.

Second, there are actions that are at the "outer perimeter" of presidential powers. In this area, there is presumptive absolute immunity, but it can be overcome. The Court wrote: "[W]e conclude that the separation of powers principles explicated in our precedent necessitate at least a *presumptive* immunity from criminal prosecution for a President's acts within the outer perimeter of his official responsibility. Such an immunity is required to safeguard the independence and effective functioning of the

[127] *Id.* at 610.
[128] *Id.* at 614.
[129] *Id.* at 607.
[130] *Id.* at 611.
[131] *Id.* at 618.

Executive Branch, and to enable the President to carry out his constitutional duties without undue caution."[132]

The Court did not offer a definition of what it meant by the "outer perimeter" of presidential power.

Finally, according to the Court, there are acts of the president that do not fit into either of these categories. Such conduct is not protected by immunity. The Court declared: "As for a President's unofficial acts, there is no immunity."[133] Toward the end of the majority opinion, the Court reiterated: "The President enjoys no immunity for his unofficial acts, and not everything the President does is official. The President is not above the law."[134] In other words, the private acts of the president, conduct that is not carrying out the powers of the office, are not safeguarded by any immunity.

Justice Thomas wrote a concurring opinion strongly endorsing absolute presidential immunity, but then went further and addressed an issue not presented by the parties: Whether it violates separation of powers to have a special counsel who is appointed by the attorney general, but without specific legislative authority. Justice Barrett wrote a concurring opinion that urged a narrower view of absolute presidential immunity than taken by the majority. She said that she would have the Court "assess the validity of criminal charges predicated on most official acts—*i.e.*, those falling outside of the President's core executive power—in two steps. The first question is whether the relevant criminal statute reaches the President's official conduct. Not every broadly worded statute does. If the statute covers the alleged official conduct, the prosecution may proceed only if applying it in the circumstances poses no 'dange[r] of intrusion on the authority and functions of the Executive Branch.'"[135] She described this as similar to the approach urged by the special counsel.[136]

Justice Sotomayor wrote a vehement dissent, joined by Justices Kagan and Jackson. Her first paragraph made clear her strong disagreement with the majority opinion: "Today's decision to grant former Presidents criminal immunity reshapes the institution of the Presidency. It makes a mockery of the principle, foundational to our Constitution and system of Government, that no man is above the law. Relying on little more than its own misguided wisdom about the need for 'bold and unhesitating action' by the President, the Court gives former President Trump all the immunity he asked for and more. Because our Constitution does not shield a former President from answering for criminal and treasonous acts, I dissent."[137]

Justice Sotomayor argued that there is no authority for absolute presidential immunity in the text of the Constitution or its history. The Constitution provides members of Congress immunity in the "Speech and Debate" clause, but there is no comparable provision protecting the president. She said that there is also no

[132] *Id.* at 614.
[133] *Id.* at 615.
[134] *Id.* at 642.
[135] *Trump*, 603 U.S. at 652 (Barrett, J., concurring).
[136] *Id.*
[137] *Id.* at 657 (Sotomayor, J., dissenting).

historical support for broad presidential immunity from criminal prosecutions. To the contrary, she says, the "historical evidence reinforces that, from the very beginning, the presumption in this Nation has always been that no man is free to flout the criminal law."[138]

Justice Sotomayor saw great dangers in according a president absolute immunity for all official acts. She declared: "The President of the United States is the most powerful person in the country, and possibly the world. When he uses his official powers in any way, under the majority's reasoning, he now will be insulated from criminal prosecution. Orders the Navy's Seal Team 6 to assassinate a political rival? Immune. Organizes a military coup to hold onto power? Immune. Takes a bribe in exchange for a pardon? Immune. Immune, immune, immune."[139] She powerfully concluded, "With fear for our democracy, I dissent."[140]

Finally, Justice Jackson also wrote a dissent that stressed the rule of law. She lamented the Court's broad scope of absolute presidential immunity from criminal prosecution. She wrote: "The Court has now declared for the first time in history that the most powerful official in the United States can (under circumstances yet to be fully determined) become a law unto himself. . . . For my part, I simply cannot abide the majority's senseless discarding of a model of accountability for criminal acts that treats every citizen of this country as being equally subject to the law—as the Rule of Law requires."[141]

Ultimately, the majority and the dissent fundamentally disagreed over how to strike the balance between the need for presidential immunity and the need for presidential accountability. The majority strongly favored immunity; the dissent emphatically saw the need for accountability. Each side read its view into the Constitution. The majority saw the Constitution's granting authority to a president as justifying its conception of immunity. The dissent saw the checks and balances of the Constitution, the rejection of royal prerogatives, as support for allowing liability.

Other Officers' Claims for Absolute Immunity

Although the Court has only recognized absolute immunity for judges, legislators, prosecutors, police serving as witnesses, and the president, other officeholders contend that they, too, should be accorded absolute immunity. The Court has rejected many of these claims,[142] but others are left to be resolved. For instance, it

[138] *Id.* at 663-664.

[139] *Id.* at 685.

[140] *Id.* at 686.

[141] *Id.* at 705 (Jackson, J., dissenting).

[142] *See, e.g.,* Cleavinger v. Saxner, 474 U.S. 193 (1985) (senior corrections officers who sat as part of an "Institution Disciplinary Committee" to hear charges that inmates had violated prison rules are not entitled to absolute immunity); Ferri v. Ackerman, 444 U.S. 193 (1979) (court-appointed attorneys are not entitled to absolute immunity); Butz v. Economou, 438 U.S. 478 (1978) (federal executive officials are entitled to qualified immunity); Scheuer v. Rhodes, 416 U.S. 232 (1974) (governors are entitled to only qualified immunity).

is likely that at some point the Court will be called on to decide the nature of the immunity to be accorded to officials such as social workers,[143] probation officers,[144] government mediators,[145] and members of professional licensing boards.[146]

§8.6.3 *Qualified Immunity*

If officers are not performing a function accorded absolute immunity, they are then entitled to good-faith immunity, which is commonly termed "qualified immunity." Because absolute immunity is applied in relatively few circumstances, most executive branch and administrative officials can claim only qualified immunity.[147] The Supreme Court has declared that qualified immunity "represents the norm" for executive branch officials.[148] Qualified immunity exists only as to suits for damages, not as to suits for injunctive relief.[149]

Qualified immunity is an affirmative defense that the officer must raise; the plaintiff's complaint need not allege the absence of good faith.[150] Also, the

[143] *See, e.g.,* Cox v. Dep't of Social and Health Services, 913 F.3d 831 (9th Cir. 2019) (affording social workers qualified immunity); Brent v. Wayne County Dep't of Human Services, 901 F.3d 656 (6th Cir. 2018) (finding differing conduct afforded social workers varying levels of immunity); Kovacic v. Cuyahoga County Dept. of Children and Family Services, 724 F.3d 687 (6th Cir. 2013); Beltran v. Santa Clara County, 514 F.3d 906 (9th Cir. 2008) (en banc); Vaughn v. Ruoff, 253 F.3d 1124 (8th Cir. 2001); Holloway v. Brush, 220 F.3d 767 (6th Cir. 2000) (en banc) (qualified immunity for social workers); *but see* B.S. v. Somerset County, 704 F.3d 250 (3d Cir. 2013); Dornheim v. Sholes, 430 F.3d 919 (8th Cir. 2005); Abdouch v. Berger, 426 F.3d 982 (8th Cir. 2005). *See also* Gray v. Poole, 275 F.3d 1113 (D.C. Cir. 2002) (level of immunity for social workers depends on tasks performed).

[144] *Compare* Dettellis v. Sharbaugh, 919 F.3d 161 (2d Cir. 2019) (affording qualified immunity); Rose v. Flairty, 772 F.3d 552 (8th Cir. 2014) (affording quasi-judicial immunity); Peay v. Ajello, 470 F.3d 65 (2d Cir. 2006) (affording absolute immunity); Anton v. Genty, 78 F.3d 393, 396 (8th Cir. 1996) (absolute immunity to parole and probation officers), *with* Galvan v. Garmon, 710 F.2d 214 (5th Cir. 1983), *cert. denied,* 466 U.S. 949 (1984) (no absolute immunity for a probation officer's reports of parole violations).

[145] *See* Savoie v. Martin, 673 F.3d 488 (6th Cir. 2012) (affording judge quasi-judicial immunity for comments made as a mediator); Mills v. Killebrew, 765 F.2d 69 (6th Cir. 1985).

[146] *See, e.g.,* Buckwalter v. Nev. Bd. of Medical Examiners, 678 F.3d 737 (9th Cir. 2012) (affording absolute immunity); O'Neal v. Mississippi Board of Nursing, 113 F.3d 62, 66 (5th Cir. 1997) (absolute immunity for members of nurse licensing authority); Watts v. Burkhart, 978 F.2d 269, 278 (6th Cir. 1992) (members of state medical licensing board are protected by absolute immunity); Bettencourt v. Bd. of Registration in Medicine of the Commonwealth of Mass., 904 F.2d 772, 782 (9th Cir. 1990) (members of the medical board have absolute immunity).

[147] *See, e.g.,* Procunier v. Navarette, 434 U.S. 555 (1978) (prison officials have good-faith immunity); Wood v. Strickland, 420 U.S. 308 (1975) (school officials have good-faith immunity); Pierson v. Ray, 386 U.S. 547 (1967) (police officers have good-faith immunity).

[148] Buckley v. Fitzsimmons, 509 U.S. 259, 271 (1993).

[149] *See, e.g.,* Kanuszweski v. Mich. Dep't of Health and Human Services, 927 F.3d 396 (6th Cir. 2019); Neely-Bey Tarik-El v. Conley, 912 F.3d 989 (7th Cir. 2019); Montanez v. Sec'y Pa. Dep't of Corrections, 773 F.3d 472 (3d Cir. 2014); Valley v. Rapides Parish School Bd., 118 F.3d 1047 (5th Cir. 1997); Yang Jing Gan v. City of New York, 996 F.2d 522 (2d Cir. 1993).

[150] Nelson v. City of Madison Heights, 845 F.3d 695 (6th Cir. 2017); Oliver v. Roquet, 858 F.3d 180 (3d Cir. 2017); Story v. Foote, 782 F.3d 968 (8th Cir. 2015); Siegert v. Gilley, 500 U.S. 226 (1991); Gomez v. Toledo, 446 U.S. 635 (1980); Brooks v. Gaenzle, 614 F.3d 1213 (10th Cir. 2010).

Court has held that the denial of qualified immunity is an immediately appealable order.[151]

In recent years, the Court's qualified immunity decisions have been subjected to significant criticism.[152] Since *Harlow v. Fitzgerald*, discussed below, articulated the test for qualified immunity, there have been over 30 Supreme Court decisions dealing with the issue. Plaintiffs have prevailed only three times.[153] Some lower courts have criticized the Court for making the test for qualified immunity so difficult for plaintiffs whose constitutional rights have been violated to overcome. Judge Don Willett, on the United States Court of Appeals for the Fourth Circuit, wrote: "I write separately to register my disquiet over the kudzu-like creep of the modern immunity regime. . . . Section 1983 meets Catch-22. Plaintiffs must produce precedent even as fewer courts are producing precedent. Important constitutional questions go unanswered precisely because those questions are yet unanswered. Courts then rely on that judicial silence to conclude there's no equivalent case on the books. No precedent = no clearly established law = no liability. An Escherian Stairwell. Heads defendants win, tails plaintiffs lose. . . . I add my voice to a growing, cross-ideological chorus of jurists and scholars urging recalibration of contemporary immunity jurisprudence and its 'real world implementation.'"[154] Although there has been both conservative and liberal criticism of qualified immunity, and proposals in Congress to abolish it at least in police excessive force cases, no changes have yet occurred.[155]

Problem with Defining Qualified Immunity

The fundamental question concerning qualified immunity concerns the definition of "good faith." The ability of many injured plaintiffs to recover will turn on the standard for determining qualified immunity. The definition of qualified immunity must strike a balance between protecting the officer's exercise of discretion, while still compensating and deterring violations of federal law.

The standard for determining qualified immunity has evolved over many years. Interestingly, although the Court generally emphasizes a historical approach to immunities questions, neither the existence of qualified immunity nor the legal test devised by the Court has any support in the common law.

The Court's first attempt to define qualified immunity was in *Scheuer v. Rhodes.*[156] On May 4, 1970, the Ohio National Guard killed four students participating in an antiwar demonstration at Kent State University. Litigation was commenced on

[151] Mitchell v. Forsyth, 472 U.S. 511 (1985).

[152] Alexander A. Reinert, Qualified Immunity's Flawed Foundation, 111 Cal. L. Rev. 201 (2023); F. Andrew Hessick & Katherine C. Richardson, Qualified Immunity Laid Bare, 56 Wake Forest L. Rev. 501 (2021); William Baude, Is Qualified Immunity Unlawful? 106 U. Cal. L. Rev. 45 (2018); Joanna C. Schwartz, The Case Against Qualified Immunity, 93 Notre Dame L. Rev. 1797 (2018).

[153] Hope v. Pelzer, 536 U.S. 730 (2002); Groh v. Ramirez, 540 U.S. 551 (2004).

[154] Zadeh v. Robinson, 902 F.3d 483, 499 (5th Cir. 2018) (Willett, J., concurring).

[155] For an excellent analysis of the implications of eliminating qualified immunity, *see* Joanna C. Schwartz, After Qualified Immunity, 120 Colum. L. Rev. 309 (2020).

[156] 416 U.S. 232 (1974).

behalf of three of the students against the governor of Ohio and several state officials. The complaint alleged that the defendants "intentionally, recklessly, willfully and wantonly" deployed the National Guard and instructed them to act illegally.

The Supreme Court ruled that the governor lacked absolute immunity and could claim only qualified immunity. The Court stated that in determining whether an act is in good faith, "[i]t is the existence of reasonable grounds for the belief formed at the time and in light of all the circumstances, coupled with good faith belief, that affords a basis for qualified immunity of executive officers."[157] The *Scheuer* test contained both an objective component (was the act reasonable?) and a subjective component (did this officer believe it was reasonable?). Under *Scheuer*'s approach, a plaintiff could refute the existence of good faith *either* by demonstrating that a reasonable officer would find the action impermissible or by showing that this particular officer knew his or her action was unreasonable. A purely subjective standard, equating bad faith solely with malice or intent, apparently was rejected because it might encourage perjury and would not set a high enough standard for officer conduct. A purely objective standard, excluding liability based on the officer's actual state of mind, apparently was rejected because of a desire to deter and punish those who knowingly act in a wrongful manner.

The second major case developing the definition of qualified immunity was *Wood v. Strickland*.[158] Students who were expelled from school for the possession of alcohol claimed that they were denied procedural due process and sued school officials. The Supreme Court concluded that school officials are entitled to qualified immunity and then clarified the test for determining whether an action was in good faith. The Court emphasized that the test included both objective and subjective elements. An official is not immune if "he knew or reasonably should have known that the action . . . would violate . . . constitutional rights . . . , or if he took the action with the malicious intention to cause a deprivation of constitutional rights or other injury."[159] Under this standard, liability exists against an individual officer either by demonstrating that the officer acted unreasonably or with impermissible intent. Interestingly in light of subsequent developments, there was a vehement dissent criticizing the *objective* component of the legal test because of the difficulty of defining the law that an officer should be expected to know.[160]

Harlow v. Fitzgerald test

In 1982, in *Harlow v. Fitzgerald*, the Court substantially reformulated the test for determining whether the officer acted in good faith.[161] A. Ernest Fitzgerald, an analyst in the Air Force, sued claiming that his job was eliminated in retaliation for his exposing cost overruns in the Defense Department. Although in a companion

[157] *Id.* at 247-248.

[158] 420 U.S. 308 (1975).

[159] *Id.* at 321-322.

[160] *Id.* at 329 (Powell, J., dissenting; Justices Burger, Blackmun, and Rehnquist concurred in Powell's dissent).

[161] 457 U.S. 800 (1982).

case the Supreme Court found the president to possess absolute immunity, the other executive officials were accorded only qualified immunity.[162] However, the Court held that malice was no longer relevant in overcoming a claim of immunity. The Court expressly discarded the subjective component of the *Scheuer* and *Wood* cases. The Court articulated the test that still controls: "[G]overnment officials performing discretionary functions generally are shielded from liability for civil damages insofar as their conduct does not violate clearly established statutory or constitutional rights of which a reasonable person would have known."[163]

The Court said that the subjective element—allowing recovery upon proof of malice—was too disruptive of government operations. The Court felt that it was too easy for plaintiffs to allege malice with the hope of finding evidence during discovery. Such discovery was time-consuming for the officer and, additionally, it was difficult for trial courts to grant summary judgment on the malice question because subjective intent is a factual question that generally requires a trial.[164] The Court felt that the efficiency costs of the subjective component of the *Wood* test outweighed its benefits.

The effect of the Court's decision in *Harlow* "may be to allow an unscrupulous official to engage in malicious misuse of public authority whenever the relevant legal standards are objectively unclear."[165] The Court's concern is more with protecting officers from the additional costs of defending essentially meritless suits than with ensuring that injured individuals receive compensation for the wrongs they have suffered.

Ashcroft v. al-Kidd

In the 2011 case *Ashcroft v. al-Kidd*, the Court modified the phrasing of the *Harlow* test for qualified immunity.[166] Abdullah al-Kidd, a United States citizen and a married man with two children, was arrested at a Dulles International Airport ticket counter. Over the next 16 days, he was confined in high-security cells lit 24 hours a day in Virginia, Oklahoma, and then in Idaho, during which he was strip-searched on multiple occasions. Each time he was transferred to a different facility, al-Kidd was handcuffed and shackled about his wrists, legs, and waist. He was released on "house arrest" and subjected to numerous restrictions on his freedom. By the time al-Kidd's confinement and supervision ended, 15 months after his arrest, al-Kidd had been fired from his job as an employee of a government contractor and had separated from his wife.

Al-Kidd was not arrested and detained because he had committed a crime or even because there was probable cause that he had committed a crime. Rather, al-Kidd was held under the federal material witness statute, which allows the government to hold a material witness who has essential testimony and who otherwise

[162] Nixon v. Fitzgerald, 457 U.S. 731 (1982); discussed at text accompanying notes 122-125, *supra*.
[163] 457 U.S. at 818.
[164] *Id.* at 816-817.
[165] Low & Jeffries, *supra* note 17, at 871.
[166] 563 U.S. 731 (2011).

is likely to be unavailable to testify. But the government was not holding al-Kidd because they wanted to secure his testimony, as that statute requires. His detention had nothing to do with obtaining testimony from him. Rather, al-Kidd was detained to investigate him and the material witness statute was used because the government did not have enough evidence to arrest him on suspicion of any crime.

Al-Kidd was never charged with any crime, nor ever used as a material witness. He sued Attorney General John Ashcroft, who had authorized the detention. Ashcroft claimed that he was protected by qualified immunity and moved to dismiss the lawsuit. The federal court of appeals rejected this saying that any government official, and especially the attorney general of the United States, should know that it violates the Fourth Amendment to arrest and detain a person as a material witness if there is no desire to use the person as a witness and no probable cause to suspect that the person has committed any crime.[167]

The Supreme Court, however, reversed and held that al-Kidd had no claim upon which he could recover. Justice Scalia wrote for the Court and said that former Attorney General John Ashcroft was protected by qualified immunity because there was not clearly established law that his conduct was unconstitutional. The Court declared: "A Government official's conduct violates clearly established law when, at the time of the challenged conduct, '[t]he contours of [a] right [are] sufficiently clear' that *every* '*reasonable official* would have understood that what he is doing violates that right.' We do not require a case directly on point, but existing precedent *must have placed the statutory or constitutional question beyond debate*."[168] Justice Scalia concluded his opinion by very broadly defining the protection of qualified immunity. He wrote: "Qualified immunity gives government officials breathing room to make reasonable but mistaken judgments about open legal questions. When properly applied, it protects 'all but the plainly incompetent or those who knowingly violate the law.' "[169]

District of Columbia v. Wesby

In *District of Columbia v. Wesby*, the Court found that police did not violate the Fourth Amendment when they arrested people who were at a party in an unoccupied house.[170] The Court also concluded that even if there had been a Fourth Amendment violation, the officers were protected by qualified immunity. Justice Thomas, writing for the Court, summarized the law of qualified immunity:

> Under our precedents, officers are entitled to qualified immunity under §1983 unless (1) they violated a federal statutory or constitutional right, and (2) the unlawfulness of their conduct was "clearly established at the time." "Clearly established" means that, at the time of the officer's conduct, the law was "sufficiently clear" that every "reasonable official would understand that what he is doing" is

[167] Al-Kidd v. Ashcroft, 580 F.3d 949, 973 (9th Cir. 2009).
[168] 563 U.S. at 741 (emphasis added).
[169] *Id.* at 743.
[170] 583 U.S. 48 (2018).

unlawful. In other words, existing law must have placed the constitutionality of the officer's conduct "beyond debate." This demanding standard protects "all but the plainly incompetent or those who knowingly violate the law." To be clearly established, a legal principle must have a sufficiently clear foundation in then-existing precedent. The rule must be "settled law," which means it is dictated by "controlling authority" or "a robust consensus of cases of persuasive authority." It is not enough that the rule is suggested by then-existing precedent. The precedent must be clear enough that every reasonable official would interpret it to establish the particular rule the plaintiff seeks to apply. Otherwise, the rule is not one that "every reasonable official" would know. The "clearly established" standard also requires that the legal principle clearly prohibit the officer's conduct in the particular circumstances before him. The rule's contours must be so well defined that it is "clear to a reasonable officer that his conduct was unlawful in the situation he confronted." This requires a high "degree of specificity." We have repeatedly stressed that courts must not "define clearly established law at a high level of generality, since doing so avoids the crucial question whether the official acted reasonably in the particular circumstances that he or she faced." A rule is too general if the unlawfulness of the officer's conduct "does not follow immediately from the conclusion that [the rule] was firmly established."[171]

The Sequence of Analysis

Although the Court prescribed a two-step analysis for a court in evaluating whether an officer is protected by qualified immunity, it is now clear that it is not required that this be followed. In *Saucier v. Katz*,[172] the Court said that a court should first consider whether a constitutional right has been violated. If so, second, the court should determine whether it is a clearly established right that a reasonable officer should know.[173]

But in *Pearson v. Callahan*, the Court held that a court need not follow this two-step approach and can dismiss based on qualified immunity without deciding whether there has been a constitutional violation.[174] Callahan had agreed to a drug deal with an undercover police officer and invited the officer into his home. After doing so, many other officers entered. The Utah Supreme Court held that the entry by the other officers violated the Fourth Amendment because there was not consent to their presence and there was no warrant.

Callahan then sued for money damages for violation of his Fourth Amendment rights. The district court found in favor of the defendant officers on the ground that the law was not clearly established. The court of appeals reversed and found that there was a violation of clearly established federal law. The Supreme Court unanimously reversed in an opinion by Justice Alito.

The Court held that "the *Saucier* procedure should not be regarded as an inflexible requirement and that petitioners are entitled to qualified immunity on

[171] *Id.* at 62-64.
[172] 533 U.S. at 201 (2001).
[173] The Court earlier had prescribed this approach in Wilson v. Layne, 526 U.S. 603 (1999).
[174] 555 U.S. 223 (2009).

the ground that it was not clearly established at the time of the search that their conduct was unconstitutional."[175] The Court explained that if it is apparent that there is not clearly established law that a reasonable officer should know, it often would be better for a court to avoid deciding whether there is a constitutional violation. The Court stated that the *Saucier* "procedure sometimes results in a substantial expenditure of scarce judicial resources on difficult questions that have no effect on the outcome of the case. There are cases in which it is plain that a constitutional right is not clearly established but far from obvious whether in fact there is such a right. District courts and courts of appeals with heavy caseloads are often understandably unenthusiastic about what may seem to be an essentially academic exercise."[176]

The Court also said that in some instances there would be little value to a court deciding a constitutional issue, such as when the matter will soon be resolved by the Supreme Court, and often there will not be the needed facts for the constitutional ruling. The Court further said that "rigid adherence to the *Saucier* rule may make it hard for affected parties to obtain appellate review of constitutional decisions that may have a serious prospective effect on their operations. Where a court holds that a defendant committed a constitutional violation but that the violation was not clearly established, the defendant may face a difficult situation. As the winning party, the defendant's right to appeal the adverse holding on the constitutional question may be contested."[177] Also, requiring that there first be a determination of whether there is a constitutional violation, even when it is unnecessary to decide the case, is inconsistent with the Court's general desire to avoid rulings on constitutional issues.

However, the Court was clear that courts still may follow the two-step *Saucier* approach; it is just no longer required. The Court recognized that the two-step approach "is often beneficial," but "it should no longer be regarded as mandatory."[178] In fact, soon after *Pearson v. Callahan*, the Court followed the two-step approach in *Safford Unified School Dist. v. Redding* and held that school officials violated a seventh-grade girl's Fourth Amendment rights by subjecting her to a strip search but concluded that the defendants were protected by qualified immunity because the law was unclear as to when strip searches of students violate the Constitution.[179]

In *Camreta v. Greene*, the Court held that if a lower court follows the two-step approach, a defendant may appeal an adverse ruling on a constitutional issue, even if the court found him or her to be protected by qualified immunity.[180] The lower

[175] *Id.* at 227.

[176] *Id.* at 236-237. Whether the two-step *Saucier* approach is desirable in the development of the law is disputed. *Compare* Nancy Leong, The *Saucier* Qualified Immunity Experiment: An Empirical Analysis, 36 Pepp. L. Rev. 667 (2009) (the *Saucier* approach does not result in clarification of the law or development of constitutional rights), *with* Paul W. Hughes, Not a Failed Experiment: *Wilson-Saucier* Sequencing and the Articulation of Constitutional Rights, 80 U. Colo. L. Rev. 401 (2009).

[177] 555 U.S. at 240.

[178] *Id.* at 236.

[179] 557 U.S. 364 (2009).

[180] 563 U.S. 692 (2011).

court had found that school officials had violated a student's Fourth Amendment rights but that the defendants were protected by qualified immunity. Even though the defendants had prevailed, the Court said that they nonetheless could appeal. Justice Kagan, writing for the Court, explained: "This Article III standard often will be met when immunized officials seek to challenge a ruling that their conduct violated the Constitution. That is not because a court has made a retrospective judgment about the lawfulness of the officials' behavior, for that judgment is unaccompanied by any personal liability. Rather, it is because the judgment may have prospective effect on the parties."[181] The Court said that therefore qualified immunity is "in a special category when it comes to this Court's review of appeals brought by winners."[182]

On the one hand, allowing courts to dismiss based on qualified immunity without deciding whether there is a constitutional violation has the benefits identified in *Pearson*, especially of avoiding unnecessary constitutional rulings. But it also has a significant disadvantage: The constitutional right never gets established. In case after case, injured individuals, whose rights allegedly were violated, lose because there is no case establishing the right.

How Is it Determined If There Is Clearly Established Law That a Reasonable Officer Should Know?

The crucial question after *Harlow* is, what is a clearly established statutory or constitutional right of which a reasonable person would have known? Under what circumstances is a right deemed to be clearly established? How is it decided what a reasonable officer should know?[183]

The Supreme Court has addressed this in a series of cases since *Harlow*. In *Davis v. Scherer*, the Supreme Court held that the only relevant inquiry is whether the *federal* law rights are clearly established; it does not matter that the officer simultaneously violates state law rights that are clearly established.[184] The plaintiff contended that an officer who violates well-settled state law rights cannot be said to act in an objectively reasonable manner. The Court, however, felt that such an approach would impermissibly expand officer liability because recovery would be allowed any time the constitutional infringement also involved a violation of state law.[185]

The Supreme Court also clarified the *Harlow* test in *Anderson v. Creighton*.[186] In *Anderson*, the defendant, an FBI agent, conducted a warrantless search of the plaintiffs' home because the agent erroneously thought that bank robbers were hiding

[181] *Id.* at 702.

[182] *Id.* at 704.

[183] For a criticism of *Harlow* and an argument that it should be replaced by a more rules-based approach, *see* Alan K. Chen, The Ultimate Standard: Qualified Immunity in the Age of Constitutional Balancing, 81 Iowa L. Rev. 261 (1995).

[184] 468 U.S. 183 (1984).

[185] *Id.* at 195-196.

[186] 483 U.S. 635 (1987).

there. The Eighth Circuit denied the defendant qualified immunity because the law was settled that warrantless searches could not be done unless there was probable cause and exigent circumstances.

The Supreme Court, in an opinion by Justice Scalia, reversed. The Court said that qualified immunity is not lost when an officer violates the Fourth Amendment unless a reasonable officer would know that the *specific* conduct was impermissible. A "law enforcement officer who participates in a search that violates the Fourth Amendment may [not] be held personally liable for money damages if a reasonable officer could have believed that the search comported with the Fourth Amendment."[187] The inquiry appears to be whether the officer had reason to know that the specific conduct was prohibited.

The *Anderson* decision is troubling in a number of respects. First, in the facts of *Anderson,* it is clearly established that officers are not to conduct warrantless searches unless there is probable cause and exigent circumstances. Although there are cases in which the law is uncertain about the specific actions involved, *Anderson* is not such a situation. As Justice Stevens explained in dissent, the legal issue of exigent circumstances presented in the case is settled. Whether such exigent circumstances existed in this case is a factual, not a legal, issue, and therefore cannot be resolved on summary judgment or under the *Harlow* test.

Second, *Anderson* raises the question of how specific the law must be in order to deny an officer immunity. Must there be a law dealing with the exact behavior of the officer, especially when the action is unreasonable under the more general principles of law? In *Saucier v. Katz,* described above, the Court again emphasized that the determination of whether there is clearly established law must be made in a particularized sense with respect to the specific facts in the case and not as a broad, general proposition.[188]

A central issue in qualified immunity analysis is whether there needs to be a prior case on point, and how specific it must be in order to create clearly established law. On the one hand, in *Hope v. Pelzer* the Court held that there need not be a prior decision on point in order for the plaintiff to show the existence of clearly established law.[189] Rather, officers can be held liable as long as they had "fair warning" that their conduct was impermissible.[190] This standard makes it much easier for civil rights plaintiffs, as compared with an approach that would have required that there be cases on point to say that there is clearly established law.

In 1995, Larry Hope was a prisoner at the Limestone Prison in Alabama. At the time, Alabama was the only state in the country that handcuffed prisoners to "hitching posts" if they disrupted work squads or refused to work. Twice, Hope was tied to a hitching post by prison guards. On May 11, 1995, Hope was tied to a hitching post for two hours because of an altercation with another inmate. During this time, he was offered drinking water and a bathroom break every 15 minutes. On June 7, 1995, Hope was again tied to a hitching post for getting into a scuffle with a prison

[187] *Id.*
[188] 533 U.S. at 206.
[189] 536 U.S. 730 (2002).
[190] *Id.* at 741.

guard. This time, he was tied to the hitching post for seven hours. During this time, he was given no access to a bathroom and was given water only once or twice. Officers taunted him by giving water to some dogs and pouring water on the ground. Guards took away Hope's shirt and left him to burn in the hot sun.

Hope sued the three guards responsible for tying him to the hitching post. The district court dismissed Hope's case based on qualified immunity, and the U.S. Court of Appeals for the Eleventh Circuit affirmed. The Eleventh Circuit emphasized that there was not a case on point with facts materially similar to Hope's allegations.[191]

Courts, at all levels, had struggled with how to determine whether there is clearly established law that a reasonable officer should know. Some decisions, like the Eleventh Circuit in *Hope*, stressed the need for cases on point.[192]

In *United States v. Lanier*, five years before *Hope v. Pelzer*, the Supreme Court seemed to approve this approach to determining qualified immunity.[193] *Lanier* was not a civil suit under §1983, but rather was a criminal prosecution under 18 U.S.C. §242. Both §1983 and §242 were enacted as part of the Civil Rights Act of 1871; the former creates civil liability and the latter criminal liability for those acting under color of state law who deprive a person of rights protected by the Constitution.

Lanier involved a state court judge, Lanier, who had sexually assaulted and harassed women in his chambers. The U.S. Court of Appeals for the Sixth Circuit ruled in favor of Lanier, emphasizing the absence of prior decisions explicitly deeming such conduct to be a violation of constitutional rights. The Supreme Court reversed and stressed that a reasonable person surely would know that such behavior is a violation of a woman's constitutional rights.

In *Hope v. Pelzer*, in a 6-3 decision, the Supreme Court ruled that the officers who tied Hope to a hitching post were not entitled to qualified immunity. Justice Stevens, writing for the Court, followed the now familiar two-step approach described above: First, the Court determines whether the plaintiff's allegations, if true, would establish a constitutional violation, and if so, second, the Court decides whether the government officer's action violates clearly established law that a reasonable officer should know.[194]

The Supreme Court, like the Eleventh Circuit, found that the use of the hitching post was unconstitutional. The Court long has held that "the unnecessary and wanton infliction of pain . . . constitutes cruel and unusual punishment forbidden by the Eighth Amendment."[195] The Court said that based on the facts alleged by Hope, "the Eighth Amendment violation is obvious. . . . Despite the clear lack of

[191] 240 F.3d 975, 981 (11th Cir. 2001).

[192] On the other hand, some courts expressly ruled that cases on point were not necessary for there to be clearly established law. In *Burgess v. Lowery*, 201 F.3d 942 (7th Cir. 2000), the Seventh Circuit held that the existence of a decision within the circuit is not necessary for a court to find that there is clearly established law. Judge Richard Posner, writing for the court, explained that such a requirement would protect behavior that was so outrageous that no court would have had occasion to disapprove it in a published opinion.

[193] 520 U.S. 259 (1997).

[194] Saucier v. Katz, 533 U.S. 194, 201 (2001).

[195] Whitley v. Albers, 475 U.S. 312, 319 (1986).

an emergency situation, the respondents knowingly subjected him to a substantial risk of physical harm, to unnecessary pain caused by the handcuffs and the restricted position of confinement for a seven-hour period, to unnecessary exposure to the heat of the sun, and to a deprivation of bathroom breaks that created a risk of particular discomfort and humiliation."[196] The Court said that "[t]his punitive treatment amounts to gratuitous infliction of 'wanton and unnecessary' pain that our precedent clearly prohibits."[197]

The Court then turned its attention to whether the officers were protected by qualified immunity. Justice Stevens said that the Eleventh Circuit's insistence on prior decisions on point was a "rigid gloss" unsupported by Supreme Court precedents.[198] The Court stressed that qualified immunity operates "to ensure that before they are subjected to suit, officers are on notice that their conduct is unlawful."[199] Thus, the key inquiry is whether the officer had "fair notice" that the conduct was a violation of rights. Justice Stevens explained that the central question in determining whether the prison officials could be held liable to Hope was "whether the state of the law in 1995 gave [them] fair warning that their alleged treatment of Hope was unconstitutional."[200] The Court then reviewed the law as it existed in 1995 and said that the officers had fair warning that their conduct was unconstitutional.

In the years following *Hope v. Pelzer,* the decision was virtually never cited or even acknowledged by the Supreme Court until *Taylor v. Riojas* in 2020.[201] Trent Taylor was a prisoner in Texas. For a period of six days, he was confined in a pair of what the Court rightly described as "shockingly unsanitary cells."[202] The Court explained that "[t]he first cell was covered, nearly floor to ceiling, in 'massive amounts' of feces: all over the floor, the ceiling, the window, the walls, and even 'packed inside the water faucet.'"[203] Over a period of four days, Taylor could not eat or drink for fear of contamination.

Taylor was then moved to a very cold cell, "with only a clogged drain in the floor to dispose of bodily wastes."[204] The Court said: "Taylor held his bladder for over 24 hours, but he eventually (and involuntarily) relieved himself, causing the drain to overflow and raw sewage to spill across the floor. Because the cell lacked a bunk, and because Taylor was confined without clothing, he was left to sleep naked in sewage."[205]

Taylor sued the corrections officers, alleging that they violated the Eighth Amendment because their treatment of him was cruel and unusual punishment. The district court ruled in favor of the defendants based on qualified immunity,

[196] 536 U.S. at 737.
[197] *Id.*
[198] *Id.*
[199] *Id.* at 740.
[200] *Id.*
[201] 592 U.S. 7 (2020) (per curiam).
[202] Taylor v. Riojas, 592 U.S. 7, 7 (2020) (per curiam).
[203] *Id.* at 7-8.
[204] *Id.* at 8.
[205] *Id.*

holding that they could not be held liable because they did not violate clearly established law that every reasonable officer should know.

The United States Court of Appeals for the Fifth Circuit affirmed the dismissal of Taylor's case.[206] Although the Court of Appeals concluded that Taylor's constitutional rights had been violated—confinement in these cells constituted cruel and unusual punishment—it also concluded that the officers were protected by qualified immunity. It said that the officers could not be held liable because "[t]he law wasn't clearly established" that "prisoners couldn't be housed in cells teeming with human waste" for only six days.[207]

The Supreme Court, in a 7-1 decision, with only Justice Thomas dissenting (and Justice Barrett not participating), the Court reversed the Fifth Circuit in a *per curiam* opinion. The Court held that the officers were not protected by qualified immunity because "no reasonable correctional officer could have concluded that, under the extreme circumstances of this case, it was constitutionally permissible to house Taylor in such deplorably unsanitary conditions for such an extended period of time."[208] The Court said: "Confronted with the particularly egregious facts of this case, any reasonable officer should have realized that Taylor's conditions of confinement offended the Constitution."[209]

Justice Thomas did not write a dissenting opinion. The *per curiam* opinion simply states, "Justice Thomas dissents."[210]

The case is important in that it is a rare affirmation by the Court that there does not need to be a case on point to overcome qualified immunity.

On the other hand, in many qualified immunity decisions the Court has stressed the absence of cases on point as a basis for dismissing a case based on qualified immunity. In *Brosseau v. Haugen*,[211] a police officer, Brosseau, was chasing a suspect, Haugen, who was wanted on a warrant. Haugen got into a car and began backing it out of a driveway to get away from the officer. Brosseau raised her gun and ordered Haugen to get out of the car. When Haugen refused and continued to back out, Brosseau shot and seriously wounded Haugen.

Haugen sued for the use of excessive force, and Brosseau raised qualified immunity as a defense. The district court granted the defendant's motion to dismiss, but the Ninth Circuit reversed. The Supreme Court granted certiorari and decided the case based entirely on the petition and opposition for certiorari; the case was never briefed or argued.

In a per curiam opinion, with only Justice Stevens dissenting, the Supreme Court held that the officer was protected by qualified immunity. The Court declared: "We therefore turn to ask whether, at the time of Brosseau's actions, it was 'clearly established' in this more 'particularized' sense that she was violating Haugen's Fourth Amendment right. The parties point us to only a handful of cases

[206] Taylor v. Stevens, 946 F.3d 211 (2019).
[207] *Id.* at 222.
[208] 592 U.S. at 8-9.
[209] *Id.* at 9.
[210] *Id.* at 10.
[211] 543 U.S. 194 (2004).

relevant to the situation Brosseau confronted: whether to shoot a disturbed felon, set on avoiding capture through vehicular flight, when persons in the immediate area are at risk from that flight."[212] The Court stressed the lack of cases on point in ordering the case dismissed for lack of qualified immunity. The Court concluded its opinion by stating: "These three cases taken together undoubtedly show that this area is one in which the result depends very much on the facts of each case. None of them squarely governs the case here; they do suggest that Brosseau's actions fell in the 'hazy border between excessive and acceptable force.' The cases by no means 'clearly establish' that Brosseau's conduct violated the Fourth Amendment."[213]

In *Ashcroft v. al-Kidd*, discussed above, the Court again found qualified immunity based on the absence of cases on point.[214] Al-Kidd was arrested on a material witness warrant, even though there was no desire to ever use him as a material witness. He was held in maximum-security prisons and on his release was placed under house arrest. He never was charged with any crime and never used as a material witness. He sued the attorney general, John Ashcroft, contending that the material witness warrant was a pretext for holding him to question him in the absence of any probable cause for his arrest.

The Supreme Court ruled that the attorney general was protected by qualified immunity and stressed the absence of cases on point holding that such conduct violates the Fourth Amendment. Justice Scalia, writing for the Court, said, "At the time of al-Kidd's arrest, not a single judicial opinion had held that pretext could render an objectively reasonable arrest pursuant to a material-witness warrant unconstitutional."[215] Justice Scalia emphasized that more general principles of the Fourth Amendment were not sufficient to overcome qualified immunity: "The Court of Appeals also found clearly established law lurking in the broad 'history and purposes of the Fourth Amendment.' We have repeatedly told courts . . . not to define clearly established law at a high level of generality. The general proposition, for example, that an unreasonable search or seizure violates the Fourth Amendment is of little help in determining whether the violative nature of particular conduct is clearly established."[216]

In three cases in 2014, the Court found qualified immunity based on the absence of a case on point. All were unanimous. In *Lane v. Franks*, the Court unanimously held that a government employee's First Amendment rights were violated when he was fired for truthful testimony he gave in court pursuant to a subpoena.[217] This seems obvious; of course, it is wrong to fire a person for testifying honestly in a criminal trial, especially when the individual had no choice but to testify because of a subpoena.

[212] *Id.* at 199.
[213] *Id.* at 201.
[214] 563 U.S. 731 (2011).
[215] *Id.* at 741.
[216] *Id.* at 742.
[217] 573 U.S. 228 (2014).

Nonetheless, the Court found that the defendant responsible for the firing was protected from liability by qualified immunity. Justice Sotomayor, writing for the Court, said that "[t]he relevant question for qualified immunity purposes is this: Could Franks reasonably have believed, at the time he fired Lane, that a government employer could fire an employee on account of testimony the employee gave, under oath and outside the scope of his ordinary job responsibilities?"[218] The Court reviewed precedents, especially from the Eleventh Circuit, and found that none had clearly held that this violates the First Amendment.

In *Plumhoff v. Rickard*, the Court also found that government officials were protected by qualified immunity.[219] Police officers pulled over a white Honda Accord because the car had only one operating headlight. Donald Rickard was the driver of the Accord, and Kelly Allen was in the passenger seat. The officer asked Rickard if he had been drinking, and Rickard responded that he had not. Because Rickard failed to produce his driver's license upon request and appeared nervous, the officer asked Rickard to step out of the car. Rather than comply with the officer's request, Rickard sped away.

A high-speed chase then occurred that lasted five minutes and reached speeds over 100 miles per hour. At one point, the officers appeared to have Rickard's car pinned. But when the car pulled away, officers fired three shots into the car. As the car attempted to speed away, another 12 shots were fired by the police. Both the driver and the passenger were killed. The United States Court of Appeals for the Sixth Circuit concluded that the police used excessive force and violated the Fourth Amendment.

The United States Supreme Court unanimously reversed, ruling in favor of the police. Justice Samuel Alito wrote for the Court and held that there was no violation of the Fourth Amendment. The Court said that the driver's conduct posed a "grave public safety risk" and that the police were justified in shooting at the car to stop it.[220] The Court said "[i]t stands to reason that, if police officers are justified in firing at a suspect in order to end a severe threat to public safety, the officers need not stop shooting until the threat has ended."[221] Moreover, the Court said that even if there were a Fourth Amendment violation, the officers were protected by qualified immunity in that the law was not clearly established that the conduct violated the Fourth Amendment. The Court concluded: "[W]e hold that the Fourth Amendment did not prohibit petitioners from using the deadly force that they employed to terminate the dangerous car chase that Rickard precipitated. In the alternative, we note that petitioners are entitled to qualified immunity for the conduct at issue because they violated no clearly established law."[222]

Finally, in *Wood v. Moss*, the Court found that Secret Service agents were protected by qualified immunity when they engaged in viewpoint discrimination with

[218] *Id.* at 243.
[219] 572 U.S. 765 (2014).
[220] *Id.* at 777.
[221] *Id.*
[222] *Id.* at 781.

regard to speakers.[223] President George W. Bush was in Oregon and the Secret Service agents allowed supporters of President Bush to be closer and pushed opponents further away. The law is clear that the government cannot discriminate among speakers based on their views unless strict scrutiny is met.

Nonetheless, the Court, in a unanimous decision with the majority opinion written by Justice Ginsburg, found that the Secret Service agents were protected by qualified immunity because there were no cases on point concerning when Secret Service agents violate the First Amendment. The Court explained: "No decision of which we are aware, however, would alert Secret Service agents engaged in crowd control that they bear a First Amendment obligation 'to ensure that groups with different viewpoints are at comparable locations at all times.' "[224]

In a per curiam opinion in *City of Escondido, California v. Emmons*, in 2019, the Court said that a body of case law is usually needed to have clearly established law: "[W]e have stressed the need to identify a case where an officer acting under similar circumstances was held to have violated the Fourth Amendment. . . . While there does not have to be a case directly on point, existing precedent must place the lawfulness of the particular [action] beyond debate. . . . Of course, there can be the rare obvious case, where the unlawfulness of the officer's conduct is sufficiently clear even though existing precedent does not address similar circumstances. . . . But a body of relevant case law is usually necessary to clearly establish the answer. . . ."[225]

In more recent cases, too, the Court has stressed the absence of a case on point as a basis for finding qualified immunity. Both *Rivas-Villegas v. Cortesluna* and *City of Tahlequah v. Bond* involved claims against police officers for excessive force. In each, the Court reversed a federal court of appeals and found qualified immunity, stressing the absence of a case with sufficiently similar facts.

In *Rivas-Villegas v. Cortesluna*, police responded to a domestic violence call.[226] Ramon Cortesluna, the suspect, came out of the house and was shot twice by the police when he put his hands down after being told not to do so. Officer Daniel Rivas-Villegas then pushed him onto the ground and pressed his knee against Cortesluna's back so that a colleague could handcuff him.

Cortesluna sued the officers for excessive force. The federal district court concluded that the force used by both officers was reasonable and that the officers were entitled to qualified immunity. The Ninth Circuit found that the firing of the shots with beanbag rounds was protected by qualified immunity, but that it was excessive force for a police officer to press his knee into the back of a suspect lying face down on the ground hard enough to cause an injury.

The Supreme Court unanimously reversed in a per curiam opinion and concluded that the officer was protected from liability by qualified immunity. The Court stressed the absence of a case with sufficiently similar facts. The Court declared: "Even assuming that controlling Circuit precedent clearly establishes law

[223] 572 U.S. 744 (2014).
[224] *Id.* at 759-760.
[225] 586 U.S. 38, 43-44 (2019).
[226] 595 U.S. 1 (2021).

for purposes of §1983, [prior precedent] did not give fair notice to Rivas-Villegas. He is thus entitled to qualified immunity."[227] The Court said: "Although 'this Court's case law does not require a case directly on point for a right to be clearly established, existing precedent must have placed the statutory or constitutional question beyond debate.' "[228]

Although the Court says that there does not need to be a case "directly on point," it then finds qualified immunity entirely because no prior decision had sufficiently similar facts.

The Court's other decision, *City of Tahlequah v. Bond*, similarly arose from a domestic violence situation.[229] Police were called by a woman to remove her ex-husband, Dominic Rollice, from her home. The police confronted Rollice in a garage. While talking to the police, Rollice picked up a hammer. When Rollice disobeyed the police order to drop the hammer, police shot and killed him.

Rollice's estate sued the police for excessive force. The federal district court ruled in favor of the officers, but the United States Court of Appeals for the Tenth Circuit reversed. The Court of Appeals found that the police used excessive force and were not protected by qualified immunity. The Court of Appeals found that the officers were not in danger from the hammer, and the use of deadly force was unreasonable under the circumstances.

The Supreme Court again reversed in a per curiam opinion. Once more, the Court stressed the absence of a case with sufficiently similar facts. It stated: "Not one of the decisions relied upon by the Court of Appeals . . . comes close to establishing that the officers' conduct was unlawful."[230] The Court concluded its decision by declaring: "Neither the panel majority nor the respondent have identified a single precedent finding a Fourth Amendment violation under similar circumstances. The officers were thus entitled to qualified immunity."[231]

It is notable that both of these decisions were unanimous and that the justices saw them as sufficiently clear as to not even need briefing and oral argument. At the very least, they show that in police excessive force cases, the Court insists that there be a case with very similar facts or the officers must be deemed to be protected by qualified immunity. There thus is a high hurdle for plaintiffs seeking to recover for claims of excessive use of force by the police.

There is an obvious tension between *Hope v. Pelzer* and *Taylor v. Riojas*, declaring that there need not be a case on point to overcome qualified immunity, and the subsequent cases, finding qualified immunity based on the lack of a case on point. It is striking that the Court in the subsequent cases does not discuss or even cite *Hope v. Pelzer*. Not surprisingly, there is great confusion in the lower courts as to whether and when cases on point are needed to overcome qualified immunity.

In a number of cases, the Court has ordered cases dismissed based on qualified immunity because the right was not established at a sufficient degree of specificity.

[227] *Id.* at 5.
[228] *Id.*
[229] 595 U.S. 9 (2021).
[230] *Id.* at 13.
[231] *Id.* at 14.

It is unclear how this is different from the inquiry as to whether there is a case sufficiently on point. For example, in *City & Cnty. of San Francisco, Calif. v. Sheehan*, the Court said that police officers who shot an obviously mentally disturbed woman were protected by qualified immunity because the right was not established at a sufficiently specific level of abstraction: "The real question . . . is whether, despite these dangerous circumstances, the officers violated the Fourth Amendment when they decided to reopen Sheehan's door rather than attempting to accommodate her disability. . . . Rather, we simply decide whether the officers' failure to accommodate Sheehan's illness violated clearly established law. It did not. To begin, nothing in our cases suggests the constitutional rule applied by the Ninth Circuit. The Ninth Circuit focused on *Graham v. Connor*, . . . but *Graham* holds only that the 'objective reasonableness' test applies to excessive-force claims under the Fourth Amendment. . . . That is far too general a proposition to control this case. 'We have repeatedly told courts—and the Ninth Circuit in particular—not to define clearly established law at a high level of generality.' . . . Qualified immunity is no immunity at all if 'clearly established' law can simply be defined as the right to be free from unreasonable searches and seizures."[232] In other cases, too, the Court has ordered cases dismissed because the right was not established at a specific enough level of generality.[233]

The Court has repeatedly emphasized the importance of determining qualified immunity as a question of law early in the proceedings.[234] In *Siegert v. Gilley*, the Court held that it is for the trial court to determine whether the law was clearly established at the time of the defendant's conduct and that discovery should be allowed only if the court finds that the officers' conduct violated a clearly established right.[235] In other words, the analytical framework of §1983 cases requires the trial court to decide that there was a violation of a clearly established right before permitting discovery to proceed.

In *Hunter v. Bryant*, the Court stressed that qualified immunity is generally a question of law, not fact, for the judge to resolve.[236] James Bryant delivered a letter to administrators of the University of Southern California that stated that there was a plot to assassinate President Reagan by "Mr. Image." The Secret Service arrested

[232] City & Cty. of S.F. v. Sheehan, 575 U.S. 600 (2015).

[233] *See, e.g.*, White v. Pauly, 580 U.S. 73 (2017) ("Today, it is again necessary to reiterate the longstanding principle that 'clearly established law' should not be defined 'at a high level of generality.' As this Court explained decades ago, the clearly established law must be 'particularized' to the facts of the case. Otherwise, '[p]laintiffs would be able to convert the rule of qualified immunity . . . into a rule of virtually unqualified liability simply by alleging violation of extremely abstract rights.' "); *see also* Kisela v. Hughes, 584 U.S. 100 (2018).

[234] Because the question of whether there is clearly established law is a question of law, a court of appeals can determine the state of the law on its own even if the appropriate precedents were not raised by the parties below. In Elder v. Holloway, 510 U.S. 510, 511 (1994), the Supreme Court unanimously declared: "Whether an asserted federal right was clearly established at a particular time, so that a public official who allegedly violated the right has no qualified immunity from suit, presents a question of law, not one of 'legal facts.' That question of law . . . must be resolved *de novo* on appeal. A court in engaging in a review of a qualified immunity judgment should therefore use its 'full knowledge of its own and other relevant precedents.'"

[235] 500 U.S. 226 (1991).

[236] 502 U.S. 224 (1991).

Bryant for making threats against the president, although ultimately the complaint was dismissed. Bryant then sued the Secret Service officers for several constitutional violations, including arresting and searching him without probable cause or a warrant. The Supreme Court held that the officers had qualified immunity because their actions were reasonable. In a per curiam opinion, the Court stated that "[i]mmunity ordinarily should be decided by a court long before trial."[237] The Court said that "[t]he qualified immunity standard gives ample room for mistaken judgments by protecting all but the plainly incompetent and those who knowingly violate the law."[238]

The Court also has clarified an additional important procedural aspect of §1983: A heightened proof standard is not appropriate when an improper motive must be demonstrated in order to prevail on a constitutional claim. In *Crawford-El v. Britton,* the Court held that improper motive need be proven only per the usual requirement in civil cases of proof, by a preponderance of the evidence.[239] *Crawford-El* involved a prisoner who claimed that prison officials intentionally lost his possessions in retaliation for his being outspoken to the press. The U.S. Court of Appeals for the District of Columbia Circuit in an en banc opinion concluded that protecting *Harlow*'s objective standard requires that subjective motivation be proven by clear and convincing evidence when it is a part of the constitutional claim.

The U.S. Supreme Court, in a 5-4 decision, reversed and held that nothing in the text of §1983 or its legislative history supports imposing a heightened proof requirement. Indeed, Justice Kennedy in a concurring opinion indicated support for such a requirement, but said that it should come from Congress and not the judiciary.[240] Justice Stevens's majority opinion emphasized that district courts should use case management techniques to protect officers from frivolous suits, rather than imposing a heightened proof requirement.[241]

Chief Justice Rehnquist, in a dissenting opinion joined by Justice O'Connor, argued that a defendant should be entitled to qualified immunity if he or she offers a legitimate reason for the actions and the plaintiff is unable to establish by "objective evidence" that the reason is a pretext.[242] Justice Scalia, joined by Justice Thomas, went even further and contended that a defendant should prevail if he or she can provide any conceivable permissible motive for the conduct.[243] Justice Scalia sharply criticized *Monroe v. Pape*'s allowing officers to be held liable for wrongful conduct not authorized by law and said that "once the trial court finds that the asserted grounds for the official action were objectively valid . . . , it would not admit any proof that something other than these reasonable grounds was the genuine motive."[244]

[237] *Id.* at 228.

[238] *Id.* (citations omitted).

[239] 523 U.S. 574 (1998).

[240] *Id.* at 601 (Kennedy, J., concurring).

[241] For a discussion of the problems in handling qualified immunity issues on summary judgment, *see* Alan Chen, The Burdens of Qualified Immunity: Summary Judgment and the Role of Facts in Constitutional Tort Law, 47 Am. U. L. Rev. 1 (1997).

[242] 523 U.S. at 609 (Rehnquist, C.J., dissenting).

[243] *Id.* at 611-612 (Scalia, J., dissenting).

[244] *Id.*

Crawford-El is important because many constitutional claims require proof of an impermissible government purpose or motive. For instance, equal protection challenges to laws that are facially race- or gender-neutral, but that have a discriminatory impact, require proof of a discriminatory purpose.[245] Likewise, a government employee suing an employer for violating his or her free speech rights must prove that retaliation for expression was a substantially motivating factor for the adverse employment action.[246] *Crawford-El* would have imposed a substantial obstacle to recovery in such suits had it approved a heightened pleadings standard.

Private Individuals Sued Under §1983

Although §1983 usually is used only against government officers because of its requirement that the defendant act "under color of state law," sometimes private individuals who exercise government power or act in concert with government officers also are sued under this statute. Private individuals may be sued under §1983 if they are acting under color of law. But may private individuals sued under §1983 claim the immunities accorded to government officers? The Court initially denied qualified immunity to private individual defendants, but in its subsequent decision indicated that this defense is generally available to such defendants.

In *Wyatt v. Cole*, a private individual was sued for acting together with a sheriff in seizing property pursuant to a writ of replevin.[247] The Supreme Court held that immunities are available only to government officers sued under §1983. In a majority opinion by Justice O'Connor, the Court emphasized that immunities exist to protect the "government's ability to perform its traditional functions."[248] Government officers are accorded immunities to preserve their willingness to exercise discretion without undue fear of lawsuits and to retain the attractiveness of government service. The Supreme Court explained that such considerations are not present when nongovernment actors are sued under §1983.

Justice O'Connor's opinion left open the question as to whether private individuals can claim a good-faith defense. A good-faith defense is different from immunity in several respects. First, denials of immunity are immediately appealable, whereas denial of a good-faith defense is appealable only after there has been a final judgment in the case. Second, under *Harlow*, immunity is an objective test, but the good-faith defense is more subjective: Did this individual believe that the conduct was lawful and proper? Finally, while qualified immunity is generally regarded as a question of law for the judge, the good faith of an individual in a specific situation is much more a question of fact, likely to be decided by a jury.

In *Richardson v. McKnight*, the Court ruled that prison guards at privately operated prisons are not protected by qualified immunity, but again left open the possibility of a good-faith defense.[249] *Richardson* involved a §1983 suit brought by an

[245] *See, e.g.,* Washington v. Davis, 426 U.S. 229 (1976) (facially neutral laws deny equal protection based on race only if there is proof of both discriminatory impact and discriminatory purpose).

[246] Mt. Healthy City School Dist. v. Doyle, 429 U.S. 274 (1977).

[247] 504 U.S. 158 (1992).

[248] *Id.* at 167.

[249] 521 U.S. 399 (1997).

inmate in a Tennessee prison that had been privatized. The Court said that the question of whether a private prison guard could claim qualified immunity was to be answered by looking at both the "history and to the purposes that underlie government employee immunity."[250] Justice Breyer, writing for the majority in the 5-4 decision, stressed the absence of any historical evidence supporting immunity for private prison guards and the likely failure of market incentives to control the use of excessive force in private prisons.[251] However, the Court said that the defendants might be able to assert a "special 'good faith' defense,"[252] though again the Court did not elaborate as to its content.

But in *Filarsky v. Delia*, the Court shifted course and accorded absolute immunity to a private individual hired by a city to conduct an investigation.[253] Chief Justice Roberts, writing for the Court, said that "the common law did not draw a distinction between public servants and private individuals engaged in public service in according protection to those carrying out government responsibilities."[254] The Court thus concluded that "immunity under §1983 should not vary depending on whether an individual working for the government does so as a full-time employee, or on some other basis."[255] The Court distinguished, but did not overrule, *Wyatt v. Cole* and *Richardson v. McKnight*, the former on the ground that it did not involve a person hired by the government and the latter based on the nature of private prisons. But the conclusion from *Filarsky v. Delia* is that the Court has shifted and now generally is allowing private individuals sued under §1983 to claim qualified immunity as a defense.

§8.7 WHO IS A "PERSON" FOR PURPOSES OF §1983 LIABILITY? STATE GOVERNMENTS AND TERRITORIES

Suits Against States In State Courts

In *Quern v. Jordan*, the Supreme Court held that the Eleventh Amendment bars §1983 suits against state governments in federal court.[1] However, because

[250] *Id.* at 404. *See e.g.,* Estate of Clark v. Walker, 865 F.3d 544 (7th Cir. 2017) (ruling privately employed nurse in jail was ineligible for qualified immunity); McCullum v. Tepe, 693 F.3d 696 (6th Cir. 2012) (holding that privately employed prison psychiatrist did not qualify for immunity); Rosborough v. Mgmt. & Training Corp, 350 F.3d 459 (5th Cir. 2003) (holding private prison employees are liable under §1983). *But see* Perniciaro v. Lea, 901 F.3d 241 (5th Cir. 2018) (affording privately employed psychiatrist to state facility qualified immunity).

[251] *Id.* at 404-412.

[252] *Id.* at 413.

[253] 566 U.S. 377 (2012).

[254] *Id.* at 387.

[255] *Id.* at 389.

§8.7 [1] 440 U.S. 332 (1979); *see* §§7.5 and 7.7, *supra,* for a discussion of Quern v. Jordan.

state courts have concurrent jurisdiction over §1983 suits,[2] the issue arises as to whether states are persons who may be sued in state court under §1983.

In *Will v. Michigan Department of State Police*, the Court resolved a split among the state courts and held that state governments are not persons under §1983 and thus may not be sued in state court under this statute.[3] Interestingly, in deciding whether suits could be brought in state court, the Court said that "in deciphering congressional intent as to the scope of §1983, the scope of the Eleventh Amendment is a consideration."[4] The Court reasoned that as it had ruled in Eleventh Amendment cases, Congress may override state sovereign immunity only if it expresses a clear intent to do so. The Court said that it "cannot conclude that §1983 was intended to disregard the well-established immunity of a State from being sued without its consent."[5]

Moreover, the Court ruled that state officials could not be sued in their official capacity in state court under §1983. The Court explained that "a suit against a state official in his or her official capacity is not a suit against the official but rather a suit against the official's office."[6] However, this means only that a suit cannot be brought against the officer, in his or her official capacity, for money damages to be paid by the state treasury. The Court, in a footnote, made it clear that it was not changing the firmly established rule that state officials may be sued under §1983 for prospective relief even when in reality the remedy is against the official policies of the state and compliance will cost the state a substantial sum. The Court stated that "[o]f course a State official in his or her official capacity, when sued for injunctive relief, would be a person under §1983 because official capacity actions for prospective relief are not treated as actions against the State."[7]

On the one hand, *Will* can be defended on federalism grounds as a proper protection of a state's immunity from suit. As the majority explained, if Congress wants to create state liability—even in state court—it should express this intent clearly and unmistakably. But on the other hand, *Will* can be criticized for unduly limiting the scope of §1983. The Eleventh Amendment applies only to bar suits in federal court; the Court's reliance on it to limit state court litigation seems misplaced.[8] Moreover, as the Court has recognized on many occasions, §1983 was meant to provide a remedy against state and local governments for their constitutional violations.[9]

[2] Maine v. Thiboutot, 448 U.S. 1, 3 n.1 (1980) (federal courts do not have exclusive jurisdiction over §1983 suits; state courts have concurrent jurisdiction).

[3] 491 U.S. 58 (1989).

[4] *Id.* at 66-67.

[5] *Id.* at 67.

[6] *Id.* at 71.

[7] *Id.* at 71 n.10. For a discussion of the distinction between individual and official capacity suits, *see* text accompanying *supra* notes 47-49, §8.6.

[8] Justice Brennan began his dissenting opinion by stating, "Because this case was brought in state court, the Court concedes, the Eleventh Amendment is inapplicable. Like the guest who wouldn't leave, however, the Eleventh Amendment lurks everywhere in today's decision and, in truth, determines its outcome." 491 U.S. at 71-72 (Brennan, J., dissenting).

[9] *See, e.g.*, Patsy v. Board of Regents, 457 U.S. 496 (1982); Mitchum v. Foster, 407 U.S. 225 (1972).

Territories

The Supreme Court applied its reasoning in *Will* to conclude that territories also may not be sued under §1983. In *Ngiraingas v. Sanchez,* the Supreme Court ruled that neither the Territory of Guam nor its officers acting in their official capacity are "persons" under §1983.[10] The Court emphasized that in enacting §1983, Congress was not concerned with remedying constitutional violations in the territories. Because the territories were under federal control—with territorial courts created by Congress and staffed by judges appointed by the president—they were not analogous to states whose court systems were failing to protect the rights of former slaves.[11]

In 1874, Congress amended the Civil Rights Act of 1871 to add "Territory" to the statute and created liability for every person acting under color of law of any territory. But the Court reasoned that this did not make territories directly liable under §1983. Rather, it provided that territories would be treated like states for purposes of §1983 liability. In light of *Will,* the Court concluded that "neither the Territory of Guam nor its officers acting in their official capacity are 'persons' under §1983."[12]

§8.8 WHAT FEDERAL LAWS MAY BE ENFORCED VIA §1983 ACTIONS?

Section 1983 creates liability for any person who violates the rights, privileges, or immunities secured by the Constitution and laws of the United States. Thus, a question arises about which federal laws may be the basis for a §1983 suit. Is §1983 available only to redress violations of federal laws that implement the Fourteenth Amendment, or may it be used to enforce all federal laws pertaining to civil rights, or can it be used to enforce every federal law, regardless of its content? The issue is important because there are a great many federal laws that do not create a cause of action to prevent or remedy violations of those laws.[1] Because the Supreme Court

[10] 495 U.S. 182 (1990).

[11] *Id.* at 189.

[12] *Id.* at 190. In a different context, the Supreme Court has ruled that Native American tribes are not "persons" and thus cannot initiate suits under §1983. *See* Inyo County v. Paiute-Shoshone Indians, 538 U.S. 701 (2003).

§8.8 [1] Professors Low and Jeffries state that laws that do not create a remedy fall into three broad categories: "(1) joint federal-state regulatory programs—e.g., The Historic Sites, Buildings, and Antiquities Act, the Fish and Wildlife Coordination Act, and the Surface Mining Control and Reclamation Act; (2) resource management programs administered cooperatively by federal and state agencies . . . and (3) federal grant programs, programs . . . [such as welfare programs] under the Social Security Act, . . . grant programs under the Food Stamp Act, the Small Business Investment Act, the Energy Conservation Act, . . . and the Urban Mass Transportation Act, among others." Peter W. Low & John C. Jeffries, Federal Courts and the Law of Federal-State Relations 1081-1082 (4th ed. 1998).

has made it increasingly difficult to infer causes of action directly from federal statutes,[2] the availability of §1983 as a basis for suits to remedy statutory violations by those acting under color of law is quite important.

Maine v. Thiboutot

The seminal case concerning the availability of §1983 to redress violations of federal statutes is *Maine v. Thiboutot.*[3] The plaintiffs filed suit in state court against the state of Maine and its officers, alleging that they had violated federal statutory provisions concerning calculation of welfare benefits. The state argued that there was no cause of action under §1983 because that statute was available only to remedy violations of statutes intended to enforce the Fourteenth Amendment. Specifically, the state argued that the legislative history of §1983 reveals only a concern with protecting civil rights. Moreover, the state contended that the 1871 Civil Rights Act, of which §1983 was a part, was quite clearly focused on civil rights issues. For example, the jurisdictional provision of the 1871 Civil Rights Act, now codified as 28 U.S.C. §1343(3), provided federal courts authority to hear claims for the denial of "any right, privilege, or immunity secured by the Constitution of the United States or by any Act of Congress providing for equal rights of citizens."[4] In fact, previously, the Supreme Court held that §1343(3) only created jurisdiction for civil rights laws, and not for other federal statutes, such as the Social Security Act.[5]

The Supreme Court, in *Thiboutot,* rejected these arguments. The Court concluded that under the literal language of the statute, §1983 suits are available whenever any federal law has been allegedly violated. Justice Brennan, writing for the majority, stated: "The question before us is whether the phrase 'and laws,' as used in §1983, means what it says or whether it should be limited to some subset of laws. Given that Congress attached no modifiers to the phrase, the plain language of the statute undoubtedly embraces respondents' claim that petitioners violated the Social Security Act."[6] The Court dismissed the legislative history because it "does not permit a definitive answer."[7]

The Court's approach in *Thiboutot* is thus somewhat different from that employed in other §1983 contexts. For instance, in recognizing immunities, the Court does not limit itself to the literal language of §1983 (which is written in seemingly absolute terms) or ignore the history because it is unresolvable.[8]

[2] *See, e.g.,* Transamerica Mortgage Advisors, Inc. v. Lewis, 444 U.S. 11 (1979); *see* §6.3, *supra.*

[3] 448 U.S. 1 (1980).

[4] 28 U.S.C. §1343(3).

[5] Chapman v. Houston Welfare Rights Org., 441 U.S. 600 (1979). Before the jurisdictional amount requirement was eliminated from §1331, §1343(3) was an important alternative basis for jurisdiction because it had no minimum amount requirement.

[6] 448 U.S. at 4.

[7] *Id.* at 7.

[8] For a detailed criticism of *Thiboutot, see* George D. Brown, Whither *Thiboutot*? Section 1983, Private Enforcement, and the Damages Dilemma, 33 DePaul L. Rev. 31 (1983).

As the dissent argued, *Thiboutot* is a major expansion in the scope of §1983.[9] By seemingly recognizing a cause of action for all violations of federal laws by state and local governments and their officers, §1983 lessens the need to infer a cause of action under a statute in such circumstances. Also, because *Thiboutot* expressly allows recovery of attorneys' fees for statutory suits, plaintiffs have an incentive to sue under §1983 instead of using alternative remedies available under federal law that likely do not contain a fees award provision.

As written by the Court, *Thiboutot* appears to create a cause of action for violations of all federal statutes by those acting under color of state law. Subsequently, the Supreme Court has narrowed the effect of *Thiboutot*, creating two exceptions where §1983 may not be used in connection with statutory violations. These exceptions have grown increasingly broad.

In *Health and Hospital Corporation of Marion County v. Talevski*,[10] the Court was asked to overrule *Maine v. Thiboutot* and end such litigation. The case involved a lawsuit brought on behalf of a patient in a county-owned nursing home claiming that its treatment of the patient violated rights guaranteed him under the Federal Nursing Home Reform Act.

The Act requires that nursing homes that receive Medicaid funding respect and protect their residents' health, safety, and dignity. The law refers to rights of nursing-home residents to be free from unnecessary physical or chemical restraints and to be discharged or transferred only when certain preconditions are satisfied.

The Supreme Court in an opinion, by Justice Ketanji Brown Jackson, expressly reaffirmed *Maine v. Thiboutot* and held that laws adopted under the spending clause can be enforced through §1983 suits. Moreover, the Court said that the Federal Nursing Home Reform Act (FNHRA) creates enforceable rights and thus can be the basis for suits under §1983. Justice Jackson concluded the majority opinion by declaring: "Section 1983 is available to enforce every right that Congress validly and unambiguously creates; we will not impose a categorical font-of-power condition that the Reconstruction Congress did not. And, here, the test that our precedents establish leads inexorably to the conclusion that the FNHRA secures the particular rights that Talevski invokes."[11]

Justice Clarence Thomas wrote a dissenting opinion urging the overruling of *Maine v. Thiboutot*, while Justice Samuel Alito wrote a dissent urging further narrowing of the ability to sue under §1983 to enforce spending clause laws.

Implicit or Explicit Statutory Preclusion

First, §1983 may not be used to enforce statutes that explicitly or implicitly preclude §1983 litigation. In *Middlesex County Sewerage Authority v. National Sea Clammers Association*, commercial fishermen brought suit against several government entities

[9] 448 U.S. at 12 (Powell, J., dissenting). Justice Powell, in an appendix, listed 23 statutes that could arguably give rise to §1983 causes of action after the majority's decision.

[10] 599 U.S. 166 (2023).

[11] *Id.* at 192.

to halt pollution in violation of the Federal Water Pollution Control Act and the Marine Protection, Research, and Sanctuaries Acts.[12] The Supreme Court found that the "comprehensive enforcement mechanisms" contained in these statutes demonstrated "congressional intent to preclude the remedy of suits under §1983."[13]

Because §1983 is a federal statute, obviously Congress can override it in other statutes and specify that for some laws §1983 is not available as an enforcement mechanism. In *Middlesex County*, the Court made it clear that Congress need not be explicit in order to preclude §1983 suits; a congressional intent to prevent §1983 enforcement would be inferred from a comprehensive enforcement mechanism within a federal statute. The environmental protection statutes contained provisions authorizing citizen suits, administrative remedies, and enforcement actions by the Environmental Protection Agency. The Court concluded that "the existence of these express remedies demonstrates not only that Congress intended to foreclose implied private actions but also that it intended to supplant any remedy that otherwise would be available under §1983."[14]

The Court's application of this principle to prevent §1983 litigation in *Middlesex County* is questionable because the statutes in issue had specific "savings clauses" that preserve "any right which any person (or class of persons) may have under any statute or common law."[15] It is curious to find an implicit preclusion of litigation when there is an explicit provision preserving all other remedies.

The Court applied the *Middlesex County* decision in *Smith v. Robinson.*[16] In *Smith*, the Court found that the comprehensive enforcement mechanisms contained in the Education of the Handicapped Act reflected congressional intent to preclude §1983 litigation. The Court emphasized that allowing §1983 actions would encourage circumvention of the procedural requirements contained in the act.

The Supreme Court clarified this exception in *Wright v. City of Roanoke Redevelopment and Housing Authority.*[17] The plaintiffs, public housing authority tenants, sued a public housing authority for violating the Brooke Amendment, which created a ceiling on the rents and utility charges. In a 5-4 decision, the Court held that a §1983 suit was available to enforce the Brooke Amendment. The statute provided for administrative remedies through formal and informal hearings by local housing authorities. The Court held that this was not the type of comprehensive enforcement mechanism necessary to preclude §1983 litigation.

Wright is a particularly significant decision in a couple of respects. First, it makes clear that the presumption is in favor of the availability of §1983 to enforce a federal statute. The Court emphasized that the burden is on the defendant to demonstrate "by express provision or other specific evidence from the statute itself that Congress intended to foreclose [§1983 litigation]."[18] The Court found

[12] 453 U.S. 1 (1981).
[13] *Id.* at 20.
[14] *Id.* at 21.
[15] *Id.* at 29 (Stevens, J., dissenting).
[16] 468 U.S. 992 (1984).
[17] 479 U.S. 418 (1987).
[18] *Id.* at 424.

no indication that Congress intended to preclude §1983 actions to enforce the Brooke Amendment. Second, *Wright* indicates that the existence of administrative remedies alone does not preclude §1983 litigation absent a more specific congressional intent to prohibit §1983 suits. In both *Middlesex County* and *Smith,* Congress had created alternative vehicles for access to the courts. None were present in *Wright.* Thus, it appears that a statutory enforcement scheme will be deemed comprehensive only when it provides for both administrative and judicial remedies.

The Court took a very different approach from *Wright* in its subsequent decision concerning this exception: *City of Rancho Palos Verdes v. Abrams.*[19] A lawsuit was brought under §1983 to enforce a provision of the federal Telecommunications Act that limited the authority of state and local governments to impede the installation of wireless communications technology. The act authorizes a private remedy for violations of the statute. The issue was whether this provision precluded a §1983 action.

Justice Scalia, writing for the Court, noted that the private remedy provided under the statute was narrower than relief under §1983. He said that "[t]he provision of an express, private means of redress in the statute is ordinarily an indication that Congress did not intend to leave open a more expansive remedy under §1983."[20] He said that to use §1983, the plaintiffs must demonstrate "by textual indication, express or implicit, that the remedy is to complement, rather than supplant, §1983."[21]

Thus, in *Rancho Palos Verdes,* the Court puts a presumption against allowing §1983 to be used to enforce a federal law, at least in circumstances where the federal statute is more restrictive than §1983 in the remedies it allows. This is a dramatic departure from *Wright,* which had placed the presumption in favor of allowing §1983 suits unless Congress had indicated otherwise.

Federal Statutes Must Create Rights

The Supreme Court also recognized a second major exception to *Thiboutot*: §1983 is available only to enforce federal statutes that create rights. In *Pennhurst State School & Hospital v. Halderman,* one issue was whether the plaintiffs had a cause of action under §1983 to enforce provisions of the Developmentally Disabled Assistance and Bill of Rights Act of 1975.[22] Justice Rehnquist indicated that the act in question appeared to merely declare policy and not create substantive rights.

In *Golden State Transit Corp v. City of Los Angeles,* the Court articulated a three-part test for determining whether a statute creates enforceable rights.[23] In *Golden State,* the Court held that the plaintiff was entitled to maintain a §1983 suit for compensatory damages against the city because it allegedly illegally intervened in

[19] 544 U.S. 113 (2005).
[20] *Id.* at 121.
[21] *Id.* at 122.
[22] 451 U.S. 1 (1981). For a more detailed description of the *Pennhurst* litigation, *see* §7.5, *supra.*
[23] 493 U.S. 103 (1989).

a private labor dispute in violation of the National Labor Relations Act. The Court said that a federal statute is enforceable under §1983 if the statute creates a binding obligation, if the interest created by the statute is sufficiently specific as to be judicially enforceable, and if the provision was intended to benefit the plaintiff.

Since *Golden State*, four Supreme Court decisions have considered whether a statute creates a right and is enforceable in a §1983 suit. In *Virginia Hospital Association v. Wilder*, the Supreme Court ruled that §1983 can be used by medical care providers to collect funds owed to them by state governments under the Medicaid Act.[24] Under the Medicaid Act, states must secure approval from the Department of Health and Human Services for a plan for reimbursing health care providers. In 1980, Congress enacted the Boren Amendment, which requires that reimbursement be "reasonable and adequate" to meet the costs of "efficiently and economically operated facilities."[25] The Virginia Hospital Association, a nonprofit corporation composed of both public and private hospitals, filed suit in federal court against several Virginia officials, contending that the Virginia system for reimbursement did not provide "reasonable and adequate" compensation. Because the Boren Amendment does not create a cause of action, the plaintiff sued pursuant to §1983.

The Court split along ideological lines, with Justice Brennan writing a majority opinion joined by Justices White, Marshall, Blackmun, and Stevens, holding that the Boren Amendment did create a legally enforceable right. The key for the Court in concluding that there is a legal right is that the Boren Amendment creates a "binding obligation."[26] Although a state has flexibility in designing its method for reimbursement, health care providers have a right to reasonable and adequate payment.

Wilder appeared to expand the use of §1983 to enforce federal laws by finding statutes to create a right whenever there is a binding duty. In contrast, the subsequent decision in *Suter v. Artist M.* restricted the application of §1983.[27] *Suter* concerned the use of §1983 to enforce the Adoption Assistance and Child Welfare Act of 1980. The law provides that a state will be reimbursed for expenses it incurs in administering foster care and adoption programs if it has a plan approved by the secretary of health and human services. The law requires that the approved plan be "mandatory" upon all jurisdictions in the state and that under it "reasonable efforts will be made" to prevent children from being removed from their homes and to facilitate reunification of families.[28]

In a 7-2 opinion, with only Justices Blackmun and Stevens dissenting, the Court held that this act did not create an enforceable right. The Court held that "[t]he term 'reasonable efforts' in this context is at least as plausibly read to impose only a rather generalized duty on the State, to be enforced not by private individuals, but by the Secretary in the manner previously discussed."[29]

[24] 496 U.S. 498 (1990).
[25] 42 U.S.C. §1396a(a).
[26] 496 U.S at 510-511.
[27] 503 U.S. 347 (1992).
[28] 42 U.S.C. §§671(a)(3), 671(a)(5).
[29] 503 U.S. at 363.

There is an obvious tension between *Wilder* and *Suter.* In *Wilder,* the law called for "reasonable" reimbursement and was deemed enforceable; in *Suter,* the statute spoke of "reasonable efforts" and was deemed nonenforceable. The Court in *Suter* distinguished *Wilder* on the ground that there the statute and regulations set forth "[h]ow the State was to comply with [the act]," whereas in *Suter* it "was, within broad limits, left up to the State."[30] Yet in both instances there was a clear duty imposed on states, and in each there was a range of discretion left to state governments.

The Court in *Suter* gave an additional reason for its conclusion, one that is even more restrictive of §1983 suits. The Court indicated that federal laws that require state plans to be developed create a requirement only for the writing and approval of state plans. Once the state has created a plan and it is approved, no §1983 litigation is allowed even if the plan is in total contravention to the federal statute or even if the state blatantly fails to comply with the plan. The Court said that "the Act does place a requirement on the States, but that requirement only goes so far as to ensure that the State have a plan approved by the Secretary."[31]

In other words, *Suter v. Artist M.* provides that federal courts cannot enforce federal statutes which mandate the development of state plans and impose requirements on their content. The Court explained that the only remedy to enforce such statutory provisions in the face of state government violations is for the Secretary of Health and Human Services to reduce or eliminate payments based on a finding that the state plan or the administration of the plan does not comply with federal law.

Suter v. Artist M. thus would have had a detrimental effect on judicial enforcement of the many parts of the Social Security Act—and other federal statutes—that impose requirements through the device of necessitating the creation of state plans. Subsequently, however, Congress passed legislation to overturn *Suter* and to allow a private right of action to enforce provisions of the Social Security Act that require state and local plans for meeting federal mandates.[32] The congressional action is significant in preserving §1983 as an enforcement mechanism for key provisions of the Social Security Act.

In *Blessing v. Freestone,* the Supreme Court held that Title IV-D of the Social Security Act, which creates a duty for states to provide child support services, does not create an across-the-board private right to enforce substantial compliance with its provisions.[33] The Court emphasized that a plaintiff who seeks to enforce a federal statute under §1983 must demonstrate a violation of a specific federal statutory provision that creates an enforceable right, "not merely a violation of federal law."[34] To create an enforceable right, the statutory provision "must be written in mandatory rather than precatory terms."[35]

[30] *Id.* at 360.

[31] *Id.* at 358.

[32] 42 U.S.C. §1320a-2. *See* Stanberry v. Sherman, 75 F.3d 581, 583-584 (10th Cir. 1996) ("The Congress disavowed *Suter's* approach, while not purporting to change the decision. It also reaffirmed the approach taken in Supreme Court decisions prior to *Suter.*").

[33] 520 U.S. 329 (1997).

[34] *Id.* at 340.

[35] *Id.* at 341.

The Court ruled that the provisions in Title IV-D that required substantial state compliance with federal law were too general to create enforceable rights. However, the Court concluded that other aspects of Title IV-D might create enforceable rights and remanded the case for further consideration. *Blessing* thus follows the earlier decisions in holding that a federal law is enforceable under §1983 only if it creates an enforceable right.

The Court addressed which laws can be enforced via §1983 action was *Gonzaga University v. Doe.*[36] For plaintiffs seeking to enforce federal laws against violations by state and local governments via §1983 actions, *Gonzaga University v. Doe* indeed may pose a substantial obstacle to litigation. The Supreme Court held that a federal law adopted by Congress under the spending power may be enforced through a §1983 action only if Congress clearly intended to create a private right of action. The Court concluded that §1983 may not be used to enforce the provisions of the Family Educational Rights and Privacy Act.[37]

John Doe is a former undergraduate at Gonzaga University, a private university in Spokane, Washington. Doe sought to become a public school teacher and needed to obtain an affidavit of good moral character from a dean at Gonzaga. A university official had overheard one student tell another student of sexual misconduct by Doe. The university official contacted the state agency responsible for teacher certification and discussed the allegations against Doe. Subsequently, Doe was informed that the university would not provide him the affidavit required for certification as a Washington schoolteacher.

Doe sued Gonzaga and the school official in state court for torts and breach of contract, as well as for violating the provisions of the Family Educational Rights and Privacy Act (FERPA). The act prohibits educational institutions receiving federal funds from releasing educational records to unauthorized persons. A jury found for Doe on all counts, awarding him $1,155,000, including $150,000 in compensatory damages and $300,000 in punitive damages on the FERPA claim.

Although FERPA does not expressly create a cause of action, Doe sued pursuant to §1983.[38] The Washington Supreme Court, like every federal court of appeals that had considered the issue, ruled that §1983 could be used to enforce FERPA.[39]

The Supreme Court reversed, and in an opinion by Chief Justice Rehnquist, held that FERPA does not unambiguously confer a right on individuals and thus cannot be enforced via a §1983 action. The Court stated: "We now reject the notion that our cases permit anything short of an unambiguously conferred right to support a cause of action brought under §1983."[40] The Court concluded that

[36] 536 U.S. 273 (2002).

[37] 20 U.S.C. §1232g.

[38] Although §1983 applies only if there is state action and Gonzaga University is a private entity, the Washington courts found that the university acted "under color of state law" when it disclosed Doe's personal information to state officials in connection with the state-law teacher certification requirements. The Supreme Court did not grant certiorari on this issue and said that it was assuming, without deciding, that the actions occurred under color of state law. 536 U.S. at 277 n.1.

[39] *Id.* at 299 (Stevens, J. dissenting) ("all of the Federal Courts of Appeals expressly deciding the question have concluded that FERPA creates enforceable rights under §1983").

[40] *Id.* at 283.

"FERPA's nondisclosure provisions fail to confer enforceable rights."[41] The Court explained that the statute says that the federal government may not provide funds to educational institutions that have a "policy or practice" of releasing student educational records in violation of the Act's requirements. The Court said that this is not sufficient to bestow enforceable rights on individuals.

The greatest significance of the decision is in the Court's expressly tying the availability of a §1983 suit to the question of whether there would be a private right of action to enforce the federal statute. Chief Justice Rehnquist wrote: "[W]e further reject the notion that our implied right of action cases are separate and distinct from our §1983 cases. To the contrary, our implied right of action cases should guide the determination of whether a statute confers rights enforceable under §1983."[42] Chief Justice Rehnquist explained that "[a] court's role in discerning whether personal rights exist in the §1983 context should therefore not differ from its role in discerning whether personal rights exist in the implied right of action context."[43] Chief Justice Rehnquist concluded the majority opinion by declaring, "In sum, if Congress wishes to create new rights enforceable under §1983, it must do so in clear and unambiguous terms—no less and no more than what is required for Congress to create new rights enforceable under an implied private right of action."[44]

This is troublesome for civil rights plaintiffs because the Supreme Court has been very restrictive in its willingness to infer private rights of action for statutes that do not expressly authorize suits.[45] *Gonzaga University v. Doe* thus will be a barrier for plaintiffs seeking to use §1983 to enforce federal laws that do not create a private right of action.

There are, however, some important ways in which the impact of the decision might be limited. First, *Gonzaga University v. Doe* concerns a law adopted by Congress under its spending power; arguably its impact is restricted to statutes enacted under this congressional authority. Second, in considering whether there is a private right of action under a law, courts must consider both whether there is an enforceable right and whether the law was meant to provide a remedy. Section 1983 expressly creates a remedy in its authorization for both money damages and injunctive relief. Therefore, there may be statutes where there is no private right of action, not because of the absence of a right but for the lack of a remedy, which still can be enforced via a §1983 action.

In *Health & Hosp. Corp. v. Talevski*, discussed above, the Court distinguished *Gonzaga v. Doe* and held that a §1983 action could proceed based on the Federal Nursing Home Reform Act (FNHRA) that provides "rights of nursing-home residents to be free from unnecessary physical or chemical restraints and to be

[41] *Id.* at 287.

[42] *Id.*

[43] *Id.* at 282.

[44] *Id.* at 290.

[45] *See, e.g.*, Alexander v. Sandoval, 532 U.S. 275 (2001); Touche Ross & Co. v. Redington, 442 U.S. 560 (1979). *See* Elizabeth Earle Beske, The Court and the Private Plaintiff, 58 Wake Forest L. Rev. 1 (2023).

discharged or transferred only when certain preconditions are satisfied."[46] The Court explained: "We have held that the *Gonzaga* test is satisfied where the provision in question is 'phrased in terms of the persons benefited' and contains 'rights-creating,' individual-centric language with an 'unmistakable focus on the benefited class.' Conversely, we have rejected §1983 enforceability where the statutory provision 'contain[ed] no rights-creating language'; had 'an aggregate, not individual, focus'; and 'serve[d] primarily to direct the [Federal Government's] distribution of public funds.'"[47]

The Court analyzed the two provisions of the law and found that the provisions consistently refer to "rights" for "residents." Additionally, "these two provisions also establish who it is that must respect and honor these statutory rights; namely, the Medicaid-participant nursing homes in which these residents reside."[48] This was sufficient for the law to be deemed one that creates rights and that can be enforced in a Section 1983 suit.

§8.9 WHEN MAY §1983 BE USED FOR CONSTITUTIONAL CLAIMS?

Section 1983 creates a cause of action for anyone whose constitutional rights have been violated by a person acting under color of state law. Hence, §1983 is the basis for most constitutional litigation against local governments and state and local officers in the United States.

Dormant Commerce Clause Claims Enforceable

The Supreme Court has held that §1983 is broadly available when there is a state or local violation of the Constitution. In *Dennis v. Higgins*, the Supreme Court held that suits for violation of the dormant commerce clause may be brought under §1983.[1] The plaintiff, a motor carrier, brought a suit in state court challenging state taxes on motor carriers as imposing an unconstitutional undue burden on interstate commerce. The Court concluded that the plaintiff asserted a proper cause of action because §1983 should be "broadly construed" to provide a remedy "against all forms of official violation of federally protected rights."[2] The Court explained that the commerce clause creates a "right" to engage in interstate commerce free from undue interference by individual states.[3]

[46] 599 U.S. 166, 171 (2023).
[47] *Id.* at 183-184.
[48] *Id.* at 185.
§8.9 [1] 498 U.S. 439 (1991).
[2] *Id.* at 445.
[3] However, in National Private Truck Council v. Oklahoma Tax Commn., 515 U.S. 582 (1995), the Supreme Court held that §1983 could not be used to challenge state taxes as violating the dormant

Preemption Claims Not Necessarily Enforceable

In contrast, in *Golden State Transit Corp. v. City of Los Angeles*, the Court held that claims that a state or local law is preempted by federal law are not necessarily enforceable in a §1983 suit.[4] The Court concluded that the supremacy clause does not create rights enforceable under §1983. The Court noted, "Given the variety of situations in which preemption claims may be asserted, in state court and in federal court, it would obviously be incorrect to assume that a federal right of action pursuant to §1983 exists every time a federal rule of law preempts state regulatory authority."[5]

However, the Court recognized that federal law can create a federal right that is enforceable through §1983 litigation, and in this context §1983 can be the basis for suits to invalidate preempted state laws.[6] The distinction is a subtle one. Section 1983 is not automatically available for every preemption claim. Rather, the analysis involves a two-step approach: first, does the federal law create a federal right, and second, has Congress specifically foreclosed a §1983 remedy? In other words, to bring a preemption claim via a §1983 suit, the plaintiff must justify the use of §1983 to enforce the particular federal law that is alleged to preempt the state or local action.

In a subsequent decision, *Armstrong v. Exceptional Child Center*, the Court held that there cannot be a lawsuit directly under the supremacy clause of Article VI.[7] In an opinion by Justice Scalia, the Court said that the supremacy clause creates "a rule of decision: Courts 'shall' regard the 'Constitution,' and all laws 'made in Pursuance thereof,' as 'the supreme Law of the Land.' They must not give effect to state laws that conflict with federal laws. It is equally apparent that the Supremacy Clause is not the 'source of any federal rights,' and certainly does not create a cause of action."[8] This then means that enforcing the supremacy clause requires either fitting within §1983 or finding another statute that creates a cause of action.

Section 1983 Suits Not Available for Violations of *Miranda v. Arizona*

In *Chavez v. Martinez*,[9] the Supreme Court held that there is no cause of action for money damages for the failure of the police to properly warn a suspect as required by *Miranda v. Arizona* when the statements gained by the police are never introduced in court.[10] There was no majority opinion of the Court. Justice Thomas

---

commerce clause. The Court explained that principles of federalism, as reflected in the Tax Injunction Act, 28 U.S.C. §1341, preclude federal courts from enjoining state taxes even when they are alleged to be unconstitutional. The Tax Injunction Act and the *National Private Truck Council* decision are discussed in more detail in §11.3.

[4] 493 U.S. 103 (1989).

[5] *Id.* at 107-108.

[6] *Id.* at 108.

[7] 575 U.S. 320 (2015).

[8] *Id.* at 324-325.

[9] 538 U.S. 760 (2003).

[10] 384 U.S. 436 (1966).

wrote for a plurality and explained: "Statements compelled by police interrogations of course may not be used against a defendant at trial, but it is not until their use in a criminal case that a violation of the Self-Incrimination Clause occurs."[11]

Justice Souter, joined by Justice Breyer, concurred in the judgment. They found that there was a violation of the Fifth Amendment's protection against self-incrimination, but they saw no need to provide a civil remedy for such infringements.[12] Justice Souter, however, said that Martinez might have a claim for such violations under substantive due process, though not under the self-incrimination clause.[13] A majority of the justices agreed to remand the case on that basis.

In *Chavez v. Martinez*, the Court held that civil suits are not possible if the statements are not introduced into evidence against the suspect. But what if the statements are introduced? That was the issue this term in *Vega v. Tekoh*, and the Court, in a 6-3 decision, held that civil suits for money damages are not permissible for *Miranda* violations, even when the statements are admitted at trial against the defendant.[14]

Terrence Tekoh was working as a certified nursing assistant at a Los Angeles medical center. When a female patient accused him of touching her inappropriately, the police were called and Los Angeles County Sheriff's Deputy Carlos Vega responded.

Vega took Tekoh into a small room and questioned him at length in an aggressive manner. After extensive and intimidating questioning, Tekoh provided a written statement apologizing for inappropriately touching the patient's genitals. Although Tekoh seems to have been unquestionably in custody, in that a reasonable person under these circumstances would not have felt free to leave under the circumstances, Vega never administered *Miranda* warnings.

Tekoh was arrested and charged in California state court with unlawful sexual penetration. Tekoh was tried and acquitted. Tekoh then brought this action under 42 U.S.C. §1983 against Vega and several other defendants seeking damages for alleged violations of his constitutional rights, including his Fifth Amendment right against compelled self-incrimination.

The issue was whether there could be a civil suit for money damages against a police officer for violating the Fifth Amendment by failing to administer *Miranda* warnings.

The Court, in a 6-3 decision split along ideological lines, ruled that no such suits are permissible. Justice Samuel Alito wrote the opinion for the Court. He said that *Miranda* does not create a constitutional right, but instead, "[s]ince *Miranda*, the Court has repeatedly described the rules it adopted as 'prophylactic.'"[15]

Justice Elena Kagan wrote for the dissent. She said, "The Court's decision in *Miranda v. Arizona* (1966) affords well-known protections to suspects who are interrogated by police while in custody. Those protections derive from the

[11] 538 U.S. at 767.
[12] *Id.* at 779 (Souter, J., concurring in the judgment).
[13] *Id.* at 779-780.
[14] 597 U.S. 134 (2022).
[15] *Id.* at 143 (internal citations omitted).

Constitution."[16] The dissent saw *Miranda* as creating a Fifth Amendment right for those questioned in custody to be given the required warnings. Sharply disagreeing with the majority, she said that "*Dickerson v. United States* tells us in no uncertain terms that *Miranda* is a 'constitutional rule.' And that rule grants a corresponding right: If police fail to provide the *Miranda* warnings to a suspect before interrogating him, then he is generally entitled to have any resulting confession excluded from his trial. From those facts, only one conclusion can follow—that *Miranda*'s protections are a 'right[]' 'secured by the Constitution' under the federal civil rights statute."[17] Justice Kagan was especially concerned about how those like Tekoh, whose Fifth Amendment rights have been violated, are left with no remedy.

Thus, it is now clear that there is no cause of action for money damages for violations of *Miranda.*

What Torts are Constitutional Violations?

The central issue confronting the courts in considering the use of §1983 to redress constitutional infringements concerns what torts committed by state and local officers and local governments constitute constitutional violations actionable under §1983.[18] A large number of potential §1983 suits can be characterized as involving both unconstitutional conduct and torts under state law. For instance, when a police officer or a prison guard uses excessive force, there is both a tort law claim for battery and constitutional claims for cruel and unusual punishment and a deprivation of liberty without due process of law.[19] Similarly, a false arrest is potentially actionable as a tort and as a violation of the Fourth Amendment's prohibition against unreasonable seizures.[20] Even negligence by government officers—such as malpractice by a prison doctor or poor driving causing an accident by a state or municipal employee—might be characterized as both a tort and an unconstitutional deprivation of life, liberty, or property without due process of law.[21] When, in these and similar circumstances, is a §1983 suit available?

During the 1980s, the Supreme Court restricted the availability of the Constitution and §1983 as a remedy for government conduct that also is actionable as a tort. The Court has based its decisions on the explicitly stated premise that §1983 is not a "font of tort law to be superimposed upon whatever systems may

[16] *Id.* at 152. (Kagan, J., dissenting).

[17] *Id.* at 152-153.

[18] For an excellent discussion of the concept of constitutional torts, *see* Christina B. Whitman, Constitutional Torts, 79 Mich. L. Rev. 5 (1980); Christina B. Whitman, Government Responsibility for Constitutional Torts, 85 Mich. L. Rev. 225 (1986).

[19] Perhaps the most famous case dealing with when excessive force is a basis for a §1983 claim is the frequently cited opinion in Johnson v. Glick, 481 F.2d 1028 (2d Cir. 1973), *cert. denied sub nom.* John v. Johnson, 414 U.S. 1148 (1973) (excessive force is a §1983 action when it "shocks the conscience"), discussed more fully below at text accompanying notes 36-39 *infra.*

[20] *See, e.g.,* Baker v. McCollan, 443 U.S. 137 (1979) ("False imprisonment does not become a violation of the Fourteenth Amendment merely because the defendant is a state official.").

[21] *See, e.g.,* Estelle v. Gamble, 429 U.S. 97 (1976) (prisoner must show deliberate indifference to serious medical needs to demonstrate a constitutional violation based on inadequate medical care).

already be administered by the States."[22] Because some of the most serious constitutional violations also might be characterized as a state law tort, the Court's newly created restrictive principles risk substantial erosion of federal court protection of constitutional rights.

Specifically, the Court has articulated three major limitations on constitutional claims under §1983. Each of these restrictions arises when there are allegations that a state or local government or its officers has deprived a person of due process of law. It must be emphasized that these decisions do not simply limit federal court jurisdiction or the scope of §1983; rather, they are restrictive interpretations of the Constitution itself.

Negligence Insufficient

First, the Court held that allegations and proof of negligence are not sufficient to demonstrate a deprivation of due process; establishing a denial of due process requires demonstrating more than negligent deprivation of liberty or property. This was the holding in two companion cases decided in 1986, *Daniels v. Williams*[23] and *Davidson v. Cannon.*[24] In *Daniels,* a prisoner claimed that his freedom from bodily harm, a protected liberty interest, was denied without due process when he tripped on a pillow that was negligently left on a staircase by a prison guard. In *Davidson,* a prisoner claimed that prison authorities violated his due process rights by failing to protect him from attack by another prisoner. The prisoner had been threatened and informed the prison authorities, but they inadvertently forgot about the message, and the prisoner subsequently was seriously injured by the attack. Under New Jersey law, the prisoner could not bring an action to recover for the injuries against the guards or prison officials in state court.[25]

The Supreme Court ruled that neither prisoner presented a constitutional claim, and hence, neither stated a cause of action under §1983. In earlier decisions the Court indicated that negligent deprivations of liberty and property without due process of law constituted violations of the Fourteenth Amendment and could be the basis for §1983 litigation.[26] In *Davidson* and *Daniels,* the Court overruled these precedents and concluded that "the Due Process Clause is simply not implicated by a *negligent* act of an official causing unintended loss of or injury to life, liberty, or property. . . . Not only does the word 'deprive' in the Due Process Clause connote more than a negligent act, but we should not open the federal courts to lawsuits where there has been no affirmative abuse of power."[27] The effect of *Daniels* and *Davidson* extends beyond prisoner cases, beyond §1983 suits, to all due

[22] Paul v. Davis, 424 U.S. 693, 701 (1976).

[23] 474 U.S. 327 (1986).

[24] 474 U.S. 344 (1986).

[25] N.J. Stat. Ann. §59:5-2(b)(4) ("Neither public entity nor a public employee is liable for . . . any injury caused by a prisoner to any other prisoner.").

[26] Parratt v. Taylor, 451 U.S. 527, 541-542 (1981).

[27] Daniels v. Williams, 474 U.S. at 328, 330.

process claims: A deprivation of due process exists only if there is an allegation of an intentional violation by government or government officers.

The *Daniels* and *Davidson* holdings are troubling for several reasons. First, especially in *Davidson,* why is the absence of a state remedy not a denial of due process? In *Davidson,* state law prohibited the plaintiff from suing the prison or its employees to recover for the injuries inflicted by another prisoner. There is a strong argument that the state deprived liberty without due process by failing to provide any remedy for prisoners injured in this manner.[28] The Court said that the absence of proceedings is irrelevant because there is no denial of due process,[29] but this ignores the fact that the absence of proceedings itself is arguably a denial of due process.

Second, the distinction between negligent and intentional deprivations of life, liberty, and property should be questioned. The term "deprivation" signifies a loss; the Court cannot justify limiting the due process clause to intentional deprivations based on a textual analysis of the Constitution. Nor can the Court justify its conclusions based on an assumption that injuries inflicted by intentional conduct are inherently more serious than negligent actions. Negligent government conduct can be tremendously violative of rights, such as, to give an extreme example, if the government executes the wrong person.

Third, as Justice Blackmun noted in dissent in *Davidson,* the Court does not give sufficient weight to the government's responsibility in the infliction of the injuries.[30] Individuals who are not incarcerated can protect themselves from these types of dangers, but prisoners are "stripped [by the state] of all means of self-protection."[31] Accordingly, the government has a special responsibility for the harms incurred and can be said, through its negligence, to have caused a deprivation of the liberty to be free from bodily harm.[32]

Several important questions remain unresolved after *Daniels* and *Davidson.* One such issue is whether other states of mind—such as recklessness, deliberate indifference, or gross negligence—are sufficient to constitute a deprivation of due process. The Supreme Court has not answered this question, although *County of Sacramento v. Lewis,* discussed below, strongly indicates that in nonemergency situations, deliberate indifference is a basis for liability.[33] Although there is some division among lower courts, lower courts are generally in accord and have held that deliberate indifference or recklessness is sufficient to constitute a due process violation.[34]

[28] *See* Whitman, Government Responsibility for Constitutional Torts, *supra* note 18, at 274.

[29] 474 U.S. at 348.

[30] *Id.* at 350 (Blackmun, J., dissenting).

[31] *Id.* at 349.

[32] *See* Whitman, Government Responsibility for Constitutional Torts, *supra* note 18, at 272.

[33] 523 U.S. 833 (1998).

[34] For decisions finding a due process violation based on recklessness, deliberate indifference, or gross negligence, *see* Burke v. Regaldo, 935 F.3d 960 (10th Cir. 2019) (finding deliberate indifference); M.D. by Stukenberg v. Abbott, 907 F.3d 237 (5th Cir. 2018) (finding deliberate indifference); Selby v. Caruso, 734 F.3d 554 (6th Cir. 2013); Stemler v. City of Florence, 126 F.3d 856 (6th Cir. 1997) (deliberate indifference); Hill v. Shobe, 93 F.3d 418 (7th Cir. 1996) (recklessness or deliberate indifference); Davis v. Fulton County, 90 F.3d 1346 (8th Cir. 1996) (rejecting gross negligence).

This state of mind issue is particularly important in the context of §1983 suits against prison officials and police officers for excessive use of force. It is estimated that the "largest number of §1983 cases consists of claims of excessive force against state and local law enforcement officials."[35] In the oft-cited case of *Johnson v. Glick*, the Second Circuit said that excessive force constitutes a denial of due process, and hence a basis for a §1983 action, when it "shocks the conscience."[36] Although most circuits adopted the *Johnson* test for deciding whether excessive force violates the due process clause,[37] the Supreme Court in *Graham v. Connor* rejected this approach.[38] The Court held that "*all* claims that law enforcement officers have used excessive force—deadly or not—in the course of an arrest, investigatory stop, or other seizure of a free citizen should be analyzed under the Fourth Amendment and its 'reasonableness' standard, rather than under a 'substantive due process' approach."[39]

The crucial underlying question is whether *Graham* substantively changed the analysis or whether it simply shifted the discussion from a due process issue to a Fourth Amendment question. Under *Graham*, to prevail a plaintiff must demonstrate: (1) significant injury; (2) that resulted from the use of clearly excessive force; and (3) that the force used was objectively unreasonable.[40] Under the earlier approach, articulated in *Johnson v. Glick*, a jury could look to the nature of the injury and the force used and find liability because the actions of the officer "shocked the conscience." Under *Graham v. Connor*, however, there is the additional step of determining whether the actions were objectively unreasonable.[41] In this way, *Graham* changes the law and makes recovery in excessive force cases somewhat more difficult.

The Court has indicated that in emergency situations even proof of deliberate indifference or recklessness is not sufficient; the government can be held liable only if its conduct "shocks the conscience." In *County of Sacramento v. Lewis*,

[35] Martin A. Schwartz & John E. Kirklin, Section 1983 Litigation: Claims, Defenses, and Fees 227 (3d ed. 1997). *See, e.g.*, Couser v. Gay, 959 F.3d 1018 (10th Cir. 2020); Rodriguez v. County of Los Angeles, 891 F.3d 776 (9th Cir. 2018); Wilborn v. Ealey, 881 F.3d 998 (7th Cir. 2018).

[36] 481 F.2d 1028 (2d Cir.), *cert. denied sub nom.* John v. Johnson, 414 U.S. 1033 (1973). *See, e.g.*, Edrei v. Maguire, 892 F.3d 525 (2d Cir. 2018) (ruling that the *Johnson* factors continue to guide excessive force analysis despite reorganization under *Graham*).

[37] *See, e.g.*, Abdelfattah v. U.S. Dep't of Homeland Sec., 787 F.3d 524 (D.C. Cir. 2015); Bolmer v. Oliveira, 594 F.3d 134 (2d Cir. 2010); Gilmere v. City of Atlanta, 774 F.2d 1495 (11th Cir. 1985), *cert. denied*, 476 U.S. 1115 (1986); Gumz v. Morrisette, 772 F.2d 1395 (7th Cir. 1985), *cert. denied*, 475 U.S. 1123 (1986); Norris v. District of Columbia, 737 F.2d 1148 (D.C. Cir. 1984). It should be noted that the Supreme Court approved of a Fourth Amendment claim for excessive use of force by police. Tennessee v. Garner, 471 U.S. 1 (1985). As such, the Fourth Amendment might supplant due process claims in this area. One court of appeals has expressly reaffirmed the "shock the conscience" standard after *Daniels* and *Davidson*: New v. Minneapolis, 792 F.2d 724 (8th Cir. 1986).

[38] 490 U.S. 386 (1990).

[39] *Id.* at 395 (emphasis in original).

[40] This approach is articulated in Johnson v. Morel, 876 F.2d 477 (5th Cir. 1989).

[41] By creating a purely objective test for excessive force claims, *Graham* adopts an approach similar to the Harlow v. Fitzgerald, 457 U.S. 800 (1982), test for determining qualified immunity. *See* §8.6.3, *supra*. In Saucier v. Katz, 533 U.S. 194 (2001), the Supreme Court held that excessive force and qualified immunity are distinct questions and a finding of excessive force does not preclude a finding of qualified immunity.

the Court held that there can be liability for injuries resulting from a high-speed police chase only if there is proof that the police conduct was so egregious as to shock the conscience.[42] *Lewis,* like so many high-speed chase cases, had tragic facts. A police officer misunderstood another officer and initiated a high-speed chase of a boy on a motorcycle. The pursuit ended in a crash, which killed a passenger on the motorcycle, a teenage boy.

The Supreme Court, in an opinion by Justice Souter, held that substantive due process can be used for such claims, but that the government should be liable only if there is an abuse of power "shocking to the conscience."[43] The Court adopted a very restrictive definition of what behavior would meet this test, requiring that the plaintiff prove that the police officer intended to harm the victim. Therefore, although the Court left open substantive due process as a basis for suit, the test that it articulated is so limited that it is difficult to imagine many instances of police behavior being found to create liability under it. However, the Court emphasized that the shocks the conscience test only applies in emergency-type situations where there is not time for deliberation before action. Implicitly, *Lewis* supports deliberate indifference as a basis for liability in other cases.

Adequate State Law Post-Deprivation Remedies Sufficient for Random Procedural Due Process Violations: *Parratt v. Taylor*

Daniels and *Davidson* embody the first major way in which the Court has limited due process claims and §1983 suits. A second and at least equally important restriction on due process suits is that there is no denial of due process if a plaintiff seeks a post-deprivation remedy for the loss of property as a result of a random and unauthorized act of a government officer and the state provides adequate post-deprivation redress. This principle was articulated in the landmark case of *Parratt v. Taylor.*[44]

In *Parratt,* a prisoner ordered a $23.50 hobby kit, which was lost by prison guards. The prisoner filed a §1983 suit contending that he was deprived of property without due process of law. The Court held that the allegation of negligence was sufficient to constitute a "deprivation" under the due process clause—a holding that was subsequently overruled in *Daniels* and *Davidson.* However, the Court concluded that the plaintiff did not allege a violation of the due process clause because he was seeking only a post-deprivation remedy for the lost hobby kit, and the state provided such a remedy through its tort law. The Court emphasized that this case did not involve an issue of inadequate pre-deprivation due process; there is nothing the state could have done to prevent the hobby kit from being lost. Nor was it a claim that the state itself was responsible for the injury. Instead, the loss resulted from the random and unauthorized act of a government officer, and due process could mean only a chance for a remedy after the loss. Justice Rehnquist

[42] 523 U.S. 833 (1998).
[43] *Id.* at 836.
[44] 451 U.S. 527 (1981).

said that this was a request for "procedural due process simpliciter" and was fulfilled by the existence of adequate state law remedies.[45]

While *Parratt* involved a negligent deprivation of property, its holding was extended to intentional losses of property in *Hudson v. Palmer*.[46] In *Hudson*, prison guards searched a prisoner's cell and intentionally destroyed some of his non-contraband personal property. The Court ruled that there was no basis for a due process claim. As in *Parratt*, the plaintiff was not challenging a government policy nor was the plaintiff requesting a pre-deprivation hearing. Because the plaintiff was seeking only a post-deprivation remedy, and the state provided one, there was no denial of due process even though an intentional act caused the destruction of the property. Chief Justice Burger, writing for the majority, stated:

> The underlying rationale of *Parratt* is that when deprivations of property are effected through random and unauthorized conduct of a state employee, pre-deprivation procedures are simply "impracticable" since the state cannot know when such deprivations will occur. We can discern no logical distinction between negligent and intentional deprivations of property insofar as the "practicability" of affording pre-deprivation process is concerned. The state can no more anticipate and control in advance the random and unauthorized intentional conduct of its employees than it can anticipate similar negligent conduct.[47]

Thus, the principle that emerges is that when a random and unauthorized act of a government official causes a deprivation of property, there is no deprivation of due process when the plaintiff seeks a post-deprivation remedy and the state provides an adequate post-deprivation remedy.

The tension between *Parratt* and *Monroe* must be noted. *Monroe* holds that officers act under color of law for purposes of §1983 regardless of whether they are acting pursuant to an official policy or in a random and unauthorized manner.[48] Furthermore, *Monroe* says that federal courts are available to hear such suits irrespective of the potential adequacy of state procedures.[49] Technically, *Parratt* is not in conflict with these holdings. *Monroe* states that *if there is a constitutional violation*, it occurs under color of law even if it is not pursuant to official policy and even if the state provides adequate remedies. *Parratt* holds that *there is no constitutional violation* when an individual seeks a post-deprivation remedy for property lost through a random and unauthorized act and the state provides adequate post-deprivation redress. Thus, *Monroe* and *Parratt* can be reconciled as interpreting two different things: *Monroe* considers the meaning of "under color of state law" in analyzing §1983; *Parratt* deals with what constitutes a "deprivation" of due process.

[45] *Id.* at 543-544. For an excellent argument that the Court mischaracterized the claim as a procedural due process issue, *see* Martin H. Redish, Abstention, Separation of Powers, and the Limits of the Judicial Function, 94 Yale L.J. 71, 100-101 (1984).

[46] 468 U.S. 517 (1984).

[47] *Id.* at 533.

[48] 365 U.S. 167 (1961); *see* §8.3, *supra*.

[49] *See* §8.3, *supra*.

This meshing of the two decisions, while correct, masks the underlying tension between the cases. *Parratt* reflects a belief that suits against individual officers for their random and unauthorized acts should be in state court. The majority in *Monroe* quite explicitly rejected this position in interpreting §1983 to include even actions by officers in violation of state policy.

After *Parratt,* there were many unanswered questions, including whether the rule applies to deprivations of liberty, whether it applies to substantive due process claims or only to procedural due process, and whether it applies to all government actions or only random and unauthorized acts. The Supreme Court answered these questions and greatly clarified the scope of *Parratt*'s application in *Zinermon v. Burch.*[50]

The plaintiff, Burch, voluntarily committed himself to a state mental hospital. After his release he sued hospital officials, maintaining that they should have known that he was incompetent to give informed consent to his admission. The plaintiff argued that the failure of hospital administrators and doctors to initiate the state's involuntary commitment proceedings deprived him of liberty without due process. The question before the Supreme Court was whether, in light of *Parratt v. Taylor,* the existence of remedies in the state court system precluded constitutional claims under §1983.

The Court resolved uncertainty and ruled that *Parratt* applies to claims of deprivation of liberty as well as for loss of property.[51] However, the Court articulated several limits on the application of *Parratt.*

First, the Court made it clear that *Parratt* applies only when the plaintiff is objecting to a failure to provide adequate procedural due process. *Parratt* does not apply if the plaintiff claims a violation of a substantive constitutional right, whether it is a right secured by the Bill of Rights or one protected under substantive due process. The Court declared that a plaintiff "may invoke §1983 regardless of any state tort remedy that might be available to compensate him for the deprivation of these [substantive] rights."[52]

This distinction makes sense. In procedural due process cases, the issue is whether the government has provided adequate mechanisms such as notice and hearing. But in substantive due process cases, the question is whether the government's action is justified by a sufficiently important purpose. If a plaintiff seeks procedural due process, the inquiry is whether the state remedy adequately supplies the procedures that are needed. But if the plaintiff complains of an infringement of a substantive right, due process is an inquiry of whether there is a sufficiently important (depending on the level of scrutiny) justification for the government's action. In other words, if the constitutional violation is a lack of adequate procedures, state procedures can remedy the infringement, but if the constitutional violation is a lack of an adequate justification for the government's action, then the existence of state procedures is not relevant. Moreover, the extension of *Parratt* to

[50] 494 U.S. 113 (1990).
[51] *Id.* at 132.
[52] *Id.* at 125.

substantive violations "would virtually nullify section 1983."[53] As the Fifth Circuit declared: "*Parratt v. Taylor* is not a magic wand that can make any section 1983 action resembling a tort suit disappear into thin air. *Parratt* applies only when the plaintiff alleges a deprivation of procedural due process, it is irrelevant when the plaintiff has alleged a violation of some substantive constitutional proscription."[54]

Moreover, the *Zinermon* Court emphasized *Parratt* applies only to the failure to provide procedural due process that results from the random and unauthorized acts of government officials. In both *Parratt* and *Hudson*, the Court emphasized that the deprivations of property were the result of random and unauthorized acts, not official policy.[55]

Furthermore, in *Logan v. Zimmerman Brush Co.*, the Court declared that *Parratt* was limited to instances of a "random and unauthorized act by a state employee."[56] In *Logan*, an employee claimed that he was terminated from his job because of a physical handicap. He challenged his firing through the proper state administrative agency, but the agency negligently failed to hold a hearing within the statutorily prescribed time limit. The employer secured a dismissal of the plaintiff's claim with prejudice. The defendant argued that the case had to be dismissed based on *Parratt*. The Supreme Court disagreed, stating that "[u]nlike the complainant in *Parratt*, Logan is challenging not the [agency's] error, but the 'established state procedure' that destroys his entitlement without according him proper procedural safeguards."[57]

In *Zinermon*, the Court held that the government's action was not random and unauthorized because officials with the authority to supply a hearing failed to provide one even though they should have foreseen the need for such procedural protections. The Court explained that the plaintiff "was deprived of a substantial liberty interest . . . by the very state officials charged with the power to deprive mental patients of their liberty and the duty to implement procedural safeguards. Such a deprivation is foreseeable, due to the nature of mental illness, and will occur, if at all, at a predictable point in the process."[58]

Thus, *Parratt* applies solely to allegations that the random and unauthorized acts of individual officers have inflicted harm. This distinction reflects a belief that the latter—actions of individual officers—are generally suited to resolution

[53] Susan Bandes, *Monell, Parratt, Daniels,* and *Davidson*: Distinguishing a Custom or Policy from a Random, Unauthorized Act, 72 Iowa L. Rev. 101, 123 (1986).

[54] Augustine v. Doe, 740 F.2d 322, 329 (5th Cir. 1984). In Williamson County Regional Planning Commission v. Hamilton Bank, 473 U.S. 172, 195 (1985), the Court extended *Parratt* to takings claims and held that an individual cannot claim that the *state* has taken private property for public use until the property owner has "unsuccessfully attempted to obtain just compensation through the procedures provided by the State for obtaining such compensation." But in 2019, in Knick v. Township of Scott, Pennsylvania, 588 U.S. 180 (2019), the Court expressly overruled *Williamson County*. *Knick* is discussed in §2.4.

[55] *Parratt,* 451 U.S. at 541; *Hudson,* 468 U.S. at 533.

[56] 455 U.S. 422, 435-436 (1982).

[57] *Id.* For a discussion of the relationship of *Parratt* and *Logan, see* Rodney A. Smolla, The Displacement of Federal Due Process Claims by State Tort Remedies: Parratt v. Taylor and Logan v. Zimmerman Brush Company, 1982 U. Ill. L. Rev. 831.

[58] 494 U.S. at 138-139.

through the state's tort law. In contrast, the former—claims of unconstitutional policy or inadequate procedures—should be addressed by federal courts because of their potential to affect a larger number of people in the future.

After *Zinermon,* when does *Parratt v. Taylor* apply? That is, when does the existence of adequate state remedies preclude a due process claim? *Parratt* applies only when (1) the plaintiff seeks a post-deprivation remedy (2) for a random and unauthorized act of a government official (3) that resulted in the deprivation of liberty or property without adequate *procedural* due process, (4) and the officials responsible could not have provided a hearing to prevent foreseeable harms, and (5) adequate state remedies exist.

Or, phrased differently, *Parratt* does *not* apply and a §1983 suit is available for the deprivation of due process if the plaintiff objects to the failure to provide a post-deprivation remedy, or the harms resulted from an official government policy, or there is an alleged violation of a substantive right, or the officials responsible could have provided a hearing to prevent foreseeable harm, or there are inadequate state remedies.

Although *Zinermon* resolved many unanswered questions about the scope and application of *Parratt,* many questions remain to be answered. For example, the Court has not yet defined what constitutes an adequate state remedy under *Parratt.* In *Parratt,* Justice Rehnquist, writing for the majority, indicated that state remedies need not be coextensive with those available under §1983 to be deemed adequate. For instance, the absence of punitive damages and the lack of a jury trial under state law did not render state remedies inadequate.[59] However, other than this, the Court has given little guidance as to the standard for determining whether the state remedy is adequate. Does the lack of availability of attorneys' fees under state law, which are recoverable for successful §1983 suits, render state remedies inadequate?[60] Should state remedies be deemed inadequate if most or all of the defendants would be absolutely immune from liability under state law?[61] When are procedural differences between the federal and state court, such as the absence of injunctive relief or the lack of the class action mechanism, a basis for finding state remedies to be inadequate?[62]

[59] Parratt v. Taylor, 451 U.S. at 544. For a discussion of the standard for determining the adequacy of state remedies, *see* Note, Parratt v. Taylor Revisited: Defining the Adequate Remedy Requirement, 65 B.U. L. Rev. 607 (1985).

[60] *See, e.g.,* Simpson v. Brown County, 860 F.3d 1001 (7th Cir. 2017) (noting past circuit precedent that the absence of attorney's fee did not make state remedy inadequate); Davey v. Tomlinson, 627 F. Supp. 1458 (E.D. Mich. 1986) (absence of attorneys' fees does not render state law remedies inadequate).

[61] *See* Juliana v. Hanna, 732 F.3d 842 (7th Cir. 2013); Ausley v. Mitchell, 748 F.2d 224 (4th Cir. 1984) (inadequacy of state remedies if all defendants are absolutely immune under state law); Irshad v. Spann, 543 F. Supp. 922 (E.D. Va. 1982), *vacated and remanded,* 673 F.2d 1311 (4th Cir. 1982) (sovereign immunity does not render state remedies inadequate).

[62] *See, e.g.,* Roman v. City of Richmond, 570 F. Supp. 1554 (N.D. Cal. 1983) (lack of injunctive relief in state courts); Vickers v. Trainor, 546 F.2d 739 (7th Cir. 1976) (discussing lack of class action mechanism under state law). An interesting case where the court found remedies to be inadequate was Pena v. Mattox, 84 F.3d 894 (7th Cir. 1996), where the court found that state remedies were inadequate when the police held an individual, on charges that he did not commit, so as to give the mother time to put a child up for adoption.

Nor is it clear how state proceedings may be proven inadequate after their completion. As Professor Bandes explains, "Although theoretically, at least, the plaintiff may return to federal court if state remedies prove inadequate, there is no authority on how the plaintiff could avoid the res judicata effect of an adverse state judgment and the apparent loss of the federal question."[63]

Perhaps most important, the Court has not clarified how state remedies can be proven inadequate when they are theoretically available and potentially sufficient, but in practice prove nonexistent. In *Monroe v. Pape*, the Court emphasized that §1983 was adopted, in large part, "to provide a federal remedy where the state remedy, although adequate in theory, was not available in practice."[64] Yet thus far, the Supreme Court and lower courts seem to focus exclusively on whether the remedies created on paper are sufficient.

In *Albright v. Oliver*,[65] Justice Kennedy, in a concurring opinion, urged a revival of *Parratt v. Taylor* and its more aggressive use to limit constitutional tort claims. In *Albright*, a plurality of the Court concluded that claims for malicious prosecution must be brought under the Fourth Amendment and not substantive due process.[66] Justice Kennedy, in an opinion concurring in the judgment, urged the application of *Parratt*. Justice Kennedy observed that the "common sense teaching of *Parratt* is that some questions of property, contract, and tort law are best resolved by state legal systems without resort to the federal courts, even when a state actor is the alleged wrongdoer."[67] Justice Kennedy complained, however, that "courts, including our own, have been cautious in invoking the rule of *Parratt*. . . . But the price of our ambivalence over the outer limits of *Parratt* has been its dilution and, in some respects, its transformation into a mere pleading exercise."[68] Justice Kennedy argued that *Parratt* should apply in any case where a right violated by random and unauthorized act can be remedied through state law. This would be a dramatic expansion of *Parratt* and have a radical effect on constitutional litigation. Only Justice Thomas joined Justice Kennedy's opinion.

Generally, No Government Duty to Prevent Private Harms

A third major limit on due process claims was articulated by the Supreme Court in *DeShaney v. Winnebago County Department of Social Services*, which broadly held that the government generally has no duty to protect individuals from privately inflicted harms. The guardians of a four-year-old child sued the Department of Social Services for its failure to protect the child from beatings his father inflicted that ultimately resulted in irreversible brain damage. The plaintiffs maintained

[63] Bandes, *supra* note 53, at 124 n.159.

[64] 365 U.S. 167, 173-174 (1961).

[65] 510 U.S. 266 (1994).

[66] The plurality opinion was written by Chief Justice Rehnquist and joined by Justices O'Connor, Scalia, and Ginsburg. The Court subsequently reaffirmed that malicious prosecution claims can be brought in a §1983 suit for violation of Fourth Amendment rights. *See* Chiaverini v. City of Napoleon, 602 U.S. 556 (2024); Thompson v. Clark, 596 U.S. 39 (2022).

[67] 510 U.S. at 284 (Kennedy, J., concurring in the judgment).

[68] *Id.* at 285.

that over a 26-month period, the department was informed of the abuse but failed to act.

The Supreme Court held that there was no constitutional violation because the child was not in the custody of the government and because the abuse occurred at the hands of a private party. Chief Justice Rehnquist, writing for the Court, stated:

> [N]othing in the language of the Due Process Clause itself requires the State to protect the life, liberty, and property of its citizens against invasion by private actors. The Clause is phrased as a limitation on the State's power to act, not as a guarantee of certain minimal levels of safety and security.[69]

The Court expansively declared that "[a]s a general matter . . . a state's failure to protect an individual against private violence simply does not constitute a violation of due process."[70] The Court recognized narrow situations where the state has a duty to provide protection: when the state acts affirmatively to limit the individual's ability to protect himself or herself, such as when there is incarceration or institutionalization.[71]

DeShaney reflects a deeply entrenched belief that the Constitution is a charter of negative liberties—rights that restrain the government—and not a creator of affirmative rights to government services.[72] But *DeShaney* also can be criticized as resting on faulty distinctions and premises. In a strongly worded dissent, Justice Blackmun accused the majority of gross insensitivity and of resorting to "formalistic reasoning" in drawing an artificial distinction between action and inaction.[73] Characterizing the Department of Social Service's conduct as inaction seems arbitrary; the Court could have described the government's failure to protect Joshua DeShaney as "the active, if reckless, management of a case in which it was deeply involved."[74] Justice Blackmun argued that, at a minimum, once the government began to investigate the case, especially because the child had no other protection, it had the obligation to do so carefully and competently.

The Supreme Court followed and extended *DeShaney* in *Town of Castle Rock v. Gonzales.*[75] Like *DeShaney*, the case had truly tragic facts. Jessica Gonzales obtained a restraining order limiting contact between her estranged husband and their three daughters. Colorado has a law requiring enforcement of restraining orders, and the order itself included language mandating enforcement by the police. One night, Gonzales discovered that her three daughters were missing. She immediately suspected her husband had taken them and called the police. The police refused to help her. Five times that evening she contacted the police, including

[69] 489 U.S. 189, 195 (1989).

[70] *Id.* at 197.

[71] *Id.* at 201.

[72] For a thorough exploration of this view and a discussion of its flaws, *see* Susan Bandes, The Negative Constitution: A Critique, 88 Mich. L. Rev. 2271 (1990); *see also* Barbara A. Armacost, Affirmative Duties, Systemic Harms and the Due Process Clause, 94 Mich. L. Rev. 982 (1996).

[73] 489 U.S. at 212 (Blackmun, J., dissenting).

[74] The Supreme Court, 1988 Term: Leading Cases, 103 Harv. L. Rev. 137, 173 (1989).

[75] 545 U.S. 748 (2005).

once by going to the station house, and each time they were unhelpful. Later that night, her husband killed the three girls and died in a shoot-out with the police.

Jessica Gonzales sued under the due process clause for the failure of the police to enforce the restraining order. The U.S. Court of Appeals for the Tenth Circuit, in an en banc decision, ruled in her favor and expressly distinguished *DeShaney*. The court explained that Gonzales's claim was for procedural due process, the state law and the restraining order being written in mandatory language created a property interest, and Gonzales was deprived of this property without due process of law. *DeShaney*, in contrast, was a substantive due process case.

The Supreme Court, in a 7-2 decision, with Justice Scalia writing for the Court, reversed. The Court reaffirmed that there is a property interest only if there is an entitlement. The Court said that a "benefit is not a protected entitlement if government officials may grant or deny it in their discretion."[76] The Court explained that police always have discretion as to how to enforce a law and prosecutors always have discretion as to whether to initiate a criminal action. Thus, the Court concluded that there is no property interest for purposes of due process. Moreover, the Court noted that "it is by no means clear that an individual entitlement to enforcement of a restraining order could constitute a 'property' interest for purposes of the Due Process Clause. Such a right would not, of course, resemble any traditional conception of property."[77]

The bottom line is that it does not matter whether the claim is called substantive or procedural due process or whether the law is written in mandatory or discretionary terms. The government generally has no duty to provide protection from private inflicted harms. Only if the government literally creates the danger or a person is in government custody is there any constitutional duty for the government to provide protection. State and local governments may create duties and remedies under their law, but they do not exist under the Constitution.

After *DeShaney*, the key issue is under what circumstances the government has a special relationship with an individual that imposes an affirmative duty to provide protection. Many lower courts have applied *DeShaney* to dismiss suits and have refused to impose such an obligation on the government. For example, in *Tucker v. Callahan*, the Sixth Circuit held that *DeShaney* barred a suit against a police officer who watched an individual being beaten (and as a result was rendered a quadriplegic) but took no action.[78] In *Archie v. City of Racine*, the Seventh Circuit held that a dispatcher could not be held liable for the failure to send a fire department rescue squad to respond promptly to a person with breathing difficulties who subsequently died.[79] In *McKee v. City of Rockwall, Texas*, the Fifth Circuit rejected a constitutional claim for an injury

[76] *Id.* at 756.

[77] *Id.* at 766.

[78] 867 F.2d 909 (6th Cir. 1989). Jones v. Reynolds, 439 F.3d 685 (6th Cir. 2006) (holding officers had no duty to stop a drag race that they came upon before it started).

[79] 847 F.2d 1211 (7th Cir. 1988) (en banc), *cert. denied*, 489 U.S. 1065 (1989). *See also* Wilson-Trattner v. Campbell, 863 F.3d 589 (7th Cir. 2017) (holding that there was no substantive due process claim against police who did not stop domestic abuse despite numerous incidents and calls).

that a woman suffered after police failed to make an arrest at a domestic assault call.[80] The court concluded, "This is the lesson of *DeShaney*: that law enforcement officers have authority to act does not imply that they have any constitutional duty to act."[81] In *Stevens v. City of Green Bay*, a police officer who left an intoxicated individual on the street after briefly taking him into custody was not liable for his death.[82]

Some cases denying relief have especially moving and tragic facts. In *Pinder v. Johnson*, police officers responded to a domestic dispute and promised the victim that the perpetrator would be arrested and confined.[83] Instead, the police immediately released the suspect, and he returned to the house, burned it down, and killed three children. Yet the Fourth Circuit found no liability for the government or its officers. In *Doe v. Hillsboro Independent School District*, the court ruled that school officials had no duty to protect a student from rape by a custodian.[84]

Some lower courts have been willing to find a government duty to provide protection when the government took an affirmative step to place the person in danger. In *Kallstrom v. City of Columbus*, the Sixth Circuit found that releasing undercover officers' names, addresses, and phone numbers would foreseeably place them and their families at risk.[85] The Ninth Circuit's decision in *Wood v. Ostrander* is illustrative.[86] The police arrested a driver of a car and impounded the vehicle. The police left the passenger stranded in a high-crime area at 2:30 A.M. The passenger, the plaintiff in the suit, was subsequently raped by a man who offered her a ride home. The court emphasized that the police officers had placed her in danger and thus had an affirmative duty to protect her. But other courts have refused to apply or follow this principle.[87]

Lower courts also have distinguished *DeShaney* when individuals are in government custody or control. For example, a federal district court found that elementary school students required to attend school were entitled to protection from physical

[80] 877 F.2d 409 (5th Cir. 1989), *cert. denied*, 493 U.S. 1023 (1990). *See* Morrow v. Balaski, 719 F.3d 160 (3d Cir. 2013) (ruling that a school did not have the affirmative duty to protect student from bullies physically attacking her).

[81] *Id.* at 414.

[82] 105 F.3d 1169 (7th Cir. 1997). *See* Estate of Her v. Hoeppner, 939 F.3d 872 (7th Cir. 2019) (finding no *DeShaney* relationship between a girl that drowned and the lifeguards on duty).

[83] 54 F.3d 1169 (4th Cir. 1995) (en banc). *See also* Graves v. Lioi, 930 F.3d 307 (4th Cir. 2019) (finding no liability for officer who allowed a husband to postpone self-surrender who then went to go stab and kill his wife outside of the court).

[84] 113 F.3d 1412 (5th Cir. 1997) (en banc). Doe v. Covington County Sch. Dist., 675 F.3d 849 (5th Cir. 2012) (finding the school was not liable for releasing an elementary student several times to man, who was not on her authorized release list, who molested her).

[85] 136 F.3d 1055 (6th Cir. 1998). *But see* Hart v. City of Little Rock, 432 F.3d 801 (8th Cir. 2005) (holding that releasing officers' personal information did not violate due process).

[86] 879 F.2d 583 (9th Cir. 1989). *See also*, T.D. v. Patton, 868 F.3d 1209 (10th Cir. 2017) (holding that social worker affirmatively created the harm by knowingly placing child with his sex offender father who then abused the child); Kennedy v. City of Ridgefield, 439 F.3d 1055 (9th Cir. 2006) (finding officer affirmatively created dangerous situation).

[87] *See, e.g.*, Keller v. Fleming, 952 F.3d 216 (5th Cir. 2020) (holding that an officer was not liable after he dropped off a mentally handicapped man on the side of the road and then the man was hit and killed by a car); Stevens v. City of Green Bay, 105 F.3d 1169 (7th Cir. 1997) (a police officer who left an intoxicated individual on street not liable for his death).

and verbal abuse inflicted by other students.[88] Other courts, however, have rejected any such duty.[89]

An issue dividing lower courts after *DeShaney* concerns the government's duty to protect children in foster homes from harms inflicted by private (nongovernment) individuals. The majority in *DeShaney* did not resolve the question of foster care, but recognized that it might be a situation "sufficiently analogous to incarceration or institutionalization to give rise to an affirmative duty to protect."[90]

The principle that appears to be emerging from the lower court decisions (though not all cases can be explained by this approach) is that the government has an affirmative duty to protect children in foster care when the government placed them there. But the government has no such obligation to provide protection when the children are voluntarily put in foster care without active government involvement. For example, a federal district court noted that "a child has a §1983 action against the state for injuries suffered while in foster care where the state is deliberately indifferent to the likelihood that a foster home is unsafe, yet places a child there or allows a child to remain there."[91] In contrast, a court of appeals found that *DeShaney* barred a suit against a state for injuries suffered by a child who was voluntarily placed in a foster home by his parents.[92]

Summary

In sum, the Court has attempted to limit the use of the Constitution and §1983 as a remedy for tortious conduct by governments and government officers. This restriction has been accomplished by narrowing the scope of the due process clause of the Fourteenth Amendment. Specifically, the Court has held that negligent conduct cannot constitute a deprivation of due process, that random and unauthorized deprivation of property and liberty are not due process violations where the plaintiff seeks a post-deprivation remedy and an adequate one is available under state law, and that the government generally has no duty to protect individuals from privately inflicted harms.

[88] Pagano by Pagano v. Massapequa Pub. Schools, 714 F. Supp. 641, 642-643 (E.D.N.Y. 1989); *see also* Stoneking v. Bradford Area School Dist., 882 F.2d 720, 723 (3d Cir. 1989), *cert. denied,* 493 U.S. 1044 (1990).

[89] *See, e.g.,* Morrow v. Balaski, 719 F.3d 160 (3d Cir. 2013); Patel v. Kent School Dist., 648 F.3d 965 (9th Cir. 2011); Doe v. Taylor Indep. School Dist., 15 F.3d 443, 465 (5th Cir. 1994).

[90] 489 U.S. at 201 n.9. *See also,* M.D. by Stukenberg v. Abbott, 907 F.3d 237 (5th Cir. 2018) (ruling that Texas's foster care system violated children's substantive due process); Doe ex rel. Johnson v. S.C. Dep't of Social Services, 597 F.3d 163 (4th Cir. 2010) (holding that state social service agency had duty to not place children in dangerous situations).

[91] B.H. v. Johnson, 715 F. Supp. 1387, 1396 (N.D. Ill. 1989); *see also* Henry A. v. Willden, 678 F.3d 991 (9th Cir. 2012); Artist M. v. Johnson, 726 F. Supp. 690, 699-700 (N.D. Ill. 1989).

[92] Milburn v. Anne Arundel County Dept. of Social Servs., 871 F.2d 474 (4th Cir.), *cert. denied,* 493 U.S. 1044 (1989). *See also* Doe ex rel. Johnson v. S.C. Dep't of Social Services, 597 F.3d 163 (4th Cir. 2010) (emphasizing duty to children is not present when children are voluntarily placed in foster care).

§8.10 PRECLUSIVE EFFECTS OF STATE COURT JUDGMENTS AND PROCEEDINGS

Preclusion Applies in §1983 Suits

During the 1980s, the Supreme Court decided several important cases concerning the preclusive effects of state court judgments and proceedings on subsequent federal §1983 suits.[1] Until these Supreme Court rulings, there was substantial division among the lower courts as to whether state court proceedings should have res judicata and collateral estoppel effects in later federal court civil rights actions.[2]

There was a strong argument that state court litigation should not, at least in some circumstances, preclude federal court review. The Supreme Court repeatedly has stated that §1983 was meant to give federal courts a preeminent role in protecting constitutional rights.[3] If, as the Court declared, "[t]he very purpose of §1983 was to interpose the federal courts between the States and the people, as guardians of the people's federal rights,"[4] then state court proceedings should not be able to frustrate this role. Especially in circumstances where the federal court plaintiff did not choose to conduct the litigation in state court, and particularly when there is no other access to the federal courts, a strong case can be made for limiting the res judicata and collateral estoppel effects of the state proceedings.

The Supreme Court, however, has rejected this argument and clearly has held that state court proceedings are preclusive in subsequent federal court §1983 litigation. Specifically, the Supreme Court held that 28 U.S.C. §1738 requires federal courts to give the same effect to prior state court decisions as would the courts in the state where the decisions were rendered.[5] The Court refused to find an exception to §1738 for federal civil rights litigation. In fact, federal courts must accord collateral estoppel and res judicata effects to both state judicial and administrative proceedings.

§8.10 [1] *See, e.g.,* University of Tenn. v. Elliott, 478 U.S. 788 (1986); McDonald v. City of West Branch, 466 U.S. 284 (1984); Migra v. Warren City Sch. Dist. Bd. of Educ., 465 U.S. 75 (1984); Haring v. Prosise, 462 U.S. 306 (1983); Allen v. McCurry, 449 U.S. 90 (1980).

[2] For a review of the conflicting authority, *see* William H. Theis, Res Judicata in Civil Rights Act Cases: An Introduction to the Problem, 70 Nw. U. L. Rev. 859 (1976).

[3] *See, e.g.,* Patsy v. Board of Regents of Fla., 457 U.S. 496, 502-503 (1982); Monroe v. Pape, 365 U.S. 167, 180 (1961).

[4] Mitchum v. Foster, 407 U.S. 225, 242 (1972).

[5] 28 U.S.C. §1738 provides: "The . . . judicial proceedings of any court of any such State . . . shall have the same full faith and credit in every court within the United States and its Territories and Possessions as they have by law or usage in the courts of such state." The act dates from the act of May 26, 1790, ch. 11, 1 Stat. 122.

Collateral Estoppel

Collateral estoppel is the doctrine that "once a court decides an issue of fact or law necessary to its judgment, that decision precludes relitigation of the same issue on a different cause of action between the same parties."[6] In *Allen v. McCurry*, the Supreme Court held that state court litigation has collateral estoppel effect in subsequent §1983 litigation.[7] McCurry, a defendant in a state court criminal proceeding, challenged the admissibility of evidence gained through an allegedly unconstitutional search and seizure. After a suppression hearing, the state court ruled that the search was lawful and admitted the seized drugs into evidence. McCurry was convicted. Subsequently, McCurry filed a §1983 action for money damages against the officers who conducted the search and the St. Louis Police Department.

The issue before the Supreme Court was whether the state court ruling that the search was lawful precluded federal court relitigation of that issue and thus, in effect, foreclosed the §1983 suit. Even if collateral estoppel generally attaches to state court decisions, there is a strong argument for allowing relitigation in the facts of *Allen v. McCurry*. McCurry was a state court defendant; he did not choose to litigate in state court and had no ability to remove the case to federal court. Furthermore, the Supreme Court had ruled that Fourth Amendment issues could not be relitigated on habeas corpus in federal court as long as the state provided a full and fair opportunity for a hearing.[8]

Nonetheless, the Supreme Court held the state court determination that the search was lawful had collateral estoppel effect and precluded relitigation of the issue in the §1983 litigation. The Court said that §1738 requires federal courts to accord preclusive effects to state court judgments and proceedings and that "nothing in the language of §1983 remotely expresses any congressional intent to contravene the common law rules of preclusion or to repeal . . . §1738."[9] The Court said that §1983 does not ensure a federal forum to all litigants presenting constitutional claims and that the Court rejects any assertion that state courts are unwilling or unable to adequately protect federal rights. *Allen v. McCurry* thus is a broad holding that state court decisions have collateral estoppel effect in subsequent federal court §1983 litigation as long as the state court provided a full and fair opportunity for a hearing on the constitutional issue.

The relevant inquiry under *Allen* is whether the state court would accord collateral estoppel effect to the earlier state court decision; if so, preclusion also applies in the federal court. This rule was applied in *Haring v. Prosise*, where the Court considered whether a state court guilty plea prevented a subsequent federal §1983 suit.[10] In *Haring*, the defendant pled guilty in state court to making a controlled substance in

[6] Kremer v. Chemical Constr. Corp., 456 U.S. 461, 467 n.6 (1982).
[7] 449 U.S. 90 (1980).
[8] Stone v. Powell, 428 U.S. 465 (1976), discussed in §15.5, *infra*.
[9] 449 U.S. at 97-98.
[10] 462 U.S. 306 (1983).

his apartment and then later filed a federal court §1983 action. The Supreme Court unanimously held that the guilty plea did not preclude the federal suit because under Virginia law the doctrine of collateral estoppel could not be invoked under such circumstances in Virginia courts. Hence, under §1738, there was no preclusion in federal court. Under traditional collateral estoppel principles, preclusion applies only to the matter actually litigated between the parties. Because the legality of the search was not contested or decided, the matter could be raised in a §1983 case.[11]

It is unresolved after *Haring* whether state court guilty pleas ever can have preclusive effects in federal court. The Seventh Circuit ruled that a state court guilty plea prevented an individual from arguing in a federal court §1983 action that the police fired the first shot,[12] yet other courts read *Haring* as establishing a broader proposition that guilty pleas do not preclude §1983 litigation.[13] To a large extent, the inquiry is a question of law in the particular state because §1738 requires that federal courts follow the state law of preclusion.

Res Judicata Effects of State Court Proceedings

Allen v. McCurry establishes that matters litigated and decided in state court cannot be relitigated in federal court because of collateral estoppel. Additionally, the Supreme Court has applied res judicata to state court proceedings, holding that parties may not raise in federal court §1983 litigation issues that could have been litigated in state court. Res judicata is the doctrine that bars parties from litigating issues in a subsequent action that were or could have been litigated in an earlier proceeding.[14] The Court applied res judicata in a §1983 context in *Migra v. Warren City School District Board of Education.*[15]

Ethel Migra was employed by the Warren Board of Education as a supervisor of elementary education. Her contract was renewed on an annual basis. After the 1979-1980 school year, she was informed that her contract would not be renewed, and she filed a lawsuit in state court for breach of contract and wrongful interference with her employment contract. Migra won in both the trial court and the court of appeals and was reinstated. She then filed a §1983 suit in federal court, contending that her firing violated the First Amendment because the school board acted in retaliation for a desegregation plan she had authored.

The Supreme Court unanimously ruled that Migra's §1983 suit was precluded by the earlier state court litigation. Because Migra's constitutional claim arose from the same set of facts as the state court suit and because it could have been raised at the same time, res judicata barred the federal court litigation. The Court said that it "is

[11] *Id.* at 319 ("Prosise's decision not to exercise his right to stand trial cannot be regarded as a concession of any kind that a Fourth Amendment evidentiary challenge would fail.").

[12] *See* Rodriguez v. Schweiger, 796 F.2d 930 (7th Cir. 1986), *cert. denied,* 481 U.S. 1018 (1987). *See also* United States v. Porter, 933 F.3d 226 (3d Cir. 2019).

[13] *See, e.g.,* Wells v. Coker, 707 F.3d 756 (7th Cir. 2013); Watts v. Graves, 720 F.2d 1416 (5th Cir. 1983).

[14] Kremer v. Chemical Constr. Corp., 456 U.S. 461, 466-467 n.6 (1982).

[15] 465 U.S. 75 (1984).

difficult to see how the policy concerns underlying §1983 would justify a distinction between the issue preclusive and claim preclusive effects of state court judgments."[16] The Court said that §1738 embodies the view that it is more important to give full faith and credit to state court judgments than it is to ensure separate forums for state and federal claims.[17]

Migra poses a special problem for litigants suing state government officers on both federal and state law claims. As discussed in Chapter 7, in *Pennhurst State School & Hospital v. Halderman,* the Supreme Court held that the Eleventh Amendment bars federal courts from hearing pendent state law claims against state officers in federal court.[18] After *Pennhurst,* a litigant with both federal and state law claims against the state officer has relatively few options. One might be to bring the federal claims in federal court and the state claims in state court. However, in light of *Migra,* if the state court decides first, res judicata will prevent the federal court from deciding the federal law issues because they could have been brought in state courts. Alternatively, a §1983 litigant might bring the federal claims in federal court and, if unsuccessful, initiate state court proceedings on the state law issues. Although res judicata would not bar the state court litigation, because the state claims could not have been raised in federal court, the federal court decision will have collateral estoppel effect in state court as to any facts found or common issues decided. The combination of *Pennhurst* and *Migra* creates a substantial litigation problem for plaintiffs with both state and federal claims against state officers.[19]

Allen and *Migra* hold that state court judgments and proceedings have res judicata and collateral estoppel effect in federal court §1983 litigation.

State Court Review of Agency Decisions

In *Kremer v. Chemical Construction Corp.,* the Supreme Court said that state court judicial review of a state administrative agency's action is entitled to full faith and credit.[20] Although *Kremer* involved a claim under Title VII of the Civil Rights Act of 1964, its holding is fully applicable to §1983 litigation as well. Kremer filed a charge of employment discrimination with the Equal Employment Opportunity Commission. As required under the statute, the commission referred the matter to the appropriate state agency. The New York State Division of Human Rights investigated and issued a report that the charge was unfounded. Kremer sought judicial review of the agency's decision in the state courts. Simultaneously, Kremer, after receiving a right-to-sue letter from the Equal Employment Opportunity Commission, filed a Title VII suit in federal court. The state court affirmed the

[16] *Id.* at 83.

[17] For a criticism of this holding, *see* Stephen J. Shapiro, The Application of State Claim Preclusion Rules in a Federal Civil Rights Action, 10 Ohio N.U. L. Rev. 223 (1983) (arguing for a distinction between claim and issue preclusion rules).

[18] 465 U.S. 89 (1984). *See* §7.5.3, *supra.*

[19] Possible solutions to this litigation problem are discussed in §7.5.3, *supra.*

[20] 456 U.S. 461 (1982).

state agency's determination. The issue then was whether the federal court was obligated to dismiss the Title VII case based on collateral estoppel and res judicata.

The Supreme Court concluded that the federal litigation was precluded by the state proceedings. The Court found "[n]othing in the legislative history of the 1964 [Civil Rights] Act suggest[ing] that Congress considered it necessary or desirable to provide an absolute right to relitigate in federal court an issue resolved by a state court."[21] The Court said that it was irrelevant that the state court proceeding was in the form of judicial review of an administrative agency because there is no requirement that judicial review must proceed de novo if it is to be preclusive.[22]

Preclusive Effects of State Agency Proceedings

The Supreme Court extended preclusion even further in 1986, in *University of Tennessee v. Elliott*.[23] An employee of the University of Tennessee claimed that he was fired because of his race and filed an administrative appeal within the state system and a federal court suit under §1983 and Title VII. The state administrative proceedings finished first, with the agency concluding that the discharge was not racially motivated. The issue was whether the *unreviewed* agency decision had preclusive effect in federal court. In *Kremer*, the Court held that a judicial decision affirming an agency ruling was preclusive of federal court litigation. In *Elliott* the question concerned preclusion from a state agency decision where there had not been judicial review. The Court held that "when a state agency acting in a judicial capacity . . . resolves disputed issues of fact properly before it which the parties have had an adequate opportunity to litigate, federal courts must give the agency's factfinding the same preclusive effect to which it would be entitled in the State's courts."[24]

On the one hand, *Elliott* can be viewed as a narrow holding according preclusive effect to agency *fact-finding* and only when the agency holds judicial-type hearings. On the other hand, §1738 mandates preclusion based on state *court* proceedings; nothing in it suggests a need to defer to agency proceedings. Even if state courts are presumptively trusted to adequately protect rights, there is no reason for this confidence to extend to state administrative bodies. Moreover, as the dissenting opinions suggested, the effect of *Elliott* might be to discourage individuals from using available state administrative mechanisms.[25] If agency fact finding is preclusive even when not reviewed in state court, a litigant may be foreclosing federal court litigation by using the administrative proceedings.

It should be emphasized that not every state agency proceeding is preclusive of federal court litigation. In *McDonald v. City of West Branch*, the Court held

[21] *Id.* at 473.

[22] *Id.* at 473-474. For a discussion of employment discrimination litigation after *Kremer*, *see* Andrea Catania, Access to the Federal Courts for Title VII Claimants in the Post-*Kremer* Era: Keeping the Doors Open, 16 Loy. U. Chi. L.J. 209 (1985).

[23] 478 U.S. 788 (1986).

[24] *Id.* at 799 (citations omitted).

[25] *Id.* at 801-802 (Stevens, J., concurring in part and dissenting in part).

that §1738 does not require federal courts to give preclusive effects to unappealed arbitration awards.[26] In *McDonald,* a fired police officer lost in an arbitration proceeding that was created pursuant to a collective bargaining agreement. The officer then filed a federal court §1983 suit. The Court unanimously held that in "a §1983 action, a federal court should not afford res judicata or collateral estoppel effect to an award in an arbitration proceeding brought pursuant to the terms of a collective-bargaining agreement."[27]

Likewise, in a case not involving §1983, the Supreme Court held that judicially unreviewed state administrative findings have no preclusive effect on age discrimination proceedings in federal court.[28] The plaintiff, Angelo Solimino, filed with the Equal Employment Opportunity Commission (EEOC) an age discrimination suit against the defendant savings and loan where he had worked for 40 years. The EEOC referred the matter to the New York State Division of Human Resources. The agency found no probable cause under state law to believe that the plaintiff had been discriminated against, and its decision was upheld on administrative review. Rather than appealing the ruling to state court, Solimino filed a suit in federal court under the Age Discrimination in Employment Act of 1967.

The issue before the Supreme Court was whether the decision by the New York State Division of Human Resources had a preclusive effect in federal court on a claim concerning the same facts. The Supreme Court unanimously ruled that the judicially unreviewed administrative findings should not have preclusive effect. The Court emphasized that this was not an agency ruling that would require preclusive effect under state law, thus distinguishing cases such as *Kremer.* Indeed, the Court concluded that allowing such preclusive effect to unreviewed agency findings would undermine the goals of the federal age discrimination statute.

Thus, although all state court proceedings will have preclusive effects in federal court as long as there was a full and fair opportunity to litigate the federal claims, only some unreviewed agency proceedings will be preclusive. The application of res judicata and collateral estoppel will turn on factors such as how the issue would be treated in state courts, whether the state proceedings can be characterized as judicial in nature, and whether allowing preclusion would undermine the goals of the federal statute.

The decisions applying preclusion are not inconsistent with the earlier rulings in *Monroe v. Pape*[29] and *Patsy v. Board of Regents.*[30] *Monroe* and *Patsy* establish, respectively, that a plaintiff need not exhaust available state judicial and administrative remedies before initiating §1983 litigation. The preclusion decisions described above do not impose an exhaustion requirement. However, the preclusion cases establish that once a matter is decided by state courts and quasi-judicial state agencies, collateral estoppel and res judicata exist in subsequent §1983 litigation.

[26] 466 U.S. 284 (1984).

[27] *Id.* at 292.

[28] Astoria Fed. Sav. & Loan Assn. v. Solimino, 501 U.S. 104 (1991).

[29] *See, e.g.,* Monroe v. Pape, 365 U.S. 167 (1961).

[30] Patsy v. Board of Regents of Fla., 457 U.S. 496, 502-503 (1982).

If anything, the preclusion cases might have the effect of decreasing the use of state proceedings because a state tribunal's ruling likely will foreclose federal court review.

Perhaps most of all, the preclusion decisions reflect the Supreme Court's current belief that there is no reason why federal courts need be available if state court proceedings seem adequate. The decisions reflect the Court's underlying assumption that there is parity between federal and state courts, making federal court litigation unnecessary and wasteful. Thus, there is an obvious inconsistency with other Supreme Court decisions that interpret §1983 as resting on a profound distrust of state judiciaries.[31]

Heck v. Humphrey Preclusion

Finally, the Supreme Court has articulated a significant new preclusion rule: For a plaintiff to recover damages for an allegedly unconstitutional conviction or imprisonment, a plaintiff must first have the conviction or sentence reversed on appeal or expunged by executive pardon.[32] This rule can be properly characterized as a rule of preclusion or as a rule of exhaustion and is discussed in detail above in the section on exhaustion.[33] *Heck v. Humphrey* involved a civil suit for money damages brought by a state prison inmate who had been convicted of voluntary manslaughter and was serving a 15-year sentence. The inmate sued the state prosecutor and police investigator for malicious prosecution.

The Supreme Court nonetheless held that the suit was barred and held that "in order to recover damages for allegedly unconstitutional conviction or imprisonment, or for other harms caused by actions whose unlawfulness would render a conviction or sentence invalid, a §1983 plaintiff must prove that the conviction or sentence has been reversed on direct appeal, expunged by executive order, declared invalid by a state tribunal authorized to make such determination, or called into question by a federal court's issuance of a writ of habeas corpus."[34]

In *Edwards v. Balisok*, the Court applied *Heck* to prisoner disciplinary proceedings.[35] *Balisok* involved an inmate in a Washington prison who was serving a 20-year sentence for attempted murder. In a prison disciplinary proceeding, he was found to have blackmailed another inmate, and his punishment included revocation of 30 days of good-time credits. After an unsuccessful appeal to the prison warden, the inmate filed a §1983 suit for money damages, claiming that the hearing examiner violated due process by refusing to consider key evidence at the hearing. The Supreme Court applied *Heck* and unanimously ruled that Balisok's claim was not cognizable under §1983 until he first succeeded in having the good-time credits

[31] *See, e.g.*, Mitchum v. Foster, 407 U.S. 225 (1972); *see also* Gene R. Nichol, Federalism, State Courts, and Section 1983, 73 Va. L. Rev. 959 (1987) (discussing inconsistent interpretations of the legislative history of §1983).

[32] Heck v. Humphrey, 512 U.S. 477 (1994).

[33] *See* §8.4.

[34] 512 U.S. at 486-487.

[35] 520 U.S. 641 (1997).

restored.[36] Justice Scalia's majority opinion applied *Heck* and explained that "[t]he principal procedural defect complained of by respondent would, if established, necessarily imply the invalidity of his good-time credits."[37] Thus, the Court concluded that the "claim for declaratory relief and money damages, based on allegations of deceit and bias on the part of the decision-maker that necessarily imply the invalidity of the punishment imposed is not cognizable under §1983."[38]

Although *Heck* can be understood as a case about preclusion, it is much more difficult to characterize *Edwards* in that manner. In *Heck*, the criminal conviction had issued preclusive effect in any civil litigation until and unless the conviction was overturned. But in *Edwards*, the issue of whether the prison disciplinary proceeding violated due process had not ever been litigated and could not have been raised earlier. Moreover, Balisok was not seeking to collaterally attack the revocation of the good-time credits, but instead wanted damages for procedural violations.

In 1998 in *Spencer v. Kenna*, five justices took the position, though they did not join in a single opinion, that *Heck* and *Edwards* apply only when the prisoner is in custody and has habeas corpus available as a remedy.[39] Under this view, *Heck* and *Edwards* are applicable only to prisoner litigation.

Subsequently, in *Skinner v. Switzer*, the Court said that *Heck* did not preclude a §1983 suit seeking access to biological evidence for the purpose of DNA testing.[40] The Court distinguished *Heck* and explained that "[s]uccess in his suit for DNA testing would not 'necessarily imply' the invalidity of his conviction."[41] The test results could exonerate the defendant, but they also could be inconclusive or incriminate him. This, the Court, said was sufficient to distinguish *Heck v. Humphrey*.

§8.11 THE REMEDIES AVAILABLE IN §1983 LITIGATION

Section 1983 creates broad authority for courts to fashion remedies needed to prevent and redress violations of federal law by those acting under color of law. The statute explicitly authorizes both legal and equitable remedies, along with any other proper redress.

In addition to traditional equity principles that restrict the availability of injunctive relief, many jurisdictional doctrines limit the ability of federal courts to impose injunctions. These are discussed throughout this book. For example,

[36] Justice Ginsburg, joined by Justices Souter and Breyer, wrote a short concurring opinion to emphasize that the Court's holding applies only to civil suits that "necessarily imply the invalidity of the punishment imposed." *Id.* at 649-650.

[37] *Id.* at 646.

[38] *Id.* at 648.

[39] 523 U.S. 1 (1998). Justice Souter's opinion was joined by Justices O'Connor, Ginsburg, and Breyer. *Id.* at 990. Justice Stevens, in dissent, took the same view. *Id.* at 24.

[40] 562 U.S. 521 (2011).

[41] *Id.* at 534.

the Supreme Court has created special standing requirements when plaintiffs seek injunctive relief,[1] has limited the ability of federal courts to enjoin municipal police departments,[2] and has prevented federal courts from enjoining pending state judicial and administrative proceedings.[3]

What Damages May Be Awarded?

Additionally, two major questions have arisen with regard to the remedies available under §1983. First, what damages may be recovered in successful §1983 actions? Second, how should matters not specifically covered in §1983 or its legislative history, such as survivability of a §1983 action or the statute of limitations, be decided?

As to the former, it is clearly established that damages exist under §1983 to provide compensation for actual injuries suffered. In *Carey v. Piphus,* the Court considered the damages to be awarded to students who were denied procedural due process when they were suspended by their schools.[4] The district courts found a constitutional violation but refused to award damages because no evidence existed documenting any harms suffered. The Seventh Circuit reversed, holding that the students were entitled to damages for the denial of due process, even though there was no proof of actual injury. The Supreme Court agreed with the district court's position, concluding that absent evidence of actual injury, a plaintiff can recover only nominal damages in the amount of one dollar.

The Court emphasized that the purpose of damage awards under §1983 is to compensate people for particular injuries suffered.[5] The Court said that compensation principles often can be derived from the tort law, though this approach is not useful when the constitutional violation, such as a denial of procedural due process, has no analogue in the common law.[6] The Court rejected the plaintiffs' claim that presumed damages, like those permitted in defamation cases, should be allowed for the violations of procedural due process. Instead, the Court said that plaintiffs are restricted to recovering for the actual harms they have incurred, including compensation for emotional and mental distress.[7] Also, as discussed

§8.11 [1] *See* City of Los Angeles v. Lyons, 461 U.S. 95 (1983) (federal court could not enjoin use of allegedly unconstitutional police chokehold because plaintiff could not demonstrate likelihood that he would be choked again); *see* §2.3.2, *supra.*

[2] *See* Rizzo v. Goode, 423 U.S. 362 (1976) (comity restricts ability of federal courts to restrain police department); *see* §13.3.5, *infra.*

[3] *See* Younger v. Harris, 401 U.S. 37 (1971) (federal courts may not enjoin pending state criminal proceedings); Ohio Civil Rights Commn. v. Dayton Christian Schools, 477 U.S. 619 (1986) (applying Younger v. Harris to preclude federal court injunctions of state administrative proceedings); *see* §13.3.4, *infra.*

[4] 435 U.S. 247 (1978). For a critical discussion of Carey v. Piphus, *see* Note, Damage Awards for Constitutional Torts: A Reconsideration of Carey v. Piphus, 93 Harv. L. Rev. 966 (1980).

[5] 435 U.S. at 254.

[6] *Id.* at 258.

[7] *Id.* at 263-264.

below, even if compensatory damages are unavailable, punitive damages still might be recovered.[8]

Carey v. Piphus concerns only limits on damages for violations of procedural due process. After *Carey*, there was substantial division among the lower courts as to whether presumed damages might be recovered for other constitutional violations.[9] A subsequent Supreme Court decision, *Memphis Community School District v. Stachura*, appears to have resolved this uncertainty and applied the *Carey* principle to all constitutional violations.[10] In *Stachura*, a teacher sued claiming violation of his First Amendment and procedural due process rights. The judge's jury instructions permitted an award of damages based on the importance of the constitutional rights involved. Specifically, the judge told the jury: "[B]ecause these constitutional rights are not capable of precise evaluation does not mean that an appropriate monetary award should not be awarded. The precise value you place upon any constitutional right . . . is within your discretion. You may wish to consider the importance of the right in our system of government . . . [and] in the history of our republic."[11]

The Supreme Court reversed, concluding that the jury instructions were improper because damages under §1983 exist solely to provide compensation for actual injuries suffered. The Court specifically rejected the contention that *Carey* was limited to procedural due process cases and was inapplicable to particular constitutional provisions such as the First Amendment. The Court said that there is not a "two tier system of constitutional rights" with substantive rights treated differently than procedural rights.[12] Rather, in all instances "damages based on the 'value' or 'importance' of constitutional rights are not authorized by §1983 because they are not truly compensatory."[13]

Thus, it seems clearly established that recovery of damages under §1983 is limited to compensation for actual injuries suffered. Actual injuries include, of course, not only financial harms incurred, such as lost wages or medical bills, but also emotional and psychological harms. Lower courts are unanimous in allowing actual damages for emotional distress and humiliation.[14]

The central question concerning *Carey* and *Stachura* is whether they too narrowly define the purposes of §1983. Although compensation is an important

[8] *Id.* at 257 n.11; Smith v. Wade, 461 U.S. 30 (1983) (punitive damages permitted in §1983 suits).

[9] For example, there was a division among the lower courts as to whether presumed damages could be recovered for violations of the First Amendment. *Compare* Crawford v. Garnier, 719 F.2d 1317 (7th Cir. 1983) (proof of actual damages is required in First Amendment cases) *with* Campos-Orrego v. Rivera, 175 F.3d 89 (1st Cir. 1999) (nominal damages are available in First Amendment cases).

[10] 477 U.S. 299 (1986).

[11] *Id.* at 302-303.

[12] *Id.* at 309.

[13] *Id.* at 309 n.13.

[14] *See, e.g.*, Price v. City of Charlotte, North Carolina, 93 F.3d 1241 (4th Cir. 1996); Sykes v. McDowell, 786 F.2d 1098 (11th Cir. 1986); Stewart v. Furton, 774 F.2d 706 (6th Cir. 1985). Additionally, some circuits have held that presumed damages are available for some constitutional violations; that the effect of *Stachura* is to prevent damages based on the importance or value of the constitutional right. *See, e.g.*, Trevino v. Gates, 99 F.3d 911, 921-922 (9th Cir. 1996); Parrish v. Johnson, 800 F.2d 600 (6th Cir. 1986).

objective, deterrence of constitutional violations also is a goal that has been explicitly recognized by the Supreme Court.[15] Because it is often difficult to quantify the monetary value of a constitutional right, such as voting or free speech, it is arguable that permitting compensation only for actual damages is insufficient to achieve adequate deterrence. In fact, precisely for this reason, one commentator has suggested that §1983 be amended to provide a liquidated damage sum to compensate for the value of the constitutional right infringed.[16] For example, the proposal was that "[a]ny deprivation of a constitutional right should be valued at not less than $1,000; any time wrongfully spent in jail, no matter how brief, should be valued at not less than $2,500."[17] Especially in light of the difficulties in securing federal court injunctive relief, restrictions on the availability of damages threaten to lessen the ability of §1983 to prevent and redress constitutional violations. The concern is that *Carey* and *Stachura* excessively limit damage awards.

Punitive Damages

The Supreme Court has concluded that punitive damages may be recovered from individual officers, although not from government entities. In *Smith v. Wade*, the Court held that punitive damages are available when the official's "conduct is shown to be motivated by evil motive or intent, or when it involves reckless or callous indifference to the federally protected rights of others."[18] The majority, in a 5-4 decision, held that §1983 implicitly adopted the common law of torts as of 1871 and hence included its standard for punitive damages. The Court rejected the argument that "recklessness or callous indifference" is too vague a standard.

Three dissenting justices—Justices Rehnquist, Burger, and Powell—disagreed with the majority's reading of the common law history and argued that Congress did not intend punitive damages to be available. Justice O'Connor also dissented but challenged both the majority's and the other dissenters' use of common law history in determining modern §1983 doctrines. Justice O'Connor contended that punitive damages should be available only for malicious conduct.[19]

Although punitive damages may be recovered from individual officers, as discussed earlier in this chapter, municipal governments may not be sued for punitive damages under §1983.[20] In *City of Newport v. Fact Concerts*, the Supreme Court held that while cities are generally liable under §1983 for their unconstitutional policies or customs, recovery of punitive damages from municipalities is not permitted.[21]

[15] Owen v. City of Independence, 445 U.S. 622, 651 (1980).

[16] Jon O. Newman, Suing the Lawbreakers: Proposals to Strengthen the Section 1983 Damage Remedy for Law Enforcers' Misconduct, 87 Yale L.J. 447, 465 (1978).

[17] *Id.*

[18] 461 U.S. 30, 56 (1983).

[19] *Id.* at 92.

[20] *See* §8.5.3, *supra*.

[21] 453 U.S. 247 (1981).

What Law Where §1983 is Silent?

In addition to the availability of damages, the second major issue concerning remedies under §1983 involves instances where the statute is silent and the legislative history nonexistent concerning the appropriate rule of law. For example, how should it be decided whether §1983 actions survive the death of the victim, or how should the statute of limitations for §1983 cases be determined?

Congress anticipated the incompleteness of federal civil rights laws and provided, in 42 U.S.C. §1988, that when the federal law is "deficient," a federal court should apply the state law of the forum as long as it is not "inconsistent with the Constitution and laws of the United States." Thus, the Supreme Court has held that in light of §1988, state law is controlling when there is no basis for determining a legal standard under federal law.

Many commentators are critical of this approach. Professor Eisenberg, for example, argues that §1988 only was meant to apply in cases that were removed from state to federal court.[22] Similarly, other commentators argue that it "requires an incongruous historical vision to picture the Reconstruction Congress establishing the local law of recently rebelling states as the linchpin of an avowedly nationalist enforcement program."[23]

Nonetheless, the Supreme Court has held that state law is used when §1983 is "deficient." The major question is when should federal courts develop federal law under §1983, such as they have done for questions of officer immunities and the availability of punitive damages, and when should federal courts deem §1983 deficient and use state federal law? Although §1983 is silent as to issues such as immunities and punitive damages, the Supreme Court has not relied on state law but instead has developed federal law. There is no clear rule as to when §1983's gaps should be filled in with state law or with the development of federal standards.[24]

Most notably, the Court has held that state law should be used to determine the survivorship in §1983 actions and the statute of limitations. In *Robertson v. Wegmann*, the Supreme Court concluded that survivorship of §1983 claims is not determined by federal law but instead is decided, under §1988, by state law.[25] In *Robertson*, the federal district court used Louisiana's survivorship law to deny the plaintiff recovery. The Supreme Court held that, in general, it is appropriate to use state law to resolve survivorship questions. The Court then considered whether the state law is inconsistent with §1983; under §1988, state law is not to be used if

[22] *See* Theodore Eisenberg, State Law in Federal Civil Rights Cases: The Proper Scope of §1988, 128 U. Pa. L. Rev. 499 (1980).

[23] Seth F. Kreimer, The Source of Law in Civil Rights Actions: Some Old Light on Section 1988, 133 U. Pa. L. Rev. 601, 616 (1985). *See also* William H. Theis, Shaw v. Garrison: Some Observations on 42 U.S.C. §1988 and Federal Common Law, 36 La. L. Rev. 681 (1976) (arguing that §1988 refers to the federal common law developed pursuant to Swift v. Tyson, 41 U.S. 1 (1842), and not to state law).

[24] The Supreme Court has stated that under §1988, first federal law is applied; if there is none, state law is determined and applied, unless state law would frustrate the achievement of the federal objective. Burnett v. Grattan, 486 U.S. 42, 47-48 (1984). However, there is no specification as to when the courts should create federal standards in §1983 suits where none exist.

[25] 436 U.S. 584 (1978).

it is inconsistent with the Constitution and laws of the United States. The Court noted that a "state statute cannot be considered 'inconsistent' with federal law merely because the statute causes the plaintiff to lose the litigation."[26] Specifically, the Court found that Louisiana law permits survivorship in most instances and the denial of recovery in this instance did not frustrate §1983's goals of compensation and deterrence.[27]

The Court has not spelled out criteria for determining when a state statute is inconsistent with federal law and hence need not be applied under §1988. *Robertson* makes it clear that inconsistency is not limited to situations where the state law is unconstitutional or preempted by federal law. A state law is inconsistent if it frustrates the underlying policy objectives of §1983.

Another area where the Supreme Court applies state law is in determining the statute of limitations. Interestingly, not all statute of limitations questions are decided by state law. For instance, federal law determines when a §1983 action accrues.[28] But the statute of limitations itself is determined by state law, specifically by using the state's statute of limitations for personal injury cases. In *Wilson v. Garcia,* the Court said that statutes of limitations in §1983 should not be determined based on the facts in the particular case.[29] Nor should the state's statute of limitations for actions against government officers be used, because "it was the very ineffectiveness of state remedies that led Congress to enact the Civil Rights Acts in the first place."[30] Rather, the Court felt that §1983 is most closely analogous to tort claims for personal injuries and, hence, the state's statute of limitations for such suits is applicable in §1983 litigation.

Subsequently, the Court refined the *Wilson* approach and held that "where state law provides multiple statutes of limitations for personal injury actions, courts considering §1983 claims should borrow the general or residual statute for personal injury actions."[31] In *Owens v. Okure,* the Court held that New York's one-year statute of limitations for intentional torts should not be applied because not all §1983 actions involve intentional acts.[32] Instead, the Court said that the state's general three-year statute of limitations was applicable and thus a suit against police officers for an illegal arrest was allowed to be brought 22 months after the action occurred.[33]

[26] *Id.* at 593.

[27] The Supreme Court granted certiorari, but subsequently dismissed the writ as having been improvidently granted, on the question of whether the Alabama wrongful death statute, which authorizes only punitive damages, could be applied. *See* Jefferson v. City of Tarrant, 522 U.S. 75 (1997).

[28] Chardon v. Fernandez, 454 U.S. 6 (1981).

[29] 471 U.S. 261, 275 (1985). Also, state law determines issues concerning the tolling of statutes of limitations. *See* Chardon v. Fumero Soto, 462 U.S. 650 (1983).

[30] 471 U.S. at 279.

[31] Owens v. Okure, 488 U.S. 235, 249-250 (1989).

[32] *Id.*

[33] Additionally, the Court has held that the length of time to bring a §1983 lawsuit is extended by state statutes that toll the statute of limitations while prisoners are incarcerated. Hardin v. Straub, 490 U.S. 538 (1989).

However, state statutes of limitations are applied only if they do not frustrate the enforcement of federal law. In *Burnett v. Grattan*, the Supreme Court rejected a six-month statute of limitations that the state used for judicial review of state administrative employment discrimination proceedings.[34] The Court held that the state's interest in prompt review of administrative decisions conflicted with §1983's objective of assuring a forum for those whose constitutional rights have been violated. The six-month statute of limitations was deemed too short and thus, under §1988, was ruled inconsistent with federal law.[35]

In *Reed v. Goertz*, the Court resolved a Circuit split over when the statute of limitations for a 42 U.S.C. §1983 claim seeking DNA testing of crime-scene evidence begins to run.[36] The Fifth Circuit had held that the statute of limitations began to run when the state *trial* court denied DNA testing, while the Eleventh Circuit held that it did not begin to run until the end of the entire state-court litigation had run its course, including appeals.[37] In a 6-3 decision, Justice Kavanaugh wrote for the majority ruling in favor of Reed that the statute of limitations begins when the entire litigation ends.[38]

The Court stressed that a plaintiff must have a "complete and present cause of action," which the Court determines by focusing on the specific constitutional right alleged to have been infringed.[39] Here, the right in question is Reed's liberty interest in DNA testing. Because this right hinges on the state process for considering the request, the failure to provide the fair process could not be complete until Texas was done considering the request.[40] Therefore, the Court found that the statute of limitations could not begin to run until the Texas Court of Criminal Appeals denied Reed's motion for rehearing in October 2017.[41]

The majority further justified the decision by emphasizing the consequences of the alternative approach.[42] It would be inefficient for a plaintiff to file a federal claim while the state appeals process was still ongoing.[43]

In *Felder v. Casey*, the Supreme Court ruled states may not apply state notice of claim laws to §1983 suits brought in state courts.[44] Many states have laws requiring government officers and public bodies to be given notice of claims prior to filing of suit against them in state courts. The Supreme Court held that states may not require compliance with these statutes as a prerequisite to the commencement of a §1983 action.

[34] 468 U.S. 42 (1984).

[35] It is also worth noting that in Wallace v. Kato, 594 U.S. 384 (2007), the Court held that the statute of limitations on a §1983 false arrest claim begins to run at the time that legal process is initiated.

[36] *Reed v. Goertz*, 598 U.S. 230, 237 (2023).

[37] *Id.* at 232.

[38] *Id.*

[39] *Id.* at 235-236.

[40] *Id.* at 236.

[41] *Id.*

[42] *Id.* at 236-237.

[43] *Id.* at 237.

[44] 487 U.S. 131 (1988).

§8.11 The Remedies Available in §1983 Litigation

Cases such as *Robertson v. Wegmann* and *Wilson v. Garcia* set out a general approach to issues where §1983 is deficient: Pursuant to §1988, state law is used as long as it is not inconsistent with federal law. However, many questions, both general and specific, are unresolved. Generally, as mentioned above, it is not clear when §1983 should be deemed deficient or when the Court should find federal law based on common law history or policy considerations. Also, there are not clear criteria for deciding when state law would frustrate the achievement of a federal objective and hence when federal courts should fashion federal common law. More particular questions also remain open. For example, when a state has varying statutes of limitations for different personal injury torts, which should apply?[45]

Moreover, the Supreme Court held that a prosecutor and an arrestee may enter into an agreement under which the prosecutor dismisses all charges in exchange for the individual agreeing to forgo any claims that might exist against the city or its police officers.[46] The Supreme Court held that the agreement was enforceable and rejected a claim that such agreements inherently violate public policy. Here, and in many areas discussed throughout this chapter, the underlying question is whether the Court is sufficiently sensitive to the need for §1983 actions and especially to the availability of federal courts for such litigation.

Thus, overall, §1983 authorizes a full panoply of remedies, but many restrictions often prevent federal courts from granting either injunctive or damage relief.

[45] *See, e.g.*, Silva v. Cain, 169 F.3d 608 (9th Cir. 1999) (one-year general statute of limitations applies and not its special statute of limitations for claims against public entities); Farrell v. McDonogh, 966 F.2d 279 (7th Cir. 1992) (two-year personal injury statute controls and not five-year general statute of limitations).

[46] Town of Newton v. Rumery, 480 U.S. 386 (1987).

CHAPTER 9

Federal Court Relief Against Federal Officers and the Federal Government

§9.1 SUITS AGAINST FEDERAL OFFICERS

§9.1.1 Introduction

Authority for Suits Against Federal Officials

No federal statute authorizes federal courts to hear suits or give relief against federal officers who violate the Constitution of the United States. Although 42 U.S.C. §1983 authorizes suits against state and local officers, it has no application to the federal government or its officers.[1] Nor is there any analogous statute pertaining to violations of federal law by federal officials.

Despite the absence of a statute creating a cause of action against federal officers for constitutional transgressions, the Supreme Court long has held that federal officers may be sued for injunctive relief to prevent future infringements of federal laws.[2] Also, Congress amended the Administrative Procedure Act to provide that suits against federal agencies, officers, or employees "seeking relief other than money damages" shall not be dismissed on account of the United States being a necessary party.[3] The statute even allows the United States to be named as the defendant in a suit for prospective relief. In short, when the federal government acts unconstitutionally, assuming all other jurisdictional requirements are met, the plaintiff may sue the officer or the United States for an injunction.

In contrast, the ability of federal courts to entertain suits seeking money damages against federal officers is much more controversial. In the landmark 1971 decision of *Bivens v. Six Unknown Named Agents of Federal Bureau of Narcotics*, the Supreme Court said that it would infer a cause of action for damages directly from constitutional provisions.[4] This section analyzes the *Bivens* cause of action.

Subsection 9.1.2 examines the Supreme Court's decision creating the authority of federal courts to hear suits against federal officers for money damages based on causes of action inferred from the Constitution. The exceptions to the *Bivens* doctrine are discussed in subsection 9.1.3. Over the last 40 years, the exceptions to *Bivens* have grown greatly, and the availability of *Bivens* suits has been significantly narrowed. The cases narrowing the availability of *Bivens* suits are described in detail. Subsection 9.1.4 considers the ability to bring *Bivens* suits directly against federal, state, or local government entities. Finally, subsection 9.1.5 examines procedural issues that arise in *Bivens* litigation.

Limitations on Recovery

Two important qualifications need to be remembered in considering the liability of individual federal officers. First, the discussion in this section considers only whether and when a cause of action exists under *Bivens*. Even if a cause of action is recognized, the defendant still can raise immunity as a defense. The rules for immunities of federal officers are identical to those that have been recognized

§9.1 [1] *See* Wheeldin v. Wheeler, 373 U.S. 647 (1963) (federal officers are not liable under §1983). Federal officers may be sued under §1983 only if they act in concert with state or local officers to violate the Constitution or laws of the United States. *See* Dombrowski v. Eastland, 387 U.S. 82 (1967).

[2] *See, e.g.,* Larson v. Domestic & Foreign Commerce Corp., 337 U.S. 682 (1949) (federal officers may be enjoined). An important issue that has not yet been directly addressed by the Supreme Court concerns when nationwide injunctions are appropriate. *See* Amanda Frost, In Defense of Nationwide Injunctions, 93 N.Y.U. L. Rev. 1065 (2018); Samuel L. Bray, Multiple Chancellors: Reforming the National Injunction, 131 Harv. L. Rev. 417 (2017).

[3] 5 U.S.C. §702, 90 Stat. 2721 (1976). *See* §9.2.2, *infra.*

[4] 403 U.S. 388 (1971).

for state and local officers under §1983.[5] The topic of officers' immunities is discussed in §8.6, and it must be emphasized that it is a very important limit on the ability to recover from federal officers.

Second, *Bivens* creates a cause of action for constitutional violations; hence, limits on the scope of constitutional protections have the obvious effect of restricting *Bivens* suits. For example, the Supreme Court's decisions narrowing the scope of the due process clause—such as *Daniels v. Williams, Davidson v. Cannon,* and *Parratt v. Taylor*—apply in suits against federal officers.[6] *Bivens* provides a cause of action for a constitutional violation by a federal officer; whether there is a constitutional violation is obviously a separate question. Likewise, all of the usual rules of federal procedure, such as pleading requirements, apply in *Bivens* suits.[7]

Shifting Law

There is no way to understand the law concerning *Bivens* suits except in the context of how the Court's attitude toward such claims has changed. For the first decade after *Bivens,* the Court expanded its availability.[8]

Over the past four decades, however, the Supreme Court has consistently narrowed the availability of *Bivens.*[9] In fact, every Supreme Court decision in the past 40 years about the availability of *Bivens* suits has ruled against their availability. Justice Scalia, joined by Justice Thomas, expressed a clear desire to overrule *Bivens* and declared: "I would not extend *Bivens* even if its reasoning logically applied to this case. *Bivens* is a relic of the heady days in which the Court assumed common-law powers to create causes of action. Accordingly in my view, *Bivens* and its progeny should be limited to the precise circumstances involved."[10]

In *Ziglar v. Abassi,* discussed below,[11] the Court "made clear that expanding the *Bivens* remedy is now a 'disfavored' judicial activity" and that it would hesitate to extend *Bivens* to new contexts.[12] "[A] case can present a new context for *Bivens*

[5] *See, e.g.,* Harlow v. Fitzgerald, 457 U.S. 800, 809 (1982) (immunities under §1983 and under *Bivens* are identical); *see also* Butz v. Economou, 438 U.S. 478 (1978) (immunities for federal officers in *Bivens* suits). *See* discussion in §8.6, *supra.*

[6] Daniels v. Williams, 474 U.S. 327 (1986) (negligence is insufficient for a claim under due process); Davidson v. Cannon, 474 U.S. 344 (1986) (negligence is insufficient for a claim under due process); Parratt v. Taylor, 451 U.S. 527 (1981) (there is no claim for deprivation of due process if the plaintiff is seeking a post-deprivation remedy for the denial of procedural due process and the state provides an adequate remedy). These cases are discussed in detail in §8.9, *supra.*

[7] Indeed, Ashcroft v. Iqbal, 556 U.S. 662 (2009), an important case with regard to pleading in federal court arose in the context of a *Bivens* claim against the U.S. Attorney General. In *Iqbal,* the Supreme Court held that a plaintiff must plead enough that a court can say that it is "plausible" that the plaintiff can recover.

[8] *See* Carlson v. Green, 446 U.S. 14 (1980); Davis v. Passman, 442 U.S. 228 (1979), discussed below.

[9] *See, e.g.,* Ziglar v. Abbasi, 582 U.S. 120 (2017); Hui v. Castaneda, 555 U.S. 799 (2010); Wilkie v. Robbins, 551 U.S. 537 (2007); Correctional Services Corp. v. Malesko, 534 U.S. 61 (2001), all discussed below.

[10] Wilkie v. Robbins, 551 U.S. 537, 568 (2007) (Scalia, J., concurring) (citations omitted).

[11] 582 U.S. 120 (2017).

[12] *Id.* at 136 ("a *Bivens* remedy will not be available if there are 'special factors counselling hesitation in the absence of affirmative action by Congress.'") (internal citations omitted); *id.* at 139 ("The

purposes if it implicates a different constitutional right; if judicial precedents provide a less meaningful guide for official conduct; or if there are potential special factors that were not considered in previous *Bivens* cases."[13] In *Egbert v. Boule*, also discussed below, the Court noted that it had "declined 11 times to imply a similar cause of action for other alleged constitutional violations" and that "in all but the most unusual circumstances, prescribing a cause of action is a job for Congress, not the courts."[14]

Bivens suits certainly continue to exist and to be filed, but there is no doubt that the Supreme Court has significantly narrowed their availability, and lower courts are often following this lead.[15]

§9.1.2 The Cause of Action Against Federal Officers for Monetary Relief

Law Prior to *Bivens*

In *Bivens v. Six Unknown Named Agents of the Federal Bureau of Narcotics*, the Supreme Court allowed a plaintiff to seek money damages from individual federal officers for their alleged violation of the plaintiff's rights arising under the Fourth Amendment to the U.S. Constitution.[16] Prior to this decision, although courts protected constitutional rights through injunctive relief and doctrines such as the exclusionary rule, plaintiffs were not allowed to sue federal officers for monetary remedies in federal court. Plaintiffs seeking such compensation were relegated to state common law causes of action in tort.

The Court's holding in *Bivens* was foreshadowed in the 1947 decision in *Bell v. Hood*.[17] Bell sought damages in the amount of $3,000 from agents of the Federal Bureau of Narcotics for the violation of his Fourth and Fifth Amendment rights. The federal district court dismissed the case for lack of subject matter jurisdiction on the ground that the action did not arise under the Constitution or laws of the United States. The Supreme Court reversed, holding that jurisdiction was alleged because the case arose under the Constitution; the Court remanded for a determination of whether there was a cause of action for relief. The Court did

---

proper test for determining whether a case presents a new *Bivens* context is . . . If the case is different in a meaningful way from previous *Bivens* cases decided by this Court, then the context is new.")

[13] *Id.* at 148.

[14] 596 U.S. 482, 487 (2022).

[15] *See, e.g.*, Quinones-Pimentel v. Cannon, 85 F.4th 63 (1st Cir. 2023) (declining to allow *Bivens* claims to proceed because of factual differences between the claims presented and *Bivens*, even though both cases involved unlawful searches and seizures); Mays v. Smith, 70 F.4th 198 (4th Cir. 2023) (denying *Bivens* actions asserting racial discrimination and claims under the Due Process and Equal Protection Clauses against prison officials); Logsdon v. United States Marshal Service, 91 F.4th 1352, 1357 (10th Cir. 2024) (declining to extend *Bivens* to apply to U.S. Marshall Service officers for excessive force, concluding that the officers are a new class of defendant and that there would be consequences of extending a cause of action to apply to them).

[16] 403 U.S. 388 (1971).

[17] 327 U.S. 678 (1946).

not resolve this question, but certainly intimated a positive view toward causes of action inferred directly from the Constitution. The Court stated that although the Court never has decided whether money damages could be awarded for violations of the Fourth and Fifth Amendments, "where federally protected rights have been invaded, it has been the rule from the beginning that courts will be alert to adjust their remedies so as to grant the necessary relief."[18]

Facts and Holding in *Bivens*

The Supreme Court did not address the issue again until *Bivens*, 25 years later. In *Bivens*, the plaintiff alleged that he had been subjected to an illegal and humiliating search by agents of the Federal Bureau of Narcotics. Bivens sought money damages as compensation for the harms suffered. The district court dismissed the case for failure to state a claim, and the Court of Appeals for the Second Circuit affirmed, holding "that the Fourth Amendment does not provide a basis for a federal cause of action for damages arising out of an unreasonable search and seizure."[19] According to the Second Circuit, the remedy against the federal officers was under state tort law, not pursuant to a judicially created federal law cause of action.

The U.S. Supreme Court reversed. The Court held that a federal law cause of action for money damages could be inferred directly from the Fourth Amendment. The majority, in an opinion by Justice Brennan, emphasized that individuals whose rights have been violated should not be relegated to state law remedies, which might be inadequate or hostile to the federal constitutional interest.[20] The Court stated that the "Fourth Amendment operates as a limitation upon the exercise of federal power regardless of whether the State in whose jurisdiction that power is exercised would prohibit or penalize the identical act if engaged in by a private citizen."[21] Furthermore, the Court felt that the judiciary has the authority and the duty to adjust its remedies so as to ensure the necessary relief for violations of federal rights.[22]

Exceptions Recognized in *Bivens*

The majority opinion suggested two situations in which it would not recognize causes of action for constitutional violations; both were deemed absent in *Bivens*. First, the Court suggested that there would be no cause of action if there are "special factors counselling hesitation in the absence of affirmative action by Congress."[23] The Court found no such special factors in *Bivens*. Nor did the Court

[18] *Id.* at 684. On remand, the district court found that there was no cause of action for money damages under the Constitution. Bell v. Hood, 71 F. Supp. 813 (S.D. Cal. 1947).

[19] 409 F.2d 718, 719 (2d Cir. 1969), *rev'd*, 403 U.S. 388 (1971).

[20] 403 U.S. at 394-395.

[21] *Id.* at 392.

[22] *Id.*

[23] *Id.* at 396.

elaborate as to what would constitute "special factors" in other instances. Second, the Court suggested that it would not create a cause of action if Congress has specified an alternative mechanism that Congress believes provides an equally effective substitute.[24] Again, the Court found no such alternative mechanism available for Bivens and did not elaborate as to what might be deemed a sufficient substitute for a cause of action under the Constitution.

Harlan's Concurrence in *Bivens*

In an important and often-cited concurring opinion, Justice Harlan explained that the federal courts long have devised remedies for violations of federal law.[25] For example, federal courts have created damage remedies under federal statutes that do not specify the availability of such relief. Justice Harlan said that it does not make sense that "the fact that the interest is protected by the Constitution rather than statute or common law justifies the assertion that federal courts are powerless to grant damages in the absence of explicit congressional action authorizing the remedy."[26] Furthermore, Justice Harlan suggested that it is essential that federal courts be able to provide such relief because "it is apparent that some form of damages is the only possible remedy for someone in Bivens' alleged position. . . . For people in Bivens' shoes, it is damages or nothing."[27]

Justice Harlan rejected the claim that the Court violates separation of powers when it creates such a cause of action and remedy. In his view, the Court is responsible for upholding and enforcing the Bill of Rights, and, hence, the judiciary need not wait for the legislature in order to act.[28]

Dissents in *Bivens*

Justices Burger, Black, and Blackmun dissented. Chief Justice Burger contended that separation of powers meant that Congress, and not the Court, should create a cause of action for damages against federal officers.[29] Furthermore, Chief Justice Burger used his dissent as an occasion for a lengthy attack on the desirability of the exclusionary rule, a judicially created remedy whereby illegally obtained evidence is inadmissible at trial. Justices Black and Blackmun also argued that it is for Congress alone to authorize suits against federal officers for money damages.[30] Justice Black explained that "[s]hould the time come when Congress desires such lawsuits, it has before it a model of valid legislation, 42 U.S.C. §1983, to create a damage remedy against federal officers."[31] Until then, in his view, no such cause of

[24] *Id.* at 397.
[25] *Id.* at 402-403 (Harlan, J., concurring).
[26] *Id.* at 403.
[27] *Id.* at 409-410.
[28] *Id.* at 410-411.
[29] *Id.* at 412 (Burger, C.J., dissenting).
[30] *Id.* at 427-428 (Black, J., dissenting).
[31] *Id.* at 429 (Black, J., dissenting).

action should exist. Similarly, Justice Blackmun argued that "it is the Congress and not this Court that should act."[32]

Expansion of *Bivens* Suits Availability

Although in *Bivens* the Court explicitly created a cause of action for damages against federal officers only for violations of the Fourth Amendment, in subsequent decisions the Court recognized the existence of causes of action for infringements of the Fifth,[33] Eighth,[34] and First Amendments.[35] Lower federal courts have recognized *Bivens* suits for violations of the First,[36] Fourth,[37] Fifth,[38] Eighth,[39] Ninth,[40] and Fourteenth Amendments.[41]

Does *Bivens* Offend Separation of Powers?

The central policy question in evaluating *Bivens* and its progeny is whether the Court exceeded its proper role in creating a cause of action for money damages against federal officers.[42] There is a fundamental disagreement about the respective

[32] *Id.* at 430 (Blackmun, J., dissenting).

[33] Davis v. Passman, 442 U.S. 228 (1979). Discussed more fully at text accompanying notes 66-70, *infra.*

[34] Carlson v. Green, 446 U.S. 14 (1980). Discussed more fully at text accompanying notes 71-79, *infra.*

[35] Bush v. Lucas, 462 U.S. 367 (1983). Although the Court in *Bush* refused to allow a *Bivens* suit because it felt that Congress had created adequate alternative remedies, the Court accepted the general existence of such causes of action for violations of the First Amendment. Discussed more fully at text accompanying notes 80-84, *infra.*

[36] *See, e.g.,* Martin v. Naval Criminal Investigative Serv., 539 F. App'x 830, 831 (9th Cir. 2013); Bistrian v. Levi, 696 F.3d 352, 376 n.9 (3d Cir. 2012); Trulock v. Freeh, 275 F.3d 391, 406 (4th Cir. 2001); King v. Fed. Bureau of Prisons, 415 F.3d 634, 639 (7th Cir. 2005).

[37] *See, e.g.,* Rodriguez v. Swartz, 899 F.3d 719, 748 (9th Cir. 2018); Big Cats of Serenity Springs, Inc. v. Rhodes, 843 F.3d 853, 864 (10th Cir. 2016); Martinez-Aguero v. Gonzalez, 459 F.3d 618, 625 (5th Cir. 2006).

[38] *See, e.g.,* Lanuza v. Love, 899 F.3d 1019, 1034 (9th Cir. 2018); Magluta v. Samples, 375 F.3d 1269, 1276 (11th Cir. 2004); Williams v. Meese, 926 F.2d 994, 998 (10th Cir. 1991); Lyttle v. United States, 867 F. Supp. 2d 1256, 1278 (M.D. Ga. 2012).

[39] *See, e.g.,* Koprowski v. Baker, 822 F.3d 248, 250 (6th Cir. 2016); Scinto v. Stansberry, 841 F.3d 219, 224 (4th Cir. 2016); Caldwell v. Warden, FCI Talladega, 748 F.3d 1090, 1102 (11th Cir. 2014); Thomas v. Ashcroft, 470 F.3d 491, 497 (2d Cir. 2006).

[40] *See, e.g.,* Kotarski v. Cooper, 799 F.2d 1342 (9th Cir. 1986).

[41] *See, e.g.,* Jones v. City of Memphis, 586 F.2d 622 (6th Cir. 1978), *cert. denied,* 440 U.S. 914 (1979) (allowing *Bivens* suits under the Fourteenth Amendment); Rhodes v. City of Wichita, 516 F. Supp. 501 (D. Kan. 1981) (allowing suit against city based on Fourteenth Amendment and allowing respondeat superior liability); *but see* Turpin v. Mailet, 591 F.2d 426 (2d Cir. 1979), *cert. denied,* 449 U.S. 1016 (1980); Cale v. Covington, 586 F.2d 311 (4th Cir. 1978); Battaglia v. County of Schenectady, 1993 WL 404096 (N.D.N.Y. 1993) (no *Bivens* suits under the Fourteenth Amendment); the issue of *Bivens* suits under the Fourteenth Amendment against local governments is discussed more fully in §9.1.3, *infra.*

[42] The issue of *Bivens* and separation of powers, of course, was discussed in the *Bivens* decision and was the key difference between the majority and the dissenting justices. *See* text accompanying notes 29-32, *supra. See* John C. Jeffries, Jr., The Right-Remedy Gap in Constitutional Law, 109 Yale L.J. 87 (1999) (discussing implied remedies under the Constitution).

roles of the judiciary and legislature in American society. Critics of *Bivens* contend, as did the dissenting justices, that legislative action is required before suits for money damages can be brought in federal court for violations of constitutional rights.[43] Their contention is that state law tort remedies exist and that Congress must act if federal law is to provide an independent remedy. The argument is that separation of powers is violated when the Court replicates through judicial action what §1983 provides against state and local officers.

The defenders of *Bivens* suits argue that the judicial role is to provide a remedy for violations of rights.[44] The argument is that courts traditionally have fashioned remedies in the absence of legislative action, including the exclusionary rule and damage remedies under federal statutes. Moreover, as Justice Harlan argued, the protection of federal rights should not depend on the vagaries of state law. Federal courts must safeguard and enforce constitutional rights.

Is *Bivens* Constitutional Law or Common Law?

A crucial legal question left open in *Bivens* is whether the existence of a cause of action against federal officers for money damages is required by the Constitution or whether it is federal common law.[45] For example, could Congress, by statute, abolish the *Bivens* cause of action in some or all instances?[46] Such a law would be unconstitutional if the Constitution requires the existence of damage suits against federal officers. But if *Bivens* is only federal common law—the Court acting interstitially in the absence of legislation—then Congress could eliminate or restrict such suits. Lower court judges are divided on the question of whether *Bivens* is constitutionally required or whether it is common law.[47] As discussed below, the issue is crucial in many areas of *Bivens* litigation, such as in determining the exceptions

[43] *See also* Carlson v. Green, 446 U.S. 14, 51 (1980) (Rehnquist, J., dissenting) (arguing against the *Bivens* cause of action).

[44] For an excellent defense of the *Bivens* cause of action, *see* Stephen I. Vladeck, The Inconsistent Originalism of Judge-Made Remedies Against Federal Officers, 96 Notre Dame L. Rev. 1869, 1872 (2021); Susan Bandes, Reinventing *Bivens*: The Self-Executing Constitution, 68 S. Cal. L. Rev. 289 (1995).

[45] In fact, the Court expressly left open the question of whether *Bivens* is constitutionally required or common law. *See* Bush v. Lucas, 462 U.S. at 378 n.14.

[46] See, e.g., John Harrison, Jurisdiction, Congressional Power and Constitutional Remedies, 86 Geo. L.J. 2513 (1998) (arguing that Congress may eliminate federal remedies and leave enforcement of federal rights to state law); *but see* Daniel J. Meltzer, Congress, Courts and Constitutional Remedies, 86 Geo. L.J. 2537 (1998) (disagreeing with Professor Harrison's approach and conclusions). *See also* Lawrence G. Sager, The Supreme Court 1980 Term—Foreword: Constitutional Limitations on Congress' Authority to Regulate the Jurisdiction of the Federal Courts, 95 Harv. L. Rev. 17, 76 (1981) ("Our evolving constitutional tradition had come to recognize the right of constitutional litigants to a fair and independent judicial hearing."). For an argument that *Bivens* reflects common law development by the Supreme Court, *see* Henry P. Monaghan, The Supreme Court 1974 Term—Foreword: Constitutional Common Law, 89 Harv. L. Rev. 1 (1975); *but see* Thomas Schrock & Robert Welsh, Reconsidering the Constitutional Common Law, 91 Harv. L. Rev. 1117 (1978).

[47] *Compare* Davis v. Passman, 571 F.2d 793, 809 (5th Cir. 1978) (Goldberg, J., dissenting), *rev'd*, 442 U.S. 228 (1979) (*Bivens* constitutionally required), *with* Molina v. Richardson, 578 F.2d 846, 850 (9th Cir. 1978), *cert. denied*, 439 U.S. 1048 (1978).

when *Bivens* suits are not allowed and in deciding whether *Bivens* suits should be permitted against local governments when §1983 remedies are unavailable.

The initial Supreme Court decisions following *Bivens* seemed to assume that a cause of action for money damages against federal offices was constitutionally required and denied *Bivens* suits only where there is either an alternative remedy that is equally effective or special factors justifying the absence of such litigation.[48] Subsequent cases, however, have denied *Bivens* suits even when there likely was not an adequate alternative remedy.[49] These indicate that *Bivens* is a form of federal common law and that Congress can restrict such suits, or the Court can deny them, even in the absence of an adequate alternative remedy. The willingness of the Supreme Court to restrict *Bivens* suits based on federal statutes, or even state tort liability, indicates that the current Court does not see the Constitution as requiring the availability of such suits.

Rehnquist and Roberts Courts' Attitudes Toward *Bivens* Suits

In the past four decades, the Supreme Court has consistently refused to expand, and indeed has substantially limited, the availability of *Bivens* suits.[50] In *Correctional Services Corporation v. Malesko*,[51] both Chief Justice Rehnquist's majority opinion and Justice Scalia's concurring opinion noted and praised this trend. The issue in *Malesko* was whether a privately operated prison could be sued in a *Bivens* action.[52] In holding that such suits are not permitted, Chief Justice Rehnquist noted, "Since *Carlson*, we have consistently refused to extend *Bivens* liability to any new context or new category of defendants."[53] He explained: "In 30 years of *Bivens* jurisprudence we have extended its holding only twice, to provide an otherwise nonexistent cause of action against *individual officers* alleged to have acted unconstitutionally, or to provide a cause of action for a plaintiff who lacked *any alternative remedy* for harms caused by individual officer's unconstitutional conduct. Where such circumstances are not present, we have consistently rejected invitations to extend *Bivens*, often for reasons that foreclose its extension here."[54]

Justice Scalia, in a concurring opinion joined by Justice Thomas, went even further and strongly suggested that he would consider overruling

[48] *See, e.g.*, Bivens v. Six Unknown Named Agents of Fed. Bureau of Narcotics, 403 U.S. at 397; Carlson v. Green, 446 U.S. at 18-19. For example, in Bush v. Lucas, 462 U.S. 367 (1983), the Court refused to recognize a cause of action because of the alternative remedies created by Congress for federal workers under the Civil Service Reform Act. Likewise, in Schweiker v. Chilicky, 487 U.S. 412 (1988), the Court refused to recognize a cause of action because of alternative remedies Congress created under the Social Security Act.

[49] *See, e.g.*, Hui v. Castaneda, 559 U.S. 799 (2010); Wilkie v. Robbins, 551 U.S. 537 (2007); Correctional Services Corp. v. Malesko, 534 U.S. 61 (2001), all discussed below.

[50] Elizabeth Earle Beske, The Court and the Private Plaintiff, 58 Wake Forest L. Rev. 1, 10 (2023) ("While the Rehnquist Court withdrew from *Bivens* gradually, the Roberts Court sounded a full-scale retreat.")

[51] 534 U.S. 61 (2001).

[52] This aspect of the decision is discussed more fully below in text accompanying notes 144-145.

[53] 534 U.S. at 69.

[54] *Id.* at 70.

Bivens.[55] Four justices dissented in *Correctional Services Corp. v. Malesko* and lamented that "the driving force behind the Court's decision is a disagreement with the holding of *Bivens* itself."[56]

In the two decades since *Malesko*, the Court has continued to narrow the availability of *Bivens* suits and has held that they should be allowed by the courts only where they are, on balance, desirable.[57] Moreover, the Court has held that a federal statute creating immunity from suit for government officials precludes *Bivens* suits and that the existence of a state tort remedy is sufficient to preclude a *Bivens* suit against guards at a private prison.[58] Subsequently, the Court held that *Bivens* suits are not available to challenge government policies or matters implicating national security[59] or to a border officer who killed someone in a cross border shooting.[60]

In *Egbert v. Boule*, the Court stressed that recognizing a *Bivens* cause of action "is 'a disfavored judicial activity.'"[61] The Court said that "'the most important question is who should decide whether to provide for a damages remedy, Congress or the courts?' If there is a rational reason to think that the answer is 'Congress'—as it will be in most every case,—no Bivens action may lie. Our cases instruct that, absent utmost deference to Congress' preeminent authority in this area, the courts 'arrogat[e] legislative power.'"[62]

The Court then laid out the framework for Bivens claims going forward. Usually, Bivens is guided by a two-step inquiry:

> "First, we ask whether the case presents 'a new Bivens context'—i.e., is it 'meaningful[ly]" different from the three cases in which the Court has implied a damages action. Second, if a claim arises in a new context, a Bivens remedy is unavailable if there are 'special factors' indicating that the Judiciary is at least arguably less equipped than Congress to 'weigh the costs and benefits of allowing a damages action to proceed.' *If there is even a single 'reason to pause before applying Bivens in a new context,' a court may not recognize a Bivens remedy.*[63]

This is a test that puts a very strong presumption against recognizing *Bivens* claims.

[55] *Id.* at 75 (Scalia, J., concurring).
[56] *Id.* at 82 (Stevens, J., dissenting).
[57] Wilkie v. Robbins, 551 U.S. 537 (2007), discussed below.
[58] Hui v. Castaneda, 559 U.S. 799 (2010); Minneci v. Pollard, 565 U.S. 118 (2012), both discussed below.
[59] Ziglar v. Abbasi, 137 S. Ct. 1843 (2017), discussed below.
[60] Hernandez v. Mesa, 589 U.S. 93 (2020).
[61] 596 U.S. at 491.
[62] *Id.* at 491-492.
[63] *Id.* at 492 (emphasis added).

§9.1.3 Exceptions: Situations Where Bivens *Suits are Not Allowed*

Exceptions to *Bivens*

In *Bivens*, and again in *Carlson v. Green*, the Supreme Court identified two situations in which damage suits against federal officers for money damages will not be permitted. First, *Bivens* suits are not available "when defendants show that Congress has provided an alternative remedy which it explicitly declared to be a *substitute* for recovery directly under the Constitution and viewed as equally effective."[64] Second, *Bivens* suits are not allowed when there are "special factors counselling hesitation in the absence of affirmative action by Congress."[65] Each exception has been developed by the Supreme Court in several cases.

Although initially articulated as two distinct exceptions, they have been blurred as the Court has found the existence of congressionally created remedies to be a special factor counseling hesitation and preventing the availability of *Bivens* suits. In fact, the Court has completely ignored the first exception and has focused entirely on the latter, even in cases where it is considering whether the existence of a federal statute precludes a *Bivens* cause of action. Thus, for the sake of clarity, analysis can be divided into two questions: When is the existence of a congressionally created remedy sufficient to prevent a *Bivens* suit? And what other special factors counsel hesitation and preclude *Bivens* remedies?

Davis v. Passman

In *Davis v. Passman*, the Court considered whether a female aide could sue a congressman for gender discrimination based on a cause of action inferred directly from the Fifth Amendment.[66] Congressman Otto Passman fired his administrative assistant, Shirley Davis, because he wanted a male to fill the position. The Court held that generally federal officers could be sued for money damages for violations of the Fifth Amendment. In allowing the suit against the congressman, the Court emphasized the judiciary's role in ensuring effective protection of constitutional rights. The Court stated:

> [W]e presume that justiciable constitutional rights are to be enforced through the courts. And, unless such rights are to become merely precatory, the class of those litigants who allege that their own constitutional rights have been violated, and who at the same time have no effective means other than the judiciary to enforce these rights, must be able to invoke the existing jurisdiction of the courts for the protection of their justiciable constitutional rights.[67]

[64] Carlson v. Green, 446 U.S. at 18-19 (emphasis in original); *see also* Bivens v. Six Unknown Named Agents of Fed. Bureau of Narcotics, 403 U.S. at 397.

[65] 446 U.S. at 18.

[66] 442 U.S. 228 (1979).

[67] *Id.* at 242.

A crucial issue was whether Congress's exemption of its own members from federal employment discrimination legislation constituted a preclusion of all such suits against senators and representatives. When Congress amended Title VII of the Civil Rights Act of 1964 to protect federal employees from employment discrimination, it specifically exempted congressional employees.[68] The defendant alleged that this was a congressional determination that representatives and senators should not be subject to such suits.

The Court, however, rejected this argument, concluding that Congress did not mean to foreclose other remedies not included in Title VII.[69] In other words, the Court narrowly construed the exemption of congressional employees as solely removing them from liability under Title VII and not precluding all suits for employment discrimination. As such, in *Davis v. Passman*, the plaintiff had a cause of action for money damages against the former congressman for gender discrimination in violation of the Fifth Amendment.[70]

Carlson v. Green

In *Carlson v. Green*, the Supreme Court for the first time considered *Bivens* relief in an instance where an alternative federal law remedy existed.[71] A mother sued federal prison officials on behalf of her deceased son, claiming that he was the victim of gross inadequacies of medical facilities and staff, which caused his death and constituted cruel and unusual punishment. A remedy was available under the Federal Tort Claims Act; thus, the issue before the Court was whether a *Bivens* suit should be allowed in light of this alternative.[72]

The Court concluded that *Bivens* suits were a "counterpart" to the Federal Tort Claims Act because the act creates liability for the federal government and a *Bivens* cause of action permits recovery from the officers.[73] The Court found no indication that Congress intended for the act to preempt *Bivens* suits. Although some portions of the Federal Tort Claims Act specified it to be the exclusive remedy, no such provision was applicable in *Carlson v. Green*.[74]

The Court also concluded that the remedies available under the Federal Tort Claims Act were not as effective as a *Bivens* suit. For instance, punitive damages and

[68] 42 U.S.C. §2000e-16(a).

[69] 442 U.S. at 247.

[70] The Court also considered whether the immunity accorded members of Congress under the speech or debate clause constituted a "special factor counselling hesitation" preventing a *Bivens* suit. The Court concluded that the speech or debate clause did not automatically prevent a *Bivens* suit for allegedly unconstitutional employment discrimination. *Id.* at 246. The Court did remand the issue back to the court of appeals for a determination of whether or not Passman's actions were protected by the speech or debate clause. There is no reported opinion for the case on remand.

[71] 446 U.S. at 14.

[72] 28 U.S.C. §2680. The Federal Tort Claims Act was amended in 1974 to permit suits against law enforcement officers for intentional torts. Pub. L. No. 93-253, §1, 88 Stat. 50, 28 U.S.C. §2680(h). The Federal Tort Claims Act is discussed in detail in §9.2.

[73] 446 U.S. at 19.

[74] *Id.* at 20.

jury trials are available in *Bivens* litigation, but not under the act.[75] Also, the Court emphasized that damages against individual officers would serve as a more effective deterrent to constitutional violations.[76] Finally, the Court noted that under the Federal Tort Claims Act a cause of action exists only if liability arises under the state's law where the wrong occurred. In the absence of congressional direction, the Court felt that the protection of federal rights should not depend on state law.[77] Justice Rehnquist vehemently dissented, disagreeing with every aspect of the majority's decision and arguing against the very existence of judicially created causes of action for constitutional violations.[78] At the least, Justice Rehnquist felt that "the fact that Congress has created a tort remedy against federal officials at all, as it has done here under the [Federal Tort Claims Act], is dispositive."[79]

Bush v. Lucas

For the first time, in *Bush v. Lucas*, the Court found that the existence of an alternative remedy foreclosed a *Bivens* suit.[80] In *Bush*, an aerospace engineer employed at the Marshall Space Flight Center operated by the National Aeronautics and Space Administration claimed that he was demoted because of his public statements, which were highly critical of the agency. Bush appealed his demotion to the Federal Employee Appeals Authority, which ruled against him. The authority held that Bush's statements were misleading and that they exceeded the protections of the First Amendment. Two years later, Bush asked the Civil Service Commission Appeals Review Board to reopen the case. The commission did so, found in Bush's favor on First Amendment grounds, and recommended reinstatement with back pay. The recommendation was accepted.

During the pendency of the administrative appeals, Bush filed suit in state court against his superiors, seeking damages for defamation and for violation of his First Amendment rights. The defendants removed the case to federal court. The district court found that a *Bivens* suit did not exist because of the existence of alternative remedies under the Civil Service Commission regulations. The Supreme Court agreed. The Court stated at the outset that it assumed that Bush's First Amendment rights were violated, that the civil service remedies were not as effective as a damages remedy, and that Congress had not explicitly precluded the creation of a *Bivens* suit. Nonetheless, the Court found that the existence of comprehensive civil service remedies prevented Bush from bringing a cause of action directly under the First Amendment.

[75] *Id.* at 22.

[76] *Id.* at 21.

[77] *Id.* at 23.

[78] *Id.* at 31-32, 43-44, 46 (Rehnquist, J., dissenting). Justice Burger also dissented, *id.* at 30 (Burger, C.J., dissenting). Justices Powell and Stewart concurred in the result, concluding that Congress did not intend to foreclose *Bivens* suits, but disagreeing with the majority's reasoning that Congress must explicitly state its intent to displace the *Bivens* remedy. *Id.* at 26-28 (Powell, J., concurring).

[79] *Id.* at 51 (Rehnquist, J., dissenting).

[80] 462 U.S. 367 (1983).

Previously, the Court had said that to preclude *Bivens* suits, Congress must expressly declare that it had provided an alternative remedy that it deemed to be an equally effective substitute for *Bivens* suits. In *Bush*, however, the Court said that Congress could "indicate its intent [to prevent judicial remedies] by statutory language, by clear legislative history, or perhaps even by the statutory remedy itself."[81] The Court said that the question of whether a cause of action should be allowed "cannot be answered simply by noting that existing remedies do not provide complete relief for the plaintiff."[82] Rather, the Court said that Congress was in the best position to make policy judgments about what remedies should be available for federal employees. The Court found that these policy considerations were "special factors counselling hesitation"; therefore, the Court refused to allow *Bivens* suits.

Although the Supreme Court did not hold that all *Bivens* suits are precluded by the Civil Service Reform Act, lower courts consistently have applied *Bush* to bar *Bivens* suits by federal employees for matters covered by civil service act remedies.[83] Indeed, one court concluded that "[i]n the field of federal employment, even if no remedy at all has been provided by the Civil Service Reform Act, courts will not create a *Bivens* remedy."[84]

Schweiker v. Chilicky

Similarly, in *Schweiker v. Chilicky*, the Supreme Court again found congressionally created remedies to be a special factor counseling hesitation and precluding a *Bivens* cause of action.[85] *Chilicky* arose from the Reagan administration's illegal policy of disqualifying large numbers of Social Security disability recipients. Pursuant to a congressionally created program of Continuing Disability Review, the Social Security Administration wrongfully discontinued benefits to almost 200,000 individuals.[86] Congress concluded that the Social Security Administration was abusing the review process and adopted emergency legislation to stop the disqualifications. However, many individuals—such as James Chilicky—experienced months of financial hardship and the loss of medical benefits before the benefits were restored.

Chilicky filed suit claiming a violation of his due process rights by one state and two federal officers. The issue before the Supreme Court was whether there was a cause of action for money damages against government officers who allegedly violated the Due Process Clause by improperly denying Social Security benefits.

The Supreme Court concluded that the existence of a congressionally created remedial scheme was a special factor counseling hesitation and precluding a *Bivens* suit. The Court stated, "When the design of a government program suggests

[81] *Id.* at 378.

[82] *Id.* at 388.

[83] *See, e.g.,* Gonzalez v. Velez, 864 F.3d 45, 54 (1st Cir. 2017); Davis v. Billington, 681 F.3d 377, 388 (D.C. Cir. 2012).

[84] Jones v. Tennessee Valley Auth., 948 F.3d 258, 264 (6th Cir. 1991).

[85] 487 U.S. 412 (1988). For an excellent discussion of *Chilicky, see* Gene R. Nichol, *Bivens, Chilicky,* and Constitutional Damage Claims, 75 Va. L. Rev. 1117 (1989).

[86] 487 U.S. at 416.

that Congress has provided what it considers adequate remedial mechanisms for constitutional violations that may occur in the course of administration, we have not created additional *Bivens* remedies."[87] After reviewing the administrative and judicial procedures that exist to correct wrongful denials of Social Security disability benefits, the Court declared, "The case before us cannot reasonably be distinguished from *Bush v. Lucas*."[88]

Justices Brennan, Marshall, and Blackmun filed a strong dissenting opinion. They argued that "it is inconceivable that Congress meant by such mere silence to bar all redress for such injuries."[89] The dissent described the inadequacies of the existing procedures to remedy the injuries suffered and emphasized the absence of any indication that Congress meant to deny recovery for constitutional violations.

Hui v. Castaneda

In *Hui v. Castaneda*, the Court also found the preclusion of a *Bivens* suit because of the existence of a federal statute.[90] Francisco Castaneda was detained by U.S. Immigration and Customs Enforcement authorities. He repeatedly sought treatment for a lesion on his penis that was growing, frequently bleeding, and emitting a discharge. It became increasingly painful, and a lump developed in his groin. A Public Health Service physician assistant and three outside specialists said that he needed to have a biopsy to determine whether he had cancer. However, he was told that the procedure was "elective," and he was denied the biopsy, treated with ibuprofen, and given an additional ration of boxer shorts.[91]

Almost a year after Castaneda complained of the lesion, a biopsy was performed. It disclosed that he had penile cancer. His penis was amputated, and he was treated with chemotherapy, but he died a year later. Before Castaneda died, he brought a *Bivens* suit against the Public Health Service officials who had denied him a biopsy and medical treatment.

The Supreme Court unanimously ruled that a *Bivens* suit was not available because of a federal statute that created immunity from liability for Public Health Service officers. Justice Sotomayor, writing for the Court, stated, "Our inquiry in this case begins and ends with the text of §233(a). The statute provides in pertinent part that

> [t]he remedy *against the United States* provided by sections 1346(b) and 2672 of title 28 . . . for damage for personal injury, including death, resulting from the performance of medical, surgical, dental, or related functions, including the conduct of clinical studies or investigation, by any commissioned officer or employee of the Public Health Service while acting within the scope of his office or employment, *shall be exclusive of any other civil action or proceeding by reason of the same subject-matter against the officer or employee* (or his estate) whose act or omission gave rise to the claim."[92]

[87] *Id.* at 423.
[88] *Id.* at 425.
[89] *Id.* at 432 (Brennan, J., dissenting).
[90] 599 U.S. 799 (2010).
[91] *Id.* at 803.
[92] *Id.* at 805.

The Court held that since the statute creates absolute immunity for Public Health Service officers, there could be no *Bivens* claims against them. The Court concluded its opinion by declaring that the suit had to be dismissed because "§233(a) plainly precludes a *Bivens* action against petitioners for the harms alleged in this case."[93] *Carlson v. Green*, another case that involved a claim against prison officials, was distinguished on the ground that it did not involve a statute creating immunity.

On the one hand, *Hui v. Castaneda* follows from *Bush v. Lucas* and *Schweiker v. Chilicky* in finding that the existence of a federal statute precludes a *Bivens* remedy. On the other hand, *Hui v. Castaneda* goes further than these earlier decisions in allowing Congress to preclude *Bivens* suits. In the prior cases, the Court emphasized the existence of alternative remedies. In *Hui v. Castaneda*, the Court stressed Congress precluding liability of individual government officials. It thus indicates that Congress, by statute, can preclude *Bivens* claims.

Hernandez v. Mesa

In *Hernandez v. Mesa*, the Court again rejected a *Bivens* claim.[94] A border agent in El Paso, Texas fired his gun across the border and killed a 15-year-old boy on the Mexican side. The Court ruled, 5-4, that there was not a cause of action under *Bivens*. Justice Alito wrote for the majority and began his opinion by stating: "We are asked in this case to extend *Bivens v. Six Unknown Fed. Narcotics Agents* and create a damages remedy for a cross-border shooting. As we have made clear in many prior cases, however, the Constitution's separation of powers requires us to exercise caution before extending *Bivens* to a new 'context,' and a claim based on a cross-border shooting arises in a context that is markedly new. Unlike any previously recognized *Bivens* claim, a cross-border shooting claim has foreign relations and national security implications. In addition, Congress has been notably hesitant to create claims based on allegedly tortious conduct abroad."[95]

The Court said that it follows a two-step approach in deciding whether to recognize a *Bivens* cause of action: "We first inquire whether the request involves a claim that arises in a 'new context' or involves a 'new category of defendants.' And our understanding of a 'new context' is broad. We regard a context as 'new' if it is 'different in a meaningful way from previous *Bivens* cases decided by this Court.' When we find that a claim arises in a new context, we proceed to the second step and ask whether there are any 'special factors [that] counse[l] hesitation' about granting the extension."[96] The Court concluded that this case presented a new context that had not been addressed before by the Court and that there were reasons to not allow *Bivens* because of the relation to foreign policy and national security.

[93] *Id.* at 813.
[94] 589 U.S. 93 (2020)
[95] *Id.* at 96.
[96] *Id.* at 102.

Justice Thomas, joined by Justice Gorsuch, concurred and wrote separately to urge the overruling of *Bivens*.[97] He wrote that "[o]ur continued adherence to even a limited form of the *Bivens* doctrine appears to 'perpetuat[e] a usurpation of the legislative power.' "[98]

Justice Ginsburg wrote for the dissenters and said that the case did not involve an extension of *Bivens*; like *Bivens* it involved a claim of excessive police force in violation of the Fourth Amendment. Besides, she wrote, "Even accepting, *arguendo*, that the setting in this case could be characterized as 'new,' there is still no good reason why Hernández's parents should face a closed courtroom door. As in *Bivens*, plaintiffs lack recourse to alternative remedies. And not one of the 'special factors' the Court identifies weigh any differently based on where a bullet happens to land."[99]

Egbert v. Boule

The Court's decision in *Egbert vs. Boule* further limits *Bivens* suits—this time for Fourth Amendment violations for illegal searches and seizures.[100] Robert Boule owns a bed-and-breakfast called The Smuggler's Inn in Blaine, Wash., near the Canadian border. Erik Egbert, a U.S. Border Patrol Agent, followed Boule and a passenger in his car to the inn. According to Boule's complaint, Boule asked Egbert to leave, but Egbert refused, became violent, and threw Boule to the ground. Egbert then checked the immigration paperwork for Boule's guest and left after finding nothing illegal.

Boule filed a grievance against Egbert with the border patrol. Boule alleged that Egbert then retaliated by contacting the Internal Revenue Service and state agencies, prompting an investigation and audit of Boule's tax returns. Boule sued Egbert for excessive force in violation of the Fourth Amendment and for violating the First Amendment by retaliating against him for his complaint.

The Court of Appeals for the Ninth Circuit held that these allegations were sufficient to allow Boule to sue. But Justice Clarence Thomas, writing for the majority in the 6-3 opinion, said that *Bivens* suits are "a disfavored judicial activity."[101] As such, he wrote, these suits should not be allowed at all in the border policing context. The Court concluded that it would be an extension of *Bivens* to allow suits against border agents or for retaliation, and such an extension would be undesirable.

As described above, the Court reformulated the test for when *Bivens* suits are available. The Court was explicit: "*If there is even a single 'reason to pause before applying Bivens in a new context,' a court may not recognize a Bivens remedy.*"[102]

Justice Sonia Sotomayor wrote in dissent that the court's decision "will strip many more individuals who suffer injuries at the hands of other federal officers,

[97] *Id.* at 114 (Thomas, J., concurring).
[98] *Id.* at 117.
[99] *Id.* at 126 (Ginsburg, J., dissenting).
[100] 596 U.S. 482 (2022).
[101] *Id.* at 491.
[102] *Id.* (emphasis added).

and whose circumstances are materially indistinguishable from those in *Bivens,* of an important remedy."[103]

But Justice Gorsuch noted in a separate opinion that Congress can easily resolve this problem.[104] It could pass a statute—like the one authorizing suits against state and local officials—that expressly permits federal officers to be sued when they violate the Constitution. However, like a statute to fix qualified immunity, it seems unlikely such a bill will pass Congress in the foreseeable future.

The Cases Compared: The Exception Expands Greatly

The contrast between *Davis* and *Carlson* on the one side and *Bush, Chilicky, Hui, Mesa,* and *Egbert* on the other is striking. In *Davis* and *Carlson,* the Court permitted *Bivens* suits because there were not explicit congressional declarations precluding such actions. But in *Bush, Chilicky, Hui, Mesa,* and *Egbert* the Court denied *Bivens* suits despite the assumed inadequacy of other remedies and the absence of an express declaration from Congress. In *Carlson,* the unavailability of punitive damages or a jury trial under the Federal Tort Claims Act was part of the justification for the Court's permitting a *Bivens* suit. But in *Bush* the absence of punitive damages and a jury trial under the Civil Service procedures did not justify a *Bivens* suit.

Bush, Chilicky, Hui, Mesa, and Egbert reflect the Court's retreat from the *Bivens* cause of action. In *Chilicky,* Justice O'Connor, writing for the majority, said that the Court's most "recent decisions have responded cautiously to suggestions that *Bivens* remedies be extended into new contexts."[105] Additionally, *Bush, Chilicky,* and *Hui* mark the blending of the two exceptions where *Bivens* suits are not allowed. The Court in these cases found the existence of alternative remedies to be a "special factor counselling hesitation," precluding a *Bivens* suit. Originally, the Court said that Congress had to declare the existence of alternative remedies to be an adequate substitute for a *Bivens* cause of action. No longer is this necessary, because the Court has found congressionally created remedial schemes to be a special factor counseling hesitation and precluding *Bivens* actions.

Underlying the disagreement between the conservative and the liberal justices is a difference about the importance of there being a remedy for a constitutional violation by federal officers. Also, there are different views about the role of the federal judiciary, with the conservatives wanting to leave to Congress whether to allow a cause of action against federal officials, but the liberal justices seeing it as the Court's role to provide a remedy for constitutional violations.

Bivens suits still exist; the Court has not eliminated them.[106] But it has been clear that *Bivens* is not to be extended. So even when it comes to Fourth Amendment

[103] 596 U.S. at 505 (Sotomayor, J., dissenting).

[104] *Id.* at 503-504 (Gorsuch, J., dissenting).

[105] 487 U.S. at 422.

[106] Although the vast majority of federal court of appeals decisions concerning *Bivens* dismiss the suits, occasionally they are allowed to go forward. *See, e.g.,* Hicks v. Ferreyra, 64 F.4th 156 (4th Cir. 2023) (allowing a *Bivens* suit against two U.S. Park Police officers, arguing they violated his "rights under the Fourth Amendment by unlawfully seizing him during two traffic stops." Snowden

search and seizure claims, the focus of *Bivens*, the lower courts are split as to when to allow them.[107]

Suits Arising from Military Service and Matters Involving National Security

The second major exception to *Bivens* is if there are "special factors counselling hesitation" in the judicial creation of a cause of action. In addition to its use in *Bush* and *Chilicky*, the Supreme Court has applied this exception to prevent suits arising from military service and also, subsequently, in matters involving national security.

In *Chappell v. Wallace*, the Court addressed an allegation of discriminatory practices by superior officers directed at minority enlisted personnel of the U.S. Navy.[108] The Court, in an opinion by Chief Justice Burger, concluded that the special nature of the military was a factor counseling hesitation. The Court reasoned:

> [C]enturies of experience have developed a hierarchical structure of discipline and obedience to command, unique in its application to the military establishment and wholly different from civilian patterns. Civilian courts must, at the very least, hesitate long before entertaining a suit which asks the court to tamper with the established relationship between enlisted military personnel and their superior officers; that relationship is at the heart of the necessarily unique structure of the Military Establishment.[109]

After *Chappell*, there was uncertainty among the lower courts as to whether the Court had barred all *Bivens* suits arising out of military service or whether instances may arise in which competing factors militate in favor of allowing such suits.[110] The Supreme Court resolved this uncertainty in 1987 in *United States v. Stanley*.[111]

---

v. Henning, 72 F.4th 237, 239 (7th Cir. 2023) (allowing a *Bivens* suit for excessive force against a DEA agent because "Snowden's claim does not arise in a new context.")

[107] The 7th and 10th Circuits are willing to consider *Bivens* claims even if they were warranted searches, even though the original *Bivens* case involved a warrantless search. *See* Snowden v. Henning, 72 F.4th 237 (7th Cir. 2023); Logsdon v. United States Marshal Serv., 91 F.4th 1352 (10th Cir. 2024). Meanwhile, the 1st, 4th, 5th, and 6th Circuits believe *Bivens* remedies are only available for warrantless searches. *See* Quinones-Pimentel v. Cannon, 85 F.4th 63 (1st Cir. 2023); Hicks v. Ferreyra, 64 F.4th 156 (4th Cir. 2023); Cantu v. Moody, 933 F.3d 414, 423 (5th Cir. 2019). Similarly, the 1st, 5th, 6th, 8th, and 9th Circuits believe *Bivens* claims are only viable if a violation occurs at a person's home because that was the facts of *Bivens*. Quinones-Pimentel v. Cannon, 85 F.4th 63 (1st Cir. 2023); Byrd v. Lamb, 990 F.3d 879, 882 (5th Cir. 2021); Hower v. Damron, No. 21-5996, 2022 U.S. App. LEXIS 24676 (6th Cir. Aug. 31, 2022); Ahmed v. Weyker, 984 F.3d 564 (8th Cir. 2020); Mejia v. Miller, 61 F.4th 663, 668 (9th Cir. 2023). But the 4th, 7th, 10th Circuits may still consider a *Bivens* claim even if a violation occurred elsewhere. Hicks v. Ferreyra, 64 F.4th 156 (4th Cir. 2023); Snowden v. Henning, 72 F.4th 237 (7th Cir. 2023); Logsdon v. United States Marshal Serv., 91 F.4th 1352 (10th Cir. 2024).

[108] 462 U.S. 296 (1983).

[109] *Id.* at 300.

[110] *See, e.g.*, Mollnow v. Carlton, 716 F.2d 627, 629-630 (9th Cir.), *cert. denied*, 465 U.S. 1100 (1984) (*Chappell* precludes all suits arising from military service); Stanley v. United States, 786 F.2d 1490 (11th Cir. 1986), *rev'd*, 483 U.S. 669 (1987) (*Chappell* does not preclude all suits arising from military service).

[111] 483 U.S. 669 (1987).

In *Stanley*, a former serviceman sued because of severe injuries he allegedly sustained as a result of having been given LSD, without his knowledge or consent, in an army experiment in 1958. The Supreme Court held that the U.S. government was immune from suit under the Federal Tort Claims Act because of the *Feres* doctrine, which prohibits suits against the government arising from military service.[112] Moreover, the Court concluded that *Bivens* suits also were not possible against the government officers who subjected Stanley to the medical experimentation without his permission. In an opinion by Justice Scalia, the Court flatly declared "that no *Bivens* remedy is available for injuries that 'arise out of or are in the course of activity incident to service.' "[113] The Court concluded that under *Chappell v. Wallace*, all *Bivens* suits arising from military service were precluded by the need to preserve the military hierarchy.

Several justices wrote scathing dissents to this part of the Court's opinion. Justice O'Connor said that while she agrees with *Chappell*, "conduct of the type alleged in this case is so far beyond the bounds of human decency that as a matter of law it simply cannot be considered a part of the military mission."[114] Justice O'Connor contended that the defendants did not need insulation from liability resulting from the deliberate exposure of healthy individuals to medical tests without their consent. Likewise, Justice Brennan drew parallels to the Nazis' medical experimentations and argued that victims such as Stanley must have a remedy for violations of their constitutional rights.[115]

The law is now settled that *Bivens* suits are never permitted for constitutional violations arising from military service, no matter how severe the injury or how egregious the rights infringement.[116] The crucial question in evaluating *Chappell*, and especially *Stanley*, is whether a total bar on suits is necessary to achieve the Court's objective of protecting military discipline and hierarchical authority.[117] Although the military presents a unique context counseling hesitation in the creation of remedies, there is a strong argument that suits should be available at least in instances of deliberate and willful violations of constitutional rights. It is not clear that liability for blatant, intentional constitutional violations would disrupt the military or that immunity should exist for such grossly unconstitutional behavior.

In *Ziglar v. Abbasi*, the Court said that there are special factors counseling hesitation and precluding suits when policies involving national security are implicated.[118] Six men, all of Arab or South Asian descent, were arrested on immigration

[112] For a discussion of the Federal Tort Claims Act and the *Feres* doctrine, *see* §9.2, *infra*.

[113] 483 U.S. at 683.

[114] *Id.* at 709 (O'Connor, J., concurring and dissenting).

[115] *Id.* at 710-711 (Brennan, J., dissenting).

[116] *See, e.g.,* Klay v. Panetta, 758 F.3d 369 (D.C. Cir. 2014) (denying a *Bivens* suit to women in the military who were raped and subjected to sexual harassment).

[117] Scholars are virtually unanimous in strongly criticizing *Chappell* and *Stanley*. *See, e.g.,* Jonathan Tomes, *Feres* to *Chappell* to *Stanley*: Three Strikes and Service Members Are Out, 25 U. Rich. L. Rev. 93 (1990); Barry Kellman, Judicial Abdication of Military Tort Accountability: But Who Is to Guard the Guards Themselves?, 1989 Duke L.J. 1597.

[118] 582 U.S. 120 (2017).

charges and held without bail in a maximum-security prison. They were subjected to physical and verbal abuse: "Guards allegedly slammed detainees into walls; twisted their arms, wrists, and fingers; broke their bones; referred to them as terrorists; threatened them with violence; subjected them to humiliating sexual comments; and insulted their religion."[119] They sued the executive officials responsible for their detention and treatment for constitutional claims, including for race and religious discrimination and the use of excessive force.

In a 4-2 decision—Justices Sotomayor and Kagan were recused, and Justice Scalia had not yet been replaced—the Court concluded that there were special factors counseling hesitation that precluded a *Bivens* suit. Justice Kennedy wrote for the majority and said that the Court had made clear "that expanding the *Bivens* remedy is now a 'disfavored' judicial activity."[120] The Court explained: "The proper test for determining whether a case presents a new *Bivens* context is as follows. If the case is different in a meaningful way from previous *Bivens* cases decided by this Court, then the context is new. Without endeavoring to create an exhaustive list of differences that are meaningful enough to make a given context a new one, some examples might prove instructive. A case might differ in a meaningful way because of the rank of the officers involved; the constitutional right at issue; the generality or specificity of the official action; the extent of judicial guidance as to how an officer should respond to the problem or emergency to be confronted; the statutory or other legal mandate under which the officer was operating; the risk of disruptive intrusion by the Judiciary into the functioning of other branches; or the presence of potential special factors that previous *Bivens* cases did not consider."[121]

The Court said that *Bivens* suits against executive branch officials are not appropriate for "altering an entity's policy."[122] Nor are they permitted when they involve matters of national security: "National-security policy is the prerogative of the Congress and President."[123]

Justice Breyer dissented, joined by Justice Ginsburg, and argued that this case did not require an extension of *Bivens*, but instead just involved application of well-established principles to these facts. He wrote: "The Court, in my view, is wrong to hold that permitting a constitutional tort action here would 'extend' *Bivens*, applying it in a new context. To the contrary, I fear that the Court's holding would significantly shrink the existing *Bivens* contexts, diminishing the compensatory remedy constitutional tort law now offers to harmed individuals."[124]

[119] *Id.* at 128.

[120] *Id.* at 135.

[121] *Id.* at 139-140.

[122] *Id.* at 140.

[123] *Id.* at 142. For an excellent criticism of this decision, and the refusal to allow *Bivens* suits to challenge government policies, *see* Joanna C. Schwartz, Alexander Reinert & James E. Pfander, Going Rogue: The Supreme Court's Newfound Hostility to Policy-Based *Bivens* Claims, 96 Notre Dame L. Rev. 1835, 1838 (2021).

[124] *Id.* at 162 (Breyer, J., dissenting). For an excellent scholarly discussion of this topic, *see* James E. Pfander, Constitutional Torts and the War on Terrorism (2017); Leah Litman, Remedial Convergence and Collapse, 106 Cal. L. Rev. 1477 (2018).

Bivens Suits Must Be on Balance Desirable

The Court has recognized one other "special factor counseling hesitation" and precluding *Bivens* suits: such claims are not allowed if, on balance, it is not desirable to permit them. *Wilkie v. Robbins* articulated this new, potentially very significant limit on the availability of *Bivens* suits.[125]

Robbins was a Wyoming landowner who claimed that Wilkie and other employees of the Federal Bureau of Land Management (BLM) had unconstitutionally harassed and persecuted him for refusing to give the government an easement on his land. As Justice Ginsburg expressed in her dissent, when Robbins refused to grant the requested easement, "the BLM officials mounted a seven-year campaign of relentless harassment and intimidation to force Robbins to give in. They refused to maintain the road providing access to the ranch, trespassed on Robbins's property, brought unfounded criminal charges against him, canceled his special recreational use permit and grazing privileges, interfered with his business operations, and invaded the privacy of his ranch guests on cattle drives."[126]

The Court, however, said that a *Bivens* suit was not available *even if there were not alternative remedies*, because it, on balance, was not desirable to allow such a claim. Justice Souter, writing for the Court, explained: "[T]he decision whether to recognize a *Bivens* remedy may require two steps. In the first place, there is the question whether any alternative, existing process for protecting the interest amounts to a convincing reason for the Judicial Branch to refrain from providing a new and freestanding remedy in damages. But even in the absence of an alternative, a *Bivens* remedy is a subject of judgment: the federal courts must make the kind of remedial determination that is appropriate for a common-law tribunal, paying particular heed, however, to any special factors counselling hesitation before authorizing a new kind of federal litigation."[127]

The Court said that it was uncertain whether Robbins had an alternative remedy. The Court therefore said, "This, then, is a case for *Bivens* step two, for weighing reasons for and against the creation of a new cause of action, the way common law judges have always done."[128] The Court concluded that it would be undesirable to allow a *Bivens* cause of action because permitting a damages claim could lead to a flood of litigation and because of the difficulty of proving whether government officers were acting out of a retaliatory motive. The Court stated: "The point here is not to deny that Government employees sometimes overreach, for of course they do, and they may have done so here if all the allegations are true. The point is the reasonable fear that a general *Bivens* cure would be worse than the disease."[129]

Wilkie v. Robbins is thus important in indicating that there is a two-step inquiry in deciding whether there are special factors counseling hesitation and precluding a *Bivens* suit: First, are there are alternative remedies available, and second, if not,

[125] 551 U.S. 537 (2007).
[126] *Id.* at 568-569 (Ginsburg. J., dissenting).
[127] *Id.* at 550.
[128] *Id.* at 554.
[129] *Id.* at 560.

is it, on balance, desirable to allow a *Bivens* claim? *Wilkie v. Robbins* thus creates a new and potentially significant additional limit on *Bivens* causes of action.

§9.1.4 Bivens *Suits Against Government and Private Entities and Private Individuals*

In *Bivens*, the Court recognized a cause of action against individual government officers for constitutional violations. Under what circumstances, if any, can a cause of action be inferred from the Constitution for suits against government entities?

No *Bivens* Suits Against Federal Agencies

In *Federal Deposit Insurance Company v. Meyer*, the Court unanimously ruled that a federal agency is not subject to liability for damages under *Bivens.*[130] A discharged employee of a failed savings and loan sued the Federal Savings and Loan Insurance Corporation, claiming that due process was violated when it had ordered his firing. The Court held that *Bivens* actions may not be asserted against federal agencies. The Court explained that *Bivens* recognized suits against officers because of the absence of any other remedy, whereas the Federal Tort Claims Act provides a cause of action directly against the federal government.[131] The Court concluded that "[a]n extension of *Bivens* to agencies of the Federal Government is not supported by the logic of *Bivens* itself" and that it is up to Congress to decide the available remedies against the United States.[132]

Eleventh Amendment Bars *Bivens* Suits Against State Governments

Moreover, *Bivens* suits against state governments are not allowed because the Eleventh Amendment precludes states from being sued in federal court.[133] However, it might be argued that a *Bivens* cause of action brought under the Fourteenth Amendment should override a state's Eleventh Amendment immunity. In *Fitzpatrick v. Bitzer*, the Supreme Court allowed state governments to be sued for employment discrimination in violation of Title VII of the Civil Rights Act of 1964.[134] The Court held that Title VII was adopted pursuant to the Fourteenth Amendment and that the amendment was specifically intended as a limit on state sovereignty. Thus, the contention is that the Fourteenth Amendment of its own force overrides the Eleventh

[130] 510 U.S. 471 (1994).

[131] *Id.* at 485.

[132] *Id.* at 486. For an excellent criticism of *Meyer, see* Susan Bandes, Reinventing *Bivens*: The Self-Executing Constitution, 68 S. Cal. L. Rev. 289 (1995).

[133] *See, e.g.,* Alabama v. Pugh, 438 U.S. 781 (1978); *see also* Morris v. Washington Metro. Area Transit Auth., 702 F.2d 1037 (D.C. Cir. 1983); Kostka v. Hogg, 560 F.2d 37 (1st Cir. 1977); Burton v. Waller, 502 F.2d 1261 (5th Cir. 1974), *cert. denied,* 420 U.S. 964 (1975); Pagano v. Hadley, 535 F. Supp. 92 (D. Del. 1982).

[134] 427 U.S. 445 (1976). *See* §7.7, *supra.*

Amendment; thus, *Bivens* suits against states are permitted under the Fourteenth Amendment.[135] Although the Supreme Court has not directly addressed the question, at least one lower court has rejected this argument, holding that *Fitzpatrick* requires a congressional statute expressly making states liable.[136]

Bivens Suits Against Local Governments?

There are many cases considering *Bivens* suits against municipal governments. Prior to the Supreme Court's decision in *Monell v. Department of Social Services*, municipalities could not be sued under §1983 because of the Supreme Court's interpretation of the legislative history of that statute.[137] During this time when local governments were immune from suit under §1983, there were many attempts to create municipal liability in *Bivens* suits. Lower courts were divided as to whether *Bivens* suits could be brought against municipal governments for violations of the Fourteenth Amendment.[138] The Supreme Court did not address this question, though some justices expressed their belief that municipal governments could be sued via *Bivens* causes of action for constitutional violations.[139]

After *Monell* held that municipalities could be sued under §1983, *Bivens* actions against local governments became far less important. However, the issue still arises because there are instances in which cities cannot be sued under §1983 because of the Court's interpretation of that statute. Specifically, in *Monell*, the Court held that municipal entities could be sued only for their unconstitutional policies; local governments may not be sued based on respondeat superior liability.[140] Thus, the question arises concerning whether *Bivens* suits can be brought against municipalities based on respondeat superior liability.

The Supreme Court has not considered this question. Because *Monell's* limitation on respondeat superior liability is based on the Court's understanding of §1983's legislative history, no inherent reason exists for precluding such liability

[135] *See* Paul R. Verkuil, Immunity or Responsibility for Unconstitutional Conduct: The Aftermath of Jackson State and Kent State, 50 N.C. L. Rev. 548, 606-610 (1978) (arguing that the Fourteenth Amendment overrides the Eleventh Amendment).

[136] Vakas v. Rodriquez, 728 F.2d 1293, 1296 (10th Cir.), *cert. denied*, 469 U.S. 981 (1984).

[137] 436 U.S. 658 (1978); *see* Monroe v. Pape, 365 U.S. 167 (1961) (interpreting the legislative history of §1983 to prevent suits against municipal governments). *See* §8.5, *supra*.

[138] For authority refusing to allow *Bivens* suits against cities, *see* Kostka v. Hogg, 560 F.2d 37 (1st Cir. 1977); Jamison v. McCurrie, 565 F.2d 483 (7th Cir. 1977); Perzanowski v. Salvio, 369 F. Supp. 223 (D. Conn. 1974). For authority permitting *Bivens* suits against cities, *see* Gentile v. Wallen, 562 F.2d 193 (2d Cir. 1977); Cox v. Stanton, 529 F.2d 47 (4th Cir. 1975); Gray v. Union County Intermediate Educ. Dist., 520 F.2d 803 (9th Cir. 1972).

[139] City of Kenosha v. Bruno, 412 U.S. 507, 516 (1973) (concurring opinion of Justices Brennan and Marshall). *But see also* Aldinger v. Howard, 427 U.S. 1 (1976) (federal courts could not hear pendent state law claims against municipal governments because Congress did not mean to include local governments within the scope of §1983). *Aldinger* is discussed in §5.4.2, *supra*. For commentary suggesting that municipal governments should be liable in *Bivens* suits, *see* Reed Hundt, Suing Municipalities Directly Under the Fourteenth Amendment, 70 Nw. U. L. Rev. 770, 780-782 (1975); Note, Damage Remedies Against Municipalities for Constitutional Violations, 89 Harv. L. Rev. 922 (1976).

[140] Monell v. Department of Social Servs., 436 U.S. at 690.

in suits brought directly under the Constitution. In fact, one federal district court explicitly held that municipal governments may be sued directly under the Fourteenth Amendment and that they may be held liable on a respondeat superior basis for the unconstitutional acts of their officers.[141] The weight of lower court authority, however, is that the availability of relief against cities under §1983 bars *Bivens* actions and that municipalities may not be sued for respondeat superior liability.[142] The Supreme Court's decision in *Federal Deposit Insurance Corporation v. Meyer*,[143] that *Bivens* provides relief against federal officers and not federal agencies, indicates that the Court is unwilling to extend *Bivens* to suits against government entities.

No *Bivens* Suits Against Private Entities

The Court followed and extended *FDIC v. Meyer* in *Correctional Services Corp. v. Malesko*,[144] in which it held that a private entity that operates a prison cannot be sued in a *Bivens* action. The issue was whether a *Bivens* suit could be brought against a private company operating a halfway house under a contract with the Federal Bureau of Prisons. John Malesko, an inmate in the halfway house, suffered a heart attack as a result of the facility's refusal to allow him to use an elevator despite a serious heart condition. He brought a *Bivens* claim against the halfway house.

The Supreme Court, in a 5-4 decision, held that private entities may not be sued under *Bivens*. Chief Justice Rehnquist's majority opinion stressed that *Bivens* suits are available against individual federal officers, not against government or private entities. The Court stated: "Respondent instead seeks a marked extension of *Bivens*, to contexts that would not advance *Bivens*' core purpose of deterring individual officers from engaging in constitutional wrongdoing. The caution toward extending *Bivens* remedies into any new context, a caution consistently and repeatedly recognized for three decades, forecloses such an extension here."[145] The Court noted the availability of remedies under state tort law and Bureau of Prisons' procedures. As discussed above, the decision strongly indicates that there is a majority of the current Court unwilling to extend *Bivens*.

Bivens Suits Against Private Individuals

In *Minneci v. Pollard*, the Court considered whether prison guards at a private prison could be sued in a *Bivens* action.[146] Pollard was a prisoner at a private prison

[141] Rhodes v. City of Wichita, 516 F. Supp. 501 (D. Kan. 1981).

[142] *See, e.g.*, Abate v. Southern Pacific Transportation Co., 993 F.2d 107, 110-111 (5th Cir. 1993) (availability of suits under §1983 against local governments bars *Bivens* claims); Turpin v. Mailet, 591 F.2d 426, 427 (2d Cir. 1979) (en banc), *cert. denied*, 449 U.S. 1016 (1980) ("There is no place for a cause of action against a municipality directly under the 14th Amendment because the plaintiff may proceed against the [city under §1983]."); Tarpley v. Greene, 684 F.2d 1, 10 (D.C. Cir. 1982).

[143] 510 U.S. 471 (1994).

[144] 534 U.S. 61 (2001).

[145] *Id.* at 69.

[146] 565 U.S. 118 (2012).

that operated under a contract with the federal government. He broke his arm while in prison and claimed that the prison guards did not provide the needed recommended follow-up treatment and it caused him great pain. He sued them in a *Bivens* action under the Eighth Amendment, claiming deliberate indifference to his medical needs.

The Court, in an eight-to-one decision, held that no *Bivens* action was available. Justice Breyer, writing for the majority, stressed that under *Wilkie v. Robbins,* a *Bivens* suit is permitted only if it is on balance desirable. The Court concluded that no *Bivens* suit was allowed here because state tort law provided an adequate remedy to Pollard. The Court explained: "[W]e conclude that Pollard cannot assert a *Bivens* claim . . . primarily because Pollard's Eighth Amendment claim focuses upon a kind of conduct that typically falls within the scope of traditional state tort law. And in the case of a privately employed defendant, state tort law provides an 'alternative, existing process' capable of protecting the constitutional interests at stake. The existence of that alternative here constitutes a 'convincing reason for the Judicial Branch to refrain from providing a new and freestanding remedy in damages.' "[147]

The Court thus held that no *Bivens* suit can be brought against private defendants, at least if there is state tort liability. The Court concluded that "where, as here, a federal prisoner seeks damages from privately employed personnel working at a privately operated federal prison, where the conduct allegedly amounts to a violation of the Eighth Amendment, and where that conduct is of a kind that typically falls within the scope of traditional state tort law (such as the conduct involving improper medical care at issue here), the prisoner must seek a remedy under state tort law. We cannot imply a *Bivens* remedy in such a case."[148]

Only Justice Ginsburg dissented, and she would not bar a *Bivens* suit on the grounds that state tort remedies existed.[149] A tort remedy almost always exists. Wesley Bivens could have sued the agents of the Federal Bureau of Narcotics under state tort law. She therefore concluded that the Supreme Court's goal was to make sure that there is a federal cause of action for violations of constitutional rights by federal officers. *Minneci v. Pollard* is the first case to preclude *Bivens* suits based on the existence of state tort remedies.[150]

§9.1.5 *Procedures in* Bivens *suits*

Subject Matter Jurisdiction, Venue, Service of Process

A few aspects of procedure under *Bivens* suits are worth noting. First, in terms of subject matter jurisdiction, if federal officers are sued in state court they

[147] *Id.* at 125-126 (citations omitted).
[148] *Id.* at 131.
[149] *Id.* at 132-133 (Ginsburg, J., dissenting).
[150] *See* Alexander N. Reinert & Lumen N. Mulligan, Asking the First Question: Reframing *Bivens* After *Minneci,* 90 Wash. U. L.Q. 1473 (2013) (criticizing *Minneci* for precluding *Bivens* based on state tort remedies).

may remove the case to federal court.[151] Second, venue and service of process in *Bivens* litigation must comply with the usual rules under the Federal Rules of Civil Procedure and federal statutes; the provisions of the Mandamus and Venue Act of 1962 are inapplicable.[152] The Mandamus and Venue Act of 1962 provides, in part, that when the defendant is an officer or employee of the United States acting in his or her official capacity, suit may be brought in the judicial district where the defendant resides, where the cause of action arose, or where the plaintiff resides if no real property is involved in the action. The Supreme Court, however, held that this statute is inapplicable in *Bivens* actions.[153] The Court concluded that this provision was intended to apply only in instances in which the individual was the nominal defendant and the suit was "in reality against the Government."[154] Despite the literal language of the statute that seems to apply whenever individual officers are sued, the Supreme Court found that the interests of justice would not be served if a *Bivens* suit could be brought against an officer anywhere the plaintiff happened to reside.[155]

No Exhaustion of Administrative Remedies Required

Third, in *McCarthy v. Madigan*, the Supreme Court resolved a conflict among the circuits and held that a prisoner seeking solely money damages in a *Bivens* suit does not need to exhaust administrative remedies.[156] In *McCarthy*, a federal prisoner brought a damages action under *Bivens* claiming that prison officials violated his Eighth Amendment rights by their deliberate indifference to his medical problems.

Although the Court identified the important interests served by requiring exhaustion of administrative remedies, it also recognized the "virtually unflagging obligation [of federal courts] to exercise the jurisdiction given them."[157] The Court said that "[i]n determining whether exhaustion is required, federal courts must balance the interest of the individual in retaining prompt access to a federal judicial forum against countervailing institutional interests favoring exhaustion."[158] The Court said that this balancing is "intensely practical," looking at "both the nature of the claim presented and the character of the administrative procedure involved."[159] The Court found that exhaustion was not required for *Bivens* claims solely for money damages by prisoners because Congress had not required it, because the administrative procedures could not authorize an award of money

[151] 28 U.S.C. §1442(a)(1).
[152] 28 U.S.C. §1391(e).
[153] Stafford v. Briggs, 444 U.S. 527 (1980).
[154] *Id.* at 542.
[155] *Id.* at 544.
[156] 503 U.S. 140 (1992).
[157] *Id.* at 145, *quoting* Colorado River Water Conservation Dist. v. United States, 424 U.S. 800, 817 (1976).
[158] 503 U.S. at 140.
[159] *Id.* at 145.

damages, and because requiring exhaustion would heavily burden the interests of the inmate.

Attorneys' fees?

Fourth, it is unresolved whether plaintiffs prevailing in *Bivens* suits are entitled to recover attorneys' fees. In *Bush v. Lucas,* the Court expressly left this question open for future consideration.[160] The Equal Access to Justice Act allows a court to award attorneys' fees to the prevailing party in a civil action against the United States or any employee acting in official capacity.[161] Also, 28 U.S.C. §2812(d)(1)(A) provides that courts shall award prevailing parties attorneys' fees in suits against the United States, unless the action arose from a tort or the action of the United States was substantially justified. It is unresolved whether *Bivens* plaintiffs can recover attorneys' fees under these statutes.[162] The courts of appeals, however, unanimously agree that courts may not award attorneys' fees to *Bivens* plaintiffs under 42 U.S.C. §1988.[163]

§9.2 SUITS AGAINST THE FEDERAL GOVERNMENT

§9.2.1 The Principle of Sovereign Immunity

U.S. Government May Not Be Sued Without its Consent

The United States may not be sued unless federal legislation specifically authorizes the suit. The sovereign immunity of the U.S. government is firmly established. Long ago, Chief Justice John Marshall declared that "[t]he universally

[160] 462 U.S. at 372 n.9.

[161] 28 U.S.C. §2412(b).

[162] *See, e.g.,* Kreines v. United States, 33 F.3d 1105, 1109 (9th Cir. 1994) (attorneys' fees unavailable under either EAJA's §2412(b) or §2412(d)); Couden v. Duffey, 826 F. Supp. 2d 711, 717 (D. Del. 2011) ("Because plaintiffs' *Bivens* claim against Agent Duffey is a claim against him in his individual capacity, an award of attorneys' fees and costs is not recoverable under §2412"); GasPlus, L.L.C. v. U.S. Dep't of Interior, 593 F. Supp. 2d 80, 84 (D.D.C. 2009) (awarding plaintiff GasPlus attorneys' fees "incurred in suing the United States but not the costs and fees it incurred in suing government officials in their individual capacities under *Bivens* because those are not claims against the United States and, therefore, not covered by EAJA."); *but see* Estate of McIntyre v. United States, 739 F. Supp. 2d 70, 75 (D. Mass. 2010) (allowing fees related to Bivens action where plaintiff "was required to maintain suits against the individual defendants in order to ensure the possibility of obtaining necessary evidence—evidence that likely would have been unnecessary but for the government's bad faith conduct."); Lucas v. White, 63 F. Supp. 2d 1046, 1052–1053 (N.D. Cal. 1999) (awarding attorneys' fees under EAJA in *Bivens* action where "plaintiffs' action was clearly 'aimed primarily at' obtaining equitable relief against government officials to end practices in the federal prison system" even though *Bivens* claim was originally brought but dismissed before settlement).

[163] *See, e.g.,* Unus v. Kane, 565 F.3d 103, 127 (4th Cir. 2009) (holding §1988 does not authorize a fee award for *Bivens* claims).

received opinion is, that no suit can be commenced or prosecuted against the United States."[1] Many times the Supreme Court has reiterated this principle, holding that "the United States cannot be lawfully sued without its consent in any case."[2] Only Congress can consent to suits against the United States; the executive is powerless to waive the federal government's sovereign immunity.[3] The waiver of sovereign immunity by Congress must be explicit.[4]

The principle of sovereign immunity is derived from English law, which assumed that "the King can do no wrong."[5] Since the time of Edward the First, the crown of England has not been suable unless it has specifically consented to suit.[6] Throughout American history, U.S. courts have applied this principle, although they often have admitted that its justification in this country is unclear.[7]

Justifications for Sovereign Immunity

Several rationales are offered for why the United States should have complete immunity to liability without its consent. First, some believe that the operation of government would be hindered if the United States were liable for every injury it inflicted.[8] The argument is that sovereign immunity is necessary to protect the government from undue interference by the judiciary.[9] Sovereign immunity preserves the unhampered exercise of discretion and limits the amount of time the government must spend responding to lawsuits. The Supreme Court declared that the "Government, as representative of the community as a whole, cannot be stopped

§9.2 [1] Cohens v. Virginia, 19 U.S. (6 Wheat.) 264, 411-412 (1821). The sovereign immunity of state governments is discussed in Chapter 7. This, of course, has been the area where the Supreme Court has primarily addressed the concept of sovereign immunity in recent years. The relationship between the sovereign immunity of the federal and state governments is unclear because the Supreme Court has focused on federalism principles in justifying the latter.

[2] United States v. Lee, 106 U.S. 196, 205 (1882); *see also* Kennecott Copper Corp. v. State Tax Commn., 327 U.S. 573, 580 (1946) (Frankfurter, J., dissenting); Hill v. United States, 50 U.S. (9 How.) 386, 389 (1850); United States v. Clarke, 33 U.S. (8 Pet.) 436 (1834).

[3] *See, e.g.,* United States v. Shaw, 309 U.S. 495 (1940); Munro v. United States, 303 U.S. 36 (1938); Finn v. United States, 123 U.S. 227 (1887).

[4] *See, e.g.,* Lane v. Pena, 518 U.S. 187 (1996) (Rehabilitation Act lacked "unequivocal expression" of congressional intent required for a waiver of sovereign immunity).

[5] *See* 5 Kenneth Davis, Administrative Law Treatise 6-7 (2d ed. 1984) (quoting Blackstone); 2 Charles H. Koch, Jr., Administrative Law and Practice 210 (1985).

[6] United States v. Lee, 106 U.S. at 205.

[7] *Id.* at 207 ("The principle has never been discussed or the reasons for it given, but it has always been treated as an established doctrine.") (citations omitted).

[8] *See* The Siren, 74 U.S. (7 Wall.) 152, 154 (1868) ("The public service would be hindered, and the public safety endangered if the supreme authority could be subjected to suit at the instance of every citizen.").

[9] James S. Sable, Comment, Sovereign Immunity: A Battleground of Competing Considerations, 12 Sw. U. L. Rev. 457, 465 (1981); Littell v. Morton, 445 F.2d 1207, 1214 (4th Cir. 1971) ("The rationale for sovereign immunity essentially boils down to substantial bothersome interference with the operation of government.").

in its tracks by any plaintiff who presents a disputed question of property or contract right."[10]

Moreover, sovereign immunity furthers the separation of powers by limiting judicial oversight of executive conduct. In fact, by limiting judicial review, sovereign immunity avoids situations where the courts will impose orders on the other branches of government that might be disregarded.[11]

A second argument for the federal government's sovereign immunity is offered by Justice Oliver Wendell Holmes: Liability cannot exist unless the law provides for it.[12] Justice Holmes said that claiming a right to sue the government is "like shaking one's fist at the sky, when the sky furnishes the energy that enables one to raise the fist."[13] From this viewpoint, rights do not exist independent of positive law. The right to sue must be grounded in a statute for it to exist.

Finally, and not to be discounted, there are efficiency arguments for sovereign immunity. There is fear that without it there would be a flood of litigation against the United States and that money would be diverted from other government uses to pay off damage judgments against the federal government.[14] Especially in an era of large budget deficits and demands to reduce federal spending, there is concern that damage suits against the government would drain resources necessary for more important public purposes.[15]

Criticisms of Federal Sovereign Immunity

However, many commentators reject these justifications for sovereign immunity and are critical of the doctrine. Many believe that sovereign immunity is an anachronistic relic, that it is derived from centuries-old English law principles, and that it probably was imported into this country's legal system at a time when the government was fragile and unable to afford the costs of money judgments.[16] The attack on sovereign immunity is not new. President Abraham Lincoln declared, "It is . . . as much the duty of Government to render prompt justice against itself in favor of citizens as it is to administer the same between private individuals."[17]

Opponents of sovereign immunity contend that it is inconsistent with a central maxim in this country: that no one, not even the government, is above the law.

[10] Larson v. Domestic & Foreign Commerce Corp., 337 U.S. 682, 704 (1949).

[11] Koch, *supra* note 5, at 211-212.

[12] Kawananakoa v. Polyblank, 205 U.S. 349, 353 (1907).

[13] *Id.*

[14] *See* Clark Byse, Proposed Reforms in Federal "Nonstatutory" Judicial Review: Sovereign Immunity, Indispensable Parties, Mandamus, 75 Harv. L. Rev. 1479, 1526 (1962); Noel Fox, The King Must Do No Wrong: A Critique of the Current Status of Sovereign and Official Immunity, 25 Wayne L. Rev. 177, 187 (1979).

[15] James S. Sable, Comment, The Supreme Court and the Tort Claims Act: End of an Enlightened Era?, 27 Clev. St. L. Rev. 267, 270 (1978). For a defense of sovereign immunity, *see* Alfred Hill, In Defense of Our Law of Sovereign Immunity, 42 B.C. L. Rev. 485 (2001).

[16] Sable, *supra* note 9, at 458; Koch, *supra* note 5, at 212.

[17] 7 James D. Richardson, A Compilation of Messages and Papers of the Presidents 3245, 3252, *quoted in* Kennecott Copper Corp. v. State Tax Commn., 327 U.S. 573, 580 (1946) (Frankfurter, J., dissenting).

The effect of sovereign immunity is to place the government above the law and to ensure that some individuals who have suffered egregious harms will be unable to receive redress for their injuries.[18] The U.S. government can blatantly violate the most basic constitutional rights and the federal courts, absent congressional legislation, are powerless to halt or redress the wrong. The judicial role of enforcing and upholding the Constitution is rendered illusory when the government has complete immunity to suit. Although abolishing sovereign immunity would impose financial burdens on the government, some argue that it is better to spread the costs of injuries among the entire citizenry than to make the wronged individual bear the entire loss.

Furthermore, sovereign immunity is difficult to reconcile with the U.S. Constitution. Nowhere does the document mention or even imply that the federal government has complete immunity to suit. Accordingly, it would appear that sovereign immunity is a *common law* principle borrowed from the English common law. However, Article VI of the Constitution states that the Constitution is the supreme law, and, as such, it should be supreme over sovereign immunity. By this view, sovereign immunity should not preclude suits against the United States for constitutional violations.[19]

Also, the effect of sovereign immunity is to cause lawsuits to be filed against the individual government officers. The Supreme Court long has held that sovereign immunity prevents suits against the government entity, but not against the officers.[20] Hence, individuals seeking redress from the federal government must sue its officers for money damages to be paid from their own pockets.[21] Many believe that this is undesirable and that it would be preferable to have the government entity sued rather than its officers.[22] For example, it is argued that the exercise of discretion is more likely to be chilled if officers are personally liable than if the government entity is held responsible.

Statutes Creating Federal Government Liability

Despite the strong criticisms of sovereign immunity, the principle is firmly entrenched and the Supreme Court has shown no signs of abandoning it.

[18] John E.H. Sherry, The Myth That the King Can Do No Wrong: A Comparative Study of the Sovereign Immunity Doctrine in the United States and the New York Courts of Claims, 22 Admin. L. Rev. 39, 56 (1969). For criticisms of sovereign immunity, *see* Erwin Chemerinsky, Against Sovereign Immunity, 53 Stan. L. Rev. 1201 (2001); James Pfander, Sovereign Immunity and the Right to Petition: Toward a First Amendment Right to Pursue Judicial Claims Against the Government, 91 Nw. U. L. Rev. 899 (1997).

[19] Justice Frankfurter has suggested that sovereign immunity is, itself, "embodied in the Constitution." Kennecott Copper Corp. v. State Tax Commn., 327 U.S. at 580.

[20] Schneider v. Smith, 390 U.S. 17 (1968); Larson v. Domestic & Foreign Commerce Corp., 337 U.S. 682 (1949); Land v. Dollar, 330 U.S. 731 (1947); *see also* Ex parte Young, 209 U.S. 123 (1908).

[21] If the monetary relief, in reality, would be against the government, the suit is barred, even though the individual officer is named as the defendant. Larson v. Domestic & Foreign Commerce Corp., 337 U.S. at 687 ("The crucial question is whether the relief sought in a suit nominally addressed to the officer is relief against the sovereign."). *See also* Hawaii v. Gordon, 373 U.S. 57, 98 (1963).

[22] *See* Davis, *supra* note 5, at 22-24; Peter H. Schuck, Suing Government 90-91 (1983).

Accordingly, any expansion of the United States' liability must occur through federal statutes. As of now, three major statutes waive the United States' sovereign immunity and are thus a basis for relief against the federal government. First, in 1976, Congress amended the Administrative Procedure Act to allow the U.S. government to be sued for injunctive relief.[23] Second, the Federal Tort Claims Act generally allows the federal government to be sued for the negligent torts of its employees.[24] Third, the Tucker Act permits the United States to be sued for breach of contract and other monetary claims not arising in tort.[25] These three statutes are discussed in §§9.2.2, 9.2.3, and 9.2.4, respectively.

Additionally, federal statutes creating some federal government bodies waive sovereign immunity by stating that the entities may sue and be sued.[26] The Court has explained that "such waivers of governmental immunity . . . should be liberally construed."[27] In essence, such provisions allow the particular agencies to be sued in the same manner as private parties.[28] For example, the Court held that the provision permitting the Postal Service to sue or be sued allowed it to be sued for prejudgment interest in a suit alleging impermissible employment discrimination.[29] There also are federal statutes that waive sovereign immunity for claims under them. For example, in *Dep't of Agric. Rural Dev. Rural Hous. Serv. v. Kirtz*, the Court unanimously found that the Fair Credit Reporting Act (FCRA) authorizes a consumer to "sue 'any' federal agency for defying the law's terms."[30] Sovereign immunity thus cannot shield the federal government from lawsuits under the FCRA. The Court explained: "Although the Executive Branch may question the wisdom of holding federal agencies accountable for their violations of the Fair Credit Reporting Act, the Court concluded that Congress's judgment commands our respect and the law it has adopted speaks clearly: A consumer may sue 'any' federal agency for defying the law's terms."[31]

§9.2.2 *Injunctive Relief Against the United States*

Injunctive Relief Allowed Against Federal Officers

An extremely important and well-established exception to the principle of sovereign immunity is that suits against government officers are not barred.

[23] 5 U.S.C. §702, Pub. L. No. 94-574, 90 Stat. 2721.

[24] 28 U.S.C. §§1346, 2671-2678, 2680. For an excellent discussion of how Federal Tort Claims Act suits can replace *Bivens* suits in many circumstances, *see* Olivia Goldberg, (Extra)ordinary Tort Law: Evaluating the Federal Tort Claims Act as a Constitutional Remedy, 76 Stan. L. Rev. 481 (2024).

[25] 28 U.S.C. §§1346(a), 1491.

[26] Loeffler v. Frank, 486 U.S. 549, 554 (1988).

[27] FHA v. Barr, 309 U.S. 242, 245 (1939); *see also* Franchise Tax Bd. of Cal. v. USPS, 467 U.S. 512, 517-518 (1984).

[28] 486 U.S. at 555; *see also* Library of Congress v. Shaw, 478 U.S. 310, 317 n.5 (1986).

[29] Loeffler v. Frank, 486 U.S. at 555 (1988).

[30] 601 U.S. 42, 64 (2024).

[31] *Id.* at 64.

The Supreme Court long has allowed suits against officers who are allegedly acting in excess of their legal authority or pursuant to an unconstitutional statute.[32] Thus, unconstitutional government actions can be halted by seeking an injunction against the individual officer responsible for executing the government's policy.[33]

However, if the officer is acting within the terms of his or her statutory authority, and the action is not alleged to be unconstitutional, then no injunction is permitted, even though the conduct is tortious. For example, in *Larson v. Domestic & Foreign Commerce Corp.*, the Supreme Court held that sovereign immunity prevented a suit against the War Assets Administrator to keep him from canceling a contract for the sale of coal.[34] Chief Justice Vinson, writing for the Court, stated, "[I]f the actions of an officer do not conflict with the terms of his valid statutory authority, then they are the actions of the sovereign, whether or not they are tortious under general law, if they would be regarded as the actions of a private principal under the normal rules of agency."[35]

Injunctive Relief Against the Federal Government

After *Larson*, courts struggled to determine when the injunction would operate against the United States and therefore would be barred absent an allegation of unconstitutional or ultra vires officer activity.[36] In response to this problem, Congress amended the Administrative Procedure Act to specifically allow suits for injunctive relief to be brought against the United States.[37] As amended, 5 U.S.C. §702 provides:

> An action in a court of the United States seeking relief other than money damages and stating a claim that an agency or an officer or employee thereof acted or failed to act in an official capacity or under color of legal authority shall not be dismissed nor relief therein be denied on the ground that it is against the United States or that the United States is an indispensable party. The United States may be named as a defendant in any such action, and a judgment or decree may be entered against the United States.

The statute is clear: the United States has waived its sovereign immunity in suits requesting other than monetary relief. Thus, federal court suits for injunctive and declaratory relief are permitted, either against federal officers or directly

[32] *See, e.g.,* Schneider v. Smith, 390 U.S. 17 (1968); Larson v. Domestic & Foreign Commerce Corp., 337 U.S. 682 (1949); Land v. Dollar, 330 U.S. 731 (1947); *see also* Ex parte Young, 209 U.S. 123 (1908).

[33] *See, e.g.,* Schneider v. Smith, 390 U.S. 17 (1968); Philadelphia Co. v. Stimson, 223 U.S. 605 (1912).

[34] 337 U.S. 682 (1949).

[35] *Id.* at 695.

[36] *See, e.g.,* Hawaii v. Gordon, 373 U.S. 57 (1963) (denying declaratory relief on the basis of sovereign immunity).

[37] *See* Koch, *supra* note 5, at 211 (§702 amended in response to "overwhelming academic and judicial criticism"). But it should be noted that while "[i]mmunity was abolished in the federal courts, . . . the United States still cannot be found liable in any state court action." *Id.* at 216.

against the U.S. government.[38] This is a major exception to the doctrine of sovereign immunity because it allows the judiciary, assuming all other jurisdictional requirements are met, to halt illegal government conduct.

Section 702 expressly does not include suits for monetary relief. However, the Supreme Court held that a suit by a state government for reimbursement from a federal program was not a suit for money damages, and thus was permitted under §702.[39] The Court reasoned that §702 was intended to exclude suits for compensatory money damages; equitable suits for specific relief, even if requiring monetary payments, are allowed.[40]

§9.2.3 The Federal Tort Claims Act

Historical Absence of Relief

An injustice through much of American history was the inability of injured individuals to recover damages from the government for the tortious conduct of its employees. For example, if a federal postal truck struck an innocent pedestrian, the victim's recourse was to sue the driver, who likely had minimal assets to satisfy a judgment. If the negligent driver worked for anyone other than the government, the injured individual could recover from the employer based on respondeat superior, but sovereign immunity prevented any suit against the United States. The victim's only other hope for recovery was to try to get a private bill passed through Congress awarding compensation.[41]

Federal Tort Claims Act Creates Government Liability

It was not until 1946 that Congress rectified this situation and adopted the Federal Tort Claims Act, which made the United States liable for the negligent acts of its employees. The crucial provision of the act specifies that the "United States

[38] There is a scholarly debate over when nationwide injunctions are appropriate against the federal government. *See* Amanda Frost, In Defense of Nationwide Injunctions, 93 N.Y.U. L. Rev. 1065 (2018); Samuel L. Bray, Multiple Chancellors: Reforming the National Injunction, 131 Harv. L. Rev. 417 (2017).

[39] Bowen v. Massachusetts, 487 U.S. 879 (1988).

[40] *See also* Zellous v. Broadhead Assocs., 906 F.2d 94 (3d Cir. 1990) (plaintiffs seeking an allowance that they were entitled to are not barred from suit); Texas American Bancshares v. Clarke, 740 F. Supp. 1243 (N.D. Tex. 1990) (where plaintiff is seeking to recover funds to which there is an entitlement under federal law the APA does not preclude suit); *but see* Hubbard v. Administrator, E.P.A., 739 F. Supp. 654 (D.D.C. 1990) (suit for back pay barred by the APA).

[41] 1 Basil J. Mezines, Jacob A. Stein, Jules Gruff, Administrative Law 6A-6-6A-7 (rev. ed. 1986) ("The only relief available to an injured party was through the enactment by Congress of a private bill. The process was slow, cumbersome and frequently inequitable since identical claims could receive vastly different treatment by different Congresses."); J. Thomas Morina, Note, Denial of Atomic Veterans' Tort Claims: The Enduring Fallout from Feres v. United States, 24 Wm. & Mary L. Rev. 259, 261 (1983) (Federal Tort Claims Act motivated by desire to avoid "time-consuming, inefficient, and often inequitable process of reviewing these private bills").

shall be liable . . . to tort claims in the same manner and to the same extent as a private individual under like circumstances."[42] The terms of the act create liability for the U.S. government if the act is a tort in the state where the conduct occurred. That is, the Federal Tort Claims Act does not create a new body of tort law; rather, it makes the government liable if the existing law would provide a remedy.

For a short time, the Court interpreted the act as creating liability only for those government activities that also are performed by private entities. That is, no liability existed where the action was of a type done solely by the government. In one case, the Court held that the act was inapplicable because the liability that the plaintiff sought to impose on the government had no private analogue.[43] Subsequently, however, the Court disavowed this position and now allows liability for torts that only the government can inflict. For instance, in the landmark case, *Indian Towing Co. v. United States*, the Supreme Court held that the United States could be held liable for the Coast Guard's negligent maintenance of a lighthouse.[44] The Court concluded that a liberal interpretation of the act was intended and held that no parallel private liability need exist in order for a claim against the government to be permitted.

Westfall Act Limits Suits Against Government Officials

The Westfall Act[45] establishes the Federal Tort Claims Act as the exclusive remedy for any tort claim resulting from the act or omission of a government employee acting within the scope of their employment, with the exception of *Bivens* remedies for constitutional tort claims.[46] If the attorney general or their designee certifies that a federal employee was acting within the scope of employment "at the time of the incident out of which the claim arose," the individual employee is granted immunity from suit, the United States is substituted for the employee, and the action proceeds as one against the United States.[47]

In other words, tort suits against individual government employees, for acts within the scope of their employment, are barred if the Attorney General certifies that the individual was acting within the scope of his or her employment. The only

[42] 28 U.S.C. §2674.

[43] Dalehite v. United States, 346 U.S. 15 (1953); *see also* Feres v. United States, 340 U.S. 135 (1950).

[44] 350 U.S. 61 (1955). *See also* Rayonier, Inc. v. United States, 352 U.S. 315, 319 (1957) (rejecting the government's claim that liability exists only for activities performed by private parties as well).

[45] 29 U.S.C. §2679.

[46] The Westfall Act was enacted to override a judicial decision, Westfall v. Erwin, 484 U.S. 292 (1988), which added a "discretionary function" requirement as a criterion for personal immunity separate and apart from the scope-of-employment test.

[47] *Id.* §2679(d)(2). *See* Osborn v. Haley, 549 U.S. 225 (2007) (once the attorney general certified that federal employee named as defendant was acting within scope of employment, and once cause of action was removed, district court has no authority to return case to state court on ground that the attorney general's certification was unwarranted; attorney general could validly certify that federal employee named as defendant was acting within scope of his employment, so as to warrant substitution of United States as defendant pursuant to the Westfall Act, even though the attorney general's certification rested on understanding of facts that differed from plaintiff's allegations).

remedy then is against the United States under the FTCA. This, however, does not apply to constitutional claims brought under *Bivens.*[48]

Only For Claims Arising in the United States

The FTCA creates an exception for "[a]ny claim arising in a foreign country."[49] In *Sosa v. Alvarez-Machain,* the Court held that this exception applies even if the planning and direction of the tortious activity occurred in the United States as long as the wrongful conduct occurred in another country.[50] The case involved a doctor who was illegally kidnapped in Mexico at the direction of agents of the Drug Enforcement Agency. He sued the United States under the Federal Tort Claims Act, contending that the "headquarters" for the wrongful act were in the United States. The Supreme Court rejected this and held "that the FTCA's foreign country exception bars all claims based on any injury suffered in a foreign country, regardless of where the tortious act or omission occurred."[51]

Several procedural aspects of the act are worth noting. First, the statute explicitly states that the United States shall not be "liable for interest prior to judgment or punitive damages."[52] Second, jury trials are not available for claims under the act.[53]

Requirement for Presenting a Claim Before Suit

Third, before a suit can be filed under the Federal Tort Claims Act, a claim must be presented to the responsible agency.[54] The act was amended in 1966 to permit agency heads or their designees to settle any claim, except that settlements greater than $25,000 must be approved by the attorney general. However, if suit is filed, the United States, and not the agency, is the appropriate defendant. The Supreme Court held that the requirement for exhaustion prior to bringing a suit under the Federal Tort Claims Act means that a case must be dismissed where an individual exhausts administrative remedies while the suit is pending in federal court.[55]

[48] Similarly, the Gonzalez Act makes claims against the United States under the FTCA the "exclusive" remedy for injuries resulting from malpractice committed by medical personnel of the armed forces and other specified agencies. 10 U.S.C. §1089(a). In Levin v. United States, 568 U.S. 503 (2013), the Court held that the Gonzalez Act allows suits based on battery against medical personnel (such as in this case, a medical procedure without consent of the patient).

[49] §2680(k).

[50] 542 U.S. 692 (2004).

[51] *Id.* at 712.

[52] 28 U.S.C. §2674.

[53] *See* Carlson v. Green, 446 U.S. 14, 22 (1980) (jury trials not available under Federal Tort Claims Act, though they are permitted in *Bivens* suits).

[54] 28 U.S.C. §2675.

[55] McNeil v. United States, 508 U.S. 106 (1993).

Statute of Limitations

Fourth, the Federal Tort Claims Act provides that a tort claim against the United States "shall be forever barred" unless it is presented to the "appropriate Federal agency within two years after such claim accrues" and then brought to federal court "within six months" after the agency acts on the claim.[56] In other words, there are two statutes of limitations: one for presenting the claim and one for filing suit after the claim is denied.

In *United States v. Wong*, the Court held that both of these statutes of limitations are subject to equitable tolling, allowing some claims to proceed after the limitation period has expired if a plaintiff was not able to discover the injury despite due care and dilligence.[57] The Court, in a 5-4 decision, explained that the presumption is that statutes of limitations are not jurisdictional and are subject to equitable tolling. The Court said that the FTCA "provided no clear statement indicating that [it] is the rare statute of limitations that can deprive a court of jurisdiction. Neither the text nor the context nor the legislative history indicates (much less does so plainly) that Congress meant to enact something other than a standard time bar."[58] Justice Alito, writing for the four dissenting justices, strongly disagreed and declared: "The statutory text, its historical roots, and more than a century of precedents show that this absolute bar is not subject to equitable tolling. I would enforce the statute as Congress intended and reverse."[59]

Limit on Attorneys' Fees

Fifth, attorneys' fees are limited under the act to 25 percent of a judgment and 20 percent of a settlement.[60] Sixth, recovery against the United States is a "complete bar" to a suit against the employee "whose act or omission gave rise to the claim."[61] In other words, the act, in effect, imposes an election of remedies: Suit cannot be brought against both the United States under the Federal Tort Claims Act and against the individual employee under a *Bivens* cause of action.

Broad Range of Damages Allowed

The Supreme Court has interpreted the act broadly in terms of the types of damages that are recoverable. In *Molzof v. United States*, the Court held that damage awards could include compensation for the loss of enjoyment of life as a result of

[56] 28 U.S.C. §2401(b).

[57] 575 U.S. 402 (2015).

[58] *Id.* at 410.

[59] *Id.* at 421 (Alito, J., dissenting).

[60] 28 U.S.C. §2678.

[61] 28 U.S.C. §2676. Additionally, the act provides that a remedy against the United States for operation of a motor vehicle within the scope of an employee's job is "exclusive of any other civil action . . . against the employee or his estate whose act or omission gave rise to the claim." 28 U.S.C. §2679(b). *See also* Carr v. United States, 422 F.2d 1007 (4th Cir. 1970) (upholding the constitutionality of this limit on liability).

irreversible brain damage.[62] Robert Molzof suffered irreversible brain damage as a result of negligence at a government veterans' hospital. He sought compensation for, among other things, medical expenses and loss of enjoyment from life. The lower courts rejected these claims because Molzof was receiving free medical care from the government and because damages for lost enjoyment of life would constitute punitive damages in violation of the Federal Tort Claims Act.

The Supreme Court unanimously rejected this view and held that damages for lost enjoyment of life were recoverable under the Federal Tort Claims Act. Justice Thomas's opinion for the Court explained that punitive damages are designed to punish, whereas the award to Molzof was to compensate for the harms suffered.

Recovery for Negligence

The act creates liability for the negligence of government employees. Recovery cannot be had on a theory of strict liability. The Supreme Court has expressly declared that the "statute requires a negligent act."[63] For example, in *Laird v. Nelms,* the plaintiffs sued the government for the injuries they suffered as a result of sonic booms caused by military planes. No negligence was alleged in either the planning or the conduct of the flights.[64] The Supreme Court denied liability, concluding that negligence is a prerequisite to recovery under the Federal Tort Claims Act.

Exception for Intentional Torts

The act states 13 exceptions where the United States may not be sued for tort liability. Several are of major significance in limiting the scope of the act. Of particular significance is an exemption of liability for the United States for most intentional torts. The act states that the federal courts are denied jurisdiction over "[a]ny claim arising out of assault, battery, false imprisonment, false arrest, malicious prosecution, abuse of process, libel, slander, misrepresentation, deceit or interference with contract rights."[65] Not all intentional torts are exempted; liability is possible for some, such as trespass and conversion.[66]

Most important, the act was amended in 1974 to permit recovery against the United States for assault, battery, false imprisonment, false arrest, abuse of process, or malicious prosecution *committed by federal law enforcement officers.*[67] The amendment was adopted in response to many instances of illegal behavior, especially by federal narcotics agents, and the injustice of injured individuals being unable to receive

[62] 502 U.S. 711 (1992).

[63] Dalehite v. United States, 346 U.S. 15, 45 (1953).

[64] 406 U.S. 797 (1972).

[65] 28 U.S.C. §2680(h). *See, e.g.,* Wilson v. United States, 959 F.2d 12 (2d Cir. 1992) (applying the intentional torts exception to bar a suit against parole employees for false imprisonment, abuse of process, and malicious prosecution).

[66] Davis, *supra* note 5, at 29.

[67] 88 Stat. 50 (1974); 28 U.S.C. §2680(h).

compensation for their losses.[68] The Court has held that this exception allowing suits for intentional wrongs of law enforcement is not limited to investigative acts. In *Millbrook v. United States,* the Court unanimously ruled that a prisoner who was sexually assaulted by corrections officials while in custody could sue under the FTCA.[69] The Court concluded: "[T]he waiver effected by the law enforcement proviso extends to acts or omissions of law enforcement officers that arise within the scope of their employment, regardless of whether the officers are engaged in investigative or law enforcement activity, or are executing a search, seizing evidence, or making an arrest."[70]

The exemption of intentional torts cannot, however, be overcome by alleging negligent failure to adequately supervise the personnel responsible for the wrong. Commentators had suggested that for intentional torts where suit against the United States was not possible, recovery could be obtained by suing for the negligence of the superiors of the employee who committed the tort.[71] The Supreme Court expressly rejected this view in *United States v. Shearer.*[72] The issue was whether the survivor of a serviceman who was murdered by another serviceman could recover from the government under the Federal Tort Claims Act for negligently failing to prevent the murder. Apart from its discussion of the government's immunity to suits arising from military service,[73] the Court held that the act precluded government liability for a supervisor's failure to prevent harms caused by a subordinate.[74]

But the United States may be held liable for the actions of individual employees who were not in supervisory capacities and who were negligent in failing to prevent an assault and battery. In *United States v. Sheridan,* the Court held that the government may be held liable when federal officers negligently permit a foreseeable assault and battery to occur.[75] In *Sheridan,* several naval corpsmen knew that a fellow corpsman was drunk and armed with a rifle but did not stop him or inform anyone about him. The corpsman shot and injured someone, and a suit was filed alleging negligence on the part of the individuals who did not act to prevent the harm from occurring. The Supreme Court concluded that the United States could be held liable for the corpsmen's negligence, even though the underlying cause of action involved an assault and battery. Unlike *Shearer,* in *Sheridan* there was no claim of a negligent failure to supervise.[76]

[68] S. Rep. No. 588, 93d Cong., 2d Sess. 3 (1973), *reprinted in* 1974 U.S. Code Cong. & Admin. News 2789, 2791.

[69] 569 U.S. 50 (2013).

[70] *Id.* at 1446.

[71] Davis, *supra* note 5, at 29.

[72] 473 U.S. 52 (1985).

[73] *See* discussion at text accompanying notes 104-109, *infra* (discussing the government's immunity for injuries incurred by soldiers).

[74] 473 U.S. at 57.

[75] 487 U.S. 392 (1988). *See also* Sandoval v. United States, 980 F.2d 1057 (5th Cir. 1993) ("Government may be held liable for negligently failing to prevent the intentional tort of a non-employee under its supervision.").

[76] 487 U.S. at 396-397.

Discretionary Functions Exception

A second major exception to the act is for "discretionary functions" of government employees. Specifically, the Federal Tort Claims Act provides an exemption to liability for claims "based upon the exercise or performance or the failure to exercise or perform a discretionary function or duty on the part of a federal agency or an employee of the Government, whether or not the discretion involved be abused."[77] This exception reflects, in part, a desire to prevent the government from being held liable for errors in making policy or formulating laws.[78] The act focuses on creating liability for the tortious conduct of government employees; it is not meant to provide a basis for judicial review of government policies.[79]

The difficulty in applying this exception is in determining what constitutes a discretionary function. The Supreme Court has attempted in several cases to formulate a distinction between, on the one hand, policy or planning activities for which no liability is permitted and, on the other, operational activities, for which liability is allowed. Still, the line is often difficult to draw.

The first major case under this exception was *Dalehite v. United States.*[80] A large cargo ship loaded with fertilizer manufactured by the federal government exploded, killing 500 people, injuring more than 3,000, and causing millions of dollars of property damage. The district court found the United States negligent in many respects, but the Supreme Court reversed based on the discretionary functions exception to the Federal Tort Claims Act. The Court stated that the "decisions held culpable were all responsibly made at a planning rather than operational level."[81]

Subsequently, the Supreme Court reiterated this distinction in *Indian Towing Co. v. United States.*[82] The United States was sued for damage caused to a ship by the Coast Guard's negligent maintenance of a lighthouse. The Court held that the discretionary functions exception was inapplicable because the government was sued not for its policy decision to maintain lighthouses, but for its negligent performance of this task. The Court concluded: "The Coast Guard need not undertake the lighthouse service. But once it exercised its discretion to operate a light . . . and engendered reliance on the guidance afforded by the light, it was obligated to use due care to make certain that the light was kept in good working order."[83]

In contrast, the Supreme Court refused to allow a suit against the United States for negligence by the Federal Aviation Administration in implementing a system of

[77] 28 U.S.C. §2680(a).

[78] Davis, *supra* note 5, at 65.

[79] Also, the Administrative Procedure Act limits judicial review of matters committed to agency discretion. The discretionary functions exception is meant to prevent review of such unreviewable matters through tort suits. *Id.*

[80] 346 U.S. 15 (1953).

[81] *Id.* at 42.

[82] 350 U.S. 61 (1955).

[83] *Id.* at 69. *See also* Rayonier, Inc. v. United States, 352 U.S. 315 (1957) (liability allowed for negligent failure of the forest service in fighting a fire).

spot-checking planes for compliance with federal safety standards.[84] The Court held that the creation and implementation of a system for compliance review is a discretionary activity and that judicial intervention in such decision making through private tort suits would require the court to second-guess the political, social, and economic judgments of an agency exercising its regulatory functions.[85]

Emphasis on Judgment or Choice

Two cases have clarified the discretionary functions exception. In *Berkovitz v. United States*, the Supreme Court held that the discretionary functions exception was inapplicable to a claim that the government had violated federal laws regarding the inspection and approval of polio vaccines.[86] The Court again explained that "conduct cannot be discretionary unless it involves an element of judgment or choice. . . . The exception, properly construed, therefore protects only governmental actions and decisions based on considerations of public policy."[87] The Court expressly rejected the argument that the United States was immune for all acts arising out of federal regulatory programs. The Court said that the plaintiff's claims were directed at government action that allegedly involved no discretion—the release of vaccines that did not meet federal safety standards—and unanimously held that liability would be permissible.[88]

In *United States v. Gaubert*, the Supreme Court applied the discretionary functions exception to prevent a suit against the United States for the negligence of federal regulators of a bankrupt savings and loan.[89] A shareholder of an insolvent savings and loan brought an action under the Federal Tort Claims Act contending that there had been negligent supervision of directors and officers by federal regulators.

The Supreme Court held that the discretionary functions exception "covers only acts that are discretionary in nature, acts that involve an element of judgment or choice."[90] The Court concluded that overseeing the day-to-day operations of savings and loan establishments "regularly require[s] judgment as to which of a range of permissible courses is the wisest. Discretionary conduct is not confined to the policy or planning level."[91]

Gaubert is potentially an expansion of the discretionary functions exception because it holds that any decisions involving "judgment" or "choice" are included, regardless of the decision maker involved. A large number of decisions, if not most, involve some choices.

[84] United States v. S.A. Empresa de Viacao Aerea Rio Grandense, 467 U.S. 797 (1984); *see also* United States v. Olson, 546 U.S. 43 (2005) (holding that the liability for the United States could not be based on state law rules in claims brought for the alleged negligence of mine inspectors).

[85] *Id.*

[86] 486 U.S. 531 (1988).

[87] *Id.* at 536.

[88] *Id.* at 531.

[89] 499 U.S. 315 (1991).

[90] *Id.* at 322.

[91] *Id.*

Together *Berkovitz* and *Gaubert* establish a two-part test for the discretionary functions exception. First, the government action must involve an element of judgment or choice for the exception to apply. Second, the judgment or choice involved must be based on considerations of public policy.

Lower courts struggle with the Court's distinction between planning, for which there is no liability, and operations, for which recovery is allowed.[92] Although obvious examples of each category exist, many situations can be characterized as either planning or operations. Professor Kenneth Culp Davis suggests that the distinction might be clarified by highlighting the difference between those "who make law or governmental policy and those who do not."[93] Immunity would exist only for the discretionary decisions of the former.

No Liability for Implementation of Statutes or Regulations

Yet another important exception to the Federal Tort Claims Act is for acts or omissions of government employees "exercising due care in the execution of a statute or regulation, whether or not such statute or regulation be valid."[94] The effect of this provision is to prevent liability arising from unconstitutional statutes or regulations. The Court has explained this provision as reflecting the intent that the constitutionality of legislation or the legality of a regulation should not be tested through a tort suit.[95] Yet policy questions arise as to whether the government should avoid liability for its unconstitutional acts. In fact, generally, the Federal Tort Claims Act does not allow recovery against the United States for unconstitutional actions of government officers unless they also constitute a tort. The Supreme Court, however, has held that individual officers may be sued for constitutional violations through *Bivens* causes of action.[96] Of course, recovery from the officer requires overcoming the officer's absolute or qualified immunity to suit.[97]

[92] *See, e.g.*, Evans v. United States, 876 F.3d 375, 384 (1st Cir. 2017) (holding tree removal on private property to combat beetle infestation without owner's permission was part of policy determination); Rinaldi v. United States, 904 F.3d 257, 274 (3d Cir. 2018) (Bureau of Prisons housing and cellmate assignments are "of the kind that the discretionary function exception was designed to shield"); Seaside Farm, Inc. v. United States, 842 F.3d 853, 860 (4th Cir. 2016) (FDA's decision to issue a contamination warning that devalued plaintiff's crop covered by exception); Spotts v. United States, 613 F.3d 559, 572 (5th Cir. 2010) (decision not to evacuate high-security inmates from prison damaged by Hurricane Rita, leaving them without electricity or potable water for extended period of time, was policy decision protected by exception); Anestis v. United States, 749 F.3d 520, 529 (6th Cir. 2014) (exception did not apply because VA policies requiring personnel to provide care to person in "emergency state" regardless of veteran's status as enrollee, or even as a veteran, were mandatory); Milligan v. United States, 670 F.3d 686, 695 (6th Cir. 2012) (exception applied because police procedures did not mandate officer have copy of warrant while executing an arrest and identification of the arrestee was rooted in policy considerations); Compart's Boar Store, Inc. v. United States, 829 F.3d 600, 605 (8th Cir. 2016) (testing of pigs destined for China implicated policy analysis even though some provisions of policy were mandatory, and action remained discretionary because judgment or choice involved).

[93] Davis, *supra* note 5, at 73.

[94] 28 U.S.C. §2680.

[95] Dalehite v. United States, 346 U.S. at 27.

[96] Suits against individual federal officers are discussed in §9.1, *supra.*

[97] The immunities of individual officers are discussed in §8.6, *supra.*

Other Exceptions

The other exceptions to the Federal Tort Claims Act can be more briefly stated. Suits may not be brought against the United States for negligence by the postal service in the delivery of the mails or for claims arising from the collection of customs taxes or duties.[98] Nor may suits be brought for admiralty matters, for claims arising from the Trading with the Enemy Act of 1917, for quarantines imposed by the United States, or for claims against the Tennessee Valley Authority or the Panama Canal Company.[99] Also prevented are suits against the United States for the fiscal operations of the Treasury Department in regulating the monetary system or against federal land or credit banks.[100] The United States is not liable for any claim arising in a foreign country.[101] The Supreme Court applied this exception and ruled that the act does not allow suits for claims arising in Antarctica, "a sovereignless region without civil tort law of its own."[102] Finally, in an exception substantially enlarged by the judiciary and discussed in detail below, liability is precluded for any claims arising out of military combat.[103]

Exception for Injuries Arising from Military Service

Although a strong argument can be made that these 13 exceptions specified in the act should be exclusive, the judiciary has created an additional extremely important limitation on United States liability under the Federal Tort Claims Act. Specifically, the federal government may not be sued for injuries suffered by members of the armed services arising from activities incident to military service. The act creates exemptions for injuries suffered in foreign countries or in the course of combat. The Supreme Court, however, has gone much further and created a broad exception for all injuries incurred by an individual while serving in the military. This exception is known as the *Feres* doctrine, a title taken from the seminal case of *Feres v. United States.*[104]

Feres involved three cases that were consolidated before the U.S. Supreme Court. One involved a serviceman who died in a barracks fire that allegedly resulted from the government's negligence. The other two cases concerned individuals who

[98] 28 U.S.C. §2680(b) (postal matters); (c) (customs). In Ali v. Federal Bureau of Prisons, 552 U.S. 214 (2008), the Supreme Court held that the language in (c)—"[a]ny claim arising in respect of the assessment or collection of any tax or customs duty, or the detention of any . . . property by any officer of customs or excise or any other law enforcement officer"—applies to the actions of *all* law enforcement officers and thus precluded a suit by a federal prisoner who claimed that officials of the Federal Bureau of Prisons lost his possessions.

[99] 28 U.S.C. §2680(d) (admiralty suits); (e) (Trading with the Enemy Act of 1917); (f) (quarantines); (l) (Tennessee Valley Authority); (m) (Panama Canal Company).

[100] *Id.* (i) (Treasury); (n) (federal land and credit banks).

[101] *Id.* (k) (foreign countries).

[102] Smith v. United States, 507 U.S. 197 (1993) (denying recovery to the spouse of an American killed while working for a construction company under contract to the National Science Foundation).

[103] 28 U.S.C. §2680(j) (combat-related claims).

[104] 340 U.S. 135 (1950).

received negligent medical treatment from military personnel while serving in the armed forces. One of the plaintiffs died as a result of alleged malpractice; the other plaintiff had surgery, during which a towel marked "Medical Department U.S. Army," measuring 30 inches by 18 inches, was left in his abdomen. The Supreme Court ruled that none of the plaintiffs could recover under the Federal Tort Claims Act, despite the absence of an applicable exception denying relief. Instead, the Court fashioned a new exception to the act, holding that "the Government is not liable . . . for injuries to servicemen where the injuries arise out of or are in the course of activity incident to service."[105]

This holding has been reaffirmed repeatedly by the Supreme Court, creating a broad immunity for the United States to suits by members of the armed services for all injuries they incur while in the military. For example, in 1987, the Supreme Court held that members of the armed forces cannot sue the United States for injuries they suffer as a result of the negligence of civilian, nonmilitary members of the government.[106] In 1985, the Court held that the *Feres* doctrine barred a suit against the United States for the off-duty, off-base murder of one soldier by another.[107] Frequently, courts have held that members of the armed forces cannot recover against the government for the malpractice of military doctors, no matter how egregious the negligence.[108] In short, the United States has complete immunity for injuries inflicted by the military, even if they are willful and wanton. Even when the U.S. Army gave LSD to unsuspecting soldiers—an action that had no relation to military service and violated international human rights accords prohibiting human experimentation—the *Feres* doctrine precluded recovery against the government and the responsible officers.[109]

Criticism of *Feres* Doctrine

Not surprisingly, the *Feres* doctrine has been sharply criticized.[110] For example, Justice Clarence Thomas has repeatedly called for reconsideration of the *Feres* doctrine.[111] In part, the criticisms have focused on the injustice of denying compensation to individuals injured while serving their country. Many lower courts have commented on the manifest injustices that are caused by the *Feres* doctrine.[112] Also, the criticisms have focused on the inappropriateness of the

[105] *Id.* at 146.

[106] United States v. Johnson, 481 U.S. 681 (1987) (suit barred by military member's survivors for death caused by alleged negligence of FAA).

[107] United States v. Shearer, 473 U.S. 52 (1985).

[108] Feres v. United States, 340 U.S. at 146; *see* Army Times, Mar. 12, 1984, at 1-2 (no recovery for man who died as a result of malpractice during simple urological surgery; no recovery for woman who suffered permanent brain damage during routine gynecological surgery).

[109] United States v. Stanley, 483 U.S. 669 (1987).

[110] *See* Jonathan Tomes, *Feres* to *Chappell* to *Stanley:* Three Strikes and Servicemembers Are Out, 25 U. Rich. L. Rev. 93 (1990); Barry Kellman, Judicial Abdication of Military Tort Accountability: But Who Is to Guard the Guards Themselves?, 1989 Duke L.J. 1597.

[111] *See, e.g.,* Justice Thomas's dissent from the denial of certiorari in Clendening v. United States, 143 S. Ct. 11 (2022); Doe v. United States, 141 S. Ct. 1498 (2021).

[112] *See, e.g.,* Ritchie v. United States, 733 F.3d 871, 879 (9th Cir. 2013) (Nelson, J., concurring) (this case reveals the questionable validity of the *Feres* doctrine), *cert. denied,* 572 U.S. 1100 (2014);

Court's adding to the exceptions enumerated in the Federal Tort Claims Act. The act specifies 13 exemptions from liability, and the Supreme Court itself declared in interpreting the Federal Tort Claims Act in another context: "There is no justification for this Court to read exemptions into the Act beyond those provided by Congress. If the Act is to be altered, that is a function for the same body that adopted it."[113] In fact, Congress specifically considered and did not include in the Federal Tort Claims Act exemptions identical to those created by the Court in *Feres*.[114]

Justifications for *Feres* Doctrine

Several justifications for the *Feres* doctrine have been offered. Interestingly, the Court's explanation has shifted over time. Originally, in *Feres*, the Court emphasized that the government could be held liable under the Federal Tort Claims Act only for activities that also are undertaken by private entities; because only the government has a military, no suits could be brought by service personnel.[115] But as explained above, the Supreme Court expressly discarded this limitation on recovery under the act, permitting suits even for activities done solely by the federal government.[116]

Additionally, the Supreme Court in *Feres* stated that it would be undesirable to make the soldier's recovery depend on state law, which may vary from state to state. The soldier's relationship with the government was said to be distinctly federal.[117] Yet this same argument was rejected when the Court considered whether federal prisoners could bring suits under the Federal Tort Claims Act.[118] The government urged that a federal prison has a uniquely federal relationship with inmates and that it would be inappropriate for recovery to vary depending on state law. The Supreme Court dismissed this concern saying that no recovery for injuries would be worse than inconsistent recovery.[119]

One other justification mentioned in the *Feres* case continues to be relied on sometimes by the Court: the Veterans Administration was intended to be the

---

O'Neill v. United States, 140 F.3d 564, 566 (3d Cir. 1998) (Becker, J., statement concerning the denial of the petition for rehearing) (describing the injustices of the *Feres* doctrine); Hinkie v. United States, 715 F.2d 96, 97 (3d Cir. 1983), *cert. denied,* 465 U.S. 1023 (1984) (speaking of the "injustice of the result" because of the *Feres* doctrine).

[113] Rayonier, Inc. v. United States, 352 U.S. at 320.

[114] Many of the bills that were introduced into Congress to create government liability for torts would have exempted recovery for injuries that occurred incident to military service. Congress consciously chose not to adopt such a provision. Brooks v. United States, 337 U.S. 49, 51-52 (1949). *See also* Note, The Cancer Spreads: Atomic Veterans Powerless in the Aftermath of Feres v. United States, 6 Cardozo L. Rev. 391, 409 (1984).

[115] 340 U.S. at 141.

[116] *See* discussion accompanying notes 43-44, *supra*; *see* Rayonier, Inc. v. United States, 352 U.S. 315 (1957); Indian Towing Co. v. United States, 350 U.S. 61 (1955).

[117] 340 U.S. at 142-143.

[118] United States v. Muniz, 374 U.S. 150 (1963).

[119] *Id.* at 162.

exclusive source of compensation for injured soldiers.[120] Yet in some cases, the Supreme Court has expressly disavowed this rationale. For example, in *Brooks v. United States,* the Supreme Court held that military personnel could receive compensation from the government for injuries received not incident to service.[121] The Court said that benefits paid under other compensation acts should be deducted from any recovery under the Federal Tort Claims Act, but that the existence of other compensation schemes was not a reason to prevent all recovery under tort suits.

Subsequent to the *Feres* decision, the Court began emphasizing a different rationale for precluding recovery for injuries received incident to military service: the need to preserve military discipline.[122] This has been the primary justification offered for the *Feres* doctrine. The military has a need for discipline and hierarchical authority that is not present in the civilian arena. The Court contends that permitting lawsuits would be destructive of military order.

Critics, however, challenge whether all lawsuits need to be precluded in order to protect military discipline. They argue, for example, that suits for medical malpractice do not undermine military discipline or risk second-guessing of military orders.[123] Furthermore, suits against civilian authorities responsible for tortious acts and resultant injuries would not adversely affect military operations.[124] Thus, some critics of the *Feres* doctrine contend that the need to preserve military discipline justifies immunity only when there is some nexus to commands or orders.[125] Defenders of the *Feres* doctrine claim that military discipline requires that the possibility of lawsuits be completely precluded; thus, they support the *Feres* doctrine's total ban on all liability.[126]

Determining What Injuries are Incident to Military Service

The primary unsettled issue in applying the doctrine involves the definition of injuries "incident to military service." It is firmly established that the *Feres* doctrine exempts only liability for injuries incident to military service. In *Brooks v. United States,* a serviceman on leave, off base, and in a private car was killed in a collision with an army truck.[127] The Supreme Court held that the injury was not incident

[120] 340 U.S. at 144; *see also* Stencel Aero Engineering Corp. v. United States, 431 U.S. 666, 671 (1977).

[121] 337 U.S. at 53 (1949). *See* Note, From *Feres* to *Stencel*: Should Military Personnel Have Access to FTCA Recovery?, 77 Mich. L. Rev. 1099, 1118 (1979).

[122] United States v. Brown, 348 U.S. 110 (1954); Stencel Aero Engineering Corp. v. United States, 431 U.S. at 671; Chappell v. Wallace, 462 U.S. 296 (1983).

[123] Barry Bennett, The *Feres* Doctrine, Discipline and the Weapons of War, 29 St. Louis U. L.J. 383, 403 (1985).

[124] United States v. Johnson, 481 U.S. 681 (1987) (suit by military member's survivors for death caused by alleged negligence of FAA barred).

[125] Bennett, *supra* note 123, at 404.

[126] *See* United States v. Johnson, 481 U.S. 681 (1987); United States v. Stanley, 483 U.S. 669 (1987).

[127] 337 U.S. 49 (1949).

to service and allowed recovery against the United States. Although *Brooks* was decided before *Feres*, the Court subsequently reaffirmed *Brooks*'s holding.

In *United States v. Brown*, a former soldier was allowed to sue the government for injuries he received from a military doctor after his discharge from the Army.[128] Although the injury was initially suffered during active service, the Court held that the post-discharge surgery "was not incident to service" and hence the suit was not prohibited by the *Feres* doctrine. Similarly, members of the family of service personnel may sue the government for injuries that the family members personally suffer, such as from malpractice by base doctors, because their injuries are not incident to their service in the military.[129] However, family members may sue for their personal injuries only; they cannot litigate as survivors for harms suffered by a member of their family who died during military service.[130]

Alternative Tests for Determining "Incident to Service"

Thus, the key to recovery against the United States is successfully claiming that the injury received was not incident to service. Some lower federal courts have used a "but for" test.[131] If the injured party was in active duty in the military and the injury occurred in a military vehicle or on a military installation, the claim is barred by *Feres*. If the injury was not suffered in this manner, the court determines if the injury would have occurred but for the victim's military status. For instance, if the soldier is exercising a privilege stemming from military service, suit would be barred. The "but for" test bars almost all recovery because courts reason that virtually any injury would not have occurred but for the person's presence and conduct, which was tied to being in the military.

Other lower courts use a "military discipline" test; service personnel are barred from suing if they were subject to military discipline at the time the injury was suffered.[132] Thus, recovery is denied if the soldier was actually acting under orders or even if orders potentially could have been given. The courts have determined that military officers in a service hospital exercise a command function over all service

[128] 348 U.S. 110 (1954).

[129] *See* Robert Rhodes, The *Feres* Doctrine After Twenty-Five Years, 18 A.F. L. Rev. 24, 35 (1976).

[130] Stencel Aero Engineering Corp. v. United States, 431 U.S. 666 (1977). However, the family cannot sue for injuries that they suffered as a result of harms incurred by the soldier. For example, a soldier's exposure to toxic chemicals or radiation that produces birth defects or cancer in an offspring cannot be the basis for the suit, even when it is brought by the child who is suffering the harm and never served in the military. *See, e.g.*, Hinkie v. United States, 715 F.2d 96 (3d Cir. 1983), *cert. denied*, 465 U.S. 1023 (1984); In re Agent Orange Prod. Liab. Litig., 506 F. Supp. 737 (E.D.N.Y. 1979), *cert. denied*, 454 U.S. 1128 (1981).

[131] *See, e.g.*, Ortiz v. United States ex rel. Evans Army Cmty. Hosp., 786 F.3d 817, 831 (10th Cir. 2015) (applying "genesis" test to find that injuries to service member were but-for cause of child's brain injury in utero and therefore barred under *Feres*); Ritchie v. United States, 733 F.3d 871, 875 (9th Cir. 2013) (barring suit based on genesis test); Minns v. United States, 155 F.3d 445, 449 (4th Cir. 1998) (adopting genesis test).

[132] *See, e.g.*, Parker v. United States, 611 F.2d 1007 (5th Cir. 1980) (allowing recovery for death occurring while soldier was leaving base).

personnel in the hospital, thus precluding all malpractice cases. Courts similarly have found that the pilot or driver of a military vehicle exercises command control over all passengers in the vehicle, preventing suits for injuries caused by the driver's negligence.

Other courts have used a "line of duty" test: Recovery is denied for all injuries incurred during the soldier's "line of duty."[133] The crucial distinction in applying this test is between work-related and non-work-related injuries. In practice, however, courts applying this test often look to whether the situation possibly involves military discipline.[134]

The lack of a clear test for determining what is incident to service produces inconsistent results among the lower courts and a great deal of uncertainty about the application of the *Feres* doctrine in particular cases. Overall, however, the conclusion is inescapable that the *Feres* doctrine precludes suits against the United States for virtually all injuries suffered by military personnel. Without a doubt, the *Feres* doctrine is one of the most important and one of the most controversial exceptions to the Federal Tort Claims Act.

§9.2.4 The Tucker Act

Creation of the Court of Claims

The U.S. government's first significant waiver of sovereign immunity occurred in 1855 when Congress enacted the Court of Claims Act. The act created the Court of Claims and gave it authority to hear all claims based upon any act of Congress or regulation of an executive department, "or for any contract, express or implied, with the government of the United States." However, the court's power was quite limited; it only could issue advisory recommendations, which Congress could follow or ignore.[135] In 1887, the Tucker Act was amended to allow the Court of Claims to make binding judgments, to permit the Court of Claims to hear suits against the United States for breach of contract, and to create concurrent jurisdiction between the district courts and courts of claims over many matters.[136]

[133] *See, e.g.,* Regan v. Starcraft Marine, LLC, 524 F.3d 627, 640-645 (5th Cir. 2008) (undertaking detailed analysis to determine whether boat accident occurred in line of duty and concluding it did not occur incident to military service for purposes of the *Feres* doctrine); Wake v. United States, 89 F.3d 53, 60 (2d Cir. 1996).

[134] Bennett, *supra* note 123, at 390. *See, e.g.,* McMahon v. Presidential Airways, Inc., 502 F.3d 1331, 1348-1354 (11th Cir. 2007) (holding derivative *Feres* immunity does not exist for military contractors primarily because *Feres*'s discipline strand does not apply in the context of private contractors); Meister v. Texas Adjutant Gen.'s Dep't, 233 F.3d 332, 338 (5th Cir. 2000) (holding *Feres* bar inapplicable because civilian employee of Texas National Guard was "not subject to military discipline or the military hierarchy" and could quit whenever she wanted).

[135] 1 Mezines, Stein & Gruff, *supra* note, at 6A-7.

[136] *Id.*

Federal Courts Improvement Act of 1982

In 1982, the Federal Courts Improvement Act of 1982 was enacted.[137] It abolished the existing Court of Claims and Court of Customs and Patent Appeals and created two new courts: a U.S. Claims Court and the U.S. Court of Appeals for the Federal Circuit. The Claims Court assumed the trial jurisdiction of the old Court of Claims and its decisions are reviewable in the Federal Circuit.

Most importantly, the Claims Court retains authority to award money damages against the U.S. government. The current law provides that "[t]he United States Claims Court shall have jurisdiction to render judgment upon any claim against the United States founded upon either the Constitution, or any Act of Congress or any regulation of an executive department, or upon any express or implied contract with the United States, or for liquidated or unliquidated damages in cases not sounding in tort."[138]

The U.S. district courts have concurrent jurisdiction with the Claims Court for suits against the United States for recovery of any internal revenue tax alleged to have been erroneously or illegally assessed or collected.[139] Also, the district courts have concurrent jurisdiction for claims of less than $10,000 (the Claims Court has exclusive jurisdiction for cases involving greater value), except for cases covered by the Contract Disputes Act of 1978, which cannot be filed in the district courts.[140]

No Simultaneous Jurisdiction

The Supreme Court held that the Claims Court cannot exercise jurisdiction if a lawsuit is simultaneously pending in federal district court. In *Keene v. United States*, the Supreme Court held that federal law "bar[s] jurisdiction over the claim of a plaintiff who, upon filing, has an action pending in any other court 'for or in respect to' the same claim."[141]

Suits for Contracts Express or Implied in Fact

The Tucker Act grants federal courts jurisdiction for claims against the United States that are founded in "express or implied" contracts. In *Hercules, Inc. v. United States*, the Court held that this applies only to contracts that are either express or implied in fact, not to contracts that are implied in law.[142] Chemical manufacturers that produced Agent Orange—a defoliant purchased by the United States and used during the Vietnam War—sued the federal government to recover substantial litigation expenses and settlement costs incurred in tort claims by veterans

[137] Pub. L. No. 97-164, 96 Stat. 25.
[138] 28 U.S.C. §1491(a)(1).
[139] 28 U.S.C. §1346(a)(1).
[140] 28 U.S.C. §1346(a)(2).
[141] 508 U.S. 200, 208 (1993).
[142] 516 U.S. 417 (1996).

alleging injuries resulting from exposure. The manufacturers sued the government on alternative theories of contractual indemnification and warranty of specifications provided by the government.

The Supreme Court rejected these claims. The Court explained that because the contracts at issue do not contain express warranty or indemnification provisions, the plaintiffs must establish, based on the circumstances at the time of contracting, that there was an implied agreement between the parties. The Court found no such implied contract and that there is no government liability for post-performance third-party costs.

Types of Relief

The Supreme Court has held that suits against the United States for reimbursement of funds owed under a government program are not within the exclusive jurisdiction of the Claims Court under the Tucker Act.[143] In *Bowen v. Massachusetts*, the issue was whether the state of Massachusetts could challenge in federal court the federal government's denial of a claim for reimbursement. The United States contended that because money was sought, the Claims Court had exclusive jurisdiction. The Supreme Court disagreed and concluded that because the suit was for reimbursement—an equitable remedy—the district court had jurisdiction.[144]

Lower courts appear to be unanimous that the Tucker Act does not preclude federal district court suits for declaratory relief.[145] Even though the ultimate effect of a declaratory judgment might be monetary liability of the federal government, the federal court can hear the suit requesting a declaratory judgment.

The Tucker Act is clearly a waiver of sovereign immunity for suits for money damages against the United States.[146] Two important limitations exist on the ability of the Claims Court and the district courts to impose relief under the Tucker Act. First, the claims must not arise from torts. Accordingly, the primary effect of the Tucker Act is to permit suits for breach of contract to be initiated directly against the United States.

Second, the Claims Court has authority only to hear cases that primarily seek money damages. The Claims Court may not impose other remedies unless they are tied and subordinate to a monetary award.[147] There are some notable exceptions,

[143] 487 U.S. 879 (1988).

[144] *Id.* at 882.

[145] *See, e.g.,* Bay View, Inc. v. Ahtna, Inc., 105 F.3d 1281 (9th Cir. 1998); Charter Federal Sav. Bank v. O.T.S., 976 F.2d 203 (4th Cir. 1992); Southeast Kansas Community Action Program, Inc. v. Secretary of Agric. of the U.S., 967 F.2d 1452 (10th Cir. 1992).

[146] United States v. Testan, 424 U.S. 392, 399 (1976). A recent application of this is Me. Cmty. Health Options v. United States, 590 U.S. 296 (2020), where the Court concluded that §1342 of the Affordable Care Act established a money-mandating obligation, that Congress did not repeal this obligation, and that petitioners may sue the Government for damages in the Court of Federal Claims.

[147] There is authority that the Act prohibits declaratory relief for contract claims, if not *constitutional* claims. As an example, the Tenth Circuit has held that the "Tucker and Little Tucker Acts 'impliedly forbid' federal courts from ordering declaratory or injunctive relief, at least in the form of specific performance, for contract claims against the government, and that the APA thus does not

however, where the statute permits the Claims Court to award injunctive or declaratory remedies. For instance, the 1982 Federal Courts Improvement Act states that "[t]o afford complete relief on any contract claim brought before the contract is awarded, the [Claims Court] shall have exclusive jurisdiction to grant declaratory judgments and such equitable and extraordinary relief as it deems proper, including but not limited to injunctive relief."[148] Also, the Claims Court has broad authority to give complete relief to government employees, including reinstatement, placement in appropriate duty or retirement status, or correction of applicable records.[149] However, these remedies to employees can be awarded only in a case for money damages that is already within the Claims Court's jurisdiction.[150] That is, an employee could not sue in the Claims Court seeking only equitable and declaratory remedies.

Given the size of the U.S. government's business operations, the ability to sue it for breach of contract and other nontort losses is crucial. Hence, the Tucker Act remains a vital statute.

---

waive sovereign immunity for such claims." Robbins v. U.S. Bureau of Land Mgmt., 438 F.3d 1074, 1082 (10th Cir. 2006). The Tenth Circuit later cabined that holding to contract claims. *See* Normandy Apartments, Ltd. v. U.S. Dep't of Hous. & Urban Dev., 554 F.3d 1290, 1299 (10th Cir. 2009) ("we—like other circuits—have limited the application of the 'impliedly forbids' exception to the APA waiver of sovereign immunity to contract claims."). The D.C. Circuit has held that "[i]nsofar as the plaintiffs seek specific injunctive and declaratory relief . . . the government has waived its sovereign immunity under [5 U.S.C. §702]. Cobell v. Norton, 240 F.3d 1081, 1094 (D.C. Cir. 2001). But the Court of Federal Claims has expressly disagreed, noting: "The United States Court of Appeals for the District of Columbia Circuit—we think incorrectly—has nonetheless held that §§702 and 704 of the APA do not bar a suit in the district court for an equitable accounting and the award of monetary relief, though it has agreed that some forms of monetary relief are unavailable in the district court and must be sought in the Court of Federal Claims." E. Shawnee Tribe of Oklahoma v. United States, 582 F.3d 1306, 1308-1309 (Fed. Cir. 2009), *cert. granted, judgment vacated on other grounds,* 563 U.S. 971, 131 S. Ct. 2872, 179 L. Ed. 2d 1184 (2011). For a discussion of trends in this area, *see* Gregory C. Sisk, The Jurisdiction of the Court of Federal Claims and Forum Shopping in Money Claims Against the Federal Government, 88 Ind. L.J. 83, 94-100 (2013).

[148] 28 U.S.C. §1491(a)(3).

[149] 28 U.S.C. §1491(a)(2).

[150] United States v. Testan, 424 U.S. at 404.

Part III

Federal Court Review of State Court Judgments and Proceedings

Some of the most difficult questions concerning federal court jurisdiction involve the relationship between the federal and state judiciaries. The chapters that follow examine the circumstances under which federal courts are able to review the judgments and proceedings of state courts.

Chapter 10 considers the jurisdiction of the U.S. Supreme Court and especially focuses on the Court's review of decisions of the highest state court. The chapter also discusses Supreme Court review of federal court decisions.

Chapter 11 focuses on federal statutes that define the relationship between federal and state courts. Four statutes are considered: the Anti-Injunction Act, the Tax Injunction Act, the Johnson Act (which prevents federal court injunctions of state utility rate-setting proceedings), and the Civil Rights Removal Act.

Chapters 12, 13, and 14 examine a series of principles known as the abstention doctrines. These are judicially created rules defining circumstances in which federal courts should refrain from hearing and deciding cases even though all jurisdictional and justiciability requirements are met. Chapter 12 considers abstention because of unclear state law—circumstances in which federal courts abstain to allow state courts to clarify uncertain questions of state law. The chapter examines both the instances in which such abstention is appropriate and the procedures followed when such abstention occurs. Chapter 13 discusses abstention to avoid interference with pending state court proceedings. The Supreme Court has held that federal district courts may not review decisions of state courts and generally may not enjoin pending state court proceedings due to equity and comity considerations. Chapter 14 discusses abstention to prevent duplicative state and federal court proceedings. In many circumstances the same issues involving the same parties are simultaneously litigated in state and federal court. This chapter analyzes the circumstances in which federal courts should abstain to avoid duplicative litigation.

Finally, Chapter 15 discusses federal court habeas corpus relief. Federal courts have the authority to grant habeas corpus to any person who is held in custody in violation of the Constitution and laws of the United States. Although the primary focus of this chapter is on federal habeas corpus review of state court criminal convictions, the chapter also examines federal court relief for federal prisoners.

Each of these chapters raises issues concerning the two themes that recur throughout this volume: separation of powers and federalism. Separation of powers issues arise when asking whether it is ever appropriate for federal courts to refuse to exercise jurisdiction granted by Congress. For example, is it a violation of separation of powers for the federal courts to abstain when jurisdiction is granted by federal statutes? Likewise, should the Supreme Court impose additional restrictions on the availability of habeas corpus beyond those contained in federal statutes?

Federalism issues arise frequently in considering the ability of federal courts to review state court judgments and proceedings. For instance, the Supreme Court repeatedly speaks, in a number of doctrinal areas, of the need to avoid friction with state judiciaries and the need to defer to state judicial proceedings. Should the promotion of harmony between federal and state courts be a major consideration in defining federal court jurisdiction? What is the appropriate degree of deference owed to the state courts? Many of the jurisdictional doctrines adopted over the past several decades, especially in the area of abstention and habeas corpus, are based on the Supreme Court's assumption that state courts are equal to federal courts in their ability and willingness to protect federal constitutional rights. The appropriateness of this assumption of parity is central to many of the doctrines discussed in the following chapters.

CHAPTER 10

U.S. Supreme Court Review

§10.1 INTRODUCTION

The primary focus of this chapter is on U.S. Supreme Court review of state court judgments and proceedings. The chapter also examines Supreme Court review of lower federal court decisions.

Specifically, §10.2 discusses the constitutional and statutory authority for Supreme Court review of state court decisions. Section 10.3 considers how cases come to the U.S. Supreme Court, considering the Court's original and appellate jurisdiction. Section 10.4 examines the final judgment rule: the principle that, in general, the Supreme Court may review only the final judgment of a state's highest court or the final judgment of a U.S. Court of Appeals. The many exceptions to the usual rule of finality are also discussed in this section. Finally, §10.5 describes the principle that the Supreme Court is prevented from reviewing state court decisions if there are independent and adequate state grounds of decision. The related though distinct question of Congress's ability to create exceptions to the Supreme Court's appellate jurisdiction is discussed in Chapter 3.

Functions of the Supreme Court

There is relatively little disagreement about the function of the Supreme Court in the American system of government, although there obviously is a great divergence of views about how the Court should carry out its tasks. Specifically, the Court serves a number of important functions. First, it serves as the authoritative voice as to the meaning of the U.S. Constitution. Long ago, Chief Justice John Marshall declared that "it is emphatically the province and duty of the judicial department to say what the law is."[1] Thus, jurisdictional rules should facilitate the ability of the Supreme Court to decide important constitutional questions through its review of state court and lower federal court rulings.

A second and related function of the Supreme Court is to ensure the supremacy of federal law. In *Cooper v. Aaron*, the Court rejected a state's attempt to disregard Supreme Court precedent, concluding that *Marbury v. Madison* established "the basic principle that the federal judiciary is supreme in the exposition of the law of the Constitution, and that principle has ever since been respected by this Court and the Country as a permanent and indispensable feature of our constitutional system."[2] Without Supreme Court review of state court decisions, states would be free to disregard federal statutes and even the Constitution. Because state court decisions generally are not reviewable in the lower federal courts, only the Supreme Court can ensure the supremacy of federal law.

Third, the Supreme Court resolves conflicting interpretations of federal law among the various state and federal courts. The Court thus serves to ensure the uniformity of federal law. Although differences in local law are an advantage of a

§10.1 [1] 5 U.S. (1 Cranch) 137, 177 (1803).
[2] Cooper v. Aaron, 358 U.S. 1, 19 (1958).

federalist system of government, it is widely believed that federal law should mean the same thing in all parts of the country.

Fourth, the Supreme Court is the definitive voice in interpreting federal statutes. There are obvious advantages to having a final resolution of difficult questions of statutory construction.

This brief description of the Supreme Court's functions reveals several things. The Court may decide only questions of federal law. The Court has no authority to decide matters of state law in reviewing the decisions of state courts. The state courts are the ultimate interpreters of state law, absent the presence of a federal issue.[3] In fact, it is firmly established that the Court will grant review only if there is a substantial federal question.[4]

Workload of the Supreme Court

Also, the many functions the Court is expected to serve, along with the volume of litigation in the United States, create the problem of how to allocate a scarce resource. Of the hundreds of thousands of proceedings in state and federal courts, the U.S. Supreme Court now hears and decides under 75 cases per year. In October Term 2023, the Supreme Court decided 59 cases with signed opinions after briefing and oral argument. This is typical of the caseload in recent years. Over the past 25 years, there has been a substantial decrease in the size of the Court's docket; during the 1980s, the Court often decided more than 150 cases per Term, whereas now the Court is hearing not even half that number.[5] Recurring questions are how the Court should select these cases to best achieve its institutional mission and how jurisdictional rules might maximize the Court's effective functioning.[6]

As discussed below, the trend over the course of American history has been to accord the Court greater discretion in choosing what cases to hear. But attempts at reform continue. For example, when the Court's docket was much larger, there was substantial attention to proposals to create a National Court of Appeals.[7] This court would occupy a place in between the current courts of appeals and the U.S. Supreme Court and, depending on the proposal, might serve to select cases for Supreme Court review or to resolve conflicts among the federal courts of appeals. Strong opposition to the creation of this new court revealed the enormous divergence of viewpoints regarding how the system should be structured to best fulfill

[3] *See* Murdock v. City of Memphis, 87 U.S. (20 Wall.) 590 (1875), discussed in §10.2, *infra*.

[4] *See, e.g.*, Zucht v. King, 260 U.S. 174 (1922); *see* discussion in §10.3, *infra*.

[5] Arthur Hellman, The Shrunken Docket of the Rehnquist Court, 1996 Sup. Ct. Rev. 403, 403.

[6] For an excellent evaluation of the Supreme Court's workload, *see* Peter S. Menell & Ryan Vaca, Revisiting and Confronting the Federal Judiciary Capacity "Crisis": Charting a Path for Federal Judiciary Reform,108 Cal. L. Rev. 789 (2020). For an earlier discussion of the functions of the Supreme Court and proposals for how it should manage its workload, *see* Samuel Estreicher & John Sexton, Redefining the Supreme Court's Role (1986).

[7] Federal Judicial Center, Report of the Study Group on the Caseload of the Supreme Court, 57 F.R.D. 573 (1972); Paul A. Freund, Why We Need the National Court of Appeals, 59 A.B.A. J. 247 (1973).

the Supreme Court's functions in the American system of government.[8] The dramatic reduction in the size of the Supreme Court's docket in the past two decades has alleviated concern over the need to reduce its workload by creating a new court.

§10.2 THE SUPREME COURT'S AUTHORITY TO REVIEW STATE COURT JUDGMENTS AND PROCEEDINGS

Section 25 of the 1789 Judiciary Act

The Constitution of the United States does not explicitly say that the Supreme Court may review the decisions of state courts. However, the Judiciary Act of 1789 provided for Supreme Court review of state court judgments. Section 25 of the act allowed the Supreme Court to review state court decisions by a writ of error to the state's highest court in several specific situations. The Act did not provide jurisdiction for all types of cases or controversies enumerated in Article III, nor did it even provide Supreme Court review of state courts in all cases involving federal questions. In general, §25 granted the Supreme Court authority to review state court decisions that ruled against federal law or federal government interests. For example, the Act granted the Court power to hear cases where the state court declared invalid a federal statute, treaty, or an act of the U.S. government or ruled against any title, right, privilege, or exemption claimed under federal law.[1] Also, §25 provided for review where the highest state court ruled in favor of a state statute or state authority when there was a challenge based on federal law.

Martin v. Hunter's Lessee

The constitutional basis for such Supreme Court review was firmly stated by the Court in several early decisions. *Martin v. Hunter's Lessee* is widely recognized as the first case to establish the Supreme Court's constitutional authority to review state court judgments.[2] In *Martin,* there were two conflicting claims to certain land within the state of Virginia. Martin claimed title to the land based on inheritance from Lord Fairfax, a British citizen who owned the property. The United States and England had entered into two treaties protecting the rights of British subjects to own land in the United States. However, Hunter claimed that Virginia had taken

[8] For criticisms of the proposal to create a National Court of Appeals, *see* Charles Black, The National Court of Appeals: An Unwise Proposal, 83 Yale L.J. 883 (1974); William Brennan, Justice Brennan Calls National Court of Appeals Proposal "Fundamentally Unnecessary and Ill Advised," 59 A.B.A. J. 835 (1973); Eugene Gressman, The National Court of Appeals: A Dissent, 59 A.B.A. J. 253 (1973). The proposal for the National Court of Appeals and criticisms of the idea are discussed in detail in §10.3, *infra.*

§10.2 [1] Act of Sept. 24, 1789, ch. 20, 1 Stat. 73, 85-87.

[2] 14 U.S. (1 Wheat.) 304 (1816).

the land before the treaties came into effect and, hence, Martin did not have a valid claim to the property.

The Virginia Court of Appeals ruled in favor of Hunter and, in essence, in favor of the state's authority to have taken and disposed of the land. The U.S. Supreme Court issued a writ of error and reversed the Virginia decision. The Supreme Court held that the federal treaty was controlling and it established Lord Fairfax's ownership and thus the validity of inheritance pursuant to his will. The Virginia Court of Appeals, however, declared that the Supreme Court lacked the authority to review state court decisions. The Virginia court stated that the "Courts of the United States, therefore, belonging to one sovereignty, cannot be appellate Courts in relation to the State Courts, which belong to a different sovereignty—and, of course, their commands or instructions impose no obligation."[3]

The U.S. Supreme Court again granted review and, in a famous opinion by Justice Joseph Story, articulated the Court's authority to review state court judgments. Chief Justice John Marshall did not participate because he and his brother had contracted to purchase a large part of the Fairfax estate that was at issue in the litigation.[4] Justice Story persuasively argued that the Constitution presumed that the Supreme Court could review state court decisions. For example, the Constitution creates a Supreme Court and gives Congress discretion whether to create lower federal courts. But if Congress chose not to establish such tribunals, then the Supreme Court would be powerless to hear any cases, except for the few fitting within its original jurisdiction, unless it could review state court rulings.[5]

Additionally, Justice Story explained the importance of Supreme Court review of state courts. Justice Story said that although he assumed that "judges of the state courts are, and always will be, of as much learning, integrity, and wisdom as those of the courts of the United States," the Constitution is based on a recognition that "state attachments, state prejudices, state jealousies, and state interests might sometimes obstruct, or control, or be supposed to obstruct or control, the regular administration of justice."[6] Furthermore, Justice Story observed that Supreme Court review is essential to ensure uniformity in the interpretation of federal law. Justice Story concluded that the very nature of the Constitution, the contemporaneous understanding of it, and many years of experience all established the Supreme Court's authority to review state court decisions.

Review of Criminal Cases

The Supreme Court has never questioned its constitutional authority to take appeals from state courts or to command state judiciaries to follow federal law. An important elaboration of the Court's power to take cases from state

[3] *Quoted in* Gerald Gunther, Constitutional Law 32 (11th ed. 1985).
[4] *Id.* at 30.
[5] 14 U.S. at 329.
[6] *Id.* at 346-347.

courts was *Cohens v. Virginia.*[7] Two brothers were convicted in Virginia state court for selling District of Columbia lottery tickets in violation of Virginia law. The defendants sought review in the U.S. Supreme Court because they claimed the Constitution prevented them from being prosecuted for selling tickets authorized by Congress. Virginia argued that the Supreme Court had no authority to review state court decisions in general, and in particular, review was not allowed in criminal cases and in cases where a state government was a party.

The Supreme Court, in an opinion by John Marshall, reaffirmed the constitutionality of §25 of the Judiciary Act and the authority of the Supreme Court to review state court judgments. The Court emphasized that state courts often could not be trusted to adequately protect federal rights because "[i]n many States the judges are dependent for office and for salary on the will of the legislature."[8] In language similar to that often heard in modern debates about whether there is parity between federal and state courts, Chief Justice Marshall stated, "When we observe the importance which [the] Constitution attaches to the independence of judges, we are the less inclined to suppose that it can have intended to leave these constitutional questions to tribunals where this independence may not exist."[9] The Court thus declared that criminal defendants could seek Supreme Court review when they claimed that their conviction violated the Constitution. Additionally, the Court held that the Eleventh Amendment did not bar Supreme Court appellate review of cases involving the state as a party because such review did not constitute a "suit" against the state.[10]

Authority for and Limits of Review

The constitutional authority for Supreme Court review of state court decisions is not open to serious question. Even the staunchest defenders of state courts recognize the need for Supreme Court review to ensure the supremacy of federal law and to provide uniform interpretations of the Constitution.

The primary limitation on the Supreme Court's constitutional authority to review state court judgments is that such review is limited to questions of federal law. This, too, is hardly surprising or controversial because the Supreme Court's authority to hear appeals from state courts is based entirely on its role in upholding and interpreting federal law. In *Murdock v. City of Memphis*, in 1875, the Supreme Court held that it could review only questions of federal law and that the decisions of the state's highest court are final on questions of state law.[11] The Court explained that §25 of the Judiciary Act was based on a belief that the Supreme Court must be available to ensure state compliance with the U.S. Constitution,

[7] 19 U.S. (6 Wheat.) 264 (1821). For an excellent discussion of Martin v. Hunter's Lessee and Cohens v. Virginia, *see* David Currie, The Constitution in the Supreme Court: The Powers of the Federal Courts, 1801-1835, at 49 U. Chi. L. Rev. 646 (1982).

[8] 19 U.S. at 386-387.

[9] *Id.* at 387.

[10] *Id.* at 407-409, 412. For a fuller discussion of the Eleventh Amendment, *see* Chapter 7, *supra.*

[11] 87 U.S. (20 Wall.) 590 (1875).

but that there was no indication that Congress intended the Court to oversee state court decisions as to state law matters. Nor from a policy perspective was there any reason for the Supreme Court to examine and decide questions of state law.

Thus, a commonsense approach emerged: the Supreme Court is the authoritative arbiter of the meaning of federal law, but state courts play that role concerning state law. The Supreme Court can review state court decisions of all federal law questions, but state court decisions regarding state law are unreviewable.

In application, however, this rule poses important problems in defining the Supreme Court's constitutional authority to review state court decisions. One issue is how the Court should handle cases posing both state and federal questions, particularly in instances where a reversal of the state court's interpretation of federal law will not change the results in the case because state law is an independent and adequate ground supporting the decision. This topic is discussed in detail in §10.5.

The issue of the Supreme Court's authority to decide state law questions, rather than remand to the state's highest court for a ruling, was at the core of *Bush v. Gore.*[12] Five justices—Chief Justice Rehnquist and Justices O'Connor, Scalia, Kennedy, and Thomas—concluded that counting uncounted votes in Florida, without preset standards, violated equal protection.[13] Justices Souter and Breyer, albeit in dissenting opinions, agreed that there were equal protection problems with counting votes without preset standards. But the Court split five to four as to the appropriate solution. The dissent argued that the case should be remanded to the Florida courts to decide how to proceed under Florida law, including the possibility of the Florida Supreme Court setting standards for the recount. The majority, in a per curiam opinion, said that *based on Florida law* the Supreme Court should end the recount.

The Court, in its per curiam opinion, said that Florida indicated that it wished to observe the December 12 date set by federal law, which created a conclusive presumption that a state's electors chosen by that date would be recognized by Congress. The Court thus ordered an end to the counting, stating:

> The Supreme Court of Florida has said that the legislature intended the State's electors to "participat[e] fully in the federal electoral process," as provided in 3 U.S.C. §5. That statute, in turn, requires that any controversy or contest that is designed to lead to a conclusive selection of electors be completed by December 12. That date is upon us, and there is no recount procedure in place under the State Supreme Court's order that comports with minimal constitutional standards.

[12] 531 U.S. 98 (2000).

[13] The per curiam opinion stated: "The problem inheres in the absence of specific standards to ensure its equal application. The formulation of uniform rules to determine intent based on these recurring circumstances is practicable and, we conclude, necessary." The Court said that this results in similar ballots being treated differently. The Court also objected to the procedures being followed in the recount: "In addition to these difficulties the actual process by which the votes were to be counted under the Florida Supreme Court's decision raises further concerns. That order did not specify who would recount the ballots. The county canvassing boards were forced to pull together ad hoc teams comprised of judges from various Circuits who had no previous training in handling and interpreting ballots. Furthermore, while others were permitted to observe, they were prohibited from objecting during the recount." *Id.* at 106.

> Because it is evident that any recount seeking to meet the December 12 date will be unconstitutional for the reasons we have discussed, we reverse the judgment of the Supreme Court of Florida ordering a recount to proceed.
>
> Seven Justices of the Court agree that there are constitutional problems with the recount ordered by the Florida Supreme Court that demand a remedy. The only disagreement is as to the remedy. Because the Florida Supreme Court has said that the Florida Legislature intended to obtain the safe-harbor benefits of 3 U.S.C. §5, Justice Breyer's proposed remedy—remanding to the Florida Supreme Court for its ordering of a constitutionally proper contest until December 18—contemplates action in violation of the Florida election code, and hence could not be part of an "appropriate" order authorized by Fla. Stat. §102.168(8) (2000).[14]

Thus, the per curiam ordered an end to the counting of votes in Florida based on its interpretation of the Florida election law.

Each of the other four dissenting justices wrote opinions and disagreed with the Supreme Court deciding the case based on a question of state law. Justice Stevens said that if the lack of standards for counting is the problem, the solution is to send the case back to Florida for the creating of standards and the subsequent counting.[15] Justice Souter's dissenting opinion, joined by the other three dissenting justices, objected to the Court hearing the case at all. Justice Souter argued that there were no significant federal issues raised and that the case should have been left to the Florida courts to resolve.[16] Justice Ginsburg's dissent argued that there was no denial of equal protection and that, in any event, the appropriate solution was to have the case sent back to Florida for the counting to continue.[17]

Finally, Justice Breyer acknowledged that there were equal protection problems with counting votes without standards, but argued that the Court was wrong in ending the counting rather than remanding the case for counting with standards. He stressed that there is nothing magical about the December 12 deadline; states could still choose their electors after that date and could be confident that Congress would recognize them. He ended his opinion forcefully: "I fear that in order to bring this agonizingly long election process to a definitive conclusion, we have not adequately attended to that necessary 'check upon our own exercise of power,' 'our own sense of self-restraint.' Justice Brandeis once said of the Court, 'The most important thing we do is not doing.' What it does today, the Court should have left undone. I would repair the damage done as best we now can, by permitting the Florida recount to continue under uniform standards."[18]

In light of the basic principle that state courts have the final say as to questions of state law, was the Court justified in ending the counting in Florida? The Court, in its per curiam opinion, said that the Florida Supreme Court had indicated that it wanted to follow the December 12 deadline set by the federal "safe harbor" statute. Because it was December 12, the Supreme Court ordered an end to the

[14] *Id.* at 111.
[15] *Id.* at 123 (Stevens, J., dissenting).
[16] *Id.* at 129 (Souter, J., dissenting).
[17] *Id.* at 135 (Ginsburg, J., dissenting).
[18] *Id.* at 159 (Breyer, J., dissenting).

counting. The dissent argued that because it was an issue of Florida state law, the Supreme Court should have remanded the case for the Florida Supreme Court to decide the content of Florida law under the unprecedented circumstances.

State Law Intertwined with Federal Issues

Another issue concerns instances in which the federal and state law questions are intertwined, such as when the federal Constitution protects a right created by state law. Under such circumstances, the Supreme Court may review state court decisions as to state law to ensure the protection of federal rights. For example, in *Indiana ex rel. Anderson v. Brand*, a teacher claimed that the local government's decision to fire her violated the Constitution's prohibition, in Article I, §10, of state impairments of the obligations of contracts.[19] The central issue in the case was whether there was a contract under state law. The Court engaged in a lengthy analysis of state law and concluded, contrary to the earlier decision of the Indiana Supreme Court, that there was a contract under Indiana law and that it was impaired by the government's action.

The question is when is the Supreme Court permitted to decide state law questions because of their integral relationship to a federal law question before the Court. The Court explained, "Even though the constitutional protection invoked be denied on non-federal grounds, it is the province of this Court to inquire whether the decision of the state court rests upon a fair or substantial basis."[20] For example, in *Standard Oil Co. of California v. Johnson*, the Supreme Court interpreted a state law taxing gasoline sales that exempted sales to the United States government and its departments.[21] The question was whether Army post exchanges fit within the statutory exemptions. The Supreme Court concluded that such exchanges are instrumentalities of the United States and, therefore, should be exempt under the California law. The Court might have based its decision directly on the Constitution, holding it unconstitutional for California to tax federal military base exchanges. Instead, the Court avoided the constitutional question by interpreting the California law to not impose such a tax.

Thus, the general rule that the Supreme Court may not review state court decisions on state law grounds has a narrow exception where the state law issue is integrally tied to a federal question. Such cases are relatively rare, but still constitute an important exception to the usual rule articulated in *Murdock v. City of Memphis* limiting Supreme Court review to federal law issues.

Changes in Statutory Authority and Methods of Review

Although the Court's constitutional authority to review state court decisions has not been altered since the earliest days of American history, there have been modifications in its statutory authority. As discussed below, for example, in 1914

[19] 303 U.S. 95 (1938).

[20] Broad River Power Co. v. South Carolina, 281 U.S. 537, 540 (1930).

[21] 316 U.S. 481 (1942).

the Supreme Court's jurisdiction to review state court decisions was expanded to allow the Court to hear cases where the state's highest court invalidated a state law on federal law grounds or upheld a federal law.[22]

The method of Supreme Court review was modified early in this century. Whereas previously cases came to the Supreme Court by writ of error, the Judiciary Act was revised to provide that cases come to the Supreme Court by appeal or by certiorari. Now virtually all cases come to the Supreme Court by writ of certiorari. The mechanisms for Supreme Court review are discussed in detail in the next section.

§10.3 HOW CASES COME TO THE U.S. SUPREME COURT

The three primary ways that cases come to the Supreme Court are (1) pursuant to its original jurisdiction, (2) on review of a final judgment of a decision of the highest court of a state, and (3) on review of a final judgment of a U.S. Court of Appeals. Subsection 10.3.1 examines the Court's original jurisdiction. The distinction between appeal and certiorari, until a decade ago crucial to the procedures for review of both state courts and lower federal courts, is discussed in §10.3.2. Subsections 10.3.3 and 10.3.4 discuss, respectively, Supreme Court review of judgments of the state's highest court and of federal courts of appeals. Subsection 10.3.5 considers the Supreme Court's emergency docket, often referred to as the "shadow docket." Finally, §10.3.6 examines proposals to create an intermediate court between the Supreme Court and the U.S. Court of Appeals, such as a National Court of Appeals.

§10.3.1 The Supreme Court's Original Jurisdiction

Article III's Authorization for Original Jurisdiction

Article III of the Constitution describes the Supreme Court's jurisdiction both in terms of original jurisdiction—cases filed initially in the Supreme Court—and appellate jurisdiction. In defining the Court's original jurisdiction, Article III provides that the Supreme Court shall have original jurisdiction "in all cases affecting ambassadors, other public ministers and consuls, and those in which the State shall be a party." A central question concerns the relationship between this provision and congressional statutes defining the Supreme Court's jurisdiction.

[22] Act of Dec. 23, 1914, ch. 2, 38 Stat. 790.

Congress's Authority to Change Original Jurisdiction

The Supreme Court has interpreted Article III as creating a ceiling on the Court's original jurisdiction. In *Marbury v. Madison*, the Supreme Court held that the categories of original jurisdiction enumerated in Article III are exhaustive; it is unconstitutional for Congress to expand the Supreme Court's original jurisdiction beyond the Constitution's text.[1] In *Marbury*, the Court read the Judiciary Act of 1789 as permitting original jurisdiction in cases in which a writ of mandamus was sought against federal government officers. The Supreme Court held this portion of the Judiciary Act unconstitutional because Article III defines the extent of the Court's original jurisdiction. As such, the Court dismissed Marbury's suit for a writ of mandamus because it held that it lacked constitutional authority to hear such a suit as part of its original jurisdiction.

Although it long has been established that Congress cannot add to the Court's original jurisdiction, an unresolved issue is whether Congress can subtract from it. Can Congress deny original jurisdiction simply by refusing to enact statutes providing for it? Or may the Supreme Court hear cases fitting within the enumerated categories of original jurisdiction even in the absence of a jurisdictional statute? The latter seems to be the view endorsed by the Court in most of its opinions. On many occasions, the Court has expressed the position that Article III directly vests the Supreme Court with authority to hear cases.[2] Thus, the jurisdictional statutes are superfluous in defining the Court's original jurisdiction: Congress cannot add or subtract from the original jurisdiction.[3] Additions are impermissible under *Marbury v. Madison*, and subtractions are irrelevant because the Court can hear the cases despite the absence of statutory authority.

However, it is clearly established that Congress may establish concurrent jurisdiction in lower federal courts or in state judiciaries for questions arising within the Court's original jurisdiction. In *Marbury v. Madison*, the Court implied that the categories of appellate and original jurisdiction were completely distinct and that the Court could not, for example, exercise appellate review over cases falling within the categories of original jurisdiction. The Court, however, quickly repudiated this position and stated that the Court could hear appeals in cases that also fit within its original jurisdiction.[4] This opened the door for Congress to vest concurrent jurisdiction over matters within the original jurisdiction in the state and lower federal courts.[5] Such concurrent jurisdiction is desirable because, in the vast majority of cases, it is preferable for the Court to hear cases on appeal and not serve as a trial court. The Supreme Court lacks the time and

§10.3 [1] 5 U.S. (1 Cranch) 137 (1803).

[2] *See, e.g.*, Arizona v. California, 373 U.S. 546, 564 (1963); Wisconsin v. Pelican Ins. Co., 127 U.S. 265, 300 (1888); Kentucky v. Dennison, 65 U.S. (24 How.) 66, 98 (1860).

[3] For a more detailed argument that Congress cannot limit the Court's original jurisdiction, *see* Richard Fallon, John F. Manning, Daniel Meltzer & David Shapiro, Hart & Wechsler's The Federal Courts and the Federal System 267-271 (7th ed. 2015).

[4] *See* Cohens v. Virginia, 19 U.S. (6 Wheat.) 264, 392-405 (1821).

[5] *See, e.g.*, California v. Arizona, 440 U.S. 59 (1979); Illinois v. City of Milwaukee, 406 U.S. 91, 100-101 (1972); Ohio ex rel. Popovici v. Agler, 280 U.S. 379 (1930).

resources to function effectively as a court of original jurisdiction. Compelling the Court to hear all cases fitting within its original jurisdiction would impose a substantial burden on it.[6]

Where such concurrent jurisdiction exists, the Court has discretion to refuse to hear cases within its original jurisdiction and instead to require that the matters be brought first in a federal or state trial court.[7] This, too, is based on a recognition of the difficulty in having the U.S. Supreme Court function as a court of original jurisdiction. The Court simply is not equipped to sit effectively as a trial court. In fact, in the relatively rare instances that the Court's original jurisdiction is invoked and the Court does not remand the matter to a lower court, the Court appoints special masters to conduct any necessary fact-finding procedures.

28 U.S.C. §1251

The current statute providing for the original jurisdiction of the U.S. Supreme Court reflects these principles and policy considerations. Specifically, 28 U.S.C. §1251 states:

> (a) The Supreme Court shall have original and exclusive jurisdiction of all controversies between two or more states;
> (b) The Supreme Court shall have original but not exclusive jurisdiction of:
> (1) All actions or proceedings to which the ambassadors, other public ministers or consuls, or vice consuls of foreign states are involved;
> (2) All controversies between the United States and a State;
> (3) All actions or proceedings by a State against citizens of another State or against aliens.[8]

Thus, the only instance in which the Supreme Court must exercise original jurisdiction is for suits between two states; in all other situations, the Court's original jurisdiction is concurrent with the jurisdiction of other courts. As such, it is hardly surprising that virtually all cases that are decided as matters of original jurisdiction arise from actions between two or more states.[9] Even these cases are relatively rare; there are not more than a few original jurisdiction cases on the Court's docket in any year.[10]

[6] *See, e.g.,* Ames v. Kansas ex rel. Johnston, 111 U.S. 449, 464 (1884) (allowing concurrent jurisdiction for suits by ambassadors, and expressing the view that forcing the Court to hear such cases would impose a "burden").

[7] *See, e.g.,* Ohio v. Wyandotte Chemicals Corp., 401 U.S. 493, 499 (1971); Georgia v. Pennsylvania R.R., 324 U.S. 439, 464 (1945); Massachusetts v. Missouri, 308 U.S. 1, 44 (1939).

[8] 28 U.S.C. §1251.

[9] 17 Charles A. Wright, Arthur R. Miller & Edward H. Cooper, Federal Practice and Procedure 192 (1988).

[10] *Id.* at 167 n.1.

Suits Between State Governments

There are compelling reasons for vesting in the Supreme Court original and exclusive jurisdiction over cases involving two or more states. Without a tribunal to resolve their differences, states might resort to armed conflicts with one another or other forms of coercive behavior. Moreover, no lower court is likely to be perceived as sufficiently independent to handle the matter. Any state's own courts would be regarded as too parochial. Lower federal courts sit within states and federal judges are likely to have been drawn from that state's bar. The Supreme Court alone is in a position to resolve disputes between state governments. Nonetheless, even for suits between states where the Court has original and exclusive jurisdiction, the Court has stated that it has discretion to refuse to hear such cases if necessary to ensure "the most effective functioning of this Court within the overall federal system."[11] For example, if no important federal interest is involved—such as in one case involving a breach of contract suit arising from one state university's failure to play a football game against another state university—the Court has exercised its discretion to refuse to hear the matter.[12]

Suits between states before the Supreme Court most frequently have involved boundary disputes.[13] In fact, in the *Federalist Papers*, Alexander Hamilton indicated that the purpose of vesting original jurisdiction in the Supreme Court for suits between states was to resolve likely boundary disputes.[14] Also, a number of original jurisdiction cases have concerned water rights, including issues such as the allocation of water from interstate rivers and control over pollution by one of the states.[15] Another source of such cases has been disputes arising from one state's alleged discrimination against another state in matters of commerce, taxation, or resource allocation.[16] Additionally, many of the original jurisdiction cases have involved commercial matters, such as breach of contract suits between the states or litigation concerning enforcement of one state's financial obligations to another.[17]

The Eleventh Amendment does not bar a state from suing another state before the U.S. Supreme Court.[18] The Supreme Court has reasoned that states consented to such suits when they joined the union.[19] Of course, it could be argued that the

[11] Texas v. New Mexico, 462 U.S. 554, 570 (1983).

[12] California v. West Virginia, 454 U.S. 1027 (1981).

[13] *See, e.g.,* North Dakota v. Minnesota, 263 U.S. 583 (1924); Rhode Island v. Massachusetts, 37 U.S. (12 Pet.) 657, 723-725 (1838). The power of the Supreme Court to fashion federal common law to resolve disputes among the states is discussed in §6.2.5, *supra.*

[14] The Federalist No. 80, at 477-478 (C. Rossiter ed. 1961).

[15] Colorado v. New Mexico, 467 U.S. 310 (1984); Ohio v. Kentucky, 410 U.S. 641 (1973); Nebraska v. Wyoming, 325 U.S. 589 (1945); Missouri v. Illinois, 180 U.S. 208 (1901).

[16] *See, e.g.,* Maryland v. Louisiana, 451 U.S. 725 (1981) (Louisiana tax on offshore natural gas passed on to non-Louisiana customers); Pennsylvania v. West Virginia, 262 U.S. 553 (1923) (West Virginia law prohibiting transportation of natural gas to other states).

[17] *See, e.g.,* Kentucky v. Indiana, 281 U.S. 163 (1930) (breach of contract); South Dakota v. North Carolina, 192 U.S. 286 (1904) (enforce financial obligation of state bonds).

[18] *See, e.g.,* Kansas v. Colorado, 533 U.S. 1, 8 (2001); Principality of Monaco v. Mississippi, 292 U.S. 313, 328-329 (1934); Virginia v. West Virginia, 206 U.S. 290, 319 (1907).

[19] *See, e.g.,* Virginia v. West Virginia, 206 U.S. 290, 319 (1907).

states consented to all suits in federal court based on the Constitution and federal laws when they ratified the Constitution.[20] Although the Court has rejected this expansive exception to the Eleventh Amendment, it has recognized the need for states to be able to sue other states and hence held that the Eleventh Amendment is no bar to suits between states filed in the Supreme Court.

The authority for original jurisdiction for suits between states requires that the parties be the states themselves. The Supreme Court explained that for it to exercise original jurisdiction, "it must appear that the complaining State has suffered a wrong through the action of the other State, furnishing ground for judicial redress, or is asserting a right against the other State which is susceptible of judicial enforcement according to the accepted principles of the common law or equity systems of jurisprudence."[21] For example, in *Kansas v. Colorado,* the Court held that a state may not sue just to present the claims of its citizens who could not sue because of the Eleventh Amendment.[22] But the Court said that when the state itself has suffered an injury, the Eleventh Amendment does not bar a suit in which the damages are measured, in part, by the loss to the individual citizens.

Political subdivisions of states, such as local governments, cannot invoke this basis for original jurisdiction.[23] Nor may a state invoke the Supreme Court's original jurisdiction where it is not the real party in interest, but instead is suing on behalf of particular citizens who have been injured.[24] However, a state "may act as the representative of its citizens in original actions where the injury alleged affects the general population of a State in a substantial way."[25] Additionally, of course, the state may sue when its own interests are at stake in the litigation.

Original But Concurrent Jurisdiction

As mentioned above, 28 U.S.C. §1251 creates original but not exclusive jurisdiction over three categories of cases. First, the Supreme Court can exercise original jurisdiction over "actions or proceedings to which ambassadors, other public ministers, consuls, or vice consuls of foreign states are parties."[26] This provision almost never has been invoked. In over 200 years, there have been only three cases in which Supreme Court jurisdiction was based on this authority.[27] Such cases generally are brought in federal district courts that have concurrent jurisdiction.

[20] Some have endorsed this view. *See, e.g.,* Martha A. Field, The Eleventh Amendment and Other Sovereign Immunity Doctrines (parts I and II), 126 U. Pa. L. Rev. 515, 538-539, 1261-1278 (1977); *see* discussion of this theory in §7.3, *supra.*

[21] Wyoming v. Oklahoma, 502 U.S. 437, 447 (1992), *quoting* Maryland v. Louisiana, 451 U.S. 725, 735-736 (1981).

[22] 533 U.S. 1, 8 (2001).

[23] Illinois v. City of Milwaukee, 406 U.S. 91, 94-98 (1972).

[24] *See, e.g.,* Maryland v. Louisiana, 451 U.S. 725, 737 (1981).

[25] *Id. See also* Georgia v. Tennessee Copper Co., 206 U.S. 230 (1907); Missouri v. Illinois & the Sanitary Dist. of Chicago, 200 U.S. 496 (1906).

[26] 28 U.S.C. §1251(b)(1).

[27] *See* Ex parte Gruber, 269 U.S. 302 (1925); Casey v. Galli, 94 U.S. 673 (1877); Jones v. Le Tombe, 3 U.S. (3 Dall.) 384 (1798).

The state courts, however, are denied jurisdiction to hear civil actions against consuls or vice consuls of foreign states or members of a diplomatic mission or their families.[28]

Second, the Supreme Court has original but not exclusive jurisdiction for "[a]ll controversies between the United States and a State."[29] Article III states that the Supreme Court has original jurisdiction over cases to which the state shall be a party. In 1948, Congress revised §1251 to specify that cases between the United States and a state government may be brought within the Court's original jurisdiction. The lower federal courts have concurrent jurisdiction over such suits,[30] and the Court generally has been reluctant to hear such suits under its original jurisdiction because of the existence of an alternative forum that is better suited to serve as a trial court.[31] Nonetheless, there have been suits before the Supreme Court as part of its original jurisdiction involving both the United States suing state governments and states suing the federal government.[32]

Finally, §1251 provides for original but not exclusive jurisdiction in the Supreme Court for "[a]ll actions or proceedings by a State against the citizens of another State or against aliens."[33] Although Article III vests original jurisdiction in the Supreme Court for all suits in which the state is a party, the Eleventh Amendment bars suits against a state without its consent. Generally, the Eleventh Amendment does not apply in the U.S. Supreme Court. For example, the Eleventh Amendment does not bar the Court from hearing appeals from state courts in which the state is a party; nor does the Eleventh Amendment preclude a state government from suing another state in the Supreme Court.[34] However, the Eleventh Amendment does apply in the Supreme Court when the state is sued, as part of the Court's original jurisdiction, by individual citizens, aliens, or foreign governments.[35]

Thus, the Court's original jurisdiction pursuant to §1251(b)(3) involves suits in which the state government is the plaintiff. Again, the Court will hear such cases only if the state is the real party in interest, such as if it is suing to protect its own interests or the welfare of its general population. The Court will not permit the state to sue on behalf of particular individuals.[36] Also, as described above, the Court's jurisdiction over such suits is concurrent with federal district courts and the Supreme Court will refuse to hear suits brought by a state where it believes that the matter would be better handled by remand to a trial court. For instance, in

[28] 28 U.S.C. §1351.

[29] 28 U.S.C. §1251(b)(2).

[30] 28 U.S.C. §§1345, 1346 (jurisdiction to hear cases where the United States is plaintiff or defendant).

[31] *See, e.g.,* California v. Nevada, 447 U.S. 125, 133 (1980).

[32] *See, e.g.,* Oregon v. Mitchell, 400 U.S. 112 (1970); United States v. Louisiana, 339 U.S. 699 (1950); United States v. California, 332 U.S. 19 (1947).

[33] 28 U.S.C. §1251(b)(3).

[34] *See, e.g.,* Maine v. Thiboutot, 448 U.S. 1, 9 n.7 (1980); Nevada v. Hall, 440 U.S. 410, 418-421 (1979).

[35] The Eleventh Amendment is discussed in detail in Chapter 7, *supra.*

[36] *See, e.g.,* Oklahoma ex rel. Johnson v. Cook, 304 U.S. 387 (1938); New Hampshire v. Louisiana, 108 U.S. 76 (1883). The standing of governmental entities to sue on behalf of their citizens is discussed in §2.3.7, *supra.*

Ohio v. Wyandotte Chemicals Corp., the Court refused to hear a case brought by the state of Ohio to enjoin pollution of rivers that flow into Lake Erie.[37] Although the case was within the Court's original jurisdiction, the Court felt that because of the factual complexity of the case it would be better dealt with in a trial court.

Thus, the original jurisdiction of the Supreme Court is a small part of the Court's workload. In general, a party wishing to invoke it must demonstrate not only that the Court has the legal authority to hear the matter in its original jurisdiction but also that there are important reasons why the Court should hear the case in that fashion.[38]

§10.3.2 The Distinction Between Appeal and Certiorari

The statutes defining the Supreme Court's jurisdiction draw a distinction between "appeal" and "certiorari" as vehicles for appellate review of the decisions of state and lower federal courts. Where the statute provides for "appeal" to the Supreme Court, the Court is obligated to take and decide the case when appellate review is requested. Where the state provides for review by "writ of certiorari," the Court has complete discretion whether to hear the matter; the Court takes the case if there are four votes to grant certiorari. Effective September 25, 1988, the distinction between appeal and certiorari as a vehicle for Supreme Court review was virtually entirely eliminated. Now almost all cases come to the Supreme Court by writ of certiorari.[39]

History of the Appeal/Certiorari Distinction

The distinction has its origins in the late nineteenth and early twentieth centuries. Under the Judiciary Act of 1789, review was available in the Supreme Court by writ of error and the Court was obligated to hear all such cases. In 1891, the Court's jurisdiction was modified when the U.S. Circuit Courts of Appeals were created. The Supreme Court was given authority to review decisions from these courts in diversity, admiralty, patent, and revenue cases by writ of certiorari. Unlike the writ of error, where jurisdiction was mandatory, the writ of certiorari was completely discretionary with the Court. In 1914, the Supreme Court was given authority for the first time to review state court decisions upholding a federal statute or invalidating a state statute. Review in such cases also was discretionary with the Court and was by writ of certiorari.

[37] 401 U.S. 493 (1971). The ability of the federal courts to fashion federal common law to resolve disputes over interstate waters is discussed in §6.2.5, *supra.*

[38] For a discussion of the procedural rules for original jurisdiction cases, *see* Robert L. Stern, Eugene Gressman, Stephen M. Shapiro & Kenneth S. Geller, Supreme Court Practice 549-566 (9th ed. 2007). For a discussion of original jurisdiction in state supreme courts, and how it differs from the United States Supreme Court, *see* Zachary D. Clopton, Power and Politics in Original Jurisdiction, 91 U. Chi. L. Rev. 83 (2024).

[39] Pub. L. No. 100-352, 102 Stat. 662 (1988).

In 1925, an act known as the "Judges' Bill" was adopted in order to reduce the workload of the Supreme Court. It articulated the distinction between appeal and certiorari and made most of the Court's jurisdiction pursuant to certiorari.[40] Until 1988, there were only minor changes. In general, final judgments from a state court came by appeal only if the state court invalidated a federal statute or upheld a state statute. Final judgments of a federal court of appeals came by appeal only if the court invalidated a state statute or declared a federal law unconstitutional in a civil action to which the U.S. government is a party. All other cases came to the U.S. Supreme Court by certiorari.

A law enacted in 1988 eliminated appeals in these cases; now almost all cases from courts of appeals or state highest courts come to the Supreme Court by writ of certiorari. Review by appeals remains in the limited circumstances where three-judge courts make decisions and where specific statutes authorize appeals to the Supreme Court.[41]

Distinctions Between Appeal and Certiorari

There are several important distinctions between appeal and certiorari. The most crucial difference is that appeals jurisdiction is obligatory—that is, the Court is supposed to hear and decide cases defined as appeals under the relevant statutes—but certiorari jurisdiction is completely discretionary. The Supreme Court's Rules specifically state, "A review on writ of certiorari is not a matter of right, but of judicial discretion, and will be granted only where there are important and specific reasons therefor."[42]

However, this distinction between appeals and certiorari has more meaning on paper than in practice because the Court has held that it will hear cases on appeal only if they present a substantial federal question.[43] In *Zucht v. King*, the Court said, "[I]t is our duty to decline jurisdiction whenever it appears the constitutional question presented is not, and was not at the time of granting the writ, substantial in character."[44] In *Zucht*, a challenge was brought to a state's compulsory vaccination law. Because the issue was clearly settled by prior cases, the Court refused to hear the case, although there was jurisdiction as of right.

Thus, the Court does not feel obligated to decide all cases falling within its appeals jurisdiction, even though there is ostensibly jurisdiction in the Supreme Court as a matter of right. The Court frequently dismissed appeals for lack of a substantial federal question. Chief Justice Earl Warren remarked, "It is only

[40] For a criticism of the Judges' Bill and the move toward a discretionary Supreme Court docket, *see* Edward A. Hartnett, Questioning Certiorari: Some Reflections Seventy-Five Years After the Judges' Bill, 100 Colum. L. Rev. 1643 (2000). For a history of its adoption, *see* Benjamin B. Johnson, The Origins of Supreme Court Question Selection, 122 Colum. L. Rev. 793, 835-839 (2022) (describing justices' lobbying for the Judges' Bill as a way to reduce their caseload).

[41] For a description of these statutes, *see* text accompanying notes 71-78, *infra*.

[42] Supreme Court Rule 17; Stern, Gressman, Shapiro & Geller, *supra* note 38, at 306.

[43] *See, e.g.*, Zucht v. King, 260 U.S. 174 (1922) (cases may be dismissed, though on appeal, for want of a substantial federal question).

[44] *Id.* at 176.

accurate to a degree to say that our jurisdiction in cases on appeal is obligatory as distinguished from discretionary on certiorari."[45]

Another difference between certiorari and appeal is the significance of the Court's denial of review. A denial of a writ of certiorari by the Supreme Court has no precedential value. The Court grants certiorari if four justices vote to hear the case and the denial of certiorari signifies nothing except the lack of four votes to hear that case. If the Court grants certiorari it can hear all of the issues presented or it can limit review to particular questions raised. But when an appeal is filed with the Court, it often acts by summarily affirming the lower court decision. That is, if the Court does not dismiss for want of a substantial federal question and it does not hear and decide the case, it often upholds the lower court decision by what is termed a summary affirmance. Summary affirmances have been much rarer since 1988 when almost all of the Supreme Court's appellate jurisdiction was eliminated.

What Is the Precedential Significance of a Summary Affirmance?

A vexing question is what precedential value should be accorded to a summary affirmance. The Supreme Court has indicated that lower courts should treat summary affirmances as decisions on the merits. For example, the Court declared that "lower courts are bound by summary decisions by this Court until such time as the Court informs [them] that [they] are not."[46] However, the Court itself has stated that "summary actions do not have the same authority" as decisions reached after briefing and arguments.[47] The distinction seems to be that lower courts should treat summary affirmances as precedents, but the Supreme Court need not feel bound by them in its later rulings.

Moreover, the precedential significance of summary affirmances is clouded because the Court also has indicated that a summary affirmance should be viewed as approving the lower court's result, but not necessarily its reasoning. In one case the Court expressly said that the federal district court "erred in believing that our affirmance . . . adopted the reasoning as well as the judgment [in the prior case]."[48] On another occasion, the Court said that a "summary disposition affirms only the judgment of the court below . . . and no more may be read into our action than was essential to sustain that judgment."[49] The result is to leave lower courts with substantial discretion to decide the significance of particular summary affirmances.[50]

[45] *Quoted in* Frederick B. Weiner, The Supreme Court's New Rules, 68 Harv. L. Rev. 20, 51 (1954).

[46] Hicks v. Miranda, 422 U.S. 332 (1975).

[47] Metromedia, Inc. v. City of San Diego, 453 U.S. 490, 500 (1981). *See also* Edelman v. Jordan, 415 U.S. 651, 671 (1974) ("[Summary affirmances] obviously are of precedential value, [but it is] [e]qually obvious that they are not of the same precedential value as would be an opinion of this Court treating the question on the merits.").

[48] Mandel v. Bradley, 432 U.S. 173, 176 (1977).

[49] Illinois State Bd. of Elections v. Socialist Workers Party, 440 U.S. 173, 182-183 (1979) (citations omitted).

[50] *Hicks*, it should be noted, involved the duty of lower courts to follow summary affirmances; *Edelman* involved their binding effect on the Supreme Court.

Procedural Differences Between Appeal and Certiorari

Practically, there is a difference in the procedures that are followed in seeking review for a case depending on whether it is a matter of appeal or certiorari. The Court's jurisdiction in appeals cases is invoked by filing a "Jurisdictional Statement." In contrast, when review by certiorari is sought, a "petition for writ of certiorari" is filed.[51] However, federal statutes provide that if appeal is sought in a case for which appeal is not proper, the papers filed shall be treated as a petition for a writ of certiorari.[52] Moreover, because essentially the Court's jurisdiction is discretionary even in appeals cases, one seeking Supreme Court review always needs to demonstrate an important federal question warranting the Court's hearing and deciding the case.

§10.3.3 Supreme Court Review of the Final Judgments of a State's Highest Court

28 U.S.C. §1257

The statutory authority for Supreme Court appellate review of state court decisions is found in 28 U.S.C. §1257. That provision states that the Court may review the "final judgments or decrees rendered by the highest court of a State in which review of a decision could be had." Previously, §1257 drew a distinction between appeals and certiorari review by the Supreme Court. Specifically, §1257 provided that review was by appeal where the state court ruled against the validity of a federal statute or treaty or where the state court rejected a challenge to a state statute as being repugnant to the Constitution, laws or treaties of the United States. In all other cases, such as when the state court upheld a federal law or invalidates a state law, review was by writ of certiorari. In 1988, however, this distinction was eliminated and all review of state highest court decisions is now by the discretionary writ of certiorari.[53]

The two most important issues concerning Supreme Court review of state court judgments are: What is a final judgment of a state's highest court? What constitutes independent and adequate state law grounds of decision preventing Supreme Court review? These topics are addressed in §§10.4 and 10.5, respectively.

[51] For a discussion of particular content and form of these documents, *see* Stern, Gressman, Shapiro & Geller, *supra* note 38, at 339-492.

[52] 28 U.S.C. §2103.

[53] Pub. L. No. 100-352, 102 Stat. 662 (1988).

§10.3.4 *Supreme Court Review of the Decisions of Lower Federal Courts*

There are two primary mechanisms for Supreme Court review of the decisions of the U.S. courts of appeals: certiorari and certification. Additionally, there are a few situations in which the Supreme Court can directly review the decisions of federal district courts.

Certiorari

The vast majority of cases come to the U.S. Supreme Court from the courts of appeals by writs of certiorari. Section 1254 grants the Court authority to hear cases "[b]y writ of certiorari . . . upon the petition of any party to any civil or criminal case, before or after rendition of judgment or decree."[54] In other words, a petition for certiorari can be filed in literally every case in the courts of appeals, as §1254 allows any party to any civil or criminal case to seek Supreme Court review.

Although §1254 permits review of a court of appeals decision either before or after judgment, the general practice is for the Court to grant certiorari only after a court of appeals decision has been rendered. The Supreme Court has observed that the authority to grant certiorari before judgment is a "power not ordinarily to be exercised."[55] Rule 11 of the Supreme Court's rules provides that a "petition for writ of certiorari to review a case pending in a federal court of appeals, before judgment is given in such court, will be granted only upon a showing that the case is of such imperative public importance as to justify the deviation from normal appellate practice and to require immediate settlement in this Court."[56] In this way, the Court benefits from the review and decision of the court of appeals.

Certiorari Before Judgment

However, the rule provides for certiorari before a judgment by the court of appeals in cases involving matters of great national significance where a fast resolution by the Supreme Court is particularly desirable.[57] For example, the Court granted certiorari before judgment in *United States v. Nixon*—the White House tapes case where speed in deciding the matter was of crucial importance for the pending criminal trials and, indirectly, for the ongoing impeachment proceedings.[58] Other examples of certiorari before judgment are *Youngstown Sheet & Tube*

[54] 28 U.S.C. §1254(1).

[55] The Three Friends, 166 U.S. 1, 49 (1897).

[56] Stern, Gressman, Shapiro & Geller, *supra* note 38, at 262.

[57] For an excellent discussion of this topic, *see* James Lindgren & William P. Marshall, The Supreme Court's Extraordinary Power to Grant Certiorari Before Judgment in the Court of Appeals, 1986 Sup. Ct. Rev. 259. In addition to the examples discussed below, in Students for Fair Admission v. President and Fellows of Harvard College, 600 U.S. 181 (2023), the Supreme Court granted certiorari after a decision of the United States Court of Appeals for the First Circuit. At the same time, the Supreme Court granted certiorari before judgment in Students for Fair Admission v. University of North Carolina before the Fourth Circuit had issued a decision.

[58] 418 U.S. 683 (1974).

Co. v. Sawyer,[59] where President Truman seized and operated the steel mills during a labor strike, and *Dames & Moore v. Regan,*[60] where the Court considered the constitutionality of President Carter's executive order releasing a freeze on Iranian assets to secure freedom for American hostages. Even in these cases, however, some have criticized the Court for not waiting until after a court of appeals decision before granting review.[61]

Certiorari before judgment also is occasionally used to consolidate cases involving similar issues.[62] As Professors Lindgren and Marshall observe, although "[t]he text of Supreme Court Rule 18 recognizes only one class of certiorari before judgment, the 'imperative public importance case' . . . the writ is more often granted to consolidate a case with another case pending before the Supreme Court."[63] Consolidation of cases provides the Court several factual contexts within which to consider difficult legal questions. Also, consolidation serves as a way of disposing of a number of cases posing the same question within the federal court system.

Certification

In addition to certiorari, the Supreme Court also may hear cases from the U.S. courts of appeals via certification. This provision dates back to 1802, where Congress first enacted authority for the lower federal courts to certify questions to the U.S. Supreme Court. Section 1254 provides that certification is available "at any time by a court of appeals of any question of law in any civil or criminal case as to which instructions are desired."[64] Upon certification, the Supreme Court can give "binding instructions or require the entire record to be sent up for decision of the entire matter in controversy."[65]

The Supreme Court is generally reluctant to accept matters via certification. In part, this reflects the Court's view that it generally benefits from having a court of appeals decision before it hears or rules on a matter. Also, certification presents an issue divorced from the entire case and the Court believes that usually it is better to decide legal questions in a well-developed factual context. If nothing else, the Court is jealous of its prerogative of deciding what cases are worthy of its attention and certification allows other courts to determine what matters will be decided by the Supreme Court. Thus, the Court has expressed its reluctance to hear matters pursuant to certification. The Court, for instance, stated, "It is

[59] 343 U.S. 579 (1952).

[60] 453 U.S. 654 (1981).

[61] Gerald Gunther, Judicial Hegemony and Legislative Autonomy: The *Nixon* Case and the Impeachment Process, 22 UCLA L. Rev. 30, 31-33, 39 (1974) (criticizing the Court's grant of certiorari before judgment in United States v. Nixon). In Trump v. United States, 144 S. Ct. 2312 (2024), the Supreme Court denied certiorari before judgment, but granted review after the decision of the United States Court of Appeals for the District of Columbia Circuit.

[62] Lindgren & Marshall, *supra* note 57, at 297; *see, e.g.,* Taylor v. McElroy, 360 U.S. 709 (1959); Porter v. Dicken, 328 U.S. 252 (1946).

[63] Lindgren & Marshall, *supra* note 57, at 297.

[64] 28 U.S.C. §1254(3).

[65] *Id.*

also the task of a Court of Appeals to decide all properly presented cases coming before it, except in the rare instances, as for example the pendency of another case before this Court raising the same issue, where certification may be advisable in the proper administration and expedition of judicial business."[66]

The Court has stated that it will accept certification of issues only as to questions of law, only if the questions are not too abstract or general, and only if there is a substantial reason for certification rather than the usual appellate procedures.[67] In light of these restrictions, it is hardly surprising that there have been only three instances in modern times in which certification has been allowed.[68]

Review of District Court Decisions

Finally, there are a few instances in which the Supreme Court can review the decisions of federal district courts. There is still direct appeal to the Supreme Court from decisions of three-judge courts. Until the early 1970s, federal jurisdictional statutes provided for three-judge courts whenever there were suits to enjoin enforcement of allegedly unconstitutional federal or state statutes. Direct appeal from these multimember courts to the Supreme Court was available. In 1976, in response to many proposals to eliminate the three-judge court format, Congress repealed the statutes that allowed for three-judge courts when there were constitutional challenges to statutes.[69] There have been proposals in Congress to require three-judge courts whenever there is a constitutional challenge to a law enacted through a voter-approved initiative.[70]

However, there remain a few federal statutes that provide for continued use of three-judge district courts in particular circumstances. For example, federal laws require three-judge courts when there is a challenge to the apportionment of congressional districts or any statewide legislative body.[71] Also, the Civil Rights Act of 1964 provides for a three-judge court upon application by the attorney general of the United States.[72] Additionally, the Voting Rights Act of 1965 provides for three-judge courts including for legal challenges to election districting.[73] The Regional Rail Reorganization Act[74] and the Presidential Election Campaign Fund Act also have provisions authorizing use of three-judge courts.[75] The Bipartisan Campaign Finance Reform Act of 2002 also provided for review of only constitutional challenges in a three-judge federal district court.[76] When such three-judge courts are

[66] Wisniewski v. United States, 353 U.S. 901, 902 (1957).

[67] *See, e.g.,* NLRB v. White Swan Co., 313 U.S. 23 (1941).

[68] *See* Iran Natl. Airlines Corp. v. Marschalk Co., 453 U.S. 919 (1981); Moody v. Albemarle Paper Co., 417 U.S. 622 (1974); United States v. Barnett, 316 F.2d 236 (5th Cir. 1963).

[69] Act of Aug. 12, 1976, Pub. L. No. 94-381, 90 Stat. 1119.

[70] State Initiative Fairness Act, H.R. 1170, 105th Cong. (1997).

[71] 28 U.S.C. §2284.

[72] 42 U.S.C. §2000a-5(b).

[73] *See, e.g.,* 42 U.S.C. §1971(g).

[74] 45 U.S.C. §701.

[75] 26 U.S.C. §9001.

[76] *See* McConnell v. Federal Election Commission, 540 U.S. 93 (2003) (reviewing the decision of the three-judge federal court).

used there remains direct appeal to the U.S. Supreme Court.[77] In fact, this is now the only instance in which the Supreme Court still possesses appeals jurisdiction.[78]

§10.3.5 *The Supreme Court's Emergency Docket*

There always has been the ability to go to the Supreme Court, in a matter within its jurisdiction, and ask for an emergency stay of a lower court decision or other emergency relief. For example, there have been many instances of those facing execution going to the Supreme Court for an emergency stay of their death sentence being carried out, sometimes receiving relief only minutes before the scheduled execution.

But in recent years there has been much more attention to matters coming to the Supreme Court on this emergency docket and it has been labelled "the shadow docket." University of Chicago Law Professor William Baude is credited with coining this phrase.[79] Professor Stephen Vladeck has described the growth in the shadow docket: "Since 2017, the justices have been utilizing these orders far more often, and with far broader effects, than ever before, sometimes instead of resolving similar legal questions on the merits docket (where, of course, they'd have to explain their reasoning)."[80]

The increased use of the shadow docket has been criticized in that the Supreme Court is deciding important issues of constitutional law without full briefing and oral arguments.[81] There is concern that these decisions often nonetheless are regarded as binding precedent.[82] Also, there is the objection that the Supreme Court does not follow the requisite standard of appellate review, which, for example, provides that a preliminary injunction (or its denial) should be overturned only if there is an abuse of discretion.

[77] 28 U.S.C. §1253 provides for direct appeal from three-judge courts. Also, many of the specific statutes provide for direct appeal to the Supreme Court.

[78] Pub. L. No. 100-352, 102 Stat. 662 (1988). Bennett Boskey & Eugene Gressman, The Supreme Court Bids Farewell to Mandatory Appeals, 109 Sup. Ct. Rev. LXXI, XCVII (1988).

[79] Stephen Vladeck, The Shadow Docket xii (2023).

[80] *Id.*

[81] As an example, during the COVID pandemic the Court decided important questions of free exercise of religion in rulings on its emergency docket. *See, e.g.,* South Bay United Pentecostal Church v. Newsom, 140 S. Ct. 1613 (2020) (denying relief to church challenging closure orders limiting assembly for religious purposes); Calvary Chapel Dayton Valley v. Sisolak, 140 S. Ct. 2603 (2020) (denying relief to church challenging closure orders limiting assembly for religious purposes); Roman Catholic Diocese of Brooklyn v. Cuomo, 592 U.S. 14 (2020) (granting preliminary injunction to stop enforcement of orders restricting size of attendance for religious worship); Tandon v. Newsom, 593 U.S. 61 (2021) (prohibition on gatherings of more than three households in homes is unconstitutional as applied to worship services.)

[82] Vladeck, *supra* note 79, at xii ("Worse, they are also insisting, for the first time, that at least some of these unexplained rulings are precedents that lower courts and government officials are bound to follow.")

Some, such as Professor Vladeck, are very critical of what they see as abuses of the shadow docket. Others, including Justice Samuel Alito, have responded and defended the Court's emergency docket as necessary and not improper in any way.[83] Whatever one's views about the shadow docket, it is likely that important matters will come to the Court in this way.

§10.3.6 The Proposals for a National Court of Appeals

Development of Proposals

In 1971, then Chief Justice Warren Burger appointed a Study Commission on the Caseload of the Supreme Court. The commission, chaired by Professor Paul Freund and composed of eminent scholars and practitioners, made many recommendations.[84] For example, it proposed the elimination of three-judge district courts, a recommendation largely adopted in 1976. Also, it proposed abolishing specific instances of direct appeals to the Supreme Court and suggested generally replacing all appeals with certiorari. Undoubtedly, its most controversial proposal was for the creation of a National Court of Appeals. The new court would consist of seven judges, drawn from existing federal court of appeals judges, who would serve three-year terms. The National Court of Appeals would review all petitions for writs of certiorari and select the most worthy for the Supreme Court, from which the Court would choose the cases on its docket. Additionally, the National Court of Appeals would decide cases where there was a split among the circuits, when the case was not sufficiently noteworthy to justify Supreme Court review.

About the same time as the Freund Commission issued its report, a similar set of recommendations was made by another group: the Commission on Revision of the Federal Court Appellate System. Chaired by Senator Roman Hruska, this commission also recommended the creation of a National Court of Appeals.[85] The Hruska Commission, however, would have permitted the National Court of Appeals to decide only matters referred to it by the Supreme Court or other courts of appeals. It would not have performed the screening function envisioned by the Freund Commission.

[83] Adam Liptak, Alito Responds to Critics of the Supreme Court's 'Shadow Docket,' New York Times (September 30, 2024), https://www.nytimes.com/2021/09/30/us/politics/alito-shadow-docket-scotus.html.

[84] Federal Judicial Center, Report of the Study Group on the Caseload of the Supreme Court, 57 F.R.D. 573 (1972). For a discussion of these proposals and an analysis of why they failed, *see* Peter S. Menell & Ryan Vaca, Revisiting and Confronting the Federal Judiciary Capacity "Crisis": Charting a Path for Federal Judiciary Reform, 108 Cal. L. Rev. 789 (2020).

[85] Commission on Revision of the Federal Court Appellate System, Structure, and Internal Procedures: Recommendations for Change, 67 F.R.D. 195 (1975).

Criticism of Proposals

These proposals drew sharp criticisms, most importantly from several current and former members of the Supreme Court.[86] The severest attacks were directed at the Freund Commission's proposal that would have allowed the National Court of Appeals to screen cases for the Supreme Court. Critics argued that one of the Court's most important powers is setting its agenda; giving control over its docket to another body has the potential to drastically change the Court's authority. Moreover, it was argued that creating an intermediate court of appeals would lessen the prestige of the existing courts of appeals. The Hruska Commission's proposal was challenged as likely to fail in reducing the Court's docket. It was argued that the Court would need to take substantial extra time in deciding what cases to refer to the new court and in later reviewing its decisions.[87] Underlying the controversy was disagreement over the nature of the current problem and, consequently, what types of solutions were in order.[88] For example, after a lengthy study of the Supreme Court's caseload, professors Samuel Estreicher and John Sexton concluded that an intermediate court of appeals was unnecessary because the Court's "problem is not one of workload, . . . but of role definition."[89]

The proposals for a National Court of Appeals drew a great deal of attention but did not come close to enactment by Congress. During the 1980s, Senators Dole, Heflin, and Thurmond introduced a bill into Congress to create an Intercircuit Tribunal of the U.S. Court of Appeals.[90] The Intercircuit Tribunal would be composed of a group of U.S. court of appeals judges who would decide cases involving conflicts among the circuits. The hope was that this would remove a number of cases from the Supreme Court's docket. Former Chief Justice Burger, a major advocate of such a proposal, contended that it would take 35 to 50 cases a year off the Court's docket.[91]

The proposal for an Intercircuit Tribunal was controversial. Some Supreme Court justices, such as White, Rehnquist, and O'Connor, endorsed it, while others, such as Justices Stevens, Brennan, and Marshall, opposed it, claiming that it "would do nothing to alleviate the workload of the Court" and would "increase the workload of our already overworked Courts of Appeals."[92]

[86] *See, e.g.*, William Brennan, Justice Brennan Calls National Court of Appeals Proposal "Fundamentally Unnecessary and Ill Advised," 59 A.B.A. J. 835 (1973); Earl Warren, Let's Not Weaken the Supreme Court, 60 A.B.A. J. 677 (1974).

[87] *See* William Alsup, Reservations on the Proposal of the Hruska Commission to Establish a National Court of Appeals, 7 U. Tol. L. Rev. 431 (1976).

[88] In response to the proposals, important studies were done of the Supreme Court's caseload; *see* Gerhard Casper & Richard A. Posner, The Workload of the Supreme Court (1976); Samuel Estreicher & John Sexton, Redefining the Supreme Court's Role 14-24 (1986) (reviewing proposals for change in the Supreme Court's jurisdiction).

[89] Estreicher & Sexton, *supra* note 88, at 7.

[90] S. 645, 98th Cong., 1st Sess. (1983).

[91] Warren Burger, Annual Report on the State of the Judiciary, 69 A.B.A. J. 442, 447 (1983).

[92] *Quoted in* Estreicher & Sexton, *supra* note 88, at 23.

For now, the debate over these proposals has faded, in large part because the significant reduction in the size of the Supreme Court's docket has ended concern over a workload crisis. As mentioned above, in October Term 2018, the Court decided 66 cases after briefing and oral arguments. No longer is there the general perception the Court has too great a workload.[93]

§10.4 THE FINAL JUDGMENT RULE

§10.4.1 Introduction

The Supreme Court generally may review only the final judgment of a state's highest court or the final judgment of a U.S. court of appeals. Subsection 10.4.2 considers the former, review of final judgments of a state's highest court, and §10.4.3 examines the latter, review of court of appeals decisions. The underlying policies are quite similar in both situations.

Benefits of the Final Judgment Rule

First, the final judgment rule promotes judicial efficiency. If the system allowed appeals of individual issues prior to the entry of a final judgment, the Supreme Court would decide many issues unnecessarily. Where the party seeking interlocutory review ultimately prevails even without it, hearing such appeals wastes judicial resources. For example, a criminal defendant might try to appeal many specific rulings of the trial judge, but appellate review is unnecessary if it turns out that the defendant would have been acquitted even without interlocutory review.

Second, requiring final judgments before Supreme Court review promotes expeditious resolution of proceedings. Halting lower court proceedings to permit interlocutory appeals inevitably delays the litigation. In virtually every case, one side benefits from delay; permitting interlocutory review creates a powerful tool that can be used for this strategic advantage.

Third, requiring final judgments benefits the Supreme Court by providing a fully developed record, including the reasoning and conclusions of the lower court judges.[1] Interlocutory review asks the Court to decide particular issues divorced from the entire case, which is a practice the Court consistently avoids.

Fourth, in the context of Supreme Court review of state court decisions, the final judgment rule promotes federalism.[2] The disruption of state proceedings is avoided by requiring them to be completed prior to Supreme Court review. In many

[93] For a recent argument that there is a workload crisis in the Supreme Court and the lower federal courts, *see* Peter S. Menell & Ryan Vaca, Revisiting and Confronting the Federal Judiciary Capacity "Crisis": Charting a Path for Federal Judiciary Reform, 108 Cal. L. Rev. 789 (2020).

§10.4 [1] Note, The Finality Rule for Supreme Court Review of State Court Orders, 91 Harv. L. Rev. 1004, 1006 (1978).

[2] Cox Broadcasting Corp. v. Cohn, 420 U.S. 469, 502-505 (1975).

other doctrines, the Supreme Court has emphasized that considerations of equity and comity require that the federal courts avoid interfering with ongoing state court litigation.[3]

Justifications for Review Without a Final Judgment

However, despite the importance of these policy considerations, there are circumstances where there are compelling reasons for providing review even though there is not a final judgment. For example, review prior to a final judgment is important when there is a lower court decision that infringes on important constitutional rights, and later review is either unavailable or ineffective in repairing the harms.[4] Thus, the Court has been particularly willing to review lower court decisions imposing prior restraints on expression because such orders are inimical to the First Amendment and later appellate review often cannot restore the lost speech.[5] The Supreme Court has recognized a number of exceptions to the final judgment rule, discussed below, where important objectives are served by allowing earlier review.

Review of Federal and State Court Decisions Compared

For the most part, there is a great similarity in the doctrines concerning the final judgment rule as it applies to Supreme Court review of state court decisions and those of lower federal courts. In fact, the Supreme Court frequently uses precedents interchangeably, and also in both areas uses cases arising in the context of the rule limiting federal courts of appeals to reviewing only final judgments of district courts.[6] However, this is not to say that the doctrines are identical for Supreme Court review of state courts and for lower federal courts. There is a difference in the statutory requirements for finality. Whereas §1257 limits the Court to reviewing only the final judgments of the highest court in which review can be had, §1254 allows the Supreme Court to grant certiorari even before final judgment of the federal court of appeals and to take issues certified to it by a court of appeals.[7] Also, §1292 provides for the court of appeals to accept interlocutory appeals from the district courts under specified circumstances. Hence, the final judgment rule varies depending on whether the context is Supreme Court review of a state court decision, Supreme Court review of a federal court of appeals decision, or a federal court of appeals review of a district court decision.

[3] *See, e.g.*, Younger v. Harris, 401 U.S. 37 (1971) (federal courts may not enjoin pending state court proceedings). The requirement that federal courts abstain rather than enjoin state proceedings is discussed in Chapter 13, *infra*.

[4] *See* Cox Broadcasting Corp. v. Cohn, 420 U.S. at 485; Note, *supra* note 1, at 1007.

[5] *See, e.g.*, National Socialist Party of Am. v. Village of Skokie, 432 U.S. 43, 44 (1977); Organization for a Better Austin v. Keefe, 402 U.S. 415, 418 n.* (1971).

[6] Charles Alan Wright, The Law of Federal Courts 740 (4th ed. 1983) (precedents are often cited interchangeably).

[7] For a discussion of certiorari before judgment and certification, *see* §10.3.4, *supra*.

Also, there are somewhat different policy considerations when the Court seeks to review a state court decision prior to a final judgment. Considerations of federalism—especially concerns of comity militating against federal court interruptions of ongoing state proceedings—influence application of the final judgment rule when review is sought of state court rulings.[8]

§10.4.2 Review of the Final Judgment of a State's Highest Court

The jurisdictional statute authorizing Supreme Court review of state court decisions, 28 U.S.C. §1257, provides for review of the final judgments of the highest court of a state in which a decision can be had. This provision poses two independent issues: What constitutes the highest court of a state in which review can be had? What constitutes a final judgment sufficient to permit Supreme Court jurisdiction?[9]

Review in Highest State Court in Which Review Can Be Had

Section 1257 does not limit the Supreme Court to reviewing only the decisions of the highest court in a state; rather, it says that the Court can review judgments of the highest court *in which review can be had.* That is, an individual seeking Supreme Court review must exhaust all available appeals within the state court system.[10] The decisions of lower state courts are reviewable by the Supreme Court when there is no appellate review of such rulings within the state and when they thus constitute the judgment of the highest courts in which review can be had. For example, in *Thompson v. City of Louisville,* the Supreme Court reviewed decisions of the police court of Louisville, Kentucky.[11] The fines imposed by this court were so small that appellate review was not available in the Kentucky courts; therefore, the police court's decisions were the highest court in which review could be had. Similarly, when a state's highest court declines to review a lower state court decision, the U.S. Supreme Court can review that lower court decision. The requirement that an individual exhaust all appeals in the state system to seek Supreme Court review does not require seeking rehearing in a court that already has decided the matter.[12] If the state court deciding the matter was a panel of the highest court consisting

[8] Cox Broadcasting Corp. v. Cohn, 420 U.S. at 502-505. *But see* Martin H. Redish, Federal Jurisdiction: Tensions in the Allocation of Judicial Power 248-249 (2d ed. 1990) (arguing that federalism considerations deserve less weight when the Supreme Court seeks to review federal law issues).

[9] For a thorough examination of the final judgment rule and how it has evolved, *see* Robert J. Martineau, Defining Finality and Appealability by Court Rule: Right Problem, Wrong Solution, 54 U. Pitt. L. Rev. 717 (1993).

[10] Individuals must pursue appeals within the state even when the appeals court has discretion as to whether or not to hear the case. *See* Parker v. Illinois, 333 U.S. 571 (1948).

[11] 362 U.S. 199 (1960).

[12] *See, e.g.,* Local 174, Teamsters Union v. Lucas Flour Co., 369 U.S. 95 (1962).

of less than all of its members, en banc review need be sought prior to Supreme Court review only if it is available as a matter of right.[13]

What Is a "Final Judgment or Decree"?

The more difficult question concerns what constitutes the "final judgments or decrees" of the highest court in which review can be had. The Court has articulated a simple definition of "final judgment": A decision is final if it "ends the litigation on the merits and leaves nothing for the court to do but execute the judgment."[14] For example, in criminal cases, there is not a final judgment prior to the rendering of a verdict or the imposition of a sentence.[15]

In *Jefferson v. City of Tarrant, Alabama*,[16] the Court said that for a state court judgment to be final it must be (a) subject to no further review or correction in any other state tribunal, and (b) it also must be final as an effective determination of the litigation and not of merely interlocutory or intermediate steps within it. *Jefferson* involved a claim by an estate following the death of an African American woman in a fire. The estate claimed that the death occurred because the fire department inadequately provided services to the minority community and as a result failed to rescue her promptly after arriving at the scene.

The trial court found that federal common law rather than the Alabama Wrongful Death Act governed the survivability of the decedent's cause of action, and the city sought interlocutory review. The Alabama Supreme Court held that the Alabama Wrongful Death Act's allowance of only punitive damages governed recovery on federal civil rights claims and remanded the case for further proceedings on the remaining state law claims. The U.S. Supreme Court held that the Alabama decision was not a final judgment and was therefore not proper for review.

The Supreme Court said that the Alabama Supreme Court decision was not final, but only an interlocutory ruling. Instead of terminating the litigation, the state court had answered a single certified question that addressed only two of the four counts in the plaintiff's complaint. The case was remanded for further proceedings, and absent settlement or dispositive motions, there will be a trial on the merits. Thus, there was no final judgment, and Supreme Court review was not available.

[13] *Compare* Gorman v. Washington Univ., 316 U.S. 98 (1942) (denying review of a panel of four of the seven judges of the Missouri Supreme Court because en banc review was available as a matter of right in cases involving federal questions), *with* Local 174, Teamsters Union v. Lucas Flour Co., 369 U.S. 95 (1962) (the Court reviewed a decision of a panel of the Supreme Court of Washington because en banc review is not granted as a matter of right).

[14] Catlin v. United States, 324 U.S. 229, 233 (1945).

[15] *See, e.g.*, Flynt v. Ohio, 451 U.S. 619 (1981) (no final judgment because there was not a conviction or a sentence).

[16] 522 U.S. 75 (1997).

Cox Broadcasting Corp. v. Cohn: Four Exceptions to Finality Rule

The complexity arises because the Supreme Court has recognized four situations in which it will grant review even though additional state proceedings remain. Although the Supreme Court has recognized exceptions to the finality rule since relatively early in American history,[17] it was in *Cox Broadcasting Corp. v. Cohn* that the Court clarified the law and articulated four exceptions to the traditional rule of finality.[18] Because §1257 requires a final judgment or decree, the Court does not label these four categories as exceptions to finality, but instead as situations in which it finds there to be sufficient finality even though there are further proceedings on the merits of the case in state court.

In *Cox Broadcasting,* a man whose daughter was raped and murdered sued for damages based on the violation of a state statute preventing the disclosure of a rape victim's identity. The plaintiff was granted summary judgment by the trial court; the defendants' claims of First Amendment protection were rejected. On appeal, the Georgia Supreme Court reversed the trial court, concluding that the statute preventing publication of a rape victim's identity did not create a cause of action for money damages. The Georgia Supreme Court remanded the case for consideration of relief based on common law privacy rights. The Georgia Supreme Court agreed with the trial court that the Georgia statute did not violate the First Amendment and that the Constitution did not prevent relief. The defendants then sought U.S. Supreme Court review, even though there obviously still were additional state court proceedings pursuant to the remand.

The Supreme Court granted review, reversed the Georgia courts, and held that the First Amendment precluded sanctions for publication of true information from court records. The Court clarified the law concerning the final judgment rule by observing there were four situations in which review could be had when state courts decided federal issues, but additional state proceedings on state law issues remained.[19]

Exception: If No Doubt As to Outcome of Remaining Proceedings

First, the Court will grant review when the state courts have decided federal issues and there is no doubt as to the outcome of the remaining state court proceedings on the state law issues. Justice White, writing for the majority in *Cox Broadcasting,* explained that "[i]n the first category are those cases in which there are further proceedings—even entire trials—yet to occur in the state courts but where for one reason or another the federal issue is conclusive or the outcome of the further proceedings preordained."[20] The Court said that "because the case is

[17] *See, e.g.,* Forgay v. Conrad, 47 U.S. (6 How.) 201 (1848).

[18] 420 U.S. 469 (1975).

[19] *Id.* at 479-483.

[20] *Id.* at 479.

for all practical purposes concluded, the judgment of the state court on the federal issue is deemed final."[21]

Two cases cited by the Court in *Cox Broadcasting* are instructive as to this exception. In *Mills v. Alabama*, the editor of a newspaper was criminally prosecuted for publishing an editorial on election day encouraging voters to vote in favor of a proposal for a new form of city government.[22] The editor's sole defense in the trial court was that his prosecution violated the First Amendment. The trial court agreed that the prosecution was unconstitutional, but the Alabama Supreme Court reversed and remanded the matter for trial. The Supreme Court granted review at this stage because it believed that the pending trial "would be no more than a few formal gestures leading inexorably towards a conviction."[23] Because Mills's sole defense was based on the Constitution, and the state supreme court already ruled on and rejected the constitutional argument, the outcome of the trial was a foregone conclusion. The Court concluded that denying review until after the completion of all of the state proceedings would improperly delay resolution of the constitutional issues and waste the time and energy of the parties and the state's judicial system.

Another case cited by the *Cox Broadcasting* Court as illustrative of the first exception was *Organization for a Better Austin v. Keefe*.[24] The Organization for a Better Austin circulated leaflets accusing Keefe of using real estate selling tactics that fueled panic selling and obstructed maintenance of a racially integrated community. Keefe sued for an injunction in Illinois state courts to halt the leafleting. The Illinois trial court issued a preliminary injunction, enjoining the organization "from passing out pamphlets, leaflets or literature of any kind, and from picketing, anywhere in the City of Westchester, Illinois."[25] The Illinois court of appeals sustained the preliminary injunction, and the Illinois Supreme Court denied review. The matter then was scheduled for return to the trial court for proceedings concerning the request for a permanent injunction.

Although further proceedings in the state courts remained, the Supreme Court nonetheless granted review. The Court explained that the sole issue was the constitutional question of whether an injunction violated the First Amendment, and that already had been decided by the Illinois courts. The Court observed that there is "nothing in the record that would indicate that the Illinois courts applied a less rigorous standard in issuing and sustaining [the preliminary] injunction than they would with any permanent injunction in the case."[26] Nor was there any indication of a factual dispute that might cause the request for a permanent injunction to be denied. Accordingly, the outcome of the further state proceedings was a foregone conclusion. Moreover, prompt review by the Supreme Court was particularly important because freedom of speech was restricted by the state court's injunction.

[21] *Id.*
[22] 384 U.S. 214 (1966).
[23] *Id.* at 217.
[24] 402 U.S. 415 (1971).
[25] *Id.* at 417.
[26] *Id.* at 418 n.1.

Another case applying this exception was *Duquesne Light Co. v. Barasch.*[27] The Pennsylvania Supreme Court denied a utility company's claim to allow recovery of certain costs either by inclusion in the rate base or amortization. Although state proceedings remained, the U.S. Supreme Court nonetheless found the case to fit within the first exception articulated in *Cox Broadcasting.* The Court explained that the Pennsylvania Supreme Court decision resolved all of the legal issues in the case, and "all that remains is the straightforward application of its clear directive to otherwise complete rate orders."[28] Thus, because the Pennsylvania court "left the outcome of further proceedings preordained," the Court had jurisdiction to decide the constitutional issue.[29]

Thus, the first situation described in *Cox Broadcasting* applies when the state courts have decided the federal issue and where the outcome of the remaining proceedings on the state law questions are virtually certain because there is neither a factual dispute nor a defense based on state law. This exception makes great sense, especially in cases where important constitutional rights, such as freedom of speech, are lost by delaying Supreme Court review. When it is clear that the remaining proceedings are a mere formality with the results preordained, there is no reason for the Court to postpone review.

The problem that arises in applying this exception is deciding in any particular case whether further proceedings truly would be a mere formality.[30] After all, in *Mills* or *Keefe,* the defendant might have contested the facts or presented state law defenses on remand even though initially only constitutional defenses were asserted. One commentator urged that to alleviate uncertainty the Court should "predicate interlocutory appeal . . . upon the appellant's renunciation of any additional claims and defenses and to insist that this stipulation be binding in the absence of extraordinary subsequent developments."[31] This proposal, however, seems both unnecessary and undesirable. It is unnecessary because the Court appears to have had little trouble applying this exception.[32] In cases where the federal issue has been decided and there is not a foreseeable challenge to the facts or a likely state law defense, the Court allows review, especially where there is an important reason for an expeditious resolution of the matter. The proposal is undesirable because it penalizes people who exercise Supreme Court review by denying them the opportunity to try to defend themselves should the matter return to state court.

[27] 488 U.S. 299 (1989).

[28] *Id.* at 307.

[29] *Id.* (citations omitted).

[30] *See* Note, *supra* note 1, at 1016; Redish, *supra* note 8, at 255.

[31] Note, *supra* note 1, at 1016-1017.

[32] The Court in *Cox Broadcasting* cited to several other cases where review was allowed under the circumstances of the first category; *see, e.g.,* Local No. 438, Constr. & Gen. Laborers' Union v. Curry, 371 U.S. 542 (1963); Pope v. Atlantic Coast Line R.R., 345 U.S. 379, 382 (1953); Richfield Oil Corp. v. State Bd. of Equalization, 329 U.S. 69, 73-74 (1946).

Exception: Federal Law Issues Will Survive and Necessitate Supreme Court Review

The second exception to the usual rule of finality is where the state court's decision as to the federal law issues will survive any further state judicial proceedings and ultimately will warrant Supreme Court review. Justice White observed that these are cases "in which the federal issue, finally decided by the highest court in the State, will survive and require decision regardless of the outcome of future state court proceedings."[33]

Again, two cases cited by the Court in *Cox Broadcasting* are illustrative of this exception. *Brady v. Maryland* is a paradigm example of this second category.[34] Brady and a companion were convicted of a murder that occurred during a robbery they committed and were sentenced to death. Brady's defense, which was not accepted at trial, was that he committed the robbery but that his companion did the killing. Subsequent to his trial, conviction, and sentencing, Brady learned that his companion admitted to the murder. Brady challenged the prosecutor's withholding of this information as a denial of due process. The Maryland court of appeals held that the prosecutor's action was unconstitutional but remanded the case solely on the issue of punishment. The Supreme Court granted review, even though there were still state proceedings pursuant to the remand.

The Court reasoned that regardless of the modification of the punishment, Brady still would have an appeal of his conviction based on the U.S. Constitution. The Court explained that review of the constitutional question was appropriate prior to the completion of the state proceedings because the issue is "'independent of, and unaffected by,' what may transpire in a trial at which petitioner can receive only a life imprisonment or a death sentence. [The federal issue] cannot be mooted by such a proceeding."[35]

Another case cited in *Cox Broadcasting* that illustrates this exception is *Radio Station WOW, Inc. v. Johnson.*[36] In *Johnson,* the Federal Communications Commission approved the transfer of a radio station license, but the Nebraska Supreme Court invalidated the transaction. The Nebraska court remanded the case to the trial court for a determination of damages. The U.S. Supreme Court granted review notwithstanding the remaining state proceedings because the federal issue—whether Nebraska could invalidate the transfer—would survive the future state court proceedings and ultimately would have to be resolved by the Supreme Court.

Since *Cox Broadcasting,* there have been other cases where this exception has been applied. For example, in *NAACP v. Claiborne Hardware Co.*, the Mississippi Supreme Court upheld the liability of individuals and civil rights organizations who organized a boycott of businesses in Claiborne County, Mississippi.[37] The Mississippi court, however, remanded the matter to the state trial court for a

[33] Cox Broadcasting Corp. v. Cohn, 420 U.S. at 480.
[34] 373 U.S. 83 (1963).
[35] *Id.* at 85 n.1.
[36] 326 U.S. 120 (1945).
[37] 458 U.S. 886 (1982). *See also* American Export Lines, Inc. v. Alvez, 446 U.S. 274 (1980).

modification of the damages award. The Supreme Court granted review of the federal law questions, even though additional state judicial proceedings were planned. The Court explained that the federal law issues—the First Amendment protection for the boycott—were separate from the recomputation of damages and that these questions would need to be decided regardless of the state's computation of damages on remand.

The Court applied this in *Moore v. Harper*, in 2023, to hold that it could review a decision of the North Carolina Supreme Court that partisan gerrymandering of congressional districts violated the North Carolina Constitution.[38] The issue was whether the United States Constitution leaves this entirely to the legislature, making state judicial review of gerrymandering of congressional districts unreviewable in courts. After its decision and as a result of an election, the composition of the North Carolina Supreme Court changed and it overruled its earlier decision. Nonetheless, the Supreme Court said that this was reviewable under the second exception in *Cox Broadcasting*: "[This case] fits within this second category of cases described in *Cox Broadcasting*. By striking down the 2021 congressional plans enacted by the General Assembly, *Harper I* 'finally decided' the 'federal issue' whether the Elections Clause insulates state legislatures from review by state courts for compliance with state law. That issue both has survived and requires decision because subsequent proceedings have neither altered *Harper I* 's[39] analysis of the federal issue nor negated the effect of its judgment striking down the 2021 plans."

Again, this is a desirable exception to the usual rule of finality. Because there is a distinct federal issue that ultimately will have to be decided, there is no efficiency reason for the Supreme Court to wait until the state court proceedings are completed. Also, this exception is particularly desirable where there is an interest in a speedy resolution of a matter.

Exception: When Review is Now or Never

The third exception to the usual finality requirement is when the Supreme Court's only opportunity for reviewing the state court's federal law rulings is prior to the proceedings on remand. Justice White explained that "[i]n the third category are those situations where the federal claim has been finally decided, with further proceedings on the merits in the state courts to come, but in which later review of the federal issue cannot be had, whatever the ultimate outcome of the case."[40] In other words, it is a now or never situation; either the Court takes the case at this stage, or it never will be able to review the state court's decision on federal law issues.

The Supreme Court cited to its earlier decision in *North Dakota State Board of Pharmacy v. Snyder's Drug Stores, Inc.* as illustrative of this exception.[41] North Dakota law required that companies own pharmacies where licensed pharmacists held

[38] 600 U.S. 1 (2023).

[39] *Id.*

[40] 420 U.S. at 481.

[41] 414 U.S. 156 (1973).

the majority of stock. Snyder's Drug Stores was denied a permit to open a pharmacy in North Dakota because its parent company was not owned by pharmacists licensed in North Dakota. Snyder's appealed, and ultimately the state supreme court held that the North Dakota law violated the U.S. Constitution. The North Dakota Supreme Court remanded the case for an administrative hearing to determine whether the company was entitled to a license based on other aspects of the state law.

Although additional state proceedings remained, the U.S. Supreme Court granted review. The Court reasoned that the constitutional issue would not be addressed except at this stage of the proceedings. If Snyder's Drug Store was denied a license on state law grounds, it would not appeal the earlier constitutional ruling in its favor. Conversely, if Snyder's was granted a license, North Dakota law prevented the state from appealing. Either way, the constitutional issue could be reviewed only at this point, after the North Dakota Supreme Court's remand and prior to the further proceedings.[42]

A similar case was *Florida v. Meyers*.[43] Meyers's automobile was searched at the time of his arrest. Eight hours later, the car, which had been impounded, was searched again. The trial judge concluded that the searches were legal and refused to suppress the evidence. The court of appeals reversed, finding that the second search violated the Constitution and remanded the matter for a new trial. The Florida Supreme Court denied a petition for review. At that point, prior to the new trial, the Supreme Court granted certiorari. The Court explained that its only opportunity for review was at that stage in the proceedings. The Court, in a per curiam opinion, stated, "[The] decision on the federal constitutional issue is reviewable at this time because if the State prevails at the trial, the issue will be mooted; and if the State loses, governing State law . . . will prohibit it from presenting the federal claim for review."[44]

In *Kansas v. Marsh*, the Supreme Court applied this exception to permit review of a decision by the Kansas Supreme Court that had declared that state's death penalty law to be facially unconstitutional.[45] Marsh had been convicted of murder and sentenced to death. The Kansas Supreme Court overturned his death sentence on the grounds that the state's death penalty law was flawed in that it allowed a jury to impose a capital sentence if it was in equipoise between aggravating and mitigating circumstances. The case was remanded for a new trial. Thus, there was no final judgment in the state courts.

Nonetheless, the Supreme Court granted review. The Court explained: "Here, although Marsh will be retried on the capital murder and aggravated arson charges, the Kansas Supreme Court's determination that Kansas' death penalty statute is facially unconstitutional is final and binding on the lower courts. Thus, the State will be unable to obtain further review of its death penalty law later in this case.

[42] *Id.* at 163-164.
[43] 466 U.S. 380 (1984).
[44] *Id.* at 381 n.*.
[45] 548 U.S. 163 (2006).

If Marsh is acquitted of capital murder, double jeopardy and state law will preclude the State from appealing. If he is reconvicted, the State will be prohibited under the Kansas Supreme Court's decision from seeking the death penalty, and there would be no opportunity for the State to seek further review of that prohibition."[46] In other words, Supreme Court review was "now or never"; if it did not hear the issue at that point, there would be no later opportunity for review.

This is the most questionable of the four exceptions to the traditional finality rule. The underlying basis for this exception is to ensure that the Supreme Court will be able to review a state court's decision on a federal law issue. Yet in many other contexts the Supreme Court is unconcerned over the fact that procedural rules foreclose its ability to review state court rulings even on federal constitutional questions. For example, the Supreme Court refuses to review state court decisions on federal law issues when there is an independent and adequate state ground of decision.[47] Likewise, the Court allows state procedural rules to foreclose federal court review of criminal convictions on habeas corpus.[48] Yet in this area the Court deviates from the usual rule of finality to ensure that it will be able to decide the federal law issue when the state's procedural rules likely would foreclose later review.[49]

Exception: Preserving Supreme Court Review of Important Federal Issues

The Court's statement of the fourth exception to the traditional finality requirement is by far the most confusing. Justice White, writing for the Court, explained the fourth category by stating:

> Lastly, there are those situations where the federal issue has been finally decided in the state courts with further proceedings pending in which the party seeking review here might prevail on the merits on nonfederal grounds, thus rendering unnecessary review of the federal issue by this Court, and where reversal of the state court on the federal issue would be preclusive of any further litigation on the relevant cause of action rather than merely controlling the nature and character of, or determining the admissibility of evidence in, the state proceedings still to come. In these circumstances, if a refusal immediately to review the state-court decision might seriously erode federal policy, the Court has entertained and decided the federal issue . . .[50]

In other words, this fourth category applies when several requirements are met: (1) The state courts have completed all proceedings on the federal issue and reached a decision on it; (2) the party seeking Supreme Court review of the federal law issue might prevail on the state law grounds upon remand and such

[46] *Id.* at 168.
[47] The independent and adequate state grounds rule is discussed in the next section, §10.5, *infra.*
[48] *See, e.g.,* Wainwright v. Sykes, 433 U.S. 72 (1977); *see* §15.5, *infra.*
[49] *See* Note, *supra* note 1, at 49-50.
[50] 420 U.S. at 482-483.

a victory would prevent Supreme Court review of the federal questions; (3) the Supreme Court's decision on the federal law issues might end the litigation; and (4) there are important federal interests to be served by allowing Supreme Court review prior to the completion of the state court proceedings. Thus, the third category differs from the fourth because in the former it is certain that Supreme Court review will be unavailable except at that point, whereas in the fourth exception Supreme Court review might be had later if the party appealing the federal issues also loses on the state law questions. Also, the fourth category, unlike the third, expressly requires that an important federal interest be served by allowing Supreme Court review prior to the completion of the state proceedings.

The Court found that the *Cox Broadcasting* case itself fit in this fourth exception. The Georgia Supreme Court upheld the constitutionality of the Georgia statute preventing publication of the rape victim's identity and remanded the case for a trial on common law privacy causes of action. It is possible that the defendants would win at trial, in which case the Supreme Court would not have the opportunity to determine the constitutionality of the Georgia statute. If the statute is unconstitutional, then the defendants should not have to bear the costs of the trial. Moreover, First Amendment values would be served by invalidating the statute as soon as possible.

The *Cox Broadcasting* Court cited three prior decisions as illustrating this fourth category. First, in *Local No. 438 Construction & General Laborers' Union v. Curry*, the Georgia Supreme Court issued a preliminary injunction halting labor picketing, rejecting claims that the order was preempted by federal labor statutes.[51] The case was remanded to the state trial court to determine whether to issue a permanent injunction. The Supreme Court granted review, prior to the proceedings on remand, because the federal preemption issue was distinct from the unresolved state law questions and because "postponing review would seriously erode the national labor policy."[52]

In *Mercantile National Bank of Dallas v. Langdeau*, two national banks were sued in a Texas state court in Travis County, Texas.[53] The banks argued that a federal statute protected them from suit in that court and pursuant to the federal venue statute, the case had to be brought elsewhere. The Texas courts ruled against the banks and the case was set for a trial on the merits. The Supreme Court granted review on the venue question. The Court reasoned that the venue question was a "separate and independent matter, anterior to the merits and not enmeshed in the factual and legal issues comprising the plaintiff's cause of action."[54] Furthermore, the Court said that allowing review before completion of the state court proceedings would serve the policy of the federal statute, which was to protect the banks from long and complex litigation in an inconvenient forum.[55]

[51] 371 U.S. 542 (1963).

[52] *Id.* at 550. Also, the Court found that the results on the hearing for the permanent injunction were a foregone conclusion and thus the case also could be fit into the first category described above.

[53] 371 U.S. 555 (1963).

[54] *Id.* at 558.

[55] *Id.*

A third illustration of this fourth category is *Miami Herald Publishing Co. v. Tornillo.*[56] The case involved a challenge to a Florida statute that created a right to reply for political candidates criticized in newspaper editorials. The trial court accepted the Miami Herald's claim that the statute was unconstitutional, but the Florida Supreme Court reversed, upholding the statute, and remanded the case to the lower court for a trial. Prior to the proceedings on remand, the Supreme Court granted review and declared unconstitutional the Florida statute. The Court explained the propriety of hearing the case prior to a final judgment by observing that "[w]hichever way we were to decide on the merits, it would be intolerable to leave unanswered, under these circumstances, an important question of freedom of the press under the First Amendment; an uneasy and unsettled constitutional posture of [the state statute] could only further harm the operation of a free press."[57]

Another case involving this fourth exception was *Southland Corp. v. Keating.*[58] Owners of a 7-Eleven franchise sued the Southland Corporation for violating a California law regulating franchising. The defendant, pursuant to the terms of the franchise contract, requested arbitration to resolve the dispute. The California Supreme Court found the Federal Arbitration Act inapplicable and concluded that the matter should be decided within the courts rather than in arbitration. The case was then remanded for a trial. The Supreme Court granted review at that point to determine whether the federal act was violated by the California Supreme Court's decision. The Court justified the grant of review by explaining that "failure to accord immediate review of the decision of the California Supreme Court might 'seriously erode [the] federal policy' [embodied in the Federal Arbitration Act]."[59] Furthermore, "Without immediate review of the California holding by this Court there may be no opportunity to pass on the federal issue and as a result there would remain in effect the unreviewed decision of the State Supreme Court [limiting the application of the Federal Act]."[60]

A subsequent case involving this exception was *Fort Wayne Books, Inc. v. Indiana.*[61] Two individuals were prosecuted for violating Indiana's obscenity law and the Indiana Racketeer Influenced and Corrupt Organization Act (RICO). The state trial court dismissed the RICO charges, holding that the state RICO law was impermissibly vague in its application to obscenity materials. The court of appeals reversed and reinstated the charges, and the Indiana Supreme Court denied review.

Although there was not a final judgment because trial court proceedings remained, the Supreme Court nonetheless granted review. The Court explained that the defendants could prevail on nonfederal grounds at their trial, thus preventing appeal as to the constitutionality of the application of Indiana's RICO law to obscenity. Accordingly, the Court concluded that the "only debatable question

[56] 418 U.S. 241 (1974).
[57] *Id.* at 247 n.6.
[58] 465 U.S. 1 (1984).
[59] *Id.* at 7.
[60] *Id.* at 6.
[61] 489 U.S. 46 (1989).

is whether a refusal to grant immediate review of petitioner's claim might seriously erode federal policy."[62] The Court concluded that the First Amendment issues raised necessitated resolution and justified immediate review. Justice White, writing for the Court, declared that "[r]esolution of this important issue of the possible limits the first amendment places on state and federal efforts to control organized crime should not remain in doubt."[63]

The fourth exception is criticized as being inconsistent with other procedural principles that prevent Supreme Court review of federal law issues, such as the independent and adequate state grounds doctrine discussed below. Moreover, it is argued that the exception is inconsistent with the text and purposes of §1257 and that the Court should not have fashioned this exception on its own.[64] These criticisms seem misplaced. The fourth category applies only if there is a final ruling from the state court on the federal law issues. Furthermore, an important federal interest is required to justify prompt Supreme Court review. Under such circumstances, resources are saved and the social good is served by allowing the Supreme Court to provide a definitive resolution of important federal law questions.

§10.4.3 Supreme Court Review of Final Judgments of the U.S. Courts of Appeals

Review Without a Final Judgment of a Federal Court of Appeals

The Supreme Court's general practice is to review lower federal court decisions only after a final judgment of a U.S. court of appeals.[65] However, there are a number of situations in which the Supreme Court hears cases prior to the entry of a final judgment.

One instance in which the Supreme Court reviews cases prior to the entry of a final judgment by the court of appeals is when federal jurisdictional statutes provide for appeals from federal district court decisions. For example, a few instances remain in which three-judge federal courts are used.[66] In such situations there is direct review in the U.S. Supreme Court.[67] Also, there is Supreme Court review of

[62] *Id.* at 55.

[63] *Id.* at 56.

[64] *See* Redish, *supra* note 8, at 216.

[65] *See* Hamilton-Brown Shoe Co. v. Wolf Bros. & Co., 240 U.S. 251, 258 (1916) (articulating policy of only reviewing final judgments).

[66] Three-judge courts are available for the following: reapportionment cases, 28 U.S.C. §2284; cases under the Civil Rights Act of 1964 at the request of the attorney general, 42 U.S.C. §2000a-5(b), 2000e-6(b); the Voting Rights under the Civil Rights Act of 1964 at the request of the attorney general, 42 U.S.C. §2000a-5(b), 2000e-6(b); the Voting Rights Act of 1965, *see, e.g.,* 42 U.S.C. §1971(g); the Railroad Reorganization Act, 45 U.S.C. §719(b); and the Presidential Election Campaign Fund Act, 26 U.S.C. §9001.

[67] 28 U.S.C. §1253. Actually, §1253 only applies for reapportionment cases; the other statutes have their own provisions concerning appeals to the U.S. Supreme Court. *See also* Robert L. Stern, Eugene Gressman, Stephen M. Shapiro & Kenneth S. Geller, Supreme Court Practice 90-112 (8th ed. 2002).

federal district court decisions if there is a specific federal statute authorizing such review. For example, the Flag Protection Act of 1989 provided for a direct appeal to the Supreme Court of any district court decision ruling on the constitutionality of the law.[68] Indeed, the statute provided that the Court shall "if it has not previously ruled on the question, accept jurisdiction over the appeal and advance on the docket and expedite to the greatest extent possible."[69] After two federal district courts declared the Flag Protection Act unconstitutional, the Supreme Court granted review, provided for expedited briefing and arguments, and affirmed the lower court rulings invalidating the law.[70]

Second, the Supreme Court may review cases docketed in the court of appeals prior to the entry of a final judgment by the appeals court. Section 1254 provides that cases in the courts of appeals may be reviewed by certiorari upon the petition of any party "before or after rendition of judgment or decree."[71] Although the grant of certiorari before judgment is relatively uncommon, it has occurred in many instances, including several important cases such as *United States v. Nixon*,[72] *Dames & Moore v. Regan*,[73] and *Youngstown Sheet & Tube Co. v. Sawyer*.[74] Similarly, in *Gratz v. Bollinger*, the Supreme Court granted review in a case pending before the Sixth Circuit concerning the constitutionality of a University of Michigan affirmative action program for undergraduate admissions even though the court of appeals had not yet issued a decision.[75] Review likely was granted so as to consider the case together with *Grutter v. Bollinger*, a challenge to the University of Michigan Law School's affirmative action program, which had been upheld by the Sixth Circuit.[76] Likewise, the Supreme Court granted certiorari before judgment in *Students for Fair Admission v. University of North Carolina* before the Fourth Circuit had issued a decision. This was to consolidate it with *Students for Fair Admission v. President and Fellows of Harvard College*,[77] since both cases posed the issue of whether colleges and universities may engage in affirmative action.

The Supreme Court's Rules make it clear that certiorari before judgment is restricted to the exceptional case that is "of such imperative public importance . . . to require immediate settlement in this Court."[78] The Court generally has adhered

[68] Pub. L. No. 101-131, amending 18 U.S.C. §700.

[69] *Id.* at subsection (d)(2).

[70] United States v. Haggerty, 731 F. Supp. 415 (W.D. Wash. 1990); United States v. Eichman, 731 F. Supp. 1123 (D.D.C.), *aff'd*, 496 U.S. 300 (1990).

[71] For an excellent discussion of certiorari before judgment, *see* James Lindgren & William P. Marshall, The Supreme Court's Extraordinary Power to Grant Certiorari Before Judgment in the Court of Appeals, 1986 Sup. Ct. Rev. 259.

[72] 418 U.S. 683 (1974) (executive privilege did not justify President Nixon's refusal to comply with subpoena for White House tapes).

[73] 453 U.S. 654 (1981) (approving President Carter's executive agreement with Iran to release frozen Iranian assets in exchange for release of American hostages).

[74] 343 U.S. 579 (1952) (declaring unconstitutional President Truman's seizure of the steel mills during a labor strike).

[75] 539 U.S. 244 (2003).

[76] 539 U.S. 306 (2003).

[77] 600 U.S. 181 (2023).

[78] Supreme Court Rule 11; Stern, Gressman, Shapiro & Geller, *supra* note 38, at 262-263.

to this rule and has granted certiorari before judgment in cases of pressing national significance where a speedy resolution is important.[79] Nonetheless, some criticize the Supreme Court's granting of certiorari before judgment, contending that the Court's decision-making process would be enhanced by waiting for a court of appeals decision.[80] However, there undoubtedly are cases where a definitive decision from the Supreme Court is essential and time is of the essence, justifying the provision for certiorari before judgment for exceptional cases.

Despite the absence of a specific rule providing for it, the Supreme Court also grants certiorari before judgment to consolidate a case pending in a court of appeals with a case before the Supreme Court.[81] Consolidation might be done to provide the Court with another factual context within which to decide a legal question or to enhance efficiency by disposing of multiple cases posing the same issue.[82]

A third and final situation where the Supreme Court hears cases before a final judgment is rendered is when the U.S. court of appeals issues a decision before the district court grants a final judgment. In general, the U.S. court of appeals can review only final decisions of district courts.[83] However, in two major situations a court of appeals may grant interlocutory review: the collateral order doctrine and pursuant to statutes permitting such appeals. In such instances, the Supreme Court can review the court of appeals decisions and, hence, will be hearing and deciding matters before there is a final judgment.

The Collateral Order Doctrine

The collateral order doctrine refers to the authority of a court of appeals to review a ruling of a district court that is unrelated to the merits of the case and that allegedly threatens an important right, thus justifying immediate appellate review. The seminal case concerning the collateral order doctrine is *Cohen v. Beneficial Industrial Loan Corp.*[84] *Cohen* posed a choice of law question for the federal district court. The case involved a shareholder's derivative action against a corporation. Jurisdiction was based on diversity of citizenship and the pertinent state law required the shareholders to post a security bond. The district court

[79] *See* Lindgren & Marshall, *supra* note 57, at 277-297 (reviewing cases where certiorari before judgment has been granted).

[80] *See, e.g.*, Gerald Gunther, Judicial Hegemony and Legislative Autonomy: The *Nixon* Case and the Impeachment Process, 22 UCLA L. Rev. 30, 31-33 (1974) (criticizing the grant of certiorari before judgment).

[81] *See, e.g.*, Bolling v. Sharpe, 347 U.S. 497 (1954). *See also* Lindgren & Marshall, *supra* note 57, at 308.

[82] Professors Lindgren and Marshall also point out two other situations, even rarer, in which certiorari before judgment has been granted. One is where a case was previously before the U.S. Supreme Court; *see* Lindgren & Marshall, *supra* note 57, at 308-312. Second, certiorari before judgment has been granted in some instances where a direct appeal from a district court was requested; although the Court found that an appeal was not proper under the circumstances, it nonetheless took the case by granting certiorari before judgment; *see id.* at 312-316.

[83] 28 U.S.C. §1291.

[84] 337 U.S. 541 (1949).

refused to require the posting of the security and the defendant sought immediate appeal. The Supreme Court unanimously held that the district court's order was appealable, even though the merits of the case were yet to be decided. The Court explained that there is a "small class [of cases] which finally determine claims of right separable from and collateral to, rights asserted in the action, too important to be denied review and too independent of the cause itself to require that appellate consideration be deferred until the whole case is adjudicated."[85]

Thus, a ruling of a district court is appealable to a court of appeals prior to the entry of a final judgment when the district court has issued an order that is truly separate from the elements of the plaintiff's cause of action or the defendant's defenses and where there is an important reason for immediate appellate review.[86] In subsequent cases, the Supreme Court has emphasized that this is a very narrow exception.[87]

For example, in *Coopers & Lybrand v. Livesay,* the Court held that a district court's ruling denying certification for a class action is not immediately appealable under the collateral order doctrine.[88] The Court deemed it irrelevant that the effect of denying class certification likely meant an end to the litigation. The Court stated that "the fact that an interlocutory order may induce a party to abandon his claim before final judgment is not a sufficient reason for considering it a 'final decision' within the meaning of §1291."[89] In denying the interlocutory appeal, even though it likely caused an end to the lawsuit and thus meant that the district court's order never would be reviewed, the Court restated the collateral order doctrine: "To come within the 'small class' of decisions excepted from the final-judgment rule by *Cohen,* the order must conclusively determine the disputed question, resolve an important issue completely separate from the merits of the action, and be effectively unreviewable on appeal from a final judgment."[90]

Similarly, in *Will v. Hallock,* the Supreme Court found that the requirements of the collateral order doctrine were not met.[91] In this case, a district court refused

[85] *Id.* at 546.

[86] For a proposal to modify this approach, advocating the use of a balancing test, *see* Martin H. Redish, The Pragmatic Approach to Appealability in the Federal Courts, 75 Colum. L. Rev. 89 (1975).

[87] In one post-*Cohen* case, the Court took an approach that would have allowed many more appeals under the collateral order doctrine. Gillespie v. United States Steel Corp., 379 U.S. 148 (1964). The Supreme Court, however, subsequently said that the case is limited to its facts. Coopers & Lybrand v. Livesay, 437 U.S. 463, 477 n.30 (1978) ("If *Gillespie* were extended beyond the unique facts of that case, §1291 would be stripped of all significance."). In many cases, the Court has refused to allow interlocutory review under the collateral order doctrine. *See, e.g.,* Midland Asphalt Corp. v. United States, 489 U.S. 794 (1989) (holding that interlocutory review was not available of a district court's denial of a motion to dismiss because of prosecutorial violations of federal rules providing for secrecy of grand jury materials); Van Cauwenberghe v. Biard, 486 U.S. 517 (1988) (denying interlocutory review of a district court's denial of a motion to dismiss a civil suit on grounds of immunity from civil process or forum non conveniens).

[88] 437 U.S. at 463.

[89] *Id.* at 477.

[90] *Id.* at 468. The Supreme Court reaffirmed this three-part test in Van Cauwenberghe v. Biard, 486 U.S. 517 (1988).

[91] 546 U.S. 345 (2006).

to dismiss a suit for constitutional violations against federal officers when it dismissed the suit against the U.S. government. The case involved a man who suffered identity theft and whose stolen credit card was used to purchase child pornography. Federal agents seized the man and his wife's computers, software, and disk drives. No charges were brought against them and everything was returned, but several disk drives were severely damaged, and all the stored data was lost. The man's wife ran a computer software business from her home, and it was ruined by the destruction of the computers and loss of information.

They sued the United States and several officers. The district court found that the suit against the United States was barred, but the constitutional claims against the officers could go forward. The officers objected and pointed to a federal statute, the Westfall Act, which they argued required dismissal of the suit against them.[92] They sought to appeal the refusal of the district court to dismiss the case under the collateral order doctrine.

The Supreme Court unanimously held that the collateral order doctrine did not apply. Justice Souter wrote for the Court and said that the collateral order doctrine requires that the order "(1) conclusively determine the disputed question, (2) resolve an important issue completely separate from the merits of the action, and (3) be effectively unreviewable on appeal from a final judgment."[93] The Court said that these are "stringent requirements" and were not met in this case. Any decision of the district court concerning the officers' liability, including as to whether they were protected by qualified immunity, would be reviewable on appeal.

In other cases, as well, the Court has adhered to a narrow view of the collateral order doctrine. For example, the Court has said that interlocutory appeals are unavailable for district court orders refusing to disqualify counsel in civil cases,[94] and for district court orders disqualifying counsel in both civil and criminal cases.[95] The Supreme Court also has held the collateral order doctrine inapplicable when a court denies an extradited person's motion to dismiss based on immunity from civil process,[96] when a district court refuses to stay its proceedings because of simultaneous litigation of the matter in state court,[97] and when a district court refuses to dismiss a civil case because of immunity to civil process or

[92] 28 U.S.C. §2676.

[93] 546 U.S. at 349.

[94] Firestone Tire & Rubber Co. v. Risjord, 449 U.S. 368 (1981).

[95] Richardson-Merrell, Inc. v. Koller, 472 U.S. 424 (1985) (orders disqualifying counsel in civil cases are not appealable until a final judgment is entered); Flanagan v. United States, 465 U.S. 259 (1984) (orders disqualifying counsel in criminal cases are not appealable until a final judgment is entered).

[96] Van Cauwenberghe v. Biard, 486 U.S. 517 (1988).

[97] Gulfstream Aerospace v. Mayacamas, 485 U.S. 271 (1988). In *Gulfstream Aerospace*, the Court also overruled the *Enelow-Ettelson* doctrine that orders granting or denying stays of "legal" proceedings on "equitable" grounds were considered to be immediately appealable. *Id.* at 283-289, *overruling* Enelow v. New York Life Ins. Co., 293 U.S. 379 (1935) and Ettelson v. Metropolitan Life Ins. Co., 317 U.S. 188 (1942). However, the *Gulfstream* decision was itself overruled within several months by 9 U.S.C.A. §16(a). *See, e.g.*, Microchip Tech. Inc. v. U.S. Philips Corp., 367 F.3d 1350, 1355 (Fed. Cir. 2004) ("section 16 renders appealable under section 1292(a)(1) the denial of an injunctive order (i.e., motions to compel arbitration) that otherwise would not be appealable under *Gulfstream*").

forum non conveniens.[98] The Court emphasized the strong presumption against interlocutory review and the limited exception created by the collateral order doctrine. In *Cunningham v. Hamilton County, Ohio,* the Court ruled that an order imposing sanctions on an attorney and disqualifying her from further participation in the case was not immediately appealable under the collateral order doctrine.[99] The Court stressed that the sanctions order was not wholly distinct from the merits of the case and that appellate review was available after a final judgment.

In a subsequent decision on the collateral order doctrine, the Court once again emphasized its narrow scope and refused to find that it applied to allow an interlocutory appeal. In *Mohawk Industries v. Carpenter,* the Court unanimously held that the collateral order doctrine did not apply to allow an individual to have an interlocutory appeal of a federal district court decision denying the protection of the attorney-client privilege.[100]

Mohawk Industries challenged a district court order that it disclose material that it believed was protected by the attorney-client privilege. It argued that this was "collateral" to the merits of the lawsuit and that appellate review was "now or never": Once information is revealed, it never can be made secret again. The Court, in an opinion by Justice Sotomayor, rejected this. The Court said, "The crucial question, however, is not whether an interest is important in the abstract; it is whether deferring review until final judgment so imperils the interest as to justify the cost of allowing immediate appeal of the entire class of relevant orders. We routinely require litigants to wait until after final judgment to vindicate valuable rights, including rights central to our adversarial system."[101]

The Court rejected the argument that denial of interlocutory review would risk irreparable injury. In part, this was because the Court rejected Mohawk's argument that forcing litigants to wait until final judgment to appeal discovery orders would unduly chill attorney-client communications.[102] But the Court also stressed the adequacy of postjudgment appeals: "In our estimation, postjudgment appeals generally suffice to protect the rights of litigants and assure the vitality of the attorney-client privilege. Appellate courts can remedy the improper disclosure of privileged material in the same way they remedy a host of other erroneous evidentiary rulings: by vacating an adverse judgment and remanding for a new trial in which the protected material and its fruits are excluded from evidence."[103]

Although the Court's unwillingness to allow interlocutory appeals is understandable in light of the benefits of the final judgment rule, it is questionable in cases where the district court's decision will be the "death knell" for the lawsuit.

[98] Van Cauwenberghe v. Biard, 486 U.S. 517 (1988). *See also* Lauro Lines, S.R.L. v. Chasser, 490 U.S. 495 (1989) (no collateral review of district court's refusal to dismiss a case on the ground that a contractual forum selection clause required that the matter be litigated in another jurisdiction).

[99] 527 U.S. 198 (1999).

[100] 558 U.S. 100 (2009).

[101] *Id.* at 108.

[102] *Id.* at 109.

[103] *Id.* at 108.

For example, in *Coopers & Lybrand*, the district court's order refusing to certify the class action meant that the lawsuit would end. As such, in practical terms the order really was the final decision in the case and should have been reviewable. Even as to *Mohawk Industries*, the Court gave little weight to the harms to the attorney-client privilege of requiring disclosure without the possibility of interlocutory appeal.

28 U.S.C. §1292: Interlocutory Review

The other situation in which a court of appeals will review a case before the district court grants a final judgment is pursuant to 28 U.S.C. §1292, which provides for interlocutory review under specific circumstances.[104] Section 1292 outlines a number of situations in which courts of appeals can grant interlocutory review.[105] For example, §1292(a)(1) allows the court of appeals to review interlocutory orders of the district courts "granting, continuing, modifying, refusing or dissolving injunctions, or refusing to dissolve or modify injunctions, except where a direct review may be had in the Supreme Court." In other words, decisions of district courts granting or refusing injunctions are appealable. Section 1292(a)(2) allows interlocutory review for "orders appointing receivers or refusing orders to wind up receiverships." Section 1292(a)(3) provides review of district court orders "determining the rights and liabilities of the parties to admiralty cases from which final decrees are allowed."

Also, §1292 provides that when a district court judge enters an order that is not appealable on an interlocutory basis, the judge may refer the question to the U.S. court of appeals. Such certification is limited to instances in which the judge is "of the opinion that such order involves a controlling question of law as to which there is substantial ground for difference of opinion and that an immediate appeal from the order may materially advance the ultimate termination of the litigation."[106] Under such circumstances, the district court must present the question in writing to the court of appeals within ten days of entering the order. The court of appeals then has discretion as to whether to review the issue on an interlocutory basis.

Thus, an important exception to the usual rule that the Supreme Court only reviews final judgments is when it hears and decides cases in which the U.S. court of appeals provided interlocutory relief.

[104] Professors Low, Jeffries, and Bradley correctly point out that there are other ways in which to obtain interlocutory review as well. Rule 54(b) of the Federal Rules of Civil Procedure allows a district court to make an express determination of appealability when the judge decides that the decision of some of the claims is sufficiently separable from the remainder of the case. Also, the writ of mandamus can be used in extraordinary circumstances where it is shown that the district court has abused its discretion. For mandamus to be available there must be a showing of a need for immediate appeals court intervention.

[105] The Supreme Court recently held that §1292 applies to authorize court of appeals interlocutory review of district court decisions reviewing bankruptcy court decisions. Connecticut Natl. Bank v. Germain, 503 U.S. 249 (1992).

[106] 28 U.S.C. §1292(b).

§10.5 THE SUPREME COURT'S REFUSAL TO REVIEW HIGHEST STATE COURT DECISIONS IF THERE ARE INDEPENDENT AND ADEQUATE STATE LAW GROUNDS SUPPORTING THE RESULT

§10.5.1 The Independent and Adequate State Grounds Doctrine

An important and complex limitation on Supreme Court review of state court decisions is the independent and adequate state grounds doctrine. Simply stated, the Supreme Court will not hear a case if the decision of the state's highest court is supported by a state law rationale that is independent of federal law and adequate to sustain the result. Phrased slightly differently, the Court must decline to hear the case if its reversal of the state court's federal law ruling will not change the outcome of the case because the result is independently supported by the state court's decision on state law grounds.

Origin of the Independent and Adequate State Grounds Doctrine

The independent and adequate state grounds doctrine has its basis, analytically if not historically, in the Supreme Court decision in *Murdock v. City of Memphis*, which held that the Court may not review state court decisions on state law matters.[1] Murdock's ancestors conveyed land to Memphis for the purpose of creating a naval depot. The deed of sale provided that the land would revert to the grantors or their heirs if the United States did not use the land for the specified purpose. Although the city transferred the property to the federal government, the land never was used for the construction of a naval depot. Ten years after acquiring the property, the United States returned it to the city. Murdock sued the city, requesting that it return the property to him under the terms of the conveyance.

The Supreme Court held that the issue presented did not involve federal law, but instead was a state law matter concerning whether Murdock retained a reversionary interest based on the original conveyance instrument. The Court held that it lacked any authority to review state court rulings as to state law. The Judiciary Act of 1789, in §25, quite explicitly prevented Supreme Court review of state court decisions on state law questions.[2] Although the revision of the Judiciary Act in 1867 omitted this provision, the Court concluded that Congress's unmistakable intent was to prevent Supreme Court review of state court interpretations of state laws. The Court explained that the Supreme Court review long had been predicated on the assumption that its "jurisdiction was limited to the correction of errors relating

§10.5 [1] 87 U.S. (20 Wall.) 590 (1875).

[2] Section 25 of the Judiciary Act of 1789 provided: "But no other error shall be assigned or regarded as a ground of reversal in any such case as aforesaid than such as appears on the face of the record and immediately respects the before-mentioned questions of validity or construction of the said Constitution, treaties, statutes, commissions, or authorities in dispute."

solely to Federal law."[3] The Court said that the protection of the Constitution and federal laws did not warrant an examination and decision of "other questions not of a federal character."[4] In other words, a state's highest court is the authoritative interpreter of state law and the Supreme Court's power to review state courts is limited to the latter's decisions as to federal questions.

An important question arises when a state's highest court bases its decision on both federal law and on state law grounds. If the Supreme Court's reversal of the state court's decision as to federal law would change the outcome in the case, then quite obviously the Court can hear and decide the matter. But the Court cannot hear the case if the Court's reversal of the federal law ruling will not alter the result because the state court's decision as to state law will mandate the same outcome. In other words, because in light of *Murdock v. City of Memphis* the Court cannot review state court decisions on state law questions, it may not grant review when state law would lead to the same conclusion irrespective of the Supreme Court's decision on the federal law issues. As the Supreme Court explained, "The settled rule [is] that where the judgment of a state court rests upon two grounds, one of which is federal and the other non-federal in character, our jurisdiction fails if the non-federal ground is independent of the federal ground and adequate to support the judgment."[5]

Illustrations

A simple example is illustrative. If a state's highest court declares a municipal ordinance unconstitutional as independently violating both the state constitution and the U.S. Constitution, the Supreme Court must deny review because the statute would be invalidated on state law grounds even if the state court's federal law ruling were reversed. In contrast, if the municipal ordinance were declared *constitutional* under both the state and federal Constitutions, then the Court can grant review because a reversal of the state court's federal law decision would change the outcome of the case; instead of the statute being upheld, it would be declared unconstitutional.

Another example illustrates the principle in a different context. Imagine that a person is beat up by a municipal police officer and brings a suit in federal court based on both federal law, specifically 42 U.S.C. §1983, and on the state law of battery. The plaintiff seeks $100,000 in compensatory damages; the recovery is identical under either federal or state law.

There are four possible scenarios for Supreme Court review. One is for the state's trial court to find a violation of both federal law and the state's tort law and to conclude that the plaintiff is entitled to $100,000 in damages under either federal or state law. The state's highest court affirms on both grounds, thus upholding a $100,000 judgment for the plaintiff. Given the assumption in this hypothetical that the recovery is identical under state and federal law, the Supreme Court

[3] 87 U.S. at 630.
[4] *Id.* at 633.
[5] Fox Film Corp. v. Muller, 296 U.S. 207, 210 (1935).

would not review the state highest court decision. Even if the state court's decision concerning §1983 were reversed, the plaintiff would still collect $100,000 based on the state law claim—a claim that the Court, of course, cannot review because of *Murdock v. Memphis.*

A second possibility would be if the state court awarded $100,000 based on the state law claim, but found no violation of federal law. Assuming that the maximum damages under the federal claim also was $100,000 and the plaintiff would not collect a penny more if recovery was allowed under federal law as well, the Supreme Court should not hear the case. Again, because of *Murdock* it cannot review the state court's state law ruling, and it should not hear the case since allowing federal liability would not alter the judgment.

In contrast, a third situation is where the state court found no violation of state law but awarded $100,000 for the §1983 violation. In that case, the Supreme Court should hear the case because reversing the state court's interpretation of federal law could change the result—for example, from $100,000 to zero.

Similarly, a fourth possibility is if the state court ruled against the plaintiff as to both the state law and the federal law claims. Again, the Supreme Court can grant review because a reversal as to the federal law issue would shift from the plaintiff recovering nothing to the plaintiff's being able to collect for the injuries suffered.

The Basic Rule and Its Justifications

These examples illustrate the basic rule: where a state court decision rests on two grounds, one of which is federal law and the other is state law, the Supreme Court will not review the case if the state law ground is independent of the federal law ground and is adequate by itself to support the result.[6] There are many justifications for this rule.

The Court often has observed that the prohibition against advisory opinions prevents it from hearing cases when there is an independent and adequate state law ground for the decision. For example, in *Herb v. Pitcairn,* the Court stated, "We are not permitted to render an advisory opinion, and if the same judgment would be rendered by the state court after we corrected its views of federal laws, our review would amount to nothing more than an advisory opinion."[7] In other words, if a reversal of the state court's interpretation of federal law would not alter the

[6] For a relatively early statement of this rule, *see* Eustis v. Bolles, 150 U.S. 361, 366 (1893) ("It is likewise settled law that, where the record discloses that if a question has been raised and decided adversely to a party claiming the benefit of a provision of the Constitution or laws of the United States, another question, not Federal, has been also raised and decided against such party, and the decision of the latter question is sufficient, notwithstanding the Federal question to sustain the judgment, this court will not review the judgment.").

[7] 324 U.S. 117, 126 (1945) (citations omitted); *see also* Florida v. Meyers, 466 U.S. 380, 381-382 n.* (1984).

result in the case, such a ruling would be no more than an impermissible advisory opinion.[8]

Also, the independent and adequate grounds doctrine allows the Court to avoid unnecessary constitutional rulings. The Court frequently stresses the desirability of avoiding constitutional questions wherever possible.[9] When the state court rules on both federal constitutional grounds and on state law grounds, the Court avoids the former when the state law is independent and adequate to support the result in the case.

The doctrine also promotes harmony between the federal and state systems by minimizing Supreme Court review of state court decisions. The argument is that any federal court reversal of a state court ruling is a possible source of friction. By confining review to instances where the Supreme Court decision might make a difference, the Court avoids unnecessary tension between federal and state courts.

Additionally, by preventing Supreme Court review in some cases, the doctrine has the effect of conserving the Court's finite resources for cases more deserving of its attention.[10] The doctrine is in accord with the Court's customary role in reviewing state court decisions. As the Court observed, "Our only power over state judgments is to correct them to the extent that they incorrectly adjudge federal rights. And our power is to correct wrong judgments, not to revise opinions."[11]

Criticism of the Independent and Adequate Grounds Doctrine

Not all commentators support the existence of the independent and adequate state grounds doctrine. For example, Professors Matasar and Bruch argue that the doctrine should be abolished and the Supreme Court should review state court decisions irrespective of whether a state law basis exists for the ruling.[12] Professors Matasar and Bruch, and others, point to a number of undesirable consequences of the doctrine.

For example, the doctrine permits inconsistent and incorrect interpretations of federal law to remain unreviewed. A state court decision wrongly interpreting federal law will remain on the books, potentially influencing other courts around the country, if there is an independent and adequate state law basis for the decision. Likewise, inconsistent state interpretations of federal law will not be resolved if they are accompanied by state law grounds. Accuracy and consistency in the application of federal law are sacrificed.[13] The importance of Supreme Court review of state decisions in

[8] For a discussion of the prohibition against advisory opinions, *see* §2.2, *supra*. *But see* Richard A. Matasar & Gregory S. Bruch, Procedural Common Law, Federal Jurisdictional Policy, and Abandonment of the Adequate and Independent State Grounds Doctrine, 86 Colum. L. Rev. 1291, 1302-1310 (1986) (arguing that review would not be an advisory opinion).

[9] *See, e.g.,* Ashwander v. TVA, 297 U.S. 288, 246 (1936) (Brandeis, J., concurring); Railroad Commn. of Texas v. Pullman Co., 312 U.S. 496 (1941) (discussed in detail in §12.2, *infra*).

[10] *See generally* Samuel Estreicher & John Sexton, Redefining the Supreme Court's Role (1986) (defining the Court's workload and the need for more careful allocation of its resources).

[11] Herb v. Pitcairn, 324 U.S. at 125-126.

[12] Matasar & Bruch, *supra* note 8, at 1292-1294.

[13] *See, e.g., id.* at 1314-1315.

such instances is reflected in an exception the Court created to the final judgment rule. The Court said that review is permitted in the absence of a final judgment from the state's highest court when the Court otherwise would not have the chance to correct a state court's errors regarding federal law.[14]

Also, the independent and adequate state grounds doctrine invites state courts to try to immunize their decisions from Supreme Court review by manufacturing a state basis for the decision. In many civil rights cases during the 1960s, the state courts tried to prevent Supreme Court review of their anti-civil rights rulings by invoking a state law ground of decision.[15] As discussed below, one of the exceptions to the doctrine is when the state law ground was created or imposed for the purpose of frustrating Supreme Court review.[16]

Despite the criticisms of the doctrine, it is well entrenched in current law and the Supreme Court has given no indication that it is about to abandon it. The precise legal basis for the doctrine is uncertain, but most commentators regard it not as constitutionally required but instead as a prudential rule of judicial self-restraint.[17]

Overview of Issues

In examining the independent and adequate state grounds doctrine, this section focuses on two questions. First, §10.5.2 examines when a state ground of decision is to be deemed "adequate" to support the result. Particular attention is paid to the issue of when state procedural rules can prevent Supreme Court review of state court decisions. Second, §10.5.3 considers when a state ground of decision is "independent" of federal law. The especially difficult question, and one that has received a great deal of attention, is how the Court should handle cases where the state court is unclear about whether it is relying on an independent state law basis for its decision.

Finally, by way of introduction, it should be noted that it is for the U.S. Supreme Court to decide whether there is an independent and adequate state ground for the decision.[18] The Court is not bound to accept a state court's conclusion that there is an independent and adequate state law basis for its decision.

[14] *See, e.g.,* Cox Broadcasting Corp. v. Cohn, 420 U.S. 469, 481 (1975); North Dakota State Bd. of Pharmacy v. Snyder's Drug Stores, Inc., 414 U.S. 156 (1973); *see* §10.4, *supra.*

[15] *See, e.g.,* Henry v. Mississippi, 379 U.S. 443 (1965); NAACP v. Alabama ex rel. Flowers, 377 U.S. 288 (1964); Wright v. Georgia, 373 U.S. 284 (1963); NAACP v. Alabama ex rel. Patterson, 357 U.S. 449 (1958); Williams v. Georgia, 349 U.S. 375 (1955).

[16] *See* §10.5.2, *infra.*

[17] *See, e.g.,* Thomas E. Baker, The Ambiguous Independent and Adequate State Ground in Criminal Cases: Federalism Along a Mobius Strip, 19 Ga. L. Rev. 799, 806-807 (1985) ("The independent and adequate state ground doctrine is best explained on a prudential level."); Matasar & Bruch, *supra* note 8, at 1295-1355 (refuting constitutional basis for the doctrine).

[18] *See, e.g.,* Street v. New York, 394 U.S. 576, 583 (1969); Abie State Bank v. Bryan, 282 U.S. 765, 772-773 (1931).

§10.5.2 What is an Adequate *State Ground of Decision?*

A state court's decision on a state law issue is deemed adequate to support its result if the Supreme Court's reversal of the state court's federal law ruling will not alter the outcome of the case. An adequate state law ground exists where the state law basis for the decision is sufficient by itself to support the judgment, regardless of whether the federal law issue is affirmed or reversed. As Professors Matasar and Bruch observe, "A decision based on state law is adequate if the judgment in the case would necessarily be affirmed even if any decision on federal law were reversed."[19]

Unconstitutional State Law Inadequate

State law obviously is not adequate to support the result when there is a claim that the state law itself violates the U.S. Constitution. An unconstitutional state law cannot support the state court's holding. For example, in *Staub v. City of Baxley*, a city ordinance made it an offense to solicit membership in any organization without a permit.[20] Appellant was convicted of violating the ordinance notwithstanding her claims that the law violated the First Amendment. The state court of appeals affirmed, refusing to decide the merits of the case because it concluded that, under state law, the failure to request a permit prevented the appellant from raising constitutional issues on appeal. The Court held that the state law was not adequate to support the judgment because it was unconstitutional. The Court observed that "[t]he decisions of this Court have uniformly held that the failure to apply for a license under an ordinance which on its face violated the Constitution does not preclude review in this Court of a judgment of conviction under such an ordinance."[21]

State Law Inadequate If No Support for Decision in the Record

Nor is state law adequate when there is no fair and substantial basis in the record supporting the state court's state law ruling. In *Ward v. Board of Commissioners of Love County, Oklahoma*, members of the Choctaw Indian Tribe who received land from the federal government objected to the state's taxation of the property.[22] The Indians were informed that the land was about to be sold unless they paid the taxes. Subsequently, the Indians sued for recovery of the money paid. The Oklahoma Supreme Court held that it would not hear the Indians' constitutional claim because of state law preventing a person who voluntarily paid a tax from suing to recover the amount paid. Because it concluded that the Indians voluntarily paid

[19] Matasar & Bruch, *supra* note 8, at 1292-1293 n.2 (emphasis omitted).

[20] 355 U.S. 313 (1958).

[21] *Id.* at 319. *See also* Xerox Corp. v. County of Harris, Tex., 459 U.S. 145, 149 (1982) (state law ground not adequate if it is allegedly unconstitutional).

[22] 253 U.S. 17 (1920).

the taxes, the Oklahoma court refused to hear the federal law claim. The Supreme Court reversed, concluding that the "decision that the taxes were voluntarily paid was without any fair or substantial support."[23] Since it was clear that the Indians paid the taxes because they were coerced to do so, the record contained no basis for concluding that the taxes were voluntarily paid.

When Is the Failure to Comply with State Procedures "Adequate"?

The most important controversy in determining the adequacy of state grounds concerns the failure to comply with state *procedural* requirements as an independent and adequate state ground of decision. A simple example is illustrative. Imagine that a state's highest court ruled against an appellant presenting a constitutional claim because the appellant failed to file a notice of appeal within the required 90 days. The state court did not reach the merits, but instead based its decision entirely on the state law procedural requirement. Is the procedural ruling, then, an adequate ground for the decision precluding Supreme Court review of the federal constitutional question?

The general answer is that decisions on state procedural grounds are deemed "adequate" and are sufficient to prevent the Supreme Court from reviewing substantive constitutional issues. The Supreme Court observed that "[f]ailure to present a federal question in conformance with state procedure constitutes an adequate and independent state ground of decision barring review in this Court, so long as the State has a legitimate interest in enforcing its procedural rules."[24] For example, in one case the Supreme Court held that it could not hear the plaintiff's constitutional claim because under state law all constitutional issues are to be appealed directly from the trial court to the state supreme court; appeal to the court of appeals is deemed a waiver of constitutional issues.[25] The Supreme Court said that the state supreme court's decision that the constitutional issues were waived constituted an independent and adequate ground preventing review. Similarly, the Court ruled that a criminal defendant could not challenge the constitutionality of jury instructions that resulted in a death sentence because the Florida Supreme Court had deemed the issue nonreviewable because there had not been a timely objection at trial.[26]

Situations in Which State Procedural Rules Do Not Preclude Review

Although generally state procedural grounds are deemed adequate to support the result, the Court correctly is unwilling to allow states to manufacture procedural rules in order to preclude Supreme Court review. Nor is the Court willing to allow trivial state rules—procedural requirements where there is at best only

[23] *Id.* at 23.

[24] Michigan v. Tyler, 436 U.S. 499, 512 n.7 (1978).

[25] Parker v. Illinois, 333 U.S. 571 (1948). *See also* Parker v. North Carolina, 397 U.S. 790 (1970); Johnson v. New Jersey, 384 U.S. 719 (1966).

[26] Sochor v. Florida, 504 U.S. 527, 533 (1992).

a minimal state interest—to prevent the vindication of important constitutional rights.[27] Thus, the Court has recognized three types of situations in which it will not allow state procedural rulings to preclude Supreme Court review of the federal law issues raised.

State Procedural Rules Inadequate If They Deny Due Process

First, and most obviously, state procedural rules are not adequate if they deny due process of law. This is simply a restatement of the rule described above: a state law cannot be adequate if it is unconstitutional. For example, in *Reece v. Georgia*, the state court refused to allow a defendant to challenge the racial composition of a grand jury because of a state law requiring such challenges to be made prior to the issuance of an indictment.[28] The Court, however, found that this rule denied due process because the state refused to provide counsel until after an indictment was made.

Another example is *Brinkerhoff-Faris Trust & Savings Co. v. Hill*, where the Court held that there was not an independent and adequate state ground of decision because the state law violated the due process clause.[29] The plaintiffs brought suit on behalf of their shareholders to enjoin the county treasurer from collecting taxes assessed against shares of its stock. The argument was that the County denied equal protection by assessing bank stock at full value while assessing other types of property at less. The state court refused to hear the claim because it held that the state board of equalization, where the matter was filed, lacked jurisdiction and that contrary to its previous rulings, the plaintiffs should have filed the complaint in the state tax commission. The state court, however, found that laches prevented the plaintiffs from proceeding before the latter tribunal. The Supreme Court reversed, holding that the state denied due process by interpreting its law to prevent all forums from hearing the case.[30] The state court's rulings were not adequate to support the judgment because they were unconstitutional in extinguishing all remedies for the plaintiffs.

Procedural Rules Failing to Further an Important State Interest

The second situation in which state procedural rules do not constitute adequate grounds supporting the state court's decision is where the rules fail to promote a sufficiently important state interest, but do prevent the vindication of federal rights. That is, the Supreme Court will grant review even though state

[27] *See* Terrance Sandalow, Henry v. Mississippi and the Adequate State Ground: Proposals for a Revised Doctrine, 1965 Sup. Ct. Rev. 187, 218-219 (need for doctrine to prevent state courts from inventing rules to frustrate federal court review and to balance state and federal interests).

[28] 350 U.S. 85 (1955).

[29] 281 U.S. 673 (1930).

[30] *Id.* at 681-682.

procedures were not followed if the state's rules "heavily burden the assertion of federal rights without significantly advancing any important state policy."[31]

An early example of this principle was *Rogers v. Alabama*, in 1904.[32] In *Rogers*, a defendant moved to quash an indictment for murder on the ground that Black people were excluded from the grand jury on account of their race and because a provision of the state constitution denied Black people the right to vote in violation of the Fourteenth Amendment. The motion was stricken by the state court because of "prolixity," apparently because the allegations of disenfranchisement had little direct relevance to the subject of the trial. The Civil Code of Alabama allowed for pleadings to be stricken if "unnecessarily prolix, irrelevant or frivolous." Although the state courts used this procedural basis to prevent a consideration of the merits of the defendant's federal claim, the Supreme Court nonetheless heard the case and found that the exclusion of Black people from the grand jury violated the equal protection clause. The Court emphasized that the state's interest in efficiency was not substantially furthered by striking a two-page motion and that the effect of the procedural ruling was to prevent the vindication of an important constitutional claim. The Court explained that "[i]t is a necessary and well settled rule that the exercise of jurisdiction by this court to protect constitutional rights cannot be declined when it is plain that the fair result of a decision is to deny the rights."[33]

Henry v. Mississippi

The most important case holding that state procedural rules preclude Supreme Court review only if they serve an important state purpose is *Henry v. Mississippi*.[34] Aaron Henry, a civil rights activist, was arrested by the Mississippi police for having made "indecent proposals" to and having had "offensive contact" with an 18-year-old hitchhiker whom he allegedly given a ride. Henry's conviction was based in large part on the testimony by a police officer concerning what was observed during a search of Henry's car, which was done pursuant to the consent of Henry's wife. Henry's attorney did not object to the evidence at the time it was admitted during the trial but did object later in a motion for a directed verdict at the conclusion of the state's case.

The Mississippi Supreme Court reversed Henry's conviction, holding that the wife's consent did not waive Henry's constitutional rights. The court reversed the conviction despite a state rule requiring a contemporaneous objection to evidence at the time of its admission. The court concluded that the fact that Henry was not represented by local counsel justified the deviation from the procedural rule. Subsequently, the Mississippi Supreme Court learned that Henry actually was

[31] Daniel J. Meltzer, State Court Forfeitures of Federal Rights, 99 Harv. L. Rev. 1130, 1142 (1986).

[32] 192 U.S. 226 (1904).

[33] *Id.* at 230.

[34] 379 U.S. 443 (1965). For a discussion of *Henry*, its relationship to civil rights struggles, and its significance, *see* Robert Jerome Glennon, The Jurisdictional Legacy of the Civil Rights Movement, 61 Tenn. L. Rev. 869 (1994).

represented by local counsel. The court then withdrew its earlier opinion and issued a new one affirming the conviction.

The U.S. Supreme Court vacated the conviction and remanded the case for a determination of whether Henry knowingly waived his federal claim when no objection was made at the time the evidence was offered. The Court emphasized the need to distinguish between state substantive and procedural law in determining whether there is an independent and adequate state ground of decision. Whereas a state substantive ground always is deemed adequate if reversal of the federal law holding would not alter the outcome of the case, a procedural ground should be deemed adequate only if it serves a "legitimate state interest."[35] The Court explained that the "question of when and how defaults in compliance with state procedural rules can preclude our consideration of a federal question is itself a federal question."[36] As such, in every case, it is the Supreme Court's rule to "inquire whether the enforcement of a procedural forfeiture serves such a [legitimate] state interest."[37]

The Court recognized that state courts have an important interest in requiring litigants to make contemporaneous objections to the introduction of evidence. However, the Court observed that the state's interests might have been served equally well by the objection made in the course of the motion for the directed verdict. The Court said that "[i]f this is so, and enforcement of the rule here would serve no substantial state interest, then settled principles would preclude treating the state ground as adequate; giving effect to the contemporaneous-objection rule for its own sake 'would be to force resort to an arid ritual of meaningless form.'"[38]

Under the law of waiver in effect at the time of the *Henry* decision, a waiver required demonstrating that the defendant deliberately bypassed the available procedures; that is, showing that the defendant made a strategic decision to not make a contemporaneous objection.[39] The Court remanded the case to the state court for a determination of whether a waiver occurred under this standard.

Henry remains an important case because of its distinction between state substantive and procedural grounds of decision. Although the Court must give effect to state substantive law that would support the judgment, the Court need not respect state procedural rulings unless they serve a legitimate state interest. Some commentators, most notably Professor Terence Sandalow, have criticized this substance-procedure distinction.[40] Professor Sandalow argued that both state substantive and procedural rulings can adequately support a state court's judgment and that both can frustrate the vindication with the federal right while providing little benefit to the state. Thus,

[35] *Id.* at 447.

[36] *Id.*

[37] *Id.*

[38] *Id.* at 449.

[39] The Court articulated the deliberate bypass standard in Fay v. Noia, 372 U.S. 391, 439 (1963). The Supreme Court subsequently abandoned this test. *See* Wainwright v. Sykes, 433 U.S. 72 (1977). *See* discussion in §15.5, *infra.*

[40] Sandalow, *supra* note 27, at 197-198. *See also* Alfred Hill, The Inadequate State Ground, 65 Colum. L. Rev. 943 (1965) (discussing Henry v. Mississippi).

Professor Sandalow would prefer an approach that discards the artificial distinction between substance and procedure and openly balances the state's interest in its ground of decision and the federal right at stake.[41]

What Is a Legitimate State Interest?

The crucial question after *Henry* is what constitutes a legitimate state interest in a procedural rule as opposed to an "arid ritual of meaningless form." The Supreme Court has not articulated any clear criteria for this determination, instead proceeding on a case-by-case basis.[42] For example, in *Henry,* the Court's aggressive scrutiny of the state's procedural interest might have been motivated by the facts of the case: Henry, a civil rights activist, was being prosecuted in Mississippi in 1962. Cases after *Henry* reveal the Court's careful attention to a case's factual setting and its analysis of the importance of the particular rule in question.

For instance, in *Douglas v. Alabama,* a defendant's attorney objected to the reading of a codefendant's confession.[43] However, the objection was not repeated at the time the confession was actually put into evidence, and the Alabama Supreme Court deemed this a procedural forfeiture that prevented it from hearing the defendant's constitutional claim. The Supreme Court reversed. The Court explained that the defense counsel already had objected three times to the introduction of the confession and that "[n]o legitimate state interest would have been served by requiring repetition of a patently futile objection, already thrice rejected, in a situation in which repeated objection might well affront the court or prejudice the jury beyond repair."[44]

In contrast, in *Parker v. North Carolina,* the state defendant was convicted of burglary pursuant to his guilty plea.[45] Subsequently, the defendant attempted to have the conviction reversed on the grounds that Black people had been excluded from the grand jury that indicted him.[46] The state courts refused to hear this constitutional argument because of a state procedural rule requiring that such a contention must be raised in a motion to quash the indictment before the entry of a guilty plea. The Supreme Court declined to review the constitutional claim because it concluded that the state had a legitimate interest in ensuring timely objections to grand jury composition.

In considering what state procedural rules are sufficiently important to prevent Supreme Court review, it should be noted that the Court now is far more deferential to such rules—especially those requiring contemporaneous objections—than was the situation at the time *Henry* was decided. For example, in defining

[41] Sandalow, *supra* note 27, at 218.

[42] For an excellent discussion of what constitutes a procedural forfeiture preventing federal court review, *see* Meltzer, *supra* note 31.

[43] 380 U.S. 415 (1965).

[44] *Id.* at 422.

[45] 397 U.S. 790 (1970).

[46] The defendant also argued that his confession had been coerced. The state courts reviewed this claim on the merits and ruled against the defendant.

the availability of federal habeas corpus relief for state prisoners, the Court has stressed the importance of state contemporaneous objection rules.[47] When *Henry* was decided, federal courts could hear claims raised in habeas corpus petitions that were not presented in state court unless it was shown that the defendant "deliberately bypassed" state procedures. Under current law, in contrast, a defendant in a habeas corpus proceeding can present matters not raised in state court only if it is demonstrated that there was "cause" for the omission and that there is "prejudice" in being precluded from being able to litigate the matter in federal court.[48] The Supreme Court has held that the test when there is a procedural forfeiture should be the same whether the matter comes to the federal court via a habeas corpus petition or on direct review to the Supreme Court.[49]

State Procedural Rules Manufactured to Preclude Review

The third major situation in which a state procedural rule does not constitute an adequate state law ground for the decision is when the Court concludes that the state court tried to prevent review of a federal constitutional claim by creating a new procedural hurdle or by applying a rule that is not consistently followed. The Court obviously is concerned that state courts might try to insulate their rulings from Supreme Court review by manufacturing or manipulating procedural doctrines in an effort to create independent and adequate state grounds of decision. Thus, the Court long has recognized that a procedural rule will not prevent Supreme Court review, even if it serves a legitimate state interest, if it "is an obvious subterfuge to evade consideration of a federal issue."[50]

For example, the Court has held that there is not an independent and adequate state ground of decision when the state court creates a new procedural rule that would foreclose Supreme Court review. In *NAACP v. Alabama ex rel. Patterson*, the state of Alabama sued the National Association for the Advancement of Colored People to halt its activities in the state.[51] The organization was held in contempt of court because of its failure to comply with an order requiring it to produce its membership lists. The Alabama Supreme Court refused to hear the NAACP's appeal because it said that the organization did not comply with the procedural rule that writs of mandamus were the only basis for challenging contempt orders. The U.S. Supreme Court refused to allow this procedure to constitute an independent and adequate state ground of decision because there was "nothing in the prior [state] cases which suggests that mandamus is the exclusive remedy for reviewing state court orders after disobedience of them has led to contempt judgments."[52]

[47] *See, e.g.*, Murray v. Carrier, 477 U.S. 478 (1986); Wainwright v. Sykes, 433 U.S. 72 (1977).

[48] *See* discussion in §15.5, *infra*.

[49] Harris v. Reed, 489 U.S. 255 (1989), discussed in §15.5.1. For an argument that the procedural forfeiture rules should be identical in habeas corpus review and in independent and adequate state grounds analysis, *see* Meltzer, *supra* note 31, at 1151.

[50] Radio Station WOW, Inc. v. Johnson, 326 U.S. 120, 129 (1945).

[51] 357 U.S. 449 (1958).

[52] *Id.* at 457 (emphasis omitted).

After the Supreme Court reversed, the state court reinstated its contempt judgment, and the Supreme Court reversed again, all without reaching the merits of the contempt order. The NAACP then sued in federal court, alleging the failure of the state courts to provide a hearing on the merits. The Supreme Court ordered such a hearing. The Alabama trial court then ruled against the NAACP on the merits and permanently enjoined it from operating in the state. The Alabama Supreme Court affirmed, refusing to consider the NAACP's federal constitutional claims, solely on the basis of a procedural rule regarding the NAACP's brief. The Alabama Supreme Court said that when unrelated issues are argued together and one is without merit, the others will not be considered.

The U.S. Supreme Court reversed and remanded, ordering prompt entry of a decree vacating the injunction and permitting the NAACP to operate in Alabama.[53] The Court refused to allow the Alabama procedural rule to bar Supreme Court review because it previously never had been applied in that manner. The Court explained, "Novelty in procedural requirements cannot be permitted to thwart review in this Court applied for by those who, in justified reliance upon prior decisions, seek vindication in state courts of their federal constitutional rights."[54]

Also, the Court has held that it will not deem a state procedural rule to be an adequate ground for the decision if the rule is inconsistently followed by the state courts. The Court has observed that "state procedural requirements which are not strictly or regularly followed cannot deprive us of the right to review."[55] *James v. Kentucky* is instructive.[56] The defendant requested an "admonition" to the jury that no inference could be drawn from his failure to testify at the trial. The trial court denied the request and the Kentucky Supreme Court affirmed, holding that Kentucky law draws a distinction between instructions and admonitions. The Supreme Court, however, refused to allow the Kentucky procedural rule to bar review. The Court explained that "Kentucky's distinction between admonitions and instructions is not the sort of firmly established and regularly followed state practice that can prevent implementation of federal constitutional rights."[57] Furthermore, the Court explained that to insist on the defense counsel's use of a particular label would "force resort to an arid ritual of meaningless form and would further no perceivable state interest."[58]

In *Lee v. Kemna*, in the context of a petition for a writ of habeas corpus, the Supreme Court held that a defendant's failure to comply with a state procedural rule did not bar consideration of his constitutional claims.[59] A defendant in a murder trial in Missouri state court was precluded from presenting his key alibi witnesses because they were inexplicably absent from the courtroom, even though they had traveled from California and had been subpoenaed. The defendant requested a continuance of the trial until the next day, but the judge refused, saying that his

[53] NAACP v. Alabama ex rel. Flowers, 377 U.S. 288 (1964).

[54] *Id.* at 301 (citations omitted).

[55] Barr v. City of Columbia, 378 U.S. 146, 149 (1964).

[56] 466 U.S. 341 (1984).

[57] *Id.* at 348-349.

[58] *Id.* at 349 (citations omitted).

[59] 534 U.S. 362 (2002).

family commitments and another scheduled trial required that the case proceed without the witnesses. After the defendant was convicted, he appealed and argued that the denial of the continuance violated due process. The Missouri court of appeals ruled against the defendant on procedural grounds, concluding that he had failed to comply with a state procedural rule requiring that motions for a continuance be in writing and accompanied by an affidavit.

The federal court dismissed the defendant's habeas corpus petition based on the procedural default. The Supreme Court, however, said that "[t]here are . . . exceptional cases in which exorbitant application of a generally sound rule renders the state ground inadequate."[60] Justice Ginsburg's majority opinion stressed that the defendant's compliance with the Missouri rule would have made no difference because the trial judge did not rely on it in denying the continuance; the continuance was denied because of the judge's personal and professional obligations. Also, Justice Ginsburg noted that nothing in the Missouri rule, or Missouri law, directed how the sudden, unexplained disappearance of a key witness is to be handled. Finally, "and most important . . . [the defendant] substantially complied with Missouri's rules" by clearly requesting and explaining the need for a continuance.[61] Justice Ginsburg said that requiring a written motion and an affidavit in the middle of the trial and under the circumstances "would be so bizarre as to insert an Alice-in-Wonderland quality into the proceedings."[62] Thus, *Lee v. Kemna* is an of the Court excusing the failure to comply with state procedural rules based on a determination that they unnecessarily impeded vindication of a federal claim.

Discretionary State Rules Do Not Preclude Review

In fact, the Supreme Court has held that a state procedural rule cannot constitute an adequate state ground for decision if the rule is discretionary rather than mandatory. In other words, if the state court is not required to follow a particular rule, then that rule will not foreclose Supreme Court review. The Court's obvious concern is that state courts might use such discretionary rules to prevent review of federal claims. For example, in *Williams v. Georgia*, the Court explained that "where a State allows [constitutional challenges] to be raised at a late stage and be determined by its courts as a matter of discretion, we are not precluded from assuming jurisdiction and deciding whether the state court action in the particular circumstances is, in effect, an avoidance of the federal right."[63]

Sullivan v. Little Hunting Park, Inc. is one of the most famous cases in which the Supreme Court held that a state court's application of discretionary procedural requirements does not preclude federal review.[64] In *Sullivan*, a recreational association expelled a member for renting a home in the community to a Black man in violation of an agreement. The trial court ruled in favor of the recreational

[60] *Id.* at 376.
[61] *Id.* at 383.
[62] *Id.*
[63] 349 U.S. 375, 383 (1955).
[64] 396 U.S. 229 (1969).

association, concluding that it was a private club and therefore did not need to comply with the Constitution or federal civil rights laws. The Virginia court of appeals denied review based on a procedural rationale that the plaintiffs did not give the recreation association's attorneys sufficient time to examine and correct the trial transcripts.

The Supreme Court held that this procedural rule did not bar review. Although it was not a novel requirement created for the first time in this case, it also was not a rule that was uniformly followed by the Virginia court of appeals. The Court concluded that "[s]uch a rule, more properly deemed discretionary than jurisdictional, does not bar review."[65]

Another application of this principle that discretionary rules do not bar Supreme Court review is *Hathorn v. Lovorn,* decided in 1982.[66] In *Hathorn,* the Mississippi Supreme Court reversed the trial court's conclusion that a county had violated the Voting Rights Act. The Mississippi Supreme Court concluded that the trial court's decision was inconsistent with "the law of the case"; that is, the trial court erred by relying on federal law because prior rulings in the litigation had focused on state law issues. The Supreme Court reversed and concisely explained the requirement that a state procedural rule must be regularly followed to constitute an independent and adequate state ground of decision. The Court stated, "[A] state procedural ground is not 'adequate' unless the procedural rule is 'strictly or regularly followed.' State courts may not avoid deciding federal issues by invoking procedural rules that they do not apply evenhandedly to all similar claims."[67]

In *Ford v. Georgia,* the Supreme Court reversed a Georgia Supreme Court refusal to hear a challenge to the discriminatory use of peremptory challenges.[68] The Georgia court claimed that the jury strikes were not reviewable because there had not been an objection between the jury members' selection and the administration of their oaths. The Supreme Court held that the Georgia rule was not a bar to review because it "does not even remotely satisfy the requirement of *James* that an adequate and independent state procedural bar to the entertainment of constitutional claims must have been firmly established and regularly followed."[69] The Court emphasized that no such rule existed prior to this case, thus preventing the rule from being an independent and adequate state ground of decision.[70]

Summary

The law is complex concerning when state procedural grounds constitute independent and adequate grounds precluding Supreme Court review. In summary, state procedural rules are independent and adequate state grounds unless

[65] *Id.* at 234.

[66] 457 U.S. 255 (1982).

[67] *Id.* at 262-263 (citations omitted).

[68] 498 U.S. 411 (1991).

[69] *Id.* at 424.

[70] *See also* Johnson v. Mississippi, 486 U.S. 578 (1988) (procedural rule does not bar Supreme Court review because there is no evidence that it has been consistently or regularly applied).

they violate the Constitution, fail to serve a legitimate state interest, or are used by the state court to frustrate a hearing on a federal constitutional claim. The latter is deemed to exist if the state creates a novel procedural rule, uses a procedural rule that it does not consistently follow, or employs a discretionary procedural rule. In any of these situations, the state procedural ground of decision is deemed inadequate to support the state court's decision and the Supreme Court may hear and decide the federal law question presented in the case.

§10.5.3 *What Is an* Independent *State Ground of Decision?*

Requirement for "Independence"

The Supreme Court is precluded from reviewing a state court's judgment only if the state grounds of decision are both adequate to support the judgment and independent of federal law. A state ground is deemed independent if it is based entirely on state law and is not tied to federal law.[71] For example, a state highest court decision that relies solely on federal law is reviewable by the Supreme Court because there are no independent state law grounds for the ruling.[72] The Court has explained that when the state court's decision "was based on an interpretation of federal law, we have jurisdiction notwithstanding the fact that the same decision, had it rested on state law, would be unreviewable here."[73]

It should be noted that to constitute an independent state ground of decision, the state's highest court must have explicitly relied on it as a basis for its ruling. The Court has explained that the "mere existence of a basis for a state procedural bar does not deprive this Court of jurisdiction; the state court must actually have relied on the procedural bar as an independent basis for its disposition of the case."[74]

Not Independent If State Incorporates Federal Law

The Court has held that there is not an independent state ground of decision if the state law incorporates federal law. In *Delaware v. Prouse*, the Delaware Supreme Court ruled that a search by police officers violated both the Fourth Amendment and the Delaware Constitution.[75] Although there was a state law ground of decision, the U.S. Supreme Court nonetheless granted review because it was convinced that the sole basis for the Delaware court's decision was its interpretation of federal

[71] Matasar & Bruch, *supra* note 8, at 1292-1293 n.2 ("A decision based on state law is not *independent* of federal law if the state ground is tied to federal law.") (emphasis in original).

[72] For examples of instances in which the Supreme Court reviewed a case because it concluded that the state court relied entirely on federal law, *see* City of Revere v. Massachusetts Gen. Hosp., 463 U.S. 239 (1983); California v. Ramos, 463 U.S. 992 (1983).

[73] City of Revere v. Massachusetts Gen. Hosp., 463 U.S. at 242.

[74] Caldwell v. Mississippi, 472 U.S. 320, 327 (1985).

[75] 440 U.S. 648 (1979).

law. The Court stated: "This is one of those cases where 'at the very least, the [state] court felt compelled by what it understood to be federal constitutional considerations to construe . . . its own law in the manner it did.' . . . If the state court misapprehended federal law, '[i]t should be freed to decide . . . these suits according to its own local law.' "[76]

In other words, where state law incorporates federal law, the Supreme Court will review the state court's decision even though there is a state law ground for the decision. *South Dakota v. Neville* is particularly instructive.[77] In *Neville*, a state statute allowed the defendant to refuse to take a blood alcohol test, but authorized revocation of the driver's license for the failure to do so and permitted the refusal to take the test to be used as evidence at the trial. The trial court granted the defendant's motion to suppress the evidence, and the South Dakota Supreme Court affirmed on the basis that the statute violated the privilege against self-incrimination.

The Supreme Court said that although the South Dakota Supreme Court held that the statute violated both the state and the federal Constitutions, nonetheless it would hear the case because the state law issue was not an "independent state ground."[78] The Court said that the South Dakota Supreme Court's opinion focused on federal law and "then concluded without further analysis that the state privilege was violated as well."[79] As such, the Court held that the state law grounds were not independent of federal law, but instead were based on the South Dakota court's interpretation of federal law.[80]

Although some commentators believe that this rule rests on "shaky theoretical ground,"[81] it is consistent with the purposes of the independent and adequate state grounds doctrine. If a state law incorporates federal law, then logically it is not independent of federal law. Moreover, if the state court misinterprets federal law and mistakenly feels itself bound by federal precedents, a Supreme Court ruling can free the state court to fashion its own law in the area. Similarly, the Supreme Court has held that a state court decision is not independent if it is based on a misunderstanding of federal law.[82]

How to Proceed When State Court Is Unclear? Uncertainty Before *Michigan v. Long*

A crucial problem that has received a great deal of attention is how the Supreme Court should proceed when it is unclear whether the state law ground was meant to incorporate federal law or whether it was intended to be an independent

[76] *Id.* at 662-663 (citations omitted).

[77] 459 U.S. 553 (1983).

[78] *Id.* at 556-557 n.5 (emphasis omitted).

[79] *Id.*

[80] On remand, the South Dakota court held that the South Dakota Constitution was not violated. State v. Neville, 346 N.W.2d 425 (S.D. 1984). *See also* Montana v. Jackson, 460 U.S. 1030 (1983); Texas v. Brown, 460 U.S. 730 (1983) (decisions finding no independent state ground because state law incorporates federal law).

[81] Charles Alan Wright, The Law of Federal Courts 790 (5th ed. 1994).

[82] Smith v. Texas, 550 U.S. 297 (2007).

basis for the decision. Prior to the Supreme Court's decision in 1983 in *Michigan v. Long*, the Supreme Court had used several inconsistent approaches.[83] In some cases, the Court appeared to create a presumption that the discussion of state law constituted an independent ground of decision precluding Supreme Court review.[84] At minimum, the Court would carefully examine the state court's opinion to decide whether it was likely that the state court intended to rely on independent state law grounds.

In other cases, the Court refused to hear the matter until the state court clarified whether its decision was meant to rest on an independent state law basis. For example, in some instances the Court vacated the state court judgment and remanded the matter to the state court for a clarification of whether the ruling was based on state law.[85] In other instances, the Court retained the case on its docket while the matter was sent back to state court for a clarification as to whether there was an independent state law ground.[86]

In yet other cases, the Court presumed that there was no independent state basis for the decision unless the state court expressly stated that it had relied on state law.[87] In other words, under this approach, unless the state court explicitly invoked state law, the Court assumed that the decision was based on federal law and heard the case.

Michigan v. Long

In *Michigan v. Long*, the Court reconsidered this area and adopted the latter approach: the Supreme Court will presume that there is not a state law basis for a decision unless the state's highest court provides a clear statement that its decision was grounded on state law.[88] The facts of *Michigan v. Long* are not complex. Long was stopped by the police while driving his car. When the police noticed a hunting knife in the car, they subjected Long to a pat-down search and removed an object that they saw protruding from an armrest in the front seat. The object contained marijuana; Long was arrested for possession, and his car was impounded. Subsequently, more marijuana was found in his trunk. The state trial court denied Long's motion to suppress, holding that the search of the vehicle was lawful pursuant to the pat down and that the search of the trunk was valid as an inventory search. The Michigan Supreme Court reversed, holding the passenger

[83] 463 U.S. 1032 (1983). For a discussion of the alternative approaches to how the Court should proceed when it is unclear whether there is an independent state ground of decision, *see* Ann Althouse, How to Build a Separate Sphere: Federal Courts and State Power, 100 Harv. L. Rev. 1485, 1500-1507 (1987).

[84] *See, e.g.*, Memphis Natural Gas Co. v. Beeler, 315 U.S. 649, 651 (1942).

[85] *See, e.g.*, Paschall v. Christie-Stewart, 414 U.S. 100 (1973); Minnesota v. National Tea Co., 309 U.S. 551 (1940).

[86] *See, e.g.*, Herb v. Pitcairn, 324 U.S. 117 (1945).

[87] *See, e.g.*, Zacchini v. Scripps-Howard Broadcasting Co., 433 U.S. 562 (1977); Stembridge v. Georgia, 343 U.S. 541 (1952).

[88] 463 U.S. 1032 (1983).

compartment search invalid and the marijuana found in the trunk inadmissible as the fruit of an illegal search.

The U.S. Supreme Court reversed and remanded, concluding that the search of the inside of the car and the trunk did not violate the Fourth Amendment. It was argued that the Supreme Court should not review the Michigan Supreme Court decision because it was based on the Michigan Constitution as well as the U.S. Constitution. Because states can accord greater rights under their constitutions than are provided under the U.S. Constitution, it was claimed that the determination that the search violated the Michigan Constitution was an independent and adequate state law grounds for the decision.

The Supreme Court rejected the application of the independent and adequate state grounds doctrine. The Court observed that it was unclear whether the Michigan Supreme Court intended to rely separately on the Michigan Constitution because the Michigan court's decision referred twice to the state constitution, but otherwise relied exclusively on federal law.[89] The Court, in an opinion by Justice O'Connor, noted that prior decisions were inconsistent as to the proper approach when it was unclear whether the state court relied on independent state law grounds. The Court said that in the future it would assume that there is not a separate state law basis for the state court decision unless the state court clearly indicates that it is relying on state law. The Court held:

> Accordingly, when, as in this case, a state court decision fairly appears to rest primarily on federal law, or to be interwoven with the federal law, and when the adequacy and independence of any possible state law ground is not clear from the face of the opinion, we will accept as the most reasonable explanation that the state court decided the case the way it did because it believed that federal law required it to do so. . . . If the state court decision indicates clearly and expressly that it is alternatively based on bona fide separate, adequate, and independent grounds, we, of course, will not undertake to review the decision.[90]

In other words, the Supreme Court will review state court decisions unless there is a plain statement from the state's highest court that its decision was based on independent state law grounds. Justice O'Connor explained that this approach was preferable to having the Supreme Court guess the intended basis for the state court opinion or remand the case to the state court for a clarification. Because state courts can prevent Supreme Court review by clearly indicating that their decision is based on state law, the rule adopted in *Michigan v. Long* would, according to the Court, "provide state judges with a clearer opportunity to develop state jurisprudence unimpeded by federal interference."[91]

Justice Stevens dissented in *Michigan v. Long* and argued that the Supreme Court should not review cases where there is no allegation that the state court

[89] *Id.* at 1037.
[90] *Id.* at 1040-1041.
[91] *Id.* at 1041.

prevented the vindication of federal rights.[92] Justice Stevens contended that when the state court rules in favor of the criminal defendant there is no reason for the Supreme Court to hear the case. He explained that "[i]n this case, the State of Michigan has arrested one of its citizens and the Michigan Supreme Court has decided to turn him loose. . . . [S]ince there is no claim that he has been mistreated by the State of Michigan, the final outcome of the state processes offended no federal interest whatever."[93] Under Justice Stevens's approach, the purpose of Supreme Court review is to assure the vindication of federal rights. As such, there is no reason for review absent a claim that the state is infringing on someone's constitutional liberties.

Defense and Criticism of *Michigan v. Long*

Because *Michigan v. Long* creates a presumption in favor of Supreme Court review, not surprisingly it has attracted a great deal of attention from legal scholars and even Supreme Court justices.[94] Many scholars have defended the decision on federalism grounds. For example, Professor Laurence Tribe observed that "by making clear that state courts may avoid Supreme Court review by clearly separating their discussion of state and federal law, *Long* advances interests which lie at the root of our federal system."[95] In other words, *Long* is said to advance federalism because it encourages states to develop independent state law doctrines, such as under state constitutions.[96] State courts can immunize their decisions from Supreme Court review as long as there is a plain statement that the state court relied on state law, unless, of course, there is a constitutional challenge to the state law ground.[97] State constitutions can provide more rights than exist under the U.S. Constitution, but the state court must make it clear that the decision is based on the state constitution. At the same time, when a state court is relying on federal law, Supreme Court review advances federalism because the state might wrongly believe that there is federal law binding its judgment; Supreme Court review correcting such an error restores state discretion to fashion its own law.[98] In *Arizona*

[92] *Id.* at 1066-1072 (Stevens, J., dissenting). Justice Stevens also explained these views in Stevens, Some Thoughts on Judicial Restraint, 66 Judicature 177 (1982).

[93] 463 U.S. at 1068 (Stevens, J., dissenting).

[94] *See, e.g.*, Althouse, *supra* note 83; Thomas E. Baker, The Ambiguous Independent and Adequate State Ground in Criminal Cases: Federalism Along a Mobius Strip, 19 Ga. L. Rev. 799 (1985); Robert C. Welsh, Reconsidering the Constitutional Relationship Between State and Federal Courts: A Critique of Michigan v. Long, 59 Notre Dame L. Rev. 1118 (1984).

[95] Laurence Tribe, American Constitutional Law 165 (2d ed. 1987).

[96] *See* Ann Althouse, Variations on a Theory of Normative Federalism: A Supreme Court Dialogue, 42 Duke L.J. 979 (1993) (defending *Long* as advancing federalism interests).

[97] Althouse, *supra* note 83, at 1506-1507; *see also* Baker, *supra* note 94, at 836-838.

[98] Professor Martin Redish develops an alternative defense of Michigan v. Long. He contends that the *Long* approach will help state courts to understand federal law and, subsequently, "choose to fashion parallel state law in an entirely divergent manner. . . . In this manner, the interactive dialogue between representatives of the state and federal judicial systems can enrich the substantive development of the law of both jurisdictions." Martin H. Redish, Supreme Court Review of State Court "Federal" Decisions: A Study in Interactive Federalism, 19 Ga. L. Rev. 861, 865 (1985).

v. Evans, the Supreme Court declared, "*Michigan v. Long* properly serves its purpose and should not be disturbed. Under it, state courts are absolutely free to accord greater protection to individual rights than do similar provisions of the United States Constitution. They also are free to serve as experimental laboratories."[99]

Many commentators are sharply critical of the Court's holding and approach in *Michigan v. Long*.[100] The Court in *Long* places a strong presumption in favor of Supreme Court jurisdiction. Federal courts, however, are tribunals of limited jurisdiction and the general presumption is against federal court review. For example, the Supreme Court has held that federal courts should abstain when there is an unclear issue of state law and clarification might avoid a federal court ruling on a constitutional question.[101] But in *Michigan v. Long*, the Court took jurisdiction rather than allowing the state court to provide clarification that might obviate the need for a Supreme Court ruling on a federal constitutional issue. If nothing else, it seems strange that a Supreme Court, which repeatedly has limited federal court jurisdiction and has emphasized deference to state courts, should create a strong presumption in favor of federal court review of state court proceedings. Thus, it is not surprising that some might read *Long* in a more cynical way as a conservative Supreme Court going out of its way to fashion a doctrine that will permit it to reverse state supreme court decisions that are more liberal in protecting individual liberties.

Indeed, in *Arizona v. Evans*, Justice Ginsburg, in a dissenting opinion, expressly called for the Court to overrule *Michigan v. Long*. Justice Ginsburg argued that "the *Long* presumption . . . impedes the States' ability to serve as laboratories for testing solutions to novel legal situations."[102] Moreover, Justice Ginsburg argued that the *Michigan v. Long* rule wastes Supreme Court time because in many of the cases the state court simply reinstates its earlier ruling based on state law grounds. Justice Ginsburg declared: "Application of the *Long* presumption has increased the incidence of nondispositive United States Supreme Court determinations—instances in which state courts, on remand, have reinstated their prior judgments after clarifying their reliance on state grounds. . . . Even if those reinstatements do not render the Supreme Court's opinion technically 'advisory,' they do suggest that the Court unnecessarily spent its resources on cases better left, at the time in question, to state-court solution."[103] However, Justice Stevens joined Justice Ginsburg's call to overrule *Michigan v. Long*.

Many of the cases after *Michigan v. Long* have involved instances in which the Supreme Court reversed state court rulings, like that in *Long*, in favor of criminal defendants.[104] For example, in *Delaware v. Van Arsdall*, the Delaware Supreme Court reversed a murder conviction because the defendant was denied the opportunity

[99] 514 U.S. 1, 8 (1995).

[100] For a detailed criticism of Michigan v. Long, *see* Matasar & Bruch, *supra* note 8, at 1368-1374.

[101] Railroad Commn. of Texas v. Pullman Co., 312 U.S. 496 (1941); *see* §12.2, *infra*.

[102] 514 U.S. at 23 (Ginsburg, J., dissenting).

[103] *Id.* at 54.

[104] For a review of the Supreme Court's use of Michigan v. Long, *see* Patricia Fahlbusch & Daniel Gonzalez, Note, Michigan v. Long: The Inadequacies of Independent and Adequate State Grounds, 42 U. Miami L. Rev. 159 (1987).

to cross-examine a witness about a deal the witness made with the prosecutor whereby criminal charges were dropped in exchange for the testimony.[105] The U.S. Supreme Court reversed, holding that review was appropriate because the Delaware Supreme Court's opinion "lacks the requisite 'plain statement' that it rests on state grounds."[106]

Similarly, in another case the Supreme Court reversed a New York court of appeals decision affirming the dismissal of obscenity charges.[107] The Supreme Court held that its review was appropriate because "in the absence of a 'plain statement' to the contrary, [it is presumed] that the decision of the Court of Appeals was premised on federal, not state, law."[108] In a number of other cases as well, the Supreme Court has reversed state court decisions protecting individual liberties based on its assumption that decisions are always based on federal law absent a clear contrary statement from a state court.[109]

Arizona v. Evans[110] and *Pennsylvania v. Labron*[111] are also examples where the Court used *Michigan v. Long* to overrule state court rulings in favor of criminal defendants. In *Arizona v. Evans*, the Arizona Supreme Court applied the exclusionary rule when a police search resulted from a clerical computer error that mistakenly caused the police to believe that there was an outstanding misdemeanor warrant. The Supreme Court said that it was not clear that the Arizona Supreme Court was relying on Arizona law, and indeed it referred to federal law, and thus the case was proper for review. On the merits, the Court then concluded that the exclusionary rule does not preclude the use of evidence obtained in violation of the Fourth Amendment where the erroneous information resulted from good-faith clerical errors of court employees.

In *Pennsylvania v. Labron*, the Pennsylvania Supreme Court applied the exclusionary rule to evidence obtained in a search of the defendant's immobile car; the court explained that a warrantless search was unjustified because the police had ample time to obtain a warrant. The Supreme Court reversed and explained that the Pennsylvania Supreme Court mistakenly applied federal law concerning warrantless automobile searches. The Court followed *Michigan v. Long* and stressed that the adequacy and independence of any possible state law ground was not clear from the facts of the opinion.

In *Kansas v. Carr*, the justices again considered the desirability of Supreme Court review of state court decisions providing greater protection for criminal defendants.[112] The Kansas Supreme Court ruled in favor of criminal defendants based on unclear jury instructions about mitigating factors and about whether there should have been separate sentencing procedures for the defendants

[105] 475 U.S. 673 (1986).

[106] *Id.* at 689 n.3 (citations omitted).

[107] New York v. P. J. Video, Inc., 475 U.S. 868 (1986).

[108] *Id.* at 972 n.4.

[109] *See, e.g.,* Montana v. Hall, 481 U.S. 400 (1987); Florida v. Meyers, 466 U.S. 380 (1984); Ohio v. Johnson, 467 U.S. 493 (1984).

[110] 514 U.S. 1 (1995).

[111] 518 U.S. 938 (1996).

[112] 577 U.S. 108 (2016).

who had been jointly tried. The Supreme Court, in an opinion by Justice Scalia, reversed and stressed that the state court had relied on federal law. He wrote: "The Kansas Supreme Court's opinion leaves no room for doubt that it was relying on the Federal Constitution. . . . It generally would have been 'none of our business' had the Kansas Supreme Court vacated Gleason's and the Carrs' death sentences on state-law grounds. But it decidedly did not. . . . The state courts may experiment all they want with their own constitutions, and often do in the wake of this Court's decisions. But what a state court cannot do is experiment with our Federal Constitution and expect to elude this Court's review so long as victory goes to the criminal defendant. 'Turning a blind eye' in such cases would change the uniform 'law of the land' into a crazy quilt. And it would enable state courts to blame the unpopular death-sentence reprieve of the most horrible criminals upon the Federal Constitution when it is in fact their own doing."[113]

Justice Sotomayor dissented and echoed Justice Stevens's concerns from *Michigan v. Long* saying she dissents "because . . . I see no reason to intervene in cases like these—and plenty of reasons not to. Kansas has not violated any federal constitutional right. If anything, the State has overprotected its citizens based on its interpretation of state and federal law. For reasons ably articulated by my predecessors and colleagues and because I worry that cases like these prevent States from serving as necessary laboratories for experimenting with how best to guarantee defendants a fair trial."[114]

Although *Long* has been most frequently applied in the criminal cases, the Court has also followed it in civil cases.[115] In *Quinn v. Millsap*, the Court refused to find an independent and adequate state ground because there was not an express statement from the state court that its decision was based on a state law ground.[116] The Missouri Supreme Court invalidated a requirement that members of a county board had to own property in the area. Though the state court discussed both the federal and state law issues, the Supreme Court deemed review appropriate because there was not a "plain statement of the court's reliance on alternative state law holding."[117] The Court declared, "In the absence of such a plain statement, we have jurisdiction to review the federal ground on which the Missouri Supreme Court's judgment rests."[118]

In one notable case, *Bush v. Palm Beach County Canvassing Board*,[119] the Supreme Court did not rely on *Michigan v. Long*, but instead invoked its predecessor, *Minnesota v. National Tea Co.*[120] After the presidential election in November 2000, Al Gore asked for a recount in four counties in Florida. The secretary of state, however, said that under Florida law the recounts had to be completed within seven days. Gore then filed suit arguing that the failure to accept the recounts

[113] *Id.* at 117-118.

[114] *Id.* at 127 (Sotomayor, J., dissenting)

[115] *See, e.g.*, Asarco v. Kadish, 490 U.S. 605, 625 (1989) (allowing Supreme Court review because the Arizona Supreme Court did not "divorce the state constitutional issues from the questions of federal law").

[116] 491 U.S. 95 (1989).

[117] *Id.* at 102 n.6.

[118] *Id.*

[119] 531 U.S. 70 (2000).

[120] 309 U.S. 551 (1940).

from these counties violated Florida law. The trial court ruled against Gore, but the Florida Supreme Court reversed and extended the deadline for the recounts.

The Supreme Court granted certiorari and held an expedited hearing, but then remanded the case for the clarification of two issues. First, the Court said that it was unclear whether the Florida Supreme Court decision was based on the Florida Constitution or Florida statutes; the Court indicated that the former would be impermissible because Article II of the Constitution requires that state laws define procedures in presidential elections.[121] Also, the Court said that it was uncertain whether the decision was based on a desire to comply with a federal statute, 3 U.S.C. §5, which creates a conclusive presumption in favor of electors chosen by December 12.[122]

The Supreme Court vacated and remanded the Florida Supreme Court decision based on *Minnesota v. National Tea Co.* The Court said that the "considerable uncertainty as to the precise grounds for the decision" was "sufficient reason for us to decline at this time to review the federal questions asserted to be present."[123]

On the one hand, vacating a state court decision and remanding it for clarification is an approach rejected in *Michigan v. Long.* On the other hand, unlike *Michigan v. Long,* the issue was not whether the state court relied on a state ground of decision, but rather, uncertainty about the content of the state grounds. In the end, *Bush v. Palm Beach County Canvassing Board* was made irrelevant by subsequent developments. After the election was certified in favor of George W. Bush, Al Gore invoked a different procedure of Florida law to challenge the result and to request a counting of uncounted votes. This, of course, culminated in *Bush v. Gore* and the Supreme Court ending the vote counting in Florida.[124]

It might be argued more generally that the Supreme Court manipulates the independent and adequate state grounds doctrine when it serves its purpose to facilitate or frustrate review. For example, during the 1960s, the Supreme Court was deeply concerned about state obstruction of civil rights efforts, and the Court went out of its way to ensure that state procedural grounds would not prevent review of important civil rights issues.[125] During the 1980s, some see *Michigan v. Long* and its progeny as establishing a doctrine to facilitate Supreme Court reversals of state court decisions expanding protection of individual liberties. But it must be remembered that *Michigan v. Long* does invite states to fashion their own legal principles, and the Court says that it will respect them as long as the state court expressly declares its purpose to rely on a state law ground.

At minimum, *Michigan v. Long* clarified the law. When there is uncertainty as to whether there is an independent state ground of decision, the Supreme Court will assume that there is not and will decide the case. A state court can prevent such uncertainty via a plain statement that it was relying on state law as an independent basis for its judgment.

[121] 531 U.S. at 78.

[122] *Id.*

[123] *Id.*

[124] Bush v. Gore is discussed above at text accompanying notes 119-122, §10.2.

[125] *See, e.g.,* Henry v. Mississippi, 379 U.S. 443 (1965); Fay v. Noia, 372 U.S. 391, 439 (1963).

CHAPTER 11

Statutory Control of the Relationship Between Federal Courts and the States

§11.1 INTRODUCTION

Many doctrines and principles define the relationship between federal and state courts. Some are judicially created. For example, Chapters 12, 13, and 14 examine various abstention doctrines devised by the Supreme Court—situations where the Court has held that federal courts may not hear and decide cases even though all jurisdictional and justiciability requirements are met. This chapter, in contrast, focuses on *statutes* that define the relationship between federal courts and the states.

Congressional Authority to Control Federal Court Jurisdiction

There is no doubt that Congress has broad power to determine the authority of the federal courts, especially in relation to state judiciaries.[1] The Supreme Court has held that Congress determines the jurisdiction of the lower federal courts.[2] On several occasions, the Court concluded that because Congress has discretion whether to create lower federal courts, it also has the authority to determine their jurisdiction.[3] To the extent that Congress has enacted statutes defining federal jurisdiction, it would violate separation of powers for the courts to disregard them unless they are unconstitutional.[4] Additionally, because the issue of federal court review of state court judgments and proceedings is a question of federalism, Congress is the appropriate institution to decide the scope of federal court jurisdiction.[5] Likewise, it can be argued that Congress should allocate power between federal and state courts.

Federal Statutes Examined

In this chapter, four specific federal statutes that define the relationship between federal courts and the states are examined. Section 11.2 considers the Anti-Injunction Act, a federal law that prevents federal courts from enjoining pending state court proceedings unless the case fits into a specific exception contained in the act.[6] The Tax Injunction Act, a federal statute generally preventing

§11.1 [1] For a discussion of Congress's power to restrict federal court jurisdiction over particular types of cases, *see* Chapter 3.

[2] *See, e.g.*, Lauf v. E.G. Shinner & Co., 303 U.S. 323 (1938); Sheldon v. Sill, 8 How. 441 (1850). The scope of Congress's authority to control federal court jurisdiction is examined in detail in Chapter 3.

[3] *See, e.g.*, Palmore v. United States, 411 U.S. 389 (1973); Lauf v. E.G. Shinner & Co., 303 U.S. 323 (1938); Sheldon v. Sill, 8 How. 441 (1850).

[4] Martin H. Redish, Abstention, Separation of Powers, and the Judicial Function, 94 Yale L.J. 71, 74 (1985).

[5] Professor Herbert Wechsler, in a famous article, argued that the national political process best determines the relationship between the federal and state governments. Herbert Wechsler, The Political Safeguards of Federalism: The Role of the States in the Composition and Selection of the National Government, 54 Colum. L. Rev. 543 (1954).

[6] 28 U.S.C. §2283.

federal courts from enjoining the collection of taxes under state law, is examined in §11.3.[7] There also is another federal statute that limits the ability of federal courts to enjoin the collection of federal taxes. This also is called the Anti-Injunction Act, though it is a different law from the one discussed in §11.2. Section 11.4 discusses the Johnson Act—a federal law that prevents federal courts from enjoining, suspending, or restraining the utility rates entered by a state or local rate-making agency.[8] As is discussed in the subsequent sections of this chapter, each of these statutes reflects federalism concerns and a limit on the power of federal courts to enjoin important aspects of state and local governance.

Although each of the above-mentioned statutes provides for federal court deference to state court proceedings, the final statute discussed here—the Civil Rights Removal Act—has the opposite effect.[9] The act provides for the removal from state to federal court of civil and criminal proceedings of specified civil rights matters. The act, adopted soon after the Civil War, is based on a distrust of the state courts' willingness and ability to adequately protect the rights of Black people. The Civil Rights Removal Act is discussed in §11.5.

These, of course, are not the only statutes that define the relationship of federal and state courts. For example, the habeas corpus statutes, discussed in detail in Chapter 15, determine the authority of the federal courts to provide relief to individuals convicted by a state court.[10] Likewise, the federal civil rights laws, especially 42 U.S.C. §1983, crucially bear on the relationship between federal and state courts. This is discussed in detail in Chapter 8.

Thus, the focus of this chapter is on four specific statutes that define federal-state relations: the Anti-Injunction Act, the Tax Injunction Act, the Johnson Act, and the Civil Rights Removal Act.

§11.2 THE ANTI-INJUNCTION ACT

§11.2.1 Overview and Background of the Anti-Injunction Act

Historical Background

The Supreme Court frequently has observed that the Anti-Injunction Act dates back to a federal statute adopted in 1793.[1] This law, enacted early in America's history, provided that no "writ of injunction [shall] be granted to stay

[7] 28 U.S.C. §1341.

[8] 28 U.S.C. §1342.

[9] 28 U.S.C. §1443.

[10] 28 U.S.C. §§2241 et seq.; *see especially* 28 U.S.C. §2254 (habeas corpus relief for individuals in state custody).

§11.2 [1] *See* Mitchum v. Foster, 407 U.S. 225, 231-236 (1972) (Anti-Injunction Act's origins are in statute adopted in 1793); Atlantic Coast Line R.R. v. Brotherhood of Locomotive Engrs., 398 U.S. 281, 285-286 (1970).

proceedings in any court of a state."[2] Because there is no legislative history for the statute, it is unknown why Congress chose to enact this restriction.[3] The provision limiting injunctions was "but one sentence in one section of a two page statute."[4] Commentators have persuasively demonstrated that the terms of the 1793 statute only limited the power of a single Supreme Court Justice to enjoin state court proceedings.[5] As written, the statute did not apply to the lower federal courts. In fact, the provision was almost completely ignored and rarely even mentioned by any court.[6]

In 1874, as part of the codification of federal laws into the Revised Statutes, the provision was placed in a separate section and modified. Although the codification was not supposed to alter substantively the existing law, the provision was substantially changed so as to limit the power of all federal courts.[7] Specifically, §720 of the Revised Statutes stated: "The writ of injunction shall not be granted by any court of the United States to stay proceedings in any court of a State, except in cases where such injunction may be authorized by any law relating to proceedings in bankruptcy."[8]

Purpose of the Anti-Injunction Act

Though again there is little explanation of the purpose behind this provision, the Supreme Court frequently has said that the "statute is designed to prevent conflict between federal and state courts."[9] The underlying idea is that a federal injunction of ongoing state proceedings is likely to breed resentment and hostility in the state judiciaries and even risk disobedience of the federal court's orders. Therefore, avoiding injunctions of state courts is a way of limiting friction between state and federal courts.[10] However, it might be argued that in most cases the injunction of pending state court proceedings usually would apply to cases listed on the

[2] Act of Mar. 2, 1793, ch. 22, §5, 1 Stat. 335. *See* James E. Pfander & Nassim Nezemi, Morris v. Allen and the Lost History of the Anti-Injunction Act of 1793, 108 Nw. U. L. Rev. 187 (2013).

[3] *See* Mitchum v. Foster, 407 U.S. at 232 ("The precise origins of the legislation are shrouded in obscurity."). For an interesting theory that the act was meant to allow federal court interference with state proceedings by any means except for injunctions, *see* Comment, Federal Court Stays of State Court Proceedings: A Re-Examination of Original Congressional Intent, 38 U. Chi. L. Rev. 612 (1971).

[4] John Daniel Reaves & David S. Golden, The Federal Anti-Injunction Statute in the Aftermath of *Atlantic Coast Line Railroad*, 5 Ga. L. Rev. 294, 296 (1971).

[5] *See* William T. Mayton, Ersatz Federalism Under the Anti-Injunction Statute, 78 Colum. L. Rev. 330, 346 (1978).

[6] Prior to its revision in 1876, the only case to mention the act was Watson v. Jones, 80 U.S. (13 Wall.) 679 (1871).

[7] Mayton, *supra* note 5, at 346.

[8] Rev. Stat. of 1874, ch. 12, §720, 18 Stat. 134.

[9] Vendo Co. v. Lektro-Vend Corp., 433 U.S. 623, 630 (1977); Leiter Minerals v. United States, 352 U.S. 220, 225 (1957).

[10] James E. Pfander and Nassim Nazemi argue that the Anti-Injunction Act was adopted with the assumption that if a state court obtained jurisdiction first and a party went to federal court for an injunction on equitable grounds, the federal action was barred. But when the federal court obtained

docket in the clerk's office and would not even be visible to judges. Moreover, the benefits of harmony and avoiding friction are seldom explained.

The Supreme Court did not treat the prohibition against injunctions as an absolute bar to such relief. Quite the contrary, the Court recognized a number of situations in which federal courts could stay state proceedings. For instance, the Court held that the act did not prevent a federal court from enjoining state proceedings concerning real property if the federal court first acquired jurisdiction.[11] Nor did the act prevent a federal court from enjoining state proceedings that threatened to undermine a previous federal judgment or harass successful litigants in federal court proceedings.[12] In fact, by the 1930s, so many exceptions to the Act had been recognized that some commentators remarked that "except for the prohibition, in some cases, of injunction before judgment, the statute has long been dead."[13]

Toucey v. New York Life Insurance Co. Narrowed Exceptions

In 1941, however, in *Toucey v. New York Life Insurance Co.*, the Supreme Court changed its view of the act and ruled that the statute generally would be viewed as a firm prohibition against federal court injunctions of state court proceedings.[14] In *Toucey*, the plaintiff sued the New York Life Insurance Company in state court to collect monthly disability insurance payments. The company removed the case to federal court based on diversity of citizenship. The federal court ruled against the plaintiff on the merits. The plaintiff, Toucey, then assigned his benefits to another individual who initiated a new lawsuit over the exact same matter in state court. The defendant, New York Life Insurance Company, requested and received an injunction from the federal court to halt the state court proceedings.

The Supreme Court, in an opinion by Justice Frankfurter, reversed and held that an injunction against the state court proceedings was inappropriate. After carefully reviewing the history of the act, Justice Frankfurter concluded that the statute should be narrowly construed to prevent federal courts from enjoining state court litigation. Justice Frankfurter said, "We must be scrupulous in our regard for the limits within which Congress has confined the authority of the courts of its own creation."[15] The Court certainly recognized that this view was a departure

---

jurisdiction first and a matter was then brought in state court, the federal court could enjoin the state proceeding where necessary as a matter of effectuating its jurisdiction. James E. Pfander & Nassim Nazemi, The Anti-Injunction Act and the Problem of Federal-State Jurisdictional Overlap, 92 Tex. L. Rev. 1 (2013).

[11] *See, e.g.*, Princess Lida v. Thompson, 305 U.S. 456, 465-466 (1939). In fact, the only time state courts can enjoin federal proceedings is when the state courts first acquire in rem or quasi in rem jurisdiction before the federal courts. *See* Donovan v. City of Dallas, 377 U.S. 408 (1964). *See* discussion in §14.2, *infra*.

[12] *See, e.g.*, Sovereign Camp Woodmen of the World v. O'Neill, 266 U.S. 292 (1924); Supreme Tribe of Ben-Hur v. Cauble, 255 U.S. 356 (1921).

[13] Edgar Noble Durfee & Robert L. Sloss, Federal Injunction Against Proceedings in State Court: The Life History of a Statute, 30 Mich. L. Rev. 1145, 1169 (1932).

[14] 314 U.S. 118 (1941).

[15] *Id.* at 141.

from precedent, but it stated that "[l]oose language and a sporadic, ill-considered decision cannot be held to have imbedded in our law a doctrine which so patently violates the expressed prohibition of Congress."[16]

1948 Revision of the Act

In 1948, Congress amended the Anti-Injunction Act, specifically to overrule *Toucey* and permit federal courts to enjoin state court proceedings that threaten to undermine earlier federal court judgments. The legislative history of the 1948 act states that "the revised section restores the basic law as generally understood and interpreted prior to the *Toucey* decision."[17] The act has remained unchanged since 1948. It provides, "A court of the United States may not grant an injunction to stay proceedings in a State court except as expressly authorized by Act of Congress, or where necessary in aid of its jurisdiction, or to protect or effectuate its judgments."[18]

Although many aspects of the act are unclear and ambiguous,[19] some are quite straightforward. First, the act prohibits federal courts from enjoining state proceedings either directly by enjoining state courts or indirectly by enjoining the parties from proceeding with litigation in the state courts.[20] Second, the act applies only if there are proceedings actually pending in the state courts; it does not prevent federal courts from issuing injunctions in the absence of ongoing state court litigation.[21]

Third, the Court repeatedly has stated that the exceptions contained in the act are exclusive and that the Court may not create additional situations in which injunctions can be issued.[22] In fact, the Court declared that "since the statutory prohibition against such injunctions in part rests on the fundamental constitutional independence of the States and their courts, the exceptions should not be enlarged by loose statutory construction."[23] The following three subsections, §§11.2.2, 11.2.3, and 11.2.4, respectively, consider the three exceptions in the act: where injunctions are expressly authorized by statute; where they are necessary in aid of federal court jurisdiction; and where they are needed to effectuate a judgment of the federal court. Additionally, despite the Court's words to the contrary, it has recognized several exceptions that are not mentioned in the act. Subsection 11.2.5 examines these situations where federal courts may issue

[16] *Id.* at 139.

[17] H. Rep. No. 308, 80th Cong., 1st Sess., A181-182 (1947).

[18] 28 U.S.C. §2283.

[19] Professor Redish, for example, observed that "[i]t is generally recognized that the anti-injunction statute is rife with inadequacies and ambiguities." Martin H. Redish, The Anti-Injunction Statute Reconsidered, 44 U. Chi. L. Rev. 717, 760 (1977). These remain largely unresolved even a half century after Professor Redish wrote this.

[20] *See, e.g.,* Atlantic Coast Line R.R. v. Brotherhood of Locomotive Engrs., 398 U.S. 281, 286 (1970).

[21] *See, e.g.,* Dombrowski v. Pfister, 380 U.S. 479, 484 n.2 (1965).

[22] *See, e.g.,* Vendo Co. v. Lektro-Vend Corp., 433 U.S. 623, 630 (1977); Amalgamated Clothing Workers v. Richman Bros., 348 U.S. 511, 515-516 (1955).

[23] Atlantic Coast Line R.R. v. Brotherhood of Locomotive Engrs., 398 U.S. at 287.

injunctions, notwithstanding the absence of specific authorization in the Anti-Injunction Act.

Unresolved Issues

Several issues remain unanswered about the scope of the Anti-Injunction Act. For example, although the Supreme Court has not yet ruled on the question, most lower federal courts have held that federal courts may not issue declaratory judgments that would have essentially the same effect as an injunction.[24] As the Third Circuit explained, "Where . . . declaratory relief would produce the same effect as an injunction, a declaratory judgment is barred if §2283 would have prohibited an injunction."[25]

Another unresolved question is what constitutes a judicial proceeding. The Anti-Injunction Act prohibits federal courts from enjoining proceedings in any court of a state. The question, of course, is what constitutes a proceeding in a state court.[26] For example, lower courts have held that arbitration proceedings should be considered state court proceedings that cannot be enjoined under the act.[27]

Relationship to *Younger* abstention

In addition to the Anti-Injunction Act, the Supreme Court created a parallel abstention doctrine based on concerns for equity and comity. In *Younger v. Harris,* the Supreme Court held that federal courts may not enjoin pending state court criminal prosecutions.[28] The Court expressly declared that its decision was not based on the Anti-Injunction Act, but instead rested on federalism considerations and on the availability of adequate state court proceedings to resolve the constitutional challenges. In subsequent cases, the Supreme Court extended the *Younger* abstention doctrine to prevent federal courts from issuing declaratory judgments that would have the effect of injunctions;[29] to preclude federal court injunctions

[24] *See, e.g.,* People v. Randtron, 284 F.3d 970-975 (9th Cir. 2001); Clay Regional Water v. City of Spirit Lake, Iowa, 193 F. Supp. 2d 1129, 1149 (N.D. Iowa 2002); United States Steel Corp. Plan for Employee Ins. Benefits v. Musisko, 885 F.2d 1170, 1175 (3d Cir. 1989), *cert. denied,* 453 U.S. 1074 (1990); *but see* Prudential Insurance Co. of America v. Doe, 140 F.3d 785, 788 (8th Cir. 1998) (federal courts have discretion in deciding whether to hear declaratory judgment actions and may look to whether the petitioner is the first litigant and at what stage the federal suit was filed).

[25] United States Steel Corp. Plan for Employee Ins. Benefits v. Musisko, 885 F.2d 1170, 1175 (3d Cir. 1989), *cert. denied,* 453 U.S. 1074 (1990).

[26] *See, e.g.,* Roudebush v. Hartke, 405 U.S. 15, 20 (1972) (recount of election results is not a judicial proceeding within the meaning of the Anti-Injunction Act).

[27] Empire Blue Cross & Blue Shield v. Janet Greeson's A Place for Us, Inc., 985 F.2d 459 (9th Cir. 1993); Kelly v. Merrill Lynch, Pierce, Fenner & Smith, Inc., 985 F.2d 1067 (11th Cir. 1993); *but see* Six Clinics Holding Co., II v. CAFCOMP Systems, Inc., 119 F.3d 393, 398 (6th Cir. 1997) (holding that arbitration proceedings are private and consensual and that therefore are not "state court proceedings").

[28] 401 U.S. 37 (1971).

[29] *See, e.g.,* Samuels v. Mackell, 401 U.S. 66 (1971).

of state-initiated enforcement proceedings in state court;[30] to bar injunctions that involve the integrity of the state judiciary;[31] and even to limit federal injunctions of state administrative proceedings where important state interests are at stake.[32] The *Younger* abstention doctrine and its application in each of these areas are discussed in detail in Chapter 13.[33]

The *Younger* abstention doctrine, where it applies, creates a separate and independent barrier to federal court injunctions of pending state court proceedings. In other words, for a federal court to enjoin ongoing state court litigation, the case must fit within *both* an exception to the Anti-Injunction Act and an exception to the *Younger* doctrine. The fact that the case falls within an exception to the Anti-Injunction Act is necessary, but not sufficient, to permit the federal court to issue an injunction. For example, as discussed below, the Supreme Court has held that 42 U.S.C. §1983 is an exception to the Anti-Injunction Act in that it constitutes an express authorization for injunctions.[34] However, where the *Younger* doctrine applies, it bars injunctions of state proceedings in §1983 cases unless one of the narrow exceptions to the *Younger* doctrine also is present.[35]

§11.2.2 Injunctions that are Expressly Authorized by Statute

The first exception contained in the Anti-Injunction Act is when injunctions are "expressly authorized by Act of Congress." This exception incorporates the law prior to the act's revision in 1948, when the Supreme Court allowed federal courts to enjoin state proceedings pursuant to specific federal statutes. The exception is simply explained: Congress created the bar against injunctions contained in the act; therefore, Congress may override its own limitation and authorize stays of state court proceedings.

In order to constitute an express authorization of an injunction, a statute need not specifically state that it constitutes an exception to §2283. In one of its first interpretations of the 1948 act, the Court observed that "no prescribed formula is required; an authorization need not expressly refer to §2283."[36]

[30] *See, e.g.,* Huffman v. Pursue, Ltd., 420 U.S. 592 (1975).

[31] Pennzoil Co. v. Texaco, Inc., 481 U.S. 1 (1987).

[32] *See, e.g.,* Ohio Civil Rights Commn. v. Dayton Christian Schools, 477 U.S. 619 (1986).

[33] In one of its most recent decisions on *Younger* abstention, the Court described when it applies: "First, precluded federal intrusion into ongoing state criminal prosecutions. Second, certain 'civil enforcement proceedings' warranted abstention. Finally, federal courts refrained from interfering with pending 'civil proceedings involving certain orders . . . uniquely in furtherance of the state courts' ability to perform their judicial functions.'" Sprint Communications, Inc. v. Jacobs, 571 U.S. 584, 591 (2013).

[34] Mitchum v. Foster, 407 U.S. 225 (1972).

[35] The exceptions to the *Younger* doctrine are discussed in §13.4, *infra.*

[36] Amalgamated Clothing Workers v. Richman Bros., 348 U.S. 511, 516 (1955).

Statutes Expressly Authorizing Injunctions

Some federal statutes explicitly authorize federal court injunctions of state proceedings. For example, the Interpleader Act allows federal courts in an interpleader action to issue injunctions "against instituting or prosecuting any proceeding in any State or United States court."[37] The purpose of the Interpleader Act is to allow all conflicting claims to a limited fund to be decided in one action; enjoining all other suits facilitates the objective of a unitary adjudicatory process. Another instance of a federal statute expressly authorizing injunctions is the bankruptcy law.[38] In fact, the pre-1948 version of the Anti-Injunction Act specifically exempted bankruptcy suits from the prohibition against injunctions of state court proceedings. Other federal statutes also quite explicitly state that the federal judiciary may enjoin state court litigation.[39]

How Explicit Must a Statute Be? *Mitchum v. Foster*

The difficult question in interpreting this exception is how explicit a statute must be in authorizing injunctions of state proceedings. The Supreme Court has held that a statute need not even mention injunctions of state proceedings if the purposes of the statute would be frustrated if injunctions were not allowed. The key case so holding is *Mitchum v. Foster*.[40] In *Mitchum*, the question before the Court was whether 42 U.S.C. §1983 constituted an express authorization of injunctions of state proceedings.

Although §1983 permits courts to award both monetary and injunctive relief, the provision never specifically mentions injunctions of state court proceedings. The Court, however, deemed this omission irrelevant in deciding whether §1983 constituted an express authorization of injunctions. The Court said that "a federal law need not expressly authorize an injunction of a state proceeding in order to qualify as an exception."[41] The Court said that a statute would be deemed to allow injunctions if it "created a specific and uniquely federal right or remedy, enforceable in a federal court of equity, which could be frustrated if the federal proceeding were not empowered to enjoin a state court proceeding."[42]

The Court explained that the legislative history of §1983 clearly indicated that it could be given its intended effect only if federal courts could stay state court proceedings. The Court emphasized that the very purpose of §1983 was to protect people from state governments and especially from state judiciaries. The Court, in a unanimous opinion, declared:

[37] 28 U.S.C. §2361.

[38] 11 U.S.C. §362.

[39] Such statutes expressly authorizing injunctions include the removal statutes, 28 U.S.C. §1446(e), and the habeas corpus statute, 28 U.S.C. §2251. *See* McFarland v. Scott, 512 U.S. 849 (1994) (federal district court has jurisdiction to enter a stay of execution where necessary to give effect to the defendant's statutory right to appointed habeas corpus counsel).

[40] 407 U.S. 225 (1972).

[41] *Id.* at 237.

[42] *Id.*

> The legislative history makes evident that Congress clearly conceived that it was altering the relationship between the States and the Nation with respect to the protection of federally created rights; it was concerned that state instrumentalities could not protect those rights; it realized that state officers might, in fact, be antipathetic to the vindication of those rights; and it believed that these failings extended to the state courts. . . . The very purpose of §1983 was to interpose the federal courts between the States and the people as guardians of the people's federal rights.[43]

Relationship of *Mitchum* and *Younger*

Although the Court's reading of the legislative history of §1983 seems unassailably correct, *Mitchum* remains a puzzling decision, especially in light of *Younger v. Harris,* which was decided only a year earlier.[44] In *Younger,* the Court held that considerations of equity and comity, completely independent of the Anti-Injunction Act, prevent federal courts from enjoining pending state court criminal proceedings. Although in *Younger* the plaintiff's federal law complaint was based on §1983 and alleged violations of the First Amendment, the Court nonetheless held that the federal court could not enjoin the state court. *Younger* is based on an explicit assumption of trust in state courts to properly adjudicate constitutional claims; *Mitchum* is based on an express distrust of state courts in constitutional cases.

The relationship of the two decisions is puzzling because of the Court's construction of the Anti-Injunction Act in *Mitchum.* The Court concluded that the act's requirement for express statutory authorizations for injunctions does not actually require express statutory authorizations. The Court could easily have avoided the paradoxical relationship between *Mitchum* and *Younger* simply by holding in *Younger* that the injunction was barred by the Anti-Injunction Act because §1983 does not contain an express authorization for stays of state court proceedings. If the Court had taken this approach, it would not have needed to create an independent bar to federal court injunctions. Additionally, it could have avoided the major separation of powers issues raised by *Younger*: What authority does the federal court have to abstain from issuing relief, particularly when there is a specific federal statute defining when injunctions are allowed and when they are prohibited?[45]

Ultimately, the effect of *Younger* and *Mitchum* taken together is that there are two independent barriers to federal court injunctions of state court proceedings: the judicially created abstention doctrine and the Anti-Injunction Act. Both must be overcome. Section 1983 constitutes an exception to the Anti-Injunction Act, but not to the *Younger* doctrine. Accordingly, a federal court can enjoin state proceedings pursuant to §1983 only if the case also fits within one of the exceptions to *Younger* abstention.[46]

[43] *Id.* at 242.

[44] 401 U.S. 37 (1971). Younger v. Harris is discussed in detail in §13.2, *infra.*

[45] Martin H. Redish, Abstention, Separation of Powers, and the Judicial Function, 94 Yale L.J. 71, 91-95 (1984).

[46] For a discussion of the exceptions of the *Younger* doctrine, *see* §13.4, *infra.*

Other Express Authorizations

Mitchum v. Foster opens up the possibility that other federal statutes might be read as expressly authorizing injunctions of state court proceedings even though the laws do not explicitly mention such relief. The Court has not yet found other instances in which injunctions are allowed because they are necessary to effectuate a statute's purposes. The Court's only other case dealing with the "expressly authorized" exception to the Anti-Injunction Act was *Vendo Co. v. Lektro-Vend Corp.*[47]

Vendo Co. is a confusing decision because of the absence of a majority opinion. The Vendo Company filed a lawsuit in state court accusing the defendants of breaching a contractual agreement to not compete with Vendo Company's machines. While the state court suit was pending, the defendants in that litigation filed a lawsuit in federal court alleging that the agreement not to compete violated the federal antitrust laws, particularly the Clayton Act. After lengthy litigation, the state court found in favor of the plaintiff and awarded more than $7 million in damages. Although there were no federal proceedings while the state litigation was ongoing, once the state court judgment was upheld by the state supreme court, Vendo sought a federal court preliminary injunction preventing enforcement of the state court judgment. The district court awarded the injunction and the Seventh Circuit affirmed, concluding that §16 of the Clayton Act should be treated as an express authorization for injunctions.

The Supreme Court reversed. Justice Rehnquist wrote the plurality opinion in which Justices Stewart and Powell concurred. Justice Rehnquist concluded that §16 of the Clayton Act was not an express authorization of injunctions. Although the statute created a "uniquely federal right or remedy," Justice Rehnquist argued that the case was unlike *Mitchum* in that there was not a statute that "could be given its intended scope only by the stay of a state court proceeding."[48] Whereas the legislative history of §1983 indicated a strong distrust of state judiciaries, no similar purposes motivated §16 of the Clayton Act.

Justice Blackmun, joined by Chief Justice Burger, concurred in the result. Justice Blackmun argued that §16 is an express authorization for injunctions, but only in circumstances where the "pending state court proceedings . . . are themselves part of a 'pattern of baseless repetitive claims' that are being used as an anticompetitive device."[49]

Justice Stevens wrote a dissenting opinion, in which Justices Brennan, White, and Marshall joined. The dissent argued that the Clayton Act permitted federal courts to enjoin state court litigation that was itself an antitrust violation. Unlike Justice Blackmun, the dissent argued that even a single instance of state court litigation could violate the federal antitrust laws. Under such circumstances, federal courts could enjoin state proceedings.

What makes the *Vendo Co.* case confusing is that while five justices ruled that an injunction was impermissible in that instance, six of the justices held that, at

[47] 433 U.S. 623 (1977).
[48] *Id.* at 632.
[49] *Id.* at 644 (Blackmun, J., concurring in the result).

least in some situations, the Clayton Act was an express authorization for injunctions of state court proceedings. At the very least, the *Vendo Co.* decision does little to clarify the question of when federal statutes that do not explicitly provide for injunctive relief should be regarded as express authorizations of injunctions. Nor has the Supreme Court provided any guidance as to the meaning of this exception to the Anti-Injunction Act since *Vendo Co.* The result is that there is a substantial split among the lower courts as to whether specific statutes, such as the federal securities laws and the federal environmental laws, should be regarded as expressly authorizing injunctions of state court proceedings.[50]

§11.2.3 Injunctions in Aid of Jurisdiction

The second exception contained in the Anti-Injunction Act is where a federal court injunction is "necessary in aid of its jurisdiction." As interpreted, this exception applies in only two circumstances: where a case is removed from state court to federal court and where the federal court first acquires jurisdiction over a case involving the disposition of real property.

Injunction When Case Is Removed From State to Federal Court

When the current version of the Anti-Injunction Act was adopted in 1948, the Reviser's Note explained that the purpose of this exception was "to make clear the recognized power of the Federal courts to stay proceedings in State cases removed to the district courts."[51] In other words, if a case is removed from state court to federal court pursuant to the removal statute and the state court does not properly relinquish jurisdiction, the federal court may enjoin further state judicial proceedings. However, there was little need for a separate exception for removal cases because the Supreme Court always had regarded the removal statute as an express authorization for staying state proceedings.[52]

[50] *See, e.g.,* Stockslager v. Carroll Elec. Coop. Corp., 528 F.2d 949 (8th Cir. 1976) (National Environmental Policy Act constitutes an express authorization of injunctions); Jennings v. Boenning & Co., 482 F.2d 1128 (3d Cir.), *cert. denied,* 414 U.S. 1025 (1973) (Securities and Exchange Act does not constitute an express authorization of injunctions); Studebaker Corp. v. Gittlin, 360 F.2d 692 (2d Cir. 1966) (Securities and Exchange Act constitutes an express authorization of injunctions); Board of Supervisors of Dickenson County v. Circuit Court of Dickenson County, 500 F. Supp. 212 (E.D. Va. 1980) (National Environmental Policy Act does not constitute an express authorization of injunctions).

[51] 28 U.S.C. §2283 (Reviser's Note).

[52] *See, e.g.,* Mitchum v. Foster, 407 U.S. 225, 234-237 (1972) (removal as a situation where there is an express authorization of injunctions); Dietzsch v. Huidekoper, 103 U.S. 494 (1880) (removal as an exception to the Anti-Injunction Act).

Real Property Exception

A second and more important effect of this exception is to permit federal courts to enjoin state judicial proceedings where the federal court first acquires jurisdiction over a case involving real property. It is long established that whatever court initially acquires in rem or quasi in rem jurisdiction over a matter involving property can enjoin all other courts from hearing the matter. Even in *Toucey v. New York Life Insurance Co.*, where Justice Frankfurter articulated a very narrow view of the exceptions to the Anti-Injunction Act, the Court recognized the well-settled view that if an action is in rem the court first obtaining jurisdiction over the res could enjoin suits in other courts involving the same res.[53] In other words, the general rule is that whichever court first gains jurisdiction in a case concerning the disposition of property has exclusive jurisdiction to decide claims to that property and may enforce its jurisdiction with injunctions if necessary.[54]

The rationale for allowing such injunctions is not completely clear. The Court has indicated that it reflects a desire to avoid inconsistent dispositions over property; for example, to prevent a situation where different courts award conflicting titles to the same land.[55] Yet it is unclear why injunctions are necessary to prevent inconsistent decisions because traditional principles of preclusion, res judicata, and collateral estoppel, should ensure that the decision of the court that decides first will be followed by all other courts.

Moreover, the need to prevent inconsistent results is not limited to cases involving real property. In in personam actions, one court's decision might effectively prevent all other courts from providing relief. Imagine, for example, a situation in which a defendant with limited monetary assets is sued in several courts. Whichever court decides first will dispose of all the assets, effectively rendering the remaining litigation meaningless. It might be argued that in such situations federal courts should be able to enjoin other proceedings in order to preserve meaningful authority and jurisdiction. In fact, more generally, because of res judicata and collateral estoppel, a decision of one court as to a controversy between parties will prevent all other courts from exercising their jurisdiction and deciding the matter.

Real Property Exception Does Not Include in Personam Cases

However, the Supreme Court has been firm that the "in aid of jurisdiction" exception applies only in real property situations and not in in personam cases. In the leading case of *Atlantic Coast Line Railroad v. Brotherhood of Locomotive Engineers*, it was argued that permitting the state court to decide an issue would have the effect of robbing the federal court of jurisdiction because of preclusion

[53] 314 U.S. 118, 135-136 (1948). *See also* Kline v. Burke Constr. Co., 260 U.S. 226 (1922) (articulating the distinction between in rem and in personam proceedings). *See* Donovan v. City of Dallas, 377 U.S. 408 (1964). However, under *Donovan* it is impermissible for a state court to enjoin a party from proceeding in a federal court. Baker v. General Motors Corp., 522 U.S. 222, 236 n.9 (1998).

[54] *Id.* at 412; Princess Lida v. Thompson, 305 U.S. 456, 465-468 (1939).

[55] *See* Colorado River Water Conservation Dist. v. United States, 424 U.S. 800, 819 (1976).

doctrines.[56] Thus, it was urged that the federal court, in aid of its jurisdiction, should be able to restrain the state proceedings. The Court explicitly rejected this argument. Justice Black, writing for the majority, stated that "the state and federal courts had concurrent jurisdiction in this case, and neither court was free to prevent either party from simultaneously pursuing claims in both courts. . . . Therefore the state court's assumption of jurisdiction over the state law claims and the federal preclusion issue did not hinder the federal court's jurisdiction so as to make an injunction *necessary* to aid that jurisdiction."[57]

There is one case in which the Supreme Court allowed an injunction "in aid of jurisdiction" of state proceedings in an in personam action. Subsequently, however, the Court said that the decision was based not on this exception but instead was pursuant to an express congressional authorization of injunctions. In *Capital Services, Inc. v. National Labor Relations Board*, the Supreme Court affirmed an injunction issued by a federal district court.[58] Capital Services obtained an injunction from a state court preventing a union from picketing and then filed an unfair labor practices charge against the union with the National Labor Relations Board. The board issued a formal complaint and sought a federal court injunction to halt the union picketing and also an injunction to stay any further state court proceedings until after the federal court resolved the matter on the merits. The Supreme Court upheld the injunction of the state court as being in aid of the federal court's jurisdiction.

Conceivably, *Capital Services* might be read as a major expansion of the "in aid of jurisdiction" exception to the Anti-Injunction Act. Arguably, it stands for the proposition that federal courts have the authority to enjoin state courts where a state decision likely would end the federal court's ability to decide a particular case within its jurisdiction. However, one year after *Capital Services*, the Court said that the case was decided under the "expressly authorized" exception and not the "in aid of jurisdiction" exception.[59] Moreover, subsequent cases have not followed up on the *Capital Services* opinion, which contrary to the reinterpretation, suggested that the "in aid of jurisdiction" exception could be applied in contexts other than cases involving real property.

The effect of the narrow construction of this exception is to foster duplicative litigation in state and federal courts.[60] In many situations, the exact same issue between the same parties is simultaneously litigated in both forums. For example, a defendant in a state court proceeding, who cannot remove a diversity case to federal court because he or she is sued in his or her home state, might retaliate by filing a suit in federal court naming the state court plaintiff as the defendant. Sometimes duplicative litigation arises because the plaintiff simultaneously

[56] 398 U.S. 281 (1970) (discussed more fully in this section in text accompanying notes 64-66, *infra*).

[57] *Id.* at 295-296 (emphasis added) (citations omitted).

[58] 347 U.S. 501 (1954).

[59] Amalgamated Clothing Workers v. Richman Bros., 348 U.S. 511, 514 (1955).

[60] For an argument that the relitigation exception should be broadened to prevent duplicative litigation in the mass torts context, *see* Bryan J. Schillinger, Preventing Mass Tort Litigation Through the Limited Resources Doctrine, 14 Rev. Litig. 465 (1995).

files the same suit in federal and state court. In cases involving the disposition of real property, as explained above, whichever court acquires jurisdiction first can enjoin all other courts. But in all other matters, the federal court may not stay the state proceedings; nor, of course, may the state court stay the federal proceedings. The result is duplicative litigation, which is totally wasteful because ultimately only one court will actually issue a decision; whichever court decides first will preclude the other from rendering a judgment. The problem of duplicative litigation and the possibility of federal court abstention as a solution are discussed in detail in Chapter 14.

§11.2.4 Injunctions to Promote or Effectuate a Federal Court's Judgment

Injunctions to Prevent Relitigation

The third and final exception to the Anti-Injunction Act is when injunctions are necessary to promote or effectuate an earlier judgment by a federal court. This is usually referred to as the "relitigation exception" because it permits federal courts to enjoin state proceedings if necessary to ensure the preclusive effect of an earlier federal court decision. This exception was meant to overrule the Supreme Court's decision in *Toucey v. New York Life Insurance Co.*, which denied a federal court the power to enjoin a state proceeding that threatened to undermine an earlier federal court decision.[61] As described above, in *Toucey*, after an insurance company was sued in federal court and prevailed, the company was then sued on the same grounds in state court. The company sought to effectuate the federal court judgment by enjoining the state court litigation, but the Supreme Court refused to permit the injunction. The Reviser's Note made it clear that the primary purpose of the 1948 revision of the Anti-Injunction Act was to overrule *Toucey*.[62]

In other words, the relitigation exception provides that when a federal court decides an issue, it can prevent that same issue from being relitigated in state court where principles of preclusion should bind the state court. This exception prevents the harassment of federal court litigants by repetitive state court proceedings and ensures the finality of the federal courts' decisions. Thus, the relitigation exception applies only in situations where because of res judicata the state court should not hear a case, but does so anyway.[63]

[61] 314 U.S. 118 (1941). *Toucey* is discussed in detail in this section, in text accompanying notes 14-16, *supra*.

[62] 28 U.S.C. §2283 (Reviser's Note).

[63] The Supreme Court held that a case may not be removed from state to federal court to prevent relitigation. *See* Rivet v. Regions Bank of Louisiana, 522 U.S. 470 (1998). In other words, for a case to be removed from state to federal court, there must be a basis for federal court jurisdiction apart from the need to enforce the res judicata effect of the prior federal court ruling.

Was the Prior Decision a Ruling on the Merits?

Occasionally, issues arise as to whether an earlier federal court decision was a judgment on the merits that should be preclusive or whether it was entirely a procedural ruling. If the federal court ruled on the merits, then its decision should be upheld by an injunction if necessary, but if the federal court dismissed the case on procedural grounds, then the state court should be free to hear the matter. An example of this arose in *Atlantic Coast Line Railroad v. Brotherhood of Locomotive Engineers.*[64]

In *Atlantic Coast Line,* a federal court refused to issue an injunction to halt labor picketing. Subsequently, the state court enjoined the labor activity. The union then sought a federal court injunction staying enforcement of the state court's order halting the labor demonstrations. The federal court had to resolve the meaning of the earlier federal decision refusing an injunction of the labor activity. Did the federal court deny an order halting the picketing because it believed that the union had a right to picket? If so, the federal court should enjoin the state to keep it from stopping the legally protected labor demonstration. Or did the federal court refuse to enjoin the labor picketing because it lacked jurisdiction to hear such a claim under the Norris-LaGuardia Act, which generally denies federal courts jurisdiction to enjoin labor activities?[65] If so, the federal court's dismissal for lack of jurisdiction should not preclude a later state court decision and could not be the basis for an injunction of the state proceedings.

The Court concluded that it was the latter—that the federal court had dismissed for lack of jurisdiction and had not ruled that there was a right to engage in the activity—and thus refused to allow the federal court to enjoin the state litigation. The dissent, however, argued that the federal court had decided that the union "had a federally protected right to picket . . . and by necessary implication, that this right could not be subverted by resort to state proceedings."[66]

Earlier Federal Court Ruling Must Have Been on the Merits

Thus, a federal court may not enjoin state court proceedings under the relitigation exception if the earlier federal court ruling was based on federal court procedures and not on the merits of the case. The Supreme Court reaffirmed this in *Choo v. Exxon Corp.*[67] A federal court suit was initiated by the widow of a Singapore resident who died while working for Exxon Corp. The district court granted summary judgment for the defendant on some of the plaintiff's claims and dismissed the remainder on forum non conveniens grounds after Exxon Corp. agreed to submit them to the jurisdiction of Singapore's courts. After the dismissal, the widow filed suit in Texas state court. Exxon Corp. then sought a federal court

[64] 398 U.S. 281 (1970).

[65] The Norris-LaGuardia Act is codified in 29 U.S.C. §101. The act is discussed in more detail in §3.3, *supra.*

[66] 398 U.S. at 299 (Brennan, J., dissenting).

[67] 486 U.S. 140 (1988).

injunction to halt the state court proceedings. The Supreme Court held that the Anti-Injunction Act prevented enjoining the Texas court from hearing the claims that had been dismissed from federal court. The Supreme Court deemed the relitigation exception inapplicable because the federal court's forum non conveniens ruling meant only that federal court litigation was inappropriate; it was not a judgment about the appropriateness of the state court's hearing the matter.[68]

After *Choo*, the lower courts have been divided as to what the relitigation exception applies to. Specifically, the issue is whether the relitigation exception applies to only those matters that were actually litigated in state courts or whether it applies to all that could have been litigated and thus is precluded from litigation by res judicata. Most lower courts have taken the former approach and concluded that the relitigation exception is limited to issues actually litigated in federal court.[69] Other courts, most notably the Ninth Circuit, have held that the relitigation exception applies not only to matters that were actually litigated but also to anything that would be barred from relitigation by res judicata.[70]

Timing for Seeking Injunctions

Another important decision concerning the relitigation exception involved the timing for when the parties must request a federal court injunction to successfully obtain a stay of state judicial proceedings. In *Parsons Steel, Inc. v. First Alabama Bank*, the plaintiff sued the defendant bank simultaneously in federal and state court on the same causes of action.[71] The federal court decided first, ruling in favor of the defendant. The plaintiff then pursued the state court suit. The defendant raised res judicata as a defense in state court, but the state court held that the earlier federal court decision did not preclude the state proceedings. The state court entered a judgment for the plaintiff and awarded $4 million in damages. At that point, the defendant sought an injunction from the federal court to prevent enforcement of the state judgment to effectuate the earlier ruling by the federal court.

The Supreme Court unanimously held that the federal court could not enjoin the state court under such circumstances. The Court said that the "relitigation exception" was limited "to those situations in which the state court has not yet ruled on the merits of the res judicata issue."[72] That is, once the res judicata issue was raised in state court and decided, then the federal court had to accept the state's determination that there is not preclusion. In other words, the bank might have obtained an injunction of the state court proceedings while they were pending, but once they were completed, and especially once the res judicata issue was

[68] *Id.* at 144-145.

[69] *See, e.g.,* Carey v. Sub Sea International, Inc., 121 F. Supp. 2d 1073 (E.D. Tex. 2000); In re G.S.F. Corp., 938 F.2d 1467, 1478 (1st Cir. 1991); Farias v. Bexar County Board of Trustees, 925 F.2d 866, 879-880 (5th Cir.), *cert. denied,* 502 U.S. 866 (1991); American Town Hall Center v. Hall 83 Assocs., 912 F.2d 104, 112 n.2 (6th Cir. 1990).

[70] Western Sys., Inc. v. Ulloa, 958 F.2d 869 (9th Cir. 1992).

[71] 474 U.S. 518 (1986).

[72] *Id.* at 524.

ruled on by the state court, then the federal court was bound by the state court's determinations.

On the one hand, this unanimous decision follows the traditional rule that a state court's determination of an issue, such as res judicata, is binding on the federal courts. At the same time, however, the effect is to allow states to undermine federal judgments. The bank's victory in federal court was rendered nugatory by the state court's multimillion-dollar verdict against it.

Moreover, the *Parsons Steel* decision will have the effect of increasing the frequency of federal court injunctions of state proceedings. Usually, if someone is sued in state court after prevailing on the same issues in federal court, he or she will raise res judicata as a defense to the state judicial proceedings. In most cases, the state court will accord preclusive effect to the earlier federal judgment and that will end the state proceedings. In such instances, the federal courts need not enjoin the state court litigation; the state, on its own, will dismiss the matter because of claim and issue preclusion.

However, *Parsons Steel* creates a strong incentive to not litigate the preclusion issue in state court. If the question is presented there and lost, it will bar a subsequent federal injunction. Hence, after *Parsons Steel,* the person subjected to a repetitive suit in state court should immediately seek a federal court injunction. The result will be federal court injunctions in many instances where the state court would have dismissed the case anyway on preclusion grounds. This seems inconsistent with the Supreme Court's general preference that matters be litigated in state court where possible and its general desire to avoid injunctions of state judicial proceedings.

§11.2.5 Additional Exceptions to the Anti-Injunction Act

Suits by the United States and to Preserve Status Quo

The Supreme Court has emphasized that the three exceptions contained in §2283 are exclusive; the Court should not create additional exceptions permitting federal courts to enjoin the pending state proceedings.[73] Nonetheless, the Court has recognized some additional situations where injunctions are allowed.

For example, in *Leiter Minerals, Inc. v. United States,* the Supreme Court held that the Anti-Injunction Act does not apply to suits brought by the United States.[74] Justice Frankfurter, writing for a unanimous court, said that the "frustration of superior federal interests that would ensue from precluding the federal government from obtaining a stay of state court proceedings except under the severe restrictions of §2283 would be so great that we cannot reasonably impute such

[73] Atlantic Coast Line R.R. v. Brotherhood of Locomotive Engrs., 398 U.S. 281, 297-298 (1970); Amalgamated Clothing Workers v. Richman Bros., 348 U.S. 511 (1955).

[74] 352 U.S. 220 (1957); *see also* United States v. Village of Palatine, Ill., 845 F. Supp. 540 (N.D. Ill. 1993) (neither the Anti-Injunction Act nor *Younger* abstention (discussed in Chapter 13) bars the United States from obtaining an injunction of state court proceedings).

a purpose to Congress."[75] Subsequently, the Court broadened this exception to exempt all suits brought by federal government agencies from the prohibition against injunctive relief.[76]

Also, lower courts are in agreement that federal courts may issue preliminary injunctions to preserve the status quo until it can be decided whether the case fits within one of the exceptions to the Anti-Injunction Act.[77]

§11.3 STATUTES LIMITING ENJOINING THE COLLECTION OF TAXES: THE TAX INJUNCTION ACT AND THE ANTI-INJUNCTION ACT

The Tax Injunction Act, 28 U.S.C. §1341, provides that the "District Courts shall not enjoin, suspend or restrain the assessment, levy or collection of any tax under State law where a plain, speedy and efficient remedy may be had in the courts of such State." The act, adopted in 1937, has been interpreted as creating a jurisdictional bar to federal courts interfering with the collection of state or local taxes.[1] Because the act is viewed as a limit on the subject matter jurisdiction of the federal courts, jurisdiction may not be obtained by the consent of the state or local governments.[2]

There is another federal statute, confusingly also called "the Anti-Injunction Act," 26 U.S.C. §7421(a), which bars federal court jurisdiction over preenforcement suits that would restrain "the assessment or collection of any [federal] tax." There is an obvious similarity to this and the Tax Injunction Act, which applies as to state and local taxes. This statutory provision is discussed at the conclusion of this section.

Purposes of the Tax Injunction Act

The Tax Injunction Act embodies considerations of federalism: deference to state and local governments in the collection of revenues. As the Supreme Court expressed, the act reflects the "scrupulous regard for the rightful independence of state governments . . . and a proper reluctance to interfere by injunction with

[75] 352 U.S. at 226.

[76] NLRB v. Nash-Finch Co., 404 U.S. 138 (1971).

[77] *See, e.g.,* Barancik v. Investors Funding Corp. of N.Y., 489 F.2d 933 (7th Cir. 1973); Baines v. City of Danville, 337 F.2d 579, 593 (4th Cir. 1964), *aff'd,* 364 U.S. 890 (1966).

§11.3 [1] *See* Moe v. Confederated Salish & Kootenai Tribes of the Flathead Reservation, 425 U.S. 463, 470 (1976). Also, the federal Anti-Injunction Act, discussed below, precludes federal courts from enjoining the collection of federal taxes. 26 U.S.C.A. §7421(a).

[2] *See, e.g.,* Burris v. City of Little Rock, 941 F.2d 717 (8th Cir. 1991); Hardwick v. Cuomo, 891 F.2d 1097 (3d Cir. 1989); City of Burbank v. State of Nev., 658 F.2d 708, 709 (9th Cir. 1981).

their fiscal operations."[3] Thus, the Court has spoken of the act as recognizing "the imperative need of a State to administer its own fiscal operations."[4] In fact, the act parallels a statute prohibiting federal courts from interfering with the collection of federal revenues.[5]

Four major issues arise in interpreting the Tax Injunction Act. First, what constitutes "the levy, assessment or collection" of a tax by a state or local government? Second, what is the meaning of the act's exception, permitting federal courts to issue injunctions if there is not a "plain, speedy and efficient" state court remedy? Third, what federal court actions constitute an impermissible injunction, suspension, or restraint of state taxes? For example, may federal courts issue declaratory judgments that state taxes are unconstitutional or may federal courts award monetary relief for the unconstitutional collection of taxes? Fourth, are there any additional exceptions to the act recognized by the Court although not mentioned in the statute? Finally, may a state court hear a suit under §1983 to enjoin a state tax? Each of these questions is analyzed in turn.

What is a Tax?

Courts have broadly interpreted the act as preventing federal courts from interfering with virtually all forms of state and local taxes. Thus, the act prohibits injunctions of gross receipts, income, property, sales, license, and special assessment taxes.[6] Because local governments tax pursuant to state government authority, the act prevents federal courts from enjoining both local and state taxes.

The issue of what is a tax arises primarily in deciding whether a particular fee should be characterized as a regulation, in which case the act is inapplicable, or as a tax, in which case injunctions are barred. Although the characterization is decisive in determining whether an injunction is allowed, there is no easy test for deciding the proper way to treat a particular state or local law. The U.S. Court of Appeals for the Eleventh Circuit said that the question is whether the state or local law is intended "to raise revenue for the city or to regulate licensees."[7] The distinction is problematic because regulatory measures often also raise revenue and tax measures often have the effect of regulating conduct. Nonetheless, lower courts generally have followed a commonsense approach, finding, for example,

[3] Hillsborough Twp. v. Cromwell, 326 U.S. 620, 622 (1946) (citation omitted). For a criticism of the Tax Injunction Act, arguing a neutral federal forum to resolve constitutional issues is more important than deference to state courts, *see* Stephanie Teroni, Comment, The Tax Injunction Act: A Call for Change, 95 Temple L. Rev. 501 (2024).

[4] Tully v. Griffin, 429 U.S. 68, 73 (1976).

[5] 26 U.S.C. §7421(a).

[6] *See, e.g.,* Schneider Transp., Inc. v. Cattanach, 657 F.2d 128 (7th Cir. 1981), *cert. denied,* 455 U.S. 909 (1982) (registration fees); A Bonding Co. v. Sunnuck, 629 F.2d 1127 (5th Cir. 1980) (bonding fees); Tramel v. Schrader, 505 F.2d 1310, 1315 (5th Cir. 1975) (special assessment); *but see* Hager v. City of West Peoria, 84 F.3d 865 (7th Cir. 1996) (finding permit fee raised as part of a regulatory program is not a tax); Southeastern Pennsylvania Transportation Authority v. Board of Revision of Taxes of the City of Philadelphia, 49 F. Supp. 2d 778, 780-781 (E.D. Pa. 1999) (the act prohibits injunction of gross receipts, income, property, sales, license, and special assessment taxes).

[7] Miami Herald Publishing Co. v. City of Hallandale, 734 F.2d 666, 670 (11th Cir. 1984).

that registration fees, license fees, and special improvement assessments have the primary purpose of raising revenue and thus should be classified as taxes.[8]

The broad approach followed in defining taxes is illustrated by a Sixth Circuit opinion, which held that a parolee's monthly payments to a supervision fund and to a victim's compensation fund are a tax.[9] A parolee initiated a federal court suit challenging the constitutionality of the requirement for contributions to these funds. The court, however, found that the Tax Injunction Act barred the suit because the purpose of the charges was to raise revenue and defray the cost to the public. Thus, although the revenues were earmarked rather than placed in general revenue, the levies were nonetheless taxes.

In *Direct Marketing Association v. Brohl*, the Court held that the Tax Injunction Act did not bar the federal courts from hearing a challenge to a state law requiring retailers who do not collect taxes to inform consumers of their tax obligation.[10] The Court explained that "[i]n an effort to improve the collection of sales and use taxes for items purchased online, the State of Colorado passed a law requiring retailers that do not collect Colorado sales or use tax to notify Colorado customers of their use-tax liability and to report tax-related information to customers and the Colorado Department of Revenue."[11] The issue before the Court was whether the Tax Injunction Act applied to this reporting and notice requirement.

The Court said that "the question becomes whether the enforcement of the notice and reporting requirements is an act of 'assessment, levy or collection.' We need not comprehensively define these terms to conclude that they do not encompass enforcement of the notice and reporting requirements at issue."[12] Although the Colorado law was intended to improve the collection of taxes, it was not an "assessment, levy or collection" within the meaning of the Tax Injunction Act.[13]

Is a Challenge to a Tax Credit Barred?

In *Hibbs v. Winn*, the Supreme Court considered whether the Tax Injunction Act bars a federal court from enjoining a tax credit as violating the establishment

[8] *See, e.g.*, Schneider Transp., Inc. v. Cattanach, 657 F.2d 128 (7th Cir. 1981), *cert. denied*, 455 U.S. 909 (1982) (registration fees); A Bonding Co. v. Sunnuck, 629 F.2d 1127 (5th Cir. 1980) (bonding fees); Alnoa Corp. v. City of Houston, 563 F.2d 769 (5th Cir. 1977), *cert. denied*, 435 U.S. 970 (1978) (special assessment fees); *but see* Wells v. Malloy, 510 F.2d 74 (2d Cir. 1975) (request for an injunction preventing suspension of driver's license for failure to pay tax due on purchase of motor vehicle was not seeking to enjoin collection of a tax).

[9] Wright v. McClaim, 835 F.2d 143 (6th Cir. 1987).

[10] 575 U.S. 1 (2015).

[11] *Id.* at 4.

[12] *Id.* at 8.

[13] Interestingly, the Court said that it took no position as to whether comity—discussed below—might bar the federal court from reviewing this challenge to the Colorado law. The Court stated: "We take no position on whether a suit such as this one might nevertheless be barred under the 'comity doctrine' which 'counsels lower federal courts to resist engagement in certain cases falling within their jurisdiction.' . . . Unlike the TIA, the comity doctrine is nonjurisdictional. And here, Colorado did not seek comity from either of the courts below." *Id.* at 15 (citations omitted).

clause of the First Amendment.[14] Arizona law allowed taxpayers to receive tax credits for contributions to organizations that could disburse money to parochial schools. A challenge was brought to this in federal court on the grounds that it violated the establishment clause. The state moved to dismiss based on the Tax Injunction Act.

The Supreme Court, in a 5-4 decision, concluded that the Tax Injunction Act did not bar injunctive relief. Justice Ginsburg wrote the opinion for the Court and said that the Tax Injunction Act was designed to prevent federal court review of claims by taxpayers who were trying to avoid paying their tax obligations. The Court expressly rejected the state's claim that the Tax Injunction Act was "a sweeping congressional directive to prevent federal court interference with all aspects of state tax administration."[15] The Court thus distinguished a challenge to a state tax and to a state tax credit and pointed to many cases where federal courts had reviewed the constitutionality of tax breaks for religious entities.

Undoubtedly, the majority was concerned that applying the Tax Injunction Act in these circumstances would preclude federal courts from being able to review constitutional challenges to state taxes as violating the establishment clause. The dissent, by contrast, was not at all troubled by this and said that applying the Tax Injunction Act would mean that the challenges would go to state rather than federal court.[16]

Ultimately, the disagreement between the majority and the dissent seems less about the language of the Tax Injunction Act, or even the distinction between a tax and a tax credit, and more about how important it is that federal courts be able to enforce the establishment clause.

What Is a "Plain, Speedy and Efficient Remedy"?

The most frequently litigated question under the Tax Injunction Act is, what constitutes a "plain, speedy and efficient remedy in State court"? In the years immediately following the enactment of the Tax Injunction Act, the Supreme Court expansively interpreted this exception, frequently finding state judicial review to be inadequate. Subsequently, however, the Supreme Court has adopted a strikingly different approach by narrowly interpreting the circumstances where state remedies will be deemed inadequate.

In *Spector Motor Service, Inc. v. McLaughlin*, in 1944, the plaintiff challenged Connecticut's tax on intrastate trucking operations.[17] The plaintiff contended that the tax could not be lawfully applied to it because it was involved solely in interstate business. The Supreme Court held that the federal district court was not required to dismiss the case under the Tax Injunction Act "because of the uncertainty surrounding the adequacy of the Connecticut remedy."[18] The Court emphasized that

[14] 542 U.S. 88 (2004).
[15] *Id.* at 90.
[16] *Id.* at 117 (Kennedy, J., dissenting).
[17] 323 U.S. 101 (1944).
[18] *Id.* at 106.

the absence of state court interpretations of the tax law created sufficient uncertainty to justify federal jurisdiction under the exception to the Tax Injunction Act.[19]

In *Hillsborough Township v. Cromwell*, in 1946, the plaintiff brought an action to have declared unconstitutional tax assessments on intangible personal property.[20] The Supreme Court found that there was no "plain, speedy and efficient remedy in State court." Previous New Jersey state court decisions held that an equal protection challenge to a state or local tax had to be in the form of an action to increase the taxes paid by those who benefited from the alleged discrimination. The state courts had ruled that equal protection suits could not seek a decrease in an individual's taxes. The Court concluded that on "the basis of that rule, it is plain that the state remedy is not adequate to protect respondent's rights under the federal Constitution."[21] Although the state contended that the law in New Jersey was unsettled, the Supreme Court decided that, at the very least, "there was such uncertainty surrounding the adequacy of the state remedy as to justify the District Court in retaining jurisdiction of the case."[22]

Yet another instance in which state remedies were deemed to be inadequate, and federal jurisdiction upheld, was the 1952 decision in *Georgia Railroad & Banking Co. v. Redwine*.[23] A railroad company brought suit to enjoin the assessment and collection of ad valorem taxes. The Supreme Court concluded that state remedies were not sufficient and reversed the district court's dismissal of the case. Under state law, the company would have been required to file more than 300 separate claims in 14 different counties to present the issue asserted in federal court.[24]

These early cases under the act reflected a willingness to narrowly construe the circumstances in which federal jurisdiction would be precluded. The Court emphasized that even uncertainty about the effectiveness of the state remedies was enough to permit federal court review.

Subsequent decisions, however, reflect a very different view. Now it is clear that the exception when there are not "plain, speedy and efficient" state remedies is rarely to be applied; that is, there is a strong presumption that state remedies are adequate.[25] For example, in *Tully v. Griffin*, in 1976, the Court considered a requirement that an individual prepay or post a bond for the amount of the assessment in order to challenge the tax in state administrative and judicial proceedings.[26] The Court concluded that this requirement did not render the state system inadequate, even though there were situations where the individual could not pay and thus could not challenge the state tax.[27]

[19] *Id.*

[20] 326 U.S. 620 (1946).

[21] *Id.* at 624.

[22] *Id.* at 626.

[23] 342 U.S. 299 (1952).

[24] *Id.* at 303.

[25] *See, e.g.*, California v. Grace Brethren Church, 457 U.S. 393, 413 (1982).

[26] 429 U.S. 68 (1976).

[27] *Id.* at 73. The Court also found it immaterial that the plaintiff would have had to cross state borders (here an additional six miles of travel) in order to challenge the tax law. *Id.*

In *Rosewell v. LaSalle National Bank*, the Court emphasized the strong presumption against federal court jurisdiction.[28] In *Rosewell*, the Court considered an Illinois statute that required individuals challenging property taxes to exhaust administrative remedies before filing judicial proceedings. Also, to initiate litigation, individuals were required to pay the taxes owed and then sue for refunds. The average delay was two years; even then, successful plaintiffs were not entitled to obtain interest on the money that was wrongfully collected from them.

Despite these limitations on challenges, the Court concluded that the state remedies were plain, speedy, and efficient. The majority emphasized that the act was concerned solely with the adequacy of the *procedures* established by the state.[29] The Court said that the *substantive* inadequacy of the state remedies was irrelevant. Thus, the Court found that the state's failure to pay interest on the amounts wrongfully collected was a substantive defect of the law, which could not be the basis for finding a state remedy to be inadequate. Moreover, the Court concluded that the requirement that the individual exhaust remedies or pay in advance did not justify federal court jurisdiction under the Tax Injunction Act. In fact, the Court found the state system to be "speedy" despite the two-year average delay because docket congestion of that sort was not unusual.[30]

Rosewell is a troubling decision because of its extremely narrow construction of the exception to the Tax Injunction Act. The distinction between procedural and substantive inadequacy seems ephemeral at best; distinctions between procedure and substance are virtually always artificial and difficult to draw. Furthermore, there is no reason under the act why a substantive defect is not enough to render the state procedures inadequate. For example, if a state law provided that a successful challenger to a state tax law could recover a maximum of one dollar, no matter how much was improperly taken, that could be categorized as a substantive defect; nonetheless, surely it would be enough to justify concluding that the state remedy is not plain or efficient. Ultimately, *Rosewell* must be read as signaling the Court's great reluctance to interfere with state and local tax systems even where there are substantial defects in the state review system.

In another case concerning this aspect of the Tax Injunction Act, *Franchise Tax Board of California v. Alcan Aluminum*, the Supreme Court held that the Tax Injunction Act barred a foreign company from challenging in federal court the constitutionality of the method the state of California used in calculating locally taxable income of its subsidiary.[31] The specific issue was whether the foreign parent company could seek federal court review because it could not challenge the tax in state court in its own name. The Supreme Court concluded that the Tax Injunction Act applied because the parent company's wholly owned subsidiary could challenge the tax in state proceedings. The Court noted that there was no evidence that the state claims could not be raised in state court and said that "mere

[28] 450 U.S. 503 (1981).
[29] *Id.* at 514-515.
[30] *Id.* at 518-519.
[31] 493 U.S. 331 (1990).

speculation" that the state courts would not entertain the claims was insufficient to prevent application of the Tax Injunction Act.[32]

Federal Courts Will Ensure Availability of Promised Remedy

However, it should be emphasized that federal courts will exercise jurisdiction when a state promises the availability of a remedy and then makes it unavailable. In *Reich v. Collins*, the Court held that a state must abide by its statute that provides for a refund of illegally collected taxes.[33] *Reich* involved a Georgia taxpayer who filed for a refund of a tax that had been declared unconstitutional. The taxpayer filed under a state law that provided: "A taxpayer shall be refunded any and all taxes or fees which are determined to have been illegally assessed and collected from him under the laws of this state, whether paid voluntarily or involuntarily."[34] The Georgia Supreme Court denied relief under this law because it concluded that the taxpayer had predeprivation remedies that were not used.

The U.S. Supreme Court unanimously reversed. Justice O'Connor, writing for the Court, explained, "In a long line of cases, this Court has established that due process requires a 'clear and certain' remedy for taxes collected in violation of federal law. A state has flexibility to provide that remedy before the disputed taxes are paid (predeprivation) or after they are paid (postdeprivation), or both. But what it may not do, and what Georgia does here, is to hold out what plainly appears to be a 'clear and certain' postdeprivation remedy and then declare, only after the disputed taxes have been paid, that no such remedy exists."[35]

The Court followed and applied *Reich* in *Newsweek, Inc. v. Florida Department of Revenue*.[36] A magazine publisher sought a refund of sales taxes following a determination that the exemption available for newspapers, but not magazines, was unconstitutional. The magazine publisher relied on the longstanding availability of a postpayment refund after a tax was deemed impermissible. The Court held that the state could not change its policy to preclude the availability of this remedy that had been promised by state law.

What Remedies are Precluded?

The third major issue arising under the act concerns which remedies are precluded. The act specifically prohibits injunctions; are declaratory judgments and monetary remedies also forbidden? The law is now clear that federal courts may not provide such relief in cases involving challenges to state tax systems.

Early in the history of the Tax Injunction Act, the Supreme Court indicated that suits seeking declaratory relief were to be treated like requests for injunctions. In *Great Lakes Dredge & Dock Co. v. Huffman*, in 1943, the Court said that declaratory

[32] *Id.* at 341.
[33] 513 U.S. 106 (1994).
[34] Ga. Code Ann. §4-2-35(a).
[35] 513 U.S. at 111.
[36] 522 U.S. 442 (1998) (per curiam).

judgments in "every practical sense operate to suspend collection of the state taxes until the litigation is ended."[37] The Court, however, did not base its decision on the words of the Tax Injunction Act because it concluded that principles of equitable restraint, by themselves, justified denying declaratory relief.[38]

Not surprisingly, the Court later decided the issue left open in *Great Lakes* and concluded that the Tax Injunction Act barred declaratory judgments by federal courts that would have the effect of suspending the collection of state taxes. In *California v. Grace Brethren Church,* the Court considered a challenge to the Federal Unemployment Tax Act, a joint federal-state scheme that requires employers to pay an excise tax on wages paid to employees.[39] The act exempts employees of organizations operated mostly for religious purposes, such as churches or associations of churches. Several California churches and religious schools claimed that the First Amendment's establishment clause was violated by the failure to accord them an exemption from the tax. The federal district court found the Tax Injunction Act inapplicable because of the constitutional challenge and permanently enjoined the state from collecting such taxes from the plaintiffs.

The Supreme Court vacated the district court's decision on the ground that the court lacked subject matter jurisdiction because of the Tax Injunction Act. The Court said that it was plain that the act "prohibits a federal district court in most circumstances from issuing an injunction enjoining the collection of state taxes. Although this Court once reserved the question [in *Great Lakes*], we now conclude that the Act also prohibits a district court from issuing a declaratory judgment holding state tax laws unconstitutional."[40] The Court said that the purpose of the Tax Injunction Act was to prevent federal court interference with the collection of taxes by state and local governments. Because declaratory judgments invalidating taxes would have the effect of suspending tax assessment and collection, such relief was deemed barred by the act.[41]

The *Grace Brethren Church* decision also resolved another question that divided lower federal courts: whether the Tax Injunction Act barred federal courts from deciding constitutional challenges to state and local taxes. The Court previously had indicated a bar to federal court jurisdiction of even constitutional challenges in *Fair Assessment in Real Estate Association v. McNary.*[42] The issue in *McNary* was whether the Tax Injunction Act barred a federal court from awarding monetary damages stemming from an allegedly unconstitutional tax.

In *McNary,* state taxpayers and an association representing owners of realty brought a suit under 42 U.S.C. §1983 against county officials, claiming a denial of

[37] 319 U.S. 293, 299 (1943).

[38] *Id.*

[39] 457 U.S. 393 (1982).

[40] *Id.* at 408.

[41] In other instances as well, the Court has equated the effect of declaratory judgments with injunctive relief. *See* Samuels v. Mackell, 401 U.S. 66 (1971) (the prohibition against federal court injunctions of state court proceedings also prevents declaratory relief; discussed in §13.3, *infra*). *But see* Steffel v. Thompson, 415 U.S. 452 (1974) (Rehnquist, J., concurring) (arguing for a distinction between declaratory and injunctive relief; discussed in §13.3, *infra*).

[42] 454 U.S. 100 (1981).

due process and equal protection by the unequal taxing of property. The Court found it unnecessary to decide whether the Tax Injunction Act precluded the federal court from awarding damage relief because it concluded that the principle of comity barred the federal court from deciding challenges to state tax laws. The Court concluded that irrespective of the Tax Injunction Act, comity independently limited federal court power to decide challenges to state and local taxes. The Court said that comity, a principle based on federalism and the need for federal deference to state proceedings, precluded damage relief for even unconstitutional state and local taxes. The Court stated, "[W]e hold that taxpayers are barred by the principle of comity from asserting §1983 actions against the validity of state tax systems in federal courts. Such taxpayers must seek protection of their federal rights by state remedies."[43]

McNary is a troubling decision in that it effectively renders the Tax Injunction Act meaningless. The Court said that entirely apart from the act, federal courts lack the power to hear challenges to state and local taxes. In other words, the act is superfluous.[44] This is a questionable approach because it was unnecessary; the Court easily could have applied the Tax Injunction Act to bar damage actions. Moreover, the Court can be criticized for precluding federal courts from hearing constitutional challenges, at least absent a more explicit declaration from Congress that such suits are barred.

McNary, however, left open the question of whether federal courts could decide constitutional claims that would not require any scrutiny of state tax assessment practices.[45] For instance, it remains unresolved whether the principle of comity would prevent a federal court from deciding a "facial attack on tax laws claimed to be discriminatory as to race."[46]

In subsequent cases, though, the Supreme Court has followed *McNary* and extended comity as a bar to preventing federal courts from enjoining the collection of state and local taxes. In *Levin v. Commerce Energy, Inc.*, the Court noted that "[m]ore embracive than the Tax Injunction Act, the comity doctrine applicable in state taxation cases restrains federal courts from entertaining claims for relief that risk disrupting state tax administration."[47] *Levin* involved an attempt by a gas company to increase the taxes paid by a commercial competitor. The Court said that the Tax Injunction Act did not apply because the requested relief would not interfere with the collection of taxes or disrupt the revenue flow to the state.

Nonetheless, the Court concluded that comity barred the federal court from hearing this challenge. Justice Ginsburg, writing for the Court, explained: "Comity considerations . . . preclude the exercise of lower federal-court adjudicatory authority over this controversy, given that an adequate state-court forum is available

[43] *Id.* at 116.

[44] In fact, the Second Circuit held that there is no significant difference between the standards under the Tax Injunction Act and the comity principle of *McNary*. Bernard v. Village of Spring Valley, N.Y., 30 F.3d 294, 297 (2d Cir. 1994).

[45] *Id.* at 107 n.4.

[46] *Id.*

[47] 560 U.S. 413, 417 (2010).

to hear and decide respondents' constitutional claims."[48] The Court noted that "[c]omity's constraint has particular force when lower federal courts are asked to pass on the constitutionality of state taxation of commercial activity."[49]

The Court said that a number of factors caused it to find that comity required that the federal court dismiss the matter: "First, respondents seek federal-court review of commercial matters over which Ohio enjoys wide regulatory latitude; their suit does not involve any fundamental right or classification that attracts heightened judicial scrutiny. Second, while respondents portray themselves as third-party challengers to an allegedly unconstitutional tax scheme, they are in fact seeking federal-court aid in an endeavor to improve their competitive position. Third, the Ohio courts are better positioned than their federal counterparts to correct any violation because they are more familiar with state legislative preferences and because the TIA does not constrain their remedial options. Individually, these considerations may not compel forbearance on the part of federal district courts; in combination, however, they demand deference to the state adjudicative process."[50]

Judicially Created Exceptions

The fourth and final major issue concerning the Tax Injunction Act concerns judicially created exceptions. The act allows federal court relief against state and local taxes only in the absence of a plain, speedy, and efficient state remedy. The Supreme Court, however, has recognized other exceptions to the act.

For example, the Court has concluded that the act does not bar federal courts from hearing challenges to state and local taxes brought by the U.S. government. In *Department of Employment v. United States*, the Supreme Court allowed the American Red Cross, a federal instrumentality, to sue to enjoin the collection of taxes.[51] The Court concluded that "in accord with an unbroken line of authority, and convincing evidence of legislative purpose, that §1341 does not act as a restriction upon suits by the United States to protect itself and its instrumentalities from unconstitutional state exactions."[52] Permitting the United States to sue for injunctions is consistent with the general presumption against consigning the federal government to state courts.[53]

However, in *Arkansas v. Farm Credit Services of Central Arkansas*, the Court held that Production Credit Associations may not sue under this exception to the Tax Injunction Act.[54] Although the federal statute deems these associations to be federal instrumentalities, this does not bestow upon them the same ability that federal agencies and departments have to invoke this exception to the Tax Injunction Act.

[48] *Id.* at 421.
[49] *Id.* at 422.
[50] *Id.* at 431-432.
[51] 385 U.S. 355 (1966).
[52] *Id.* at 358 (citations omitted).
[53] *Id.*
[54] 520 U.S. 821 (1997).

In other words, not all federal "instrumentalities" can invoke this exception; only the U.S. government, and its departments and agencies, may do so. The Court, however, did not explain why the Red Cross, a federal instrumentality, could invoke this exception, but not Production Credit Associations.

The Supreme Court also has created an exception to the Tax Injunction Act for suits brought directly before the Supreme Court pursuant to its original jurisdiction.[55] The Supreme Court has original jurisdiction over suits between two states. Because of the need for an impartial and authoritative resolution of such disputes, it is logical that the Supreme Court should hear such cases rather than have them decided in the courts of either state.

Finally, it is clear that other federal statutes can create exceptions to the Tax Injunction Act. That is, Congress can specify situations in which the federal courts may enjoin the collection of state and local taxes.[56]

Suits in State Court

A related question, not answered by the terms or history of the Tax Injunction Act, is whether state courts can issue injunctions or declaratory relief under 42 U.S.C. §1983 against state taxes when an adequate state legal remedy exists. In *National Private Truck Council v. Oklahoma Tax Commission*, the Court held that such suits could not be brought under §1983 in state court.[57] The Court explained that it "must interpret §1983 in light of the strong background principle against federal interference with state taxation."[58] Accordingly, the Court concluded that allowing a state court injunction of a state tax would be just as disruptive as a federal court order. The Court explained: "Just as *Fair Assessment* relied upon a background principle in interpreting §1983 to preclude damage actions in tax cases brought in federal court, so we rely on the same principle in interpreting §1983 to provide no basis for courts to award injunctive relief when an adequate legal remedy exists."[59] State law may empower state courts to issue such a remedy, but the claim cannot be brought under §1983.

On the one hand, this ruling can be defended as resting on the premise that federal law should not be the basis for enjoining state taxes when there is an adequate state remedy. On the other hand, the Tax Injunction Act's purpose is to prevent *federal* courts from interfering with state tax systems. Such federalism concerns are not present when the suit is brought in state court.

[55] Maryland v. Louisiana, 451 U.S. 725, 745 n.21 (1981).

[56] Burlington Northern R.R. v. Oklahoma Tax Commn., 481 U.S. 454 (1987) (§306 of the Railroad Revitalization and Regulatory Reform Act of 1976 prohibits state discrimination against railroad property and authorizes injunctions of violative taxes). The Supreme Court, for example, has left open the question of whether the Employment Retirement Income Security Act of 1974 (ERISA) constitutes such a statutory exception to the Anti-Injunction Act. *See* Franchise Tax Bd. v. Construction Laborers Vacation Trust, 463 U.S. 1, 20 (1983).

[57] 515 U.S. 582 (1995).

[58] *Id.* at 589.

[59] *Id.* at 590.

Removal of Proceedings from State to Federal Court

In *Jefferson County v. Acker*, the Supreme Court considered whether the Tax Injunction Act precluded a federal court from exercising removal jurisdiction when defendants challenging a tax removed a proceeding against them from state to federal court.[60] A county sued two federal judges for failure to pay an occupational tax. The defendants removed the case, pursuant to 28 U.S.C. §1442, and argued that the application of the local tax to them violated federal law. The county argued that the Tax Injunction Act barred the exercise of federal court jurisdiction.

The Supreme Court unanimously ruled that the Tax Injunction Act did not bar removal. The Court stressed that the Tax Injunction Act bars suits initiated against the government to stop tax collection; the law does not preclude federal courts from deciding federal defenses to state and local efforts to collect their taxes. The Court explained that the Tax Injunction Act was "shaped by state and federal provisions barring anticipatory actions by taxpayers to stop the tax collector from initiating collection proceedings. It was not the design of these provisions to prohibit taxpayers from defending suits brought by a government to obtain collection of a tax."[61]

The Anti-Injunction Act

Another federal statute, the Anti-Injunction Act, bars federal courts from enjoining the collection of federal taxes.[62] This is a different law from the Anti-Injunction Act discussed above that prevents federal courts from enjoining pending state court proceedings. This provision, enacted in 1867, with a few exceptions, denies courts jurisdiction over preenforcement suits that would restrain "the assessment or collection of any tax."[63] Under this provision, a taxpayer seeking to challenge a tax law must first pay the disputed tax and then bring a refund suit, at which time the courts will consider the taxpayer's legal arguments. A taxpayer also may raise legal arguments in defending against an IRS enforcement action. But a taxpayer may not bring a preenforcement suit to enjoin the collection of taxes.

This provision was important in the adjudication of the constitutionality of the Patient Protection and Affordable Care Act. The question arose as to whether a challenge to the individual mandate—the requirement that an individual purchase insurance or pay a penalty to the Internal Revenue Service—was barred by the Anti-Injunction Act. The Supreme Court concluded that the individual mandate was not a tax within the meaning of the statute.[64] The Court stressed that it is not labeled a "tax," but rather a "penalty," and that it was not treated by Congress as a tax. Thus, the Court stated: "The Affordable Care Act does not require that

[60] 527 U.S. 423 (1999).
[61] *Id.* at 435.
[62] 26 U.S.C. §7421(a).
[63] *Id.*
[64] National Federation of Independent Business v. Sebelius, 567 U.S. 519 (2012).

the penalty for failing to comply with the individual mandate be treated as a tax for purposes of the Anti-Injunction Act. The Anti-Injunction Act therefore does not apply to this suit, and we may proceed to the merits."[65]

Interestingly, the Court nonetheless held that the individual mandate was constitutional as an exercise of Congress's taxing and spending power. The Court explained: "It is up to Congress whether to apply the Anti-Injunction Act to any particular statute, so it makes sense to be guided by Congress's choice of label on that question. That choice does not, however, control whether an exaction is within Congress's constitutional power to tax."[66] More recently in *CIC Servs., LLC v. IRS*, the Court unanimously concluded that the Anti-Injunction Act did not bar a federal court suit challenging the Internal Revenue Service for adopting a rule in violation of the Administrative Procedure Act. The IRS rule imposed a reporting requirement on certain transactions, with both criminal and tax penalties for violations.

The Court held that this did not fall under the Anti-Injunction Act. Justice Kagan, in a unanimous decision, said that the regulation "imposes affirmative reporting obligations, inflicting costs separate and apart from the statutory tax penalty."[67] The Court also stressed that "violation of the Notice is punishable not only by a tax, but by separate criminal penalties."[68]

The decision is important in that it allows suits concerning regulations backed by tax penalties to proceed. It is not enough for a regulation to impose tax penalties for it to be shielded from litigation under the Anti-Injunction Act. Rather, the regulation must actually concern the collection of taxes.

§11.4 THE JOHNSON ACT: A PROHIBITION OF FEDERAL COURT INJUNCTIONS OF STATE RATE ORDERS

Statutory Provision

The Johnson Act, 28 U.S.C. §1342, prevents federal courts from enjoining utility rates set by state and local rate-making agencies. Specifically, the Johnson Act, adopted in 1934, provides:

> The District Courts shall not enjoin, suspend or restrain the operation of, or compliance with, any order affecting rates chargeable by a public utility and made

[65] *Id.* at 546.
[66] *Id.* at 564.
[67] 593 U.S. 209, 220 (2021).
[68] *Id.* at 221.

by a state administrative agency or a rate-making body of a State political subdivision, where:

(1) Jurisdiction is based solely on diversity of citizenship or repugnance of the order to the Federal Constitution; and,
(2) The order does not interfere with interstate commerce; and,
(3) The order has been made after reasonable notice and hearing; and,
(4) A plain, speedy and efficient remedy may be had in the courts of such State.[1]

The act requires that the federal courts generally avoid interfering with state and local rate setting for utilities. That is, challenges to rate regulations usually must be brought in state and not in federal courts. The act precludes federal courts from hearing all challenges to utility rate regulations, as long as the four conditions specified are met, regardless of whether the plaintiff is the utility company itself or the utility's customers.[2] The act reflects federalism concerns: a desire to avoid federal court disruption of the important state activity of regulating utilities.

The act applies only to prevent federal courts from interfering with rate regulations by state and local governments. Other forms of utility regulations are not covered by the Johnson Act. For instance, federal courts may hear challenges to state or local laws concerning security deposits,[3] or to orders identifying permissible airline routes,[4] or to procedures for terminating service.[5] The Supreme Court held, for example, that a statute requiring utilities to submit their rates for approval was not included in the act, and thus the federal court had jurisdiction to decide a challenge to the law.[6] Likewise, a federal court of appeals ruled that the Johnson Act was inapplicable when the plaintiff challenged a utility commission's order terminating service because of the content of recorded messages.[7] Because the regulatory commission's action did not pertain to rates, the federal court was allowed to hear and decide the case.

Preconditions that Must Be Met for Application of Johnson Act

The act specifies four preconditions that must be met for the Johnson Act to prevent federal court review. First, federal jurisdiction must be based on either diversity of citizenship or the alleged unconstitutionality of the rate order. Although this precludes review of most suits concerning rate regulations, it does

§11.4 [1] 28 U.S.C. §1342.

[2] *See, e.g.*, Tennyson v. Gas Serv. Co., 506 F.2d 1135 (10th Cir. 1974) (suits by customers, as well as suits by utilities, are barred).

[3] Cody v. Union Elec. Co., 545 F.2d 610 (8th Cir. 1976).

[4] Island Airlines, Inc. v. CAB, 352 F.2d 735, 744 (9th Cir. 1965).

[5] Dawes v. Philadelphia Gas Commn., 421 F. Supp. 806, 826 (E.D. Pa. 1976).

[6] Public Utils. Commn. of Cal. v. United States, 355 U.S. 534, 540 (1958).

[7] Carlin Communication, Inc. v. Southern Bell Tel. & Tel., 802 F.2d 1352 (11th Cir. 1986).

not bar jurisdiction if the rate order is challenged as violating a federal statute. Thus, lower federal courts have held that the Johnson Act does not bar jurisdiction when rate regulations are challenged as being preempted by federal laws.[8]

Second, the Johnson Act applies only if the rate order does not interfere with interstate commerce. For example, in *Public Utilities Commission of Ohio v. United Fuel Gas Co.*, the Supreme Court found the Johnson Act inapplicable to a challenge to orders fixing rates for natural gas transported and sold in interstate commerce.[9] The Court said that "to the extent that they constitute an attempt to regulate matters in interstate commerce which Congress has lodged exclusively with the Federal Power Commission," federal jurisdiction exists.[10] However, most attempts to avoid the Johnson Act by claiming that the state regulation controls interstate commerce have failed.[11]

Third, for the Johnson Act to apply and prevent federal court review, there must be adequate notice and hearing within the state regulatory system. Thus, in *Petroleum Exploration, Inc. v. Public Service Commission*, the Court held that the federal court could enjoin state proceedings because "the order complained of . . . was entered without notice or hearing."[12] However, no hearing is required in instances where there is no factual dispute and the sole question posed is a legal issue as to whether the regulatory agency had the legal authority to issue the order in question.[13]

Fourth, the Johnson Act requires federal nonintervention only if the state remedy is "plain, speedy and efficient." This is language that was subsequently copied in the Tax Injunction Act, described above in §11.3. In fact, because the statutes contain the same language and it is clear that this aspect of the Tax Injunction Act was modeled after the Johnson Act, the terms are given identical meaning in interpreting the two statutes.[14]

Also, as with the Tax Injunction Act, the Johnson Act does not bar suits brought by the U.S. government.[15] Again, the underlying philosophy seems to be that the federal government always should be able to litigate its claims in federal court.

[8] New Orleans Pub. Serv., Inc. v. New Orleans, 782 F.2d 1236, 1242 (5th Cir. 1986), *cert. denied,* 481 U.S. 1023 (1987).

[9] 317 U.S. 456 (1943).

[10] *Id.* at 469-470.

[11] 17 Charles Alan Wright, Arthur R. Miller & Edward H. Cooper, Federal Practice and Procedure 633-634 (1988).

[12] 304 U.S. 209, 214 (1938). *See also* City of Meridian v. Mississippi Valley Gas Co., 214 F.2d 525 (5th Cir. 1954) (Johnson Act does not prevent injunctions if state agency failed to provide notice and hearing).

[13] Wright, Miller & Cooper, *supra* note 11, at 636.

[14] *See, e.g.,* Tennyson v. Gas Serv. Co., 506 F.2d 1135, 1139 (10th Cir. 1974).

[15] *See, e.g.,* Public Utils. Comm'n. of Cal. v. United States, 355 U.S. 534, 540 (1958); United States v. Public Serv. Comm. of Maryland, 422 F. Supp. 676, 678 (D. Md. 1976).

§11.5 THE CIVIL RIGHTS REMOVAL ACT

§11.5.1 Introduction

Statutory Provision and Its Origins

In the days and months following the Civil War, Congress expressed great distrust in the ability or willingness of Southern states and their courts to protect the rights of newly freed slaves. One manifestation of this distrust was the enactment of the Civil Rights Removal Act, 28 U.S.C. §1443. Unlike the other statutes discussed in this chapter that mandate federal court deference to state proceedings, the Civil Rights Removal Act creates situations in which both criminal and civil proceedings pending in state court can be removed to federal court. The act, which was included in the first major civil rights law adopted after the Civil War, was intended to protect the rights of Black people by preventing the use of state judicial proceedings to harass.[1] The act was motivated by a perception that Black people and those aiding them were being prosecuted or sued in state courts and that these courts were strongly biased against the former slaves and their newly recognized rights.[2] Protection against such persecution was provided by allowing removal to the more sympathetic federal forum.

The act, in its current form, states:

> Any of the following civil actions or criminal prosecutions, commenced in a State court may be removed by the defendant to the district court of the United States for the district and division embracing the place where it is pending:
>
> (1) Against any person who is denied or cannot enforce in the courts of such State a right under any law providing for the equal civil rights of citizens of the United States, or of all persons within the jurisdiction thereof;
> (2) For any act under color of authority derived from any law providing for equal rights, or for refusing to do any act on the ground that it would be inconsistent with such law.[3]

In other words, the act identifies two situations in which cases can be removed from state to federal court. First, a defendant in state court can remove a case if he or she can demonstrate that the state court proceedings will deny rights created by federal civil rights statutes. Alternatively, a case can be removed to federal court if a person's defense is that the action was required by federal civil rights laws or

§11.5 [1] Martin H. Redish, Federal Jurisdiction: Tensions in the Allocation of Judicial Power 377 (2d ed. 1990).

[2] Anthony G. Amsterdam, Criminal Prosecutions Affecting Federally Guaranteed Civil Rights: Federal Removal and Habeas Corpus Jurisdiction to Abort State Court Trial, 113 U. Pa. L. Rev. 793, 823-824 (1965).

[3] 28 U.S.C. §1443.

that the person is being sued or prosecuted for failing to act in a manner that was prohibited by such a law.

Statutory Revisions Since 1866

The act has changed relatively little since its adoption in the Civil Rights Act of 1866. As originally enacted, the law permitted removal of cases both before and after judgments by state courts. In 1875, the Civil Rights Removal Act was amended to permit removal only before a judgment was entered.[4] This was an important revision because it required federal courts to determine in advance of state proceedings whether they will be inadequate to safeguard federal rights.[5] Such predictions are inevitably difficult, and federal courts are understandably reluctant to label state courts inferior absent truly exceptional circumstances. Conversely, permitting removal after judgment would be inconsistent with the traditional principle that decisions are to be reviewed through the appellate process and not by collateral attack in federal courts.

In 1887, the Civil Rights Removal Act was amended to prevent parties from appealing a federal court's decision to deny removal and remand a case back to state court. The obvious effect was to greatly limit the ability of the Supreme Court to construe the statute and to review situations in which removal was improperly denied. Congress, as part of the Civil Rights Act of 1964, eliminated this limitation and authorized courts of appeals to review decisions of federal district courts denying removal of cases from state to federal courts under the Civil Rights Removal Act.[6] There is compelling evidence that this revision was intended to facilitate Supreme Court review in order to broaden the circumstances under which removal would be allowed.[7]

Although the Civil Rights Removal Act was intended to offer substantial protection of civil rights, because of very restrictive interpretations by the Supreme Court, the act has had little effect. As one commentator expressed, "In the wake of [the Supreme Court's decisions], the privilege promised by the civil rights removal statute has become relatively moribund."[8]

The following two subsections examine the provisions of the Civil Rights Removal Act. Subsection 11.5.2 considers instances in which cases can be removed to federal court because state courts will not adequately protect rights secured by federal civil rights laws. Subsection 11.5.3 examines situations in which cases can be removed because of a defense that the action or omission complained of was a result of compliance with federal civil rights statutes.

[4] Redish, *supra* note 1, at 378. Congress limited removal to "before judgment" in the face of a Supreme Court decision that "after judgment" removal violated the Seventh Amendment. The Justices v. Murray, 76 U.S. (9 Wall.) 274 (1870).

[5] Redish, *supra* note 1, at 377-378.

[6] 28 U.S.C. §1447(d); Act of July 2, 1964, Pub. L. No. 88-352, §901, 78 Stat. 266.

[7] Amsterdam, *supra* note 2, at 911.

[8] Stevan C. Dittman, Removal in Civil Rights Cases Under 28 U.S.C. Section 1443(2), 31 Loy. L. Rev. 855, 888 (1986).

§11.5.2 *Removal Because of the Denial in State Court of Rights Secured by Federal Civil Rights Laws*

Narrow Construction of Removal Authority

The first clause of the Civil Rights Removal Act provides that a defendant in state court can remove a case to federal court if he or she "is denied or cannot enforce in the courts of such State a right under any law providing for the equal civil rights of citizens of the United States, or of all persons within the jurisdiction thereof."[9] In a series of decisions in the late nineteenth century and again during the 1960s, the Supreme Court interpreted this provision quite narrowly. Specifically, these decisions establish that a case can be removed under this clause only if two conditions are met. First, a person must be deprived of a right secured by a federal law dealing with racial equality. That is, removal cannot be based on a violation of a right that stems from other than a specific federal law, nor can removal be based on rights that do not pertain to racial equality. Second, the person must be deprived of his or her rights pursuant to a state statute or state constitutional provision. Both individually and cumulatively, these restrictions greatly limit the instances in which removal is possible.

Strauder and *Rives*

The Court first articulated the latter of these restrictions in two decisions in 1879, *Strauder v. West Virginia*[10] and *Virginia v. Rives.*[11] In *Strauder,* the plaintiff was convicted of murder in a West Virginia state court. The West Virginia Supreme Court affirmed the conviction. Before the trial began, the defendant sought to remove the case to federal court on account of a state law that provided that no Black people were eligible to serve on juries in the state. The Supreme Court held that removal should have been granted. The Court said that the Fourteenth Amendment was intended to prevent discrimination against Black people and that the state law preventing Black people from serving on juries clearly violated this constitutional provision.[12] Moreover, the Court said that Congress had authority pursuant to §5 of the Fourteenth Amendment to protect civil rights and that the Civil Rights Removal statute was lawfully enacted under this power.[13] Accordingly, the Court reversed the conviction and held that removal of the case to federal court should have been allowed.

By contrast, in *Rives,* the Supreme Court refused to allow removal because the denial of civil rights was not the result of a specific state law. Two Black men who were accused of murdering a white man objected to the jury panel that included only whites. The defendants moved the court to modify the jury panel to include

[9] 28 U.S.C. §1443(1).
[10] 100 U.S. (10 Otto) 303 (1879).
[11] 100 U.S. (10 Otto) 313 (1879).
[12] Strauder v. West Virginia, 100 U.S. at 308-309.
[13] *Id.* at 310-311.

one-third Black people. The state trial court denied the motion, and the defendants sought to remove the case to federal court. Unlike the discriminatory West Virginia law in *Strauder*, in *Rives* the state statute permitted all citizens, irrespective of race, to sit on juries.

In considering whether removal to federal court should have been allowed, the Court said that the issue was whether the Civil Rights Removal Act "applies to all cases in which equal protection of the laws may be denied to a defendant."[14] The Court answered emphatically that the act "clearly does not" apply to all denials of equal protection.[15] Instead, the Court said that the act pertains "primarily, if not exclusively, [to] a denial of such rights, or an inability to enforce them, resulting from the Constitution or laws of the State, rather than a denial first made manifest at the trial of the case."[16]

In other words, to remove a case, the defendant must demonstrate before trial that a specific *state law* will cause the denial of his or her constitutional rights. The Court said that in the absence of a state constitutional or statutory provision, it is not possible to demonstrate that the defendant's rights will be denied in state court.[17] The *Rives* Court said that unless there is a specific state law denying civil rights, it is assumed that the state court will remedy any alleged deprivation of civil rights.

Reaffirmations of *Strauder* and *Rives*

The distinction articulated in *Strauder* and *Rives* was frequently reaffirmed by the Court throughout the late nineteenth and early twentieth centuries. For example, in *Neal v. Delaware*, the Supreme Court refused to allow removal of a case to federal court despite a longstanding state practice of excluding Black people from serving on juries.[18] In fact, Delaware's Constitution provided that only white males could vote in elections and state courts had interpreted this clause as limiting jury service to whites. Nonetheless, the Supreme Court found *Rives* to be controlling. The Court reasoned that the Fifteenth Amendment, which guaranteed the right to vote, superseded the contrary Delaware law and that the state could be assumed to comply with federal law. Because there was no Delaware *law* violating rights, removal was held to be unavailable. The Court, however, did reverse the conviction on direct review of the state supreme court decision because of impermissible discrimination in jury selection.[19]

Likewise, in *Gibson v. Mississippi*, the Court refused to allow removal of a case despite a state practice of refusing to call Black people for jury service.[20] The

[14] Virginia v. Rives, 100 U.S. at 319.

[15] *Id.*

[16] *Id.*

[17] *Id.* at 320.

[18] 103 U.S. 370 (1880).

[19] Interestingly, Justices Field and Waite dissented from this reversal, contending that proof of discrimination in jury selection was not sufficient to justify overturning the state court's decision. 103 U.S. at 398, 401 (Waite, J., and Field, J., dissenting).

[20] 162 U.S. 565 (1896).

defendant, accused of murder, argued that even though Black people eligible for jury service in the county outnumbered whites by an almost five-to-one ratio, no Black people had been called for jury service. The Court said that this did not justify removal because the discrimination did not result from a specific state law. The Court again said that the Civil Rights Removal Act was not available to remedy discrimination by state courts; rather, the act was limited to instances where there was a specific state statute or constitutional provision discriminating against Black people.[21]

Kentucky v. Powers was a dramatic example of the application of this rule.[22] A man was convicted of murder, and the Supreme Court admitted that "it is impossible for the accused to obtain a fair trial in the locality where the prosecution is pending."[23] There was incontrovertible evidence that the court officials responsible for supervising jury selection had systematically excluded every potential juror who was of the same political party as the defendant.[24] Nonetheless, the Court ruled that removal was unavailable because there is "no right of removal . . . where the alleged discrimination against the accused, in respect of his equal rights, was due to the illegal or corrupt acts of administrative officers, unauthorized by the constitution or laws of the State."[25] The defendant's only recourse was appellate review in the state courts and the possibility of direct review in the U.S. Supreme Court.

Defense and Criticism of the Narrow Interpretation

This narrow interpretation of the Civil Rights Removal Act has the advantage of not placing federal courts in the role of evaluating state courts. Removal cannot be gained by demonstrating the state court to be biased, no matter how strong the evidence of prejudice and discrimination. Rather, removal is limited to situations in which there is a provision of law that can be identified, either in state statutes or the state constitution, that mandates discrimination.

Yet this interpretation restricts the Civil Rights Removal Act in a manner inconsistent with congressional intent and in a fashion that makes it ineffective in remedying the problem of discrimination in state courts. After a lengthy review of the legislative history of the Civil Rights Removal Act, Professor Amsterdam concluded that "there is affirmative evidence that Congress was aware of and intended to redress nonstatutory denials of federal constitutional rights."[26] In fact, in general, in enacting the post-Civil War civil rights laws, Congress was motivated by the existence of hostility of state courts to civil rights, even where the state's laws

[21] *See also* Williams v. Mississippi, 170 U.S. 213 (1898) (no removal for jury discrimination because no state law mandated discrimination); Murray v. Louisiana, 163 U.S. 101 (1896) (no removal for jury discrimination because no state law mandated discrimination); Charley Smith v. Mississippi, 162 U.S. 592 (1896) (no removal for jury discrimination because no state law mandated discrimination).

[22] 201 U.S. 1 (1906).

[23] *Id.* at 33.

[24] *Id.*

[25] *Id.* at 31 (emphasis omitted).

[26] Amsterdam, *supra* note 2, at 816.

were adequate as written.[27] The Civil Rights Removal Act was intended to remedy discrimination in state courts. The Supreme Court's interpretation limited it to instances where state laws violated civil rights and thus prevented it from serving as a vehicle for protecting Black people from prejudice in state courts.

Rachel and *Peacock*

During the 1960s, the Supreme Court again construed the Civil Rights Removal Act and again reaffirmed the limitations announced in the nineteenth century. Specifically, in two decisions handed down the same day—*Georgia v. Rachel*[28] and *City of Greenwood v. Peacock*[29]—the Court explained the scope of the Civil Rights Removal Act.

In *Georgia v. Rachel*, Thomas Rachel and 19 other individuals were prosecuted in state court for criminal trespass for their actions in attempting to obtain service at privately owned restaurants open to the general public in Atlanta, Georgia. The defendants sought to remove the case from the state to the federal court. The Supreme Court held that removal was appropriate because the two requirements of the first provision of the act were met: The defendants complained of a violation of federal laws guaranteeing equal rights, and the deprivation was certain to occur if the proceedings continued in state court.

In explaining the first of these requirements, the Court said that removal is allowed only if there is a violation of a federal law pertaining to racial equality. The Court emphasized that the Civil Rights Removal Act was "intended to protect a limited category of rights, specifically defined in terms of racial equality."[30] Therefore, "broad contentions under the First Amendment and the Due Process Clause of the Fourteenth Amendment cannot support a valid claim for removal under §1443."[31] However, this requirement was met in *Rachel* because Title II of the Civil Rights Act of 1964 prohibited discrimination by restaurants and other places of public accommodations.

But the *Rachel* Court made it clear that removal could not be predicated solely on a state's denial of federal laws protecting civil rights. Rather, the defendant seeking removal usually must demonstrate that there is a specific state law mandating the discrimination. In *Rachel*, the Court explicitly reaffirmed the earlier distinction articulated in *Strauder* and *Rives*. The Court said, "*Strauder* and *Rives* . . . teach that removal is not warranted by an assertion that a denial of rights of equality may take place and go uncorrected at trial. Removal is warranted only if it can be predicted by reference to a law of general application that the defendant will be denied or cannot enforce the specified federal rights in the state courts."[32]

[27] *See* discussion in Patsy v. Board of Regents of Fla., 457 U.S. 496 (1982); Mitchum v. Foster, 407 U.S. 225 (1972); Monroe v. Pape, 365 U.S. 167 (1961); *see also* §8.2, *supra.*

[28] 384 U.S. 780 (1966).

[29] 384 U.S. 808 (1966).

[30] Georgia v. Rachel, 384 U.S. at 791.

[31] *Id.* at 792.

[32] *Id.* at 800.

The Court explained that by requiring the existence of a discriminatory state statute, removal would be limited to instances where it could be predicted before trial that there would be a deprivation of rights. Also, permitting removal solely on the basis of specific state laws avoided involving "federal judges in the unseemly process of pre-judging their brethren of the state courts."[33]

In *Rachel*, however, there was no state law mandating discrimination against blacks. Nonetheless, the *Rachel* Court upheld removal because the very existence of the state court prosecution was a violation of civil rights secured by federal law. The Court explained:

> The [*Rives*] Court . . . gave some indication that removal might be justified, even in the absence of a discriminatory state enactment, if an equivalent basis could be shown for an equally firm prediction that the defendant would be "denied or cannot enforce" the specified federal rights in state court. Such a basis for prediction exists in the present case. In the narrow circumstances of this case, *any* proceedings in the courts of the State will constitute a denial of the rights conferred by the Civil Rights Act of 1964.[34]

Thus, *Rachel* reaffirmed the earlier decision, but also broadened the category of situations in which state courts might be found to deny federal civil rights. The most common instance is where a specific state law is facially discriminatory. Alternatively, under *Rachel*, such a denial can be found where the prosecution itself is inherently unconstitutional.

The narrowness of this expansion of the Civil Rights Removal Act was revealed in the companion case of *City of Greenwood v. Peacock*. *Peacock* involved state prosecutions of 29 people who had engaged in civil rights activities in Mississippi in 1964. The defendants claimed that they were being harassed for their work on behalf of equal rights and that the state courts were likely to deny their civil rights. Accordingly, the defendants sought to remove the prosecutions to federal court.

The Supreme Court held that removal was inappropriate and distinguished *Rachel*. First, the Court stated that civil rights removal was unavailable for claims based on freedom of speech or assembly. The statute was limited to denials of statutory guarantees of equal civil rights.[35]

Second, unlike *Rachel*, there was not a federal statute creating a specific right to engage in the activity that was the basis for the prosecution and arrest. In *Rachel*, the 1964 Civil Rights Act created a right to patronize the restaurant. In *Peacock*, there was no federal statute protecting the right to protest. Moreover, in *Rachel*, the defendants contended that the prosecution itself violated federal law; no such claim was available to the defendants in *Peacock*. The Court said that removal could not be predicated on proof that state officials denied federal rights, that the charges against the defendant are false, or that the defendant could not obtain a fair trial in state court.[36] Rather, removal requires demonstrating either the existence of

[33] *Id.* at 803-804.
[34] *Id.* at 804 (emphasis in original).
[35] City of Greenwood v. Peacock, 384 U.S. at 825, 826.
[36] *Id.* at 827.

a discriminatory state law or that the very prosecution in state court inherently violates federal law. The Court feared that a more expansive interpretation would impermissibly "permit the judges of the federal courts to put their brethren of the state judiciary on trial."[37]

The Court defended its holding against removal by explaining that alternative avenues for federal court review were available. If convicted, the defendants ultimately could seek review in the U.S. Supreme Court or habeas corpus relief in federal district court. Additionally, the defendants could bring civil actions against the state officers.[38] Even criminal prosecutions of the officers for violating constitutional rights were a possibility.[39]

Furthermore, the Court argued that allowing removal in situations such as *Peacock* would open the door to removal of "every criminal case in every court in every state" if the defendant alleged either that a fair trial was unavailable in state court or that the prosecution was racially motivated and the defendant was innocent of the charges.[40] The Court said that permitting such widespread removal would require "hundreds of new federal judges . . . to cope with the vastly increased caseload."[41]

Dissents in *Peacock*: An Alternative Approach

Four justices—Justices Douglas, Brennan, Fortas, and Chief Justice Warren—dissented in *Peacock* and urged a different interpretation of the Civil Rights Removal Act. The dissent argued that Congress, in enacting the act, was motivated by a distrust of state courts in civil rights cases.[42] As such, removal should be available upon proof that the state courts likely would be hostile to the federal civil rights claims. Thus, Justice Douglas, writing for the dissent, argued that the first clause of the Civil Rights Removal Act speaks of two different situations when it refers to instances where the defendant "is denied or cannot enforce in the courts of such State" federally guaranteed civil rights. The phrase "is denied" refers to "*present*" deprivations of rights, such as by virtue of an unconstitutional statute or ordinance.[43] In contrast, the phrase "cannot enforce in the courts of such State" speaks to "*anticipated* state court frustration of equal civil rights."[44]

In other words, according to the dissent, removal should be permissible under §1443(1) in two separate circumstances: (1) if the defendant demonstrates that rights have been denied by the state, such as through an unconstitutional

[37] *Id.* at 828.

[38] However, decisions subsequent to *Peacock* indicate that the state court's fact-finding would have collateral estoppel effect in subsequent civil proceedings in federal court for violations of civil rights and liberties. *See* Allen v. McCurry, 449 U.S. 90 (1980); *see also* discussion in §8.10, *supra.*

[39] City of Greenwood v. Peacock, 384 U.S. at 828.

[40] *Id.* at 832.

[41] *Id.* at 834.

[42] *Id.* at 836 (Douglas, J., dissenting).

[43] *Id.* at 841 (emphasis in original).

[44] *Id.* (emphasis in original).

statute or an unconstitutional prosecution, or (2) if the defendant demonstrates that rights are likely to be denied by the state court because of that tribunal's hostility to federal civil rights. The latter, permitting removal on proof of state court bias, would depart from previous Supreme Court interpretations of the Act dating back to *Rives.* The dissent recognized that this would place federal courts in the role of evaluating state courts, but said that removal "would occur only in the unusual case" and that generally state courts could be assumed to "conscientiously . . . apply the law of the land."[45] Moreover, the dissent said that when there are allegations of state court bias, evaluation of the state courts is essential to ensure the protection of federal rights and serve the underlying objectives of the Civil Rights Removal Act.

Rachel and *Peacock* Followed

The dissent's position in *Peacock* has never been accepted by a majority of the Court. In the subsequent case of *Johnson v. Mississippi,*[46] the Court reaffirmed the earlier holdings in *Rachel* and *Peacock.* In *Johnson,* the petitioners, six Black residents of Vicksburg, Mississippi, together with other citizens, protested the lack of employment of Black people by local merchants and city officials. Soon thereafter these six individuals, together with 43 other Black people, were arrested for conspiracy to unlawfully boycott. The defendants sought removal to the federal court under the Civil Rights Removal Act, alleging that their prosecution was pursuant to a facially unconstitutional statute and that their arrest was motivated by a desire to deprive them of their federally protected rights.

The district court refused to allow removal, remanding the case to state court, and both the court of appeals and the U.S. Supreme Court affirmed. The Court said that *Rachel* and *Peacock* articulate a two-part test for removal under §1443(1). First, the defendants must allege that they are deprived rights guaranteed by federal laws pertaining to racial equality. Allegations of violations of First Amendment rights or due process rights are insufficient to permit removal.[47] Second, the defendants must show that they will be denied their rights in state court; usually this requires the existence of a specific state statute or constitutional provision.[48] The *Johnson* defendants were deemed to meet neither of these requirements because they did not allege a violation of a specific federal statute dealing with civil rights and there was no state law mandating discrimination.

Thus, the Supreme Court has consistently adopted a narrow interpretation of §1443(1). Removal is permissible only if there is both an allegation of a federal law pertaining to racial equality *and* clearly violative state conduct, which almost always requires showing that there is a specific state statute or constitutional provision mandating discrimination. Proof of blatant discrimination by prosecutors or court personnel is never sufficient to justify removal. Nor can removal be gained

[45] *Id.* at 851.
[46] 421 U.S. 213 (1975).
[47] *Id.* at 219.
[48] *Id.*

by proving discrimination by state courts, no matter how extreme or repeated. Moreover, the statute must deal specifically with *racial* equality; allegations of gender discrimination or violations of federal statutes dealing generally with civil rights are insufficient.[49]

Criticism of the Court's Approach

The Court's approach to this section of the Civil Rights Removal Act is troublesome. Certainly, it has the benefit of avoiding federal court review of state court judges and it does articulate a definite test that is relatively easy to apply.[50] However, it is curious that the Court essentially limits removal to instances in which there is a specific state statute that denies equal rights guaranteed by federal law. The Court's approach to the Civil Rights Removal Act is premised on a trust of state courts. If such courts are trustworthy, why cannot they be expected to declare the violative state laws invalid? In fact, if state courts fail to act properly in this manner, their error can be corrected on appeal when a statute is facially unconstitutional.

On the other hand, the Civil Rights Removal Act was inspired by a distrust of state courts; there was a substantial fear that such tribunals, on occasion, would be biased against civil rights claims. Such prejudice might infect fact-finding and rulings on numerous motions that would be very difficult to review on appeal or even in subsequent collateral proceedings. By totally precluding removal based on proof of state court bias, the Court ignored the underlying basis for the very enactment of the civil rights removal statute. Phrased differently, the Court essentially limited removal to the instances where it is least likely to be needed.[51]

The four justices dissenting in *Peacock* articulate a desirable alternative: interpreting the statute to permit removal either if there is a present deprivation of rights, such as through an unconstitutional state statute, or an anticipated deprivation because of a biased state judiciary.[52] Although the latter would require an inquiry into the nature of the state courts, it is not unlike that already undertaken by the federal courts when they are forced to consider whether the state courts

[49] *See, e.g.*, Wilkins v. Rogers, 581 F.2d 399, 403 (4th Cir. 1978) (allegations of sex discrimination are not cognizable under §1443(1)); United States ex rel. Sullivan v. State, 588 F.2d 579, 580 (8th Cir. 1978) (§1443 applies only to rights involving racial equality and not all federal rights); Iowa v. Johnson, 976 F. Supp. 812 (N.D. Iowa 1997) (allegations regarding a criminal prosecution not claiming racial inequality are not removable pursuant to §1443(1)); Wright v. London Grove Township, 567 F. Supp. 768, 771 (E.D. Pa. 1983) (the statute deals with racial equality; allegations of gender discrimination are insufficient).

[50] *See* Martin H. Redish, Revitalizing Civil Rights Removal Jurisdiction, 64 Minn. L. Rev. 523, 530 (1980) (explaining Court was seeking an "easily applied standard to define the scope of civil rights removal jurisdiction").

[51] Amsterdam, *supra* note 2, at 857-858.

[52] For a defense of this approach, *see* Redish, *supra* note 1, at 389-393; for an alternative proposal, *see* Amsterdam, *supra* note 2 (arguing for broad removal for substantive violations of rights, but narrow removal for procedural inadequacies in state courts).

provided a full and fair hearing of federal constitutional claims.[53] If the Supreme Court's assumption of parity between federal and state courts is true, then in relatively few instances would defendants be able to prove state court bias and remove cases. But if defendants were able to actually demonstrate state court hostility to federal civil rights, then the additional burden on federal courts would be justified.

§11.5.3 Removal Because the Defendant's Conduct was Required by Federal Civil Rights Laws

Narrow Interpretation

The second section of the Civil Rights Removal Act permits removal "[f]or any act under color of authority derived from any law providing for equal rights, or for refusing to do any act on the ground that it would be inconsistent with such law."[54] In other words, removal is allowed if the defendant alleges that his or her action or failure to act was required by a federal civil rights law. Here too, the Court has adopted a very restrictive interpretation. In order to remove a case to federal court pursuant to this clause the defendant must be a government officer, or someone assisting an officer in the performance of his or her official duty, and there must be a violation of a federal law dealing with racial equality.[55]

In *City of Greenwood v. Peacock*, the Court considered the meaning of §1443(2).[56] The Court said that the language in this section allowing removal for a defendant accused of "any act under color of authority derived from any law providing for equal rights" only applied to federal officers and persons assisting federal officers in the performance of their duties.[57] The Court based this narrow interpretation on a review of the legislative history of the 1866 Civil Rights Act. The Court concluded that this portion of §1443(2) essentially duplicated the provision codified in §1442(a)(1), which allows federal officers to remove cases to federal court if they are defendants in state court proceedings arising from their official duties. In other words, only federal officers (or those assisting such officers) can remove cases to federal court based on a defense that their conduct was required by federal laws concerning racial equality.

The *Peacock* Court also considered the latter portion of §1443(2), which provides for removal if the defendant is prosecuted or sued in state court for a refusal "to do any act on the ground that it would be inconsistent with" a law providing for racial equality. The *Peacock* Court said that "removal under that language is available

[53] *See, e.g.,* Parratt v. Taylor, 451 U.S. 527 (1981) (no due process violation if plaintiff seeks a postdeprivation remedy for the deprivation of property and the state provides an adequate postdeprivation remedy); Stone v. Powell, 428 U.S. 465 (1976) (Fourth Amendment claims can be raised on habeas corpus only if there is not a full and fair hearing in state court).

[54] 28 U.S.C. §1443(2).

[55] *See* Dittman, *supra* note 8, at 869.

[56] 384 U.S. 808, 814 (1966).

[57] *Id.*

only to state officers."[58] The Court again relied on the legislative history of the Civil Rights Removal Act. Specifically, the Court quoted the floor manager of the bill in the House of Representatives, who stated that the provision is "intended to enable State officers, who shall refuse to enforce State laws discriminating . . . on account of race or color, to remove their cases to the United States courts when prosecuted for refusing to enforce those laws."[59]

Lower courts have adhered to this interpretation and limited §1443(2) to government officers. For example, in one case the U.S. Court of Appeals for the Tenth Circuit permitted the U.S. attorney general to remove a case from state to federal court when he was sued by a local school board attempting to enjoin the Justice Department's school desegregation efforts.[60] In another instance, the Second Circuit permitted city officials to remove a case to federal court when they were sued for discontinuing the use of a test required by state law.[61] The officials contended that the test discriminated against Black people in violation of Title VII of the Civil Rights Act of 1964. Removal was justified because the failure to use the test was a result of a good-faith belief that the test violated federal civil rights laws. Likewise, lower courts have denied removal in instances where the defendants seeking access to the federal courts were not government officers.[62] As with §1443(1), the defendant seeking removal must allege that the federal statute involved is one dealing with racial equality.[63]

Again, the Court's narrow interpretation of the Civil Rights Removal Act is troubling. The literal language of §1443(2) makes it available to any individual who claims that he or she is being sued or prosecuted for actions taken in compliance with federal civil rights laws. The Court, however, has restricted the statute's use to government officers and thereby largely has made it redundant of other jurisdictional statutes. Overall, the Supreme Court's decisions have rendered the Civil Rights Removal Act a statute that rarely can be used.

[58] *Id.* at 824 n.22.

[59] *Id.* (*quoting* Representative Wilson).

[60] Bohlander v. Independent School Dist. No. 1 of Tulsa County, Okla., 420 F.2d 693 (10th Cir. 1969) (per curiam).

[61] White v. Wellington, 627 F.2d 582 (2d Cir. 1980). *See also* Bridgeport Educ. Assn. v. Zinner, 415 F. Supp. 715 (D. Conn. 1976) (members of a board of education were allowed to remove a case to federal court because they alleged that they were sued for their failure to make certain appointments when doing so would have violated federal civil rights laws); *but see* Dodd v. Rue, 478 F. Supp. 975 (S.D. Ohio 1979) (refusing to allow removal on similar facts).

[62] *See, e.g.,* Detroit Police Lieutenants & Sergeants Assn. v. City of Detroit, 597 F.2d 566, 568 (6th Cir. 1979) ("defendants are not persons assisting federal officers and, therefore, removal is not proper under the first phrase of subsection (2)"); Fosdick v. Dunwoody, 420 F.2d 1140 (1st Cir. 1970) (defendants are not federal officers or agents and hence cannot remove). *But see* Buffalo Teachers Fedn. v. Board of Educ., 477 F. Supp. 691 (W.D.N.Y. 1979) (allowing removal where school board was sued for actions taken pursuant to order of a federal court).

[63] *See, e.g.,* Doe v. Berry, 967 F.2d 1255 (8th Cir. 1992); South Carolina v. Lindsey, 741 F. Supp. 1217 (D.S.C. 1990).

CHAPTER 12

Federal Court Abstention Because of Unclear State Law

§12.1 INTRODUCTION: ABSTENTION DEFINED

The Supreme Court has identified certain circumstances in which the federal courts must abstain and refuse to decide cases that are properly within their jurisdiction. The term "abstention" refers to judicially created rules whereby federal courts may not decide some matters before them even though all jurisdictional and justiciability requirements are met. This chapter examines one set of abstention doctrines: those requiring federal courts to decline review in order to allow state courts to clarify unclear state law. This chapter focuses on two questions. First, when is abstention because of unclear state law necessary? Second, what procedures are followed when there is such abstention?

Section 12.2 addresses the former question, examining three separate situations when abstention because of unclear state law is appropriate. Abstention because a state court's clarification of state law might avoid a federal court ruling on constitutional grounds—commonly referred to as *Pullman* abstention because of the name of the leading case[1]—is discussed in §12.2.1. Abstention in diversity cases because of unclear state law—often termed "*Thibodaux* abstention"[2]—is examined in §12.2.2. Finally, §12.2.3 discusses abstention because of complex state administrative procedures—frequently labeled "*Burford* abstention."[3]

The procedures followed in abstention cases are discussed in §12.3. When a federal court abstains, under what circumstances may the case return to federal court after the state court clarifies the state law issues? Also, when may federal courts certify questions to state courts?

Underlying Policy Issues

The central policy question concerning abstention is whether the Supreme Court was justified in fashioning these doctrines. Long ago, Chief Justice John Marshall wrote, "It is most true that this Court will not take jurisdiction if it should not: but it is equally true, that it must take jurisdiction, if it should."[4] In *Sprint Communications v. Jacobs*, the Court reiterated this and declared, "In the main, federal courts are obliged to decide cases within the scope of federal jurisdiction."[5] Congress created the lower federal courts and specified their jurisdiction. In fact, where Congress desired federal court abstention it enacted particular statutes such as those discussed in the previous chapter—the Anti-Injunction Act, the Tax Injunction Act, and the Johnson Act. As such, it is contended that the Supreme Court acted impermissibly in creating the abstention doctrines. In an important article, Professor Martin Redish forcefully argued that the doctrines are "a judicial usurpation of legislative authority in violation of separation of powers."[6]

On the other hand, abstention doctrines are defended as the judicial creation of common law rules necessary to serve essential interests, especially the protection of states in the system of federalism.[7] As is discussed in detail in this chapter and the following two chapters, which consider other judicially created

§12.1 [1] Railroad Commn. of Texas v. Pullman Co., 312 U.S. 496 (1941).

[2] Louisiana Power & Light Co. v. City of Thibodaux, 360 U.S. 25 (1959).

[3] Burford v. Sun Oil Co., 319 U.S. 315 (1943).

[4] Cohens v. Virginia, 19 U.S. (6 Wheat.) 264, 404 (1821). *Accord* Bacon v. Rutland R.R., 232 U.S. 134, 137 (1914); Ex parte Young, 209 U.S. 123, 143 (1908).

[5] 571 U.S. 584, 588 (2013). *See also* Federal Bureau of Investigation v. Fikre, 601 U.S. 234, 240 (2024) ("A court with jurisdiction has a 'virtually unflagging obligation' to hear and resolve questions properly before it.")

[6] Martin H. Redish, Abstention, Separation of Powers and the Limits of the Judicial Function, 94 Yale L.J. 71, 76 (1984).

[7] *See* Michael Wells, Why Professor Redish Is Wrong About Abstention, 19 Ga. L. Rev. 1097 (1985). Professor Wells argues that federal jurisdiction in civil liberties cases is largely a result of judicially created doctrines. Hence, he maintains that it is appropriate for the judiciary to fashion limits on its authority. *See also* David L. Shapiro, Jurisdiction and Discretion, 60 N.Y.U. L. Rev. 543 (1985) (within the Anglo-American structure, jurisdictional grants include an inherent discretion to decline jurisdiction in any number of settings, including those covered by *Pullman*, *Burford*, and *Colorado River*). *See also* Richard H. Fallon, Jr., Why Abstention Is Not Illegitimate: An Essay on the Distinction Between "Legitimate" and "Illegitimate" Statutory Interpretation and Judicial Lawmaking, 107 Nw. U. L. Rev.

abstention requirements, abstention doctrines uniformly reflect a desire to allow state courts to decide certain matters instead of federal courts.[8] In short, abstention is defended as promoting federalism and harmony between federal and state courts. Furthermore, abstention is defended as representing the judiciary's traditional equitable discretion and authority to refuse to issue injunctions where strong policy considerations militate against the imposition of such remedies.[9]

This theme, whether abstention is an unjustified violation of separation of powers or an appropriate protection of federalism, recurs throughout the following sections and chapters. It is an issue that raises fundamental questions about the proper relationship between the Supreme Court and Congress and between the federal courts and the state governments.

§12.2 WHEN IS ABSTENTION BECAUSE OF UNCLEAR STATE LAW APPROPRIATE?

§12.2.1 Abstention to Avoid Federal Court Constitutional Rulings: **Pullman** *Abstention*

Railroad Commission of Texas v. Pullman Company

Federal court abstention is required when state law is uncertain and a state court's clarification of state law might make a federal court's constitutional ruling unnecessary. Under such circumstances, the federal court should not resolve the federal constitutional question until the matter has been sent to state court for a determination of the uncertain issue of state law.

This doctrine is commonly termed "*Pullman* abstention," taking its title from the seminal case of *Railroad Commission of Texas v. Pullman Co.*[1] The Texas Railroad Commission issued a regulation preventing the operation of sleeping cars unless there was a conductor, and not only a porter, present. In Texas, at this

---

847 (2013); William P. Marshall, Abstention, Separation of Powers, and Recasting the Meaning of Judicial Restraint, 107 Nw. U. L. Rev. 881 (2013).

[8] Professor Barry Friedman rejects Professor Redish's criticism of abstention doctrines and argues that abstention doctrines should be reformulated to focus directly on the competing substantive concerns: the need for federal protection of constitutional rights versus the need for sensitivity to state court proceedings. Barry Friedman, A Revisionist Theory of Abstention, 88 Mich. L. Rev. 530 (1989). Professor Friedman suggests that in deciding whether to abstain federal courts should consider whether federal interests require lower federal court decision-making, whether state courts will provide an adequate means of raising and preserving federal issues for Supreme Court review, and whether direct review by the Supreme Court is likely to be adequate to protect federal interests. *Id.* at 547.

[9] *See, e.g.*, Douglas v. City of Jeannette, 319 U.S. 157, 163 (1943).

§12.2 [1] 312 U.S. 496 (1941). For an excellent discussion of the context and background of this case, *see* Lauren Robel, Riding the Color Line: The Story of *Railroad Commission of Texas v. Pullman Co.*, *in* Federal Courts Stories (Vicki Jackson & Judith Resnik eds. 2010) 163.

time, conductors were white and porters were Black. The commission's regulation was subjected to a broad-based challenge, including the allegation that it was unconstitutional racial discrimination in violation of the Fourteenth Amendment. Additionally, there was a pendent state law claim that the railroad commission lacked legal authority under Texas law to issue the regulation.

The Supreme Court unanimously held that the federal district court erred by deciding the challenge to the Texas regulation. The Court said that it was unclear under Texas law whether the commission had authority to issue the rule. The Court further stated that the federal court should have abstained from deciding the case until the state courts had the chance to clarify the state law. If the state court ruled in favor of the plaintiffs, holding that the commission acted improperly in promulgating the regulation, then the matter would be resolved. However, if the state court upheld the regulation, then the matter could return to federal court for a determination of the constitutional issue. In other words, the Supreme Court held that where state law is uncertain and a clarification of state law might make a federal court's determination of a constitutional question unnecessary, the federal court should abstain until the state court has had an opportunity to resolve the uncertainty as to state law.

Rationales for the Holding in *Pullman*

The Supreme Court offered three major rationales for its holding; each has been questioned in the years since *Pullman.* First, the Court said that abstention avoided friction between federal and state courts. Justice Frankfurter, writing for the Court, stated that "[f]ew public interests have a higher claim upon the discretion of a federal chancellor than the avoidance of needless friction with state policies."[2] Friction is greater if the federal court invalidates a state law than if the state court voids its own statute. Additionally, misinterpretations of state law by a federal court are a potential source of friction between federal and state judiciaries.[3]

Commentators question whether this rationale justifies abstention. For example, Professor Martha Field challenges whether *Pullman* abstention actually lessens friction between federal and state courts.[4] There are, Professor Field suggests, two possible outcomes when a federal court decides the state law issue instead of allowing the state court to rule. The federal court could come to the same conclusion as the state court would. For example, both might have invalidated the Texas law, or both might have upheld it. In such circumstances, friction is minimal or nonexistent because the result is identical regardless of which court decides the case. Alternatively, the federal court might reach a conclusion that differs from that of the state court. Under *Pullman* abstention, this would occur if the state court upheld the regulation on state law grounds, but the federal court invalidated it

[2] *Id.* at 500.

[3] Julie A. Davies, *Pullman* and *Burford* Abstention: Clarifying the Roles of Federal and State Courts in Constitutional Cases, 20 U.C. Davis L. Rev. 1, 9-10 (1986).

[4] Martha A. Field, Abstention in Constitutional Cases: The Scope of the *Pullman* Abstention Doctrine, 122 U. Pa. L. Rev. 1071, 1090 (1974).

on constitutional grounds when the matter returned to federal court. In this situation, abstention increases rather than decreases friction because the state court's decision is rendered superfluous and, in effect, is overruled.

Another response to the friction argument is to question whether promoting harmony between the federal and state courts should be a consideration in defining federal court jurisdiction. The Court never explains what it means by friction. Is it simply some anger directed at the federal courts? If so, why should that matter? The argument is that friction is inherent to the very existence of federal courts possessing the authority to declare state laws unconstitutional.

Defenders of *Pullman* abstention respond that it is desirable to lessen tensions between federal and state governments whenever possible and that one way to do this is to minimize situations in which federal courts invalidate state laws. Ultimately, the disagreement between *Pullman*'s critics and its defenders involves both an empirical question (does *Pullman* abstention lessen friction?) and a normative issue (should friction matter in fashioning jurisdictional rules?).

A second justification offered by the *Pullman* Court is that abstention reduces the likelihood of erroneous interpretations of state law. State courts are the authoritative voice as to the meaning of state laws. Apart from the tensions caused by mistakes in construing state law, there is an independent value in correct interpretation of the law and in avoiding situations where the federal court's view of state law is later overruled by the state court.[5] Thus, it is argued that it is preferable to allow state courts to interpret state law, rather than have federal courts guess as to how state courts would do so. Indeed, the Supreme Court observed that federal court errors in interpreting state law are themselves a source of friction. Justice Ginsburg remarked that "[w]arnings against premature adjudication of constitutional questions bear heightened attention when a federal court is asked to invalidate a State's law, for the federal tribunal risks friction-generating error when it endeavors to construe a novel state Act not yet reviewed by the State's highest court."[6]

This rationale has also been criticized. Federal courts often are entrusted with resolving uncertain questions of state law. For example, under *Erie Railroad v. Tompkins*, federal courts apply state law in all diversity cases.[7] Frequently, this involves federal courts interpreting state laws that are unclear.[8] Likewise, pendent jurisdiction often requires federal courts to decide state law questions that state courts have not yet resolved. There is an inherent risk of error whenever federal courts interpret state law, yet that risk is commonly accepted.

[5] 312 U.S. at 499-500.

[6] Arizonans for Official English v. Arizona, 520 U.S. 43, 78 (1997).

[7] 304 U.S. 64 (1938); *see* §5.3.5, *supra*. *See also* James C. Rehnquist, Taking Comity Seriously: How to Neutralize the Abstention Doctrines, 46 Stan. L. Rev. 1049, 1096-1098 (1994) (arguing that abstention is appropriate only when there are pending state court proceedings).

[8] *See* England v. Louisiana State Bd. of Medical Examiners, 375 U.S. 411, 426 (1964) (Douglas, J., concurring) (criticizing *Pullman* abstention; under *Erie*, federal courts decide state law questions; the "fact that those questions are complex and difficult is no excuse for a refusal by the District Court to entertain the suit").

Moreover, the likelihood of error is uncertain. Federal district court judges sit in the same state as the state's judiciary. In most instances, the federal judges practiced law in that state and frequently decide cases under state law. Hence, it is questionable whether they are less capable of correctly interpreting state law than are state court judges.[9]

Some respond that state judges are more experienced in handling state law matters and hence are less likely to make mistakes in interpreting the state's law.[10] Because ultimately it is the state's highest court that will get the last word, some contend that it is better to let state courts decide a question rather than to have a federal court speculate how the state judiciary might rule.

Finally, the Supreme Court defended its *Pullman* holding as a way of avoiding unnecessary constitutional rulings.[11] If the state court invalidates the state law, then there is no need for the federal court to reach the constitutional question. It is well established that, when possible, constitutional rulings are to be avoided.[12] The Supreme Court remarked that "[f]ederal courts, when confronting a challenge to the constitutionality of a federal state, follow a 'cardinal principle': They 'will first ascertain whether a construction. . . is fairly possible' that will contain the statute within constitutional bounds."[13]

However, the argument against this rationale is that constitutional rulings can be avoided simply by having the federal court decide the state law issue first and then reach the constitutional question only if necessary.[14] In fact, this was the approach endorsed by the Supreme Court before *Pullman.* In *Siler v. Louisville & Nashville Railroad,* the Court held that the federal district court should have initially decided the case on the state law grounds, thereby potentially avoiding the constitutional questions.[15]

Without a doubt, requiring the federal court to decide state law questions before resolving constitutional issues would achieve the objective of avoiding constitutional rulings. Defenders of *Pullman* abstention, therefore, must fall back on the earlier described argument that it is better to have state courts decide state law questions than it is to have federal courts do so.

Criticisms of *Pullman* Abstention

Critics of *Pullman* abstention do not simply challenge the underlying rationale offered for it by the Court. They also point to the substantial costs created by the doctrine. Abstention causes enormous delays as cases are shifted from federal to state court and then, often, back to federal court. Delays of six or eight years

[9] Field, *supra* note 4, at 1092.

[10] *See* Paul J. Mishkin, The Federal Question in the District Courts, 53 Colum. L. Rev. 157 (1953).

[11] 312 U.S. at 501.

[12] *See* Ashwander v. TVA, 297 U.S. 288, 346-347 (1936) (Brandeis, J., concurring).

[13] Arizonans for Official English v. Arizona, 520 U.S. at 78 (*quoting* Ashwander v. TVA).

[14] Some commentators have criticized the principle that federal courts should avoid constitutional rulings. *See* Frederick Schauer, *Ashwander* Revisited, 1995 Sup. Ct. Rev. 71; Lisa A. Kloppenberg, Avoiding Constitutional Questions, 35 B.C. L. Rev. 1003 (1994).

[15] 213 U.S. 175 (1909).

before the resolution of cases are common when abstention is ordered, though this has become less of a problem as now virtually all states have some form of certification statutes that allow federal courts, at least in some circumstances, to certify issues to the state courts.[16] The increase in costs and time probably causes some litigants to give up and not pursue their claims.[17] If nothing else, the long delay is frustrating and undesirable unless there is a particularly compelling justification for it.

It should be noted, however, that this criticism is directed at the procedure that sends the case to state court for a ruling as to the state law issue and then permits the case to return to federal court, if necessary, for a determination of the constitutional question.[18] The delay and attendant increases in costs could be avoided either by eliminating the abstention requirement or by sending the entire case, including all federal issues, to the state court for a decision. Alternatively, certification of specific issues to the state court, pursuant to a state certification statute, is a way of lessening the delay caused by abstention. Indeed, the Supreme Court has declared that "[c]ertification today covers territory once dominated by a deferral device called *Pullman* abstention."[19] Yet some judges and scholars criticize whether certification actually succeeds in reducing delay and producing the desired clarification of state law.[20] The desirability of the current abstention procedures, and alternatives such as certification, are discussed in detail in §12.3.

Despite the debate over the wisdom of *Pullman* abstention, the doctrine is firmly entrenched and frequently arises in federal court litigation. Justice Thomas declared, "*Pullman* recognizes the importance of state sovereignty by limiting federal judicial intervention in state affairs to cases where intervention is necessary."[21] Although there are some earlier cases extending abstention to lawsuits for money damages,[22] the Supreme Court subsequently indicated that the abstention doctrines are derived from the discretion inherent to courts of equity and thus cannot be used to dismiss suits for money damages.[23] The Court indicated that a stay may be permissible in suits for money damages, but that only suits for equitable or injunctive relief could be dismissed or remanded based on abstention doctrines. Federal district courts may abstain in

[16] Martin H. Redish, Federal Jurisdiction: Tensions in the Allocation of Judicial Power 235 (1980).

[17] Field, *supra* note 4, at 1086.

[18] This procedure is created in England v. Louisiana State Bd. of Medical Examiners, 375 U.S. 411 (1964), discussed in §12.3, *infra*.

[19] Arizonans for Official English v. Arizona, 520 U.S. at 75-76.

[20] *See* Bruce Selya, Certified Madness: Ask a Silly Question, 29 Suffolk L. Rev. 677 (1995); M. Bryan Schneider, But Answer Came There None: The Michigan Supreme Court and the Certified Question of State Law, 41 Wayne L. Rev. 273 (1995).

[21] Virginia Office for Prot. & Advocacy v. Stewart, 563 U.S. 247, 255 (2011) (Thomas, J., concurring).

[22] *See* Clay v. Sun Ins. Office, 363 U.S. 207 (1960); Davies, *supra* note 3, at 4-5.

[23] Quackenbush v. Allstate Insurance Co., 517 U.S. 706, 722-726 (1996). Although *Quackenbush* involved *Burford* abstention—abstention to defer to complex state administrative procedures—the Court spoke generally of all the abstention doctrines being derived from the discretion inherent to courts of equity.

response to a motion from either party or the court may decide on its own to abstain.[24]

Prerequisites for *Pullman* Abstention

Two factors must be present for *Pullman* abstention to be warranted: (1) There must be substantial uncertainty as to the meaning of the state law, and (2) there must be a reasonable possibility that the state court's clarification of state law might obviate the need for a federal constitutional ruling. The Court repeatedly has stated that abstention is confined to situations where these "special circumstances" are present.[25]

For example, the Supreme Court has explained that abstention is appropriate if the state statute is "susceptible of a construction by the state judiciary which might avoid in whole or in part the necessity for federal constitutional adjudication, or at least materially change the nature of the problem."[26] Thus, abstention is required only if the state's law is "fairly subject to an interpretation which will render unnecessary" a ruling on the federal constitutional issue.[27] Abstention is not necessary if a state law is patently unconstitutional, even if the state court has not yet construed it, because a saving construction by the state judiciary is unlikely. As the Supreme Court stated, abstention is inappropriate when "the unconstitutionality of the particular state action under challenge is clear."[28]

The Supreme Court has offered relatively little guidance about how unclear the state law must be or how great the possibility has to be that the state court ruling might avoid a federal constitutional decision.[29] Under the Supreme Court's formulations, it must be sufficiently likely that the federal court decision could be avoided by a state court ruling;[30] in other words, it must be shown that the state law is fairly subject to an interpretation that could render a federal constitutional decision unnecessary.[31] There are, however, differing degrees of uncertainty and differing degrees of likelihood that the state court would choose a construction that would forestall the need for a federal court ruling. It is not clear where on these continuums abstention is appropriate.[32]

[24] Bellotti v. Baird, 428 U.S. 132, 143 n.10 (1976) (court can abstain on its own motion); Quinn v. Aetna Life & Casualty Co., 616 F.2d 38, 41 n.4 (2d Cir. 1980) (either party can request abstention); *but see* Mazanec v. North Judson San Pierre School Corp., 763 F.2d 845, 847-849 (7th Cir. 1985) (presumption against abstention where neither party requested abstention before trial).

[25] Kusper v. Pontikes, 414 U.S. 51, 54 (1973) (citations omitted); Baggett v. Bullitt, 377 U.S. 360, 375 (1964) (citations omitted).

[26] Bellotti v. Baird, 428 U.S. 132, 146-147 (1976), *quoting* Harrison v. NAACP, 360 U.S. 167, 177 (1959).

[27] Harman v. Forssenius, 380 U.S. 528, 534-535 (1965).

[28] Thornburgh v. American College of Obstetricians, 476 U.S. 747, 756 (1986). *See also* Davies, *supra* note 3, at 7.

[29] Field, *supra* note 4, at 1088-1089; Davies, *supra* note 3, at 7.

[30] Reetz v. Bozanich, 397 U.S. 82, 86-87 (1970).

[31] 380 U.S. at 535.

[32] The Court indicated that the degree of uncertainty in state law might be lessened if a state has a certification procedure that entails less costs and delays than abstention without certification. Arizonans for Official English v. Arizona, 520 U.S. at 75-76.

§12.2 When Is Abstention Because of Unclear State Law Appropriate?

The Supreme Court has decided that abstention is not warranted simply because a state law is challenged as being unconstitutionally vague unless there is a substantial likelihood that the state court's clarification would avoid the federal constitutional ruling. In *Baggett v. Bullitt*, the Supreme Court considered a challenge to a Washington state law that required loyalty oaths of state employees.[33] Although the state courts had never construed or reviewed the statute that was challenged as being unconstitutionally vague, the Court deemed abstention inappropriate. The Court said that it doubted that "a construction of the oath provisions, in light of the vagueness challenge, would avoid or fundamentally alter the constitutional issue raised in this litigation."[34] The uncertain issue could not be resolved through a choice made by the state court between two or three competing understandings of the state's law.[35] Rather, the claim was that the statute was so vague that it provided inadequate notice about which conduct was allowed and which was impermissible; no likely narrowing construction could resolve the "indefinite number" of unclear issues under the statute.

In other words, abstention is appropriate when a statute is challenged as being unconstitutionally vague only if there is a substantial possibility that the state court could provide a narrowing construction that would save the statute from being invalidated.[36] As the Supreme Court explained:

> Where the case turns on the applicability of a state statute or regulation to a particular person or a defined course of conduct, resolution of the unsettled question of state law may eliminate any need for constitutional adjudication. Abstention is therefore appropriate. Where, however,. . . the statute or regulation is challenged as vague because individuals to whom it plainly applies simply cannot understand what is required of them and do not wish to forswear all activity arguably within the scope of the vague terms, abstention is not required.[37]

Also, the Supreme Court has held that abstention is not appropriate, and state law is not to be deemed uncertain, merely because the state has not yet considered the law's constitutionality under the state's constitution. State constitutions usually contain provisions safeguarding individual liberties that are similar or identical to those in the U.S. Constitution. Should a federal court refuse to hear a challenge under, for example, the First Amendment in order to allow a state court the opportunity to review the matter under the identical provision of the state constitution? Generally, the answer is no; federal courts need not abstain to allow state courts to construe state laws under state constitutional provisions.

[33] 377 U.S. 360 (1964).

[34] *Id.* at 375-376.

[35] *Id.* at 378.

[36] *See* Hawaii Housing Authority v. Midkiff, 467 U.S. 229, 236 (1984) (federal courts need not abstain "when a state statute is not fairly subject to an interpretation which will render unnecessary the adjudication of the federal constitutional question"); *see also* S & S Pawn Shops Inc. v. City of Del City, 947 F.2d 432, 442 (10th Cir. 1991) (*Pullman* abstention appropriate when a statute is challenged on vagueness grounds and the statute was "sufficiently ambiguous that the Oklahoma court could reasonably interpret it" as being constitutional).

[37] Procunier v. Martinez, 416 U.S. 396, 401 n.5 (1974).

In *Wisconsin v. Constantineau*, the Supreme Court considered the constitutionality of a state law that allowed a chief of police to post a person's picture in liquor stores and thereby prevent the individual from purchasing alcoholic beverages for one year.[38] Three justices, in dissent, argued that abstention was warranted to allow the Wisconsin courts to review that state law under the Wisconsin Constitution. Chief Justice Burger, in a dissenting opinion joined by Justice Blackmun, argued, "For all we know, the state courts would find this statute invalid under the State Constitution. . . . Since no one could reasonably think that the judges of Wisconsin have less fidelity to due process requirements of the federal constitution than we do, this case is. . . a classic illustration of one in which we should decline to act until resort to state courts has been exhausted."[39]

The majority of the Court rejected abstention. The Court emphasized that abstention is not appropriate simply to give state courts the chance to decide a question first.[40] Requiring abstention every time a state has a provision identical to the one in the U.S. Constitution would create an abstention requirement in most constitutional cases. The presence of the federal district courts as guarantors of constitutional rights would be lost. In essence, there would be an exhaustion requirement imposed such that federal constitutional challenges could be decided only after possible state constitutional issues were resolved by the state courts. The Supreme Court, however, repeatedly has ruled that such an exhaustion requirement would conflict with Congress's intent in adopting 42 U.S.C. §1983, which is the basis for most constitutional litigation against state and local governments and their officers.[41]

Federal court abstention is required, however, when the state has a constitutional provision unlike any that exists in the U.S. Constitution and the state court's construction of that clause might make the federal court ruling unnecessary. In *Reetz v. Bozanich*, Alaska's fishing laws were challenged as being unconstitutional under the federal Constitution and as violating specific provisions of the Alaska Constitution dealing with fishing rights.[42] The Supreme Court held that abstention was appropriate because the meaning of the unique fishing provisions in the Alaska Constitution was unclear and because the state court's ruling on these issues might obviate the need for a constitutional ruling by a federal court. Thus, what emerges from *Constantineau* and *Reetz* is that abstention is not proper if the federal and state constitutional provisions are identical, even if a state court decision on state constitutional grounds might render a federal court decision unnecessary. But abstention is justified if there is a unique state constitutional provision and a state court interpretation of it could make a federal constitutional decision unnecessary.[43]

[38] 400 U.S. 433 (1971).

[39] *Id.* at 440 (Burger, C.J., dissenting).

[40] *Id.* at 439; *see also* Zwickler v. Koota, 389 U.S. 241, 251 (1967).

[41] *See* §8.4, *supra.*

[42] 397 U.S. 82 (1970).

[43] An interesting unresolved question is whether the federal court should abstain if a state, in interpreting its own constitutional provision, which is a mirror image of one in the federal Constitution, provides greater protections of individual liberties than exist under the U.S. Constitution. *See* Fields

Unresolved Issues as to When *Pullman* Abstention is Appropriate

Many issues remain unresolved concerning when *Pullman* abstention is appropriate. First, it is unclear whether federal courts should weigh the costs of delaying a constitutional ruling in deciding whether to abstain. In some instances, the Supreme Court has concluded that abstention was inappropriate because of the importance of the constitutional claims involved. For example, on several occasions, the Supreme Court has noted the undesirability of delaying adjudication of freedom of speech claims because of fear that speech will be chilled while the matter was pending in the state courts.[44] Likewise, in a case involving a challenge to an allegedly unconstitutional interference with the right to vote, the Court held, in part, that abstention was unjustified because of the crucial importance of voting in the American democracy.[45] However, in a subsequent decision, *Growe v. Emison,* the Court held that the federal district court should have deferred to the state court's timely efforts to redraw the malapportioned districts.[46] The Court emphasized that federal judges should defer to state courts concerning the highly political reapportionment process if the state already has begun to handle the apportionment problem.

There is little agreement among the lower courts as to what interests are sufficiently important to justify refusing abstention or the weight to be given such interests in deciding when abstention is appropriate.[47] Professor Davies remarked that "the greatest area of interpretive confusion occurs in cases. . . [involving] abstention when sensitive social policy issues exist. The lower courts' dilemma in deciding what constitutes a sensitive social policy issue, and its effect on an abstention decision, is attributable to the Supreme Court's failure to address the question."[48]

Similarly, it is not clear whether a federal court should consider the economic consequences abstention has on the parties. For instance, should a federal court refuse to abstain if the effect of abstention would be to force the plaintiff to abandon the lawsuit because of the additional costs? The United States Court of Appeals for the Third Circuit specifically held that abstention was inappropriate because of the substantial economic harm it would cause the plaintiff.[49] A vehement dissent

---

v. Rockdale County, 785 F.2d 1558 (11th Cir. 1986) (abstention is proper if state provides greater protections than exist under the U.S. Constitution, even if the state provision is a mirror image of the federal one).

[44] *See, e.g.,* Zwickler v. Koota, 389 U.S. at 241, 252; Baggett v. Bullitt, 377 U.S. at 379.

[45] Harman v. Forssenius, 380 U.S. 528, 537 (1965).

[46] 507 U.S. 25 (1993).

[47] *See, e.g.,* Eastport Assocs. v. City of Los Angeles, 935 F.2d 1071 (9th Cir. 1991) (land-use planning is a sensitive area justifying refusal to abstain); Almodovar v. Reiner, 832 F.2d 1138 (9th Cir. 1987) (challenge to state anti-obscenity ordinance is a sensitive area of social policy); Brooks v. Walker County Hosp., 688 F.2d 334 (5th Cir. 1982), *cert. denied,* 462 U.S. 1105 (1983) (state health care law is a sensitive area).

[48] Davies, *supra* note 3, at 19.

[49] Stretton v. Disciplinary Bd. of the Sup. Ct. of Pa., 944 F.2d 137 (3d Cir. 1991); United Servs. Auto. Assn. v. Muir, 792 F.2d 356, 362 (3d Cir. 1986), *cert. denied,* 479 U.S. 1031 (1987); Presbytery of New Jersey of the Orthodox Presbyterian Church v. Florio, 902 F. Supp. 492 (D.N.J. 1995); American Inst. of Foot Medicine v. N.J. State Bd. of Medical Examiners, 807 F. Supp. 1170 (D.N.J. 1992) (delay is a relevant factor in deciding whether to abstain).

was filed arguing that the majority had misapplied *Pullman* and had created an exception that threatened to swallow the rule.[50]

A second related area of uncertainty concerns whether *Pullman* abstention is mandatory or discretionary. In some instances, the Supreme Court has spoken as if federal district courts must abstain if a state court's clarification of state law might avoid a constitutional ruling.[51] In other decisions, the Court treated abstention as a discretionary doctrine that need not be applied if there are substantial reasons for not abstaining.[52] The Court has spoken of abstention as being derived from "discretion historically enjoyed by courts of equity."[53]

The preferable approach is to treat abstention as discretionary and to allow federal courts to hear the case, even if the *Pullman* criteria are met, provided substantial reasons for avoiding abstention are present.[54] For example, as the Supreme Court has indicated, if there are sensitive constitutional rights, such as voting and freedom of speech, which will be harmed by delay, abstention should be avoided. Similarly, if abstention will have a devastating effect on the parties, precluding continuation of the litigation or forcing them to completely forgo access to the federal courts, the court should consider this in deciding whether to abstain. Abstention is not mandated by statute; it was created by the Court to achieve certain policy objectives.[55] Hence, it should not be applied when there are more important countervailing considerations.

Third, it is unclear whether federal courts may abstain in a case where jurisdictional statutes create exclusive federal jurisdiction. The Fifth Circuit expressly declared that abstention was inappropriate in such circumstances because when federal courts "have exclusive jurisdiction. . . abstention to permit adjudication of the entire case in a state forum defeats the purpose of that legislation."[56] Although several justices have noted that this is an unanswered question, no resolution has yet been forthcoming from the Supreme Court.[57]

[50] 792 F.2d at 367. *See also* Georgevich v. Strauss, 772 F.2d 1078 (3d Cir. 1985), *cert. denied,* 475 U.S. 1028 (1986); Coast City Truck Sales, Inc. v. Navistar International Transportation Co., 912 F. Supp. 747 (D.N.J. 1995); Barber v. State of Wis. Ethics Bd., 815 F. Supp. 1216 (W.D. Wis. 1993) (the possibility of delay alone is not a sufficient basis for refusing to abstain); Buchanan, *supra* note 29, at 1254.

[51] *See, e.g.,* City of Meridian v. Southern Bell Tel. & Tel. Co., 358 U.S. 639, 640 (1959).

[52] *See, e.g.,* Baggett v. Bullitt, 377 U.S. at 360, 375; NAACP v. Bennett, 360 U.S. 471 (1959).

[53] Quackenbush v. Allstate Insurance Co., 517 U.S. 706, 728 (1996). Although *Quackenbush* did not concern *Pullman* abstention, its statement about abstention being derived from the discretion inherent to courts of equity concerned all types of abstention. *Quackenbush* is discussed more fully below in §12.2.3.

[54] *See* Baran v. Port of Beaumont Navigation District of Jefferson County, Tex., 57 F.3d 436 (5th Cir. 1995); American Bank & Trust Co. v. Dent, 982 F.2d 917 (5th Cir. 1993) (abstention is discretionary).

[55] *See* Rex E. Lee & Richard G. Wilkins, An Analysis of Supplemental Jurisdiction and Abstention with Recommendations for Legislative Action, 1990 BYU L. Rev. 321 (arguing that a statute should be adopted codifying *Pullman* abstention and making it clear that it is discretionary).

[56] Key v. Wise, 629 F.2d 1049, 1059 (5th Cir. 1980), *cert. denied,* 454 U.S. 1103 (1981).

[57] Key v. Wise, 454 U.S. 1103, 1106 (1981) (Brennan, Marshall, Blackmun, JJ., dissenting from denial of certiorari).

Fourth, although abstention is permissible only if the state provides procedures that permit a speedy resolution of the state law issues, it is not clear what constitutes adequate state procedures. In *Pullman,* the Court in ordering abstention noted that "[t]he law of Texas appears to furnish easy and ample means for determining the Commission's authority."[58] Many courts have indicated that abstention is not appropriate if significant questions exist about the ability of state procedures to resolve the uncertainties concerning state law.[59]

Finally, there is even disagreement among the lower federal courts as to the legal test to be used in deciding whether abstention is appropriate. The Second Circuit, for example, has articulated a three-part test: the state law must be uncertain; the resolution of the federal law issue must depend on the construction of the state law; and the state law must be susceptible to a reasonable interpretation that would avoid the constitutional issue.[60] In contrast, the Fifth Circuit has ruled that abstention is appropriate if any of the following factors are present: if there is a difficult or unclear issue of state law; if the decision on the state law issue would eliminate the constitutional question; or if federal court review risks substantial friction with a state's program.[61] The Fifth Circuit's test thus goes much further in requiring abstention than does that adopted by the Second Circuit. In fact, it is difficult to reconcile the Fifth Circuit's approach with the Supreme Court's decisions; the Supreme Court never has indicated that abstention is appropriate solely to avoid friction with state policies or on the basis of unclear state law.

Many commentators urge that the Supreme Court completely discard the *Pullman* abstention doctrine. Professor David Currie argued that abstention has a "*Bleak House* aspect that in my mind is too high a price to pay for the gains in avoiding error, friction and constitutional questions."[62] Others, such as Professor Martha Field, propose limiting abstention to instances in which federal courts would disrupt important state policies, particularly in areas where states have created tribunals for uniform review of state regulatory agency decisions.[63] The American Law Institute suggests that the procedures for abstention be altered such that all issues, including federal constitutional questions, would be litigated in state court when

[58] 312 U.S. at 501.

[59] United States v. Borneo, Inc., 971 F.2d 244 (9th Cir. 1992); Winston v. Children & Youth Services of Del. County, 948 F.2d 1380 (3d Cir. 1991), *cert. denied,* 504 U.S. 956 (1992); *see also* Allen v. City of Los Angeles, 92 F.3d 842 (9th Cir. 1996) ("Proceedings in other courts may be taken into consideration in the decision to abstain if those proceedings have a direct connection to the issues in question.").

[60] *See, e.g.,* Expressions Hair Design v. Schneiderman, 808 F.3d 118, 137 (2d Cir. 2015). Other circuits also apply a similar three-prong test. *See, e.g.,* Burdick v. Takushi, 846 F.2d 587 (9th Cir. 1988); Vinyard v. King, 655 F.2d 1016 (10th Cir. 1981); Record Revolution No. 6, Inc. v. City of Parma, 638 F.2d 916 (6th Cir. 1980); D'Iorio v. County of Delaware, 592 F.2d 681, 685-686 (3d Cir. 1978).

[61] *See, e.g.,* Word of Faith Outreach Center Church v. Morales, 986 F.2d 962 (5th Cir. 1993); Buchanan, *supra* note 29, at 1255.

[62] David P. Currie, The Federal Courts and the American Law Institute, Part II, 36 U. Chi. L. Rev. 268, 317 (1969).

[63] Field, *supra* note 4, at 1126-1129.

abstention has been ordered.[64] In light of these calls for abolition or reform, the Supreme Court very well might rethink the *Pullman* abstention doctrine in the years ahead.

§12.2.2 Abstention because of Unclear State Law in Diversity Cases: **Thibodaux** *Abstention*

Abstention Generally not Required in Diversity Cases

Under the Supreme Court's landmark decision in *Erie Railroad v. Tompkins*, federal courts apply state law in diversity cases.[65] Frequently, therefore, federal courts must decide questions of state law that are unclear and unresolved in the state court system. When, if at all, is abstention in such circumstances appropriate in diversity cases?

In *Meredith v. Winter Haven*, the Supreme Court held that federal courts should not abstain in diversity cases when state law is unclear.[66] *Meredith* involved a diversity suit that was filed against a city by owners and holders of bonds who claimed that the city was obligated to pay them interest. Florida's law was unclear as to the city's obligations. Nonetheless, the Supreme Court ruled that abstention was inappropriate in diversity cases, even when state law was uncertain. The Court explained, "Congress having adopted the policy of opening the federal courts to suitors in all diversity cases involving the jurisdictional amount, we can discern in its action no recognition of a policy which would exclude cases from the jurisdiction merely because they involve state law or because the law is uncertain or difficult to determine."[67]

The *Meredith* conclusion that abstention is inappropriate in diversity cases makes sense in light of the policy rationales supporting the existence of diversity jurisdiction. Federal courts were given diversity jurisdiction largely because of the fear that state courts might be biased against out-of-state litigants. As such, it is not reasonable for federal courts to refuse to exercise their jurisdiction and send diversity cases to state courts.[68]

Furthermore, in *Pullman* abstention situations the case is sent to state court for a determination of the state law question but can return to federal court, if necessary, for a ruling on the federal law issue. Thus, the Supreme Court is fond of saying that *Pullman* abstention is the "postponement" of jurisdiction, not its "abdication."[69] However, in diversity cases in which there are only state law questions,

[64] American Law Institute, Study of Division of Jurisdiction Between Federal and State Courts, §1371(c) 288-290 (1981). The procedures for abstention and this proposal are discussed in more detail in §12.3, *infra.*

[65] 304 U.S. 64 (1938); discussed in §5.3.5, *supra.*

[66] 320 U.S. 228 (1943).

[67] *Id.* at 236.

[68] *See* Note, Abstention and Certification in Diversity Suits: "Perfection of Means and Confusion of Goals," 73 Yale L.J. 850, 858 (1964).

[69] Allen v. McCurry, 449 U.S. 90, 101 n.17 (1980); Harrison v. NAACP, 360 U.S. 167, 177 (1959).

abstention often would mean that the case is sent permanently to the state court. The effect would be a judicial nullification of the diversity jurisdiction statute.

Circumstances Justifying Abstention in Diversity Cases

Although the *Meredith* rule remains in force and abstention is generally not required in diversity cases when there is unclear state law, the Supreme Court subsequently held that there are some situations where abstention is appropriate in diversity litigation. The seminal case is *Louisiana Power and Light Co. v. City of Thibodaux.*[70] In *Thibodaux*, the city initiated an eminent domain proceeding in state court to take property that was owned by the power company, a Florida corporation. The company removed the case to federal court, based on the existence of diversity jurisdiction. The federal district court, on its own, chose to abstain by staying the pending action to allow the state courts to determine whether the city had the legal authority under state law to use eminent domain in this manner. The Supreme Court upheld the propriety of abstention.

The Court reaffirmed the general rule of *Meredith* that "the mere difficulty of state law does not justify a federal court's relinquishment of jurisdiction in favor of state court action."[71] Nonetheless, the Court concluded that abstention was appropriate because of the "special and peculiar nature" of eminent domain proceedings.[72] The Court emphasized that eminent domain is "intimately involved with [the government's] sovereign prerogative" and thus justifies abstention when there are important issues of unclear state law.[73]

In another decision handed down the same day as *Thibodaux*, the Court made it clear that abstention is not required in all diversity cases involving the eminent domain power. In *Allegheny County v. Frank Mashuda Co.*, an individual challenged the city of Pittsburgh's authority to take land that was subsequently leased to private corporations.[74] Although the property was initially taken for the construction of an airport, the landowner later learned that the property was being rented to private business concerns. The state law was unambiguous: Governments could not use their eminent domain power to take property for private uses. Justice Brennan, writing for the Court, explained that abstention is "an extraordinary and narrow exception to the duty of a District Court to adjudicate a controversy properly before it" and is appropriate only in "exceptional circumstances."[75] The Court explained that there is nothing inherent to eminent domain that requires abstention whenever such issues come to federal court. In fact, the Court said that "eminent domain is no more mystically involved with sovereign prerogative" than numerous other interests that federal courts frequently adjudicate.[76]

[70] 360 U.S. 25 (1959).
[71] *Id.* at 27.
[72] *Id.* at 28.
[73] *Id.*
[74] 360 U.S. 185 (1959).
[75] *Id.* at 188-189.
[76] *Id.* at 192 (citations omitted).

Mashuda can be reconciled with *Thibodaux* because the latter involved both eminent domain and unclear law, whereas there were no issues of uncertain state law in *Mashuda.* It should be noted, however, that relatively few of the justices were persuaded by this distinction. Four justices—Justices Black, Clark, Frankfurter, and Harlan—dissented in *Mashuda,* finding the case indistinguishable from *Thibodaux.* Conversely, three justices—Chief Justice Warren and Justices Brennan and Douglas—dissented in *Thibodaux,* believing it to be indistinguishable from the proper denial of abstention in *Mashuda.* Thus, it was the two justices who joined the majority in both *Thibodaux* and *Mashuda*—Justices Stewart and Whittaker—who cast the decisive votes distinguishing the two cases. Justice Stewart explicitly stated that the difference he perceived was that in *Thibodaux,* but not in *Mashuda,* there were unclear issues of state law.[77]

The decisions in *Thibodaux* and *Mashuda* thus establish that federal courts should abstain in diversity cases if there is uncertain state law *and* an important state interest that is "intimately involved" with the government's "sovereign prerogative." But the Court has provided little guidance as to what state interests are sufficiently important to justify abstention in diversity cases.

Subsequently, the Supreme Court said that the distinction between *Thibodaux* and *Mashuda* is that the case was stayed in the former, but dismissed in the latter. In *Quackenbush v. Allstate,* the Court said, "Unlike in *Thibodaux,* however, the District Court in [*Mashuda*] had not merely stayed adjudication of the federal action pending the resolution of an issue in state court, but rather had dismissed the federal action altogether. Based in large measure on this distinction, we reversed the District Court's order."[78] This distinguishes the cases entirely based on the procedures followed, rather than the government's interests. If followed, this could substantially expand the scope of abstention in diversity cases as federal courts could abstain, even if there was not some special state interest, as long as the case was stayed and not dismissed. This seems problematic in light of the Court's clear command in *Meredith* that unclear state law is not sufficient by itself for abstention in diversity cases.

When is Abstention Appropriate in Diversity Cases?

There is only one Supreme Court case dealing with such abstention since *Thibodaux* and that was in a brief, per curiam opinion. In *Kaiser Steel Corp. v. W. S. Ranch Co.,* Kaiser claimed authority under a state statute to use water located on the ranch company's land.[79] The ranch company claimed that such a state law would violate the state constitution's limits on takings of private property. The Supreme Court summarily held that the district court erred in deciding the case

[77] 360 U.S. at 31 (Stewart, J., concurring). *See also* Field, *supra* note 4, at 1150-1151 (describing difference in uncertainty of state law as the best way of reconciling *Thibodaux* and *Mashuda*). Another possible distinction between *Thibodaux* and *Mashuda* is that in *Mashuda* the district court dismissed the case, whereas in *Thibodaux* the federal district court stayed the federal proceedings.

[78] Quackenbush v. Allstate, 517 U.S. 706, 721 (1996).

[79] 391 U.S. 593 (1968).

and that it should have abstained. The Court explained that "[t]he state law issue which is crucial in this case is one of vital concern in the arid State of New Mexico, where water is one of the most valuable natural resources."[80] Because the issue is a "truly novel one. . . [s]ound judicial administration requires" abstention.[81] Justices Brennan, Douglas, and Marshall concurred, emphasizing the "special circumstances" because of the state's great interest in the allocation of water resources.[82]

Lower courts are substantially divided over when abstention is appropriate in diversity cases. For example, one Fifth Circuit decision indicated that abstention should be used whenever a diversity case presents important, unsettled questions of state law.[83] On the other hand, other Circuits held that abstention in diversity cases is reserved for extraordinary situations where the uncertain state law issues "are considerably complex and. . . their incorrect resolution will threaten important state policies."[84]

As with *Pullman* abstention, many commentators are sharply critical of the *Thibodaux* decision and urge the elimination of abstention in diversity cases. Critics contend that as long as diversity jurisdiction continues to exist, federal courts must decide such cases that are properly before them. The argument is that abstention is inconsistent with the very rationale behind diversity jurisdiction: the importance of providing a neutral federal forum when litigants are from different states.[85] Other critics argue that the criteria for *Thibodaux* abstention should be more clearly stated and the occasions for its occurrence should be limited.[86] Other scholars take a very different approach and argue that abstention in diversity cases should be much more common when there is unclear state law, as long as the state has a certification procedure that would allow for relatively expeditious state court clarification of its law.[87]

[80] *Id.* at 594.

[81] *Id.*

[82] *Id.* at 595 (Brennan, J., concurring).

[83] *See, e.g.,* United Servs. Life Ins. Co. v. Delaney, 328 F.2d 483 (5th Cir.), *cert. denied,* 377 U.S. 935 (1964). The *Delaney* decision has been substantially criticized; *see* Burton C. Agata, *Delaney,* Diversity, and Delay: Abstention or Abdication, 4 Hous. L. Rev. 422 (1966); William C. Bednar, Comment, Abstention Under *Delaney:* A Current Appraisal, 49 Tex. L. Rev. 247 (1971). Subsequent Fifth Circuit decisions seem less willing to allow abstention; *see* Sayers v. Forsyth Bldg. Corp., 417 F.2d 65, 72 (5th Cir. 1969).

[84] *See, e.g.,* Peridot Tree Inc. v. City of Sacramento, 94 F.4th 416 (9th Cir. 2024).

[85] Charles L. Gowen & William H. Izlar, Federal Court Abstention in Diversity of Citizenship Litigation, 43 Tex. L. Rev. 194, 194 (1964).

[86] *See* Kelly D. Hickman, Note, Federal Court Abstention in Diversity of Citizenship Cases, 62 S. Cal. L. Rev. 1237 (1989) (arguing that federal courts should not abstain unless the highest state court never has dealt with the issue, the lower state courts provide no discernible trend as to how the law would be interpreted in the state court, the legislative history of the statute in question does not answer the issue with any degree of uncertainty, and there is a state interest as important to state sovereignty as eminent domain).

[87] *See* Deborah J. Challener, Distinguishing Certification from Abstention in Diversity Cases: Postponement Versus Abdication of the Duty to Exercise Jurisdiction, 38 Rutgers L.J. 847 (2007).

§12.2.3 *Abstention to Defer to Complex State Administrative Procedures:* Burford *Abstention*

Burford v. Sun Oil Co.

A third situation in which abstention is appropriate because of unclear state law is when there is a need to defer to complex state administrative procedures. The landmark case, from which this branch of the abstention doctrine takes its name, is *Burford v. Sun Oil Co.*[88] The Sun Oil Company initiated a lawsuit in federal court challenging the validity of a Texas Railroad Commission order granting Burford a permit to drill four oil wells on a plot of land in an East Texas oil field. The plaintiff sought to enjoin the commission's order as a denial of due process and as a violation of state law.

The Supreme Court, in an opinion by Justice Black, held that the federal district court should have dismissed the case. The Court emphasized the existence of complex state administrative machinery and of the need for centralized decision-making in allocating oil drilling rights. The Court explained that a single agency was best equipped to deal with the complicated issues "[s]ince oil moves through the entire field, one operator can not only draw the oil from under his own surface area but can also, if he is advantageously located, drain oil from the most distant parts of the reservoir."[89] Accordingly, the Court felt that each oil and gas field must be regulated as a unit, by one entity. Furthermore, the Court noted that Texas had created a comprehensive system of administrative and judicial review, consolidating all cases in one state district court and providing appellate review within the state judicial system.[90] Abstention was particularly justified in light of the importance of gas and oil to Texas's economy and the general significance of "conserving gas and oil, two of our most important national resources."[91]

The *Burford* Court held that the federal district court should have completely dismissed the case. This is unlike *Pullman* or *Thibodaux* abstention, where the Court sends the case to state court for a clarification of state law issues but permits the case to return to federal court if necessary. Thus, abstention because of complex state administrative procedures does not merely "postpone" federal court jurisdiction; it completely displaces federal court review.[92]

It should be emphasized that the Court in *Burford* justified abstention because of the presence of both unclear questions of state law and of a need for centralized administration. Justice Black's opinion repeatedly spoke of the uncertainties in

[88] 319 U.S. 315 (1943). For a review of *Burford* abstention, *see* Gordon Young, Federal Court Abstention and State Administrative Law from *Burford* to *Ankenbrandt*: Fifty Years of Judicial Federalism Under Burford v. Sun Oil Co. and Kindred Doctrines, 42 DePaul L. Rev. 859 (1993).

[89] 319 U.S. at 319.

[90] *Id.* at 320, 324.

[91] *Id.* at 320.

[92] Field, *supra* note 4, at 1153.

interpreting and applying the state statute and the desirability of allowing the state courts to perform this task because of their greater expertise in the area.[93]

Alabama Public Service Commission v. Southern Railway

Burford provides little guidance as to how uncertain the state law must be or what kinds of state procedures and interests would justify such abstention. An important case expanding the scope of *Burford* abstention is *Alabama Public Service Commission v. Southern Railway*.[94] The railway applied to discontinue certain local train service, but the state commission denied the request. Although procedures existed for state court review of the administrative decision, the railway filed suit in federal court. The railway claimed that it was an unconstitutional deprivation of property without due process to force it to operate a railroad at a financial loss.

The Court found that abstention was appropriate, but emphasized that it was not applying *Pullman* abstention—this was not a situation in which the state court's clarification of its law might avoid a federal court ruling on a constitutional issue. Also, unlike *Pullman* abstention situations in which federal review is stayed, the federal district court in the *Alabama Public Service Commission* case was instructed to dismiss the case.

The Court justified abstention because of the presence of an important local interest and the existence of a state regulatory structure.[95] The Court specifically analogized to *Burford* in justifying abstention.[96] However, the case seems to be a substantial expansion of the *Burford* abstention principle. In *Burford*, the Court pointed to the need for unified allocation of oil drilling rights and the existence of a comprehensive state administrative system. There was no similar requirement for solitary decision-making and no detailed regulatory structure in the *Alabama Public Service Commission* case, yet the Court concluded that abstention was appropriate because "[a]s adequate state court review of an administrative order based upon predominantly local factors is available. . . , intervention of a federal court is not necessary for the protection of federal rights."[97]

This language conceivably could be used to justify abstention whenever there is a federal constitutional challenge to a state administrative decision that also could be reviewed in state court. For instance, when local school boards are sued for impermissible race discrimination in assigning pupils, it could be argued under

[93] 319 U.S. at 327-328. Professor Field argues that the presence of unclear state law is not a prerequisite for *Burford* abstention. Her view is that the existence of complex state administrative proceedings requiring centralized decision-making is sufficient to justify abstention. Field, *supra* note 4, at 1153-1154. However, the Supreme Court has not yet approved of *Burford* abstention in the absence of unclear law. Thus, at this point it must be regarded as an unresolved question whether *Burford* abstention might be appropriate when there is settled state law. The Fifth Circuit, though, has found *Burford* abstention appropriate based on the existence of complex administrative proceedings. In the Matter of Entrust Energy, Inc., 101 F.4th 368 (5th Cir. 2024).

[94] 341 U.S. 341 (1951).

[95] *Id.* at 347-348.

[96] *Id.* at 350.

[97] *Id.* at 349.

Alabama Public Service Commission that federal court review is unavailable because of the local interest in schools and the opportunity for review in state court. Such an exhaustion requirement would extinguish federal court review in a large number of cases and conflict with 42 U.S.C. §1983, which imposes no requirement for exhausting state remedies before the initiation of federal court proceedings.[98]

The Supreme Court has given no indication that it intends such a broad reading of *Alabama Public Service Commission.* To the contrary, in four major cases that subsequently came before the Supreme Court, *Burford* abstention was refused. In *McNeese v. Board of Education,* the Court held that Black students could bring a federal court suit challenging a segregated school system without first invoking the state's administrative procedures.[99] The Court specifically rejected a request to apply *Burford* abstention.

Similarly, in *Zablocki v. Redhail,* the Court refused to require the lower court to abstain.[100] *Zablocki* involved a Wisconsin state statute that prevented individuals from obtaining a marriage license unless they were current in their child support payments for children not in their custody. The Court explicitly distinguished *Burford*: "Unlike *Burford*. . . this case does not involve complex issues of state law, resolution of which would be disruptive of state efforts to establish coherent policy with respect to a matter of substantial public concern."[101] The Court flatly rejected abstention, declaring that "there is, of course, no doctrine requiring abstention merely because resolution of a federal question may result in the overturning of a state policy."[102]

Must Be Danger of Disrupting Uniform State Procedures

In *New Orleans Public Service, Inc. v. Council of City of New Orleans (NOPSI),* the Court emphasized that *Burford* abstention is appropriate only where there is a danger that federal court review would "disrupt the State's attempt to ensure uniformity in the treatment of an essentially local problem."[103] After the Federal Energy Regulatory Commission allocated costs for the Grand Gulf Reactor to several utility companies, including NOPSI, the utility company attempted to obtain a rate increase to cover the additional costs. The New Orleans City Council, the rate-making body, refused to allow rate increases to provide full reimbursement because it concluded that NOPSI had been negligent in its managerial decisions concerning the potential liability for the Grand Gulf Reactor.

The district court abstained on both *Burford* and *Younger* abstention grounds. The Supreme Court reversed on both holdings. As to *Burford* abstention, the Court stated that the existence of complex state administrative procedures did not necessitate abstention. Justice Scalia, writing for the majority, explained, "While *Burford*

[98] *See* §8.4, *supra.*
[99] 373 U.S. 668 (1963).
[100] 434 U.S. 374 (1978).
[101] *Id.* at 379 n.5 (citation omitted).
[102] *Id.*
[103] 491 U.S. 350, 364 (1989).

is concerned with protecting complex state administrative processes from undue federal interference, it does not require abstention where there is a potential for conflict with state regulatory law or policy."[104] Because electricity is not primarily bought and sold within a predominantly local market, federal court review of the city council's decision "will not disrupt state resolution of distinctively local regulatory facts or policies."[105]

NOPSI is a welcome clarification of *Burford* abstention. *NOPSI* makes clear that the mere existence of state administrative procedures, or even a complex state administrative apparatus, does not necessarily warrant abstention. *Burford* abstention requires that the administrative system have a primary purpose of achieving uniformity within a state and that there be the danger that judicial review would disrupt the proceedings and undermine the desired uniformity.

Burford Limited to Suits for Declaratory and Equitable Relief

Quackenbush v. Allstate Insurance Co. made it clear that *Burford* abstention is appropriate not in suits for monetary damages but rather only as to claims for injunctive or declaratory relief.[106] The petitioner, Charles Quackenbush, the California insurance commissioner, sued Allstate Insurance Company seeking money damages for breach of contract and torts. Specifically, Quackenbush was suing as trustee for another insurance company, Mission Insurance Company, alleging that Allstate had breached reinsurance agreements. Although the case had been filed in state court, Allstate removed the matter to federal court based on diversity jurisdiction.

The federal district court remanded the case to state court based on *Burford* abstention, concluding that "California has an overriding interest in regulating insurance insolvencies and liquidations in a uniform and orderly manner" and that "this important state interest could be undermined by inconsistent rulings from the federal and state courts."[107] The U.S. Supreme Court unanimously reversed. The Court concluded that "the power to dismiss under the *Burford* doctrine, as with other abstention doctrines, derives from the discretion historically enjoyed by courts of equity."[108] Thus, abstention was inappropriate in the suit for money damages. The Court again emphasized that *Burford* abstention is appropriate only in rare circumstances. Justice O'Connor, writing for the Court, said that the "balance only rarely favors abstention, and the power to dismiss recognized in *Burford* represents an extraordinary and narrow exception to the duty of the District Court to adjudicate a controversy properly before it."[109]

[104] *Id.* at 362.

[105] *Id.* at 364.

[106] Quackenbush v. Allstate Insurance Co., 517 U.S. 706 (1996). For an analysis of this decision, *see* Lewis Yelin, *Burford* Abstention in Actions for Damages, 99 Colum. L. Rev. 1871 (1999).

[107] 517 U.S. at 710.

[108] *Id.* at 727-728.

[109] *Id.* (citations omitted).

Uncertainty in Lower Courts

Despite these clarifications from the Supreme Court concerning the appropriateness of *Burford* abstention, lower courts continue to disagree as to when this type of abstention is appropriate. On the one hand, some lower courts have refused *Burford* abstention except in extraordinary circumstances where federal court review would disrupt a coordinated state regulatory structure.[110] On the other hand, some lower courts have allowed *Burford* abstention as long as a matter is deemed to be of local interest, even where there is no showing that the federal court would disrupt state administrative proceedings.[111]

Professor Martin Redish has offered a straightforward proposal for deciding when *Burford* abstention is appropriate. Professor Redish suggests that "[w]here no significant question of federal law is involved, then, *Burford* abstention appears easily justified."[112] However, if there is a substantial federal question, *Burford* abstention should be invoked only if: "(1) the subject of regulation is of significant and special concern to the state; (2) the state regulatory scheme is, in fact, detailed and complex; and (3) the federal issue cannot be resolved without requiring the federal court to immerse itself in the technicalities of the state scheme."[113] This formula provides for abstention in rare cases, such as *Burford*, where federal court review would disrupt coordinated administration by a state regulatory agency, but still preserves federal court jurisdiction in most instances.

[110] *See, e.g.,* Neufeld v. City of Baltimore, 964 F.2d 347 (4th Cir.), *cert. denied,* 517 U.S. 1222 (1992) (challenge to city ordinance regulating television antennas did not warrant *Burford* abstention because the case did not involve difficult questions of state law involving peculiarly local concerns and exercising federal jurisdiction would not disrupt an important state policy); *compare* Pomponio v. Fauquier City Board of Supervisors, 21 F.3d 1319 (4th Cir. 1994) ("In cases in which plaintiffs' federal claims stem solely from construction of state or local land use or zoning law, not involving the constitutional validity of the same and absence exceptional circumstances not present here, the district courts should abstain under the *Burford* doctrine to avoid interference with the State's or locality's land use policy.").

[111] *See, e.g.,* Bethphage Lutheran Serv., Inc. v. Weicker, 965 F.2d 1239 (2d Cir. 1992) (approving *Burford* abstention because state law provided an adequate remedy to enable provider to challenge the state action in state courts); Lac D'Amiante du Quebec, Ltee. v. American Home Assurance Co., 864 F.2d 1033 (3d Cir. 1988) (approving *Burford* abstention based on a desire to avoid disrupting state regulatory proceedings). *See generally* Charles S. Treat, Comment, Abstention by Federal Courts in Suits Challenging State Administrative Decisions: The Scope of the *Burford* Doctrine, 46 U. Chi. L. Rev. 971, 971, 980-988 (1979) (scope of *Burford* remains "unclear"; divergence among lower court cases).

[112] Martin H. Redish, Federal Jurisdiction: Tensions in the Allocation of Judicial Power 246 (1980).

[113] *Id. See also* Hamlin Group v. Power Auth. State of N.Y., 703 F. Supp. 305, 307-310 (S.D.N.Y. 1989), *aff'd,* 923 F.2d 844 (2d Cir. 1990) (articulating criteria for when *Burford* abstention is appropriate). *See also* Charles R. Wise & Robert K. Christensen, Sorting Out Federal and State Judicial Roles in State Institutional Reform: Abstention's Potential Role, 29 Fordham Urb. L.J. 387 (2001) (arguing that in considering whether to grant *Burford* abstention, courts should analyze three functions: judicial capacity, federalism, and administrative responsibility).

§12.3 THE PROCEDURES WHEN THERE IS FEDERAL COURT ABSTENTION

Procedures Depend on Type of Abstention

The procedures followed vary somewhat depending on what type of abstention is involved. For example, *Burford* abstention—abstention out of deference to centralized state administrative proceedings—requires the federal court to dismiss the case. The effect of *Burford* abstention is thus not to postpone federal court review but to prevent it entirely.[1] Even though federal jurisdiction exists and perhaps constitutional issues are presented (as they were in *Burford*), the case is permanently consigned to the state court system.[2] Thus, *Burford* abstention most acutely raises the policy question discussed at the outset of this chapter: Should federal courts refuse jurisdiction that was constitutionally vested in them by Congress?

By contrast, in *Pullman* abstention situations—where federal courts abstain because state court clarification of uncertain state law might avoid a federal constitutional ruling—the federal court retains jurisdiction over the case. The federal court stays its proceedings and sends the case to state court for a ruling on the state law question. In most states, certification statutes exist that the federal court can use to ask for a state court ruling on a particular issue. If the state court decision does not resolve the matter, the parties can return to federal court for a ruling on the constitutional issue.

England v. Louisiana State Board of Medical Examiners

The central case outlining the procedure to be followed in *Pullman* abstention situations is *England v. Louisiana State Board of Medical Examiners*.[3] In *England*, a group of chiropractors brought a challenge to the Louisiana Medical Practices Act, which limited their practice. The federal court abstained because it was unclear under state law whether the act applied to chiropractors. The plaintiffs submitted their entire case, including all constitutional claims, to the state court for decision. They lost in the trial and appeals courts, and the Louisiana Supreme Court denied review. The plaintiffs then sought to return to federal court. The district court, however, dismissed the case because all issues had been resolved in the state courts.

§12.3 [1] However, the Sixth Circuit ruled that *Burford* does not provide a basis for surrendering, as opposed to potentially suspending, jurisdiction. Gray v. Bush, 628 F.3d 779 (6th Cir. 2010); Superior Beverage Co., Inc. v. Shiefflin & Co., 488 F.3d 910, 913-914 (6th Cir. 2006) (in the context of a complaint seeking both equitable and money relief, "a federal court's discretion to abstain from exercising jurisdiction does not extend so far as to permit a court to dismiss or remand, as opposed to stay, an action at law").

[2] An unresolved question is whether *Burford* abstention is jurisdictional or whether it is waived if it is not raised at the trial court level. *See* Grimes v. Crown Life Ins. Co., 857 F.2d 699 (10th Cir. 1988), *cert. denied*, 489 U.S. 1096 (1989) (*Burford* abstention is not waived if it is not raised at the trial court level).

[3] 375 U.S. 411 (1964).

The Supreme Court reversed. The Court began with the premise that there are "fundamental objections to any conclusion that a litigant who has properly invoked the jurisdiction of a Federal District Court. . . can be compelled, without his consent and through no fault of his own, to accept instead a state court's determination of those claims."[4] The Court emphasized that abstention merely postpones federal court rulings on constitutional issues; it does not foreclose federal jurisdiction.[5]

Accordingly, the Court held that when federal courts abstain, the parties need try only the state law issues in state court and they may return to federal district court to litigate the federal constitutional issues. The state court's decision, in other words, will not have res judicata effect precluding the splitting of claims between the state and federal courts. The Supreme Court in *England* spoke of the need for federal court availability to decide constitutional issues.[6] The Court said that appellate review by the Supreme Court of the state court's decision did not offer enough of a chance of a federal court ruling on the constitutional question. Furthermore, the Court found federal court fact-finding on constitutional issues to be an important reason for allowing parties back into federal court. Thus, the *England* Court implicitly rejected the assumption that federal and state courts are identical when it comes to deciding constitutional claims. Rather, it recognized the importance of having federal courts available to resolve constitutional issues.

England is clear that trying the state law issues in state court following federal court abstention will not preclude later litigation of the federal issues in federal court. In other words, the traditional res judicata rule against splitting claims is inapplicable. However, it is uncertain as to whether collateral estoppel would bind the federal court to any fact-finding conduct by the state court. Although *England* indicated the importance of federal court fact-finding on constitutional issues, subsequent decisions (although not involving abstention)—such as *Allen v. McCurry*—apply collateral estoppel in constitutional cases and prevent relitigation of facts.[7]

The Court in *England* explained the procedures to be followed when *Pullman* abstention occurs. The parties can choose to litigate all of their issues, including federal constitutional claims, in state court. In that event, the party relinquishes the right to return to federal court.[8] However, a party can expressly reserve the right to return to federal court for a determination, if necessary, of the federal law questions.[9] Furthermore, the Court held that "[s]uch an explicit reservation is

[4] *Id.* at 415.

[5] *Id.* at 415-416, *quoting* Harrison v. NAACP, 360 U.S. 167, 177 (1969).

[6] 375 U.S. at 417.

[7] *Id.* at 416-417 (importance of federal fact-finding). *But see* Allen v. McCurry, 449 U.S. 90 (1980) (federal courts in deciding §1983 cases must accord collateral estoppel to state court fact-finding). Allen v. McCurry is discussed in detail in §8.10, *supra*.

[8] 375 U.S. at 419.

[9] Los Altos El Granada Investors v. City of Capitola, 583 F.3d 674 (9th Cir. 2009) (a California court's striking of a mobile home park owner's *England* reservation in its federal takings claims as irrelevant does not have any preclusive effect on the claims owner could assert before a federal court, even though federal courts are required to give full faith and credit to the California court's decision to strike the reservation); *but see* Geiger v. Foley Hoag LLP Retirement Plan, 521 F.3d 60 (1st Cir.

not indispensable; the litigant is in no event to be denied his return to the District Court unless it clearly appears that he voluntarily. . . fully litigated his federal claims in the state courts. When the reservation has been made, however, his right to return will in all events be preserved."[10]

Subsequently, the Court discussed the *England* reservation procedure and considered its application in takings cases. In *San Remo Hotel, L.P. v. City & County of San Francisco,* the Court found that the *England* reservation did not allow a party challenging a taking to relitigate a matter in federal court that had been fully litigated in state court.[11] Under *Williamson County Regional Planning Commission v. Hamilton Bank of Johnson City,* a takings claim was not ripe for review in federal court until it has been litigated in state court; there is no taking by the state until the state courts have ruled in favor of the government.[12] If the challenger bringing a takings claim does not exhaust state remedies, then the case is barred from federal court. But if the challenger litigates these claims in state court, even based on abstention from federal court, *San Remo Hotel* holds that the state court litigation is preclusive of federal law.

But in *Knick v. Township of Scott, Pennsylvania,* in 2019, the Court explicitly overruled *Williamson County.*[13] Chief Justice Roberts, writing for the Court, pointed to the problems posed by *San Remo Hotel*: "The takings plaintiff thus finds himself in a Catch-22: He cannot go to federal court without going to state court first; but if he goes to state court and loses, his claim will be barred in federal court. The federal claim dies aborning. The *San Remo* preclusion trap should tip us off that the state-litigation requirement rests on a mistaken view of the Fifth Amendment."[14] *Knick* holds that there is no need to exhaust administrative or judicial remedies before bringing a takings claim to federal court, eliminating the need to worry about how *England* would apply while exhausting state procedures.

Problems with *England* Procedure

The implementation of the *England* procedure poses several problems. First, it often is difficult to determine whether a party has waived the right to return to federal court. Ideally, litigants who wish to preserve their access to the federal judiciary should say so expressly on the record in the state court. Such an explicit reservation would always allow the litigants to return to federal court at the conclusion of the state court proceedings. However, when such express reservations are not made, the federal court often must struggle to determine the intent of the parties based on the issues raised and litigated in the state court.

2008) (the *England* reservation does not prevent the application of preclusion where the state court has in fact resolved the issues that plaintiff seeks to (re)litigate in the stayed federal action).

[10] 375 U.S. at 421-422.

[11] 545 U.S. 323 (2005).

[12] 473 U.S. 172 (1985).

[13] 588 U.S. 180 (2019), discussed in §2.4.3.

[14] *Id.* at 184-185.

Second, a problem arises when state courts refuse to decide the state law questions because of state constitutional provisions that prevent advisory opinions. When federal courts abstain, the case remains on the docket of the federal court and the matter is stayed while it is pending in state court. Some state courts have perceived this as a request for a state advisory opinion because the state court cannot be assured that it is rendering the final judgment in the matter. For example, the Texas Supreme Court ruled that it cannot grant declaratory relief under state law if a federal court retains jurisdiction over the matter.[15]

The Supreme Court responded to this problem by holding that under such circumstances federal courts should dismiss the case without prejudice. In *Harris County Commissioners Court v. Moore*, the Court ruled that abstention was appropriate and outlined the procedures to be followed in states like Texas that refuse to rule if the case remains on the federal court's docket.[16] The Court said, "In order to remove any possible obstacles to state court jurisdiction, we direct the District Court to dismiss the complaint. The dismissal should be without prejudice so that any remaining federal claim may be raised in a federal forum after the Texas courts have been given the opportunity to address the state law questions in this case."[17] One must wonder whether this alternate procedure will really satisfy the state court's concerns. As long as the matter can return to federal court—whether or not it remains on the docket while the case is in state court—the state is not issuing the final decision in the case.[18]

A third problem with the *England* procedure, and undoubtedly the most serious, is the cost and delay it creates. Following abstention, parties must litigate their state law claims in the state trial court, appeal through the state system, possibly face remand back to the state trial court and more appeals, and only then return to federal court to litigate the constitutional question through the federal system. The procedure commonly takes many years and imposes substantially increased costs on the litigants.[19] Without a doubt, many less affluent individuals cannot afford the cost of litigating through two systems and thus are priced out of the federal court system by the abstention procedure. In fact, because defendants usually benefit from delaying the ultimate judgment, abstention is a powerful tool that defendants can use to delay the proceedings and impose additional costs on plaintiffs.[20]

In *Thibodaux* abstention—abstention in diversity cases because of unclear law and an important state interest related to state sovereignty—the case is sent to state court for a clarification of state law, but can return to federal court for a resolution of any remaining issues. As is the practice in *Pullman* abstention, the federal

[15] *See* United Servs. Life Ins. Co. v. Delaney, 396 S.W.2d 855 (Tex. 1965).

[16] 420 U.S. 77 (1975).

[17] *Id.* at 88-89.

[18] It should be noted that Texas has adopted a certification procedure that will eliminate the need, at least in Texas, of using the dismissal procedure. *See* Tex. Const. Ann., art. V, §3-c; Tex. R. App. Proc. 58, 74.

[19] For example, the *England* litigation came to an end only after nine years of proceedings. *Thibodaux* took seven years to be completed.

[20] Martha A. Field, The Abstention Doctrine Today, 125 U. Pa. L. Rev. 590, 602 (1977).

court retains jurisdiction over the case, but stays the proceedings pending a determination of state law. However, in most instances there will be nothing remaining to be decided in the federal court after the state proceedings are completed.[21] In *Pullman* abstention situations, the case can return to federal court for a decision on constitutional issues; but in diversity cases, there are only state law questions to be decided. Hence, in *Thibodaux* abstention situations, the effect of sending the case to state court is likely a permanent end to the federal court proceedings.

Certification as an Alternative to *England* Procedures

The *England* procedure is thus the basic approach in both *Pullman* and *Thibodaux* situations. There is, however, an alternative. Almost all states now have statutes that permit federal courts to "certify" questions to state courts for a decision on a particular question of state law.[22] In all of these states, the United States Supreme Court or a federal court of appeals can certify issues to the state court system. In most of these states, federal district courts also may certify questions. Florida adopted the first state certification statute in 1945, and there has been a steady trend toward enactment of such laws throughout the country.

Certification greatly simplifies the abstention procedure and therefore reduces the delays and increased costs usually accompanying abstention.[23] The Supreme Court has explicitly praised certification on this basis. In one case, the Supreme Court spoke of how certification saves "time, energy, and resources and helps build a cooperative judicial federalism."[24] The Supreme Court has said that "[c]ertification procedure, in contrast [to the *England* procedure] allows a federal court faced with a novel state-law question to put the question directly to the State's highest court, thereby reducing the delay, cutting the cost, and increasing the assurance of gaining an authoritative response."[25]

[21] *See* Charles S. Treat, Comment, Abstention by Federal Courts in Suits Challenging State Administrative Decisions: The Scope of the *Burford* Doctrine, 46 U. Chi. L. Rev. 971, 992-993 n.113 (1979) ("It is unclear just what function is intended to be served by retention of jurisdiction in *Thibodaux* cases. In neither *Thibodaux* nor *Kaiser* was there any federal question to reserve.").

[22] Only two states, Arkansas and North Carolina, do not have a certification procedure. While Missouri has a certification statute, Mo. Rev. Stat. §477.004 (2007), the Missouri Supreme Court has declined to answer certified questions on the ground that the Missouri Constitution does not permit it to do so. *See* Zeman v. V.F. Factory Outlet, Inc., 911 F.2d 107, 109 (8th Cir. 1990). *See* Deborah J. Challener, Distinguishing Certification from Abstention in Diversity Cases: Postponement Versus Abdication of the Duty to Exercise Jurisdiction, 38 Rutgers L.J. 847, 866 n.133 (2007).

[23] Thomas G. Buchanan, Note, *Pullman* Abstention: Reconsidering the Boundaries, 59 Temp. L.Q. 1243, 1261-1262 (1986); Comment, Abstention and Certification in Diversity Suits: Perfection of Means and Confusion of Goals, 73 Yale L.J. 850, 869 (1964).

[24] Lehman Bros. v. Schein, 416 U.S. 386, 391 (1974); *see also* Bellotti v. Baird, 428 U.S. 132, 150-151 (1976). For an example of certification in a constitutional case, *see* Virginia v. American Booksellers Assn., Inc., 484 U.S. 383, 394-396 (1988).

[25] Arizonans for Official English v. Arizona, 520 U.S. at 75-76 (1997). In fact, because of the benefits of certification, Professor Field has suggested that abstention should occur only when states have certification statutes. Field, *supra* note 20, at 605-609.

But these benefits of certification procedures should not be overstated. Although certification is more efficient than the customary *England* abstention procedure, certification certainly adds costs and delays that are not incurred when the case is allowed to remain in federal court. Also, in some states, such as California, only the federal court of appeals can certify a question to the California Supreme Court; district courts cannot use the certification procedure. Some commentators have observed that state courts often fail to decide certified questions,[26] while others conclude that certification fails to live up to its promise of significantly reducing the costs and delays attendant to abstention.[27]

One important issue concerning certification is whether its availability alters the standard for when abstention is appropriate or if it only changes the procedure. There is a strong argument that the existence of certification should not increase the frequency of abstention. Certification modifies the procedure by which a case is returned to state court, but certification does not provide an additional reason for abstention. However, there is a strong indication that the Supreme Court believes that the existence of certification procedures changes both the circumstances where abstention is warranted and the procedures. In *Lehman Brothers v. Schein*, the Supreme Court permitted abstention and certification in a diversity case even though there were no issues related to state sovereignty as *Thibodaux* requires.[28]

Likewise, in a *Pullman* abstention context the Court, in ordering abstention, noted the availability of certification procedures. In *Bellotti v. Baird*, the Supreme Court considered a constitutional challenge to a state law requiring parental consent for abortions.[29] The Court held that abstention and certification were appropriate. The Court stated, "The importance of speed in resolution of the instant case is manifest. . . . Although we do not mean to intimate that abstention would be improper in this case were certification not possible, the availability of certification greatly simplifies the analysis."[30]

Likewise, in *Arizonans for Official English v. Arizona*, the Court stressed that certification should be used when there are "novel, unsettled questions" of state law.[31] The Court said that "[t]aking advantage of certification made available by a State may greatly simplify an ultimate adjudication in federal court."[32] The Court thus indicated that federal courts should be more willing to abstain when certification procedures exist. The Court emphasized that "certification does not involve the delays, expense, and procedural complexity that generally attend the abstention decision."[33]

[26] M. Bryan Schneider, But Answer There Came None: The Michigan Supreme Court and the Certified Question of State Law, 41 Wayne L. Rev. 273, 325 (1995).

[27] Bruce M. Selya, Certified Madness: Ask a Silly Question, 29 Suffolk U. L. Rev. 677 (1995). *But see* Judith Kaye & Kenneth Weissman, Interactive Judicial Federalism: Certified Questions in New York, 69 Fordham L. Rev. 373 (2000) (arguing that certifications work well in New York).

[28] 416 U.S. 386 (1974).

[29] 428 U.S. 132 (1976).

[30] *Id.* at 151.

[31] 520 U.S. 43, 78 (1997).

[32] *Id.* at 79.

[33] *Id.*

In *Houston v. Hill,* however, the Supreme Court stated that the availability of certification "is not in itself sufficient to render abstention appropriate."[34] Thus, it is likely the Court would conclude the existence of certification procedures is an important factor to be considered in a court's deciding whether to abstain, but the opportunity for certification does not independently justify abstention. Not surprisingly, given these inconsistent directions, there is inconsistency among the lower courts as to when they prescribe certification as a form of abstention when there is unclear state law.[35]

ALI Proposal

Many alternatives to the *England* and certification procedures have been suggested. The most famous of these was a proposal by the American Law Institute (ALI) for a federal statute to eliminate the *England* procedure and require all issues to be litigated in state court following abstention.[36] The ALI expressed a dislike for the *England* approach whereby cases are "shuttle[d]. . . back and forth from state to federal court,. . . requiring piecemeal adjudication. . . thereby delaying ultimate adjudication on the merits."[37] Thus, as long as adequate state procedures exist, the ALI proposed to eliminate the ability to return to federal district court after abstention. Instead, all issues, including federal constitutional questions, would have to be tried in the state court. Recourse to the federal courts would be limited to possible Supreme Court review of the decision by the highest state court. The ALI concluded, "[T]here remains no justification for a return to the federal court after a state court determination, and as exotic a rule of federal procedure as that defined by. . . *England v. Louisiana State Board of Medical Examiners* will no longer be needed."[38]

The ALI proposed eliminating abstention in cases involving alleged infringement of the right to vote or discrimination on the basis of race, creed, or national origin.[39] Also, it endorsed certification procedures, encouraging their use whenever possible.[40]

The ALI proposal again raises the fundamental question of whether there is parity between state and federal courts. If the two judicial systems are fungible, then little would be lost by sending cases from federal to state court. If, however, it is believed that federal courts might produce better results, then the complete loss of the federal forum would be extremely undesirable. The *England* Court

[34] Houston v. Hill, 482 U.S. 451 (1987).

[35] Molly Thomas-Jensen, Certification After Arizonans for Official English v. Arizona: A Survey of Federal Appellate Courts' Practices, 87 Denv. U. L. Rev. 139 (2009) (surveys the circuits' approaches to certification in *Pullman*-type cases and concludes that the courts are inconsistent and frequently at odds with *Arizonans*).

[36] American Law Institute, Study of the Division of Jurisdiction Between State and Federal Courts 48-51 (1969).

[37] *Id.* at 283.

[38] *Id.* at 286.

[39] *Id.* at 50.

[40] *Id.*

emphasized the importance of fact-finding in federal district courts and of the insufficiency of having a federal forum available only through the possibility of Supreme Court review. These benefits would be lost under the ALI proposal. Although the ALI's recommendations were made more than 50 years ago, in 1969, Congress never has shown an indication that they are likely to be adopted.

Are Abstention Orders Appealable?

A final procedural point concerning abstention involves the appealability of a district court order to abstain or refuse abstention. The Supreme Court has held that a district court's decision to abstain is immediately appealable. In *Quackenbush v. Allstate Insurance Co.*, in a *Burford* abstention context, the Court noted that an "abstention-based stay order was appealable as a 'final-decision' because it put the litigants 'effectively out of court.'"[41] The Court acknowledged that stay orders do not meet the traditional demands of finality, but nonetheless should be immediately appealable.[42]

In *Quackenbush*, the Court relied on earlier decisions holding that for *Colorado River* abstention—abstention because of duplicative state proceedings (discussed in Chapter 14)—a district court's decision to abstain is immediately appealable.[43] These cases also held that the refusal to abstain is not appealable until a final judgment is entered in the case. Therefore, in light of the Court's reliance on these precedents, it is likely that for all of the abstention doctrines, a federal court's decision to abstain is immediately appealable, but its refusal to abstain is not appealable until there is a final judgment.

This seems a sensible approach for all of the abstention doctrines. Allowing appeal of abstention orders risks further delay, but prohibiting appeal might wrongly deny litigants their opportunity to litigate in federal court.

The Court has not articulated a clear standard for appellate review. Lower courts, however, appear to agree that an abuse of discretion standard should be used; that is, a district court's decision concerning abstention will not be overturned unless it is an abuse of discretion.[44]

In the end, few are satisfied with the current abstention procedures. Some suggest eliminating abstention, while others propose abolishing the *England* approach. No matter what the particular modification, it is likely that the Court will be asked to rethink the current abstention procedures, which remain both time consuming and potentially abusive.

[41] Quackenbush v. Allstate Insurance Co., 517 U.S. 706, 713 (1996).

[42] *Id.* at 714.

[43] *See* Gulfstream Aerospace Corp. v. Mayacamas Corp., 485 U.S. 271 (1988) (denial of a motion to abstain on *Colorado River* grounds not immediately appealable); Moses H. Cone Memorial Hosp. v. Mercury Constr. Corp., 460 U.S. 1 (1983) (granting of a motion to abstain on *Colorado River* grounds is immediately appealable); *see also* discussion in §14.4, *infra.*

[44] *See, e.g.*, Cedar Shake and Shingle Bureau v. City of Los Angeles, 997 F.2d 620 (9th Cir. 1993); Kollsman v. City of Los Angeles, 737 F.2d 830, 833 (9th Cir. 1984), *cert. denied*, 469 U.S. 1211 (1985) (abuse of discretion standard used); *but see* Moe v. Dinkins, 635 F.2d 1045, 1048 n.7 (2d Cir. 1980), *cert. denied*, 459 U.S. 827 (1982).

CHAPTER 13

Federal Court Abstention to Avoid Review of State Court Judgments or Interference with Pending State Proceedings

§13.1 INTRODUCTION

This chapter considers two other judicially created abstention doctrines. The *Rooker-Feldman* doctrine says that federal district courts cannot review state court decisions.[1] Except for habeas corpus, discussed in Chapter 15, the only vehicle for federal court review of state court decisions is via United States Supreme Court review.

The other doctrine is a judicially created principle that federal courts cannot enjoin pending state court proceedings. In 1971, in *Younger v. Harris*, the Supreme Court held that federal courts may not enjoin pending state court criminal proceedings.[2] The Court expressly declared that its decision was not based on the Anti-Injunction Act (discussed in Chapter 11). Rather, the Court fashioned a separate abstention doctrine preventing federal courts from interfering with pending state criminal prosecutions, even if there is an allegation of a constitutional violation and even though all jurisdictional and justiciability requirements are met.

Since 1971, the Court has made it clear that *Younger* abstention is not a narrow doctrine confined to criminal matters. Quite the contrary, the Court has applied the *Younger* principle to prevent federal courts from interfering with state civil and even state administrative proceedings.[3] In fact, the Supreme Court has suggested that the rationale of *Younger* might be applied to prevent the federal courts from interfering with the actions of state and local executive agencies, such as police departments.[4]

However, in *Sprint Communications, Inc. v. Jacobs*, the Court was explicit that *Younger* abstention is limited to three circumstances: preventing federal intrusion into ongoing state criminal prosecutions, into state-initiated civil enforcement proceedings, and into civil proceedings that involve the ability of courts

§13.1 [1] Rooker v. Fidelity Trust Co., 263 U.S. 413 (1923); District of Columbia Court of Appeals v. Feldman, 460 U.S. 462 (1983).

[2] 401 U.S. 37 (1971). Also, as John Harland Giammatteo explained, "In the past ten years, lower federal courts have quietly but regularly abstained from hearing federal claims challenging state court procedures, citing concerns of comity and federalism." He argues that these decisions "exemplify" the "new comity abstention." John Harland Giammatteo, The New Comity Abstention, 111 Cal. L. Rev. 1705, 1705 (2023). He writes: "This new form of abstention requires federal courts to abstain from hearing litigation challenging state court procedures or granting remedies that would affect state court proceedings. According to these circuits, abstention is required in these cases because of comity, i.e., an equal respect for state institutions, and 'Our Federalism,' which requires properly balancing state and federal institutions and interests in a federal system. However, even as they invoke the words of Younger v. Harris, these circuits generally acknowledge that their opinions are not controlled by Younger." *Id.* at 1708.

[3] *See* discussion in §13.4.3, *infra. See, e.g.,* Pennzoil Co. v. Texaco, Inc., 481 U.S. 1 (1987) (federal courts may not enjoin pending state court civil proceedings between private parties); Ohio Civil Rights Comm'n v. Dayton Christian Schools, Inc., 477 U.S. 619 (1986) (federal courts may not enjoin pending state administrative proceedings involving important state interests).

[4] *See* discussion in §13.4.5, *infra. See, e.g.,* Rizzo v. Goode, 423 U.S. 362 (1976) (federalism considerations limit federal court review of police department practices).

to perform their judicial functions.[5] The Court said that these three categories "define *Younger*'s scope."[6]

Section 13.2 focuses on the *Rooker-Feldman* doctrine and the preclusion of federal district court review of state court judgments. The remainder of the chapter focuses on the *Younger* abstention doctrine: the judicially created bar to federal court interference with ongoing state proceedings. Section 13.3 examines the seminal case of *Younger v. Harris*. The extension of *Younger* beyond a prohibition against injunctions of criminal proceedings is described in §13.4. Finally, §13.5 discusses the exceptions to the *Younger* doctrine, situations where federal courts may issue injunctions or declaratory judgments notwithstanding the existence of pending state court proceedings.

Interestingly, the *Rooker-Feldman* doctrine has not generated a great deal of controversy, whereas, as described in detail in this chapter, *Younger* abstention is quite controversial and has provoked a heated debate among scholars as to its desirability.[7] The debate over *Younger* abstention centers on the two themes, separation of powers and federalism, which are common to almost all disagreements over federal court jurisdiction. Critics of *Younger* argue that the Court usurped legislative prerogatives in creating a new abstention doctrine.[8] Especially in light of the Anti-Injunction Act, which already prohibits federal court injunctions of state proceedings, some argue that the Court should not have created a new, independent barrier to federal court jurisdiction.

The defenders of *Younger* abstention see it as the Court's exercising the traditional powers possessed by a court of equity to refuse to issue injunctions. Also, it is contended that the *Younger* abstention doctrine, like the abstention principles discussed in the previous chapter, reflects the Court's power to fashion common law rules for the federal courts.[9] The *Younger* doctrine is defended on federalism grounds as providing proper deference and respect to state judiciaries.

Critics of *Younger* abstention respond that the effect of this doctrine is to leave crucial constitutional law issues in state court, subject only to the relatively remote

[5] 571 U.S. 69, 77 (2013).

[6] *Id.*

[7] For criticism of the *Younger* doctrine, *see, e.g.,* Donald H. Zeigler, Federal Court Reform of State Criminal Justice Systems: A Reassessment of the *Younger* Doctrine from a Modern Perspective, 19 U.C. Davis L. Rev. 31 (1985); Donald H. Zeigler, A Reassessment of the *Younger* Doctrine in Light of the Legislative History of Reconstruction, 1983 Duke L.J. 987; Martin H. Redish, The Doctrine of Younger v. Harris: Deference in Search of a Rationale, 63 Cornell L. Rev. 463 (1978). For a defense of the *Younger* doctrine, *see, e.g.,* Ann Althouse, How to Build a Separate Sphere: Federal Courts and State Power, 100 Harv. L. Rev. 1485, 1488-1489, 1531-1534 (1987); Paul M. Bator, The State Courts and Federal Constitutional Litigation, 22 Wm. & Mary L. Rev. 605, 608-622 (1981). A recent article powerfully argues that *Younger* abstention is inappropriate in cases involving systemic or structural flaws in state and local criminal justice systems, such as suits challenging fines, fees, collection practices, and bail. Fred Smith, Abstention in the Time of Ferguson, 131 Harv. L. Rev. 2283 (2018).

[8] *See, e.g.,* Martin H. Redish, Abstention, Separation of Powers, and the Limits of the Judicial Function, 94 Yale L.J. 71 (1984); *but see* Michael Wells, Why Professor Redish Is Wrong About Abstention, 19 Ga. L. Rev. 1097 (1985); David L. Shapiro, Jurisdiction and Discretion, 60 N.Y.U. L. Rev. 543 (1985).

[9] Wells, *supra* note 8, at 1099-1100.

chance of review by the U.S. Supreme Court. For those who believe that federal courts are superior to state courts in their ability and willingness to protect constitutional rights, *Younger* is based on an incorrect assumption of parity between federal and state courts. Not surprisingly, the *Younger* doctrine was created and expanded by a conservative Court that frequently has proclaimed a belief that there is parity between federal and state courts and often has expressed a need to be guided by federalism concerns in its decision-making.[10]

Thus, the disagreement over the *Younger* doctrine raises familiar themes: When is it appropriate for the Supreme Court to create rules denying federal courts jurisdiction they possess pursuant to Article III and federal statutes? How important is the availability of a federal forum in constitutional adjudication; is there parity between federal and state courts?

§13.2 ABSTENTION TO AVOID FEDERAL COURT REVIEW OF STATE COURT JUDGMENTS: THE *ROOKER-FELDMAN* DOCTRINE

The *Rooker-Feldman* doctrine expressly bars federal district courts from reviewing state court decisions. The doctrine takes its name from two Supreme Court cases, *Rooker v. Fidelity Trust Co.*[1] and *District of Columbia Court of Appeals v. Feldman.*[2] In *Rooker*, a federal court plaintiff sought to have a state court judgment declared "null and void" and the Supreme Court held that federal courts do not have jurisdiction to "entertain a proceeding to reverse or modify" a state court judgment. In *Feldman*, the Court again concluded that a federal district court has "no authority to review the final judgments of a state court in judicial proceedings."[3]

Thus, the *Rooker-Feldman* doctrine provides that "a party losing in state court is barred from seeking what in substance would be appellate review of the state judgment in a United States District Court based on the losing party's claim that the state judgment itself violates the loser's federal rights."[4]

The Supreme Court has stressed that the *Rooker-Feldman* doctrine is limited to preventing federal courts from reviewing completed state court proceedings. In *Exxon Mobil Corp. v. Saudi Basic Industries Corp.*, the Supreme Court held that the doctrine is "confined to cases of the kind from which [it] derived its name: cases

[10] *See* discussion in §1.5, *supra; see, e.g.*, Stone v. Powell, 428 U.S. 465, 493-494 n.35 (1976); Allen v. McCurry, 449 U.S. 90, 96 (1980); *see* James C. Rehnquist, Taking Comity Seriously: How to Neutralize the Abstention Doctrines, 46 Stan. L. Rev. 1049 (1994) (arguing that Supreme Court should be neutral as to choice between federal and state forums and criticizing abstention doctrines that fail this neutrality).

§13.2 [1] 263 U.S. 413, 414, 416 (1923).

[2] 460 U.S. 462 (1983).

[3] 460 U.S. at 482.

[4] Johnson v. De Grandy, 512 U.S. 997, 1005-1006 (1994).

brought by state-court losers complaining of injuries caused by state-court judgments rendered before the district court proceedings commenced and inviting district court review and rejection of these judgments."[5]

The case involved a suit in state court by Saudi Basic Industries against Exxon Mobil subsidiaries seeking a declaratory judgment concerning royalties. Exxon Mobil then filed a suit against Saudi Basic Industries in federal court alleging that the royalties constituted improper overcharging, and Saudi Basic Industries filed counterclaims. Saudi Basic Industries moved to dismiss the federal district court case based on the Foreign Sovereign Immunities Act.[6] The district court denied this motion and Saudi Basic Industries sought interlocutory review in the Third Circuit. While this appeal was pending, the state court ruled in favor of Exxon Mobil's subsidiaries. The Third Circuit then dismissed the case based on the *Rooker-Feldman* doctrine.

The Supreme Court unanimously reversed. The Court, in an opinion by Justice Ginsburg, explained that the *Rooker-Feldman* doctrine was limited to circumstances where the loser in a state court proceeding was seeking to have the federal court overturn that judgment. In other words, *Rooker-Feldman* is limited to situations where the state court judgment has been rendered before the federal proceedings have been commenced. Justice Ginsburg noted that the federal court may have to give preclusive effect to the state court decision, but that is different from the *Rooker-Feldman* doctrine, which denies jurisdiction.

In *Lance v. Dennis*, the Court held that *Rooker-Feldman* applies only when a party from a state court proceeding is seeking to have the federal court overturn the state court's judgment.[7] In *Lance*, a state attorney general successfully sued a secretary of state in state court to have the legislature's redistricting plan overturned. Other plaintiffs then sued in federal court to have the secretary of state's plan reinstated. The federal district court ordered the case dismissed based on the *Rooker-Feldman* doctrine.

The Supreme Court, in a per curiam opinion, reversed. The Court concluded that the *Rooker-Feldman* doctrine "does not bar actions by nonparties to the earlier state court judgment simply because, for purposes of preclusion law, they could be considered in privity with a party to the judgment."[8]

In *Skinner v. Switzer*, the Court held that the *Rooker-Feldman* doctrine did not bar a convicted state prisoner's §1983 action challenging the constitutionality of Texas's postconviction DNA statute.[9] The Court explained that while a state court decision is not reviewable by lower federal courts, a statute or rule governing the decision may still be challenged in a federal action. The Court declared, "If a federal plaintiff 'present[s] [an] independent claim,' it is not an impediment to the exercise of federal jurisdiction that the 'same or a related question' was earlier aired between the parties in state court."[10]

[5] 544 U.S. 280, 284 (2005).
[6] 28 U.S.C. §§1602 et seq.
[7] 546 U.S. 459 (2006).
[8] *Id.* at 466.
[9] 562 U.S. 521 (2011).
[10] *Id.* at 1297.

The Court applied *Skinner v. Switzer* in *Reed v. Goertz* to hold that the statute of limitations for a §1983 suit challenging the denial of testing runs from the end of the state court proceedings.[11] The Court expressly rejected the state's argument that the suit was barred by the *Rooker-Feldman* doctrine. The Court explained: "[E]ven though a 'state-court decision is not reviewable by lower federal courts,' a 'statute or rule governing the decision may be challenged in a federal action.' Here, as in *Skinner*, Reed does 'not challenge the adverse' state-court decisions themselves, but rather 'targets as unconstitutional the Texas statute they authoritatively construed.'"[12]

These cases have made clear that the *Rooker-Feldman* doctrine is limited to preventing a loser in a state court proceeding from seeking review in a federal district court.[13] But the relationship to *Younger* abstention remains important. While proceedings are pending in state court, a party generally cannot seek to enjoin them via a federal court action. After state court proceedings are completed, *Rooker-Feldman* means that a party cannot seek review in a federal district court (except in a criminal case via a writ of habeas corpus).[14]

On the one hand, this rule implements the principle that federal court review of state court rulings is limited to appellate review in the U.S. Supreme Court. There are very limited circumstances in which federal district courts may collaterally review state court decisions, most notably via writs of habeas corpus. Section 1983, however, is not a basis for federal district court review of state court proceedings. On the other hand, it is unclear what the *Rooker-Feldman* doctrine adds to other doctrines, such as the requirement that the federal courts give res judicata effect to state court decisions and that federal courts not interfere with pending state court proceedings.

[11] 598 U.S. 230 (2023).

[12] *Id.* at 235 (citations omitted).

[13] Commentators have noted the effect of these recent decisions in limiting the *Rooker-Feldman* doctrine. *See, e.g.*, Stephen I. Vladeck, The Increasingly "Unflagging Obligation": Federal Jurisdiction After *Saudi Basic* and *Anna Nicole*, 42 Tulsa L. Rev. 553, 566 (2007) (discussing the "twin killing" of *Rooker-Feldman* doctrine as part of a larger trend of expanding federal court jurisdiction and limiting its exceptions); Samuel Bray, *Rooker-Feldman* (1923-2006), 9 Green Bag 2d 317 (2006).

[14] Unresolved issues remain as to the application of the *Rooker-Feldman* doctrine. *See* Dustin E. Buehler, Revisiting *Rooker-Feldman*: Extending the Doctrine to State Court Interlocutory Orders, 36 Fla. St. U. L. Rev. 373 (2009) (following *Exxon Mobil* and *Lance*, the Supreme Court has not addressed whether *Rooker-Feldman* doctrine permits review of state interlocutory orders, and circuits have split on the issue); Allison B. Jones, The *Rooker-Feldman* Doctrine: What Does It Mean to Be Inextricably Intertwined?, 56 Duke L.J. 643, 660 (2006) (without much guidance from the Supreme Court concerning the meaning and application of the "inextricably intertwined" concept, federal courts have formulated their own criteria and rules, resulting in a large body of diverse standards).

§13.3 *YOUNGER V. HARRIS*: ABSTENTION TO AVOID FEDERAL COURT INTERFERENCE WITH PENDING STATE COURT PROCEEDINGS

Pre-*Younger* Precedents

Before *Younger*, there were seemingly conflicting precedents concerning when federal courts could enjoin state court criminal proceedings. Pre-*Younger* precedents prevented federal courts from interfering with ongoing state prosecutions. For example, in *Douglas v. City of Jeannette*, in 1943, the Supreme Court affirmed the federal district court's dismissal of a suit brought by Jehovah's Witnesses to enjoin the threatened enforcement of a city ordinance that prohibited solicitation without a license.[1] Although in a companion case to *Douglas* the Supreme Court declared the ordinance unconstitutional,[2] the Court nonetheless held that an injunction of the state proceedings was inappropriate. In *Douglas*, the Court emphasized traditional principles of equity; specifically, that the existence of adequate alternative procedures for constitutional review of the ordinance made a federal court injunction of state proceedings unnecessary.[3] The Court, in language that was quite similar to that later used in *Younger*, held that "courts of equity in the exercise of their discretionary powers should . . . refus[e] to interfere with or embarrass threatened proceedings in state courts save in those exceptional cases which call for the interposition of a court of equity to prevent irreparable injury which is clear and imminent."[4]

Other pre-*Younger* precedents indicated that federal courts could enjoin unconstitutional state court proceedings. Professor Burton Wechsler remarked that "prior to *Younger* the Supreme Court consistently encouraged the use of lower federal court declaratory and injunctive relief against unconstitutional state criminal laws."[5] *Dombrowski v. Pfister* is the most notable example of a Supreme Court decision approving such an injunction.[6] The plaintiffs in *Dombrowski*, members of a civil rights organization, filed a suit in federal court seeking declaratory and injunctive relief restraining state officials from prosecuting them for alleged violations of the Louisiana Subversive Activities and Communist Control Law. The

§13.3 [1] 319 U.S. 157 (1943). *See also* Stefanelli v. Minard, 342 U.S. 117 (1951); Fenner v. Boykin, 271 U.S. 240 (1926).

[2] Murdock v. Pennsylvania, 319 U.S. 105 (1943).

[3] Douglas v. City of Jeannette, 319 U.S. at 163.

[4] *Id.*

[5] Burton D. Wechsler, Federal Courts, State Criminal Law and the First Amendment, 49 N.Y.U. L. Rev. 740 (1974).

[6] 380 U.S. 479 (1965). For an excellent analysis of this case, *see* Owen M. Fiss, *Dombrowski*, 86 Yale L.J. 1103, 1106-1107 (1977). Perhaps the most famous case in which the Supreme Court held that federal courts may enjoin state court proceedings was Ex parte Young, 209 U.S. 123 (1908), discussed in detail in §7.5, *supra*. However, in *Young*, the Court noted that the federal court could not "interfere in a case where the proceedings were already pending in a state court." *Id.* at 162 (citation omitted).

plaintiffs alleged that the statutes were facially overbroad in violation of the First Amendment and that the statutes were unconstitutionally being used to harass and threaten civil rights activists. The plaintiffs previously had been arrested for allegedly violating the statute, and their offices had been raided and their files and records seized. Although a judge dismissed the charges against them, the plaintiffs were subsequently indicted by a grand jury for the same offenses, and the prosecutors constantly threatened them.

The Supreme Court in *Dombrowski* held that a federal court injunction of state court proceedings was appropriate. In an opinion by Justice Brennan, the Court emphasized the need for federal court action to enjoin the enforcement of overbroad statutes that might chill the exercise of First Amendment rights. The Court stated: "When the statutes also have an overbroad sweep, as is here alleged, the hazard of loss or substantial impairment of those precious rights might be critical. . . . The assumption that defense of a criminal prosecution will generally assure ample vindication of constitutional rights is unfounded in such cases. . . . [F]or the threat of sanctions may deter . . . almost as potently as the actual application of sanctions."[7]

Under *Dombrowski*, at minimum, federal courts had authority to enjoin state court prosecutions under statutes that were unconstitutionally overbroad in violation of the First Amendment. Following *Dombrowski*, hundreds of cases were filed in federal courts seeking injunctions of state court proceedings.[8] Lower courts understandably were divided as to when federal court injunctions were appropriate.[9]

Against this background, the Supreme Court decided six cases on the same day in 1971 that made clear that *Dombrowski* was the exception and the principles of *Douglas* were the rule.[10] The most important of these decisions was *Younger v. Harris*, from which this type of abstention takes its name.

Younger v. Harris

The plaintiff in *Younger v. Harris* was indicted in state court for distributing leaflets alleged to violate the California Criminal Syndicalism Act. The plaintiff sought a federal court injunction against the state criminal prosecution on the grounds that the existence of the act and the prosecution under it violated the First and Fourteenth Amendments. Subsequently, three other persons intervened as plaintiffs claiming that Harris's prosecution inhibited their teaching and their political activities as members of the Progressive Labor Party. A three-judge federal court, relying on *Dombrowski v. Pfister*, held that the Criminal Syndicalism Act was unconstitutionally vague and overbroad and awarded injunctive relief.

[7] 380 U.S. at 486.

[8] *See* Frank L. Maraist, Federal Injunctive Relief Against State Court Proceedings: The Significance of *Dombrowski*, 48 Tex. L. Rev. 535, 606 (1970).

[9] For a review of this case law, *see* Wechsler, *supra* note 5, at 861.

[10] The six cases were Younger v. Harris, 401 U.S. 37 (1971); Boyle v. Landry, 401 U.S. 77 (1971); Samuels v. Mackell, 401 U.S. 66 (1971); Perez v. Ledesma, 401 U.S. 82 (1971); Dyson v. Stein, 401 U.S. 200 (1971); Byrne v. Karalexis, 401 U.S. 216 (1971).

On direct appeal from the three-judge court, the U.S. Supreme Court concluded that the injunction "must be reversed as a violation of the national policy forbidding federal courts to stay or enjoin pending state court proceedings except under special circumstances."[11] Justice Black, writing for the Court, first dismissed the claims of the intervening plaintiffs as not presenting a ripe controversy. Because the intervenors had not been indicted, arrested, or even threatened by a prosecutor, Justice Black concluded that "persons having no fears of state prosecution except those that are imaginary or speculative, are not to be accepted as appropriate plaintiffs in such cases."[12]

Although the Court concluded that Harris presented a live controversy because he was currently being prosecuted in state court, he was nonetheless denied injunctive relief because of considerations of equity and comity. Specifically, Justice Black spoke of "the basic doctrine of equity jurisprudence that courts of equity should not act, and particularly should not act to restrain a criminal prosecution, when the moving party has an adequate remedy at law and will not suffer irreparable injury if denied equitable relief."[13] The federal court plaintiff could have raised his constitutional claims as a defense to the state court criminal prosecution; hence, there was a preexisting remedy that made the injunction unnecessary.

Justice Black then identified a separate, albeit interrelated, consideration: comity. Justice Black stated that "[t]his underlying reason for restraining courts of equity from interfering with criminal prosecutions is reinforced by an even more vital consideration, the notion of 'comity,' that is, a proper respect for state functions."[14] Justice Black explained that this idea could best be captured in the phrase "Our Federalism"—a belief that "the National Government will fare best if the states and their institutions are left free to perform their separate functions in their separate ways."[15]

The Court spent a good deal of time distinguishing *Dombrowski.* In the *Younger* Court's view, *Dombrowski* represented a limited exception to the general rule against injunctions. State officials subjected the federal court plaintiffs in *Dombrowski* to repeated bad-faith prosecutions that did not offer them a chance to raise their constitutional challenges in state court. The *Younger* Court expressly rejected the assertion that the presence of First Amendment issues is sufficient to modify the general rule against federal courts enjoining state courts. Justice Black stated, "It is undoubtedly true . . . that [a] criminal prosecution under a statute regulating expression may inhibit the full exercise of First Amendment freedoms. But this sort of chilling effect . . . should not by itself justify federal intervention."[16]

[11] Younger v. Harris, 401 U.S. at 41.

[12] *Id.* at 42.

[13] *Id.* at 43-44.

[14] *Id.* at 44.

[15] *Id.*

[16] *Id.* at 50 (citation omitted). Also, it must be noted that *Dombrowski* involved actions against civil rights protesters at the height of the civil rights movement of the 1960s, when the Supreme Court was especially sensitive to protecting civil rights.

Younger thus announced a firm bar to federal courts enjoining *pending* state court criminal prosecutions.[17] The application of *Younger* to prevent declaratory judgments when there are pending criminal proceedings and its extension to civil and even administrative proceedings are discussed in §13.4. The relatively limited exceptions to the *Younger* doctrine are discussed in §13.5.

Relationship to the Anti-Injunction Act

The *Younger* Court explicitly stated that its decision was based on considerations of equity and comity and not on the Anti-Injunction Act.[18] This raises important questions about the relationship between the *Younger* doctrine and the Anti-Injunction Act, and particularly about how to reconcile *Younger* with the Court's decision a year later in *Mitchum v. Foster.*[19] The Anti-Injunction Act prohibits federal courts from enjoining state court proceedings unless one of three specific exceptions is fulfilled. One exception is if injunctions are "expressly authorized by an Act of Congress." In *Mitchum,* the Court held that 42 U.S.C. §1983 was an express authorization for injunctions, such that federal courts could enjoin state courts pursuant to a §1983 suit. The Court in *Mitchum* emphasized that "[t]he very purpose of §1983 was to interpose the federal courts between the States and the people, as guardians of the people's federal rights—to protect the people from unconstitutional action under color of state law."[20]

Although the litigation in *Younger* was brought under §1983, the Court refused to allow the federal courts to enjoin the state court proceedings. Thus, *Younger* abstention is best understood as creating a separate and independent barrier to federal court injunctions. That is, for a plaintiff to obtain an injunction where the *Younger* doctrine applies, the case must fit within *both* an exception to the Anti-Injunction Act *and* an exception to the *Younger* principle. Although suits under §1983 constitute an exception to the Anti-Injunction Act, they are not automatically an exception to *Younger* abstention.

Therefore, *Younger* and *Mitchum* are not technically inconsistent; they deal with differing barriers to injunctions. However, on a policy level the cases are harder to reconcile. *Mitchum* is based on the express premise that it is the role of the federal courts to protect people from state and local government violations of constitutional rights. *Mitchum* declares that the Congress that adopted §1983 distrusted state courts and hence federal courts may enjoin unconstitutional state court proceedings. In contrast, *Younger* is based on the view that federal courts

[17] *See, e.g.,* Ankenbrandt v. Richards, 504 U.S. 689, 705 (1992) ("Absent any *pending* proceeding in state tribunals, therefore, application by the lower courts of *Younger* abstention was clearly erroneous.") (emphasis in original).

[18] 401 U.S. at 54. Justice Black stated, "Because our holding rests on the absence of the factors necessary under equitable principles to justify federal intervention, we have no occasion to consider whether 28 U.S.C. §2283 . . . would in and of itself be controlling under the circumstances of this case." The Anti-Injunction Act, 28 U.S.C. §2283, is discussed in §11.2, *supra.*

[19] 407 U.S. 225 (1972).

[20] *Id.* at 242.

should not interfere with state courts and that the availability of state court proceedings is sufficient to protect constitutional rights. *Younger* rests firmly on an assumption that state courts are to be trusted to adequately uphold civil rights and civil liberties—an assumption rejected in *Mitchum.*

Is *Younger* Abstention Constitutional or Prudential?

The interplay between *Younger* and *Mitchum* raises another important question: Is *Younger* abstention federal common law that can be eliminated by federal statute, or does *Younger* reflect a constitutional limit on the powers of the federal judiciary?[21] If *Younger* is a prudential doctrine, then a specific congressional statute should be able to authorize federal court injunctions of state court proceedings. In fact, the Supreme Court ruled in *Mitchum* that §1983 is an "express authorization" of such injunctions. Accordingly, if *Younger* abstention is federal common law, it should be inapplicable in §1983 litigation, yet *Younger v. Harris* was itself a §1983 suit.

Alternatively, if *Younger* is a constitutional restriction on federal court power, then the Court can be criticized for deciding the case on constitutional grounds before considering possible nonconstitutional approaches. The Court long has emphasized the importance of deciding constitutional questions only as a last resort if nonconstitutional bases are unavailable.[22] In *Younger,* the Court had a possible nonconstitutional rationale for its decision: the Anti-Injunction Act. Because *Mitchum* had not yet been decided, the Court should have considered the statutory grounds for decision, §2283, before it turned to a constitutional rationale.

In fact, the *Younger* doctrine would have been unnecessary had the Court concluded that §2283 requires "*express*" authorizations for injunctions and nothing in §1983 expressly permits federal courts to enjoin state court proceedings. This approach would have permitted Congress to amend §2283 if it decided such injunctions were desirable.[23] Under *Younger,* Congress's authority is uncertain because the Court did not clearly announce a constitutional bar to federal court relief.

Criticism and Defense of the Equity and Comity Rationales

Many commentators have sharply criticized the *Younger* decision and questioned whether considerations of equity and comity justify the Court's conclusions.

[21] *See, e.g.,* Steven G. Calabresi & Gary Lawson, Equity and Hierarchy: Reflections on the *Harris* Execution, 102 Yale L.J. 255, 261-265 (1992) (arguing that *Younger* abstention is an equitable doctrine not required by the Constitution); Calvin R. Massey, Abstention and the Constitutional Limits of the Judicial Power of the United States, 1991 BYU L. Rev. 811 (arguing that abstention doctrines are constitutionally based and not prudential).

[22] *See* Ashwander v. TVA, 297 U.S. 288, 346-348 (1936) (Brandeis, J., concurring); Railroad Comm'n of Texas v. Pullman Co., 312 U.S. 496 (1941). *Pullman,* and its premise that it is desirable to avoid federal constitutional rulings, is discussed in §12.2.1, *supra.*

[23] Martin H. Redish, Abstention, Separation of Powers, and the Limits of the Judicial Function, 94 Yale L.J. 71 (1984) (arguing that *Younger* is a violation of separation of powers).

For example, the traditional principle of equity is that a court should not issue an injunction if an adequate remedy at law exists. In *Younger*, however, the Supreme Court said that a federal court should not issue an injunction if a state court has proceedings available where it can review the constitutionality of the state statute. The usual equity maxim relates to refusing injunctions if money damages are sufficient; it has no direct relevance to one court refusing to hear an issue because another court can do so. In fact, 20 years before *Younger*, in *Alabama Public Service Commission v. Southern Railway*, the Supreme Court declared, "An adequate remedy at law as a bar to equitable relief in the federal courts refers to a remedy on the law side of federal courts. It was never a doctrine of equity that a federal court should exercise its judicial discretion to dismiss a suit merely because a state court could entertain it."[24]

Moreover, critics of the equity rationale question whether the state court remedy should be viewed as adequate. In part, their argument centers on a challenge to the assumption of parity between federal and state courts in deciding constitutional issues.[25] In part, too, the claim is that a statute that is unconstitutionally overbroad in violation of the First Amendment chills speech and a later state court invalidation of the statute is not an adequate substitute for a federal court injunction because it is not possible to restore the speech that was lost.

More generally, Professor Douglas Laycock has argued that the opportunity to raise constitutional claims in state court is not, in many cases, a substitute for federal court review because state courts often lack the ability to provide relief available in federal courts, such as interlocutory, class-wide, or prospective remedies.[26] Professor Laycock concludes, "[E]ven if one accepts the core of *Younger*—that federal relief should be withheld where the pending state remedy is adequate—a pending prosecution should not be a near automatic bar to a federal action. The federal court should consider whether the state remedy is actually adequate on each set of facts and provide supplemental relief where needed."[27]

Defenders of *Younger* respond that there is a longstanding principle that courts of equity should not enjoin pending criminal prosecutions.[28] *Younger*, along with the earlier decision in *Douglas*, is merely a reflection of this tradition. Moreover, defenders of *Younger* emphasize the importance of "Our Federalism"

[24] 341 U.S. 341 (1951).

[25] Anne R. Traum, Distributed Federalism: The Transformation of Younger, 106 Cornell Law Review 1759, 1777-1778 (2021) ("Younger abstention exacts a high toll, cutting off the availability of federal courts to articulate and enforce constitutional rights in state criminal proceedings. Younger abstention is forum-shifting in that it denies plaintiffs the forum and civil remedies they sought in federal court.")

[26] Douglas Laycock, Federal Interference with State Prosecutions: The Need for Prospective Relief, 1977 Sup. Ct. Rev. 193.

[27] *Id.* at 194. For a powerful criticism of the application of *Younger* abstention in the area of challenges to the child welfare and foster care systems, *see* Peter R. O'Neill, Note, *Younger* and the Youth: The *Younger* Abstention Doctrine in the Child Welfare Context, 76 Stan. L. Rev. 1323 (2024).

[28] Ann Althouse, How to Build a Separate Sphere: Federal Courts and State Power, 100 Harv. L. Rev. 1485, 1487 (1987); Fred O. Smith Jr., Abstaining Equitably, 97 Notre Dame L. Rev. 2095, 2114 (2022).

and of federal courts avoiding interference with state judiciaries.[29] The *Younger* abstention doctrine promotes harmony between federal and state courts in many ways. Injunctions of state proceedings represent an implicit affront to the ability and willingness of state court judges to adequately resolve constitutional questions. Additionally, federal court injunctions are disruptive of state proceedings and thus are likely to breed hostility toward federal judges.[30]

Critics of *Younger*, however, question the comity rationale for the decision. Is permitting federal court review and remedies necessarily perceived as an affront to the competence of state judges? The claim that injunctions breed friction is based on an assumption about the likely psychological reactions of state court judges. However, in most instances state judges probably will not even know that an injunction has been issued. Professor Wells explains that usually "federal relief will consist of removal of a state case from a list of unheard cases kept in the clerk's office. There will be no more disruption than if the state case had been settled and state judges may scarcely be aware of the insult visited upon them."[31]

In fact, even if state judges are aware of the injunctions, they possibly may welcome the lessening of their caseload and particularly appreciate the removal of controversial cases from their dockets. After all, since most states have some form of electoral review of judges, it is at least plausible that state court judges would prefer to have federal judges take the heat of declaring state laws unconstitutional.

Moreover, it can be argued that state judges might have the view that just as state courts are the preeminent interpreters and enforcers of state laws, so do federal courts occupy that role with regard to federal law. This view is one of mutual respect and role specialization; no insult, other than whatever is inherent to the existence of the federal courts, is implied. Alternatively, state court judges might view the jurisdictional statutes as creating a choice of forum for constitutional litigants.[32] From this perspective, permitting federal court relief when there are pending state proceedings is no more of an affront to state courts than is the existence of removal jurisdiction.

Furthermore, the argument is that just as federal courts interrupt their proceedings under *Pullman* abstention to allow state courts to interpret and apply state law, so may they appropriately interrupt state proceedings to allow federal courts to interpret federal law. However, defenders of *Younger* are quick to point out that there is a difference between federal courts halting their own proceedings, as in *Pullman* abstention, and federal courts interfering with another court, as would be the case without the *Younger* doctrine.

Finally, there is the normative question as to whether avoiding friction between federal and state courts should be a basis for crafting jurisdictional rules. Critics of *Younger* contend that the Court never explained the value of harmony,

[29] *See* Ralph U. Whitten, Federal Declaratory and Injunctive Interference with State Court Proceedings: The Supreme Court and the Limits of Judicial Discretion, 53 N.C. L. Rev. 591 (1975).

[30] Martin H. Redish, Federal Jurisdiction: Tensions in the Allocation of Judicial Power 344-345 (2d ed. 1990).

[31] Michael Wells, The Role of Comity in the Law of Federal Courts, 60 N.C. L. Rev. 59, 70 n.65 (1981).

[32] Redish, *supra* note 30, at 345.

and it is a far less important value than assuring protection of constitutional rights. Professors Soifer and Macgill argue, for example, that the Reconstruction-era civil rights laws were based on a distrust of state courts, and considerations of comity do not justify federal courts ignoring this legislative history.[33] Defenders of *Younger*, however, emphasize the importance of federalism and deference to state governments and applaud *Younger* as a proper limit on the power of federal courts.

Implicit in each side's arguments are assumptions about whether there is parity between federal courts and state courts in deciding constitutional issues. Defenders of *Younger* argue that deference to the state courts involves no costs because constitutional claims can be fully and fairly resolved before state tribunals. Critics of *Younger* base their arguments on the assumption that federal forums should be available to resolve constitutional issues.

Although the debate over the *Younger* doctrine is likely to continue, there is no doubt that the doctrine is firmly entrenched. In fact, *Younger* abstention has been extended far beyond the specific question presented in *Younger*, whether a federal court may enjoin a pending criminal prosecution.

§13.4 THE EXTENSION OF *YOUNGER V. HARRIS*

Younger v. Harris was limited to considering the propriety of federal courts enjoining state criminal proceedings. In subsequent cases the Court has considered the application of *Younger* to (1) declaratory judgments when there are pending state proceedings; (2) declaratory and injunctive relief when there are no pending state proceedings; (3) state civil cases both involving the government as a party and between private litigants; (4) state administrative proceedings involving important state interests; and (5) injunctive relief against state and local executive officers, such as police departments.

However, in *Sprint Communications, Inc. v. Jacobs*, the Court said that *Younger* abstention applies in only "three types of proceedings." First, *Younger* precluded federal intrusion into ongoing state criminal prosecutions. Second, certain "civil enforcement proceedings" warranted abstention. Finally, federal courts refrained from interfering with pending "civil proceedings involving certain orders . . . uniquely in furtherance of the state courts' ability to perform their judicial functions."[1] Therefore, the cases are organized around these three categories. After these are discussed, other Supreme Court decisions that don't fit into these categories are considered.

[33] Aviam Soifer & H.C. Macgill, The *Younger* Doctrine: Reconstructing Reconstruction, 55 Tex. L. Rev. 1141 (1977).

§13.4 [1] 571 U.S. 69, 77 (2013).

§13.4.1 Preclusion of Intrusion into Ongoing State Criminal Prosecutions

Application to Suits for Declaratory Judgments

In *Samuels v. Mackell*, a companion case to *Younger*, the Court held that federal courts may not provide a plaintiff with declaratory relief when he or she is subject to a pending state court criminal prosecution.[2] Arguably, a declaratory judgment interferes with state judiciaries less than an injunction and thus might be distinguished from the *Younger* holding.[3] Unlike an injunction, a declaratory judgment is not a direct command to the state court to cease its proceedings. Also, a declaratory judgment is not punishable by contempt.[4]

The Supreme Court, however, rejected these distinctions and held that the principles of *Younger* are fully applicable to requests for declaratory relief. Justice Black, again writing for the majority, concluded that "ordinarily a declaratory judgment will result in precisely the same interference with and disruption of state proceedings that the long-standing policy limiting injunctions was designed to avoid."[5] The Court explained that under the Declaratory Judgment Act, declaratory judgments are enforceable by injunctions and, moreover, declaratory relief has the same practical effect as an injunction. Thus, Justice Black concluded, "We therefore hold that, in cases where the state criminal prosecution was begun prior to the federal suit . . . where an injunction would be impermissible under these principles, declaratory relief should ordinarily be denied as well."[6] In other words, a person being prosecuted in state court may not seek a federal court declaratory judgment invalidating the statute that is the basis for the prosecution.

The Court, however, recognized the possibility of situations where declaratory relief might be allowed while an injunction would be forbidden. The Court noted that there might be exceptional situations in which the injunctive remedy "seemed particularly intrusive or offensive," but declaratory judgments would be permissible.[7] The Court did not elaborate as to what might constitute such situations, but it emphasized that such instances would be rare because "[o]rdinarily . . . the practical effect of the two forms of relief will be virtually identical."[8]

Critics of *Samuels* contend that the Court should have drawn a sharper distinction between injunctive and declaratory relief. For example, Professor Ralph Whitten, a defender of the *Younger* doctrine, argues that the drafters of the Declaratory Judgment Act did not wish it to be administered in accord with traditional equity

[2] 401 U.S. 66 (1971).

[3] *See, e.g.*, Steffel v. Thompson, 415 U.S. 452, 481 (1974) (Rehnquist, J., concurring) (distinguishing between declaratory and injunctive relief).

[4] Martin H. Redish, Federal Jurisdiction: Tensions in the Allocation of Judicial Power 309 (2d ed. 1990).

[5] Samuels v. Mackell, 401 U.S. at 72.

[6] *Id.* at 73.

[7] *Id.*

[8] *Id.*

rules.[9] Professor Whitten thus criticizes the Court's failure to adhere to the traditional distinction between injunctive and declaratory remedies. Defenders of *Samuels*, however, argue that the central thesis of *Younger* is that state courts should decide constitutional issues when there are pending state criminal prosecutions. Because declaratory judgments would deprive state courts of the ability to determine the constitutional question before them, the Court held that declaratory judgments should be treated in the same manner as injunctions.

Monetary Relief

An unresolved question is whether a federal court may provide *monetary* relief to an individual who is a state court criminal defendant when the damages claim arises out of the same matter as is pending in state court. For example, if a person is prosecuted under an allegedly unconstitutional statute, could he or she receive money damages for injuries suffered from the enforcement of the statute while, at the same time, defending a prosecution under the law in state court?

The Supreme Court has noted that this is an unresolved issue but approved of federal courts staying suits for money damages when there are pending state court criminal prosecutions concerning the same issues. In *Deakins v. Monaghan*, individuals who were the subject of a state grand jury investigation initiated a federal court action seeking injunctive and monetary relief.[10] The request for equitable remedies was moot before the Supreme Court, but there remained the question of whether the federal district court acted properly in dismissing the suit for damages. The Court said, "We need not decide the extent to which the *Younger* doctrine applies to a federal action seeking only monetary relief."[11] On other occasions as well, the Court has noted but not resolved the question of whether *Younger* precludes federal court litigation of damage suits when the same matter is the subject of a state criminal proceeding.[12] In *Deakins*, the Court held that the district court erred in dismissing the federal court plaintiffs' claims for monetary relief. The Court said that because the state proceedings could not have awarded damages, the federal court should have stayed, not dismissed, the federal litigation.

In a subsequent decision, *Quackenbush v. Allstate Insurance Co.*, the Court indicated that abstention doctrines are derived from the discretion inherent to a federal court's equity powers.[13] Although the case involved an issue of *Burford* abstention—whether a federal court should abstain to defer to complex state administrative procedures—and not *Younger* abstention,[14] the Court spoke generally of the basis for abstention doctrines. A unanimous Court concluded that "the

[9] Ralph U. Whitten, Federal Declaratory and Injunctive Interference with State Court Proceedings: The Supreme Court and the Limits of Judicial Discretion, 53 N.C. L. Rev. 591, 655 (1971).

[10] 484 U.S. 193 (1988).

[11] *Id.* at 202.

[12] Tower v. Glover, 467 U.S. 914, 923 (1984); Juidice v. Vail, 430 U.S. 327, 339 n.16 (1977).

[13] 517 U.S. 706 (1996). *Quackenbush* is discussed in detail in §12.2.3.

[14] *Burford* abstention is discussed in §12.2.3.

power to dismiss under the *Burford* doctrine, *as with other abstention doctrines*, derives from the discretion historically enjoyed by courts of equity."[15] This is a strong indication that the Court is likely to find that *Younger* abstention applies only to suits for injunctive or declaratory relief and not to claims for money damages.

The lower courts are divided as to whether federal courts can provide damage remedies when there are ongoing state court criminal proceedings.[16] The Third Circuit has held that federal courts should stay, but not dismiss, suits for monetary relief in instances where *Younger* would prohibit injunctive relief.[17] The Second Circuit, however, has concluded that federal courts generally may adjudicate damage suits, even though there are pending criminal prosecutions in state court concerning the same matter.[18]

It can be argued that a federal court suit for money damages might have the same effect as a declaratory judgment. As part of deciding the damages claim, the federal court might declare the state law unconstitutional, thus in effect depriving the state court of the opportunity to resolve the issue.

However, the better view is that the principles of *Younger* do not prevent federal courts from providing monetary relief when the same matter is the subject of a criminal proceeding in state court. The *Younger* Court justified abstention by emphasizing that the state court could provide all of the relief requested in federal court, making an injunction unnecessary. Likewise, in *Samuels* the state court could declare the statute unconstitutional, obviating the need for a federal declaratory judgment, but money damages are not available in a state court criminal proceeding. Accordingly, the federal court's adjudication of a damages claim does not reflect distrust of the state courts and should not be perceived as an affront by state court judges. Also, in *Younger* and in subsequent cases such as *Quackenbush v. Allstate*, the Court emphasized that abstention is based on principles of equity.[19] Hence, the existence of state proceedings should not prevent the federal court from awarding monetary relief, even though the effect may be to decide an issue before the state court.

[15] 517 U.S. at 728 (emphasis added).

[16] For cases holding *Younger* bars damage suits, *see* Herrera v. City of Palmdale, 918 F.3d 1037 (9th Cir. 2019) (holding that, under *Younger* abstention, suits for damages should be stayed until state court proceedings finish); D.L. v. Unified School Dist. No. 497, 392 F.3d 1223 (10th Cir. 2004) (holding that *Younger* abstention applied to damage suits when ruling would have a preclusive effect on ongoing state proceedings); Simpson v. Rowan, 73 F.3d 134, 138 (7th Cir. 1995); Gwynedd Properties, Inc. v. Lower Gwynedd Township, 970 F.2d 1195 (3d Cir. 1992); Williams v. Hepting, 844 F.2d 138 (3d Cir. 1988). For cases holding that *Younger* does not bar damage suits, *see* Kirschner v. Klemons, 225 F.3d 227 (2d Cir. 2000); Alexander v. Ieyoub, 62 F.3d 709 (5th Cir. 1995); Lewis v. Beddingfield, 20 F.3d 123 (5th Cir. 1994); Koohi v. United States, 976 F.2d 1328 (9th Cir. 1992). *See also* Schilling v. White, 58 F.3d 1081 (6th Cir. 1995) (holding that the relevant inquiry for *Younger* analysis is the nature and degree of the state's interest in its judicial proceedings rather than whether a party is seeking injunctive relief or monetary damages).

[17] *See* Monaghan v. Deakins, 798 F.2d 632 (3d Cir. 1986), *aff'd*, 484 U.S. 193 (1988).

[18] *See* Giulini v. Blessing, 654 F.2d 189 (2d Cir. 1981).

[19] There is a split among the circuits as to whether *Younger* abstention applies where a criminal defendant is seeking pretrial habeas corpus relief rather than equitable relief. *Compare* In re Justices of the Supreme Court, 218 F.3d 11 (1st Cir. 2000), *with* Brown v. Ahren, 676 F.3d 899 (9th Cir. 2012); Carden v. Montana, 626 F.2d 82 (9th Cir. 1980).

§13.4.2 Federal Court Declaratory and Injunctive Relief in the Absence of Pending State Proceedings

Steffel v. Thompson

The *Younger* Court expressed no view on the availability of federal injunctive or declaratory relief in the absence of a pending state proceeding. The Supreme Court resolved a part of this issue in *Steffel v. Thompson,* where it unanimously held that declaratory relief could be provided by a federal court when there was no ongoing state prosecution.[20] In *Steffel,* the plaintiff and his companion were threatened with arrest for violating Georgia criminal trespass laws while distributing handbills at a local shopping center. Although they left to avoid arrest, they returned a few days later and again were threatened with prosecution for trespass. While the plaintiff left, his companion remained and was arrested. The plaintiff then filed a suit in federal court seeking both declaratory and injunctive relief. The federal district court dismissed the suit based on the principles of *Younger v. Harris.*

The Supreme Court reversed, focusing on the appropriateness of declaratory relief in the absence of ongoing state prosecutions. The Court held that the rationale of *Younger* was inapplicable if there were not pending state proceedings. Justice Brennan, writing for the Court, noted that "[w]hen no state criminal proceeding is pending at the time the federal complaint is filed, federal intervention does not result in duplicative legal proceedings or disruption of the state criminal justice system."[21] Moreover, in the absence of a pending state proceeding, federal court action cannot "be interpreted as reflecting negatively upon the state court's ability to enforce constitutional principles."[22]

Although the Court did not address the question of whether federal courts could issue injunctions in the absence of pending state court proceedings, several of the justices offered opinions on the subject. For instance, Justice Rehnquist, in a concurring opinion, drew a sharp distinction between injunctions and declaratory relief. He stated, "A declaratory judgment is simply a statement of rights, not a binding order supplemented by continuing sanctions. State authorities may choose to be guided by the judgment of a lower federal court, but they are not compelled to follow the decision by threat of contempt or other penalties."[23] The problem with Justice Rehnquist's description of declaratory judgments is that it is hard to see how they avoid being nonjusticiable advisory opinions under his view. Moreover, his position seems inconsistent with the Court's reasoning in *Samuels v. Mackell,* described above, which held that declaratory judgments are indistinguishable from injunctions when there are pending state court proceedings.[24]

[20] 415 U.S. 452 (1974).

[21] *Id.* at 462.

[22] *Id. See* Barry Friedman, Under the Law of Federal Jurisdiction: Allocating Cases Between State and Federal Court, 104 Colum. L. Rev. 1211, 1248-1254 (2004) (explaining why litigants who have not yet violated a law should have access to a federal court to determine the constitutionality of the law).

[23] 415 U.S. at 482 (Rehnquist, J., concurring).

[24] 401 U.S. 66 (1971); *see* §13.4.1, *supra.*

Justice White, in a separate concurring opinion, disagreed with Justice Rehnquist and offered his view that a federal court's declaratory judgment must be complied with by state courts and, if it is not followed, can be enforced by a subsequent injunction.[25] Thus, Justice White expressed his view that federal courts can provide both injunctive and declaratory relief when there are no pending state proceedings.

Steffel stands for the proposition that federal courts may issue declaratory relief if state criminal proceedings are threatened, but not pending. If *Steffel* had been decided differently, the Court indeed would have placed "the hapless plaintiff between Scylla of intentionally flouting state law and the Charybdis of forgoing what he believes to be constitutionally protected activity in order to avoid becoming enmeshed in a criminal proceeding."[26] In fact, had *Steffel* precluded federal court declaratory relief even in the absence of state court proceedings, the effect would have been to almost completely close the federal courts to constitutional challenges to state statutes. Federal courts would have been obligated to abstain when there was a pending state proceeding, as long as state courts had available potentially adequate procedures to decide the issues raised. Thus, it is not surprising that the *Steffel* Court was unanimous in allowing declaratory judgments in the absence of state procedures. Of course, a case must meet the requirements for ripeness and standing, something that often is difficult in the absence of actual arrest and prosecutions.[27]

After *Steffel*, and in light of *Samuels v. Mackell*, a clear rule concerning federal court declaratory judgments emerged: Declaratory relief is available if there is not a pending state court criminal prosecution.[28] Of course, this legal test requires determining what constitutes a pending state proceeding. From the facts of *Younger*

[25] 415 U.S. at 477 (White, J., concurring).

[26] *Id.* at 462.

[27] For example, in Younger v. Harris, plaintiffs who had not been arrested but challenged the California Criminal Syndicalism statute had their claims dismissed as not ripe. 401 U.S. 37, 42 (1971). For a discussion of ripeness, *see* §2.4, *supra*. In MedImmune, Inc. v. Genentech, Inc., 549 U.S. 118, 128-129 (2007), the Court, relying on *Steffel* and other cases, stated: "Where threatened action by *government* is concerned, we do not require a plaintiff to expose himself to liability before bringing suit to challenge the basis for the threat—for example, the constitutionality of a law threatened to be enforced. The plaintiff's own action (or inaction) in failing to violate the law eliminates the imminent threat of prosecution, but nonetheless does not eliminate Article III jurisdiction. . . . In each of these cases, the plaintiff had eliminated the imminent threat of harm by simply not doing what he claimed the right to do. That did not preclude subject-matter jurisdiction because the threat-eliminating behavior was effectively coerced."

[28] One commentator explained this by saying, "The small subset of cases that federal courts may hear under *Steffel* are those in which the state's interest in administering its statutes is at its nadir and the federal plaintiff's interest in having his constitutional claim heard is at its zenith. Taken together, the justiciability and equitable restraint doctrines establish bookends around a narrow range of cases—those involving a genuine threat of imminent prosecution or requiring an actor to forgo constitutionally protected conduct, but where prosecution has not actually begun—in which federal courts may interfere with state legislative prerogatives. This class of cases is sufficiently narrow for the federal courts to act without unnecessarily upsetting the federalism and separation of powers boundaries between the federal courts and the states." Ryan Griffin, Litigating the Contours of Constitutionality: Harmonizing Equitable Principles and Constitutional Values When Considering Preliminary Injunctive Relief, 94 Minn. L. Rev. 839, 858-859 (2010).

and *Samuels* it was apparent that an indictment in state court was deemed to constitute a pending prosecution. Some lower courts have ruled that an arrest commences state court proceedings for purposes of the *Younger* doctrine.[29] In *Deakins,* the existence of a state grand jury investigation was regarded as sufficient to justify the federal court's staying a damage action concerning the same subject matter.[30]

Hicks v. Miranda

Although *Steffel* allows declaratory relief if no state proceedings were pending when the federal suit was initiated, the Court subsequently held that federal courts may not provide declaratory judgments if a state prosecution is commenced before the federal court procedures are substantially completed. In *Hicks v. Miranda,* the state prosecuted an individual the day after he had filed a civil suit for declaratory relief in federal court.[31] Despite the fact that the federal suit was filed first, the principles of *Younger* and *Samuels* were applied and the Court ordered the case dismissed from the federal docket.

In *Hicks,* the police seized copies of the film *Deep Throat* from a movie theater and arrested two of the theater's employees. The state also began legal proceedings to have the movie declared obscene. After a hearing, the film was judged to be obscene. At that point, the theater owner, who was not a defendant in the state court criminal prosecutions, filed a lawsuit in federal court to have the state's obscenity law declared unconstitutional. The federal district court exercised its jurisdiction and declared the state law unconstitutional.

The Supreme Court reversed. In part, the Court noted that the theater owner's interests were already being litigated in the pending state court proceedings against the theater's employees.[32] More important, the Supreme Court held that the initiation of state proceedings against the owner provided him a forum to adjudicate his constitutional claims. Because the federal court suit was at its initial stages, federal abstention and deference to the state courts was appropriate. Justice White, writing for the majority in a 5-4 decision, observed that "[n]either *Steffel v. Thompson,* nor any other case in this Court has held that for *Younger v. Harris* to apply, the state criminal proceedings must be pending on the day the federal case is filed."[33] To the contrary, the Court held that "where state criminal proceedings are begun against the federal plaintiffs after the federal complaint is filed but

[29] *See, e.g.,* Rialto Theatre Co. v. City of Wilmington, 440 F.2d 1326 (3d Cir. 1971), *cert. denied,* 409 U.S. 1109 (1973); Eve Prods., Inc. v. Shannon, 439 F.2d 1073 (8th Cir. 1971); *but see* Hoye v. City of Oakland, 653 F.3d 835 (9th Cir. 2011) (holding that a charging document not yet filed in state court was not enough to trigger *Younger* abstention); Agriesti v. MGM Grand Hotels, Inc., 53 F.3d 1000 (9th Cir. 1995) (holding that arrests are executive, not judicial acts, and there were no ongoing criminal proceedings because under Nevada law the commencement of a prosecution begins when a charge is filed).

[30] 484 U.S. 193 (1988).

[31] 422 U.S. 332 (1975).

[32] *Id.* at 349.

[33] *Id.* (citations omitted).

before any proceedings of substance on the merits have taken place in the federal court, the principles of *Younger v. Harris* should apply in full force."[34]

Debate over *Hicks*

Concern has been expressed that *Hicks* offers prosecutors a tool to remove cases from federal court by retaliating against federal plaintiffs by initiating state prosecutions.[35] Justice Stewart, in a dissenting opinion, remarked that the *Hicks* decision "virtually instructs state officials to answer federal complaints with state indictments."[36] Professors Soifer and Macgill contend that *Hicks* "laid waste the century-old canon of federalism that the filing of an action in state court could not oust a federal court first obtaining jurisdiction of the case."[37] In essence, *Hicks* gave the state district attorney the power to remove a case from federal court to state court by initiating a prosecution while the federal suit was still in its earliest stages.[38] Thus, Professor Owen Fiss remarked that "*Hicks* fundamentally altered the structure of the federal jurisdictional scheme: it vested the district attorney—not the aggrieved citizen—with the power to choose the forum, and indeed, the nature of the proceeding in which the federal constitutional claim would be litigated."[39]

But *Hicks* can be defended as accomplishing *Younger*'s purpose of preventing federal court interference with state court criminal prosecutions. If the federal court were to issue a declaratory judgment while a state prosecution was pending, the effect would be to deprive the state judiciary of an opportunity to decide the issue. Regardless of which case was filed first, if the federal case was decided before the state one, the impact would be the same as that prohibited in *Samuels v. Mackell.* However, *Hicks* reveals that the Court's comity rationale is not a principle of mutuality but one of unilateral deference to state courts. State judiciaries need not defer to the federal court's interest in deciding constitutional claims that are properly within their jurisdiction, but federal courts must dismiss cases as soon as state litigation is commenced.

Hicks holds that federal courts must dismiss suits if there are not "proceedings of substance on the merits" prior to the initiation of state criminal prosecutions. Yet it remains unclear how much must transpire in federal court in order to resist a motion for dismissal after a state prosecution is commenced. The Supreme Court has addressed a few specifics. A federal court's denial of a request for a temporary restraining order does not constitute sufficient "proceedings of substance on the merits" to keep the case in federal court.[40] By contrast, a federal court's granting

[34] *Id.*

[35] *Id.* at 357 (Stewart, J., dissenting).

[36] *Id.*

[37] Aviam Soifer & H.C. Macgill, The *Younger* Doctrine: Reconstructing Reconstruction, 55 Tex. L. Rev. 1141, 1192 (1977).

[38] Owen M. Fiss, *Dombrowski,* 86 Yale L.J. 1103, 1135-1136 (1977).

[39] *Id.* at 1135.

[40] In *Hicks,* the federal court plaintiffs had requested and been denied a temporary restraining order, but the Court held that this was not enough to prevent federal court abstention once state criminal proceedings were initiated.

of a preliminary injunction is enough to prevent dismissal when subsequent state criminal charges are lodged.[41] Apart from these particulars, it is unclear at what point in federal proceedings *Hicks* does not apply and the federal court can refuse abstention.[42]

Injunctions When no State Proceedings are Pending

The above discussion focused on federal court declaratory relief in the absence of pending state prosecutions; a separate though related question concerns injunctions under such circumstances. Since the plaintiffs in *Steffel* did not seek an injunction on appeal, the Court explicitly left unanswered the question of whether federal courts could enjoin state court prosecutions before they were initiated.

In light of *Samuels*'s conclusion that declaratory and injunctive relief are indistinguishable, it would appear that injunctions are permissible in situations where declaratory judgments can be issued. If no state proceedings are pending, an injunction does not interrupt the state's judiciary nor does it deprive state courts of the ability to decide matters properly before them. Yet the majority in *Steffel v. Thompson*, while expressing no view on the propriety of injunctions, observed "that a declaratory judgment will have a less intrusive effect on the administration of state criminal laws" than would an injunction.[43] If the Court adopts this view, it might distinguish injunctions from declaratory judgments when there are no pending state proceedings.

Doran v. Salem Inn, Inc.

Although the Supreme Court has declared, "Absent any pending proceeding in state tribunals, therefore, application by the lower courts of *Younger* abstention was clearly erroneous,"[44] it appears that federal courts may issue injunctions in the absence of ongoing state prosecutions. In *Doran v. Salem Inn, Inc.*, the Supreme Court upheld a preliminary injunction against threatened prosecutions.[45] In *Doran*, three bar owners brought a federal action seeking declaratory relief and a preliminary injunction preventing enforcement of a newly enacted ordinance

[41] *See* Hawaii Hous. Auth. v. Midkiff, 467 U.S. 229, 238 (1984) ("A federal court action in which a preliminary injunction is granted has proceeded well beyond 'the embryonic stage' . . . and considerations of economy, equity, and federalism counsel against *Younger* abstention at that point.") (citation omitted).

[42] In dicta, the Supreme Court indicated that *Younger* abstention might apply if there are about to be pending state court proceedings. Morales v. Trans World Airlines, Inc., 504 U.S. 374, 381-382 n.1 (1992) ("Younger v. Harris . . . imposes heightened requirements for an injunction to restrain an already-pending or an about-to-be-pending state criminal action, or civil action involving important state interests.").

[43] Steffel v. Thompson, 415 U.S. at 469.

[44] Ankenbrandt v. Richards, 504 U.S. 689, 705 (1992).

[45] 422 U.S. 922 (1975).

prohibiting topless dancing. After the federal suit was filed and a temporary restraining order denied, one of the bar owners resumed the prohibited conduct. Criminal proceedings then were begun against him and his employees in state court. Subsequently, the federal district court granted preliminary injunctive relief to all three bar owners.

The Supreme Court affirmed the preliminary injunction granted to the two owners who had complied with the ordinance pending a decision from the federal court. As to the individual who was being prosecuted in state court, the principles of *Younger*, *Samuels*, and *Hicks* were declared applicable, and the individual was denied access to the federal courts. The Court said that when there is no pending state court proceeding, individuals may receive a preliminary injunction because it does not disrupt the state courts and because there is no available forum in which to raise the constitutional claims.[46]

The Court, however, implied that its approval of preliminary injunctions in the absence of state proceedings might not extend to permanent injunctions. Justice Rehnquist, writing for the Court, stated, "At the conclusion of a successful federal challenge to a state statute or local ordinance, a district court can generally protect the interests of a federal plaintiff by entering a declaratory judgment, and therefore the stronger injunctive medicine will be unnecessary."[47] Of course, this seems inconsistent with *Samuels*'s conclusion that injunctive and declaratory relief have an indistinguishable effect on state courts. Also, it is not clear whether Justice Rehnquist suggested a limit on the availability of permanent injunctions or simply expressed a view that usually they would be unnecessary.

Doran is important in other respects as well. *Doran* clarifies that federal courts need not dismiss a case under *Younger* principles simply because the same issue is pending before the state courts in proceedings involving different, unrelated parties.[48] In *Doran*, all three theater owners were challenging the same ordinance. The existence of a criminal prosecution against one did not keep the other two out of federal court.

[46] *See also* Ankenbrandt v. Richards, 504 U.S. at 705 (1992) (holding that it was clearly erroneous for a federal district court to apply *Younger* abstention in the absence of a pending state prosecution).

[47] 422 U.S. at 931.

[48] *See* Mass. Delivery Ass'n v. Coakley, 671 F.3d 33 (1st Cir. 2012) (holding that *Younger* abstention was not warranted for an action brought by a business trade association despite several of its members being subject to ongoing state proceedings); Canatella v. Cal., 404 F.3d 1006 (9th Cir. 2005) (holding that *Younger* abstention did not apply despite two unrelated lawyers being involved in similar state bar sanctions); FOCUS v. Allegheny County Court of Common Pleas, 75 F.3d 834 (3d Cir. 1996) (*Younger* abstention not applicable where federal plaintiffs were denied intervention in state court matter); Hoover v. Wagner, 47 F.3d 845 (7th Cir. 1995); Rivera-Puig v. Garcia-Rosario, 983 F.2d 311 (1st Cir. 1992) (improper to apply *Younger* abstention when there are pending proceedings against different parties); *but see* Citizens for a Strong Ohio v. Marsh, 123 Fed. Appx. 630 (6th Cir. 2005) (holding that *Younger* was warranted for donors to political organizations who raised federal claims related to state proceedings against the political organizations); Casa Marie, Inc. v. Superior Court of Puerto Rico, 988 F.2d 252 (1st Cir. 1993) (holding that *Younger* abstention applies where non intervenor interests are sufficiently intertwined with federal plaintiff's interests).

Wooley v. Maynard

In *Wooley v. Maynard,* the Supreme Court upheld a permanent injunction in the absence of pending state court proceedings.[49] George Maynard, a Jehovah's Witness, was prosecuted and convicted three times for violating a New Hampshire statute that made it a misdemeanor to obscure the state motto, "Live Free or Die," on state license plates. Before another prosecution was commenced against him, Maynard and his wife brought suit in federal court challenging the statute on First Amendment grounds and seeking declaratory and injunctive relief.

The Supreme Court declared the state's statute unconstitutional and upheld the injunction. Although the Court said that there is a general policy against federal courts enjoining enforcement of criminal statutes, it held that injunctions are appropriate in "exceptional circumstances" upon "a clear showing that an injunction is necessary in order to afford adequate protection of constitutional rights."[50] The Court found that such "exceptional circumstances" existed because Maynard had been subjected to three prosecutions within five weeks.

Does *Wooley* Authorize Injunctions Absent State Proceedings?

Some commentators and lower courts read *Wooley* as extending *Steffel* and *Doran* and permitting federal courts to issue permanent injunctions in the absence of ongoing state court litigation.[51] Others read *Wooley* in a more limited way. Professor Redish, for example, argues that *Wooley* is only incidentally about permanent injunctions; according to Redish the case fits within the established exception to *Younger* for bad-faith prosecutions.[52] Either view can be justified on the basis of the Court's opinion in *Wooley*. Professors Soifer and Macgill noted the ambiguity in *Wooley* by remarking that the "opinion does not reveal whether the *Maynard* test was good for that day only, whether it was good for those facts only, or even which of those facts were dispositive."[53]

The prevailing view in the lower courts is that permanent injunctions are allowed in the absence of ongoing state proceedings. This seems the best view in light of the Supreme Court's decisions in *Steffel* and *Doran* permitting declaratory judgments and preliminary injunctions. A distinction between permanent

[49] 430 U.S. 705 (1977).

[50] *Id.* at 712 (citation omitted).

[51] Fiss, *supra* note 38, at 1145. *See, e.g.,* Malhan v. Secretary U.S. Dep't of State, 938 F.3d 453 (3d Cir. 2019) (holding that *Wooley* allowed the District Court to investigate if injunction was appropriate as wage garnishment and proceedings had ended); Moore v. City of Asheville, N.C., 396 F.3d 385 (4th Cir. 2005) (holding that prospective injunctions were allowed in the absence of pending proceedings); Ealy v. Littlejohn, 569 F.2d 219, 232 (5th Cir. 1978); Collin v. Smith, 447 F. Supp. 676, 701 (N.D. Ill. 1978).

[52] Redish, *supra* note 30, at 361. *See, e.g.,* Blazier v. Larson, 443 Fed. Appx. 334 (10th Cir. 2011) (emphasizing the injunctions, like in *Wooley,* were only allowed in exceptional circumstances that necessitated them); Standard Oil Co. v. Federal Energy Admin., 440 F. Supp. 328, 367-368 n.101 (N.D. Ohio 1977).

[53] Soifer & Macgill, *supra* note 37, at 1206.

injunctions as opposed to declaratory judgments and preliminary injunctions would be ephemeral. If no such proceedings are pending, however, federal court relief is appropriate.

§13.4.3 The Application of Younger *Abstention to State-Initiated Civil Enforcement Proceedings*

As initially developed, the Younger doctrine limited the power of the federal courts to interfere with pending state *criminal* proceedings. Subsequently, however, the Court applied *Younger* to state-initiated enforcement proceedings in state court. This is the second category where *Sprint Communications, Inc. v. Jacobs* says that *Younger* abstention applies.

Huffman v. Pursue, Ltd.

The Court first considered the application of *Younger* abstention to civil cases in *Huffman v. Pursue, Ltd.*,[54] a decision heralded as "Our Federalism's great leap forward."[55] In *Huffman*, state officials instituted a civil nuisance proceeding against an adult movie theater for violating an Ohio statute declaring the exhibition of obscene films to be a nuisance. The state prevailed and obtained a judgment in the county court of common pleas closing the theater for a year. Rather than appealing the judgment within the state court system, the theater management sought injunctive and declaratory relief in federal court under 42 U.S.C. §1983. A three-judge federal court ruled in favor of the plaintiffs' claim that the Ohio statute and the proceedings against them violated their First Amendment rights.

The Supreme Court reversed, holding that the district court should have abstained under the principles of *Younger v. Harris*. Justice Rehnquist, writing for the Court, emphasized that the state's nuisance proceeding was "more akin to a criminal prosecution than are most civil cases."[56] The Court noted that the state was a party to the civil nuisance proceeding, which was "both in aid of and closely related to criminal statutes which prohibit the dissemination of obscene materials."[57] Thus, the Court concluded that federal court injunctive and declaratory relief was "likely to be every bit as great as it would be were this a criminal proceeding."[58]

Justices Brennan, Marshall, and Douglas dissented. They argued that criminal and civil proceedings are very different. Criminal proceedings are not initiated until after "the completion of steps designed to safeguard . . . against spurious

[54] 420 U.S. 592 (1975).

[55] Soifer & Macgill, *supra* note 37, at 1173. *See also* Jeffrey M. Shaman & Richard C. Turkington, Huffman v. Pursue, Ltd.: The Federal Courthouse Door Closes Further, 56 B.U. L. Rev. 907 (1976).

[56] 420 U.S. at 604.

[57] *Id.*

[58] *Id.*

prosecution—arrest, charge, information, or indictment."[59] In civil cases, however, the state can initiate an action simply by filing a complaint. Thus, the dissenters argued that it is too easy for the state to "strip [someone] of a forum and a remedy that federal statutes were enacted to assure him."[60] Although *Huffman* was a limited holding involving quasi-criminal state nuisance proceedings, Justice Brennan correctly predicted that it was "obviously only the first step" to applying *Younger* abstention to all civil cases in state court.[61]

Trainor v. Hernandez

In *Trainor v. Hernandez*, the Supreme Court clarified that *Younger* and *Huffman* apply in all civil proceedings to which the state is a party.[62] In *Trainor*, the Illinois Department of Public Aid instituted a civil fraud proceeding in state court to recover the welfare benefits obtained by Hernandez and his wife, who allegedly had concealed their personal assets while applying for and receiving public assistance. The department obtained a writ of attachment pursuant to the Illinois Attachment Act against the defendants' savings in a credit union. After the attachment, Hernandez brought a federal court action challenging the constitutionality of the attachment statute and seeking declaratory and injunctive relief.

In reversing the district court's invalidation of the statute, the Court held that *Younger* abstention should apply even though the proceeding was wholly civil. The Court emphasized that "the State was a party to the suit in its role of administering its public assistance programs. . . . [The state] was vindicat[ing] important state policies such as safeguarding the fiscal integrity of those programs."[63] The Court analogized *Trainor* to *Huffman* on the grounds that in both cases the state might have initiated criminal enforcement actions.[64] The Court's conclusion, however, was broader than state-initiated civil suits where there are parallel criminal statutes. Justice White, writing for the Court, stated, "[T]he principles of *Younger* and *Huffman* are broad enough to apply to interference by a federal court with an ongoing civil enforcement action such as this, brought by the State in its sovereign capacity."[65] The Court, however, expressly stated that it was not deciding the question of whether *Younger* principles apply in all civil litigation.[66]

Moore v. Sims

Yet another important case that applied *Younger* to civil proceedings in which the government was a party was *Moore v. Sims*.[67] In *Moore*, the Texas Department

[59] *Id.* at 615 (Brennan, J., dissenting).
[60] *Id.*
[61] *Id.* at 613.
[62] 431 U.S. 434 (1977).
[63] *Id.* at 444.
[64] *Id.*
[65] *Id.*
[66] *Id.* at 445 n.8.
[67] 442 U.S. 415 (1979).

of Human Resources removed children from their parents, who were suspected of child abuse, pursuant to an emergency ex parte order giving the department temporary custody. The parents filed suit in federal court challenging the constitutionality of the Texas law concerning the authority of the Department of Human Resources to protect children. A three-judge district court held Texas's law to be unconstitutional because it failed to provide adequate notice to parents and because it did not ensure a prompt hearing after removal of the children from their home.

The Supreme Court reversed, concluding that the lower court should have abstained and dismissed the case. Justice Rehnquist, writing for the Court, observed that earlier decisions had established that *Younger* is "fully applicable to civil proceedings in which important state interests are involved."[68] Justice Rehnquist concluded that a federal court should abstain as long as proceedings exist in the state system to adjudicate the constitutional claim. He wrote that "abstention is appropriate unless state law clearly bars the interposition of the constitutional claim."[69]

Four justices—Justices Stevens, Brennan, Stewart, and Marshall—filed a vehement dissent. They contended that the parents in *Moore* lacked a state forum in which they could have brought their constitutional challenges to the state law. The dissent argued that *Younger* should be deemed inapplicable where "there is no single pending state proceeding in which the constitutional claims may be raised 'as a defense' and effective relief secured."[70] The dissent contended that there was no reason why a court should relinquish jurisdiction over all claims simply because some of the issues are simultaneously pending in state court.

[68] *Id.* at 423.

[69] *Id.* at 425-426. *See also* Thomas v. Disanto, 762 Fed. Appx. 770, 775 n.4 (11th Cir. 2019); Oglala Sioux Tribe v. Fleming, 904 F.3d 603, 613 (8th Cir. 2018) (holding abstention was warranted because plaintiffs had not established that South Dakota courts were "unwilling or unable to adjudicate" constitutional claims); Gonzalez v. Waterfront Commn. of New York Harbor, 755 F.3d 176 (3d Cir. 2014) (holding that *Younger* abstention is warranted when a state court can review administrative proceedings); Morkel v. Davis, 513 Fed. Appx. 724, 728-729 (10th Cir. 2013) (ruling that it was plaintiff's burden to show that state law prevented bringing of federal claims); Chapman v. Oklahoma, 472 F.3d 747 (10th Cir. 2006) (holding that a parent could not bring a constitutional challenge to pending state court family law proceedings); Hirsh v. Justices of the Supreme Court of California, 67 F.3d 708, 713 (9th Cir. 1995) ("Judicial review is inadequate only when state procedural law bars presentation of the federal claims"); Liedel v. Juvenile Court of Madison County, Ala., 891 F.2d 1542 (11th Cir. 1990) (holding that parents could not bring a federal court civil rights action challenging state child abuse proceedings). *But see* Bunting ex rel. Gray v. Gray, 2 Fed. Appx. 443 (6th Cir. 2001) (holding that *Younger* abstention was inappropriate because divorce proceedings did not allow for raising constitutional claims); LaShawn A. v. Kelly, 990 F.2d 1319 (D.C. Cir. 1993) (ruling *Younger* inapplicable in a class action case involving foster care because none of the administrative proceedings constituted an adequate forum).

[70] 442 U.S. at 436-437 (Stevens, J., dissenting).

§13.4.4 The Application of Younger *Abstention in Civil Cases Where Important Judicial Interests are Involved*

The third situation in which the Supreme Court in *Sprint Communications, Inc. v. Jacobs* said that *Younger* abstention is appropriate is that "federal courts refrain[] from interfering with pending 'civil proceedings involving certain orders . . . uniquely in furtherance of the state courts' ability to perform their judicial functions.'"[71] The Court cited to two cases as illustrating this: *Juidice v. Vail* and *Pennzoil v. Texaco.*

Juidice v. Vail

In *Juidice v. Vail,* the Supreme Court for the first time applied *Younger* to a civil proceeding in which the government was not a party.[72] In *Juidice,* individuals were held in contempt of court by state court judges for refusing to comply with subpoenas to appear in supplemental proceedings brought by their judgment creditors. The individuals then filed suit in federal court seeking injunctive and declaratory remedies against the state's contempt proceedings.

The Supreme Court held that *Younger* was applicable even though the actual parties to the suit were private litigants. However, the Court emphasized the importance of the state's interest in state court contempt proceedings. The Court said that "the contempt process, through which it vindicates the regular operation of its judicial system . . . lies at the core of the administration of a State's judicial system."[73] Again, the Court refused to express an opinion as to whether *Younger* applies to all civil litigation, though the dissent found this disclaimer to be unpersuasive.[74]

Pennzoil Co. v. Texaco, Inc.

Getty Oil and Pennzoil entered into a contract for the sale of Pennzoil's oil interests. Subsequently, Texaco purchased Getty Oil and a lawsuit was filed in state court against Texaco asserting that it had tortiously induced Getty Oil to breach its contract with Pennzoil. A jury ruled in favor of Pennzoil and awarded $7.53 billion in actual damages and $3 billion in punitive damages. Under Texas law, if Texaco wanted to appeal, it had to post a bond; the required bond exceeded $13 billion. It was clear that Texaco could not afford such a bond.

Texaco initiated suit in federal district court in New York, at the site of the company's headquarters, seeking to enjoin the enforcement of the bond requirement as a prerequisite to an appeal. The lower federal courts ruled in favor of Texaco and enjoined the Texas state proceedings. The Supreme Court unanimously reversed.

[71] Sprint Communications, Inc. v. Jacobs, 571 U.S. 69 (2013).

[72] 430 U.S. 327 (1977).

[73] *Id.* at 335 (citation omitted).

[74] *Id.* at 336 n.13 (Court left open the question of the applicability of *Younger* to all civil proceedings). *See also id.* at 345 (Brennan, J., dissenting) (questioning that the Court really was leaving open the application of *Younger* to all civil actions).

Five justices held that the lower court erred because it "should have abstained under the principles of federalism enunciated in *Younger v. Harris*."[75] The Court emphasized that the rationales behind *Younger* were fully applicable in civil cases. An injunction of state courts offends comity, regardless of the content of the case, and a federal forum is unnecessary as long as there are state proceedings in which to raise the issues. The Court analogized to *Juidice v. Vail*, noting that both cases involved deference to state courts. In fact, the Court concluded that the "reasoning of *Juidice* controls" and that federal court abstention was warranted.[76]

A narrow reading of *Pennzoil* is possible: It involves an area, judicial enforcement of court orders, where an important state interest exists—one already recognized in *Juidice v. Vail.* The Court, however, implied that *Younger* applies to all civil proceedings. Justice Powell stated, "So long as those challenged statutes relate to pending state proceedings, proper respect for the ability of state courts to resolve federal questions presented in state court litigation mandates that the federal court stay its hand."[77]

§13.4.5 Refusal to Extend Younger *to Other Private Civil Litigation*

NOPSI Decision

Thus, the key question after *Pennzoil* was whether *Younger* applies in all civil cases or only those where an important state interest is present. In *New Orleans Public Service, Inc. v. Council of City of New Orleans* (*NOPSI*), the Court rejected an expansive interpretation of *Pennzoil* that would apply *Younger* to all civil litigation.[78] The utility company, NOPSI, sought a rate increase in the New Orleans City Council to recover costs that it was ordered to assume by the Federal Energy Regulatory Commission. The council concluded that NOPSI's negligence resulted in some of the costs it had incurred and refused to allow the full rate increase sought by NOPSI. The council then filed a declaratory judgment action in state court to establish the validity of its rate order. The utility contested this suit in state court and also initiated litigation in federal court challenging the constitutionality of the council's denial of the full rate increase. The district court abstained, in part, based on *Younger v. Harris* because of the existence of pending state court proceedings. The court of appeals affirmed the abstention.

The Supreme Court, however, reversed and declared that federal court abstention is not warranted in all instances where there are pending state court proceedings. Justice Scalia, writing for the majority, stated:

> Although our concern for comity and federalism has led us to expand the protection of *Younger* beyond state criminal prosecutions, to civil enforcement proceedings,

[75] 481 U.S. 1, 10 (1987).
[76] *Id.* at 13.
[77] *Id.*
[78] 491 U.S. 350 (1989).

> and even to civil proceedings involving certain orders that are uniquely in furtherance of the state courts' ability to perform their judicial functions, it has *never been suggested that* Younger *requires deference to a state judicial proceeding reviewing legislative or executive action.* Such a broad abstention requirement would make a mockery of the rule that only exceptional circumstances justify a federal court's refusal to decide a case in deference to the States.[79]

Indeed, the Court recognized that a federal court ruling would likely prevent the state court from deciding the issues before it. Nonetheless, the Court held that this was not enough to warrant *Younger* abstention. The Court noted, "It is true, of course, that a federal court's disposition of such a case may well affect, or for practical purposes preempt, a future—or, as in the present circumstances, even a pending state court action. But there is no doctrine that the availability or even the pendency of state judicial proceedings excludes the federal courts."[80]

The Court said that even if it assumed that the rate-setting process was a unitary one with all administrative and judicial proceedings as part of a single rate-making procedure, abstention still was inappropriate. The Court reasoned that rate-setting, especially as conducted by the New Orleans City Council, was essentially a legislative task and that *Younger* never had been applied to prevent review of matters other than judicial proceedings.

NOPSI is quite important in making it clear that federal courts need not abstain in all instances where there are pending state court civil proceedings.

Sprint Communications, Inc. v. Jacobs

In *Sprint Communications, Inc. v. Jacobs,* the Court was explicit that *Younger* abstention is not to be extended beyond the three categories described above.[81] A dispute developed between Sprint Communications and Windstream Iowa Communications, Inc. as to whether Sprint had to pay fees to Windstream for long distance Voice over Internet Protocol (VoIP) calls. The Iowa Utilities Board ruled that intrastate fees applied to VoIP calls.

Sprint sued Windstream and the Iowa Utility Board members in federal district court seeking a declaration that the Telecommunications Act of 1996 preempted the Utility Board decision and an injunction against its enforcement. The district court said that abstention was appropriate and the United States Court of Appeals for the Eighth Circuit affirmed. The Supreme Court unanimously reversed.

Justice Ginsburg, writing for the Court, observed: "Circumstances fitting within the *Younger* doctrine, we have stressed, are 'exceptional'; they include . . . 'state criminal prosecutions,' 'civil enforcement proceedings,' and 'civil proceedings involving certain orders that are uniquely in furtherance of the state courts' ability to perform their judicial functions.' Because this case presents none of the circumstances the Court has ranked as 'exceptional,' the general rule governs: '[T]he

[79] *Id.* at 367-368 (emphasis added).

[80] *Id.* at 373.

[81] 571 U.S. 69 (2013).

pendency of an action in [a] state court is no bar to proceedings concerning the same matter in the Federal court having jurisdiction.' "[82]

Thus, *NOPSI* and *Sprint Communications* resolve an issue that had divided the lower courts and hold that *Younger* abstention is generally not applicable in civil cases. But there are some other situations where the Court has considered *Younger* abstention that do not fit into the three *Sprint Communications* categories. These are discussed below.

§13.4.6 The Application of Younger *Abstention to Pending State Administrative Proceedings*

Younger abstention is based on the relationship between the federal and state judiciaries: the need for federal courts to trust state courts and avoid interfering with them. The Court, however, has extended *Younger* abstention beyond federal deference to state judicial proceedings and required federal courts to abstain when there are pending state *administrative* proceedings. The Court in *Middlesex County Ethics Committee v. Garden State Bar Association* first applied *Younger* abstention to state administrative proceedings.[83]

Middlesex County Ethics Committee

In *Middlesex*, the plaintiffs brought an action in the federal district court contending that their First Amendment rights were violated by ongoing investigations by a state bar ethics committee. A New Jersey attorney, who also was executive director of the National Conference of Black Lawyers, criticized a judge's fairness and referred to proceedings in that judge's courtroom as a "travesty," a "legalized lynching," and a "kangaroo court."[84] Charges were brought against the attorney for acting in a manner "prejudicial to the administration of justice" in the New Jersey administrative bar discipline system. The attorney then filed suit in federal court, contending that the pertinent regulations and the bar proceedings were unconstitutional.

The Supreme Court, in an opinion by Chief Justice Burger, upheld the federal district court's decision to dismiss the proceedings out of deference to the pending state proceedings. The Court explained, "The policies underlying *Younger* are fully applicable to noncriminal judicial proceedings when important state interests are involved."[85] The bar disciplinary actions were considered judicial because they were supervised and ultimately reviewed by the state supreme court and because they were closely related to the functioning of the state's judicial system. Moreover, the state's

[82] *Id.* at 588. The effect of *Sprint Communications v. Jacobs* has been to decrease the application of *Younger* in civil litigation. Anne R. Traum, Distributed Federalism: The Transformation of Younger, 106 Cornell Law Review 1759, 1759 (2021).

[83] 457 U.S. 423 (1982).

[84] *Id.* at 428.

[85] *Id.* at 432.

interest was deemed "extremely important" because of the need to maintain and ensure the "professional conduct" of attorneys.[86]

The *Middlesex County* case raises troubling questions. In *Younger*, the Court emphasized that federal court relief was unnecessary because constitutional claims could be raised in the pending state judicial proceedings. Yet in *Middlesex County*, there was no indication that the state administrative bodies were empowered to hear and decide the attorney's constitutional claims. In *Younger*, the Court emphasized the need for federal deference to state judicial proceedings; comity is the respect owed to the court system of another sovereign. But the extension of deference to state administrative actions cannot be justified without substantial explanation, which was absent in *Middlesex County*.

By itself, the *Middlesex County* decision might be viewed as a narrow expansion of *Younger* abstention principles because bar disciplinary proceedings are a part of the state judicial system. A distinction might be drawn between administrative matters that are handled pursuant to authority delegated by the state judiciary and those that are pending in other state agencies. *Younger* abstention, based on deference to the state judiciary, would be applied to the former, which is a part of the court system, but not the latter. This then would fit within the third category from *Sprint Communications, Inc. v. Jacobs*, where the matter involves important interests of the state judiciary.

Ohio Civil Rights Commission v. Dayton Christian Schools

But *Ohio Civil Rights Commission v. Dayton Christian Schools, Inc.* is much harder to fit into these three categories of *Sprint Communications* or to reconcile with a narrow view of *Middlesex County*.[87] A teacher at a church-run school was told that her contract would not be renewed when she informed school officials that she was pregnant. The principal of the school informed her that it was the school's religious doctrine that mothers should stay home with their preschool children.[88] After the teacher contacted an attorney, she was immediately fired for not following the dispute resolution provisions contained in her contract.

The teacher filed a complaint with the Ohio Civil Rights Commission, contending that her nonrenewal was unlawful sex discrimination in violation of Ohio law and that her firing was impermissible retaliation for attempting to exercise her rights. The

[86] *Id.* at 434. *See also* Clowdis v. Silverman, 666 Fed. Appx. 267 (4th Cir. 2016) (holding that the district court was correct to apply *Younger* abstention to a doctor's claims against the Virginia Medical Board for revoking his license); Williams v. Gov't of V.I. Bd. of Med. Exam'rs, 360 Fed. Appx. 297 (3d Cir. 2010) (holding that *Younger* abstention was warranted for a doctor's complaint against the Virgin Islands Board of Medical Examiners for suspending his license); Am. Family Prepaid Legal Corp. v. Columbus Bar Ass'n, 498 F.3d 328 (6th Cir. 2007) (holding that the district court was correct to apply *Younger* abstention when American Family filed a complaint against in federal court against the Columbus Bar Association); Gilbertson v. Albright, 381 F.3d 965 (9th Cir. 2004) (holding that the district court, under *Younger*, should have stayed damages for a land surveyor who brought claims against the State Board of Examiners for Engineering and Land Surveying for revoking his license); Spargo v. N.Y. State Commn. on Judicial Conduct, 351 F.3d 65 (2d Cir. 2003) (ruling that the district court should have abstained under *Younger* abstention when a state judge brought claims challenging state administrative sanctions against his conduct).

[87] 477 U.S. 619 (1986).

[88] *Id.* at 623.

commission concluded that there was probable cause to believe that the teacher had been wrongfully terminated and initiated administrative proceedings. The school raised the First Amendment as a defense to the initiation of the state proceedings and also filed suit in federal district court seeking to enjoin the administrative action.

The Supreme Court held that the federal court "should have abstained from adjudicating this case under *Younger v. Harris*."[89] The Court stated that *Younger* principles apply when there are state administrative proceedings "in which important state interests are vindicated, so long as in the course of those proceedings the federal plaintiff would have a full and fair opportunity to litigate his constitutional claim."[90] Justice Rehnquist, writing for the majority, concluded that the state's interest in eliminating gender discrimination justified the application of *Younger* and *Middlesex County*. The Court also found that the availability of state judicial review of the commission's decisions ensured an adequate opportunity to raise constitutional issues.

The Court emphasized that it was not altering existing doctrines providing that state administrative proceedings need not be exhausted before civil rights suits can be filed in federal court.[91] The Court explained that if no administrative proceedings are pending, a plaintiff may go to federal court without using available state administrative remedies. But once administrative actions are initiated, federal court interference is impermissible if important state interests are at stake.

Four justices—Justices Stevens, Brennan, Marshall, and Blackmun—concurred in the judgment based on their belief that the school's constitutional claims were not ripe for review because the commission's investigation was not, by itself, a violation of the First Amendment.[92] In a footnote, these justices stated that they disagreed with the majority's conclusion that abstention was required under the *Younger* doctrine. They explained that "*Younger* abstention has never been applied to subject a federal court plaintiff to an allegedly unconstitutional state administrative order when the constitutional challenge to that order can be asserted, if at all, only in state court judicial review of the administrative proceeding."[93]

[89] *Id.* at 625 (citation omitted).

[90] *Id.* at 627.

[91] *Id.* at 627 n.2. *See, e.g.*, Patsy v. Board of Regents of Fla., 457 U.S. 496 (1982). *See* §8.4, *supra*.

[92] 477 U.S. 619, 633 n.5 (Stevens, J., concurring in the judgment).

[93] *Id.* Some lower courts drew a distinction between "remedial" as opposed to "coercive" state administrative proceedings, concluding that a federal court can issue an injunction if the state proceeding is remedial. Planned Parenthood of Kansas v. Anderson, 882 F.3d 1205 (10th Cir. 2018) (relying on the remedial-coercive distinction to hold that *Younger* abstention did not apply to remedial actions); Moore v. City of Asheville, 396 F.3d 385, 397 n.4 (4th Cir. 2005); Devin v. Kalm, 594 F.3d 893 (6th Cir. 2010) (holding that *Younger* did not apply to a plaintiff seeking remedial relief, who initiated both the state and federal proceedings); O'Neill v. City of Philadelphia, 32 F.3d 785, 791 n.13 (3d Cir. 1994); Brown v. Day, 555 F.3d 882 (10th Cir. 2009) (relying on that distinction and holding that courts may issue an injunction when the state proceeding at issue is remedial). *But see* Hudson v. Campbell, 633 F.3d 985 (8th Cir. 2011) (choosing not to rely on remedial-coercive distinction because plaintiff had adequate opportunity to raise federal claims in state proceedings). *See* Eric Turner, You Say Remedial, I Say Coercive, Let's Call the Whole Thing Off: Why the Remedial/Coercive Distinction Is Not Critical in *Younger* Abstention, 49 Washburn L.J. 629 (2010). But after Sprint Communications, Inc. v. Jacobs this distinction seems irrelevant to the Court.

The reach of the holdings in *Middlesex County* and *Dayton Christian Schools* is unclear because it is not known what will be deemed to constitute an "important state interest."[94] However, the very application of *Younger* abstention to nonjudicial state proceedings has been challenged. Professor Laurence Tribe, for example, argues, "*Younger* should not be extended beyond a context where deference to a state *judicial* system is owed."[95] Even if comity requires trust and respect for state judicial proceedings, there is no reason why there must be corresponding trust and respect for administrative proceedings. *Younger* abstention is based on the existence of an ongoing state judicial action where constitutional issues can be raised. But when the pending proceedings are administrative, the victim of an alleged unconstitutional state action must litigate all through the agency proceedings before getting to raise the constitutional issues in a state court. Also, it is unclear how the Court will reconcile these cases, and especially *Dayton Christian Schools*, with its narrow reading of the extensions of *Younger* in *Sprint Communications, Inc. v. Jacobs.*

§13.4.7 The Application of Younger *Abstention to Prevent Federal Court Injunctive and Declaratory Relief Against the Executive Branches of State and Local Governments*

O'Shea v. Littleton

The most dramatic extension of *Younger* is the Court's suggestion that it might be applied to limit a federal court's ability to adjudicate constitutional challenges to state and local executive conduct. The first suggestion of this extension of *Younger* came in *O'Shea v. Littleton.*[96] A lawsuit was filed in federal district court claiming that a municipal court system intentionally discriminated against Black people in setting bail and in sentencing. The Supreme Court, in an opinion by Justice White, denied relief on ripeness grounds.[97] The Court, however, also suggested that the

[94] *See, e.g.,* Sirva Relocation, LLC v. Richie, 794 F.3d 185 (1st Cir. 2015) (ruling that a state had an important interest in eliminating workplace discrimination); Verizon New England, Inc. v. R.I. Dept. of Labor and Training, 723 F.3d 113 (1st Cir. 2013) (holding that enforcing unemployment benefits was an important state interest); Kendall v. Russell, 572 F.3d 126 (3d Cir. 2009) (holding that judicial accountability and regulating the judiciary were important state interests); Am. Family Prepaid Legal Corp. v. Columbus Bar Ass'n, 498 F.3d 328 (6th Cir. 2007) (holding that Ohio had an important interest in regulating unauthorized practice of law); O'Neill v. City of Philadelphia, 32 F.3d 785, 792 (3d Cir. 1994) (city has "a significant and substantial interest" in the regulation of on-street parking, and in the vindication of the system it has implemented to adjudicate violations of those regulations); Mission Oaks Mobile Home Park v. City of Hollister, 989 F.2d 359 (9th Cir. 1993), *overruled on other grounds,* Green v. City of Tucson, 255 F.3d 1086, 1092 (9th Cir. 2001) (*Younger* abstention appropriate in light of city's interest in administering mobile home rent control).

[95] Laurence Tribe, American Constitutional Law 207 (2d ed. 1988) (emphasis in original).

[96] 414 U.S. 488 (1974). For an excellent argument that *Younger* abstention should not apply in cases challenging structural flaws in state or local criminal justice systems, *see* Fred Smith, Abstention in the Time of Ferguson, 131 Harv. L. Rev. 2283 (2018).

[97] The Court found an insufficient probability that the plaintiffs would be brought again before the municipal courts on criminal charges. *Id.* at 495-499. *See also* §2.4, *supra.*

principles of *Younger v. Harris* should be applied to prevent federal court review. The Court observed that the periodic monitoring of state courts by a federal court would violate the notion of "Our Federalism."[98]

The application of *Younger* in this manner is questionable. *Younger* and its progeny involve federal courts needing to defer to pending state proceedings; in *O'Shea,* there were no pending state proceedings. Moreover, as Professor Tribe observed, "plaintiffs' allegations challenged the constitutionality of the very judicial processes to which the ordinary *Younger* rules would remand them, so that the case fell within an otherwise well-established exception to the *Younger* doctrine."[99]

On the other hand, the *O'Shea* Court might not have been applying *Younger* as much as using it as an example of federalism considerations as a limit on federal judicial power. Even from this perspective, however, *O'Shea* raises troubling questions about the ability of federal courts to refuse to hear constitutional claims in their jurisdiction because of a desire to avoid interfering with state and local governments. Perhaps *O'Shea*'s reliance on *Younger* can best be understood as representing a concern that constant federal court monitoring of state courts would inevitably entail federal judicial interference with ongoing state proceedings of a sort clearly prohibited in *Younger.*

Rizzo v. Goode

The possible extension of *Younger* to limit federal court review of state and local executive actions was most clearly suggested in Justice Rehnquist's opinion for the Court in *Rizzo v. Goode.*[100] In *Rizzo,* the district court had issued an injunction against the Philadelphia Police Department after finding substantial evidence of racially motivated police brutality. The lower court found the police disciplinary proceedings to be inadequate and issued an injunction overhauling the city's internal police procedures. The Supreme Court reversed, concluding that the suit was not justiciable. The Court noted that there was no claim of a "real and immediate injury," but instead a conjecture about what a "small, unnamed minority of policemen might do to them in the future because of that unknown policeman's perception of departmental disciplinary procedures."[101]

Justice Rehnquist, writing for the majority, went further, however, and suggested that the principles of *Younger* would justify abstention even if the case were

[98] *Id.* at 500. *See also* Disability Rights N.Y. v. New York, 916 F.3d 129 (2d Cir. 2019) (holding that *Younger* abstention was warranted because relief sought would have amounted to a continuing audit of New York Surrogate's Court proceedings); Luckey v. Miller, 976 F.2d 673 (11th Cir. 1992) (*Younger* abstention was appropriate in a class action suit challenging the adequacy of Georgia's indigent criminal defense system even though the plaintiffs did not contest any single conviction nor seek to restrain any individual prosecution).

[99] Tribe, *supra* note 95, at 207.

[100] 423 U.S. 362 (1976).

[101] *Id.* at 372.

justiciable. In broad language, Justice Rehnquist indicated a possible limit on the power of federal courts to review state and local executive actions:

> Thus the principles of federalism which play such an important part in governing the relationship between federal courts and state governments, though initially expounded and perhaps entitled to their greatest weight in cases where it was sought to enjoin a criminal prosecution in progress, have not been limited to that situation or indeed to a criminal proceeding itself. We think these principles likewise have applicability where injunctive relief is sought, not against the judicial branch of the state government, but against those in charge of an executive branch of an agency of state or local governments such as petitioners here.[102]

The Court did not indicate when such federal court abstention is appropriate, nor have subsequent Supreme Court decisions clarified this aspect of the *Rizzo* decision.[103]

The Court's suggested expansion of abstention in *Rizzo* has been sharply criticized. *Younger* is based on an assumption of parity between federal and state courts—that federal court relief is unnecessary when state proceedings exist to resolve a constitutional claim. But it is a totally different matter for federal courts to defer to executive officers, particularly when the lawsuit is a challenge to the constitutionality of the conduct of those very officers.[104] *Younger* could be understood as postponing federal court review until state proceedings were completed; Supreme Court review and even federal district court habeas corpus proceedings remained available at the completion of the state litigation. In *Rizzo*, however, access to the federal courts was totally foreclosed.[105]

At least since *Ex parte Young*, federal courts have possessed the unquestioned authority to enjoin unconstitutional acts by state and local officers.[106] If *Rizzo* is a suggestion to the contrary, then it threatens a major change in the constitutional system, for it would immunize unconstitutional actions from judicial review. The Supreme Court has not given any indication that *Rizzo* began such a revolution and lower courts generally have treated *Rizzo* simply as a reminder that federal courts should proceed carefully when intruding into important state and local government activities.[107]

[102] *Id.* at 380.

[103] The Court, on occasion, has approvingly cited to Rizzo v. Goode, but without elaborating on the abstention principle suggested there. *See, e.g.*, City of Los Angeles v. Lyons, 461 U.S. 95, 111-113 (1983).

[104] *See* Redish, *supra* note 30, at 370.

[105] *See* S. Stephen Rosenfeld, The Place of State Courts in the Era of Younger v. Harris, 59 B.U. L. Rev. 597, 624 (1979).

[106] 209 U.S. 123 (1908).

[107] Redish, *supra* note 30, at 370. *See, e.g.*, Dodds v. Richardson, 614 F.3d 1185 (10th Cir. 2010) (showing the necessary investigation, under *Rizzo*, for an injunction against state enforcement agencies); Thomas v. County of Los Angeles, 978 F.2d 504 (9th Cir. 1992) (elaborating that *Rizzo* represents that a rigorous review is necessary when evaluating injunction against a state enforcement agency); Morales v. Turman, 562 F.2d 993, 996 (5th Cir. 1977) (*Rizzo* means courts "should refrain from interference in state affairs unless necessary."); Welsh v. Likins, 550 F.2d 1122, 1131 (8th Cir. 1977).

Once more, it is unclear how the Court's limited view of *Younger* abstention in *Sprint Communications, Inc. v. Jacobs* relates to this far broader view of the reach of *Younger*.

§13.4.8 *The Attempted Application of* **Younger** *to Prevent Federal Court Review of the Legality of Military Tribunals*

In 2006, in *Hamdan v. Rumsfeld*, the Court considered an unusual potential application of *Younger* abstention: whether the federal court should abstain from considering the legality of military tribunals created pursuant to presidential executive order.[108] *Younger* abstention, of course, is about keeping federal courts from interfering with pending *state* court proceedings. But the United States argued that its rationale applied to prevent the federal courts from reviewing the legality of ongoing proceedings in a military tribunal. The claim was that Hamdan, who had been designated for trial in a military proceeding, should raise his objections there and if convicted seek appellate review.

The Supreme Court, in a 5-3 decision, rejected this analogy and held that no abstention was warranted. Although Americans in the military cannot invoke federal jurisdiction when there is an ongoing court-martial proceeding, the Supreme Court said that Hamdan's situation was different. Justice Stevens, writing for the majority, explained, "First, Hamdan is not a member of our Nation's Armed Forces, so concerns about military discipline do not apply. Second, the tribunal convened to try Hamdan is not part of the integrated system of military courts, complete with independent review panels, that Congress has established."[109]

The Court also stressed that review for Hamdan, if convicted, would be within the executive branch and that these proceedings did not have the same assurance of independence as state court proceedings. The Court stated, "Nonetheless, these review bodies clearly lack the structural insulation from military influence that characterizes the Court of Appeals for the Armed Forces, and thus bear insufficient conceptual similarity to state courts to warrant invocation of abstention principles."[110] Thus, the Court concluded that the "circumstances of this case . . . simply do not implicate the 'obligations of comity' that, under appropriate circumstances, justify abstention."[111]

[108] 548 U.S. 557 (2006).

[109] *Id.* at 587.

[110] *Id.*

[111] *Id.* Justice Scalia dissented and argued that "considerations of interbranch comity weigh heavily against judicial intervention." *Id.* at 676-677 (Scalia, J., dissenting). He also argued that the system provided by Congress for review of decisions by military tribunals warranted abstention and deference to that system. *Id.* at 675-676.

§13.5 EXCEPTIONS TO THE *YOUNGER* DOCTRINE

Statement of Exceptions in *Younger*

In *Younger v. Harris*, the Supreme Court stated that in "extraordinary circumstances" federal courts may enjoin pending state court proceedings.[112] The *Younger* Court indicated that injunctions were not appropriate simply because the federal court plaintiff brought a suit under §1983, alleged a violation of the Constitution, or even claimed that the exercise of First Amendment rights were chilled. Rather, the Court specified the type of limited circumstances that would justify federal court injunctions of ongoing state litigation. The Court identified three particular exceptions to the *Younger* abstention doctrine: bad-faith state prosecutions, patently unconstitutional state laws, and the absence of an adequate state forum in which to raise the constitutional issues.[113] Subsequent Supreme Court cases have revealed how narrow these exceptions are and how truly extraordinary the case must be to fit within them.[114]

Bad-Faith Prosecutions

The first exception recognized by the Court was for bad-faith state prosecutions. The *Younger* Court distinguished *Dombrowski v. Pfister* by observing that the latter case involved successive state court prosecutions for the purpose of harassment and not conviction.[115] In *Dombrowski*, the plaintiffs, civil rights activists, alleged that they repeatedly were arrested and indicted even though the state officials did not intend to actually prosecute and convict them. Instead, the plaintiffs alleged, the state's criminal justice system was being used to harass them and dissuade them from continuing to work for the civil rights of Black people within Louisiana. The *Younger* Court viewed *Dombrowski* as representing an exception to the general ban against federal court injunctions of state prosecutions. If prosecutors arrest and indict, but dismiss charges before trial, the individual has no opportunity to assert

[112] 401 U.S. 37, 53-54 (1971).

[113] Additionally, some lower courts have suggested a fourth exception: that *Younger* need not be followed in an emergency situation where denying review could cause irreparable injury. *See* Arevalo v. Hennessy, 882 F.3d 763 (9th Cir. 2018); Diamond "D" Constr. Corp. v. McGowan, 282 F.3d 191 (2d Cir. 2002) (acknowledging that irreparable harm is an exception to *Younger*, but that it is a high standard to meet); Olde Discount Corp. v. Tupman, 1 F.3d 202, 214 (3d Cir. 1993); Hoylake Invs. Ltd. v. Washburn, 723 F. Supp. 42, 50 (N.D. Ill. 1989). Also, one commentator has suggested two other exceptions: a colorable claim of double jeopardy, and waivers by the state of *Younger* abstention. Brian Stagnet, Avoiding Abstention: The *Younger* Exceptions, 29 Tex. Tech L. Rev. 137 (1998).

[114] Some commentators have suggested that the lower courts have also created an exception for preemption cases. Daniel Jordan Simon, Abstention Preemption: How the Federal Courts Have Opened the Door to the Eradication of "Our Federalism," 99 Nw. U. L. Rev. 1355 (2005) (for 20 years, lower federal courts have quietly developed a "preemption exception" to *Younger*).

[115] 380 U.S. 479 (1965).

his or her constitutional claim. Hence, bad-faith prosecutions may be challenged and enjoined in federal court.

The definition of a bad-faith prosecution is when "a prosecution has been brought without reasonable expectation of obtaining a valid conviction."[116] However, since *Younger*, there is not a single instance in which the Supreme Court has applied this exception and found a state action to constitute a bad-faith prosecution. In fact, commentators have observed that "the universe of bad-faith-harassment claims that can be established is virtually empty."[117] In several cases, the Court rejected claims of bad-faith prosecutions and revealed the narrowness of this exception.

In *Allee v. Medrano*, the federal district court enjoined Texas police officials from harassing and brutalizing farmworkers.[118] The Supreme Court reversed and remanded for a determination of whether the district court intended its order as a restraint upon any pending prosecutions under state statutes, and, if so, whether *Younger* was satisfied. In a concurring opinion, Chief Justice Burger addressed the claim that there was a pattern of bad-faith prosecutions in state court. Chief Justice Burger totaled the number of proven incidents and divided by the number of days in which they had occurred. He concluded that there was not a sufficient pattern of wrongful acts because the misconduct occurred only once per month over a one-year period.[119] Moreover, Chief Justice Burger wrote that "[w]illful, random acts of brutality by police, although abhorrent in themselves, and subject to civil remedies, will not form a basis for a finding of bad faith."[120]

This conclusion—that establishing bad faith requires showing the absence of fair state judicial proceedings—was subsequently adopted by a majority of the Court. In *Juidice v. Vail*, a challenge was brought to the use of contempt proceedings by state court judges.[121] The Court emphasized that bad faith was alleged on the part of creditors, not on the part of the judges who issued the contempt orders. The Court concluded that the bad-faith "exception may not be utilized unless it is alleged and proved that [the judges] are enforcing the contempt procedures in bad faith or are motivated by a desire to harass."[122]

In other cases as well, the Supreme Court refused to find the existence of a bad-faith prosecution. In *Hicks v. Miranda*, the district court had found the existence of bad faith on the basis of repeated seizures of the movie *Deep Throat*,[123] but the Supreme Court reversed the lower court's decision, concluding that there was not harassment because the prosecuting officials, in each instance, were acting pursuant to judicial warrants and there was no allegation of bad faith on the part

[116] Kugler v. Helfant, 421 U.S. 117, 126 n.6 (1975).

[117] Owen M. Fiss, *Dombrowski*, 86 Yale L.J. 1103, 1115 (1977); C. Keith Wingate, The Bad-Faith-Harassment Exception to the *Younger* Doctrine: Exploring the Empty Universe, 5 Rev. Litig. 123 (1986).

[118] 416 U.S. 802 (1974).

[119] *Id.* at 845 (Burger, C.J., concurring in part).

[120] *Id.* at 838.

[121] 430 U.S. 327 (1977).

[122] *Id.* at 338.

[123] 422 U.S. 332 (1975).

of the judges.[124] Likewise, in *Moore v. Sims*, the Supreme Court held that there were not bad-faith prosecutions because all of the claims could be presented in state proceedings and there was no allegation of impermissible bias on the part of the state judiciary.[125]

Hence, the bad-faith prosecutions exception appears limited to facts such as those present in *Dombrowski*: repeated prosecutions initiated by state officials solely for the purpose of harassment without the opportunity to raise the claims in state court because of the unavailability or bias of the state judiciary. Thus, it is not surprising that there have been no Supreme Court cases since *Younger* applying this exception and that commentators label the cases fitting in this exception as constituting an "empty universe."

Although lower courts generally have rejected claims of harassment and bad-faith prosecution, some lower courts have applied the exception to reject abstention.[126] For example, some courts have found bad-faith harassment of the owners of adult bookstores when there have been repeated arrests or the seizure of materials under a statute of questionable constitutionality.[127]

Patently Unconstitutional Laws

A second exception recognized in *Younger* was for statutes that are patently unconstitutional. Justice Black, writing for the Court in *Younger*, said that injunctions would be appropriate if there was a statute that was "flagrantly and patently violative of express constitutional provisions in every clause, sentence and paragraph, and in whatever manner and against whomever an effort might be made to apply it."[128] This is a curious exception to the *Younger* doctrine because federal court action seems especially unnecessary when a state statute is so completely unconstitutional. If state courts are ever to be trusted in constitutional cases, surely it is when the state statute is unconstitutional in every clause, sentence, and paragraph. Perhaps the Court's reasoning was that if a statute is so thoroughly

[124] *Id.* at 350-351.

[125] 442 U.S. 415, 432 (1979).

[126] *See, e.g.*, Gates v. Strain, 885 F.3d 874 (5th Cir. 2018); Tony Alamo Christian Ministries v. Selig, 664 F.3d 1245 (8th Cir. 2012); Baffert v. Cal. Horse Racing Bd., 332 F.3d 613 (9th Cir. 2003); Wightman v. Texas Supreme Court, 84 F.3d 188 (5th Cir. 1996); Fieger v. Thomas, 74 F.3d 740 (6th Cir. 1996); Doe v. Connecticut, 75 F.3d 81 (2d Cir. 1996); Arkebauer v. Kiley, 985 F.2d 1351 (7th Cir. 1993) (en banc) (no bad-faith prosecution). *But see* Mulholland v. Marion Cty. Election Bd., 746 F.3d 811 (7th Cir. 2014) (emphasizing that even though the court did not need to reach the issue of bad faith, these facts would have placed the case within the bad faith exception to *Younger*); Lewellen v. Raff, 843 F.2d 1103 (8th Cir. 1987); Fitzgerald v. Peek, 636 F.2d 943 (5th Cir.), *cert. denied,* 452 U.S. 916 (1981).

[127] *See, e.g.,* Nobby Lobby, Inc. v. City of Dallas, 970 F.2d 82 (5th Cir. 1992) (bad faith based on police repeated seizures of questionable constitutionality); Video Store, Inc. v. Holcomb, 729 F. Supp. 579 (S.D. Ohio 1990) (existence of 12 simultaneously pending lawsuits evidences bad faith). *See also* Cullen v. Fliegner, 18 F.3d 96 (2d Cir. 1993) (finding determination that disciplinary proceedings against a teacher were in bad faith was not clearly erroneous); Word of Faith World Outreach Ctr. Church, Inc. v. Morales, 787 F. Supp. 689 (W.D. Tex. 1992) (finding bad faith by Texas attorney general in harassment of religious group).

[128] 401 U.S. 37, 53-54 (1971) (*quoting* Watson v. Buck, 313 U.S. 387 (1941)).

unconstitutional, then the result is obvious and there is little interference with state courts' decision-making because the outcome is preordained.

Yet again, there is not a single instance since *Younger* in which the Court has applied this exception to justify federal court action in light of pending state proceedings. The narrowness of this exception is revealed in *Trainor v. Hernandez.*[129] In *Trainor*, the plaintiffs challenged a state attachment statute that the state was using to recover welfare payments that allegedly had been fraudulently made. The district court found the state attachment statute to be patently violative of due process. The Supreme Court reversed, holding that not all state attachment statutes are unconstitutional and that therefore the district court was wrong in applying this exception and failing to abstain.

Justice Stevens dissented, arguing that the Court had eradicated this exception to the *Younger* doctrine. Justice Stevens explained that under the majority's reasoning "the 'patently and flagrantly unconstitutional' exception to *Younger*-type abstention is unavailable whenever a statute has a legitimate title, or a legitimate severability clause, or some other equally innocuous provision."[130] Justice Stevens thus concluded that the majority effectively "eliminates one of the exceptions from the doctrine."[131] Nothing since *Trainor* has indicated that there is more content to this exception.[132]

However, lower courts have applied this exception to permit federal courts to enjoin state court criminal proceedings that would violate double jeopardy.[133] As the Tenth Circuit concluded, "[I]t is clear that federal intervention is justified where prospective state prosecutions run afoul of the Double Jeopardy Clause."[134]

Unavailability of an Adequate State Forum

The third exception to the *Younger* doctrine is when an adequate state forum is unavailable. In *Younger*, Justice Black stated that when there are pending state proceedings, constitutional issues should be raised there "unless it plainly appears that this course would not afford adequate protection."[135] The Court, however, did

[129] 431 U.S. 434 (1977).

[130] *Id.* at 463 (Stevens, J., dissenting).

[131] *Id.*

[132] Likewise, lower court decisions applying this exception are rare. *See* Tolbert v. City of Memphis, 568 F. Supp. 1285 (W.D. Tenn. 1983) (patently unconstitutional Memphis ordinance declared unconstitutional).

[133] *See, e.g.*, Seay v. Canon, 927 F.3d 776 (4th Cir. 2019); Dominguez v. Kernan, 906 F.3d 1127 (9th Cir. 2018); Walck v. Edmondson, 472 F.3d 1227 (10th Cir. 2007); Gilliam v. Foster, 75 F.3d 881, 903 (4th Cir. 1996).

[134] 472 F.3d at 1233. There may be another circumstance under which federal courts apply this exception: for "speedy trial claims." Daniel Jordan Simon, Abstention Preemption: How the Federal Courts Have Opened the Door to the Eradication of "Our Federalism," 99 Nw. U. L. Rev. 1355, 1364-1365 (2005) ("Where a defendant sues for violation of her right to a speedy trial, the federal courts have found that, if the requested relief is the trial itself, abstention is not required.").

[135] 401 U.S. at 45 (citation omitted).

not elaborate as to what factors would justify a conclusion that a state court was inadequate and therefore a federal court could enjoin the state proceedings.

The Supreme Court first found a state forum to be inadequate under the *Younger* doctrine in *Gibson v. Berryhill.*[136] In *Gibson,* the plaintiffs, who were licensed optometrists, brought an action in the federal district court seeking an injunction to halt proceedings before the Alabama Board of Optometry. The Alabama Board of Optometry, which consisted entirely of optometrists who were self-employed, brought proceedings to rescind the licenses of all optometrists who worked for others. The district court issued an injunction because it concluded that the State Board of Optometry was biased because its members would benefit by suspending a large number of optometrists from practice.

Without deciding whether *Younger* properly applied to administrative proceedings, the Supreme Court held that the district court's conclusion of bias justified federal court intervention. In other words, *Gibson* suggests that federal courts may give relief, notwithstanding the existence of pending state proceedings, if state tribunals are biased and are not to be trusted on the particular issue.

The Court also has indicated that proof of bias is quite difficult, especially when the challenge is to state courts. In *Kugler v. Helfant,* the plaintiff, a state court judge, alleged that members of the state supreme court were so involved in his case that an unbiased hearing was impossible.[137] The Supreme Court disagreed, concluding that there was insufficient evidence that the state courts would not provide a fair hearing. The Court emphasized that the procedures for disqualification of judges and the recent changes in the state supreme court's membership made it impossible to conclude that the state courts could not adequately resolve the constitutional claims.

The other instance in which the Supreme Court found that state proceedings were inadequate was in *Gerstein v. Pugh.*[138] In *Gerstein,* the plaintiffs were held in custody while awaiting trial. They alleged that they were deprived of liberty without due process of law because no judicial officer ever had made a finding of probable cause. The prisoners did not seek release, but rather sought mandatory preliminary hearings. The Court dismissed the relevance of *Younger* in a footnote. The whole thrust of the federal court plaintiffs' argument was that they lacked a state forum in which to present their constitutional claims because of the absence of preliminary hearings. Some commentators have read *Gerstein* as allowing injunctive relief when state courts are very unlikely to remedy the constitutional violations.[139]

Thus, state proceedings will be deemed inadequate if either impermissible bias is shown or if there is no available state remedy. Such findings, however, are likely to be very rare.

[136] 411 U.S. 564 (1973).

[137] 421 U.S. 117 (1975).

[138] 420 U.S. 103 (1975).

[139] William H. Theis, Younger v. Harris: Federalism in Context, 33 Hastings L.J. 103, 159-169 (1981).

Overall, although *Younger* suggests three situations when injunctions of state proceedings are permissible, each of them is very limited. *Younger* is not an absolute ban on federal court injunctions, but it is quite close.

Waiver

A final exception to *Younger* is waiver. It was generally thought that *Younger* abstention must be raised by the parties and that federal courts are not to raise it on their own, but some subsequent cases have allowed courts to raise this sua sponte.[140] Also, a state government can waive its *Younger* abstention argument. If the state "voluntarily chooses to submit to a federal forum, principles of comity do not demand that the federal court force the case back into the State's own system."[141] Likewise, now that *Younger* applies to civil proceedings, there is no reason why the same waiver rules will not be followed in private civil litigation.

However, the underlying rationale behind allowing waivers is questionable. If *Younger* abstention exists to protect state courts from interference and to thereby promote federalism, it is unclear why consent of the *parties* is sufficient to justify interference.

[140] Swisher v. Brady, 438 U.S. 204, 213 n.11 (1978); Time Warner Cable v. Doyle, 66 F.3d 867 (7th Cir. 1995); *but see* Arevalo v. Hennessy, 882 F.3d 763 (9th Cir. 2018) (showing the circuit court did not take issue with the district court raising *Younger* sua sponte); Geier v. Missouri Ethics Commn., 715 F.3d 674 (8th Cir. 2013) (affirming the district court raising *Younger* abstention sua sponte); O'Neil v. Coughlan, 511 F.3d 638 (6th Cir. 2008) (holding court may raise *Younger* abstention sua sponte); Morrow v. Winslow, 94 F.3d 1386 (5th Cir. 1996) (court may raise *Younger* abstention sua sponte).

[141] Ohio Bureau of Employment Servs. v. Hodory, 431 U.S. 471, 480 (1977).

CHAPTER 14

Abstention to Avoid Duplicative Litigation

§14.1 THE PROBLEM OF DUPLICATIVE LITIGATION

The issue

This chapter considers the question of what a federal court should do when an action filed in federal court essentially duplicates litigation simultaneously occurring in state court. When state and federal courts are confronted with virtually identical lawsuits—litigation involving the same parties and issues—the federal court has several possible options. Because of the Anti-Injunction Act and the *Younger* abstention doctrine, the federal court generally may not enjoin the pending state court action.[1] But should the federal court abstain, dismissing or staying its own proceedings in deference to the state court? Or should the federal court allow the two identical suits to proceed simultaneously, with the knowledge that

§14.1 [1] 28 U.S.C. §2283 (discussed in §11.2, *supra*); Younger v. Harris, 401 U.S. 37 (1971) (discussed in Chapter 13).

whichever court rules first will preclude the other from deciding the case because of the doctrine of res judicata?

How Duplicative Litigation Occurs

Duplicative litigation arises in several ways. One common situation might be termed "reactive suits."[2] A party sued in state court might react by filing suit over the same subject matter in federal court, or the reverse: The federal action might be initiated first, and the defendant from that proceeding might file suit in state court. Parties might bring a reactive suit because they perceive that the other forum would be more sympathetic to their claims, because of the strategic and tactical advantages available in the other forum, or because the second court system might offer a speedier resolution for the dispute.[3] For example, in one case, when a New York corporation sued an Illinois company in New York state court for breach of contract, the Illinois business reacted by suing the New York company in federal district court in Illinois for breach of contract.[4] The subject matter of the lawsuits and the parties were identical.

Similarly, the requirement for complete diversity promotes duplicative litigation.[5] For instance, if a California resident sues two Arizona companies in federal court in California, one of the Arizona defendants might file suit against the other two parties (the California resident and the other Arizona defendant) in state court. Because there is not complete diversity, the case cannot be removed from state to federal court. The result is that the exact same matter is simultaneously litigated in federal and state court.

Also, limits on removal jurisdiction in diversity cases foster duplicative litigation. A defendant may not remove a case from state to federal court, even if the other requirements for diversity jurisdiction are met, if the person is sued in his or her own state.[6] However, a person may file a diversity suit in federal court in one's home state. Therefore, a person sued in state court who prefers to litigate the matter in federal court might file a reactive suit in the federal forum, assuming all of the requirements for diversity jurisdiction are met.

Reactive suits arise in the context of federal question jurisdiction as well. For instance, a defendant sued in state court on a state law cause of action cannot remove a case from state to federal court because of a defense based on federal law.[7] Therefore, under some circumstances, the state court defendant might choose to initiate a federal court suit based on federal question jurisdiction against the state court plaintiff. For example, in one case, a group of nonunion teachers were sued in state court for the contribution that they owed, under state law,

[2] *See* Allan D. Vestal, Reactive Litigation, 47 Iowa L. Rev. 11 (1961); *see also* Michael M. Wilson, Comment, Federal Court Stays and Dismissals in Deference to Parallel State Court Proceedings: The Impact of *Colorado River*, 44 U. Chi. L. Rev. 641, 644 (1977).

[3] *Id.* at 644.

[4] Microsoftware Computer Sys., Inc. v. Ontel Corp., 686 F.2d 531 (7th Cir. 1982).

[5] Strawbridge v. Curtiss, 7 U.S. (3 Cranch) 267 (1806) (discussed in §5.3.3, *supra*).

[6] 628 U.S.C. §1441(b).

[7] Louisville & Nashville R.R. v. Mottley, 211 U.S. 149 (1908) (discussed in §5.2.3, *supra*).

in representation fees.[8] Their defense was that collecting fees from them constituted a violation of their First and Fourteenth Amendment rights. They could not remove the case to federal court because the plaintiff's complaint did not present a federal question. The state court defendants, however, reacted by filing a suit in federal court alleging a violation of their constitutional rights because of the state law requiring them to pay union dues.

Duplicative litigation might also result from what might be termed "repetitive suits."[9] A state court plaintiff may bring suit in federal court against the state court defendant on similar or identical causes of action. For example, in one case, a person who wanted to open an adult bookstore filed a suit in state court against the city after he was refused a permit.[10] While the matter was still pending in state court, the potential bookstore operator filed a suit in federal court requesting declaratory and injunctive relief. Repetitive suits might be filed to harass the defendant, because of impatience with the delay in getting a resolution in a court, or in reaction to an adverse ruling that foreshadows a decision on the merits but is not a final resolution that must be accorded res judicata effect.

Desirability of Litigation Occurring in Only One Forum

This chapter examines how federal courts handle duplicative litigation as a result of reactive and repetitive suits. Specifically, the issue is when, if at all, must federal courts abstain to avoid pending concurrent suits. Allowing the litigation to proceed simultaneously in federal and state courts is wasteful because ultimately only one of the jurisdictions will actually decide the case. Once one court renders a ruling, the other court will be obliged to halt its proceedings and give res judicata effect to the decision. This gives the parties an incentive to attempt to manipulate the timing of the decisions. The state court plaintiff will try to speed up the decision-making process in state court and delay the federal court's ruling; for the federal court plaintiff, the opposite will be true.

Therefore, ideally the litigation would proceed in only one court, not in both jurisdictions simultaneously.[11] Under current law, however, there is no way to achieve this unless the federal court abstains. The federal court may not enjoin the state court proceedings because of the Anti-Injunction Act and the *Younger* doctrine, and the state court is under no obligation to abstain and defer to the federal court. But to require the federal court to abstain every time there is a duplicative proceeding in state court would give federal court defendants a powerful tool for defeating federal jurisdiction and, in essence, for removing cases from federal to state court. Moreover, Congress has defined the power of the federal courts through its jurisdictional statutes, and it has offered no indication that it

[8] Oliver v. Fort Wayne Educ. Assn., Inc., 820 F.2d 913 (7th Cir. 1987).

[9] *See* Allan D. Vestal, Repetitive Litigation, 45 Iowa L. Rev. 525 (1960); *see also* Wilson, *supra* note 2, at 643.

[10] Tovar v. Billmeyer, 609 F.2d 1291 (9th Cir. 1979).

[11] *See* James C. Rehnquist, Taking Comity Seriously: How to Neutralize the Abstention Doctrine, 46 Stan. L. Rev. 1049 (1994) (arguing that federal courts should follow a "first filed" rule and that the court that acquires jurisdiction first should decide the matter).

wants federal courts to relinquish jurisdiction when there are parallel proceedings in state court.[12]

Overview of Chapter

Section 14.2 examines the current law concerning abstention to avoid duplicative proceedings. In general, the Supreme Court has held that federal courts should not stay or dismiss proceedings merely because the same matter is being litigated in state court. Rather, only in truly exceptional circumstances must a federal court relinquish jurisdiction because of simultaneous proceedings in state court.[13] Section 14.3 considers the many unresolved issues concerning federal court abstention to avoid duplication of parallel state litigation. Finally, §14.4 discusses procedural issues that arise when federal courts abstain because of the existence of concurrent state court proceedings.

This chapter focuses solely on duplication between federal and state court proceedings. This, of course, is not the only way in which duplicative litigation can occur. The same matter might be simultaneously pending in two suits in the same federal district or, more likely, in two suits in different federal district courts. In such circumstances, federal law permits federal courts to transfer and consolidate proceedings to avoid duplication. Specifically, 28 U.S.C. §1407 provides that "[w]hen civil actions involving one or more common questions of fact are pending in different districts, such actions may be transferred to any district for coordinated or consolidated pretrial proceedings."[14] However, no such provision exists for consolidation of cases between federal and state courts, thus posing the problem discussed in this chapter of how duplicative litigation between such judiciaries should be handled.

§14.2 WHEN SHOULD FEDERAL COURTS ABSTAIN BECAUSE OF DUPLICATIVE LITIGATION IN STATE COURTS?

No General Rule for Abstention

In general, the rule has long been established that the existence of a case in one court does not defeat jurisdiction in another. For example, in 1877, the Supreme Court declared, "[T]he pendency of a prior suit in another jurisdiction is not a

[12] The Ninth Circuit recently made clear that abstention because of duplicative proceedings must meet the requirements of *Colorado River*, discussed below, and does not fall under the district court's general case management authority. Ernest Bock, LLC v. Steelman, 76 F.4th 827 (9th Cir. 2023).

[13] Moses H. Cone Memorial Hosp. v. Mercury Constr. Corp., 460 U.S. 1, 13-14 (1983); Colorado River Water Conservation Dist. v. United States, 424 U.S. 800, 818-819 (1976). These cases are discussed in §14.2, *infra*.

[14] The procedures for consolidation of multidistrict litigation are described in 28 U.S.C. §1407.

bar . . . even though the two suits are for the same cause of action."[1] The Supreme Court often has reiterated this and stated: "Jurisdiction existing, . . . a federal court's 'obligation' to hear and decide a case is 'virtually unflagging.' Parallel state-court proceedings do not detract from that obligation."[2]

Real Property Exception: First Court with Jurisdiction Decides

There is one firmly entrenched exception to this rule: in actions concerning real property, whichever court has jurisdiction first is entitled to exclusive jurisdiction over the matter and even can enjoin other courts from hearing the case. As the Supreme Court explained, "[I]n cases where a court has custody of property, that is, proceedings in rem or quasi in rem . . . the state or federal court having custody of such property has exclusive jurisdiction to proceed."[3] An exception to the Anti-Injunction Act permits federal courts to enjoin state proceedings when the federal court first acquires jurisdiction over property.[4] Moreover, the only situation in which state courts may enjoin parties from proceeding in federal court is when an in rem or a quasi in rem proceeding is pending in state court prior to the initiation of federal litigation.[5]

Thus, there is a clear rule preventing duplicative proceedings in cases involving real property: the court that acquires jurisdiction first decides the matter. This procedure was designed to avoid inconsistent dispositions of property.[6] Of course, inconsistent decisions also could be avoided as they are in in personam cases by according res judicata effect as soon as one court decides. The real benefit of creating exclusive jurisdiction in cases involving property is less in avoiding inconsistent outcomes, and more in terms of increased efficiency. The parties and the judicial system as a whole save resources because a case is litigated in only one court.

The American Law Institute (ALI) offered an alternative explanation for the ability of a court to enjoin other courts that later acquire jurisdiction over an identical property issue. The ALI said that the rule is based on the premise "that commencement of an action in one court, be it state or federal, results in the unavailability of the res for control or disposition by a second court."[7] The idea is that for a court to decide an in rem or quasi in rem case, it must

§14.2 [1] *See, e.g.*, Stanton v. Embrey, 93 U.S. 548, 554 (1877); McClellan v. Carland, 217 U.S. 268 (1910); M'Kim v. Voorhies, 11 U.S. (7 Cranch) 279 (1812); Diggs v. Wolcott, 8 U.S. (4 Cranch) 179 (1807).

[2] Sprint Communications, Inc. v. Jacobs, 571 U.S. 584, 591 (2013) (citation omitted); *see also* Federal Bureau of Investigation v. Fikre, 601 U.S. 234, 240 (2024) ("A court with jurisdiction has a 'virtually unflagging obligation' to hear and resolve questions properly before it.")

[3] Donovan v. City of Dallas, 377 U.S. 408, 412 (1964); Princess Lida v. Thompson, 305 U.S. 456, 465-468 (1939).

[4] 28 U.S.C. §2283, discussed in §11.2, *supra.*

[5] *See* General Atomic Co. v. Felter, 434 U.S. 12 (1977) (per curiam) (property cases are the only situation where state courts may enjoin federal courts).

[6] Colorado River Water Conservation Dist. v. United States, 424 U.S. 800, 819 (1976). *See also* Hagan v. Lucas, 35 U.S. (10 Pet.) 400, 403 (1836).

[7] American Law Institute, Study of the Division of Jurisdiction Between State and Federal Courts 304 (1969).

first acquire jurisdiction over the property in dispute. Once a lawsuit concerning property is filed in one court, that court automatically gets jurisdiction over the property, and other courts cannot hear the case because they cannot remove jurisdiction from the first court. This argument, however, seems to be based entirely on the fiction that only one court can hear disputes over a given piece of property at any point in time. There is no reason why this is true.

No Preclusion of Concurrent Jurisdiction in Other Areas

Although there is a rule creating exclusive jurisdiction for whatever court first obtains jurisdiction over a case concerning real property, no similar principle exists for other types of litigation.[8] Nor are there any other rules to prevent duplicative litigation in state and federal courts. In in personam actions, federal courts may not enjoin pending state proceedings over the same subject matter. In fact, even if there is a danger that the state court might decide first and thereby deprive the federal judiciary from resolving the matter because of res judicata, injunctions of state court actions still are not allowed.[9] Moreover, state courts never may enjoin federal courts in in personam proceedings, even if the state court acquired jurisdiction first and even if a federal court decision effectively would end the state court proceedings.[10]

The result is that frequently the same matter involving the same parties is simultaneously litigated in federal and state courts at a great expenditure of additional resources. The expenses of duplicative litigation are wasteful because whichever court decides first will bind the other. Thus, under current law, the only way to avoid duplicative litigation is for the federal court to stay or dismiss its proceedings and allow the state court action to continue.

Federal Courts Generally Need Not Abstain to Avoid Duplication

The Supreme Court, in general, has held that federal courts need not dismiss or stay an action on account of the existence of parallel litigation in state court.[11] In part, this reflects the view that requiring federal court dismissal would give litigants a powerful tool to keep cases out of federal court or remove cases to state court simply by filing a parallel suit in state court. Also, requiring federal courts to relinquish jurisdiction when there are concurrent proceedings in state

[8] Some lower federal courts have extended the in rem exception to issue antisuit injunctions to protect complex class action proceedings, which are almost always in personam. The courts analogized their efforts at coordinating complex cases to the creation of a judicial res, particularly at advanced stages of litigation. Tobias Barrington Wolff, Federal Jurisdiction and Due Process in the Era of the Nationwide Class Action, 156 U. Pa. L. Rev. 2035, 2047-2052 (2008).

[9] Atlantic Coast Line R.R. v. Brotherhood of Locomotive Engrs., 398 U.S. 281 (1970), discussed in §11.2, *supra*.

[10] Donovan v. City of Dallas, 377 U.S. 408 (1964).

[11] *See* Sprint Communications, Inc. v. Jacobs, 571 U.S. at 588. The Ninth Circuit has recently ruled the fact that the state court decision would have preclusive effect is not a reason for the federal court to abstain when there is duplicative litigation in federal and state court. Ernest Bock, LLC v. Steelman, 76 F.4th 827 (9th Cir. 2023).

court would favor state courts over federal courts—a presumption inconsistent with Congress's creation of federal jurisdiction and one that is not supported by any statutory authority.

However, in 1942, in *Brillhart v. Excess Insurance Co.*, the Supreme Court indicated that under some circumstances federal court deference to pending state proceedings might be appropriate.[12] In *Brillhart*, a federal district court dismissed a diversity suit requesting a declaratory judgment because similar litigation was pending in state court. The Supreme Court held that it was appropriate for the federal court to abstain if it was convinced that the controversy would be adequately settled by the state court proceeding. The Court emphasized that it was dealing with a declaratory judgment proceeding and that "[o]rdinarily it would be uneconomical as well as vexatious for a federal court to proceed in a declaratory judgment suit where another suit is pending in a state court presenting the same issues, not governed by federal law, between the same parties."[13]

Subsequently, lower courts expanded the situations in which federal courts may abstain because of the existence of simultaneous litigation in another tribunal. In fact, a trend emerged that in diversity cases federal courts would abstain out of deference to duplicative concurrent state proceedings.[14] The Supreme Court, however, in two major decisions—*Colorado River Water Conservation District v. United States*[15] and *Moses H. Cone Memorial Hospital v. Mercury Construction Co.*[16]—declared that such abstention is appropriate only in very limited, exceptional circumstances. Also, in *Wilton v. Seven Falls Co.*, the Court held that in suits for declaratory judgments federal courts have more discretion to choose whether to abstain than exists in other types of cases.[17]

Colorado River Water Conservation District v. United States

In *Colorado River*, the United States brought suit in federal district court seeking a declaration of water rights. More than 1,000 defendants were named. Subsequently, one of the defendants in the federal court suit filed a motion in state court to make the United States a party to a state court proceeding concerning

[12] 316 U.S. 491 (1942).

[13] 316 U.S. at 495; *see also* Provident Tradesmens Bank & Trust Co. v. Patterson, 390 U.S. 102, 126 (1968). As discussed below, the Supreme Court reaffirmed *Brillhart* in Wilton v. Seven Falls Co., 515 U.S. 277 (1995), holding that federal courts have discretion in suits for declaratory judgments as to whether to abstain. In MedImmune, Inc. v. Genentech, Inc., 549 U.S. 118, 136 (2007), citing *Brillhart* and *Wilton* and speaking of the Declaratory Judgment Act, the Court emphasized that federal courts have "unique and substantial discretion in deciding whether to declare the rights of litigants."

[14] *See, e.g.*, Amdur v. Lizars, 372 F.2d 103 (4th Cir. 1967); P. Beiersdorf & Co. v. McGohey, 187 F.2d 14 (2d Cir. 1951); Mottolese v. Kaufman, 176 F.2d 301 (2d Cir. 1949) (upholding federal court abstention in light of duplicative state proceedings). *See also* Michael M. Wilson, Comment, Federal Court Stays and Dismissals in Deference to Parallel State Court Proceedings: The Impact of *Colorado River*, 44 U. Chi. L. Rev. 641, 659 (1977) (prior to the *Colorado River* decision, the trend in the lower courts was toward broad stay power).

[15] 424 U.S. 800 (1976).

[16] 460 U.S. 1 (1983).

[17] 515 U.S. 277 (1995).

the same water rights. Although the United States generally may not be sued in state court, the McCarran Amendment provides that the United States consents to being sued in state court in actions to determine the rights to water in a river system.[18] At the same time, several defendants in the federal proceeding filed a motion in federal court seeking to dismiss the federal action for lack of subject matter jurisdiction. They claimed that the McCarran Amendment precluded the district court from assuming jurisdiction over a matter to decide water rights in a river system. Instead of dismissing the action, the district court stayed its proceedings because of the existence of the parallel state proceedings. The U.S. Court of Appeals for the Tenth Circuit reversed, finding abstention under such circumstances to be inappropriate.

The Supreme Court reversed the Court of Appeals decision and reinstated the district court's stay. The Court carefully explained that the case did not fit within any of the traditional abstention doctrines. Moreover, the Court emphasized that federal courts have a virtually unflagging obligation to exercise jurisdiction and, therefore, a federal court usually may not abstain simply because of parallel proceedings in state court. The Court stated that "[g]enerally . . . the pendency of an action in the state court is no bar to proceedings concerning the same matter in the Federal court having jurisdiction."[19]

However, the Court recognized that under truly exceptional circumstances, such as the McCarran Amendment here, federal courts may abstain out of deference to pending state court proceedings.[20] The Court noted that the "circumstances permitting the dismissal of a federal suit due to the presence of a concurrent state proceeding for reasons of wise judicial administration are considerably more limited than the circumstances appropriate for abstention."[21]

Colorado River's Factors in Evaluating Abstention

The Court identified four factors that a federal court should consider when determining whether the interests of wise judicial administration and a comprehensive disposition of the litigation outweigh the duty to exercise jurisdiction. Specifically, the Court stated that federal courts should consider the problems that occur when a state and federal court assume jurisdiction over the same res, the relative inconvenience of the federal forum, the need to avoid piecemeal litigation, and the order in which the state and federal proceedings were filed.[22]

In *Colorado River*, the Court found that the federal district court's abstention was proper because the McCarran Amendment reflected a congressional policy decision to avoid piecemeal litigation in the adjudication of river water rights.[23] The Court concluded that the adjudication of water rights is best conducted in

[18] The McCarran Amendment is codified in 43 U.S.C. §666.

[19] Colorado River Water Conservation Dist. v. United States, 424 U.S. at 817 (citations omitted).

[20] *Id.* at 818.

[21] *Id.*

[22] *Id.* at 818-819.

[23] *Id.* at 819.

"unified proceedings," such as those provided under the state's law. In ruling in favor of abstention, the Court noted the absence of any proceedings in the federal district court other than the filing of the complaint; the case's potentially extensive implications for water rights in the state; the proximity of the state court and the distance of the federal court to the water site; and the existing participation by the U.S. government in ongoing state proceedings. Together, these factors constituted exceptional circumstances warranting abstention.

Colorado River thus clarified the law with regard to abstention because of parallel state proceedings. The Supreme Court emphasized that the existence of duplicative state litigation was not, by itself, sufficient to justify federal court abstention.

Even after *Colorado River* there was confusion among the lower courts as to what constituted sufficiently exceptional circumstances as to justify deference to concurrent state court litigation.[24] Professor David Sonenshein observed that "within a few years after the Court decided *Colorado River*, the lower federal courts were in disarray; some resisted deference in the absence of 'exceptional circumstances,' while others indicated that *Colorado River* might have freed them to clear their dockets merely because a parallel, and thus duplicative, state court action had been filed."[25]

Will v. Calvert Fire Insurance Co.: Divided Opinion

The Supreme Court's next decision concerning parallel state and federal proceedings exacerbated, rather than resolved, the confusion. In *Will v. Calvert Fire Insurance Co.*, the Court was divided 4-1-4 as to whether the federal court should have abstained.[26] Calvert Fire Insurance Company rescinded its membership in a reinsurance pool with American Mutual Reinsurance Company. American Mutual filed suit in state court seeking a declaratory judgment that the pool agreement between it and Calvert was still effective. Calvert's answer in state court alleged that the reinsurance pool contract was not enforceable because American Mutual had violated the Federal Securities Act of 1933, the Securities and Exchange Act of 1934, various state securities laws, and the state common law of fraud. Calvert filed a counterclaim for $2 million in state court, seeking damages for each of the above actions, except for the violations of the federal securities laws. Federal courts have exclusive jurisdiction to award monetary relief for violations of the securities acts.

Simultaneously with filing its answer in state court, Calvert initiated a lawsuit in federal court against American Mutual seeking damages for violations of the

[24] *Compare* Atkinson v. Nelson, 460 F. Supp. 1102 (D. Wyo. 1978); Private Medical Care Found., Inc. v. Califano, 451 F. Supp. 450 (W.D. Okla. 1977) (ordering abstention because of concurrent state proceedings), *with* Turf Paradise, Inc. v. Arizona Downs, 670 F.2d 813 (9th Cir.), *cert. denied*, 456 U.S. 1011 (1982); Gentron Corp. v. H.C. Johnson Agencies, Inc., 79 F.R.D. 415 (E.D. Wis. 1978) (abstention inappropriate because of pending state court proceedings).

[25] David A. Sonenshein, Abstention: The Crooked Course of *Colorado River*, 59 Tul. L. Rev. 651, 667 (1985).

[26] 437 U.S. 655 (1978).

Securities and Exchange Act of 1934. American Mutual moved to dismiss the federal suit on the grounds that the reinsurance agreement was not a security and that the federal court should defer to the pending state proceeding. The federal district court agreed to stay the federal litigation until the state court proceedings were concluded. Calvert then sought and received a writ of mandamus from the U.S. Court of Appeals for the Seventh Circuit compelling the district court judge to proceed with the federal court suit.

The Supreme Court, in a decision without a majority opinion, reversed the court of appeals. Four justices—Justices Rehnquist, Stewart, Stevens, and White—ruled that the district court acted appropriately in abstaining. Justice Rehnquist, writing for these four justices, argued that federal district courts have discretion to abstain when there is an identical case pending in state court. Although Justice Rehnquist recognized that *Colorado River* emphasized the federal courts' duty to hear cases within their jurisdiction, he stated that "[i]t is equally well settled that a district court is under no compulsion to exercise that jurisdiction where the controversy may be settled more expeditiously in state court."[27] Justice Rehnquist based this statement on the earlier Supreme Court decision in *Brillhart v. Excess Insurance Co.*[28] and concluded that it is committed to the discretion of the federal district courts to decide whether to abstain when there is parallel state court litigation.

Calvert's strongest objection to abstention was that the federal court had exclusive jurisdiction to hear and decide claims for money damages under the federal securities acts. Justice Rehnquist, however, curiously concluded that this issue was not before the Court because he read the record as indicating that the district court had not abstained on this part of the plaintiff's lawsuit. He explained that the absence of any additional proceedings in the three years since the district court's abstention decision was not a result of that ruling, but instead simply a reflection of the backlog in the district court. Thus, Justice Rehnquist took no position regarding whether federal courts could abstain because of concurrent state proceedings when a case presented an issue within exclusive federal court jurisdiction.

Justice Blackmun concurred in the judgment, but not in Justice Rehnquist's reasoning. Justice Blackmun argued that *Colorado River* had established that abstention due to pending concurrent state proceedings was allowed only in exceptional circumstances; thus, *Brillhart* was no longer valid in recognizing discretion of district court judges to abstain. Justice Blackmun stated that the court of appeals should have reversed and remanded the district court's decision in light of *Colorado River.*

Four justices—Justices Brennan, Marshall, Powell, and Chief Justice Burger—dissented. They argued that Justice Rehnquist's opinion was guilty of "[i]gnoring wholesale the analytical framework set forth in *Colorado River.*"[29] Justice Brennan, writing for these four justices, stated that *Colorado River* had established

[27] *Id.* at 662-663.

[28] 316 U.S. 491 (1942).

[29] Will v. Calvert Fire Ins. Co., 437 U.S. at 674 (Brennan, J., dissenting).

that such abstention was "rare" and limited to "exceptional circumstances."[30] The dissent strongly challenged Justice Rehnquist's conclusion that district courts have discretion to refuse to hear cases within their jurisdiction because of parallel proceedings in state court. The dissent found *Brillhart*, which Justice Rehnquist relied on, to be totally inapposite because it involved a diversity action and a request for a declaratory judgment.

Thus, in *Calvert*, five justices—Justice Blackmun and the four dissenting justices—rejected Justice Rehnquist's broad grant of authority to district courts to abstain because of pending concurrent state court litigation. The absence of a majority opinion and the fact that Justice Rehnquist's opinion was the plurality's statement caused a great deal of confusion. After *Calvert*, many lower courts believed they had increased authority to abstain to avoid duplicating state court proceedings.[31]

Moses H. Cone Memorial Hospital v. Mercury Construction Co.

The Court attempted to resolve this confusion in *Moses H. Cone Memorial Hospital v. Mercury Construction Co.*[32] The Supreme Court once again emphasized that abstention to avoid duplicative litigation is permissible only in exceptional circumstances. In *Moses Cone*, the plaintiff in the state action filed a suit seeking a determination that its contract with the defendant, Mercury Construction Company, was not subject to arbitration. Subsequently, Mercury Construction initiated federal district court proceedings seeking, pursuant to diversity jurisdiction, a declaratory judgment compelling arbitration under the Federal Arbitration Act. The district court stayed its proceedings in light of the pending state court litigation. The court of appeals reversed and held that abstention was inappropriate.

The Supreme Court affirmed the court of appeals decision and reaffirmed the holding of *Colorado River*. The Court reiterated that a federal court may abstain from exercising jurisdiction only when exceptional circumstances are present. The mere duplicativeness of parallel state and federal proceedings is insufficient to justify abstention. Additionally, the Court stated that the factors announced in *Colorado River* should not be used by a federal district court judge as a mere checklist; rather, they require a careful balancing of the considerations involved. Finally, the Court added other factors to be considered in deciding whether abstention is appropriate: whether a federal question is present, which forum's substantive law would govern the merits of the litigation, and the adequacy of the state forum to

[30] *Id.* at 673.

[31] For a description of lower court opinions seeing a broader authority to abstain after *Calvert*, *see* Thomas C. Platt III, Note, Abstention and Mandamus After Will v. Calvert Fire Insurance Co., 64 Cornell L. Rev. 566, 585 (1979).

[32] 460 U.S. 1 (1983).

protect the rights of the parties.[33] The Court said that the existence of a federal question weighs heavily against abstention.[34]

The Court stressed that federal courts generally must decide cases within their jurisdiction. The Court stated, "[W]e emphasize that our task in cases such as this is not to find some substantial reason for the exercise of federal jurisdiction by the district court."[35] Instead, the Court said, "[T]he task is to ascertain whether there exist 'exceptional' circumstances, the 'clearest of justifications,' that can suffice under *Colorado River* to justify the surrender of that jurisdiction."[36] The Court hardly could have found stronger language to communicate its message that abstention because of pending state proceedings was limited to rare, truly exceptional cases.

Arizona v. San Carlos Apache Tribe of Arizona

Nor has the Court backed away from this position in the years since the *Moses Cone* decision. The Supreme Court reaffirmed *Colorado River* in *Arizona v. San Carlos Apache Tribe of Arizona.*[37] Indian tribes brought suit on their own behalf for water rights in Arizona and Montana. As in *Colorado River,* identical suits were pending in state and federal courts. In fact, the only difference between this case and the facts of *Colorado River* was the identity of the plaintiff: American Indian tribes instead of the U.S. government. The Supreme Court held that this distinction made no difference and ruled that the case was in all respects identical to *Colorado River.* In fact, if the Court had denied abstention in *Arizona v. San Carlos Apache Tribe of Arizona,* but permitted it when the United States was a party, the Court would have taken the anomalous position that the United States is less deserving of access to federal courts.[38] Such a position would be inconsistent with federal jurisdictional statutes that are expansive in allowing the United States to proceed in federal court. Accordingly, the Court held that the same exceptional circumstances justifying federal court abstention in *Colorado River* applied in *San Carlos Apache Tribe.*

Wilton v. Seven Falls Co.

The Court, however, has limited the application of *Colorado River* and *Moses Cone* in one important respect. In *Wilton v. Seven Falls Co.*, the Court ruled that in suits for declaratory judgments federal courts have discretion whether to defer to duplicative state proceedings.[39] Seven Falls Co. was the defendant in litigation in

[33] *See, e.g.*, Steven Plitt & Aeryn Heidemann, Are State Court Garnishment Actions an Effectual Impediment to Federal Declaratory Judgment Jurisdiction: Is Timing Everything?, 15 Conn. Ins. L.J. 119, 149 & n.146 (2008); Ann M. Scarlett, A Better Approach for Balancing Authority and Accountability in Shareholder Derivative Litigation, 57 U. Kan. L. Rev. 39, n.214 (2008) (describing additional factors in analysis).

[34] *Id.* at 23.

[35] *Id.* at 25-26 (emphasis omitted).

[36] *Id.* (emphasis omitted).

[37] 463 U.S. 545 (1983).

[38] *Id.* at 566.

[39] 515 U.S. 277 (1995).

Texas state court over the ownership and operation of several oil and gas properties. After judgment was entered against it in the state court litigation, Seven Falls sought indemnification from Wilton, an insurance underwriter. Wilton had refused to provide a defense for Seven Falls or to indemnify it.

Wilton filed a suit for a declaratory judgment in federal court seeking a ruling that it was not liable under the insurance policies. Seven Falls then filed a suit in state court against Wilton and asked the federal court to dismiss or stay the state court proceedings. The district court granted the stay to avoid duplicative litigation, and both the court of appeals and the U.S. Supreme Court affirmed.

Although the exceptional circumstances warranting *Colorado River* abstention were not present, the Supreme Court unanimously concluded that the federal court had discretion to abstain under the federal Declaratory Judgment Act. The Court noted at the outset that neither *Colorado River* nor *Moses Cone* involved suits brought under the Declaratory Judgment Act.[40] The Court emphasized that the Act is written in discretionary terms, stating that federal courts "may declare the rights and other legal relations of any interested parties seeking such declaration."[41] The Court observed that "[s]ince its inception, the Declaratory Judgment Act has been understood to confer on federal courts unique and substantial discretion in deciding whether to declare the rights of litigants."[42] The Court noted that more than 50 years ago, in *Brillhart v. Excess Insurance Co.*, it held that when a declaratory judgment is requested, the district court is "under no compulsion to exercise that jurisdiction" if the controversy might be settled more expeditiously in state court.[43]

Thus, the Court concluded that the "exceptional circumstances" test of *Colorado River* was too restrictive of federal courts' discretion when applied to suits for declaratory judgments. Justice O'Connor, writing for the Court, explained that the Declaratory Judgment Act's "textual commitment to discretion, and the breadth of leeway we have always understood it to suggest, distinguish the declaratory judgment context from other areas of the law in which concepts of discretion surface."[44] District courts therefore have "discretion to stay or to dismiss an action seeking a declaratory judgment before trial or after all arguments have drawn to a close."[45] The Court said that this grant of discretion to trial courts necessarily meant that appellate review was by an abuse of discretion standard.[46]

The Supreme Court, however, offered little guidance as to the criteria that a federal court should apply in deciding whether to defer to state proceedings when there is a request for a federal declaratory judgment.[47] Justice O'Connor's majority

[40] *Id.* at 285.

[41] *Id.* (*quoting* 28 U.S.C. §2201(a)).

[42] 515 U.S. at 285.

[43] 316 U.S. 491, 494 (1942).

[44] Wilton v. Seven Falls Co., 515 U.S. at 286-287.

[45] *Id.* at 287.

[46] *Id.* at 289.

[47] One place where this confusion has manifested itself is in employment law in litigation over covenants not to compete. *See* Gillian Lester & Elizabeth Ryan, Choice of Law and Employee Restrictive Covenants: An American Perspective, 31 Comp. Lab. L. & Poly. J. 389, 408-413 (2010) (examining enforcement of employee covenants not to compete when the parties or issues involved

opinion said that district courts are in the best position to "grasp" the "usefulness of the declaratory judgment remedy and the fitness of the case for resolution."[48] This hardly gives any sense of when federal courts should or should not abstain in declaratory judgment suits because of pending state court proceedings. For example, can a federal court choose to abstain and defer to the state court simply because of the pressures of the other cases on its docket?[49] The better approach would be to require that federal courts identify particular reasons why it is preferable that the case be heard in state court rather than federal court. However, the very deferential abuse of discretion standard of review would make this very difficult to monitor and enforce.

Some circuits have developed criteria in the absence of clear guidance from the Supreme Court. For example, the Eleventh Circuit, adopting factors developed by the Fourth and Sixth Circuits, articulated the following nonexhaustive list of "guideposts":

(1) the strength of the state's interest in having the issues raised in the federal declaratory action decided in the state courts;
(2) whether the judgment in the federal declaratory action would settle the controversy;
(3) whether the federal declaratory action would serve a useful purpose in clarifying the legal relations at issue;
(4) whether the declaratory remedy is being used merely for the purpose of "procedural fencing"—that is, to provide an arena for a race for res judicata or to achieve a federal hearing in a case otherwise not removable;
(5) whether the use of a declaratory action would increase the friction between our federal and state courts and improperly encroach on state jurisdiction;
(6) whether there is an alternative remedy that is better or more effective;
(7) whether the underlying factual issues are important to an informed resolution of the case;
(8) whether the state trial court is in a better position to evaluate those factual issues than is the federal court; and

---

have connections to multiple jurisdictions, a situation that is rife with incentives for parties to seek tactical advantages by manipulating courts' jurisdiction. Within the context of the variety of parallel proceedings that may arise in non-compete disputes, the authors describe that the "facially contradictory holdings" in *Brillhart* and *Colorado River* have led to inconsistency in the lower courts and confusion over what presumptions ought to inform federal courts faced with a pending parallel state suit.).

[48] 515 U.S. at 287. *See* Government Employees Ins. Co. v. Dizol, 133 F.3d 1220 (9th Cir. 1998) (en banc) (a district court with jurisdiction over a declaratory judgment may decide it without raising sua sponte the question of whether it should exercise its discretion to refuse to hear the matter).

[49] *See* Grace M. Giesel, The Expanded Discretion of Lower Courts to Regulate Access to the Federal Courts After Wilton v. Seven Falls Co.: Declaratory Judgment Acts and Implications Far Beyond, 33 Hous. L. Rev. 393 (1996) (suggesting that docket pressures may determine abstention in cases). *See also* Great Am. Ins. Co. v. Gross, 468 F.3d 199, 207 n.6 (4th Cir. 2006) ("This court . . . and several other circuits have amplified the general policy against concurrent federal litigation expressed in *Colorado River.* Basically, these decisions suggest that a district court may stay or dismiss a suit that is duplicative of another federal court suit as part of its general power to administer its docket.").

(9) whether there is a close nexus between the underlying factual and legal issues and state law and / or public policy, or whether federal common or statutory law dictates a resolution of the declaratory judgment action.[50]

Summary

The current law concerning abstention to avoid duplicative proceedings can be stated succinctly. As a general rule, federal courts may not abstain when there is identical concurrent litigation in state court. Without a doubt, it is economically wasteful to have the same litigation occurring in two courts when only one will actually decide the issues of the case. Also, the simultaneous litigation induces parties to try to manipulate the timing of the decisions to benefit themselves strategically. Nonetheless, the Supreme Court rightly has refused to allow those who prefer to litigate in state court to have the power to prevent federal court review simply by filing a suit in state court. Absent a congressional statute mandating abstention, the Court has insisted that federal jurisdiction be exercised except in the truly exceptional case. However, in suits for declaratory judgments, because the Declaratory Judgment Act gives federal courts broad discretion, abstention can occur without a finding of exceptional circumstances.[51]

Perhaps the best solution to the problem of duplicative litigation would be a statute mandating that the court that acquires jurisdiction over a matter first would

[50] Ameritas Variable Life Ins. Co. v. Roach, 411 F.3d 1328, 1331 & n.4 (11th Cir. 2005). *See* Katherine A. Gustafson, To Hear or Not Hear: Resolving a Federal Court's Obligation to Hear a Case Involving Both Legal and Declaratory Judgment Claims, 50 U. Balt. L. Rev. 383 (2023) (arguing that "when a federal court is faced with a case seeking both declaratory judgment and a legal remedy, it should determine its obligation to exercise jurisdiction by applying the Independent Claim test. . . . If the legal claim is independent, the court must adjudicate the legal claim absent extraordinary circumstances.")

[51] The Supreme Court has not yet addressed whether the same discretion should apply when a federal court is asked to issue a declaratory judgment under authority other than the Declaratory Judgment Act. *See* National Union Fire Ins. Co. of Pittsburgh v. Karp, 108 F.3d 17 (2d Cir. 1997). *Springfield Hosp.* comments that *Karp* is not being followed by district courts in the 2nd Circuit: "However, no cases in this Circuit, or elsewhere, have followed Karp's lead in ostensibly allowing DJA claims for relief to stand on their own, rather than as 'added to claims for relief brought under other auspices.' *Id.* To the contrary, the distinct trend in the law is to hold that HN3 the DJA does not create a separate cause of action." Springfield Hosp. v. Hofmann, No. 5:09-cv-254, 2011 U.S. Dist. LEXIS 86466, at *9 (D. Vt. Aug. 4, 2011). *See* Plitt & Heidemann, *supra* note 33, at 119 (Insurance claims often result in parallel proceedings, but it is not clear under *Brillhart* and *Wilton* whether a state garnishment action—a derivative of a concluded state court liability and damages claim—can be removed to federal court attendant with a federal declaratory judgment action, or whether such an action, having properly been removed to federal court, can be used as a basis for a federal district court judge to abstain from the exercise of jurisdiction under the discretionary Federal Declaratory Judgment Act. This article notes the trend to view the presence of a parallel court proceeding as only one factor, rather than a prerequisite, for applying *Wilton*.); *id.* at 151-152, 179.

have exclusive jurisdiction.[52] Until then, however, the Court's insistence on federal court jurisdiction should be maintained.

§14.3 THE FUTURE COURSE OF *COLORADO RIVER* ABSTENTION: UNRESOLVED QUESTIONS CONCERNING ABSTENTION TO AVOID DUPLICATIVE LITIGATION

What are Sufficiently "Exceptional Circumstances"?

Although the Supreme Court has declared that federal courts generally should not abstain to avoid duplication with concurrent state proceedings, many questions remain unresolved concerning when such abstention is appropriate. First, what constitutes sufficiently "exceptional circumstances" to justify this type of abstention? Despite the Court's statement in *Moses H. Cone Memorial Hospital v. Mercury Construction Co.* that such abstention is to be rare and limited to "exceptional" circumstances,[1] some lower courts continue to order abstention when there are parallel proceedings pending in state courts even in the absence of exceptional circumstances.[2] But other lower federal courts refuse *Colorado River* abstention unless there are truly exceptional circumstances.[3]

Lower courts are in agreement that abstention is to be considered only if there are pending state court proceedings that are truly duplicative of the federal ones—that is, the same parties are litigating the same issues in both

[52] It should be remembered, of course, that *Colorado River* abstention applies only if there is a proceeding pending in state court. *See* Illinois School Dist. Agency v. Pacific Ins. Co., 471 F.3d 714, 724 n.4 (7th Cir. 2006).

§14.3 [1] 460 U.S. 1 (1983).

[2] *See, e.g.,* Tyler v. City of South Beloit, 456 F.3d 744 (7th Cir. 2006) (finding extraordinary circumstances to warrant *Colorado River* abstention); Rivera-Féliciano v. Acevedo-Vila, 438 F.3d 50 (1st Cir. 2006); Nakash v. Marciano, 882 F.2d 1411 (9th Cir. 1989) (approving *Colorado River* abstention to avoid piecemeal litigation and duplication with state proceedings); De Cisneros v. Younger, 871 F.2d 305 (2d Cir. 1989) (approving *Colorado River* abstention when there were duplicative proceedings in federal and state court over a suit to recover damages suffered as a result of a fire).

[3] *See, e.g.,* Great American Ins. Co. v. Gross, 468 F.3d 199 (4th Cir. 2006) (*Colorado River* abstention requires extraordinary circumstances); Mountain Pure, LLC v. Turner Holdings, LLC, 439 F.3d 920 (8th Cir. 2006) (no exceptional circumstances); Ryan v. Johnson, 115 F.3d 193 (3d Cir. 1997) (abstention not justified in diversity cases to avoid piecemeal litigation); In re Abbott Laboratories, 51 F.3d 524 (5th Cir. 1995) (the novelty or complexity of state law issues is not a basis for abstention); Gonzalez v. Cruz, 926 F.2d 1 (1st Cir. 1991) (*Colorado River* abstention rarely justified in diversity cases); Neuchatal Swiss Gen. Ins. Co. v. Lufthansa Airlines, 925 F.2d 1193 (9th Cir. 1991) (refusing *Colorado River* abstention); New Beckley Mining Corp. v. Intl. Union, United Mine Workers of Am., 946 F.2d 1072 (4th Cir. 1991) (absence of exceptional circumstances means that *Colorado River* abstention is not justified).

forums.[4] Typically, in deciding whether to defer to pending state proceedings, lower courts examine the factors identified by the Court in *Colorado River Water Conservation District v. United States*.[5] Federal courts usually look to such considerations as the relative progress of the federal and state court litigation; the importance of avoiding piecemeal litigation; whether there is a congressionally declared policy that would be served by abstention; the relative inconvenience of the federal court to the parties; and whether there is a federal question being litigated.[6]

The application of these factors, however, reveals great disparity as to what constitutes exceptional circumstances sufficient to warrant *Colorado River* abstention. For example, does the federal interest in upholding the policies behind the removal jurisdiction statute justify dismissing or staying a federal court proceeding that is duplicative of ongoing state court litigation? This situation arises when a person is sued in his or her own state court by an out-of-state plaintiff. Under the terms of the removal jurisdiction statute, a state court defendant cannot remove such a case to federal court.[7] However, a state court defendant can initiate a federal court suit, based on diversity jurisdiction, against the state court plaintiff.

Arguably, allowing such federal court jurisdiction circumvents the limit on removal jurisdiction. Abstention might be justified as implementing the congressional policies behind the restriction on removal from state to federal court. But there is a strong argument that if Congress wants to prevent such duplicative litigation in federal courts, it could amend the jurisdictional statutes to specify such a restriction. Moreover, it can be maintained that a person should not be denied access to the federal courts for a suit within federal jurisdiction simply because the other party filed a case in state court first.[8]

A similar issue concerning abstention and removal arises when a state court defendant, who might have removed the state case to federal court, instead files a separate suit in another federal district. For example, when a plaintiff sues an out-of-state defendant in his or her own state court, the defendant might react by filing

[4] *See, e.g.*, Fox v. Maulding, 16 F.3d 1079 (10th Cir. 1994) (abstention appropriate only if there are parallel state and federal proceedings; that is, if substantially the same parties are litigating substantially the same issues in federal and state courts); Baskin v. Bath Twp. Bd. of Zoning Appeals, 15 F.3d 569 (6th Cir. 1994) (*Colorado River* abstention requires pending state court proceedings); TransDulles Center, Inc. v. USX Corp., 976 F.2d 219 (4th Cir. 1992) (abstention inappropriate because there were not parallel state court proceedings).

[5] 424 U.S. 800 (1976). For a discussion of the factors that courts should consider in applying *Colorado River* abstention, *see* Howard A. Davis, Slowing the Flow of *Colorado River*: The Doctrine of Abstention to Promote Judicial Administration, 77 Ill. B.J. 648 (1989).

[6] The Seventh Circuit listed 10 factors that a federal court should consider in deciding whether to apply *Colorado River* abstention: whether the state has assumed jurisdiction over the property involved; the inconvenience of the federal forum; the desirability of avoiding piecemeal litigation; the order in which jurisdiction was obtained; the source of governing law, state or federal; the adequacy of state court action in protecting federal rights; the relative progress of state and federal proceedings; the presence or absence of concurrent jurisdiction; the availability of removal; the contrived nature of the federal claim. Caminiti & Iatarola v. Behnke Warehousing, Inc., 962 F.2d 698 (7th Cir. 1991).

[7] 28 U.S.C. §1441(b).

[8] *But see* James C. Rehnquist, Taking Comity Seriously: How to Neutralize the Abstention Doctrine, 46 Stan. L. Rev. 1049 (1994) (arguing for an expansion of *Colorado River* abstention and for the principle that whichever court acquires jurisdiction first should decide the matter).

a suit in federal court in the defendant's home state. Under such circumstances, should the federal court abstain because the state court defendant could have obtained federal jurisdiction more appropriately through removal?[9]

The better view is that abstention is inappropriate under such circumstances. The Supreme Court in *Colorado River* and *Moses Cone* emphasized that exceptional circumstances must be present in order for abstention to occur on account of pending state court proceedings. The mere duplication of a diversity case in state court, regardless of whether it could have been removed, does not constitute sufficient exceptional circumstances to justify *Colorado River* abstention. In fact, the Supreme Court indicated that *Colorado River* abstention was not justified simply because the state court defendant chose to initiate new proceedings rather than removing the existing ones to federal court. In *Gulfstream Aerospace Corp. v. Mayacamas Corp.*, the Court declared, "This Court never has intimated acceptance of petitioner's view that the decision of a party to spurn removal and bring a separate suit in federal court invariably warrants the stay or dismissal of the suit under the *Colorado River* doctrine."[10] However, the Court said only that abstention is not "invariably" justified under such circumstances; it is left unresolved as to when, if ever, such abstention might be warranted.

Exclusive Federal Jurisdiction

A second unresolved issue arises when there is duplicative state and federal court litigation, but one of the issues pending in federal court falls within exclusive federal jurisdiction.[11] This question was raised, but not decided, in *Will v. Calvert Insurance Co.*[12] American Mutual Reinsurance Company sued Calvert Insurance Company in state court for breach of contract. Calvert filed counterclaims against American Mutual for breach of contract, common law fraud, and violations of the federal securities statutes of 1933 and 1934. Although federal courts have exclusive jurisdiction to give affirmative relief under the securities laws, state courts may decide issues that arise as a defense. Calvert also filed a separate suit in federal court against American Mutual seeking monetary relief for violations of the federal securities acts. When the federal district court abstained, the question was raised over whether such abstention was proper when there was an issue within the federal court's exclusive jurisdiction.

The Supreme Court ducked this issue by concluding that the federal court had not abstained as to the plaintiff's claims under the federal securities laws.[13] This was an unusual reading of the record, especially because there had been

[9] *See* Microsoftware v. Ontel, 686 F.2d 531, 537 (7th Cir. 1982) (upholding abstention under such circumstances), which was decided before Moses H. Cone Memorial Hospital v. Mercury Constr. Corp., 460 U.S. 1, 8-13 (1993), held that *Colorado River* abstention is limited to extraordinary circumstances.

[10] 485 U.S. 271, 290 (1988).

[11] Sharyl Walker, Note, Judicial Abstention and Exclusive Federal Jurisdiction: A Reconciliation, 67 Cornell L. Rev. 219, 233 (1981) ("The power of a federal court to exercise judicial abstention when the federal action involves a claim within the court's exclusive jurisdiction is an open question.").

[12] 437 U.S. 655 (1978).

[13] *Id.* at 667 (plurality opinion).

no further federal court proceedings in the three years since the district court ordered abstention. Yet Justice Rehnquist, writing for a plurality, said that "the delay in adjudicating the damages claim is simply a product of the normal excessive load of business in the District Court."[14]

It now appears settled that a state court decision as to matters within exclusive federal jurisdiction will be given preclusive effect in a later federal court action. In *Marrese v. American Academy of Orthopaedic Surgeons,* a version of this question was raised.[15] The plaintiffs sued because they had been allegedly wrongly excluded from the defendants' organization. The plaintiffs' claims were based entirely on state common law. No federal antitrust violations were alleged. Furthermore, because federal courts have exclusive jurisdiction over antitrust matters, the plaintiffs could not have raised them in state court. After the plaintiffs lost in state court, they then initiated suit in federal court alleging a violation of the antitrust laws. The defendants moved to dismiss based on res judicata. The district court refused to dismiss the case, but the court of appeals reversed.

The Supreme Court, in an opinion by Justice O'Connor, overturned the court of appeals decision. The Court said that the issue was "whether a state court judgment may have preclusive effect on a federal antitrust claim that could not have been raised in the state proceeding."[16] The Court held that the court of appeals erred because in deciding whether preclusion was appropriate, it should have looked first to whether the state court would have given preclusive effect to the earlier judgment. Under the federal statute giving preclusive effect to state court judgments, preclusion is appropriate when it would be applied by the state courts.[17]

In *Matsushita Elec. Indus. Co. v. Epstein,* the Court concluded that a settlement agreement approved by a state court precludes a subsequent securities act claim within the exclusive jurisdiction of federal courts.[18] This indicates that state court decisions will have preclusive effect even as to matters within exclusive federal jurisdiction.[19]

If state court decisions do preclude subsequent litigation in federal court of issues within exclusive federal jurisdiction, then the effect is to deprive federal courts of deciding matters that Congress vested in their exclusive jurisdiction.[20] Accordingly, abstention under such circumstances on account of pending state

[14] *Id.*

[15] 470 U.S. 373 (1985).

[16] *Id.* at 379.

[17] 28 U.S.C. §1738.

[18] 516 U.S. 367 (1996).

[19] "The Supreme Court made it clear that claim preclusion must be denied if state courts would deny it, but left the way open to deny claim preclusion as a matter of federal law if state courts would grant it." 18B Charles Alan Wright et al., Federal Practice and Procedure: Jurisdiction §4470.1 (2d ed.).

[20] *See* Will v. Calvert Ins. Co., 437 U.S. at 670 (Brennan, J., dissenting) (state court decisions should not have preclusive effect over matters within exclusive federal court jurisdiction); Lyons v. Westinghouse Elec. Corp., 222 F.2d 184, 189 (2d Cir. 1955) (state court decisions should not have preclusive effect over matters within exclusive federal jurisdiction). *See generally* Note, The Collateral Estoppel Effect of Prior State Court Findings in Cases Within Exclusive Federal Jurisdiction, 91 Harv. L. Rev. 1281 (1978) (problems with according preclusive effect to matters within exclusive federal jurisdiction).

court proceedings seems questionable. A strong factor militating against federal court abstention should be the existence of an issue within exclusive federal court jurisdiction. If, however, preclusive effect is not accorded to state court judgments as to matters within exclusive federal jurisdiction, then abstention is inappropriate because it would not enhance judicial efficiency. If the state court decision does not bind the federal court, then the federal court ultimately will have to litigate and decide the case. Under such circumstances, abstention would serve no purpose. Thus, either way, federal courts should not abstain when there are matters before them within their exclusive jurisdiction.[21] This conclusion is in accord with the Supreme Court's general admonition that the existence of issues of federal law will "always be a major consideration weighing against surrender" of federal court jurisdiction.[22]

Ultimately, perhaps the best solution to the problem of duplicative proceedings would be congressional guidance as to when federal courts should abstain because of ongoing state court proceedings. A federal statute might create a rule mirroring the one that is followed in real property cases: the first court to acquire jurisdiction should decide the case and may enjoin parties from proceeding in other courts. Although this approach would eliminate the waste of duplicative proceedings, it also might induce a race to the courthouse as litigants compete to ensure that the case would be heard in the forum of their choice.

Alternatively, Congress might consider distinguishing between diversity and federal question jurisdiction cases.[23] In diversity cases, where only state law questions are raised, the statute might require federal court deference to pending state court proceedings, absent exceptional circumstances justifying concurrent litigation. But in cases where the plaintiff invokes federal question jurisdiction, the federal court would have authority to decide the case and even enjoin duplicative state court litigation. This approach would solve the problem of wasteful parallel proceedings in state and federal court and would be based on the interest each level of government has in having its own courts decide its own law; a case would be litigated solely in state court when there was a state law issue, and solely in federal court when there was a federal law issue.

There are problems with this proposal, too. Many cases, of course, involve both state and federal law issues. Also, diversity jurisdiction is based on a belief that state law matters should be tried in federal court when one of the parties in a diversity suit prefers that forum. The proposal to relegate such cases to state court conflicts with this policy underlying diversity jurisdiction.

[21] *See also* Stephen B. Burbank, Interjurisdictional Preclusion, Full Faith and Credit and Federal Common Law: A General Approach, 71 Cornell L. Rev. 733, 822-829 (1986); David A. Sonenshein, Abstention: The Crooked Course of *Colorado River,* 59 Tul. L. Rev. 651, 673-681 (1985).

[22] Moses H. Cone Memorial Hosp. v. Mercury Constr. Corp., 460 U.S. 1 (1983).

[23] *See* Rex E. Lee & Richard G. Wilkins, An Analysis of Supplemental Jurisdiction and Abstention with Recommendations for Legislative Action, 1990 BYU L. Rev. 321 (arguing that Congress, by statute, should keep the rule of *Colorado River* abstention in federal question cases, but make abstention easier in diversity cases).

Despite these problems, and the likely absence of any perfect answer, Congress would be well advised to devise some solution to the problem of duplicative litigation. Until then, pending concurrent proceedings in state and federal court undoubtedly will continue to be a frequent problem confronting the judicial system.

§14.4 PROCEDURAL ASPECTS OF *COLORADO RIVER* ABSTENTION

Two important procedural issues arise concerning abstention to avoid duplicative proceedings. First, when a federal court abstains because of the existence of exceptional circumstances justifying deference to ongoing state court litigation, should the federal case be stayed or dismissed? Second, is the decision of a federal court refusing to abstain or staying its proceedings immediately appealable? In *Moses H. Cone Memorial Hospital v. Mercury Construction Corp.*, the Supreme Court expressly left open the question of whether a federal court should dismiss or stay its proceedings when ordering abstention because of duplicative state court litigation.[1] In reality, this is probably an unimportant question because there will be relatively little difference between a dismissal and a stay. Either way, the state court decision will have preclusive effect in any subsequent federal proceedings. If the federal litigation is stayed, then in most cases dismissal will occur after the state proceedings are completed.

However, there might be rare instances in which the state court proceedings do not resolve all the issues or preclude their later litigation in federal court. Because of this possibility, it would be better for the federal court to stay its proceedings rather than dismiss them. As the U.S. Court of Appeals for the Seventh Circuit observed, a stay is preferable to dismissal in order to safeguard against the running of the statute of limitations should the state litigation not dispose of all claims on the merits.[2] Moreover, there is nothing to be lost by a stay rather than a dismissal. The federal court could wait to dismiss the case until after it was clear that the state proceedings had precluded the federal ones or made them unnecessary.

A Supreme Court decision in a related area indicated its preference for stays over dismissals. In *Deakins v. Monaghan,* the subjects of a state court grand jury investigation brought a federal court proceeding for injunctive and monetary relief.[3] The request for equitable remedies was moot before the Supreme Court, but the suit for damages remained a live controversy. The Supreme Court held that because the claim for monetary relief could not be brought in the state proceedings, the federal court should stay rather than dismiss its proceedings.

§14.4 [1] 460 U.S. 1 (1983).

[2] Lumen Constr., Inc. v. Brant Constr. Co., 780 F.2d 691, 697-698 (7th Cir. 1985).

[3] 484 U.S. 193 (1988).

The Court stated that "the District Court had no discretion to dismiss rather than to stay claims for monetary relief that cannot be redressed in the state proceeding."[4] However, it should be noted that *Deakins* did not address the choice between dismissals and stays when the federal and state proceedings consider the same issues.

Also, *Deakins* likely is less indicative of a general preference for stays and more reflective of the Court's drawing a distinction between claims for money damages and suits for equitable relief. In *Quackenbush v. Allstate Insurance Co.*,[5] a case involving deference to complex state administrative procedures under *Burford*,[6] the Court said generally that abstention doctrines are derived from the equitable discretion of federal courts. In *Quackenbush*, the Court ruled that suits for money damages should therefore not be dismissed from federal courts. Although neither *Deakins* nor *Quackenbush* dealt with *Colorado River* abstention, both indicate that suits for money damages should be treated differently than suits for injunctive relief. The former only should be stayed, while dismissal is permissible for the latter.[7]

Second, the Supreme Court ruled that a party may not immediately appeal the district court's refusal to abstain. Resolving a conflict between the federal courts of appeals,[8] in *Gulfstream Aerospace Corp. v. Mayacamas Corp.*, the Supreme Court stated, "Because an order denying a *Colorado River* motion is 'inherently tentative' . . . the order is not a conclusive determination within the meaning of the collateral-order doctrine and therefore is not appealable under §1291."[9]

But the law is settled that a district court's *decision to abstain* is immediately appealable.[10] Regardless of whether the abstention takes the form of a dismissal or a stay, it is likely to end the federal court proceedings when there is duplicative state court litigation. Hence, it is desirable that the abstention decision may be appealed.

[4] *Id.* at 202.

[5] 517 U.S. 706 (1996).

[6] *Burford* abstention is discussed in detail in §12.2.3.

[7] Additionally, the subject matter of the lawsuit might be relevant in evaluating whether stay or dismissal is preferable. The Seventh Circuit ruled that in civil rights cases federal courts should stay rather than dismiss proceedings. Selmon v. Portsmouth Drive Condominium Assn., 89 F.3d 406 (7th Cir. 1996).

[8] *Compare* Richman Bros. Records, Inc. v. U.S. Sprint Communications, 953 F.2d 1431 (3d Cir. 1991); RRI Realty Corp. v. Village of Southampton, 766 F.2d 63 (2d Cir. 1985) (abstention order is not immediately appealable), *with* Microsoftware Computer Sys. v. Ontel, 686 F.2d 531, 534 (7th Cir. 1982) (abstention order is immediately appealable). *See* Gulfstream Aerospace Corp. v. Mayacamas Corp., 485 U.S. 271 (1988) (resolving a circuit split over whether a district court's decision to abstain was appealable, abolishing the Enelow-Ettelson doctrine). The *Gulfstream* decision was itself overruled within several months by 9 U.S.C.A. §16(a). *See, e.g.,* Microchip Tech. Inc. v. U.S. Philips Corp., 367 F.3d 1350, 1355 (Fed. Cir. 2004) ("section 16 renders appealable under section 1292(a)(1) the denial of an injunctive order (i.e., motions to compel arbitration) that otherwise would not be appealable under *Gulfstream.*").

[9] 485 U.S. 271, 278 (1988).

[10] Moses H. Cone Memorial Hosp. v. Mercury Constr. Corp., 460 U.S. at 8-13; *see also* Quackenbush v. Allstate Insurance Co., 517 U.S. 706 (1996) (finding decision to abstain in *Burford* abstention context was immediately appealable).

CHAPTER 15

Federal Court Collateral Review of Criminal Convictions: Habeas Corpus

§15.1 INTRODUCTION

A litigant in a state court generally may secure federal court review of the state court's judgments and proceedings only by first exhausting all available appeals within the state system and then seeking review of the final judgment in the U.S. Supreme Court. Federal district courts lack the authority to hear appeals from state judicial systems.[1] However, federal courts have the authority to review state court criminal convictions pursuant to writs of habeas corpus. Under federal law, a person who claims to be held in custody by a state government in violation of the Constitution, treaties, or laws of the United States may file a civil lawsuit in federal court seeking a writ of habeas corpus. Technically, federal court consideration of the habeas corpus petition is not considered a direct review of the state court decision; rather, the petition constitutes a separate civil suit filed in federal court and is termed "collateral relief." Pursuant to the writ of habeas corpus the federal court may order the release of a state prisoner who is held by the state in violation of federal law. Also, federal courts may hear habeas petitions of federal prisoners pursuant to 28 U.S.C. §2255.

Overview of the History of Habeas Corpus

The writ of habeas corpus has its origins in English law.[2] Blackstone referred to habeas corpus as "the most celebrated writ in English law."[3] Recognizing its importance, the Framers of the Constitution provided that "The Privilege of the Writ of Habeas Corpus shall not be suspended, unless when in Cases of Rebellion or Invasion the public Safety may require it."[4] Under the Judiciary Act of 1789, habeas corpus was available to prisoners who claimed that they were held in custody by the *federal* government in violation of the Constitution, treaties, or laws of the United States.[5] After the Civil War, at a time of great distrust in the ability and willingness of state courts to protect federal rights, Congress provided habeas corpus relief to state prisoners if they were held "in custody in violation of the Constitution or laws or treaties of the United States."[6]

The writ of habeas corpus protects individuals against arbitrary and wrongful imprisonment. It is not surprising, therefore, that habeas corpus long has been viewed as the "great writ of liberty."[7] At the same time, however, the availability

§15.1 [1] Rooker v. Fidelity Trust Co., 263 U.S. 413, 416 (1923); District of Columbia Court of Appeals v. Feldman, 460 U.S. 462 (1983) (federal courts lack jurisdiction to review state court decisions). The *Rooker-Feldman* doctrine is discussed in detail in §13.2.

[2] For a history of habeas corpus, *see* Amanda Tyler, A "Second *Magna Carta*": The English Habeas Corpus Act and the Statutory Origins of the Habeas Privilege, 91 Notre Dame L. Rev. 1949 (2016); Amanda Tyler, Habeas Corpus and the American Revolution, 103 Calif. L. Rev. 635 (2015); W. Duker, A Constitutional History of Habeas Corpus (1980).

[3] 3 Blackstone's Commentaries 129 (1791).

[4] U.S. Const. art. I, §9, cl. 2.

[5] Judiciary Act of 1789, ch. 20, 1 Stat. 73.

[6] 28 U.S.C. §2254.

[7] Duker, *supra* note 2, at 3.

of federal court relief pursuant to the writ of habeas corpus remains enormously controversial. Conservatives feel that habeas corpus is a vehicle that guilty criminals use to escape their convictions and their sentences.[8] Liberals see the writ as an essential protection of constitutional rights—ensuring that individuals are not held in custody in violation of those rights.[9] The writ of habeas corpus also is controversial because it is a source of direct confrontation between federal district courts and state judiciaries. The power of a single federal judge to overturn a decision affirmed by an entire state court system is troubling to many.[10] A reflection of this ideological split is that in 1996, the Republican-controlled Congress enacted the Antiterrorism and Effective Death Penalty Act (AEDPA), which substantially changed the law of habeas corpus and in many ways restricted its availability.[11]The controversy over habeas corpus must be put in perspective. Statistics indicate that less than 1 percent of state prisoners who file habeas corpus petitions ultimately prevail.[12]

Underlying Issues in the Debate Over Habeas Corpus

The debate about the availability and scope of relief pursuant to habeas corpus petitions raises basic questions about federalism, separation of powers, the purposes of the criminal justice system, and the nature of litigation. With regard to federalism, habeas corpus poses difficult questions about the relationship of federal and state courts. For example, critics of habeas corpus review argue that such relief is generally unnecessary because state courts should be trusted to adequately protect federal constitutional rights.[13] Defenders of habeas corpus availability for state prisoners expressly challenge the assumption of parity between federal and state courts and argue that structural differences between federal and state courts mandate that federal courts be available to protect federal rights.[14] Supreme Court opinions expanding the availability of habeas corpus relief have stressed distrust

[8] *See, e.g.,* Henry J. Friendly, Is Innocence Irrelevant? Collateral Attack on Criminal Judgments, 38 U. Chi. L. Rev. 142 (1970) (arguing that habeas corpus should be available only where there is a colorable showing of a defendant's innocence).

[9] *See, e.g.,* Stephen A. Saltzburg, Habeas Corpus: The Supreme Court and the Congress, 44 Ohio St. L.J. 367 (1983) (habeas corpus is symbolic of the ideal that no person should be convicted in violation of the fundamental law of the land).

[10] *See, e.g.,* Engle v. Isaac, 456 U.S. 107, 126 (1982).

[11] Pub. L. No. 104-132, April 24, 1996, discussed in §15.4.3.

[12] John Blume, AEDPA: The "Hype" and the "Bite," 91 Cornell L. Rev. 259, 284 (2006); *see also* Fred L. Cheesman II, Nancy J. King & Brian J. Ostrom, Final Technical Report: Habeas Litigation in U.S. District Courts: An Empirical Study of Habeas Corpus Cases Filed by State Prisoners Under the Antiterrorism and Effective Death Penalty Act of 1996, at 51-52 (2007) (district courts grant habeas petitions in 12.4 percent of capital cases and 0.29 percent of noncapital cases).

[13] *See, e.g.,* Paul M. Bator, The State Courts and Federal Constitutional Litigation, 22 Wm. & Mary L. Rev. 605, 623-627 (1981).

[14] *See, e.g.,* John H. Blume, In Defense of Non-Capital Habeas: A Response to Hoffmann and King, 96 Cornell L. Rev. 435 (2011); Gary Peller, In Defense of Federal Habeas Corpus Relitigation, 16 Harv. C.R.-C.L. L. Rev. 579, 665-669 (1982); Stephen B. Bright, Elected Judges and the Death Penalty in Texas: Why Full Habeas Corpus Review by Independent Federal Judges Is Indispensable to Protecting Constitutional Rights, 78 Tex. L. Rev. 1805 (2000).

of state courts, but decisions restricting such review have emphasized a belief that state judiciaries are equal to federal courts in their ability and willingness to protect federal rights.[15]

Additionally, because federal statutes determine the availability of and procedures for habeas corpus, separation of powers issues arise in determining the proper role of the Supreme Court in deciding habeas corpus questions. Although the Constitution prohibits Congress from suspending the writ of habeas corpus except during times of rebellion or invasion, this provision was probably meant to keep Congress from suspending the writ and preventing *state* courts from releasing individuals who were wrongfully imprisoned.[16] The constitutional provision does not create a right to habeas corpus; rather, federal statutes, specifically those adopted after the Civil War, provide the authority for federal court habeas corpus relief to state prisoners.

Because federal statutes are instrumental in providing for the availability of habeas corpus relief, there is a strong argument that the Supreme Court should interpret the habeas corpus laws in accordance with traditional principles of statutory construction and not create additional barriers to federal court relief.[17] However, there is little agreement regarding Congress's objectives in adopting the habeas corpus statutes. Some, such as Professor Paul Bator, see a limited objective of providing a federal court remedy solely in instances in which state courts lacked jurisdiction to try a defendant.[18] Others, such as Professor Gary Peller, interpret the same legislative history in a much different way and conclude that Congress intended to allow state prisoners the opportunity to relitigate their constitutional claims in federal court.[19]

A third theme in the debate over the proper scope of habeas corpus relief concerns the purpose of constitutional rights in the criminal justice system. If constitutional rights exist primarily to protect innocent individuals and ensure that only those who actually committed a crime will be convicted, then it makes sense to limit habeas relief to those who are arguably innocent.[20] But if the litigation of

[15] *Compare* Brown v. Allen, 344 U.S. 443, 511 (1953) (allowing relitigation of constitutional issues on habeas corpus because of the failure of state courts to give adequate protection to federal constitutional rights), *with* Stone v. Powell, 428 U.S. 465, 493 n.35 (1976) (generally preventing relitigation of search and seizure exclusionary rule issues because of the assumption that state courts are able and willing to adequately protect federal constitutional rights). In Brown v. Davenport, 596 U.S. 118 (2022), Justice Gorsuch's majority opinion strongly questioned Brown v. Allen and allowing matters to be relitigated on habeas corpus, while in dissent Justice Kagan defended Brown v. Allen. *See* §15.5.2, *infra*.

[16] *See* Duker, *supra* note 2, at 135-136.

[17] *Cf.* Martin H. Redish, Abstention, Separation of Powers, and the Limits of the Judicial Function, 94 Yale L.J. 71 (1984) (arguing generally that the Court should not create procedural doctrines preventing the federal courts from exercising jurisdiction granted by Congress).

[18] Paul M. Bator, Finality in Criminal Law and Federal Habeas Corpus for State Prisoners, 76 Harv. L. Rev. 441, 466, 475 (1963).

[19] Peller, *supra* note 14, at 619-621.

[20] *See, e.g.*, Friendly, *supra* note 8; Manson v. Brathwaite, 432 U.S. 98, 111-112 (1977); United States v. Janis, 428 U.S. 433, 448-449 (1976).

constitutional rights serves other purposes besides protecting the innocent—goals such as controlling police behavior and protecting individual privacy and dignity—then habeas corpus relief should be available regardless of the petitioner's guilt or innocence.[21]

Fourth, discussions and decisions about the scope of habeas corpus relief raise questions about the importance of finality and the consequences of revisions in the process of litigation. Critics of habeas corpus review contend that it prolongs litigation and undermines finality in the criminal justice system. For example, Professor Paul Bator argues that the "automatic collateral relitigation model exacts severe costs. It is profligate with resources at a time of increasing scarcity."[22] Additionally, some Supreme Court justices have complained that the loss of finality as a result of habeas corpus petitions undermines the purposes of the criminal justice system in deterring crime and rehabilitating criminals.[23] Also, it is argued that a large number of non-meritorious habeas petitions causes a judicial predisposition toward dismissal, making it more difficult for deserving individuals to gain needed relief. Justice Jackson explained, "It must prejudice the occasional meritorious application to be buried in a flood of worthless ones. He who must search a haystack for a needle is unlikely to end up with the attitude that the needle is worth the search."[24]

On the other hand, defenders of habeas corpus availability emphasize the importance of collateral review to correct errors by the state courts.[25] Professor Robert Cover argued that the "jurisdictional redundancy" provided by habeas corpus serves many functions in addition to error correction, including greater assurances of legitimacy of decisions to litigants and encouraging innovation through a dialogue between differing court systems and perspectives.[26] Moreover, defenders of habeas corpus argue that the petitions occupy a fairly small percentage of the federal courts' resources and that there is no evidence that the existence of habeas corpus has any adverse effect on the criminal justice system.[27]

Because of the divergence of views on these questions, the debate over habeas corpus inevitably will continue.[28] No area of federal jurisdiction has changed

[21] *See, e.g.,* Stone v. Powell, 428 U.S. at 524 (Brennan, J., dissenting) ("Procedural safeguards . . . are not admonitions to be tolerated only to the extent they serve functional purposes that ensure that the 'guilty' are punished and the 'innocent' freed.").

[22] Bator, *supra* note 18, at 614.

[23] *See, e.g.,* Engle v. Isaac, 456 U.S. 107, 126 (1982) (O'Connor, J., writing for the majority); Burger, Annual Report to the American Bar Association by the Chief Justice of the United States, 67 A.B.A. J. 290, 292 (1981).

[24] Brown v. Allen, 344 U.S. 443, 537 (1953) (Jackson, J., concurring).

[25] *See* Judith Resnik, Tiers, 57 S. Cal. L. Rev. 837, 855 (1984); Robert Cover, The Uses of Jurisdictional Redundancy: Interest, Ideology, and Innovation, 22 Wm. & Mary L. Rev. 639, 653 (1981).

[26] Cover, *supra* note 25, at 661-673; *see also* Robert Cover & Alexander Aleinikoff, Dialectical Federalism: Habeas Corpus and the Court, 86 Yale L.J. 1035 (1977).

[27] *See, e.g.,* Resnik, *supra* note 25, at 951-952 (habeas cases account for 5 percent of the federal docket).

[28] Some have argued for significant additional restrictions on habeas corpus. *See* Nancy J. King & Joseph L. Hoffmann, Habeas for the 21st Century: Uses, Abuses and the Future of the Great Writ (2011) ("Congress should limit habeas review of state criminal cases to two categories in which it actually can do some serious good: capital cases and cases in which the prisoner can produce persuasive

more dramatically in the past 30 years than habeas corpus. As discussed below, the Court has imposed substantial new obstacles to habeas relief, including generally preventing successive habeas petitions[29] and preventing the use of habeas corpus to develop new rules of constitutional law.[30] Even more dramatically, the Antiterrorism and Effective Death Penalty Act substantially changed many aspects of the law of habeas corpus, including creating a statute of limitations for filing petitions, precluding successive petitions except in very limited circumstances and only with the approval of a U.S. court of appeals, and narrowing the scope of federal court review.[31] Additionally, twice Congress has enacted statutes precluding habeas corpus by those held as enemy combatants.

Overview of Chapter

This chapter examines the development and scope of federal habeas corpus relief. Section 15.2 sketches the history of habeas corpus relief in the United States. Section 15.3 describes the statutory framework for federal court habeas corpus review and especially details the procedures for presenting habeas corpus petitions to the federal courts. The prerequisites for federal habeas corpus relief are discussed in §15.4; specifically, the petitioner must be in state custody, must have exhausted all available state remedies, and must not be presenting petitions that duplicate those already rejected by a federal court. Perhaps most important, §15.5 considers what issues can be litigated in federal habeas corpus review. In particular, several important questions concern the scope of habeas review: what constitutional claims can be presented on habeas corpus, when habeas petitioners may relitigate matters already litigated and decided in state court, and when petitioners may present and litigate issues that were not raised in state court. Finally, §15.6 considers appeals of the denial of habeas corpus petitions and the requirement for a certificate of appealability.

Other Uses of Habeas Corpus

The primary focus of this chapter is on federal court habeas corpus relief for state prisoners. However, habeas corpus also is available for federal prisoners.[32] Most commonly, federal prisoners seek relief pursuant to 28 U.S.C. §2255, usually referred to as §2255 proceedings. Throughout this chapter, differences in the law for federal petitioners are noted and described.

---

new evidence of his innocence. Limiting habeas to these cases will help protect the long-term future of the writ in all of its varied forms.") Others strongly disagree and defend habeas corpus availability. *See* John H. Blume, In Defense of Non-Capital Habeas: A Response to Hoffmann and King, 96 Cornell L. Rev. 435 (2011).

[29] McCleskey v. Zant, 499 U.S. 467 (1991), discussed in §15.4.3.

[30] Teague v. Lane, 489 U.S. 288 (1989), discussed in §15.5.1.

[31] Antiterrorism and Effective Death Penalty Act of 1996, Pub. L. No. 104-132, 110 Stat. 1214.

[32] *See* 28 U.S.C. §2255 (describing availability of relief for federal prisoners).

Also, although this chapter deals primarily with habeas corpus review of criminal convictions, which is by far the most frequent use of habeas corpus, it should be noted that habeas corpus is available whenever a person is in government custody. Hence, habeas corpus may be used by a person challenging civil confinement in an institution,[33] a deportation order,[34] an extradition order,[35] executive detention,[36] a conviction by a military court,[37] or the denial of parole.[38] But in *Department of Homeland Security v. Thuraissigiam,* the Supreme Court upheld a federal statute limiting habeas corpus by asylum seekers.[39] The Court held that 8 U.S.C. §1252(e)(2)—which limits the habeas review obtainable by a noncitizen detained for expedited removal—does not violate the suspension or due process clauses.

Finally, although this chapter focuses on habeas corpus to secure the release of a person from custody, habeas corpus also is available, though infrequently used, to bring a person into court to testify.[40]

§15.2 A BRIEF HISTORY OF HABEAS CORPUS IN THE UNITED STATES

Constitutional Convention

Habeas corpus existed in the American colonies prior to the adoption of the Constitution.[1] In many of the colonies, there was a common law right to habeas corpus; in others, provisions in the colonies' charters and in colonial statutes ensured the availability of the writ of habeas corpus.[2]

At the Constitutional Convention, delegate Charles Pinckney proposed a revision to ensure the availability of habeas corpus.[3] A compromise resulted and

[33] *See, e.g.,* Lake v. Cameron, 364 F.2d 657 (D.C. Cir. 1966).

[34] *See, e.g.,* Rowoldt v. Perfetto, 355 U.S. 115 (1957). In INS v. St. Cyr, 533 U.S. 289 (2001), the Supreme Court held that the preclusion of habeas review for those facing deportation would be an impermissible suspension of the writ of habeas corpus. INS v. St. Cyr is discussed in Chapter 3.

[35] *See, e.g.,* Fernandez v. Phillips, 268 U.S. 311 (1925).

[36] *See* Gerald L. Neuman, Habeas Corpus, Executive Detention, and the Removal of Aliens, 98 Colum. L. Rev. 961 (1998); Richard H. Fallon, Jr., Applying the Suspension Clause to Immigration Cases, 98 Colum. L. Rev. 1068 (1998).

[37] *See, e.g.,* Strait v. Laird, 406 U.S. 341 (1972) (habeas corpus is available to challenge an administrative refusal to allow someone to leave the military because of conscientious objection); Reid v. Covert, 354 U.S. 1 (1957) (court-martial).

[38] *See, e.g.,* Morrissey v. Brewer, 408 U.S. 471 (1972).

[39] 591 U.S. 103 (2020).

[40] 28 U.S.C. §2241(c).

§15.2 [1] Max Rosenn, The Great Writ—A Reflection of Social Change, 44 Ohio St. L.J. 337, 338 (1983); Paul D. Halliday, Habeas Corpus: From England to Empire (2010).

[2] Fay v. Noia, 372 U.S. 391, 405 (1963); W. Duker, A Constitutional History of Habeas Corpus 98-99 (1980).

[3] Duker, *supra* note 2, at 127.

instead of guaranteeing habeas corpus, the Constitution prohibited its suspension. Contemporaneous English history demonstrated to the American colonists the likelihood the writ would be suspended and the dangers from such a suspension. Parliament frequently suspended the writ of habeas corpus during the seventeenth and eighteenth centuries, allowing individuals to be imprisoned without any legal protections. William Duker, in his authoritative history of the writ of habeas corpus, argues that the Framers feared that Congress might suspend the states' ability to grant habeas corpus in the same way that Parliament had suspended habeas corpus in the colonies.[4] Thus, the Constitutional Convention prevented Congress from obstructing the state courts' ability to grant the writ but did not try to create a federal constitutional right to habeas corpus.[5]

Judiciary Act of 1789

In the Judiciary Act of 1789, Congress explicitly provided federal courts the authority to grant habeas corpus to federal prisoners.[6] Although federal courts could not grant habeas corpus relief to state prisoners, the Supreme Court upheld the federal courts' ability to review the constitutionality of state criminal convictions on direct appeal.[7]

Post-Civil War Reforms

After the Civil War, Congress feared that Southern states would persecute and even literally imprison former slaves.[8] Congressional investigations discovered that "despite a theoretical improvement in legal status, Negroes remained virtually unprotected by State criminal processes."[9] The Congressional Committee on Reconstruction concluded that former slaves were victims of "cruelty, oppression and murder, which the local authorities were at no pains to prevent or punish."[10] Thus, one of the most important provisions of the Reconstruction Act allowed federal courts to grant habeas corpus to state prisoners held in violation of the Constitution and laws of the United States.[11]

[4] *Id.* at 126-156.

[5] Excellent scholarship challenges this conventional wisdom and argues for a much broader reading of the suspension clause as a limit on Congress's ability to restrict habeas corpus. *See* Gerald Neuman, Habeas Corpus, Executive Detention, and the Removal of Aliens, 98 Colum. L. Rev. 961 (1998); Eric Freedman, The Suspension Clause in the Ratification Debate, 44 Buff. L. Rev. 451 (1996).

[6] Judiciary Act of 1789, ch. 20, 1 Stat. 73, 81-82.

[7] *See, e.g.,* Cohens v. Virginia, 19 U.S. (6 Wheat.) 264, 291-293 (1821); *see* §10.2, *supra.*

[8] Rosenn, *supra* note 1, at 342.

[9] *Id.* (*quoting* U.S. Commn. on Civil Rights, Law Enforcement: A Report on Equal Protection in the South 7 (1965)).

[10] *Id.* (*quoting* Joint Comm. on Reconstruction, Report of the Joint Comm. on Reconstruction, H.R. Rep. No. 30, 39th Cong., 1st Sess. vii, xvii (1866)).

[11] Act of Feb. 5, 1867, ch. 28, 14 Stat. 385 (codified as 28 U.S.C. §§2241-2255).

Although there is disagreement about what the drafters intended on many specific questions,[12] there is consensus that the law was based on a distrust of Southern states and was designed to allow federal courts to protect former slaves from unconstitutional confinement. Shortly after the adoption of the act, the Supreme Court noted that "[t]his legislation is of the most comprehensive character. It brings within the *habeas corpus* jurisdiction of every court and of every judge every possible case of deprivation of liberty contrary to the National Constitution, treaties, or laws. It is impossible to widen this jurisdiction."[13]

Initial Restrictive Interpretation and Subsequent Expansion

Nonetheless, in the first years after the adoption of the Reconstruction Act, the application of habeas corpus was limited to circumstances in which the defendant alleged that the sentencing court lacked jurisdiction. During the latter part of the nineteenth century, the Supreme Court progressively expanded the circumstances under which a federal court could find a lack of state court jurisdiction and grant habeas corpus to a state prisoner.[14] For example, the Court found that a state court lacked jurisdiction when there was a violation of the prohibition against double jeopardy[15] and when the statute that was the basis for the prosecution was unconstitutional.[16]

In 1915, the Supreme Court went even further, and in the landmark decision of *Frank v. Mangum* held that habeas corpus is available whenever the state "supplying no corrective process, deprives the accused of his life or liberty without due process of law."[17] However, according to *Frank*, as long as the state provided an adequate review process to hear the defendant's claims, there was no basis for habeas relief for state prisoners. *Frank* was important because it was the first time the Supreme Court recognized that federal courts could grant habeas corpus to state prisoners on grounds other than a lack of trial court jurisdiction.

[12] *Compare* Gary Peller, In Defense of Federal Habeas Corpus Relitigation, 16 Harv. C.R.-C.L. L. Rev. 579, 690-691 (1982) (arguing that the legislative history justifies relitigation of all constitutional claims on habeas corpus), *with* Paul Bator, Finality in Criminal Law and Federal Habeas Corpus for State Prisoners, 76 Harv. L. Rev. 441, 526 (1963) (arguing that the legislative history justifies restricting habeas corpus to instances in which the state court lacked jurisdiction over the defendant).

[13] Ex parte McCardle, 73 U.S. (6 Wall.) 318, 325-326 (1867).

[14] Henry M. Hart, The Supreme Court 1958 Term, Foreword: The Time Chart of the Justices, 73 Harv. L. Rev. 84, 103-104 (1959) (discusses the "long process of expansion of the concept of lack of jurisdiction"); Rosenn, *supra* note 1, at 344.

[15] Ex parte Lange, 85 U.S. (18 Wall.) 163 (1873).

[16] Ex parte Siebold, 100 U.S. 371, 376 (1879).

[17] 237 U.S. 309, 335 (1915). For a discussion of the history of this case, *see* Eric Freedman, Leo Frank Lives: Untangling the Historical Roots of Meaningful Federal Habeas Corpus Review of State Convictions, 51 Ala. L. Rev. 1467 (2000).

Great Expansion in Availability of Writ After World War II

Although many habeas corpus cases were decided during the first half of the twentieth century, it was not until after World War II that the scope of habeas corpus began to change dramatically. Several forces combined to cause a major revision in the principles of habeas corpus. First, the application of the Bill of Rights to the states through the incorporation process greatly expanded the opportunity for state violations of constitutional liberties. Early in American history, the Supreme Court held that the Bill of Rights did not apply to state government actions.[18] Slowly at first, and then at an accelerating pace, the Supreme Court held that the term "liberty" in the due process clause of the Fourteenth Amendment "incorporated" provisions of the Bill of Rights.[19] Through this incorporative process the Supreme Court has applied almost all of the Bill of Rights to the states, including most of the provisions dealing with criminal procedure.[20]

Second, the expansion of the rights of criminal defendants also created more opportunity for claims that individuals were held in violation of the Constitution. In many areas, the Warren Court interpreted the Constitution to provide additional procedural protections to criminal defendants, each of which could be the basis for a habeas petition if there was an allegation of infringement.[21]

Third, national attention on civil rights after World War II served as a reminder that Black people in the South often were unconstitutionally deprived of their rights and lacked adequate protection in state courts. As the Reconstruction Act's proponents had intended, habeas corpus was perceived as a vehicle to uphold and advance civil rights.

Finally, the growth in the size of the country and the amount of litigation meant that review by the U.S. Supreme Court was not sufficient to remedy all allegedly unconstitutional convictions. If there was to be federal court review of state court procedures, it would have to be undertaken primarily in the district courts through habeas corpus.

[18] Barron v. Mayor of Baltimore, 32 U.S. (7 Pet.) 243 (1833).

[19] *See, e.g.,* Palko v. Connecticut, 302 U.S. 319 (1937) (articulating principle of selective incorporation of the Bill of Rights); Twining v. New Jersey, 211 U.S. 78 (1908) (recognizing that some of the Bill of Rights applies to the states because they are part of the conception of due process).

[20] *See, e.g.,* Malloy v. Hogan, 378 U.S. 1 (1964) (applying Fifth Amendment right to be free from self-incrimination to the states); Gideon v. Wainwright, 372 U.S. 335 (1963) (applying Sixth Amendment right to counsel to the states); Mapp v. Ohio, 367 U.S. 643 (1961) (applying Fourth Amendment right to be free from unreasonable searches and seizures to the states); In re Oliver, 333 U.S. 257 (1948) (applying Sixth Amendment right to public trial to the states).

[21] *See, e.g.,* United States v. Wade, 388 U.S. 218 (1967) (right to counsel at lineups after initial appearance or indictment); Miranda v. Arizona, 384 U.S. 436 (1966) (protection of right against self-incrimination requires warnings to be given to criminal defendants).

Warren Court Expansion; Burger, Rehnquist, and Roberts Courts Narrowing

As described below, the Warren Court greatly liberalized the availability of habeas corpus. Two of the most important changes were accomplished in decisions holding that habeas corpus petitioners could relitigate all constitutional claims in federal court and that an individual would be barred from raising matters not litigated in state court only if it could be demonstrated that the individual deliberately bypassed state procedures.[22] In sharp contrast, the Burger Court narrowed the availability of habeas corpus, both by preventing relitigation of Fourth Amendment exclusionary rule claims and by allowing a petitioner to raise a matter not previously litigated only if there was proof of good "cause" for the omission and "prejudice" to not being able to raise the issue pursuant to habeas corpus.[23] The history of habeas corpus is thus a reflection of both society's attitudes toward individual liberties and the best way to protect those liberties.

The Rehnquist Court further narrowed the scope of federal habeas corpus availability. For example, the Court has held that an unsuccessful habeas petitioner can bring a subsequent petition only if he or she can demonstrate good "cause" for not having raised the issue earlier and "prejudice" to not being heard or a likelihood of actual innocence.[24] Also, the Court imposed a new and substantial obstacle to habeas relief by deciding, beginning in *Teague v. Lane*, that habeas petitioners generally only may assert rights that existed as of the time of their conviction.[25] Repeatedly, the Court has emphasized the costs of habeas corpus in disrupting the finality of convictions and causing friction between federal and state courts.[26]

During the decade of the Roberts Court, the justices have continued to restrict the availability of habeas corpus by consistently interpreting the Antiterrorism and Effective Death Penalty Act, discussed below, as greatly limiting federal court authority to hear and grant habeas petitions.[27] Conservatives praise these restrictions on habeas corpus, but they are decried by liberals. United States Court of Appeals Judge Stephen Reinhardt powerfully expressed this when he declared: "The collapse of habeas corpus as a remedy for even the most glaring of constitutional

[22] *See, e.g.,* Fay v. Noia, 372 U.S. 391 (1963) (claims not raised in state courts may be raised on habeas corpus unless the petitioner deliberately bypassed state procedures); Brown v. Allen, 344 U.S. 443 (1953) (all constitutional claims can be relitigated on habeas corpus). *See* §15.5, *infra.*

[23] *See, e.g.,* Wainwright v. Sykes, 433 U.S. 72 (1977) (claims not presented in state court may be raised on habeas corpus only if there is cause and prejudice); Stone v. Powell, 428 U.S. 465 (1976) (Fourth Amendment exclusionary rule claims cannot be raised on habeas corpus if the state court provided a full and fair hearing). *See* §15.5, *infra.*

[24] McCleskey v. Zant, 499 U.S. 469 (1991). This is discussed further in §15.4.3.

[25] 489 U.S. 288 (1989).

[26] Teague v. Lane, 489 U.S. 288, 309-310 (1989).

[27] *See, e.g.,* Cullen v. Pinholster, 563 U.S. 170 (2011) (federal courts cannot hold evidentiary hearings on habeas corpus and are limited to the record before the state court), discussed in §15.5.4; Harrington v. Richter, 526 U.S. 86 (2011) (federal court may grant habeas only if fair-minded jurists would not agree as to the state court position), discussed in §15.5.3.

violations ranks among the greater wrongs of our legal era. Once hailed as the Great Writ, and still feted with all the standard rhetorical flourishes, habeas corpus has been transformed over the past two decades from a vital guarantor of liberty into an instrument for ratifying the power of state courts to disregard the protections of the Constitution."[28]

Antiterrorism and Effective Death Penalty Act Further Narrowing

For many years, conservatives in Congress introduced bills to narrow the scope of habeas corpus relief. In 1996, they succeeded in enacting the Antiterrorism and Effective Death Penalty Act.[29] The provisions of the act are discussed throughout this chapter in terms of their effect on particular aspects of the law of habeas corpus. To summarize, the act creates many new restrictions on the availability of habeas corpus.[30] First, the act imposes a statute of limitations on habeas petitions. First, it provides a "one-year period of limitation shall apply to an application for a writ of habeas corpus by a person in custody pursuant to the judgment of a state court."[31] However, the act also provides that in capital cases there shall be a shorter, six-month period of limitations if a state is deemed to provide adequate representation in collateral proceedings for those sentenced to death.[32]

Second, the act prohibits successive habeas corpus petitions unless a U.S. court of appeals approves the filing. The court of appeals may allow the successive habeas petition only if the petitioner shows either that the claim relies on a new rule of constitutional law that applies retroactively[33] or that the factual predicate for the claim could not have been discovered previously and the facts underlying the claim would be sufficient to establish by clear and convincing evidence that no reasonable fact finder would have found the applicant guilty of the underlying offense.

Third, the act narrows the scope of habeas corpus review. The act provides that habeas corpus relief cannot be awarded to a state prisoner solely because a state court misapplied established constitutional principles to the facts of the case. Relief is available only when the state court determination was "contrary to, or involved an unreasonable application of clearly established federal law as determined by the Supreme Court of the United States."[34] Also, the act provides for great deference to the fact-finding of the trial court, stating, "In a proceeding

[28] Stephen Reinhardt, The Demise of Habeas Corpus and the Rise of Qualified Immunity: The Court's Ever Increasing Limitations on the Development and Enforcement of Constitutional Rights and Some Particularly Unfortunate Consequences, 113 Mich. L. Rev. 1219 (2015).

[29] Antiterrorism and Effective Death Penalty Act of 1996, Pub. L. No. 104-132, 110 Stat 1214.

[30] The U.S. Supreme Court ruled that the provisions of the act do not apply retroactively, except for those relating to capital cases where the act expressly provides for retroactivity. Lindh v. Murphy, 521 U.S. 320 (1997).

[31] Antiterrorism and Effective Death Penalty Act of 1996, §101, 28 U.S.C. §2244.

[32] Section 107(a), 28 U.S.C. §§2261-2263.

[33] The Supreme Court has held that only it can determine that a decision applies retroactively. Tyler v. Cain, 533 U.S. 656 (2001).

[34] Section 104(3), 28 U.S.C. §2254(d).

instituted by an application for a writ of habeas corpus by a person in custody pursuant to the judgment of a State court, a determination of a factual issue made by a State shall be presumed to be correct. The applicant shall have the burden of rebutting the presumption of correctness by clear and convincing evidence."[35]

These and other restrictions in the act constitute a significant change in the law of habeas corpus.[36] Although courts continue to interpret the many provisions of the law, its overall impact is clear: a dramatic restriction on the scope of the writ of habeas corpus. The provisions of the act are discussed throughout this chapter. The restrictions on habeas corpus in AEDPA are very controversial. Alex Kozinski, then a federal court of appeals judge, wrote: "AEDPA is a cruel, unjust and unnecessary law that effectively removes federal judges as safeguards against miscarriages of justice. It has resulted and continues to result in much human suffering. It should be repealed."[37]

Restrictions on Habeas Petitions by Enemy Combatants

Congress also imposed statutory restrictions on habeas corpus for petitions brought by individuals held as enemy combatants as part of the war on terrorism. In 2005, Congress enacted the Detainee Treatment Act, which provided that those held in Guantánamo shall not have access to federal courts via a writ of habeas corpus; they must go through military commissions and then seek review in the District of Columbia Circuit.[38] This was adopted in response to the Supreme Court's decision in *Rasul v. Bush*, which held that federal courts have jurisdiction to hear habeas petitions by those detained in Guantánamo.[39] In *Hamdan v. Rumsfeld*, the Supreme Court ruled that this provision applies only prospectively, not retroactively, to those petitions that already were pending in federal court at the time that the law was enacted.[40]

In the fall of 2006, Congress responded by enacting the Military Commissions Act of 2006, which makes clear that the restrictions on habeas corpus in the Detainee Treatment Act apply retroactively.[41] The act provides, "No court, justice, or judge shall have jurisdiction to hear or consider an application for a writ of habeas corpus filed by or on behalf of an alien detained by the United States who has been determined by the United States to have been properly detained as an enemy combatant or is awaiting such determination."[42] The act is explicit about its retroactive application and says that it "shall apply to all cases, without exception, pending on or after the date of the enactment of this Act which relate to any aspect

[35] Section 104(4), 28 U.S.C. §2254(e).

[36] For an excellent review of the provisions of the act, *see* Larry Yackle, A Primer on the New Habeas Corpus Statute, 44 Buff. L. Rev. 381 (1996).

[37] Alex Kozinski, Criminal Law 2.0, 44 Geo. L.J. Ann. Rev. Crim. Proc. iii, xlii (2015).

[38] 119 Stat. 2739, codified at 10 U.S.C. §801.

[39] 542 U.S. 466 (2004).

[40] 548 U.S. 557 (2006).

[41] Pub. L. 109-366, 120 Stat. 2600 (2006).

[42] 28 U.S.C. §2241(e).

of the detention, transfer, treatment, trial, or conditions of detention of an alien detained by the United States since September 11, 2001."[43]

In *Boumediene v. Bush,* the Court, in a 5-4 decision, declared this to be an unconstitutional suspension of the writ of habeas corpus.[44] Justice Kennedy wrote for the Court and emphasized that Article I, §10, creates a "constitutional privilege" of habeas corpus and that this can be suspended only in times of rebellion or invasion. He reviewed the history of habeas corpus and explained that the constitutional provision was meant to provide protection from abuses of power by the executive branch of government and ensure that courts are available to protect those who claim to be illegally detained. The Court wrote: "In our own system the Suspension Clause is designed to protect against these cyclical abuses. The Clause protects the rights of the detained by a means consistent with the essential design of the Constitution. It ensures that, except during periods of formal suspension, the Judiciary will have a time-tested device, the writ, to maintain the 'delicate balance of governance' that is itself the surest safeguard of liberty."[45]

The Court said that habeas corpus applies to those held in Guantánamo. Justice Kennedy reviewed the history of habeas corpus as to American territories and concluded: "We hold that Art. I, §9, cl. 2, of the Constitution has full effect at Guantanamo Bay. If the privilege of habeas corpus is to be denied to the detainees now before us, Congress must act in accordance with the requirements of the Suspension Clause."[46]

The Court concluded that the Military Commission Act is a suspension of the writ of habeas corpus. The alternative procedures provided in the Military Commission Act—military tribunals with review in the U.S. Court of Appeals for the District of Columbia Circuit—were not deemed to be a substitute for habeas corpus. The Court noted the limits on the ability of defendants to rebut the evidence against them. The Court stated: "Although we make no judgment whether the [Combatant Status Review Tribunals], as currently constituted, satisfy due process standards, we agree with petitioners that, even when all the parties involved in this process act with diligence and in good faith, there is considerable risk of error in the tribunal's findings of fact. This is a risk inherent in any process that . . . is 'closed and accusatorial.' And given that the consequence of error may be detention of persons for the duration of hostilities that may last a generation or more, this is a risk too significant to ignore."[47]

Justice Kennedy concluded his majority opinion by emphasizing the importance of the rule of law, especially in times of crisis, such as the war on terror: "We hold that petitioners may invoke the fundamental procedural protections of habeas corpus. The laws and Constitution are designed to survive, and remain in

[43] *Id.*

[44] 553 U.S. 723 (2008). For a discussion of this case, *see, e.g.,* Gerald L. Neuman, The Habeas Corpus Suspension Clause After Boumediene v. Bush, 110 Colum. L. Rev. 537 (2010); Daniel Meltzer, Habeas Corpus, Suspension, and Guantánamo: The *Boumediene* Decision, 2008 Sup. Ct. Rev. 1.

[45] 553 U.S. at 745.

[46] *Id.* at 771.

[47] *Id.* at 785.

force, in extraordinary times. Liberty and security can be reconciled; and in our system they are reconciled within the framework of the law. The Framers decided that habeas corpus, a right of first importance, must be a part of that framework, a part of that law."[48]

Chief Justice Roberts and Justice Scalia each wrote dissenting opinions. Chief Justice Roberts argued that the alternative procedures provided in the Military Commission Act were an adequate substitute for habeas corpus and that there was thus not a "suspension of the writ." He declared, "I believe the system the political branches constructed adequately protects any constitutional rights aliens captured abroad and detained as enemy combatants may enjoy."[49]

Justice Scalia wrote a vehement dissent in which he argued that the federal courts have no business getting involved, and the granting of habeas corpus, as a result of the Court's decision, could lead to the deaths of American citizens. He said, "The writ of habeas corpus does not, and never has, run in favor of aliens abroad; the Suspension Clause thus has no application, and the Court's intervention in this military matter is entirely *ultra vires*."[50] He concluded his dissenting opinion by declaring, "Today the Court warps our Constitution in a way that goes beyond the narrow issue of the reach of the Suspension Clause, invoking judicially brainstormed separation-of-powers principles to establish a manipulable 'functional' test for the extraterritorial reach of habeas corpus (and, no doubt, for the extraterritorial reach of other constitutional protections as well). It blatantly misdescribes important precedents. . . . It breaks a chain of precedent as old as the common law that prohibits judicial inquiry into detentions of aliens abroad absent statutory authorization. And, most tragically, it sets our military commanders the impossible task of proving to a civilian court, under whatever standards this Court devises in the future, that evidence supports the confinement of each and every enemy prisoner. The Nation will live to regret what the Court has done today."[51]

In the years since *Boumediene*, the Court has not taken another case concerning habeas corpus relief for noncitizens held as enemy combatants.[52] The Supreme Court repeatedly has denied review even though the U.S. courts of appeals have

[48] *Id.* at 798.

[49] *Id.* at 802 (Roberts, C.J., dissenting).

[50] *Id.* at 827 (Scalia, J., dissenting).

[51] *Id.* at 849.

[52] In a case decided the same term as *Boumediene*, in Munaf v. Green, 553 U.S. 674 (2008), the Court held that American citizens held in Iraq by the U.S. military had a federal statutory right to file a habeas corpus petition in federal court. The Court also held, though, that U.S. courts exercising habeas corpus jurisdiction did not have the authority to enjoin the U.S. military from transferring prisoners to Iraqi custody. The Court noted that the individuals were accused of committing crimes in Iraq and that therefore "Iraq has a sovereign right to prosecute them for crimes committed on its soil, even if its criminal process does not come with all the rights guaranteed by the Constitution." *Id.* at 677. The Court said that the claims that the prisoners might be tortured by Iraqi authorities was "in the present context . . . to be addressed by the political branches, not the judiciary." *Id.* at 700. The Court explained that it was not a situation in which the executive had determined that an individual was likely to be tortured, but transferred him anyway.

consistently ruled against habeas petitions by Guantánamo detainees, and the Supreme Court has denied review in these cases.[53]

§15.3 THE STATUTORY FRAMEWORK: THE PROCEDURES IN HABEAS CORPUS REVIEW

Statutes and Rules Governing Habeas Corpus

Federal statutes prescribe the availability of habeas corpus relief and define the procedures to be followed in federal habeas corpus proceedings.[1] Additionally, in 1977, the Rules Governing Section 2254 Cases in the District Courts went into effect.[2] The statutes and rules describe many important aspects of federal habeas corpus litigation.

First, a writ of habeas corpus may be granted by "the Supreme Court, any justice thereof, the district courts and any circuit judge within their respective jurisdictions."[3] If a petition for a writ of habeas corpus is filed with the Supreme Court, a Supreme Court justice, or a federal court of appeals judge, the petition may be transferred to the district court having jurisdiction to entertain it.[4] In *Felker v. Turpin*, the Supreme Court used the possibility of Supreme Court-issued habeas corpus review as grounds for upholding a restriction on the Court's appellate jurisdiction.[5] The Antiterrorism and Effective Death Penalty Act allows successive petitions only with the approval of a U.S. court of appeals, and the denial of such permission is not reviewable by the Supreme Court. *Felker* upheld this restriction on jurisdiction on the grounds that it was not total preclusion of Supreme Court review; the Court still could grant review via original petitions for habeas corpus.[6]

Second, habeas corpus petitions must be in writing, signed, and verified by the person for whom relief is requested or by someone acting in his or her behalf.[7] The petition must describe the facts concerning the "applicant's commitment or

[53] *See* Aziz Z. Huq, What Good Is Habeas?, 26 Const. Comment. 385 (2010) (reviewing the post-*Boumediene* habeas litigation and the consistent rulings by the D.C. Circuit against habeas petitions brought by Guantánamo detainees).

§15.3 [1] 28 U.S.C. §§2241-2256.

[2] The Rules are applicable to cases commenced on or after February 11, 1977. Browder v. Director, Dept. of Corrections, 434 U.S. 257, 265 n.9 (1978).

[3] 28 U.S.C. §2241(a).

[4] 28 U.S.C. §2241(b).

[5] 518 U.S. 651 (1996).

[6] *Felker* is discussed in more detail in §3.2, concerning the constitutionality of restrictions on jurisdiction.

[7] 28 U.S.C. §2242. Although the habeas statute expressly allows a habeas petition to be brought on behalf of another, the Ninth Circuit has ruled that this requires a showing that the incarcerated individual cannot sue on his or her own behalf and that there is a relationship between that individual and the habeas petitioner. Coalition of Clergy, Lawyers & Professors v. Bush, 310 F.3d 1153 (9th Cir. 2002).

detention," including the basis for requesting the writ. Because the writ, if granted, directs the person holding the petitioner to release him or her from custody, the petition should name the custodian—such as the warden—as the respondent.[8]

Third, a federal court may grant a habeas corpus petition if it concludes that the person is held in custody in violation of the Constitution, laws, or treaties of the United States.[9] Federal court relief for those held in state custody is pursuant to 28 U.S.C. §2254 and relief for federal prisoners is pursuant to 28 U.S.C. §2255. There also are statutory provisions permitting the use of habeas corpus to secure a person's testimony[10] or the release from custody of someone who was acting pursuant to the direction of a foreign nation and in accordance with international law.[11]

Fourth, individuals in state government custody may bring a habeas corpus petition only if they have exhausted all available state remedies.[12] The statute specifically states that "[a]n applicant shall not be deemed to have exhausted the remedies available in the courts of the State . . . if he has the right under the law of the State to raise, by any available procedure, the question presented."[13] This exhaustion requirement is discussed in detail in §15.4.2.

Fifth, federal courts may not entertain a petition for a writ of habeas corpus if a previous petition presented the same issues and the petition does not present any new ground.[14] *McCleskey v. Zant* held that successive habeas corpus petitions could not be brought unless the inmate could show "cause" for not presenting the issue in the first petition and "prejudice" to not having the successive petition heard.[15] The Antiterrorism and Effective Death Penalty Act goes much further and bars successive petitions unless approved by a U.S. Court of Appeals. A court of appeals may approve a successive petition only by finding either (1) that the claim relies on a retroactive new rule of constitutional law or (2) that the factual predicate for the claim could not have been discovered earlier and that the facts are sufficient to establish by clear and convincing evidence that no reasonable fact finder would have found the applicant guilty of the underlying offense. This limitation on habeas corpus review is discussed in §15.4.3.

Sixth, courts have authority to grant habeas corpus to individuals held in custody "within their respective jurisdictions."[16] Additionally, individuals held in custody by a state containing more than one federal judicial district may file a petition in either the district where the individual is held in custody or in the district that

[8] However, the failure to do so is considered "a procedural rather than a jurisdictional defect." 17 Charles Alan Wright, Arthur R. Miller & Edward H. Cooper, Federal Practice and Procedure 696 (2010).

[9] 28 U.S.C. §2254(a); 28 U.S.C. §2255.

[10] 28 U.S.C. §2241(c)(5).

[11] 28 U.S.C. §2241(c)(4). There also is a provision for habeas corpus for a person held in custody for actions taken in pursuance of a law of Congress. 28 U.S.C. §2241(c)(2). *See also* the Civil Rights Removal Act, 28 U.S.C. §1443, discussed in §11.5, *supra.*

[12] 28 U.S.C. §2254(b).

[13] 28 U.S.C. §2254(c).

[14] 28 U.S.C. §2244(a).

[15] 499 U.S. 467 (1991).

[16] 28 U.S.C. §2241(a).

encompasses the state court that convicted the individual.[17] Both of these district courts have jurisdiction to hear the habeas petition. One such court can transfer the matter to the other if the "interests of justice" would be served.[18]

Now it is firmly established that if a petition is filed in the wrong federal judicial district—that is, the district in which the petition is filed is neither the place of confinement nor the place where the state court is located—the court without jurisdiction may transfer the petition to the appropriate court. In other words, the statute prescribing the appropriate forum for habeas petitions is treated as a venue statute and not as a restriction on subject matter jurisdiction. This was the clear import of the Supreme Court's decision in *Braden v. 30th Judicial Circuit Court of Kentucky*.[19]

In *Braden*, an individual who was imprisoned by the state of Alabama was wanted on criminal charges in Kentucky. Kentucky prosecutors filed a detainer with Alabama prison officials, informing them that they planned to prosecute Braden as soon as his Alabama sentence was served. Braden argued, however, that he was entitled to be tried on the Kentucky charges prior to the completion of his Alabama sentence. He contended that the Kentucky charges had been pending for three years and that it denied his right to a speedy trial to delay the matter any longer.

Braden filed a petition for a writ of habeas corpus in Kentucky federal court to compel his speedy trial. The Kentucky federal court dismissed the petition because Braden was in Alabama and was not physically present within the Kentucky court's jurisdiction. The Kentucky federal district court relied on the earlier Supreme Court decision in *Ahrens v. Clark*.[20] In *Ahrens*, aliens facing deportation and held in custody on Ellis Island filed a writ of habeas corpus in the federal district court for the District of Columbia. The Supreme Court held that the District of Columbia court could not issue the writ of habeas corpus because under the federal habeas corpus statute, "the presence within the territorial jurisdiction of the District Court of the person detained is prerequisite to filing a petition for a writ of *habeas corpus*."[21]

The Supreme Court, however, reversed the lower federal court and held that *Ahrens* was overruled to the extent that it prevented the Kentucky court from exercising jurisdiction. The Court stated, "In view of these developments since *Ahrens v. Clark*, we can no longer view that decision as establishing an inflexible jurisdictional rule, dictating the choice of an inconvenient forum even in a class of cases which could not have been foreseen at the time of our decision."[22] In other words, the Court viewed the statute prescribing where habeas petitions are to be brought as a venue statute and permitted transfer of petitions to the most convenient forum. A petitioner is no longer restricted to requesting habeas corpus only in the district in which he or she is held in custody.

[17] 28 U.S.C. §2241(d).
[18] *Id.*
[19] 410 U.S. 484 (1973).
[20] 335 U.S. 188 (1948).
[21] *Id.* at 189.
[22] 410 U.S. at 499-500.

§15.3 The Statutory Framework: The Procedures in Habeas Corpus Review

In *Padilla v. Rumsfeld,* the Court reaffirmed that a habeas petition must be brought in the judicial district where a person is detained.[23] Jose Padilla was apprehended in Chicago's O'Hare Airport and detained as an enemy combatant on suspicion that he was planning to build and detonate a "dirty bomb." He was initially taken to New York, where he was held as a material witness. A habeas petition was filed on his behalf from there. He was transferred to a military prison in South Carolina, but the habeas petition continued to be litigated in the Southern District of New York and then the Second Circuit, which ruled in his favor.

The Supreme Court, in a 5-4 decision, reversed and held that the habeas petition needed to be brought in the federal district court in South Carolina, where the immediate custodian over his person was located.[24] Subsequently, Padilla refiled in the District of South Carolina, which granted his petition for habeas corpus.[25] The Fourth Circuit reversed.[26] Padilla sought review in the Supreme Court and the U.S. government then charged him with federal crimes, ending Padilla's status as an enemy combatant. The Supreme Court then dismissed the petition for certiorari.[27]

Federal prisoners must file petitions pursuant to §2255 with the court that imposed the sentence.[28] Previously, federal prisoners also could file petitions with courts located in the areas where they were confined. This proved inconvenient both for the courts and the prisoners. Courts in areas where federal prisons are located were deluged with petitions, whereas courts in areas without prisons received no petitions. Also, petitioners often were confined far from the court where the trial occurred and hence were removed from the witnesses and documents they might need for their habeas petition. Consequently, federal prisoners, pursuant to 28 U.S.C. §2255, must return to the court that sentenced them and thus have less of a choice as to where to file their habeas petitions.

A seventh major aspect of habeas corpus procedure concerns the practice for answers, summary dispositions, and discovery. Under the habeas corpus rules, a judge may dismiss a petition if it is clear from the face of the petition that there are no possible grounds for relief.[29] If the petition is not dismissed, the respondent—usually the warden holding the petitioner in custody—is required to file an answer. Of course, in reality, in many cases the warden is not the real party in interest because the alleged violations occurred at trial before the petitioner was even confined. The answer is prepared by the state's attorney who opposes the habeas corpus petition.

Federal statutes provide for evidence to be taken pursuant to habeas corpus petitions "orally or by deposition, or, in the discretion of the judge, by affidavit."[30] Additionally, documentary evidence and transcripts of prior court proceedings are

[23] 542 U.S. 426 (2004).
[24] *Id.* at 442.
[25] Padilla v. Hanft, 389 F. Supp. 2d 678 (D.S.C. 2005).
[26] 423 F.3d 386 (4th Cir. 2005).
[27] 547 U.S. 1062 (2006).
[28] 28 U.S.C. §2255.
[29] 28 U.S.C. §2254, Rules Governing Section 2254 Cases in the United States District Court, Rule 4.
[30] 28 U.S.C. §2246.

admissible as evidence.[31] The habeas corpus rules provide that discovery, pursuant to the procedures provided in the Federal Rules of Civil Procedure, is permissible "if, and to the extent that, the judge in the exercise of his discretion and for good cause shown grants leave to do so, but not otherwise."[32] Therefore, federal court judges have discretion whether to allow discovery and what discovery to permit. Generally, discovery is uncommon in habeas corpus cases.

An eighth aspect of habeas corpus procedure concerns the statute of limitations for habeas petitions. Until 1996, the federal statutes concerning habeas corpus review did not prescribe any time limit within which petitions must be filed.[33] The habeas corpus rules that went into effect in 1977 provided that a petition may be dismissed if the state is prejudiced by a delay in the filing of the petition, "unless the petitioner shows that it is based on grounds of which he could not have had knowledge by the exercise of reasonable diligence before the circumstances prejudicial to the state occurred."[34]

The Antiterrorism and Effective Death Penalty, enacted in 1996, imposes a one-year statute of limitations on the filing of habeas petitions.[35] Section 101 of the act provides, "A 1-year period of limitation shall apply to an application for a writ of habeas corpus by a person in custody pursuant to the judgment of a state court."[36] Section 101 also states that "[t]he time during which a properly filed application for State post-conviction or other collateral review with respect to the pertinent judgment or claim is pending shall not be counted toward any period of limitation under this subsection."[37] The Supreme Court has held that the statute of limitations is tolled while *state* court postconviction proceedings are pending, but not during the time when a federal court habeas petition is pending.[38] This could have a very detrimental effect on habeas petitioners, for example, in a case in which a habeas petition was pending for many months before being dismissed for failure to adequately exhaust state procedures. Under these circumstances, most or even all of the statute of limitations period could be exhausted while the matter was pending in federal court. However, as discussed below, in *Holland v. Florida,* the Supreme Court held that equitable tolling is permissible in habeas cases under AEDPA.[39] Also, as discussed below, there are other ways of alleviating the harsh aspects of the statute of limitations, at least in limited circumstances: The federal

[31] 28 U.S.C. §2247.

[32] 28 U.S.C. §2254, Rule 6(a).

[33] *See, e.g.,* United States v. Smith, 331 U.S. 469, 475 (1947). Indeed, prior to the act's going into effect, the Court ruled that there was no time limit on first habeas petitions, and they could be filed even on the day of execution. Lonchar v. Thomas, 517 U.S. 314 (1996).

[34] 28 U.S.C. §2254, Rule 9(a).

[35] The statute of limitations requirement is discussed in detail below in §15.4.4.

[36] 28 U.S.C. §2244.

[37] *Id.*

[38] Duncan v. Walker, 533 U.S. 167 (2001). Also, the Supreme Court has ruled that the statute of limitations is tolled for the time in between when a state habeas petition is filed and when review is sought of that decision in a higher state court. Carey v. Saffold, 536 U.S. 214 (2002). In many states, the dismissal of a petition for postconviction relief is not appealed to a higher court; instead, review is sought in the higher court by filing a petition in the higher court. The Supreme Court in *Carey* ruled that the time between the decision and the filing tolls the statute of limitations.

[39] 560 U.S. 631 (2010), discussed below at §15.4.4.

court can keep the case on its docket while the matter is sent to state court for exhaustion ("stay and abeyance")[40] and those who are actually innocent may file outside the statute of limitations.[41]

The act also provides that in capital cases a six-month statute of limitations shall apply if it is determined that a state has established an adequate system for providing attorneys for postconviction proceedings.[42] To this point, only Arizona has been found to have created such a system and thus be entitled to invoke the shorter statute of limitations.[43] In *Calderon v. Ashmus*, the Supreme Court unanimously dismissed as nonjusticiable a request for a declaratory judgment by death-row inmates that California was not in compliance with the act.[44] *Calderon* means that inmates cannot seek a system-wide determination of whether a state is in compliance with the act; rather, in each case, the issue must be raised and litigated.

Ninth, the federal statutes authorize the federal court in ruling on a habeas corpus petition to "dispose of the matter as law and justice require."[45] Generally, the federal court in granting a habeas corpus petition either orders the release of an individual from custody, or more commonly, the court orders the individual released unless a new trial is held within a reasonable amount of time.[46]

Finally, in general, the final order of a judge in a habeas proceeding is subject to review on appeal by the court of appeals in the circuit where the federal district court is located.[47] However, a major limitation on the right to appeal is that a state prisoner whose petition for habeas corpus is denied may appeal only if the federal district court judge or a court of appeals judge issues a certificate of appealability.[48] A court can issue a certificate of appealability only if "the applicant has made a substantial showing of the denial of

[40] Rhines v. Weber, 544 U.S. 269 (2005), discussed below at §15.4.4.

[41] McQuiggin v. Perkins, 569 U.S. 383 (2013).

[42] The act states that there will be a six-month statute of limitations "if a State establishes by statute, rules of its court of last resort, or by another agency authorized by state law, a mechanism for the appointment, compensation, and payment of reasonable litigation expenses of competent counsel in State post-conviction proceedings brought by indigent prisoners whose capital convictions and sentences have been upheld on direct appeal to the court of last resort in the State or have otherwise become final for State law purposes." 28 U.S.C. §2261.

[43] For an argument that states are unlikely to choose to comply and thus trigger the shorter statute of limitations in habeas cases, *see* John Blume, AEDPA: The "Hype" and the "Bite," 91 Cornell L. Rev. 259 (2006).

[44] 523 U.S. 740 (1998). *Calderon* is discussed more fully in §2.2, concerning its ruling that the challenge was not ripe for review.

[45] 28 U.S.C. §2243.

[46] Wright, Miller & Cooper, *supra* note 8, at 527, and cases cited therein; Irvin v. Dowd, 366 U.S. 717 (1961); Dowd v. United States ex rel. Cook, 340 U.S. 206 (1951).

[47] 28 U.S.C. §2253.

[48] Section 2253(c)(1) provides: "Unless a circuit justice or judge issues a certificate of appealability, an appeal may not be taken to the court of appeals from—(A) the final order in a habeas corpus proceeding in which the detention complained of arises out of process issued by a state court; or (B) the final order is a proceeding under section 2255. (2) A certificate of appealability may issue under paragraph (1) only if the applicant has made a substantial showing of the denial of a constitutional right. (3) The certificate of appealability under paragraph (1) shall indicate which specific issue or issues satisfy the showing required by paragraph (2)."

a constitutional right."[49] Although the text of the act seems to say that district court judges cannot issue such certificates, most courts have ruled to the contrary and concluded that either a district court or a court of appeals can authorize review.[50] In *Miller-El v. Cockrell*, the Supreme Court held that a certificate of appealability should be granted if "reasonable jurists could debate" whether the petition should have been granted.[51] This "does not require a showing that the appeal will succeed";[52] nor is there to be full consideration of the merits. But the certificate should be granted if it presents a debatable issue for the court of appeals to consider. The requirement for a certificate of appealability is discussed in §15.6.

§15.4 PREREQUISITES FOR HABEAS CORPUS: CUSTODY, EXHAUSTION, NO SUCCESSIVE PETITIONS, AND TIMELINESS

A person claiming to be held in violation of the U.S. Constitution, treaties, or laws must meet certain requirements in order to secure habeas corpus relief. The person must be "in custody," all available state remedies must have been exhausted, and the petition must not duplicate an earlier petition that was presented and rejected.[1] These three requirements are discussed in §§15.4.1, 15.4.2, and 15.4.3, respectively.

§15.4.1 The Requirement for Custody

Initial Restrictive Definition of "Custody"

The habeas corpus statutes allow federal courts to entertain the application for a writ of habeas corpus from a person "in custody." Previously, the Supreme Court narrowly interpreted the phrase "in custody." In a series of decisions that now have been reversed, the Supreme Court held that habeas corpus petitioners had to be incarcerated[2] and that review was available only if granting the petition would secure a person's release from confinement.[3]

[49] *Id.*

[50] *See, e.g.*, Hunter v. United States, 101 F.3d 1565, 1573-1583 (11th Cir. 1996) (en banc).

[51] 537 U.S. 322, 336 (2003) (citations omitted).

[52] *Id.* at 337.

§15.4 [1] For an empirical study of the impact of these rules, *see* Richard Faust, Tina J. Rubenstein & Larry W. Yackle, The Great Writ in Action: Empirical Light on the Federal Habeas Corpus Debate, 18 N.Y.U. Rev. L. & Soc. Change 637 (1990-1991).

[2] *See, e.g.*, Stallings v. Splain, 253 U.S. 339 (1920) (person released on bail could not seek habeas corpus relief).

[3] *See, e.g.*, McNally v. Hill, 293 U.S. 131 (1934) (person could not obtain habeas corpus relief unless granting the petition would release the person from incarceration).

Expanded Definition of "Custody"

However, during the 1960s, the Court's approach to habeas corpus changed. Habeas corpus was no longer viewed as an extraordinary writ limited to releasing a person from incarceration.[4] Thus, as described below, the Court held that individuals may use habeas corpus petitions to challenge any restriction of liberty, such as parole; habeas petitions may be heard even if an individual will not necessarily be released because of consecutive or concurrent sentences; and habeas petitions should not be dismissed as moot even after a person is released from prison. In *Garlotte v. Fordice*, the Court ruled that a prisoner who is serving concurrent sentences "remains 'in custody' under all of his sentences until all are served."[5]

Earlier in the twentieth century, the Supreme Court held that individuals could seek habeas corpus review only if they were actually incarcerated. So, for example, a person released on bail was ineligible to present a habeas corpus petition to a federal court.[6] Physical restraint was a prerequisite for habeas corpus review. Now, however, an individual may obtain habeas corpus relief even if on parole or released on bail.

Jones v. Cunningham, which held that a person may present a habeas corpus petition while on parole, is a crucial case liberalizing the definition of "in custody."[7] In *Jones*, an individual filed a habeas corpus petition while in prison, but was paroled while the matter was pending in federal court. The U.S. Court of Appeals for the Fourth Circuit dismissed the petition because the individual was no longer in custody, but, in fact, free on parole. The Supreme Court reversed. In an opinion by Justice Black, the Court observed that "[h]istory, usage, and precedent can leave no doubt that, besides physical imprisonment, there are other restraints on a man's liberty."[8] The Court catalogued the many restrictions on liberty suffered by a person on parole—ranging from limits on travel to required visits from and meetings with a parole officer. In fact, under the state's law, a person granted parole was "'under the custody and control of the . . . Parole Board.'"[9] The Court said that because parole imposes restraints "not shared by the public generally," a person on parole should be regarded as in custody.[10]

Similarly, the Court held in *Hensley v. Municipal Court* that individuals could seek habeas corpus even when they were released on bail or on their own recognizance.[11] The court of appeals, in accord with prior Supreme Court rulings, concluded that a person could not seek habeas corpus until incarceration began. The

[4] *See* Thomas M. Hitch, Note, Federal Habeas Corpus: The Concept of Custody and Access to Federal Court, 53 J. Urb. L. 61, 77 (1975) (change in view of habeas corpus from extraordinary writ to general postconviction remedy).

[5] 515 U.S. 39, 41 (1995).

[6] Stallings v. Splain, 253 U.S. 339 (1920); *see also* Wales v. Whitney, 114 U.S. 564, 569 (1885) (no habeas corpus unless there is "physical restraint").

[7] 371 U.S. 236 (1963).

[8] *Id.* at 240.

[9] *Id.* at 241-242.

[10] *Id.* at 240.

[11] 411 U.S. 345 (1973); *see also* Justices of Boston Mun. Court v. Lydon, 466 U.S. 294 (1984) (court could entertain a habeas petition from a person released on his or her own recognizance).

Supreme Court reversed and emphasized that because all appeals in the state court system had been exhausted incarceration was imminent. The Court said that there was no reason to require a person to spend "[ten] minutes in jail" in order to file a habeas corpus petition.[12] The Court explained that the petitioner's movement was restricted because he was required to appear at the demand of any competent court and the failure to appear was itself a crime.

Although the requirement for actual incarceration has been eliminated, habeas corpus petitions still must be brought to challenge restrictions on liberty. Habeas corpus may not be used to challenge the imposition of fines or payment of restitution as part of a sentence.[13]

Need not Lead to Immediate Release from Custody

Also, the law previously allowed habeas corpus review only if granting of the petition would secure a person's immediate release from incarceration. Thus, in *McNally v. Hill*, the Supreme Court held that a person could not challenge only a portion of his or her convictions where the sentences ran concurrently or consecutively.[14] The Court reasoned that habeas corpus is unavailable where relief would not result in an individual's "immediate release" from prison.[15] Thus, a challenge to only some of the convictions through habeas corpus was not permitted.

However, in *Peyton v. Rowe*, the Court expressly overruled *McNally* and held that individuals could obtain habeas corpus review if any of the consecutive sentences that they are scheduled to serve was imposed as a result of a constitutional deprivation.[16] The logic behind the Court's decision in *Peyton* is evidenced by the facts in another case, *Walker v. Wainwright*, decided the same Term by the Supreme Court.[17] Walker was sentenced to life imprisonment for a murder and also was sentenced to a five-year sentence for aggravated assault, the latter sentence to begin after the completion of the life term. Under the *McNally* rule, Walker could not obtain habeas corpus review of the conviction that led to the life sentence because the federal court's granting of the petition would not release him from custody on account of the separate five-year term. In light of the obvious injustice of foreclosing review of a possibly unconstitutional conviction, the Court overruled *McNally*.

Similarly, the Supreme Court has held that a person who is subject to a detainer in order to face charges in another state may file a habeas corpus petition. In *Braden v. 30th Judicial Circuit Court of Kentucky*, a prisoner in Alabama faced a detainer to stand trial in Kentucky upon completion of his Alabama sentence.[18] Although the habeas petition related to the upcoming Kentucky trial, the Supreme

[12] 411 U.S. at 353.

[13] *See* Larry W. Yackle, Explaining Habeas Corpus, 60 N.Y.U. L. Rev. 991, 1000 (1985); *see, e.g.*, Russell v. City of Pierre, 530 F.2d 840 (8th Cir.), *cert. denied*, 429 U.S. 855 (1976); Edmunds v. Won Bae Chang, 509 F.2d 39 (9th Cir.), *cert. denied*, 423 U.S. 825 (1975).

[14] 293 U.S. 131 (1934).

[15] *Id.* at 138.

[16] 391 U.S. 54, 64-65, 67 (1968).

[17] 390 U.S. 335 (1968).

[18] 410 U.S. 484 (1973).

Court nonetheless concluded that the petitioner was in custody for purposes of the Kentucky charges because a detainer had been filed against him.

Finally, a person who files a habeas petition while serving a sentence may continue to pursue habeas review even after the sentence is completed because of the collateral consequences of the criminal conviction. Previously, in *Parker v. Ellis*, the Supreme Court held that a court could not review a habeas petition of a person who had fully served his or her sentence.[19] However, in *Carafas v. LaVallee*, the Supreme Court overturned *Parker* and held that a challenge to a criminal conviction is not moot even after the sentence is completed because of the lasting disabilities attendant to a conviction record.[20] In most states, convicted felons cannot operate certain businesses, vote, or serve as jurors. Therefore, even after individuals are released from prison and parole and all aspects of the sentence are completed, they still meet the "in custody" requirement as long as they face collateral consequences of their conviction.[21]

Thus, in many different ways the Supreme Court has expanded the definition of "in custody" to facilitate the use of habeas corpus to remedy unconstitutional convictions and sentences.

§15.4.2 The Requirement for Exhaustion of State Procedures

Importance of Exhaustion Requirement

An extremely important limitation on the power of federal courts to hear habeas corpus petitions is the requirement that petitioners in state custody exhaust all available state court procedures prior to seeking federal court review. Some studies suggest that between 30 to 50 percent of habeas petitions are dismissed for failure to exhaust.[22]

Supreme Court Creation of Exhaustion Requirement

The Supreme Court originally created the exhaustion requirement, although now it is embodied in the habeas statutes. The original statutes authorizing habeas corpus review for state prisoners did not require exhaustion of state court proceedings prior to federal habeas corpus review. However, in *Ex parte Royall*, in 1886, the Court held that because of comity considerations and deference to state courts, federal courts should not entertain a claim in a habeas corpus petition until after

[19] 362 U.S. 574 (1960).

[20] 391 U.S. 234 (1968).

[21] In Lane v. Williams, 455 U.S. 624 (1982), the Supreme Court held that an individual attacking a sentence, but not the conviction, could not seek habeas corpus relief where the sentence had been fully served and there were no collateral consequences that could be eliminated by a successful attack on the sentence.

[22] *See* Richard H. Fallon, Jr., Daniel J. Meltzer & David L. Shapiro, 2018 Supplement to Hart & Wechsler's The Federal Courts and the Federal System 218 (2018).

the state courts have had an opportunity to hear the matter.[23] Royall had been indicted under two state statutes and sought habeas corpus review to have the statutes declared unconstitutional.

The Supreme Court upheld the lower court's refusal to hear the habeas corpus petition. The Court stated that habeas corpus jurisdiction "should be exercised in light of the relations existing under our system of government, between judicial tribunals of the Union and of the States, and in recognition of the fact that the public good requires that those relations be not disturbed by unnecessary conflict between courts equally bound to guard and protect rights secured by the Constitution."[24]

Statutory Creation of Exhaustion Requirement

In 1948, the habeas corpus statutes were revised, and among the changes was the inclusion of specific language requiring that individuals challenging state custody exhaust state court remedies. Specifically, 28 U.S.C. §2254(b) provides: "An application for a writ of habeas corpus on behalf if a person in custody pursuant to the judgment of a State court shall not be granted unless it appears that (A) the applicant has exhausted remedies available in the courts of the State; or (B)(i) there is an absence of available State corrective process or (ii) circumstances exist that render such process ineffective to protect the rights of the applicant."[25]

The exhaustion requirement prevents federal courts from interfering with ongoing state criminal prosecutions.[26] If there were no exhaustion requirement, then a person contending that he or she was being prosecuted under an unconstitutional statute could halt the state court litigation by filing a habeas corpus petition in federal court. But the Supreme Court has emphasized that considerations of equity and comity prevent federal courts from enjoining or otherwise interfering with pending state criminal proceedings.[27] Thus, the exhaustion requirement for federal court habeas corpus review allows state courts to interpret and enforce state criminal laws. Federal court review is delayed until the state has had a full chance to correct any errors in its law or procedures.[28]

In analyzing the exhaustion requirement, three questions are crucial: What state court procedures must be used? What must be presented to state courts?

[23] 117 U.S. 241 (1886).

[24] *Id.* at 251. For a criticism of this decision on the grounds that the Court's decision was a "flat contravention of the statutory command," *see* Anthony Amsterdam, Criminal Prosecutions Affecting Federally Guaranteed Civil Rights: Federal Removal and Habeas Corpus Jurisdiction to Abort State Court Trial, 113 U. Pa. L. Rev. 793, 901 (1965).

[25] 28 U.S.C. §2254(b).

[26] *See* Ex parte Hawk, 321 U.S. 114, 117 (1944); Davis v. Burke, 179 U.S. 399, 402 (1900) (need for federal courts to avoid interfering with pending state court proceedings).

[27] *See, e.g.,* Younger v. Harris, 401 U.S. 37 (1971) (federal courts may not enjoin pending state court criminal prosecutions); the prohibition against federal interference with state court proceedings is discussed in Chapter 13, *supra.*

[28] *See, e.g.,* Wilwording v. Swenson, 404 U.S. 249, 250 (1971) (the exhaustion requirement allows state courts an "initial 'opportunity to pass upon and correct' alleged violations of its prisoners' federal rights").

When are petitions deemed sufficient to meet the exhaustion requirement? Each question is considered in turn.

What State Court Procedures Must Be Used?

First, the petitioner must pursue all available state court remedies; that is, exhaustion of state proceedings is incomplete as long as there remains an available state court proceeding that might provide the relief sought by the petitioner. This means that a habeas corpus petition may be brought if potential state remedies once existed, but are no longer available. For example, exhaustion has occurred if the time limit for direct appeal has expired such that no state remedies are available at the time of the filing of the habeas petition.[29] However, the failure to use available state procedures likely will prevent federal habeas corpus relief, not because of exhaustion problems, but rather because state procedural defaults bar federal habeas corpus relief unless there is good "cause" for the omission and "prejudice" to the denial of review.[30] The Supreme Court has ruled that a failure to include claims in a petition for discretionary review before a state's highest court is a procedural default that precludes raising those claims on habeas corpus.[31]

A state prisoner need not seek U.S. Supreme Court review of the state court's decision to present a federal court habeas petition.[32] Nor is habeas corpus precluded when a state prisoner seeks Supreme Court review of the state court ruling via a writ of certiorari and the Supreme Court declines to hear the case.[33] Of course, if the Supreme Court hears and decides the case, the Court's decision is determinative and must be followed in subsequent habeas corpus proceedings.

A state prisoner need not use state procedures for collateral review in order for there to be exhaustion, such as state court habeas corpus mechanisms, as long as the issues have been presented and decided by the state courts on direct appeal. The Court explained that it "is not necessary . . . for the prisoner to ask the state for collateral relief, based on the same evidence and issues already decided by direct review."[34] However, a petitioner must use available state court collateral review procedures, if they exist, for issues not raised on direct appeal.[35] Conversely, a petitioner need not present a matter on direct appeal to the state courts, even if direct appeals are still available, if the issue already was raised and decided by the state court in a collateral proceeding. In other words, once an issue is raised and litigated in state court it need not be presented again even when additional state proceedings are possible.

Section 2254(b) excuses the failure to use state procedures if "circumstances render such process ineffective to protect the rights of the prisoner." The Court

[29] Fay v. Noia, 372 U.S. 391 (1963).

[30] *See, e.g.*, Wainwright v. Sykes, 433 U.S. 72 (1977) (articulating the cause and prejudice requirement), discussed in §15.5.2, *infra*.

[31] O'Sullivan v. Boerckel, 526 U.S. 838 (1999).

[32] Lawrence v. Florida, 549 U.S. 327, 337 (2007); Fay v. Noia, 372 U.S. 391, 435 (1963).

[33] *See, e.g.*, Brown v. Allen, 344 U.S. 443, 450 (1953).

[34] Brown v. Allen, 344 U.S. 443, 447 (1953); *see also* Roberts v. LaVallee, 389 U.S. 40, 42-43 (1967).

[35] *See, e.g.*, Wade v. Mayo, 334 U.S. 672, 677-678 (1948).

has interpreted this clause as creating an exception to the exhaustion requirement "only if there is no opportunity to obtain redress in state court or if the corrective process is so clearly deficient as to render futile any effort to obtain relief."[36]

For example, in *Wilwording v. Swenson*, the federal district court had dismissed a habeas corpus petition challenging conditions of prison confinement because alternatives remained in the state court system, including "a suit for injunction, a writ of prohibition, or mandamus or a declaratory judgment in the state courts."[37] The Supreme Court refused to require exhaustion of these proceedings, in part because there was not a "single instance, regardless of the remedy invoked, in which the Missouri courts have granted a hearing to state prisoners on the conditions of their confinement."[38] The Court concluded that under such circumstances, exhaustion of state remedies was futile and therefore unnecessary.

In contrast, in *Castille v. Peoples*, the Supreme Court held that the exhaustion requirement is not met when a defendant presents an issue to state courts only via a procedure that provides for discretionary review.[39] Pennsylvania has a special appeals process, termed a petition for allocatur, that requires a showing of "special and important reasons" for it to hear the appeal.[40] A defendant presented his claims via this process, and the Pennsylvania Supreme Court denied the petition without an opinion.

The Third Circuit held that this constituted exhaustion of state procedures because the state court had an opportunity to rule on the constitutional claims. The Supreme Court reversed, holding that as long as the regular appeals process remains available, presenting claims only via this special appellate process does not constitute exhausting state procedures.[41]

Lower federal courts have found state remedies to be futile when the state's highest court has recently rendered an adverse ruling in an identical case and there was no reason to believe that the court would change its position.[42] Also, lower courts have permitted review despite the failure to exhaust state remedies when there are inordinate delays in the state court's failure to rule on the federal claims.[43] Generally, however, it is quite difficult to demonstrate that state remedies are futile and few situations will meet this exception to the exhaustion requirement.

What Must Be Presented to the State Courts?

A second major issue concerning exhaustion of state remedies involves what must be presented to the state courts in order for the exhaustion requirement to be deemed fulfilled. The Supreme Court has held that the "federal claim must be

[36] Duckworth v. Serrano, 454 U.S. 1, 3 (1981).
[37] 404 U.S. 249, 249-259 (1971).
[38] *Id.* at 250.
[39] 489 U.S. 346 (1989).
[40] Pa. R.A.P. 1114.
[41] 489 U.S. at 351.
[42] *See, e.g.,* Layton v. Carson, 479 F.2d 1275, 1276 (5th Cir. 1973).
[43] *See, e.g.,* Lowe v. Duckworth, 663 F.2d 42 (7th Cir. 1981).

fairly presented to the state courts."[44] That is, the same matter raised in the federal court habeas corpus petition must have been presented to the state court or the matter will be dismissed for the failure to exhaust if state proceedings remain available where the issue can be raised. Federal courts use state court records to determine whether the petitioner raised the same issue in state court that is now presented in the habeas proceeding.[45]

However, the exhaustion requirement is deemed to have been met when the habeas petitioner supplements the evidence presented in state court, but does not raise a new issue. In *Vasquez v. Hillery*, the Supreme Court permitted a habeas corpus petitioner to present additional statistical evidence proving discrimination in the selection of the grand jury.[46] The Court explained that it had "never held that presentation of additional facts to the district court, pursuant to that court's directions, evades the exhaustion requirement when the prisoner has presented the substance of his claim to the state courts."[47] In other words, exhaustion will not present a problem to the defendant who is supplementing the evidence for a claim already presented to the state court and is not raising a new issue. However, there certainly will be cases in which it is a fine line between what constitutes a new issue as opposed to merely new evidence.

Issues must be presented to the state courts even when it is clear that the state law or procedures are unconstitutional.[48] Thus, there is no exception to the exhaustion requirement for patently unconstitutional state statutes.[49]

What Must the Petition Contain to Meet the Exhaustion Requirement?

Finally, there is the issue of what the petition must contain to meet the exhaustion requirement. The Supreme Court, in *Rose v. Lundy*, held that the federal court must dismiss a habeas corpus petition if it contains both exhausted and unexhausted claims.[50] Federal courts will hear habeas corpus petitions only if all the claims presented were raised before the state courts. Prior to *Rose v. Lundy*, eight of ten federal circuit courts of appeals held that if a petition contains both exhausted and unexhausted claims, the federal court should hear the former and dismiss the latter.[51] The Supreme Court, however, disagreed and held that "a district court must dismiss habeas petitions containing both unexhausted and exhausted claims."[52] The Court, in an opinion by Justice O'Connor, reasoned that the decision in *Rose*

[44] Picard v. Connor, 404 U.S. 270, 275 (1971); *see also* Anderson v. Harless, 459 U.S. 4 (1982).

[45] Picard v. Connor, 404 U.S. at 276.

[46] 474 U.S. 254 (1986).

[47] *Id.* at 257-258.

[48] Duckworth v. Serrano, 454 U.S. 1, 4 (1981).

[49] For example, there is an exception to the *Younger* abstention doctrine for patently unconstitutional state laws. *See* §13.4, *supra*.

[50] 455 U.S. 509, 522 (1982).

[51] *See* Mark J. Ryan, Note, Rose v. Lundy: The Supreme Court Adopts the Total Exhaustion Rule for Review of Mixed Habeas Corpus Petitions, 1984 Wis. L. Rev. 859, 862.

[52] 455 U.S. at 522.

v. Lundy will encourage habeas petitioners to litigate all their claims in state court and will facilitate the development of complete records in the state courts.[53]

Rose creates a significant problem for habeas corpus petitioners. At minimum, it imposes a substantial penalty on habeas petitioners who are often pro se litigants: If they err and include unexhausted claims, their entire petition will be dismissed. Because the determination of whether state remedies have been exhausted on a particular question is often a difficult legal issue, the total exhaustion rule imposes a substantial practical barrier to habeas corpus petitioners.[54]

Moreover, Justice O'Connor's opinion in *Rose v. Lundy* presents an additional procedural hurdle to litigants trying to meet the exhaustion requirement. If a federal court dismisses a habeas petition because it contains both exhausted and unexhausted claims, the logical reaction of a state prisoner would be to refile the petition containing only the exhausted issues. The prisoner then could simultaneously pursue the unexhausted claims in state court and return to federal court later with a new habeas petition on those issues if necessary. But Justice O'Connor's opinion suggested that a prisoner who attempted to split the claims in this manner might be later barred from presenting the subsequent habeas petition by the doctrine that prevents abuse of the writ. Justice O'Connor, in this portion of her opinion writing for a plurality, explained that "a prisoner who decides to proceed only with his exhausted claims and deliberately sets aside his unexhausted claims risks dismissal of subsequent federal petitions."[55]

Thus, after a federal court dismisses a habeas petition containing both exhausted and unexhausted claims, the petitioner faces a difficult choice. The individual could return to state court and litigate the unexhausted claims there before presenting a new habeas petition to the federal court. This, however, could mean a long delay before having the exhausted claims ruled upon. Alternatively, the prisoner could present the exhausted claims in an immediate new habeas petition, but this might mean foreclosing the chance to present the other claims in a future habeas petition.

Neither alternative seems desirable. The former imposes a long delay before exhausted claims are even ruled upon. Thus, a person might be wrongfully held in prison for a lengthy period of time. The latter alternative precludes a later return to federal court—an unjust solution absent evidence of real abuse of the system.[56]

Can the Exhaustion Requirement Be Waived?

The most important unresolved issue concerning the exhaustion requirement involves whether state governments can waive prisoners' obligation to exhaust state court remedies. Lower courts are split on this question. Some circuits have held that the exhaustion rule may not be waived by the state and may be raised

[53] *Id.* at 519-520.

[54] *See* Peter W. Low & John Calvin Jeffries, Federal Courts and the Law of Federal-State Relations 1018-1019 (9th ed. 2018).

[55] 455 U.S. at 521.

[56] *See* Ryan, Note, *supra* note 51, at 883-886.

by a district court on its own if not argued by the state's attorney.[57] These courts reason that the exhaustion rule is based on a desire to promote harmony between the federal and state governments and, therefore, it embodies concerns that transcend the wishes of the parties.[58] Other circuit courts, however, have held that the exhaustion requirement may be waived by the state.[59] These courts contend that the rule is not jurisdictional, but instead is based on deference to the state governments. Hence, if the state does not object to the petition, there is no reason for the federal court to dismiss on exhaustion grounds.[60]

The Supreme Court considered, but did not fully resolve the issue of waiver, in *Granberry v. Greer*, which held that courts could raise the issue of exhaustion on their own when the state failed to do so.[61] However, the Court also concluded that, at least under some circumstances, waiver could permit nonexhausted claims to be heard on habeas corpus. Writing for the majority, Justice Stevens said that a court is "not required to dismiss for non-exhaustion notwithstanding the state's failure to raise it, and the court is not obligated to regard the State's omission as an absolute waiver of the claim."[62] However, the court's ability to raise the exhaustion issue in such circumstances is not dispositive; rather than automatically dismiss nonexhausted claims, the court should "determine whether the interests of comity and federalism will be better served by addressing the merits forthwith or by requiring a series of additional state . . . court proceedings before reviewing the merits of the petitioner's claim."[63]

Although *Granberry* resolves the issue of whether courts can raise exhaustion problems on their own, it does not settle the waiver question. The decision, for example, does not speak to a situation in which the state explicitly consents to allowing the federal court habeas corpus petition despite the presence of nonexhausted claims. Also, the Court's opinion encourages federal courts to undertake a case-by-case investigation in deciding whether to dismiss or hear a case when the state does not raise exhaustion objections. But the Court provides little guidance for lower courts trying to decide in particular cases whether they can hear the matter notwithstanding exhaustion problems.

No §1983 Suits Challenging Confinement

Finally, with regard to the exhaustion requirement, it should be noted that individuals seeking release from confinement cannot bring a suit pursuant to 42

[57] *See, e.g.,* Snider v. Melindez, 199 F.3d 108 (2d Cir. 1999); Brown v. Fauver, 819 F.2d 395 (3d Cir. 1987); Bowen v. State of Tennessee, 698 F.2d 241 (6th Cir. 1983).

[58] Brown v. Fauver, 819 F.2d at 398.

[59] *See, e.g.,* Bradburn v. McCotter, 786 F.2d 627 (5th Cir.), *cert. denied,* 479 U.S. 847 (1986); Purnell v. Missouri Dept. of Corrections, 753 F.2d 703 (8th Cir. 1985).

[60] Bradburn v. McCotter, 786 F.2d at 629.

[61] 481 U.S. 129 (1987).

[62] *Id.* at 129.

[63] *Id.* at 134. The Supreme Court has ruled that a habeas petition that is filed after an earlier petition was dismissed for failure to exhaust is not a second or successive habeas petition. Slack v. McDaniel, 529 U.S. 473 (2000).

U.S.C. §1983. Section 1983 creates a cause of action for those claiming that a person acting under color of state law has violated the Constitution or laws of the United States.[64] Courts may award declaratory, injunctive, or monetary relief to successful §1983 claimants. The Supreme Court expressly held that state administrative and judicial remedies need not be exhausted prior to filing a federal court §1983 suit.[65] Therefore, to circumvent the exhaustion requirement in habeas corpus cases, litigants might try to bring §1983 suits to challenge the constitutionality of their confinement.

In *Preiser v. Rodriguez*, the Supreme Court held that habeas corpus was the exclusive remedy when state prisoners sought release from custody.[66] In *Preiser*, the plaintiffs challenged the revocation of their good-time credits and simultaneously sued under §1983 and filed a petition for a writ of habeas corpus. The Supreme Court ruled that §1983 could not be used when a prisoner was seeking an immediate or speedier release from prison. Such challenges to confinement only could be brought in federal courts through a writ of habeas corpus. The Court recognized that permitting §1983 suits would render the exhaustion requirement in habeas litigation meaningless. The *Preiser* Court, however, emphasized that §1983 suits could be brought when plaintiffs are challenging the conditions of confinement as being unconstitutional, but §1983 suits are not allowed when the plaintiffs are seeking release from custody.

In *Heck v. Humphrey*, the Supreme Court extended *Preiser* to hold that a prisoner may not bring a §1983 suit that would recover damages for a conviction unless the conviction has been overturned on appeal or habeas corpus.[67] In other words, a §1983 action that effectively challenges a conviction is barred until and unless the conviction is overturned. *Heck v. Humphrey* and its application are discussed in detail in §8.4.

In several cases the Supreme Court has held that prisoners facing execution may bring a §1983 suit to challenge the *method* of execution. In *Nelson v. Campbell*, the Court ruled that an inmate could challenge the procedure used for cutting veins for purposes of execution by lethal injection.[68] In *Hill v. McDonough*, the Court ruled that a prisoner could bring a §1983 suit to challenge the three-drug sequence used in the state for death by lethal injection.[69] The Court reaffirmed this in *Nance v. Ward*.[70] In all of these cases, the Court stressed that the inmates were not seeking to use §1983 suits to challenge the punishment being inflicted, but rather just its method.

[64] Section 1983 is examined in detail in Chapter 8.

[65] *See, e.g.*, Patsy v. Board of Regents of Fla., 457 U.S. 496 (1982); Monroe v. Pape, 365 U.S. 167 (1961); *see* §8.4, *supra*.

[66] 411 U.S. 475 (1973). Preiser v. Rodriguez is discussed in detail in §8.4, *supra*. For an argument that restrictions on habeas should change the availability of Section 1983 suits, *see* Dev. P. Ranjan, Collateral Effects of Habeas Retrogression, 109. Va. L. Rev. 1491 (2023).

[67] 512 U.S. 477 (1994).

[68] 541 U.S. 637 (2004).

[69] 547 U.S. 573 (2006).

[70] 597 U.S. 159, 165 (2022).

Also, in *Skinner v. Switzer*, the Court held that a §1983 suit could be brought by a person who claimed that the preclusion of postconviction DNA testing was unconstitutional.[71] Subsequently, in *Reed v. Goertz*, the Court resolved a Circuit split over when the statute of limitations for a 42 U.S.C. §1983 claim seeking DNA testing of crime-scene evidence begins to run.[72] The Court held that the statute of limitations begins when the entire litigation ends.[73]

§15.4.3 The Prohibition Against Successive Habeas Corpus Petitions

History

One of the most important changes in habeas corpus law in the 1990s was the imposition, by both the Supreme Court and Congress, of strict bans on successive habeas corpus petitions. As originally drafted, the habeas corpus statutes did not bar individuals from filing repeated petitions presenting the same claims. In the 1948 revisions of the habeas corpus laws, a provision was added excusing a federal court from ruling on a petition when the matter contained in it already had been presented and decided in a prior petition. Specifically, §2244(a) provided that a judge need not entertain a petition for a writ of habeas corpus when the legality of the detention "has been determined by a judge or court of the United States on a prior application for a writ of habeas corpus and the petition presents no new ground not theretofore presented and determined, and the judge or court is satisfied that the ends of justice will not be served by such inquiry."

The Court interpreted this provision in *Sanders v. United States.*[74] Although *Sanders* involved a §2255 petition by a federal prisoner, the Court concluded that the rules preventing successive petitions were identical for state and federal petitioners. The Court in *Sanders* said that a habeas corpus petition should be denied based on earlier petitions "only if (1) the same ground presented in the subsequent application was determined adversely to the applicant on the prior application; (2) the prior determination was on the merits; and (3) the ends of justice would not be served by reaching the merits of the subsequent application."[75] The Court emphasized that judges ruling on habeas petitions have discretion and may choose to rule on petitions even though they would appear to be barred under these criteria.[76]

[71] 562 U.S. 521 (2011). This case, and the issue more generally, is discussed in Chapter 13.

[72] Reed v. Goertz, 598 U.S. 230, 237 (2023).

[73] *Id.*

[74] 373 U.S. 1 (1963).

[75] *Id.* at 15.

[76] *Id.* at 18. *See also* 28 U.S.C. §2244(b), providing that if the federal court declines a petition for a writ of habeas corpus after an evidentiary hearing or a hearing on the merits of an issue of law, a person in state custody may not present a subsequent petition "unless the court . . . is satisfied that the applicant has not on the earlier application deliberately withheld the newly asserted ground or otherwise abused the writ."

In addition to the bar against successive suits contained in federal statutes, the Rules Governing Section 2254 Cases in the United States District Courts also prevent petitioners from presenting the matters already ruled on in previous habeas proceedings. The habeas corpus rules went into effect in 1977 and state, in part, that "[a] second or successive petition may be dismissed if the judge finds that it fails to allege new or different grounds for relief and the prior determination was on the merits or, if new and different grounds are alleged, the judge finds that the failure of the petitioner to assert those grounds in a prior petition constituted an abuse of the writ."[77] The Advisory Committee note explains that this rule was designed to implement the requirements set forth in the *Sanders* case.[78]

Thus, under both the Advisory Committee's explanation and under the *Sanders* decision, a court never would have been obligated to dismiss a successive petition from the same individual presenting identical issues. The court could dismiss or it could hear the matter based on the Court's belief as to what would best serve the interests of justice.

McCleskey v. Zant

In *McCleskey v. Zant*, the Supreme Court held that an individual who has previously filed a habeas corpus petition challenging a conviction may file a subsequent petition presenting a new issue only if the individual can show cause and prejudice from the earlier omission of the issue.[79] A criminal defendant, who had been sentenced to death, learned after the filing of his first habeas corpus petition that there had been an informant in his cell. The defendant then filed a second habeas corpus petition arguing that the government's coaching and use of the informant violated *Massiah v. United States*,[80] which held that the government may not, in the absence of counsel, deliberately elicit statements from a person under indictment.

The Supreme Court held that the defendant could not raise the issue in the second habeas petition. The Court explained that the doctrines of abuse of the writ and procedural default implicate "nearly identical concerns flowing from the significant costs of federal habeas corpus review."[81] Thus, the Court concluded, "We have held that a procedural default will be excused only upon a showing of cause and prejudice. . . . We now hold that the same standard applies to determine if there has been an abuse of the writ through inexcusable neglect."[82] The majority concluded that in this case, the petitioner knew enough without the wrongly withheld information that he should have pursued his *Massiah* claim in his earlier habeas petition.

[77] 28 U.S.C. §2254, Rule 9(b), Rules Governing Section 2254 Cases in the United States District Courts.

[78] Advisory Committee Note to Rule 9(b).

[79] 499 U.S. 467 (1991).

[80] 377 U.S. 201 (1964).

[81] 499 U.S. at 490-491.

[82] *Id.* at 493.

Justice Marshall, joined by Justices Blackmun and Stevens, strongly criticized the decision. Justice Marshall, in dissent, wrote, "Today's decision departs drastically from the norms that inform the proper judicial function. Without even the most casual admission that it is discarding long-standing legal principles, the Court radically redefines the content of the abuse of the writ doctrine."[83] The dissent objected especially to precluding a second habeas petition that was based on information that was not available when the first was filed, precisely because the government wrongly had withheld the information from the defendant.

Statutory Provision

The Antiterrorism and Effective Death Penalty Act creates a strict prohibition of successive habeas corpus petitions. An individual may file a successive petition only if he or she first obtains permission from the U.S. court of appeals. The act states, "Before a second or successive application permitted by the section is filed in the district court, the applicant shall move in the appropriate court of appeals for an order authorizing the district court to consider the application."[84]

Moreover, the act provides that "[t]he grant or denial of an authorization by a court of appeals to file a second or successive application shall not be appealable and shall not be the subject of a petition for rehearing or for a writ of certiorari."[85] In *Felker v. Turpin*, the Supreme Court upheld the constitutionality of this preclusion of its ability to review court of appeals decisions denying successive petitions.[86] The Court explained that its review was not completely foreclosed because the Court retained the ability to grant habeas corpus petitions in its original jurisdiction. The Court also stressed the broad authority of Congress to control the procedures concerning habeas corpus. Chief Justice Rehnquist, writing for the Court, said, "[W]e have long recognized that the power to award the writ by any of the courts of the United States must be found in the written law, and we have likewise recognized that judgments about the proper scope of the writ are normally for Congress to make."[87] The Court thus rejected the claim that the restrictions on successive petitions amounted to an unconstitutional suspension of the writ of habeas corpus.

Under the act, a court of appeals may allow a successive petition only in two circumstances. First, a successive petition may be allowed if "the applicant shows that the claim relies on a new rule of constitutional law, made retroactive to cases on collateral review by the Supreme Court that was previously unavailable."[88] In *Tyler v. Cain*, the Supreme Court ruled that only a decision by the Supreme Court can make a decision retroactive for purposes of allowing a successive habeas petition.[89] A criminal defendant challenged his conviction on the grounds of an

[83] *Id.* at 506 (Marshall, J., dissenting).
[84] Antiterrorism and Effective Death Penalty Act of 1996, §106(b), 28 U.S.C. §2244(3)(A).
[85] *Id.*
[86] 518 U.S. 651 (1996).
[87] *Id.* at 664 (citations omitted).
[88] *Id.* at 656.
[89] 533 U.S. 656 (2001).

impermissible jury instruction, which seemed to clearly be unconstitutional based on the Supreme Court's decision in *Cage v. Louisiana.*[90] Nonetheless, the Supreme Court held that habeas relief could not be granted because it had never declared that *Cage* applies retroactively. Justice Thomas, writing for the Court in a 5-4 decision, focused on the literal language of the habeas statute that allows a successive habeas petition based on rules "made retroactive to cases on collateral review by the Supreme Court."[91] The result, as the dissent lamented, is that people will be held in prison even though it is clear that their conviction was unconstitutional because the Supreme Court had not made the rule retroactive.

Alternatively, the petition may be permitted if "the factual predicate for the claim could not have been discovered previously through the exercise of due diligence and the facts underlying the claim, if proven and viewed in light of the evidence as a whole, would be sufficient to establish by clear and convincing evidence that, but for the constitutional error, no reasonable factfinder would have found the applicant guilty of the underlying offense."[92]

The Supreme Court ruled that a habeas petition filed after an earlier petition was dismissed for failure to exhaust is not barred as a second or successive petition.[93] Also, the Court has held that it is not a successive petition if an individual files a petition after a state court decision that follows a successful habeas petition. In *Magwood v. Patterson,* a federal court granted a petition for a writ of habeas corpus to a capital defendant and ordered a new penalty phase in state court.[94] The defendant was again sentenced to death in state court and, after exhausting his state remedies, filed a petition for habeas corpus in federal court. The issue was whether this was a "successive petition."

The Supreme Court, in a 5-4 decision, held that this was not a successive petition and that therefore the restrictions of AEDPA did not apply. Justice Thomas, writing for the Court, explained that it is a successive petition only if it is challenging the same state court judgment. The death sentence imposed after the successful habeas petition was a new judgment, and thus the habeas petition was not to be deemed successive. The Court said that the habeas petitioner can raise all claims in this petition, whether they were raised in the earlier petition or not.

In *Gonzalez v. Crosby,* the Court held that a motion under Rule 60(b) of the Federal Rules of Civil Procedure, which sought "relief from a final judgment" of a federal district court, was a successive petition so long as the motion "attacks the federal court's previous resolution of a claim on the merits."[95] But in *Banister v. Davis,* the Court held that a motion to amend or alter a judgment pursuant to Rule 59(e) is not a successive

[90] 498 U.S. 39 (1990).

[91] 28 U.S.C. §2244(b)(2)(A).

[92] 518 U.S. at 657. In Stewart v. Martinez-Villareal, 523 U.S. 637 (1998), the Court ruled that a habeas petition based on alleged incompetence to be executed was not a successive petition and thus not barred. The Court ruled that when a claim is dismissed as premature for lack of exhaustion, its refiling is not barred as a subsequent petition.

[93] Slack v. McDaniel, 529 U.S. 473 (2000).

[94] 561 U.S. 320 (2010).

[95] 545 U.S. 524, 532 (2005).

petition.[96] Justice Kagan, writing for the Court, explained: "The upshot, after AEDPA as before, is that Rule 59(e) motions are not second or successive petitions, but instead a part of a prisoner's first habeas proceeding. In timing and substance, a Rule 59(e) motion hews closely to the initial application; and the habeas court's disposition of the former fuses with its decision on the latter. Such a motion does not enable a prisoner to abuse the habeas process by stringing out his claims over the years. It instead gives the court a brief chance to fix mistakes before its (single) judgment on a (single) habeas application becomes final and thereby triggers the time for appeal."[97]

In *Jones v. Hendrix*, the Court held that a change in the interpretation of a federal statute does not justify a successive habeas petition.[98] In 2000, the United States District Court for the Western District of Missouri sentenced Marcus DeAngelo Jones to 27 years in prison for two counts of possession of a firearm as a felon. He appealed, and the sentence was affirmed. He later filed a motion to vacate his sentence, pursuant to a 28 U.S.C. §2255 motion. The district court denied his motion, but the Eighth Circuit reversed, concluding that Jones had ineffective counsel and that he should never have received two duplicate charges. Jones was resentenced, removing one count of possession of a firearm and resolving his §2255 motion.

Under 28 U.S.C §2255, Congress included clause (e), or the "saving clause," stipulating that habeas petitions would no longer be permitted unless the remedy by motion is "inadequate or ineffective to test the legality" of detention. Congress subsequently passed the Anti-Terrorism and Effective Death Penalty Act of 1996. Enacted in the wake of the Oklahoma City bombing, AEDPA bars "second and successive" §2255 motions, with exceptions for newly discovered evidence or a new rule of constitutional law made retroactive by the Supreme Court. There is no mention of statutory legal innocence claims.

In *Rehaif v. United States*, the Supreme Court said that the charge of possession of a firearm by a felon required the government to prove that the defendants knew both that they possessed a firearm and that they were prohibited from doing so.[99] The second element was never proven at Jones's trial, meaning that Jones had a claim for legal innocence: A crucial element of his crime was never proven.

But Jones had already filed his one §2255 motion, and AEDPA barred him from bringing another. Jones filed a habeas petition arguing that his inability to bring another motion to vacate meant that §2255 was "inadequate or ineffective," and he, therefore, could file for habeas corpus under §2241.

In a 6-3 decision, divided along ideological lines, the Supreme Court ruled against Jones, holding that the saving clause in §2255(e) does not allow a prisoner asserting an intervening change in the interpretation of a criminal statute to circumvent AEDPA's restrictions on second §2255 motions by filing a habeas petition under §2241. Justice Thomas saw the use of the savings clause as a circumvention,

[96] 590 U.S. 504 (2020).
[97] *Id.* at 517.
[98] 599 U.S. 465 (2023).
[99] 588 U.S. 225 (2019).

or an "end-run," around the limits created by AEDPA.[100] Because AEDPA carved out two specific exceptions to the bar on successive §2255 motions—for newly discovered facts and for changes in the law that the Supreme Court says apply retroactively—Thomas said that the bar against successive petitions also applies to previously unavailable statutory claims.

Justice Thomas read the saving clause very narrowly, arguing that Congress intended AEDPA as a filter to limit habeas claims excepting only highly unusual circumstances, such as if the sentencing court no longer exists.[101] He argued that any other view of the saving clause would make AEDPA "self-defeating" based on the Congressional purpose of limiting successive §2255 motions. Thomas wrote that "[t]he inability of a prisoner with a statutory claim to satisfy those conditions does not mean that he can bring his claim in a habeas petition under the saving clause. It means that he cannot bring it at all. Congress has chosen finality over error correction in his case."[102]

Justice Sotomayor, joined by Justice Kagan, dissented and pointed to the unfairness of not allowing a habeas petition in these circumstances. She wrote, "A prisoner who is actually innocent, imprisoned for conduct that Congress did not criminalize, is forever barred by 28 U.S.C. §2255(h) from raising that claim, merely because he previously sought postconviction relief. It does not matter that an intervening decision of this Court confirms his innocence. By challenging his conviction once before, he forfeited his freedom."[103]

Justice Jackson wrote a vehement dissent, disagreeing with the Court's reasoning and conclusion and strongly disapproving of its approach to habeas corpus. In an exhaustive history of the context and Congressional intent behind §2255, she wrote that not only is there no evidence that Congress ever considered legal innocence claims when drafting the two exceptions to the bar on successive petitions, but in fact, this type of claim was inadvertently omitted.[104]

McCleskey and the even more restrictive provisions of AEDPA are motivated by a desire for finality. Multiple habeas corpus challenges to a conviction were seen as costly and a source of significant delays, especially in capital cases. On the other hand, these restrictions on successive petitions may mean that some state prisoners never will have a meaningful hearing on their constitutional claims. Prisoners who file an initial habeas petition pro se and omit important claims because they have little understanding of the law, later will be prevented from filing another petition with the help of counsel or other inmates. The restrictions on successive petitions provide efficiency and finality but likely at the cost of justice in many cases.

[100] 599 U.S. at 477.
[101] *Id.* at 474.
[102] *Id.* at 480.
[103] *Id.* at 492-493 (Sotomayor, J., dissenting).
[104] *Id.* at 507-508 (Jackson, J., dissenting).

§15.4.4 *The Requirement for a Timely Filing of the Petition*

Prior to the Antiterrorism and Effective Death Penalty Act, there was no statute of limitations for habeas corpus petitions.[105] However, AEDPA imposes a one-year statute of limitations for filing habeas petitions. Section 101 of the act provides, "A 1-year period of limitation shall apply to an application for a writ of habeas corpus by a person in custody pursuant to the judgment of a state court."[106] The act also provides that there will be a six-month statute of limitations in capital cases if a state has provided an adequate system of providing attorneys for postconviction proceedings.

In *Day v. McDonough*, the Supreme Court held that a court may raise the statute of limitations in AEDPA sua sponte, but it is not required to do so.[107] Justice Ginsburg, writing for the Court, held that the statute of limitations is not jurisdictional and thus courts are not obligated to raise it. But the Court said that a district court, on its own, may dismiss a petition if it concludes that the limitations period has expired. In this case, the state made a computational error and did not object to the petition as untimely.[108]

The issue that has produced a tremendous amount of litigation and many Supreme Court decisions in a short period of time concerns the tolling of the limitations period. The statute provides that "[t]he time during which a properly filed application for State post-conviction or other collateral relief with respect to the pertinent judgment or claim is pending shall not be counted toward any period of limitation under this subsection."[109]

The Court has clarified many aspects of this tolling provision, though others remain uncertain. First, the Supreme Court has held that the limitations period is not tolled while a habeas petition is pending in federal court.[110] For example, imagine that a person convicted in state court files a habeas petition in federal court and the federal court does nothing with the petition for 11 months before dismissing it for failure to exhaust state remedies. Do the 11 months count toward the one-year statute of limitations, or was the statute tolled during this time? In *Duncan v. Walker*, the Supreme Court held that the statute provides for tolling only while a case is pending in *state* court. Thus, the entire time the case was sitting on the federal court docket counts against the statute of limitations.[111]

The Supreme Court subsequently applied this to hold that the statute of limitations is not tolled when a petition for certiorari from the denial of collateral review in state court is pending. In *Lawrence v. Florida*, by a 5-4 decision, the Court held that

[105] *See* Lonchar v. Thomas, 517 U.S. 314 (1996) (no statute of limitations for habeas petitions).

[106] 28 U.S.C. §2244.

[107] 547 U.S. 198 (2006).

[108] In Wood v. Milyard, 566 U.S. 463 (2012), the Court reaffirmed that courts may, though are not required to, raise the statute of limitations. But the court of appeals abused its discretion in considering sua sponte the timeliness of the state prisoner's federal habeas petition, because the state had deliberately and intelligently forfeited its limitations defense.

[109] 28 U.S.C. §2244.

[110] Duncan v. Walker, 533 U.S. 167 (2001).

[111] *Id.*

the one-year statute of limitations for seeking federal habeas corpus relief from a state court judgment is not tolled during the pendency of a petition for certiorari in the U.S. Supreme Court from the denial of postconviction relief by the state court.[112]

Second, the Court has held that a federal court may stay its proceedings to permit the exhaustion of state remedies, but that it is not required to do so and should do so only if there was good cause for the failure to exhaust. In *Rhines v. Weber*, a habeas petitioner who faced execution filed a timely habeas petition raising 35 constitutional claims.[113] The district court took 18 months to act on the petition and then found that it should be dismissed because there had not been exhaustion on eight of the 35 claims. If the petition were dismissed for failure to exhaust, the petitioner would be barred from later coming back to federal court with a habeas petition; as explained above, *Duncan v. Walker* held that the time a habeas petition is pending in federal court does not toll the statute of limitations.

The district stayed the habeas petition to permit exhaustion in state court. The Supreme Court held that district courts have authority to issue stays. Justice O'Connor, writing for the Court, held that "district courts do ordinarily have authority to issue stays, where such a stay would be a proper exercise of discretion. AEDPA does not deprive district courts of that authority, but it does circumscribe their discretion."[114] But the Court expressed concern that "[s]tay and abeyance, if employed too frequently, has the potential to undermine" the goals of AEDPA in reducing delay and in encouraging litigation in state courts first.[115]

The Court concluded that "[s]tay and abeyance should be available in only limited circumstances."[116] The Court said, "Because granting a stay effectively excuses a petitioner's failure to present his claims first to the state courts, stay and abeyance is only appropriate when the district court determines there was good cause for the petitioner's failure to exhaust his claims first in state court. Moreover, even if a petitioner had good cause for that failure, the district court would abuse its discretion if it were to grant him a stay when his unexhausted claims are plainly meritless.[117]

Third, in *Holland v. Florida*, the Court has held that equitable tolling is permissible under AEDPA.[118] The case involved egregious ineffective assistance of counsel, including a capital defendant's lawyer not informing him that the state court had ruled against him so that he could file a timely habeas petition. Justice Breyer, writing for the Court in a 7-2 decision, explained that the statute of limitations under AEDPA is not jurisdictional and that it should be presumed that equitable remedies exist under statutes unless Congress provides otherwise.

[112] 549 U.S. 327 (2007).
[113] 544 U.S. 269 (2005).
[114] *Id.* at 276.
[115] *Id.* at 277.
[116] *Id.*
[117] *Id.*
[118] 560 U.S. 631 (2010).

The Court did not specify criteria for when equitable tolling will be allowed; it explained that it is in the nature of equity that it will depend on context and circumstances. Justice Breyer did note that this was not an instance of "garden variety" lawyer neglect,[119] but the Court did not attempt to identify what types of lawyer neglect or other circumstances would justify equitable tolling. The case is quite important in unequivocally holding that equitable tolling is permissible with regard to the statute of limitations under AEDPA.

Fourth, the Court has held that a showing of actual innocence is sufficient to excuse a petition that is untimely. In *McQuiggin v. Perkins*, the Court declared: "We hold that actual innocence, if proved, serves as a gateway through which a petitioner may pass whether the impediment is a procedural bar, . . . or, as in this case, expiration of the statute of limitations. We caution, however, that tenable actual-innocence gateway pleas are rare: '[A] petitioner does not meet the threshold requirement unless he persuades the district court that, in light of the new evidence, no juror, acting reasonably, would have voted to find him guilty beyond a reasonable doubt.' "[120]

The Court explained that it had allowed a showing of a "miscarriage of justice" to excuse procedural defaults.[121] The Court said that this also should apply as to the statute of limitations. Justice Scalia wrote for the four dissenters and objected that the Court had allowed a miscarriage of justice exception to judicially created rules and that the statute of limitations is different because it is imposed by statute. He said: " 'Actual innocence' has, until today, been an exception only to judge-made, prudential barriers to habeas relief, or as a means of channeling judges' statutorily conferred discretion not to apply a procedural bar. Never before have we applied the exception to circumvent a categorical *statutory* bar to relief. We have not done so because we have no power to do so. Where Congress has erected a constitutionally valid barrier to habeas relief, a court *cannot* decline to give it effect."[122]

Another issue that has arisen concerning the tolling provision is determining what state proceedings are sufficient for tolling. The statute indicates that the time during which a "properly filed" state proceeding is pending shall toll the statute of limitations. In *Wall v. Kholi*, the Court said that a collateral review proceeding, which tolls the statute of limitations, is "a form of review that is not part of the direct appeal process."[123] The Court concluded that a motion to reduce a sentence under Rhode Island law is not a part of the direct review and is therefore deemed a "collateral proceeding" under AEDPA.

In *Artuz v. Bennett*, the Court held that a petition was properly filed in state court even though it contained claims that were procedurally barred.[124] The Court explained that even though the petition may be rejected by the state court, it still was "properly filed." However, in *Pace v. DiGuglielmo*, the Court held that state

[119] *Id.* at 652.
[120] 569 U.S. 383, 386 (2013).
[121] *Id.* at 392.
[122] *Id.* at 402 (Scalia, J., dissenting).
[123] 562 U.S. 545, 552 (2011).
[124] 531 U.S. 4 (2000).

proceedings that are dismissed by the state court as untimely are not properly filed petitions and do not toll the federal statute of limitations.[125] The case involved a death row inmate in Pennsylvania whose state habeas petition was rejected as untimely. His federal habeas petition would meet AEDPA's statute of limitations only if the state proceedings were deemed properly filed. The Supreme Court, in a 5-4 decision, held that they were not properly filed and thus the federal habeas petition was barred.

In some states, petitions for collateral relief in state court are dismissed and not appealed; rather, new petitions are filed in the appellate courts. In *Carey v. Saffold*, the Court held that there is tolling for a reasonable amount of time after the petition is dismissed in state court before a new petition is filed in the appellate court.[126]

Finally, the Supreme Court has held that if the Court finds a new rule of criminal procedure, the statute of limitations begins to run from the time of that decision and not the time at which the decision is held to apply retroactively.[127] The Court, in a 5-4 decision, found that a habeas petition was time barred, even though it had been brought within one year of the time in which the Supreme Court had held that the right applied retroactively.

Overall, these cases show a court that is strictly enforcing the statute of limitations and limiting the circumstances where tolling occurs.[128] Often these decisions have been by 5-4 margins, with the justices divided along familiar ideological lines.

§15.5 THE ISSUES THAT CAN BE LITIGATED IN FEDERAL COURT HABEAS CORPUS PROCEEDINGS

Perhaps the most important and most controversial questions concerning habeas corpus involve what issues may be raised and litigated in habeas proceedings. Specifically, five questions arise in determining the scope of review in habeas corpus litigation. First, what constitutional claims can be raised on habeas corpus?[1] In *Teague v. Lane*, and in many cases since, the Supreme Court has ruled that habeas

[125] 544 U.S. 408 (2005).

[126] 536 U.S. 214 (2002).

[127] Dodd v. United States, 545 U.S. 353 (2005).

[128] *See, e.g.*, Mayle v. Felix, 545 U.S. 644 (2005) (holding that an amended habeas corpus petition containing new claims does not "relate back" to the time of the filing of the petition and thus that the new claims are time barred).

§15.5 [1] A separate question, of course, is what statutory claims can be raised on habeas corpus. The Supreme Court has held that nonconstitutional claims can be raised on habeas corpus only if the error is "a fundamental defect which inherently results in a complete miscarriage of justice, [or] an omission inconsistent with the rudimentary demands of fair procedure." Hill v. United States, 368 U.S. 424, 428 (1962) (applying the standard to federal prisoners); Reed v. Farley, 512 U.S. 339 (1994) (applying the standard to state prisoners).

petitions cannot seek recognition of new rules of constitutional law.[2] Second, when may a defendant present issues on habeas corpus that were not raised at the time of trial? This question usually entails the issue of when a state court defendant's procedural default precludes a federal court from deciding a matter on habeas corpus review. Third, when may a defendant relitigate issues on habeas corpus that were raised and decided in state court? Fourth, when may a federal court conduct independent fact-finding in habeas corpus proceedings? Finally, what should be the standard of review on habeas corpus? These five questions are addressed in §§15.5.1, 15.5.2, 15.5.3, and 15.5.4, respectively.

§15.5.1 What Constitutional Issues May Be Raised on Habeas Corpus? The Bar Against Seeking "New" Constitutional Rules on Habeas Corpus

Teague v. Lane

Teague v. Lane is one of the Supreme Court's most important habeas corpus decisions in limiting the ability of federal courts to hear constitutional claims raised in habeas corpus petitions.[3] In *Teague,* the Supreme Court ruled that when a habeas petition asks a federal court to create a new rule recognizing a constitutional right, the court may not decide the matter unless it is a right that would be applied retroactively. The Court declared that "[r]etroactivity is properly treated as a threshold question."[4]

Until *Teague,* the Supreme Court considered habeas corpus petitions alleging constitutional violations, even when they asked the Court to recognize a new constitutional right that would not be applied retroactively to other cases. When the Court articulated a new right it benefited the habeas petitioner and future criminal defendants. The Court subsequently would decide, in another case, whether it was to be applied retroactively to others. But in *Teague,* the Supreme Court ruled that retroactivity must be determined first; federal courts may not hear habeas petitions asking the Court to recognize new rights unless such rights would be retroactively applied in all cases.

The Court broadly defined what is a "new" right, thus limiting the constitutional claims that can be presented to a federal court on habeas corpus. The Court said that a "case announces a new rule when it breaks new ground or imposes a new obligation on the States or Federal government. . . . [A] case announces new rule if the result was not *dictated* by precedent existing at the time the defendant's conviction became final."[5]

[2] 489 U.S. 288 (1989).

[3] 489 U.S. 288 (1989). For a discussion of the impact of *Teague, see* David R. Dow, *Teague* and Death: The Impact of Current Retroactivity Doctrine on Criminal Defendants, 19 Hastings Const. L.Q. 23 (1991); Barry Friedman, Habeas and Hubris, 45 Vand. L. Rev. 797 (1992); Joseph Hoffmann, Retroactivity and the Great Writ: How Congress Should Respond to Teague v. Lane, 1990 BYU L. Rev. 183.

[4] 489 U.S. at 300.

[5] *Id.* at 301.

Because very few criminal procedure rights have retroactive application, the effect will be to prevent habeas petitions from asserting claims except as to rights that have been previously established.[6] The Court recognized only two situations in which rights have retroactive effect. One is where the new rules place "certain kinds of primary, private individual conduct beyond the power of the criminal law-making authority to proscribe."[7] The other is a new rule that adopts a procedure that is "implicit in the concept of ordered liberty."[8] The latter, the Court emphasized, is "reserved for watershed rules of criminal procedure."[9]

In other words, *Teague* says that an individual cannot present a claim on habeas corpus review unless either it is an already established right or it is a right that would have retroactive application. Because the latter is rare and the Court broadly defined what is a "new right," *Teague* very substantially limits what can be raised on habeas corpus.[10] Habeas corpus long has been a primary vehicle for federal courts, and especially the Supreme Court, to identify and protect new constitutional rights.[11] After *Teague*, habeas corpus no longer can serve this function.[12]

The Supreme Court has described the steps of analysis in applying *Teague*.[13] Justice Thomas, writing for the Court, in *O'Dell v. Netherland* explained, "The *Teague* inquiry is conducted in three steps. First, the date on which the defendant's conviction became final is determined. Next, the habeas court considers whether 'a state court considering [the defendant's] claim at the time his conviction became final would have felt compelled by existing precedent to conclude that the rule [he] seeks was required by the Constitution.' If not, then the rule is new. If the rule is determined to be new, the final step in the *Teague* analysis requires the court to determine whether the rule nonetheless falls within one of the two narrow exceptions to the *Teague* doctrine."[14]

[6] The test for retroactivity used by the Court is found in Justice Harlan's opinion in Mackey v. United States, 401 U.S. 667, 675 (1971). The Court in *Teague* recognized that retroactivity is rare. 489 U.S. at 288, 304.

[7] 489 U.S. at 288, 307.

[8] *Id.*

[9] *Id.* at 311.

[10] For example, in Schriro v. Summerlin, 542 U.S. 348 (2004), the Court held that the requirement that a death sentence be imposed by a jury does not apply retroactively. The Court said that its earlier decision in Ring v. Arizona, 536 U.S. 584 (2002), neither put a matter beyond the reach of state law nor was a watershed rule of criminal procedure.

[11] In his dissenting opinion, Justice Brennan offers a long list of criminal procedure rights that were recognized for the first time on habeas corpus. *See* 542 U.S. at 334-335 (Brennan, J., dissenting).

[12] *See* Larry W. Yackle, The Habeas Hagioscope, 66 S. Cal. L. Rev. 2331 (1993); Susan Bandes, Taking Justice to Its Logical Extreme: A Comment on Teague v. Lane, 66 S. Cal. L. Rev. 2453 (1993); Barry Friedman, Pas de Deux: The Supreme Court and Habeas Corpus, 66 S. Cal. L. Rev. 2467 (1993).

[13] The Court also has held that *Teague* is not jurisdictional and must be raised by the government. Godinez v. Moran, 509 U.S. 389 (1993).

[14] 521 U.S. 151, 156 (1997). It is important to note that *Teague* applies only to criminal procedure issues and not to the Court's substantive decisions about the meaning of a federal statute. In Bousley v. United States, 523 U.S. 614 (1998), a federal prisoner challenged his guilty plea on the grounds that he did not understand the elements of the offense and that his plea was not knowing and intelligent. The Court ruled *Teague* inapplicable because the requirement that a plea be knowing and intelligent

Affirmation and Application in *Penry*

The opinion in *Teague* actually drew support from only four of the Justices. However, soon after *Teague,* a majority of the Supreme Court has affirmed and applied *Teague.* A few months after *Teague,* in *Penry v. Lynaugh,* the defendant argued on federal habeas corpus that it was unconstitutional to allow capital punishment for people with intellectual disabilities.[15] The Court's opinion, joined by a majority of the justices, began by stating: "Because Penry is before us on collateral review, we must determine, as a threshold matter, whether granting him the relief he seeks would create a new rule. Under *Teague,* new rules will not be applied or announced in cases on collateral review unless they fall within one of two exceptions."[16] The Court expressly rejected the argument that *Teague* should not apply in capital cases.

Two specific issues were presented by Penry's habeas corpus petition. One was whether the execution of people with intellectual disabilities constitutes cruel and unusual punishment in violation of the Eighth Amendment. The Court found that although this was a request to recognize a new constitutional right, it fit within the first situation where rules have retroactive application. A request for "a new rule placing a certain class of individuals beyond state power to punish by death is analogous to a new rule placing certain conduct beyond the state's power to punish at all."[17] The Court thus reached the merits and concluded that imposing death sentences on people with intellectual disabilities did not violate the Eighth Amendment.[18]

The other issue presented by Penry was whether the jury instructions properly addressed the need to consider mitigating factors in deciding the appropriate punishment. Four justices—Rehnquist, White, Scalia, and Kennedy—believed that this issue was barred from consideration by *Teague.*[19] The other five justices, however, concluded that habeas corpus review of this issue was permissible because Penry was not seeking to establish a "new rule" because precedents already had established a right to jury instructions on mitigating factors. The majority remanded the case because of the absence of clear instructions that the jury could consider and give effect to the mitigating effect of Penry's mental disability. Justice Brennan strongly objected to the application of *Teague* to capital cases.[20]

---

was not a new rule. Moreover, the Court said, "[B]ecause *Teague* by its terms applies only to procedural rules, we think it inapplicable to the situation in which this Court decides the meaning of a criminal statute decided by Congress." *Id.* at 620.

[15] 492 U.S. 302 (1989).

[16] *Id.* at 313.

[17] *Id.* at 330.

[18] In 2002, in Atkins v. Virginia, 536 U.S. 304 (2002), the Supreme Court reversed this and held that the execution of an individual with an intellectual disability is cruel and unusual punishment in violation of the Eighth Amendment.

[19] *Id.* at 350 (Scalia, J., concurring in part and dissenting in part).

[20] *Id.* at 341 (Brennan, J., concurring in part and dissenting in part).

Applications of *Teague*

Nonetheless, the Court repeatedly has applied *Teague* to bar federal courts from hearing challenges in capital cases. In 1990, the Court applied *Teague* to preclude habeas corpus review in three capital cases.

In *Butler v. McKellar,* the Supreme Court used *Teague* to bar a defendant from raising a challenge to his confession on habeas corpus.[21] After Butler was convicted for murder, the Supreme Court decided *Arizona v. Roberson,* which held that the "Fifth Amendment bars police-initiated interrogation following a suspect's request for counsel in the context of a separate investigation."[22]

In *Butler,* the Court concluded that *Roberson* established a "new rule" and thus barred the challenge to the confession. Although the *Roberson* Court said that its decision was within the "logical compass" of precedents, Chief Justice Rehnquist, writing for the majority in *Butler,* declared, "[T]he fact that a court says that its decision is within the 'logical compass' of an earlier decision, or indeed that it is 'controlled' by a prior decision, is not conclusive for the purposes of deciding whether the current decision is a 'new rule' under *Teague.*"[23]

Similarly, in *Saffle v. Parks,* the Court used *Teague* to preclude a defendant from challenging the constitutionality of the jury instructions in a capital case.[24] A defendant convicted and sentenced to death in 1983 objected that the jury was instructed to "avoid any influence of sympathy." The defendant maintained that the Eighth Amendment requires that the jury be allowed to base the sentencing decision on sympathy they might feel for the defendant after hearing the mitigating evidence.

The Court, in an opinion by Justice Kennedy, concluded that the defendant was seeking to create a new rule because precedent did not "dictate" the result urged in the habeas corpus petition. Moreover, the Court found that the case did not fit within either of the situations where rules are retroactively applied. Accordingly, the defendant could not challenge the jury instructions on habeas corpus.

In *Sawyer v. Smith,* the Supreme Court again applied *Teague* to preclude a habeas corpus challenge to a death sentence.[25] In 1985, in *Caldwell v. Mississippi,* the Supreme Court held that prosecutors, during the penalty phase of a capital case, cannot minimize the importance of the jury's responsibility by emphasizing the existence of review of the jury's decision.[26] A year before *Caldwell,* Robert Sawyer was convicted of murder and the prosecutor, at the penalty phase, told the jury that others would later review their decision. Sawyer sought habeas corpus relief on the grounds that the prosecutor's statement violated *Caldwell* and violated the Eighth Amendment.

[21] 494 U.S. 407 (1990).
[22] 486 U.S. 675 (1988).
[23] 494 U.S. at 415.
[24] 494 U.S. 484 (1990).
[25] 497 U.S. 227 (1990).
[26] 472 U.S. 320 (1985).

The Supreme Court, however, said that this issue could not be raised on habeas corpus because Sawyer was asserting a right that was not in existence at the time of his conviction. Justice Kennedy, writing for the majority, stated, "Examination of our Eighth Amendment authorities that preceded *Caldwell* shows that it was not dictated by prior precedent existing at the time the defendant's conviction became final."[27] Although *Caldwell* relied on many prior Eighth Amendment cases and many states had recognized the *Caldwell* right under their constitutions, the Court concluded that the outcome in *Caldwell* was not "dictated" by precedent and indeed "that no case prior to *Caldwell* invalidated a prosecutorial argument as impermissible under the Eighth Amendment."[28]

Subsequently, in *Gilmore v. Taylor*, the Court rescinded a grant of habeas corpus relief to an individual who was sentenced prior to the Seventh Circuit's invalidation, in another case, of the jury instructions used.[29] In *Falconer v. Lane*, the Seventh Circuit held that jury instructions are impermissible if they do not direct jurors to consider mitigating evidence and the ability to convict defendants of lesser charges.[30] The Supreme Court held that *Falconer* announced a new rule because it "was not *dictated* by precedent existing at the time the defendant's conviction became final."[31] The Court thus concluded that "[b]ecause the rule announced in *Falconer* is 'new' within the meaning of *Teague,* and does not fall into one of *Teague*'s exceptions, it cannot provide the basis for federal habeas relief in respondent's case."[32]

What is a "New Rule"?

Under *Teague* and its progeny, habeas corpus relief is only available if either the case does not request recognition of a new rule or if it is a rule that would be applied retroactively. With one exception, the Court has broadly defined what is a new rule and narrowly circumscribed the scope of habeas corpus relief. In *Stringer v. Black*, the Court found that the habeas petition was not seeking recognition of a new rule and thus it was not barred by *Teague.*[33]

In *Stringer*, an individual was sentenced to death and part of the instructions to the jury said that an appropriate aggravating factor was whether the crime was "heinous, atrocious, or cruel." Subsequent to the conviction and sentencing, the Supreme Court declared such language to be impermissibly vague.[34] The issue in *Stringer v. Black* was whether *Teague* barred a habeas corpus petition based on the later Supreme Court decisions invalidating the type of jury instructions used in sentencing. Simply put, did the Supreme Court cases create a new rule?

[27] 497 U.S. at 236.
[28] *Id.* at 231.
[29] 508 U.S. 333 (1993).
[30] 905 F.2d 1129 (7th Cir. 1990).
[31] 508 U.S. at 340, *quoting* Butler v. McKellar, 494 U.S. at 412 (emphasis in original).
[32] 508 U.S. at 345-346.
[33] 503 U.S. 222 (1992).
[34] Maynard v. Cartwright, 486 U.S. 356 (1988); Clemons v. Mississippi, 494 U.S. 738 (1990).

In an opinion by Justice Kennedy, the Court said that although there was "not . . . any single case," a "clear principle emerges" from "a long line of authority." The law in Mississippi, where Stringer was convicted, required juries in sentencing to weigh aggravating and mitigating factors. The Supreme Court's earlier invalidation of similar jury instructions was in states that required the presence of aggravating factors, but did not necessitate the balancing of aggravating and mitigating factors. The Court found that the presence of this distinction did not create a new rule and thus *Teague* was inapplicable.

Stringer v. Black is important in indicating that there need not be a case directly on point to prevent a court from concluding that there is a new rule. The application of a rule to a different circumstance does not create a new rule where the application is a logical and foreseeable extension of the law.[35]

However, subsequent cases make it clear that *Stringer* is the exception and that the Court takes a broad view of what is a "new rule." In *Gray v. Netherland*, the Court found that objections to the prosecutor's surprise presentation of evidence at the sentencing hearing were barred because they would require the creation of a new rule.[36] The defense counsel had moved the court to require the prosecutor to disclose the evidence that would be presented at the penalty phase. The prosecutor stated that it would present only the defendant's statements about involvement with two other killings. However, after the jury returned its guilty verdict, the prosecutor informed the defendant that it would present extensive evidence the next day of the defendant's involvement with other murders.

The Supreme Court did not reach the question of whether the prosecutor's misrepresentations were a basis for relief; the Court remanded the issue for a determination of whether it had been properly raised at trial or whether there had been a procedural default. However, the Court, in a 5-4 decision, found that *Teague* barred the claim that there was inadequate notice of the evidence. Chief Justice Rehnquist, writing for the majority, explained, "On these facts, for petitioner to prevail on his notice-of-evidence claim, he must establish that due process requires that he receive more than a day's notice of the Commonwealth's evidence. He must also establish that due process required a continuance whether or not he sought one, or that, if he chose not to seek a continuance, exclusion was the only remedy for the inadequate notice. We conclude that only the adoption of a new constitutional rule could establish these propositions."[37]

Justice Ginsburg vehemently dissented and said that "[t]here is nothing 'new' in a rule that capital defendants must be afforded a meaningful opportunity to defend against the State's penalty phase evidence. As the Court affirmed more

[35] In Bousley v. United States, 523 U.S. 614 (1998), the Supreme Court held that *Teague* did not bar a federal prisoner from proceeding on habeas corpus when it was claimed that his guilty plea was not knowing and intelligent because he did not understand the elements of the offense. The Court emphasized that the constitutional rule—pleas must be knowing and intelligent—was not new.

[36] 518 U.S. 152 (1996).

[37] *Id.* at 167.

than a century ago: 'Common justice requires that no man shall be condemned in his person or property without . . . an opportunity to make a defense.' "[38]

Likewise, in *O'Dell v. Netherland,* the Court adopted a very broad view of what is a "new rule."[39] *O'Dell* raised the question of whether *Simmons v. South Carolina* announced a new rule in its holding that a capital defendant must be permitted to inform his sentencing jury that he is parole-ineligible if the prosecution argues that he is a future danger.[40] In a 5-4 decision, the Court concluded that this was a new rule and could not be raised on habeas corpus by a defendant who was convicted and sentenced six years before *Simmons* was decided.

Justice Thomas, writing for the majority, reviewed the decisions prior to *Simmons* and said, "[W]e think it plain that a reasonable jurist in 1998 would not have felt *compelled* to adopt the rule later set out in *Simmons.*"[41] Saying that there is a new rule unless the trial court would have felt "compelled" to decide otherwise gives "new rule" an extremely broad scope.

Subsequently, in *Chaidez v. United States,*[42] the Court applied *Teague* to deny retroactivity to its ruling in *Padilla v. Kentucky,* which held that it was ineffective assistance of counsel to fail to correctly inform a noncitizen of the immigration consequences of a guilty plea.[43] The Court in *Chaidez* said that "when we decided *Padilla,* we answered a question about the Sixth Amendment's reach that we had left open, in a way that altered the law of most jurisdictions—and our reasoning reflected that we were doing as much."[44] The Court said that "[i]f that does not count as 'break[ing] new ground' or 'impos[ing] a new obligation,' we are hard pressed to know what would. . . . No precedent of our own '*dictated*' the answer."[45]

When does a New Rule Apply Retroactively?

Teague provides that a court may recognize a new right on habeas corpus if it is a right that would apply retroactively. The Court said that a right applies retroactively if it puts a matter beyond the reach of the criminal law, as when a court holds that the Constitution protects the right to engage in conduct, or if it is a watershed rule of criminal procedure. In *Edwards v. Vannoy,* the Court overruled the latter exception; no longer is there an exception to *Teague* for watershed rules of criminal procedure.[46]

[38] *Id.* at 181 (Ginsburg, J., dissenting) (citation omitted).
[39] 521 U.S. 151 (1997).
[40] 512 U.S. 154 (1994).
[41] 521 U.S. at 165 (emphasis added).
[42] 568 U.S. 342 (2013).
[43] 559 U.S. 356 (2010).
[44] 568 U.S. at 352.
[45] *Id.* at 353.
[46] 593 U.S. 255 (2021). In the years between *Teague* and *Edwards,* never had the Court found a decision to be a watershed rule of criminal procedure. *See, e.g.,* Wharton v. Bockting, 549 U.S. 406 (2007) ("In order to qualify as watershed, a new rule must meet two requirements. First, the rule must be necessary to prevent an 'impermissibly large risk' of an inaccurate conviction. Second, the rule must 'alter our understanding of the bedrock procedural elements essential to the fairness of a proceeding.' ")

In *Montgomery v. Louisiana,* the Court clarified the law as to retroactivity and held that substantive changes in the law apply retroactively.[47] In *Miller v. Alabama,* the Court had held that it was cruel and unusual punishment in violation of the Eighth Amendment for the government to impose a mandatory sentence of life without the possibility of parole for a homicide committed by a juvenile.[48] The issue in *Montgomery* was whether this applied retroactively. Henry Montgomery was sentenced to life without parole for a murder that he committed in 1963 at age 17.

The Court held that *Miller v. Alabama* applies retroactively. Justice Kennedy, writing for the Court, said that "*Teague* requires the retroactive application of new substantive and watershed procedural rules in federal habeas proceedings."[49] The Court declared: "The Court now holds that when a new substantive rule of constitutional law controls the outcome of a case, the Constitution requires state collateral review courts to give retroactive effect to that rule."[50]

The Court stressed the distinction between substantive rules, which apply retroactively, and procedural rules, which apply retroactively only if they are "watershed." The Court wrote: "Substantive rules, then, set forth categorical constitutional guarantees that place certain criminal laws and punishments altogether beyond the State's power to impose. It follows that when a State enforces a proscription or penalty barred by the Constitution, the resulting conviction or sentence is, by definition, unlawful. Procedural rules, in contrast, are designed to enhance the accuracy of a conviction or sentence by regulating 'the *manner of determining* the defendant's culpability'; [t]hose rules 'merely raise the possibility that someone convicted with use of the invalidated procedure might have been acquitted otherwise.' "[51] The Court concluded that *Miller v. Alabama* was a substantive rule because it put something beyond the reach of the criminal law: a mandatory sentence of life without parole for homicides committed by juveniles.

In *Welch v. United States,*[52] the Court applied *Montgomery* to find that the Court's decision in *Johnson v. United States* applied retroactively.[53] In *Johnson,* the Court declared a provision of the federal Armed Career Criminal Act unconstitutional on vagueness grounds. In *Welch,* the Court said that *Johnson* applied retroactively because it was a substantive change in the law. The Court reaffirmed that changes in the substantive law apply retroactively, while changes in procedural rules apply retroactively only if they are "watershed rules of criminal procedure."

The Court said that a "rule is substantive rather than procedural if it alters the range of conduct or the class of persons that the law punishes. This includes decisions that narrow the scope of a criminal statute by interpreting its terms, as well as constitutional determinations that place particular conduct or persons covered by the statute beyond the State's power to punish."[54]

[47] 577 U.S. 190 (2016).
[48] 567 U.S. 460 (2012).
[49] 577 U.S. at 198-199.
[50] *Id.* at 200.
[51] *Id.* at 201.
[52] 578 U.S. 120 (2016).
[53] 576 U.S. 591 (2016).
[54] Welch, 578 U.S. at 129 (citations omitted).

The Court said that *Johnson* was substantive because it "changed the substantive reach of the Armed Career Criminal Act, altering the range of conduct or the class of persons that the [Act] punishes."[55]

Montgomery and *Johnson* are a major change with regard to retroactivity and significantly expand the ability of federal courts to apply Supreme Court decisions retroactively by finding them to be substantive. But as is often seen in the law, the distinction between "substantive" and "procedural" can be elusive. Many years ago, in *Guaranty Trust v. York*, Justice Felix Frankfurter remarked on the difficulty that often arises in drawing this distinction.[56]

The Court reaffirmed this approach in *Edwards v. Vannoy* and declared: "To summarize the Court's retroactivity principles: New substantive rules alter 'the range of conduct or the class of persons that the law punishes.' Those new substantive rules apply to cases pending in trial courts and on direct review, and they also apply retroactively on federal collateral review. New procedural rules alter 'only the manner of determining the defendant's culpability.' Those new procedural rules apply to cases pending in trial courts and on direct review. But new procedural rules do not apply retroactively on federal collateral review."[57] The Court applied this to conclude that its decision in *Ramos v. Louisiana*,[58] which required unanimous jury verdicts in criminal cases, did not apply retroactively.

Is *Teague* Desirable?

The underlying question remains about whether *Teague* is desirable. The Court defends *Teague* as upholding the finality of convictions and minimizing federal intrusions into the state court systems. Justice Kennedy, for example, explained that "the application of constitutional rules not in existence at the time a conviction becomes final seriously undermines the principle of finality which is essential to the operation of our criminal justice system."[59] Likewise, Chief Justice Rehnquist explained that "[t]he new rule principle validates reasonable, good-faith interpretations of existing precedents made by state courts, and thus effectuates the States' interest in the finality of criminal convictions and fosters comity between federal and state courts."[60] But others argue that the Court has been too restrictive in allowing habeas corpus to be used by defining what is a "new rule" so broadly and refusing to find any procedural change in the law to be "watershed."

Thus, not surprisingly, the underlying normative issues about *Teague* are similar concerning all of the habeas corpus issues and most of the issues discussed in this book. Ultimately, the question is how to balance the state's interest in finality and limiting federal court review with the federal interest in upholding the

[55] *Id.*
[56] 326 U.S. 99, 107 (1945).
[57] 593 U.S. at 276.
[58] 590 U.S. 83 (2020).
[59] Teague v. Lane, 489 U.S. at 309.
[60] Gilmore v. Taylor, 508 U.S. 333, 340 (1993).

Constitution and assuring that individuals are not punished in a manner that is at odds with the Constitution.

Statutory Provision

The Antiterrorism and Effective Death Penalty Act provides that a habeas corpus petition may be granted based on a claim that the trial court misapplied the law only if "the adjudication of the claim resulted in a decision that was contrary to, or involved an unreasonable application of clearly established federal law, as determined by the Supreme Court of the United States."[61] This effectively codifies *Teague v. Lane*: No new rules can be asserted on habeas corpus; relief can be granted only on the basis of Supreme Court decisions clearly establishing rights. In *Horn v. Banks*, the Supreme Court expressly held that *Teague* analysis is required under the Antiterrorism and Effective Death Penalty Act.[62] The U.S. Court of Appeals for the Third Circuit granted habeas corpus based on a finding that the state court decision was an unreasonable application of federal law. The Supreme Court reversed, holding that a federal court must engage in *Teague* analysis and determine whether the petition is asserting a new right and, if so, whether it would be applied retroactively.

§15.5.2 When May a Defendant Present Issues on Habeas Corpus That Were Not Raised in State Court? The Effect of State Court Procedural Defaults

Is Procedural Default an Independent and Adequate State Ground?

If a habeas corpus petitioner raises an issue that was not raised in state court, the question is whether the state procedural default is an independent and adequate state grounds that precludes the federal court from hearing and deciding the issue. In *Harris v. Reed*, the Court held that the rule barring Supreme Court review when there is an independent and adequate state law ground of decision is the "historical and theoretical" basis for preventing federal court habeas review when there has been a state procedural default.[63]

The law has changed dramatically over time concerning when a defendant may present a matter on habeas corpus that was not litigated at the trial. Under the Warren Court's decisions, a defendant was allowed to raise matters not argued in the state courts unless it could be demonstrated that the defendant deliberately chose to bypass the state court procedures. In other words, there was a strong presumption that procedural defaults would not bar federal habeas corpus review.

[61] Antiterrorism and Effective Death Penalty Act of 1996, §104(3), 28 U.S.C. §2254(d)(1).
[62] 536 U.S. 236 (2002) (per curiam).
[63] 489 U.S. 255 (1989). The independent and adequate state ground rule is discussed in §10.5.

In sharp contrast, the Burger Court held that a defendant could present matters on habeas corpus that were not raised at the trial only if the defendant could demonstrate either actual innocence or good "cause" for the procedural default and "prejudice" to the federal court's refusal to hear the matter. Under the Burger Court's approach, there is a strong presumption that procedural defaults in state court will preclude habeas corpus litigation. It is important to note at the outset that the Supreme Court ruled that procedural default is not jurisdictional, but rather must be preserved by the government.[64] The Court unequivocally stated that "a procedural default, that is, a critical failure to comply with state procedural law, is not a jurisdictional matter."[65]

Fay v. Noia

In the 1963 decision of *Fay v. Noia,* the Supreme Court held that an individual convicted in state court may raise on habeas issues that were not presented at trial, unless it can be demonstrated that he or she deliberately chose to bypass the state procedures.[66] In *Fay,* three codefendants were convicted. Two of the defendants appealed and were successful in having their convictions overturned because of the manner in which their confessions were obtained. Noia, the third defendant, then tried to obtain relief in the New York state courts. The New York courts, however, denied Noia's motion to have his conviction overturned because his failure to appeal constituted a procedural default precluding review.

The U.S. Supreme Court rejected the argument that failure to comply with state procedures bars federal court review on habeas corpus. The Court concluded that "a forfeiture of remedies does not legitimize the unconstitutional conduct by which . . . [a] conviction was procured."[67] In *Fay,* the Court perceived its role and the purpose of habeas corpus as preventing the detention of individuals whose conviction resulted from unconstitutional conduct. The Court said that a habeas petitioner would be foreclosed from raising an issue on the ground that it was not presented at trial only if he or she "deliberately bypassed the orderly procedure of the state courts."[68]

The Burger Court, however, adopted a dramatically different standard. It consistently held that a habeas petition may present issues not raised at trial only if there is good cause for the omission and if the defendant was prejudiced by the failure to raise the objections. In *Davis v. United States*[69] and *Francis v. Henderson,*[70] the Supreme Court refused to allow habeas petitions challenging the composition

[64] Trest v. Cain, 522 U.S. 87 (1997). The Court, however, did not decide the question of whether a federal court can raise the issue of procedural default on its own, but the Court did conclude that because procedural default is not jurisdictional, it must be preserved in order to be raised on appeal.

[65] *Id.* at 89.

[66] 372 U.S. 391 (1963).

[67] *Id.* at 428.

[68] *Id.* at 438.

[69] 411 U.S. 233 (1973).

[70] 425 U.S. 536 (1976).

of grand juries when no challenge was made at the time of trial. The Court held in both cases that the defendants would be allowed to present the claims only if they could demonstrate "cause" and "prejudice."

Wainwright v. Sykes

In *Wainwright v. Sykes*, the Supreme Court made it clear that the "deliberate bypass" standard of *Fay* was no longer controlling; rather, the defendants must show cause and prejudice before presenting a matter on habeas corpus that was not raised at trial.[71] In *Wainwright*, an individual convicted of third-degree murder in state court filed a habeas corpus petition in federal court challenging the constitutionality of the admission of his confession at trial. On appeal, the state court refused to rule on the question because it was not raised by the defendant at trial, and under state law, a failure to make a contemporaneous objection to the admission of evidence is deemed a waiver.

The Supreme Court considered whether the procedural default prevented the petitioner from challenging the admissibility of the confession in a federal court habeas proceeding. Under the *Fay v. Noia* standard, the petitioner would have been barred from raising the issue on habeas corpus only if the state could demonstrate that there was a deliberate bypass of the state procedures. But the Court in *Wainwright* rejected this approach and instead adopted the "cause" and "prejudice" test.

Justice Rehnquist, writing for the Court, offered several reasons for substituting the cause and prejudice rule for the earlier deliberate bypass standard. Justice Rehnquist argued that the contemporaneous objection rule is very important and that the *Fay* approach does not sufficiently encourage defendants to raise all of their objections at the time of the trial.[72] Justice Rehnquist contended that the *Fay* test "may encourage 'sandbagging' on the part of defense lawyers, who may take their chances on a verdict of not guilty in a state court with the intent to raise their constitutional claims in a federal habeas court if their initial gamble does not pay off."[73] According to the Court, the deliberate bypass test encouraged both litigants and state court judges to view the state court proceedings as a " 'tryout on the road' for what will later be the determinative federal habeas proceeding."[74] By contrast, the Court believed that the "cause" and "prejudice" test would elevate the importance of the state court proceedings, prevent sandbagging, maximize efficiency, and serve the interests of justice.

Comparison of *Fay* and *Wainwright*

Fay v. Noia and *Wainwright v. Sykes* thus articulate very different tests for when a matter could be raised on habeas corpus that was not litigated in state court.

[71] 433 U.S. 72 (1977).

[72] *Id.* at 88-91.

[73] *Id.* at 89.

[74] *Id.* at 90.

Under *Fay*, state court procedural defaults foreclose federal court review only if the state could demonstrate that the defendant deliberately chose to bypass the state court procedures. But under *Wainwright*, procedural defaults in state court will foreclose federal court review unless the defendant can demonstrate good cause for not raising the matter in state court and prejudice to not having federal court review.

Fay and *Wainwright* not only articulate very different approaches, but they also are premised on radically disparate assumptions. First, the decisions are based on differing assumptions about the likely reasons for procedural defaults in state courts. The *Fay* Court assumed that the usual reason why matters are not raised in state courts is because of inadvertence or errors by attorneys. Justice Brennan, the author of the majority opinion in *Fay* and a dissenter in *Wainwright*, explained that "any realistic system of federal habeas corpus jurisdiction must be premised on the reality that the ordinary procedural default is born of the inadvertence, negligence, inexperience, or incompetence of trial counsel."[75] But the Court in *Wainwright* assumed that the usual reason for an omission in state court was a strategic decision by a defense attorney: specifically, a desire by defense counsel to sandbag claims until the later proceedings.

Preventing sandbagging is a major concern in the *Wainwright* opinion, but it is difficult to see what an attorney might gain by sandbagging. If the objection is presented at trial, there is a chance that the court will rule in the defendant's favor and that this ruling will aid in gaining an acquittal. If the court rules against the defendant, the objection is preserved and can be raised on appeal and later on habeas. But if the objection is sandbagged for the habeas petition, the defendant is giving up use of the objection at trial and on appeal for no apparent gain. In fact, even under the *Fay v. Noia* standard, the objection could not be presented on habeas corpus if it could be shown that the defendant deliberately bypassed review in state proceedings. Furthermore, given the low rate of success on habeas, it is hard to imagine attorneys strategically choosing to wait and take a chance on a possible later reversal.[76]

If nothing else, as an empirical matter, a blanket rule precluding habeas review for virtually all procedural defaults assumes that these procedural defaults are more likely to result from deliberate sandbagging rather than from attorney error. Yet the reality of criminal representation, especially by often overworked public defenders, would seem to lead to the opposite conclusion.

Second, *Fay* and *Wainwright* are based on differing assumptions about the fairness of binding defendants by strategic choices made by their attorneys. The *Fay* approach is based on the premise that a defendant should be deemed to have waived the right to present an issue only if he or she made a knowing and voluntary decision to forgo the state procedures. Justice Brennan explained that *Fay*'s

[75] *Id.* at 104 (Brennan, J., dissenting).

[76] Judith Resnik, Tiers, 57 S. Cal. L. Rev. 837, 897 (1984) (The sandbagging argument "assumes a fantastically risk-prone pool of defendants and attorneys. Given that the success rate at trial and on appeal, while low, is greater than the success rate on habeas corpus, the odds are against being able to 'sandbag' in a first procedure and emerge victorious in a second.").

"bypass test simply refuses to credit what is essentially a lawyer's mistake as a forfeiture of constitutional rights."[77] But *Wainwright* is premised on the assumption that individuals are represented by attorneys and that it is completely appropriate to bind clients by their counsel's choices. In fact, in a decision subsequent to *Wainwright, Murray v. Carrier* (discussed below), the Court held that a defense counsel's inadvertent failure to raise a matter did not justify allowing it to be heard on habeas unless the error amounted to ineffective assistance of counsel.[78]

Third, *Fay* and *Wainwright* differ as to the importance of ensuring compliance with state procedures. Although *Fay* recognizes the desirability of ensuring that defendants raise all of their objections in state court, the *Fay* Court thought that it was more important to ensure that no person is held in prison as a result of a constitutional violation. But *Wainwright* stressed the crucial importance of enforcing contemporaneous objection rules and ensuring the use of state court procedures.

Fay Expressly Overruled

Although *Wainwright* and its progeny implicitly overruled *Fay*, it was not until *Coleman v. Thompson*, in 1991, that *Fay* was explicitly overturned and the Court held that all procedural defaults are to be evaluated under the cause and prejudice test.[79] Justice O'Connor, writing for the majority, declared:

> We now make it explicit: in all cases in which a state prisoner has defaulted his federal claims in state court pursuant to an independent and adequate state procedural rule, federal habeas review of the claim is barred unless the prisoner can demonstrate cause for the default and actual prejudice as a result of the alleged violation of federal law, or demonstrate that the failure to consider the claim will result in a fundamental miscarriage of justice.[80]

In *Coleman*, a defendant in a capital case was denied appeal to the state court of appeals of his state habeas petition because he filed the notice of appeals three days late. The issue was whether the procedural error precluded federal habeas review. The Supreme Court explained that *Wainwright v. Sykes* effectively had overruled *Fay v. Noia* and that the petitioner's procedural default would preclude federal habeas review unless he could show cause and prejudice or a likelihood of actual innocence.

In May 1992, Coleman was executed in Virginia despite some evidence that he was actually innocent.[81] No federal court ever heard Coleman's claim.

[77] Wainwright v. Sykes, 433 U.S. at 105 (Brennan, J., dissenting). *See also* Robert Cover & Alexander Aleinikoff, Dialectical Federalism: Habeas Corpus and the Court, 86 Yale L.J. 1035, 1069-1086 (1977) (analyzing binding defendants to attorneys' errors).

[78] 477 U.S. 478 (1986).

[79] 501 U.S. 722 (1991).

[80] *Id.* at 750.

[81] *See* Jill Smolowe, Roger Keith Coleman: Must This Man Die?, Time, May 18, 1992, at 40.

What is "Cause"?

While the *Wainwright* decision clearly adopted the "cause" and "prejudice" test for habeas corpus review, the Court explicitly avoided defining these two terms. Subsequent cases have given content to this test.[82] Several decisions have focused on what is sufficient "cause" to excuse a state court procedural default and permit a habeas corpus petitioner to raise matters not presented in the state courts.

Engle v. Isaac indicated how difficult it is to show "cause."[83] In *Engle*, a defendant used habeas corpus to challenge the constitutionality of the jury instructions used in his trial. In a case decided subsequent to his conviction, the Ohio Supreme Court held that the type of jury instructions given violated Ohio law and that its ruling applied retroactively to all cases in which they had been used.[84] Nonetheless, the Supreme Court held that the issue could not be raised on habeas corpus because the defense counsel did not object at trial, even though at that time there was no reason to think that the instructions were unconstitutional. Justice O'Connor, writing for the majority, concluded, "[T]he futility of presenting an objection to the state courts cannot alone constitute cause for failure to object at trial. . . . Even a state court that has previously rejected a constitutional argument may decide, upon reflection, that the contention is valid."[85]

The Court in *Engle* made it clear that it took a very different view of habeas corpus than had the Warren Court. Justice O'Connor expressed great reservations about the availability of habeas corpus because it imposes "significant costs" on society, including "undermin[ing] the usual principles of finality" and "cost[ing] society the right to punish admitted offenders."[86] According to the Court, these cost considerations outweigh the value of providing relief to an individual who was convicted and incarcerated as a result of admittedly unconstitutional jury instructions.

Two years after *Engle*, in *Reed v. Ross*, the Supreme Court recognized that under limited circumstances, "where a constitutional claim is so novel that its legal basis is not reasonably available to counsel," a defendant may present matters on habeas that were not raised at trial.[87] *Reed* was a 5-4 decision, with four of the justices who were in the majority in *Engle*—Justices Burger, Blackmun, O'Connor, and Rehnquist—dissenting. Like *Engle*, *Reed* involved a challenge to jury instructions about the burden of proof for a claim of self-defense. The majority distinguished *Reed* from *Engle* based on the time the trial occurred. The trial took place in *Engle* after the Supreme Court's 1970 decision in *In re Winship*, which required the state to prove every element of a crime beyond a reasonable doubt.[88] Thus, the

[82] For an excellent discussion of the tests for procedural defaults, *see* Daniel J. Meltzer, State Court Forfeitures of Federal Rights, 99 Harv. L. Rev. 1128 (1986).

[83] 456 U.S. 107 (1982).

[84] State v. Robinson, 47 Ohio St. 2d 103, 110, 351 N.E.2d 88, 93 (1976). *See also* State v. Humphries, 51 Ohio St. 2d 95, 364 N.E.2d 1354, 1359 (1977) (jury instructions held improper but defendant waived error by failing to object).

[85] 456 U.S. at 130.

[86] *Id.* at 126-127.

[87] 468 U.S. 1, 16 (1984).

[88] 397 U.S. 358 (1970).

Engle Court concluded that in light of *Winship* and subsequent lower court cases interpreting it, the defendant's attorney should have thought to object to the jury instructions. But in *Reed,* the trial occurred in 1969, before *Winship,* and the Court decided that it would be inappropriate to require the defense attorney to anticipate a major Supreme Court decision.

In allowing the defendant to challenge the jury instruction on habeas corpus, the Supreme Court in *Reed* identified circumstances in which habeas petitioners can raise issues based on cases decided after their trial but applied retroactively. The Court's criteria indicated the breadth of the *Engle* holding and the narrowness of the *Reed* exception. Justice Brennan, writing for a plurality, said that a defendant could present claims that became apparent subsequent to the trial when there was a Supreme Court decision that explicitly overrules precedent, when the decision overturns "a longstanding and widespread practice to which the Court has not spoken," or when the decision disapproves "a practice this Court arguably has sanctioned in prior cases."[89] In short, even in distinguishing *Engle,* the *Reed* Court affirmed its conclusion that mere novelty of a claim is not sufficient cause for a defense counsel's failure to present it at trial. As Professor Resnik notes, "Although the *Ross* plurality found a crevice in the seeming impregnable 'cause' requirement of *Isaac,* the aperture is narrow. . . . Under [*Reed v.*] *Ross,* the hurdle of 'cause' only can be surmounted in rare instances."[90]

Even in these rare instances, the federal court may no longer be able to hear such novel claims because of *Teague v. Lane,* discussed above.[91] *Reed* involves a habeas petitioner relying on cases decided subsequent to his or her conviction, and *Teague* precludes the use of later decided cases on habeas corpus except in very limited circumstances.

However, in *Lee v. Kemna,* the Supreme Court found that there was a sufficient basis for allowing a federal habeas petition to be heard despite a state procedural default.[92] At a murder trial in Missouri state court, a defendant asked for an overnight continuance when key witnesses were not present in the courtroom. The trial judge denied the request for a continuance, explaining that he had a daughter in the hospital and another trial scheduled to begin the next day. After the defendant was convicted, his appeal for a violation of due process was denied on the grounds that he did not follow the Missouri law requiring that requests for continuances be in writing and supported by affidavits. The federal district court denied habeas corpus based on the failure to comply with state procedures, and the U.S. Court of Appeals for the Eighth Circuit affirmed.

[89] 468 U.S. at 17.

[90] Resnik, *supra* note 76, at 837, 904-905.

[91] 489 U.S. 288 (1989).

[92] 534 U.S. 362 (2002). *See also* Cruz v. Arizona, 598 U.S. 17 (2023) (The Arizona Supreme Court's holding below—that *Lynch v. Arizona* did not represent a "significant change in the law for purposes of permitting John Montenegro Cruz to file a successive petition for state postconviction relief under Arizona Rule of Criminal Procedure 32.1(g)—is not an adequate state-law ground supporting that judgment.")

The Supreme Court reversed. Justice Ginsburg, writing for the Court, said that "[t]here are . . . exceptional cases in which exorbitant application of a generally sound rule renders the state ground inadequate."[93] Ginsburg explained that a written motion for a continuance would not have made any difference; it would not have overcome the reasons why the judge denied the continuance. Also, the Court said that nothing in Missouri law required compliance with the procedural rules in a circumstance where there is an unexpected disappearance of a key witness. Finally, the Court emphasized that Lee had substantially complied with the state rules through his motion for a continuance and his explanation of the reasons for the request. *Lee v. Kemna* is important because it clearly holds that in some circumstances the failure to comply with state procedures will not preclude a subsequent habeas corpus petition.

Actual Innocence as An Alternative to Cause

Beginning in two decisions decided on the same day—*Murray v. Carrier*[94] and *Smith v. Murray*[95]—the Supreme Court has held that as an alternative to demonstrating cause, a habeas petitioner may raise matters not argued in the state courts by demonstrating that he or she is probably innocent of the charges.

The issue in *Murray v. Carrier* was whether a habeas petitioner could show cause for a procedural default by demonstrating that the defense counsel inadvertently failed to raise an issue. The inadvertence, however, did not amount to ineffective assistance of counsel. In *Murray*, the defense attorney inadvertently omitted an important issue from the notice of appeal. Under the pertinent state law, a failure to include an issue in the notice of appeal was deemed a waiver. Hence, the state courts refused to hear or rule on the omitted issue. The Supreme Court concluded that there was not sufficient cause to permit the defendant to raise the issue in a federal court habeas proceeding. Justice O'Connor, writing for the majority, stated, "So long as a defendant is represented by counsel whose performance is not constitutionally ineffective under the standard established in *Strickland v. Washington*, we discern no inequity in requiring him to bear the risk of attorney error that results in a procedural default."[96]

Justice O'Connor went on to elaborate the type of circumstances that might constitute sufficient cause. Although expressly disavowing an attempt to be exhaustive, she indicated that cause might be demonstrated by "showing that the factual or legal basis for a claim was not reasonably available to counsel, [as in] *Reed v. Ross*, or that 'some interference by state officials' made compliance impracticable, . . . [or that] the procedural default is the result of ineffective assistance of counsel."[97] Justice

[93] *Id.* at 376.

[94] 477 U.S. 478 (1986).

[95] 477 U.S. 527 (1986).

[96] Murray v. Carrier, 477 U.S. at 488.

[97] *Id.* (citations omitted). In Amadeo v. Zant, 486 U.S. 214 (1988), the Court found that a prosecutor's concealing of a memorandum detailing deliberate racial bias in jury selection constituted cause for failure to object at trial.

O'Connor emphasized that "[i]neffective assistance of counsel, then, is cause for a procedural default."[98]

Proving Ineffective Assistance of Counsel

Because *Engle* indicates that cause will rarely be demonstrated by showing that the factual or legal basis was not reasonably available, and because only in unusual cases will cause be demonstrated by showing interference by state officials, ineffective assistance of counsel is the primary method to demonstrate sufficient cause for a procedural default. However, in other decisions, the Supreme Court has articulated a legal test that makes it extremely difficult to prove ineffective assistance of counsel.

In *Strickland v. Washington*, the Supreme Court adopted a strong presumption that an attorney's decisions do not reflect ineffective assistance.[99] The Court explained that "[i]ntensive scrutiny of counsel . . . could dampen the ardor and impair the independence of defense counsel, discourage the acceptance of assigned cases, and undermine the trust between attorney and client."[100] In *Strickland*, the Court held that a defendant could establish ineffective assistance of counsel only by "showing that counsel's errors were so serious as to deprive defendant of a fair trial, a trial whose result is reliable."[101] Additionally, the defendant must show that but for the counsel's errors there is a reasonable probability that the results in the case would be different.[102] Under the *Strickland* test it is very difficult for a defendant to demonstrate ineffective assistance of counsel.[103]

Therefore, *Murray v. Carrier* identifies three circumstances in which sufficient cause for a state procedural default can be demonstrated: inability of counsel to reasonably know of a legal or factual issue, interference by the government's attorney with the habeas petition, and ineffective assistance of counsel. Yet all are quite difficult to establish. The *Murray* Court did indicate, however, one alternative to demonstrating cause. The Court said that a state prisoner who could show that he or she is probably actually innocent should be able to secure relief regardless of the reason for the state court procedural default. Justice O'Connor explained that "in an extraordinary case, where a constitutional violation has probably resulted in

[98] Murray v. Carrier, 477 U.S. at 488.

[99] 466 U.S. 668 (1984).

[100] *Id.* at 690.

[101] *Id.* at 668.

[102] *Id.* at 694.

[103] For example, in Cullen v. Pinholster, 563 U.S. 170 (2011), the Court rejected an ineffective assistance of counsel claim even though the trial lawyers did *no* investigation before a penalty phase that led to the defendant being sentenced to death. *Cullen* is discussed more fully in §15.5.4 in connection with its restrictions on evidentiary hearings in federal court on habeas corpus. However, in Rompilla v. Beard, 545 U.S. 374 (2005), and Wiggins v. Smith, 539 U.S. 510 (2002), the Court found ineffective assistance of counsel and that relief was appropriate under §2254(d). *But see* Thornell v. Jones, 602 U.S. 154 (2024) (defense counsel's failure to present additional mitigating evidence of mental health conditions, cognitive impairment caused by history of head trauma, childhood abuse, and drug misuse did not amount to ineffective assistance of counsel.)

the conviction of one who is actually innocent, a federal habeas court may grant the writ even in the absence of a showing of cause for the procedural default."[104]

The Supreme Court repeated this alternative route to obtaining habeas corpus relief in *Smith v. Murray*. In *Smith*, a defendant convicted for murder and rape challenged the jury's consideration of testimony by a psychiatrist of statements the defendant had made about his conduct in other instances. Although the defendant appealed, no assignment of error was made regarding the psychiatrist's testimony. An amicus curiae brief did raise the issue, but the state supreme court refused to consider it because it had not been raised by the defendant.

The defendant then sought habeas corpus relief. The federal district court denied the petition and the Supreme Court affirmed. The Court explained that "the mere fact that counsel failed to recognize the factual or legal basis for a claim, or failed to raise the claim despite recognizing it, does not constitute cause for a procedural default."[105] The Court expressly rejected the contention that more liberal habeas corpus review should be available in capital cases.[106] The Court, however, indicated that habeas corpus review would be available, even in the absence of demonstrating cause, when the defendant can show that he or she is likely actually innocent.[107]

However, the Supreme Court ruled that a defendant will be barred from raising ineffective assistance of counsel if that was not presented on state postconviction review.[108] The Court explained that "a procedurally defaulted ineffective-assistance-of-counsel claim can serve as cause to excuse the procedural default of another habeas claim only if the habeas petitioner satisf[ies] the 'cause and prejudice' standard with respect to the ineffective-assistance-of-counsel claim."[109] In other words, a prisoner must exhaust state remedies with regard to a claim of ineffective assistance of counsel that is presented as cause and prejudice for the procedural default of another constitutional claim.

The Court, though, has created an exception to this for situations where ineffective assistance of counsel could not be raised on direct review. In *Martinez v. Ryan*, the Court said that where ineffective assistance of counsel claims can be raised only on state collateral review and not on direct appeal, a habeas petitioner can challenge the ineffectiveness of counsel in a state collateral review proceeding.[110] Arizona does not allow a convicted person alleging ineffective assistance of trial counsel to raise that claim on direct review. Instead, the prisoner must bring the claim in state collateral proceedings. In this case, the claim of ineffective of assistance of counsel was not raised in the state collateral review proceeding; in

[104] Murray v. Carrier, 477 U.S. at 495.

[105] Smith v. Murray, 477 U.S. at 535 (*quoting from* Murray v. Carrier).

[106] *Id.* at 538. For an argument that habeas corpus petitions should be handled differently in capital cases, *see* Nancy J. King & Joseph L. Hoffmann, Habeas for the 21st Century: Uses, Abuses, and the Future of the Great Writ (2011).

[107] Smith v. Murray, 477 U.S. at 537 (*quoting from* Murray v. Carrier).

[108] Edwards v. Carpenter, 529 U.S. 446 (2000).

[109] *Id.* at 450-451.

[110] 566 U.S. 1 (2012).

fact, the attorney filed a statement that she found no meritorious claims helpful to petitioner.

The Court, in a 7-2 decision, held that although generally there is not a basis for claiming ineffective assistance of counsel on collateral review, there is an exception for situations where such challenges cannot be brought on direct review. Justice Kennedy, writing for the Court, explained: "Where, as here, the initial-review collateral proceeding is the first designated proceeding for a prisoner to raise a claim of ineffective assistance at trial, the collateral proceeding is in many ways the equivalent of a prisoner's direct appeal as to the ineffective-assistance claim."[111] The Court thus concluded: "Where, under state law, claims of ineffective assistance of trial counsel must be raised in an initial-review collateral proceeding, a procedural default will not bar a federal habeas court from hearing a substantial claim of ineffective assistance at trial if, in the initial-review collateral proceeding, there was no counsel or counsel in that proceeding was ineffective."[112]

In *Thaler v. Trevino*, the Court extended this to situations where the state allows ineffective assistance of counsel claims to be raised on direct review, but the "structure and design of the Texas system in actual operation, however, make it virtually impossible for an ineffective assistance claim to be presented on direct review."[113] Justice Breyer, here writing for the majority in a 5-4 decision, stated: "For the reasons just stated, we believe that the Texas procedural system—as a matter of its structure, design, and operation—does not offer most defendants a meaningful opportunity to present a claim of ineffective assistance of trial counsel on direct appeal. What the Arizona law prohibited by explicit terms, Texas law precludes as a matter of course. And, that being so, we can find no significant difference between this case and *Martinez*."[114]

Shinn v. Martinez Ramirez, however, significantly limited the ability of habeas petitioners to take advantage of *Martinez v. Ryan*.[115] *Shinn* involved two habeas petitioners who had been convicted of murder in Arizona. Arizona does not allow ineffective assistance of counsel claims to be raised on direct appeal. In these cases, it was not raised in Arizona court in postconviction proceedings. Both defendants sought to raise the claims in federal court on habeas corpus based on *Martinez v. Ryan*. In each instance, the federal district court allowed the habeas petitioner to present additional evidence to support the claim of ineffective assistance of counsel. In one of the cases, the new evidence showed a likelihood that the defendant was actually innocent and had been wrongly convicted and sentenced to death.

But the Supreme Court, in an opinion by Justice Clarence Thomas, ruled that holding the hearings was impermissible. Justice Thomas began by saying that "the availability of habeas relief is narrowly circumscribed."[116] He said that habeas

[111] *Id.* at 11.

[112] *Id.* at 17.

[113] 569 U.S. 413, 417 (2013).

[114] *Id.* at 428.

[115] 596 U.S. 366 (2022). For a criticism of this decision, *see* Lee Kovarsky, The New Negative Habeas Equity, 137 Harv. L. Rev. 2222, 2224 (2024).

[116] 596 U.S. at 375.

corpus "intrudes on state sovereignty" by allowing guilty people to go free and it "imposes significant costs on state criminal justice systems."[117]

The Court focused on a provision adopted as part of the Antiterrorism and Effective Death Penalty Act, 28 U.S.C. §2254(e)(2), which greatly limits the ability of federal courts to hold evidentiary hearings on habeas corpus. The Court said this applies even when there is a claim of ineffective assistance of counsel that could not have been raised earlier. The federal court is confined to the state court record and cannot consider additional evidence, even when it may show, as in one of the cases before it, that the defendant is innocent of the crime for which he or she was sentenced to death.

Justice Sonia Sotomayor wrote a strenuous dissent, joined by Justices Stephen Breyer and Elena Kagan.[118] She said that this "all but overrules" *Martinez v. Ryan* because almost always there will be a need for additional evidence to show ineffective assistance of counsel. She lamented that the Court "makes illusory the protections of the Sixth Amendment." She wrote: "The Court's decision will leave many people who were convicted in violation of the Sixth Amendment to face incarceration or even execution without any meaningful chance to vindicate their right to counsel."[119]

Defining "Actual Innocence"

In four cases, the Court has elaborated on the meaning of "actual innocence." In *Sawyer v. Whitley*, the issue was what "actual innocence" means in the context of challenging a sentence.[120] The Court held that for an individual to demonstrate actual innocence, the person must "show with clear and convincing evidence that but for constitutional error at his sentencing hearing, no reasonable juror would have found him eligible for the death penalty [under the applicable state] law."[121] The Court made it clear that "actual innocence" is a "very narrow exception" to the rule that cause and prejudice must be demonstrated to present successive or defaulted claims.[122]

Justices Blackmun, Stevens, and O'Connor concurred in the judgment and argued that the application of the clear and convincing evidence test is unprecedented in this context. Justice Stevens remarked that in a noncapital case a defendant need only show that the constitutional error "probably" resulted in a miscarriage of justice, while under the majority's test a capital defendant must present "clear and convincing evidence" that no reasonable juror would have imposed the death sentence.[123] Justice Stevens lamented that "[i]t is heartlessly

[117] *Id.* at 377.
[118] *Id.* at 391 (Sotomayor, J., dissenting).
[119] *Id.* at 392.
[120] 505 U.S. 333 (1992).
[121] *Id.* at 336.
[122] *Id.* at 341.
[123] *Id.* at 366 (Stevens, J., concurring in the judgment).

perverse to impose a more stringent standard of proof to avoid a miscarriage of justice in capital case than a non-capital case."[124]

Moreover, these justices criticized the Court's holding that "innocence of death" concerns only "those elements which render a defendant eligible for the death penalty, and not on additional mitigating evidence which was prevented from being introduced as a result of claimed constitutional error."[125] In imposing a death sentence, both aggravating and mitigating circumstances are to be considered. There is no reason why a habeas petition challenging a death sentence can identify only improper aggravating factors and not point to wrongly excluded mitigating evidence. By the majority's own test, mitigating evidence might be such as to show that no reasonable juror would have imposed the death sentence under the circumstances.

In another important case considering "actual innocence," the Court held that a claim of actual innocence is not sufficient by itself for habeas review; rather, actual innocence is relevant only if the habeas petitioner is claiming a violation of a federal right. In *Herrera v. Collins*, a majority of the Court joined Chief Justice Rehnquist's conclusion that " 'actual innocence' is not itself a constitutional claim, but instead a gateway through which a habeas petitioner must pass to have his otherwise barred constitutional claim considered on the merits."[126]

Ten years after his conviction and shortly before his scheduled execution, Herrera brought a habeas petition claiming that newly discovered evidence demonstrated that he was actually innocent of the murders and that, in fact, his now-deceased brother was the actual perpetrator. A Texas rule requiring that newly discovered evidence be presented within 30 days of conviction precluded the claim from being brought in state court.

Chief Justice Rehnquist's opinion stated that actual innocence is a basis for a federal court hearing successive or defaulted constitutional claims even when the cause and prejudice test is not met. Actual innocence, however, is not a basis for habeas corpus relief by itself. The Court's opinion stated that the "traditional remedy for claims of innocence based on new evidence, discovered too late in the day to file a new trial motion, has been executive clemency."[127]

However, this seemingly very harsh result—that innocent individuals could be executed because state and federal courts refuse to hear the newly discovered evidence and executive clemency is denied—is called into question by the concurring opinion of Justices O'Connor and Kennedy. Although these two justices concurred in Chief Justice Rehnquist's opinion, they declared, "[T]he execution of a legally and factually innocent person would be a constitutionally intolerable event."[128] Indeed, they concluded their opinion by stating that they understood the majority opinion as assuming "that a truly persuasive demonstration of actual innocence would render any such execution unconstitutional and that federal

[124] *Id.*
[125] *Id.* at 347 (citations omitted).
[126] 506 U.S. 390, 404 (1993).
[127] *Id.* at 417.
[128] *Id.* at 419 (O'Connor, J., concurring).

habeas relief would be warranted if no state avenue were open to process the claim."[129] Justices O'Connor and Kennedy reviewed the evidence against Herrera and concluded that it was appropriate to deny his habeas petition because he "is not innocent, in any sense of the word."[130]

In contrast, Justices Scalia and Thomas expressed the view that even if an individual presented compelling evidence demonstrating "actual innocence," that by itself would be insufficient for habeas relief.[131] Justice Scalia wrote, "There is no basis in text, tradition, or even in contemporary practice (if that were enough), for finding in the Constitution a right to demand judicial consideration of newly discovered evidence of innocence brought forward after conviction."[132]

At most, *Herrera v. Collins* stands for the proposition that a habeas petitioner seeking relief by claiming that newly discovered evidence demonstrates actual innocence has a very heavy burden to meet. Although Chief Justice Rehnquist's majority opinion appears to bar habeas claims based solely on actual innocence, there was not a majority of the justices subscribing to this position. Instead, when opinions are counted, a majority of the justices indicated that a well-supported claim of actual innocence could be the basis for habeas corpus relief.[133] Nonetheless, for Herrera, the Court's decision offered him no relief and on May 12, 1993, he was executed.

After *Herrera v. Collins,* courts have distinguished between two uses of actual innocence: One is as a "gateway" to preventing procedurally defaulted claims; the other is a "freestanding" claim of actual innocence. The former uses actual innocence to justify allowing the federal court to hear a claim that was not properly raised earlier. The latter says that actual innocence itself is the basis for relief. The Court continues to say that it has not resolved whether the latter is permissible, declaring: "We have not resolved whether a prisoner may be entitled to habeas relief based on a freestanding claim of actual innocence."[134]

Following *Herrera v. Collins,* the Court decided in *Schlup v. Delo* that to prove "actual innocence," a habeas petitioner must show that there was a constitutional violation that "probably resulted" in the conviction of one who is actually innocent.[135] The Court expressly rejected the argument, embraced by the dissent, that to prove actual innocence an individual must show with clear and convincing evidence that but for the constitutional error no reasonable juror would have convicted him.[136]

Lloyd Schlup was a prisoner in the Missouri State Penitentiary when another inmate was murdered. Schlup was convicted of this murder and sentenced to

[129] *Id.* at 427.

[130] *Id.* at 419.

[131] *Id.* at 427 (Scalia, J., dissenting).

[132] *Id.* at 427-428.

[133] For excellent criticisms of *Collins, see* Vivian Berger, Herrera v. Collins: The Gateway of Innocence for Death-Sentenced Prisoners Leads Nowhere, 35 Wm. & Mary L. Rev. 943 (1994); Barry Friedman, Failed Enterprise: The Supreme Court's Habeas Reform, 83 Cal. L. Rev. 485 (1995); Jordan Steiker, Innocence and Federal Habeas, 41 UCLA L. Rev. 303 (1993).

[134] McQuiggin v. Perkins, 569 U.S. 383, 392 (2013).

[135] 513 U.S. 298, 327 (1995).

[136] *Id.* at 329 (Rehnquist, C.J., dissenting).

death. After exhausting all direct appeals of his conviction and sentence, Schlup brought an unsuccessful habeas corpus petition in federal court. Later, Schlup filed a second federal habeas corpus petition alleging that constitutional error deprived the jury of critical evidence that would have established his innocence.

Schlup's second habeas corpus petition presented a number of claims including that Schlup was actually innocent of the murder. Schlup relied on an affidavit from another inmate who at the time of the murder was the clerk for the housing unit and who attested that he called for help shortly after the murder occurred. Schlup had a videotape showing that he was in the cafeteria 65 seconds before the guards received the distress call. Also, Schlup presented affidavits from two other inmates identifying another inmate as the assailant. While the case was pending before the U.S. Court of Appeals for the Eighth Circuit, Schlup obtained a statement from a former lieutenant at the prison who saw Schlup going to lunch on the day of the murder and who was with Schlup for at least two and a half minutes.[137] The lieutenant also stated that "Schlup was walking at a leisurely pace; and that Schlup 'was not perspiring or breathing hard, and that he was not nervous.' "[138]

At the outset, Justice Stevens' majority opinion in *Schlup v. Delo* distinguished *Herrera v. Collins*. Justice Stevens explained that Schlup alleged that his constitutional rights had been violated because of ineffective assistance of counsel and by the prosecution's failure to disclose exculpatory evidence. Therefore, Schlup was using actual innocence as a basis for having his otherwise barred constitutional claims heard. Unlike *Herrera*, Schlup was not arguing that actual innocence by itself was a basis for federal habeas corpus relief. In other words, *Schlup* involved actual innocence as a "gateway" and not a "freestanding" claim for habeas relief.

Justice Stevens explained that this distinction was of critical significance in determining the appropriate burden of proof. He wrote:

> Schlup, in contrast, accompanies his claim of innocence with an assertion of constitutional error at trial. For this reason, Schlup's conviction may not be entitled to the same degree of respect as one, such as Herrera's, that is the product of an error-free trial. . . . [I]f a petitioner such as Schlup presents evidence of innocence so strong that a court cannot have confidence in the outcome of the trial unless the court is also satisfied that the trial was free of non-harmless constitutional error, the petitioner should be allowed to pass through the gateway and argue the merits of his underlying claim. Consequently, Schlup's evidence of innocence need carry less of a burden.[139]

Justice Stevens explained the critical importance of habeas corpus relief for a petitioner who asserts a constitutional violation and makes a showing of likely actual innocence. He declared that the "quintessential miscarriage of justice is the execution of a person who is entirely innocent."[140] Thus, the Court concluded that a person

[137] *Id.* at 311-312.
[138] *Id.*
[139] *Id.* at 316.
[140] *Id.* at 299.

seeking to have an otherwise barred habeas petition heard because of "actual innocence" must show that "a constitutional violation has probably resulted in the conviction of one who is actually innocent."[141]

Chief Justice Rehnquist and Justices Kennedy, Thomas, and Scalia dissented. Chief Justice Rehnquist argued that the *Sawyer v. Whitley* standard—that a person only may challenge a sentence based on a claim of actual innocence if he or she demonstrates by clear and convincing evidence that but for a constitutional error no reasonable juror would have imposed the death sentence—also should be used in determining whether challenges to convictions can be heard based on actual innocence.[142]

The standard advocated by the dissent would have made it extremely difficult for any habeas petitioner to show "actual innocence." The majority's emphasis on the need to protect the innocent led it to choose a standard that is much more possible to satisfy. Ultimately, the difference between the five justices in the majority and the four in dissent is over the relative weight to be given to the need to protect finality, favored by the dissent, and the need to protect the innocent, more heavily weighted by the majority.

In *House v. Bell*, the Supreme Court found that the requirements for showing actual innocence were met to allow a procedurally defaulted claim of ineffective assistance of counsel to be raised.[143] A defendant who was convicted of murder and sentenced to death produced strong evidence on habeas corpus of his actual innocence. At trial, the prosecutor said that the motive for the crime was rape and pointed to the rape as the key aggravating factor justifying the death penalty. On habeas corpus, the defendant produced DNA evidence that showed conclusively that the semen on the victim's clothes, the basis for the rape charge, was from the victim's husband. Additionally, there was reason to believe that the presence of the victim's blood on the defendant's pants might have come from a spilling of a vial of blood taken from the victim at the autopsy. The defendant also produced other evidence of his innocence, including two witnesses who heard the victim's husband confess to the murder.

The Supreme Court, in a 5-4 decision in an opinion by Justice Kennedy, found that this was sufficient evidence of actual innocence to allow the defendant to raise a procedurally defaulted claim. The Court reaffirmed the standard that it articulated in *Schlup v. Delo*: "[P]risoners asserting innocence as a gateway to defaulted claims must establish that, in light of new evidence, it is more likely than not that no reasonable juror would have found petitioner guilty beyond a reasonable doubt."[144] The Court found that although this standard "is demanding and permits review only in the 'extraordinary' case,"[145] it was met in the facts of this case. The Court pointed to the DNA evidence, the lab error, and the additional witnesses as meeting the standard for actual innocence to allow the procedurally defaulted

[141] *Id.* at 326.
[142] *Id.* at 333 (Rehnquist, C.J., dissenting).
[143] 547 U.S. 518 (2006).
[144] *Id.* at 536-537.
[145] *Id.* at 537.

claim to be raised. The Court concluded "that this is the rare case where—had the jury heard all the conflicting testimony—it is more likely than not that no reasonable juror viewing the record as a whole would lack reasonable doubt."[146]

Finally, as to actual innocence as an alternative to cause and prejudice, it is important to note that all of the cases discussed above involved defendants who were sentenced to death. In *Dretke v. Haley*, the Supreme Court said that it had not yet ruled on whether the exception applies when a habeas petitioner asserts actual innocence to challenge a noncapital sentence.[147] The Court did not decide the issue, but remanded the case for consideration of the question first by the lower federal courts. However, it is difficult to see why death penalty cases would be different here, since imprisonment of an innocent person also would be an important reason for allowing procedurally defaulted claims to be heard.

Definition of "Prejudice"

Although several Supreme Court cases define "cause" and even "actual innocence," the Court has found less occasion to determine the meaning of "prejudice." In *United States v. Frady*, the Supreme Court indicated that "prejudice" could be demonstrated by showing that the results in the case likely would have been different absent the complained-of violation of the Constitution or federal laws.[148] Although *Frady* involved the claim of a federal prisoner, the Supreme Court declared that the cause and prejudice test was to be used for §2255 petitions in addition to habeas petitions by those held in state custody. The Court in *Frady*, again in an opinion by Justice O'Connor, stated that to demonstrate prejudice the defendant "must shoulder the burden of showing, not merely that the error at his trial created a *possibility* of prejudice, but that they worked to his actual and substantial disadvantage, infecting his entire trial with errors of constitutional dimensions."[149] In other words, a demonstration of prejudice likely will require a showing that the alleged constitutional violation affected the outcome of the trial or the appeal—that the results probably would have been different but for the violation of federal law.

The Supreme Court has emphasized that *both* cause and prejudice must be demonstrated to permit a defendant to raise on habeas corpus matters not presented in state court.[150] In practice, these elements are often less distinct. For

[146] *Id.* at 554. The Court said that it would not reach the question of whether there was a "freestanding" claim of actual innocence that required reversal of the conviction, instead holding that there was a sufficient showing to allow the procedurally defaulted claim to be raised.

[147] 541 U.S. 386 (2004).

[148] 456 U.S. 152 (1982).

[149] 456 U.S. at 170 (emphasis in original).

[150] *See* Murray v. Carrier, 477 U.S. at 496. An illustration of the need to prove both *cause* and *prejudice* is Strickler v. Greene, 527 U.S. 263 (1999). The Court found that the failure of the prosecution to disclose information under Brady v. Maryland, 373 U.S. 83 (1963), even inadvertently, was sufficient cause for the federal court to hear a habeas petition. However, the Court concluded that habeas relief could not be granted because prejudice was not demonstrated; the defendant had not shown that "there is a reasonable probability that the result of the trial would have been different if the suppressed documents had been disclosed to the defense." 527 U.S. at 289.

example, proving ineffective assistance of counsel itself requires demonstrating prejudice; thus, demonstrating ineffective assistance would fulfill both the cause and prejudice tests.

Overall, the Court's approach to this issue reveals its strong deference to state proceedings and its belief that habeas corpus relief under such circumstances should be quite rare. The Court has severely restricted defendants' ability to present matters on habeas corpus that were not raised in state court.

§15.5.3 *When May a Defendant Relitigate on Habeas Corpus Issues That Were Raised and Litigated in State Court?*

As described above, the Antiterrorism and Effective Death Penalty Act revised the law to provide that habeas corpus relief can be granted based on a claim of an error in a trial court only if it was "a decision that was contrary to, or involved an unreasonable application of clearly established federal law, as determined by the Supreme Court of the United States."[151] If a habeas petition presents such a claim, is the prior determination preclusive of the ability to relitigate the issue in federal court? As described below, preclusion generally does not bar relitigation of questions of law on habeas corpus except for Fourth Amendment exclusionary rule claims. This section concludes by considering when a decision is "contrary to" or an "unreasonable application" of "clearly established federal law."

Brown v. Allen

The principles of res judicata and collateral estoppel generally preclude a party from relitigating a matter already presented to a court and decided upon. *Brown v. Allen*, decided in 1953, created an important exception to collateral estoppel and res judicata for habeas petitions.[152] The Supreme Court, in an opinion by Justice Frankfurter, held that a constitutional claim may be raised on habeas even though it had been raised, fully litigated, and decided in state court. Justice Frankfurter observed that "even the highest State courts" had failed to give adequate protection to federal constitutional rights.[153] Because the *Brown* Court believed that habeas corpus exists to remedy state court disregard of violations of the defendant's rights, the Court established that a state prisoner should have the chance to have a hearing in federal court on federal constitutional claims.[154]

In fact, the Warren Court so valued the importance of the opportunity to relitigate constitutional issues to ensure correct decisions that it held that a prisoner

[151] Antiterrorism and Effective Death Penalty Act of 1996, §104(3), 28 U.S.C. §2254(d)(1).

[152] 344 U.S. 443 (1953). For an excellent discussion of *Brown*, *see* Eric M. Freedman, Milestones in Habeas Corpus III: Brown v. Allen, 51 Ala. L. Rev. 1541 (2000).

[153] 344 U.S. at 511.

[154] Henry Hart, The Supreme Court 1958 Term: Foreword: The Time Chart of the Justices, 73 Harv. L. Rev. 84, 106-107 (1959).

convicted by a federal court also may raise issues on habeas that had been presented and decided at trial.[155] The Court concluded that "[t]he provision of federal collateral remedies rests . . . fundamentally upon a recognition that adequate protection of constitutional rights . . . requires the continuing availability of a mechanism for relief."[156]

West v. Wright's Refusal to Overrule *Brown v. Allen*

In 1992, in *West v. Wright*, Justice Thomas, in an opinion joined by Chief Justice Rehnquist and Justice Scalia, devoted several pages arguing against de novo review on habeas corpus.[157] The issue in *West* was whether federal courts should engage in de novo review of the application of law to fact on habeas corpus. Justice Thomas's opinion left no doubt that there are three justices now on the Court who would like to overrule *Brown v. Allen* and its progeny, and only allow relitigation if the petitioner was denied a full and fair hearing in state court.

Justice O'Connor, in an opinion joined by Justices Stevens and Blackmun, responded directly to Justice Thomas and presented a nine-point reply, challenging Justice Thomas's description of the history of habeas corpus, his use of precedents, and his analysis.[158] Ultimately, Justice O'Connor, like Justice Thomas, concluded that the evidence supported the conviction in this case.[159] Thus, in *West* there were only three votes willing to overrule *Brown v. Allen.*

In 2022, in *Brown v. Davenport*, Justice Gorsuch writing for the majority sharply criticized *Brown v. Allen.*[160] Ervine Davenport was tried for murder in Michigan. During his trial, he was shackled at his hands, waist, and ankles. It is unclear whether this was visible to the jury. In *Deck v. Missouri* (2005), the Court held that the due process forbids shackling a criminal defendant at trial absent "a special need."[161] On habeas corpus, Davenport argued that his conviction violated due process because there was no finding of a special need by the trial court.

In *Brecht v. Abrahamson*, the Court held that a state prisoner seeking to challenge his conviction on federal habeas corpus must show that the error had a "substantial and injurious effect or influence" on the outcome of his trial.[162] The issue in *Brown v. Davenport* was whether this is sufficient or whether the habeas petitioner must also meet the requirement created in the Anti-Terrorism and Effective Death Penalty Act, 28 U.S.C. §2254(d)—which are discussed below—and demonstrate that the

[155] Kaufman v. United States, 394 U.S. 217 (1969).

[156] *Id.* at 226.

[157] 505 U.S. 277 (1992).

[158] *Id.* at 297 (O'Connor, J., concurring in the judgment).

[159] *Id.* at 305. Justice White wrote a one-sentence opinion concurring in the judgment, simply stating that the evidence was sufficient to support West's conviction. *Id.* at 297. Justice Souter, in an opinion concurring in the judgment, argued that *Teague* barred the federal court from hearing the claim. *Id.* at 310. In contrast, Justice Kennedy, also in an opinion concurring in the judgment, argued that *Teague* did not apply and that the evidence supported the conviction. *Id.* at 306.

[160] *See* 596 U.S. 118 (2022).

[161] 544 U.S. 622, 626 (2005).

[162] 507 U.S. 619, 623 (1993).

conviction was (1) "contrary to" or an "unreasonable application of " clearly established federal law, as determined by the decisions of this Court, or (2) based on an "unreasonable determination of the facts" presented in the state-court proceeding.

In *Brown v. Davenport*, the Court concluded that a habeas petitioner must meet *both* the standard for harmful error from *Brecht v. Abrahamson* and the requirements of Section 2254(d). Justice Gorsuch, writing for a 6-3 majority, went beyond that and suggested that habeas corpus should be available only in instances where the court lacked the jurisdiction to try the defendant. Justice Gorsuch said that historically, "[u]sually, a prisoner could not use it to challenge a final judgment of conviction issued by a court of competent jurisdiction."[163]

Justice Gorsuch noted that in *Brown v. Allen*, the Court changed the law to allow a person convicted in state court to relitigate constitutional claims in federal habeas corpus.[164] As he did a year earlier in a concurrence in *Edwards v. Vannoy*, Justice Gorsuch argued that *Brown v. Allen* was wrongly decided.[165] Here, though, five justices joined him.

Justice Kagan wrote a vehement dissent, joined by Justices Breyer and Sotomayor. She objected to the Court even discussing whether *Brown* was wrongly decided and said that if it were overruled, little would be left of habeas corpus. Justice Kagan declared: "Because the majority begins with some law-chambers history, I do too—though fair warning: My discussion is no more relevant than the majority's to the issue before us. . . . [T]he majority, unprompted, embarks on that project, perhaps hoping that the seeds it sows now will yield more succulent fruit in cases to come."[166] She said that Justice Gorsuch's "theory, in its fundamentals is wrong. Federal courts long before *Brown* extended habeas relief to prisoners held in violation of the Constitution—even after a final conviction." She reviewed the history of habeas corpus and said that, "[c]ontrary to the majority, then, our decision in Brown built on decades and decades of history."[167]

The question is whether Justice Gorsuch's majority opinion will presage a reconsideration of *Brown v. Allen*. The difference between the majority and the dissent in *Shinn* reflects the huge difference between how the conservative and the liberal justices see habeas corpus.[168]

Stone v. Powell

There is one major exception to *Brown v. Allen*. The Burger Court held that claims that a state court improperly failed to exclude evidence as being the product of an illegal search or seizure could not be relitigated on habeas corpus if the state court provided a full and fair opportunity for a hearing. In *Stone v. Powell*,

[163] 596 U.S. at 128.

[164] *See* 344 U.S. 443 (1953).

[165] *See generally* 593 U.S. 255 (2021).

[166] 596 U.S. at 146 (Kagan, J., dissenting).

[167] *Id.* at 151.

[168] For a criticism of *Brown v. Davenport*, *see* Lee Kovarsky, The New Negative Equity, 137 Harv. L. Rev. (2024).

the Supreme Court concluded that generally Fourth Amendment claims that had been raised and decided in state courts could not be heard in federal habeas corpus review.[169] The Court stated that "where the State has provided an opportunity for full and fair litigation of a Fourth Amendment claim, a state prisoner may not be granted federal habeas corpus relief on the ground that the evidence obtained in an unconstitutional search or seizure was introduced at his trial."[170]

The Court emphasized that exclusionary rule claims do not relate to the accuracy of the fact-finding process. Rather, the Court said that the exclusionary rule exists to deter illegal police practices. The Court, however, concluded that deterrence would be increased marginally, if at all, by allowing exclusionary rule claims to be raised on habeas corpus.[171] Moreover, the Court stressed the costs of the exclusionary rule in permitting guilty defendants to go free and in undermining respect for the criminal justice system.[172]

The Court also rejected the assertion that state judges would be less vigilant than federal court judges in upholding the Fourth Amendment. Whereas the Court in *Brown v. Allen* had explicitly noted frequent state court disregard of the Constitution, Justice Powell, writing for the majority in *Stone*, said that they were "unwilling to assume that there now exists a general lack of appropriate sensitivity to constitutional rights in the trial and appellate courts of the several States."[173] The Court said that there is no "intrinsic reason" why the fact that someone is a federal judge rather than a state judge "should make him more competent or conscientious or learned" with respect to Fourth Amendment claims.[174]

Criticisms of *Stone v. Powell*

The holding in *Stone v. Powell* that Fourth Amendment claims cannot generally be relitigated on habeas corpus has been subjected to several criticisms.[175] First, there is a separation of powers criticism of *Stone*: The Court exceeded the proper judicial role in deciding that certain constitutional claims could not be heard on habeas corpus review. Federal statutes make habeas corpus available for any denial of a constitutional right.[176] Accordingly, it is argued that the Court should not have decided on its own that certain claims of constitutional violations could not be raised on habeas corpus.[177]

[169] 428 U.S. 465 (1976).

[170] *Id.* at 494.

[171] *Id.* at 495.

[172] *Id.* at 490-491.

[173] *Id.* at 493-494 n.35.

[174] *Id.*

[175] *See* Gary Peller, In Defense of Federal Habeas Corpus Relitigation, 16 Harv. C.R.-C.L. L. Rev. 579 (1982).

[176] *See* 28 U.S.C. §§2241, 2254.

[177] *See* Stone v. Powell, 428 U.S. at 535-536 (Brennan, J., dissenting). For a development of the separation of powers criticism of *Stone v. Powell*, *see* Mark Tushnet, Constitutional and Statutory Analysis in the Law of Federal Jurisdiction, 25 UCLA L. Rev. 1301 (1978).

The separation of powers argument requires analysis of Congress's purpose in enacting the federal habeas corpus statutes and the extent to which Congress intended for constitutional claims to be relitigated pursuant to habeas review. Commentators disagree over Congress's objectives. For example, Professor Paul Bator argues that the Reconstruction Act, which authorizes habeas for state prisoners, had limited objectives.[178] Professor Bator contends that the drafters of the Act thought that the issues raised on habeas would be limited to challenges to the jurisdiction of the tribunal.[179] Bator argues that "[i]t would . . . require rather overwhelming evidence to show that it was the purpose of the legislature to tear habeas corpus entirely out of the context of its historical meaning and . . . convert it into an ordinary writ of error with respect to all federal questions."[180]

Other commentators disagree with Professor Bator's reading of the historical record. They argue that Congress greatly distrusted state courts and therefore allowed state prisoners access to federal courts to ensure protection of constitutional rights.[181] For example, after carefully reviewing the legislative history and the early case law, Professor Gary Peller disagrees with Professor Bator and argues that Congress, in enacting the Reconstruction Act, meant to allow state prisoners to relitigate their constitutional claims in federal court via petitions for habeas corpus.[182]

If nothing else, *Stone* is criticized from a separation of powers perspective on the ground that there is no indication that Congress intended for Fourth Amendment claims to be treated differently from other constitutional issues. While Professor Bator reads the legislative record as precluding all relitigation where the state provided a fair hearing and Professor Peller views the legislative history as justifying relitigation, there is no support in the congressional debates for singling out one constitutional right from the rest.

A second criticism of *Stone* focuses on its express assumption of parity between federal and state courts in the protection of constitutional rights. Critics of *Stone* argue that federal courts are uniquely situated to provide effective vindication of constitutional claims, justifying relitigation of constitutional issues on habeas corpus.[183] Defenders of the Court's analysis in *Stone* contend that the Court was correct in its assumption that state courts are equal to federal courts in their ability and willingness to vindicate constitutional rights.[184]

[178] Paul M. Bator, Finality in Criminal Law and Federal Habeas Corpus for State Prisoners, 76 Harv. L. Rev. 441 (1963).

[179] *Id.* at 466.

[180] *Id.* at 475.

[181] *See, e.g.,* Louis Michael Seidman, Factual Guilt and the Burger Court: An Examination of Continuity and Change in Criminal Procedure, 80 Colum. L. Rev. 436, 462 n.155 (1980) ("The Reconstruction Congress, suspicious of state attempts to subvert federal rights, intended to provide a forum in the lower federal courts for their vindication.").

[182] Peller, *supra* note 175, at 662-663.

[183] *See, e.g.,* Burt Neuborne, The Myth of Parity, 90 Harv. L. Rev. 1105 (1977); Peller, *supra* note 175, at 665-669; *see* discussion in §1.5, *supra* (describing the issue of parity).

[184] *See, e.g.,* Paul M. Bator, The State Courts and Federal Constitutional Litigation, 22 Wm. & Mary L. Rev. 605 (1981).

A presumption of parity between federal and state courts would seem to have broad implications for allowing habeas corpus relitigation of any constitutional claims. If state courts are equal to federal courts in their protection of constitutional rights, there would seem to be little justification for ever allowing relitigation in federal courts when there has been a full and fair hearing in state courts.

Third, critics of *Stone* challenge its assumption that habeas corpus review of exclusionary rule claims would serve little purpose. The Supreme Court emphasized that the exclusionary rule does not bear on the actual guilt or innocence of the petitioner. In fact, in another decision, a plurality of the Court stated that the "central reason for habeas corpus [was to afford] a means . . . of redressing an *unjust* incarceration."[185] But critics of *Stone v. Powell* challenge this limited objective for habeas corpus. They argue that although the primary purpose of individual liberties is to prevent the conviction of innocent persons, rights also are enforced as a way of deterring unlawful police practices and of protecting individual privacy and dignity from government infringement. Justice Brennan stated this view forcefully in his dissent in *Stone*: "[P]rocedural safeguards . . . are not admonitions to be tolerated only to the extent they serve functional purposes that ensure that the 'guilty' are punished and the 'innocent' freed."[186] Under this view, habeas corpus exists to ensure that no person is in custody in violation of the Constitution of the United States.

Failure to Extend *Stone*

For a time it appeared that *Stone* might represent a first step to overruling *Brown v. Allen* and thus would prevent relitigation of constitutional claims on habeas corpus. After all, if the legislative history of the habeas corpus statutes is read as preventing relitigation, or if state courts are generally equal to federal courts in their protection of constitutional rights, relitigation appears unnecessary. However, the Supreme Court has not extended *Stone* to other constitutional rights or further limited the application of *Brown v. Allen.*

In *Rose v. Mitchell,* the Supreme Court held that habeas petitioners could challenge the racial composition of grand juries even when the claim had been litigated and rejected in the state court.[187] Although on the merits the Court found that there was no discrimination, the Court emphasized the availability of habeas corpus review to determine the issue. The Court, in an opinion by Justice Blackmun, said that federal habeas review was "necessary to ensure that constitutional defects in the state judiciary's grand jury selection procedure are not overlooked by the

[185] Schneckloth v. Bustamonte, 412 U.S. 218, 257-258 (1973). *See generally* Henry Friendly, Is Innocence Irrelevant? Collateral Attack on Criminal Judgments, 38 U. Chi. L. Rev. 142 (1970) (arguing for a limit of habeas corpus to cases where there is a colorable showing of innocence).

[186] Stone v. Powell, 428 U.S. at 524 (Brennan, J., dissenting); *see also* Ira P. Robbins & James E. Sanders, Judicial Integrity, the Appearance of Justice, and the Great Writ of Habeas Corpus: How to Kill Two Thirds (or More) with One Stone, 15 Am. Crim. L. Rev. 63 (1977).

[187] 443 U.S. 545 (1979).

very judges who operate that system."[188] Thus, the Court concluded that a claim of discrimination in grand jury selection is not rendered harmless by a subsequent determination of guilt beyond a reasonable doubt by a petit jury and that *Stone* did not apply to foreclose federal court habeas review.

Likewise, the Supreme Court held that the constitutionality of jury instructions concerning the standard of proof to be applied could be challenged on habeas corpus even though the issue had been presented and decided at trial. In *Jackson v. Virginia,* the Court held that habeas corpus review is available for a petitioner who claims that "no rational trier of fact" could have concluded that the state presented sufficient evidence to establish each element of the crime beyond a reasonable doubt.[189] The Court expressly stated that this contention could be relitigated on habeas corpus even though it had been rejected by the state courts.

In *Kimmelman v. Morrison,* the Supreme Court held that a Sixth Amendment claim of ineffective assistance of counsel could be relitigated on habeas corpus, even where the attorney's error was a failure to raise Fourth Amendment objections to the introduction of evidence.[190] In *Kimmelman,* the defendant was convicted of rape largely on the basis of evidence obtained in an allegedly illegal search. The defendant sought habeas corpus relief both on the grounds that illegally seized evidence was admitted and that the defense attorney's failure to object to the introduction of the evidence constituted ineffective assistance of counsel.

The Supreme Court held that although *Stone v. Powell* barred litigating the Fourth Amendment claim on habeas corpus, the Sixth Amendment issue of ineffective assistance of counsel could be relitigated in federal court. The Court, in an opinion by Justice Brennan, observed that "[t]he right to counsel is a fundamental right of criminal defendants; it assures the fairness, and thus the legitimacy of our adversary process."[191] As such, the Court concluded that "while respondent's defaulted Fourth Amendment claim is one element of proof of his Sixth Amendment claim, the two claims have separate identities and reflect different constitutional values."[192]

In *Withrow v. Williams,* the Court refused to extend *Stone v. Powell* to *Miranda* claims.[193] In *Withrow,* a defendant confessed to a double murder before the police administering the warnings required under *Miranda v. Arizona.*[194] The state court refused to exclude the confession, but the federal district court on habeas corpus found a violation of the Fifth Amendment. The government urged the Court to extend *Stone v. Powell,* but the Court, in a 5-4 decision, refused.

188 *Id.* at 563.

189 443 U.S. 307, 324 (1979).

190 477 U.S. 365 (1986).

191 *Id.* at 374.

192 *Id.* at 375. Three justices—Justices Powell, Burger, and Rehnquist—concurred in the judgment but expressed doubt as to whether the admission of illegally seized evidence could ever constitute prejudice for Sixth Amendment purposes under the test for ineffective assistance of counsel. *Id.* at 391 (Powell, J., concurring).

193 507 U.S. 680 (1993).

194 384 U.S. 436 (1966).

Justice Souter, writing for the majority, distinguished Fourth and Fifth Amendment claims on a number of grounds. Perhaps most important, the Court noted that *Miranda*'s goal of decreasing improperly obtained confessions was related to the reliability of the confessions, whereas Fourth Amendment exclusionary rule claims were almost always unrelated to the reliability of the evidence.[195] Moreover, the Court emphasized that "eliminating review of *Miranda* claims would not significantly benefit the federal courts in their exercise of habeas jurisdiction, or advance the cause of federalism in any way."[196] Justice Souter explained that Fifth Amendment claims still would be presented to the Court as challenges to the voluntariness of the confessions and that, ultimately, the Court was better off with the bright-line test articulated in *Miranda.*

Justice O'Connor, in an opinion joined by Chief Justice Rehnquist, and Justice Scalia, in an opinion joined by Justice Thomas, strongly dissented.[197] In an earlier case, *Duckworth v. Eagan,* Justices O'Connor and Scalia had advanced this position.[198] The dissents emphasized the costs of habeas corpus in disturbing finality and in causing friction between federal and state courts. The dissents maintained that the exclusionary rule and *Miranda* warnings are both judicially created remedies and that neither should be cognizable on habeas corpus.

Thus, under the Supreme Court's decisions, a habeas corpus petitioner may relitigate all constitutional issues on habeas corpus *except* for claims that the trial court violated the Fourth Amendment by admitting illegally seized evidence.[199] Such exclusionary rule claims may not be relitigated as long as the state courts provided a full and fair opportunity for a hearing on the issue. The Supreme Court has provided little guidance as to what constitutes a full and fair hearing, and lower courts have required a finding of a serious flaw in the state procedures that prevented the defendant from having a meaningful hearing on a Fourth Amendment claim.[200]

When is a State Court Decision "Contrary To" or an "Unreasonable Application" of Clearly Established Federal Law?

The Antiterrorism and Effective Death Penalty Act imposed a significant new restriction on the ability of a federal court to grant relief to state prisoners: Habeas

[195] 507 U.S. at 692.

[196] *Id.* at 693.

[197] O'Connor, J., concurring in part and dissenting in part, 507 U.S. at 697; Scalia, J., concurring in part and dissenting in part, *id.* at 715.

[198] 492 U.S. 195, 208-209 (1989) (O'Connor, J., concurring).

[199] In Lackawanna County District Attorney v. Coss, 532 U.S. 394 (2001), the Supreme Court held that a criminal defendant who received an enhanced sentence because of prior convictions could not challenge the prior convictions on habeas corpus. The Court recognized a narrow exception in situations in which the defendant was denied his right to counsel. *See also* Daniels v. United States, 532 U.S. 374 (2001) (a defendant in federal court could not challenge prior state court convictions that were the basis for an enhanced sentence).

[200] For a review of the lower court decisions, *see* Phillip Halpern, Federal Habeas Corpus and the *Mapp* Exclusionary Rule After Stone v. Powell, 82 Colum. L. Rev. 1 (1982).

may be granted only if the state court "decision . . . was contrary to, or involved an unreasonable application of clearly established federal law, as determined by the Supreme Court." Unquestionably, this is meant to create greater deference to state courts, but there is still uncertainty over when this new standard is met.

The most important case addressing this provision is *Williams v. Taylor*.[201] Terry Williams was convicted of murder and sentenced to death in Virginia state court. A state trial court on a motion for postconviction relief found that there was ineffective assistance of counsel, but the Virginia Supreme Court disagreed, finding that there was not sufficient prejudice. The federal district court on habeas corpus found that there was ineffective assistance of counsel, but the Fourth Circuit reversed. The Fourth Circuit found that §2254(d)(1) precluded habeas review unless the state court "decided the question by interpreting or applying the relevant precedent in a manner that reasonable jurists all would agree is unreasonable."

The Supreme Court reversed the Fourth Circuit and expressly rejected the Fourth Circuit's conclusion that a state court judgment is unreasonable only if all reasonable jurists would agree that the state court was unreasonable. The Court stated:

> But the statute says nothing about "reasonable judges," presumably because all, or virtually all, such judges occasionally commit error; they make decisions that in retrospect may be characterized as "unreasonable." Indeed, it is most unlikely that Congress would impose such a requirement of unanimity on federal judges. As Congress is acutely aware, reasonable lawyers and lawgivers regularly disagree with one another. Congress surely did not intend that the views of one such judge who might think that relief is not warranted in a particular case should always have greater weight than the contrary, considered judgment of several other judges.[202]

Justice O'Connor, writing for five justices, emphasized that "contrary to" and "unreasonable application" are independent bases for habeas relief. For a state court's decision to be reviewable because it is "contrary to" clearly established federal law, the decision must be "substantially different" from the relevant Supreme Court precedent; "the word 'contrary' is commonly understood to mean 'diametrically different' or 'mutually opposed.'"[203] A state court decision is contrary to Supreme Court precedent if it contradicts that decision or reaches a different result on facts that are materially indistinguishable. As for the second phrase, in assessing whether a state court decision involves "an unreasonable application of . . . clearly established" federal law, the question is "whether the state court's application of federal law was objectively unreasonable."[204] Justice O'Connor stressed that "the most important point is that an *unreasonable* application of federal law is different from an *incorrect* application of federal law."[205]

[201] 529 U.S. 362 (2000).
[202] *Id.* at 377-378.
[203] *Id.* at 405.
[204] *Id.* at 409.
[205] *Id.* at 410.

Justice Stevens, writing for the dissenting four justices, addressed the phrases "contrary to" and "unreasonable application of" federal law. He argued that "[t]he prevailing view in the Circuits is that the former phrase requires de novo review of 'pure' questions of law and the latter requires some sort of 'reasonability' review of so-called mixed questions of law and fact."[206] Justice Stevens said, though, that these two categories are not mutually exclusive and that "there will be a variety of cases, like this one, in which both phrases may be implicated."[207]

Justice Stevens wrote for the majority in finding that Williams was entitled to habeas corpus review. The Court concluded that the Virginia Supreme Court decision was both contrary to and an unreasonable application of clearly established federal law. The Court held that the state court failed to apply controlling Supreme Court precedent that clearly established that ineffectiveness of counsel deprives a defendant of rights accorded by the Constitution.

The Supreme Court reaffirmed its interpretation of §2254(d)(1) in *Bell v. Cone*.[208] The Court held that ineffectiveness of counsel in all cases, including capital cases, is to be evaluated based on *Strickland v. Washington*.[209] The Court restated its interpretation of §2254(d)(1):

> A federal habeas court may issue the writ under the "contrary to" clause if the state court applies a different rule from the governing law set forth in our cases, or if it decides a case differently than we have done on a materially indistinguishable set of facts. The Court may grant relief under the "unreasonable application" clause if the state court correctly identifies the governing legal principle from our decision but unreasonably applies it to the facts of the particular case. The focus of the latter inquiry is on whether the state court's application of clearly established law is objectively unreasonable, and we stressed in *Williams* that an unreasonable application is different from an incorrect one.[210]

In *Lockyer v. Andrade*, the Supreme Court again repeated and applied this standard.[211] Leandro Andrade was sentenced to life imprisonment with no possibility of parole for 50 years for stealing nine videotapes from Kmart stores in San Bernardino, California. He received this sentence under California's three strikes law even though he had never committed a violent felony.

After the California courts upheld his sentence, Andrade filed a petition for habeas corpus and argued that his sentence was cruel and unusual punishment in violation of the Eighth Amendment. The U.S. Court of Appeals for the Ninth Circuit ruled in his favor, but the Supreme Court, in a 5-4 decision, reversed.

[206] *Id.* at 384 (Stevens, J., dissenting).
[207] *Id.* at 385-386.
[208] 535 U.S. 685 (2002).
[209] 466 U.S. 668 (1984).
[210] 535 U.S. at 694.
[211] 538 U.S. 63 (2003). I discuss this case in more detail in Erwin Chemerinsky, The Conservative Assault on the Constitution (2010).

Justice O'Connor, writing for the Court, focused on the standard under §2254(d). She said that the Supreme Court's decisions concerning cruel and unusual punishment "have not been a model of clarity" and "have not established a clear or consistent path for courts to follow."[212] Justice O'Connor said that the only "clearly established" doctrine is a "gross disproportionality principle, the precise contours of which are unclear, applicable only in the 'exceedingly rare' and 'extreme case.' "[213] The Court said that there thus was not clearly established law.

The Court also rejected the argument that the state court decision was objectively unreasonable. The Court said that the Ninth Circuit used a "clear error" standard and that this was not the same as "objectively unreasonable."[214] The Court, however, did not clarify the differences between these two standards.

Nor was the Court amenable to the petitioner's argument that the state court decision was "contrary to" a Supreme Court decision. Earlier, in *Solem v. Helm*, the Court held that it was cruel and unusual punishment to sentence a person to life in prison with no possibility of parole for passing a bad check worth $100.[215] But in *Lockyer v. Andrade*, the Court said that *Solem* was distinguishable because in that case there was no possibility of parole, but Andrade was eligible for parole in the year 2046, when he would be 87 years old.[216]

In *Renico v. Lett*, the Court again discussed what is an "unreasonable" application of federal law for the purposes of §2254(d).[217] The issue was whether the state court had erred in deciding that a retrial did not violate the prohibition of double jeopardy. The Court emphasized the deference to be given to state court decisions on federal habeas corpus. Chief Justice Roberts, writing for the Court, stated: "It is important at the outset to define the question before us. That question is not whether the trial judge should have declared a mistrial. It is not even whether it was an abuse of discretion for her to have done so—the applicable standard on direct review. The question under AEDPA is instead whether the determination of the Michigan Supreme Court that there was no abuse of discretion was 'an unreasonable application of . . . clearly established Federal law.' "[218] The Court concluded that the state court decision could not be said to be "unreasonable" and therefore could not be overturned on habeas corpus. Chief Justice Roberts wrote, "AEDPA prevents defendants—and federal courts—from using federal habeas corpus review as a vehicle to second-guess the reasonable decisions of state courts. Whether or not the Michigan Supreme Court's opinion reinstating Lett's conviction in this case was *correct*, it was clearly *not unreasonable*."[219]

In *Harrington v. Richter*, the Supreme Court held that the deferential standard of §2254(d) applies even if the state court does not issue an opinion explaining its

[212] *Id.* at 72.
[213] *Id.* at 73.
[214] *Id.* at 75.
[215] 463 U.S. 277 (1983).
[216] *See also* Yarborough v. Alvarado, 541 U.S. 652 (2004) (finding that the standard under §2254(d) was not met).
[217] 559 U.S. 766 (2010).
[218] *Id.* at 772-773.
[219] *Id.* at 779.

decision.[220] The California Supreme Court denied a constitutional claim in a one-sentence summary order. The Court held that relief could be granted only if the requirements of §2254(d) were met. Justice Kennedy, writing for the Court, explained, "[D]etermining whether a state court's decision resulted from an unreasonable legal or factual conclusion does not require that there be an opinion from the state court explaining the state court's reasoning."[221]

The Court then went on and found that habeas corpus relief was unwarranted because the state court decision was not an unreasonable application of clearly established federal law. The Court elaborated the analysis under §2254(d): "As a condition for obtaining habeas corpus from a federal court, a state prisoner must show that the state court's ruling on the claim being presented in federal court was so lacking in justification that there was an error well understood and comprehended in existing law beyond any possibility for fairminded disagreement."[222] This seems to be similar to the standard that the Court rejected in *Williams v. Taylor*, where it rejected the Fourth Circuit's approach that habeas relief could be granted only if no reasonable jurist could come to the conclusion of the state court. Under *Harrington v. Richter*, relief can be granted only if it is an error where there is not the possibility for "fair-minded disagreement."

In the cases since *Harrington*, the Court has continued to adhere to this approach for defining when habeas relief is permissible under §2254(d). In *White v. Woodall*, the judge at the penalty phase of a capital case did not instruct the jury that it could not draw an adverse inference from the defendant's failure to testify at that stage.[223] The Sixth Circuit granted habeas relief, but the Supreme Court reversed. The Court quoted the language from *Harrington v. Richter*, that habeas relief can be granted only if a state prisoner "show[s] that the state court's ruling on the claim being presented in federal court was so lacking in justification that there was an error well understood and comprehended in existing law beyond any possibility for fairminded disagreement." The Court stressed that it had never directly ruled that there is a right to such an instruction at the penalty phase and thus concluded that it could not be said that the state court decision was "beyond any possibility for fairminded disagreement."[224]

In *Wilson v. Sellers*, the Court considered how federal habeas courts should apply §2254(d) when a state appellate court summarily affirms, without any opinion, a lower court's opinion.[225] The Court, in an opinion by Justice Breyer, said that a federal habeas court should " 'look through' the unexplained decision to the last related state-court decision that does provide a relevant rationale" and "presume that the last-related state court decision adopted the same reasoning."[226] But the Court was explicit that this is a presumption that can be rebutted. The Court explained: "[T]he State may rebut the presumption by showing that the unexplained affirmance relied

[220] 526 U.S. 86 (2011).
[221] *Id.* at 98.
[222] *Id.* at 103.
[223] 572 U.S. 415 (2014).
[224] *Id.* at 421.
[225] 584 U.S. 122 (2018).
[226] *Id.* at 125.

or most likely did rely on different grounds than the lower state court's decision, such as alternative grounds for affirmance that were briefed or argued to the state supreme court or obvious in the record it reviewed."[227]

The Court has acknowledged that its standard for §2254(d) is "difficult to meet."[228] The question is whether the Court has adopted too restrictive a view of §2254(d), even in light of Congress's desire to limit habeas corpus in enacting AEDPA.

§15.5.4 When Can Facts Be Retried on Federal Habeas Corpus Review?

Presumption for Correctness of Facts

As described above, *Brown v. Allen* held that res judicata and collateral estoppel do not preclude relitigation of constitutional claims in federal court.[229] *Brown,* however, did not require federal courts to retry issues of fact. The Court indicated that although the federal court had the power to hold a new trial, generally a federal habeas court should accept the trial court's factual determination, unless "a vital flaw may be found in the process of ascertaining such facts in the state court."[230] The Court said that "[w]here the record of the application affords an adequate opportunity to weigh the sufficiency of the allegations and the evidence, and no unusual circumstances calling for a hearing are presented, a repetition of the trial is not required."[231]

The Antiterrorism and Effective Death Penalty Act changed the law to make it significantly more restrictive in relitigating facts. The act provides:

> In a proceeding instituted by an application for a writ of habeas corpus by a person in custody pursuant to the judgment of a State court, a determination of a factual issue made by a State shall be presumed to be correct. The applicant shall have the burden of rebutting the presumption of correctness by clear and convincing evidence. If the applicant has failed to develop the factual basis of a claim in State court proceedings, the court shall not hold an evidentiary hearing on the claim unless the applicant shows that (A) the claim relies on (i) a new rule of constitutional law, made retroactive on collateral review by the Supreme Court, that was previously unavailable; or (ii) a factual predicate that could not have been previously discovered through the exercise of due diligence; and (B) the facts underlying the claim would be sufficient to establish by clear and convincing evidence that but for constitutional error, no reasonable factfinder would have found the applicant guilty of the underlying offense.[232]

[227] *Id.* at 125-126.
[228] Metrish v. Lancaster, 569 U.S. 351, 358 (2013).
[229] 344 U.S. 443 (1953).
[230] *Id.* at 506.
[231] *Id.* at 463.
[232] Antiterrorism and Effective Death Penalty Act of 1996, §104(4), 28 U.S.C. §2254(e).

Even before application of the act, factual hearings on habeas petitions were very rare. In the year between October 1, 2000, and September 30, 2001, only 39 of 19,010, or 0.2 percent, of habeas petitions were terminated during or after trial.[233]

Townsend v. Sain

The new act makes it substantially more difficult to relitigate factual issues and changes the standard articulated by the Court in *Townsend v. Sain* and codified in federal statutes.[234] After *Brown v. Allen,* there was uncertainty in the lower courts as to when federal courts could hold new evidentiary proceedings pursuant to writs of habeas corpus. In *Townsend v. Sain,* in 1963, the Supreme Court articulated criteria for when federal courts could ignore state court fact-findings and conduct independent evidentiary hearings.[235] *Townsend* involved a challenge to a murder conviction obtained on the basis of a confession that was given after the police injected the defendant with "truth serum." The Supreme Court held that federal courts have the power to hold new factual hearings when facts are in dispute and the defendant did not receive a full and fair hearing in state court.[236] More specifically, the Court said:

> [A] federal court must grant an evidentiary hearing to a habeas applicant under the following circumstances: If (1) the merits of the factual dispute were not resolved in the state hearing; (2) the state factual determination is not fairly supported by the record as a whole; (3) the fact-finding procedure employed by the state court was not adequate to afford a full and fair hearing; (4) there is a substantial allegation of newly discovered evidence; (5) the material facts were not adequately developed at the state-court hearing; or (6) for any reason it appears that the state trier of fact did not afford the habeas applicant a full and fair fact hearing.[237]

The *Townsend* Court indicated that a presumption is given to state court fact-finding and that federal courts should hold new evidentiary hearings only if there is some reason to doubt the state court's factual record. But *Townsend* is particularly important because it requires federal courts to engage in independent fact-finding under specific circumstances.

[233] Richard H. Fallon, Daniel J. Meltzer & David L. Shapiro, 2018 Supplement to Hart and Wechsler's The Federal Courts and the Federal System 220 (2018) (*quoting* Annual Report of the Director of the Administrative Office of the United States Courts, Table C-4 (2001)).

[234] *See* Larry Yackle, Federal Evidentiary Hearings Under the New Habeas Corpus Statute, 6 B.U. Pub. Int. L.J. 135 (1996).

[235] 372 U.S. 293 (1963).

[236] *Id.* at 313.

[237] *Id.*

Section 2254(d)

In 1966, in revising the federal habeas corpus statutes, Congress adopted many aspects of the *Townsend* Court's approach as part of §2254(d).[238] The Antiterrorism and Effective Death Penalty Act revised this, as described above, to provide that "a determination of a factual issue made by a State shall be presumed to be correct. The applicant shall have the burden of rebutting the presumption of correctness by clear and convincing evidence."[239]

Sumner v. Mata

Even under the new act the issue will continue to arise as to the distinction between questions of law and fact. The Court has acknowledged that the "characterization of a question as one of fact or law is somewhat slippery."[240] The most important Supreme Court decisions on this issue were in *Sumner v. Mata.*[241] In *Sumner,* the habeas corpus petitioner contended that he was convicted on the basis of an impermissibly suggestive photo identification. The Supreme Court reversed the court of appeals decision granting the habeas corpus petition.

The Court said that §2254(d) was a jurisdictional limitation on federal judicial power and thus the lower courts erred in not applying it even though it was not raised by the state's attorney. Also, the Court held that pursuant to §2254(d) a finding of a state court could not be overturned on the basis of a preponderance of the evidence. To facilitate appellate review, a federal district court granting a habeas petition must provide a written justification for not deferring to state court fact-finding. Justice Rehnquist, writing for the majority, said, "In order to ensure that this mandate of Congress is enforced, we now hold that a habeas court should include in its opinion granting the writ the reasoning which led it to conclude that any of the first seven factors were present, or the reasoning which led it to conclude that the state finding was 'not fairly supported by the record.' "[242]

On remand, the court of appeals again found the photo identification to be impermissibly suggestive.[243] The appeals court concluded that the issue was a mixed question of fact and law and that in such circumstances §2254(d) was inapplicable. The Supreme Court again granted review and again reversed.[244] The Court agreed that §2254(d) did not apply to mixed questions of law and fact. In other words, as to issues involving both matters of law and fact, *Brown v. Allen* is controlling and the federal court can hold de novo proceedings. The Supreme

[238] After *Townsend,* the statute was changed to state that a state court finding of fact, if "evidenced by a written finding, written opinion, or other reliable and adequate written indicia, shall be presumed to be correct."

[239] 28 U.S.C. §2254(e)(1).

[240] Thompson v. Keohane, 516 U.S. 99 (1996).

[241] 449 U.S. 539 (1981).

[242] *Id.* at 551.

[243] 649 F.2d 713 (9th Cir. 1981).

[244] Sumner v. Mata, 455 U.S. 591 (1982).

Court, however, believed that there were several purely factual questions and that the court of appeals did not adequately justify departing from the state court's fact-finding on these issues.

Again on remand the court of appeals granted the habeas corpus petition. For a third time, the state's attorney sought review in the U.S. Supreme Court. This time, however, while the case was pending the defendant pled guilty to a lesser charge and was released from custody based on the time already served. The litigation then ended.

Sumner v. Mata is important, in part, because it establishes that §2254(d) is inapplicable to questions of law or to mixed questions of law and fact. The cases subsequent to *Sumner* have struggled with drawing distinctions between legal and factual questions. In *Marshall v. Lonberger*, a defendant was charged with murder in Ohio.[245] The defendant on habeas corpus challenged the introduction at the trial of evidence concerning an earlier conviction in Illinois. The defendant contended, as he had in the trial court, that the plea was involuntary and that he had not been aware of the charges to which he had entered his guilty plea. The Supreme Court held that the issue of the voluntariness of the plea was a question of law that could be relitigated on habeas corpus, but that the matter of his knowledge in entering the plea was a factual issue where deference to the state court was indicated. In *Brumfield v. Cain*, the Court rejected a state court's factual findings as unreasonable under §2254(d)(2).[246] The state court had denied a factual hearing as to whether the defendant, who had been sentenced to death, was intellectually disabled such that imposition of capital punishment would be cruel and unusual punishment. The Court said that the denial of a hearing was unreasonable in light of the evidence in the record.

Cases Applying the Distinction between Law and Fact

The distinction between questions of law and fact is further illustrated by two cases decided in the 1983-1984 Term. In *Patten v. Yount*, the constitutional challenge concerned whether jurors with certain views should be disqualified.[247] The Supreme Court said that whether particular views justify disqualification is a mixed question of law and fact; the federal court need not defer to the state court on this issue. But the actual views of a particular juror are a factual inquiry and a federal court generally should not second-guess the state court's conclusions.

Similarly, in *Rushen v. Spain*, the question was whether there was prejudice to the defendant as a result of ex parte communications between the trial judge and a juror.[248] The Supreme Court said that the nature and content of the particular communications is a question of fact, and the federal court must adhere

[245] 459 U.S. 422 (1983).
[246] 576 U.S. 305 (2015).
[247] 467 U.S. 1025 (1984).
[248] 464 U.S. 114 (1983).

to §2254(d). But the issue of whether the communications constitute harmless error is a matter of law that the federal court can decide independently on habeas corpus.

A subsequent Supreme Court case dealing with §2254(d) was *Miller v. Fenton.*[249] The issue in *Miller* was whether the voluntariness of a confession is a factual question, where the federal court generally should defer to the state judge's conclusions, or a legal issue, where the federal judiciary decides the matter on its own. Justice O'Connor explained that "[i]n the §2254(d) context, as elsewhere, the appropriate methodology for distinguishing questions of fact from questions of law has been, to say the least, elusive."[250] The Court, however, concluded that the federal court should decide de novo whether a confession is voluntary. However, the subsidiary facts—such as the precise police practices, including the length and nature of the questioning—are matters of fact where §2254(d) is applicable.

A classic distinction between fact and law emerges from these cases.[251] Factual questions—what occurred when, involving whom, and under what circumstances—may be relitigated only if the criteria in §2254(d) are met. But legal questions, including legal issues closely tied to the facts, may be decided de novo, unless they pertain to Fourth Amendment exclusionary rule claims.

The Court applied this distinction in *Thompson v. Keohane,* which held that whether a person is "in custody" for the purpose of the requirement that *Miranda* warnings be administered is a question of law, not fact.[252] The Court contrasted factual issues involving questions of "what happened" from the "uniquely legal dimension presented by issues such as the voluntariness of a confession and the effectiveness of counsel's assistance."[253] The Court concluded that the determination of whether a person was in custody and should have been given *Miranda* warnings is of the latter type. The Court explained that whether "a reasonable person would have felt that he or she was not at liberty to terminate the interrogation and leave . . . calls for the application of the controlling legal standard to the historical facts and thus presents a 'mixed question of law and fact' qualifying for independent review."[254]

[249] 474 U.S. 104 (1985).

[250] *Id.* at 112.

[251] In Amadeo v. Zant, 486 U.S. 214 (1988), the Court invoked the law-fact distinction in defining the appropriate scope of review by courts of appeals of district court decisions on habeas corpus petitions. In *Amadeo,* the district court found that the prosecutor had concealed a memo documenting racial bias in jury selection. The district court found this to be sufficient "cause" to permit the defendant to raise a challenge to jury selection on habeas corpus, even though it was not objected to at trial. The court of appeals reversed. The Supreme Court said that the court of appeals disagreed not with the legal conclusion as to whether concealment constituted "cause," but as to the factual question of whether concealment had occurred. The Supreme Court reversed the court of appeals and held that a court of appeals should reverse a district court's factual findings only if they are "clearly erroneous." *Id.* at 223.

[252] 516 U.S. 99 (1996).

[253] *Id.* at 100.

[254] *Id.* at 112-113.

Keeney v. Tamayo-Reyes

In *Keeney v. Tamayo-Reyes,* the Court narrowed the availability of factual hearings under §2254 and *Townsend v. Sain.*[255] Based on advice from a defense attorney, a Cuban immigrant with little education and almost no knowledge of English pleaded nolo contendere to first-degree manslaughter. Subsequently, the defendant brought a state and then a federal habeas corpus petition arguing that he did not know that he was pleading no contest to manslaughter but instead thought that he was agreeing to be tried on that charge. The Ninth Circuit decided that he should have been given an evidentiary hearing as to the adequacy of his understanding at the time of his plea, unless it could be shown that the defendant deliberately bypassed the orderly procedure of state courts.

The Supreme Court reversed, holding that a factual hearing is permissible for matters not raised at the state trial only if the habeas petitioner can show "cause and prejudice." The Court stressed that the cause and prejudice standard is appropriate because it contributes to the finality of state convictions, it encourages full factual development in state court, and it creates uniformity in the law by applying the same test as in other areas of habeas corpus law.

Justice O'Connor dissented, joined by Justices Blackmun, Kennedy, and Stevens.[256] Justice O'Connor drew a sharp distinction between the availability of habeas corpus review and the standard used when that review occurs. She explained that the cause and prejudice test has been used to determine when a litigant can present matters on habeas corpus, such as when issues can be raised that were not presented in state court. But the issue in *Tamayo-Reyes* was different; it focused not on whether there will be federal court review, but rather how the court will conduct that review. The dissent maintained that §2254(d) delineates the circumstances in which a federal court can grant a de novo hearing and that the majority acted improperly in grafting an additional requirement on to the statute.

Williams v. Taylor and *Cullen v. Pinholster*

The Antiterrorism and Effective Death Penalty Act provides that an evidentiary hearing is available only if: "(A) the claim relies on (i) a new constitutional rule, made retroactive on collateral review by the Supreme Court, or (ii) a factual predicate that could not previously, with due diligence have been discovered; and (B) the facts underlying the claim would establish, by clear and convincing evidence, that but for the constitutional error, no reasonable factfinder would have found the applicant guilty of the underlying offense."[257]

This standard is even more restrictive than that in *Tamayo-Reyes.* The habeas petition must show both cause and actual innocence. Moreover, demonstrating actual innocence requires that the habeas petitioner demonstrate *by clear and*

[255] 504 U.S. 1 (1992).

[256] Justice Kennedy also wrote a separate dissenting opinion. 504 U.S. at 24.

[257] 28 U.S.C. §2254(e)(2).

convincing evidence that no reasonable judge or jury would have found the defendant guilty.

The restrictiveness of the new statutory provision is shown by *Williams v. Taylor*[258] and especially *Cullen v. Pinholster*. In *Williams v. Taylor*, a habeas petitioner sought an evidentiary hearing in federal court. The Supreme Court ruled that an evidentiary hearing was not warranted. Justice Kennedy, writing for the Court, said that "a failure to develop a factual basis for a claim is not established unless there is a lack of diligence, or some greater fault, attributable to the prisoner or the prisoner's counsel."[259] The Court explained that "diligence . . . depends upon whether the prisoner made a reasonable attempt, in light of the information available at the time, to investigate and pursue claims in state court; it does not depend . . . upon whether those efforts could have been successful."[260]

Ultimately, the issues concerning §2254(d) and all of habeas corpus involve—as do almost all of the issues considered throughout this book—questions of federalism and separation of powers. Should the state courts generally be trusted to conduct adequate fact-finding in deciding constitutional issues? Should the Court create additional requirements restricting habeas corpus in light of the detailed federal habeas statutes? What is Congress's authority to restrict the jurisdiction of the federal courts to grant habeas corpus relief?

Cullen v. Pinholster went even further in limiting the ability of a federal court to hold an evidentiary hearing on habeas corpus.[261] Scott Lynn Pinholster was convicted of murder. His defense lawyers had not been notified that the prosecutor planned to present aggravating circumstances in a penalty phase and therefore did not prepare to present mitigating evidence. Nonetheless, the judge allowed the penalty phase to go forward, and the defense lawyers presented only one witness, Pinholster's mother.

After Pinholster was sentenced to death and exhausted his appeals in California state court, his new lawyers filed a writ of habeas corpus in federal court. The lawyers provided declarations showing substantial new evidence that supported the claim of ineffective assistance of counsel. The federal court granted a hearing, and the new evidence documented that the defense counsel at trial had undertaken no investigation of mitigating circumstances and had they done so they would have learned that Pinholster suffered from a brain injury, a seizure disorder, and personality disorders. The evidence also included testimony from family members and school officials about Pinholster's abuse as a child. All of this is powerful mitigating evidence that might have caused the jury to refrain from imposing the death penalty.

[258] 529 U.S. 420 (2000). It should be noted that there were two cases, decided on the same day, with the same caption, Williams v. Taylor. Discussed above is the case involving Terry Williams, which concerned the meaning of the requirement that a habeas petition demonstrate that a state court decision is contrary to or an unreasonable application of clearly established federal law. The case discussed here involved Michael Williams, who sought an evidentiary hearing.

[259] *Id.* at 432.

[260] *Id.* at 435.

[261] 563 U.S. 170 (2011).

The federal district court granted the writ of habeas corpus, and ultimately the Ninth Circuit affirmed in an en banc decision. The Supreme Court, though, in an opinion by Justice Clarence Thomas, reversed. The Court held that the federal district court should not have held the hearing on ineffective assistance of counsel. The Court ruled that the federal court on habeas corpus is limited to considering the evidence that was before the state court and cannot hold an evidentiary hearing. The Court stated, "We now hold that review under §2254(d)(1) is limited to the record that was before the state court that adjudicated the claim on the merits."[262] The Court said that §2254(e)(2) was a limit on evidentiary hearings and did not authorize the hearing held in this case.[263]

It is difficult to reconcile this with §2254(e)(2), which specifies situations in which federal courts can hold an evidentiary hearing on habeas corpus, including if "the factual predicate . . . could not have been previously discovered through the exercise of due diligence." Justice Sotomayor, in a forceful dissent, argued that the result is that individuals who have substantial evidence of ineffective assistance of counsel, of a prosecutor's failure to disclose exculpatory evidence, or even of actual innocence, will be unable to present this material on habeas corpus. In theory, the criminal defendants can go to state court, but often state courts are unwilling to hear the evidence or simply deny claims without a hearing and with no more than a postcard.

§15.6 APPELLATE REVIEW OF THE DENIAL OF HABEAS CORPUS

In general, the final order of a judge in a habeas proceeding is subject to review on appeal by the court of appeals in the circuit where the federal district court is located.[1] However, a major limitation on the right to appeal is that a state prisoner whose petition for habeas corpus is denied may appeal only if the federal district court judge or a court of appeals judge issues a certificate of appealability.[2]

[262] *Id.* at 181.

[263] In a cryptic footnote, the Court said, "The focus of that section is not on 'preserving the opportunity' for hearings, but rather on *limiting* the discretion of federal district courts in holding hearings. We see no need in this case to address the proper application of §2254(e)(2)." *Id.* at 185 n.8. After Cullen v. Pinholster, however, it is unclear as to when, if at all, evidentiary hearings can be held under this provision.

§15.6 [1] 28 U.S.C. §2253.

[2] Section 2253(c)(1) provides: "Unless a circuit justice or judge issues a certificate of appealability, an appeal may not be taken to the court of appeals from—(A) the final order in a habeas corpus proceeding in which the detention complained of arises out of process issued by a state court; or (B) the final order is a proceeding under section 2255. (2) A certificate of appealability may issue under paragraph (1) only if the applicant has made a substantial showing of the denial of a constitutional right. (3) The certificate of appealability under paragraph (1) shall indicate which specific issue or issues satisfy the showing required by paragraph (2)."

Before the Antiterrorism and Effective Death Penalty Act, this was termed a "certificate of probable cause." A court can issue a certificate of appealability only if "the applicant has made a substantial showing of the denial of a constitutional right."[3] In other words, absent a certification of appealability, a state prisoner may not appeal the denial of habeas corpus.[4] Although the text of the act seems to say that district court judges cannot issue such certificates, most courts have ruled to the contrary and concluded that either a district court or a court of appeals can authorize review.[5]

In *Miller-El v. Cockrell*, the Supreme Court held that a certificate of appealability should be granted if "reasonable jurists could debate" whether the petition should have been granted.[6] This "does not require a showing that the appeal will succeed",[7] nor is there to be full consideration of the merits. But the certificate should be granted if it presents a debatable issue for the court of appeals to consider.

The Supreme Court has stated that the standard for a certificate of appealability is that a petitioner must "sho[w] that reasonable jurists could debate whether (or, for that matter, agree that) the petition should have been resolved in a different manner or that the issues presented were 'adequate to deserve encouragement to proceed further.' "[8] The Supreme Court has stressed that this is not to be a review on the merits of the habeas petition and that a certificate of appealability is not to be denied just because the court thinks that the petitioner will not prevail on the merits. The Court explained: "This threshold inquiry does not require full consideration of the factual or legal bases adduced in support of the claims. In fact, the statute forbids it. When a court of appeals sidesteps this process by first deciding the merits of an appeal, and then justifying its denial of a COA based on its adjudication of the actual merits, it is in essence deciding an appeal without jurisdiction."[9] The key is whether there is a debatable issue, in which case the certificate of appealability should be granted.[10]

[3] *Id.*

[4] *See, e.g.,* McCarthy v. Harper, 449 U.S. 1309 (1981).

[5] *See, e.g.,* Hunter v. United States, 101 F.3d 1565, 1573-1583 (11th Cir. 1996) (en banc).

[6] 537 U.S. 322, 336 (2003) (citations omitted).

[7] *Id.* at 337.

[8] *Id.* (citations omitted).

[9] *Id.* at 336-337.

[10] *Id.* at 338 ("We do not require petitioner to prove, before the issuance of a COA, that some jurists would grant the petition for habeas corpus. Indeed, a claim can be debatable even though every jurist of reason might agree, after the COA has been granted and the case has received full consideration, that petitioner will not prevail."). Also, the Court has held that the provision of the Antiterrorism and Effective Death Penalty Act of 1996 (AEDPA), requiring the certificate of appealability (COA) to indicate which specific issue or issues satisfy AEDPA's requirement that a petitioner make a substantial showing of the denial of a constitutional right, is not jurisdictional. Gonzales v. Thaler, 565 U.S. 134 (2012).

APPENDIX A

The Constitution of the United States of America

We the People of the United States, in Order to form a more perfect Union, establish Justice, insure domestic Tranquility, provide for the common defence, promote the general Welfare, and secure the Blessings of Liberty to ourselves and our Posterity, do ordain and establish this Constitution for the United States of America.

ARTICLE I

SECTION 1. All legislative Powers herein granted shall be vested in a Congress of the United States, which shall consist of a Senate and House of Representatives.

SECTION 2. The House of Representatives shall be composed of Members chosen every second Year by the People of the several States, and the Electors in each State shall have the Qualifications requisite for Electors of the most numerous Branch of the State Legislature.

No Person shall be a Representative who shall not have attained to the Age of twenty five Years, and been seven Years a Citizen of the United States, and who shall not, when elected, be an Inhabitant of that State in which he shall be chosen.

Representatives and direct Taxes shall be apportioned among the several States which may be included within this Union, according to their respective Numbers, which shall be determined by adding to the whole Number of free Persons, including those bound to Service for a Term of Years, and excluding Indians not taxed, three fifths of all other Persons. The actual Enumeration shall be made within three Years after the first Meeting of the Congress of the United States, and within every subsequent Term of ten Years, in such Manner as they shall by Law direct. The Number of Representatives shall not exceed one for every thirty Thousand, but each State shall have at Least one Representative; and until such enumeration shall be made, the State of New Hampshire shall be entitled to chuse three, Massachusetts eight, Rhode Island and Providence Plantations one, Connecticut five, New York six, New Jersey four, Pennsylvania eight, Delaware one, Maryland six, Virginia ten, North Carolina five, South Carolina five, and Georgia three.

When vacancies happen in the Representation from any State, the Executive Authority thereof shall issue Writs of Election to fill such Vacancies.

The House of Representatives shall chuse their Speaker and other Officers; and shall have the sole Power of Impeachment.

SECTION 3. The Senate of the United States shall be composed of two Senators from each State, chosen by the Legislature thereof, for six Years; and each Senator shall have one Vote.

Immediately after they shall be assembled in Consequence of the first Election, they shall be divided as equally as may be into three Classes. The Seats of the Senators of the first Class shall be vacated at the Expiration of the second Year, of the second Class at the Expiration of the fourth Year, and of the third Class at the Expiration of the sixth Year, so that one third may be chosen every second Year; and if Vacancies happen by Resignation, or otherwise, during the Recess of the Legislature of any State, the Executive thereof may make temporary Appointments until the next Meeting of the Legislature, which shall then fill such Vacancies.

No Person shall be a Senator who shall not have attained to the Age of thirty Years, and been nine Years a Citizen of the United States, and who shall not, when elected, be an Inhabitant of that State for which he shall be chosen.

The Vice President of the United States shall be President of the Senate, but shall have no Vote, unless they be equally divided.

The Senate shall chuse their other Officers, and also a President pro tempore, in the Absence of the Vice President, or when he shall exercise the Office of President of the United States.

The Senate shall have the sole Power to try all Impeachments. When sitting for that Purpose, they shall be on Oath or Affirmation. When the President of the United States is tried, the Chief Justice shall preside: And no Person shall be convicted without the Concurrence of two thirds of the Members present.

Judgment in Cases of Impeachment shall not extend further than to removal from Office, and disqualification to hold and enjoy any Office of honor, Trust or Profit under the United States: but the Party convicted shall nevertheless be liable and subject to Indictment, Trial, Judgment and Punishment, according to Law.

SECTION 4. The Times, Places and Manner of holding Elections for Senators and Representatives, shall be prescribed in each State by the Legislature thereof; but the Congress may at any time by Law make or alter such Regulations, except as to the Places of chusing Senators.

The Congress shall assemble at least once in every Year, and such Meeting shall be on the first Monday in December, unless they shall by Law appoint a different Day.

SECTION 5. Each House shall be the Judge of the Elections, Returns and Qualifications of its own Members, and a Majority of each shall constitute a Quorum to do Business; but a smaller Number may adjourn from day to day, and may be authorized to compel the Attendance of absent Members, in such Manner, and under such Penalties as each House may provide.

Each House may determine the Rules of its Proceedings, punish its Members for disorderly Behaviour, and, with the Concurrence of two thirds, expel a Member.

Each House shall keep a Journal of its Proceedings, and from time to time publish the same, excepting such Parts as may in their Judgment require Secrecy; and the Yeas and Nays of the Members of either House on any question shall, at the Desire of one fifth of those Present, be entered on the Journal.

Neither House, during the Session of Congress, shall, without the Consent of the other, adjourn for more than three days, nor to any other Place than that in which the two Houses shall be sitting.

SECTION 6. The Senators and Representatives shall receive a Compensation for their Services, to be ascertained by Law, and paid out of the Treasury of the United States. They shall in all Cases, except Treason, Felony and Breach of the Peace, be privileged from Arrest during their Attendance at the Session of their respective Houses, and in going to and returning from the same; and for any Speech or Debate in either House, they shall not be questioned in any other Place.

No Senator or Representative shall, during the Time for which he was elected, be appointed to any civil Office under the Authority of the United States, which shall have been created, or the Emoluments whereof shall have been encreased during such time; and no Person holding any Office under the United States, shall be a Member of either House during his Continuance in Office.

SECTION 7. All Bills for raising Revenue shall originate in the House of Representatives; but the Senate may propose or concur with amendments as on other Bills.

Every Bill which shall have passed the House of Representatives and the Senate, shall, before it become a Law, be presented to the President of the United States; If he approve he shall sign it, but if not he shall return it, with his Objections to that House in which it shall have originated, who shall enter the Objections at large on their Journal, and proceed to reconsider it. If after such Reconsideration two thirds of that House shall agree to pass the Bill, it shall be sent, together with the Objections, to the other House, by which it shall likewise be reconsidered, and if approved by two thirds of that House, it shall become a Law. But in all such Cases the Votes of both Houses shall be determined by Yeas and Nays, and the Names of the Persons voting for and against the Bill shall be entered on the Journal of each House respectively. If any Bill shall not be returned by the President within ten Days (Sunday excepted) after it shall have been presented to him, the Same shall be a Law, in like Manner as if he had signed it, unless the Congress by their Adjournment prevent its Return, in which Case it shall not be a Law.

Every Order, Resolution, or Vote to which the Concurrence of the Senate and House of Representatives may be necessary (except on a question of Adjournment) shall be presented to the President of the United States; and before the Same shall take Effect, shall be approved by him, or being disapproved by him, shall be repassed by two thirds of the Senate and House of Representatives, according to the Rules and Limitations prescribed in the Case of a Bill.

SECTION 8. The Congress shall have Power To lay and collect Taxes, Duties, Imposts and Excises, to pay the Debts and provide for the common Defence and general Welfare of the United States; but all Duties, Imposts and Excises shall be uniform throughout the United States;

To borrow Money on the credit of the United States;

To regulate Commerce with foreign Nations, and among the several States, and with the Indian Tribes;

To establish an uniform Rule of Naturalization, and uniform Laws on the subject of Bankruptcies throughout the United States;

To coin Money, regulate the Value thereof, and of foreign Coin, and fix the Standard of Weights and Measures;

To provide for the Punishment of counterfeiting the Securities and current Coin of the United States;

To establish Post Offices and post Roads;

To promote the Progress of Science and useful Arts, by securing for limited Times to Authors and Inventors the exclusive Right to their respective Writings and Discoveries;

To constitute Tribunals inferior to the supreme Court;

To define and punish Piracies and Felonies committed on the high Seas, and Offences against the Law of Nations;

To declare War, grant Letters of Marque and Reprisal, and make Rules concerning Captures on Land and Water;

To raise and support Armies, but no Appropriation of Money to that Use shall be for a longer Term than two Years;

To provide and maintain a Navy;

To make Rules for the Government and Regulation of the land and naval Forces;

To provide for calling forth the Militia to execute the Laws of the Union, suppress Insurrections and repel Invasions;

To provide for organizing, arming, and disciplining, the Militia, and for governing such Part of them as may be employed in the Service of the United States, reserving to the States respectively, the Appointment of the Officers, and the Authority of training the Militia according to the discipline prescribed by Congress;

To exercise exclusive Legislation in all Cases whatsoever, over such District (not exceeding ten Miles square) as may, by Cession of particular States, and the Acceptance of Congress, become the Seat of the Government of the United States, and to exercise like Authority over all Places purchased by the Consent of the Legislature of the State in which the Same shall be, for the Erection of Forts, Magazines, Arsenals, dock-Yards, and other needful Buildings;—And

To make all Laws which shall be necessary and proper for carrying into Execution the foregoing Powers, and all other Powers vested by this Constitution in the Government of the United States, or in any Department or Officer thereof.

SECTION 9. The Migration or Importation of such Persons as any of the States now existing shall think proper to admit, shall not be prohibited by the Congress prior to the Year one thousand eight hundred and eight, but a Tax or duty may be imposed on such Importation, not exceeding ten dollars for each Person.

The Privilege of the Writ of Habeas Corpus shall not be suspended, unless when in Cases of Rebellion or Invasion the public Safety may require it.

No Bill of Attainder or ex post facto Law shall be passed.

No Capitation, or other direct, Tax shall be laid, unless in Proportion to the Census or Enumeration herein before directed to be taken.

No Tax or Duty shall be laid on Articles exported from any State.

No Preference shall be given by any Regulation of Commerce or Revenue to the Ports of one State over those of another; nor shall Vessels bound to, or from, one State, be obliged to enter, clear, or pay Duties in another.

No Money shall be drawn from the Treasury, but in Consequence of Appropriations made by Law; and a regular Statement and Account of the Receipts and Expenditures of all public Money shall be published from time to time.

No Title of Nobility shall be granted by the United States: And no Person holding any Office of Profit or Trust under them, shall, without the Consent of the Congress, accept of any present, Emolument, Office, or Title, of any kind whatever, from any King, Prince or foreign State.

SECTION 10. No State shall enter into any Treaty, Alliance, or Confederation; grant Letters of Marque and Reprisal; coin Money; emit Bills of Credit; make any Thing but gold and silver Coin a Tender in Payment of Debts; pass any Bill of Attainder, ex post facto Law, or Law impairing the Obligation of Contracts, or grant any Title of Nobility.

No State shall, without the Consent of the Congress, lay any Imposts or Duties on Imports or Exports, except what may be absolutely necessary for executing its inspection Laws: and the net Produce of all Duties and Imposts, laid by any State on Imports or Exports, shall be for the Use of the Treasury of the United States; and all such Laws shall be subject to the Revision and Controul of the Congress.

No State shall, without the Consent of Congress, lay any Duty of Tonnage, keep Troops, or Ships of War in time of Peace, enter into any Agreement or Compact with another State, or with a foreign Power, or engage in War, unless actually invaded, or in such imminent Danger as will not admit of delay.

ARTICLE II

SECTION 1. The executive Power shall be vested in a President of the United States of America. He shall hold his Office during the Term of four Years, and, together with the Vice President, chosen for the same Term, be elected, as follows:

Each State shall appoint, in such Manner as the Legislature thereof may direct, a Number of Electors, equal to the whole Number of Senators and Representatives to which the State may be entitled in the Congress: but no Senator or Representative, or Person holding an Office of Trust or Profit under the United States, shall be appointed an Elector.

The Electors shall meet in their respective States, and vote by Ballot for two Persons, of whom one at least shall not be an Inhabitant of the same State with themselves. And they shall make a List of all the Persons voted for, and of the Number of Votes for each; which List they shall sign and certify, and transmit sealed to the Seat of the Government of the United States, directed to the President of the Senate. The President of the Senate shall, in the Presence of the Senate and House of Representatives, open all the Certificates, and the Votes shall then be counted. The Person having the greatest Number of Votes shall be the President, if such Number be a Majority of the whole Number of Electors appointed; and if there be more than one who have such Majority, and have an equal Number of Votes, then the House of Representatives shall immediately chuse by Ballot one of them for President; and if no Person have a Majority, then from the five highest on the List the said House shall in like Manner chuse the President. But in chusing the President, the Votes shall be taken by States, the Representation from each State having one Vote; a quorum for this Purpose shall consist of a Member or Members from two thirds of the States, and a Majority of all the States shall be necessary to a Choice. In every Case, after the Choice of the President, the Person having the greatest Number of Votes of the Electors shall be the Vice President. But if there should remain two or more who have equal Votes, the Senate shall chuse from them by Ballot the Vice President.

The Congress may determine the Time of chusing the Electors, and the Day on which they shall give their Votes; which Day shall be the same throughout the United States.

No Person except a natural born Citizen, or a Citizen of the United States, at the time of the Adoption of this Constitution, shall be eligible to the Office of President; neither shall any Person be eligible to that Office who shall not have attained to the Age of thirty five Years, and been fourteen Years a Resident within the United States.

In Case of the Removal of the President from Office, or of his Death, Resignation, or Inability to discharge the Powers and Duties of the said Office, the Same shall devolve on the Vice President, and the Congress may by Law provide for the Case of Removal, Death, Resignation or Inability, both of the President and Vice President, declaring what Officer shall then act as President, and such Officer shall act accordingly, until the Disability be removed, or a President shall be elected.

The President shall, at stated Times, receive for his Services, a Compensation, which shall neither be encreased nor diminished during the Period for which he shall have been elected, and he shall not receive within that Period any other Emolument from the United States, or any of them.

Before he enter on the Execution of his Office, he shall take the following Oath or Affirmation:—"I do solemnly swear (or affirm) that I will faithfully execute the Office of President of the United States, and will to the best of my Ability, preserve, protect and defend the Constitution of the United States."

SECTION 2. The President shall be Commander in Chief of the Army and Navy of the United States, and of the Militia of the several States, when called into the actual Service of the United States; he may require the Opinion, in writing, of the principal Officer in each of the executive Departments, upon any Subject relating to the Duties of their respective Offices, and he shall have Power to grant Reprieves and Pardons for Offences against the United States, except in Cases of Impeachment.

He shall have Power, by and with the Advice and Consent of the Senate, to make Treaties, provided two thirds of the Senators present concur; and he shall nominate, and by and with the Advice and Consent of the Senate, shall appoint

Ambassadors, other public Ministers and Consuls, Judges of the supreme Court, and all other Officers of the United States, whose Appointments are not herein otherwise provided for, and which shall be established by Law: but the Congress may by Law vest the Appointment of such inferior Officers, as they think proper, in the President alone, in the Courts of Law, or in the Heads of Departments.

The President shall have Power to fill up all Vacancies that may happen during the Recess of the Senate, by granting Commissions which shall expire at the End of their next Session.

SECTION 3. He shall from time to time give to the Congress Information of the State of the Union, and recommend to their Consideration such Measures as he shall judge necessary and expedient; he may, on extraordinary Occasions, convene both Houses, or either of them, and in Case of Disagreement between them, with Respect to the Time of Adjournment, he may adjourn them to such Time as he shall think proper; he shall receive Ambassadors and other public Ministers; he shall take Care that the Laws be faithfully executed, and shall Commission all the Officers of the United States.

SECTION 4. The President, Vice President and all Civil Officers of the United States, shall be removed from Office on Impeachment for, and Conviction of, Treason, Bribery, or other high Crimes and Misdemeanors.

ARTICLE III

SECTION 1. The judicial Power of the United States, shall be vested in one supreme Court, and in such inferior Courts as the Congress may from time to time ordain and establish. The Judges, both of the supreme and inferior Courts, shall hold their Offices during good Behaviour, and shall, at stated Times, receive for their Services, a Compensation, which shall not be diminished during their Continuance in Office.

SECTION 2. The judicial Power shall extend to all Cases, in Law and Equity, arising under this Constitution, the Laws of the United States, and Treaties made, or which shall be made, under their Authority;—to all Cases affecting Ambassadors, other public Ministers and Consuls;—to all Cases of admiralty and maritime Jurisdiction;—to Controversies to which the United States shall be a Party;—to Controversies between two or more States;—between a State and Citizens of another State;—between Citizens of different States;—between Citizens of the same State claiming Lands under Grants of different States, and between a State, or the Citizens thereof, and foreign States, Citizens or Subjects.

In all Cases affecting Ambassadors, other public Ministers and Consuls, and those in which a State shall be Party, the Supreme Court shall have original Jurisdiction. In all the other Cases before mentioned, the supreme Court shall have appellate Jurisdiction, both as to Law and Fact, with such Exceptions, and under such Regulations as the Congress shall make.

The Trial of all Crimes, except in Cases of Impeachment, shall be by Jury; and such Trial shall be held in the State where the said Crimes shall have been committed; but when not committed within any State, the Trial shall be at such Place or Places as the Congress may by Law have directed.

SECTION 3. Treason against the United States, shall consist only in levying War against them, or in adhering to their Enemies, giving them Aid and Comfort. No Person shall be convicted of Treason unless on the Testimony of two Witnesses to the same overt Act, or on Confession in open Court.

The Congress shall have Power to declare the Punishment of Treason, but no Attainder of Treason shall work Corruption of Blood, or Forfeiture except during the Life of the Person attained.

ARTICLE IV

SECTION 1. Full Faith and Credit shall be given in each State to the public Acts, Records, and judicial Proceedings of every other State. And the Congress may by general Laws prescribe the Manner in which such Acts, Records and Proceedings shall be proved, and the Effect thereof.

SECTION 2. The Citizens of each State shall be entitled to all Privileges and Immunities of Citizens in the several States.

A Person charged in any State with Treason, Felony, or other Crime, who shall flee from Justice, and be found in another State, shall on Demand of the executive Authority of the State from which he fled, be delivered up, to be removed to the State having Jurisdiction of the Crime.

No Person held to Service or Labour in one State, under the Laws thereof, escaping into another, shall, in Consequence of any Law or Regulation therein, be discharged from such Service or Labour, but shall be delivered up on Claim of the Party to whom such Service or Labour may be due.

SECTION 3. New States may be admitted by the Congress into this Union; but no new State shall be formed or erected within the Jurisdiction of any other State; nor any State be formed by the Junction of two or more States, or Parts of States, without the Consent of the Legislatures of the States concerned as well as of the Congress.

The Congress shall have Power to dispose of and make all needful Rules and Regulations respecting the Territory or other Property belonging to the United States; and nothing in this Constitution shall be so construed as to Prejudice any Claims of the United States, or of any particular State.

SECTION 4. The United States shall guarantee to every State in this Union a Republican Form of Government, and shall protect each of them against Invasion; and on Application of the Legislature, or of the Executive (when the Legislature cannot be convened) against domestic Violence.

ARTICLE V

The Congress, whenever two thirds of both Houses shall deem it necessary, shall propose Amendments to this Constitution, or, on the Application of the Legislatures of two thirds of the several States, shall call a Convention for proposing Amendments, which, in either Case, shall be valid to all Intents and Purposes, as Part of this Constitution, when ratified by the Legislatures of three fourths of the several States, or by Conventions in three fourths thereof, as the one or the other Mode of Ratification may be proposed by the Congress; Provided that no Amendment which may be made prior to the Year One thousand eight hundred and eight shall in any Manner affect the first and fourth Clauses in the Ninth Section of the first Article; and that no State, without its Consent, shall be deprived of its equal Suffrage in the Senate.

ARTICLE VI

All Debts contracted and Engagements entered into, before the Adoption of this Constitution, shall be as valid against the United States under this Constitution, as under the Confederation.

This Constitution, and the Laws of the United States which shall be made in Pursuance thereof; and all Treaties made, or which shall be made, under the Authority of the United States, shall be the supreme Law of the Land; and the Judges in every State shall be bound thereby, any Thing in the Constitution or Laws of any State to the Contrary notwithstanding.

The Senators and Representatives before mentioned, and the Members of the several State Legislatures, and all executive and judicial Officers, both of the United States and of the several States, shall be bound by Oath or Affirmation, to support this Constitution; but no religious Test shall ever be required as a Qualification to any Office or public Trust under the United States.

ARTICLE VII

The Ratification of the Conventions of nine States, shall be sufficient for the Establishment of this Constitution between the States so ratifying the Same.

ARTICLES IN ADDITION TO, AND AMENDMENT OF, THE CONSTITUTION OF THE UNITED STATES OF AMERICA, PROPOSED BY CONGRESS, AND RATIFIED BY THE SEVERAL STATES, PURSUANT TO THE FIFTH ARTICLE OF THE ORIGINAL CONSTITUTION

AMENDMENT I [1791]

Congress shall make no law respecting an establishment of religion, or prohibiting the free exercise thereof; or abridging the freedom of speech, or of the press; or the right of the people peaceably to assemble, and to petition the Government for a redress of grievances.

AMENDMENT II [1791]

A well regulated Militia, being necessary to the security of a free State, the right of the people to keep and bear Arms, shall not be infringed.

AMENDMENT III [1791]

No Soldier shall, in time of peace be quartered in any house, without the consent of the Owner, nor in time of war, but in a manner to be prescribed by law.

AMENDMENT IV [1791]

The right of the people to be secure in their persons, houses, papers, and effects, against unreasonable searches and seizures, shall not be violated, and no Warrants shall issue, but upon probable cause, supported by Oath or affirmation, and particularly describing the place to be searched, and the persons or things to be seized.

AMENDMENT V [1791]

No person shall be held to answer for a capital, or otherwise infamous crime, unless on a presentment or indictment of a Grand Jury, except in cases arising in the land or naval forces, or in the Militia, when in actual service in time of War or public danger; nor shall any person be subject for the same offence to be twice put in jeopardy of life or limb; nor shall be compelled in any criminal case to be a witness against himself, nor be deprived of life, liberty, or property, without due process of law; nor shall private property be taken for public use, without just compensation.

AMENDMENT VI [1791]

In all criminal prosecutions, the accused shall enjoy the right to a speedy and public trial, by an impartial jury of the State and district wherein the crime shall have been committed, which district shall have been previously ascertained by law, and to be informed of the nature and cause of the accusation; to be confronted with the witnesses against him; to have compulsory process for obtaining Witnesses in his favor, and to have the Assistance of Counsel for his defence.

AMENDMENT VII [1791]

In Suits at common law, where the value in controversy shall exceed twenty dollars, the right of trial by jury shall be preserved, and no fact tried by a jury, shall be otherwise re-examined in any Court of the United States, than according to the rules of the common law.

AMENDMENT VIII [1791]

Excessive bail shall not be required, nor excessive fines imposed, nor cruel and unusual punishments inflicted.

AMENDMENT IX [1791]

The enumeration in the Constitution, of certain rights, shall not be construed to deny or disparage others retained by the people.

AMENDMENT X [1791]

The powers not delegated to the United States by the Constitution, nor prohibited by it to the States, are reserved to the States respectively, or to the people.

AMENDMENT XI [1798]

The Judicial power of the United States shall not be construed to extend to any suit in law or equity, commenced or prosecuted against one of the United States by Citizens of another State, or by Citizens or Subjects of any Foreign State.

AMENDMENT XII [1804]

The Electors shall meet in their respective states and vote by ballot for President and Vice-President, one of whom, at least, shall not be an inhabitant of the same state with themselves; they shall name in their ballots the person voted for as President, and in distinct ballots the person voted for as Vice-President, and they shall make distinct lists of all persons voted for as President, and of all persons voted for as Vice-President, and of the number of votes for each, which lists they shall sign and certify, and transmit sealed to the seat of the government of the United States, directed to the President of the Senate;—The President of the Senate shall, in the presence of the Senate and House of Representatives, open all the certificates and the votes shall then be counted;—The person having the greatest number of votes for President, shall be the President, if such number be a majority of the whole number of Electors appointed; and if no person have such majority, then from the persons having the highest numbers not exceeding three on the list of those voted for as President, the House of Representatives shall choose immediately, by ballot, the President. But in choosing the President, the votes shall be taken by states, the representation from each state having one vote; a quorum for this purpose shall consist of a member or members from two-thirds of the states, and a majority of all the states shall be necessary to a choice. And if the House of Representatives shall not choose a President whenever the right of choice shall devolve upon them, before the fourth day of March next following, then the Vice-President shall act as President, as in the case of the death or other constitutional disability of the President—The person having the greatest number of votes as VicePresident, shall be the Vice-President, if such number be a majority of the whole number of Electors appointed, and if no person have a majority, then from the two highest numbers on the list, the Senate shall choose the Vice-President; a quorum for the purpose shall consist of two-thirds of the whole number of Senators, and a majority of the whole number shall be necessary to a choice. But no person constitutionally ineligible to the office of President shall be eligible to that of Vice-President of the United States.

AMENDMENT XIII [1865]

SECTION 1. Neither slavery nor involuntary servitude, except as a punishment for crime whereof the party shall have been duly convicted, shall exist within the United States, or any place subject to their jurisdiction.

SECTION 2. Congress shall have power to enforce this article by appropriate legislation.

AMENDMENT XIV [1868]

SECTION 1. All persons born or naturalized in the United States, and subject to the jurisdiction thereof, are citizens of the United States and of the State wherein they reside. No State shall make or enforce any law which shall abridge the privileges or immunities of citizens of the United States; nor shall any State deprive any person of life, liberty, or property, without due process of law; nor deny to any person within its jurisdiction the equal protection of the laws.

SECTION 2. Representatives shall be apportioned among the several States according to their respective numbers, counting the whole number of persons in each State, excluding Indians not taxed. But when the right to vote at any election for the choice of electors for President and Vice President of the United States, Representatives in Congress, the Executive and Judicial officers of a State, or the members of the Legislature thereof, is denied to any of the male inhabitants of such State, being twenty-one years of age, and citizens of the United States, or in any way abridged, except for participation in rebellion, or other crime, the basis of representation therein shall be reduced in the proportion which the number of such male citizens shall bear to the whole number of male citizens twenty-one years of age in such State.

SECTION 3. No person shall be a Senator or Representative in Congress, or elector of President and Vice President, or hold any office, civil or military, under the United States, or under any State, who, having previously taken an oath, as a member of Congress, or as an officer of the United States, or as a member of any State legislature, or as an executive or judicial officer of any State, to support the Constitution of the United States, shall have engaged in insurrection or rebellion against the same, or given aid or comfort to the enemies thereof. But Congress may by a vote of two-thirds of each House, remove such disability.

SECTION 4. The validity of the public debt of the United States, authorized by law, including debts incurred for payment of pensions and bounties for services in suppressing insurrection or rebellion, shall not be questioned. But neither the United States nor any State shall assume or pay any debt or obligation incurred in aid of insurrection or rebellion against the United States, or any claim for the loss of emancipation of any slave; but all such debts, obligations and claims shall be held illegal and void.

SECTION 5. The Congress shall have power to enforce, by appropriate legislation, the provisions of this article.

AMENDMENT XV [1870]

SECTION 1. The right of citizens of the United States to vote shall not be denied or abridged by the United States or by any State on account of race, color, or previous condition of servitude.

SECTION 2. The Congress shall have power to enforce this article by appropriate legislation.

AMENDMENT XVI [1913]

The Congress shall have power to lay and collect taxes on incomes, from whatever source derived, without apportionment among the several States, and without regard to any census or enumeration.

AMENDMENT XVII [1913]

The Senate of the United States shall be composed of two Senators from each State, elected by the people thereof, for six years; and each Senator shall have one vote. The electors in each State shall have the qualifications requisite for electors of the most numerous branch of the State legislatures.

When vacancies happen in the representation of any State in the Senate, the executive authority of such State shall issue writs of election to fill such vacancies: Provided, That the legislature of any State may empower the executive thereof to make temporary appointments until the people fill the vacancies by election as the legislature may direct.

This amendment shall not be so construed as to affect the election or term of any Senator chosen before it becomes valid as part of the Constitution.

AMENDMENT XVIII [1919]

SECTION 1. After one year from the ratification of this article the manufacture, sale, or transportation of intoxicating liquors within, the importation thereof into, or the exportation thereof from the United States and all territory subject to the jurisdiction thereof for beverage purposes is hereby prohibited.

SECTION 2. The Congress and the several States shall have concurrent power to enforce this article by appropriate legislation.

SECTION 3. This article shall be inoperative unless it shall have been ratified as an amendment to the Constitution by the legislatures of the several States, as provided in the Constitution, within seven years from the date of the submission hereof to the States by the Congress.

AMENDMENT XIX [1920]

The right of citizens of the United States to vote shall not be denied or abridged by the United States or by any State on account of sex.

Congress shall have power to enforce this article by appropriate legislation.

AMENDMENT XX [1933]

SECTION 1. The terms of the President and Vice President shall end at noon on the 20th day of January, and the terms of Senators and Representatives at noon on the 3d day of January, of the years in which such terms would have ended if this article had not been ratified; and the terms of their successors shall then begin.

SECTION 2. The Congress shall assemble at least once in every year, and such meeting shall begin at noon on the 3d day of January, unless they shall by law appoint a different day.

SECTION 3. If, at the time fixed for the beginning of the term of the President, the President elect shall have died, the Vice President elect shall become President. If a President shall not have been chosen before the time fixed for the beginning of his term, or if the President elect shall have failed to qualify, then the Vice President elect shall act as President until a President shall have qualified; and the Congress may by law provide for the case wherein neither a President elect nor a Vice President elect shall have qualified, declaring who shall then act as President, or the manner in which one who is to act shall be selected, and such person shall act accordingly until a President or Vice President shall have qualified.

SECTION 4. The Congress may by law provide for the case of the death of any of the persons from whom the House of Representatives may choose a President whenever the right of choice shall have devolved upon them, and for the case of the death of any of the persons from whom the Senate may choose a Vice President whenever the right of choice shall have devolved upon them.

SECTION 5. Sections 1 and 2 shall take effect on the 15th day of October following the ratification of this article.

SECTION 6. This article shall be inoperative unless it shall have been ratified as an amendment to the Constitution by the legislatures of three-fourths of the several States within seven years from the date of its submission.

AMENDMENT XXI [1933]

SECTION 1. The eighteenth article of amendment to the Constitution of the United States is hereby repealed.

SECTION 2. The transportation or importation into any State, Territory, or possession of the United States for delivery or use therein of intoxicating liquors, in violation of the laws thereof, is hereby prohibited.

SECTION 3. This article shall be inoperative unless it shall have been ratified as an amendment to the Constitution by conventions in the several States, as provided by the Constitution, within seven years from the date of the submission hereof to the States by the Congress.

AMENDMENT XXII [1951]

SECTION 1. No person shall be elected to the office of the President more than twice, and no person who has held the office of President, or acted as President, for more than two years of a term to which some other person was elected President shall be elected to the office of the President more than once. But this Article shall not apply to any person holding the office of President when this Article was proposed by the Congress, and shall not prevent any person who may be holding the office of President, or acting as President, during the term within which this Article becomes operative from holding the office of President or acting as President during the remainder of such term.

SECTION 2. This article shall be inoperative unless it shall have been ratified as an amendment to the Constitution by the legislatures of three-fourths of the several States within seven years from the date of its submission to the States by the Congress.

AMENDMENT XXIII [1961]

SECTION 1. The District constituting the seat of Government of the United States shall appoint in such manner as the Congress may direct:

A number of electors of President and Vice President equal to the whole number of Senators and Representatives in Congress to which the District would be entitled if it were a State, but in no event more than the least populous State; they shall be in addition to those appointed by the States, but they shall be considered, for the purposes of the election of President and Vice President, to be electors appointed by a State; and they shall meet in the District and perform such duties as provided by the twelfth article of amendment.

SECTION 2. The Congress shall have power to enforce this article by appropriate legislation.

AMENDMENT XXIV [1964]

SECTION 1. The right of citizens of the United States to vote in any primary or other election for President or Vice President, for electors for President or Vice President, or for Senator or Representative in Congress, shall not be denied or abridged by the United States or any State by reason of failure to pay any poll tax or other tax.

SECTION 2. The Congress shall have power to enforce this article by appropriate legislation.

AMENDMENT XXV [1967]

SECTION 1. In case of the removal of the President from office or of his death or resignation, the Vice President shall become President.

SECTION 2. Whenever there is a vacancy in the office of the Vice President, the President shall nominate a Vice President who shall take office upon confirmation by a majority vote of both Houses of Congress.

SECTION 3. Whenever the President transmits to the President pro tempore of the Senate and the Speaker of the House of Representatives his written declaration that he is unable to discharge the powers and duties of his office, and until he transmits to them a written declaration to the contrary, such powers and duties shall be discharged by the Vice President as Acting President.

SECTION 4. Whenever the Vice President and a majority of either the principal officers of the executive departments or of such other body as Congress may by law provide, transmit to the President pro tempore of the Senate and the Speaker of the House of Representatives their written declaration that the President is unable to discharge the powers and duties of his office, the Vice President shall immediately assume the powers and duties of the office as Acting President.

Thereafter, when the President transmits to the President pro tempore of the Senate and the Speaker of the House of Representatives his written declaration that no inability exists, he shall resume the powers and duties of his office unless the Vice President and a majority of either the principal officers of the executive department or of such other body as Congress may by law provide, transmit within four days to the President pro tempore of the Senate and the Speaker of the House of Representatives their written declaration that the President is unable to discharge the powers and duties of his office. Thereupon Congress shall decide the issue, assembling within forty-eight hours for that purpose if not in session. If the Congress, within twenty-one days after receipt of the latter written declaration, or, if Congress is not in session, within twenty-one days after Congress is required to assemble, determines by two-thirds vote of both Houses that the President is unable to discharge the powers and duties of his office, the Vice President shall continue to discharge the same as Acting President; otherwise, the President shall resume the powers and duties of his office.

AMENDMENT XXVI [1971]

SECTION 1. The right of citizens of the United States, who are eighteen years of age or older, to vote shall not be denied or abridged by the United States or by any State on account of age.

SECTION 2. The Congress shall have power to enforce this article by appropriate legislation.

AMENDMENT XXVII [1992]

No law, varying the compensation for the services of the Senators and Representatives, shall take effect, until an election of Representatives shall have intervened.

APPENDIX B

Selected Federal Statutes

28 U.S.C.

§1251. Original jurisdiction

(a) The Supreme Court shall have original and exclusive jurisdiction of all controversies between two or more States.

(b) The Supreme Court shall have original but not exclusive jurisdiction of:

(1) All actions or proceedings to which ambassadors, other public ministers, consuls, or vice consuls of foreign states are parties;

(2) All controversies between the United States and a State;

(3) All actions or proceedings by a State against the citizens of another State or against aliens.

§1253. Direct appeals from decisions of three-judge courts

Except as otherwise provided by law, any party may appeal to the Supreme Court from an order granting or denying, after notice and hearing, an interlocutory or permanent injunction in any civil action, suit or proceeding required by any Act of Congress to be heard and determined by a district court of three judges.

§1254. Courts of appeals; certiorari; certified questions

Cases in the courts of appeals may be reviewed by the Supreme Court by the following methods:

(1) By writ of certiorari granted upon the petition of any party to any civil or criminal case, before or after rendition of judgment or decree;

(2) By certification at any time by a court of appeals of any question of law in any civil or criminal case as to which instructions are desired, and upon such certification the Supreme Court may give binding instructions or require the entire record to be sent up for decision of the entire matter in controversy.

§1257. State courts; certiorari

(a) Final judgments or decrees rendered by the highest court of a State in which a decision could be had, may be reviewed by the Supreme Court by writ of certiorari where the validity of a treaty or statute of the United States is drawn in question or where the validity of a statute of any State is drawn in question on the ground of its being repugnant to the Constitution, treaties, or laws of the United States, or where any title, right, privilege, or immunity is specially set up or claimed under the Constitution or the treaties or statutes of, or any commission held or authority exercised under, the United States.

(b) For the purposes of this section, the term "highest court of a State" includes the District of Columbia Court of Appeals.

§1258. Supreme Court of Puerto Rico; certiorari

Final judgments or decrees rendered by the Supreme Court of the Commonwealth of Puerto Rico may be reviewed by the Supreme Court by writ of certiorari where the validity of a treaty or statute of the United States is drawn in question or where the validity of a statute of the Commonwealth of Puerto Rico is drawn in question on the ground of its being repugnant to the Constitution, treaties, or laws of the United States, or where any title, right, privilege, or immunity is specially set up or claimed under the Constitution or the treaties, or statutes of, or any commission held or authority exercised under, the United States.

§1259. Court of Appeals for the Armed Forces; certiorari

Decisions of the United States Court of Appeals for the Armed Forces may be reviewed by the Supreme Court by writ of certiorari in the following cases:

(1) Cases reviewed by the Court of Appeals for the Armed Forces under section 867(a)(1) of title 10.

(2) Cases certified to the Court of Appeals for the Armed Forces by the Judge Advocate General under section 867(a)(2) of title 10.

(3) Cases in which the Court of Appeals for the Armed Forces granted a petition for review under section 867(a)(3) of title 10.

(4) Cases, other than those described in paragraphs (1), (2), and (3) of this subsection, in which the Court of Appeals for the Armed Forces granted relief.

§1291. Final decisions of district courts

The courts of appeals (other than the United States Court of Appeals for the Federal Circuit) shall have jurisdiction of appeals from all final decisions of the district courts of the United States, the United States District Court for the District of the Canal Zone, the District Court of Guam, and the District Court of the Virgin Islands, except where a direct review may be had in the Supreme Court. The jurisdiction of the United States Court of Appeals for the Federal Circuit shall be limited to the jurisdiction described in sections 1292 (c) and (d) and 1295 of this title.

§1292. Interlocutory decisions

§1292. Interlocutory decisions

(a) Except as provided in subsections (c) and (d) of this section, the courts of appeals shall have jurisdiction of appeals from:

(1) Interlocutory orders of the district courts of the United States, the United States District Court for the District of the Canal Zone, the District Court of Guam, and the District Court of the Virgin Islands, or of the judges thereof, granting, continuing, modifying, refusing or dissolving injunctions, or refusing to dissolve or modify injunctions, except where a direct review may be had in the Supreme Court;

(2) Interlocutory orders appointing receivers, or refusing orders to wind up receiverships or to take steps to accomplish the purposes thereof, such as directing sales or other disposals of property;

(3) Interlocutory decrees of such district courts or the judges thereof determining the rights and liabilities of the parties to admiralty cases in which appeals from final decrees are allowed.

(b) When a district judge, in making in a civil action an order not otherwise appealable under this section, shall be of the opinion that such order involves a controlling question of law as to which there is substantial ground for difference of opinion and that an immediate appeal from the order may materially advance the ultimate termination of the litigation, he shall so state in writing in such order. The Court of Appeals which would have jurisdiction of an appeal of such action may thereupon, in its discretion, permit an appeal to be taken from such order, if application is made to it within ten days after the entry of the order: *Provided, however,* That application for an appeal hereunder shall not stay proceedings in the district court unless the district judge or the Court of Appeals or a judge thereof shall so order.

(c) The United States Court of Appeals for the Federal Circuit shall have exclusive jurisdiction—

(1) of an appeal from an interlocutory order or decree described in subsection (a) or (b) of this section in any case over which the court would have jurisdiction of an appeal under section 1295 of this title; and

(2) of an appeal from a judgment in a civil action for patent infringement which would otherwise be appealable to the United States Court of Appeals for the Federal Circuit and is final except for an accounting.

(d) (1) When the chief judge of the Court of International Trade issues an order under the provisions of section 256(b) of this title, or when any judge of the Court of International Trade, in issuing any other interlocutory order, includes in the order a statement that a controlling question of law is involved with respect to which there is a substantial ground for difference of opinion and that an immediate appeal from that order may materially advance the ultimate termination of the litigation, the United States Court of Appeals for the Federal Circuit may, in its discretion, permit an appeal to be taken from such order, if application is made to that Court within ten days after the entry of such order.

(2) When the chief judge of the United States Court of Federal Claims issues an order under section 798(b) of this title, or when any judge of the United

Tariff Schedule of the United States (relating to importation of instruments or apparatus);

(8) of an appeal under section 71 of the Plant Variety Protection Act (7 U.S.C. 2461);

(9) of an appeal from a final order or final decision of the Merit Systems Protection Board, pursuant to sections 7703(b)(1) and 7703(d) of title 5;

(10) of an appeal from a final decision of an agency board of contract appeals pursuant to section 7107(a)(1) of title 41;

(11) of an appeal under section 211 of the Economic Stabilization Act of 1970;

(12) of an appeal under section 5 of the Emergency Petroleum Allocation Act of 1973;

(13) of an appeal under section 506(c) of the Natural Gas Policy Act of 1978; and

(14) of an appeal under section 523 of the Energy Policy and Conservation Act.

(b) The head of any executive department or agency may, with the approval of the Attorney General, refer to the Court of Appeals for the Federal Circuit for judicial review any final decision rendered by a board of contract appeals pursuant to the terms of any contract with the United States awarded by that department or agency which the head of such department or agency has concluded is not entitled to finality pursuant to the review standards specified in section 7101(b) of Title 41. The head of each executive department or agency shall make any referral under this section within one hundred and twenty days after the receipt of a copy of the final appeal decision.

(c) The Court of Appeals for the Federal Circuit shall review the matter referred in accordance with the standards specified in section 7101(b) of Title 41. The court shall proceed with judicial review on the administrative record made before the board of contract appeals on matters so referred as in other cases pending in such court, shall determine the issue of finality of the appeal decision, and shall, if appropriate, render judgment thereon, or remand the matter to any administrative or executive body or official with such direction as it may deem proper and just.

§1330. Actions against foreign states

(a) The district courts shall have original jurisdiction without regard to amount in controversy of any nonjury civil action against a foreign state as defined in section 1603(a) of this title as to any claim for relief in personam with respect to which the foreign state is not entitled to immunity either under sections 1605-1607 of this title or under any applicable international agreement.

(b) Personal jurisdiction over a foreign state shall exist as to every claim for relief over which the district courts have jurisdiction under subsection (a) where service has been made under section 1608 of this title.

(c) For purposes of subsection (b), an appearance by a foreign state does not confer personal jurisdiction with respect to any claim for relief not arising out of any transaction or occurrence enumerated in sections 1605-1607 of this title.

§1331. Federal question

The district courts shall have original jurisdiction of all civil actions arising under the Constitution, laws, or treaties of the United States.

§1332. Diversity of citizenship; amount in controversy; costs

(a) The district courts shall have original jurisdiction of all civil actions where the matter in controversy exceeds the sum or value of $75,000, exclusive of interest and costs, and is between—

(1) citizens of different States;

(2) citizens of a State and citizens or subjects of a foreign state, except that the district courts shall not have original jurisdiction under this subsection of an action between citizens of a State and citizens or subjects of a foreign state who are lawfully admitted for permanent residence in the United States and are domiciled in the same State;

(3) citizens of different States and in which citizens or subjects of a foreign state are additional parties; and

(4) a foreign state, defined in section 1603(a) of this title, as plaintiff and citizens of a State or of different States.

(b) Except when express provision therefor is otherwise made in a statute of the United States, where the plaintiff who files the case originally in the Federal courts is finally adjudged to be entitled to recover less than the sum or value of $75,000, computed without regard to any setoff or counterclaim to which the defendant may be adjudged to be entitled, and exclusive of interest and costs, the district court may deny costs to the plaintiff and, in addition, may impose costs on the plaintiff.

(c) For the purposes of this section and section 1441 of this title—

(1) a corporation shall be deemed to be a citizen of every State and foreign state by which it has been incorporated and of the State or foreign state where it has its principal place of business, except that in any direct action against the insurer of a policy or contract of liability insurance, whether incorporated or unincorporated, to which action the insured is not joined as a party-defendant, such insurer shall be deemed a citizen of—

(A) every State and foreign state of which the insured is a citizen;

(B) every State and foreign state by which the insurer has been incorporated; and

(C) the State or foreign state where the insurer has its principal place of business; and

(2) the legal representative of the estate of a decedent shall be deemed to be a citizen only of the same State as the decedent, and the legal representative of an infant or incompetent shall be deemed to be a citizen only of the same State as the infant or incompetent.

(d) (1) In this subsection—

(A) the term "class" means all of the class members in a class action;

(B) the term "class action" means any civil action filed under rule 23 of the Federal Rules of Civil Procedure or similar State statute or rule of judicial procedure authorizing an action to be brought by 1 or more representative persons as a class action;

(C) the term "class certification order" means an order issued by a court approving the treatment of some or all aspects of a civil action as a class action; and

(D) the term "class members" means the persons (named or unnamed) who fall within the definition of the proposed or certified class in a class action.

(2) The district courts shall have original jurisdiction of any civil action in which the matter in controversy exceeds the sum or value of $5,000,000, exclusive of interest and costs, and is a class action in which—

(A) any member of a class of plaintiffs is a citizen of a State different from any defendant;

(B) any member of a class of plaintiffs is a foreign state or a citizen or subject of a foreign state and any defendant is a citizen of a State; or

(C) any member of a class of plaintiffs is a citizen of a State and any defendant is a foreign state or a citizen or subject of a foreign state.

(3) A district court may, in the interests of justice and looking at the totality of the circumstances, decline to exercise jurisdiction under paragraph (2) over a class action in which greater than one-third but less than two-thirds of the members of all proposed plaintiff classes in the aggregate and the primary defendants are citizens of the State in which the action was originally filed based on consideration of—

(A) whether the claims asserted involve matters of national or interstate interest;

(B) whether the claims asserted will be governed by laws of the State in which the action was originally filed or by the laws of other States;

(C) whether the class action has been pleaded in a manner that seeks to avoid Federal jurisdiction;

(D) whether the action was brought in a forum with a distinct nexus with the class members, the alleged harm, or the defendants;

(E) whether the number of citizens of the State in which the action was originally filed in all proposed plaintiff classes in the aggregate is substantially larger than the number of citizens from any other State, and the citizenship of the other members of the proposed class is dispersed among a substantial number of States; and

(F) whether, during the 3-year period preceding the filing of that class action, 1 or more other class actions asserting the same or similar claims on behalf of the same or other persons have been filed.

(4) A district court shall decline to exercise jurisdiction under paragraph (2)—

(A) (i) over a class action in which—

(I) greater than two-thirds of the members of all proposed plaintiff classes in the aggregate are citizens of the State in which the action was originally filed;

(II) at least 1 defendant is a defendant—

(aa) from whom significant relief is sought by members of the plaintiff class;

(bb) whose alleged conduct forms a significant basis for the claims asserted by the proposed plaintiff class; and

(cc) who is a citizen of the State in which the action was originally filed; and

(III) principal injuries resulting from the alleged conduct or any related conduct of each defendant were incurred in the State in which the action was originally filed; and

(ii) during the 3-year period preceding the filing of that class action, no other class action has been filed asserting the same or similar factual allegations against any of the defendants on behalf of the same or other persons; or

(B) two-thirds or more of the members of all proposed plaintiff classes in the aggregate, and the primary defendants, are citizens of the State in which the action was originally filed.

(5) Paragraphs (2) through (4) shall not apply to any class action in which—

(A) the primary defendants are States, State officials, or other governmental entities against whom the district court may be foreclosed from ordering relief; or

(B) the number of members of all proposed plaintiff classes in the aggregate is less than 100.

(6) In any class action, the claims of the individual class members shall be aggregated to determine whether the matter in controversy exceeds the sum or value of $5,000,000, exclusive of interest and costs.

(7) Citizenship of the members of the proposed plaintiff classes shall be determined for purposes of paragraphs (2) through (6) as of the date of filing of the complaint or amended complaint, or, if the case stated by the initial pleading is not subject to Federal jurisdiction, as of the date of service by plaintiffs of an amended pleading, motion, or other paper, indicating the existence of Federal jurisdiction.

(8) This subsection shall apply to any class action before or after the entry of a class certification order by the court with respect to that action.

(9) Paragraph (2) shall not apply to any class action that solely involves a claim—

(A) concerning a covered security as defined under 16(f)(3)1 of the Securities Act of 1933 (15 U.S.C. 78p(f)(3)2) and section 28(f)(5)(E) of the Securities Exchange Act of 1934 (15 U.S.C. 78bb(f)(5)(E));

(B) that relates to the internal affairs or governance of a corporation or other form of business enterprise and that arises under or by virtue of the laws of the State in which such corporation or business enterprise is incorporated or organized; or

(C) that relates to the rights, duties (including fiduciary duties), and obligations relating to or created by or pursuant to any security (as defined under section 2(a)(1) of the Securities Act of 1933 (15 U.S.C. 77b(a)(1)) and the regulations issued thereunder).

(10) For purposes of this subsection and section 1453, an unincorporated association shall be deemed to be a citizen of the State where it has its principal place of business and the State under whose laws it is organized.

(11) (A) For purposes of this subsection and section 1453, a mass action shall be deemed to be a class action removable under paragraphs (2) through (10) if it otherwise meets the provisions of those paragraphs.

(B) (i) As used in subparagraph (A), the term "mass action" means any civil action (except a civil action within the scope of section 1711(2)) in which monetary relief claims of 100 or more persons are proposed to be tried jointly on the ground that the plaintiffs' claims involve common questions of law or fact, except that jurisdiction shall exist only over those plaintiffs whose claims in a mass action satisfy the jurisdictional amount requirements under subsection (a).

(ii) As used in subparagraph (A), the term "mass action" shall not include any civil action in which—

(I) all of the claims in the action arise from an event or occurrence in the State in which the action was filed, and that allegedly resulted in injuries in that State or in States contiguous to that State;

(II) the claims are joined upon motion of a defendant;

(III) all of the claims in the action are asserted on behalf of the general public (and not on behalf of individual claimants or members of a purported class) pursuant to a State statute specifically authorizing such action; or

(IV) the claims have been consolidated or coordinated solely for pretrial proceedings.

(C) (i) Any action(s) removed to Federal court pursuant to this subsection shall not thereafter be transferred to any other court pursuant to section 1407, or the rules promulgated thereunder, unless a majority of the plaintiffs in the action request transfer pursuant to section 1407.

(ii) This subparagraph will not apply—

(I) to cases certified pursuant to rule 23 of the Federal Rules of Civil Procedure; or

(II) if plaintiffs propose that the action proceed as a class action pursuant to rule 23 of the Federal Rules of Civil Procedure.

(D) The limitations periods on any claims asserted in a mass action that is removed to Federal court pursuant to this subsection shall be deemed tolled during the period that the action is pending in Federal court.

(e) The word "States", as used in this section, includes the Territories, the District of Columbia, and the Commonwealth of Puerto Rico.

§1333. Admiralty, maritime, and prize cases

The district courts shall have original jurisdiction, exclusive of the courts of the States, of:

(1) Any civil case of admiralty or maritime jurisdiction, saving to suitors in all cases all other remedies to which they are otherwise entitled.

(2) Any prize brought into the United States and all proceedings for the condemnation of property taken as prize.

§1334. Bankruptcy cases and proceedings

(a) Except as provided in subsection (b) of this section, the district courts shall have original and exclusive jurisdiction of all cases under title 11.

(b) Except as provided in subsection (e)(2), and notwithstanding any Act of Congress that confers exclusive jurisdiction on a court or courts other than the district courts, the district courts shall have original but not exclusive jurisdiction of all civil proceedings arising under title 11, or arising in or related to cases under title 11.

(c) (1) Except with respect to a case under chapter 15 of title 11, nothing in this section prevents a district court in the interest of justice, or in the interest of comity with State courts or respect for State law, from abstaining from hearing a particular proceeding arising under title 11 or arising in or related to a case under title 11.

(2) Upon timely motion of a party in a proceeding based upon a State law claim or State law cause of action, related to a case under title 11 but not arising under title 11 or arising in a case under title 11, with respect to which an action could not have been commenced in a court of the United States absent jurisdiction under this section, the district court shall abstain from hearing such proceeding if an action is commenced, and can be timely adjudicated, in a State forum of appropriate jurisdiction.

(d) Any decision to abstain or not to abstain made under subsection (c) (other than a decision not to abstain in a proceeding described in subsection (c)(2)) is not reviewable by appeal or otherwise by the court of appeals under section 158(d), 1291, or 1292 of this title or by the Supreme Court of the United States under section 1254 of this title. Subsection (c) and this subsection shall not be construed to limit the applicability of the stay provided for by section 362 of title 11, United States Code, as such section applies to an action affecting the property of the estate in bankruptcy.

(e) The district court in which a case under title 11 is commenced or is pending shall have exclusive jurisdiction—

(1) of all the property, wherever located, of the debtor as of the commencement of such case, and of property of the estate; and

(2) over all claims or causes of action that involve construction of section 327 of title 11, United States Code, or rules relating to disclosure requirements under section 327.

§1337. Commerce and antitrust regulations; amount in controversy, costs

(a) The district courts shall have original jurisdiction of any civil action or proceeding arising under any Act of Congress regulating commerce or protecting trade and commerce against restraints and monopolies: *Provided, however,* That the district courts shall have original jurisdiction of an action brought under section 11706 or 14706 of title 49, only if the matter in controversy for each receipt or bill of lading exceeds $10,000, exclusive of interest and costs.

(b) Except when express provision therefor is otherwise made in a statute of the United States, where a plaintiff who files the case under section 11706 or 14706 of title 49, originally in the Federal courts is finally adjudged to be entitled to recover less than the sum or value of $10,000, computed without regard to any setoff or counterclaim to which the defendant may be adjudged to be entitled, and exclusive of any interest and costs, the district court may deny costs to the plaintiff and, in addition, may impose costs on the plaintiff.

(c) The district courts shall not have jurisdiction under this section of any matter within the exclusive jurisdiction of the Court of International Trade under chapter 95 of this title.

§1338. Patents, plant variety protection, copyrights, mask works, designs, trademarks, and unfair competition

(a) The district courts shall have original jurisdiction of any civil action arising under any Act of Congress relating to patents, plant variety protection, copyrights and trademarks. No State court shall have jurisdiction over any claim for relief arising under any Act of Congress relating to patents, plant variety protection, or copyrights. For purposes of this subsection, the term "State" includes any State of the United States, the District of Columbia, the Commonwealth of Puerto Rico, the United States Virgin Islands, American Samoa, Guam, and the Northern Mariana Islands.

(b) The district courts shall have original jurisdiction of any civil action asserting a claim of unfair competition when joined with a substantial and related claim under the copyright, patent, plant variety protection or trademark laws.

(c) Subsections (a) and (b) apply to exclusive rights in mask works under chapter 9 of title 17, and to exclusive rights in designs under chapter 13 of title 17, to the same extent as such subsections apply to copyrights.

§1340. Internal revenue; customs duties

The district courts shall have original jurisdiction of any civil action arising under any Act of Congress providing for internal revenue, or revenue from imports or tonnage except matters within the jurisdiction of the Court of International Trade.

§1341. Taxes by States

The district courts shall not enjoin, suspend or restrain the assessment, levy or collection of any tax under State law where a plain, speedy and efficient remedy may be had in the courts of such State.

§1342. Rate orders of State agencies

The district courts shall not enjoin, suspend or restrain the operation of, or compliance with, any order affecting rates chargeable by a public utility and made by a State administrative agency or a rate-making body of a State political subdivision, where:

(1) Jurisdiction is based solely on diversity of citizenship or repugnance of the order to the Federal Constitution; and,

(2) The order does not interfere with interstate commerce; and,

(3) The order has been made after reasonable notice and hearing; and,

(4) A plain, speedy and efficient remedy may be had in the courts of such State.

§1343. Civil rights and elective franchise

(a) The district courts shall have original jurisdiction of any civil action authorized by law to be commenced by any person:

(1) To recover damages for injury to his person or property, or because of the deprivation of any right or privilege of a citizen of the United States, by any act done in furtherance of any conspiracy mentioned in section 1985 of Title 42;

(2) To recover damages from any person who fails to prevent or to aid in preventing any wrongs mentioned in section 1985 of Title 42 which he had knowledge were about to occur and power to prevent;

(3) To redress the deprivation, under color of any State law, statute, ordinance, regulation, custom or usage, of any right, privilege or immunity secured by the Constitution of the United States or by any Act of Congress providing for equal rights of citizens or of all persons within the jurisdiction of the United States;

(4) To recover damages or to secure equitable or other relief under any Act of Congress providing for the protection of civil rights, including the right to vote.

(b) For purposes of this section—

(1) the District of Columbia shall be considered to be a State; and

(2) any Act of Congress applicable exclusively to the District of Columbia shall be considered to be a statute of the District of Columbia.

§1345. United States as plaintiff

Except as otherwise provided by Act of Congress, the district courts shall have original jurisdiction of all civil actions, suits or proceedings commenced by the United States, or by any agency or officer thereof expressly authorized to sue by Act of Congress.

§1346. United States as defendant

(a) The district courts shall have original jurisdiction, concurrent with the United States Court of Federal Claims, of:

(1) Any civil action against the United States for the recovery of any internal-revenue tax alleged to have been erroneously or illegally assessed or collected, or any penalty claimed to have been collected without authority or any sum alleged to have been excessive or in any manner wrongfully collected under the internal-revenue laws;

(2) Any other civil action or claim against the United States, not exceeding $10,000 in amount, founded either upon the Constitution, or any Act of Congress, or any regulation of an executive department, or upon any express

or implied contract with the United States, or for liquidated or unliquidated damages in cases not sounding in tort, except that the district courts shall not have jurisdiction of any civil action or claim against the United States founded upon any express or implied contract with the United States or for liquidated or unliquidated damages in cases not sounding in tort which are subject to sections 7104(b)(1) and 7107(a)(1) of title 41.. For the purpose of this paragraph, an express or implied contract with the Army and Air Force Exchange Service, Navy Exchanges, Marine Corps Exchanges, Coast Guard Exchanges, or Exchange Councils of the National Aeronautics and Space Administration shall be considered an express or implied contract with the United States.

(b) (1) Subject to the provisions of chapter 171 of this title, the district courts, together with the United States District Court for the District of the Canal Zone and the District Court of the Virgin Islands, shall have exclusive jurisdiction of civil actions on claims against the United States, for money damages, accruing on and after January 1, 1945, for injury or loss of property, or personal injury or death caused by the negligent or wrongful act or omission of any employee of the Government while acting within the scope of his office or employment, under circumstances where the United States, if a private person, would be liable to the claimant in accordance with the law of the place where the act or omission occurred.

(2) No person convicted of a felony who is incarcerated while awaiting sentencing or while serving a sentence may bring a civil action against the United States or an agency, officer, or employee of the Government, for mental or emotional injury suffered while in custody without a prior showing of physical injury or the commission of a sexual act (as defined in section 2246 of title 18).

(c) The jurisdiction conferred by this section includes jurisdiction of any set-off, counterclaim, or other claim or demand whatever on the part of the United States against any plaintiff commencing an action under this section.

(d) The district courts shall not have jurisdiction under this section of any civil action or claim for a pension.

(e) The district courts shall have original jurisdiction of any civil action against the United States provided in section 6226, 6228(a), 7426, or 7428 (in the case of the United States district court for the District of Columbia) or section 7429 of the Internal Revenue Code of 1986.

(f) The district courts shall have exclusive original jurisdiction of civil actions under section 2409a to quiet title to an estate or interest in real property in which an interest is claimed by the United States.

(g) Subject to the provisions of chapter 179, the district courts of the United States shall have exclusive jurisdiction over any civil action commenced under section 453(2) of title 3, by a covered employee under chapter 5 of such title.

§1349. Corporation organized under federal law as party

The district courts shall not have jurisdiction of any civil action by or against any corporation upon the ground that it was incorporated by or under an Act of Congress, unless the United States is the owner of more than one-half of its capital stock.

§1350. Alien's action for tort

The district courts shall have original jurisdiction of any civil action by an alien for a tort only, committed in violation of the law of nations or a treaty of the United States.

§1351. Consuls, vice consuls, and members of a diplomatic mission as defendant

The district courts shall have original jurisdiction, exclusive of the courts of the States, of all civil actions and proceedings against—

(1) consuls or vice consuls of foreign states; or

(2) members of a mission or members of their families (as such terms are defined in section 2 of the Diplomatic Relations Act).

§1353. Indian allotments

The district courts shall have original jurisdiction of any civil action involving the right of any person, in whole or in part of Indian blood or descent, to any allotment of land under any Act of Congress or treaty.

The judgment in favor of any claimant to an allotment of land shall have the same effect, when properly certified to the Secretary of the Interior, as if such allotment had been allowed and approved by him; but this provision shall not apply to any lands held on or before December 21, 1911, by either of the Five Civilized Tribes, the Osage Nation of Indians, nor to any of the lands within the Quapaw Indian Agency.

§1354. Land grants from different states

The district courts shall have original jurisdiction of actions between citizens of the same state claiming lands under grants from different states.

§1355. Fine, penalty or forfeiture

(a) The district courts shall have original jurisdiction, exclusive of the courts of the States, of any action or proceeding for the recovery or enforcement of any fine, penalty, or forfeiture, pecuniary or otherwise, incurred under any Act of Congress, except matters within the jurisdiction of the Court of International Trade under section 1582 of this title.

(b) (1) A forfeiture action or proceeding may be brought in—

(A) the district court for the district in which any of the acts or omissions giving rise to the forfeiture occurred, or

(B) any other district where venue for the forfeiture action or proceeding is specifically provided for in section 1395 of this title or any other statute.

(2) Whenever property subject to forfeiture under the laws of the United States is located in a foreign country, or has been detained or seized pursuant to legal process or competent authority of a foreign government, an action or proceeding for forfeiture may be brought as provided in paragraph (1), or in the United States District court for the District of Columbia.

(c) In any case in which a final order disposing of property in a civil forfeiture action or proceeding is appealed, removal of the property by the prevailing party shall not deprive the court of jurisdiction. Upon motion of the appealing party, the district court or the court of appeals shall issue any order necessary to preserve the right of the appealing party to the full value of the property at issue, including a stay of the judgment of the district court pending appeal or requiring the prevailing party to post an appeal bond.

(d) Any court with jurisdiction over a forfeiture action pursuant to subsection (b) may issue and cause to be served in any other district such process as may be required to bring before the court the property that is the subject of the forfeiture action.

§1356. Seizures not within admiralty and maritime jurisdiction

The district courts shall have original jurisdiction, exclusive of the courts of the States, of any seizure under any law of the United States on land or upon waters not within admiralty and maritime jurisdiction, except matters within the jurisdiction of the Court of International Trade under section 1582 of this title.

§1357. Injuries under Federal laws

The district courts shall have original jurisdiction of any civil action commenced by any person to recover damages for any injury to his person or property on account of any act done by him, under any Act of Congress, for the protection or collection of any of the revenues, or to enforce the right of citizens of the United States to vote in any State.

§1358. Eminent domain

The district courts shall have original jurisdiction of all proceedings to condemn real estate for the use of the United States or its departments or agencies.

§1359. Parties collusively joined or made

A district court shall not have jurisdiction of a civil action in which any party, by assignment or otherwise, has been improperly or collusively made or joined to invoke the jurisdiction of such court.

§1361. Action to compel an officer of the United States to perform his duty

The district courts shall have original jurisdiction of any action in the nature of mandamus to compel an officer or employee of the United States or any agency thereof to perform a duty owed to the plaintiff.

§1366. Construction of references to laws of the United States or Acts of Congress

For the purposes of this chapter, references to laws of the United States or Acts of Congress do not include laws applicable exclusively to the District of Columbia.

§1367. Supplemental jurisdiction

(a) Except as provided in subsections (b) and (c) or as expressly provided otherwise by Federal statute, in any civil action of which the district courts have original jurisdiction, the district courts shall have supplemental jurisdiction over all other claims that are so related to claims in the action within such original jurisdiction that they form part of the same case or controversy under Article III of the United States Constitution. Such supplemental jurisdiction shall include claims that involve the joinder or intervention of additional parties.

(b) In any civil action of which the district courts have original jurisdiction founded solely on section 1332 of this title, the district courts shall not have supplemental jurisdiction under subsection (a) over claims by plaintiffs against persons made parties under Rule 14, 19, 20, or 24 of the Federal Rules of Civil Procedure, or over claims by persons proposed to be joined as plaintiffs under Rule 19 of such rules, or seeking to intervene as plaintiffs under Rule 24 of such rules, when exercising supplemental jurisdiction over such claims would be inconsistent with the jurisdictional requirements of section 1332.

(c) The district courts may decline to exercise supplemental jurisdiction over a claim under subsection (a) if—

(1) the claim raises a novel or complex issue of State law,

(2) the claim substantially predominates over the claim or claims over which the district court has original jurisdiction,

(3) the district court has dismissed all claims over which it has original jurisdiction, or

(4) in exceptional circumstances, there are other compelling reasons for declining jurisdiction.

(d) The period of limitations for any claim asserted under subsection (a), and for any other claim in the same action that is voluntarily dismissed at the same time as or after the dismissal of the claim under subsection (a), shall be tolled while the claim is pending and for a period of 30 days after it is dismissed unless State law provides for a longer tolling period.

(e) As used in this section, the term "State" includes the District of Columbia, the Commonwealth of Puerto Rico, and any territory or possession of the United States.

§1441. Removal of civil actions

(a) Generally.—Except as otherwise expressly provided by Act of Congress, any civil action brought in a State court of which the district courts of the United States have original jurisdiction, may be removed by the defendant or the defendants, to the district court of the United States for the district and division embracing the place where such action is pending.

(b) Removal based on diversity of citizenship.—(1) In determining whether a civil action is removable on the basis of the jurisdiction under section 1332(a) of this title, the citizenship of defendants sued under fictitious names shall be disregarded.

(2) A civil action otherwise removable solely on the basis of the jurisdiction under section 1332(a) of this title may not be removed if any of the parties in interest properly joined and served as defendants is a citizen of the State in which such action is brought.

(c) Joinder of Federal law claims and State law claims.—(1) If a civil action includes—

(A) a claim arising under the Constitution, laws, or treaties of the United States (within the meaning of section 1331 of this title), and

(B) a claim not within the original or supplemental jurisdiction of the district court or a claim that has been made nonremovable by statute,

the entire action may be removed if the action would be removable without the inclusion of the claim described in subparagraph (B).

(2) Upon removal of an action described in paragraph (1), the district court shall sever from the action all claims described in paragraph (1)(B) and shall remand the severed claims to the State court from which the action was removed. Only defendants against whom a claim described in paragraph (1)(A) has been asserted are required to join in or consent to the removal under paragraph (1).

(d) Actions against foreign States.—Any civil action brought in a State court against a foreign state as defined in section 1603(a) of this title may be removed by the foreign state to the district court of the United States for the district and division embracing the place where such action is pending. Upon removal the action shall be tried by the court without jury. Where removal is based upon this subsection, the time limitations of section 1446(b) of this chapter may be enlarged at any time for cause shown.

(e) Multiparty, multiforum jurisdiction.—(1) Notwithstanding the provisions of subsection (b) of this section, a defendant in a civil action in a State court may remove the action to the district court of the United States for the district and division embracing the place where the action is pending if—

(A) the action could have been brought in a United States district court under section 1369 of this title; or

(B) the defendant is a party to an action which is or could have been brought, in whole or in part, under section 1369 in a United States district court and arises from the same accident as the action in State court, even if the action to be removed could not have been brought in a district court as an original matter.

The removal of an action under this subsection shall be made in accordance with section 1446 of this title, except that a notice of removal may also be filed before trial of the action in State court within 30 days after the date on which the defendant first becomes a party to an action under section 1369 in a United States district court that arises from the same accident as the action in State court, or at a later time with leave of the district court.

(2) Whenever an action is removed under this subsection and the district court to which it is removed or transferred under section 1407(j)1 has made a liability determination requiring further proceedings as to damages, the district court shall remand the action to the State court from which it had been removed for the determination of damages, unless the court finds that, for the convenience of parties and witnesses and in the interest of justice, the action should be retained for the determination of damages.

(3) Any remand under paragraph (2) shall not be effective until 60 days after the district court has issued an order determining liability and has certified its intention to remand the removed action for the determination of damages. An appeal with respect to the liability determination of the district court may be taken during that 60-day period to the court of appeals with appellate jurisdiction over the district court. In the event a party files such an appeal, the remand shall not be effective until the appeal has been finally disposed of. Once the remand has become effective, the liability determination shall not be subject to further review by appeal or otherwise.

(4) Any decision under this subsection concerning remand for the determination of damages shall not be reviewable by appeal or otherwise.

(5) An action removed under this subsection shall be deemed to be an action under section 1369 and an action in which jurisdiction is based on section 1369 of this title for purposes of this section and sections 1407, 1697, and 1785 of this title.

(6) Nothing in this subsection shall restrict the authority of the district court to transfer or dismiss an action on the ground of inconvenient forum.

(f) Derivative removal jurisdiction.—The court to which a civil action is removed under this section is not precluded from hearing and determining any claim in such civil action because the State court from which such civil action is removed did not have jurisdiction over that claim.

§1442. Federal officers or agencies sued or prosecuted

(a) A civil action or criminal prosecution that is commenced in a State court and that is against or directed to any of the following persons may be removed by them to the district court of the United States for the district and division embracing the place wherein it is pending:

(1) The United States or any agency thereof or any officer (or any person acting under that officer) of the United States or of any agency thereof, in an official or individual capacity, for or relating to any act under color of such office or on account of any right, title or authority claimed under any Act of Congress for the apprehension or punishment of criminals or the collection of the revenue.

(2) A property holder whose title is derived from any such officer, where such action or prosecution affects the validity of any law of the United States.

(3) Any officer of the courts of the United States, for or relating to any act under color of office or in the performance of his duties;

(4) Any officer of either House of Congress, for or relating to any act in the discharge of his official duty under an order of such House.

(b) A personal action commenced in any State court by an alien against any citizen of a State who is, or at the time the alleged action accrued was, a civil officer of the United States and is a nonresident of such State, wherein jurisdiction is obtained by the State court by personal service of process, may be removed by the defendant to the district court of the United States for the district and division in which the defendant was served with process.

(c) Solely for purposes of determining the propriety of removal under subsection (a), a law enforcement officer, who is the defendant in a criminal prosecution, shall be deemed to have been acting under the color of his office if the officer—

(1) protected an individual in the presence of the officer from a crime of violence;

(2) provided immediate assistance to an individual who suffered, or who was threatened with, bodily harm; or

(3) prevented the escape of any individual who the officer reasonably believed to have committed, or was about to commit, in the presence of the officer, a crime of violence that resulted in, or was likely to result in, death or serious bodily injury.

(d) In this section, the following definitions apply:

(1) The terms "civil action" and "criminal prosecution" include any proceeding (whether or not ancillary to another proceeding) to the extent that in such proceeding a judicial order, including a subpoena for testimony or documents, is sought or issued. If removal is sought for a proceeding described in the previous sentence, and there is no other basis for removal, only that proceeding may be removed to the district court.

(2) The term "crime of violence" has the meaning given that term in section 16 of title 18.

(3) The term "law enforcement officer" means any employee described in subparagraph (A), (B), or (C) of section 8401(17) of title 5 and any special agent in the Diplomatic Security Service of the Department of State.

(4) The term "serious bodily injury" has the meaning given that term in section 1365 of title 18.

(5) The term "State" includes the District of Columbia, United States territories and insular possessions, and Indian country (as defined in section 1151 of title 18).

(6) The term "State court" includes the Superior Court of the District of Columbia, a court of a United States territory or insular possession, and a tribal court.

§1442a. Members of armed forces sued or prosecuted

A civil or criminal prosecution in a court of a State of the United States against a member of the armed forces of the United States on account of an act done under color of his office or status, or in respect to which he claims any right, title, or authority under a law of the United States respecting the armed forces thereof, or under the law of war, may at any time before the trial or final hearing thereof be removed for trial into the district court of the United States for the district where it is pending in the manner prescribed by law, and it shall thereupon be entered on the docket of the district court, which shall proceed as if the cause had been originally commenced therein and shall have full power to hear and determine the cause.

§1443. Civil rights cases

Any of the following civil actions or criminal prosecutions, commenced in a State court may be removed by the defendant to the district court of the United States for the district and division embracing the place wherein it is pending:

(1) Against any person who is denied or cannot enforce in the courts of such State a right under any law providing for the equal civil rights of citizens of the United States, or of all persons within the jurisdiction thereof;

(2) For any act under color of authority derived from any law providing for equal rights, or for refusing to do any act on the ground that it would be inconsistent with such law.

§1444. Foreclosure action against United States

Any action brought under section 2410 of this title against the United States in any State court may be removed by the United States to the district court of the United States for the district and division in which the action is pending.

§1445. Nonremovable actions

(a) A civil action in any State court against a railroad or its receivers or trustees, arising under sections 1-4 and 5-10 of the Act of April 22, 1908 (45 U.S.C. 51-54, 55-60), may not be removed to any district court of the United States.

(b) A civil action in any State court against a carrier or its receivers or trustees to recover damages for delay, loss, or injury of shipments, arising under section 11706 or 14706 of title 49, may not be removed to any district court of the United States unless the matter in controversy exceeds $10,000, exclusive of interest and costs.

(c) A civil action in any State court arising under the workmen's compensation laws of such State may not be removed to any district court of the United States.

(d) A civil action in any State court arising under section 40302 of the Violence Against Women Act of 1994 may not be removed to any district court of the United States.

§1446. Procedure for removal of civil actions

(a) Generally.—A defendant or defendants desiring to remove any civil action from a State court shall file in the district court of the United States for the district and division within which such action is pending a notice of removal signed pursuant to Rule 11 of the Federal Rules of Civil Procedure and containing a short and plain statement of the grounds for removal, together with a copy of all process, pleadings, and orders served upon such defendant or defendants in such action.

(b) Requirements; generally.—(1)The notice of removal of a civil action or proceeding shall be filed within 30 days after the receipt by the defendant, through service or otherwise, of a copy of the initial pleading setting forth the claim for relief upon which such action or proceeding is based, or within 30 days after the service of summons upon the defendant if such initial pleading has then been filed in court and is not required to be served on the defendant, whichever period is shorter.

(2) (A) When a civil action is removed solely under section 1441(a), all defendants who have been properly joined and served must join in or consent to the removal of the action.

(B) Each defendant shall have 30 days after receipt by or service on that defendant of the initial pleading or summons described in paragraph (1) to file the notice of removal.

(C) If defendants are served at different times, and a later-served defendant files a notice of removal, any earlier-served defendant may consent to the removal even though that earlier-served defendant did not previously initiate or consent to removal.

(3) Except as provided in subsection (c), if the case stated by the initial pleading is not removable, a notice of removal may be filed within 30 days after receipt by the defendant, through service or otherwise, of a copy of an amended pleading, motion, order or other paper from which it may first be ascertained that the case is one which is or has become removable.

(c) Requirements; removal based on diversity of citizenship.—(1) A case may not be removed under subsection (b)(3) on the basis of jurisdiction conferred by section 1332 more than 1 year after commencement of the action, unless the district court finds that the plaintiff has acted in bad faith in order to prevent a defendant from removing the action.

(2) If removal of a civil action is sought on the basis of the jurisdiction conferred by section 1332(a), the sum demanded in good faith in the initial pleading shall be deemed to be the amount in controversy, except that—

(A) the notice of removal may assert the amount in controversy if the initial pleading seeks—

(i) nonmonetary relief; or

(ii) a money judgment, but the State practice either does not permit demand for a specific sum or permits recovery of damages in excess of the amount demanded; and

(B) removal of the action is proper on the basis of an amount in controversy asserted under subparagraph (A) if the district court finds, by the preponderance of the evidence, that the amount in controversy exceeds the amount specified in section 1332(a).

(3) (A) If the case stated by the initial pleading is not removable solely because the amount in controversy does not exceed the amount specified in section 1332(a), information relating to the amount in controversy in the record of the State proceeding, or in responses to discovery, shall be treated as an "other paper" under subsection (b)(3).

(B) If the notice of removal is filed more than 1 year after commencement of the action and the district court finds that the plaintiff deliberately failed to disclose the actual amount in controversy to prevent removal, that finding shall be deemed bad faith under paragraph (1). (d) Notice to adverse parties and State court.—Promptly after the filing of such notice of removal of a civil action the defendant or defendants shall give written notice thereof to all adverse parties and shall file a copy of the notice with the clerk of such State court, which shall effect the removal and the State court shall proceed no further unless and until the case is remanded.

(e) Counterclaim in 337 proceeding.—respect to any counterclaim removed to a district court pursuant to section 337(c) of the Tariff Act of 1930, the district court shall resolve such counterclaim in the same manner as an original complaint under the Federal Rules of Civil Procedure, except that the payment of a filing fee shall not be required in such cases and the counterclaim shall relate back to the date of the original complaint in the proceeding before the International Trade Commission under section 337 of that Act.

[(f) redesignated (e)]

(g) Where the civil action or criminal prosecution that is removable under section 1442(a) is a proceeding in which a judicial order for testimony or documents is sought or issued or sought to be enforced, the 30-day requirement of subsection (b) of this section and paragraph (1) of section 1455(b) is satisfied if the person or entity desiring to remove the proceeding files the notice of removal not later than 30 days after receiving, through service, notice of any such proceeding.

§1447. Procedure after removal generally

(a) In any case removed from a State court, the district court may issue all necessary orders and process to bring before it all proper parties whether served by process issued by the State court or otherwise.

(b) It may require the removing party to file with its clerk copies of all records and proceedings in such State court or may cause the same to be brought before it by writ of certiorari issued to such State court.

(c) A motion to remand the case on the basis of any defect other than lack of subject matter jurisdiction must be made within 30 days after the filing of the notice of removal under section 1446(a). If at any time before final judgment it appears that the district court lacks subject matter jurisdiction, the case shall be remanded. An order remanding the case may require payment of just costs and any actual expenses, including attorney fees, incurred as a result of the removal. A certified copy of the order of remand shall be mailed by the clerk to the clerk of the State court. The State court may thereupon proceed with such case.

(d) An order remanding a case to the State court from which it was removed is not reviewable on appeal or otherwise, except that an order remanding a case to the State court from which it was removed pursuant to section 1442 or 1443 of this title shall be reviewable by appeal or otherwise.

(e) If after removal the plaintiff seeks to join additional defendants whose joinder would destroy subject matter jurisdiction, the court may deny joinder, or permit joinder and remand the action to the State court.

§1448. Process after removal

In all cases removed from any State court to any district court of the United States in which any one or more of the defendants has not been served with process or in which the service has not been perfected prior to removal, or in which process served proves to be defective, such process or service may be completed or new process issued in the same manner as in cases originally filed in such district court.

This section shall not deprive any defendant upon whom process is served after removal of his right to move to remand the case.

§1449. State court record supplied

Where a party is entitled to copies of the records and proceedings in any suit or prosecution in a State court, to be used in any district court of the United States, and the clerk of such State court, upon demand, and the payment or tender of the legal fees, fails to deliver certified copies, the district court may, on affidavit reciting such facts, direct such record to be supplied by affidavit or otherwise. Thereupon such proceedings, trial, and judgment may be had in such district court, and all such process awarded, as if certified copies had been filed in the district court.

§1450. Attachment or sequestration; securities

Whenever any action is removed from a State court to a district court of the United States, any attachment or sequestration of the goods or estate of the defendant in such action in the State court shall hold the goods or estate to answer the final judgment or decree in the same manner as they would have been held to answer final judgment or decree had it been rendered by the State court.

All bonds, undertakings, or security given by either party in such action prior to its removal shall remain valid and effectual notwithstanding such removal.

All injunctions, orders, and other proceedings had in such action prior to its removal shall remain in full force and effect until dissolved or modified by the district court.

§1451. Definitions

For purposes of this chapter—

(1) The term "State court" includes the Superior Court of the District of Columbia.

(2) The term "State" includes the District of Columbia.

§1452. Removal of claims related to bankruptcy cases

(a) A party may remove any claim or cause of action in a civil action other than a proceeding before the United States Tax Court or a civil action by a governmental unit to enforce such governmental unit's police or regulatory power, to the district court for the district where such civil action is pending, if such district court has jurisdiction of such claim or cause of action under section 1334 of this title.

(b) The court to which such claim or cause of action is removed may remand such claim or cause of action on any equitable ground. An order entered under this subsection remanding a claim or cause of action, or a decision to not remand, is not reviewable by appeal or otherwise by the court of appeals under section 158(d), 1291, or 1292 of this title or by the Supreme Court of the United States under section 1254 of this title.

§1491. Claims against United States generally; actions involving Tennessee Valley Authority

(a) (1) The United States Court of Federal Claims shall have jurisdiction to render judgment upon any claim against the United States founded either upon the Constitution, or any Act of Congress or any regulation of an executive department, or upon any express or implied contract with the United States, or for liquidated or unliquidated damages in cases not sounding in tort. For the purpose of this paragraph, an express or implied contract with the Army and Air Force Exchange Service, Navy Exchanges, Marine Corps Exchanges, Coast Guard Exchanges, or Exchange Councils of the National Aeronautics and Space Administration shall be considered an express or implied contract with the United States.

(2) To provide an entire remedy and to complete the relief afforded by the judgment, the court may, as an incident of and collateral to any such judgment, issue orders directing restoration to office or position, placement in appropriate duty or retirement status, and correction of applicable records, and such orders may be issued to any appropriate official of the United States. In any case within its jurisdiction, the court shall have the power to remand appropriate matters to any administrative or executive body or official with such direction as it may deem proper and just. The Court of Federal Claims shall have jurisdiction to render judgment upon any claim by or against, or dispute with, a contractor arising under section 7104(b)(1) of title 41, including a dispute concerning termination of a contract, rights in tangible or intangible property, compliance with cost accounting standards, and other nonmonetary disputes on which a decision of the contracting officer has been issued under section 61 of that Act.

(b) (1) Both the United States Court of Federal Claims and the district courts of the United States shall have jurisdiction to render judgment on an action by an interested party objecting to a solicitation by a Federal agency for bids or proposals for a proposed contract or to a proposed award or the award of a contract or any alleged violation of statute or regulation in connection with a procurement or a proposed procurement. Both the United States Court of Federal Claims and the district courts of the United States shall have jurisdiction to entertain such an action without regard to whether suit is instituted before or after the contract is awarded.

(2) To afford relief in such an action, the courts may award any relief that the court considers proper, including declaratory and injunctive relief except that any monetary relief shall be limited to bid preparation and proposal costs.

(3) In exercising jurisdiction under this subsection, the courts shall give due regard to the interests of national defense and national security and the need for expeditious resolution of the action.

(4) In any action under this subsection, the courts shall review the agency's decision pursuant to the standards set forth in section 706 of title 5.

(5) If an interested party who is a member of the private sector commences an action described in paragraph (1) with respect to a public-private competition conducted under Office of Management and Budget Circular A-76 regarding the performance of an activity or function of a Federal agency, or a decision to convert a function performed by Federal employees to private sector performance without a competition under Office of Management and Budget Circular A-76, then an interested party described in section 3551(2)(B) of title 31 shall be entitled to intervene in that action.

(6) Jurisdiction over any action described in paragraph (1) arising out of a maritime contract, or a solicitation for a proposed maritime contract, shall be governed by this section and shall not be subject to the jurisdiction of the district courts of the United States under the Suits in Admiralty Act (chapter 309 of title 46) or the Public Vessels Act (chapter 311 of title 46).

(c) Nothing herein shall be construed to give the United States Court of Federal Claims jurisdiction of any civil action within the exclusive jurisdiction of the Court of International Trade, or of any action against, or founded on conduct of, the Tennessee Valley Authority, or to amend or modify the provisions of the Tennessee Valley Authority Act of 1933 with respect to actions by or against the Authority.

§1492. Congressional reference cases

Any bill, except a bill for a pension, may be referred by either House of Congress to the chief judge of the United States Court of Federal Claimsfor a report in conformity with section 2509 of this title.

§1495. Damages for unjust conviction and imprisonment; claim against United States

The United States Court of Federal Claims shall have jurisdiction to render judgment upon any claim for damages by any person unjustly convicted of an offense against the United States and imprisoned.

§1500. Pendency of claims in other courts

The United States Court of Federal Claims shall not have jurisdiction of any claim for or in respect to which the plaintiff or his assignee has pending in any other court any suit or process against the United States or any person who, at the time when the cause of action alleged in such suit or process arose, was, in respect thereto, acting or professing to act, directly or indirectly under the authority of the United States.

§1501. Pensions

The United States Court of Federal Claims shall not have jurisdiction of any claim for a pension.

§1658. Time limitations on the commencement of civil actions

§1502. Treaty cases

Except as otherwise provided by Act of Congress, the United States Court of Federal Claims shall not have jurisdiction of any claim against the United States growing out of or dependent upon any treaty entered into with foreign nations.

§1651. Writs

(a) The Supreme Court and all courts established by Act of Congress may issue all writs necessary or appropriate in aid of their respective jurisdictions and agreeable to the usages and principles of law.

(b) An alternative writ or rule nisi may be issued by a justice or judge of a court which has jurisdiction.

§1652. State laws as rules of decision

The laws of the several states, except where the Constitution or treaties of the United States or Acts of Congress otherwise require or provide, shall be regarded as rules of decision in civil actions in the courts of the United States, in cases where they apply.

§1653. Amendment of pleadings to show jurisdiction

Defective allegations of jurisdiction may be amended, upon terms, in the trial or appellate courts.

§1657. Priority of civil actions

(a) Notwithstanding any other provision of law, each court of the United States shall determine the order in which civil actions are heard and determined, except that the court shall expedite the consideration of any action brought under chapter 153 or section 1826 of this title, any action for temporary or preliminary injunctive relief, or any other action if good cause therefor is shown. For purposes of this subsection, "good cause" is shown if a right under the Constitution of the United States or a Federal Statute (including rights under section 552 of title 5) would be maintained in a factual context that indicates that a request for expedited consideration has merit.

(b) The Judicial Conference of the United States may modify the rules adopted by the courts to determine the order in which civil actions are heard and determined, in order to establish consistency among the judicial circuits.

§1658. Time limitations on the commencement of civil actions arising under Acts of Congress

(a) Except as otherwise provided by law, a civil action arising under an Act of Congress enacted after the date of the enactment of this section may not be commenced later than 4 years after the cause of action accrues.

(b) Notwithstanding subsection (a), a private right of action that involves a claim of fraud, deceit, manipulation, or contrivance in contravention of a regulatory requirement concerning the securities laws, as defined in section 3(a)(47) of the Securities Exchange Act of 1934 (15 U.S.C. 78c(a)(47)), may be brought not later than the earlier of—

(1) 2 years after the discovery of the facts constituting the violation; or

(2) 5 years after such violation.

§2071. Rule-making power generally

(a) The Supreme Court and all courts established by Act of Congress may from time to time prescribe rules for the conduct of their business. Such rules shall be consistent with Acts of Congress and rules of practice and procedure prescribed under section 2072 of this title.

(b) Any rule prescribed by a court, other than the Supreme Court, under subsection (a) shall be prescribed only after giving appropriate public notice and an opportunity for comment. Such rule shall take effect upon the date specified by the prescribing court and shall have such effect on pending proceedings as the prescribing court may order.

(c) (1) A rule of a district court prescribed under subsection (a) shall remain in effect unless modified or abrogated by the judicial council of the relevant circuit.

(2) Any other rule prescribed by a court other than the Supreme Court under subsection (a) shall remain in effect unless modified or abrogated by the Judicial Conference.

(d) Copies of rules prescribed under subsection (a) by a district court shall be furnished to the judicial council, and copies of all rules prescribed by a court other than the Supreme Court under subsection (a) shall be furnished to the Director of the Administrative Office of the United States Courts and made available to the public.

(e) If the prescribing court determines that there is an immediate need for a rule, such court may proceed under this section without public notice and opportunity for comment, but such court shall promptly thereafter afford such notice and opportunity for comment.

(f) No rule may be prescribed by a district court other than under this section.

§2072. Rules of procedure and evidence; power to prescribe

(a) The Supreme Court shall have the power to prescribe general rules of practice and procedure and rules of evidence for cases in the United States district courts (including proceedings before magistrate judges thereof) and courts of appeals.

(b) Such rules shall not abridge, enlarge or modify any substantive right. All laws in conflict with such rules shall be of no further force or effect after such rules have taken effect.

(c) Such rules may define when a ruling of a district court is final for the purposes of appeal under section 1291 of this title.

§2241. Power to grant writ

§2241. Power to grant writ

(a) Writs of habeas corpus may be granted by the Supreme Court, any justice thereof, the district courts and any circuit judge within their respective jurisdictions. The order of a circuit judge shall be entered in the records of the district court of the district wherein the restraint complained of is had.

(b) The Supreme Court, any justice thereof, and any circuit judge may decline to entertain an application for a writ of habeas corpus and may transfer the application for hearing and determination to the district court having jurisdiction to entertain it.

(c) The writ of habeas corpus shall not extend to a prisoner unless—

(1) He is in custody under or by color of the authority of the United States or is committed for trial before some court thereof; or

(2) He is in custody for an act done or omitted in pursuance of an Act of Congress, or an order, process, judgment or decree of a court or judge of the United States; or

(3) He is in custody in violation of the Constitution or laws or treaties of the United States; or

(4) He, being a citizen of a foreign state and domiciled therein is in custody for an act done or omitted under any alleged right, title, authority, privilege, protection, or exemption claimed under the commission, order or sanction of any foreign state, or under color thereof, the validity and effect of which depend upon the law of nations; or

(5) It is necessary to bring him into court to testify or for trial.

(d) Where an application for a writ of habeas corpus is made by a person in custody under the judgment and sentence of a State court of a State which contains two or more Federal judicial districts, the application may be filed in the district court for the district wherein such person is in custody or in the district court for the district within which the State court was held which convicted and sentenced him and each of such district courts shall have concurrent jurisdiction to entertain the application. The district court for the district wherein such an application is filed in the exercise of its discretion and in furtherance of justice may transfer the application to the other district court for hearing and determination.

(e) (1) No court, justice, or judge shall have jurisdiction to hear or consider an application for a writ of habeas corpus filed by or on behalf of an alien detained by the United States who has been determined by the United States to have been properly detained as an enemy combatant or is awaiting such determination.

(2) Except as provided in paragraphs (2) and (3) of section 1005(e) of the Detainee Treatment Act of 2005 (10 U.S.C. 801 note), no court, justice, or judge shall have jurisdiction to hear or consider any other action against the United States or its agents relating to any aspect of the detention, transfer, treatment, trial, or conditions of confinement of an alien who is or was detained by the United States and has been determined by the United States to have been properly detained as an enemy combatant or is awaiting such determination.

§2242. Application

Application for a writ of habeas corpus shall be in writing signed and verified by the person for whose relief it is intended or by someone acting in his behalf.

It shall allege the facts concerning the applicant's commitment or detention, the name of the person who has custody over him and by virtue of what claim or authority, if known.

It may be amended or supplemented as provided in the rules of procedure applicable to civil actions.

If addressed to the Supreme Court, a justice thereof or a circuit judge it shall state the reasons for not making application to the district court of the district in which the applicant is held.

§2243. Issuance of writ; return; hearing; decision

A court, justice or judge entertaining an application for a writ of habeas corpus shall forthwith award the writ or issue an order directing the respondent to show cause why the writ should not be granted, unless it appears from the application that the applicant or person detained is not entitled thereto.

The writ, or order to show cause shall be directed to the person having custody of the person detained. It shall be returned within three days unless for good cause additional time, not exceeding twenty days, is allowed.

The person to whom the writ or order is directed shall make a return certifying the true cause of the detention.

When the writ or order is returned a day shall be set for hearing, not more than five days after the return unless for good cause additional time is allowed.

Unless the application for the writ and the return present only issues of law the person to whom the writ is directed shall be required to produce at the hearing the body of the person detained.

The applicant or the person detained may, under oath, deny any of the facts set forth in the return or allege any other material facts.

The return and all suggestions made against it may be amended, by leave of court, before or after being filed.

The court shall summarily hear and determine the facts, and dispose of the matter as law and justice require.

§2244. Finality of determination

(a) No circuit or district judge shall be required to entertain an application for a writ of habeas corpus to inquire into the detention of a person pursuant to a judgment of a court of the United States if it appears that the legality of such detention has been determined by a judge or court of the United States on a prior application for a writ of habeas corpus, except as provided in section 2255.

(b) (1) A claim presented in a second or successive habeas corpus application under section 2254 that was presented in a prior application shall be dismissed.

(2) A claim presented in a second or successive habeas corpus application under section 2254 that was not presented in a prior application shall be dismissed unless—

(A) the applicant shows that the claim relies on a new rule of constitutional law, made retroactive to cases on collateral review by the Supreme Court, that was previously unavailable; or

(B) (i) the factual predicate for the claim could not have been discovered previously through the exercise of due diligence; and

(ii) the facts underlying the claim, if proven and viewed in light of the evidence as a whole, would be sufficient to establish by clear and convincing evidence that, but for constitutional error, no reasonable factfinder would have found the applicant guilty of the underlying offense.

(3) (A) Before a second or successive application permitted by this section is filed in the district court, the applicant shall move in the appropriate court of appeals for an order authorizing the district court to consider the application.

(B) A motion in the court of appeals for an order authorizing the district court to consider a second or successive application shall be determined by a three-judge panel of the court of appeals.

(C) The court of appeals may authorize the filing of a second or successive application only if it determines that the application makes a prima facie showing that the application satisfies the requirements of this subsection.

(D) The court of appeals shall grant or deny the authorization to file a second or successive application not later than 30 days after the filing of the motion.

(E) The grant or denial of an authorization by a court of appeals to file a second or successive application shall not be appealable and shall not be the subject of a petition for rehearing or for a writ of certiorari.

(4) A district court shall dismiss any claim presented in a second or successive application that the court of appeals has authorized to be filed unless the applicant shows that the claim satisfies the requirements of this section.

(c) In a habeas corpus proceeding brought in behalf of a person in custody pursuant to the judgment of a State court, a prior judgment of the Supreme Court of the United States on an appeal or review by a writ of certiorari at the instance of the prisoner of the decision of such State court, shall be conclusive as to all issues of fact or law with respect to an asserted denial of a Federal right which constitutes ground for discharge in a habeas corpus proceeding, actually adjudicated by the Supreme Court therein, unless the applicant for the writ of habeas corpus shall plead and the court shall find the existence of a material and controlling fact which did not appear in the record of the proceeding in the Supreme Court and the court shall further find that the applicant for the writ of habeas corpus could not have caused such fact to appear in such record by the exercise of reasonable diligence.

(d) (1) A 1-year period of limitation shall apply to an application for a writ of habeas corpus by a person in custody pursuant to the judgment of a State court. The limitation period shall run from the latest of—

(A) the date on which the judgment became final by the conclusion of direct review or the expiration of the time for seeking such review;

(B) the date on which the impediment to filing an application created by State action in violation of the Constitution or laws of the United States is removed, if the applicant was prevented from filing by such State action;

(C) the date on which the constitutional right asserted was initially recognized by the Supreme Court, if the right has been newly recognized by the Supreme Court and made retroactively applicable to cases on collateral review; or

(D) the date on which the factual predicate of the claim or claims presented could have been discovered through the exercise of due diligence.

(2) The time during which a properly filed application for State post-conviction or other collateral review with respect to the pertinent judgment or claim is pending shall not be counted toward any period of limitation under this subsection.

§2245. Certificate of trial judge admissible in evidence

On the hearing of an application for a writ of habeas corpus to inquire into the legality of the detention of a person pursuant to a judgment the certificate of the judge who presided at the trial resulting in the judgment, setting forth the facts occurring at the trial, shall be admissible in evidence. Copies of the certificate shall be filed with the court in which the application is pending and in the court in which the trial took place.

§2246. Evidence; depositions; affidavits

On application for a writ of habeas corpus, evidence may be taken orally or by deposition, or, in the discretion of the judge, by affidavit. If affidavits are admitted any party shall have the right to propound written interrogatories to the affiants, or to file answering affidavits.

§2247. Documentary evidence

On application for a writ of habeas corpus documentary evidence, transcripts of proceedings upon arraignment, plea and sentence and a transcript of the oral testimony introduced on any previous similar application by or in behalf of the same petitioner, shall be admissible in evidence.

§2248. Return or answer; conclusiveness

The allegations of a return to the writ of habeas corpus or of an answer to an order to show cause in a habeas corpus proceeding, if not traversed, shall be accepted as true except to the extent that the judge finds from the evidence that they are not true.

§2249. Certified copies of indictment, plea and judgment; duty of respondent

On application for a writ of habeas corpus to inquire into the detention of any person pursuant to a judgment of a court of the United States, the respondent shall promptly file with the court certified copies of the indictment, plea of petitioner and the judgment, or such of them as may be material to the questions raised, if the petitioner fails to attach them to his petition, and same shall be attached to the return to the writ, or to the answer to the order to show cause.

§2250. Indigent petitioner entitled to documents without cost

If on any application for a writ of habeas corpus an order has been made permitting the petitioner to prosecute the application in forma pauperis, the clerk of any court of the United States shall furnish to the petitioner without cost certified copies of such documents or parts of the record on file in his office as may be required by order of the judge before whom the application is pending.

§2251. Stay of State court proceedings

(a) In general.—

(1) Pending matters.—A justice or judge of the United States before whom a habeas corpus proceeding is pending, may, before final judgment or after final judgment of discharge, or pending appeal, stay any proceeding against the person detained in any State court or by or under the authority of any State for any matter involved in the habeas corpus proceeding.

(2) Matter not pending.—For purposes of this section, a habeas corpus proceeding is not pending until the application is filed.

(3) Application for appointment of counsel.—If a State prisoner sentenced to death applies for appointment of counsel pursuant to section 3599(a)(2) of title 18 in a court that would have jurisdiction to entertain a habeas corpus application regarding that sentence, that court may stay execution of the sentence of death, but such stay shall terminate not later than 90 days after counsel is appointed or the application for appointment of counsel is withdrawn or denied.

(b) No further proceedings.—After the granting of such a stay, any such proceeding in any State court or by or under the authority of any State shall be void. If no stay is granted, any such proceeding shall be as valid as if no habeas corpus proceedings or appeal were pending.

§2252. Notice

Prior to the hearing of a habeas corpus proceeding in behalf of a person in custody of State officers or by virtue of State laws notice shall be served on the attorney general or other appropriate officer of such State as the justice or judge at the time of issuing the writ shall direct.

§2253. Appeal

(a) In a habeas corpus proceeding or a proceeding under section 2255 before a district judge, the final order shall be subject to review, on appeal, by the court of appeals for the circuit in which the proceeding is held.

(b) There shall be no right of appeal from a final order in a proceeding to test the validity of a warrant to remove to another district or place for commitment or trial a person charged with a criminal offense against the United States, or to test the validity of such person's detention pending removal proceedings.

(c) (1) Unless a circuit justice or judge issues a certificate of appealability, an appeal may not be taken to the court of appeals from—

(A) the final order in a habeas corpus proceeding in which the detention complained of arises out of process issued by a State court; or

(B) the final order in a proceeding under section 2255.

(2) A certificate of appealability may issue under paragraph (1) only if the applicant has made a substantial showing of the denial of a constitutional right.

(3) The certificate of appealability under paragraph (1) shall indicate which specific issue or issues satisfy the showing required by paragraph (2).

§2254. State custody; remedies in Federal courts

(a) The Supreme Court, a Justice thereof, a circuit judge, or a district court shall entertain an application for a writ of habeas corpus in behalf of a person in custody pursuant to the judgment of a State court only on the ground that he is in custody in violation of the Constitution or laws or treaties of the United States.

(b) (1) An application for a writ of habeas corpus on behalf of a person in custody pursuant to the judgment of a State court shall not be granted unless it appears that—

(A) the applicant has exhausted the remedies available in the courts of the State; or

(B) (i) there is an absence of available State corrective process; or

(ii) circumstances exist that render such process ineffective to protect the rights of the applicant.

(2) An application for a writ of habeas corpus may be denied on the merits, notwithstanding the failure of the applicant to exhaust the remedies available in the courts of the State.

(3) A State shall not be deemed to have waived the exhaustion requirement or be estopped from reliance upon the requirement unless the State, through counsel, expressly waives the requirement.

(c) An applicant shall not be deemed to have exhausted the remedies available in the courts of the State, within the meaning of this section, if he has the right under the law of the State to raise, by any available procedure, the question presented.

(d) An application for a writ of habeas corpus on behalf of a person in custody pursuant to the judgment of a State court shall not be granted with respect to any claim that was adjudicated on the merits in State court proceedings unless the adjudication of the claim—

(1) resulted in a decision that was contrary to, or involved an unreasonable application of, clearly established Federal law, as determined by the Supreme Court of the United States; or

(2) resulted in a decision that was based on an unreasonable determination of the facts in light of the evidence presented in the State court proceeding.

(e) (1) In a proceeding instituted by an application for a writ of habeas corpus by a person in custody pursuant to the judgment of a State court, a determination of a factual issue made by a State court shall be presumed to be correct. The applicant shall have the burden of rebutting the presumption of correctness by clear and convincing evidence.

(2) If the applicant has failed to develop the factual basis of a claim in State court proceedings, the court shall not hold an evidentiary hearing on the claim unless the applicant shows that—

(A) the claim relies on—

(i) a new rule of constitutional law, made retroactive to cases on collateral review by the Supreme Court, that was previously unavailable; or

(ii) a factual predicate that could not have been previously discovered through the exercise of due diligence; and

(B) the facts underlying the claim would be sufficient to establish by clear and convincing evidence that but for constitutional error, no reasonable factfinder would have found the applicant guilty of the underlying offense.

(f) If the applicant challenges the sufficiency of the evidence adduced in such State court proceeding to support the State court's determination of a factual issue made therein, the applicant, if able, shall produce that part of the record pertinent to a determination of the sufficiency of the evidence to support such determination. If the applicant, because of indigency or other reason is unable to produce such part of the record, then the State shall produce such part of the record and the Federal court shall direct the State to do so by order directed to an appropriate State official. If the State cannot provide such pertinent part of the record, then the court shall determine under the existing facts and circumstances what weight shall be given to the State court's factual determination.

(g) A copy of the official records of the State court, duly certified by the clerk of such court to be a true and correct copy of a finding, judicial opinion, or other reliable written indicia showing such a factual determination by the State court shall be admissible in the Federal court proceeding.

(h) Except as provided in section 408 of the Controlled Substances Act, in all proceedings brought under this section, and any subsequent proceedings on review, the court may appoint counsel for an applicant who is or becomes financially unable to afford counsel, except as provided by a rule promulgated by the Supreme Court pursuant to statutory authority. Appointment of counsel under this section shall be governed by section 3006A of title 18.

(i) The ineffectiveness or incompetence of counsel during Federal or State collateral post-conviction proceedings shall not be a ground for relief in a proceeding arising under section 2254.

§2255. Federal custody; remedies on motion attacking sentence

(a) A prisoner in custody under sentence of a court established by Act of Congress claiming the right to be released upon the ground that the sentence was imposed in violation of the Constitution or laws of the United States, or that the court was without jurisdiction to impose such sentence, or that the sentence was in excess of the maximum authorized by law, or is otherwise subject to collateral attack, may move the court which imposed the sentence to vacate, set aside or correct the sentence.

(b) Unless the motion and the files and records of the case conclusively show that the prisoner is entitled to no relief, the court shall cause notice thereof to be served upon the United States attorney, grant a prompt hearing thereon, determine the issues and make findings of fact and conclusions of law with respect thereto. If the court finds that the judgment was rendered without jurisdiction, or that the sentence imposed was not authorized by law or otherwise open to collateral attack, or that there has been such a denial or infringement of the constitutional rights of the prisoner as to render the judgment vulnerable to collateral attack, the court shall vacate and set the judgment aside and shall discharge the prisoner or resentence him or grant a new trial or correct the sentence as may appear appropriate.

(c) A court may entertain and determine such motion without requiring the production of the prisoner at the hearing.

(d) An appeal may be taken to the court of appeals from the order entered on the motion as from a final judgment on application for a writ of habeas corpus.

(e) An application for a writ of habeas corpus in behalf of a prisoner who is authorized to apply for relief by motion pursuant to this section, shall not be entertained if it appears that the applicant has failed to apply for relief, by motion, to the court which sentenced him, or that such court has denied him relief, unless it also appears that the remedy by motion is inadequate or ineffective to test the legality of his detention.

(f) A 1-year period of limitation shall apply to a motion under this section. The limitation period shall run from the latest of—

(1) the date on which the judgment of conviction becomes final;

(2) the date on which the impediment to making a motion created by governmental action in violation of the Constitution or laws of the United States is removed, if the movant was prevented from making a motion by such governmental action;

(3) the date on which the right asserted was initially recognized by the Supreme Court, if that right has been newly recognized by the Supreme Court and made retroactively applicable to cases on collateral review; or

(4) the date on which the facts supporting the claim or claims presented could have been discovered through the exercise of due diligence.

(g) Except as provided in section 408 of the Controlled Substances Act, in all proceedings brought under this section, and any subsequent proceedings on review, the court may appoint counsel, except as provided by a rule promulgated by the Supreme Court pursuant to statutory authority. Appointment of counsel under this section shall be governed by section 3006A of title 18.

(h) A second or successive motion must be certified as provided in section 2244 by a panel of the appropriate court of appeals to contain—

(1) newly discovered evidence that, if proven and viewed in light of the evidence as a whole, would be sufficient to establish by clear and convincing evidence that no reasonable factfinder would have found the movant guilty of the offense; or

(2) a new rule of constitutional law, made retroactive to cases on collateral review by the Supreme Court, that was previously unavailable.

§2261. Prisoners in State custody subject to capital sentence; appointment of counsel; requirement of rule of court or statute; procedures for appointment

(a) This chapter shall apply to cases arising under section 2254 brought by prisoners in State custody who are subject to a capital sentence. It shall apply only if the provisions of subsections (b) and (c) are satisfied.

(b) Counsel.—This chapter is applicable if—

(1) the Attorney General of the United States certifies that a State has established a mechanism for providing counsel in postconviction proceedings as provided in section 2265; and

(2) counsel was appointed pursuant to that mechanism, petitioner validly waived counsel, petitioner retained counsel, or petitioner was found not to be indigent.

(c) Any mechanism for the appointment, compensation, and reimbursement of counsel as provided in subsection (b) must offer counsel to all State prisoners under capital sentence and must provide for the entry of an order by a court of record—

(1) appointing one or more counsels to represent the prisoner upon a finding that the prisoner is indigent and accepted the offer or is unable competently to decide whether to accept or reject the offer;

(2) finding, after a hearing if necessary, that the prisoner rejected the offer of counsel and made the decision with an understanding of its legal consequences; or

(3) denying the appointment of counsel upon a finding that the prisoner is not indigent.

(d) No counsel appointed pursuant to subsections (b) and (c) to represent a State prisoner under capital sentence shall have previously represented the prisoner at trial in the case for which the appointment is made unless the prisoner and counsel expressly request continued representation.

(e) The ineffectiveness or incompetence of counsel during State or Federal post-conviction proceedings in a capital case shall not be a ground for relief in a proceeding arising under section 2254. This limitation shall not preclude the appointment of different counsel, on the court's own motion or at the request of the prisoner, at any phase of State or Federal post-conviction proceedings on the basis of the ineffectiveness or incompetence of counsel in such proceedings.

§2262. Mandatory stay of execution; duration; limits on stays of execution; successive petitions

(a) Upon the entry in the appropriate State court of record of an order under section 2261(c), a warrant or order setting an execution date for a State prisoner shall be stayed upon application to any court that would have jurisdiction over any proceedings filed under section 2254. The application shall recite that the State has invoked the post-conviction review procedures of this chapter and that the scheduled execution is subject to stay.

(b) A stay of execution granted pursuant to subsection (a) shall expire if—

(1) a State prisoner fails to file a habeas corpus application under section 2254 within the time required in section 2263;

(2) before a court of competent jurisdiction, in the presence of counsel, unless the prisoner has competently and knowingly waived such counsel, and after having been advised of the consequences, a State prisoner under capital sentence waives the right to pursue habeas corpus review under section 2254; or

(3) a State prisoner files a habeas corpus petition under section 2254 within the time required by section 2263 and fails to make a substantial showing of the denial of a Federal right or is denied relief in the district court or at any subsequent stage of review.

(c) If one of the conditions in subsection (b) has occurred, no Federal court thereafter shall have the authority to enter a stay of execution in the case, unless the court of appeals approves the filing of a second or successive application under section 2244(b).

§2263. Filing of habeas corpus application; time requirements; tolling rules

(a) Any application under this chapter for habeas corpus relief under section 2254 must be filed in the appropriate district court not later than 180 days after final State court affirmance of the conviction and sentence on direct review or the expiration of the time for seeking such review.

(b) The time requirements established by subsection (a) shall be tolled—

(1) from the date that a petition for certiorari is filed in the Supreme Court until the date of final disposition of the petition if a State prisoner files the petition to secure review by the Supreme Court of the affirmance of a capital sentence on direct review by the court of last resort of the State or other final State court decision on direct review;

(2) from the date on which the first petition for post-conviction review or other collateral relief is filed until the final State court disposition of such petition; and

(3) during an additional period not to exceed 30 days, if—

(A) a motion for an extension of time is filed in the Federal district court that would have jurisdiction over the case upon the filing of a habeas corpus application under section 2254; and

(B) a showing of good cause is made for the failure to file the habeas corpus application within the time period established by this section.

§2264. Scope of Federal review; district court adjudications

(a) Whenever a State prisoner under capital sentence files a petition for habeas corpus relief to which this chapter applies, the district court shall only consider a claim or claims that have been raised and decided on the merits in the State courts, unless the failure to raise the claim properly is—

(1) the result of State action in violation of the Constitution or laws of the United States;

(2) the result of the Supreme Court's recognition of a new Federal right that is made retroactively applicable; or

(3) based on a factual predicate that could not have been discovered through the exercise of due diligence in time to present the claim for State or Federal post-conviction review.

(b) Following review subject to subsections (a), (d), and (e) of section 2254, the court shall rule on the claims properly before it.

§2265. Certification and judicial review

(a) Certification.—

(1) In general.—If requested by an appropriate State official, the Attorney General of the United States shall determine—

(A) whether the State has established a mechanism for the appointment, compensation, and payment of reasonable litigation expenses of competent counsel in State postconviction proceedings brought by indigent prisoners who have been sentenced to death;

(B) the date on which the mechanism described in subparagraph (A) was established; and

(C) whether the State provides standards of competency for the appointment of counsel in proceedings described in subparagraph (A).

(2) Effective date.—The date the mechanism described in paragraph (1)(A) was established shall be the effective date of the certification under this subsection.

(3) Only express requirements.—There are no requirements for certification or for application of this chapter other than those expressly stated in this chapter.

(b) Regulations.—The Attorney General shall promulgate regulations to implement the certification procedure under subsection (a).

(c) Review of certification.—

(1) In general.—The determination by the Attorney General regarding whether to certify a State under this section is subject to review exclusively as provided under chapter 158 of this title.

(2) Venue.—The Court of Appeals for the District of Columbia Circuit shall have exclusive jurisdiction over matters under paragraph (1), subject to review by the Supreme Court under section 2350 of this title.

(3) Standard of review.—The determination by the Attorney General regarding whether to certify a State under this section shall be subject to de novo review.

§2266. Limitation periods for determining applications and motions

(a) The adjudication of any application under section 2254 that is subject to this chapter, and the adjudication of any motion under section 2255 by a person under sentence of death, shall be given priority by the district court and by the court of appeals over all noncapital matters.

(b) (1) (A) A district court shall render a final determination and enter a final judgment on any application for a writ of habeas corpus brought under this chapter in a capital case not later than 450 days after the date on which the application is filed, or 60 days after the date on which the case is submitted for decision, whichever is earlier.

(B) A district court shall afford the parties at least 120 days in which to complete all actions, including the preparation of all pleadings and briefs, and if necessary, a hearing, prior to the submission of the case for decision.

(C) (i) A district court may delay for not more than one additional 30-day period beyond the period specified in subparagraph (A), the rendering of a determination of an application for a writ of habeas corpus if the court issues a written order making a finding, and stating the reasons for the finding, that the ends of justice that would be served by allowing the delay outweigh the best interests of the public and the applicant in a speedy disposition of the application.

(ii) The factors, among others, that a court shall consider in determining whether a delay in the disposition of an application is warranted are as follows:

(I) Whether the failure to allow the delay would be likely to result in a miscarriage of justice.

(II) Whether the case is so unusual or so complex, due to the number of defendants, the nature of the prosecution, or the existence of novel questions of fact or law, that it is unreasonable to expect adequate briefing within the time limitations established by subparagraph (A).

(III) Whether the failure to allow a delay in a case that, taken as a whole, is not so unusual or so complex as described in subclause (II), but would otherwise deny the applicant reasonable time to obtain counsel, would unreasonably deny the applicant or the government continuity of counsel, or would deny counsel for the applicant or the government the reasonable time necessary for effective preparation, taking into account the exercise of due diligence.

(iii) No delay in disposition shall be permissible because of general congestion of the court's calendar.

(iv) The court shall transmit a copy of any order issued under clause (i) to the Director of the Administrative Office of the United States Courts for inclusion in the report under paragraph (5).

(2) The time limitations under paragraph (1) shall apply to—

(A) an initial application for a writ of habeas corpus;

(B) any second or successive application for a writ of habeas corpus; and

(C) any redetermination of an application for a writ of habeas corpus following a remand by the court of appeals or the Supreme Court for further proceedings, in which case the limitation period shall run from the date the remand is ordered.

(3) (A) The time limitations under this section shall not be construed to entitle an applicant to a stay of execution, to which the applicant would otherwise not be entitled, for the purpose of litigating any application or appeal.

(B) No amendment to an application for a writ of habeas corpus under this chapter shall be permitted after the filing of the answer to the application, except on the grounds specified in section 2244(b).

(4) (A) The failure of a court to meet or comply with a time limitation under this section shall not be a ground for granting relief from a judgment of conviction or sentence.

(B) The State may enforce a time limitation under this section by petitioning for a writ of mandamus to the court of appeals. The court of appeals shall act on the petition for a writ of mandamus not later than 30 days after the filing of the petition.

(5) (A) The Administrative Office of the United States Courts shall submit to Congress an annual report on the compliance by the district courts with the time limitations under this section.

(B) The report described in subparagraph (A) shall include copies of the orders submitted by the district courts under paragraph (1)(B)(iv).

(c) (1)(A) A court of appeals shall hear and render a final determination of any appeal of an order granting or denying, in whole or in part, an application brought under this chapter in a capital case not later than 120 days after the date on which the reply brief is filed, or if no reply brief is filed, not later than 120 days after the date on which the answering brief is filed.

(B) (i) A court of appeals shall decide whether to grant a petition for rehearing or other request for rehearing en banc not later than 30 days after the date on which the petition for rehearing is filed unless a responsive pleading is required, in which case the court shall decide whether to grant the petition not later than 30 days after the date on which the responsive pleading is filed.

(ii) If a petition for rehearing or rehearing en banc is granted, the court of appeals shall hear and render a final determination of the appeal not later than 120 days after the date on which the order granting rehearing or rehearing en banc is entered.

(2) The time limitations under paragraph (1) shall apply to—

(A) an initial application for a writ of habeas corpus;

(B) any second or successive application for a writ of habeas corpus; and

(C) any redetermination of an application for a writ of habeas corpus or related appeal following a remand by the court of appeals en banc or the Supreme Court for further proceedings, in which case the limitation period shall run from the date the remand is ordered.

(3) The time limitations under this section shall not be construed to entitle an applicant to a stay of execution, to which the applicant would otherwise not be entitled, for the purpose of litigating any application or appeal.

(4) (A) The failure of a court to meet or comply with a time limitation under this section shall not be a ground for granting relief from a judgment of conviction or sentence.

(B) The State may enforce a time limitation under this section by applying for a writ of mandamus to the Supreme Court.

(5) The Administrative Office of the United States Courts shall submit to Congress an annual report on the compliance by the courts of appeals with the time limitations under this section.

CHAPTER 155—INJUNCTIONS; THREE-JUDGE COURTS

Sec.

§2283. Stay of State court proceedings

A court of the United States may not grant an injunction to stay proceedings in a State court except as expressly authorized by Act of Congress, or where necessary in aid of its jurisdiction, or to protect or effectuate its judgments.

§2284. Three-judge court; when required; composition; procedure

(a) A district court of three judges shall be convened when otherwise required by Act of Congress, or when an action is filed challenging the constitutionality of the apportionment of congressional districts or the apportionment of any statewide legislative body.

(b) In any action required to be heard and determined by a district court of three judges under subsection (a) of this section, the composition and procedure of the court shall be as follows:

(1) Upon the filing of a request for three judges, the judge to whom the request is presented shall, unless he determines that three judges are not required, immediately notify the chief judge of the circuit, who shall designate two other judges, at least one of whom shall be a circuit judge. The judges so designated, and the judge to whom the request was presented, shall serve as members of the court to hear and determine the action or proceeding.

(2) If the action is against a State, or officer or agency thereof, at least five days' notice of hearing of the action shall be given by registered or certified mail to the Governor and attorney general of the State.

(3) A single judge may conduct all proceedings except the trial, and enter all orders permitted by the rules of civil procedure except as provided in this subsection. He may grant a temporary restraining order on a specific finding, based on evidence submitted, that specified irreparable damage will result if the order is not granted, which order, unless previously revoked by the district judge, shall remain in force only until the hearing and determination by the district court of

three judges of an application for a preliminary injunction. A single judge shall not appoint a master, or order a reference, or hear and determine any application for a preliminary or permanent injunction or motion to vacate such an injunction, or enter judgment on the merits. Any action of a single judge may be reviewed by the full court at any time before final judgment.

§2671. Definitions

As used in this chapter and sections 1346(b) and 2401(b) of this title, the term

"Federal agency" includes the executive departments, the judicial and legislative branches, the military departments, independent establishments of the United States, and corporations primarily acting as instrumentalities or agencies of the United States, but does not include any contractor with the United States.

"Employee of the government" includes (1) officers or employees of any federal agency, members of the military or naval forces of the United States, members of the National Guard while engaged in training or duty under section 115, 316, 502, 503, 504, or 505 of title 32, and persons acting on behalf of a federal agency in an official capacity, temporarily or permanently in the service of the United States, whether with or without compensation, and (2) any officer or employee of a Federal public defender organization, except when such officer or employee performs professional services in the course of providing representation under section 3006A of title 18.

"Acting within the scope of his office or employment", in the case of a member of the military or naval forces of the United States or a member of the National Guard as defined in section 101(3) of title 32, means acting in line of duty.

§2672. Administrative adjustment of claims

The head of each Federal agency or his designee, in accordance with regulations prescribed by the Attorney General, may consider, ascertain, adjust, determine, compromise, and settle any claim for money damages against the United States for injury or loss of property or personal injury or death caused by the negligent or wrongful act or omission of any employee of the agency while acting within the scope of his office or employment, under circumstances where the United States, if a private person, would be liable to the claimant in accordance with the law of the place where the act or omission occurred: Provided, That any award, compromise, or settlement in excess of $25,000 shall be effected only with the prior written approval of the Attorney General or his designee.

Notwithstanding the proviso contained in the preceding sentence, any award, compromise, or settlement may be effected without the prior written approval of the Attorney General or his or her designee, to the extent that the Attorney General delegates to the head of the agency the authority to make such award, compromise, or settlement. Such delegations may not exceed the authority delegated by the Attorney General to the United States attorneys to settle claims for money damages against the United States. Each Federal agency may use arbitration, or other alternative means of dispute resolution under the provisions of subchapter IV of chapter 5 of title 5, to settle any tort claim against the United States, to the extent of the agency's authority to award, compromise, or settle such claim without the prior written approval of the Attorney General or his or her designee.

Subject to the provisions of this title relating to civil actions on tort claims against the United States, any such award, compromise, settlement, or determination shall be final and conclusive on all officers of the Government, except when procured by means of fraud.

Any award, compromise, or settlement in an amount of $2,500 or less made pursuant to this section shall be paid by the head of the Federal agency concerned out of appropriations available to that agency. Payment of any award, compromise, or settlement in an amount in excess of $2,500 made pursuant to this section or made by the Attorney General in any amount pursuant to section 2677 of this title shall be paid in a manner similar to judgments and compromises in like causes and appropriations or funds available for the payment of such judgments and compromises are hereby made available for the payment of awards, compromises, or settlements under this chapter.

The acceptance by the claimant of any such award, compromise, or settlement shall be final and conclusive on the claimant, and shall constitute a complete release of any claim against the United States and against the employee of the government whose act or omission gave rise to the claim, by reason of the same subject matter.

§2674. Liability of United States

The United States shall be liable, respecting the provisions of this title relating to tort claims, in the same manner and to the same extent as a private individual under like circumstances, but shall not be liable for interest prior to judgment or for punitive damages.

If, however, in any case wherein death was caused, the law of the place where the act or omission complained of occurred provides, or has been construed to provide, for damages only punitive in nature, the United States shall be liable for actual or compensatory damages, measured by the pecuniary injuries resulting from such death to the persons respectively, for whose benefit the action was brought, in lieu thereof.

With respect to any claim under this chapter, the United States shall be entitled to assert any defense based upon judicial or legislative immunity which otherwise would have been available to the employee of the United States whose act or omission gave rise to the claim, as well as any other defenses to which the United States is entitled.

With respect to any claim to which this section applies, the Tennessee Valley Authority shall be entitled to assert any defense which otherwise would have been available to the employee based upon judicial or legislative immunity, which otherwise would have been available to the employee of the Tennessee Valley Authority whose act or omission gave rise to the claim as well as any other defenses to which the Tennessee Valley Authority is entitled under this chapter.

§2675. Disposition by federal agency as prerequisite; evidence

(a) An action shall not be instituted upon a claim against the United States for money damages for injury or loss of property or personal injury or death caused by the negligent or wrongful act or omission of any employee of the Government while acting within the scope of his office or employment, unless the claimant shall have first presented the claim to the appropriate Federal agency and his claim shall have been finally denied by the agency in writing and sent by certified or registered mail. The failure of an agency to make final disposition of a claim within six months after it is filed shall, at the option of the claimant any time thereafter, be deemed a final denial of the claim for purposes of this section. The provisions of this subsection shall not apply to such claims as may be asserted under the Federal Rules of Civil Procedure by third party complaint, cross-claim, or counterclaim.

(b) Action under this section shall not be instituted for any sum in excess of the amount of the claim presented to the federal agency, except where the increased amount is based upon newly discovered evidence not reasonably discoverable at the time of presenting the claim to the federal agency, or upon allegation and proof of intervening facts, relating to the amount of the claim.

(c) Disposition of any claim by the Attorney General or other head of a federal agency shall not be competent evidence of liability or amount of damages.

§2676. Judgment as bar

The judgment in an action under section 1346(b) of this title shall constitute a complete bar to any action by the claimant, by reason of the same subject matter, against the employee of the government whose act or omission gave rise to the claim.

§2677. Compromise

The Attorney General or his designee may arbitrate, compromise, or settle any claim cognizable under section 1346(b) of this title, after the commencement of an action thereon.

§2678. Attorney fees; penalty

No attorney shall charge, demand, receive, or collect for services rendered, fees in excess of 25 per centum of any judgment rendered pursuant to section 1346(b) of this title or any settlement made pursuant to section 2677 of this title, or in excess of 20 per centum of any award, compromise, or settlement made pursuant to section 2672 of this title.

Any attorney who charges, demands, receives, or collects for services rendered in connection with such claim any amount in excess of that allowed under this section, if recovery be had, shall be fined not more than $2,000 or imprisoned not more than one year, or both.

§2679. Exclusiveness of remedy

(a) The authority of any federal agency to sue and be sued in its own name shall not be construed to authorize suits against such federal agency on claims which are cognizable under section 1346(b) of this title, and the remedies provided by this title in such cases shall be exclusive.

(b) (1) The remedy against the United States provided by sections 1346(b) and 2672 of this title for injury or loss of property, or personal injury or death arising or resulting from the negligent or wrongful act or omission of any employee of the Government while acting within the scope of his office or employment is exclusive of any other civil action or proceeding for money damages by reason of the same subject matter against the employee whose act or omission gave rise to the claim or against the estate of such employee. Any other civil action or proceeding for money damages arising out of or relating to the same subject matter against the employee or the employee's estate is precluded without regard to when the act or omission occurred.

(2) Paragraph (1) does not extend or apply to a civil action against an employee of the Government—

(A) which is brought for a violation of the Constitution of the United States, or

(B) which is brought for a violation of a statute of the United States under which such action against an individual is otherwise authorized.

(c) The Attorney General shall defend any civil action or proceeding brought in any court against any employee of the Government or his estate for any such damage or injury. The employee against whom such civil action or proceeding is brought shall deliver within such time after date of service or knowledge of service as determined by the Attorney General, all process served upon him or an attested true copy thereof to his immediate superior or to whomever was designated by the head of his department to receive such papers and such person shall promptly furnish copies of the pleadings and process therein to the United States attorney for the district embracing the place wherein the proceeding is brought, to the Attorney General, and to the head of his employing Federal agency.

(d) (1) Upon certification by the Attorney General that the defendant employee was acting within the scope of his office of employment at the time of the incident out of which the claim arose, any civil action or proceeding commenced upon such claim in a United States district court shall be deemed an action against the United States under the provisions of this title and all references thereto, and the United States shall be substituted as the party defendant.

(2) Upon certification by the Attorney General that the defendant employee was acting within the scope of his office or employment at the time of the incident out of which the claim arose, any civil action or proceeding commenced upon such claim in a State court shall be removed without bond at any time before trial by the Attorney General to the district court of the United States for the district and division embracing the place in which the action or proceeding is pending. Such action or proceeding shall be deemed to be an action or proceeding brought against the United States under the provisions of this title and all references thereto, and the United States shall be substituted as the party defendant. This certification of the Attorney General shall conclusively establish scope of office or employment for purposes of removal.

(3) In the event that the Attorney General has refused to certify scope of office or employment under this section, the employee may at any time before trial petition the court to find and certify that the employee was acting within

the scope of his office or employment. Upon such certification by the court, such action or proceeding shall be deemed to be an action or proceeding brought against the United States under the provisions of this title and all references thereto, and the United States shall be substituted as the party defendant. A copy of the petition shall be served upon the United States in accordance with the provisions of Rule 4(d)(4) of the Federal Rules of Civil Procedure. In the event the petition is filed in a civil action or proceeding pending in a State court, the action or proceeding may be removed without bond by the Attorney General to the district court of the United States for the district and division embracing the place in which it is pending. If, in considering the petition, the district court determines that the employee was not acting within the scope of his office or employment, the action or proceeding shall be remanded to the State court.

(4) Upon certification, any action or proceeding subject to paragraph (1), (2), or (3) shall proceed in the same manner as any action against the United States filed pursuant to section 1346(b) of this title and shall be subject to the limitations and exceptions applicable to those actions.

(5) Whenever an action or proceeding in which the United States is substituted as the party defendant under this subsection is dismissed for failure first to present a claim pursuant to section 2675(a) of this title, such a claim shall be deemed to be timely presented under section 2401(b) of this title if—

(A) the claim would have been timely had it been filed on the date the underlying civil action was commenced, and

(B) the claim is presented to the appropriate Federal agency within 60 days after dismissal of the civil action.

(e) The Attorney General may compromise or settle any claim asserted in such civil action or proceeding in the manner provided in section 2677, and with the same effect.

§2680. Exceptions

The provisions of this chapter and section 1346(b) of this title shall not apply to—

(a) Any claim based upon an act or omission of an employee of the Government, exercising due care, in the execution of a statute or regulation, whether or not such statute or regulation be valid, or based upon the exercise or performance or the failure to exercise or perform a discretionary function or duty on the part of a federal agency or an employee of the Government, whether or not the discretion involved be abused.

(b) Any claim arising out of the loss, miscarriage, or negligent transmission of letters or postal matter.

(c) Any claim arising in respect of the assessment or collection of any tax or customs duty, or the detention of any goods, merchandise, or other property by any officer of customs or excise or any other law enforcement officer, except that the provisions of this chapter and section 1346(b) of this title apply to any claim based on injury or loss of goods, merchandise, or other property, while in the possession of any officer of customs or excise or any other law enforcement officer, if—

(1) the property was seized for the purpose of forfeiture under any provision of Federal law providing for the forfeiture of property other than as a sentence imposed upon conviction of a criminal offense;

(2) the interest of the claimant was not forfeited;

(3) the interest of the claimant was not remitted or mitigated (if the property was subject to forfeiture); and

(4) the claimant was not convicted of a crime for which the interest of the claimant in the property was subject to forfeiture under a Federal criminal forfeiture law..

(d) Any claim for which a remedy is provided by chapter 309 or 311 of title 46, relating to claims or suits in admiralty against the United States.

(e) Any claim arising out of an act or omission of any employee of the Government in administering the provisions of sections 1-31 of Title 50, Appendix.

(f) Any claim for damages caused by the imposition or establishment of a quarantine by the United States.

[(g) Repealed. Sept. 26, 1950, c. 1049, § 13(5), 64 Stat. 1043.]

(h) Any claim arising out of assault, battery, false imprisonment, false arrest, malicious prosecution, abuse of process, libel, slander, misrepresentation, deceit, or interference with contract rights: *Provided,* That, with regard to acts or omissions of investigative or law enforcement officers of the United States Government, the provisions of this chapter and section 1346(b) of this title shall apply to any claim arising, on or after the date of the enactment of this proviso, out of assault, battery, false imprisonment, false arrest, abuse of process, or malicious prosecution. For the purpose of this subsection, "investigative or law enforcement officer" means any officer of the United States who is empowered by law to execute searches, to seize evidence, or to make arrests for violations of Federal law.

(i) Any claim for damages caused by the fiscal operations of the Treasury or by the regulation of the monetary system.

(j) Any claim arising out of the combatant activities of the military or naval forces, or the Coast Guard, during time of war.

(k) Any claim arising in a foreign country.

(l) Any claim arising from the activities of the Tennessee Valley Authority.

(m) Any claim arising from the activities of the Panama Canal Company.

(n) Any claim arising from the activities of a Federal land bank, a Federal intermediate credit bank, or a bank for cooperatives.

42 U.S.C.

§1983. Civil action for deprivation of rights

Every person who, under color of any statute, ordinance, regulation, custom, or usage, of any State or Territory or the District of Columbia, subjects, or causes to be subjected, any citizen of the United States or other person within the jurisdiction thereof to the deprivation of any rights, privileges, or immunities secured by the Constitution and laws, shall be liable to the party injured in an action at law, suit in equity, or other proper proceeding for redress, except that in any action brought against a judicial officer for an act or omission taken in such officer's judicial capacity, injunctive relief shall not be granted unless a declaratory decree was violated or declaratory relief was unavailable. For the purposes of this section, any Act of Congress applicable exclusively to the District of Columbia shall be considered to be a statute of the District of Columbia.

§1988. Proceedings in vindication of civil rights; attorney's fees

(b) Attorney's fees

In any action or proceeding to enforce a provision of sections 1981, 1981a, 1982, 1983, 1985, and 1986 of this title, title IX of Public Law 92-318, the Religious Freedom Restoration Act of 1993, the Religious Land Use and Institutionalized Persons Act of 2000, title VI of the Civil Rights Act of 1964, or section 12361 of Title 34, the court, in its discretion, may allow the prevailing party, other than the United States, a reasonable attorney's fee as part of the costs, except that in any action brought against a judicial officer for an act or omission taken in such officer's judicial capacity such officer shall not be held liable for any costs, including attorney's fees, unless such action was clearly in excess of such officer's jurisdiction.

Table of Cases

Alphabetization is letter-by-letter (e.g., "Mobile" precedes "Mobil Oil Corp.").

Table of Cases

Table of Cases

Index